I0881520

THE MIEGUNYAH PRESS

The general series of the
Miegunyah Volumes
was made possible by the
Miegunyah Fund
established by bequests
under the wills of
Sir Russell and Lady Grimwade.

'Miegunyah' was the home of
Mab and Russell Grimwade
from 1911 to 1955.

These Are the Names

These Are the Names

Jewish Lives in Australia, 1788–1850

Second Edition

John S. Levi

THE
MIEGUNYAH
PRESS

THE MIEGUNYAH PRESS
An imprint of Melbourne University Publishing Limited
11–15 Argyle Street South, Carlton, Victoria 3053, Australia
mup-info@unimelb.edu.au
www.mup.com.au

First published 2006
This edition published 2013
Text © John Simon Levi 2013
Design and typography © Melbourne University Publishing Ltd 2013

This book is copyright. Apart from any use permitted under the *Copyright Act 1968* and subsequent amendments, no part may be reproduced, stored in a retrieval system or transmitted by any means or process whatsoever without the prior written permission of the publishers.

Edited by Sally Nicholls
Designed by Alice Graphics
Typeset in Bembo 11/12.5 point
by diacriTech Client Service
Printed by ABC in China

National Library of Australia Cataloguing-in-Publication entry

Levi, J. S. (John Simon), 1934– .
These are the names: Jewish lives in Australia, 1788–1850.

Bibliography.
Includes index.
9780522862294 (hbk.).

1. Jews—Australia—Registers. 2. Australia—History—1788–1851—Sources. I. Title.

305.8924094

Foreword

CONVICTS AND FREE, FAMILIES and friends, villains and professional, healthy and sick, maimed and whole, wily and worthy, short and tall, all is revealed in this amazing book detailing Australia's first Jewish settlers. From the departure of the First Fleet in 1787 and for the sixty-three years thereafter, John Levi has produced a record detailing all the Jewish migrants, both voluntary and less so, who came to what is now Australia. It is as comprehensive, entertaining and educative but less divine than the Book of Exodus, despite being written by an emeritus Rabbi. I have no doubt that, in time, it will be treated as authoritatively. Fortunately this is not a book of 'begats' but a scholarly composition about the more than 1600 Jews who were transported or who chose Australia as a home, from the very first moment of European settlement up to 1850, just before the face of Australia changed for ever with the discovery of gold.

Australia was founded as an outpost of a British government department, the present-day equivalent of the Office of Corrections. Those to be 'corrected' were tutored by the marines and navy who, it could be said, were from just the other side of the law. Being militarily bureaucratic all noteworthy acts, together with personal details of the perpetrators, were written down in beautiful copperplate. The convict records are particularly ample. Details such as complexion, height, individual mutilations, tattoos and scars are all noted. Free settlers were not so thoroughly treated. Nevertheless the ship indents recorded all passengers, and government land and licence records enable their passages through life to be traced. Using primary sources, supplemented by newspaper reports and occasional articles, this book cascades with facts. Every lash applied to a Jewish back, every act of recalcitrance and almost every *mitzvah* is set down. The book itself will become source and prime material for future generations of historians.

Basic source though this book is, some of the subtexts and the necessary implications they raise are just as beguiling. For example, the skeins of chain migration can be unravelled. How is it that one family member enticed others to follow and in what order? The factors that pushed them out of Britain, as well as those that pulled them to Australia are revealed. Why, among those who were materially successful, did some return to Britain and others remain? Even the details of the states of health of the convicts raise interesting questions. The survival rates of adults and, more significantly, of children can be traced. The book raises the issue of what effect upon family life, especially upon women, was the fact that most could reasonably expect their children to live into maturity and beyond that to old age? These are the questions the book provokes, and it provides us with the foundation to continue to ask demanding questions.

The book exposes an astounding story of Jewish fortitude and resilience. One per cent of the convicts on the First Fleet were Jews—a population percentage not since matched. Within a short time the structures of Jewish survival were in place. The book refers to the benevolent societies, the appropriate burial rituals and the formal list of synagogue donors. A further fascinating issue is unmasked, that of why so many Jews sought to establish Jewish life in difficult circumstances and why so many did not. How many Australians of our present generation must have Jewish antecedents? This book partially answers the question—hundreds of thousands. This is a unique picture of a whole community—rich and poor, emancipist, male and female, free settler and convict. So often history is reserved for the powerful or the wealthy. Australia's extraordinary wealth of records gives us a fresh perspective on the past.

The author has given new meaning to the words 'industry' and 'competence'. In my view this book surpasses his previous publications. Rabbi Levi has transformed the dry records of colonial history into a series of engaging personal stories. Here you will meet Australia's first musician, a wizard, our first actors and theatrical producers, many of Australia's first business men and women. There are pastoral pioneers, brewers and farmers. There are convicts who made good and convicts who suffered terrible punishments and whose lives were forever shattered. There are Jewish converts to Christianity and Gentiles who became Jews. In this book we meet the hapless Raphael Harris who, it is noted, 'may well have been the first Hungarian to arrive in Australia'. He understood 'distilling in all its branches'. He had 'thick lips', but 'no whiskers'. Raphael was transported for seven years for stealing a watch. In May 1831 he was given ten lashes for cutting up his blanket, and later another twelve for refusing to work. He capped his life by drowning at New Norfolk in Tasmania on Christmas Eve 1832. There is much to read about Raphael, and thousands upon thousands of facts about the other arrivals.

John Levi has given life to our history and in the telling of an entire community has bestowed dignity and meaning to our forefathers and mothers. It adorns Jewish learning wherever and whenever it is read. It has been the greatest honour to have written this foreword.

The Hon. Howard Nathan QC

Contents

Acknowledgements

MY THANKS TO THE Pratt Cultural Fund, chaired by Mr Sam Lipski AO. I am grateful for the sympathetic friendship of Mrs Jeannie Pratt AO. Their support of educational, cultural and charitable projects in Australia and in Israel has no parallel.

I extend my gratitude to the Australian Jewish Historical Society with its branches in Victoria and New South Wales and presidents Dr Howard Freeman and Mrs Helen Bersten respectively. The painstaking work of Ms Jeannette Tsoulos and Ms Rieke Nash of the Australian Jewish Genealogical Society in New South Wales was invaluable. My thanks to the enthusiastic support of Mr Lionel Sharpe OAM, President of the Australian Jewish Genealogical Society in Victoria and Ms Sophie Caplan OAM, President of the Australian Jewish Historical Society in New South Wales. The Archives of the New South Wales Genealogical Society are housed at Mandelbaum House at the University of Sydney and the help of Ms Naomi Winton is acknowledged together with the support of Mrs Helen Bersten. The archives of the Great Synagogue were generously made available to me and my thanks go to Rabbi Emeritus Raymond Apple AO. I acknowledge the support of the Hyde Park Museum, its curator at the time, Mr John Petersen, and the Historic Houses Trust of New South Wales. Over the past forty or so years I have studied the records of the Hobart Hebrew Congregation and the Archives of Tasmania, which are now online. This edition is the result of an initiative envisaged by my friend, Mr Peter M Schiftan.

There are dozens of people from around the world who have supplied me with family information. Rather than lose their connection with their family research I have tried to acknowledge them within the body of the notes. I hope I have repaid their trust and done justice to their discoveries.

The first edition of this book was written as part of a requirement for doctoral studies at Monash University.

Melbourne University Press and its Miegunyah division have been tolerant, supportive and enthusiastic. My thanks to the CEO and Publisher of Melbourne University Publishing Ltd, Ms Louise Adler, Publishing Editors Kirsty Manning-Wilcox and Catherine Cradwick. My editor for the first edition was Sally

Nicholls who patiently and vigilantly brought order and discipline into the work of this unruly author. The editor of this Second Edition is Diane Leyman, and I am very grateful for her deft expertise.

The Hon. Howard Nathan of the Victorian Supreme Court was eminently qualified to write the Foreword. His family's remarkable story, which begins with the arrival of the Third Fleet in 1791, is embedded in this text.

This book is the result of a lifetime's fascination with Australian history and the Jews of the colonial period. Apart from Israel, there are few, if any, other countries in the world in which Jews have been part of a nation's history from its settlement on its very first day. I will always be grateful for my partnership with the late Dr George Bergman of Sydney who was the scholarly pioneer in this field.

For more than fifty years my wife Robyn has been my partner. She is a woman of valour who, with untiring grace and patience, has been 'my right hand' patiently providing literary analysis, reading manuscripts, dealing with dusty documents, trawling through newspapers and exploring snake-infested rural cemeteries to help in the search for the long forgotten and often neglected records of colonial Australia's Jews.

We both dedicate this book to our grandchildren, Joshua Levi Sylvan and Amy Grace Sylvan, and to all the children at Melbourne's King David School.

Rabbi John Simon Levi

Introduction

FOR THOUSANDS OF YEARS the inhabitants of the vast Australian continent marked the passage of life by their awareness of an intimate and spiritual identity with their environment. This sense was incomprehensible to the first European exiles who found themselves dumped on the edge of an alien world. On 26 January 1788 the great southern continent's destiny changed forever with the arrival at Sydney Cove of the First Fleet carrying 759 miserable convicts and an assorted contingent of officers, soldiers and marines. Among those first arrivals were Australia's first Jews. There is no other Jewish community in the Diaspora that can trace its origins back to its country's first day of European settlement.

This early colonial chapter of Australian history is the subject of this study. The period came to an abrupt end with the discovery of gold in 1850, after which the rapid increase in population transformed the Australian colonies. This biographical dictionary includes details of the lives of all the Jewish immigrants to Australia during the first sixty-two years of European settlement. It is therefore a portrait of an entire Jewish community in the latter decades of the eighteenth century and the first half of the nineteenth century. During that time a penal colony was dominated by a military clique with an agrarian population that clung to the south-eastern edge of a vast continent. Apart from the indigenous Australians, the Jews constituted the only non-Christian minority. They formed a small urban class of 'outsiders'. They were the traders, auctioneers and dealers who made up a primitive, putative middle class.

Between 1788 and 1850 virtually half the almost 1500 Jews who arrived in Australia were convicts; only three or four individuals brought any financial capital with them. To succeed financially in the new Australian colonies took extraordinary skill and, of course, luck. Only in the final decade of the period would Jewish free settlers outnumber Jewish convicts and emancipists (former convicts) and their experiences provide us with illuminating contrasts.

It has been possible to collect the biographical data from a wide variety of sources. These details often begin with the printed records of trials conducted at the Old Bailey and the individuals reappear in the indents of the convict transport ships. For those who survived the long journey to the other side of the world, there are records of colonial musters, ration books and detailed police dossiers. The Australian convict system bred a complicated system of bureaucratic checks. The files of the governors, lieutenant governors and colonial secretaries in all the colonies are useful sources of information. Church records, cemetery registers, tombstone inscriptions, synagogue minute books and existing correspondence files yield valuable information. Official government gazettes grew into colonial newspapers and, especially in the earlier decades, kept track of births, deaths, executions, tickets of leave, certificates of freedom and pardons, departures from the colony, bankruptcies and criminal trials. Most biographies conclude with a basic list of references to assist further research.

The first Jews to arrive in Australia came with a cultural and historical background that was radically different from that of other exiles from the United Kingdom. Almost all were the children of Jewish families who were recent arrivals in England, having escaped from a deeply hostile continental European environment. By the conclusion of the eighteenth century, two million Jews, or four-fifths of all the Jews of the world, were to be found in Europe.[1] Less than one-tenth of that number lived in the developing mercantile economies of Western Europe—England, the Netherlands, France and Italy. In the German-speaking states and principalities of central Europe there may have been half a million Jews whose origins extended back to the days of the Roman Empire.[2]

History and geography had shaped two distinct European Jewish worlds. The Jewish refugees from the Iberian Peninsula fled from the Inquisition and took with them a proud tradition of involvement with the culture of Spain and Portugal. Their sophisticated world had collapsed in 1492 when Ferdinand and Isabella signed the edict of expulsion that purged Spain of both Jews and Muslims. These Jews were known as Sephardim. Most European Jews described themselves as Ashkenazim and their ethnic origins could be traced back to a community of some ten thousand Jews who lived peacefully in the Rhineland until the onslaught of the Crusades.[3] Suddenly the Jews found themselves victimised for being the nearest available infidels by those on their way to rescue the Holy Land from the Saracens. The centuries of persecution of the unbelievers who were close at hand had begun.[4]

The Jews of mediaeval Europe were only permitted to survive subject to complex legal restrictions imposed upon them by both secular and ecclesiastical authorities. The Jews of Europe could not own land, hire servants or employ serfs. They could not join trade guilds or become apprentices. They were permitted to be rag dealers and to purchase the noxious clothes of the dead. They could change and lend small amounts of money. Urban Jewish residence came to be strictly limited by law to the squalid sections of the town. Walls were built around these ghettos.

1 H. M. Sachar, *The Course of Modern Jewish History*, p. 33f.

2 R. Mahler, *A History of Modern Jewry 1780–1815*, p. xv.

3 I. A. Agus, *Urban Civilization in Pre-Crusade Europe*, p. 9.

4 H. H. Ben-Sasson (ed.), *A History of the Jewish People*, p. 477f.

When venturing beyond these restrictive walls and gates, Jews were forced to wear absurdly coloured clothes and hats and conspicuous badges on their outer garments. They were blamed for the Black Death, which they had caused by poisoning the wells. They were known to have desecrated the Host when the wafer on the altar became discoloured. The Jews were paying the price for having crucified the Lord.

The squalor of the ghetto generated both isolation and corporate autonomy. The compensation for daily humiliation was the Jewish conviction that they were God's witnesses and guardians of the sacred texts. They had stood at Mt Sinai. Their humiliation was proof of the truth of the new Israel that had superseded the old stock of Abraham. A biblical calendar governed their lives and sustained the dream that one day they would return to the Holy Land and rebuild the Holy Temple in Jerusalem.

During the seventeenth and eighteenth centuries a mercantile revolution swept through Europe. The gold and silver of the New World fed the development of capitalism, and wealth could no longer be measured only by the accumulated ownership of land. In a world in which status and rank came through financial success, it became increasingly impractical to suppress a religious community for theological reasons. The era of mercantilism or capitalism ushered in a new age of grudging tolerance for some of the Jews of Western Europe, who were catapulted into a new world of business and finance.[5]

Through long centuries of mediaeval darkness the Jews had become experts in surviving in hostile urban environments. In contrast to most of their contemporaries they were literate. Even the poorest boy could read his Hebrew bible and prayer book and conduct a service of worship. The stringent restrictions that had been placed upon the number of Jews who could live in any particular town or village meant that members of the same family were scattered geographically, allowing the creation of a rudimentary commercial network. (The Rothschild family of the Frankfurt Ghetto is the most impressive example of the utilisation of family networking that functioned above and beyond national and linguistic boundaries.)

The first members of the Jewish community of London were Sephardim who had settled in England unobtrusively during the first half of the sixteenth century. Communal and commercial ties linked these refugees to the flourishing Jewish community that had emerged in the Netherlands. The pace of Jewish emancipation in Europe began to accelerate, and its impact was felt in England.[6]

In 1657 in London a rented house was adapted for use as a synagogue. In 1701 the Spanish and Portuguese Jews dedicated the Bevis Marks Synagogue, which is carefully located beyond the boundary of the City of London. Timidly and cautiously the Jews of England emerged from obscurity. Following the precedent set by the Sephardim, in Duke's Place, just around the corner from Bevis Marks, the Ashkenazi Jews built their own synagogue. As several other smaller congregations existed, its rabbi came to be called the Chief Rabbi of the Great Synagogue. The

5 E. Rivkin, *The Shaping of Jewish History*, p. 140.
6 T. M. Endelman, *The Jews of Georgian England*, p. 2f.

statutes of the City of London demanded that the owners of retail businesses take up the freedom of the city 'upon the true faith of a Christian', which effectively excluded Jews. Up to 1830, Jews in England were barred from Parliament, from high rank in the navy and army, from membership of the University of Oxford and from degrees and fellowships at the University of Cambridge. It was not until 1831 that the restrictions imposed by the City of London were removed, after which other barriers rapidly fell. In 1833 Lincoln's Inn called Francis Goldsmid to the Bar and, in 1835, David Salomons was elected Sheriff of London and Middlesex.

By the end of the eighteenth century the Jewish community of England had grown to number some ten thousand individuals, most of whom were of Ashkenazi descent. They chose to dress distinctively. The men were bearded, adorned with large black hats that crowned their gaberdine cloaks, and they spoke Yiddish or Judeo-German, the Jewish dialects of central Europe. They settled in London's squalid East End, close to the docks and near the markets and fairs that flourished near the waterways. Imbued with an unquenchable optimism, they had dreamed that somewhere in the world they would find a safe haven. They were not the merchants and the financiers who were easily accepted by the English. They were penniless migrants who brought very few skills and no money with them. The Jewish pedlars, dressed in clothes that seemed bizarre, carried their meagre stock into the lanes of rural England in search of customers. Both in London and in the countryside they were walking targets for taunts and violence. The impression they unwittingly created was so outlandish that, in 1786, when the infamous Lord George Gordon of the anti-Catholic Gordon Riots converted to Judaism, it was assumed he was insane.

The Jews constituted an alien, poverty-stricken and puzzling presence and so it appeared as though London's East End was awash with Jews who overflowed the courts, the gaols and the prison hulks. Exaggerated as this picture may be, an anonymous essay on *The Commercial Habits of the Jews*, published in London in 1809, clearly describes a community in crisis:

> The number of intricate lanes and alleys near Whitechapel and other parts of the town entirely occupied by these [Jewish] miscreants and their associates, render them formidable to the officers of justice, and at the same time impervious to the public eye. From these depositors of filth and iniquity, the approach of morning sends them in herds over the whole face of the capital ... the baneful and immoral effects upon society with such a race of men need not be insisted upon.

In 1796 the Police Magistrate Patrick Colquhoun believed that 20 000 Jews lived in the metropolis.[7] This figure was an exaggerated one, and would not be reached until the mid-1840s. Colquhoun estimated that there were 100 000 criminals in London out of a total population of 640 000, of whom 2000 (or 10 per cent of the

7 R. D. Barnett, 'Anglo-Jewry in the Eighteenth Century', in V. D. Lipman (ed.), *Three Centuries of Anglo-Jewish History*, p. 61.

total Jewish population) were 'itinerant Jews, wandering from street to street, holding out temptation to pilfer and to steal, and Jew Boys carrying bad shillings, who purchase items stolen by Servants, Stable boys etc. etc. generally paying in base money'.

These were the first Jews in Australia. As the years passed they would be joined by their cousins and brothers and sometimes by their parents and members of their extended families. First cousin married first cousin. Men found wives among their sisters-in-law. Intercolonial marriages were common and miniature commercial dynasties came into being.

The Jews of Australia have rarely numbered more that half of 1 per cent of the country's population. Their heritage differed radically from the rest of the population. We can now ask whether the Jews constituted a distinct segment of the community in colonial Australia and whether their religious and ethnic identity remained viable in an entirely new social environment. Are we describing the lives of hundreds of unconnected individuals who have nothing in common with each other, or was there a sense of corporate identity that survived the long journey from England?

The answers to these questions can be found within these pages, in the stories of the people. Briefly, the first Jews of colonial Australia did not leave their Judaism behind in London or in Amsterdam. They struggled, at great cost, to maintain their identity. They had no clear precedent to prepare themselves for life in a new and open society and they lacked an understanding of their own history. When they built Australia's first synagogues they saw no need to provide space for communal interaction or for the education of their children. They had no trained spiritual leadership throughout the entire period. The imbalanced ratio of men to women made it impossible for the early Jewish arrivals to find a Jewish partner. A lack of religious leadership and knowledge, exacerbated by intermarriage, and residual social prejudice ravaged the first Australian-born Jewish generation. However, looking back, it may well have been the contrast with the painful memories of Jewish life in Europe that gave these new Australians some hope that the community would survive and be treated with dignity. They clearly constituted a distinct segment of colonial society and became a tightly knit community that developed a mechanism for survival.

Jewish status is a complicated matter. Being a Jew is not primarily determined by belief. According to rabbinic tradition Jewish identity is matrilineal. In the new Australian colonies this definition was often dealt with pragmatically, and the earliest Jewish congregations recognised as Jews the children of Jewish fathers. A convert to Judaism is required to be immersed in a ritual bath (*mikveh*) and to be accepted by a rabbinical court. This procedure could not be followed in Australia. Somehow or other, the wives of Jewish men were accepted by the congregations. Women changed their first names to those with a biblical resonance and were permitted to join the synagogue. Practical considerations won the day.

Given the paucity of direct data, how is it possible to identify the Jews of colonial Australia? 'Jewish' surnames provide a start. In Europe the Jews of the period of political emancipation were often forced to purchase surnames in place of the traditional Hebrew name system, which identified individuals as the son or daughter of their father. Upon arrival in England these German, Polish or Russian surnames were dropped in favour of English biblical names, such as Abrahams, Benjamin, Jacobs and Solomon. Other migrants translated their Hebrew or Yiddish name into English, while some became integrated with adopted names, such as Anderson, David or Brown. Surnames (and first names) are therefore a useful but not infallible guide to Jewish identity. There were many Elijahs, Zadoks, Cowens and Jacobs who were good and pious churchmen.

In London the transcripts of trials frequently identify who was Jewish by their place of residence, their (alleged) trade, by their place of birth and by the names of those friends and relatives who came to court to beg for mercy on behalf of the accused. In Australia Jews went to great lengths to ensure that they would not be buried as Christians. Jewish cemeteries were established in all the colonial centres before synagogues were built. The existing synagogue records provide us with basic data while letter books, marriage documents and birth books (which include the names of parents) supplement the list of names. Beginning in the 1820s parents registered their children at birth and recorded their religion. In some cases the choice of the description 'Hebrew' or 'Israelite' had nothing to do with the Jewish community but reflected membership of a Protestant sect. Nevertheless, it is clear that a number of Jewish women insisted on registering their newborn children as Jews even though the children, in later life, would have no association with the community. Trades and professions are also useful indicators of Jewish identity. Not every dealer was Jewish, but many were. George Street in Sydney came to be lined with the shops of Jewish dealers, drapers, pawnbrokers and auctioneers. Long before the search for gold opened up the outback, Jews set up general stores and pubs on country tracks and in rural villages. Those families who remained Jewish would, in time, drift back to the metropolis for social and family reasons, and during the early colonial period as many Jews lived in the rural districts as in the towns.

The British defeat of the French in 1815 led to widespread social unrest and unemployment in the United Kingdom, and consequently to a dramatic increase in the number of convicts sent to Australia. From 1816 to 1825 the average number of those sentenced to transportation was 2000 each year. From 1826 to 1836 it was 4900.[8] The colonial authorities began to pay attention to their ratio of Catholics and Protestants who were being sent to the Antipodes. The crimes of the Irish were nearly all related to poverty and hunger, and these convicts had no reason to love the Crown or to respect the British military. The need to identify convicts according to their religious affiliation was certainly not a theological necessity but constituted political caution, lest republicanism lead to an Australian colonial rebellion that would mimic the American War of Independence. In addition, as the population increased so too did the need for the accumulation of personal data on

8 A. G. L. Shaw, *Convicts and the Colonies*, p. 147.

the convict population. Convict escapees needed to be identified by their physical characteristics. We therefore know how tall the convicts were, the colour of their eyes, the shape of their face, what tattoos they had, what trades or skills they said they possessed, details about family, education, literacy, marital status, nicknames, behaviour in prison, in the hulks and on board ship, the number of children, place of birth, length of sentence and subsequent behaviour in gaol, and time of release.

Not all colonial documents agree with one another and not all colonial records still exist. Nevertheless an immense amount of information does exist and every attempt has been made to record these sources. The biographical material is biased in favour of men. Women were often treated as chattels, and children received even less attention. Even free female migrants were simply recorded as 'Mrs So and So', and when they died they were known as 'relict' of their husband with no mention of their first name.

New South Wales eventually became 'too settled' and 'too civilised' for transportation to be an effective punishment.[9] The last convict transport ship to New South Wales arrived in Sydney Harbour on 18 November 1840. The ratio of convicts to free settlers quickly altered, so that convicts and emancipists were outnumbered by free settlers and their families who had chosen to try their luck in a new world. In Van Diemen's Land the transportation of prisoners lingered until the discovery of gold on the mainland made a mockery of transportation. By that time very few Jews were being transported to Australia as the Jewish community of London had begun to educate its own children, care for the poverty-stricken immigrants and ease a great deal of the sense of alienation that had led its young people into a life of crime. As the *Cumberland Times* of Parramatta reported on 1 November 1845:

> The Hebrews of the colony, as of every other locality in the British dominions, have established for themselves as a body a reputation of general morality, integrity and munificent generosity ... We conscientiously opine the Hebrew to be in error; but wherever the gift of the religion is guaranteed by the morality of its professors we can see no reason why they should suffer disabilities.

The Jews of early Australia were not paragons of religious virtue but they defined themselves through consistent acts of self-identification. So synagogues were built, children were named and registered, and funerals were arranged even when there was no synagogue. Poverty, inexperience and one colonial economic recession after another deeply affected this small and exposed group of entrepreneurs, most of whom could only accumulate meagre assets. In colonial Australia, Jews were often damned if they succeeded and damned when they failed. Wealthy Jewish free immigrants, such as Michael Phillips, Walter Levi and Joseph Barrow Montefiore, who brought sufficient capital with them to warrant grants of land, were ignored or denied their rights. Officialdom could not believe that a Jew could own land and cultivate crops. In London the emancipist Solomon Levey bankrolled

9 ibid., p. 275.

and encouraged Thomas Peel's plans to settle at Swan River but was kept out of public view as much because of his Jewish identity as because of his convict past.

Australia rapidly engendered a sense of security and identity within the newly evolving society. On 2 December 1835 the *Sydney Herald* drew the attention of the public to the number of Jewish stall-holders at the newly built town market. The wealthy emancipist Samuel Lyons thundered: 'Why have Gentiles a deed of settlement more than infidels, or do they pay more taxes, are they more patriotic? But those days of religious persecution belong to the last century, the banner of religious toleration floats triumphantly and the Hebrew ranks with his fellow citizen in spite of a bigoted clergy'.

The 'bigoted clergy' were the Anglican bishops of the House of Lords in Westminster who, for one hundred years, had blocked every parliamentary move towards Jewish political emancipation. Far away from Europe a new social reality was being created in which the Jewish community instinctively felt they would play a full and equal part. They knew that Jews had been part of Australia since the arrival of the First Fleet.

Fifteen Jews sailed with the First Fleet in 1788. Their names should be recorded at the beginning of this book. There were seven men, seven women and one child.

> Henry Abrahams, Daniel Daniels, John Harris, John Hart, David Jacobs, Joseph Levy and Peter Opley.
>
> Esther Abrahams and her infant daughter Rosanna, Sarah Burdo, Rebecca Davison, Frances Hart, Flora Larah, Amelia Levy and Leah (Mary) Levy.

Author's Note

THE SECOND BOOK OF the Hebrew Bible (Exodus) begins with the words *V'Eleh Shemot—And These Are the Names*. Having co-authored a book called *Australian Genesis* it seemed appropriate for the second book about the first Jews in Australia to echo the name of the second book of the Torah. I hasten to add that this is not a book of revelation. It is an attempt to include the names and memories of more than 1600 pioneers. *These Are the Names* is an alphabetical list. It will be seen that family relationships often override the distinction between those who were transported and those who came as free settlers. There were many who were known by their nicknames and there were some who changed their names. These extra names, aliases and maiden names appear in brackets after the 'official' names at the head of each entry.

Where the person was born, and the years of birth and death are also recorded at the beginning of each entry. The early indents did not give the age of those transported, but later indents described the age and religion of each individual. However, both age and religion were recorded differently at time of marriage, death or subsequent trial. The degree of literacy of the transported convicts was often noted and, in the latter years of the transportation system an attempt was made to record English family relationships.

Whenever possible the name of the transport or passenger ship is listed, followed by its year of arrival. The method of designating which ship was used and which voyage it may have been follows the system used by Charles Bateson in his book *The Convict Ships 1787–1868* (1969). Following the name of the ship the number in brackets indicates the ship, its voyage, and notes the use of the same name for a new ship.

The status of each individual, 'Convict' or 'Free', is listed, and for convicts, the place of trial and the sentence handed down are also noted. It was important for the authorities to know the marital status of the convict and the settler at the time of arrival. This is followed by the number of children the individual is known to have had in the course of their lifetime. Jews were anxious to affirm the Jewish status of their children and the synagogue (and cemetery) lists kept track of the Jewish children. However, the children of 'mixed' marriages cannot be traced with the same degree of accuracy. Finally, the trade or occupation of the settlers and convicts is recorded.

This dictionary of biography of colonial Jewry is a picture of an entire community. The convicts are included together with the free settlers. Wherever possible, the names of the children introduce us to the second generation of Jewish Australians. The 'little people' have been treated with as much care as the famous and the wealthy.

Once again, I need to add that I know that there must be errors and significant omissions. I am certain that this text will generate further research. I therefore begin with an apology to those who, for family reasons, know more about these early Australians than I do.

Colonial documents are often fragmentary and obstinately contradictory. There are cases where a number of people bear the same names. There are entries, for example, for five different Samuel Jacobs, seven individuals called Abraham Levy, twelve called Samuel Levy, and seven named Abraham Cohen. There are many instances where the spelling of a person's name varied between official documents. In the text of the entries these different spellings are maintained.

These Are the Names is written for the layman to pick up and read. I hope the references will lead investigators to do their own research. I have tried to provide the clues.

A

AARON, Abraham

b. London, 1807–1828
Phoenix (2), 1824; Convict; Sentenced to 7 years, London, 1823.
Single; Labourer.

Aaron was seventeen years old when he stole a silver Torah scroll pointer from the Duke's Place (Ashkenazi) Synagogue in London. The pointer was made of gilt and set with diamonds and its value was estimated at £32. Aaron had hidden himself in the synagogue, emerging after an evening service, and subsequently attempted to sell the stolen ritual object. He was immediately denounced to the police. Aaron was unable to read or write and had no legal representation in court. He begged the court to bring his rabbi to defend him but to no avail. The convict transport ship's surgeon reported that Aaron had gone mad during the voyage and, in order to bring him to his senses, he received 200 lashes. The official colonial report estimated that the pointer was worth between £4000 and £5000. That scribal mistake would ultimately prove to be Aaron's doom.

Aaron's Australian police dossier in Van Diemen's Land is brief and tragic. On 18 January 1825 he was found out after hours and when he was caught, attempted to escape from the policeman's grasp. He was sentenced to fifty lashes. On the next day a piece of stolen silk was found in his possession and he was sentenced to a further twenty-five lashes. On 30 March 1826 Aaron refused to go out to work and for his 'insolence' was sentenced to fifty lashes. On 24 July 1826 he was deemed guilty of 'improper conduct and neglect of duty' and received another twenty-five lashes. On 29 October 1827 he was found guilty of the offence of stealing a quantity of yarn from the clothing factory in Hobart Town and was sentenced to receive another fifty lashes. A further charge of theft condemned him to colonial transportation and he was sent to Maria Island where, on 18 July 1828, he stole some clothes from Archibald McLachlan at the Colonial Hospital and was sentenced to death. Aaron was brought back to Hobart Town, persuaded to convert to Christianity, and was baptised. As noted by the Rev. Knopwood in his diary, he was hanged in Hobart Town on Friday morning, 1 August 1828, and the next day the colonial press reported:

> This morning at 8 o'clock the awful sentence of the law was carried into execution on Abraham Aaron who was lately convicted of robbery at Maria Island. He was attended by the Rev. Bedford and Rev. Carvosso and appeared to meet his fate with

> resignation. He shortly addressed the spectators, particularly the Jews, and assured them there is no salvation but through the redeeming blood of our Lord Jesus Christ.
> He appeared to be about twenty-seven years of age, but extremely frail and emaciated.

He was twenty-one years old.

OBSP, 1822–23, case 1387, p. 511; CON 31/1, and ML 189; CSO 1/336/7715, and CSO 1/292/7122; *Tasmanian*, 2 August 1828; *Hobart Town Courier*, 2 August 1828; *AG*, p. 68.

AARON, Abraham

b. Sheerness
Cumberland, 1825; Free.
Married; Dealer.

Abraham Aaron came steerage on the Cumberland, arriving in Hobart Town on 24 January 1825.

Aaron's arrival in Van Diemen's Land is surprising. There is no doubt that he was the police informer in Sheerness (Kent) responsible for the arrest and subsequent transportation of the brothers Judah and Joseph Solomon (qq.v.). Aaron brought with him a letter from Downing Street, dated 14 July 1824, regarding a grant of land—which had been carefully left unsigned (by Lord Bathurst)! The Justices of the Peace met in Launceston to consider whether the licence held by Henry Davis (q.v.) at the Commercial Inn could be transferred to Aaron. It was agreed to issue the licence.

Aaron next enquired of the Colonial Secretary whether 'a certain convict's record' could help him identify the culprit responsible for burning down his house in Launceston. The convict under suspicion had previously looked after a farm owned by Mr (George) Russell (q.v.) where there had been a mysterious fire. The Police Magistrate declined 'from the opinion I entertain of that Person's character'. Aaron was recorded as being of the Globe Tavern.

Evidently Aaron suspected John Fawkner (snr) of the arson and he subsequently challenged him to a duel: 'Sir—You having used me unbecoming to a gentleman therefore will You meet me tomorrow and fight me for any sum you may pleases. You will recollect that I came free to this country and You came here as a Convict'. Fawkner replied, 'Mr Aaron. I have received your Polite challenge—and the Convict accepts. Therefore come out and fight. Otherwise I will come into you and Pay you in your own Coin. If not I may give [you] in charge of the police or prosecute you for Libel. J. F.'

Aaron may have had reason to suspect Fawkner because the latter was a loyal friend of the extended families of Judah and Joseph Solomon. According to the police, Aaron had been a servant of Henry Davis (a brother of George Russell), who had travelled to Sydney in order to escape from his creditors. Davis was in gaol for debt and Aaron had his power of attorney. The police reported:

> His behaviour has been anything but respectable. He had visited Davis in Sydney and his house burned down just before he returned home. The sheep owned by Russell and Aaron are most of them supposed to be the property of Davis and they are

> about slaughtering and salting a hundred yearlings which Aaron is to take to Sydney. The three men are Jews born at Sheerness. Aaron's father was a foreigner who kept a clothes' shop. Aaron has a wife and family residing with his, reputedly wealthy, father-in-law who is the pawnbroker Jonas Michael at Leith.

Aaron applied to the Colonial Secretary for assistance in recovering money owed his wife's uncle, stating that Mr Michael Michaels (q.v.) had lived many years in Hobart Town where he had accumulated several thousand pounds. In 1812 he had left the colony, handing over his businesses to Mr James Lord and appointed him as his agent to collect notes of hand, mortgages and so forth to the value of £1333 to be delivered to Michaels' agent, Dr Bowden. After Mr Lord died, Mr Michaels had appointed the Rev. Knopwood as his agent. However, this gentleman had 'refused to hand over such money and notes entrusted to him'. Knopwood, a parson and a magistrate, was a powerful figure in Van Diemen's Land and the money could not be recovered.

The following month Abraham Aaron applied to the authorities for a grant of land, claiming to have assets of £186 14s and that he was doing business with Cooper and Levey (Solomon Levey q.v.) worth £800. His application was refused because 'Aarons has been running sheep on George Russell's property contrary to regulations'. Defeated, Aaron sailed for Swan River and then to England on the ship *Ephimina* on 3 September 1829, without his uncle-in-law's money.

Sydney Gazette, 3 March 1825; *Hobart Town Gazette*, 28 January 1825; LSD 1/1/, pp. 61–75; CSO 1/214/5163, dated 11 February 1828, with the address 'Police Office Launceston'; CSO, 1/242/5844, dated 14 January 1827, with the address 'The Globe Tavern, Launceston'; *Hobart Town Courier*, 3 September 1829.

AARON, David (AARONS)

b. Holland, 1792
Lady Nugent (1), 1835; Convict; Sentenced to 7 years, Lancaster, 1834.
Married; Soldier; 5 children.

'A converted Jew.' Dark ruddy complexion, dark brown hair, brown eyes, nearly bald at top of head. Scar under left ear. Can read. No previous convictions. Aaron had three male children and two female children (in England).

David Aaron was forty-one when he arrived in Sydney on the *Lady Nugent* on 9 April 1835. The family was listed in the New South Wales Muster of 1837. Aaron was assigned to David Hitchcock at Sutton Forest. He was granted a ticket of leave in 1839.

Lady Nugent (1) Printed Indent, p. 62; TL in Governors' Despatches 1840, ML A1222, p. 591.

AARON, Esther

Convict.

Esther Aaron was sentenced for theft in Sydney on 18 February 1809.

Sydney Gazette, 19 February 1809.

AARON, Joseph (AARONS)

b. London, 1816
Lady Nugent (2), 1836; Convict; Sentenced to life, Central Criminal Court, 1836.
Single; Furrier; Height: 165 cm; 1 child.

Dark complexion, black hair. Transported for burglary on the same boat as his fellow thieves, Solomon Hyams (aged nineteen), Aaron Moses, nineteen (q.v.), and David Martin (q.v.), who were convicted of the same offence. The four men broke into the house of dressmaker Jane Hart at 33 Gravel Lane, Houndsditch, on 18 March 1836, with intent to steal. They were sentenced to death on 9 May 1836 and then, 'on account of their youth', the sentence was commuted to transportation for life.

Joseph Aaron arrived in Van Diemen's Land on 12 November 1836. On 1 April 1840 he was sentenced to two months hard labour on the treadmill for disobedience. Two days later, the Lieutenant Governor directed that a record be made of his having 'courageously' extinguished a fire in the premises adjoining his master. In 1841 Aarons was working as a constable in Launceston. On 9 August 1841 an accusation of felony was discharged, and on 24 September he was fined 10 shillings for 'misconduct'.

Also that year, Joseph Aaron was asked to give evidence at the inquest into the death of the convict Benjamin Cohen (q.v.). Aaron had been asked to meet with Cohen, who was suffering from the delusion that he had been brought to Launceston to be burnt at the stake by the Inquisition.

Aaron received permission to marry 'Hannah' Cokely, twenty years of age, who had come out as a convict on the *Majestic* in 1839. They married in Launceston on 27 May 1844. Aaron received his ticket of leave on 8 March 1844 and a conditional pardon on 15 January 1846.

His signature ('Joseph Aarons') appears on the petition of 20 May 1843 asking for permission to establish a synagogue in Launceston. There is a note in the Hobart Town Congregational Minutes, dated 20 June 1847, that he 'had married a Christian woman in the Church'. He requested that the congregation 'sanction his child by her, being circumcised and also permit her to become a proselyte'. The circumcision was permitted, the child was named Mordecai, and the mother took the name 'Hannah'. By 1850, Joseph and Hannah Aarons had settled in South Australia, where he was a 'general dealer'.

OBSP, 1836, case 1134, pp. 5–6; CON 18/14; CON 31/2, no. 741; CON 52/1/2, p. 4; Launceston Synagogue Petition, CO 280/157.

AARON, Samuel Hyam

b. 1807
Warrior, 1835; Free.
Single; Dealer.

Samuel Aaron arrived in Sydney on 27 February 1835, aged twenty-eight. He became a servant of the wife of Nathan Mandelson (q.v.) of George Street, Sydney, and was revealed to have stolen clothes and other articles from the Mandelson family in December 1835. He was dismissed from work and put into police custody.

His case was heard at Sydney's Central Criminal Court on 8 December 1835. At the trial Aaron pleaded 'not guilty', but was remanded to complete his 'former sentence'.

Warrior Indent, 4/5208; *Sydney Gazette*, 3 November 1835; Central Criminal Court, Sydney, 8 December 1835, AO.

AARONS, Aaron (see ANDERSON, John Henry and James Henri (Aaron) Anderson)

AARONS, Hyam (Hiam)

b. London, 1801
Guildford (7), 1827; Convict; Sentenced to life, Surrey, 1826.
Single; Furrier and cap-maker; Height: 163 cm; 1 child.

'Jew.' Sallow pock-pitted face, dark brown hair, black or very dark brown whiskers, small eyes. Could read. 'HBH' tattooed on right arm.

Aarons arrived in New South Wales on 25 July 1827 and was assigned to G. Townsend Trevellyn. 'Higham Aaron' appears in the Newcastle Magistrates' Book on 8 May 1828. He already held a ticket of leave and was found in Newcastle without a pass. He was reprimanded and discharged from custody. He was listed in the 1828 Census as a 'Protestant' working on Road Party no. 20. Aarons was convicted with Lewis Lazarus (q.v.) in Sydney. He was described at the Hyde Park Barracks as a 'troublesome character. Disobedient. Abusive language'. After ten days on the treadmill he was to be sent to a distant road party. He was admitted to the *Phoenix* hulk on 3 September 1833 from Sydney Gaol, to serve a twelvemonth sentence in the iron gang, but was returned to the Hyde Park Barracks on 29 June 1834 after having absconded from custody. The General Muster of 1837 listed him as an assigned convict servant of James Bloodworth of Cassilis.

Aarons received his ticket of leave on 29 May 1839. Hiam Aarons received permission to marry Jean Taylor (aged twenty-seven), who had come on the *George Hibbert* (sentenced to fourteen years). Both held tickets of leave when they were married at Bathurst by the Rev. Smythe on 24 April 1841. They had a child, John, in 1842, whose birth was registered at the Presbyterian Church, in Bathurst. A conditional pardon was issued in the District of Bathurst in June 1846.

Guildford Indent 4/6282, no. 738; TL 39/1008; Permission to Marry Book, 1841, p. 226, 4/4513; ML A1241, p. 141; *Phoenix* (hulk) Entrance Book, 4/6282, no. 738; *Hyde Park Barracks Index*, X825, 8 March 1833.

AARONS, (AARON) JOSEPH jnr

Mary, 1823, Free.

The English born son of Joseph and Rachel Aarons (qq.v.) who arrived with his mother and sisters on the *Mary* at the age of two. On the 1828 census he is listed as Joseph Aarons aged 7. He flourished in the colony and, as an adult, went on to become an extremely successful pastoralist and the mayor of the rural town of Wellington. He died in 1904 leaving a widow and eight children.

Family information from Bronwyn Russell.

AARONS, Isaac

Hashemy, 1839; Free.
Married; 2 children.

Isaac Aarons arrived in Port Jackson on 25 January 1839, from London, with his wife, son and daughter. They were recorded as having travelled 'Cabin Class'. They may not have been Jewish.

Hashemy Indent, ML 4/5214.

AARONS, Joseph

b. Germany, 1763
Fortune (2), 1813; Convict; Sentenced to 14 years, Old Bailey, 1811.
Pedlar; Height: 155 cm.

Dark sallow complexion. Black hair. Eyes dark (sore eyes). Aarons was seen acting suspiciously at St Paul's Old Churchyard when a stolen bundle of silver 'cuttings' was handed over to him by a thief. Aarons was heard to say: 'There is someone watching us. Give me the bundle'. When he failed to elude his pursuer, he dropped the bundle in the street. Eight character witnesses were called before the verdict was delivered.

Aarons arrived in Sydney on 11 June 1813. He was fifty years old. The captain of the *Fortune* placed a notice in the *Sydney Gazette* on 23 October 1813 telling him that he had forgotten to pick up some money entrusted to the captain at the beginning of the voyage. Aarons, however, was ill and a patient in the Sydney General Hospital. He was granted a ticket of leave.

OBSP, 1811 case 207, p. 129; HO 10/1; CO 207/1; *Sydney Gazette*, 23 October 1813; TL no. 1046.

AARONS, Joseph

b. Holland, 1787–1865
Princess Royal (1), 1823; Convict; Sentenced to life, Old Bailey, 1821.
Married; Shopkeeper; Height: 163 cm; 12 children.

Brown pock-pitted complexion, brown hair and brown eyes. Sentenced, together with his wife, on 12 September 1821. They had attempted to steal cloth from a London warehouse. While Joseph pretended to look at some cloth displayed for sale, Rachel (q.v.), who was pregnant, attempted to hide 18 yards of cloth (worth £18) under her skirt. She was caught while leaving the warehouse when she accidentally dropped the cloth.

Both spoke very little English. Joseph defended himself (through an interpreter), saying: 'What my wife did I know nothing about. I am a merchant. The prosecutors did not see my wife take it any more than I did. I gave her two slaps on the bonnet for doing it.' Rachel declared: 'What I did was unknown to my husband'. The story 'seems true' but both were transported for life. Joseph and Rachel (née Schlesinger) had married in Hamburg in 1813.

Joseph Aarons arrived in New South Wales on 11 March 1823 and was assigned to the Jewish emancipist Joseph Raphael (q.v.). He claimed to have worked for him with 'diligence and care and honesty', in his application to be with his own family. Aarons was told to take his wife Rachel (q.v.) and four children to Emu Plains. Aarons wrote again (20 January 1824): 'Joseph Raphael makes [me] work from sunrise to sunset which severity obliges your petitioner's wife and helpless offspring to become burthens on the generosity of a humane public'. His wife, he reported, was obliged to become 'a common washerwoman. Recently received a remittance from his friends in England which will enable him to support his family independent'. Aarons was told that if he was to complain again, his wife would be sent to the Female Factory. However, he was given permission to work for himself.

In the *Sydney Gazette* of 7 October 1826 he advertised that he would pay a reward for the return of a pocket book lost on a road near Windsor and which contained four promissory notes.

By February 1827 Aarons owned a shop at 70 George Street and advertised that he sold 'piece goods', and 'Gents and Ladies' Stockings'. By 1828 he was also acting as an agent for the ship *Monitor*, which traded between Sydney and Newcastle. Aarons wrote a new petition to the Governor asking for a conditional pardon on 5 November 1827, stating that he had six children and that he worked 'in the best honest manner he could with many contracts in Local Government very large dealings with merchants'. A conditional pardon was granted on 27 May 1828.

Aarons and his family were listed in the General Muster of New South Wales of November 1828 and in the official list of convicts in the colony. He was described as a 'dealer'. Aarons was granted a pass permitting him to extend his business to the Hunter River and asked for permission to proceed from Sydney to Newcastle for the purpose of disposing of goods.

In a note addressed to the editor of the *Sydney Gazette* on 18 August 1828, a subscriber wrote: 'that at a distance of 100 miles from the capital 80 roods have been sold for £60 sterling … an honest Israelite yclept Joseph Aarons has commenced building a large brick store at Wallis Plains … We know of no one more industrious in his attention to "Advance Australia" … we can only wish him success'. At the end of the year Aarons became the owner of the Emu Inn at the corner of George and Bathurst streets in Sydney. A publican's licence was granted in July 1830. He faced near bankruptcy when a severe hail storm damaged his inn and its furniture on 13 January 1829, but he recovered and the hotel's licence was renewed until 1834.

The *Australian* of 16 October 1829 recorded that: 'On Tuesday last the rite of circumcision was performed for the second time in this colony. An infant boy of Mr Joseph Aarons, dealer of George St, was the subject of this antient rite. Mr Michael Hyam [q.v.] performed the office of High Priest'.

George Yeomans of Wallis Plains (near Newcastle) appointed Aarons his agent. It was noted that 'Aarons has a quantity of solid Pork' (*Sydney Gazette*, 9 June 1828). Aarons received a rare absolute pardon in 1838. He then sold his house in York Street and travelled with his wife and two children to England, returning to Australia in 1839. That year, Joseph Aarons and family gave £85 to the Sydney Synagogue building appeal. Aarons was a member of the synagogue committee in 1839.

Joseph Aarons 'of Pitt St' was declared insolvent on 30 March 1842, with debts of £3678 and assets of £319. He was discharged from bankruptcy on 8 March 1844, and was listed in the first Sydney municipal election voters' list with a dwelling house in Castlereagh Street. In 1845 Rachel Aarons was sentenced to two years in prison for larceny from Isaac Levey (q.v.), and Joseph was convicted of receiving stolen property and sent to prison for one year. On 16 June 1846, their daughter, Mrs Hannah Moses, received a reply to her appeal to the government to have mercy on her parents. (Hannah had married Isaac Moses [q.v.] at Yass on 28 February 1839.)

Joseph Aarons died in Sydney on 4 December 1865 and was buried at the Devonshire Street cemetery. His wife Rachel died on 20 July 1866. Their son, Isaac Aarons, arranged for the graves to be moved to Rookwood in 1901. Joseph was survived by three sons (Joseph (born in London in 1821), Henry and Isaac) and five daughters, Rosina, Sarah, Rebecca, Louisa and Hannah. His Australian-born children were Sarah (1826 at Sydney), Rebecca (1828), Henry (1829), Isaac (1831), Louisa (1834).

OBSP, 1820–21, case 1123, p. 444; *Princess Royal* Indent 4/4004, p. 459; Petition to Governor Brisbane, 20 October 1823, 4/1872; CS, petition 4/3549, p. 102, 4/3550, p. 87, 4/3692, p. 14, and 4/4432, p. 29; *Sydney Morning Herald*, 6 January 1845, 8 March 1846; *Sydney Record*, 16 March 1844; *Morning Chronicle*, 3 May 1845; G. F. J. Bergman, 'Joseph Aarons Snr', *AJJHS*, vol. 7, no. 3 (1972), pp. 234–5; CS, 30 March 1827, 4/1927; Free Pardon 015; ML A1270, p. 259; HO 10/28; *AG*, pp. 141, 153, 168, 183. Family information from Bronwyn Russell.

AARONS, Rachel (Rachael SCHLESINGER)

b. Hamburg, 1790–1866
Mary, 1823; Convict; Sentenced to life, Old Bailey, 1822.
Married; Shopkeeper; Height: 160 cm; 12 children.

Florid, freckled and pock-pitted complexion. Light brown hair, hazel grey eyes. Rachel Aarons was sentenced to transportation twice. The first trial was in company with her husband, Joseph Aarons (q.v.), at the Old Bailey for stealing 18 yards of woollen cloth valued at £15. The second trial was at the Lancaster Quarter Sessions held at Manchester on 21 October 1822, where she was convicted of stealing five dresses and sixty silk handkerchiefs.

The convict ship *Mary* arrived on 5 October 1823. Rachel and her 'four small children', Rachel (aged seven), Rosina (five), Hannah (four), and Aaron Joseph (two), were sent to the Female Factory in Parramatta. Her husband wrote to her that he 'arrived in the colony eight months previously under sentence of transportation for life and is off the stores a fortnight ago' (letter, dated 17 November 1823). On 26 April 1824 Rachel petitioned the Colonial Secretary that her husband

Joseph be assigned into her custody. Joseph Aarons prospered, and by 1828 was the owner of the Emu Inn at the corner of Bathurst and George streets in Sydney. In that year Rachel Aarons, owner of a small vessel employed in the colonial trade, assaulted a former captain who owed her money. Rachel was granted a ticket of leave in 1828 and a certificate of freedom in 1830.

In 1837 Rachel petitioned to 'support and adopt the illegitimate female child of Mary Ann Downs, a Convict per the *Elizabeth* who died in the Parramatta Factory and is now in the Female Orphan School. The Police Magistrate testified that Rachael Aarons was very decently well conducted', and the chaplain wrote that Rachel had been baptised in the Christian faith.

In March 1845 Rachel Aarons was sentenced to two years in the Female Factory for stealing goods from Isaac Levey (q.v.), who suspected that she had stolen about £500 worth of goods over a long period of time. Her daughter Hannah petitioned for her release from Parramatta Gaol, claiming her mother was in bad health. The Colonial Secretary replied to Mrs Hannah Moses saying that the government could not interfere. Hannah wrote again on 22 September 1846 and the rest of the sentence was remitted. Rachel was listed in the Female Factory at Parramatta on 11 November 1847.

Despite her obviously expedient conversion, Rachel Aarons was buried in Sydney at Lidcombe as a Jew on 24 July 1866.

Ship Indent 4/4009, p. 94; 4/4303; 4/3692; CF 30/730, dated 27/10/1830; *Sydney Gazette*, 23 April 1827; *Atlas* (Sydney), 8 February 1845; G. F. J. Bergman, 'Joseph Aarons Snr', *AJJHS*, vol. 7, no. 3 (1972), pp. 234–5; CS, 37/11645, in 4/2361.1; *AG*, pp. 153, 168.

ABRAHAM, Elizabeth

Baring, 1815; Convict; Sentenced to 7 years, 1814.
Single; 1 child.

Elizabeth Abraham arrived in New South Wales on 7 September 1815. She was listed in the 1828 Census as Jewish and with her de facto name 'Elizabeth Stephens'. Her child, Robert, was born in 1823 and in September 1826 was admitted into the Orphan Institute. His mother was listed then as 'Elizabeth Abraham'.

Male Orphan Admission Book, vol. 2, 4/352; 2/8243 p. 163.

ABRAHAM, Isaac (ABRAHAMS, Abraham DAVIS, Abraham DAVIES)

b. Maidstone, 1798
Earl St Vincent, 1826; Convict; Sentenced to 7 years, Old Bailey, 1825.
Married; Musician; 1 child.

Dark brown hair. Dark brown eyes. Behaviour on the hulk 'indifferent'. Abraham had appeared at the Middlesex Sessions and was convicted of fraud for going to Rachel Lazarus and undertaking upon receipt of £5 to provide bail for her son who had been imprisoned for passing counterfeit coins and who would not be 'enlarged' until he found security for his future good conduct. He was sentenced for 'defrauding the unfortunate'.

On 15 August 1826, when the *Earl St Vincent* was off Hobart Town, Isaac Abrahams, Abraham Davies and six others cut their iron chains and attempted to escape. They were deemed to be 'men of depraved minds and not to be trusted amid the multitude' and Abrahams (aka Davis) was transferred to Norfolk Island and then sent on to Van Diemen's Land.

His record shows a long series of minor breaches of discipline with a total of twenty-two days on the treadmill. On 5 November 1827 he was caught at the Ship's Inn public house at a quarter past eight and was reprimanded. On 31 December 1827 he was absent from his master's premises all night without leave and sent to the Prisoners' Barracks. He was absent from the muster at the barracks and sent to the treadwheel for two days. On 10 April he was returned to the treadmill for three days for being absent from the barracks without leave. On 12 April 1828 he was found with a pair of scissors, which he had for the purpose of cutting hair, and was sent back to the treadmill for seven days. On 17 May he was caught taking a loaf of bread to his fellow prisoners on the treadmill and was reprimanded. On 12 December 1831, Abraham absconded from the service of G. C. Clark Esq. and a reward of £2 was offered. He was apprehended the following week and his sentence was extended by six months.

Abrahams received a certificate of freedom on 8 March 1833 and opened a boarding house. On 3 October 1834 he allowed two convicts to remain on his premises and was fined £5. On 30 November an 'Isaac Abraham' was fined £10 for having an escaped female convict in his lodging house in Launceston. He was said to have run the lodging house for several years. The woman was only in the house for 'a few moments' when discovered by the Chief Constable. Abrahams had 'suffered great losses through the expense of a death in the family' and asked, through a petition, for a remission of his fine. This was refused because 'The character of this individual is very bad'. On 14 May 1841 Abrahams was fined £25 for a breach of the Publicans Act.

Isaac Abrahams had married Bridget Green in Launceston in 1840 and they had a child, Isaac, in 1842. Abrahams was listed on the petition for the Launceston Synagogue of 20 May 1843.

Bell's Life, 25 September 1825; ML, A1059–2, pp. 5, 11; CON 31/1, A226, CON 70/1; Launceston Police Book, p. 13; CSO 5/160/3186–8; *Hobart Town Courier*, 10 December 1831, 11 August 1837.

ABRAHAM, Leon (ABRAHAMS)

Free.

Leon and Mary Abraham(s) were recorded as having three children in New South Wales in the second half of the 1840s. They were Samuel (1845), Mary (1850) and Leon (1848).

ABRAHAM, Levi (ABRAHAMS, Levy ABRAHAMS)

b. Leghorn, Italy, 1784
Morley (1), 1817; Convict; Sentenced to life, London, 1816.
Married; Cook; Height: 157 cm; 1 child.

Dark complexion, dark hair, hazel eyes. Edward Briant, William Foreman and Levi Abrahams broke into a house about half a mile from Whitechapel, and stole goods worth £13. Levi was arrested with Esther Jonas, his sister-in-law, and Sarah Levi, his daughter, aged sixteen. They were busy picking out the linen markings when the police arrested them. Among the linen was other stolen property. Abrahams and Esther Jonas were sentenced to death (later commuted to life) and Sarah Levi to fourteen years transportation. They were sentenced on 3 April 1816. He may have arrived on the Shipley.

Levy Abrahams was listed in the General Muster of New South Wales in 1818 as a 'Settler's Man'. In 1820 Levi Abraham, a government servant assigned to Mr Jacob Josephson (q.v), jeweller, was a witness in a trial and deposed that the prisoner William Smith had brought in various articles of jewellery, which Josephson suspected had been stolen. The following year Abraham was listed as being at large with a false ticket-of-leave certificate. He was described as 'Manservant to Mr [Jacob] Josephson'. On 13 January 1821 the *Sydney Gazette* announced that he had escaped from prison and presumably from New South Wales.

OBSP, 1816, case 288, p. 169 (10 March 1816); Ship Indent 4/4005; HO 10/1; CO 207/1, no. 263.1; *Sydney Gazette*, 25 November 1820, 13 January 1821.

ABRAHAM, Phoebe

Duke of Roxburgh, 1849; Free.
Married; 4 children.

Phoebe was the wife of Samuel Abraham (q.v.), who arrived in the same ship.

Letter Book of the Sydney Synagogue.

ABRAHAM, Samuel

b. Poland, 1807–1849
Duke of Roxburgh, 1849; Free.
Married; Dealer; 4 children.

Samuel Abraham, an assisted immigrant and described as a "dealer and farm labourer" arrived with his wife Phoebe (q.v.), forty-three, and children Alfred, eighteen, Matilda, seventeen, Robert, nine, and Esther, six, on the *Duke of Roxburgh*. Samuel Abraham was buried as a Jew at the Devonshire Street Jewish Cemetery. A few months after his arrival it was noted that he had been a member of Sydney's York Street Synagogue.

First Letter Book of the Sydney Synagogue.

ABRAHAM, Solomon

Free.
Married; 1 child.

A son, Benjamin Joseph Abraham, was born to Solomon and his wife, Rosa, in Hobart Town on 27 February 1834, and was registered as a Jew.

ABRAHAMS, Aaron (John ABRAHAM)

b. London, 1808
Midas (2), 1827; Convict; Sentenced to 7 years, Hick's Hall (London), 1826.
Single; Dealer; Height: 175.5 cm.

'A Jew.' Ruddy, pock-pitted complexion, dark brown hair, dark hazel eyes. Small scar on forehead and cut on outside left hand. No education. Transported for stealing handkerchiefs. This was not his first offence. In 1824, at the age of nineteen, he had been convicted at the Old Bailey for having stolen a watch.

The *Midas* arrived in Port Jackson on 15 February 1827. In the 1828 Census, Aaron Abrahams was listed as 'no religion' and a member of the no. 6 Iron Gang. He was assigned to M. H. Redfern, a settler in Campbellfield, Airds. In 1832, Aaron Abrahams, a 'dealer', was assigned to Henry Abrahams (q.v.) in Sydney. A certificate of freedom was issued on 18 February 1833 and Abrahams returned to England in 1837.

OBSP. 7 April 1824, case 650. Sydney Gazette, 14 June 1832; Ship Indent 4/4012, p. 52; CF, 4/4314–33/93.

ABRAHAMS, Abraham

b. London, 1761
Ganges, 1797; Convict; Sentenced to life, London, 1795.
Married; Watchmaker; Height: 163 cm; 2 children.

Ruddy and pockmarked complexion. Dark brown to grey hair and bald. Brown eyes. Abrahams was observed 'lurking outside a shop' in a district where robberies had taken place. Some shop assistants set a trap leaving some material in easy reach and Abrahams stole a bolt of linen worth sixteen shillings. In his own defence, Abrahams said 'I have got two witnesses. I have got nothing but a wife and two children'. He was sentenced to death at the Old Bailey Sessions of 16 July 1795, and this was later commuted to transportation for life.

Abrahams was granted a conditional pardon by Governor King on 11 June 1803. In the Muster of 1806 he was listed as in the employment of Joseph Smallsalts, and 'free by servitude'. He then received permission to work as a whaler in Bass Strait and King Island, which he did from 1808 to 1810. His name was then crossed off the list of those with a permit to sail with the whalers. Abrahams was listed in the 1811 General Muster. In the General Muster of 1814 he appeared as a 'constable' in Sydney and as 'Free' and on government rations. The *Sydney Gazette* reported on 11 March 1815 that he had been dismissed as a constable at Sydney. In the 1818 Muster of the Colony, Abrahams was listed as a 'labourer'.

Abrahams received a conditional pardon on 26 September 1823 and it is noted in the General Muster List for 1825 that he was a 'waterman' working in Sydney. On 15 July 1826 Abrahams applied for a land grant, but was refused. In the 1828 Census of New South Wales he was listed as seventy-seven years old and a resident of Sydney.

OBSP, 1794–95, case 337, p. 735; Ship Indent CO 207.1; HO 11/1; *Sydney Gazette*, 19 June 1803, 9 September 1810; Proceedings of the Bench of Magistrates, 1808–1810, 1/301, 9 October 1810; Land Correspondence. ML A1942/2, p. 172, 2/7787; CS reel 6038, SZ 759, p. 49; *Sydney Gazette*, 19 June 1803, 5 May 1810.

ABRAHAMS, Abraham

b. London, 1790
Recovery, 1836; Convict; Sentenced to 7 years, Central Criminal Court, 1835.
Dealer; Height: 163 cm.

Can read and write. Dark sallow complexion. Dark brown and grey hair. Brown eyes. Roman nose. Small mole on left cheek. Convicted in London, 6 April 1835, for 'false pretences'.

The *Recovery* arrived in Sydney Harbour on 25 February 1836. In the *Phoenix* (hulk) Entrance Book Abrahams was described as a 'Jew' who was transferred from the Hyde Park Barracks and sent to Port Macquarie on 21 March 1836. He was listed in the Muster of 1837 as working for the government at Port Macquarie. Abrahams paid five shillings to be registered as a Jew in the Sydney Synagogue in July 1839. Abraham Abrahams received a ticket of leave in 1840 for the district of Port Macquarie, which was altered for Maitland on 25 June 1840.

A certificate of freedom was issued by a clerical error on 13 April 1842 and his ticket of leave was cancelled for absence from the district in September. On 1 March 1842 he was ordered to work on the road gang.

Recovery Printed Indent, p. 45; *Phoenix* (hulk) Entrance Book, 4/6286, p. 81; 4/4139; TL 40/983, in 4/4139; CF 4/4373–42/0572; Sydney Synagogue Minute Book, 3 July 1839; *Sydney Morning Herald*, 5 September 1842.

ABRAHAMS, Abraham

b. London, 1800–1827
Lady Castlereagh, 1821; Convict; Sentenced to 7 years, London, 1817.
Single; Carter–dealer in metals; Height: 163 cm.

Blue eyes, flaxen hair, fair pale complexion. A Jew. Abraham Abrahams and George Nichols were convicted for stealing two pairs of boots valued at £3 each. The police, acting on information received, surprised the pair in a house in Black Lion Court dividing up a bundle of stolen clothes, scissors and boots. Abrahams was seventeen years old and Nichols was twenty-one.

Abrahams was sent out to New South Wales in April 1818 and then transferred to Van Diemen's Land. On 7 July 1821 he was charged with sheep stealing, his ticket of leave was forfeited and he was returned to government service.

On 16 October 1824 he was fined five shillings for swearing a profane oath while under examination before the Superintendent of Police. He was granted a certificate of freedom in 1824. Abrahams worked as the stock keeper for Mr Livermore and was sentenced to death at the Criminal Court in Launceston on 25 October 1827, for the very serious offence of 'horse stealing' and 'diverse other felonies'. He had hidden a mare valued at £20, belonging to Thomas Gourley, a Clyde settler. The mare was found in the hills opposite Sorrel Creek. 'When the awful sentence of death was passed Abrahams prayed earnestly for a mercy.' He was executed in Hobart Town, three weeks after the verdict was delivered, on 15 November 1827.

OBSP, case 651, p. 242; HO 10/1; CON 31/1, p. 79, no. 30; NS 742/25, p. 19, Col. 2, AOT; *Hobart Town Gazette*, 14 May 1824; *Hobart Town Courier*, 25 October 1827, 3 November 1827; Anne McKay, *Journals of the Land Commissioners for Van Diemen's Land 1826–28*.

ABRAHAMS, Abraham

b. London, 1797–1865
Caroline, 1839;
Free. Married; Dealer; 9 children.

Son of Meir Abrahams of Goodmanfields of London. He married Elizabeth Jacobs (q.v.) and they had nine children: Fanny, Joseph, Caroline, Rachael, Sarah, Elina, Malita, Rosa and Adelaide all of whom, with the exception of Fanny, were born in London. Abrahams was a shipping merchant and ship owner. His craft was the brig which was built in Malta in 1831 and where Fanny was born. He, his wife Elizabeth and all nine children came to Sydney on the *Caroline*, arriving on 28 May 1839. Abrahams was recorded as giving £55 to the Sydney Synagogue building fund in the names of himself, his wife, Sarah, and his children, Caroline (q.v.), Rachael (q.v.), and 'Mr J(oseph) Abrahams', in 1844. Rachel married Phillip (van) Millingen (q.v.) at the Sydney Synagogue on 15 November 1843. She was fifteen years old and Phillip had been a passenger aboard the *Caroline* when it arrived in Melbourne in 1840. In October 1853 Abrahams was recorded as buying land in Coogee and Randwick.

Abraham Abrahams was in Melbourne by 1841, and was described as a 'merchant' of Lonsdale Street when he donated the ground for the first Jewish burial site at Merri Creek. In September that year, Abraham Abrahams, 'merchant', was admitted to the Chamber of Commerce, and became a member of a group of twelve backers (nicknamed the 'Twelve Apostles') who rallied to the aid of W. F. A. Rucker after he had incurred debts to the Union Bank of £10 000. A commercial scam destroyed some of the Apostles, though Abrahams appears to have emerged unscathed and, on 7 March 1842, was appointed Trustee to the Estate of the Langhorne Brothers. His debts at that time amounted to £3792 and his assets to £3655.

Abrahams soon moved to Sydney where, in January 1843, he was listed as 'late of Port Phillip, now of Sydney, merchant, insolvent'. The bankruptcy case appears to have taken some time because three years were to pass before the trustees were authorised to collect £100 of uncollected assets in the Port Phillip District.

As a consequence of his financial problems he was forced to sell the ship *Caroline* and the shipwright's business in William's Town which had been managed by his son Joseph. Abrahams had owned a shop in William's Town in which the town's first Anglican services were held. To the discomfiture of the congregation Abrahams claimed back-rent from the church. The shop had been leased to the church until 1854.

During the greater part of 1847, Abrahams was involved in a long-running court case that involved the purchase of a mansion, Yarra House, for £5000. He had sold it to settle his debts but it was alleged that he still owed some money to his creditors. Abrahams' wife, Elizabeth, died on 6 May 1850, aged fifty-five.

Abrahams re-married in 1860 to Ellen Early. His new wife was considerably younger than he was. They lived in Little Nelson Street in William's Town. There were two children. Abraham Abrahams was born in 1856 and died in 1862 and Sarah who was born that same year. Abraham Abrahams died 18 October 1865 at 246 Victoria Street, Richmond. It is believed that he died at a house owned by his son Joseph, who owned a number of properties in the area.

Family information from Martin Toone of Melbourne. W. P. Evans, *The Port of Many Prows*, Hawthorn Press, Melbourne, 1969, p. 170; L. M. Goldman, *The Jews in Victoria in the Nineteenth Century*, p. 24; *Port Phillip Patriot*, 1 May 1847; *Port Phillip Gazette*, 4 September 1841, 1 March 1842; *Sydney Morning Herald*, 16 September 1842, 26, 31 January 1843, 16 February 1844, 1 January 1846.

ABRAHAMS, Abraham

1814–1851
Free
Single; Dealer; 4 children.

The 27-year-old Abraham Abrahams married the 14-year-old Rachel Hains (q.v.) on 12 September 1841 at 'Sarah Valley', Illawarra. It was a Jewish marriage ceremony performed by Michael Hyam (q.v.). They had four children: Sophia (16 June 1842), Isaac (1844), Hyam (1848, at Paterson, Scone) and Henry (1851, in Sydney).

Abraham Abrahams was a member of the Sydney Synagogue in 1845. He died, aged thirty-seven, on 15 May 1851 and was buried at Bunnerong.

Sydney Morning Herald, 15 September 1842.

ABRAHAMS, Caroline

Caroline, 1839; Free.

Caroline Abrahams married the dentist Jacob Emanuel (q.v.) in Sydney in 1843. Caroline was the daughter of Abraham and Sarah Abrahams (qq.v.).

ABRAHAMS, Catherine

b. London, 1819–1901
1849; Free.
Single.

Catherine Abrahams was thirty years old when she married Emanuel Solomon (q.v.), then fifty-two, at his home, Temple Tavern, Gilles Arcade in Adelaide. She had been in the colony for three years. She was Solomon's third wife. Catherine Solomon died on 2 July 1901 at the age of eighty-two at the residence of her step-daughter, Mrs Joel Moss, of Trinity Street, College Town.

Pritchard Index; Obituary, *South Australian Register*, 4 July 1901.

ABRAHAMS, Charles

b. London, 1823
Free
6 children.

Charles Abrahams married Sarah Phillips, daughter of Emanuel Phillips (q.v.), in a Jewish ceremony in Sydney on 8 August 1849. They had three children, Michael (1850) at Paterson, Scone, Phillip (1851) and Rachel (1853) in Sydney. On 13 January 1853 Abrahams was confined to the Tarban Creek Lunatic Asylum although he did not need to be placed in the Refactory Division. He was still at Tarban Creek in June 1853, when news reached his family that he had inherited property valued at almost £200.

Sarah died at the family home in Riley Street, South Woolloomooloo, on 16 May 1861 at the age of twenty-nine, 'a kind and affectionate wife, faithful and loving daughter'. Abrahams evidently returned to England, where he married his second wife, Julia. He had two more children, Lewis (1864) and Catherine (1866), in Sydney. The family lived at 205 Castlereagh Street (which was the address of Emanuel Phillips).

CS 4/3183, 4/3201–53/5278; Notes from Jeannette Tsoulos (Sydney).

ABRAHAMS, Daniel

Convict.
Single; 1 child.

On 11 March 1809 Daniel Abrahams was charged at the Bench of Magistrates for 'stealing a box of candles, the property of Lieutenant Governor Collins from on board the transport ships' at anchor in Sydney Harbour. On 20 October, James Abrahams, the son of Daniel Abrahams and Mary Carrol, was baptised at St Philip's, Sydney.

Mutch Index; Proceedings of the (Sydney) Bench of Magistrates, SZ770.

ABRAHAMS, Edward

Born 1801.
Lord Lyndoch, 1831; Convict; Sentenced to 7 years, Old Bailey, 1830.
Single.

Edward Abrahams, a groom and coachman, was convicted at the Old Bailey for stealing a greatcoat. Jew. Hulk report 'indifferent'. He was described as being 163 cms tall, with a fresh complexion, large round head, a grey eye (and one eye missing), small sharp nose, pockpitted face and heavily tattooed arms.

Abrahams arrived in Hobart Town (from the Sheerness hulks) on 18 November 1831. On 7 January 1833 Abrahams was working at the Bonded Store, when he was found guilty of 'disgraceful conduct' in his ward and sentenced to a month's hard labour in prison. He was then assigned to work with the Survey Party on the roads. On 20 November 1833, Abrahams was sentenced to thirty lashes for having been in a public house at 10 o'clock at night. In 1834 he was suspected of having stolen the Oatlands Mail Bag. In April 1835 he was absent without leave from the Grass Tree Hill Road Party with a forged pass in his possession, and on 27 May 1835 he was sentenced to twelve months imprisonment and hard labour in the Bridgewater Chain Gang for 'highly improper conduct'. He received a ticket of leave on 14 April 1837.

Edward Abrahams resigned from the police force in September 1838. On 4 January 1839 he was fined five shillings for being drunk. By then Abrahams was in Launceston and was free by servitude.

CON 31/2, no. 470; Launceston Police Book, CON 70/1, p. 43; CON 18/12; CON 18/1/12 p. 245; CON 27/5; *Hobart Town Courier*, 14 April 1837, 28 September 1838.

ABRAHAMS, Emilia (Emelia)

b. London, 1816–1891
Lady Raffles, 1839; Free.
Single; Housemaid; 7 children.

Born in Hackney, to Lewis Abrahams and Rebecca, Emilia was the younger sister of Rachel Abrahams (q.v.). Emilia arrived in Sydney on 12 September 1839. She and her sister pledged £5 each to the Sydney Synagogue building appeal in 1839. Both sisters soon married, Rachel to Solomon Solomon (q.v.) in 1840, and Emilia to Samuel Shannon (q.v.), in the Sydney Synagogue, on 10 February 1841. Emilia spent the rest of her life in the Bunyan, Nimmitabel and Cooma districts. When her husband died in 1868, she became the administrator of the estate and of Shannon's Victoria Hotel in Cooma, until a hired manager took over in 1871. In May 1882 the hotel was sold.

Emilia Shannon died on 19 May 1891, and was buried the next day. In the absence of a rabbi, her Jewish funeral in a 'private cemetery Cooma' in the grounds of 'The Wren's Nest'—the Shannon family home—was conducted by Charles

Solomon JP, the brother of Solomon Solomon. Her estate was valued at £80 and was administered by her son, Eli.

Family notes by John Stanhope.

ABRAHAMS, Esther (JULIAN)

b. London, 1771–1846
Lady Penrhyn, 1788; Convict; Sentenced to 7 years, Old Bailey 1786.
Single; 8 children.

On 27 July 1786, Esther, aged fifteen, took two cards of black silk lace, valued at fifty shillings, from an open box that lay on the counter of a shop. A few seconds after the lace was missed, the shop assistant ran after Esther, who was now in a shop two doors down the street. Esther was accused of the theft. She nervously put her hands under her cloak and the missing lace fell to the floor. The shop assistant said: 'There you wicked devil, you have dropped two cards of lace'. Esther was sentenced at the Old Bailey on 30 August 1786, for shoplifting, for stealing 24 yards of black silk lace.

On 18 March 1787, Esther Abrahams gave birth to a female child, Rosanna (q.v.), within the walls of Newgate Gaol, and, on 3 May, they were sent on the Prince of Wales and subsequently transferred to the *Lady Penryhn*, bound for New South Wales. On board was First Lieutenant George Johnston, aged twenty-three. He formed a liaison with Esther, who became pregnant again. Johnston bought a she-goat at the Cape of Good Hope in order to provide milk for Esther. Their baby was born in Sydney and was baptised as George on 4 March 1790. (The link between Esther and George Johnston on board ship is challenged by Alan Roberts in his historical study of the Johnstons of Annandale. He persuasively argues that their relationship did not begin until the arrival of the First Fleet in January 1788.)

Two days after the birth of the baby George, Johnston and Esther set sail for Norfolk Island with Esther's two children. Johnston's diary records that he embarked from the Cascade with 'Hett and the two children, February 1791'. There is no record that Rosanna was ever baptised. Esther returned to Sydney in May 1791, and in 1792 gave birth to a stillborn girl. In March 1793, her second son, Robert, was born. Robert was given the rare recognition of being Governor Phillips' godson, and would become the first Australian-born officer in the Royal Navy. A third son, David, was born in 1797. Maria was born in 1800 and died in 1827, Julia was born in 1796, Isabella was born in 1804 and died two years later, and Blanche was born in 1806.

Annandale, the family farm in Sydney, was established in 1793 and the house in 1799. Johnston rapidly accumulated considerable wealth and power. He became the commanding officer of the New South Wales Corps in Sydney when Governor William Bligh was deposed and for six months was Lieutenant Governor of the colony. The consequence of this antipodean rebellion was a trial in England in 1811. He was cashiered from the army which brought about a serious loss of status and money. He was fortunate to have escaped the death penalty and he returned to Australia in 1813. In the General Muster of New South Wales of 1811, Esther was listed as 'Esther Julian', reflecting the alias of 'Mrs Julian' she had been using for some years. However, by 1812 the Muster listed her as Esther Abrahams who came on the *Prince of Wales*. Johnston family tradition suggests that George Johnston discovered that 'Mr Julian' was no longer living, and that there was no impediment to his marriage to Esther. In any event, Governor Macquarie was anxious that social proprieties be observed, and Esther became Mrs Johnston in 1814. Present at Esther's wedding was her daughter Rosanna, who was, by then, the wife of the prominent emancipist Isaac Nichols. The marriage licence was granted by Governor Macquarie to George Johnston of Annandale and Mrs Esther Julian 'of the same place'.

Johnston died on 3 January 1823. Esther Johnston was mentioned in the 1828 Census as a 'free settler' in possession of 2000 acres of land and living at the Annandale estate in Petersham with her son Robert, then thirty-five, who owned 430 acres of the land and daughters Julia, thirty-two, and Blanche, twenty-two. Esther was listed as fifty-four years of age, though she was fifty-seven. In 1829 Esther attempted to return to England and advertised that she would mortgage her property. In order to prevent this happening, her son Robert took legal steps to have her declared insane. At the trial a Jewish neighbour, Jacob Isaacs (q.v.), related that Esther had often taken refuge in his home and complained to him about her children. Even though she wasn't declared insane, she was not allowed to mortgage the property. It was noted that she had a handsome annual income of £489. Esther went to live with her son David, who owned a farm bequeathed to him by his father at George's Hall, Johnston's Flat and David's Bank on the George's River. Esther died fifteen years later at George's Hall, on 26 August 1846, and was buried in the family vault at Annandale. Esther's portrait, painted in 1814, is the only existing likeness of any convict who was sent to Australia on the First Fleet.

There are extensive family ramifications to Esther's background and use of different surnames. In 1832, Michael Abrahams (q.v.) migrated to Australia. Following his conviction in a Sydney court, his mother, Mrs Phoebe Abrahams, wrote to the court from London, invoking her son's relationship with her eminent grandson George Robert Nichols as a mitigating factor. It was also noted that a second convict, 'Mary Jones', who arrived in 1825 on the *Grenada* (3), and who had married Barnet Emanuel (q.v.), was a niece of Esther's. Mary Jones became known as Julia Emanuel (q.v.). When her son married for the third time, the marriage document stated that his mother's maiden name was Julia Ann Julien.

OBSP, 1786, vol. 7, part 1, case 664, p. 994; CO 201/202; G. F. J. Bergman, 'Esther Johnston, the Lieutenant-Governor's Wife', *AJJHS*, vol. 6, no. 2, pp. 90–1 (1966); HO 10/5, HO 10/6; Roberts, Alan, *Marine Officer, convict wife. The Johnstons of Annandale.* Annandale Urban Research in association with Barbara Beckett Publishing, 2008, NSW. Family notes from a direct descendant, Calvin Johnston, Victoria; Marea Stenmark, *Sir David Martin*; Geoffrey Lemcke, *Reluctant Rebel: Lt Col. George Johnston*; Morris Forbes, 'Esther Johnston Revisited: Revisionism in her Story', *AJJHS*, vol. 17, no. 2, pp. 137–8 (2004); *AG*, pp. 26–39. James Hugh Donohoe has suggested in *Captain Bligh's Petticoat Mutiny* (2011) that Esther prepared the January petition in 1808 that led to the unseating of Governor Bligh.

ABRAHAMS, Esther

b. London, 1812
Layton, 1833; Free.
Single; Servant.

Arriving as a bounty immigrant on the *Layton*, on 17 December 1833, Esther was employed by Mrs W. Solomons of Hunter Street at six shillings per week. She married Phillip Hart (q.v.) in a Jewish ceremony in Sydney, on 9 May 1834.

Layton Ship Indent, 4/5205; List of women who were employed from the lumberyard, 4/43255.

ABRAHAMS, Esther

b. Sheerness
Mayflower, 1841; Free.

The daughter of Judah Solomon (q.v.) and the wife of Lewis Abrahams (q.v.), Esther came to Van Diemen's Land with Henry Abrahams and his wife Hannah (qq.v.).

CSO 92/6; *Hobart Town Courier*, 26 March 1841.

ABRAHAMS, Frederick

b. London 1804
Countess of Harcourt (1), 1821; Convict; Sentenced to 7 years, Middlesex, 1820.
Single: Height: 155 cm.

Brown hair and brown eyes. Frederick Abrahams stole twenty iron bars from a house about to be demolished and was arrested as he took them into an old-iron shop. The bars were valued at two shillings. He was with a gang of 'boys', who ran away, though Abrahams was apprehended. He was aged sixteen. Gaol Report: not known. Behaviour: orderly. Abrahams stated that his father and mother lived in Whitcomb Street, and that his father was a shoemaker.

Abrahams was assigned to Mr Simpson and charged with neglect of duty and disobedience of orders, for which he was reprimanded. He was free by servitude by 5 April 1828, when he was fined six shillings for being disorderly on the streets. On 8 September 1828 he was fined five shillings for repeating the same offence. It can be assumed that he returned to England, after having completed his sentence.

OBSP, 1819–20, case 1357, p. 655; Ship Indent 2/8254, p. 218; HO 11/4 (Indent); CON 31/1, no. 106.

ABRAHAMS, George

Free.

In late 1848, 'A young man named George Abrahams was charged with creating a disturbance at the Waterloo Inn' in Melbourne. He assaulted the landlord and called him 'a vagabond, scamp and a Sunday School Teacher'! He was bound over to keep the peace at the cost of £5. In 1867, a George Abrahams of Ballarat planted the garden around the goldfields synagogue at the time of its renovation and painted the interior, including a trompe l'oeil of clouds and an unblinking eye above the Ark.

Melbourne Morning Herald, 6 January 1849; L. M. Goldman, *The Jews in Victoria*, p. 215.

ABRAHAMS, George Samuel

b. Whitechapel, 1783–1846
Palmyra, 1846; Convict; Sentenced to 7 years, Central Criminal Court, 1846.
Married; Auctioneer and Brazier; Height: 155 cm; 4 children (in England).

Ruddy complexion, grey hair, grey bushy whiskers, high forehead. Large nose. Bald on top of head. 'A Jew.' George Abrahams had received a stolen scarf knowing it to have been stolen. He was aged sixty-three. It was his first conviction.

On arrival, George Samuel Abrahams was assigned to the work gang at Rocky Hills on 3 September 1846. He died there twenty-six days later.

CON 33/81, no. 18700; HO 11/15.

ABRAHAMS, Hannah

b. Sheerness, 1802–1864
Mayflower, 1841; Free.
Married; 2 children.

Hannah was the daughter of Judah and Esther Solomon (qq.v.). She arrived from London on the *Mayflower* on 26 March 1841, with her children Sarah (q.v.) and Lewis (q.v.) and her husband, Henry Abrahams (q.v.). They sailed steerage class from England.

Four years earlier Hannah Abrahams of London had written to the Colonial Secretary's Office on 26 June 1837. She said that she was writing on behalf of her mother, Mrs Esther Solomon, because her stepfather, Judah Solomon, 'refuses to acknowledge my mother as his wife'. Esther had followed her convict husband to the colonies in 1832. By November 1843, Hannah lived at Liverpool Street in Hobart Town. She was listed as a 'clothier' of Liverpool Street in the 1847 *Hobart Town Directory and General Guide*. Hannah died on 23 April 1864 and was buried in the Harrington Street Jewish cemetery in Hobart.

CSO 92/6. *The Courier*, 30 March 1841.

ABRAHAMS, Henry (ABRAMS)

b. 1759
Alexander, 1788; Convict; Sentenced to life, Chelmsford, Essex, 1785.
Waterman.

Henry Abrahams was convicted on three counts of highway robbery. He was arrested in London and brought back to Chelmsford for trial. While in gaol he informed the authorities of a plot by several other prisoners who had planned to escape. His death sentence was changed to transportation for life to Africa, and he subsequently travelled to Australia on the First Fleet.

In Sydney Cove, Henry Abrahams gave evidence at the Fourth Sitting of the Criminal Court on 26 May 1788, where John Trace was accused of stealing a pound and a half of flour. 'Abrams' said he had been given some by the prisoner. Trace was found guilty and sentenced to 200 lashes on his back with a cat-o'nine-tails. On 6 September 1788 he gave evidence in a case before the magistrates when Elizabeth Kelly and Mary Leary were accused of disturbing the peace. 'James Abram' said the two women were continually abusing each other.

On 23 October 1788 Henry Abrahams gave evidence in the trial of James White, who was charged with abusing an overseer and threatening to beat him. 'Abrams', an overseer of a gang, came upon stakes put across a road as ordered by White. Abrahams ordered them removed. White challenged him. White said he would 'kick Abrams' arse'. He also said Captain Tench would not be pleased if the stakes were pulled up. Abrams said 'Damn and Bougre Captain Tench and Mr Long. I would knock their blocks off'. White was found guilty and was to be reprimanded publicly on the Saturday. On 29 October, Henry Abrams was charged with making use of disrespectful words when speaking of Captain Tench and Lieutenant Long. The captain of his convict ship testified that 'Abrams had kept himself distant from the other convicts and was always very clean. He came out with a single iron'. Lieutenant Kellow said: 'He behaved reasonably well'. Lieutenant Davey said he was 'best and quietest'. On 1 November the Bench found him not guilty, 'suffering that good character to weigh against so contradictory a testimony ... Had there been any clear proof ... he would have met with the severest punishment'.

Abrahams was sent to Norfolk Island on the *Supply* on 14 February 1789. He was listed as Convict No.12 in the Norfolk Island Victualling Book. By 1 July 1791 he was maintaining himself, and sold quantities of pork to the commissariat. He was still on Norfolk Island in 1796, after which he appears to have returned to England.

ML A1147; 1/296, Magistrates Records, pp. 242–3; HO 10/6; M. Gillen, *The Founders of Australia*, pp. 2–3; *Norfolk Island Victualling Book*, King's Papers C189, pp. 61, 62, 65. *AG*, pp. 19–21.

ABRAHAMS, Henry (Hymie)

b. Westminster, 1780
Batavia, 1818; Convict; Sentenced to 14 years, Middlesex, 1817.
Married; Labourer; Height: 165 cm.

Sallow complexion, dark brown hair, dark eyes. The letters 'HAR' tattooed on right arm and a small anchor and a mermaid on left arm. Hymie Abrahams was convicted of receiving a stolen watch. He swore that he was not home when the goods were delivered. He had a wife and a servant at home both of whom were mentioned in court. The accused claimed that he was 'in Whitechapel' at the time.

On 14 April 1818, after disembarking in Sydney, Henry Abrahams was sent to Windsor, where he worked as an assigned convict servant. He was granted a ticket of leave on 7 November 1822, and this was renewed in 1827. Henry Abrahams appeared in the List of Convicts in New South Wales in November 1828. He was described as a Jew and a dealer who lived in Sydney. Abrahams married Eliza Brown, aged twenty-six, at St John's at Parramatta, with the Rev. Samuel Marsden officiating, in 1828.

On 21 July 1830 Abrahams asked for a ticket of leave for the district of Sydney. He lived in George Street and said that he was frequently required to go to Parramatta where, at times, he held auctions in his capacity as a general dealer. He wrote that he would have served his sentence time in May 1831. The request was refused by the Colonial Secretary; however, a certificate of freedom was issued on 23 May 1831, when his trade was listed as 'pedlar'. In 1831 he owned the coach that ran between Sydney and Parramatta. Abrahams had obviously made some money because by the end of that year he had become the publican of the Jews' Harp Hotel in Upper George Street. In 1833 his licence was transferred from the Jew's Harp to the Fox and Hounds Hotel at the corner of King and Elizabeth streets.

In June 1838 he attempted to move once again, and requested the publican's licence for the Royal Waterman in Sussex Street. His application was rejected. On 21 April 1842, 'Hymie Abrahams signed a petition to the government complaining about the state of the road from Windsor to Parramatta. Henry Abrahams had a house in Sussex Street, according to the *Sydney Morning Herald* of 17 September 1842, and the *Registry of Flash Men* alleged that it was a 'disorderly house', where men could purchase a dance with a woman for fifteen pence a turn.

In 1845 Abrahams gave £5 to the Sydney Synagogue appeal, even though he was not a seat holder.

OBSP, 1816–18, case 315, p. 312; Ship Indent and TL 4/4063, 4/3498, p. 152; Petition for CF, CS 30/5876; CF 31/500; *Sydney Gazette*, 29 April 1824, 3 October 1833, 28 June 1838; HO 10/28; *Commercial Journal and Advertiser*, 10 June 1838; W. A. Miles, *Registry of Flash Men*, p. 69, 2/673.

ABRAHAMS, Henry

b. London 1794
Somersetshire, 1814; Convict; Sentenced to life, Old Bailey, 1813.
Single; Shoemaker.

Dark complexion, black hair. Brown eyes. The 19-year-old Henry Abrahams and the 21-year-old Barnett Levy (q.v.) violently assaulted and robbed a passerby, who instantly recognised them because they had grown up opposite his bakery in Houndsditch. The witness said that he knew that for the previous three or four years they had been reputed thieves.

Henry Abrahams was listed on the General Muster of New South Wales in 1818 as a government labourer. A ticket of leave was granted on 29 April 1824, and renewed in 1833. Henry Abrahams had a shop in Sydney during the 1820s, and Aaron Abrahams (q.v.) was assigned to work for him in 1832.

OBSP, 1813, case 861, p. 463; Ship Indent 4/4005, p. 19; *Sydney Gazette*, 29 April 1824; TL 33/547.

ABRAHAMS, Henry

d. 1842
Mayflower, 1841; Free.
Married; Dealer.

Henry Abrahams and his wife Alice arrived on the *Mayflower*, steerage class, from London on 26 March 1841. He was the brother of Isaac (Israel) Abrahams (q.v.). Henry gave £2 to the Launceston Synagogue building appeal in June 1842 and five shillings to the Hobart Synagogue for S(amuel) Levy 'of Launceston', 4 October 1842. In 1844 Alice Abrahams married Morris Whyle (q.v.).

CSO 92/6; Launceston Synagogue Petition, CO 280/157; *Launceston Examiner*, 29 June 1844.

ABRAHAMS, Hyam (Henry)

b. Colchester, 1802
Governor Ready, 1827; Convict; Sentenced to life, Old Bailey, 1826.
Single; Labourer; Height: 160 cm.

'Henry' Abrahams was indicted at the Old Bailey on 26 October 1826 for breaking and entering a house in Stepney at seven in the evening and ransacking the home of a couple while they were at church. Abrahams stole six silver tablespoons valued at twelve shillings and a variety of household items. The victim knew Abrahams' widowed mother who was 'very respectable' and the accused had been in his house a number of times. Abrahams was sentenced to death but recommended for mercy by the prosecutor. He had been in gaol before.

'Jewish countenance.' Heavily tattooed: with two sprigs, WM, scar above elbow point, mermaid, two fishes, HM, AL, LA, NY, LE, NH and 'without hope man is nothing' on lower left arm. A tattooed bird between finger and thumb on left hand, with right hand 'Home Sweet Home be it ever so lowly'. A mermaid, man and woman and hearts tattooed on right arm. Scar running from outer corner of left eye under the eye. Pockmark centre of left cheek.

Hyam Abrahams arrived in Hobart Town on 2 August 1827. His colonial convict record begins 25 July 1828 when he was 'found at a Public House about 5 o'clock with intent to commit a felony and threatening to stick a knife into James Patterson.' He was sentenced to three months in gaol and fourteen days on the treadwheel. On 21 October 1818 he was found outside the Barracks. He was sentenced to work in irons and three days on the treadwheel. On 18 March 1829 he was found to be in the bakehouse of the Prisoner's Barracks and sentenced to twelve lashes and hard labour in the chain gang. On 28 April 1829 he was caught stealing a loaf of bread and also having a number of loaves in his possession and given three years hard labour to be worked in irons. On 20 March 1830 he absconded from the chain gang and was given fifty lashes and sentenced to be sent to Macquarie Harbour for three years.

By 31 December 1833, while assigned to Mr Hobbs, he absconded and was sentenced to four months imprisonment with the Hulk Chain Gang. On 5 March 1834 Abrahams was sentenced for 'forcibly breaking out of H. M. Gaol in Bothwell'.

He was transferred to the Oatlands Gaol from which he attempted to escape and on 14 May 1834 he was sentenced to one hundred lashes. Later that year he was sent to the prison at Port Arthur. There he became a 'trusty' and, in April 1838, was officially loaned to Commander Fletcher as an assigned servant. On 1 June 1838 he was issued with a ticket of leave. This was suspended on 11 June 1841 and he was told to leave Hobart Town and given two months hard labour for 'not leaving town according to the conditions of his Pass'. He was sent to the Bridge Party in New Norfolk and then to Richmond, where in June 1841 his ticket of leave was restored. His final police dossier entry was for 17 February 1845, when a fine of five shillings was imposed for being drunk. At that time he still held his ticket of leave.

Later in 1845 Abrahams was granted a conditional pardon. The official recommendation stated that he had spent seventeen and a quarter years in the colony and six and a half years with a ticket of leave: 'His behaviour having shown his fitness for a conditional pardon'. The pardon was approved 26 February 1846.

OBSP 26 October 1826. CON 32/1, no. 680; CON 23/1, no. 245; HO 10/59.

ABRAHAMS, Isaac (Israel)

b. Maidstone
Earl St Vincent, 1826; Convict; Sentenced to 7 years, Middlesex, 1825.
Musician; Height: 166.5 cm.

The brother of Henry Abrahams (q.v.). Described as a musician, and 'used to clean clothes and hats'. 'Has been at sea.' Had a scar on his forehead over left eyebrow and another on his left arm. Isaac Abrahams was sentenced on 12 September 1825 at the Middlesex Sessions.

Isaac Abrahams arrived in Hobart Town on 13 August 1826. He was granted a free certificate, no. 212, on 1 May 1835. 'Isaac Abrahams of Launceston, a labourer', was listed as a supporter of the petition for a memorial of Henry Davis (q.v.), written on 24 October 1836, which would utilise a block of land at Cataract Hill for a Jewish cemetery. Abrahams appeared on the Launceston Synagogue petition as 'Israel Abrahams' on 20 May 1843.

CON 31/1; CON 23/1, no. 226; MM 33/1; CO 280/157.

ABRAHAMS, Jacob

b. London, 1778
Royal Admiral I (2), 1800; Convict; Sentenced to 7 years, London, 1799.
Labourer.

Abrahams stole raw sugar, valued at two shillings, from a broken hogshead at the wharves as he was unloading it. He attempted to hide the sugar in his hat. He was sentenced at the London Gaol Delivery in October 1799.

When his sentence ended Abrahams received permission to leave New South Wales on the *Argo* in December 1806.

OBSP, 1798–99, case 543, p. 612; *Sydney Gazette*, 28 November 1806; CSO 5/160, 3816–18.

ABRAHAMS, Jacob (Robert JONES, Robert COX)

b. London, 1773
Royal Admiral I (1), 1792; Convict; Sentenced to 7 years, Old Bailey, 1792.

Jacob Abrahams, alias Robert Jones, alias Robert Cox, was sentenced at the Old Bailey on 23 February 1792 for the theft of a gown and a petticoat and using a knife against his captor. His female associate was fined one shilling and given a year in gaol.

Abrahams arrived in Port Jackson on 7 October 1792. He became the notorious Norfolk Island gaoler under the name of Robert Jones, and wrote an account of the regime of Lieutenant Colonel Joseph Foveaux. The Irish political exile Joseph Holt wrote: 'This Bob Jones, his brothers and himself was concerned in many robberies and a reward was offered and this wretch went and prosecuted the father and two brothers and all three died and he was transported under the name of Bob Jones, thinking that he would not be known'.

'George Abrams' was listed in the 1811 General Muster and he received a Certificate of Freedom on 1 October 1810. By the 1822 Muster, he appeared as 'George Abrahams', free by servitude and a carpenter by trade.

Recollections of 13 Years Residence in Norfolk Island and Van Diemen's Land, by Robert Jones Buckley, last Chief Gaoler at Norfolk Island; M. Gillen, *The Founders of Australia*, pp. 3, 412.

ABRAHAMS, John

b. London, 1793–1824
Ocean II (1), 1818; Convict; Sentenced to life, Old Bailey, 1817.
Single; Attorney's clerk; Height: 163 cm.

Dark ruddy complexion, black hair, black eyes. Abrahams stole ten pieces of ribbon (210 yards) from a warehouse and was initially sentenced to death at the London Gaol Delivery on 19 February 1817.

The *Ocean* arrived in New South Wales on 10 January 1818, and on 18 January Abrahams was sent to Windsor. Abrahams was listed in the 1818 Muster as a 'settler's man' and appeared in the records of the Windsor prisoners' rations. On 19 October 1818 John Abrahams was sent to the prison station at Newcastle on the *Lady Nelson*. The *Sydney Gazette* advertised that Abrahams had absconded from service on 6 November 1823. On 25 November 1823 he was sent as a convict to Port Macquarie on the *Lady Nelson*. He had been working with Mr Chandler's clearing party. Abrahams was buried at Port Macquarie on 14 November 1824.

OBSP, 1816–17, case 389, p. 154; Ship Indent 4/4005; HO 10/1; Windsor Prisoners' Rations, ML, A803 p. 326; *Sydney Gazette*, 6 November 1823, supplement 1, p. 1; 4/3497, p. 307; 4/3499, p. 107; 4/3503, p. 221.

ABRAHAMS, Joseph

b. Aldgate, 1793
Caledonia (2), 1822; Convict; Sentenced to life, Bristol, 1822.
Cotton wick maker; Height: 173 cm.

Brown eyes. Black and grey hair. Joseph Abrahams was living at Partridge Court, London. His brother-in-law was a pedlar at the Clare Market.

According to the *Australian* of 5 January 1825, there was a letter awaiting Joseph Abrahams at Hobart Town GPO. On 14 July 1826, while assigned to Mr Walker, he was found guilty of neglect of duty and insolence and sentenced to twenty-five lashes. On 18 September 1828 he was accused of stealing a quantity of shoemaker's tools but was discharged. On 4 August 1835, Abrahams had £15 worth of wearing apparel in his possession 'for which he cannot account'. He was discharged from his master's service and returned to Hobart Town. A conditional pardon was granted on 29 February 1836.

Abrahams was tried and convicted at Hobart Town Supreme Court on 3 September 1839 for aiding a burglary and was given a colonial sentence of fourteen years in prison. Abrahams was also found guilty of two offences that were committed on 3 September and 10 September and was sent to Port Arthur Penitentiary for five years. On 15 May 1844, at Hobart Town Prisoners' Barracks, Abrahams was sentenced to two months hard labour for gambling in a public house, and on 29 October 1844, at New Norfolk Farm, he was sentenced to seven days solitary confinement for 'misconduct'.

Despite these harsh sentences a ticket of leave was granted on 20 January 1846, which came into official force on 27 May 1847.

CON 32/4, Supplementary Volume; Ship Indent 4/4008, p. 177; Muster Roll, ML 2/8249, p. 170; *Hobart Town Courier*, 13 September 1839; CP 833; CSO 49/3 (133), p. 162; CSO 50/10/83–4.

ABRAHAMS, Joseph

b. Sheerness
Free.
Married; Dealer; 2 children.

Joseph Abrahams' birthplace suggests that he was related by marriage to the family of Judah and Joseph Solomon (qq.v.).

Joseph Abrahams was in Melbourne in 1841 working as a ships' chandler. He had two daughters and was the brother of Abraham Abrahams (q.v.) of Lonsdale Street. In 1844 the *Port Phillip Patriot* published a long letter Abrahams had written to his father in London about an adventure in which he had been involved on a British ship travelling from Macao to Borneo. Abrahams had hoped to sell clothes and materials to the sultan. On the way down the river the ship had been ambushed by hundreds of native warriors and many of the Europeans on board were injured, including his associate Benjamin Hart (q.v).

In 16 September 1846 Abrahams was working as a clerk for Mr Healey in Melbourne and was described as a general dealer. A man named Thomas Richmond purchased an opossum skin rug, which was for sale in the shop.

Port Phillip Patriot, 26 August 1844; VPR, Series 30, Box 190P-NCR 249 (SLV).

ABRAHAMS, Joseph (ABRAMS)

b. Bath, 1805
Exmouth, 1831; Convict; Sentenced to life, Chester City, 1830.
Indoor servant and soldier; Height: 170 cm.

Ruddy complexion, pock-pitted; dark brown hair.

Joseph Abrahams was listed as thirty-two years old in the 1837 General Muster of Convicts in New South Wales. In July 1839 he applied to join the Sydney Synagogue. Abrahams absconded from the service of Dr John Kinchella JP, in Bathurst, on 30 December 1840, but was recaptured and returned to government service. A ticket of leave was issued in 1843 and a conditional pardon later that same year. On 24 February 1840 he was withdrawn from penal servitude. Joseph and Rosetta Abrahams had a son, Phillip, in Sydney in 1849, who was registered as a 'Hebrew'. 'Rosetta' was the acquired name of his non-Jewish wife. Joseph Abrahams signed the petition to establish a Jews' Burial Ground in Yass, on 20 December 1844.

List of Convicts 2/8258, p. 195; FitzRoy Papers, ML, A1234, no. 43/1607, vol. 53, p. 469; HO 10/32; *New South Wales Government Gazette*, 1841, p. 34; TL 43/1067; CP 43/1607, in 4/4178; CS Petition, 4/2650.4, dated 20 December 1844; CS 4/3687, 40/593, 24 February 1840; TL 43/1607, in 4/4178.

ABRAHAMS, Joseph (Lewis, Joshua)

b. London, 1806–1849
Hercules II (1), 1825; Convict; Sentenced to 7 years, London, 1824.
Single; Fruit dealer; Height: 160 cm.

Fresh complexion. Dark brown hair, chestnut eyes, roman nose. Joseph Abrahams was transported for taking a package from a cart and selling it to Abraham Wolfe, a 'fence'. He was sentenced on 28 October 1824. Bell's Life *(London) of 16 January 1825 carried the detailed story of the arrest and trial of 'Lewis Abrahams', who appears to be the same individual. He was indicted for stealing a watch and several other valuable articles to the value of £100. The newspaper reported:*

> *a pursuit was commenced and the prisoner followed into Albion St. He went into a house, he was followed there but not found; but on the fire was seen a trunk broken up and beginning to burn. The prisoner was found in the house next door. Several witnesses were called to the good character of the prisoner. He was found guilty. In the judgement of the court: He is a daring, experienced thief. He should therefore no longer expect to remain in this country.*

Joseph Abrahams arrived in New South Wales on 7 May 1825. It was reported that he had behaved 'very well' on board the convict transport ship. He was initially assigned to the District of Evan. Abrahams was sent to Norfolk Island, and returned to Sydney on 22 November 1829 to be housed in the Hyde Park Barracks. He received a certificate of freedom on 16 November 1831. The following year, on 6 February 1832, the *Sydney Herald* reported: 'Joseph Abrahams, being a slippery gentleman but not able to slide over glass was, in default thereof, sent three days to gaol'. In 1835 he received permission to travel between Windsor and Fitzgerald Plains in the assigned service of R. Fitzgerald Esq.

Abrahams was transported to Norfolk Island (again!) for fourteen years for receiving stolen property and was listed on 26 August 1835 among the 'Men in Irons' sent from Norfolk Island to Sydney's Hyde Park Barracks. On 30 November 1839 Abrahams was a member of a chain gang in Woolloomooloo and was sent to Cockatoo Island. In 1844 the *Registry of Flash Men* described 'Joe Abrahams, a Jew thief and notorious scoundrel [who] lives in Sussex St'.

OBSP, 1823/4 case 1408. p. 634; *Hercules II* (1) Indent 4/3687, and 4/4010, p. 122; *Bell's Life*, 16 January 1825; CF 31/1117; *Sydney Gazette*, 6 December 1831; *Sydney Herald*, 6 February 1832; 4/6271, 7 January 1840; Windsor Bench of Magistrates, 4/4259-45/909; Woolloomooloo Stockade, Iron Gang Returns, 1836–1840, 7 January 1840, ML, 4/6271; CS Outward Letters 4/3687.

ABRAHAMS, Leah

Free.
Single.

Leah Abrahams married George Moss (q.v.) in Sydney in 1840.

ABRAHAMS, Levi (Levy)

b. Manchester, 1798
Marquis of Hastings, 1826; Convict; Sentenced to life, Old Bailey, 1824.
Single; Jeweller's clerk; Height: 160 cm.

Pale complexion, hazel eyes, black curly hair. Levi Abrahams was caught breaking into a house in St Clements Lane and stealing some silver. The house terrier awoke the household. Abrahams killed the dog with a knife and attempted to escape. He claimed to have been in London for about four weeks and was looking for work. His parents lived in Manchester. He claimed that other men did the burglary while he stood guard and the blood on his clothes had come from his nose. He was sentenced to death, which was later commuted to transportation for life.

Levy Abrahams arrived in Sydney on 3 January 1826 and was almost immediately issued with a ticket of leave. Within six months the ticket of leave was taken away for 'assaulting in a wanton and violent manner a decent female' on 18 June. In a plea for mercy to the Colonial Secretary, Abrahams wrote: 'I came out on the same ship as the Colonial Secretary Alexander Macleay and made a good impression upon him', but 'after magisterial investigation I suffered the punishment awarded' for having taken a bribe. He wrote that he had been employed as superintendent clerk, at Newcastle, since November 1827. 'I have done the convict engineer and coal mine duty for three years and eight months satisfactory work though on the lowest type of prisoner gratuity.'

On 17 February 1828 Levi Abrahams appeared before the Newcastle Magistrates for 'conniving at the absence of prisoners from Divine Service' and was put in solitary confinement for seven days. On 12 April he was convicted for 'conniving at prisoners remaining out of barracks and receiving a bribe for doing so'. Abrahams was sentenced to fifty lashes. On 9 June, ten days were added to his sentence after he was found 'tippling' in a Public House on a Sunday morning.

On 1 December 1831 the Superintendent of Public Works, Mr Buchanan, took him to Sydney and asked that he be assigned there. This was refused. Abrahams asked 'for the sake of humanity for a higher wage and not to be subjected to such an ordeal' as Newcastle or assignment to Mr Buchanan. He claimed to be in 'delicate health spitting blood from the chest'. On 10 April 1835 Levy Abrahams had been employed for two years in the Road Office. Good conduct and attention to duty entitled him to eight pence a day, which was increased to one shilling a day. The Colonial Secretary added: 'I presume no trust is reposed in this person'. On 19 February 1836 Levi Abrahams was found to be absent from the Hyde Park Barracks and placed in solitary confinement in the cells on bread and water for five days. On 13 June 1836, he was assigned to the Surveyor General's work party. He was suspected of running away and given six weeks on the treadmill. He was sent to the House of Correction on 3 July 1837 for 'drunkenness repeated often with insolence', where he was sentenced to sixteen weeks on the treadmill and then reassigned to Sydney's Hyde Park Barracks.

The *Sydney Gazette* of 11 May 1839 reported that Levy Abrahams, an assigned servant of Mr Buchanan, the Surveyor, robbed some notes in Mr Teton's shop and that when apprehended 'it was discovered that he had some [bank] notes in his mouth, which with great difficulty, was forced open and the fifteen one pound notes were found there'. Abrahams was subsequently sent to Norfolk Island for seven years on the *Governor Phillip* in August 1839. From Norfolk Island in early 1840, Levy Abrahams wrote to the Sydney Synagogue asking for prayer books and food for Passover. Abraham described the effort made by Captain Machonachie to enable the Jewish convicts on the island to have their own religious services as part of his enlightened plan to rehabilitate criminals. Abraham wrote: 'We have experienced every encouragement from Capt Machonachie R. N., Civil Superintendent of this Island in the pursuit of our religious duties as far as practicable, in having a ward solely appropriated to our use as a place of worship and furnished with what was immediately necessary for this purpose'. Abrahams functioned as the 'reader' for the congregation, which numbered nine men—one too few for a duly constituted quorum (*minyan*) for a full Jewish prayer service.

In 1842 the *Registry of Flash Men* recorded the theft of silver plate by 'a Norfolk Islander and assigned clerk at the Liverpool Hospital Levy Abrahams'. He took the goods to an auctioneer called Cohen. The recorder of the *Registry* lamented: 'It is unfortunate that Israelitish names are so familiar in acts of suspected roguery'. On 16 September 1844 the *Sydney Morning Herald* reported that Abrahams had been committed for trial on a charge of stealing medical supplies from the Liverpool Hospital. When he was acquitted, the *Flash Men*'s author, William Augustus Miles, was horrified when one of the guards at the Hyde Park Barracks, 'in the face of the whole court', cheered the verdict. It was 'an edifying spectacle to a sympathetic public how a noble hearted free servant of the Crown honours with his friendship a convict of the same'.

Levi Abrahams was granted a conditional pardon in 1847. He had been in the colony for almost twenty-five years and for three years had held a ticket of leave.

OBSP, 1824–25, case 112, p. 4; CS 4/1793, p. 282, 31/10567; CS 4/1747, p. 70; CS 4/2124, Letters Received 1831, 4/1747, 18 June 1820, 35/2785, in 4/2299, 4/4569, p. 12; CS 4/2299 -35/2785, 10 April 1835, CS 4/3685, 39/627; CP 47/775; *Sydney Gazette*, 11 May 1839; CS 4/4213; *Registry of Flash Men*, pp. 116–17, 2/673; HO 10/55, *Hyde Park Barracks Index*, X825, 19 February 1836; *AG*, p. 315.

ABRAHAMS, Lewis

b. Warsaw
Neptune III (3), 1838; Convict; Sentenced to 7 years, Warwick, 1837.
Married; Tailor, old clothes man; Height: 158 cm; 7 children (in England).

Dark complexion. Black hair. Dark hazel eyes. Large nose. A Jew. His wife and seven children lived in Birmingham.

The *Neptune* arrived in Hobart Town on 18 January 1838. Abrahams' initial assignment, through the Marine Department, was to Mr G. Meredith of Swanport, who returned him, on 10 August 1839, to the police stating him to be 'useless'. It was recommended that he be sent to the interior. Abrahams received a ticket of leave in 1842. A conditional pardon was granted on 23 January 1843. On 2 May 1843 the Hobart Town Jewish Philanthropic Society voted to pay Abrahams five shillings a week, as a weekly pensioner, 'being deprived of the sight in both eyes'. He wrote to the congregation, on 14 January 1844, stating that he was 'a blind pensioner' and needed financial assistance to return to his wife and family in England. Abrahams was given £20 by the congregation.

Launceston Police Book, 16 April 1839, CON 70/1, p. 49, CON 18/18; *Hobart Town Courier*, 19 January 1844; Hobart Synagogue Minute Book, 1843.

ABRAHAMS, Lewis

Mayflower, 1841; Free.
Single; Dealer; 5 children.

The brother of Sarah Abrahams (q.v.), who was the son of Hannah (q.v.) (née Solomons), Lewis Abrahams arrived in Hobart Town on 26 March 1841.

A member of the Hobart Synagogue from 1842, Lewis Abrahams rented seat no. 52 in the synagogue in 1845, and gave £2 to the Sydney Synagogue building fund appeal in 1844. Abrahams was in business with his uncle, Henry Davis (q.v.), until August 1851, when the partnership was dissolved. Abrahams issued trade tokens in the name 'Lewis Abrahams, Draper, Liverpool Street, Hobart Town', to be redeemed for cash when the colonial money supply improved.

Hobart Town Courier, 26 March 1841; *Mercury*, 21 August 1851; CSO 92/6.

ABRAHAMS, Lyon (Lion)

b. London, 1797–1858
Larkins (1), 1817; Convict; Sentenced to life, Kingston, March Assizes, 1816.
Single; Labourer, groom; Height: 168 cm; 4 children.

Ruddy complexion, slightly pock-pitted, black to grey hair, hazel eyes, nearly blind of left eye.

In the 1818 Muster, Lyon Abrahams was listed as a 'settler's man'. In a petition to the Colonial Secretary in 1822 Abrahams explained that he had been 'Sometimes in Government Employ and through his good conduct received the Indulgence to go on his own hand by paying John Kidsman Coxton of the government boat *Entolope* five shillings a week and remained there nearly three years'. Major Druitt gave him a pass until he received a ticket of leave. According to the contrary records of the Colonial Secretary, Lyon Abraham had been hidden by Richard Porter, a shoemaker of Clarence Street, Sydney, for two years. Governor Goulburn sent him on to Sydney's Prisoners' Barracks on 22 August 1822.

Abrahams claimed to have been working as a labourer for many of 'the merchants and gentlemen of Sydney'. He said that he had never been brought before the Justice of the Peace nor spent one night in a watch house since his arrival in the colony. Abrahams appealed to the Governor's 'Tender consideration to Grant him the indulgence of a Ticket of Leave'. On 29 December 1825 the *Sydney Gazette* reported that Lyon Abrahams had been convicted by the Sydney Bench of Magistrates of stealing. He was sent to the convict station at Port Macquarie for three years. There he was accused by the wardsman of the Prisoners' Barracks of being seen by a constable standing by the fire near some gamblers. A fellow prisoner gave evidence that 'he had just walked over to them'. He was acquitted on 13 October 1828.

Lyon Abrahams stole some shirts and was sentenced to seventy-five lashes. He received 'only' fifty lashes and was placed in heavy irons to do heavy labour. Abrahams was subsequently allowed to change his ticket of leave from the Port Macquarie District to Windsor. Lyons was out of work in 1835 and the police suggested that his ticket of leave be withdrawn: 'He is an able Jew but so lazy as to preclude the possibility of his obtaining a call for his services from any person requiring a labouring hand'. Lyon Abrahams listed as a 'dealer', aged forty-six, applied to marry Catherine Redmond, nineteen. She had arrived free on the *Navarino*. The consent of Redmond's parents or guardians had to be obtained before the marriage could be solemnised. The wedding was noted on 24 November 1840.

A conditional pardon for the District of Port Macquarie was granted on 1 October 1841 and the Census of New South Wales in 1847 listed Abrahams at George Street, Windsor. Lyon Abrahams died at Windsor in 1858 and was said to have been seventy-four years of age. His children, who were baptised at St Matthew's, were Maria (baptised on 17 April 1842), Rosetta (born 1843), Leon Archibald (baptised 9 April 1848), Mary Ann (baptised 5 January 1851) and Rachael (baptised 10 June 1855, and who died nine months later).

Ship Indent 4/4405, p. 388; Petition, CS 1822, 4/1864, pp. 1–2; CS 4/1761, p. 138; CS 4/2256.1-34/9431; Port Macquarie Bench of Magistrates, Proceedings, 4/5686, 13 October 1828, 17 March 1829, p. 122; TL 35/252, 37/568, in 4/2353; CS 35/5239, 22 July 1835; Permission to Marry Book, 1840, p. 200, 4/4513; HO 10/53.

ABRAHAMS, Mary

b. 1783
Experiment (1), 1804; Convict; Sentenced to 7 years, Guilford, Surrey, 1802.
Single; Needlewoman; 1 child.

Mary Abrahams was sentenced on 9 August 1802.

Mary Abrahams arrived in New South Wales on 24 June 1804. Abrahams was assigned to George Pantam. Her daughter, Mary Anne, was born on 15 December 1804 and baptised at St Philip's, Sydney, on 16 January 1805. Mary Abrams lived with Charles Hancock, according to the Muster of 12 August 1806. She appeared on the Rev. Samuel Marsden's Female Muster of 1806 as a concubine with one female child. In the *Sydney Gazette* of 29 May 1808, it was reported that Mary Abrams had a petticoat and cloak stolen 'from her house' and that Hannah Cole had been arrested for the theft.

On 27 November 1808 the male friend of Mary Abrams (Laurence Lewis) stole £30 from Lieutenant Laycock. The *Sydney Gazette* reported on 1 April 1810 that Mary Abrahams had received a certificate of freedom. However, in January 1817 she was reported to be 'absent from employment and at large' and back in custody by 29 March. Mary Abrahams was found guilty of larceny and sentenced to three years transportation in March 1822. She was sent to Newcastle and, in 1823, petitioned Governor Brisbane for her freedom, stating 'her health being in an exceedingly ill state ever since her arrival on this settlement and is thereby rendered unable to do her government duty, which she would most readily do if not completely disabled from doing so allow her off stores as she could maintain herself by her own Industry being a good needlewoman'. In the 1828 Census Mary Abrahams was listed as a 'Protestant', lodging at 'Patrick Carrolls, Erskine Street, Sydney'.

ML 4/3505, 4/4004; Register of Pardons 4/4427, p. 490f.; 4/3505, p. 44; 4/1869, p. 3; St Philip's Register, 95/100; Petition 4/1869, Letter 3; *Sydney Gazette*, 22 February 1817, 22 March 1822.

ABRAHAMS, Mary Theresa (Theresa Elizabeth PEARCE)

b. London
Minstrel, 1812; Convict; Sentenced to life, Surrey Quarter Sessions, 1812.
Single; Needlewoman.

Mary Abrahams is listed as having arrived on the Minstrel, under the name of Theresa Eliza Pearce. She had been sentenced on 30 May 1812.

Mary Abrahams arrived in New South Wales on 25 October 1812 and was sent to the Factory in Parramatta. On 6 October 1817, 'Theresa Elizabeth Pearce' asked for permission to marry Edward Hatton at Parramatta.

CS 4/3497, p. 93; CS X820, p. 37.

ABRAHAMS, Michael

b. London, 1812
Merope, 1835; Free. Sentenced to 14 years, Sydney Quarter Sessions, 1836.
Single; Gentleman's servant; Height: 163 cm.

Fair complexion, dark brown hair, hazel eyes. Stated this offence: 'Swindling—obtaining paper under false pretences'. Michael Abrahams was one of four brothers: Charles, a barrister at Lincoln Inn; Samuel, an attorney; and Benjamin, a hotel keeper in Calcutta. When tried in Sydney, he was described as a Jew, single, who could read and write.

In January 1836, the *Sydney Gazette* noted: 'Michael Abrahams, a young man of respectable appearance in court for swindling'. Abrahams was sentenced at the Sydney Quarter Sessions to fourteen years transportation and was transported to Van Diemen's Land on the *Siren* for 'obtaining goods under false pretences'. He arrived in Hobart Town on 16 April 1836 and was sent to Oatlands Public Works. On 2 May 1837 he was sentenced to be removed to work with 'a distant road party' after giving false evidence against two fellow convicts. On 5 October 1837 he received three months probation for disobedience to orders and on 8 August 1838 he was tried for 'violent and threatening conduct towards his overseer'. The case was dismissed.

Michael Abrahams' mother, Mrs Phoebe Abrahams, wrote from her Regent Street address to Hobart Town pleading for her son to be sent home to England. Michael had 'fallen into bad company in Sydney'. He had quarrelled with his older brother in the East Indies. He had gone to Sydney to be with his relative, George Robert Nichols (the grandson of Esther Abrahams, q.v.). Lieutenant Governor Franklin reported that he had informed the distressed mother that Michael's conduct 'has not been marked by the degree of propriety which would either warrant me at present extending to him any indulgence, or in recommending him to your Lordship. He had unhappily deviated from a safe course of conduct and embarked in a traffic of low characters viz the sale of spirits'. Mrs Abrahams had replied that she 'entertains no doubt that the conduct of her unhappy son has been criminal', and 'humbly pleads for him upon the grounds of his youth, his being placed in a vicious society'. Michael Abrahams received an absolute pardon in 1840, and evidently returned to England.

The mention of his relationship with George Robert Nichols sheds light on the authenticity of Esther Abrahams' surname and shows that, more than fifty years after her deportation, Esther had not been forgotten by her English family.

CON 31/2, no. 718; Transportation Register, 4/4523, p. 32; CS no. 39, in *HRA*, vol. 26, p. 317, 28 March 1837, and no. 73, 17 July 1838, p. 339; CON 16/1, p. 29; CON 13/8, p. 331; CO 1/29, pp. 45–56, Glenelg to Franklin; *Hobart Town Courier*, 24 November 1840.

ABRAHAMS, Mordecai (Montague)

b. London, 1787–1856
Somersetshire (1), 1814; Convict; Sentenced to life, Old Bailey, 1813.
Single; Glass cutter; Height: 168 cm.

Dark pale complexion, black hair, black eyes. Together with accomplices Mordecai Abrahams stole £22 from a farmer who was walking down a street in Whitechapel. It was robbery with violence and witnesses saw Abrahams doing the robbery. He was twenty-six. He was sentenced to death on 14 July 1814 but this was later commuted to transportation for life.

Mordecai Abrahams was listed as an assigned government servant working for John Blaxland in the Male Muster of 1816. He was described as a 'settler's man' in the 1818 Muster. Abrahams was granted a ticket of leave on 22 May 1823. In the 1828 Census he was listed as a 'dealer' living at Mary Larkin's house in Kent Street, Sydney. Of her six tenants, four were Jews: Mordecai Abrahams, Lewis Lyons (q.v.), Isaac Moses (q.v.), and Solomon Simpson (q.v.). Mordecai Abrahams of Sydney was listed in the 1837 General Return of Convicts in New South Wales. A conditional pardon was granted on 17 October 1839, and renewed on 1 November 1839.

'Montague' Abrahams was recorded as having a dwelling house in Market Street in the Brisbane Ward, in September 1842. Mordecai Abrahams died on 1 December 1856, and was buried in Devonshire Street Jewish Cemetery.

OBSP, 1813, case 736, p. 403; Ship Indent 4/4005; HO 10/3. 4/3687, 39/801; HO 10/28; *Sydney Morning Herald*, 17 September 1842.

ABRAHAMS, Rachel (Rachael)

b. London, 1815–1900
Lady Raffles, 1839; Free.
Single; Housemaid; 9 children.

Rachel Abrahams was the elder sister of Emilia Abrahams (q.v.), and the daughter of Lewis and Rebecca Abrahams of Hackney. Both sisters were 'recruited' as house servants to travel to Australia on a migrant ship. Both sisters gave £5 to the Sydney Synagogue building appeal in September 1839.

Rachael married Saul Solomon (Solomon Solomon, q.v.) on 12 August 1840. Saul was the son of Samuel Solomon (q.v.). Her children were Lewis (Louis) (1842), Philip Charles (1843–1922), Esther (1846–1880), who married Nathan Cohen (q.v.), Michael Cleveland (1848), Rebecca (1850–1922), who married David Moses, Deborah (1853–1942), who married Nathan Cohen after Esther's death, Elizabeth (Bessie) (1855–1937), Samuel (1857–1914) and Caroline (1859–1944).

ABRAHAMS, Rachel

b. London, 1828–1861
1838; Free.
Single; 13 children.

The daughter of Abraham and Sarah Abrahams, Rachel married Phillip David Millingen (q.v.) at Sydney in 1843 at the age of fifteen.

ABRAHAMS, Rebecca

b. Sydney c. 1820

Rebecca Abrahams' father, and not her mother, was Jewish. Rebecca was formally converted to Judaism in Sydney in 1840 and married Emanuel Myers (q.v.). Rebecca may have been the daughter of Mordecai Abrahams (q.v.).

ABRAHAMS, Rosanna

b. London, 1787–1837
Lady Penrhyn, 1788; Free.
3 children.

Rosanna Abrahams was born at Newgate Prison on 18 March 1787, the daughter of Esther Abrahams (q.v.). Early documents give her first name as 'Esther', indicating that she was simply regarded as an encumbrance or appendage of her mother. Mother and infant were deported from England on 3 May 1787, and arrived in Australia in the First Fleet. Rosanna went to Norfolk Island with her mother and George Johnston following the birth of her first half-brother.

Rosanna married the emancipist Isaac Nichols at St Philip's on 18 February 1805. It was four months after the death of Isaac's first wife. (The *Sydney Gazette*, on 28 October 1804, inferred that Mary Nichols had been mentally ill.) Rosanna 'Julian' was entered into the Church register by the clerk. 'Julian' was struck out and 'Abrahams' substituted by the Rev. Samuel Marsden. The signature that followed was 'Rosanna Abrahams'. There were three sons: Isaac David (10 April 1807), George Robert (27 September 1809–1857), and Charles Hamilton (1811).

Isaac Nichols died on 8 November 1819. Rosanna married for the second time, to Mr James Stuart (Stewart), at St Philip's on 13 August 1820. Her half-sister, Blanche Johnston, was one of the witnesses at the marriage. In the 1828 Census, Rosanna Stewart was listed as living in Kent Street, Sydney. She owned 4000 acres of land, with 8 horses and 300 cattle. Her son Charles was living with her. Rosanna died in Sydney on 11 April 1837.

HO 56/21, 103/109; M. Gillen, *The Founders of Australia*, p. 2; R. Holden, *Orphans of History*, pp. 198–9; *AG*, pp. 26, 28, 35, 38.

ABRAHAMS, Samuel

1794–1814 *Surrey I* (1), 1814; Convict; Sentenced to 7 years, Old Bailey, 1812.

Samuel Abrahams was sentenced at the Middlesex Gaol Delivery on 2 December 1812. Abrahams stole a firkin (small cask) of butter from the back of a cart. In his own defence Abrahams explained 'I get my living by portering. A man asked me to carry it for him to Duke's Place. I have witnesses that saw him put it on my shoulder. They are not here now. They would be here next sessions, that is the reason I wished to put my trial off'.

Originally confined on board the *Laurel* hulk in the Thames and transferred to the Surrey for transportation, Abrahams was one of thirty-six convicts who died on board the transport ship during its journey to Australia. Abrahams died on the 5 July 1814.

OBSP. 2 December 1812. Case 87. Ship Indent 4/4004, p. 547; *Sydney Gazette*, 10 September 1814; CS SZ 758, pp. 535–6.

ABRAHAMS, Elizabeth

Caroline, 1839; Free.
Married; 9 children.

Elizabeth (née Jacobs) was the wife of Abraham Abrahams (q.v.). Her nine children were Fanny, Joseph, Caroline, Rachael, Sarah, Elina, Malita, Rosa and Adelaide. A donation was made in her name to the 1844 Sydney synagogue building appeal. Sarah died at Hobart on 6 May 1850 aged fifty-five.

Ship Indent 4/5214, List of Passengers on the *Caroline* via Hobart Town, 28 May 1839. Information Martin Toone, Melbourne.

ABRAHAMS, Sarah

Mayflower, 1841; Free.
Married; 2 children.

A daughter of Judah and Esther Solomon (qq.v.), Sarah may have been the wife of Lewis Abrahams (q.v.). She arrived from London on the *Mayflower* in March 1841. Sarah moved to Hobart Town and rented a seat in the Hobart Synagogue in 1845–48.

Hobart Town Courier, 26 March 1841; CSO 92/6.

ABRAHAMS, William

b. Holland, 1808–1843
Hooghly (2), 1828; Convict; Sentenced to 7 years, Old Bailey, 1825.
Single; Errand boy; Height: 147 cm.

'Jew.' Swarthy, ruddy and freckled complexion. Reddish hair. Hazel eyes. Sharp nose. L. F. tattooed on lower left arm. Scar on right breast and outer corner of right eye. Scar on knuckles of left hand. Lost a front tooth on right side of upper jaw. 'No education' but can read. William Abrahams stole a cap from a little child. He was transported for assault and robbery. Gaol Report: 'Imprisoned before and whipped, bad character'. Surgeon's Report: 'Good attentive to his book'. Because of his age, Abrahams had to wait for three years on a hulk before being sent out aboard the convict transport. Strangely the 17 year old Abrahams was authorised by Chief Rabbi Herschell to act as a Shochet (slaughterer of kosher meat) in Australia. The records of the London rabbinic court reads 'I have given my hand to the R. Solomon Hirschell to abide by certain rules which he has laid down on me as I am to kill poultry'.

William 'Abraham' appears on the list of convicts held in New South Wales in November 1828. He had spent at least three years on the hulks in the Thames Estuary before being deported to Australia. He was described as a Jew assigned to the Hunter River District to work for G. F. Graham in Newcastle. His name appears in the 1832 Entrance and Description Book of the Newcastle Gaol. The Newcastle Bench ordered him to be sent to Sydney. His behaviour had been 'orderly'. Sydney prison records of 1830 show that he was 160 cm tall. He received a ticket of leave in 1828 and a certificate of freedom was issued on 9 May 1832. William Abrahams died on 23 June 1843. There is no record of Abraham working as a slaughterer of poultry in Australia.

OBSP, 1824–25, case 736, p. 309; Ship Indent 4/4013, p. 47; CF 4/4311-32/0452; Newcastle Gaol, Entrance and Description Book, 1832, no. 262, 2/2004. Jeremy I. Pfeffer, *From One End of the Earth to the Other*, p. 288.

ACKMAN, Emanuel

b. Cracow, Poland, c. 1792–1876
James Dean, 1847; Free.
Married; Dealer; 10 children.

Emanuel Ackman was smuggled out of Poland at the age of six in order to avoid being called up for military service and would never see his parents again. In London he was fostered by Henry Harris, a crystal cutter, and his wife Elizabeth, and later married their daughter Rachael (q.v.) on 23 March 1836. Emanuel and Rachael arrived in Victoria on 20 June 1847 with five children: Sarah (1837–1916), Elizabeth (1839–1925), Esther (1842–1919), Samuel (1844–1922), and Abraham (1846).

Emanuel set up business in Geelong as a draper. A son, Henry, was born in Geelong on 23 May 1848. Their infant son, Abraham, was buried by the Melbourne Jewish Congregation in January 1849. Their other children were Fanny (1850), Elsie (Ailcy) (August 1853), Amelia (1855), Michael (1859), and Coleman (after 1859), who died in infancy.

The *Melbourne Morning Herald* of 17 February 1849 reported that John Davies (q.v.) had been indicted for forging a cheque made out to Emanuel Ackman. On 9 July 1849 the Chief Constable of Geelong noticed that Ackman was wearing some very attractive rings, which turned out to be stolen. He was tried in Geelong on 16 August 1849 and was acquitted. On 25 August 1849, Ackman made his first land purchase in Geelong.

In 1849 the Geelong Philanthropic and Jewish Burial Society held its first High Holydays services. Ackman became one of the three original trustees for a Jewish burial ground in Geelong and also for an 1851 land grant for a synagogue.

The Ackmans' daughter Sarah married Michael Samuel Levy at Geelong on 26 January 1853 and their baby son Emanuel died in Geelong in 1857. Emanuel Ackman died on 13 February 1876 at the age of eighty-three and was buried at the Melbourne General Cemetery.

Family history from Dr Malcolm and Mrs Barbara Fredman, Melbourne; A. Shire (ed.), *Great Synagogue Marriage Registers*, 313/32.

ACKMAN, Rachael

b. London, 1816–1913
James Dean, 1847; Free.
Married; 8 children.

Rachael was the daughter of Henry and Elizabeth Harris, who had been foster parents for their future son-in-law, Emanuel Ackman (q.v.). Rachael married Emanuel Ackman on 23 March 1836 at London's Great Synagogue. The Ackman family became pioneer settlers in Geelong. (Their children are listed in Emanuel Ackman's entry). Rachael's sister Hannah and brother-in-law Mark Marks (q.v.) had arrived in New South Wales in 1845.

By 1890, Rachael was living at 24 Regent Street, Fitzroy, in 1908 at 381 Victoria Parade, East Melbourne, and in 1913 at 18 Canterbury Road, St Kilda. Rachael Ackman died on 30 March 1913 at the age of ninety-seven.

Family history from Dr Malcolm and Mrs Barbara Fredman, Melbourne.

ADAMS, Maurice

Mariner (3), 1827; Convict; Sentenced to 7 years, Waterford City, 1826.
Labourer.

'A Jew.' Stole money at Waterford City in Ireland and was sentenced to transportation.

Adams arrived in New South Wales on 23 May 1827. A colonial conviction was recorded at the General Sessions in Bathurst on 14 August 1829 for having been at large in the bush and for committing robbery. He was sentenced to three years colonial transportation and sent to Moreton Bay, returning to Sydney on the *Elizabeth* on 28 February 1833. On 20 April 1837, Adams was free by servitude, but in 1842 was sentenced to three months in irons for theft.

Mariner (3) Indent 4/4013, p. 47; *OBSP*, 1824–25, case 736, no. 1968; Chronological Register of Convicts at Moreton Bay; CF 37/0340; *Sydney Morning Herald*, 16 May 1842.

AFFRIATT, Lydia

1813–1872
Westmoreland, 1833; Free.
Single.

Lydia Affriatt was the daughter of Joseph Affriatt (the son of Judah Affriatt of Morocco) and Dinah Leah (née Moses), and sister of Sarah Affriatt (q.v.). Joseph was a pedlar or 'chapman'. However, on Lydia's death certificate it says that her father was 'secretary to the Dey [governor] of Algiers'. Lydia arrived in New South Wales on 19 May 1833. She married Charles Abraham Wilson (q.v.) on 25 March 1835. Wilson had arrived in New South Wales on the *Lion* in 1825, and was the son of Emma Josephson (q.v.) and Henry Wilson, 'gentleman'. Jacob Josephson (q.v.) gave his consent for Lydia to marry, describing her as his sister's 'lass'. Lydia's mother,

Dinah Moses, may have been the half-sister of Emma Josephson. The marriage was witnessed by Barnett Levey (q.v.), whose wife was Sarah Emma Josephson. Lydia was baptised into the Church of England in 1841. She died on 15 April 1872.

Lydia and Charles Abraham Wilson had fourteen children. A grandchild, Jacob Affriatt Wilson, was in the first intake of students to Sydney University and completed a degree in medicine at St Bartholomew's. He returned to Australia in 1865 only to die of tuberculosis in 1867, aged thirty.

Family research by Robert Wilson, Canada and Ronnie Nichols, Sydney.

AFFRIATT, Sarah

b. London, 1819–1909
Canton, 1835; Free.
Single.

The daughter of Joseph Affriatt and Dinah Leah (née Moses), Sarah was born on 22 June 1819, a sister to Lydia Affriatt (q.v.). Her father was described as a 'chapman' or pedlar. Sarah Affriatt was allowed to travel to Australia on a government free passage to join her family in the colony. She married Henry Wilson (q.v.), brother-in-law of Barnett Levey (q.v.), in Sydney on 4 May 1835. She had been baptised at St Matthew's, Bethnal Green, on 5 June 1831. Wilson had arrived in Sydney in 1827 and was the son of Emma Josephson (q.v.) and Henry Wilson. Henry owned the Scotch Thistle Inn in 1838, and the Woolpack Inn in 1844. Sarah is said to have taken out sixty hotel licences around Sydney and the Blue Mountains during her lifetime. Sarah and Henry Wilson had seven children.

Family research by Robert Wilson, Canada and Ronnie Nichols, Sydney.

ALEXANDER, Abraham (Alexander ABRAHAM)

b. Aldgate, 1801
Chapman, 1824; Convict; Sentenced to 7 years, Old Bailey, 1823.
Single; Pedlar; Height: 165 cm.

Abraham Alexander stole a barrel of liquor from outside a public house in Nightingale Lane, an act he was seen committing with another man. Alexander was twenty-one. He was also known as 'Alexander Abraham'. He was a pedlar with the word 'bad' written in after his listed trade in the convict ship indent. His previous offences included a conviction for stealing sixpence, stealing from a cart, hawking without a licence and assault. His face was badly scarred.

The first entry in a very long police record that extends over two supplementary volumes was dated March 1825. Alexander was sent to the harsh prison outpost at Macquarie Harbour on the west coast of Van Diemen's Land, where he was convicted of 'insolence to Overseer' and sentenced to twenty-five lashes. In April 1826 as a member of the chain gang he was found to have 'defaced his Irons' for which he received 'fifty lashes and fresh ones'. On 22 August 1827, he received twenty-five lashes for 'neglect of duty'. On 7 March 1828 while working on the Government Farm, he used abusive language to an overseer and threatened to do him some bodily harm for which he was placed in the chain gang for four months and given fifty lashes. On 18 June 1828 he was forced to wear double irons, having cut his irons. In September 1828 he assaulted his overseer and was sent to the chain gang for a further four months. On 26 December he absconded from the chain gang at St Peter's Pass and was at large for three days. He was given fifty lashes and returned to work on the road gang on March 1829. There he committed a 'misdemeanour' on the way to the chain gang at New Norfolk, and was sentenced to receive twenty-five lashes upon his arrival.

Alexander was free by servitude in the Launceston District by 1830. (Ticket of Leave no. 298 granted on 25 September 1830). On 23 November 1831 he was bound over to keep the peace after he insulted Cashmore Israel (q.v.). On 28 June 1834 he was sentenced to seven years transportation for having assaulted Richard Baker and having stolen eight Spanish dollars from him. He was sent to Port Arthur, and in early 1835 he escaped and, while at large, was in touch with the bushranger Samuel Britten. A number of minor charges followed, concluding with the much more serious charge on 3 August 1838 of pilfering a biscuit from the government cart while he was in charge of the cart. He was found guilty and placed in No. 1 chain gang for three months.

On 25 November 1839, Alexander was assigned to a Mr Smith. A few hours after his service had begun he 'disrespectfully demanded a Pass to proceed to the Avoca Police Office to complain about the clothes Smith had given him to wear'. He was placed in the Avoca Town Chain Gang for three months. On 26 May 1840 he fought 'a pitched battle on the Lord's Day' and was given twelve months hard labour in chains. On 24 July 1840 his sentence was extended by two months for 'disorderly conduct' when it was discovered that he secretly took off his leg irons at night.

Alexander was free by servitude by the end of 1841. Several minor offences appear in the Launceston Police book including a fine of forty shillings imposed for assaulting a constable'. There is an affidavit, dated 10 March 1831, regarding the loss of his certificate of freedom. His signature is to be found on the 1843 Launceston Synagogue petition and he donated £2 to the synagogue building appeal.

OBSP, 1822–23, p. 519; Allport Collection, Chapman Convict List; CON 31/1, no. 197; CON 22/1, no. 197; CON 23/1/1/. CON 32/1; CO 280/157; Dixson Add. 164; *Launceston Examiner*, 29 June 1844.

ALEXANDER, Abraham Edward

b. London, 1823–1908
1835; Free.
Single; Clothier; 14 children.

Abraham Edward Alexander was the third child of Israel Alexander (q.v.) and Hannah (née Lyons). Within months of his arrival in Australia, A. E. Alexander was working with his brother Godfrey as a draper in Portland in the Western

District of Victoria. He was listed as a 'clothier'of Elizabeth Street, Melbourne, in 1841 but returned to Portland. On 16 January 1850 he married Hannah Jacobs, the daughter of Samuel Jacobs (q.v.). It was Melbourne's sixth Jewish wedding. A daughter, Miriam, was born in Geelong later that same year. In 1851 'A. E. Alexander and R. Alexander' opened the Bee Hive Drapery and Clothing Store at 27 Collins Street, Melbourne. They were 'Importers of every description of Drapery and Clothing. Mr A. E. Alexander had proceeded to England to buy drapery at least 15% cheaper than any other house in town'. In 1862, Abraham (who was known by his second name, Edward) and Hannah moved to Rockhampton, where five of their children were born. The family moved to Sydney in 1880. Abraham Edward Alexander died in Sydney on 17 April 1908 and Hannah died on 7 September 1913. Both were buried in the Jewish section of Rookwood Cemetery.

Their children were Miriam (1850–1900), Phillip Abraham (1855–1912), Rose (1856–1931), Lionel Albert (1857–1932), Frank Edward (1858–1918), Ernest Arthur (1860), Florence (1861–1916), Blanche (1862–1944), Edith Ida (1865), Maude (1866–1943), and Grace (1868). Three other children were born and died in infancy in Rockhampton.

Ken Smith (comp.), *Our Alexander Families*, privately printed, Oatlands, NSW; *Melbourne Morning Herald*, 29 November 1851.

ALEXANDER, George

b. Whitechapel, 1815
Eden I (1), 1836; Convict; Sentenced to 7 years, Central Criminal Court, 1835.
Shoemaker; Height: 160.5 cm.

Fresh complexion, dark brown hair, grey eyes, long nose. An anchor tattooed on left arm. George Alexander was transported for robbing a quantity of leather, newly made boots, sheets and clothes, from his employer. Alexander and his much older co-worker Joseph Barker stole enough leather to make twenty pairs of boots. They had already pawned a pair of boots in Brick Lane. Alexander was described as a 'Jew.'

George Alexander arrived in Hobart Town on 22 December 1836. On 10 August 1838, while he was an assigned convict servant, he was reprimanded for being in a public house in the company of prostitutes. On 8 October 1838 he was given a sentence of hard labour for two months for having been absent without leave for seven days. On 10 December 1839 he received eighteen lashes for gross insolence. Four months later, on 6 April 1840, he was found to have three shillings and sixpence in his possession for which he couldn't account. The money was forfeited. During 1841 and 1842 he was an assigned servant to Mr Archer. On 1 February 1842 he received thirty-six lashes for 'insolence'. A certificate of freedom was granted in 1842.

OBSP 26 October 1835, case 2240. CON 31/2, no. 758; CON 18/7; CF 1842, no. 918.

ALEXANDER, George (Godfrey)

b. London, 1821–1900
1837; Free. Single;
Draper, then chiropodist; 11 children.

Godfrey Alexander was one of seven children, and followed his older brother Raphael (q.v.) to Australia in 1837. Godfrey was seventeen years old. He arrived in Melbourne and proceeded to Portland in 1841, together with his brother Raphael and David Cashmore (q.v.), to establish a pioneer business, the London Mart, in Gawler Street. It was the first drapery store in the district. Alexander was an original member of the Melbourne Hebrew Congregation.

Asher Hymen Hart (q.v.) officiated at Alexander's marriage in Geelong to Miriam Levy, the 16-year-old sister of John Levy (q.v.) and Michael Samuel Levy, in May 1850. It was Geelong's first Jewish wedding ceremony. Until 1854 Godfrey Alexander's main store stood on Market Square at the south side of Malop Street. In 1849 he was appointed a trustee of the Geelong Jewish burial ground (with Benjamin Goldsmid Levien, q.v., and Emanuel Ackman, q.v.), and in 1854 was warden of the first synagogue to be built in Geelong. Godfrey Alexander gave ten guineas for the building of a synagogue in Melbourne in 1853.

Alexander left Geelong in 1858, selling his six Geelong properties in Kardinia Street and Market Square. The family briefly lived in Melbourne, possibly working with Godfrey's brother Raphael in his drapery store, before Godfrey began work as a chiropodist at 324 George Street in Sydney. He maintained his practice for the following twenty years, moving his professional rooms no less than seven times. He was the first chiropodist in New South Wales. The family lived at 400 Pitt Street. Godfrey died, aged eighty, and was buried at Rookwood cemetery on 9 September 1900. Miriam had died in 1880.

Godfrey and Miriam had eleven children. Their first four, born in Geelong, were Sarah (1851–1930), Samuel (1853–1935), Louis Godfrey (1855–1924) and Leah (1857–1924). Two children were born in Collingwood: Rose (1859), and Emmanuel Godfrey (1861). Five children were born in Sydney: Hannah (1863), Sidney John (1865–1927), Eveline (1868–1878), Abraham Ernest (1871–1936), and Ida Esther (1873–1932).

R. H. Montague, 'Godfrey Alexander: Sydney's First Chiropodist', *AJJHS*, vol. 6, no. 8 (1970), pp. 531–2; *Portland Guardian*, 1842–43; Melbourne Hebrew Congregation Birth Book, 1852.

ALEXANDER, Henry

b. London, 1822
Lloyds (2), 1837; Convict; Sentenced to 7 years, Central Criminal Court, 1836.
Single; Errand boy; Height: 150 cm.

Dark, ruddy freckled complexion. Dark brown, nearly black, hair. Brown eyes. Tattoo H:A SCTABA. 'No religion.' Fifteen years of age.

Henry Alexander was listed in the 1837 General Return of Convicts in New South Wales as an assigned convict servant of Mr O'Brien of Yass. While still a servant it was noted that 'Hyam Alexander a convict with Surveyor Wright's party at Clarendon is a witness in a court case after he had given information to the Police'. A ticket of leave was issued to him in 1841 for the district of Yass. Henry Alexander stood trial for 'robbery under arms' at Braidwood on 14 December 1842 and his ticket of leave was cancelled. He was also charged with being absent from the Yass district. His ticket of leave was restored on 8 April 1856.

Lloyds (2) Indent, p. 111; TL 41/1850, in 4/4154; *Commercial Journal and Advertiser*, 18 August 1840; *Sydney Morning Herald*, 21 January 1842.

ALEXANDER, Hyam (Alexander HYAMS) (Hyam ABRAHAMSON)

b. Southwark, 1797
John Barry (1), 1819; Convict; Sentenced to life, Middlesex, 1819.
Single; Upholsterer, groom; Height: 157 cm.

Dark sallow complexion, black hair, dark eyes. Hyam Alexander (aged twenty-two) and John Phillips (q.v.) (aged eighteen) were transported for life. They stole a watch, valued at £50, chain, seals and pocket book from the Right Hon. Thomas Lord Foley, who was attending an election meeting near Covent Garden. The thieves were observed as they cut away the noble gentleman's overcoat and undercoat and stole the articles. Alexander was sentenced on 17 February 1819.

Hyam Alexander arrived in New South Wales on 26 September 1819. On 8 September 1821 he had volunteered to work as an assigned convict as an 'overseer' at the magazine stores. On 27 September 1823 he was sent from Emu Plains to Port Macquarie on the *Lady Nelson*. Alexander was sentenced to fifty lashes for refusing to work on 16 October 1826. He was sentenced in Sydney for obtaining property under false pretences, given two years colonial transportation, and sent to Moreton Bay on 30 April 1827 on the *Alligator*. He returned to Sydney on 8 December 1828. Hyam Alexander was assigned to Aspinall and Brown. On 25 April 1831 he was found to be absent without leave and sentenced to the treadmill for seven days and then returned to service. He was then punished at the Hyde Park Barracks for being 'absent without leave late at night', given twenty-six lashes and returned to his assigned service. Alexander was sent to the *Phoenix* hulk from the Hyde Park Barracks in May 1833 and then assigned to the Rev. Giles.

The 1833 Parramatta Gaol Record Book reported that he was admonished and 'dealt with' on 13 September 1833. Hyam was listed in the 1837 General Return of Convicts in New South Wales as working for the government in Berrima. On 11 June 1838 Hyam asked 'Your Excellency to look into his case after his long servitude'. He wrote that he had never received any indulgence such as tea or sugar, and had 'received only twenty-five lashes and that crime was for being absent only twenty-five minutes'. The note on his petition stated 'False!' His request was 'refused on account of a false statement in it'.

In 1839 he was twice punished severely. On 21 June he was sent to the treadmill, where his behaviour was said to be 'insolent'. On 22 June the Parramatta Gaol

Record Book continued to note that Hyam Alexander Hyams, who had been assigned to P. Plunkett, was guilty of 'insolence, neglect of work and disobedience of orders'. He was sent to gaol for one month after which he was to be assigned to government service at the District of Wollongong. On 10 July 1839 he was moved to the Hyde Park Prisoners Barracks. On 23 August 1841 the Bathurst police officer was asked to interview the prisoner and reported that Hyam's 'conduct has been extremely good'. The Colonial Secretary responded that he 'can't sanction the case'.

Alexander's ticket of leave was issued in 1843 at Bathurst and altered for Maitland in 1847. In that year Hyam Alexander, who gave his age as forty-six, married Charlotte Wilson, aged thirty-five, who held a ticket of leave. Charlotte and Hyam Alexander had a son named Hyam in 1848. A conditional pardon was issued on 14 November 1854. He was sentenced at the Quarter Sessions, Sydney, to five years on roads in October 1857 when he was found illegally in Sydney, but was allowed to remain at Ipswich. This was altered to Maitland on 18 February 1858. According to the *Sydney Morning Herald*, 31 March 1859, he was again brought before the Water Police Court after being arrested in Castlereagh Street for claiming that his surname was Brown and that he was a free man. He was returned to government service.

OBSP, 1818–19, case 396, p. 172f.; *John Barry* (1) Indent 4/4006; Chronological Register of Convicts at Moreton Bay, no. 960 (listed as 'Ham Abrahamson. Jew'); 4/3896, 2 January 1829; Parramatta Gaol Record Book, no. 1123.4/6530; House of Correction, 22 June 1839, p. 157, 4/4569; *Sydney Gazette*, 16 October 1826; *Phoenix* (hulk) Entrance Book 4/6282; 4/4181; TL 43/2412; 4/4231; *Hyde Park Barracks Index*, X824, 30 May 1831; TL 43/2412; CP 58/67.

ALEXANDER, Isaac

b. London, d. 1859
Free.
Married; Saddler; 3 children.

Isaac and Samuel Alexander (q.v.) bought land at Molongo on 19 August 1850. Isaac died in 1859 leaving an estate of £15 000. Isaac was the father of the philosopher Samuel Alexander, who was born in Sydney the year his father died. Isaac and his wife Cecilia Alexander had three children: Mary (1848), Levi (1849) and Samuel (1859).

Land Correspondence 2/7799; Miles, *Registry of Flash Men*, 2/673.

ALEXANDER, Israel

b. Poznan, Poland, 1794–1876
Senator, 1848; Free.
Married; Tailor; 7 children.

Israel Alexander was born in Poznan. (A death notice in the *Sydney Morning Herald* indicates that he was born in 1794). He married Hannah Lyons in London in 1833 where their seven children were born.

Israel and Hannah Alexander followed their sons Raphael and Godfrey to Australia, arriving in Melbourne on 12 October 1848. It appears that they came with their two youngest children, Michael and Rosa, arriving in Melbourne on 12 October 1848.

Hannah died on 14 September 1871 aged seventy-five, having lived at 98 Young Street, Fitzroy, in Melbourne. Israel was living at Green Street, Prahran, in Melbourne, when he died on 7 November 1876 at the age of eighty-two. Both were buried in unmarked graves in the Jewish section of the Melbourne General Cemetery.

Ken Smith (comp.), *Our Alexander Families*, privately printed, Oatlands, NSW.

ALEXANDER, Jacob

b. London
Free.
Single.

Jacob Alexander was the brother of Maurice Alexander (q.v.). Jacob married Emily Yates, the daughter of Saul Yates (q.v.).

ALEXANDER, Lewis

b. London, 1806
Charles Kerr, 1837; Convict; Sentenced to 7 years, Central Criminal Court, 1836.
Married; Horse dealer, stage coach proprietor; 8 children.

Fair ruddy complexion. Dark brown hair. Grey eyes. Diagonal scar on left cheekbone. Scar inner corner left eyebrow. Can read and write. 'Jew.' Aged thirty-one. Lewis Alexander was transported for stealing a ticket for property that was being kept in a pawn shop. Alexander was married and had four children at the time of his deportation. Two were males and two were females.

'Louis' Alexander was listed in the service of the government in Sydney in the 1837 General Return of Convicts in New South Wales. The Hyde Park Barracks convict list registered him as an 'Auctioneer and Horse Dealer'. A ticket of leave was issued in 1841 and a certificate of freedom on 2 December 1843.

His wife, Flora, was not Jewish. Four children were born in Sydney: Elizabeth Eve (2 July 1840), Beaufort Somerset (3 February 1842), Matilda Selina (3 August 1843), and Benjamin (1848). All children were registered at birth as 'Hebrew'. Alexander advertised in the *Sydney Morning Herald* on 13 April 1844: 'Lewis Alexander (bred to the business in London). City Horse Depository, Saddle and Harness Manufacturer. Pitt St North'. Additional advertisements followed in the *Sydney Morning Herald* during 1844 and 1845.

Lewis Alexander, his wife and four children sailed for San Francisco and the Californian goldfields on the barque *Victoria* on 9 November 1849.

Charles Kerr Indent, 9 October 1837, p. 147; 4/4387; TL 41/1968; CP 42/2086.

ALEXANDER, Maurice (Morris)

b. London, 1820–1874
Hercules, 1834; Free.
Single; Dealer.

Maurice (Morris) Alexander was the eldest son of Isaac Alexander and Susannah née Levey, and the nephew of Solomon Alexander, Barnett Alexander, Rebecca Ellis (q.v.), Samuel Levey (q.v.), and Isaac Levey (q.v.). He arrived in Sydney aged fourteen with his uncle, Isaac Levey, and his first cousin Jacob Marks (q.v.).

Maurice worked for his uncle, Isaac Levey, who developed general stores in Sydney, Goulburn, and a number of other country towns. On 20 October 1847 Maurice married his first cousin, Isabella Dinah Levey, the youngest daughter of Isaac Levey of the Australian Warehouse in George Street, Sydney. Maurice was the brother of Jacob Alexander (q.v.) of Davis, Alexander & Co. of Goulburn. In the *Sydney Morning Herald* of 15 April 1845 and 9 December 1845 his advertisements were emblazoned 'Advance Australia', announcing the store in Yass of Myers and Alexander, which also functioned as 'Real Estate Agents'.

Maurice became a partner in his father-in-law's business. In the course of time he became a director of several public companies, City Bank, United Insurance Co., and the Sydney Gas Co. He was also a trustee of the New South Wales Savings Bank. Alexander owned the pastoral Norwood Station near Goulburn.

Active in public life, Maurice Alexander was a member of the Board of the York Street Synagogue from 1855 until his death. Alexander was a Justice of the Peace and the Member for Goulburn in 1861–72 (over three terms) in the New South Wales Legislative Assembly.

Alexander died at his home at 48 Wynyard Street, on 27 January 1874. Aged fifty-four and leaving an estate of £18 050, he was buried at the Devonshire Street Jewish Cemetery. Among his beneficiaries were his wife, Isabella, his mother, Mrs Susannah Nathan of London, his sisters, Fanny of London, Elizabeth (the wife of Charles Moses) of Melbourne, and Catherine (the wife of Woolf Lazarus) of Melbourne, and his brother, Jacob Alexander of Sydney. Isabella died on 27 October 1885 leaving an estate of £13 045. She was buried in the Devonshire Street Cemetery and subsequently reburied at Rookwood. Maurice Alexander's very elaborate memorial has the Hebrew inscription 'one of the noted men of the city'.

Ship Indent 4/5209; *Sydney Morning Herald*, 28 January 1874; Land Correspondence 2/7799; Memoir by family, ML 042/Pa 205; *Town and Country Journal*, 7 March 1874. AJHSJ, Vol 17, part 4, (2005) Morris Forbes *The Jews of Goulburn 1835–1881, A Revision of the History*, p. 500 ff.

ALEXANDER, Michael

b. London, c. 1831
Senator, 1848; Free.
Single; Dealer; 7 children.

Michael Alexander married Miriam Aarons in 1856 in Melbourne. They had seven children: Lewis (1857) in Ballarat, Rosetta (1859) in Beechworth, Israel Jacob

(1861) in Melbourne, Elizabeth (1862), Joseph (1864), Edward Abraham Solomon (1867), and Alice Hannah (1869).

Michael Alexander was listed as a dealer at 59 Johnston Street, East Collingwood, in 1861, and at 133 Kerr Street, Fitzroy (where his father lived), in 1863. He subsequently lived in North Melbourne and Fitzroy and appears to have died after 1888.

ALEXANDER, Moss (Morris, Moses)

b. London, c. 1825–1910
1837; Free.
Single; Dealer; 9 children.

Moss Alexander arrived in Melbourne with his brother Godfrey Alexander (q.v.). He was the fourth child of Israel Alexander (q.v.) and Hannah (née Lyons). Moss established the first drapery store in Portland in 1841 before moving to Geelong. Moss Alexander married Mary McNamara in 1855 in Melbourne. They had five children. Mary Alexander died in 1867, and in 1869 Alexander married his sister-in-law, Elizabeth MacNamara, and they had four children. Morris Alexander, a 'draper's assistant', was listed as insolvent in October 1860. He died on 5 June 1910, and Elizabeth (Bridget) died in 1941, aged ninety-five.

ALEXANDER, Rachel

b. London, 1809
Lady MacNaghten, 1836; Free.
Single; Dressmaker.

An assisted bounty migrant. Jewess. Could read and write.

'Mrs Simmons of Sydney' was listed on Rachel Alexander's documents as a 'friend or relative in New South Wales'. It was also noted that she had been 'ill on the ill fated voyage'. Rachel arrived in Sydney on 26 February 1837. The ship's passengers had suffered from an outbreak of scarlet fever.

Lady MacNaghten papers A1267-15, p. 226.

ALEXANDER, Raphael

b. London, 1817–1892
Alexander, 1835; Free.
Single; Tailor; 12 children.

Raphael Alexander travelled steerage on the *Alexander*, arriving in Sydney on 30 August 1835. He was travelling with Michael Samuel (q.v.), who also appeared in the ship's passenger list as a tailor.

Alexander was a clothier in Collins Street, Melbourne, in 1841. He was granted a confectioner's licence in Melbourne on 10 September 1842. Alexander was a founding member of the Melbourne Hebrew Congregation in 1844 but, by April 1845, had fallen behind in his payments to the congregation. On 24 June 1845, Raphael Alexander married Agnes Thomson at the Wesleyan Methodist Church in Melbourne. They had twelve children. In 1848 he was listed as a householder and a voter because he had a property in Elizabeth Street. 'A. E. Alexander and R. Alexander' were owners of the Bee Hive Drapery and Clothing Store in Collins Street, Melbourne, by the end of 1851.

Alexander Indent 4/5209; *Melbourne Morning Herald*, 29 November 1851; *Port Phillip Gazette*, 10 September 1842.

ALEXANDER, Rosa

b. London, c. 1838
Senator, 1848; Free.
Single.

The seventh and youngest child of Israel Alexander (q.v.) and his wife Hannah (née Lyons), Rosa married Alfred Harris in Melbourne in 1852. Her date of death is unknown, but occurred after 1888.

ALEXANDER, Samuel

b. London, 1805–1859
Norfolk (1), 1825; Convict; Sentenced to 7 years, Newington, Surrey, 1824.
Single; Shoemaker, furniture cleaner; Height: 157.5 cm.

Fair, sallow complexion, dark brown hair, brown eyes. The son of Israel Alexander of London. Samuel Alexander was sentenced for shoplifting at the Surrey Quarter Sessions, 30 August 1824.

Samuel Alexander was convicted, in the colony of New South Wales, at the Windsor General Session on 21 October 1826, for stealing 'a quantity of pork'. He was sent to the Moreton Bay prison settlement and returned to Sydney on 28 December 1828. He was convicted in Sydney on 4 January 1830 for being 'incorrigible' and for 'running away from the Iron Gang', and sent back to Moreton Bay. On 5 October 1831 a certificate of freedom was granted, but Alexander was once again convicted in the Criminal Court at Sydney, this time for smuggling. He was sentenced to death, but was reprieved and sent to Norfolk Island on 25 January 1834.

Alexander was one of the nine Jews on Norfolk Island who, in May 1840, wrote to the Sydney Synagogue asking for prayer books to be sent to them. He is listed in the *Registry of Flash Men* as 'a Norfolk Islander and shoemaker and head of a gang of thieves who live at the back of the *Monitor* newspaper office [in Barrack Lane]. They are at work now' (January 1844).

OBSP, 1819–20, case 1857, p. 655; *Norfolk* Indent 2/8254, and 4/4010, p. 143; *Phoenix* (hulk) Entrance Book 4/5281, p. 18; *Lucy Ann* Indent 4/3896, p. 304; Miles, *Registry of Flash Men*, p. 70, 2/673; Land Correspondence 2/7799; CF 31/1047.

ALEXANDER, Samuel

b. London
1848; Free.
Watchmaker and jeweller.

Isaac Davis (q.v.) and Samuel Alexander commenced business in Collins Street as jewellers and watchmakers in the week of 27 April 1848. Alexander gave generously to the Melbourne Hebrew Congregation's building appeals in the early 1850s. Samuel Alexander was a shopkeeper in Ballarat in the early 1850s. He appears to have settled in Ararat and was present at the High Holyday services held there in 1858.

Port Phillip Herald, 27 April 1848.

ALEXANDER, Samuel

b. London, 1827–1911
1849; Free.
Single; 10 children.

The fifth child of Israel Alexander (q.v.) and Hannah (née Lyons), Samuel Alexander apparently arrived in Melbourne in 1849. In 1854 he married Frances (Fanny) Hartley Richards. They had ten children.

ALEXANDER, Samuel

Free.
Single; Dealer.

Samuel was the brother of Isaac Alexander (q.v.). Both men were early settlers in the 1850s in the Molongo District.

ALKIN, William

b. London, 1807
Marquis of Hastings (3), 1828; Convict; Sentenced to life, London, 1828.
Single; Pedlar, street seller; Height: 171 cm.

Ruddy complexion. Brown hair. Blue eyes. Tattoo of a woman's bust on left arm. Can read and write. William Alkin was an orange seller, who cut the window of a glass and china shop and tried to steal a decanter. Caught in the act, he was tried on 10 January 1828 and initially sentenced to death. He had no previous convictions.

William Alkin arrived in Port Jackson on 12 October 1828. He was listed as 'Protestant' in the ship's indent but, subsequently in the colonial records, as a Jew. The Parramatta Gaol Record Book recorded that Alkin was 'Tried at Sydney 19 July 1838. To be sent to the stone quarry at Liverpool'. A ticket of leave was issued on 25 March 1839. Alkin was living in the district of Campbelltown. The pass was altered for Camden in 1842 and he was allowed to travel between Sydney and Goulburn later that year. He received a conditional pardon dated 1 July 1846.

OBSP, 1827–28, case 263, p. 163; *Marquis of Hastings* (3) Indent 4/4127, 4/4013; Parramatta Gaol Record Book, 1838–1839, 4/6533 no. 1115; A/1222, no. 401, 4/4127; TL 39/401; CP 46/347.

ALLEN, David (LEMAIR)

b. Strasbourg, 1826
Triton, 1842; Convict; Sentenced to 7 years, Lancaster-Salford, 1841.
Single; Coach painter; Height: 160 cm.

Able to read French. Reads and writes English. A stout man, fair complexion, very dark brown hair, dark eyes, black whiskers, long nose, broad mouth. David Allen stole a portmanteau from his master, Mr Joseph Williams. He had twice been imprisoned for theft before his sentence of transportation. His gaol report in England stated that he was a 'bad character'. On the ship he served as clerk to the surgeon, who 'recommends' him.

David Allen's initial period of probation in Van Diemen's Land was fifteen months at Bridgewater. On 22 April 1840 he was given four days in solitary confinement for 'insolence and disrespectful language'. In May 1844 he was recommended for a ticket of leave for his meritorious conduct on the occasion of a fire at Mr Rolwegen's house and was assigned to Louis Nathan (q.v.). Before a reply could be received from London, however, he was sentenced to seven additional years transportation at the Hobart Supreme Court, on 22 October 1845, for stealing two tablecloths and various other articles from his master. He had rented seat 74 at the Hobart Synagogue in that year, had paid fifteen shillings in offerings and subscription, and had sung in the choir at the consecration service.

Following Allen's conviction, he was sent to Port Arthur, deprived of his pass, and the earlier recommendation was struck off the records. Two minor charges of pilfering added four months to his initial probationary period. In May 1849 he was sentenced to six months hard labour for larceny under £5 while an assigned servant.

On 17 December 1850 his ticket of leave was reinstated. He had been living in Launceston, but illegally travelled to Victoria, where he was arrested in Geelong. His sentence was then extended another eighteen months and he was sentenced to spend four years with the quarry gang at Port Arthur. A certificate of freedom was finally granted on 29 June 1853.

CON 33/33, no. 7926; Hobart Synagogue Minute Book no. 1.

ALLEN, Isaac

b. Spitalfields, 1807
Layton, 1826; Convict; Sentenced to 7 years, London, 1826.
Married; Hawker; 1 child (in London).

Isaac Allen, the son of Levi Allen of Spitalfields, was convicted for fraud. Allen sold a watch for 'more than its true value'; he had been convicted of a similar offence eight years earlier. 'Jew.' Brown hair.

Blue eyes. Scar on left cheek and pock-pitted. Gaol Report: 'here before'. 'Wife and child with my father and mother.'

Allen spent his first year in Van Diemen's Land at the Prisoners' Barracks in Hobart Town. On 15 October 1827 he was found to be absent without leave. As it was his first offence he was discharged. On 26 November 1827, while a member of the 'Orphan School Road Gang', he was found drunk in the streets of the town at 9:15 p.m. He was punished with fourteen days in the chain gang.

In February 1828, while a member of the New Town Road Party, he was sentenced to twenty-five lashes for 'Disobedience'. On 13 February 1829 he was judged to be 'drunk and disorderly'and given three days on the treadmill. Only ten days later, on 23 February 1829, he was given twelve lashes for being 'drunk and disorderly'. By 3 March 1829 he had been assigned to work as a servant in a private house. He was suspected of stealing eight shillings from his master's guest and given twelve months in a chain gang. In March 1830, he was absent from work and placed on the treadmill for two days. On 19 April, while a member of 'No. 2 Chain Gang', he was found to be absent from morning muster and sentenced to twelve lashes. On 14 June, while assigned to the Public Works Department, he was found guilty of 'neglect of duty', and received a further twenty-five lashes. On 11 October 1832, he was given fifty lashes for being drunk. A certificate of freedom was granted to Allen on 20 September 1833. However, on 6 December 1836, Allen was convicted and sentenced for a period of seven years and sent to the Port Arthur Penitentiary.

CON 31/1, no. 251; CON 23/1; CF 33/174.

ANDERSON, Benjamin

b. London, 1809
Lady Harewood, 1831; Convict; Sentenced to 7 years, London, 1829.
Single; Fishmonger; Height: 160 cm.

Dark sallow complexion. Dark brown hair, baldish. Dark brown eyes. SD tattooed on left arm. Small scar between eyes and on left cheek. Can read and write. 'Hebrew.' Anderson was transported for stealing a coat valued at £3 that was hanging on the door of a private house. He pleaded that he had eaten no food for two days, and that someone had given him two glasses of liquor to drink. He was sentenced on 29 October 1829.

On arrival in New South Wales on 4 March 1831, Benjamin Anderson was assigned to Major Sullivan at Williams River. In 1833 he 'misbehaves' and was sent to be imprisoned in solitary confinement for seven days. Subsequently, his behaviour was judged to be 'orderly'. He remained in the service of Major Sullivan until he received his certificate of freedom on 27 September 1836. A Benjamin Anderson had a house in Liverpool Street, Sydney, in September 1842.

OBSP, 1828–29, case 1552, p. 714; 4/4103, no. 31/430, 2/2204; *Australian*, 27 September 1836; CF 36/0753.

ANDERSON, James Henri (Henry) (Aaron AARONS)

b. London, 1823–1879
London; 1839, Free.
Single; Dealer, musician; 6 children.

The son of Samuel Aarons and Sarah (née Michaels) of London. The step-brother of John Aaron Anderson (q.v.). It is difficult to distinguish between the two men and, confusingly, they became brothers-in-law when they married sisters. James Henri Anderson was a musician brought to Hobart Town. In 1842 he performed as the pianist among a group of musicians employed to present grand opera. He was in Hobart Town by early 1842 and held a 'grand concert of the most popular music, as now performed in the principle places of fashionable report in London'. In March 1843 he gave a concert in Launceston and within a year was in Sydney. J H Anderson is reported as playing at a pianoforte recital in Sydney in April 1844 and, together with Isaac Nathan (q.v.) shared responsibility for the musical service of consecration of the new York Street synagogue. He arranged, and published, a six-page songbook, *The Lays of the Hebrews—A Selection of Hebrew Melodies as Sung at the Consecration of the Sydney Synagogue, Sydney, 1844.* In June 1844 he was listed as having pledged £10 to the Launceston Synagogue appeal and was the honorary secretary of the congregation. He was in Launceston at the time of the dedication of the synagogue, in March 1846, and wrote and performed the music at the dedication service. The *Launceston Examiner* reported: 'The greater part of the solos and the choruses we believe were composed by Mr Anderson'. Anderson gave £1 to the Sydney Synagogue appeal 'from Hobart' in 1845. In that same year, on 23 August, he was the bridegroom at Jewish wedding no. 6 in Launceston, when he married Hannah Solomon, the daughter of Mark Solomon (q.v.) and his wife Catherine. Hannah was born 15 July 1823 and had been baptised 18 August 1823 at St David's Hobart.

On 22 October 1848, J H Anderson, formerly secretary of the Launceston Synagogue was appointed by the Melbourne Synagogue as reader of the congregation. In addition to his liturgical duties, £10 was added to his salary 'for the purpose of enabling him to employ a man to clean and trim the lamps and clean the synagogue'. His period of service concluded at the end of the year and on 29 January 1849 Moses Rintel (q.v.) was employed to take his place.

Anderson was living at Collins Street, Melbourne, in 1849 when his wife Hannah gave birth to Sarah Catherine 'Kate' (Melbourne Hebrew Congregation Birth Book, 5 May 1849). He advertised, untruthfully, in the *Melbourne Morning Herald*, on 1 May 1849, that he was a professor of music who had studied at London's Royal Academy of Music. He offered lessons in pianoforte and English singing, with appointments to be made through D & S Benjamin, a store in Collins Street. In 1850 J. H. Anderson published *The Fitzroy Quadrilles* dedicated to Lieutenant Governor Charles Fitzroy.

In June 1853 Anderson played the organ at the induction service of the Rev. Herman Hoelzel at the Hobart Synagogue. By September 1859 Anderson had moved back to Sydney and advertised that he was an 'Importer of Music and Musical Instruments' while presiding at the harmonium and directing the choir at the dediction for the Macquarie Street break away synagogue. A 'very melodious Hallelujah Psalm' was sung by the composer. The Andersons' sixth child, Adolphus, was born in Newcastle and registered at the Sydney Synagogue in 1854. Anderson was involved in the music for the Macquarie Street Synagogue, serving on the board in 1867 and 1868.

John Henry Anderson died on 1 May 1879, aged fifty-six, and was buried at the Melbourne General Cemetery. According to his death certificate James Henry Anderson spent two years in Van Diemen's Land, 16 years in New South Wales, 15 years in Queensland, two years in New Zealand. (The recorded years spent in Queensland must be a mistake. Perhaps it should be months rather than years). Rachel, the 'beloved wife' of J. H. Anderson Esq. of Melbourne, late of Sydney died on 22 December 1877 at her residence, 172 Forbes Street, Woolloomooloo (*Sydney Morning Herald*). She was fifty years old.

Their children were Sarah Catherine, twins born in 1846 Abraham Frederick and Augustus Abraham, Aaron Henri (who died aged four in 1853), Joseph born c. 1853, Ada Rebecca born 1857 in Sydney, Linda Arabella born 1859 in Sydney, Lionel Sidney born 1863, Walter born 1864, Gertrude Miriam (born 1866 and died 2 November 1949), Alfred Michael (who died in Melbourne in 1876 aged 28), and Adolphus (born in Newcastle).

Sydney Morning Herald, 3 April 1844; *Launceston Examiner*, 29 June 1844, 28 March 1846, 2 December 1846; J. Aron and J. Arndt, *The Enduring Remnant*, p. 28. Graeme Skinner, *Australian Composers and Arrangers of Early Colonial Synagogue Music; New Light on Isaac Nathan, Henri Anderson, Joseph Reichenberg and Herman Hoelzel*, AJHSJ, vol 20, part 2, June 2011. p. 193f. Family research by Susan Groenhut and Dr Graeme Skinner.

ANDERSON, John Henry/Aaron (John) Aarons

Popularly known as 'the Bolter' and the stepbrother (and brother-in-law) of James Henri Anderson (q.v.). John Anderson/Aaron Aarons/Aaron. John Anderson was also probably the convict known as Jack Anderson. He served a full seven years of his sentence on the road gangs in the district of Launceston. A letter to the *Cornwall Chronicle* (21 July 1836) states that, after the finish of his sentence, 'the enterprising, dapper little Jack Anderson started a business for a few months, obtained credit (his sole aim) became insolvent and obtained a period of imprisonment.' He had married Rachel Solomon, sister of Hannah and daughter of Mark and Catherine Solomon (q.v.) on 23 August 1845 in Launceston. There may also be a fleeting note in the *Port Phillip Gazette* of 16 May 1842: 'Many of our readers will doubtless recollect a fellow of the name of Anderson, an associate and we believe a co-partner of the swindler [Henry] Davis who had made his way to Hobart Town'.

On the 18 November 1846 the *South Australian Register* wrote of John Anderson alias Aaron 'He is a dapper little fellow, about thirty years of age—a Jew but without very Jewish countenance—in height about five feet. He arrived in South Australia from Van Diemen's Land and applied for an auctioneer's licence which was refused. He was a lazy, fraudulent, insolent runaway'. The leaders of the Adelaide Jewish community Emanuel Solomon, (q.v.) E. L. Montefiore (q.v.) and Barnett Nathan (q.v.) were said to have vouched for him. The *Launceston Examiner*, on 2 December 1846, reported that Anderson, 'well known in this island, formerly an auctioneer (and a prominent member and secretary of the Jewish congregation), was apprehended on Tuesday on a Warrant from Adelaide with an inspector of the mounted police in pursuit'. The charge was 'Felony' swindled £600 by issuing bad cheques'.

On 12 December the newspaper added: 'This well known character Anderson was discharged on a technicality as the Launceston Court ruled that the South Australian warrant was illegal. The inspector returned to Adelaide and Anderson went to live in Hobart Town, where it was soon reported: 'John Anderson has gone to Mauritius by the *Alice Brooks* but his character will probably reach there before him and prevent the successful practice of further frauds'.

Rachel and Hannah were both buried in the Jewish section of the Rookwood cemetery. Hannah's epitaph stated she had been born 15 May 1828 at Hobart Town and baptised 5 June 1825 at St David's. Her gravestone reads 'Sacred to the memory of Hannah, relict of the late J. A. Anderson, who departed this life 5 February 1875, aged 52 years'. There were nine children. Both Anderson families named their first-born Alfred. There are two sons named Michael and they both had a Catherine and a Gertrude.

Research by Susan Groenhut and Dr Graeme Skinner.

ANSELL, Henry Simon

b. London, 1825
1843; Free. Single;
Watchmaker; 6 children.

The son of Hyam and Frances Ansell, and grandson to Rabbi Zalmon Ansell, the former *Av Beth Din* (Chairman of the Jewish Religious Court) of London, Henry Simon Ansell married Rosetta Casper at her father's house, at 38 Liverpool Street, Hobart Town, on 24 July 1850. Rosetta was a child of Ellis and Elizabeth Casper (qq.v.). He set up shop in Geelong and wrote to his brother Moses in England, suggesting that some young Jewish girls should be sent to Victoria to prevent intermarriage. He was the first honorary treasurer of the Geelong Hebrew Congregation.

Henry and Rosetta's children were Solomon Hyam and Rosinia (1854), Morris (1855), born in Geelong, Frances (1858), in Collingwood, Asher (1859), in Melbourne, and Rosetta (born and died in 1861) in Fitzroy. She was named after her mother, who died giving birth on 27 September 1861. After the death of his wife and infant child, Henry and his other children moved to Birmingham, England, where he married Matilda Myers.

Family information from Anne Budlender, Victoria.

ASHER, Benjamin

Benjamin Asher sailed from Sydney for California and the goldfields on the barque *Victoria* on 9 November 1849.

ASHER, Frances

b. London, 1803–1889
1842; Free.
Single.

Frances Asher married Aaron Solomons (q.v.), who arrived in Van Diemen's Land in 1841. She was his second wife, and they were to have ten children. Frances died in Melbourne on 3 August 1889, and was buried in the Melbourne General Cemetery. Her children were Phoebe (q.v.) (1827), Leah (1832), Abigail (1834), Isaac (1839), Louisa (1845), Henry John, Miriam (1847), Rachael (1849), Joseph and Sarah.

ASHER, Henry

b. Poland, 1805–1852
Westmoreland (1), 1835; Convict; Sentenced to 7 years, York/West Riding, 1835.
Single; Jeweller; Height: 155 cm.

Ruddy and a little pock-pitted complexion. Brown hair. Dark hazel eyes. Nose thick and inclining to the right. Henry Asher was convicted of house breaking.

Henry Asher arrived in Sydney on 15 July 1835 and was sent to the District of Port Macquarie. In the 1837 General Return of Convicts in New South Wales he was listed in the prisoners' work party on Goat Island in Sydney Harbour. A ticket of leave was granted in 1841 and a certificate of freedom on 22 February 1842.

Henry Asher was a member of the Sydney Synagogue in 1845. An infant child, Henry Joel Asher, was registered in 1850 and died in Sydney on 7 December 1852, being buried as a Jew.

Petition A86, p. 298, 4/4371; TL 41/1345; CF 42/0273.

ASHER, Joel Henry

Argo, 1836; Free.

Mr H. Asher 'from Hobart Town' was the only passenger travelling on the *Argo*, which arrived at Port Jackson on 30 June 1836. Asher advertised that he had commenced business as Auctioneer and Commission Agent at 16 Elizabeth Street, Hobart Town. I. H. Asher was a member of the Hobart Town Synagogue in 1842 and pledged to pay one guinea in 1844 (which he did not pay). He was not a seat holder, but in 1845 gave £3 3s to the Synagogue building appeal. Asher apparently moved to Sydney, because it was reported (*Australian*, 19 October 1842) that he had been empanelled as a juror in the Norfolk Island piracy case.

There are two other references to J. H. Asher in Van Diemen's Land. The first was an arrival on the *Sisters* (cabin class), on 31 July 1844, and the second on the *Louise* (cabin class), on 14 March 1846. Asher departed from Launceston for Sydney on 25 April 1846. Asher travelled on to Brisbane and opened the California Store in North Brisbane, near the ferry, in 1846. Subsequently he became an auctioneer and agent, selling his business at the end of 1849. He bought land in Ipswich in February 1850. By then he was listed as a 'Commission Agent' in Sussex Street, Brisbane. He was the only Jew in Brisbane at the time, and left for Sydney at the end of that year. In 1851, Joel Henry Asher was listed as a licensed pawnbroker at 363 George Street South in Ford's *Sydney Commercial Directory*. Asher returned to Brisbane, and on 31 March 1852 bought land at Sofala, where he was living.

Joel Asher and Harriet were the parents of Benjamin (1848) born in Sydney, Miriam (1848), Henry (1850), Solomon (1853), Sarah (1853), Louisa (1855), Rosetta (1857), Morris (1858), Sydney (1861), Ralph (1867), whose birth was registered at St Philip's, Sydney, Hannah (1863), at Newcastle, and Solomon (1865) at Glebe.

Joel Henry Asher died in Sydney on 11 March 1847 and was buried at the Devonshire Street Cemetery, recorded by the synagogue as a 'native of Poland' and as a member of the congregation.

ML/5210, Hobart Town Courier, 7 September 1844, Moreton Bay Courier, 1 September 1849, 10 November 1849, 29 December 1849, 6 April 1849; Petition for Land 2/7792; *AG*, p. 314.

ML 4/5210; *Hobart Town Courier*, 7 September 1844.

ASHER, Joel Henry

b. London, ca 1820–1875
Bardaster, 1839; Free.
Dealer; 11 children.

Joel Henry Asher arrived with his brother, Morris Asher (q.v.), in Sydney on 3 March 1839. His name appeared in the first voters' list in the Sydney municipal election of 1842 because he had a 'shop and rooms' in George Street. In July 1843, Joel Asher had 'relinquished his drapery and slop business and commenced work as a general agent and auctioneer in George St'. On 1 November 1843 he was declared insolvent and Walter Gray and Moses Joseph were appointed trustees of his estate. He was granted his certificate of discharge on 29 February 1844, paying tenpence ha'penny in the pound.

Asher then moved to Auckland where he opened a shop and in 1847 he was married to Harriett Keesing (1827-1881) before leaving New Zealand and beginning a business in Moreton Bay. His wife and child joined him there in 1849 and in 1850 was granted a licence to be an auctioneer in the colony. Asher travelled on to Brisbane and opened the California Store in North Brisbane, near the ferry, in 1846. Subsequently he became an auctioneer and agent, selling his business at the end of 1849. He bought land in Ipswich in February 1850. By then he was listed as a 'Commission Agent' in Sussex Street, Brisbane.

For the next fourteen or fifteen years Joel lived and worked as hotel owner, newspaper editor and shopkeeper in Sydney, Newcastle and Nelligen. His youngest son was born in Auckland in 1869.

Joel and Harriett appear to have separated. Joel died at Auckland at the age of 56 in 17 June 1875. His occupation on his death certificate was 'storekeeper'.

Moreton CSO 92/13 F17; CSO 92/16 F60 (AOT); POL 459/Q, p. 74; *Australasian Chronicle*, 8 April 1833; *Sydney Morning Herald*, 15 September 1842; *AG*, p. 314. ML 4/5210; *Hobart Town Courier*, 7 September 1844; Family history notes by Ian Nicol of Sydney.

ASHER, Morris

b. Hackney, 1818–1909
Bardaster, 1839; Free.
Single; Dealer; 14 children.

The son of Isaac Benjamin Asher and Mary née Moss (Moses), Isaac was a storekeeper on the isle of Jersey. Morris arrived in Sydney with his older brother, Joel Henry Asher (q.v.), travelling steerage, on 3 March 1839. The *Bardaster* arrived in Port Jackson from Adelaide, where Morris Asher had spent a brief time. He worked as a hawker in the Grenfell District and opened small country stores in Wombat and Grenfell. Six months after his arrival, he took charge of seven bullock teams and took them overland to the new township of Melbourne. On 24 February 1840, he opened his Sydney General Stores in Albury, announcing that he would 'sell lower than any store within a 100 miles of the settlement'. Asher then moved to Wellington, New Zealand, where he traded as a storekeeper and fitted up whaling stations at Queen Charlotte Sound and Kapiti Island. He made more than twenty-three trans-Tasman crossings, importing sheep and merchandise from New South Wales. He served in the Wellington Militia and fought in the Maori Wars.

On 11 February 1846, Mr Morris Asher of Sydney, 'late of New Zealand', married Rebecca Levey, the fifth child of Philip Levey (q.v.) and his wife, Leah (qq.v.), in a Jewish ceremony. Rebecca signed the congregational registry with a mark. Their first child was Rose (Rosetta), born in 1846 in New Zealand. They returned to Australia on the *Kelso* in 1848, and settled in Albury, where Asher built three hotels, the Rose, the Criterion and the Imperial. He opened a general store and established a boiling-down works and a flour mill. Subsequent children were Jane

(Deborah) (1848–1929), Benjamin (1848), Samuel (in Albury, 3 May 1850–1944), Sarah (1853–1924), Alice (1856), Isaac (Richard) Benjamin (1856–1937), Morris Mark in Albury (1858–1922), Henry Joel (Harry) (1860–1934), Fanny (in Sydney, 1861–1944), Miriam (Marion) (in Sydney, 1863), Phillip (1864), Sidney John (later S.J. Laidlaw) (1866–1912), and Septimus David (in Bathurst, 1869-circa 1955). The Melbourne Hebrew Congregation recorded that Morris Asher, 'storekeeper' of Albury, and his wife Rebecca brought a son to Melbourne for his circumcision on 8 December 1850.

In 1859 Asher contested the seat of Hume in the newly constituted New South Wales Parliament and won by three votes. He failed to be re-elected in 1865, and ran a store in the Lachlan goldfields. He was appointed appraiser of lands in the Riverina. Asher later worked as an auctioneer and lost most of his money through speculation. He died, at the age of ninety-one, on 29 October 1909, leaving an estate valued at £4459 7s 7d.

Melbourne Morning Herald, 13 February 1846, 24 February 1849, 9 March 1849; Minute Book Melbourne Hebrew Congregation, 3 May 1850–58, December 1850; M. Z. Forbes, 'Jewish Personalities in the Movement for Responsible Government in NSW', *AJJHS*, vol. 4, no. 6 (1957), p. 316; 'Reminiscences of an Octogenarian', *Sydney Mail*, 31 July 1907; *AG*, pp. 252, 300, 301. Family History Notes by Ian Nicol of Sydney.

ASSER, Abigail

c. 1815–1866
Westmoreland, 1833; Free.
Single; Nursemaid.

Abigail Asser, a nursemaid, arrived with the families of Barnett Aaron Phillips (q.v.) and Solomon Levien (q.v.) on 19 May 1833. Abigail died on 31 May 1866, and was buried at the Devonshire Street Jewish Cemetery in Sydney.

ASSER, Henry

Surprize (1), 1790; Convict; Sentenced to life, Old Bailey, 1786.
Single.

Henry Asser was convicted of stealing £14 worth of linen and clothes from his employer, a linen draper. Asser sold the stolen property to Barnett Levi, who realised that it was stolen and informed the draper. Asser was sentenced to death, which was then commuted because of 'his extreme youth'. The prisoner 'cried very much' when being questioned.

The *Surprize* was part of the ill-fated and badly managed Second Fleet, which arrived in Port Jackson on 26 June 1790. Henry Asser was listed on the 1814 Muster at Liverpool. He was 'free' and a landholder. Asser eventually received an absolute pardon (which is noted on the margin of the Indent).

OBSP, 1785–1786, case 486, p. 730f; *Surprize* (1) Indent 4/4004, p. 36; 1814 Muster, A1942–2, p. 146.

AUSTIN, Adolph (ARNSTEIN)

b. Lippstadt, Westphalia, 1796–1856
1847; Free.
Married; 2 children.

Adolph Arnstein and his wife Sarah (née Hertzfield) (Sarah Austin, q.v.) travelled to Sydney from London with their son, Lewis Austin. Adolph Arnstein (Austin) died, aged sixty, and was buried at the Devonshire Street Jewish Cemetery on 19 September 1856. Sarah married a second time, to Moses Mayer.

AUSTIN, Edward (Adolph ARENSTEIN)

b. Sulzbach, Westphalia, 1804–1856
Hercules II (3), 1832; Convict; Sentenced to 7 years, London, 1831.
Married; Tailor; Height: 160 cm; 5 children.

Sallow complexion. Dark brown hair. Dark eyes. 'Scar on top of right thumb, a Jew'. Could read and write German and English. Austin was indicted for stealing two brooches valued at ten shillings and one ring valued at £1. A shop assistant caught Austin coming down the stairs from the garret where she lived. He spoke 'bad English'. The prisoner therefore submitted a written defence, stating that he had come from Bavaria in search of a merchant named Masenbach, who had told him he lived on the third floor of the house in question. The court did not believe him.

Edward Austin arrived in New South Wales on 16 October 1832. Austin (Arenstein) was listed in the 1837 General Return of Convicts working as an assigned convict servant to Major General Stuart in Bathurst. In the same year he received his ticket of leave for the district of Bathurst. A certificate of freedom followed on 19 April 1839. That year, he married Mary Anne Chambers, who had been born in England.

By November 1844 he owned the St James Store in Bathurst and a 'boiling down business' yielding tallow and skins. He described himself as a 'wool broker', and in August 1845 sold his boiling-down business to Joseph Aarons. In 1843 the Sydney Synagogue had appointed Austin as its representative in Queanbeyan and, in 1845, he gave the York Street Synagogue a donation of £20.

Austin applied for naturalisation in 1846, stating that his parents were Lowe and Caroline Arenstein. He had been born in Salzbach, Bavaria. By that time, he had four children and owned 'considerable property' in Bathurst. He wished to travel to England to settle his affairs and to return. He was anxious to sell his stock in trade plus the business at Bathurst, which averaged an income of £15 000 a year, and intended to buy wool to take back to England. Austin's application for naturalisation was accepted by London.

Edward Austin died at Bathurst on 29 September 1856 and was buried at the Devonshire Street Jewish Cemetery (later reburied at Rookwood).

Children were Lewis, David, Fanny, Doris and Eve.

OBSP, 1831, case 131, p. 72; *Hercules* II (3) Indent, p. 131; Ship Indent 4/4017, p. 99; TL 37/494; CF 4/434739/0585; *Sydney Morning Herald*, 1 April 1844, 23 August 1844, 1 November 1844, 18 November 1844, 1 October 1845; Governors' Despatches, A1300, 4 July 1846, p. 17.

AUSTIN, Sarah (née HERTZFIELD) (MAYER)

1847; Free.
Married; 2 children.

Sarah arrived in Sydney, with her husband, Adolph Austin (q.v.), and son, Lewis Austin. After Adolph died in 1856, Sarah remarried, to Moses Mayer, with whom she had another child, David.

B

BADEN, Thomas (Levy Isaacs)

b. London, 1799–1867
Lady Castlereagh, 1818; Convict; Sentenced to 7 years, Old Bailey, 1817.
Single; Goldsmith; Height: 175 cm; 4 children.

Black hair, eyes dark, fair pale complexion. 'Well behaved' on board ship. Thomas Baden came from a family of jewellers in London. His name was variously spelled Beadon, Beedon, Beeton and Beaton. He was sentenced in January 1817 for stealing some printed cotton worth one shilling and fivepence from a draper in Oxford Street.

Thomas Baden was born Thomas Isaacs, but took his mother's maiden name. Baden (Beadon) was stationed in Launceston and in 1819 was appointed a constable. He was dismissed from the force in January 1821 and sentenced to hard labour in the gaol gang at Port Dalrymple for three months. On 8 June 1822, he was charged with neglect of duty while working in the Public Works Department, and was sentenced to work in irons for one month. On 8 October 1824 he was charged with having assaulted a Mr Mayley. No proof of the offence was tendered to the court, and the charge was dismissed. Baden took refuge on the islands at the western end of Bass Strait. It was said that his English family remitted 'a handsome allowance' to him through one of the Jewish residents of Launceston. By 1830 he had moved to Gun Carriage Island in Bass Strait. His common-law wife was Beth Smith, whose real name was Woreterneemerunnertatteyane. She had been forcibly removed from the Tasmanian mainland by John Harrington, and was 'owned' by Thomas Tucker until Baden (Beeton) obtained her—probably by buying her. They had four children, Lucy, Jane, James and Henry who were 'home educated' to read and write.

Baden returned to Launceston for some years, and then took his wife and his children back to live on the islands in Bass Strait, settling on Badger Island.

OBSP, 1817, case 245, p. 245; A. L. Meston, *The Half-castes of the Furneaux Group*, p. 50; CON 31/1, no. 109, p. 28; CON 13/1, p. 173; HO 10/43.

BARNARD, Samuel

Marian Watson; Free; Sentenced to 7 years, Sydney, 1841.
Dealer.

Listed as a Jew, Samuel Barnard was transported for embezzlement of £9, the property of his employer, Thomas Davis, after a trial in Sydney on 18 August 1841. Barnard was placed in the Clerks' Room Police Barracks in Hobart Town for twelve months.
CON 31/8, no. 494.

BARNET, Lazarus (Bernard LAZARUS)

b. London, 1801
Speke (2), 1821; Convict; Sentenced to 7 years, Old Bailey, 1820.
Single; Errand boy; Height: 152 cm.

Stout, dark sallow complexion, black hair, dark black eyes. Tattoo AK on right arm. Pock-pitted. Lazarus Barnet was transported for stealing a pair of stockings from a shop in Bishopsgate, having been sentenced at Middlesex on 28 February 1820.

Barnet arrived on 18 May 1821. In the 1825 General Muster list he was recorded as 'Bernard' Lazarus, in 'Government employ' in Sydney. He worked at the New Lumber Yard and in January 1822 the Colonial Secretary's records show him as a 'Basket maker'. Lazarus Barnet was listed in the 1828 Census as a gardener at William Brown's, York Street, Sydney. His religion was given as 'Protestant'and he was 'Free by Servitude'. He was granted a ticket of leave in 1829. Barnet worked as a compositor at the office of the *Sydney Gazette* in 1836, and was charged in March of that year with being absent from his hired service for three days. He was sentenced to thirty days on the treadmill. It was his third conviction in four months for absconding, and he claimed to have been 'unwell'. In August he was charged again for refusing to return to work, and sentenced to two months in gaol. A Lazarus Barnet had received a certificate of freedom on 22 February 1827, and another on 12 August 1841. The certificate was renewed in 1858, where his surname was misspelled as 'Barent'.
OBSP, 1819–20, case 498, p. 205; *Speke* (2) Indent 4/4007, p. 352; HO 10/19; *Sydney Gazette*, 20 August 1836, 3 March 1827, 6 December 1836, 20 August 1836; TL 29/398; CF 4/4368, 4/4424-41/1097, 58/6066.

BARNETT, Aaron (Aaron Moses)

b. London, 1785–1843
Glatton, 1803; Convict; Sentenced to life, Surrey, 1800.
Single; Labourer; Height: 163 cm.

Ruddy, pockmarked, yellow muddy complexion, black hair, dark brown eyes. Can neither read nor write. Aaron Barnett was sentenced at Surrey on 11 August 1800.

The *Glatton* arrived in New South Wales on 11 March 1803. In July 1804 Aaron Barnett was punished for 'theft' and whipped for stealing government provisions. He was listed in the 1806 Muster as a prisoner in Sydney assigned to P. Hibbs. By the 1814 Muster, Barnett was listed as being 'free of the government stores'. He was a labourer, living at Windsor, when he was granted a certificate of freedom on 1 January 1814.

On 31 March 1816 he married Ann Emerson (who had been transported on the *Francis Eliza* in 1815 with a seven-year sentence). By May 1820 Barnett had been appointed a constable in Sydney. He remained in the police force for the next three years. Aaron and Anne Barnett were the witnesses at the marriage of Israel Chapman (q.v.) and each signed the register with an X. In 1823 he asked for, and received, one assigned convict servant. The servant was John Daniels (q.v.), who subsequently absconded from work and was wanted by the police. By 1826 Aaron Barnett had twenty head of cattle and 'as a married man desirous of settling in the colony and free by conditional pardon', asked for a grant of land. In the Census of 1828 he was listed as 'Hebrew' (as was his wife). He was a tenant farmer with sixty acres of land, twenty cultivated acres and twenty horned cattle in the District of Botany. Barnett married, for a second time, at St Luke's, Liverpool, to Eleanor Frawley, on 12 October 1831. Aaron Barnett of George Street was granted a confectioner's licence on 13 May 1843, but nine days later was buried in the Devonshire Street Jewish Cemetery.

Sydney Gazette, 29 July 1804, 13 May 1820, 28 August 1823, 13 January 1825, 13 May 1825; Land Correspondence 2/7796, 1 February 1826; *Sydney Morning Herald*, 13 May 1843; CP Register 4/4430, p. 76, p. 188.

BARNETT, Abigail

Free.
Single.

Abigail Barnett married Emanuel Myers (q.v.) at the Sydney Synagogue on 9 June 1845.

BARNETT, Abraham

b. London, 1807–1835
Waterloo (3), 1833; Convict; Sentenced to 14 years, Middlesex, 1832.
Single; Clothes dealer; Height: 165 cm.

No education. Dark sallow complexion. Dark brown hair. Grey eyes. Large nose. Barnett worked in Petticoat Lane and, together with James Wilson (aged fifty-five), stole a watch from a passerby in Essex Street. Barnett was twenty-three at the time of his trial. He was sentenced on 18 October 1832.

Abraham Barnett arrived in New South Wales on 3 August 1833. He died at the hospital in Liverpool and was buried by St Luke's Church of England in 1835.

OBSP, 1832, case 2432; *Waterloo* Indent, p. 81, no. 1503.

BARNETT, Barnett

Free.
Married; Dealer; 1 child.

In 1847, Barnett and Sarah Barnett (née Levy) of Maitland West had a child, Folk, whom they registered as a 'Hebrew'.

BARNETT, Emanuel

Free.

Emanuel Barnett was a committee member of the Adelaide Hebrew Congregation in 1850.

BARNETT, Folk

Free.
Single.

Folk Barnett married Julia Emanuel (q.v.) at the Sydney Synagogue on 12 March 1844. Julia was the widow of Barnet Emanuel (q.v.).

BARNETT, Henry

1807–1870
1839; Free.
Single; Dealer.

The son of Barnett Barnett, 'merchant', and Sarah (née Levy), Henry Barnett was born in London, and married Charlotte Cohen (q.v.) at the Bridge Street synagogue in Sydney on 30 June 1841. On 1 April 1843 Henry Barnett, Baron B. Cohen (q.v), Francis Cohen (q.v.), and George Phillips (q.v.) were all out on bail after a quarrel with George O'Brien. As the cause of the disturbance was explained: 'Yes, Harry Barnett had better mind his wife that look at Mrs D. E. or F telling Mrs B of anything of the kind would be worse than a twice told tale. As to Mrs B's "little affair" as I call it before marriage—not a word 'tis past. Mr O'Brian denies all connection with his now defunct paper'.

Henry Barnett, 'dealer' of George Street, was listed as insolvent on 2 April 1842 with debts of £472 and only £5 of assets. He was discharged as a bankrupt on 12 March 1844. In November 1846 Henry Barnett, publican, was fined forty shillings for selling liquor after hours. Henry died 2 December 1870 and his wife, Charlotte, died in 1 July 1871, aged fifty-one. Both were buried at Lidcombe's Jewish cemetery.

Australasian Chronicle, 14 April 1843; *Omnibus and Sydney Spectator*, 1 April 1843; *Sydney Morning Herald*, 16 April 1842; *Citizen*, 7 November 1846.

BARNETT, Hiam (Hyam)

b. London, 1779–1835
America, 1829; Convict; Sentenced to 7 years, Bristol, 1828.
Married; Hatter; Height: 157 cm; 8 children.

Dark ruddy complexion, dark brown to grey hair, hazel eyes. 'No peculiar marks.' Could read and write. On 14 July 1828 Barnett was convicted for stealing brass. No previous convictions had been recorded in England. He was married with eight children in England when he was convicted at the Bristol Quarter Sessions on 13 October 1828.

On arrival in Sydney on 18 August 1829 Hiam Barnett was immediately assigned to work for Simeon Lord. Hiam Barnett was a prisoner at Newcastle Gaol in November 1832. Hyam Barnett was buried by the Church of England in Bathurst in 1835.

Ship Indent 4/4014, p. 202, no. 1457–16.

BARNETT, Isaac

b. London, 1811
Florentia (1), 1828; Convict; Sentenced to life, Southworth, 1826.
Single; Errand boy; Height: 151 cm.

Ruddy fair complexion, dark brown hair, dark hazel eyes. Could not read or write. Isaac Barnett was sentenced at Surrey, on 24 October 1826, for 'robbing a person'.

The *Florentia* arrived on 3 January 1828. Isaac Barnett was described in the 1828 Census as a Protestant. He was assigned to the Australian Agricultural Company at Port Stephens. A ticket of leave was issued in 1836 for the District of Argyle, then changed in 1838 for Berrima. A first class conditional pardon was granted in 1842. At this time, his height was recorded as 161 cm. Barnett went to Hobart Town to live with his brother in 1843 and returned to Sydney in the following year, only to be arrested in June for picking a man's pocket.

On 7 August 1847, the Colonial Secretary asked his department to prepare a pardon for Isaac Barnett. Isaac was buried at the Harrington Street Jewish cemetery. The date was not recorded,

Florentia Indent 4/4013, p. 16; Governors' Despatches 1846, A1241, A1217, p. 139; TL 36/653, 36/705; CP 43/303; HO 10/53; CS 47/204; *Sydney Morning Herald*, 3 June 1844.

BARNETT, James

b. Birmingham, 1796–1835
Isabella I (1), 1818; Convict; Sentenced to life, London, 1818.
Single; Seaman; Height: 155 cm; 2 children.

Sallow complexion, dark hair. Barnett was among a crowd of boys at Covent Garden who were pick-pockets. A stolen watch was found in Barnett's 'right-hand pocket' by a constable.

James Barnett arrived in New South Wales on 14 September 1818 and married Ann Bates at St John's Church of England in Parramatta on 2 January 1821. He was listed in the 1828 Census as a Jew, perhaps mistakenly, with a wife and two children, John (1824) and Sarah (1826). He was listed as working as a seaman at Newington.

Barnett died at Bathurst in 1835 and was buried by the Church of England.

OBSP. 12 April 1820, case 450.

BARNETT, John

b. London, 1804–1887
John (1), 1827; Convict; Sentenced to 14 years, Old Bailey, 1827.
Single; Old clothes man; Height: 168 cm; 2 children.

Sallow complexion, black hair, hazel eyes, scar on right hand. Ring on little finger of right hand. In London, John Barnett stole two sovereigns from a drunken man in Whitechapel. He was pursued and caught.

John Barnett arrived in Sydney on 25 November 1827 and was assigned to a bookbinder, Mr G. Hazard, of Prince Street, Sydney. He was listed thus in the 1828 Census. He was granted a ticket of leave in 1837. Barnett married Sarah Frances (q.v.), the daughter of Benjamin Francis (q.v.), on 21 January 1833. It was Australia's second Jewish marriage and Moses Brown (q.v.) officiated. Sarah was officially converted to Judaism in Australia (as her father was Jewish and her mother was not). The conversion was authorised on 18 January 1833 by Michael Phillips (q.v.) and J. B. Montefiore (q.v.).

Barnett's name appears on the petition asking for the establishment of a synagogue in Launceston in May 1843.

OBSP, 1826–27, case 1250, p. 479; TL 37/458, 23 February 1842; CO 2809/274; Launceston Synagogue Petition, CO 280/673.

BARNETT, John

b. London, d. 1887
Palambam, 1832; Free.
Married; Cooper; 4 children.

John Barnett arrived in Sydney on the *Palambam*, with Sarah (q.v.), his wife, and their two children, Mary Jane, aged six, and Robert Freeman, aged seven. On 2 December 1833, John and Sarah had a son, Lewis. On 10 October 1836 a daughter, Jane, was born. Both children were registered with the Jewish community. In 1836 Barnett was working as a 'collector' for the *Australian*. Mr John Barnett was recorded as having given £10 to the Sydney Synagogue building fund on 15 September 1839. A donation of £5 was recorded in the name of Master Lewis Barnett. Lewis was buried in the Devonshire Street Cemetery on 26 April 1841. In November 1842, John Barnett was listed as eligible to vote in the first Sydney municipal elections, as he had a dwelling house in Castlereagh Street. On 31 March 1842 the *Australian* announced that John Barnett had commenced a partnership with J. G. Raphael (q.v.) as an auctioneer in Lower George Street.

John Barnett was buried at Sydney's Rookwood Jewish Cemetery on 3 October 1887.

Australian, 9 April 1842.

BARNETT, Jonas Solomon (Youner)

b. London, 1794
Morley (4), 1823; Convict; Sentenced to life, Old Bailey, 1822.
Single. Watchmaker, jeweller; Height: 163 cm.

Brown hair, brown eyes. Slightly pock-pitted with mole on right side of chin and a small mole at the corner of his right eye. His alias, 'Youner', sounds like the Yiddish for 'younger' (Yinger). He often reversed his names, and was frequently identified as Solomon Joseph Barnett. Barnett had been transported for stealing sixty dozen silk stockings. He had been on the prison hulk, Retribution, in 1812, serving a seven-year sentence, which concluded, after four years, with the granting of a pardon. His dossier notes he 'has very bad connexions'. He was sentenced at the London Gaol Delivery on 20 February 1822, and had behaved 'indifferently' on board the prison hulk.

'Youner' Barnett arrived in Van Diemen's Land on 11 January 1823. After a brief period of assignment with the Public Works in Hobart Town, Solomon (as he appears to have been known in Van Diemen's Land) was granted an allotment of land in 1824 (in Hobart Town).

His rehabilitation came to an abrupt end, however. He was a messenger to the Colonial Secretary's Office when, on 9 October 1827, he was sent to a penal settlement for three years for not being able to account for a stolen silver watch that was found in his possession. A ticket of leave was granted on the Queen's birthday, 24 February 1832. In November 1833, he was appointed a constable. In March 1835 he was convicted of being drunk on duty and of allowing a prisoner in his charge to become intoxicated. He was dismissed from the police force, deprived of his ticket of leave, and transferred to a rural district. Barnett received a conditional pardon on 22 January 1838, and was permitted by the Lieutenant Governor to travel to Sydney, where he had a brother. He carried on 'a respectable business in Sydney until 1844, when business caused him to return for a visit to Van Diemen's Land'. Once he had landed in Hobart Town, he discovered he needed official permission to return to New South Wales. He therefore wrote to the Colonial Secretary, stating that he would be 'utterly ruined' if he could not obtain the necessary permit. He was then forced to ask the Hobart Hebrew Congregation to assist him to travel to the new colony of Port Phillip. The congregation agreed to help him leave and, in 1851, he was given the necessary official permission to proceed to any port save those in Great Britain.

Morley (4) Indent 4/4008, p. 249; CON 31/38, no. 485; CON 23/3; CON 23/1, no. 485; LSD 1/73/195; Dixson Library 165a, Petitions 1845, p. 353a–f; HO 10/43; CS 38/8656, rec'd 18 August 1838, 4/2432.2; *Launceston Independent*, 3 March 1832; CP 1746.

BARNETT, Joseph

b. London, 1797–1850
John I (3), 1831; Convict; Sentenced to life, Old Bailey, 1829.
Married; Jeweller; Height: 165 cm; 7 children (in England).

Dark complexioned, black hair, black whiskers, oval face, 'retreating' hair, brown eyes, long nose, medium mouth and chin. 'A Jew.' Joseph Barnett was married to Sarah Barnett, who lived at City

Road, London. They had seven children. He was convicted for 'felony' when he stole from a warehouse. He was caught carrying a basket containing stolen silver plate worth £100. He protested to the judge: 'I am innocent. It is all prejudice against me'. He had been tried previously for the theft of a five-pound note. He could read and write. Barnett brought seventeen shillings with him on board the transport ship.

Barnett arrived in Van Diemen's Land on 29 January 1831. On 17 December 1834, while assigned to Mr Burton, he was arrested for stealing a watch belonging to Isaac Solomon (q.v.), the brother of Judah and Joseph, and was sentenced to an additional seven years at the Launceston Quarter Sessions on 4 January 1835. On 8 February 1835 he absconded from the road party and on recapture was sentenced to three years hard labour, attached to the Hulk Chain Gang, and sent to the convict station at Bridgewater.

On 22 November 1838, while assigned to a Mr Solomon, he was charged with misconduct. Barnett offered to give police information about a felony if he received a ticket of leave. For his impudence he was given a sentence of six months hard labour at Grass Tree Hill; it was noted that his conduct was to be reported. On 14 September 1839 he was arrested for being at the Military Barracks at Launceston without permission and was sentenced to three weeks hard labour in chains. He received his first ticket of leave on 13 July 1841.

Barnett was employed as a police constable, and on 7 September 1842, was attacked by a woman he was arresting. Others nearby also attacked him, shouting: 'You bloody Jew. She shan't go'. Constable John Isaacs (q.v.) came to his aid and the woman was fined £2.

On 5 April 1843 Barnett was sentenced at the Supreme Court in Launceston to fourteen years for receiving stolen goods and was sent to Port Arthur. This sentence was reduced in June 1845 by two years for apprehending an absconder, and in March 1846 he was allowed to leave Port Arthur for Bridgewater. Barnett's wife must have died because on 19 August 1841 he received permission to marry Caroline Phillips, a daughter of Moses Phillips (q.v.). His second ticket of leave was issued on 29 March 1849 and a (posthumous) conditional pardon was granted on 16 November 1852.

CON 34/3, no. 1459; CON 31/4; Allport Collection; CON 18/9; CON 52/2, p. 13; *Hobart Town Courier*, 19 April 1839; CSO 22/35/1148, 7 September 1842.

BARNETT, Joseph

b. Houndsditch, 1804
Arab (1), 1822; Convict; Sentenced to life, Old Bailey, 1822.
Single; Hawker; Height: 155 cm.

Ruddy complexion, blue eyes, dark brown hair. With Thomas Johnson and John Jones, who were two other pickpockets, Barnett stole eight shillings from a man watching the changing of the guard at St James Palace. He was listed as a Jew.

Barnett arrived in Van Diemen's Land on 6 November 1822. As soon as his period of probation was over, on 29 January 1824, Joseph Barnett was convicted of hawking goods about Hobart Town without a licence and was sentenced to an additional six months hard labour. On 15 June 1825, he was caught inside a private house with the intent to steal, and was sent to Maria Island. On 13 January 1827 he was found with stolen potatoes in his possession and received twenty-five lashes. On 5 January 1828 he was absent from duty while with the boats belonging to the Public Works Department and sent to the Black Snake Road Party for three months. In the next six months he received seventy-five lashes for absence and insolence and was sent to the treadmill for two days. On 22 July 1828 he was convicted for having a stolen waistcoat in his possession at the Prisoners' Barracks in Hobart Town and sent back to Maria Island.

Barnett received a seven-year sentence at the Supreme Court in Hobart Town on 10 March 1829. He was given twenty-five lashes in May 1831 for being absent without leave from the New Town Barracks and sentenced to twelve months hard labour in the Hulk Chain Gang. In July 1835 he was given a further twenty-four lashes for neglect of duty, and on 6 August 1835 was accused of robbery and, though the charge was unproven, was put in a road party for twelve months.

On 4 July 1840, Joseph Barnett was given permission to marry Margaret Reed, who had come to Van Diemen's Land on the *Nautilus*. His conditional pardon was approved on 8 September 1842. He briefly rented seat no. 76 in the Hobart Town Synagogue in 1845.

In 1875 the Hobart Hebrew Congregation received a letter about a Joseph Barnett who was 'about to die'. The congregation refused to have anything to do with him. The Synagogue Minutes explain that he 'never was a member of the congregation and has a son living in Hobart Town'. Joseph Barnett died on 17 August 1875 at the New Norfolk Asylum and was buried by the Hobart Hebrew Congregation.

OBSP, 1821–22, case 490, p. 223; CON 31/1; CSO 1/108/27, p. 27f.(1830–31); CON 23/1; HO 11/4; CP 765.

BARNETT, Joseph (John)

b. London, 1813–1851
Free.
Married.

Joseph Barnett received a publican's licence for the Lincoln Hotel. By 1850, Barnett was involved in a series of business ventures. He sold a whale fishery at Encounter Bay after it had made a profit of £600 for the previous two years. He bought a number of houses from people who had left for the goldfields and advertised that he needed 'a respectable young man' to collect rent on them. He owned and managed the Jerusalem Coffee House in Port Adelaide.

Joseph Barnett died at Port Adelaide at the age of thirty-eight. He was described as a wine merchant at the time of his death. Pritchard queries whether it was his widow, Elizabeth Barnett, who married Henry Thomas Cullen in 1853.

South Australian Gazette and Colonial Register, 16 March 1839, 31 January 1850; 4 February 1850, 11 July 1850, 15 July 1850; Pritchard Index.

BARNETT, Joshua Lewis

b. London, 1811
Henry Porcher, 1837; Free.
Colonial conviction 14 years, Sydney, 1837.
Single; Height: 160 cm.

Fresh complexion, black hair, dark reddish hair, dark grey eyes. Literate. Henry Barnett, the father of 'Lewis' as he was known, was a coach proprietor. Lewis was said to have been able to drive a pair of horses through the metroplitan traffic.

Joshua Lewis Barnett was transported from New South Wales to Van Diemen's Land on the *Francis Freeling*, arriving 12 March 1837, after having been sentenced in Sydney to fourteen years transportation for receiving stolen tortoise shell. The case caused wide public interest. The *Sydney Gazette* of 24 January 1837 told the story of 'Two of the Hebrew Nation' who had been charged with receiving stolen goods and who were both named Lewis Barnett.

In Hobart Town on 5 August 1837, Barnett was convicted for 'idleness'and put on bread and water in solitary confinement for forty-eight hours. On 28 April 1838 he was given six months hard labour for neglecting his duty as a watchman. On 7 March 1839, while a servant of Mr John Moses (q.v.), Lewis Barnett was found to be drunk and was reprimanded. On 10 January 1839, he was reported by Mr Moses for insolence, and returned to the Public Works Department to work in the interior for three months. On 19 May 1840, having been returned to the Moses household, he was found guilty of misconduct for being in a public house after hours, and received four days in the cells on bread and water. Despite his poor conduct, on 17 June 1840, John Moses asked that Barnett be permitted to go with him on business to Sydney. Permission was refused on the grounds that his offences in Sydney had been 'very bad'.

On 27 May 1841, still assigned to Moses, he was accused of misconduct for being in the theatre after hours. He received two months hard labour. On 2 January 1844, another charge of misconduct resulted in a sentence of three days solitary confinement. A ticket of leave was issued on 12 April 1844 and it was noted that 'The Lieutenant Governor has directed a record be made in favour of this Man for his meritorious conduct at a fire, which took place in the premises of M. McGreely'. On 8 July of that year, he was found to have been drunk and sentenced to one month hard labour. However, a ticket of leave was issued on 19 August 1845 and a conditional pardon was recommended on 26 January 1847.

In September 1846 Lewis Barnett had been granted permission to marry Rachel Nathan (q.v.). On 23 May 1846 a son, Abraham, was born in Launceston and Henry was born on 11 May 1849. Barnett's absolute pardon was approved on 4 July 1848.

Sydney Gazette, 14 July 1835, 24 January 1837; Supreme Court on Circuit, 4 February, 1837, 4/6488; Assignment Lists of Convicts, CS 4/4523, p. 42; CON 31/3, no. 2606; CON 16/1, p. 47; CON 35/1/1, p. 42; CON 52/2, p. 287; CSO 5/243/6338; Permission to Marry Book, CON 52/2; *Sydney Morning Herald*, 5 December 1845.

BARNETT, Levi

b. London, 1799–1848
Elizabeth (1), 1816; Convict; Sentenced to life, Old Bailey, 1815.
Single; Old clothes man; Height: 155 cm.

Dark complexion, black hair, dark eyes. Barnett Levi was sentenced to six months in prison at the Old Bailey 6 July 1814. A constable saw 'the lad . . . slip something out of his breeches pocket and put it in his mouth. These are the two shillings I took out of his mouth'. Barnett was back in court within months of his release from gaol and was sentenced at the London Gaol Delivery on 6 December 1815. He gave his religion as 'C of E'.

Levi Barnett arrived in New South Wales on 5 October 1816. The Parramatta Magistrates Book of 30 June 1822 recorded that, on 19 April 1822, Levy Barnett was 'found in the streets away from his barracks late at night'. Barnett was sentenced to fourteen days in the gaol gang on bread and water and returned to the convict barracks. On 25 October 1823 he was transferred to Penrith from Emu Plains and in 1825 he was listed as a convict labourer at Evan. By the end of the year, the Colonial Secretary recorded that he was a convict in the service of John Scarfe of Castlereagh.

Barnett was listed in the 1828 Census as having 'no religion'. According to the list of convicts for New South Wales, he was living at Port Macquarie. He was returned from prison at Port Macquarie on 16 April 1829, to be held at the *Phoenix* hulk and then sent to the Hyde Park Barracks. Barnett was sentenced at the Sydney General Sessions on 6 August 1829 for stealing government property, and spent the next three years at the prison settlement at Moreton Bay. He later settled in the District of Berrima, receiving a ticket of leave in 1840, and a conditional pardon in 1845. He died on 20 September 1848 and was buried at the Tarban Creek Lunatic Asylum 'of Plymouth'. Barnett's body was later disinterred and buried in Sydney's Devonshire Street Jewish Cemetery.

4/3896, 16 April 1829. 8; FitzRoy Correspondence, ML A1242, p. 124, in 1847; HO 10/28; HO 10/53; TL 40/1631, in 4/4142; CP 46/161, in 4/4005, p. 193.

BARNETT, Levy

1841; Free.

An 'L. Barnett' arrived from London on 12 June 1841. According to the *New South Wales Pioneers Index* Levy Barnett had a child, 'Sarah', in 1849. (Also in the York Street Birth Register 27 January 1849).

BARNETT, Lewis (Lewis BENNETT)

b. Aldgate, 1802
Adamant, 1821; Convict; Sentenced to 7 years, London, 1821.
Single; Butcher; Height: 159 cm; 6 children.

Dark florid complexion. Black hair. Hazel eyes. Lewis Barnett was sentenced on 10 January 1821 (under the surname 'Bennett') for stealing a bundle of mohair cloth.

The convict transport ship *Adamant* arrived in Sydney on 8 September 1821. Barnett was granted a ticket of leave in 1827. In 1831, Lewis Barnett married Elizabeth, whose surname was listed as both 'Jones' and 'Solomon'. She had been married to Solomon Solomons (q.v.), who had arrived on the *Marquis of Wellington* in 1815. Elizabeth adopted a Jewish identity, calling herself 'Rebecca', and their first child, Sarah, was born in 1832.

In the 1832 *Sydney General Post Office Directory*, Barnett was listed as a publican of George Street. The coach for Parramatta started at his public house, which was called the Swan with Two Necks. He was also the publican of the Red Lion, also in George Street. He was the agent for those in Parramatta who were waiting to have assigned female servants sent to them. He also had an assigned servant of his own. In 1837 he was arrested together with a namesake. The other Lewis Barnett had 'recently arrived' in Sydney as a free settler. The *Sydney Gazette* of 24 January 1837 told the story of 'Two of the Hebrew Nation' who were charged as receivers. The stolen goods were found in the house adjoining the ex-convict, who denounced the 'free' Barnett with the words 'You have got me into a mess, you told me you took the house to keep a woman'. Despite his denials, the 'free' Barnett was convicted of receiving stolen property and was sent to Van Diemen's Land. The 'convict' Barnett stated that he knew the other man from London and had lived in his house until he took the adjoining house.

In 1835 Barnett moved to Goulburn Street. Hannah Barnett was born in 1837. Lewis and Rebecca Barnett registered their child, Henry, as a Jew following his birth in 1839. Julia was born in 1841, and Amelia in 1849, both in Sydney. An infant son, Abraham, was buried in the Devonshire Street Jewish Cemetery on 1 November 1847. Lewis Barnett appeared on the York Street Synagogue list of donors in 1839 with a donation of £20. He was a seat holder who gave a further £35 to the synagogue in the subsequent three years. In 1845 he was described as a 'hawker', and accused by Samuel Solomon (q.v.), a dealer, of not having paid his commission for a consignment of blouses and coats. Ford's *Sydney Commercial Directory*, 1851, listed two 'Lewis Barnetts', one as a merchant at 3 Jamison Street, and the other as a general dealer at 29 King Street West.

2/8240 p. 1, in 4/4007; TL 27/62; *Monitor*, 28 August 1830; *Sydney Gazette*, 15 November 1832, 24 January 1837; *Sydney Morning Herald*, 5 December 1845; *Australian*, 27 July 1832, 12 July 1835.

BARNETT, Miriam

1822–1917
Jane, 1843; Free.
Single; Dealer; 6 children.

Miriam Barnett was the daughter of Baron Barnett of London, and was born on 11 August 1822. She married the 'shopkeeper' Saul (Solomon) Solomons (q.v.) at Launceston on 20 November 1844. Three of her children, Rachel Miriam (7 October 1845), Amelia (3 October 1846), and Phoebe (11 March 1848), were born in Launceston. The family then moved to South Australia, travelling on the *Halcyon*, and arriving on 28 February 1849. Three further children, Baron Isaacar

(8 May 1849), Henry Aaron (20 March 1851), and Matilda (Tillie) (18 June 1853), were born in Adelaide.

Miriam lived at Burra Burra House in Hindley Street for thirty-seven years and then for thirty years at her home in Gover Street, North Adelaide. She died on 5 August 1917 just prior to her ninety-fifth birthday and was buried at the West Terrace Jewish Cemetery.

Pritchard Index.

BARNETT, Moses (Morris)

d. 1838
Isabella I (5), 1833; Convict.

Moses Barnett was listed on the ship's indent as 'Morris Barnett'. He arrived in Hobart Town on 14 November 1833. 'Moses' Barnett was buried in the Jewish Cemetery in Harrington Street, Hobart Town in 1838.

CON 31/5; CON 27/6; MM33/2.

BARNETT, Moses (Moss)

d. 1871
Free. 2 children.

Moses Barnett applied to the Board of the Sydney Synagogue for 'making' Miss Maria Hart (q.v.) a Jewess, as her father was Jewish, in order for them to marry. The Board responded: 'If she proves the same to the satisfaction of the committee that her father is a Jew they will exceed [*sic*] to her request'. When it came to the test, eight members of the board voted for the marriage to be performed and two against. They were married on 17 March 1841 (in Jewish wedding no. 43). Their children were Hannah (25 December 1841), born at Liverpool, and Samuel (9 September 1843), born in Sydney. Both children were registered as 'Hebrew'.

Moses was buried at the Lidcombe Jewish Cemetery on 27 May 1871. 'Margaret', the wife of 'Moss Barnett', was buried on 1 January 1844 in the Devonshire Street Jewish Cemetery. Her grave was transferred to Lidcombe in 1901.

Sydney Synagogue Minute Book, dated 24 February 1841, p. 63; Bridge Street Synagogue Letter Book, dated 6 November 1840 (Archives of AJHS Sydney).

BARNETT, Rachel (née SOLOMON)

b. Sheerness, 1811–1869
Trinity, 1839; Free.
Married; 9 children.

Rachel was the second daughter of Judah and Esther Solomon (qq.v.). She had married Samuel Barnett (q.v.) at the Great Synagogue in London on 11 December 1831. They had nine children: Isaac (1832), Judah (1833), and Esther (1834) in

London, and Michael, David, Benjamin (1840), Samuel (22 December 1841), Louisa (1845), and Louis (1847) (whose name was changed to Lewis) in Hobart Town. In 1847, the family moved from Van Diemen's Land to Melbourne. Rachel died on 3 December 1869 at 5 Napier Street, Fitzroy. She had lived for eighteen years in Van Diemen's Land and fourteen years in Victoria. Joseph Simmons, 'a friend', was recorded as present at her death. Simmons was Louisa's father-in-law, as Louisa had married Lewis Simmons in 1868.

BARNETT, Reuben (Rheuben)

b. Warsaw, Poland, 1817–1894
Mt Stewart Elphinstone, 1845; Convict; Sentenced to 7 years, Central Criminal Court, 23 October 1843.
Married; Watchmaker; Height: 152 cm; 11 children.

'Polish Jew', fresh complexion, dark brown hair, long face, brown eyes, long nose. Had been living in Harrow. His right shoulder was notably higher than his left. Could read and write 'a little'. Surgeon's report: 'Very Good'. Reuben Barnett's offence was stated as: 'Receiving India Silks valued at £100 from Mr Ellis Hetherington, St Paul's Church Yard'. Barnett had married Julia Aarons, daughter of Michael Aarons, on 25 August 1841, at 21 Tenter Ground, Spitalfields, under the auspices of the Great Synagogue in London. His mother, Esther, and a brother lived in Warsaw. At the time of his conviction at the Old Bailey, his wife and their one-year-old child, Barnet Barnett, born on 25 June 1842, were living in Spitalfields.

Barnett arrived in Hobart Town on 17 June 1845 and served as a constable during that first year. Barnett was charged with minor misdemeanours and in January 1846 spent ten days in solitary confinement for 'misconduct'. On 20 December, he was found guilty of 'taking indecent liberties with Patrick Connor' and his recently issued ticket of leave was revoked. Barnett was sentenced to nine months hard labour in chains. His ticket of leave was reissued on 11 December 1849.

Barnett's wife and son remained in London and, in 1881, were living at 3 Partridge Court, Aldgate. Reuben Barnett married a second time, on 16 September 1861, at the Free Campbell Church, Oatlands. His new wife was Julia Salmon, the daughter of Joseph Salmon and Ellen (McDonnell). There were ten children of this second marriage: Jane Helena Barnett (22 July 1862, born in Oatlands District), Mary Elizabeth (31 January 1864), William Rheuben (24 August 1865), Alfred Joseph (born in Fingal District), Rose Adelaide (13 February 1871), Julia Bertha (16 August 1872), Frances Ellen (26 June 1876, born in Hobart), Francis Henry (16 June 1878), Sarah Jane (21 August 1880), and Reuben Henry (14 June 1883, born at Launceston).

Reuben Barnett was buried in the Roman Catholic section of the Cornelian Bay Cemetery in Hobart in 1894.

CON 33/1/66, no. 249; CON 14/21, no. 15568; CON 18/45; Family research by Dianne Duncanson-Clark, great-granddaughter of Alfred Joseph (John) Barnett.

BARNETT, Richard

b. London, 1807
Heroine, 1833; Convict; Sentenced to 7 years, Old Bailey, 1833.
Single; Dealer; Height: 168 cm.

Dark ruddy complexion. Black hair. Chestnut eyes. Small mole on left side of chin. Nose large, inclining to the right. Eyebrows partially meeting. Can read and write. Jew. Barnett was found with a bolt of stolen cloth valued at £10. The cloth was stolen from a tailor who lived at St Paul's Churchyard. He was sentenced at the London Gaol Delivery on 3 January 1833.

Richard Barnett was granted a conditional pardon in 1838.

OBSP, 1832–33, case 341, p. 163; *Heroine* Printed Indent 33/963, p. 115; CP 38/317.

BARNETT, Samuel

1801–1864(?)
Free.
Married; 1 child.

Samuel and Rachael Barnett were listed in the Sydney Synagogue records with a daughter, Clara, born in Sydney on 8 September 1842. He was listed among those qualified to vote in Sydney's first municipal elections in 1842.

There were two Samuel Barnetts in business in Sydney in the latter part of the 1840s. One sold clothes at 252 George Street, and the other owned the hotel, the Cheshire Cheese, at the corner of Sussex and King streets. In July 1844, 'publican' Barnett was granted a night licence for his hotel. In 1845 Samuel Barnett gave £30 to the York Street congregation and was a seat holder throughout the 1840s. The hotel owner was, without doubt, the generous benefactor of the synagogue, though it is unclear whether he was this Samuel Barnett.

Australian, 7 April 1842; *Sydney Morning Herald*, 10 March 1843.

BARNETT, Samuel

b. London, 1793–1864(?)
Marquis of Huntley (1), 1826; Convict; Sentenced to life, Newgate, 1825.
Single; Scourer; Height: 174 cm; 6 children.

Dark sallow complexion, pock-pitted, hazel grey eyes, black hair. Scar on upper lip under right nostril. Broad scar on cap of left knee. Samuel Barnett stole a tablecloth, valued at £25, from a shopkeeper's home in the City of London. His original sentence, on 15 September 1815, was 'Death'.

Samuel Barnett arrived in New South Wales on 13 September 1826. He appeared in the 1828 Census as a 'constable' on 'government service', assigned to the Australian Agricultural Company at Port Stephens. A ticket of leave was granted on 23 August 1831 (*Sydney Gazette*), and a conditional pardon on 23 June 1838. An absolute pardon was issued on 1 February 1843. Barnett was listed in the 1837 General Return of Convicts in New South Wales as living in Sydney with a ticket of leave.

Samuel Barnett received permission to marry Mary Smith, who came free to the colony on 6 May 1833. The Rev. S. Marsden officiated at Parramatta. On 8 April 1840 Barnett wrote to the Sydney Synagogue from his home in Liverpool (NSW) asking that his wife (whose name was by then 'Rebecca') and children be admitted into the Jewish faith: 'Mine is no novel case for several parties who are now the leading members of our congregation, have been placed in the same situation'. He added 'It is better to save one sinner in a world than to turn him away'. His wife Mary/Rebecca was formally accepted as a convert ('made a *Geyrester* [*sic*] by I.S.', according to a note) on 12 August 1840, and a Jewish wedding (no. 34) was performed by Isaac Simmons (q.v.). At the time of his writing, his children were Henry Samuel, born 1834, who was uncircumcised, and Leah (Sarah), born in Sydney in 1838, and registered as a 'Hebrew' (she had been named in the synagogue). In 1838 Samuel Barnett was honoured by being called to the Torah by the secretary of the synagogue, Emanuel Crabb (q.v.), against the 'explicit wish' of the president of the congregation.

Samuel and Rebecca had four more children: Julia (1840), Hannah (1841), Abraham (1844, who died on 31 October 1847), and Moses (1844). Their son Henry Samuel drowned 'off Tugen' on 23 June 1852.

Barnett owned a shop in King Street in 1842. However, *Low's Directory of the City and District of Sydney* of 1847 listed two Samuel Barnetts. One was a clothes seller at 252 George Street and the other owned the licence for the Cheshire Cheese hotel at the corner of Sussex and King streets. On 30 June 1849, 'Samuel Barnett of Sydney' was listed as insolvent in the *Maitland Mercury*. In August 1851, Samuel Barnett, a clerk for Mr Davis, draper of George Street, Sydney, was convicted of embezzling a cheque for £4 10s, with a Thomas Murray as an accessory in the fraud.

A Samuel Barnett died in Sydney in November 1864. Mrs Rebecca Barnett, 'relict of the late Mr Samuel Barnett and beloved mother of Mrs Myer Solomon' died at her residence, at 89 Macquarie Street, on 26 April 1881 and was buried in the Jewish section of the Rookwood Cemetery.

OBSP, 1824–25, case 1579, p. 596; Ship Indent 4/4011, p. 70; HO 10/52; HO 10/53; *Commercial Journal and Advertiser*, 11 April 1840, 17 September 1842, 3, 5, 19 August 1851; Minutes of the Sydney Synagogue, 8 April 1840, p. 35, *Maitland Mercury*, 30 June 1849; *Sydney Morning Herald*, 5 April 1845, 27 April 1881.

BARNETT, Samuel

b. Sheerness, 1806–1898
Juliet, 1839; Free.
Married; Merchant; 9 children.

'Mr Barnett from London, Cabin Class', arrived (in Hobart Town) on the *Juliet* on 17 September 1839 with his wife, Rachael (q.v.) (née Solomon), the second daughter of Judah and Esther Solomon (qq.v.), and their three children, Isaac (1832), Judah (1833), and Esther (1834). Rachel had been born in Sheerness in 1811 and Rachael's sister Louisa (q.v.) and brother-in-law (John Davis) were also on board. Samuel and Rachael Solomon had married at the Great Synagogue in London on 11 December 1831.

Samuel Barnett advertised that he had taken over the inn, the Bricklayer's Arms, in Elizabeth Street, and the licence was formally transferred on 14 February 1840. In the 1842 Census ofVan Diemen's Land he was described as a 'Merchant, Owner at 4 Melville St.They live in a brick building and the family consisted of 3 boys and 2 girls under 14 two of whom were born in the colony. He has an assigned servant'. Barnett was a member of the Hobart Hebrew Congregation in 1842 and rented seat no. 57. His wife gave the synagogue £7. He promised to lend the synagogue's building fund £20 but was unable to fulfil his promise.

In 1846 Barnett briefly held the publican's licence for the Rising Sun, Bathurst Street, which was transferred to the Caledonia Hotel in Elizabeth Street in Hobart Town in early 1848. Samuel tried his luck at the gold fields in California in 1849 before returning to Van Diemen's Land by 1854. Samuel and Rachel had six children in Hobart Town: Michael, David, Benjamin (1840), Samuel (22 December 1841), Louisa (1845), and Louis (1847), whose name was changed to Lewis. Later that year the family moved from Van Diemen's Land to Melbourne.

Rachael died on 3 December 1869 at 5 Napier Street, Fitzroy. Samuel Barnett died in Fitzroy in 1898, aged ninety-two.

Hobart Town Courier, 14 February 1840, 5 September 1846; MB 2/39/4, p. 263, AOT.

BARNETT, Samuel

b. London, 1821
Anson, 1844; Convict; Sentenced to 10 years, Old Bailey, 1843.
Single; Labourer; Height: 173 cm.

Dark complexion, dark brown hair, large nose and mouth, large chin, clean shaven, oval face. A Jew. Scar under right eye. Samuel Barnett was transported for 'stealing from the person'. The offence was stated as 'picking a lady's pocket of two shillings and six pence, one penny and several half pence'. Barnett had been imprisoned for one month previously for picking pockets. Gaol report: 'Bad character and sullen'.

Samuel Barnett arrived in Van Diemen's Land on 4 February 1844, and was consigned to an initial period of eighteen months hard labour at the Fingal Depot. He was released from this initial period of probation on 4 August 1845. On 8 December 1845, at Cleveland, he was sentenced to one month hard labour for selling his victuals without permission. On 27 July 1846, as a prisoner in Launceston, he was sentenced to six weeks with hard labour and the treadwheel for having been found gambling on the Sabbath day. He was still in Launceston on 8 August 1847, when he was sentenced to two months imprisonment with hard labour for being drunk. On 24 April 1848 he was found guilty of misconduct for having slept out from the prisoners' depot. He was punished by being sent to Oatlands in the 'Interior' and sentenced to two months hard labour. Barnett was issued with his ticket of leave on 24 September 1849, and his conditional pardon on 12 August 1851.

CON 33/50, no. 14732.

BARNETT, Samuel

1801–1864
City of Edinburgh, 1838; Free.
Clerk.

Described as an 'emigrant', Samuel Barnett was indicted in April 1842 for having obtained money under false pretences and was sentenced to six months at the Newcastle Gaol. The sum of money obtained was £3 1s.

Australian, 13 December 1838.

BARNETT, Sarah

Palambam, 1832; Free.
Married; 4 children.

Sarah arrived in Sydney with her husband, John Barnett (q.v.), and their two children, Mary Jane, aged six, and Robert Freeman, aged seven. On 2 December 1833, John and Sarah had a son, Lewis. On 10 October 1836, a daughter, Jane, was born and both children were registered with the Jewish community.

BARNETT, Solomon

John Craig, 1834; Free.
Single; Dealer.

Solomon Barnett was a steerage passenger on the *John Craig*, which arrived at Port Jackson on 11 December 1834. Solomon Barnett married Esther.

Ship Indent 4/5207; *Australian*, 12 December 1834.

BARNETT, William

b. London.
Free.
Dealer.

W. Barnett, a dealer, of 66 George Street, Sydney, 'opposite the Market', advertised that he was 'about to leave the colony' and that all claims against him should be presented. On 31 January 1832, the *Sydney Gazette* recorded that he had spent £927 buying two houses and a public house. His name appeared in the November 1842 list of eligible voters for the municipal elections, with a shop and dwelling house in George Street. He was unable to withstand the economic depression, and was listed as insolvent on 10 February 1843. He was listed on the York Street Synagogue subscription list in 1845 and gave the congregation £2.

4/4006; *Sydney Gazette*, 29 January 1824, 5 February 1824, 21 January 1828, 31 January 1832; *Sydney Morning Herald*, 15 September, 4 November 1842.

BARNETT, William

b. London, 1806–1841
Marquis of Hastings, 1826; Convict; Sentenced to life, Newgate, 1825.
Single; Height: 164 cm.

Hazel grey eyes, black hair.

William Barnett was assigned to Mr Dwight Richardson. The 1828 Census listed him as Jewish and working in Sydney with the 'No. 5 Chain Gang'. Barnett died on 6 September 1841.
CO 207/2.

BARRETT, Abraham

b. London, 1823
Hindostan (3), 1841; Convict; Sentenced to 10 years, Central Criminal Court, 1840.
Single; Printer's pressman; Height: 150 cm.

Lived in the Strand, London. Could read and write. Rather dark complexion, dark brown hair, long face, 'rather large nose', and high forehead. Barrett was found guilty of stealing a lady's reticule containing two shillings, scissors and two handkerchiefs.

Barrett's initial period of probation was two years, which he spent imprisoned at Point Puer. There, although his behaviour was 'orderly' and 'good', he spent seven days in solitary confinement for insolence and received 'thirty-six stripes on the breach' for disobedience. He was released from the first stage of probation on 27 May 1844 and moved to the Prisoners' Barracks in Hobart Town. On 12 May 1846 he received his ticket of leave. On 9 April 1847 he was found guilty of misconduct by gambling at the racecourse at New Town. On 3 August 1848, in Launceston, he was found to be out of doors after curfew and received seven days imprisonment and hard labour on the treadwheel. His ticket of leave was renewed on 14 September 1849 and he received his certificate of freedom on 21 June 1850.
CON 33/4.

BARUCH, Daniel (BARUH)

1790–1875
Royal Sovereign, 1849; Free.
Single; Physician; 3 children.

Daniel Baruch was Australia's first Jewish doctor. He arrived in the province of South Australia in 1849, and had little connection with the Jewish community.

Baruch married Eleanor Reid (1823–1892), and they had three children: Daniel (1850), Louis Albert (1856), and Laura (1861).

BARUH, Uziel

1739–1790
Neptune, 1790; Convict; Sentenced to 14 years, Old Bailey, 1785.
Dealer, butcher.

Baruh's kosher butcher's shop was in Duke Street, Duke's Place, near the main Ashkenazi Synagogue in Aldgate. He married Jeudit (Judith) de Moshe Baruh at Bevis Marks (Sephardi Synagogue) on 21 September 1763. In 1785 he was convicted for receiving a large number of silver objects, knowing them to have been stolen by William Harding. The silver was hidden in the wood panelling of the main parlour. Baruh was apparently well known by the police as a receiver of stolen goods. He employed two Jewish servants, Jacob Aaron and Abraham Nathan. It was Nathan who denounced Baruh to the police. Baruh was defended by two lawyers and denied everything. Abraham Fernandez of the Sephardi 'Hebrew College' was called as a character witness. It was claimed by Baruh's barrister that Nathan had tried to extort money from Mrs Baruh, saying to her that he would not give evidence if she gave him money. The lawyer (Mr Silvester) asked: 'Why Nathan, you did not see the bag brought in? Where were you? In the synagogue?' Silvester referred to Nathan as 'that little jew boy'. On 6 April 1785 Baruh was sentenced to fourteen years transportation to Africa, and sent to the Thames Hulk Justitia. His age at the time was forty-eight.

Baruh was buried in Sydney on 13 July 1790—within two weeks of the arrival of the starving, disease-ridden convicts on the Second Fleet. The burial records of St Philip's misspelt his name as 'Huser Brewe alias Bereugh'.

OBSP, 1784–85, case 500, pp. 660–5; Michael Flynn, *The Second Fleet*, p. 152.

BELASCO, John

b. 1770
Pitt, 1792; Convict; Sentenced to 7 years, Old Bailey, 1791.
Single; Butcher's assistant.

John Belasco stole a bundle of 'scotch thread' from a cart in Cheapside and was caught running away with it. Belasco worked for a butcher. Moses Mendoza appeared in court as a character witness: 'I live in Bevis Marks near the Portugeze (sic) Synagogue; I have known him from his infancy. I really think him to be a very honest young fellow'. He was sentenced at the Old Bailey Sessions on 13 April 1791.

There is only one official mention of Belasco being in Sydney, which is a reference in the Mutch Index.

OBSP, 1790–91, case 161, p. 271; Mutch Index.

BELASCO, Samuel

b. London, 1806–1875
Layton (1), 1827; Convict; Sentenced to life, Surrey, 1825.
Single; Hawker: Height: 160 cm.

Brown hair, blue eyes. A pickpocket who stole a pocket book, several sovereigns and a silver pencil case. He was arrested at the Epsom Racecourse in May 1825. According to the ship's list of convicts, he was the brother of 'the famous pugilist Abraham Belasco who lived in Denmark Court, the Strand'. Samuel Belasco had been in gaol before for picking pockets at Epsom. His character in gaol was reported as 'bad'. He was sentenced on 12 July 1825 for stealing a pocket book containing £3.

'Aby' Belasco was charged with assault and testified that he had seen his brother shamefully beaten and kicked by the officers and by Mr Lee (whose pocket had been picked) . . . [Aby] merely stepped forward to enquire what he had done in order to prevent him being ill-treated. When he was told he had done wrong he immediately desisted from further interference. It was not likely that he should try to rescue a brother whom he had once caused to be taken before the Thames police magistrates and committed for three months to the House of Correction . . .

Belasco arrived in Hobart Town on 9 October 1827, 'with nineteen shillings and three pence, one gold ring and a breast pin'. He was assigned to Mr E. Lawrence in Launceston. He received fifty lashes in January 1829 for robbing his master's garden, forty lashes in March for fighting, and twelve months in irons for stealing some canvas in April. He was sent to work at the lime quarry near George Town.

On 7 February 1833 he was officially classified as an invalid. In April he was convicted for stealing fifty apples and he received two separate sentences of eight days in solitary confinement for assault and for being absent without leave. He was discharged from the New Norfolk Hospital on 15 March 1836 for stealing bedding. On 1 September 1836 he was placed in the cells for three days for being absent without leave from the hospital. He received a ticket of leave in April 1837 and an official warning for hawking articles 'under suspicious circumstances'.

On 25 March 1837 Samuel Belasco was baptised at New Norfolk and, on 16 February 1838, Belasco applied for permission to marry Ann Tilsed. The marriage at first was not approved as there were official objections to Tilsed being allowed to marry. Permission was finally granted and the marriage took place on 22 March 1838. A conditional pardon was issued to Belasco on 14 July 1841. According to the Schedule for Conditional Pardons, he 'had been 14 years in the colony and served the regulated period with a ticket of leave with only one offence charged against him since 1836'.

In 1842 he was granted a hawker's licence for the District of New Norfolk. In 1869 he was returned to the asylum in New Norfolk as a pauper of 'unsound mind and a proper person to be taken charge of and detained under care and treatment'. The medical certificate stated that Belasco had been 'blind now 30 years'.

Samuel Belasco died at the hospital at New Norfolk on 9 December 1875 and was buried in the churchyard of St Matthew's, where his wife was buried. Ann had died in 1864.

Susan Ballyn and Lucy Frost, 'Sephardi Convicts in Van Diemen's Land', in P. Elias and A. Elias (eds), *A Few from Afar*, p. 75f; VDL papers, ML, A1950, p. 393; *Hobart Town Courier*, 21 April 1837; CON 22/2, no. 985; CON 52/1, p. 35; CON 31/1; MM 31/1; CON 23/1; HO 10/56; HSD 285/1, Order for the reception of an insane person, 21 April 1869, AOT.

BENJAMIN, Benjamin

1775–1837

Benjamin Benjamin was buried at the old Harrington Street Hobart Town Jewish Cemetery on 12 September 1837. He was sixty-two years of age. His widow, Eve, aged sixty-eight, was buried in Hobart Town by the synagogue on 4 July 1852.

BENJAMIN, Benjamin

b. London, 1834–1905
London, 1843; Free.
16 children.

Benjamin was the eldest son of Moses Benjamin (q.v.) and Catherine (née Moses). Moses brought his wife and six children to Melbourne, intending to join his younger half-brother, Solomon Benjamin, in business. They arrived on 29 December 1843. Benjamin was the eldest child, at nine. His brothers and sisters were Rebecca, Rachel, Elias, David and Frances.

After he had finished school in Melbourne, Benjamin joined his father and brother Elias as a draper and haberdasher in his father's business, Albert House, Collins Street. The family initially lived at 7 Collins Street, three doors up from Elizabeth Street. On 5 August 1857, Benjamin married his niece, Fanny (q.v), the daughter of Abraham and Sophia Cohen (qq.v.). When Moses Benjamin retired in 1864, his son began a partnership with his brother-in-law Edward Cohen (q.v). The new business initially specialised in importing tea and operated as a general commission agency. Together, Benjamin and Cohen bought a substantial sheep station on the Murray River known as Canally. The partnership ended in 1877 with Cohen's death. Benjamin inherited £60 000 from his father's estate and in 1878 Benjamin retired from business and entered local politics.

Benjamin was treasurer of the Melbourne Hebrew Congregation from 1860 to 1865. He was president from 1868 to 1875, in 1879, and in 1885. In 1870 he built the Italianate brick mansion, Canally, in East Melbourne. He was elected to the Melbourne City Council in 1870 and served for more than twenty years. He was elected mayor in 1887 and 1888, the year of the centenary of Australia's European settlement. He played a leading role in the formal celebrations and the Great Exhibition that was held at the Melbourne Exhibition Building. As mayor he also opened the new Princes Bridge across the Yarra River. At the conclusion of the year, Benjamin became the second Australian, and the first mayor of Melbourne, to be knighted. In 1889 he was elected to the Victorian Legislative Council, representing Melbourne Province. He supported the federation movement, free trade between the colonies and the eight-hour day. The financial crash in the early 1890s, and the dishonesty of his business partners, consumed his wealth and forced him to resign from every public office and he was only able to pay his debtors one shilling in the pound. The *Bulletin* magazine nicknamed him 'Bingy Bingy' and claimed that his pursuit of glory had been his undoing.

Sir Benjamin Benjamin died on 7 March 1905. He was survived by his wife, seven sons and six daughters. The sixteen children of Sir Benjamin and Lady Fanny were Maurice Edward (1858–1914), Catherine (1860–1875), Abraham Herbert (1861–1925), Florence Sophia (1863–1924), Percy Lionel (1865–1903), Edith Fanny (1867–1924), Frank Bedford (1868–1884), Howard Elias (1870–1933), Minnie Violet (1871–1953), Ida Rose (1873–1949), May Constance (1876–1952), Leslie Ronald (1878–1942), Gerald Septimus (1879–1942), Stanley Octavius (1880–1916), Oswald Deronda (1884–1944), and Myra Lilian (1885–1958).

Rodney Benjamin, 'Early Melbourne and the Benjamin Brothers', *AJJHS*, vol. 13, no. 3 (1996), p. 385f, 'Sir Benjamin Benjamin', *AJJHS*, vol. 6, no. 3 (1967), p. 129f; G. Solomon, 'Sir Benjamin Benjamin', in *ADB*, vol. 3, pp. 139–40; *Bulletin*, 11 March 1905.

BENJAMIN, David

b. London, 1815–1885
Henry, 1838; Free.
Single; Shopkeeper; 6 children.

David Benjamin was the youngest son of Lyon Benjamin and his first wife, Miriam, of Hyde Park, London. Lyon Benjamin was a sealing-wax maker and the father of four sons, all of whom came to Australia, and two daughters. A daughter, Harriet (Hart, q.v.), migrated to South Australia in 1848 with her husband Samuel Hart (q.v.) and five children. David and his brothers, Samuel (q.v.) and Moses (q.v.), and half-brother Solomon (q.v.) came to Australia as free migrants. David arrived in Australia on the *Henry* on 6 July 1838 with Solomon and '21 cases [of clothing] and 6 bales of slops'.

David and Solomon Benjamin immediately moved to Launceston and, within a month, were trading as D. Benjamin at Tamar House on the corner of Brisbane and St John streets. Their marketing slogan was 'Small profits quick returns'. On Wednesday, 6 March 1839, David Benjamin, 'of Tamar House, Launceston', opened a (branch) store in Collins Street, Melbourne, and young Solomon was chosen to open the Melbourne store. David continued the business in Launceston, moving from Tamar House and opening the Launceston Emporium in Charles Street, in partnership with George Marks (q.v.). David Benjamin married Esther Solomon (q.v.), the second daughter of Henry Solomon (q.v.) of Hobart Town, on 15 December 1840. It was the third Jewish marriage in Van Diemen's Land. In July 1846, Benjamin and Marks sold the Launceston business to A & S. Solomons, being Aaron Solomons and his son, Saul Solomons (qq.v.).

On 28 October 1840, the brothers David and Solomon Benjamin 'of Melbourne' bought two plots of land in William's Town for £325, and an allotment of land in Portland for £361. In the 1842 Census of Launceston, David Benjamin was listed as tenant of a shop in Elizabeth Street with his partner and fellow tenant George Marks.

Benjamin took an active role in the Jewish life of the colony, donating £50 to the Launceston Synagogue in 1844 and presenting the synagogue with £25 from

'Moses and Sons and Davis of London'. He was the president of the synagogue at its consecration on 26 March 1846.

In 1846 he had begun the process of leaving Launceston by announcing that he had 'joined up with Moses and Nathan in Hobart Town to act as a ships' agents'. Within six months Benjamin was ready to cross Bass Strait and settle permanently in Melbourne:"Messrs D & S Benjamin, feeling grateful for the patronage of the last nine years thanks the inhabitants of Launceston and vicinity and recommends their successors Solomon and Watts'. David and his family moved to Melbourne in October 1846. At that time, he and Esther had two children, Miriam (11 October 1841), and Moses Henry (26 April 1845), both born in Launceston. Four more children were born in Melbourne: Jessie (December 1846), Alfred (1848), Louis (1850), and Edwin (1852).

David Benjamin was president of the Melbourne Hebrew Congregation from 1851 to 1854. In 1853 he welcomed Melbourne's small Jewish population to his 'extensive Collins St shop' for the High Holyday overflow services, and in that year laid the foundation stone for the enlarged Bourke Street Synagogue.

Benjamin became a director of the Australian Joint Stock Bank and the Bank of New South Wales. A combination of gold buying and land purchases proved to be immensely successful. He commissioned the architect who designed and built the second Bourke Street Synagogue, and gave the huge sum of £1000 to help in its construction.

In 1854 the profits generated by his Australian career enabled him to retire and he took his family 'home' to England.

MB 2/39/2, p. 280, AOT; Rodney Benjamin, 'Early Melbourne and the Benjamin Brothers', *AJJHS*, vol. 13, no. 3 (1996), p. 367f; *Port Phillip Gazette*, 2 March 1839; *Melbourne Advertiser*, 2 March 1839; *Port Phillip Patriot*, 18 February 1839, 13 March 1840, 15 December 1850; *Launceston Examiner*, 29 June 1844, 11 March 1846, 8 August 1846, 7 October 1846; *AG*, pp. 265, 275, 282, 283, 286, 293, 320.

BENJAMIN, David

b. London, 1817–1888
Island Queen, 1840; Free.
Single; Cabinet maker; 11 children.

The son of Tzaddick and Rebecca Benjamin, Benjamin arrived in Western Australia on 10 December 1840 on the *Island Queen*. He was a bonded craftsman who came out to work for the ill-fated Australind Company of Western Australia. He was the only Jew in the new colony, other than the family of Lionel Samson.

On 24 October 1841 at Australind, near Bunbury, Benjamin married Mary Anne Jane Whitely (born 1826).

The Australind settlement quickly failed and in 1844 the Benjamins lived in Busselton, where their first child was born. In 1846 they lived at Wonnerup. The Benjamins travelled to Ballarat following the discovery of gold. Benjamin and his wife left for South Australia on 12 January 1846 on the *River Chief*. They had eleven children: Samuel (1843), at Australind, Amelia (1844), at Busselton, Charles

(1846), at Wonnerup (died of dehydration on the ship and was buried in the Jewish cemetery in Adelaide), Joseph (15 November 1848), Zadock Charles (1847), and Jane (1848), in Adelaide, and, in Melbourne, Symon (1856), Lewis (1858), Abigail (1860), Rachel (1862), and Esther (1863). Their son Joseph Benjamin became a 'cigar maker', and had a stall at the Ballarat Market. He married Elizabeth Ann Amies, who was born on 6 June 1853.

In 1853 the family travelled from Australia to Europe. It was recorded that Mary Anne Jane (Whitely) who had married in Australia on 24 October 1841 had been formally converted to Judaism in Rotterdam, together with her five children, and registered as Jews in London on 20 June 1853.

David Benjamin died in Sydney on 26 May 1888 at the age of 72. Rebecca (Mary Ann Jane) died on 19 August 1912.

Family history from (the late) Mrs Haddon Storey of Melbourne. Jeremy I Pfeffer 'From One End of the Earth to the Other' p. 319.

BENJAMIN, Elizabeth

William Lockerby, 1834; Free.
Married; 5 children.

The wife of Samuel Benjamin (q.v.), Elizabeth settled in Sydney with her husband and their children, Henry, Jane, Juliet, Rachael and Caroline.

BENJAMIN, Elizabeth

b. London
Hive (1), 1834; Free.
Married; 9 children.

Elizabeth travelled with her husband, Raphael (Ralph) Benjamin (q.v.), a convict, arriving in Sydney on the *Hive* on 11 June 1834. At the time of her husband's deportation, they had seven children (two boys and five girls). Elizabeth had two more children, who were born in Sydney.

BENJAMIN, Emanuel

Palambam, 1832; Free.
Single; Trader; 1 child.

Emanuel Benjamin was the cousin of Henry Samuel Benjamin (q.v.). Emanuel was in Hobart Town in 1834 and appeared in a law suit. On 20 June 1837 he married Sarah Pellinger at New Norfolk. A child, Benjamin Morris Benjamin, was christened at New Norfolk on 24 April 1838.

Emanuel obtained the licence for the King of Prussia Inn at New Norfolk and advertised 'good beds, stabling etc'. He then became the licensee of the Old

Star and Garter Wine Vaults in New Norfolk, which then lost the word 'old' and became an inn. It was transferred to his cousin on 24 February 1843. Emanuel Benjamin had been declared insolvent on 16 December 1842. On 6 May 1842, Emanuel Benjamin had been bound over to keep the peace towards Miss Julia Gregson, who was already bound over to do the same towards him, as there was some 'ill feeling' between the two. A charge of assault had followed a ferry trip to New Norfolk.

Sarah Benjamin died on 21 February 1855 and was buried at New Norfolk.

Hobart Town Gazette, 7 October 1836, 5 October 1838, 8 October 1841; *Hobart Town Courier*, 21 October 1836, 12 October 1838, 24 February 1842, 6 May 1842, 16 December 1843.

BENJAMIN, Fanny

d. 1841
Free.

Fanny Benjamin was buried in the Devonshire Street Jewish Cemetery on 7 July 1841.

BENJAMIN, Fanny

b. London, 1822–1913
Alfred, 1841; Free.
Single.

Fanny was the daughter of Moses Benjamin (q.v.) and Susan (née Solomon), and was born on 11 December 1822. Fanny Benjamin came to Sydney in 1841, and then returned to her parents, in London. She returned to Australia on the *Sultana*, arriving in Adelaide on 10 August 1851. On 28 July 1852, aged twenty-nine, she married Samuel Cohen, aged thirty. They went to New Zealand, and her husband died at Christchurch on 11 June 1865. Fanny returned to Adelaide and, on 11 April 1869, she married Samuel Hyam Isaacs, aged forty-five, at the home of her father, who lived at Tavistock Street, Adelaide. Fanny died on 24 March 1913 at the age of ninety and was buried in the West Terrace Jewish Cemetery in Adelaide.

Pritchard Index.

BENJAMIN, Fanny (née COHEN)

b. Sydney, 1839
16 children.

Fanny, the daughter of Abraham and Sophia Cohen (qq.v.), of Port Macquarie and Sydney, was born on 22 July 1839. She married her uncle, Benjamin Benjamin (q.v.). They were to have sixteen children. See Cohen, Fanny.

BENJAMIN, Ferotcha

d. 1842
Free.

Ferotcha Benjamin was buried by the Sydney Synagogue in the Devonshire Street Cemetery on 21 September 1842.

BENJAMIN, Harty

b. London
Active, 1791; Convict; Sentenced to 7 years, Old Bailey, 1787.

Benjamin was found to be in possession of stolen goods in Petticoat Lane. Said that his mother lived in Petticoat Lane. Found guilty of possessing stolen goods but not of burglary. Sentenced to seven years transportation on 21 February 1787. The Convict Indents stated that he was transported on the William and Ann in 1791, but p. 202 of the Active Indent includes his name.

A letter awaited him in Sydney, according to the *Sydney Gazette* of 8 January 1809. In the *Sydney Monitor* of 25 February 1839 'Benjamin Harty', a ticket of leave holder for the district of Bathurst, was charged with being drunk. He was found riding on the shaft of his master's team of horses in George Street 'to the risk of his own neck'. He was severely admonished and was sentenced to serve fourteen days in solitary confinement on bread and water.

OBSP, 1786–87, case 282, p. 426; COD 9, 4/4523; CO 207/1.

BENJAMIN, Henry

William Lockerby, 1834; Free.

Henry Benjamin came to Australia with his parents, Samuel Benjamin (q.v.) and Elizabeth (q.v.), and siblings. They settled in Sydney. By 1844 Henry Benjamin was old enough to be listed as a seat holder in the York Street Synagogue together with his father.

Ship Indent 4/5207, 16 August 1834; *Sydney Gazette*, 19 August 1834.

BENJAMIN, Henry Samuel

b. London, 1810–1852
Palambam, 1832; Free.
Married; Dealer, innkeeper; 6 children.

Henry Benjamin was the son of Benjamin and Eva Benjamin, the cousin and father-in-law of Emanuel Benjamin (q.v.), and the son-in-law of Judah and Esther Solomon (qq.v.) of Hobart Town. Benjamin came to Van Diemen's Land on the

Palambam with his wife Lydia Benjamin (q.v.), and two children, Henry and Esther. Also on board the Palambam were Lydia's mother Esther Solomon (q.v.) and two young sisters Sarah and Rebecca. A rumour swept Hobart Town that an invasion of Jews had arrived although they were the only Jews to disembark.

Benjamin first settled in the inland town of Oatlands at the York and Albany Hotel. The climate disagreed with the family and, in May 1834 he advertised its sale through 'Judah & Joseph Solomon, Hobart Town', as he hoped to take his family to New South Wales for twelve months. Benjamin brought a suit, *Benjamin v. Griffiths*, against the purchaser of the hotel. Griffiths testified that 'that little Jew, Benjamin robbed me' and also 'the bloody Jew bastard took it'. Benjamin won the case, and was awarded £65 in damages. However, the family's move to Sydney was not a success and on 14 September 1835 Benjamin wrote from the Hamilton Inn to the Colonial Secretary, 'I have been lately obliged to return from Sydney on account of the climate not agreeing with my health and being about to recommence business as an Innkeeper in this Colony'. He was dismayed when his liquor stock had been seized 'owing to the hostility of a local constable'.

In January 1836, Benjamin recommenced business as an innkeeper at the Old Hamilton Inn and, in addition, opened a general store in the town. On 6 June 1839, H. S. Benjamin was permitted to employ one assigned convict servant. A notice in the *Hobart Town Courier* in 1840 announced: 'Mr and Mrs Benjamin thank customers of their inn in the Interior and inform the public that they have taken over the "Macquarie Hotel" in Hobart Town on 4 August 1840'. In 1842 the *Colonial Times* announced that H. S. Benjamin of Macquarie Street was insolvent, and that he had taken over the Ferry House Inn at New Norfolk: 'All communications are to [be] sent to Mr Judah Solomon, Temple House, Hobart Town'. In 1843 he was licensed as a hawker and changed his address to New Norfolk's Star and Garter Inn. He was involved in a court case, which resulted in a fine of five shillings for 'filthy and indecent language'. Five days later he was bound over for twelve months 'for endeavouring to excite Mr John Stevenson to commit a breach of the peace'. The family moved to Hobart Town and Benjamin was granted a licence to run the King George Inn at the New Wharf. In 1845, he was appointed the honorary auditor of the Hobart Synagogue.

Henry Benjamin died on board ship on his way to Melbourne in 1852 at the age of forty-two. His body was returned to Hobart and he was buried in the Hobart Town Jewish Cemetery in Harrington Street on 25 July 1852. Lydia then married Lewis Cohen.

Henry Samuel Benjamin and Lydia had six children: Henry (1831), Esther (c. 1832), Benjamin (c. 1835), Morris (22 August 1837), Samuel (1839) (q.v.) and Eve (1843, died 12 March 1863).

Colonial Times, 14 October 1834, 15 July 1834, 2 October 1835; *Hobart Town Gazette*, 11 October 1835, 6 June 1839, 7 October 1842, 2 October 1847; CSO 1/828/17579; *Hobart Town Courier*, 2 October 1835, 30 January 1842, 30 September 1842, 24 February 1843, 17 November 1843, 18 January 1845; Land Purchase, LSD 1/76/54.

BENJAMIN, John

b. London, 1819–1858
Andromeda, 1843; Free.
Single; Tailor; 8 children.

John Benjamin, son of Emanuel, was married to Sarah Levey, the second child of Philip Levey (q.v.) and his wife Leah (née Mordecai) (q.v.). Their marriage had been held in London on 21 July 1843 and they arrived in Australia with Sarah's family in December 1843.

John and Sarah Benjamin settled in Burra Burra in South Australia. Two children were born in South Australia, both of whom died in infancy: Henry, on 21 March 1848 at the age of two, and Deborah, on 28 March 1848, aged eight months. The couple had six more children: John Asher Benjamin (13 January 1849) in Goulburn, Philip (1 October 1850), Lydia (25 August 1852), Fanny (16 July 1854), Jane (15 March 1857), and Asher (3 April 1859) in Yass.

John Benjamin died on 11 September 1858, seven months before his last child was born. Sarah moved back to New South Wales, where her younger sister, Hannah Hart, lived in Yass. Sarah died in Yass on 22 June 1867, at the age of forty-four, 'leaving six orphaned children', according to the inscription on her headstone in the Yass Cemetery.

BENJAMIN, Joseph

b. Whitechapel, 1805–1890
Sir Godfrey Webster (1), 1823; Convict; Sentenced to 7 years, Old Bailey, 1823.
Single; Hawker; Height: 160 cm; 5 children.

Joseph Benjamin stole a watch from the Roman Catholic priest, the Rev. Emanuel Dios Santos, in the queue in front of the Drury Lane Theatre. Brown hair, light grey eyes, scar on side of forehead over left eyebrow.

Joseph Benjamin arrived in Van Diemen's Land on 30 December 1823. On 17 February 1824, in Hobart Town, Joseph Benjamin was acquitted of a charge of receiving stolen goods. On 2 April 1825 he was found to be 'absent without leave from Church' and was returned to the Department of Public Works. On 5 July 1825 he was sentenced to be confined to the watch house at night for 'enticing away from her husband and repeatedly making tipsy the wife of Simon Solomon' (q.v.). Ten days later he appeared again at the Supreme Court in Hobart Town for giving some tobacco to a runaway. While at the court, he was seen attempting to pick the pocket of a court official. He was therefore charged with 'attempting to pick the pocket of Mr Rayner' and, as a consequence, on 20 July, was sentenced to fifty lashes and sent to Maria Island. On 9 April 1827, as a prisoner at Maria Island, he was found to have stolen property in his possession and was sentenced to one hundred lashes. On 5 October of the same year he received a further fifty lashes for having stolen mutton in his possession.

Back in Hobart Town on 27 May 1830, he was arrested, brought to trial and convicted of receiving a stolen watch. Benjamin was sent to 'No. 2 Chain Gang' where, on 4 October 1831, he was found guilty of defacing his irons and his sentence was extended by six months. The *Colonial Times* reported on 12 November 1830 that two days earlier, Joseph Benjamin had been sentenced to fourteen years imprisonment at the Hobart Town Supreme Court. If this was so, Benjamin seems to have been speedily released, though he was certainly not out of trouble. A twelve-month sentence with the Public Works Department at Campbell Town on 15 July 1836 followed for 'trading with fowls and eggs'. Joseph Benjamin received his conditional pardon on 17 May 1843. He received a hawker's licence for Longford on 17 November 1843. He worked as a grocer in 1846 in Perth and as a storekeeper in 1852. His signature appears on the Launceston Synagogue petition of May 1843 and he gave £19 to the building appeal in 1845. In August 1845 he received a land grant of forty-five acres at Clarence and signed the grant with an 'X'.

Joseph Benjamin, 'aged thirty-six' (he was actually thirty-nine) and 'free' married Mary Martha Gale, aged twenty, in Launceston on 11 April 1844. Mary had arrived as a convict on the *Gilbert Henderson* in April 1840.

Benjamin and his wife remained in Perth. In 1854 he became the licensee of the Star Hotel, which was later renamed the Benjamin Hotel. He retired in 1876, and moved to the Launceston home of his daughter Elizabeth and son-in-law Alfred Jones, the governor of the local gaol. He died on 18 February 1890, and was buried as a Jew beside his wife in Perth. He was survived by his four daughters and one son: Elizabeth Mary Ann (Jones) (1844–1923), Charlotte Louisa (Kirby) (1846–1924), Elsie Maria (Markey) (1848–1930), Joseph John Benjamin (1850–1940), and Mary Ann Sarah (Taylor) (1852).

OBSP, 1822–23, case 420, p. 157; CON 31/1; Launceston Police Register, CO 280/157; CON 32/1, supplementary vol. p. 116; CP 251; CON 70/1, p. 117; *Hobart Town Courier*, 17 November 1843; Family information from Alison and Gary Pollard, and Judith C. Lyne.

BENJAMIN, Lydia (née SOLOMON)

b. Sheerness, Sheppey, 1813–1880
Palambam, 1832; Free.
Married; 6 children.

Lydia was the third child of Judah Solomon and Esther (née Levy, Russell) (qq.v.). She married Henry Samuel Benjamin (q.v.) and came to Van Diemen's Land with her mother, husband, and her two young children, Henry and Esther, in 1832. To Judah's discomfort, the family moved into Judah's large home in Argyle Street and stayed.

Lydia and Henry's children were Henry (1831), Esther (c. 1832), Benjamin (c. 1835), Morris (22 August 1837), Samuel (1839), and Eve (1843–1863). Following Henry's death, Lydia married Lewis Cohen in Hobart, on 11 November 1855, and returned with him to England. She died on 21 January 1880 in London.

Anne Rand, 'Temple House and the Judah Solomon Family', in P. Elias and A. Elias (eds), *A Few from Afar*, p. 23f.

BENJAMIN, Maria (née SIMMONS)

b. Germany, 1797
Persian, 1827; Convict; Sentenced to 7 years, Middlesex, 1826.
Widow; Straw bonnet maker; Height: 142 cm.

Dark brown hair, dark brown eyes. Can read and write. No previous conviction. Sentenced on 26 October 1826. Maria stole the clothes worn by a prostitute who had been persuaded to sleep off the after effects feeling 'very ill in the street' at her lodgings in Pump Court, Westminster. The following day Maria was caught wearing the stolen bonnet. Her accuser also knew her by the name of 'Simmonds' and the police described her rented room as 'a den of thieves'. 'Has a brother already in Australia—Solomon S(y)imons' (Solomon Simons, q.v.). Surgeon's report: 'A very orderly and well-disposed woman, and I think from her conduct she will support this character'.

The *Persian* arrived in Van Diemen's Land on 6 August 1827. Maria Benjamin's police record there is brief. On 22 October 1827, while an assigned servant to Mr Clainbone, she was reprimanded for being out after hours. On 2 March 1829, while assigned to Mr Chapman, she was found to be absent without leave and sentenced to gaol for fourteen days. On 6 August 1829, she applied to marry Thomas Mellor as a 'free' person. The marriage took place in Launceston on 22 August 1829. The 1832 Muster noted that she was again in gaol. She was free by servitude on 26 October 1833.

OBSP 26 October 1826, case 1892. VDL papers, ML A1059-1, p. 420; Launceston Police Book, CON 70/1, p. 148; CON 40/1; CON 33/1; CON 45/1.

BENJAMIN, Morris

Free.
Married; Dealer; 4 children.

Mr and Mrs Morris Benjamin ran a shop in Hobart Town and had four young sons. Mr M. Benjamin gave £2 to the Hobart Synagogue building fund on 9 June 1843.

Mrs Benjamin took her neighbour, Mr Mooney, to court for having kicked her eight-year-old son in the stomach. The Mooney children were 'making vulgar allusions to our persuasion', she said, and had compounded the aggravation by singing the well-known ditty, 'If I had a piece of pork. I would stick it on a fork. And give it to a Jew boy, Jew'. Mooney was fined ten shillings and ordered to pay costs.

Hobart Town Courier, 21 April 1846.

BENJAMIN, Moses

b. London, 1797–1876
Free.
Married; 10 children.

The son of Elijah Benjamin of London, Moses was married in London to Susan Solomon, the daughter of pencil-maker Samuel Moss Solomon (q.v.) and Betsy (née

Moses), of London. Moses and Susan Benjamin celebrated their golden wedding anniversary in Adelaide on 23 January 1871 in the presence of their ten children.

Moses Benjamin died on 24 April 1876, aged seventy-nine, at his home in Tavistock Street, Adelaide.

Pritchard Index; *Observer*, 27 January 1871.

BENJAMIN, Moses

b. London, 1805–1885
London, 1843; Free.
Married; Merchant; 7 children.

Moses Benjamin was the second son of Lyon and Miriam Benjamin of London and born 11 October 1805. His elder brother (by one year) was Samuel Benjamin (q.v.) and his younger brother was David Benjamin (q.v.). He also had a half-brother, Solomon Benjamin (q.v.).

Moses had married Catherine (née Moses) in London in 1829. In 1843 they migrated to Melbourne with their six children, Rebecca (1830–1902), Rachel (1832), Benjamin (1834–1905) (q.v.), Elias (1837–1870), David (1839–1901), and Frances (c. 1840–1909). An infant, Samuel, had died in London. The voyage was vividly recalled by a fellow passenger who wrote: 'a Jewish family in the intermediate, consisting of father, mother and numerous family, had the adjoining cabin to us; they eventually became wealthy and prominent citizens of Melbourne. One of the boys was several times recently Mayor of Melbourne and is now Sir Benjamin Benjamin'.

Evidently Moses had expected to join his younger half-brother, Solomon, in business. However, soon after he arrived he opened his own drapery store in Albert House, Collins Street. His advertised stock included 2000 pairs of trousers and 8400 shirts! He also announced 'no business transacted between 6 o'clock on Friday and 6 o'clock on Saturday evenings'.

In 1845 Moses Benjamin lived at 7 Collins Street in a wooden house of four rooms—three doors up from Elizabeth Street. He also advertised that his shop had 'no connection with any other House in Port Phillip'. Whatever the cause had been for the family quarrel, on 9 April 1846 D & S Benjamin joined forces with Moses Benjamin at 'Cheapside House, Collins St'. His name appeared on the address signed by the Jews of Port Phillip congratulating Chief Rabbi Nathan Adler on his appointment to the Melbourne Synagogue. Moses was elected treasurer of the Melbourne Hebrew Congregation shortly after his arrival, serving from 1846 to 1849. When Solomon and David left Melbourne for London following the first years of the gold rush, they sold two city blocks of land to their brother Samuel. They were in Collins Street, near Exhibition Street, where Moses had built his house (next door to that of his son-in-law, Edward Henry Cohen (q.v.), who had married his daughter Rebecca in 1847).

Moses Benjamin built a warehouse in Little Collins Street near Queen Street. M. Benjamin and Son functioned as a wholesale firm and the 'son' was Benjamin Benjamin.

Moses Benjamin became a Justice of the Peace, and was a well-known identity in the City of Melbourne. He died in Melbourne in 1885, and his very large estate was valued at £201 504.

Rodney Benjamin, 'Early Melbourne and the Benjamin Brothers', *AJJHS*, vol. 13, no. 3 (1996), p. 345f; *Port Phillip Patriot*, 29 January 1844; Alfred Joyce, *A Homestead History*, ed. G. F. James, Melbourne University Press, Carlton, Vic., 1949; *AG*, pp. 283, 320.

BENJAMIN, Moses

Katherine Stewart Forbes (2), 1832; Convict; Sentenced to 14 years, Lancaster, 1831.
Single; Pedlar.

Moses Benjamin was convicted at Lancaster on 24 October 1831 for receiving stolen silver plate.

The *Katherine Stewart Forbes* arrived in Van Diemen's Land on 16 July 1832. From December 1833 to June 1834 Moses Benjamin was an assigned servant to Mr Fitzgerald. During this time he was punished with bread and water for nine days in the cells, six days on the treadmill and twenty-five lashes for five different counts that ranged from neglect of duty to 'refusing good food supplied by his master'. He received a ticket of leave in July 1838. On 14 July 1841 he received fourteen days hard labour 'for having goods displayed outside his shop after having been warned of the consequences'.

In the 1842 Van Diemen's Land Census, Moses Benjamin (aged between forty-five and sixty) was living with another Jew (male) in Liverpool Street. The other man at the same address was recorded as being younger and having come free to the colony.

A conditional pardon was granted on 18 November 1842 and was extended to the Australian colonies on 8 July 1845.

CON 31/5, no. 1706; CON 18/10; CON 27/5; *Hobart Town Courier*, 13 July 1838; *Colonial Times*, 26 May 1834, 10 June 1834.

BENJAMIN, Moses

A 'Benjamin Moses' was listed as a storekeeper in Goulburn in 1839 in the *New South Wales and Port Phillip Directory for 1839*. It may have been a reference to two people, Samuel Benjamin (q.v.) and Elias Moses (q.v.), who were in business together in Goulburn around that time.

BENJAMIN, Phoebe

b. London, 1793
Mary Anne I (2), 1822; Convict; Sentenced to life, Middlesex, 1821.
Single; Silk glove maker: Height: 145 cm.

Florid complexion, dark hair, hazel eyes. Phoebe Benjamin was first sentenced to six months in prison after having stolen a bundle of clothes from a drunken man. She was found with the stolen goods as she walked home through Whitechapel at midnight. She was sentenced on 12 September 1821.

Phoebe arrived in Hobart Town on 20 May 1822. She was listed as having absconded from her assigned service on 12 August 1824 (*Sydney Gazette*). Phoebe married Solomon Lyons (q.v.) at St John's Parramatta in July 1826. It was the second official marriage between two Jews in Australia. On 28 October 1826, she was ordered to serve time at the Female Factory in Parramatta.

OBSP, 1819, case 1303, p. 458, Ship Indent 4/4008, p. 114.

BENJAMIN, Raphael (Ralph)

b. London, 1791–1873
Hive (1), 1834; Convict; Sentenced to 14 years, Old Bailey, 1833.
Married; Dealer; Height: 165 cm; 9 children.

Sallow complexion, freckled, brown and grey hair, grey eyes. Lost all front teeth but two. The father of seven children—two male and five female. Ralph Benjamin was convicted for selling stolen ribbon. He had 1224 yards of material valued at £39. 'The prisoner came to my home in the afternoon of 20 August [1833] and said he wished to speak to me—my young man called me down to him: he said he had some goods [to sell], would I stop home and look at them. I had bought before off him in that manner. He keeps a clothes shop in Golden Lane. He said he had bought them off a respectable man'. Benjamin told the court 'I am totally innocent. I never dealt in such [stolen] articles. I have been eighteen years in the clothes line'.

Raphael Benjamin arrived in Sydney on 11 June 1834, with his wife, Elizabeth (q.v.), and two of their children, Henry and Jane. Ralph Benjamin was assigned to the Australian Agricultural Company at Port Stephen and Mr James Barker of Sydney wrote to the Colonial Secretary concerning the employment of male convict servants. Benjamin had been assigned to him and he did not wish to accept him, because his wife and children had arrived in Australia and were in need of him. Barker wrote: 'give me another man of the name of Benjamin in exchange which will answer my service much better'. The Colonial Secretary replied on 1 January 1835 that the transfer of Ralph Benjamin to Charles Barnett was not possible. Mr Henry Dumaresq had paid for the assignment of Benjamin and the 'prison regulations forbade transfer of prisoners from the country to Sydney'. Dumeresq asked again, because Benjamin's wife and children 'have followed him to the Colony and being without the means of support or protection may seem to warrant me in so doing'. The Colonial Secretary replied that he could not 'impinge in these matters'.

Ralph was a member of the Sydney Synagogue and was honoured by being *Chatan Torah* in September 1842. 'Mr and Mrs Raphael Benjamin' had given £15 to the Sydney Synagogue building appeal on 15 September 1839. Raphael and his son Samuel were both members of the Sydney Synagogue in 1845. Family tradition recalls that Raphael was a publican and a 'merchant'.

Ralph Benjamin received a ticket of leave in 1841 and a certificate of freedom on 10 September 1847. He died at the residence of his son, at 513 George

Street. He was buried at the Lidcombe Jewish Cemetery, Sydney, on 26 February 1873, described as the father of Jane (Mrs Solomon Lazarus), Caroline (Mrs Morris Nelson), Henry Benjamin and Lewis Benjamin.

CS 35/129, 1 January 1835; TL 41/2198; CF 47/0672; *Sydney Morning Herald*, 28 February 1873; Family information from Mrs L. Walters, Melbourne.

BENJAMIN, Reuben

b. London, 1816–1856
Roslin Castle (4), 1834; Convict; Sentenced to 7 years, London, 1833.
Single; Dealer; Height: 155 cm.

Dark sallow complexion, black hair, chestnut eyes. Thick large nose. Lost canine teeth in upper jaw. Scar right cheek. Eyebrows partially meeting. Large wart lower right arm. Legs hairy. Benjamin stole a bundle of laundry valued at ten shillings from a fourteen-year-old boy in Hyde Park. Benjamin was chased and caught and brought to the police.

The *Roslin Castle* arrived in New South Wales on 15 September 1834. Reuben Benjamin received a ticket of leave for the District of Goulburn in November 1838 and a certificate of freedom on 17 November 1840. A conditional pardon followed in 1842, also for the Goulburn District. He was buried by the York Street Synagogue on 29 October 1856, at the age of forty.

OBSP, 1832–33, case 1059, p. 855; Printed Ship Indent, p. 119; Letters from Governor's Office from Goulburn District; TL 38/1879, p. 213 A664; Governors' Despatches for 1839, ML, A1220, p. 456; CF 42/1413, 40/1892—District of Goulburn, 4/4124, 4/4362.

BENJAMIN, Samuel

b. London, 1804–1854
Ann, 1833; Free.
Single; Merchant; 11 children.

Samuel Benjamin was the eldest son of Lyon Benjamin and his first wife Miriam of Hyde Park, London. His brothers were Moses (q.v.) and David (q.v.), and Solomon Benjamin (q.v.) was his half-brother.

Samuel Benjamin arrived in Sydney on the *Ann* on 13 November 1833 with Elias Moses (q.v.), and the two men went to Goulburn in order to establish a wholesale and retail business. Both men were aged twenty-four and were described as 'dealers'. Samuel was married in Sydney on 4 February 1835, at the Bridge Street Synagogue, the announcement reading: 'by the officiating minister of the Jews Synagogue (Solomon Phillips) Samuel Benjamin, of the firm Benjamin and Moses, to Rachael [Rachel Moses, q.v.] the youngest sister of Elias Moses of the above firm'. The two partners therefore became brothers-in-law.

The couple's children were Mary (born 24 October 1835 at Sydney and died 16 March 1849), Elias Abraham (1837–1838), Benjamin (1838–1912), Maurice (Moses) S. (born at Illawarra, 1840–1885), Fanny (born in Sydney in 1840, died thirty-one days later), Jane (8 June 1841), Clara (8 September 1842–1911), Rachel (born in Sydney 1844, died 13 November 1849), Elizabeth (1846–1875), David Hobart (born 1847, died 8 February 1849), and Sarah (1849–1880). The children's remains were removed from the Devonshire Street Cemetery and reburied in the Rookwood Cemetery in 1901.

In 1835 Benjamin had opened a business at Sydney House, 44 Lower George Street, and also at 321 George Street, 'opposite the Burial Ground'. In 1836, a store was established on George Street, Windsor, called the London Stores, which boasted that it was the town's 'pioneer store' and, in 1842, was the only one of its kind between Sydney and Melbourne. Benjamin also owned a boiling-down works in Goulburn, the Argyle Steam Boiling Establishment, Tourang, which employed one hundred men at the height of the season. Samuel Benjamin and Elias Moses bought two city blocks in the 1839 Melbourne land sale. They also had a general store, the Goulburn Store, in Queanbeyan in 1844.

Samuel Benjamin gave £30 to the York Street Synagogue building appeal in 1839. He joined the synagogue's board in 1840 and helped to prepare the 1845 Sydney Synagogue Report. Benjamin was an enthusiastic supporter of the Sydney edition of the *Voice of Jacob* and the early Jewish Library. Between 1836 and 1852 he and Elias Moses bought land parcels in a dozen townships, which included the first land purchases in Portland, Victoria (1840), and early purchases in Melbourne, Queanbeyan, Windsor and Braidwood. The *Sydney Morning Herald* reported on 7 January 1845 that Samuel Benjamin, along with two servants, had been held up by bushrangers while travelling to his Queanbeyan store, but had escaped unharmed.

Samuel Benjamin died in Sydney on 4 December 1854 and was buried at the Devonshire Street cemetery. Rachael died in Sydney on 15 June 1862.

Rodney Benjamin, 'Early Melbourne and the Benjamin Brothers', *AJJHS*, vol. 13, no. 3 (1996), p. 384; ML 4/5205; Great Synagogue Journal (Sydney), July 1950; Noel F. Learmonth, *The Portland Bay Settlement*; *Port Phillip Patriot*, 10 October 1840; Land Purchases 2/7799; *Sydney Morning Herald*, 7 January 1845; *AG*, pp. 182, 282, 305, 308, 314.

BENJAMIN, Samuel

William Lockerby, 1834; Free.
Married; Dealer; 5 children.

Samuel Benjamin arrived on 16 August 1834. His wife Elizabeth and their children, Henry (q.v.), Juliet, Jane, Rachel and Hannah, travelled with him in steerage. The 1842 municipal voters' list showed that Samuel Benjamin owned a shop and dwelling in George Street, Sydney. He was a seat holder in the York Street Synagogue in 1845 and gave £30 to the building fund. Samuel Benjamin signed a petition that new settlers should get more assistance from the colonial government.

William Lockerby Indent 4/5207; *Sydney Morning Herald*, 15 September 1842; Petition, Governors' Despatches, ML, A1216, p. 583.

BENJAMIN, Samuel

b. Hamilton, Van Diemen's Land, 1839–1926

The child of Henry Samuel Benjamin (q.v.) and Lydia Benjamin (q.v.), the daughter of Judah Solomon (q.v), Samuel was born on 21 July 1839. At the age of thirteen, after his bar mitzvah, Samuel went to work at Judah and Joseph Solomon's business at Temple House in Hobart Town, and remained there until the firm ceased operation in 1854. Samuel Benjamin then went to Melbourne in partnership with a cousin—a son of Joseph Solomon (q.v.). When his partner proceeded to London to establish a boot and shoe factory, Samuel remained in Melbourne to look after the business. The business grew and he moved to Sydney and saw his boot and leather business grow to produce £200 000 a year. It was in Sydney that he married Fannie Benjamin (no relative). They had a son, Montefiore Moses Benjamin, and two daughters, Eveline Rosetta and Lydia.

Benjamin lost his personal fortune in the Stock Exchange crash of 1880. He left Australia and, in 1884, started a wine and spirit business in New York. When this was burned down he moved to Cincinnati, Ohio, and it was there that he received news that he had inherited £100 000 from his uncle, Joseph Solomon. He returned to Tasmania, after an absence of thirty-five years, to live at Temple House in Argyle Street, next to the synagogue. The mansion was the home of his extended family. His daughter-in-law was Myra Lindo Levien of Melbourne and his grandchildren were Joseph, Eileen, Dorothy and Eveline.

Benjamin was elected an alderman of the Hobart City Council in 1897. He was a turbulent representative of the people. Stefan Paltrow observed: 'Unfortunately, his personality was such that independence led to isolation, and impartiality to aggressive personal criticism. Cooperation was not his style, and so he was unable to achieve any reforms unless these were already generally supported'. The Mayor of Hobart, George Davies, declared 'Benjamin threw mud at the rest of them [the aldermen] in the hope that some of it would stick, and it must stick in some places'. He served as president of the Hobart Hebrew Congregation until his death, on 5 March 1926, at the age of eighty-seven.

Mercury, 6 March 1926; L. M. Goldman, 'The History of Hobart Jewry', *AJJHS*, vol. 3, no. 5 (1951), p. 209f; S. Paltrow, 'Fearless and Independent: Jews Elected in Public Office in Tasmania 1855–1902', and Anne Rand, 'Temple House and the Judah Solomon Story', in P. Elias and A. Elias (eds), *A Few from Afar*, pp. 104f., and 25.

BENJAMIN, Sarah (née LEVEY)

b. Whitechapel, 1823–1867
Andromeda, 1843; Free.
Married; 8 children.

The barque *Andromeda* arrived in Port Jackson on 7 December 1843. On board the ship was the family of Philip Levey (q.v.), his wife Leah (q.v.) (née Mordecai), their nine unmarried children, and their daughter Sarah, who had recently married

John Benjamin (q.v.). Sarah and John Benjamin settled in Kooringa, Burra Burra, in South Australia.

BENJAMIN, Simeon

1817–1859
Free.
Single; Draper.

Simeon Benjamin was the son of Benjamin Benjamin of London. He was penalized one guinea by the Hobart Synagogue's committee for declining the honour of being a bridegroom of the Torah in October 1841. A member of the Hobart Town Synagogue in 1842 (but not in 1844), Benjamin gave £2 to the synagogue and was shown in the congregational ledger as owing two shillings in 1845. He was not a seat holder in the new synagogue. Simeon Benjamin married Elizabeth Solomon on 21 January 1846 (the tenth Jewish wedding in Van Diemen's Land), at Victoria House, Liverpool Street, in Hobart Town. It was Elizabeth's second marriage. The officiating minister was Henry Jones (q.v.). Edward Magnus (q.v.) was rebuked by the congregation's leadership for writing the traditional Hebrew marriage certificate without authorisation. At the time Benjamin's occupation was given as 'draper' and Elizabeth was described as a 'jeweller'.

In 1846 'Simeon Benjamin in Liverpool St, a jeweller', was robbed by Michael Solomon (q.v.), a 'near relative' of Mrs Benjamin. (He was her estranged son-in-law).

Benjamin died, aged forty-two, on 8 August 1859. He left an intestate estate. His principal asset was his stock in trade (drapery), which, on 24 August 1860, was offered for sale by order of the Curator, Mr Sorrell.

BENJAMIN, Simon

b. London, 1799
Malabar (1), 1819; Convict; Sentenced to life, Old Bailey, 1818.
Single; Fishmonger: Height: 165 cm.

Light brown hair, fair ruddy complexion, hazel eyes. Simon Benjamin stole a watch from a drunken man in a London street and was caught in the act. He was sentenced on 2 December 1818.

In New South Wales, Simon Benjamin was listed among the convicts on 5 November 1819 who had been sent to Parramatta. On 11 July 1821, he was sentenced to be sent to Newcastle for three years. Subsequently, the *Sydney Gazette* announced, on 27 November 1823 and 13 January 1824, that Benjamin had absconded from 'Mr Terry's Clearing Party' (in the bush). He was officially listed as an absconded prisoner from 1 April 1824.

OBSP, 1818–19, case 115, p. 49; 4/4006, p. 424; HO 11/3; *Sydney Gazette*, 27 November 1823, 1 April 1824, 13 January 1825; Convicts Sent to Parramatta, 5 November 1819, 4/3501; Convicts Sent to Newcastle, 11 July 1821, 4/3504.

BENJAMIN, Solomon

b. London, 1818–1888
Henry, 1838; Free.
Draper; 17 children.

The son of Lyon and Phirely Benjamin of London, Solomon Benjamin was born on 20 March 1818. He was the half-brother of Moses, David and Samuel Benjamin (qq.v.), and arrived in Australia in 1838 with David. They travelled to Van Diemen's Land. David established a drapery and clothing store at Brisbane and St John streets in Launceston in premises known as Tamar House. In November of that year, Solomon Benjamin appears to have visited Melbourne briefly to 'spy out the land'. On 14 February 1839 Solomon sailed from Launceston to Melbourne on the barque *Wallaby* to set up a branch of the Launceston store. David maintained the business in Launceston but Melbourne was experiencing a boom and in June 1840 the Benjamins opened Cheapside House on the northeastern corner of Collins and Queen streets.

In March 1840, after Solomon had turned twenty-one, the name of the firm became D & S Benjamin, and it was at Cheapside House that Asher Hymen Hart (q.v.) conducted the first High Holyday services in Melbourne.

At the Sydney Synagogue, on 11 August 1841, Solomon Benjamin married Miriam Nathan (q.v.) 'of George St', who was sixteen. Miriam (1825–1882) was a daughter of Nathan Lyon Nathan (q.v.) and Sarah Nathan of London. A sister, Rosetta (Nathan, q.v.), was married to Moses Joseph (q.v.) of Sydney.

The Benjamin brothers bought a block of land at William's Town at the third Port Phillip land sale in September 1840 as they hoped to build a warehouse with easy access to Port Phillip Bay. Shortly after the purchase, the mouth of the Yarra River was widened so that ships could sail up the river to the site of the new town. The *Port Philip Gazette* advertised on 12 August 1843 that 'Cheapside House . . . the oldest establishment in Melbourne' was selling off all its extensive stock 'in consequence of business of importance requiring their presence in London'. In fact, Solomon's half-brother Moses, with all his family, arrived in December 1843 and joined the business. The business itself moved up Collins Street. The gold rush brought the Benjamin brothers great wealth, not only through their drapery trade but also through extensive gold trading.

Solomon Benjamin witnessed the first three Jewish weddings in the Port Phillip district and served as first vice-president of the Melbourne Hebrew Congregation, and then became the honorary treasurer. Between 1846 and 1849 Solomon Benjamin bought £700 worth of land in the new settlement. In 1843, with Asher Hymen Hart and Michael Cashmore (q.v.), he applied for land for a Jewish cemetery in Melbourne.

The Benjamins had seventeen children. They were Miriam (7 September 1842 to 19 February 1923) (the second entry in the Melbourne Hebrew Congregation's Birth Register), Sarah (18 May 1844 to 5 April 1880), Benjamin Albert (26 February 1846 to 1942), Louis (20 July 1847, died eight and a half months later), Samuel (10 February 1849–1870), Charlotte Victoria (5 September 1850),

Nathaniel Lionel (21 June 1852), Morris (born at 44 Bedford Square, London, on 2 May 1854), Alfred Leopold (27 September 1855), Rachel Amy (26 November 1856), Rosa Kate (8 December 1857), Jacob Henry (Brunswick Place, Regents Park, 13 May 1859), David Frederick (5 June 1860), Esther (1861), Louis Stanley (Clifton Gardens, 2 March 1863–1934), Clara (16 March 1865, lived two days), and Florence Gertrude (13 October 1865).

Benjamin retired from business at the ripe old age of thirty-five in 1853, and returned to England, where he bought a house in Clifton Gardens. He died in London in 1888 and was said (in a Jewish American newspaper report) to have left an estate worth US$3 million. His Australian-born daughter Miriam (q.v.) married Lewis Sanders.

Rodney Benjamin, 'Early Melbourne and the Benjamin Brothers' *AJJHS*, vol. 13 no. 3 (1966), p. 365f; ML 2/7799; Melbourne Hebrew Congregation Birth Book; *AG*, pp. 282, 283, 286, 287, 293, 320; Ms. Family Register, written for S. Benjamin Esq. and Rev. Moses Rintel, Melbourne, held by the Jewish Museum (Melbourne).

BENTLEY, James

b. Winchester
Hyderabad, 1843; Free.
Single; Soldier.

Bentley was classified as a labourer when he enlisted in the British Army on 1 January 1843. He joined his regiment in Van Diemen's Land on 17 November 1843, arriving on the *Hyderabad*, a freight ship. Bentley was listed as being on garrison duty from July to September 1844. He was then sent to the Tasman Peninsula from October 1844 to March 1845. He remained on duty, including a period in hospital, until he was discharged from the army, on 31 October 1845. On 28 August 1845 the Commanding Officer of the 96th Regiment stationed in Hobart Town, Lieutenant Colonel Elliott, wrote to David Poole (q.v.), who at that time was acting as honorary solicitor of the Hobart Synagogue, expressing concern about the discharge 'of a Hebrew James Bentley from the Army'. The letter was received by the synagogue's committee but no action appears to have been taken.

Minutes of the Hobart Synagogue; Research by the late Dr Peter Elias, Hobart; Regimental no. 1565, Box 3183, no. 6205, pp. 69, 129, 189, no. 6207, pp. 10, 70, 130, AOT.

BERKMAN, Marcus

b. Berlin, 1814 *Roslin Castle* (4), 1834; Convict; Sentenced to life, Old Bailey, 1833. Single; Saddler, upholsterer, pedlar; Height: 165 cm.

Ruddy complexion, brown hair, grey eyes. Left leg diseased. On 11 November 1833 Berkman stole jewellery worth £20 from Samuel Jacobs, a hawker, who slept in the same room as he did at a boarding house in London. Jacobs was at synagogue when Berkman stole his stock. Berkman had been in England for a year and claimed in court that he was not able to speak English and needed an interpreter. The witnesses insisted that he could speak English.

Berkman was issued a ticket of leave on 13 September 1844 for the Cassilis District. This was altered to Moreton Bay on 5 December 1844. A conditional pardon was granted on 24 October 1848. At that time, he was allowed to remain at Darling Downs for twelve months service to Mr George Leslie by recommendation of the Brisbane Bench.

On 20 February 1851 Marcus Berkman of Darling Downs was naturalised. Almost immediately after that he was able to begin to buy land and Marcus Berkman 'of Warwick, Queensland', bought a parcel of land. In the mid-1850s, alluvial gold was found in the vicinity, and Berkman purchased this gold.

OBSP, 1833–34, case 140, p. 107; TL 44/2282, in 4/4193; HO 10/54; Land Correspondence, 2/7796.

BINDER, Barney (Bernard)

b. London, 1799
Midas, 1827; Convict; Sentenced to 7 years, Guilford, 1826.
Single; Carter and labourer; Height: 155 cm.

Dark ruddy complexion, dark brown hair, brown eyes. Tattooed with a figure of a man and the letters JB on his right arm, and the date 1826 on his left arm. Barney Binder was convicted at Guildford on 17 July 1826 for stealing poultry, and listed on the ship's indent as a Protestant.

The *Midas* arrived in Port Jackson on 15 February 1827. Binder was listed in the 1828 Census as Bendor, a government servant and a 'Jew'. He was listed as a salt boiler at John Blaxland's estate at Newington.

Ship Indent, 4/4012, p. 54.

BIRSTINGL, Lewis

b. Arad, Hungary, 1819
1842; Free.
Single; Jeweller.

The younger brother of Maurice Birstingl (q.v.), Lewis was born in the south-east of Hungary. The two brothers were orphaned in the wake of a cholera epidemic, after which they went to Paris and then London. Lewis learned to deal in glassware and glass jewellery and apparently travelled extensively through Europe developing his considerable linguistic skills.

Lewis Birstingl arrived in Sydney at a crucial time in the life of his older brother, who was standing trial for stealing the drawing-plate from his former business partner. Once the trial was over, and his brother pardoned, Lewis took over the responsibility as Maurice's 'agent' for the jewellery business of 'Birnstingle (*sic*) and Co., watch and clockmakers, jewellers, silversmiths and importers of British and foreign novelties', at 478 George Street, while Maurice journeyed to Europe on a business trip from 1843 to 1844.

In early 1845 the brothers presented the new York Street Synagogue with a silver pointer for the reading of the Torah.

During the late 1840s the jewellery shop began to be described as 'general merchants' and at the beginning of the gold rush as 'a bullion office'. The brothers imported material for the miners, such as camp ovens, paper, soap, and wines, including the 'most superior champagne'. 'L. Birstingl & Co.' opened a shop in Wynyard Lane that catered for haberdashery goods. At the same time, the brothers exported large quantities of gold to Great Britain, and imported large quantities of merchandise into New South Wales.

On 17 September 1853, Lewis Birstingl sailed on the steamship *Victoria* for England, where he married and had children. In London, at Glasshouse Street, he opened a photographic studio and experimented with the colouring of photographs.

Biography in Egon F. Kunz, *Blood and Gold: Hungarians in Australia*, p. 20f.

BIRSTINGL, Maurice

b. Arad, Hungary, 1807–1903
John, 1838; Free.
Single; Jeweller.

In 1831, following a cholera epidemic which took the lives of their parents, Maurice, aged twenty-four, left Hungary with his twelve-year-old brother, Lewis (q.v.). They made their way to London by way of Paris. Maurice worked as a jeweller and silversmith and then, together with a French jeweller, Bartholomew Guion, set off for Australia, arriving in Sydney on 1 July 1838. The two jewellers announced that they, having:

> just arrived from Paris and London, where they had been working for several years, have the honour to inform the Public that they have established a Manufactory of every kind of jewellery, at No 5 Bridge Street, Colonade, where orders will be executed after the most fashionable patterns. Jewels altered and repaired. Messrs G and B. have imported a choice assortment of Fancy Goods to an inspection of which they especially invite the ladies of Sydney.

The partnership came to an end on 25 May 1840, when Guion paid Birstingl £900 for all stock in trade, tools and debts. Maurice Birstingl then went to Europe to buy stock for a new business. Upon his return the *Australian* hoped that 'as Mr B. went away while the colony was flourishing he will not suffer because he came back when it was depressed'. An advertisement in the same paper gave the new address of the business 'M. Birstingl and Co. manufacturing watch and clock makers, jewellers and silversmith, 2 Bridge St Sydney'.

When Birstingl returned to Sydney, a jealous, and obviously nervous, former colleague charged him with having stolen a drawing-plate, which was now the property of Guion. Birstingl claimed that he had bought the plate in Paris. A handsome testimonial from Captain Innes and others allowed the Governor to issue the accused with an Absolute Pardon as 'an act of grace'. By this time, Lewis Birstingl had arrived in Sydney and the two brothers advertised for 2500 ounces of silver to fulfil orders received. Maurice then left for an extended business trip to Europe while Lewis acted as his 'agent'. Maurice sent back 'watches, clocks, musical boxes. Ornaments jewellery, looking glasses imported from Munich, Vienna and Paris' to the business, now located at 478 George Street.

Both Maurice and his brother were members of the Sydney Synagogue, contributed to the building fund, and gave a silver Torah pointer to the congregation.

In 1845 Maurice received his naturalisation certificate, which was the first issued to any Hungarian in the colony of New South Wales. By the end of the 1840s the firm had diversified into a 'general business', which, with the gold rush beginning in 1851, quickly added the description 'bullion office'. The Birstingls imported all the stock required by miners, from camp ovens to cigars and champagne. M. Birstingl and Co. was among the leading bullion exporters in the colony.

In November 1853, Maurice left New South Wales on the steamer *Chusan*, bound for Marseilles. He settled in Paris, where he married and had two children. He died in Paris in 1903, at the age of ninety-six.

Biography in Egon F. Kunz, *Blood and Gold Hungarians in Australia*, p. 20f.; Ship Indent 38/137, 4/5213 (name spelled Maurentius Bartengle); *Australian*, 10 August, 15 August, 22 August, 28 October 1842; *Sydney Morning Herald*, 10 April, 29 June 1844.

BLAU, Adolphus

b. Hungary, 1825
Prince of Wales, 1850; Free.
Single; Jeweller.

Adolphus Blau's arrival in Sydney on 21 February 1850 was connected with the Birstingl brothers, Lewis and Maurice (qq.v.), and their commercial activities. Blau brought with him four cases of watches for the firm of Birstingl. In October 1853, Blau emerged as a jeweller as the Birstingl brothers left Australia. It is likely that Blau worked for the Birstingls in his first three years in Australia before opening his own shop, at 489 George Street, which carried a wide selection of silver, rings, watches and other jewellery.

The end of 1854 saw the business of 'Blau, Adolphus, jeweller and silversmith', move to 177 George Street. Blau then left Australia and his business was taken over by Edward Morize. In 1861, Blau returned to Sydney and was an importer of jewellery and a watchmaker in Hunter Street.

Egon F. Kunz, *Blood and Gold: Hungarians in Australia*, p. 31f.

BOAZ, Joachim (BOAS)

b. Poland, 1785
Baring (1), 1815; Convict; Sentenced to life, Old Bailey, 1814.
Single; Clerk; Height: 160 cm.

Dark sallow complexion, black hair, brown eyes. Together with Moses Rockotz (q.v.), Boaz was charged with two offences. Having arrived in England on 27 May 1814, the two men had visited two drapers' stores on 14 June. In the first store they had successfully stolen twelve yards of cambric valued at thirty shillings. At the second, they stole seven pieces of cambric lace valued at £15, but their nervousness betrayed them and they were arrested. Boaz submitted a written plea: 'I did not come [to England] to rob this country or to settle'. The two thieves were unable to speak English. They were sentenced to death on 6 July 1814, their sentences subsequently commuted to transportation for life.

Boaz arrived in New South Wales on 7 September 1815. By 1821 he had rented a small farm in the District of Evan and was able to supply the government with twenty-nine bushels of wheat worth £13 1s. On 20 October 1825 he petitioned the Colonial Secretary for a mitigation of his sentence. He had 'rented a smal [*sic*] farm in the District of Evan until very recently when Memorialist was obliged to relinquish it in consequence of several times being robbed of his little all. Now a shoemaker by which he procures a comfortable maintenance'. A ticket of leave was granted. Boaz then asked for a conditional pardon, signing his name 'Joachim Boaze'. In the 1828 Census, Boaz was listed as a 'Hebrew' and shoemaker, employed by John Williams of Camden.

Boaz waited ten years for his pardon, which he received on 23 September 1834 (358), when his occupation was listed as 'pedlar'.

OBSP, cases 585, 586, pp. 315–16; Ship Indent 2/8243, p. 174; TL Register 4/4060, 441/195, in lieu of lost ticket 24/411; CP Register, 221/358, 4/4433, p. 221, 3 November 1835; CS, In Correspondence, 4/1748, p. 181; State Receipts, CS, Petitions for Mitigation of Sentence, 4/1873, p. 19.

BOCKERAH, Ann

d. 1793
Neptune, 1790; Free.
Married; 1 child.

The wife of Solomon Bockerah (q.v.), Ann arrived on the Second Fleet, and may have been the first free adult Jewish settler in Australia. She died in 1793 and was buried on 21 February 1793 by St John's, Parramatta, leaving a child, Sarah, born in Australia. Evidently, following the death of Solomon Bockerah, his widow, Ann, together with Sarah, her daughter, joined the Atkins household. In the diary of Atkins Ann's death is obliquely recorded as 'a great domestic loss'. Atkins wife, Elizabeth, arrived in New South Wales in 1802 and seems to have adopted Sarah as part of her household. In 1800 Ann became one of the first pupils of the Female Orphan Institute.

Sarah's death is commemorated by a table shaped, sandstone monument on which is inscribed:

> *Sacred to the memory of Sarah Buckrell (sic) who died Febr 21 1793. Aged 22 years. This monument is erected by Richard Atkins, Esq as a testimonial of the regard he bore her when living. Requiescat in Pace.*

Research by Justin Cahill of New South Wales who is a direct descendant of Ann.

BOCKERAH, Solomon

d. 1791
Scarborough (2), 1790; Convict; Sentenced to life, Old Bailey, 1788.
Married; 1 child.

On 1 November 1788, Solomon Bockerah and Robert Hobbs broke into a dwelling place at 7 p.m. and stole a piece of velveteen worth £8 4s. Bockerah was the leader of a gang of four or five men who broke into a shop in the City of London. The others escaped, but he was taken in a fight when the coach that was taking him to the police station was attacked by Bockerah's friends. Hobbs was found not guilty and Bockerah was sentenced to death, later commuted to transportation for life.

Bockerah was held in Newgate for more than a year before being officially discharged from the prison and put on the *Scarborough*, a ship of the Second Fleet. The *Scarborough* lost 85 of its 259 convicts through maltreatment and Bockerah survived the voyage only to die in Sydney. He was buried on Saturday, 16 July 1791, by the chaplain at St Philip's. He was officially described, at the time, as 'a Jewish convict'.

Bockerah's wife Ann (q.v.) must have accompanied him to Australia on the Second Fleet as a free woman. She was buried by St John's, Parramatta, on 21 February 1793, leaving an orphaned child, Sarah, who had been born in Australia. On 29 January 1810 Sarah Bockerah petitioned Governor Macquarie for a grant of fifty acres of land. She wrote that she had been left 'an orphan during her infant state, having been admitted into the [Orphan] Institution from which the petitioner was taken by the late Mrs Atkins, in whose employ continued three years. The Petitioner being a native of this Settlement, and a Mother, will she flatters herself Induce your Excellency to confirm the said Grant'. Macquarie wrote 'to be renewed in the name of her husband John Lawrence—now Free'. Lawrence was actually John Laurie, whom Sarah married in April 1810. If Ann was Jewish, and there is no reason to think that she was not, then her daughter, Sarah, must be numbered among the first Jewish children in the colony.

OBSP, 1788–89, case 82, p. 53; CS 4/1821, Memo to Gov. Macquarie no. 27, 4/4003.

BOTIBOL, Esther Henrietta

b. Portica, Italy, 1834–1910
Anna Maria (2), 1852; Convict; Sentenced to 7 years, Central Criminal Court, 1851.
Single; Dressmaker; Height: 136 cm; 6 children.

The dossier lists a brother, Isaac, and a sister. Fair complexion, light brown hair, small face, brown eyes, small nose, mouth and chin. Very much pockmarked. 'Jewess.' Esther Botibol was transported for stealing a gold ring and a dress valued at £5. She had previously been convicted for four minor offences, and was sentenced on 12 May 1851.

Esther Botibol was listed as being 'uncooperative and disagreeable' on board ship. Her transport arrived in Hobart Town on 26 January 1852. On 17 May 1852 she absconded. She had been an assigned servant in the household of a Mr Marks and, having absconded a second time, on 1 June 1852 she was sentenced to six months hard labour. On 28 June she was sentenced to ten days in the cells for tearing her apron, the 'property of the government'. On 22 July she repeated her 'crime' and spent fourteen days in the cells. On 25 October she was convicted of 'disorderly conduct' and sentenced to a month's hard labour, to commence at the conclusion of her previous sentence. In February 1853 she was returned to the cells for disorderly conduct, and on 1 December she was sentenced to a month's hard labour for 'refusing to keep her bed and refusing to allow the nurse to apply remedies prescribed by the Medical Officer'. A ticket of leave was issued on 17 October 1854. In November, she was sentenced to eighteen months hard labour for larceny under £5.

Her criminal career continued. By December 1855 she was once again assigned to work within a household in Hobart Town. She absconded and was sentenced to a month's hard labour. On 19 February 1856 she was sentenced to nine months hard labour for absconding, and on 26 June she was placed in solitary confinement for seven days for using profane language to the matron and her existing sentence was extended. A second ticket of leave was issued on 17 February 1857. Five weeks later she was caught 'being out after hours' and given seven days hard labour. On 18 September 1857 she was returned to the cells for ten days for 'misconduct'. On 9 October a charge of 'Misconduct' in being absent from her residence resulted in three months hard labour. In the Supreme Court in Hobart on 19 August 1876 she received a sentence of six months for 'larceny' and on 14 July 1877, a twelve-month sentence for another theft. It was decreed that she was not to reside in Hobart Town but she was unable to keep out of town.

She had become involved with Thomas Simmonds, a millwright and wood splitter and she was to bear him six children. They married at the Wesleyan Parsonage in Hobart on 12 November 1872, when their youngest child was eight months old. Esther was thirty-three and Thomas was fifty-five. In 1868 they had applied to have three of their children cared for in the Queen's Orphanage. The children were Ann Jane, aged two, Esther, aged nine, and Thomas, aged eight. Nicholas, aged five, and Susannah, aged one, were not included in the application. Their sixth child, Mary Ann Eliza, was born in Hobart Town on 29 March 1872.

On 19 August 1875 Esther was given a six-month sentence, and two years later she stole a pair of boots, resulting, on 14 July 1877, in a sentence of twelve months imprisonment. Thomas Simmonds died on 25 May 1894 and Esther Henrietta Symmonds (*sic*) died in Hobart in 1910. She was buried in the Jewish cemetery in Hobart. Esther was certainly the last Jewish convict to have been transported to eastern Australia.

CON 15/6; CON 40/1, no. 1136; Susan Ballyn and Lucy Frost, 'Sephardi Convicts in Van Diemen's Land', in P. Elias and A. Elias (eds), *A Few from Afar*, p. 79f, where it is noted that on various documents her 'place of origin' is given as 'Lisbon, Portugal, and Rathbone Place, London'. All are probably correct. She lived at Rathbone Place, she had been born in Portica, and her Sephardi family remembered that they came from Lisbon.

BRAHAM, Abraham Hart

b. London, 1789
Admiral Gambier (2), 1811; Convict; Sentenced to life, London, 1810.

Braham was convicted for a felonious assault on the highway and stealing a gold watch valued at £25. The theft occurred in Fleet Street at 10 p.m. on 30 March 1810. The victim testified: 'A man ran against me. I was walking at the time and, at the same moment, I felt my watch was gone'. Braham took the watch to a pawnbroker in Houndsditch. He returned to the pawnbroker with another man and the pawnbroker became suspicious and called for the police. Braham was later arrested in a public house at Bow Street. The police office said 'Oh Master Braham is it you? I have been looking for you a good while for a watch that you stole in Fleet St'. Braham pleaded 'I am entirely innocent of the charge. I have dealt in watches. The gentleman must be mistaken in the man. I have pledged to the amount of a £100 of watches at his shop and Mr Morris never knew any harm in my character'. Braham was sentenced at the London Gaol Delivery on 6 June 1810.

Braham arrived in New South Wales on 10 October 1811. On 3 September 1814 Abraham Hart Braham advertised in the *Sydney Gazette* for the right to administer the estate of his late brother, William Brown (q.v.), whose real name was Moses Braham.

On 13 January 1815, Braham was sentenced to one year colonial transportation for theft and sent to Newcastle. He was transported again on 21 July 1817 and was listed as being in Newcastle at the time of the 1817 Muster.

OBSP, 1810, case 414, p. 230; Ship Indent 2/8240, p. 122, AO; 4/4004, p. 380; HO 10/1; HO 11/2; *Sydney Gazette*, 28 May 1814, 3 September 1814; CS, Prisoners sent to Newcastle, 4/3493.

BROCKSTEIN, George Jacob (BROCKSTAYNE)

b. Kolo, Poland, 1819–1887
Free.
Single; Dealer; 3 children.

George Brockstein, 'late of Bishopsgate', married Esther (Hester) Cohen (née Isaacs, q.v.) at the Sydney Synagogue on 11 April 1848. Esther was the widow of Edward Daniel Cohen (q.v.). George and Esther had a son in Sydney in 1849. He was named Alfred and registered as a 'Hebrew'. A second son, Lawrence, was born probably in 1853 (died 11 February 1882), and Isaac was born in 1855.

Brockstein was a gold buyer on the Bathurst goldfields. The pioneer gold prospector, Edward Hargraves, scornfully wrote about his business dealings with the London-born Jewish businessman: 'Vell, ven you find de gold I think you get good reward'.

Esther died in Sydney in 1857 and George (who now spelled his surname 'Brockstayne'), was buried at Lidcombe Cemetery's Jewish section on 10 July 1887, survived by Alfred and Isaac. On his grave his sons inscribed that their father's 'heart was in God's Torah. His lips spoke the Torah'.

M. Z. Forbes, 'Hargraves' "Mishter Cohen": A Prelude to the Goldrushes', *AJJHS*, vol. 10, no. 1 (1986), p. 61f.

BRODZIAK, Kate

Free.
Married; 8 children.

Kate (Catherine) was the wife of Meyer Brodziak (q.v.). Together they had eight children: Rosalie (1848), Alfred (1850), Francis (1851), Mark (1852), Hannah (1853), Julia (1856), Hannah (1858), and Bertha (1859). Kate died on 10 June 1885 and was buried at Lidcombe Cemetery's Jewish section.

BRODZIAK, Lewis

b. Poland, 1823–1884
Triton, 1842; Free.
Dealer.

Lewis was the brother of Meyer Brodziak (q.v.) and the son of Abraham and Golda (Julia). Lewis Brodziak donated ten shillings to the Hobart Town Congregation on 11 April 1843 and, in 1844, an additional three shillings. He married Annie Davis, sister of Samuel and David Davis (qq.v.). In 1845 it was announced that 'Mr Brodziak, formerly of Davis and Brodziak, has recommenced business as watchmaker and jeweller at 99 King St, Sydney'. The 1845 Shipping Register recorded that Davis and Brodziak imported 'one box' from London and sent 123 bags of maize to Hobart Town. In 1846 Brodziak was given a hawker's licence for the Hunter River District.

On 2 February 1853, Lewis Brodziak, a jeweller of 9 George Street, Sydney, became a British subject and was granted a naturalisation certificate. Lewis Brodziak was buried at Lidcombe Cemetery's Jewish section on 29 August 1884.

Hobart Town Congregational First Minute Book; *Sydney Morning Herald*, 8 November 1845; *Maitland Mercury*, 31 January 1846.

BRODZIAK, Meyer (Myer)

b. Prussia, 1817–1885
Kelso, 1842; Free.
Married; Silversmith; 8 children.

The brother of Lewis Brodziak (q.v.) and son of Abraham and Golda, Meyer Brodziak was listed in the *New South Wales Almanac and Remembrancer of 1848* as a silversmith and jeweller at 106 King Street East. In 1848 his wife Kate had a baby girl, called Rosalie, who was recorded as a 'Hebrew'. Their other children were Alfred (born in Scone, 1850), Francis (1851), born in Sydney, Mark (1852), Hannah (1853, who died in infancy), Julia (1856), Hannah (1858), and Bertha (1859). 'Myer'Brodziak was naturalised in October 1850.

Kate Brodziak died on 10 June 1885 and was buried at Lidcombe Cemetery's Jewish section. Myer Brodziak died on 6 August 1885, aged sixty-eight.
Letters of Denization 1849, 4/1173.

BROWN, John (né Joseph DANIELS)

b. Petticoat Lane, 1824
Henrietta, 1843; Convict; Sentenced to 10 years, Central Criminal Court, 1843.
Single; Sail-maker; Height: 155 cm.

Black hair, head rather long, dark eyes, large nose, small mouth, medium chin. Tattoos: hearts and darts on left arm above elbow, small blue mark on back of second finger on the left hand. He could read. John Brown was convicted for picking pockets and stealing a purse containing money. Brown claimed: 'I am not guilty. I was never in prison before', but he had been convicted before. Hulk report: 'Bad. Flogged at the Hulk for swearing and quarrelling'.

The *Henrietta* arrived in Hobart Town on 19 November 1843. Brown's initial period of probation extended for two years and he was assigned to the convict station at Southport. During that time he was given four lashes on the back for being absent without leave on 25 November 1844. Charged with idleness, absence from work, pilfering, disobedience, and making use of profane language, he received twenty-four lashes on 7 March 1845. His first placement as an assigned convict began in 16 December 1846. Within three days he was found guilty of disobedience of orders and insolence and put in solitary confinement for ten days. On 13 May 1847 he was found guilty of larceny under £5 and sentenced to twelve months hard labour. On 1 October 1847, for using threatening language to an assistant superintendent, he was given seven days in solitary confinement. On 13 January 1848 he was found to have two pairs of linen trousers in his possession and his existing sentence of hard labour in chains was extended by two months. Three more acts of disobedience and general misconduct with minor punishments followed. On 26 February 1850, Brown received his ticket of leave. However, this was revoked on 19 March 1851 when he was found to be absent from the muster. A certificate of freedom was issued on 23 August 1852.
CON 33/46, no. 10880.

BROWN, Moses

1809–1859
Wellington, 1830; Free.
Single; Dealer; 1 child.

Son of Moses Brown and Hannah (née Moses) of London, Moses Brown arrived on the *Wellington* on 24 October 1830, and opened the Grand Repository in Lower George Street, selling jewellery, furniture and general merchandise. He married Matilda De Metz, who was eighteen, on 23 July 1834. Brown officiated at Sydney's fifth Jewish wedding (of Abraham Joseph Levy, q.v.) and was elected to the committee of the first general meeting of Sydney Jews.

In December 1832, Moses Brown charged Mosely Moss Cohen (q.v.) with perjury. Cohen's brother, the convict Edward Daniel Cohen (q.v.), had been set up in business by Brown, to whom he was assigned, as a watchmaker. Brown had lent him his name and advanced him money. Brown had given Edward Daniel Cohen a large antique gold ring to modernise. When M. M. Cohen arrived in Sydney, Brown 'transferred' his brother to him in exchange for £25. The ring was then handed on to M. M. Cohen who sent Brown a bill for £5 10s. Brown refused to pay, saying that Cohen was responsible for the work. The Bench dismissed the case. Brown moved his jewellery business to King Street in 1837 and, in July 1838, advertised for 'a young man who will make himself useful in business'. In September 1842 he was declared insolvent.

Brown was actively involved in the life of the Jewish community and officiated at a number of marriages. The synagogue registered that he had a child on 8 September 1842. Moses Brown died at Camden in 1859.

CON 33/46, no. 9547; *Australian*, 24 October 1830, 26 September 1842; *Sydney Gazette*, 17 February 1833, 5 July 1838; *Currency Lad*, 15 December 1832, p. 3.

BROWN, William (né Moses BRAHAM)

d. 1814
Duke of Portland, 1807; Convict; Sentenced to life, Middlesex, 1806.

William Brown was sentenced on 16 April 1806. His name was spelt 'William Bowen' in the ship's indent. He was the brother of Abraham Hart Braham (q.v.), who arrived on the Admiral Gambier in 1811.

William Brown arrived at Port Jackson on 27 July 1807. He died in early September 1814, and his brother Abraham applied for administration of his estate on 3 September.

Sydney Gazette, 3 September 1814.

BURDO, Sarah (BURDOE)

1764–1834
Lady Penrhyn, 1788; Convict; Sentenced to 7 years, Old Bailey, 1786.
Single; Mantua-maker, prostitute.

The evidence that Burdoe was Jewish is not conclusive. Her surname could have been Bordeaux (where there was a significant community of Sephardim). John Nicol, who sailed as a steward on board the Lady Juliana, believed that there were 'a number of Jewesses' on board the First Fleet. As the fleet anchored at Tenerife, 'One, Sarah Sabolah, had a crucifix, and the others soon got them and passed themselves for Roman Catholics, by which means they got many presents from the people on shore and laid up a large stock for sea'. Nicol could easily have mixed up the surname and the combination of 'Sarah and Rebecca' is interesting. Sarah's surname indicates that she may have been able to speak Spanish or Portuguese. At the Old Bailey it was charged that Burdoe, together with Rebecca Davison (q.v.) robbed a man and stole £3 13s 6d. They had taken their 'client' to the Jewish-owned Jerusalem Tavern in the East End where the robbery took place.

Burdoe's sentence expired in October 1793. She received a certificate of freedom on 8 February 1811 and was issued with a document attesting to her status. In the 1814 Muster she was listed as independent of the Government Stores, and the wife of Isaac Archer of Parramatta. She was identified as a 'midwife' in 1819, and appeared in the 1828 Census, living in Clarence Street. Her death, on 16 July 1834, was recorded in the Register of St James' Church in Sydney.

Mollie Gillen records that when Sarah married the former marine Isaac Archer she signed her name 'Bordeaux'. She also notes that in London, in 1786, a Sarah Purdoe had been involved in an attack with a knife on her former lover and almost killed him.

OBSP, 1785–86, case 811, p. 1270; T. Flannery (ed.), *The Life and Adventures of John Nicol, Mariner 1776–1891*, Text Publishing, Melbourne, 1997, p. 126; Register of Pardons, 4/4427, p. 546; Mutch Index, p. 112; M. Gillen, *The Founders of Australia*, pp. 58f.

BURNSIDES, Mary Ann

b. London, 1811.
1828; Free.
Single; 3 children.

Mary Ann, the daughter of Private Ambrose Burnsides, converted to Judaism and changed her first name to Rebecca, in order to marry Emanuel Myers (q.v.) in 1829. She was eighteen years old, and was his first wife. She had a son, Benjamin, in 1829, who was registered as a 'Hebrew'. A son, Joseph, was born in 1833, and a daughter, Hannah, at Windsor in 1836, and both were registered as 'Hebrew'. There is a synagogue record that 'E. Myers' was buried at the Devonshire Street Cemetery on 6 November 1832. This may well have been a child of Mary Ann/Rebecca and Emanuel. It can be assumed that Rebecca had died by August 1840, as Emanuel remarried at that time.

BURNSTEIN, Jacob

b. Prussia, 1827
Anna Maria (1), 1848; Convict; Sentenced to 7 years, London, 1848.
Married.

While Burnstein was listed as a Protestant, it is unlikely that he was because his parents were Isaac and Hinda Burnstein. He had six brothers and three sisters and no family in England. He was convicted for 'stealing a silver plate, spoons and forks'.

Burnstein arrived in Van Diemen's Land on 7 June 1848. Later that year and again in 1851 he was found to be hawking goods without a licence. In 1852 his sentence was extended for eighteen months when he was found attempting to leave the colony on the *Rebecca*, bound for Port Phillip. In 1853 he was stationed at the prisoners' work detail at Bridgewater, where a causeway was being built across the River Derwent.

CON 31/26, no. 20641; CON 33/89; CON 14/38.

C

CANTOR, Coleman

Free.
3 children.

Coleman and Leah Cantor had three children: Jacob (1860), Hyam (1863) and Caroline (1867).
York Street Synagogue Register.

CANTOR, Edward

Free.
Single; 3 children.

Edward Cantor was appointed a representative of the Sydney Synagogue in Queanbeyan on 13 November 1843. He was a seat holder at the Sydney Synagogue in 1845. He married Hannah Guise in 1845 and a child, Ann, was born in Queanbeyan in 1850. Hannah and Sarah were born in Sydney and were baptised at St Lawrence's, Sydney, in 1852 and 1854. Ann was born in 1859, indicating, by her name, that their first child had died. At the time, Cantor held the licence of the Barley Mow Inn in Park Street. He advertised in the *Sydney Morning Herald* (July 1851) that he was 'an old bushman and squatter'. In October 1859 Edward Cantor, a butcher, was declared to be insolvent due to medical and legal expenses. The family moved to Maitland and in May 1887 Edward Cantor died a few days after attempting to commit suicide by cutting his throat.
The Star (Ballarat) 6 October 1859. The *Maitland Mercury*, 24 May 1887.

CANTOR, Israel

Free.
Shop assistant.

Israel Cantor was employed in Sydney by Henry Harris of George Street as a 'shopman' in 1840, and stood trial when he acquired money and clothes from his

employer with a 'fictitious order'. Cantor was listed as one of the original members of the Melbourne Hebrew Congregation in 1844.
Sydney Morning Herald 30 May 1840.

CARR, John

b. Mile End Road, 1819–1851
Candahar, 1841; Convict; Sentenced to 10 years, Central Criminal Court, 1841.
Single; Gilder; Height: 155 cm.

Dark complexion, black hair, small face, brown eyes, small nose and mouth, long chin. He had lost some front teeth. Heavily tattooed, with initials S. C. J. W and A. R. A. D. E., a woman, a mermaid with glass and comb, a sailor and a flag. A Jew. He was convicted for stealing seven alderman's cloaks, the property of Mr Cox. His general conduct on board ship was 'indifferent'.

John Carr's initial period of probation was for two and a half years, which was extended by six and a half months for six different counts of 'misconduct'. These offences included striking another prisoner, making use of improper language to a fellow prisoner, and conspiring with twelve other prisoners to obstruct an assistant superintendent in the execution of his duty. He was stationed with the road gang at Jericho, and was released on 21 September 1845.

Carr received his ticket of leave on 22 February 1848. It was revoked on 11 March 1851, as Carr was absent from muster. He was returned to the chain gang, and in Ross, on 16 July 1851, was given fourteen days solitary confinement for 'mutilating a New Testament'. On 3 August 1851 he died in hospital at Ross.
CON 33/23.

CASHMORE, David

b. Houndsditch
Free.
Single; Draper.

David was the brother of Michael Cashmore (q.v.) and was one of the earliest settlers in Portland, Victoria. By 1841 he was working with George (Godfrey) Alexander (q.v.). He gave £10 to the Sydney Synagogue building appeal in 1841 and was an original member of the Melbourne Hebrew Congregation in April 1844. Together with Alexander, he moved to Geelong and opened a general store. He served as a foundation member of the Geelong Hebrew Congregation. He had a drapery in Malop Street in 1849.
AG, p. 360.

CASHMORE, Joseph

b. London
Medusa, 1842; Free.

The *Medusa* arrived in Sydney on 29 July 1842. Joseph Cashmore was reported to have worked with Edward Salamon (q.v.), a storekeeper of West Maitland, and claimed to be owed £52 17s 2d. In 1845 he took the case to court, after P.J. Cohen (q.v.) and L. Spyer (q.v.) had arbitrated in order to keep the dispute within the Jewish community, and had decided in favour of Salamon.

Morning Chronicle, 23 August 1845.

CASHMORE, Michael

b. Houndsditch, 1815–1886
1836; Free.
Single; Dealer; 8 children.

Michael's parents were Joseph and Alice (née Nathan) Cashmore. He was born on 7 March 1815 and was the eldest of six children and the first of the family to emigrate to Australia. He was followed by his mother, his brother David (q.v.) and sisters Sarah (q.v.), who married Abraham Elias Cohen (q.v.) in 1850, Rebecca, who married Alfred Abrahams in 1853, and Esther, who married Isaac Crawcour in London. The *Ketubah* is in the Jewish Museum in London.

Michael Cashmore left London at the age of twenty-one and went first to Sydney, where he opened a drapery store in Lower George Street. Cashmore donated £7 10s to the Sydney Synagogue building appeal in September 1839. On 9 December 1840 Michael Cashmore married Elizabeth (Betsy) Solomon (q.v.), the daughter of Samuel Moss Solomon and Esther Solomon (née Davis) (qq.v.) in Sydney. The young couple were shipwrecked when the steamer *Clonmel* ran aground on the way back to Melbourne and the passengers spent several weeks marooned at Wilsons Promontory. It was reported: 'All he saved was his newly won wife and an old silver watch'.

In June 1840 Cashmore went to Port Phillip, bringing with him twenty-two cases of goods for sale, and met with a commercial success. On 9 June 1841 he announced in the *Australian* that he was once again 'about to proceed to Port Phillip', to commence business as a general storekeeper, with 'an excellent assortment of Hosiery, Drapery and Haberdashery. Also every variety of ready made clothing'. Cashmore soon advertised his 'new wholesale and retail store' at the corner of Elizabeth and Great William streets (later known as Collins Street), and called the London and Manchester Warehouse, with the jingle: 'Economy being the order of the day, Thither to Cashmore's quickly wend your way, Plenty you'll there behold to please the eyes, At prices low that must create surprise. The assortment is the best that can be found, Seek Melbourne through, Seek Melbourne round'. The building Cashmore was leasing was the first brick building in Melbourne, and was also Melbourne's tallest, with four storeys. Cashmore also ran a 'branch establishment opposite Victoria House'. He performed as an amateur actor at Melbourne's Theatre Royal in 1842. In April 1843, Georgiana McCrae wrote in her diary, 'The scarcity of actual coin is remarkable. It is said that Cashmore, No 1 Collins Street East, is the only man in town who can give you the full change of a £5 note'.

Cashmore may have conducted the first Jewish religious services in Victoria in the home of Moses Lazarus (q.v.), a draper of Collins Street West. He was elected the first president of the Melbourne Hebrew Congregation and, together with Asher Hymen Hart and Solomon Benjamin (qq.v.), wrote to Sir George Gipps on 1 November 1843 asking for land for a Jewish cemetery.

On 18 December 1844 the *Port Phillip Gazette* reported that Michael Cashmore had served on the first jury panel of the Criminal Sessions in the district. On 7 April 1846 he was elected to the Melbourne City Council. He was a director of the Melbourne Gas and Coke Company and a promoter of the National Bank of Australasia. He was one of the founders of the Australia Felix Lodge.

Cashmore left Melbourne for the Ballarat goldfields in 1857 and then opened a business at Brown's Diggings. He returned to Melbourne and became Inspector of Meat for the City of Melbourne Corporation, occupying this position for seventeen years.

He died, aged seventy-one, at St Vincent's Place, South Melbourne on 17 October 1886. Elizabeth died in 1898 at the age of seventy-seven. The Cashmores had eight children: among them were Alice (1842–1873), who was the first Jewish girl to be born in Victoria, Joseph (7 September 1898), Esther (14 June 1845), Samuel (25 April 1847), Isaac (22 April 1849), Henry (25 February 1851), and Rebecca (1853).

Trevor Cohen, 'Michael Cashmore: A Melbourne Pioneer', *AJJHS*, vol. 6, no. 3 (1967), p. 144f; L. M. Goldman, *The Jews in Victoria in the Nineteenth Century*; Hilary L. Rubinstein, *The Jews in Victoria 1835–1985*, p. 8f.; *Port Phillip Patriot*, 10 September 1840; *AG*, pp. 130, 278, 283, 286–7, 290–1, 295; Letter to Sir George Gipps, 43/1563.

CASHMORE, Sarah

b. Houndsditch
Free.

Sarah was the youngest sister of Michael Cashmore (q.v.). She married Abraham Elias Cohen (q.v.), a 'bachelor of Melbourne', on 24 July 1850. It was Melbourne's eighth Jewish marriage.

CASPER, Edward (Edwin)

b. London, 1825–1910
Tasmania, 1843; Free.
Single; 2 children.

The son of Ellis and Elizabeth Casper (qq.v.), Edward Casper came out to Van Diemen's Land with his mother and seven siblings. The congregation in Hobart

Town accepted him as an active member and in 1841 he was chosen to be the Bridegroom of the Beginning on the Festival of Simchat Torah. Edward rented seat no. 16 in the Hobart Town Synagogue and on 28 August 1845 he was appointed the auditor for the synagogue's accounts. Casper married Naomi Wertheimer in Hobart Town in 1855. They had a child, Palmyra Georgina, on 6 March 1856. That year, Edward and Naomi moved to Victoria. Grace Catherine was born at Sandridge, Victoria, in 1857. Edward and family returned to England and Edward died at 30 Bedford Street, St Giles, on 19 December 1910, at the age of eighty-five. His wife had died on 18 December 1895, at Kensington, London.

CASPER, Elizabeth Miriam (Betsy) (née NATHAN)

b. London, 1783–1868
Tasmania, 1843; Free.
Married; 12 children.

Elizabeth had married Ellis Caspar (Casper, q.v.) at the Great Synagogue in Duke's Place, London, on 22 February 1809. She was the daughter of Isaac and Catherine Nathan of London. Following the conviction and transportation of her husband Ellis and her son Lewin (q.v.), after the celebrated 'Gold Dust Robbery' trial, Elizabeth came to Van Diemen's Land as a passenger on the barque *Tasmania*, travelling to Hobart Town with eight of her children, to be with her husband.

Ellis and Elizabeth moved to Melbourne in 1856. Elizabeth Casper died at 58 Gertrude Street, Fitzroy, in Victoria, on 29 June 1868. Their children were Harriet (21 December 1810 to 4 December 1898), Lewis (Lewin?) (22 July 1815 to 13 June 1842), a daughter (1814 to c. 1862), Ellen (c. 1816 to after 1862), Nathan (23 April 1817 to 1 June 1817), Henry (22 August 1818 to 17 April 1819), Grace (c. 1825–1881), Edward (Edwin) (q.v.) (12 May 1825 to 19 December 1910), Sarah (c. 1825 to 4 March 1907), Rosetta (c. 1830 to 27 September 1861), George (1831 to 24 September 1914), and Matilda (q.v.) (1834).

Sarah married Samuel Levy (q.v.) at Levy's home in Murray Street, Hobart Town, in 1846.

Matilda married Emanuel Moses Myers (q.v.) in Hobart Town on 26 May 1853, 'at the residence of Moses Casper and Henry Wolff (q.v.) in Elizabeth St'. Rosetta married Henry Simon Ansell (q.v.) in a Jewish ceremony in Hobart Town, on 24 July 1850. Grace married Henry Wolff in Hobart Town, on 23 December 1846. In 1855, Henry came to Melbourne where Ellis operated a business at the Hall of Commerce, 50 Collins Street. While the business addresses appear to have changed frequently, Grace, her husband, and their four children lived at the Casper residence in 208 King Street. Henry died in 1859, and Grace married a second time, in 1868, to Jacob Silberberg.

Family information supplied by Simon Marks-Isaacs of Sydney; *The Times* (London), 25 June 1839, 4 July 1839.

CASPER, Ellis (Elias Levy CASPAR)

b. London, 1784–1862
Lord Lyndoch (5), 1841; Convict; Sentenced to 14 years, Central Criminal Court, 1839.
Married; Jeweller and watchmaker; Height: 163.5 cm; 12 children.

Fair complexion, black to grey hair, light hazel eyes, strong featured. Jew. Can read and write. Sentenced at the Old Bailey on 17 June 1839. His behaviour on board ship was 'very good'. He was transported with Emanuel Moses (q.v.) and Lewin Casper (q.v.), his 26-year-old son. The offence was feloniously receiving stolen goods. Ellis was one of the principals in the famous 'Gold Dust Robbery' trial, which, to the fury of the jury, lasted from 25 June to 2 July 1839. Dr Solomon Herschell, 'the venerable Chief Rabbi or High Priest of the German Jews resident in London', appeared as a character witness for the Caspers in addition to fifteen other witnesses 'chiefly of the Jewish persuasion'. Casper's wife Elizabeth (q.v.) (née Nathan) and children lived in London. As the children were born the family moved from Prugen Square, next to the Old Bailey, to Mitre Court in Aldgate, to Little Prescot Street in Goodman's Fields, to Bevis Marks Street. Casper had one brother, Nathaniel, and three sisters.

While the convict dossier listed him as 'Caspar', the Birth Book of the Great Synagogue in London, which recorded the birth of his children, shows that he was named Elias Casper. Despite the official documents he was known as 'Casper' in Hobart Town. Ellis Casper served the initial period of probation on board the prison hulk on the River Derwent and at the Prisoners' Barracks in Hobart Town. He was removed to Sandy Bay in August 1842 where he spent a six-day period in solitary confinement for insolence and neglect of duty. In June 1842 the public was shocked when Casper was refused permission by Captain Forster to attend the funeral of his son Lewin. An appeal was made to Governor Franklin, who also refused permission. Ellis Casper was appointed 'javelin man' (or overseer) in gaol. A charge of 'unlawfully detaining a watch' was dismissed on 6 June 1842 while he was serving as 'javelin man' in the gaol.

Casper became a member of the Hobart Hebrew Congregation in 1842 and rented seat no. 37. By 1845, Mrs Casper and three children were listed as seat holders in the synagogue. Casper's name appears as one of the founders of the Tasmanian Hebrew Benevolent Institute in 1847, with his sons Edward (q.v.) and George Casper. Ellis Casper, 'Watch and clock maker, jeweller and silversmith, late of Finsbury Square London and now at 21 Murray St, Hobart Town', advertised that he would be moving to 'more commodious premises' in Liverpool Street by the end of 1847. He boasted of 'a clock he had installed in the Supreme Court, as well as to others in gentlemen's offices and Buildings, all having his own name on them as a guarantee for accurate performance'. (More than 150 years later, the clock inscribed 'E. Casper, Hobart Town', is still at the Tasmanian Supreme Court and keeps accurate time.)

Five family marriages are recorded by the Hobart Town Synagogue. Sarah Casper married Samuel Levy (q.v.) on 28 January 1846 at Levy's home in Murray Street. Grace Casper married Henry Wolff (q.v.) on 23 December 1846 at his home. Rosetta (Rose) Casper married Henry Simon Ansell (q.v.), watchmaker, on 24 July 1850 at Ellis Casper's home at 38 Elizabeth Street. Matilda Casper (q.v.) married

Emanuel Moses Myers (q.v.), 'a gentleman', on 26 May 1853 at Henry Wolff 's home in Elizabeth Street. Edward Casper, thirty, married Naomi Wertheimer in Hobart Town in 1855. George Casper, thirty-two, married Elizabeth Baum, twenty, on 2 July 1863 at the Melbourne Hebrew Congregation.

Ellis Casper gained his ticket of leave on 2 June 1846. Due to his 'good behaviour', he was recommended for a pardon on 14 December 1847, which was granted on 30 January 1849. Ellis and Elizabeth Casper moved to Melbourne in 1856. Ellis died at his residence, 208 King Street, in 1862 in his seventy-eighth year and was buried at the Melbourne General Cemetery at Carlton. Betsy Casper died in Melbourne on 29 June 1868 at the age of eighty-five and was also buried at Carlton.

CON 35/5; *Hobart Town Gazette*, 6 June 1845; CON 31/8, no. 2703; Camden Pelham (pseud.), *The Chronicles of Crime, or the Newgate Calendar*, vol. 2, p. 480f.

CASPER, Lewin (CASPAR)

b. London, 1815–1842
Lord Lyndoch (5), 1841; Convict; Sentenced to 7 years, Central Criminal Court, 1840.
Single; Clerk; Height: 168 cm.

Fair complexion, dark brown hair and red whiskers, a long face, hazel eyes and a large nose. Charged with inciting others to steal gold dust. Lewin Casper had been a clerk in a firm that was to be responsible for picking up some boxes of Brazilian gold dust, worth £4600, that had been landed at Falmouth, and bringing it to bullion merchants in London. Lewin recruited his father, Ellis Casper (q.v.), and associates to get to the gold first: 'Together with his father, a watchmaker, they carefully planned the robbery'. The Newgate Calendar, *in describing the robbery, wrote that the 'extraordinary robbery to which these persons were parties involved circumstances probably more singular than any other which came before a court of justice'. Lewin Casper was convicted on 2 March 1840. The* Lord Lyndoch *surgeon reported that Casper was ill twice while on board.*

Lewin arrived in Van Diemen's Land on 5 September 1841. He served a year probation at the Hobart Town Prisoners' Barracks and at Bridgewater, where his conduct was said to be 'very good'. On 13 June 1842, he died from scarlet fever at the hospital within the Prisoners' Barracks in Hobart Town.

CON 14/5 no. 2706; Camden Pelham (pseud.), *The Chronicles of Crime, or the Newgate Calendar*, vol. 2, p. 480f.

CASPER, Matilda (CASPAR)

b. London, 1834–1895
Free.
Single; 6 children.

The daughter of Ellis (q.v.) and Elizabeth Casper (q.v.), Matilda came out to Van Diemen's Land with her mother and seven of her siblings. Matilda married Emanuel Moses Myers (q.v.), aged twenty-five, in the Hobart Hebrew Congregation on 26 May 1853, 'at the residence of Moses Casper and Henry Wolff in Elizabeth St'. Matilda was nineteen. Matilda and her husband had six children: Dinah (born

1854, died in infancy), a son (1855, died in infancy), Andrew (1856), Miriam (1858), Henry (1860), and Elizabeth (1862). In 1864, the family moved to Canada, and from there to Waco, Texas, where Matilda died in 1895.

Family information from Simon Marks-Isaacs of Sydney.

CHAPMAN, Israel ('Izzy')

b. Chelsea, 1794–1868
Glory, 1818; Convict; Sentenced to life, Middlesex, 1818.
Single; Coachman and groom; Height: 162 cm.

Dark ruddy complexion, black hair, dark eyes. Transported for robbery. George Scott and Israel Chapman held up a sea captain in Aldgate and stole fourteen shillings from him on 13 December 1817. Chapman, 'a stout man', was seen running away. Both men were originally sentenced to death. Israel was the brother of Noel Chapman (q.v.).

'Izzy' Chapman arrived in Sydney on 14 September 1818. In England, before his deportation, he had been a 'resurrection man' in the business of supplying medical anatomists with stolen corpses. Within a year of his arrival in Sydney he had been appointed to be an overseer and chief wardsman of the Prisoners' Barracks in Hyde Park. On 30 November 1821 Chapman captured his first bushranger and received a reward of £1. Two days before, he had married Catherine Martin, a needle worker from London, at St Phillips. The witnesses at the marriage were Aaron Barnett (q.v.) and Anne Barnett. Catherine was twenty-five and illiterate. She had been a convict, and arrived on the *Morley* (3).

Chapman received a conditional pardon on 21 November 1821. He was dismissed from the police force in 1822, and reinstated in 1823. By this time he had acquired a reputation for catching offenders by dreams and visions. In 1827 Chapman resigned again, as the *Sydney Gazette* recorded on 9 May 1827: 'Chapman the flower of Colonial Constables, has resigned the Staff of Office. Hard work and little pay do not suit an active policeman, and he properly resolves to shew his employers the void that is created by his resignation. He is perfectly right'. Within a month of his departure he had been re-employed with a salary of £100 a year. On 5 December 1827 he received an absolute pardon for his 'indefatigable exertions'. Chapman had acquired a reputation for being 'a Hebrew dreamer'. As the Sydney Gazette reported in 26 October 1827 ' Israel Chapman, the fidelity of whose dreams has almost become proverbial, was, for three successive nights, tormented with a vision, in which he beheld a man who had been appointed guardian in the shop of Mr Dillon, carrying off sundry goods and chattels. The renowned dreamer, certain that three successive warnings were not to be disregarded, watched about the premises three nights and on the third he made a prisoner of the alleged thief and detected the stolen property.'

Catherine Chapman died on 26 January 1829 at the age of thirty-three. She was buried in the Devonshire Street Anglican Cemetery, 'Wife of Mr Isrrael [*sic*] Chapman Late Police Runner'. Chapman left Australia shortly after his wife's death. There were rumours that he was recalled to give evidence in the Sudds Thompson affair, but the *Sydney Gazette* noted 'there is no truth whatever in the report circulated'. Chapman returned to Australia in March 1833, after two years in the West Indies, bringing with him his new 'wife' Mary Ann. (In fact Chapman married Mary Slater at Scots Church on 23 October 1833). On 16 March 1833 the *Sydney Gazette* reported: 'Mr Israel Chapman has again received the staff of office. The villains who infest the town practising their delinquencies had better mind their P's and Q's. They will not be able to elude this vigiland, this very active officer for a very long period. They had better take the hint and betake themselves to honest industry'. The new Mrs Chapman brought him grief. She was twice sued by neighbours for quarrelling with them and Izzy was charged by Mary Ann for having 'thrashed her unmercifully'.

In August 1847 Chapman asked the authorities for a grant of land and a pension. He wrote from Berrima, where his brother, Noel Chapman, was the chief constable. Israel claimed to have been in the employ of the government for sixteen years, he had been a constable and overseer at the lumber yards, he had been inspector of the police in Sydney for three years and then moved to Campbelltown, and he had been forced to resign owing to wounds and injuries: 'I was shot in the head and my right hand is crippled. I am now getting very old and in proportion to the increase of age so are my pecuniary resources decreasing'. He was fifty-seven and he claimed to have captured eleven bushrangers. His petition was refused. Izzy Chapman returned to Sydney and became a bailiff. In 1852 he was convicted of theft and sent to Darlinghurst Prison for six months hard labour. Izzy had over-enthusiastically helped two of his friends to recover rent they claimed was owed by a tenant. He died in the Lunatic Asylum at Liverpool on 4 July 1868, and was buried in the Jewish section of the Rookwood Cemetery by the Sydney Synagogue's congregation as an act of charity.

OBSP, 1817–18, case 191, p. 75; Ship Indent 4/5204, 4/4006, p. 76; Mutch Index 401/27; Land Petitions, Box 37, 2/7283, no. 47/5969; G. F. J. Bergman, 'Israel Chapman, 1794–1868, Australia's First Police Detective, and Noel Chapman, Chief Constable', *AJJHS*, vol. 6, no. 7 (1969); G. F. J. Bergman and Terry Newman, 'More about Israel and Noel Chapman', *AJJHS*, vol. 7, no. 3 (1972), p. 249f; J. G. Lang, *The Forger's Wife*; *AG*, pp. 69–77, 139, 307; Nancy Keesing (Hortzberg), 'Israel Chapman in Fiction', *AJJHS*, vol. 6, no. 7 (1969), p. 411. Grace Karskens, *Resurrecting Chapman, AJJHS,* vol. 18, no 1 (2006), p. 8.

CHAPMAN, Noel

b. Chelsea, 1807–1849
Speke (2), 1826; Convict; Sentenced to 7 years, Surrey, 1825.
Single; Coach boy; Height: 156 cm; 2 children.

Fair ruddy complexion, brown hair, brown eyes. Tattoo of two pugilists on left arm and of one on right arm. Sun and seven stars on breast. Blue ring on third finger of left hand. Second and third toe of each foot contracted. Sentenced at Surrey on 10 December 1825. He was the brother of the 'celebrated detective' Israel Chapman (q.v.).

Chapman arrived in Sydney on 26 November 1826 and was assigned to be the servant of Mr James of George Street, Sydney. He had twenty-eight shillings in a savings bank and asked for permission to buy clothes. Permission was refused. In the 1828 Census, Noel Chapman was listed as lodging with Benjamin Goddard, Kent Street, Sydney—obviously awaiting government orders. Noel Chapman very quickly ingratiated himself into the favour of the administration by helping to 'apprehend six runaways'. Despite this it was decided to refuse Israel Chapman's request to have Noel assigned to his care and orders were given that Noel be sent immediately to Mr Campbell. When Campbell declined to accept him he was placed on 'the next list for assignment'. He received his ticket of leave on 21 April 1828, and on 29 December 1829 was appointed 'ordinary constable' at Windsor. On 1 February 1831 he received permission to be married to Rebecca Armfield by the Rev. Joseph Docker of Armfield. Rebecca was eighteen and had been born in the colony. She was the daughter of James Armfield and Isabella, née Ruse, the daughter of James Ruse, who was on the First Fleet and was the recipient of Australia's first land grant.

Chapman was granted a certificate of freedom on 21 December 1832. During 1835 he was registered by the Hawkesbury Benevolent Society, 'driving cattle at the Hawkesbury' for the society. Chapman moved to Windsor in early 1836 to become the district constable and worked conscientiously at that job. The *Sydney Gazette* (7 February 1839) recounts:

> Chapman, District Constable at Windsor, was giving evidence at the trial of J. Carroll for horse stealing. He observed that he had apprehended the rider on suspicion of being a runaway. In reply to a question from the Chief Justice, Chapman observed that he always apprehended strangers who came into town, if he at first could not ascertain, who they were. 'What' said his Honour, 'Would you also apprehend me?' 'Most certainly I would!' replied Chapman, 'If I suspected you'. The only answer to this by His Honour was a terrible large pinch of snuff and 'Mr Attorney General, you can go on'.

On 1 January 1840 Noel Chapman returned to Berrima to become its chief constable at the salary of £70 per annum. He also earned some income from a newspaper agency and was listed as the local agent for the *Australian* newspaper and the *Political Literary and Commercial Journal* of Launceston. In 1847 he was appointed bailiff of the Court of Requests for the Police District of Berrima, and for some of 1849 was chief constable at Yass.

Chapman died on 29 December 1849, 'after a painful illness'. He died intestate with an estate of less than £50. There were two sons, Benjamin and Henry Edward. Benjamin, born 1832 to Noel and Rebecca, married aged 24 to Harriet Warden and had twelve children. Henry Edward Chapman did not marry and lived with his brother. Both brothers died in Yass in 1917. Rebecca, his widow, became the housekeeper of Jacob Myers (q.v.) at Yass. Rebecca's younger sister, Ann, married Lewis Levy (q.v.) at Camden in August 1840.

Ship Indent 4/4067; 16 May 1828, 28/29; 4/4313, 21 December 1832; CF 32/1092; *Sydney Gazette*, 21 April 1828, 29 December 1829; Marriages Allowed 1831, 4/4512, no. 32; Principal Superintendent of Convicts, January 1831–July 1837, Hawkesbury Benevolent Society, ML, A625, p. 77; 4/3665, p. 125; Returns of the Colony, 4/282; 4/4067, 28/29; *New South Wales Government Gazette*, 10 February 1836, p. 208, 1840, p. 966; G. F. J. Bergman, 'Israel Chapman, 1794–1868, Australia's First Police Detective, and Noel Chapman, Chief Constable', *AJJHS*, vol. 6, no. 7 (1969); *AG*, pp. 73, 75.

COHEN, Aaron

b. London, 1817–1875
1849; Free.
Single; Dealer.

The child of Philip and Jane Cohen of London, Aaron Cohen arrived in South Australia and established a grocery business. He died in Adelaide on 27 March 1875.

COHEN, Abraham

b. London, 1764–1843
Lotus, 1833; Convict; Sentenced to 14 years, Old Bailey, 1832.
Married; Dealer and labourer; Height: 163 cm; 5 children (in England).

Ruddy complexion, long head, grey hair, aquiline nose. Lost several front teeth. Large mouth. A Jew. His wife, Elizabeth, lived in North London. Abraham Cohen was the father of Isaac Cohen (q.v.), who was transported on the same ship for the same offence: receiving stolen goods. He was arrested, together with Isaac, at home in the act of sorting out clothes and boots stolen from a police station in Charlotte Street, Bloomsbury. His other children and his wife remained in England.

Cohen was sixty-nine years old when he arrived as a prisoner in Hobart Town on 16 May 1833. Cohen's police dossier has no offences listed and he received a conditional pardon on 2 June 1842. He had rented seat no. 99 in the back of the Hobart Synagogue. He died at Hobart Town on 10 February 1843, at the age of seventy-nine.

OBSP 18 October 1832, case 2319. CON 31/7, no. 1511; CON 18/13; *Hobart Town Courier*, 10 June 1842; CP 490.

COHEN, Abraham Hyam

b. Brighton, 1812–1874
Warrior, 1835; Free.
Single; 12 children.

Abraham Cohen was the fifth son of Emanuel Hyam Cohen and Hannah (née Benjamin). He was the brother of Levy Emanuel Cohen, Nathan Cohen, and Raphael Cohen (q.v.), who arrived on 22 October 1839. Emanuel Hyam Cohen was the founder of the Jewish congregation in Brighton, England. Abraham Cohen migrated to Australia travelling steerage on the *Warrior*, arriving in Sydney on 27 February 1835, and married Sophia Cohen (q.v.) in Sydney on 27 July 1836. Sophia was the daughter of Henry Simeon Cohen and Elizabeth Cohen (qq.v.). Their first three children were born in Sydney between 1837 and 1839 and, late in 1839, the family moved to Port Macquarie.

Abraham and Sophia had ten surviving children: Rosa (27 July 1836) born in Sydney and died at Port Macquarie 29 October 1840; a second Rosa (12 June 1837), who was born in Sydney and named at the synagogue 8 July; Frederick (4 August 1838), born in Sydney; Fanny (q.v.) (22 July 1839), born in Sydney, who married Benjamin Benjamin (q.v.); Henry Emanuel (q.v.) and George (q.v.), twins (1 September 1840), born at Port Macquarie; Nathan (q.v.) (10 July 1842), born at Port Macquarie; Caroline (q.v.) (2 March 1844), born at Port Macquarie; Hannah (1 July 1845), at Port Macquarie; Sarah (1 July 1847), at Port Macquarie, Jane (Jenny) Matilda (1849, named on 5 January 1850), born at Castlereagh Street, Sydney, Miriam (Minnie) (27 February 1852), in Sydney, and Aaron (1866).

Abraham Cohen was in charge of the printing and accounts at the office of the *Australian* in 1836 and, in 1838, offered to print the debates of the Legislative Council. In September 1839 he sold his interest to his business partner, George Robert Nichols. Abraham Cohen had various businesses in New South Wales country towns, chiefly Port Macquarie and Goulburn. In 1840, he became the licensee of a hotel, the Speed the Plough, at the corner of William and Horton streets in Port Macquarie, taking over from his brother-in-law Solomon Marks (q.v.). In 1841 Abraham Cohen and Dr J. Fattorini formed a steam ship company to purchase a steam ship that would be able to enter the shallow harbour entrance of the port. The plan was too ambitious, undercapitalised, and failed to come to fruition.

Abraham was steward of the Lodge Australia no. 548 in 1837. In that same year he briefly served as president of the York Street Synagogue Committee. Abraham Cohen gave £15 to the Sydney Synagogue appeal in October 1839. On 13 November 1843, he was appointed the representative of the Sydney Synagogue in Port Macquarie. Cohen settled in Sydney in 1848 where he became the owner of Cohen's Family Hotel in Wynyard Square. Cohen died at Wynyard Square on 22 January 1874. Sophia, his widow, died in Sydney in December 1882.

Ship Indent 4/5208; CS 4/2397.2, 38/312; 4/2403, 38/10916; *Australian*, 1 April 1836, 13 June 1837, 19 December 1837, 9 March 1839; *Sydney Morning Herald*, 7 November 1844; *Sydney General Trade List*, 19 May 1838.

COHEN, Abraham (Thomas PHILLIPS, Samuel PHILLIPS, Emanuel COHEN)

b. Whitechapel, 1822

Equestrian (2), 1845; Convict; Sentenced to 15 years, Oxford Quarter Sessions, 7 April 1845. Single; Labourer.

Ruddy complexion, oval face, dark brown hair, black eyebrows, hazel eyes, large nose and mouth. Slight cut on lower lip and a blue mark and scar on left arm below the elbow. Scar on left jaw and scar over left eyebrow. Abraham Cohen was convicted of stealing jewellery and money. He had a previous conviction in Oxford for stealing jewellery and money and had been sent to prison for six months. Surgeon's report: 'Good'. He was described as a Protestant who could read 'a little'.

Arriving in Hobart Town on 15 October 1844, Cohen was described in the Recognition Book by the name of Thomas Phillips. His convict dossier gave three other aliases: Samuel Phillips, Abraham Cohen, and Emanuel Cohen.

Cohen's initial term of probation was for twenty-four months and he was sent to work with the prison gang at Nicholl's Rivulet. By the end of 1847 he was in service, and one of his first assignments was with Moses Joseph (q.v.) in Liverpool Street in Hobart Town. On 5 January 1848 he was found guilty of misconduct and spent fourteen days in solitary confinement at the Hobart Town Gaol. By 22 September he was assigned to Nathaniel Solomons (q.v.) in Launceston, where he was committed for trial on 6 October 1848 for stealing four pairs of trousers and other articles. He was found not guilty. In July 1849 his police record concluded with a note that he had absconded.

CON 33/72; CON 14/32; CON 18/44.

COHEN, Abraham

1825–1901
Free.
Single; Merchant; 5 children.

Abraham Cohen was the seventh son of Barent and Sierlah Cohen (née Levy), and brother of Jane Cohen, Lewis Cohen (q.v.), Samuel Cohen (q.v.), Henry Cohen (q.v.), David Cohen (q.v.) of Maitland, George Cohen (q.v.) of Gunnedah, Solomon Cohen (q.v.), Morris Cohen (q.v.), and Charles Cohen.

Abraham Cohen was one of the first Jewish settlers in Tamworth. Together with his cousin, Lewis Wolfe Levy (q.v.), he became the owner of the general store in the main street of the town. The company of Cohen & Levy became a household name in the commercial life of the important rural town and was eventually acquired by T. G. Smith & Co. Ltd, in 1906. Abraham Cohen's first wife died in November 1854, and the *Sydney Morning Herald* reported that there would be an inquest. He married Leah Mandelson, the daughter of Nathan and Phoebe Mandelson (qq.v.), on 23 January 1856. The marriage took place at the Mandelson residence in Castlereagh Street.

Abraham Cohen became an alderman of the first Municipal Council of Tamworth in 1876. When Cohen died in London in 1901, he left an estate valued at £205 000, which included properties in Tamworth, Sydney and London. The children of Abraham and Leah Cohen were Nathan, Phoebe, Sierlah, Rachel and Samuel.

Sydney Morning Herald, 7 November 1854; *Hebrew Standard*, 14 June 1901.

COHEN, Abraham

b. London, 1828–1869
1841; Free.
Single; Shoemaker.

Born in London on 9 December 1828. Abraham Cohen was the second of four children, of whom three came to Australia. He was the son of Benjamin and Sarah Cohen (qq.v.), and was named after his paternal grandfather. Benjamin, a convict, committed suicide within weeks of his wife and children arriving in Van Diemen's Land. Sarah had carried on Benjamin's confectionary shop in London, and then opened a similar shop in Hobart Town.

Abraham had been thirteen when he arrived in Van Diemen's Land. The family lived at his mother's shop, at 26 Liverpool Street, in Hobart Town, and Abraham became a seat holder at the Hobart Synagogue. In 1846, Abraham Cohen was listed among Hobart's 'Mechanics and Artificers' as a shoemaker. He died of tuberculosis and 'a cold' on 18 August 1869.

Pam Zopf and Geoff Court, *From Iberia to Van Diemen's Land. A Cohen Family Odyssey*, Privately Printed 2008.

COHEN, Abraham Elias

1849; Free.
Single; Dealer.

Abraham Elias Cohen married Sarah Cashmore (q.v.), sister of Michael Cashmore (q.v.), in Melbourne on 24 July 1850. It was Melbourne's eighth Jewish marriage.

COHEN, Ann (Hannah)

b. London
Brothers, 1833; Free.
Single; 6 children.

Ann was a daughter of Henry Simeon and Elizabeth Cohen (qq.v.). She came out to Australia with her mother and nine siblings on 21 December 1833. She married Solomon Marks (q.v.) on 3 August 1836. Their children were Adolphus (q.v.) (2 June 1837–1882), born in Sydney, Benjamin Francis (q.v.) (1846), Esther (1850), Elizabeth (1858–1914), who married Sigmond Hoffnung (q.v.), and died in England, Sarah Miriam, who died in infancy and was buried on 29 April 1850 in the Devonshire Street Cemetery, and Frank Samuel (c. 1852–1893). Solomon Marks died on 18 October 1852 at the age of 36. He was buried at Devonshire Street and in 1872 was re-interred at Rookwood where he lies alongside Elizabeth Cohen directly behind the grave of Henry Cohen.

Family research by Stephen Hanford.

COHEN, Baron Burnett (Baron Barnard COHEN)

1810–1871, Born Manchester
Persian, 1829; Free.
Single; Jeweller's clerk.

A son of Simeon Cohen of Manchester and brother of John Joel Cohen (q.v.) and Jacob Charles Cohen (q.v), Baron Burnett Cohen was declared to be insolvent on 11 June 1842. In 1843 he was listed as being out on bail with Henry Barnett (q.v.), George Phillips and his nephew Francis Cohen (q.v.), after assaulting the publisher

George O'Brien after O'Brien had printed some anti-Semitic remarks directed at J. J. Cohen, Francis Cohen's father. Baron Burnett Cohen was also charged in 1856 with violence during a political meeting that celebrated the first free election in New South Wales. He was described in the press as 'the Chief Baron of Bridge Street' who had been struck 'upon the somewhat prominent organ which he wears in the centre of his face'.

Baron B. Cohen married Ellen Selina Newton at Scots Church in Sydney in 1851. Cohen ran a hotel called the Nelson in Bridge Street. In 1852 he held the licence of the Captain Cook Hotel at the corner of Spring and Bent streets. The 1852 *Sydney Directory* lists Baron Cohen as a watchmaker and jeweller at 29 Bridge Street. A child, Simeon Joseph, was born to Baron B. Cohen and Ellen Cohen in 1853.

Cohen followed the gold rush of the late 1850s, and was at Forbes, where he briefly served as secretary of a provisional committee that maintained a little synagogue at Lambing Flats and Forbes. ('Burnett the Jew Boy' also attained dubious fame in the same district by winning a boxing match that went thirty-six rounds.)

Cohen followed the discovery of new goldfields, moving to Grenfell in 1862, then Emu Creek, or Camp Hill, and then Parkes in 1871. In 1883, at his hotel, the Parkes Inn, he fell asleep, rolled into the fire that was burning in the grate, and died. He was sixty-nine years of age and left a wife and children.

M. Z. Forbes, 'The Saga of the Cohens', *AJJHS*, vol. 10, no. 3 (1988), p. 186f; *Australasian Chronicle*, 13 April 1833; *Sydney Morning Herald*, 30 June 1842, 6 February 1851.

COHEN, Behren (Baron)

b. Liverpool, d. 1854
Jessie, 1838; Free.

'B' Cohen was a cabin class passenger on the *Jessie*, which sailed from Liverpool, arriving in Sydney on 19 January 1838. By mid-June 1842, he was listed as insolvent, with debts of £13 and assets of £3. He was described as a 'jeweller and clerk of George Street'. The *Registry of Flash Men* recorded that he was 'implicated' in a robbery at 'Daniels', committed on 23 November 1844, and that he was sent to prison.

Baron Cohen was buried in the Presbyterian section of the Old Sandhill's (Devonshire Street) Cemetery in Sydney on 19 February 1854.

Ship Indent 4/5213; *Sydney Free Press and Commercial Journal*, 14 June 1842; W. A. Miles, *Registry of Flash Men*, p. 126, 2/673.

COHEN, Benjamin

b. London, 1752–1826
Admiral Barrington, 1791; Convict; Sentenced to life, London, 1787.

Benjamin Cohen arrived in New South Wales on 16 October 1791. He was the pound keeper at Parramatta (9 April 1814) and was still there in 1818. He held a ticket of leave when he was 'appropriated' to the Van Diemen's Land Co. He had brought out with him a trunk, two coats, two waistcoats, two pairs of trousers and five shirts. He was thirty-nine years of age when he arrived in Australia. A different hand has written in the ship's indent page the numerals '26', indicating that he died in 1826. He was not listed on the 1828 Census (nor is he to be found on any of the previous Musters.)

ML, A 1059/8, VDL Papers, p. 61; *Sydney Gazette*, 9 April 1814 p. 2; Recognition Book, no. 2040.

COHEN, Benjamin

b. London, 1798–1841
Lord Lyndoch (2), 1836; Convict; Sentenced to 14 years, Central Criminal Court, 1835.
Married; Confectioner; Height: 163 cm; 5 children.

Dark complexion, with black to grey hair, black whiskers, brown eyes, a long nose, wide mouth, and a large chin. 'A Jew'. Benjamin Cohen was tried on 30 October 1835, in a session at the Old Bailey, for feloniously receiving stolen goods. Cohen 'kept a shop' making 'sweet meats' at 8 Hackney Street. He was indicted for 'feloniously receiving on behalf of a certain evil-disposed person on the 17 October at St Leonard Shoreditch 2 lbs of saffron, value 21s, 35 lbs of gamboge, value 4s, 10 lbs of isinglass value 7s and 5 lbs of scammony, value 3s well knowing them to be stolen'. Benjamin, born 22 June 1798, was the fourth of eleven children born to Hanoch and Judith Cohen (née Abendana), who were themselves confectioners. The family had come from Portugal and belonged to the Bevis Marks Synagogue. They lived at 120 Middlesex Street (Petticoat Lane). Cohen had married Sarah de Abraham Torres (Cohen, q.v) at the Bevis Marks Synagogue in 1825, and they had five children. Despite five certificates in his favour having been presented to the court in his defence, he was sentenced to transportation for life. The surgeon on the convict transport ship reported that he had 'behaved very well'.

Benjamin Cohen arrived on 20 August 1836, and was assigned to the Van Diemen's Land Co. in the north-west of the island. On 24 November 1836, Cohen was reprimanded for 'gross neglect of duty'. When Cohen 'accidently drowned' in the well in the Prisoners' Barracks at Launceston, on 8 May 1841, while still a convict, an inquest was held into his death. Suicide was suspected (10 May 1841, Inquest no. 536). His family had 'recently arrived at Hobart Town from England' and he had been shipped from Circular Head to be nearer his family. At the inquest, evidence was tendered by Joseph Aaron (q.v.), who had been called to meet with Cohen. Aaron identified a Hebrew prayerbook, Bible and *Tefillin* and said that Cohen had been convinced he was about to be arrested and burnt by the Inquisition 'between two iron stakes'. The Coroner summed up the evidence and the jury quickly returned a verdict 'that the deceased Benjamin Cohen drowned himself whilst laboring under temporary derangement of mind'.

Sarah Cohen, 'wife of Benjamin', aged fifty-three, was buried by the Hobart Hebrew Congregation at the Harrington Street cemetery, on 12 July 1857. The children of Benjamin and Sarah Cohen were Enoch (born 25 May 1827), Abraham (q.v.) (born 9 December 1828 died 18 August 1869), Isaac (q.v.)(born

11 December 1830 died 24 May 1906), Judith (born 12 January 1833 died 24 July 1834), Jacob (q.v.)(born 13 December 1834 died 22 October 1886).

CON 27/2, no. 2119; CSO 1/875/18510; MM 33/6; CON 13/8; CON 18/13; CON 31/7, no. 2040; Pam Zopf and Geoff Court, *From Iberia to Van Diemen's Land. A Cohen Family Odessey*, Privately Printed 2008.

COHEN, Caroline

b. London, 1827–1881
Brothers, 1833; Free.
Single; 7 children.

The fourth daughter of Henry and Elizabeth Cohen (qq.v.) of Port Macquarie was born in London. Caroline Cohen married Asher (Arthur) Isaac Nathan (q.v.) in Sydney in 1843 and settled in Launceston. Their children were Lewis Arthur, born in Launceston, 30 May 1844. Walter Isaac born in Launceston 27 November 1845, Arthur Hyam born in Launceston 1847, David born at Launceston 1849, Edward born Launceston 1849, Sarah born 1853 in Launceston and Sidney Jacob born in Sydney in 1860, The family moved back to London and most of the sons of Caroline and Asher Nathan emigrated to New Zealand. Asher Nathan died in 1863. Caroline died in England in March 1881 at 25 Queensborough Terrace, West London.

COHEN, Caroline

b. Port Macquarie, 1844–1921
Free.

A granddaughter of Henry and Elizabeth Cohen (qq.v.) and daughter of Sophia and Abraham Cohen (qq.v.) of Port Macquarie, in 1867 Caroline married Solomon Joseph, who was born in 1834 and had come to Melbourne in 1859. They followed the gold rush to Dunedin, New Zealand, returning to Melbourne in 1871, where Solomon Joseph edited the *Australian Israelite*. In 1875 they moved to Sydney, and in 1882 to Tamworth, where Joseph became the owner and editor of the *Tamworth News*.

COHEN, Charlotte

b. London, 1820–1871
Old England, 1840; Free.
Single.

Charlotte arrived in Sydney, having travelled cabin class, on 14 December 1840. She married Henry Barnett (q.v.) at the Bridge Street Synagogue on 30 June 1841. She died in 1871 and was buried at the Lidcombe Jewish Cemetery.

Ship Indent 4/5218.

COHEN, David

b. London, 1818–1902
1839; Free.
Single; Merchant; 8 children.

David Cohen was the fifth child of Barnett and Sierlah Cohen of Lambeth, and brother of Jane, Lewis (q.v.), Samuel (q.v.), Henry (q.v.), George (q.v.), Solomon (q.v.), Abraham (q.v.) Morris (q.v.) and Charles. Only Jane and Charles remained in England, while all the other siblings migrated to Australia. David arrived in Australia in 1839. In 1835 Samuel and Lewis Cohen had bought land in High Street, Maitland, which became the site of their warehouse. In 1836 Samuel Cohen opened a store called Lambeth House and in 1837 the partnership of L & S Cohen was established. Lewis was responsible for the stores in Campbelltown and Sydney. The partnership was short lived, ending in 1839, when David took over his brother Lewis's debts. The Cohens' first cousin, Lewis Wolfe Levy of Tamworth, joined the successful Maitland firm of David Cohen & Co.

David Cohen of West Maitland married Julia Nathan (q.v.), the fourth daughter of Nathan Lyon Nathan (q.v.), in London. Julia's sister Rachel (Nathan, q.v.) was married to David's brother Samuel. She was also sister to Louis Nathan (q.v.) and Rosetta Joseph (Nathan, q.v.). In 1842 David Cohen was listed as the owner of a shop in King Street, in Sydney. He became a synagogue seat holder in 1848. In 1849 'David Cohen of West Maitland' was listed as buying land in Armidale, New South Wales. He had a 'run' by the Peel River and wrote to Sydney complaining that a squatter had moved in on his land 'to my serious injury'.

David and Julia Cohen had five sons and three daughters. They returned to England in 1857, and he remained the representative of the business until his death on 12 March 1902. The *Sydney Morning Herald* newspapers reported that he had left an estate of £210,000.

Australian, 20 November 1841; *Sydney Morning Herald*, 16 September 1842, 18 March 1902; Land Correspondence. 2/7827 on 26 September 1849.

COHEN, Edward Aaron

b. London, 1822–1874
Brothers, 1833; Free.
Single; 8 children.

Edward Cohen was born in London and was the second son and fifth child of Henry Simeon and Elizabeth Cohen (qq.v.). When his father was deported to Australia on the *Lloyds* in 1833, Edward and nine of his siblings followed with Edward's mother. As a very young man Edward Cohen established auction rooms at Port Macquarie, where his father had been sent as an assigned convict servant. The *Australian* of 28 January 1841 announced his annual sale of stock at his auction rooms. In Sydney, Edward managed his father's grocery store at 512 George Street and moved to Melbourne in 1842.

Edward Cohen became a partner of the emancipist Benjamin Francis (q.v.), and together they ran an auctioneering firm until the partnership was dissolved in 1854. After an eight-month stay in Sydney, Cohen returned to Melbourne where he joined the auctioneering firm of his brother Samuel Henry Cohen (q.v.) and Alexander Fraser. On 1 September 1847 Edward Aaron Cohen 'of Sydney' married Rebecca, the eldest child of Moses Benjamin (q.v.). It was the third Jewish wedding in Melbourne. The witnesses were Solomon Benjamin (q.v.), David Benjamin (q.v.) and Isaac Hart (q.v.).

Cohen served as president of the Melbourne Hebrew Congregation in 1854 and in 1863. He was elected a city councillor in 1860, an alderman in 1865, and mayor of Melbourne for 1862 to 1863. He was actively involved in the congregation and Jewish community affairs throughout his life and attempted to preserve the secular character of the public education system and its textbooks.

In 1864 Cohen joined forces with his brother-in-law Benjamin Benjamin (q.v.) (they were brothers-in-law twice over for each had married a sister of the other). Together they set up in business to act as tea importers and general commission agents. They maintained the business originally occupied by the partnership of Moses and Benjamin Benjamin at 36 Collins Street. Together they bought a large sheep station known as 'Canally'. (Benjamin Benjamin named his mansion in East Melbourne 'Canally'). Cohen was elected to the Legislative Assembly for East Melbourne, serving from 1861 to 1865; he was elected again in 1868 and served until his death in 1877. He was the second Jew to be elected to the Victorian Parliament. Cohen was honorary treasurer of the Melbourne Hospital and was involved in many charities. He served as Commissioner for Trade and Customs (1869–70, and 1872–74). He was a governor of the Colonial Bank of Victoria and director of the Australasian Insurance Company. Cohen died at East Melbourne on 13 April 1877 after a long illness, leaving an estate of £29 000. The funeral of the Hon. Edward Aaron Cohen MLA funeral was one of the largest ever seen in the colony.

His children were Nathan Edward Cohen (1848–1867), Miriam (1850) who married Alexander Marks, Elizabeth (1852–1926) born at Melbourne and married Alfred David Hart, Henry (1854–1855), Benjamin (1857–1926), Catherine (Kate) born 1859, Annie (Anne) married Montague Cohen son of Simeon Cohen, Arthur Isaac Cohen (1864) who married Violet Cohen, the daughter of Edward's brother William.

Rodney Benjamin, 'Sir Benjamin Benjamin', *AJJHS*, vol. 6, no. 3 (1967), p. 135f; G. Solomon, 'Benjamin Benjamin', in *ADB*, vol. 3, p. 436f.; B. Falk, *No Other Home (1988)*; H. L. Rubinstein, *The Jews in Victoria*, p. 47f. Henry Cohen (and family) by Philip Charles Cohen and privately printed.

COHEN, Edward Daniel (Daniel COHEN)

b. Birmingham, 1803–1847
Burrell (1), 1830; Convict; Sentenced to life, Liverpool Borough Session, 1830.
Single; Jeweller; Height: 171 cm; 4 children.

Dark sallow complexion, dark brown hair, hazel eyes, small scar between eyebrows. Jew. Could read and write. Edward Daniel Cohen was the brother of Mosely M. Cohen (q.v.). Their father, Simeon, was a goldsmith in Birmingham. Edward Daniel had been in prison before, serving a six-month sentence. He was tried on 18 January 1830 and sentenced to be transported for stealing a watch case.

The convict transport ship *Burrell* arrived in New South Wales on 19 December 1830. Trouble began when Cohen was to become an assigned servant to the Australian Agricultural Company and was bartered for two other convicts by Moses Brown (q.v.), who then set him up in business as a watchmaker.

Cohen's brother Mosely Moss Cohen then paid Brown £25 to take over his brother's assignment. The government intervened and Edward Daniel Cohen was put on trial for being party to an illegal transaction. He wrote to the authorities on 3 September 1832 asking to be transferred to the supervision of his brother, 'Mr Moses Cohen'. The request was refused and he was put on the *Phoenix* hulk on 7 September 1832, where his behaviour was described as 'indifferent'. On 20 September the Colonial Secretary received a letter from the Sheriff's Office asking that Cohen, 'now on board the hulk', be granted the 'indulgence that he asks for'. This concerned 'an urgent matter essentially important to myself and my brother which absolutely requires my attention on shore for a few hours'. Mosley M. Cohen had also contributed to this plea, on 10 September 1832, stating 'I am urged as much by the feelings of a brother as by pecuniary considerations'. The visit on shore was 'allowed'. Daniel Cohen volunteered to become an overseer of convicts at Port Macquarie, and was sent there on 4 December 1832. His behaviour there was 'good' and in June 1833 he was officially appointed 'special constable'.

On 25 August 1833 Cohen was sent back to the *Phoenix* hulk to be a witness for the prosecution in the case *Rex v. Eustace*. He was subsequently returned to Port Macquarie. His despatch to Port Macquarie would lead to confusion regarding the separate identities of Henry Simeon Cohen (q.v.), who came to Australia on the *Lloyds*, and Daniel Cohen.

In a petition dated 4 December 1834 Cohen wrote to Governor Bourke stating 'that some expectation was held out to him by Sir Robert Peel in case of his good conduct for three or four years'. Bourke observed: 'It does not appear that any hope of indulgence was held out to the convict by Sir Robert Peel—no reason for interfering'.

Daniel Cohen, 'lately of Liverpool', married Esther Dinah Isaacs (q.v.), 'only daughter of widow Isaacs of Olie St, London', at Port Macquarie, on 25 October 1837, 'according to the rites of the Jews'.

Daniel Cohen was granted a ticket of leave and was permitted to live in the Windsor District from 25 June 1840. Frances was born at Port Macquarie in 1837. An infant daughter was buried at the Devonshire Street Jewish Cemetery on

22 November 1838. Three subsequent children were born in Sydney: Lewis (1839), Moses (1841), and Eleazer Keeba (1844–1849).

The *Australian* announced on 4 August 1840, that E. D. Cohen had commenced business as a maker of clocks and watches, goldsmith and silversmith, in Windsor. The *Commercial Journal and Advertiser* of 7 November 1840 tells the story from the Windsor Police Court of one of the 'tribe of Israel, carrying on a business as watchmaker, a jeweller summoned before his Worship on the complaint of his hired servant John Pritchard, a gentile of great eloquence. Case dismissed'. Cohen received permission to live and work in Sydney from 15 January 1841, and in June 1842 advertised as a watchmaker in King Street. He evidently went on to assist his brother at his jewellery shop in George Street, and, in 1844, he announced that he was an 'optician and watchmaker'. Cohen received a conditional pardon on 1 July 1842. He became a member of the Sydney Synagogue Committee in 1843 and gave £22 to the congregation in 1845, the year of its dedication. On 11 April that year the *Sydney Morning Herald* reported that he had been acquitted of a charge of receiving stolen property. In 1845 E. D. Cohen advertised that he was 'watch-maker and repairer at the City Hall of Arts in 392 George St' and that his shop was 'known by the two mechanical clocks and large looking glass at the end of his shop'. Edward Daniel Cohen became fascinated by the gold samples bought by his brother, M. M. Cohen, from a shepherd, McGregor. In 1844 he brought the samples to the attention of the Surveyor General Sir Thomas Mitchell. While officialdom did nothing, Daniel Cohen then contacted the press. The gold nugget was brought to Sydney and, with the help of Moses, his very young son, the nugget was cleaned to be turned into a ring to be presented to Queen Victoria. On 20 December 1845, the *Cumberland Times and Western Advertiser* reported on the discovery of 'Colonial Gold': 'Mr E. D. Cohen, Jeweller of the City Hall of Arts has been exhibiting a specimen of virgin gold, purchased by him from a shepherd who had found it in the mountains. It is embedded in quartz rocks and on melting down, was found to be purest gold!' It was Australia's first report of the discovery of gold.

The *Launceston Examiner* of 27 December 1845 announced: 'The New Age Dawns', and embellished the story by adding:

> Mr Cohen purchased a small specimen of gold from the same individual about 12 months ago. The specimens we saw were in the state they were found except that the quartz rock in which the gold was imbedded, had been pounded by the discov-erer for the convenience of carriage. The vein of metal appeared to be very rich and to contain a quantity of pure gold.

The discovery had even been reported in the *Port Phillip Patriot* in Melbourne on Christmas Eve. Quoting the *Sydney Morning Herald*, the newspaper told the unemployed to search for gold: 'Out of Sydney all you idlers, make engagements with the squatters, and who knows but in addition to your wages you may be rewarded by the discovery of a gold mine?' Strangely, no one paid any attention to the discovery at the time. Edward Daniel Cohen died in Sydney on 5 October 1847. He was buried at Lidcombe and his tombstone was moved to Raphael's Ground, Lidcombe in 1901.

On 11 April 1848, Esther Cohen, widow of Daniel Cohen, married George Brockstein (Brockstayne) (q.v.) at the Sydney Synagogue.

Burrell Indent, 1830, p. 153, no. 30-2655; Governors' Despatches, A1272, p. 229, A1212, p. 1307, A1290, pp. 427, 431; CS 30/2655, 32/6560, in 42/2421.1; HO 10/53; CS 32/7088, 20 September 1832; *Phoenix* (hulk) Entrance Book, 4/6282, no. 396, in 1833; TL 4/4130, 39/1463; *Currency Lad*, 15 December 1832, p. 3.

COHEN, Edward Joseph

England, 1832; Convict; Sentenced to life, Old Bailey, 1831.
Widower; Upholsterer; Height: 174.5 cm.

Dark complexion, dark brown hair, long face, hazel eyes. Straight long nose, large round chin. Edward Cohen was sentenced on 8 September 1831, and transported for burglary.

Edward Joseph Cohen was convicted on 7 February 1834 for 'neglect of duty', and sent for one month in the Launceston Chain Gang, after having been convicted for absence from his master's premises. His only other convictions while an assigned servant occurred in 1837, and were for being absent without leave. He was given six weeks hard labour and punishment in the cells. He was in possession of a ticket of leave by February 1841, when he was found in a public house after hours and given four days on the treadmill. An additional seven days on the treadmill were given for neglect of work, and in September 1841 he was fined £1 for being absent from work.

CON 31/7; CON18/6.

COHEN, Elizabeth

b. London, c.1792–1866
Brothers, 1833; Free.
Married; 12 children.

Elizabeth was the wife of Henry Simeon Cohen (q.v.), and the daughter of Nathan Simmons and Sarah (née Phillips). She arrived in Sydney on 21 December 1833. She had married in 1809. Nine of her ten children were listed as being with her as cabin passengers, travelling as free, unassisted settlers. The passenger list may have been defective, because it omits the one-year-old child William. Her other child, Nancy, was also on board, travelling with her husband, Joseph Simmons (q.v.). Other Jews on board ship were Joseph Levine (q.v.), Joseph Joseph (q.v.) and Israel Joseph (q.v.), all of whom were described as 'merchants'.

Elizabeth had followed her husband out to New South Wales. Their children, who accompanied Elizabeth, were Nancy (1814–1866), Sophia (q.v.) (1816–1882), Ann (Hannah) (q.v.), Samuel (q.v.) (1821–1877), Edward Aaron (q.v.) (1822–1877), Philip (q.v.) (1825–1898), Joseph (q.v.) (1826–1893), Caroline (q.v.) (1827), Lewis (q.v.) (1831–1903), and William (q.v.) (1832). She also brought her servant Elizabeth Solomon (q.v.) with her.

Upon arrival, Joseph Simmons applied to have his father-in-law assigned to him. His request failed and Elizabeth and the children sailed for Port Macquarie.

James Simmons (q.v.), Joseph's brother, then applied to have Henry Cohen assigned to him. The request was refused by Governor Bourke. Elizabeth and Henry had two daughters born at Port Macquarie, Frances (Fanny) (q.v.), on 17 March 1834, and Jane (1837–1907).

On 12 April 1834 Elizabeth Cohen wrote to the Police Office in Port Macquarie about a Thomas Brown who held a ticket of leave and who had agreed to do some tailoring work for her. The job was 'badly done' but the convict had asked for a second chance. Mrs Cohen gave him some more clothes. Brown absconded, leaving the following note: 'Farewell Mrs Cowan (*sic*) I have committed my body to a watery Grave sooner than be discovered. Farewell for Ever. Thomas Brown once a tailor'. The police pursued Brown and found him thirty miles away from Port Macquarie. He was sentenced to six months in irons and his ticket of leave was cancelled. Henry and Elizabeth Cohen moved to Sydney in 1845 and her husband opened a store on the eastern side of George Street between Robin Hood Lane and Hunter Street. In 1851 the *Sydney Directory* listed 'Cohen, Henry, merchant and shipowner'. Some time after 1860 Henry and Elizabeth moved to Margaret Street.

Elizabeth Cohen died 'at her residence Margaret St, Wynyard Square', aged seventy-four, on 13 February 1866 and was buried in the Jewish section of the Devonshire Street cemetery.

CS 4/2256.1–34/484.

COHEN, Ellen

1832–1854
Inchinnan, 1849; Free.
Single; Maid servant.

An assisted immigrant, Ellen Cohen was buried at the Devonshire Street Cemetery on 19 February 1854.

COHEN, Fanny

b. Sydney, 1839–1912 16 children.

Fanny Cohen was the daughter of Abraham and Sophia Cohen (qq.v.). She married Benjamin Benjamin (q.v.) in Sydney on 5 August 1857. Her husband became mayor of Melbourne and was subsequently knighted.

Their sixteen children were Maurice Edward (1858), Catherine (1860), Abraham Herbert (1861), Florence Sophia (1863), Percy Lionel (1865), Edith Fanny (1867), Frank Bedford (1868), Howard Elias (1870), Minnie Violet (1871), Ida Rose (1873), May Constance (1876), Leslie Ronald (1878), Gerald Septimus (1879), Stanley Octavius (1880), Oswald Deronda (1884), and Myra Lilian (1885).

Lady Fanny Benjamin died in Melbourne on 18 February 1912.

COHEN, Frances

b. Port Macquarie, 1834–1884
13 children.

Frances (Fanny), the fifth daughter of Henry Simeon Cohen and Elizabeth (qq.v.), was born at Port Macquarie on 17 March 1834, and named on 21 January 1835. On 17 August 1853 she married Henry Solomon (q.v.), at the Sydney Synagogue. From 1858 to 1865, Henry and Frances Solomon lived in Launceston; they returned to Sydney in 1866. Frances died, aged forty-eight, on 23 October 1884, and was buried in the Jewish section at Rookwood Cemetery. Henry died, aged sixty-five, on 24 May 1894.

Their children were Henry B. (1854), Edward (1855), Lionel (1858), Louis (1860), Percy (1861), Maud (1863), Ida Florence (1865), Ernest N. (1866), John (1867), Louisa A. E. (1868), Beatrice E. (1870), Isabel L. (1873), and Arthur (Asher) Julian (1876).

COHEN, Francis

d. 1850
Free.
Single; Dealer.

Francis Cohen was listed in the *Registry of Flash Men* and was said to be part of a criminal gang with Nathan Jacobs (q.v.), John Jacobs (q.v.), Sol Reubens (q.v. Solomon Reuben), and Barnett Davis. The *Australasian Chronicle* of 13 April 1833 listed him as out on bail with Henry Barnett (q.v.), Baron B. Cohen (q.v.) and George Phillips (q.v.), after he had quarrelled with and assaulted George O'Brien. The 1847 *Low's Directory of the City and District of Sydney* listed Francis Cohen of John Joel Cohen & Son as living in Gloucester Street.

Francis Cohen married Louisa M. Davis at Scots Church in Sydney and opened a store on George Street which he called The Temple of Fashion and, not to be outdone by his rivals, placed one of Ballarat's gold ingots for display in his shop. It was said to have cost him £857 and he declared that he would not part with it for £1000, Francis Cohen was buried in the Presbyterian Section of the Devonshire Street Cemetery on 12 March 1850.

W. A. Miles, *Registry of Flash Men*, p. 114, 2/673; *Australasian Chronicle*, 13 April 1833; *Sydney Morning Herald*, 23 August 1844, 29 October 1853.

COHEN, George

b. London, 1820–1889
Free.
Single; Dealer; 12 children.

George Cohen was the fifth son of Barent and Sierlah Cohen of London. Of the ten siblings only two remained in England. George was the brother of Lewis (q.v.), Samuel (q.v.), David (q.v.), Abraham (q.v.), Solomon (q.v.), Morris (q.v.) and Henry (q.v.). George Cohen married Rosetta, the daughter of Samuel and Rebecca Solomon (qq.v.), in Maitland. He was the first storekeeper and postmaster of Gunnedah. The *Maitland Mercury* reported on 16 September 1849 (echoing the 1848 European uprisings): 'S & G Cohen, Lambeth House, Scone, have commenced business in the late Phillip's Store as wholesale and retail general store keepers, spirit merchants and flour manufacturers. They intend to revolutionise Scone and introduce an entirely new system of government in the management of their store which the radicals of the district (of which it is hoped there are many) will pronounce a decided improvement'. It was recorded in the Land Correspondence that George Cohen bought land in the Scone District during 1850.

George and Rosetta Cohen had six sons and six daughters. They were: Elizabeth (25 November 1849–1909), Jane (1851–1857), Burnett (1854), Hannah, Samuel, Caroline (1858), Henry, Rebecca, Albert, Leah (1869–1874), David Ethel (1872, died in infancy), and Percy. George died at Tamworth on 20 October 1889. Rose died at Maitland on 27 November 1907.

Maitland Mercury, 16 September 1849; Land Correspondence, 2/7827, bought on 16 September 1850.

COHEN, George

b. Port Macquarie, 1840–1889
Single; 5 children.

George was the twin brother of Henry Emanuel Cohen (q.v.), son of Abraham and Sophia Cohen (qq.v.), and grandson of Henry and Elizabeth Cohen (qq.v.). At the age of sixteen, George was sent to Tamworth to be apprenticed to his uncle William Cohen. In 1864 George and his twin brother Henry went to Bathurst and began to trade there as general storekeepers. The business did not flourish (despite the gold rush) and was closed after two years. In 1866 George Cohen went to Goulburn, where his older brother Frederick lived. There he met Elizabeth Davis, the daughter of Isaac Davis (q.v.), who was a hotel keeper in Goulburn, and they married in the Sydney Synagogue. George Cohen and Elizabeth moved to Cooma and established a store there. This time his business prospered. In 1886 he retired to live at Port Macquarie.

George Cohen was buried at the Jewish cemetery in Maitland on 15 January 1889.

George and Elizabeth had five children: Ernest (1867) at Bathurst, Arthur (1868) at Sydney, and, at Cooma, Victor Isaac (1870), Ettie Amelia (1875), and Linda (died 1955).

COHEN, George Judah

b. Sydney, 1842–1937
7 children.

George Judah Cohen was born on 27 April 1842 in a home on the edge of the Tank Stream in Sydney. His father, Samuel Cohen (q.v.), had come to Australia in 1834 and was, at one time, the Member for Morpeth in the New South Wales Legislative Assembly.

George Judah Cohen came to be known as the 'Rothschild of Australia'. He was educated in England and in 1861 returned to Australia to take charge of David Cohen & Co., the family business. He married his cousin Rebecca, the daughter of Lewis Wolfe Levy (q.v.). They had five sons and two daughters. One son was Sir Samuel Sydney Cohen (1869–1948) and another Alroy Cohen.

George Judah Cohen spent seventy years as a director of David Cohen & Co. He was one of the directors of Tooths, the Australian Gas Light Co., and United Insurance, and served as deputy chairman and later chairman of the Commercial Bank. He served on the executive of the Great Synagogue for twenty-three years.

He died on 22 January 1937.

G. F. J. Bergman, 'George Judah Cohen', in *ADB*, vol. 8, p. 52f.

COHEN, Henry

1759–1847
Convict.
3 children.

Henry Cohen, a farmer, the owner of thirty acres of land at New Town, appeared on the Van Diemen's Land General Muster on 30 April 1809. He had been a prisoner on Norfolk Island. He appeared in the census with one wife, two children and two pigs. On 28 February 1824 the child of Henry Cohen and his wife Mary, living in Hobart Town, was baptised and named James.

At a trial before the Supreme Court in Hobart Town on 2 October 1834, Henry Cohen was acquitted of a charge of stealing a 'quantity of meat, the property of Mr Gatehouse, New Town'. The evidence was deemed to be 'defective'.

'Henry Cohen a farmer' was buried at St John's Church New Town, Hobart Town, on 24 December 1847. He was said to be eighty-eight years old.

CO 201/52.

COHEN, Henry

b. London, 1814–1860
Free.
Single; Dealer.

Henry Cohen was the third son and fourth child of Barent and Sierlah Cohen (née Levy), and the brother of Lewis (q.v.), Samuel (q.v.), David (q.v.), Abraham (q.v.), George (q.v.), Solomon (q.v.), and Morris (q.v.). Henry joined his brothers in the Cohen family business, conducted in Maitland, and died there on 6 January 1860. He did not marry.

COHEN, Henry

d. 1847
Alice, 1828; Free.
Single; Jeweller and watchmaker.

Henry Cohen arrived on 23 December 1828 and opened a shop in George Street, Sydney, 'Henry Cohen's Working Jewellery and Watchmaker. Next door to Mr Hyam, Bootmaker 7 George St'. He also advertised that he sold drawing pencils. He was granted one assigned convict in 1831. Cohen manufactured the prize medals awarded by the Agricultural and Horticultural Society. According to the *Sydney Gazette*, they were 'of massive silver and in point of workmanship are a very fair display of Colonial craft and do very great merit to the manufacturer'.

In March 1833 he advertised that he was a 'Goldsmith and Watchmaker of 5 George St, Sydney opening a shop also in Parramatta'. On 18 June 1833, Cohen was accused by John Foreman of having stolen a watch from him and also owing him rent. Cohen 'absconds' to Van Diemen's Land and a reward of £2 was offered to 'any person who will seize and detain my watch which Cohen has stolen.'

Sydney Gazette, 4 January 1831, 24 May 1832, 18 June 1833; Governors' Despatches, 1832, ML, A1210, p. 188; *Currency Lad*, 30 March 1833; *Colonial Times*, 7 October 1834; *AG*, p. 179.

COHEN, Henry Emanuel

b. Port Macquarie, 1840–1912
2 children.

The son of Abraham and Sophia Cohen (qq.v.), Henry Emanuel Cohen had a twin brother, George (q.v.), and was the grandson of Henry Simeon Cohen and Elizabeth Cohen (qq.v.) of Port Macquarie. Henry Emanuel Cohen was born at Port Macquarie on 1 December 1840 and came to Sydney with his parents at the age of eight. The family moved to Goulburn in 1855. When he was sixteen Henry joined the firm of David Cohen and Co, and was sent to West Maitland to work as a clerk. He remained there for eight years. In 1864 he joined with his brother George to open a shop in Bathurst, trading as 'Cohen & Co'. The store closed in June 1867 and Henry left for London in 1868 to study law. On 6 June 1871, Cohen was called to the Bar by the Middle Temple and shortly afterwards set out for home, surviving a shipwreck off the coast of Ceylon. He was thirty-one years old when he set up in practice in Sydney, specialising in mercantile cases.

Cohen's father died in 1874, leaving a vacancy on the board of the York Street Synagogue, which he was persuaded to fill; he was a member of the board until his death, thirty-eight years later. Cohen was active in synagogue affairs and the president or chairman of many Jewish philanthropic and educational organisations. In December 1874, Cohen became the parliamentary representative for West Maitland, and held that seat until 1880, in succession to Lewis Wolfe Levy (q.v.).

In May 1881, he was appointed Acting Judge of the District Court, returning to Parliament in 1882, and becoming the Minister of Justice. He was president of the Arbitration Court and in 1896 became the second Jew in the British Dominions to be appointed a Judge of the Supreme Court.

Cohen married Sophie Frank, the daughter of Leo Frank of Hanover, Germany, on 15 July 1884. Sophie had arrived in Australia some twelve months previously to work as a governess to the son of Sigmond Hoffnung (q.v.). Henry and Sophie had two sons, Edgar Henry (1885) and Cecil Hope (1888). Mr Justice Cohen died at sea, on 5 January 1912, and was buried in Sydney. Sophie died in Paris in 1943.

David J. Benjamin, 'Henry Emanuel Cohen', *AJJHS*, vol. 2, no. 10 (1948), p. 524f; G. F. J. Bergman, 'Henry Emanuel Cohen', in *ADB*, vol. 3, p. 437f.

COHEN, Henry Joseph (also known as Henry Josephs)

Free.
Dealer.

Henry Joseph Cohen was the brother of Phillip Joseph Cohen (q.v.) and step-brother of Simeon Joseph Cohen (q.v.). In 1836 Henry Joseph Cohen 'of Sydney' was listed as having purchased two allotments of land at Paterson for £16. A quarrel between Cohen and Lewis Samuel resulted in Cohen preferring charges against Samuel for continually threatening him.

On 18 August 1837 Henry Joseph announced in the *Australian* that he had 'removed' to Bridge Street. In March 1838 a case was heard before the Supreme Court of New South Wales of 'Joseph v. Polack' [1838 NSW SupC 22]. The plaintiff was Henry Joseph, and the defendant was Abraham Polack (q.v.) the auctioneer: the declaration stated that the plaintiff without any cuse, beat, struck and otherwise ill-used the defendant, so that he became lame, sore, sick and disordered. Damages were laid at £1000. 'It was not denied that Polack, a much younger and stronger man, had horse whipped Cohen in plain view in George Street. The Attorney General put forward the case that it would be better for Polack, whose income was estimated to be between ten and twelve thousand pounds, were to pay the sum claimed than to be at the mercy of trial by jury.

The jury awarded Cohen (alias) Joseph damages of £40.

Cohen was described as 'Mr Henry Josephs' who was a younger brother on his mother's side to P. J. Cohen, a respectable gentleman, residing at Maitland, and [who] did not arrive in the Colony until several years after his brother, when seeing his brother's respectability and finding that there were many persons in town of his own name who were of very ill repute, took his brother's name in business'.

Cohen was a seat holder at the Sydney Synagogue and on 15 September 1839 gave twenty-one guineas to the building fund.

Cohen was the licensee of the Shamrock Inn when it was reportedly robbed by bushrangers on 1 December 1840. On 27 July 1841, 'Henry Joseph Cohen, innkeeper at Black Creek' (County of Northumberland), was insolvent. Simeon Joseph Cohen and Alfred Levien (q.v.) of West Maitland were appointed the trustees of the estate. By 1848 Henry had become the landlord of the Fitzroy Hotel. The *Shipping Gazette* of September 1849 recorded that he owned the *Thistle* and he was one of the four Jewish ship owners in the colony.

Land Correspondence, 2/7827, 17 February 1836; *Sydney Gazette*, 5 July 1836, 27 July 1841; *Maitland Mercury*, 28 October 1846; *Sydney Chronicle*, 8 April 1848; *Australian*, 18 August 1837, 16 March 1838, 1 December 1840.

COHEN, Henry Simeon

b. London, 1790–1867
Lloyds (1), 1833; Convict; Sentenced to 14 years, London, 1833.
Married; Merchant, haberdasher; Height: 156 cm; 12 children.

Fair, ruddy complexion, brown hair and bald headed, blue eyes, breast hairy. Typically for a tailor he had a scar on the ball and back of his left thumb. Henry Cohen had no previous convictions. However, this was the third time stolen promissory notes were found in his possession. He had 'unlimited credit' in the City of London and his business at 126 Edgware Road, Paddington, was a prosperous one. Cohen stated:

> I return in my business between £4000 and £5000 per year. How then can I avoid those impositions imposed upon me? If I refuse to take the notes, I may as well shut up shop, as some weeks I take £60 or £70 in notes and are in the habit continually of taking country notes being near the Paddington-canal, where boats come from all parts of the country … restore me to my wife and ten helpless children.

Cohen was sentenced on 19 March 1833 and transported for being in possession of four stolen Glastonbury bank promissory notes valued at £30. Henry was the son of Nathan Cohen and Priscilla Frances (née Benjamin). His wife was Elizabeth Cohen (q.v.) (daughter of Nathan Simmons and Sarah, née Phillips). They had married in 1809. The family lived above the business in Edgware Road. His son-in-law, Joseph Simmons (q.v.), the husband of his daughter Nancy, and the remainder of the family, arrived on the Brothers in 1833.

Henry Cohen arrived in Sydney on 18 December 1833. His initial assignment was to the Mounted Police as a tailor though this was found to be a mistake, as Cohen testified that he knew 'nothing of the trade'. On being interviewed by the Principal Superintendent of Convicts he was found to be one of the class of convicts called 'special'. The Superintendent wrote 'This man is a Jew, and was tried for having stolen Bank notes, and I am informed, his family have brought a large sum of money to the colony by the *Brothers*'. Cohen was assigned on 10 January 1834 to Major Archibald Clunes Innes in Port Macquarie, in whose service he remained for six years. His wife, Elizabeth, and their ten children came out as passengers on the *Brothers*, which arrived three days after the convict transport that brought Henry to Australia. Together with the family were two servants, Elizabeth Solomon (q.v.) and Martha Lawler.

Within a few weeks the Princial Superintendent of Convicts advised the Colonial Secretary on 8 January 1834. 'The convict Henry Cohen, *Lloyds*, who was named in the muster list as a Tailor, and as such applicated (sic) to the mounted police, turns out to be a Merchant Tailor, and knows nothing of the trade, and he has been accordingly returned by Capt Williams to the Convict B[arracks]… This man is a Jew, and was tried for having stolen Bank notes, and I am informed his family have brought a large sum to the colony by the *Brothers*.' The Colonial

Secretary directed that Cohen should be sent on to Port Macquarie, a place of secondary punishment.

In June 1839 Cohen requested a pardon, stating that he was married with '12 children'. He had worked with 'unceasing endeavour to the satisfaction of his employer'. He boasted that he had 'not been unsuccessful in his efforts'and that his wife Elizabeth kept a clothing shop in Horton Street in the centre of town. Cohen's petition was accompanied by a host of glowing character references. The benevolent Major Archibald Clunes Innes testified: 'His wife and large family have gained the good opinion of all here'. Other recommendations read: 'He has gained for his family the estimation of every person who has known him … and his exemplary wife'. The Colonial Secretary noted that the petition is 'quite out of order as he has never held a ticket of leave'. Cohen was granted the ticket of leave on 14 February 1840 and he was 'Allowed to remain in the District of Port Macquarie'. He then obtained a licence for Cohen's Hotel. He received a conditional pardon, granted by the Governor, on 1 July 1842.

In the *Sydney Morning Herald* of 24 February 1845, Henry Cohen of Port Macquarie thanked the settlers for their support over the past eleven years and announced he had 'resigned the management of the store' to his sons, E. and Samuel Henry Cohen. He was to reside in Sydney. Henry watched the markets, and commenced in Sydney as a merchant and general commissions agent with office and stores in Charlotte Place. He was listed in the *Sydney Commercial Directory* of 1851 as a 'merchant and ship owner of 325 Castlereagh St north'. The family owned a small, but profitable, intercolonial schooner named the *Elizabeth Cohen*, which sailed between Port Macquarie and Sydney until its shipwreck in 1857. In the *Sydney Morning Herald* of 2 September 1854, Henry was listed as the collector for 'The Jerusalem Fund' for the maintenance of the poor in the Holy Land. He was elected president of the York Street Synagogue in 1859.

Elizabeth Cohen died at their home in Margaret Street, Wynyard Square, on 13 February 1866, at the age of seventy-four, and was buried in the Jewish section of the Devonshire Street Cemetery. Henry died on 1 August 1867 and was buried at the Jewish section of the Rookwood Cemetery. The *Sydney Morning Herald* announced his death 'Henry Cohen Esq., in his 81st year, an old and highly respected colonist. Deeply regretted by a numerous family and a large circle of friends'. His estate consisted of forty houses and cottages around Sydney and cash bequests totalling £2025.

The children of Henry and Elizabeth were: Nancy (1814–1866) (q.v.), who married her first cousin, Joseph Simmons (q.v.), in England; Sophia (q.v.) (1816–1882), who married Abraham Cohen (q.v.); Ann (Hannah) (q.v.), who married Solomon Marks (q.v.); Samuel Henry (q.v.) (1821–1899), who married Elizabeth Hyams; Edward Aaron (q.v.) (1822–1877), who married Rebecca Benjamin; Philip (q.v.) (1825–1898); Joseph (q.v.) (1826–1893), who married Mary Hart; Caroline (q.v.) (1827–1881), who married Asher (Arthur) Isaac Nathan (q.v.); Lewis (q.v.) (1831–1903); and William (q.v.) (1832–1871), who married Sarah Solomon. The last two children were born in Port Macquarie. They were

Frances (Fanny) (q.v.) (1834–1884), who married Henry Solomon, and Jane (q.v.) (1837–1907), who married David Lawrence Levy.

OBSP, 1832–33, case 1015, p. 525f; barque *Lloyds* Printed Indent, no. 33-3400; CS 34/256, 13 January 1834, 4/2240.2; CS 39/6798, X 645:TL 40/356, 14 February 1840: HO 10/53; CP 43/183; story of the Cohen family, told by Philip Charles Cohen of Sydney (formset@exemail.com.au), detailed family information from Mrs Ruth Marks and Mr Stuart Cohen, Melbourne.

COHEN, Isaac

b. London, 1801
Lotus, 1833; Convict; Sentenced to 14 years, Old Bailey, 1832.
Single; Labourer; Height: 168 cm.

Dark complexion, narrow face, dark brown hair, aquiline nose. Isaac Cohen was transported for receiving stolen goods. He was arrested with his father, Abraham Cohen (q.v.), as together they examined baskets of clothes, coats and boots stolen from a police station in Charlotte Street, Bloomsbury. Both men were defended by a barrister. Isaac Cohen stated 'I have nothing to do with my father's business, I was there by accident'. Father and son were sent to Australia on the same ship. Hulk report: 'Good'.

On 26 April 1837, Isaac Cohen was convicted of neglect of duty and gross insolence while in the service of Mr Porter. He was sentenced to six months hard labour in chains and sent to the Bagdad Road Party, and later to Green Ponds. On 11 December 1838 he was accused of 'maliciously inventing a case to obtain a fine' while serving as a constable. The case was dismissed. However, on 4 October 1839, he was convicted of gross misconduct while serving as a constable. He was 'deprived of his ticket of leave and put to hard labour on the roads for six months being assigned to the Hobart Town Surveyor's Gang'. On 25 November 1839 he was working with the Town Surveyor's Gang when he was found guilty of disobedience of orders and put in a cell for six days on bread and water. A ticket of leave was issued on 19 November 1841. His conditional pardon was approved on 17 January 1845 and a certificate of freedom granted on 16 June 1847.

OBSP, 18 October 1832, case 2319. CON 31/7, no. 1512; CON 18/13.

COHEN, Isaac

b. Houndsditch, 1814
Maria Somes (1), 1844; Convict; Sentenced to 10 years, Central Criminal Court, 1844.
Single; Tailor; Height: 173 cm.

Fresh complexion, black hair and whiskers, long face, hazel eyes, large nose and mouth and a double chin. Inoculation marks on left and right arms. Isaac Cohen's conviction for embezzling £600 was his second conviction. The previous one was for stealing a handkerchief in Cheapside.

Isaac Cohen arrived in Van Diemen's Land on 30 July 1844. His initial period of probation was for eighteen months on Maria Island, which was extended by five and a half months for three minor offences. He left the island penal settlement in May 1846. His assigned service was spent mainly in Hobart. He appears to have worked for a number of Jews including Joshua Marks (q.v.) of the New Town Road, Reuben Joseph (q.v.) of Liverpool Street, and Joshua Lyons (q.v.) of Argyle Street.

A ticket of leave was issued in March 1850 and forfeited the following month in Oatlands, where he was convicted for petty larceny and sentenced to six months imprisonment. A similar charge the following year was dismissed (11 March 1851) and, although he was supposed to be assigned to Joshua Lyons, he was judged to be without proper supervision or control and was ordered to be removed to the 'Interior'. In May 1851, he was in the service of Mr Isaacs of Oatlands where he was found to have a forged certificate of freedom in his possession and sent to the Prisoners' Barracks in Launceston for six months hard labour. On 26 August 1852 he absconded from his assigned service in Hobart and received an additional eighteen months hard labour. On 4 March 1854 he received his certificate of freedom. On 26 May 1864 at Launceston he was convicted of stealing four pairs of boots and began twelve months hard labour.

CON 33/57, no. 134950.

COHEN, Isaac

b. London, 1830–1906
1841; Free.
Single; 10 children.

The son of Benjamin and Sarah Cohen (qq.v.), Isaac Cohen was born in London on 11 December 1830. Benjamin Cohen had been transported to Van Diemen's Land in 1836 and committed suicide in 1841, which was the year his wife and three of their children arrived in Australia. Isaac was ten years old at the time.

Isaac Cohen was mentioned in the list of Mechanics and Artificers. He was a member of the Hobart Synagogue in the early 1850s. He married Eliza Vincent on 14 February 1853 at Christ Church, Geelong. They had three children, Edward, Julia and Isaac. Isaac worked on the goldfields at Ballarat.

Isaac was in Hobart Town by 1859, living with Elizabeth Saville. He was listed as a carpenter in 1861, a ship's carpenter in 1868 and as an engine driver in 1875. Isaac and Elizabeth had seven children. He died on 24 May 1906, at which time his occupation was listed as engineer.

HO 10/28. Pam Zopf and Geoff Court, *From Iberia to Van Diemen's Land. A Cohen Family Odyssey*, privately published, 2008.

COHEN, Isaac (James COHEN)

b. 1788
Martha, 1818; Convict.
Sentenced to life.

'Isaac Cohen' was counted in the List of Convicts in New South Wales of November 1828. He was a member of the '15 Road Party at Penrith' and he was forty years of age. The 1828 Census of the colony also listed him, but stated that his name was 'James'. The Census also stated that he was a Catholic. Both documents agree that he was forty years old, and working with the same road party in Parramatta. According to the General Return of Convicts in 1837, he was 'James', and was a convict in Sydney.

COHEN, Jacob

b. Alexandria, Egypt, 1775–1846
Midas (2), 1827; Convict; Sentenced to 7 years, Ipswich, 1825.
Single; Pedlar; Height: 166 cm.

Dark sallow complexion. Black to grey hair. Hazel eyes. Tattoos 'A Gillett' written in blue and printed in red. Grey flower pot on left arm. 'Success to Liberty' and three anchors on right arm. No education. 'Jew.' Jacob Cohen had been imprisoned at Clerkenwell, found guilty of larceny and fined. He was again found guilty of larceny at Ipswich, and was sentenced on 24 October 1825.

Jacob Cohen arrived in New South Wales on 15 February 1827 and was assigned to Sir John Jamieson. In November 1827 he was listed as 'absent' from the 'No. 12 Road Gang'. The 1828 Census listed him as a member of the '24 Windsor Town Gang'. However, the *Sydney Gazette* (25 May 1830) announced that he had been 'apprehended' after running away. He was sentenced to seven days on the treadwheel, and placed in 'No. 30 Road Gang'. On 19 April 1830 he 'absconded' and was again sent to the treadwheel for seven days. On 30 April he was listed as a 'runaway', given twelve lashes and sent back to his duties. On 6 July 1831 he was admitted to the Hyde Park Barracks to be sent on to Port Macquarie. His behaviour was 'good'. Cohen appeared before the Magistrate's Bench on 9 February 1832. He was accused of having fallen asleep on duty while 'watching the corn'. He had threatened the convict overseer: 'If I had a knife I would cut your guts out'. He was sentenced to be put in the cells for forty-eight hours. A certificate of freedom was issued on 14 November 1832, and Cohen returned to Sydney.

The *Australian Journal* of 4 March 1845 related that Cohen had appeared in the Police Court having in his possession, and illegally offering for sale, a stolen gold pin. The information was provided by J. J. Cohen. The newspaper described the accused as 'a dirty grey headed rogue, about the worst looking specimen of the Hebrew tribe we remember to have seen in Sydney'.

He was buried by the Poor Fund of the Sydney Synagogue on 6 June 1846. He was said to have been sixty-six years old. He died at the Sydney Dispensary and, because of his Middle Eastern origins, was described as a 'Barbary Man'.

Midas Indent 4/4012, p. 55; *Sydney Gazette*, 5 November 1827; X822 Hyde Park Barracks Trials; Port Macquarie Bench Book, 1830–32, 4/5637 p. 289; *Phoenix* (hulk) Entrance Book, 1833, 4/6282, no. 277; CF 4/4313, 32/1027; M. Z. Forbes, 'The Saga of the Cohens and Their Times', *AJJHS*, vol. 10, no. 3 (1988), p. 180f.

COHEN, Jacob

b. London, 1834–1886
1841; Free.
Single; 7 children.

Son of Benjamin and Sarah Cohen (qq.v.), Jacob was born on 13 December 1834. He arrived in Hobart Town with his mother and three of his brothers to join their convict father, who committed suicide within weeks of their arrival. Sarah established a confectionary shop in Hobart Town.

Throughout his life Jacob Cohen described himself as a 'musician'. He appeared at the Theatre Royal in October 1853 at a benefit performance as a singer, musician and dancer. In 1873 Jacob married Harriet Windover. Harriet was aged forty-seven, and Jacob thirty-nine. Harriet died four days later. Jacob then married Alice Elizabeth Surnam, aged twenty, on 7 January 1874. His address was given as 115 Argyle Street, Hobart. They had seven children.

Pam Zopf and Geoff Court: *From Iberia to Van Diemen's Land. A Cohen Family Odyssey*. Privately printed 2008.

COHEN, Jacob Charles

b. Manchester
Persian, 1829; Free.
Married; Watchmaker and jeweller; 2 children.

A brother of John Joel Cohen (q.v.) and Baron B. Cohen (q.v) Jacob Charles Cohen served on the committee of the York Street Synagogue and was later a committee member of the Macquarie Street Synagogue. In 1841 he advertised that he was in business at 500 George Street, near Hunter Street. He supplied London-made watches, jewellery and spectacles, and ready-to-purchase raw Californian gold. J. C. Cohen & Sons became an important purchaser of Australian gold in the 1850s. Jacob Charles Cohen and Sarah Cohen had two sons, Mosley, born in Sydney in 1843, and Henry, born in 1844.

COHEN, James

b. 1787
Lord Eldon, 1817; Convict; Sentenced to 7 years, Lancaster, 1816.
Cotton spinner; Height: 165.5 cm; 5 children.

Dark pale complexion, dark brown hair, hazel eyes. Apart from his surname (which could be Irish) there is no evidence that James Cohen was Jewish.

James Cohen arrived in Sydney on 30 September 1817. Cohen was listed in the 1818 General Muster working as a 'Government Labourer'. Cohen was granted a certificate of freedom on 22 January 1823. In the General Muster of 1825, Cohen was still in the service of the government, but was described as a 'shoemaker' in Sydney. In 1837 he was listed as working for the 'government' in Sydney.

In the 1841 Census, James Cohen was listed as living at Pitt Town, in the District of Windsor. The children of James and Isabella Cohen were James (1832), Elizabeth (1836), Catherine (1837), George (1842), and Jane (1846).
CS 4/424, p. 123.

COHEN, Jane (Jenny)

b. Port Macquarie, 1837–1907

Jane Cohen was born at Port Macquarie on 19 April 1837, the sixth daughter and last child of Henry Simeon Cohen and Elizabeth (qq.v.).

On 7 November 1855, Jane married David Lawrence Levy at the Sydney Synagogue. David was a solicitor. He was an active member of the Board of the Great Synagogue serving as its honorary solicitor, treasurer and a trustee from 1871 to 1877. They do not appear to have had any children. David died, aged sixty-five, on 1 December 1893. Jane died, aged seventy, on 18 September 1907. Both were buried at the Jewish section of the Rookwood Cemetery.
The family history of Henry Cohen, p. 465f., by Philip Charles Cohen, privately printed.

COHEN, John

Free.
Married; Silversmith, general dealer.

'J. Cohen, silversmith of George St', was listed in the *New South Wales Calendar and General Post Office Directory* for 1832. The *Commercial Journal and Advertiser* of 29 February 1836 published a notice that he was the agent for N. Solomon of London. His shop was in York Street and he announced that he had commenced business in a wholesale and retail warehouse, dealing in china, glass and earthenware. In 1840 John Cohen married Mary Miller at Scots Church in Sydney.

John Cohen was a founding member of the Melbourne Hebrew Congregation in 1844. By April 1845 he had fallen behind in the payment of his subscription to the congregation and his dues were 'remitted'. He signed the address to the newly appointed Chief Rabbi Adler in February 1846. On 5 September 1850, a letter was sent to John Cohen of Elizabeth Street telling him that his seat in the Synagogue 'will be disposed of' because of his failure to pay the dues.

COHEN, John

b. Houndsditch, 1821
Blenheim, 1839; Free, Sentenced to 7 years, Sydney Quarter Sessions, 1843.
Single; Farrier, whaler; Height: 174 cm.

Fresh complexion, stout, dark brown hair, black bushy eyebrows, a broad face, long thin mouth. Jew. Can read and write. Secondary colonial transportation was on the Seahorse, *arriving in Van Diemen's*

Land on 19 April 1843: 'I arrived at Sydney per Blenheim, *a convict ship, as a sailor about four years ago'.*

Cohen arrived in New South Wales in 1839 on the *Blenheim*. He was tried at the Sydney Quarter Sessions on 6 February 1843 and sentenced to seven years transportation for stealing £20. 'I was bathing near the Domain and some men swore they saw me go near Mr Ray's [of George Street] clothes and take something from his pocket and run away.' Cohen was sent to Van Diemen's Land on the *Sea Horse*. His initial two years of probation at the Cascades ended on 30 April 1845. Cohen became a constable in Hobart Town. On 11 November 1845 he was found guilty of being in a public house after hours and was sentenced to ten days solitary confinement, and in 1846 was transferred to New Norfolk. On 1 June 1846 he was fined for being disobedient while still a constable. On 3 December 1846 he was working as an assigned servant to Mr Lawrence, in Hobart Town, when he absconded, and on recapture was sentenced to one month's hard labour on the roads. On 26 January 1847 he was remanded for refusing to work on the plea of illness. On 26 February, at Jerusalem, he was sentenced to seven days solitary confinement. He was still working on the roads at Jerusalem when he was punished with three months hard labour in prison for refusing to carry a load of wood.

John Cohen received a ticket of leave on 27 June 1848 while he served as a constable in Campbell Town. His certificate of freedom was issued on 8 February 1850.

CON 16/2, p. 39; CON 37/1, no. 198; Recognition Book, 1843, 4/6297.

COHEN, John (John RITSON)

b. Cumberland, 1821
Maitland, 1844; Convict; Sentenced to 15 years, 1843.
Single; Labourer; Height: 177 cm.

Cohen adopted a non-Jewish surname and declared himself to be a member of the Church of England. Cohen, or Ritson, had been sentenced to transportation and tried with George Edgeworth. They had stolen some silver spoons and other property. Cohen said that he had been transported before and received a sentence of fifteen years for housebreaking. He had escaped from Appleby Gaol (in England) and was 'again apprehended'. He had served a previous sentence of two years for housebreaking. He said his father's name was William, his mother Frances, his brothers George and Joseph, and his sister Nancy.

John Cohen (or Ritson) arrived on the *Maitland* on 8 February 1844. He was sent to Norfolk Island and then to Van Diemen's Land on the *Pestongee Bomangee* in April 1847. John Cohen, aged twenty-eight, married Sarah Rider, aged sixteen, at Westbury on 17 April 1849.

CON 33/76; CON 17/2, p. 20.

COHEN, John Godfrey

Lotus, 1835; Free.
Single; Jeweller; 4 children.

John G. Cohen arrived cabin class on the *Lotus* in 1835. He married Mary Bradford at St James' Church of England in Sydney in 1839. He obtained a licence as an auctioneer on 22 November 1843. Cohen opened a jewellery shop at 490 George Street, moving to 365 George Street by the end of 1845. Cohen became a major gold buyer in 1852–53. He was a member of the New South Wales Constitutional Committee in 1853.

The children of John Godfrey and Mary Cohen were Frances (1840), Anne Mary (1845), John Godfrey (1850) and Wilhelmina (1852).

Ship Indent 4/5209; *Sydney Morning Herald*, 22 November 1843, 1 January 1845; *Empire*, 21 February 1852, 24 August 1853.

COHEN, John Joel

b. Manchester, 1798–1853
Jessie, 1839; Free.
Married; Silversmith, watchmaker, dealer; 7 children.

Originally known as 'Joel John Cohen', John Joel was married to Rebecca, the sister of Mosely Moss Cohen (q.v.). Rebecca died in Manchester at the age of thirty-two in 1832. By the time he reached Sydney he had remarried and had two children. Cohen had two brothers in Australia, Jacob Charles Cohen (q.v.) and Baron Cohen (q.v.). Their father was Simeon Cohen of the firm of Cohen and Son, Goldsmiths of Manchester.

Joel Cohen, his wife and two children reached Port Jackson on 19 February 1839 on the *Jessie*, travelling cabin class from Liverpool. It was later said that he had been declared bankrupt in Manchester and had come to Sydney in order to avoid his creditors. Cohen established the Temple of Fashion opposite the Old Treasury Building at 479 George Street in February 1840. He advertised on 23 December 1842 that he manufactured jewellery and dealt with watches, spectacles and silver, with a 'first rate London workman constantly employed on the premises'. He was reported to be very active in civic affairs and was a guest at the Lord Mayor's Ball in August 1844. His presence in Sydney was obviously a grave affront to his former brother-in-law, M. M. Cohen, who kept advertising that 'he had no agents of his own name' and 'no connection' with any other house in the colony. These notices multiplied following false reports of 'Embezzlement' by John Joel Cohen, published in both the *Sydney Morning Herald* and the *Australian* (14 May 1840).

Cohen was a Freemason and manufactured the prize medals for the colony's Floral Show, and produced 'very neat, elegant and appropriate Masonic emblems'. He was a member of the Sydney Synagogue, and on 30 June 1841 his daughter Charlotte married Henry Barnett (q.v.) with the Rev. Jacob Isaacs officiating.

On 12 April 1844 the *Sydney Morning Herald* reported that J. J. Cohen had appeared in court to defend his own son, Francis (q.v.), and Baron B. Cohen (q.v.), the son of Simeon Cohen (q.v.), who, together with Henry Barnett and George Phillips (q.v.), had physically attacked a publisher named O'Brien for publishing defamatory and anti-Semitic attacks on J. J. Cohen. William Augustus Miles, author of the *Registry of Flash Men*, wrote suspiciously about 'Mead, in the service of Joel Cohen, [who is] said to be a notorious thief and purchaser of stolen property'.

In 1843 J. J. Cohen's landlord Martin Gill had denounced Cohen for paying his rent with a bad cheque and Cohen moved his shop to a new address 'in more central and commodious premises' in George Street. On 1 January 1845 he was licensed as an auctioneer. On 19 September 1844 the Jewish community rallied to protest against a proposal to institute a system of general education incorporating Christian indoctrination, and, in the *Sydney Morning Herald*, Cohen wrote a stirring public defence of Jewish rights:

> Firm as we are in the religion of our forefathers, still we must not hazard an innovation of such vital importance to our civil, political and religious liberty ... We are a scattered race, it is true—not so our faith, for we are and ever were, an individual people in our religious tenets worshipping God in one form of devotion in every part of the civilised world.

A silver salver that he manufactured was presented to Sir James Dowling on 1 November 1844.

On 2 March 1846 Cohen was elected assessor for the Bourke Ward and served on the Sydney City Council as an alderman from November 1852 to February 1853, being returned 'head of the poll' in 1852. The 1847 *Low's Directory of the City and District of Sydney* listed 'John Joel Cohen & Son' as jewellers at 479 George Street. The *Sydney Morning Herald* reported on 10 October 1851 that he had sent a consignment of gold worth £569 to London.

Cohen died on 11 June 1853, his death 'regretted by his many friends', and he was buried in the Devonshire Street Jewish Cemetery. His estate was valued at £9000.

In 1859 J. J. Cohen's daughter Hannah Julia was married in a Jewish ceremony to Solomon Cohen. Phillip Joseph Cohen (q.v.), who was not a relative, wrote in the York Street Synagogue Minutes, justifying Julia's Jewish marriage. He regarded her as 'having the highest moral character and being brought up as a strict Jewess, regular in her attendance to the Synagogue, associating with Jewish families and believing and acknowledging herself as a member of the faith'. The congregation split on the issue of the Jewish status of her baby son, and the Macquarie Street Synagogue was born.

Jessie Indent 4/5214; *Colonial Observer*, 9 February 1842; *Sydney Morning Herald*, 12 April 1843, 19 September 1844, 19 October 1844, 21 December 1844, 2 March 1846; *Australian*, 20 February 1840, 10 March 1840,

23 December 1842, 19 September 1843, 1 November 1844; J. B. Hawkins, *Australian Silver, 1800–1900*; G. F. J. Bergman,'The Bizarre Life of Mordecai Moses', *AJJHS*, vol. 8, no. 3 (1988), p. 107f, and 'Phillip Joseph Cohen 1802–64', *AJJHS*, vol. 8, no. 2 (1988), p. 70f.

COHEN, Joseph

b. Ireland
Surrey (2), 1816; Convict.

Joseph Cohen arrived on 20 December 1816. Despite his surname, he was almost certainly not Jewish.

A Joseph Cohen gave evidence in a court case in Sydney regarding damages due to a ticket of leave man who had been set upon by a clergyman in Bathurst who thought he had encountered an escaped desperado. Cohen was described as being the overseer to Captain Raine's men in Bathurst. He kept Raine's accounts and supervised the work that needed to be done. Joseph Cohen received a colonial sentence, which was commuted on 29 April 1841. Cohen was on Norfolk Island and was said to have 'behaved well'.'He has been more than twenty years in the colony and almost the same number of years in England in charge and management of all species of stock'.

On 29 May 1841 the colonial sentence was remitted and on 7 May 1842 Cohen was able to visit Sydney. By that time he had become the principal overseer of stock on Norfolk Island, but was not permitted to remain in Sydney for a lengthy period of time. Cohen was still on Norfolk Island three years later and was appointed an overseer of the stock with a salary of three shillings and sixpence aday.

Ship Indent 4/4005; *Sydney Monitor*, 5 February 1831; CS, Convicts Out Correspondence, 4/3685, Letter 42/3463; 4/2582.1, 7 May 1842; CSO 22/113/2385; CS 41/4021.

COHEN, Joseph

b. London, 1826–1893
Brothers, 1833; Free.
Single; 8 children.

Joseph was the fourth son of Henry Simeon Cohen and Elizabeth Cohen (qq.v.), and came out with his mother and siblings in December 1833.

Joseph Cohen married Mary Hart at the Sydney Synagogue on 2 October 1850. Mary Hart was the fifth daughter of Asher and Phoebe Hart (qq.v.) of Sydney. At that time Joseph was living at Armidale, New England, in New South Wales. The couple settled in Armidale and purchased town lots at Tamworth.

In 1857 Joseph Cohen was appointed a Justice of the Peace in Launceston and became an alderman of the city. His business was known as Cohen Bros, Auctioneers. He was a member of the Executive Committee of the Launceston

Bank of Savings and an officer in the Launceston Artillery Corps. He served as president of the Launceston Synagogue. He was elected to the Tasmanian House of Assembly for Launceston in 1860. At that time he was the occupier of a house and store in York Street owned by Asher (Arthur) Isaac Nathan (q.v.), who was his brother-in-law. By 1866 Joseph and his family had moved to Murrurundi where he kept a store.

Joseph and Mary Cohen were the parents of Nathan (1852–1853), Henry (1853), James Lewis (14 October 1854), born at Launceston, Rose, Edward Meyer (21 November 1857) at Launceston, Florence (9 August 1859) at Launceston, Adolphus John (1863–1865), Frank (1868) at Sydney. Joseph died in Sydney at the age of sixty-seven on 9 June 1893, and was buried at Rookwood. Mary died in 1874, at the age of 42, in Melbourne.

COHEN, Joseph Edward

b. London, 1802–1854
England, 1832; Convict; Sentenced to life, Old Bailey, 1831.
Widower; Upholsterer; Height: 177 cm; 1 child (in England).

Dark complexion, dark brown hair and whiskers, long face, high forehead, dark hazel eyes, straight long nose, large round chin. Cohen's wife had died while he was imprisoned on the hulk serving a previous sentence for stealing a watch. This time it was alleged that Cohen together with an accomplice, broke into the home of Esther Collison, who kept the White Hart public house on Ratcliff Highway. He was caught stealing money and clothes. Cohen was defended in court by a barrister and initially sentenced to death. His behaviour in gaol in England was 'bad'.

Joseph Edward Cohen arrived in Hobart Town on 19 July 1832 to begin his period of probation. On 4 February 1834, while assigned to Mr Stoneham, he was found guilty of being absent without leave, and was given a month in prison with a recommendation to do hard labour with the Launceston Chain Gang. On 23 September 1834 he was 'out after hours' and in a public house and was reprimanded. On 20 February 1837, when he was the servant of Mr Bell, he was given fourteen days hard labour in chains for being absent without leave and four days in the cells on bread and water. On 20 May 1837 he was back in the cells for seven days for having been insolent to Mr Bell. On 15 November he was not only absent without leave but also insolent to his master and given seven nights in the cells and ordered to do his normal work by day. On 12 December 1837, and again, on 20 December, he was absent without leave and ordered to spend three weeks in the cells.

Cohen received his ticket of leave on 5 January 1841. On 13 February 1841 he was given four days on the treadmill for being in a public house after hours. Another seven days hard labour on the treadmill followed for neglect of work. On 16 September 1841, while a holder of a ticket of leave, Cohen was sentenced to twenty-four hours hard labour in the House of Correction and fined £1 for having absented himself from his hired service.

Cohen died at Launceston on 10 September 1854 and was 'struck off the [convict] records'.

OBSP, 8 September 1831 case 1544. CON 34/3, no. 1402; CON 18/6; CON 31/7.

COHEN, Judah

Free.
Single.

Judah Cohen married Rose Solomon in a Jewish ceremony conducted by the Rev Jacob Isaacs at West Maitland in 1849. The witneses were Samuel Solomon and Henry Solomon.

Jewish Marriage Registry Book, Sydney.

COHEN, Leah

Free.

Mrs Leah Cohen, a widow, married William Broad, a widower of Campbell Town, in Van Diemen's Land on 25 April 1835.

CSO 1/7/288, C/Arthur File 100, 2nd volume, pp. 285, 288, 289.

COHEN, Leah

Free.
Single; 3 children.

'Leah' Cohen married Samuel Phillips (q.v.) on 2 November 1842. Leah Cohen was born 'Ellen', and must have converted to Judaism. The wedding was Jewish marriage no. 54 in New South Wales. Leah and Samuel had three children: Lewis (5 October 1843) and Lydia (17 June 1845) Joshua (17 September 1847)

Birth Register of the York Street Synagogue.

COHEN, Lewis

b. London, 1811–1884
Sovereign, 1831; Free.
Single; Tailor, draper; 11 children.

Lewis was the second child, and eldest son, of Barent and Sierlah Cohen. His siblings were Jane, Samuel (q.v.), Henry (q.v.), David (q.v.), George (q.v.), Solomon (q.v.), Abraham (q.v.), Morris (q.v.), and Charles. All the brothers, apart from Charles, settled in Australia. Lewis was the first of his siblings to arrive in Australia. He was the first cousin of Lewis Wolfe Levy (q.v.).

Lewis Cohen disembarked in Sydney on 21 February 1831 and placed an advertisement in the *Sydney Herald* announcing that he was a 'tailor and Habit Maker of Denmark Place, just arrived in Sydney from London'. Cohen applied for nine assigned servants and was granted two. In 1832 he asked for and received one servant. On 10 January 1832 Cohen announced that his partnership with Kauffman Samuel (q.v.) had been dissolved: 'I will not be responsible for any debts he may contract'.

In the *Sydney Gazette* of 15 August 1833 the marriage was announced, 'at Sydney, yesterday morning Mr P. J. Cohen, after the manner of the Jewish persuasion, Mr Lewis Cohen of George St to Mrs Sarah Hymes [*sic*] of the same place'. Sarah was the daughter of a Joseph Hyams.

Lewis Cohen prospered. In August 1837 he joined his brothers David and Samuel in partnership in Maitland. In April 1839 he opened a branch of the firm in Campbelltown and in November (1839) he dissolved the partnership, carrying on the business in Campbelltown and his tailoring business in Sydney.

Lewis Cohen pledged £10 to the Sydney Synagogue building appeal in 1839. He and Sarah had a daughter, Rose, in Melbourne in 1841. In 1843 another child was registered as having been born to Lewis and Sarah Cohen. Cohen experienced financial difficulties in the depression of the 1840s and on 10 December 1842 he filed a schedule of insolvency listing £1617 of debt and assets of £1329. He had a house in Lower George Street, Sydney, land at Campbelltown, and a home in Bridge Street, Sydney. The Minute Book of the Bridge Street Synagogue (17 August 1841 and 31 October 1841) recorded that Cohen's rooms at George Street were rented by the congregation and fitted out as a place of worship when the Bridge Street Synagogue had to be vacated and the York Street Synagogue was being built. Disaster overtook Cohen when a burglar stole £150 worth of property and he offered an inadequate reward of £10. By 23 March 1843 Cohen was officially declared to be insolvent.

The *Sydney Morning Herald* of 11 May 1844 told of Lewis Cohen, a tailor, who sued Henry Cohen of Port Macquarie, Philip Cohen, his son, and Joseph Simmons for unpaid debts. The case was brought before the Court of Requests and 'a good deal of ill feeling' arose outside the court. Apparently, Edward Cohen had challenged Lewis Cohen to a fight. Simmons tried to break it up and assailed Lewis Cohen. The young Cohen joined in and the fight became a battle between Lewis and Philip. The court awarded Lewis Cohen damages of £25.

On New Year's Day in 1845 Cohen prepared to sell all his furniture. He returned to England once again and he prospered. His nephew Louis Cohen, son of Samuel and Rachel Cohen became Lord Mayor of Liverpool.

Lewis had eleven children—four sons and seven daughters. They were Selina (1840–1930), Rose (1841), Kate (1846), Charlotte, Barnet (1844–1880), Solomon (1848–1922), David (1854–1862), Samuel, Rachel, Martha, and Jane.

Sydney Herald, 14 April 1831, 18 April 1831; *Sydney Morning Herald*, 12 December 1842, 11 May 1844, 1 January 1845; *Sydney Gazette*, 21 April 1831, 10 January 1832, 4 February 1837, 18 January 1838; *Australian*,

10 January 1834; *Maitland Mercury*, 20 September 1849; Land Correspondence 2/7827, 6 May 1840; Governors' Despatches 1832, ML, A1210, p, 191, 1833, ML, A1211, p. 632.

COHEN, Lewis

Lonach, 1833; Free; Sentenced to 7 years, Hobart Town, 1833.
Married; Dealer, tailor; 3 children.

Lewis Cohen was sentenced to colonial transportation for obtaining goods under false pretences. Stated this offence: 'embezzlement'. Cohen's family was in Hobart Town.

Lewis Cohen came free to Hobart Town, bringing with him his wife Rachael and children Sarah, Sophia and Fanny (arriving on 5 December 1833). Shortly after, Lewis Cohen was sentenced to seven years transportation to Port Arthur for obtaining goods under false pretences, and his criminal dossier began.

Cohen was obviously a defiant and difficult prisoner and the authorities did their best to 'tame' him. Between 26 December 1833 and 10 April 1834 twelve separate charges were recorded for gross insolence, neglect of duty, making a noise in his cell, obstinately persisting in making a noise in his cell, improper language and making a noise, refusing to work, indecent and improper language to the Acting Chief Constable, disgraceful language, and riotous behaviour after receiving a sentence. For these offences he received a total of 200 lashes and five weeks in solitary confinement. He spent most of 1834 and 1835 at Port Arthur, where he served twenty-two days in solitary confinement for 'privately working on the Sabbath Day','privately working in the Sailor's Shop'and, on 5 November 1834, 'Obstinately persisting in leaving his Gang against the Orders of his Overseer'. He was therefore sentenced to five days in solitary confinement.

Astonishingly, his plight was brought to the attention of the general public by the 'police reporter', writing in the January issue of the *Tasmanian Review*:

> It is impossible but to pity that unfortunate man Lewis Cohen, who we find, has been punished several times for minor offences and above all flogged for insolence. Some allowances should be made for unfortunate men of the description such as Cohen, who labouring under every privation and suffering, may be expected to give way to occasional bursts of passion, at being subjected to the control of some of the characters that are too often placed over them.

On 8 June 1836 Cohen was returned to the Crown by the Van Diemen's Land Company as ruptures rendered him 'useless' for suitable work. He was assigned to Mr Thomson until, on 12 August 1836, the surgeon reported that he was fit to be returned to government service. He was sent to the Grass Tree Hill Road Party where he remained until the end of the year. He spent 1837 and 1838 as an assigned servant, with one month hard labour at Reibey's Ford in October, after which he was sent to Launceston. On 28 June 1839, while an assigned servant to Mr Fletcher, he spent six hours in the Launceston stocks for disorderly conduct. On 16 August that year Cohen sold 'a pair of trousers that were not his', and received a further sentence of six months in the chain gang at Perth. During this service he received thirty-six lashes for disobedience and an extra month's labour in chains for 'interrupting people on the roads'. On 28 June 1839 Cohen was sentenced to spend six hours of public humiliation in the stocks for 'disorderly conduct'. On 23 May 1840, as a member of a road party, he was sentenced to ten days on the treadmill for being drunk. He received a certificate of freedom in 1841.

On 27 July 1843 an embittered Cohen charged his wife with bigamy. While Cohen was in prison, Rachael had formed a relationship with a musician named Rolfe who lived in Pitt Street, Sydney. She had left Hobart Town and, on 23 August 1842, had married Mr Rolfe. Cohen promptly arrived in Sydney, accepted £20 to keep quiet about her status, and then, changing his mind, charged her with bigamy, stating that he would produce witnesses who had been at their own wedding in the Great Synagogue in London (*Australasian Chronicle*, 22 July 1843). On 4 June 1844 Cohen was still assigned to the Public Works Department when he was found to have nineteen shillings and eleven pence 'improperly in his possession'. The money was confiscated.

Surprisingly, Cohen was persuaded to run for public office in the Launceston municipal elections of 1863. He owned a drapery and dry goods store and was licensed as an auctioneer. The *Launceston Examiner* wrote of his 'long connection with the town, active business habit, and the general respect in which you are held by the burgesses'. Cohen was elected and served as an alderman for a year. In his essay in *A Few from Afar*, Stefan Petrow writes 'He rarely spoke during municipal debates and mostly seconded the motions of other aldermen. Was he reticent to talk about issues of which he had little knowledge, or was he a duck out of water, unhappy with being exposed to the public spotlight? The latter seems more likely'.

Lewis Cohen was more comfortable within the small Launceston Jewish community and served as president of the congregation from 1864 to 1871 (when the synagogue closed its doors and sent its scrolls and items of religious value to the congregation in Hobart).

CON 31/1 no. 1656; CON 32/1 no 1656; *Hobart Town Colonist*, 10 December 1833; *Tasmanian and Austral-Asiatic Review*, January 1834; CF 1848 no. 58; *Australasian Chronicle*, 22 July 1843; *Launceston Examiner*, 3 December 1863, 29 November 1864; Stefan Petrow, 'Fearless and Independent Jews Elected to Public Office in Tasmania 1855–1902', in P. Elias and A. Elias (eds), *A Few from Afar*, p. 103.

COHEN, Lewis

b. London, 1831–1903
Brothers, 1833; Free.
Single; Dealer; 12 children.

Lewis Cohen came out to Van Diemen's Land with his mother, Elizabeth Cohen (q.v.), and nine siblings (he was the fifth son in the family), to join his father Henry Simeon Cohen (q.v.), an assigned convict living in Port Macquarie. He remained in Port Macquarie until the early 1850s. On 22 March 1854 he married Mary Frankel, the eldest daughter of Jacob and Miriam Frankel (qq.v.). The family settled in Launceston where Lewis was granted an auctioneer's licence on

9 February 1857 for his business 'Lewis Cohen & Co, auctioneers, York Street, Launceston.

The family moved to Sydney in 1875. Lewis Cohen died in Sydney in 1903.

Ten of the twelve children of Lewis and Mary were Sarah (1855), Fanny (11 August 1856), Sophia (1858), Minnie (15 January 1860), Albert Henry (1862), Nathan Sidney (10 December 1863), Amy Louise (11 September 1865–1872), Edward George (1 July 1867), Elizabeth Maud (1869), Harry Percival (1871), William Lawrence (1874–1939), and Estella Myra (1876).

Henry Cohen and family by Philip Charles Cohen (privately printed).

COHEN, Mark

Free.

In 1845 Mark Cohen gave £5 to the new Sydney Synagogue in York Street.

COHEN, Mary

Free.
Single.

Mary Cohen married James Bromhall at Longford in Van Diemen's Land on 19 February 1838.

COHEN, Mary

b. London, 1787
Canada (2), 1810; Convict; Sentenced to 7 years, Old Bailey, 1809.
Married; Servant; 1 child.

Mary Cohen was a prostitute who stole two pound notes, a shilling and four sixpences from a drunken passerby she had accosted in the 'Minories'. Her husband was out of work. She had a babe in arms and was 'known to the Police'. The prosecutor begged the Lord Mayor not to prosecute on account of the child. Cohen was sentenced on 28 June 1809.

Mary Cohen arrived in Sydney on 10 September 1810 and was assigned to the Parramatta Hospital where, in 1811, she worked as a nurse. In the 1814 Muster, Mary Cohen was listed as a convict, and 'wife to Mark Russell'. At the Criminal Court in Sydney on 4 July 1829 she received a seven-year sentence of colonial transportation for 'stealing in a dwelling house' and was sent to Moreton Bay. She petitioned the Colonial Secretary for a remission of her sentence in July 1835 due to the length of her servitude and her 'good conduct'. The ticket of leave was granted and she was returned to Sydney on 7 November 1835.

OBSP, 1808–09, case 588, p. 379; Ship Indent 4/4004, p. 337; Proceedings of the (Sydney) Bench of Magistrates, 1806–1812, ML, 1/300, 23 November 1811; CS 35/4932, I/7/35, 4/2287.1; Chronological Register of Convicts at Moreton Bay, no. 1950; TL 35/247.

COHEN, Mary Ann

b. Sydney, 1829

Born in New South Wales in 1829, Mary Ann was probably the daughter of Samuel Cohen (q.v.), who arrived as a convict on the *Guildford* in 1824. Mary Cohen was apprenticed from the Parramatta Orphan School on 2 June 1846 to become a 'House Servant' to Mr R. C. Gore of Darling Downs, who was a barrister at law. She was said to be thirteen years old. However, according to the Permission to Marry Book, in 1847 she was eighteen years old, and 'of age', when she married the emancipist Henry Budge (who was thirty-three, had arrived on the *Hooghly* with a life sentence and by that time held a ticket of leave). The Windsor Church of England records stated that Mary Ann Cohen, aged eighteen, 'native of the Colony', was married on 28 May 1847 by the Rev. Adam.

Orphan Schools 1846, 4/2737.3, 46/4039; Permission to Marry Book, 1847, p. 147, ML, 4/4514.

COHEN, Michael

b. London, 1807–1845
John I (2), 1829; Convict; Sentenced to life, Westminster, 1828.
Single; Clothes dealer; Height: 160 cm.

Dark ruddy complexion, slightly pock-pitted, dark brown hair, blue eyes, Jew, perpendicular scar on left cheek, large dark mole on right arm. Convicted at Westminster on 11 September 1828 of highway robbery, Michael Cohen was one of a group of seven or eight young men and women who jostled a passerby at night and stole a watch. Cohen was caught with the watch in his hand. He was described as a 'fruit seller'. He had a previous conviction.

Michael Cohen arrived in Sydney on 13 September 1829, and was assigned to Messrs Perkins and Liddington. On 2 October 1837 he was granted a ticket of leave and the following year was permitted to move to Campbell Town. A conditional pardon was granted on 1 October 1842.

The *Registry of Flash Men* listed him as a publican of Campbell Town, alleged to be a member of bushranger Michael Cavanagh's gang of Church Hill and he was said to have made £130 buying and selling stolen linen. There is a record of a John Cooke (alias Michael Cohen) who was charged with an outrageous assault upon a female and was 'recognised' as the 'notorious bushranger Cohen who has been at large for a long period'. Cohen was remanded to the Hyde Park Barracks. The two Michael Cohens may have been confused with each other. On 5 October 1842, the *Sydney Morning Herald* referred to Michael Cohen as 'the notorious gambling barber'. This was probably a reference to Moses Cohen (q.v.) who, on 9 January 1841, was convicted of 'keeping a gambling house'.

In 1840 Michael Cohen had apparently married Elizabeth Crane at St Luke's Church of England, Liverpool. On March 1843 the *Sydney Morning Herald* reported that 'his reputed wife', Elizabeth, was charged with bigamy, as she was already married to Isaac Crane. However, she was acquitted when it was discovered that she had been 'merely' Cohen's mistress.

Michael Cohen died at Sydney on 26 February 1845.

OBSP, 1827–28, case 1754, p. 821; Ship Indent 4/4014, p. 224; 4/4115, 2 October 1837; TL 37/1472; CP 43/221; *Commercial Journal and Advertiser*, 5 February 1840; *Sydney Morning Herald*, 7 May 1844; Governors' Despatches, A1291, p. 339; HO 10/53, Reel 938, 1456–95; W. A. Miles, *Registry of Flash Men*, pp. 21, 41.

COHEN, Michael

d. 1867
Mary Ann, 1832; Free.
Single; Dealer; 8 children.

Michael Cohen arrived in Port Jackson on 15 May 1832. A publican's licence was granted to Michael Cohen on 7 May 1844 and he became the proprietor of the Glasgow Hotel at the corner of Park and Pitt streets in 1844 or 1845. He gave £5 to the Sydney Synagogue building appeal in 1839, when he was listed as living in Campbelltown. He was a seat holder in the synagogue from 1845 to 1848.

Michael Cohen married Priscilla Solomon (the eldest daughter of Elias and Fanny Solomon of Edgware Road, London) at the York Street Synagogue on 1 September 1847. The following year, Michael and Priscilla Cohen of Maitland West registered their newborn child Henry F. as a 'Hebrew'. Sarah was born in 1849 in Scone, Rachael in Paterson in 1851, Charles in 1853 in Sydney, Esther (Eveline) in 1855, Lazarus in 1857, and Nathan in 1863.

In the 1851 Sydney Directory, Michael Cohen was listed as the owner of the Glasgow Hotel at 167 Pitt Street. He died in Sydney, at his home at the Glasgow Hotel, on 28 January 1867, and his grave is to be found in the Jewish section of the Rookwood Cemetery. He was described as 'an old and respected colonist', who left a wife and eight children.

Sydney Morning Herald, 4 March 1843, 16 October 1844, 7 April 1845; *Commercial Journal and Advertiser*, 5 February 1840.

COHEN, Mordecai

b. London, 1806
Dromedary, 1820; Convict; Sentenced to 7 years, London, 1818.
Single; Pencil-maker; Height: 156 cm.

Mordecai Cohen, aged thirteen, entered a tailor's shop in Bishopsgate Street at 11:30 p.m., just as the tailor was shutting up shop for the night, and asked for a second-hand pair of braces. The tailor became suspicious and discovered eight yards of cloth hidden under the boy's apron. Cohen was sentenced on 6 May 1818 but, 'because of his youth', he remained in a London gaol for one year before being sent to Australia.

Cohen arrived in Van Diemen's Land on 10 January 1820. On 7 March Cohen was sentenced for 'neglect of duty' to fourteen days service to the government 'in his own time'. On 17 August, Cohen was found guilty of grand larceny and sentenced to seven years transportation. On 20 October 1821 he was convicted for passing counterfeit dollars, and was sentenced 'to be sent to a distant part of the colony'. From early 1822 to 1832 Cohen was a prisoner at Sarah Island in Macquarie Harbour on the west coast of Van Diemen's Land, and in that harsh environment he received twelve sentences of twenty-five to fifty lashes each, for neglect of duty, gambling, false testimony and theft. In 1825 he was returned to Hobart Town and within six months (on 20 December of that year) was sentenced at the Supreme Court to seven years imprisonment and sent back to Macquarie Harbour. On 13 October 1826 Cohen received eighteen lashes for striking a fellow prisoner. On 11 April 1827 he received fifty lashes for saying that he had been bribed by an official to give false evidence. On 23 July 1831 he received twenty-five lashes for disobedience, and on 15 October he was given twenty-five lashes for the crime of being absent from his work gang and having been 'found fishing on a catamaran in Farm Bay'.

Mordecai Cohen, a passenger on the schooner *Edward*, arrived in Launceston from Circular Head, according to the *True Colonist* of 5 August 1834. It is difficult to believe that this is the same man.

OBSP, 1817–18, case 778, p. 252; Ship Indent 2/8253, p. 219; Ship Indent 4/4007, p. 61; CON 31/6; CON 23/1; HO 10/43; *Hobart Town Gazette*, 27 October 1821; *Sydney Gazette*, 20 December 1825, 12 January 1826.

COHEN, Morrice Robertson

1820–1881
1846; Free.
Single; Dealer and Hebrew teacher.

Morrice Robertson Cohen arrived in Hobart Town in 1846, the year after the synagogue had been consecrated, and briefly served as its first minister. Three years later, on 29 August 1849, Cohen married Julia Hort, the daughter of the pious Abraham Hort (q.v.), previously of New Zealand. It was the first marriage in the new Argyle Street Synagogue. In 1853 the Hobart congregation appointed the Rev. Herman Hoelzel as their minister. He had been authorised, by the Chief Rabbi in London, to be the 'Presiding Rabbi of the Australian Colonies'.

Hoelzel's appointment caused dismay in New South Wales, as the community had been negotiating with Hoelzel and assumed it was the senior Australian Jewish community. With Hoelzel's appointment, Morrice Cohen moved to Sydney, where he acted as the 'reader' of the congregation, and applied for that recently vacated position. Cohen was not appointed to the senior post but Hoelzel stayed in Sydney for two years. With his departure, Morrice Cohen became briefly the minister of the York Street Synagogue—he stumbled into the crisis over the Jewish status of J. J. Cohen's (q.v.) child, which split the congregation in two. Arising out of this, he was soundly abused by Samuel Cohen (q.v.), who at that time was a Justice of the Peace. In January 1860, standing on the pavement opposite the synagogue Samuel

Cohen shouted: 'You dammed scoundrel, you have returned from the country have you? How many children did you bastardise there? You are the biggest liar, thief and scoundrel in New South Wales! Samuel Cohen was fined £3 by a fellow Sydney magistrate.

Morrice Cohen founded the Zion House School, a private primary day school, which was conducted in association with the York Street Synagogue and which taught both secular and religious subjects. In 1855 he published a textbook, *The Principles of Judaism*, which was the first of its kind in Australia.

A 'Morris Cohen', son of Isaac and Sarah, was buried in Sydney in 1881.

Hobart Town Chronicle, 1 September 1849.

COHEN, Morris

b. London, 1827–1878
Free.
Single; Dealer; 10 children.

The ninth child of Barent and Sierlah Cohen of London and brother to Jane, Lewis (q.v.), Samuel (q.v.), Henry (q.v.), David (q.v.), George (q.v.), Solomon (q.v.), Abraham (q.v.) and Charles, Morris Cohen married Deborah Reuben in 1856. She was the daughter of Henry Reuben (q.v.) and Emma (Hannah) (née Solomon, q.v.), and was born in Sydney in June 1839. Morris and Deborah had four sons and six daughters: Burnett, Celia, Emma, Ida, Florence, Blanche, Harry, Cecil, Vivian, and Karl.

Morris died in Maitland on 22 August 1878.

COHEN, Mosely Moss

b. Birmingham, 1812–1895
Alexander, 1828; Free.
Single; Jeweller and silversmith; 5 children.

Mosely Moss Cohen was the son of Simeon and Hannah Cohen of Birmingham, former brother-in-law of John Joel Cohen (q.v.), and brother of Edward Daniel Cohen (q.v.), who arrived as a convict in 1830. His nephew, Joseph Leader (q.v.), was sent out as a convict in 1839. Mosely travelled steerage on the *Alexander* in 1828.

Mosely M. Cohen set himself up in business as a jeweller at 3 Denmark Place in Sydney. He advertised: 'M. M. Cohen & Co. Chronometer, Watch and clock, gold and silversmith opposite to Church Hill, George St has taken over [Moses] Brown's business as new settlers in the colony'. Cohen worked from rented premises above a George Street shop. In the *New South Wales Calendar and General Post Office Directory, 1833*, he was listed as a watchmaker and jeweller at 3 Denmark Place, the former home of Lewis Cohen (q.v.), who had moved to 1 Denmark Place. On the other side was Mr Hyam (no. 5), then Henry Cohen (no. 7). In 1833 Cohen asked for an assigned servant but failed to get one. In 1834 he asked for three servants and was allotted one.

On 20 November 1832, M. M. Cohen married Caroline Pendray, the daughter of a Mr Pendray, of George Street, Sydney. The wedding was held at Sydney's Scots Church.

Cohen moved to Denmark Place, George Street, making and mending jewellery, repairing watches and musical boxes, and selling a choice selection of dress ornaments. According to the *Sydney Morning Herald* of 22 June 1843, M.M.Cohen,'a jeweller near Bridge St will sell his stock on his retirement from the retail trade'. The business prospered and Cohen invested in rural land.

John Joel Cohen, the widowed and remarried husband of Mosely's sister Rebecca, obviously caused M. M. Cohen great discomfort. J. J. Cohen owned the Temple of Fashion in George Street and was evicted from his premises in 1843 for non-payment of rent and the presentation of a dishonoured cheque.

M. M. Cohen immediately advertised that he had no connection with his former brother-in-law.

M. M. Cohen was the first to advertise the samples of gold brought into Sydney by the shepherd Hugh McGregor. The *Registry of Flash Men* tells the story of 'Kemp [a thief] who sold a splendid ring to Cohen the jeweller in George St who has a brother bye the bye at Port Macquarie. The ring is on sale at his shop for £250!'

In 1844 Cohen retired from business to live on his estate of Caridale. Cohen stood for election for the Parramatta Council (*Cumberland Times*, 2 May 1846) and was the returning officer for the first election of aldermen in 1874. M. M. Cohen had no connection with the organised Jewish community in Sydney. The children of M. M. Cohen and Caroline were George (1835), Henry (1837), Caroline (1841), Alfred (1851), and Charles (1855).

Mosely Moss Cohen died at 'Mossworth' in Cooper Street, Burwood, on 3 September 1895.

Ship Indent 4/5203; Lynette Ramsay Silver, 'The Brothers Cohen—Unlauded Entrepreneurs', *AJJHS*, vol. 10, no. 1 (1986), p. 57f; J. B. Hawkins, *Australian Silver, 1800–1900*; W. A. Miles, *Registry of Flash Men*, p. 4.

COHEN, Moses

b. Whitechapel, 1805–1881
Arab I (1), 1822; Convict; Sentenced to life, Old Bailey, 1822.
Errand boy; Height: 160 cm; 5 children.

Fresh complexion, grey eyes, brown hair. Moses Cohen stole a woman's handbag at London-fields, Hackney. Cohen was described, at the trial, as an orange seller, aged seventeen. He was sentenced on 20 February 1822. A school was formed on board the convict transport, and the teacher's records have survived for Moses Cohen and David Jacobs (q.v.). Cohen began as a 'tolerably steady' student but was rather irregular in attendance. He made progress in reading and arithmetic, and was judged to be 'orderly and much improved' by the time the ship reached Sydney.

The convict transport ship *Arab* arrived in Van Diemen's Land on 6 November 1822, where Moses Cohen spent his initial years assigned to various road gangs. On 24 July 1827 he was caught trying to steal a government boat while absent from his hut and sent for three months work on a chain gang. The sentence was extended by a month in September for 'defacing his irons'. On 13 December 1827, stolen property was found in his possession and he was sent to the Public Works at Brighton. On 1 April 1829 he was absent from the muster, sentenced to fifty lashes and placed in the 'No. 1 Chain Gang' for three months. A further twenty-five lashes were ordered when, in October 1829, he was absent from the muster of the boat's crew.

Five years later, on 20 May 1834, Cohen was found out after hours at the Green Gate public house, and even though he was in possession of a ticket of leave, he was officially reprimanded. He received a conditional pardon (no. 1616) on 27 February 1838 and a free pardon (no. 131) on 20 October 1842.

Cohen wrote to Lieutenant Governor Sir John Franklin on 3 November 1842: 'When Your Excellency was up at Mr Gibson's Epping Forest in the month of January 1838 you very kindly promised that you would do anything that lay within your power for me. I ask your gracious indulgence to proceed to Port Phillip and return'. Cohen was at the Mogul Tavern in Argyle Street, Hobart Town. On 10 June 1846 Moses Cohen married Elizabeth Lazarus, the sister of Julia (q.v.) (who was illiterate and over twenty-one years of age). They had a daughter, Elizabeth, who was born in Hobart Town on 7 December 1848. A son, Eleazar, died on 13 January 1850, the first day of his life. Hannah was born on 5 May 1854, and Simon on 18 April 1851 (died 8 January 1854). Moses was a 'dealer', who donated one guinea to the synagogue building appeal in 1845, and was a member of the synagogue from 1845 to 1847. He was listed as a founder of the Tasmanian Hebrew Benevolent Institute in 1847.

Moses Cohen, 'Free by Servitude', announced that he would leave Van Diemen's Land on 3 March 1850. However, this did not occur. 'M. Cohen' of Davey Street was listed in the 1852 *Hobart Town Directory and General Guide*. A Moses Cohen, aged seventy-nine (he was actually seventy-six), was buried in Hobart on 19 December 1881.

OBSP, 1821–22, case 452, p. 214; *Arab I* (1) Indent 2/8241, p. 140; CON 31/6; CON 23/1; HO 11/4; CS 4/1753, p. 198; CSO 8/68/1566, 3 November 1842; CSO 1/403/9104; *Hobart Town Courier*, 21 February 1840.

COHEN, Moses

b. Spitalfields, 1826

Joseph Somes (1), 1846; Convict; Sentenced to 10 years, Central Criminal Court, 1844.
Single; Cigar-maker; Height: 157.5 cm; 1 child.

Fresh complexion, brown hair, no whiskers, dark brown eyebrows, grey eyes, small mouth, small nose, long chin. Slightly pock-pitted. Moses Cohen was charged with the offence of 'Stealing clothes from Mr Brien at Aldgate for a pair of boots'. He had served a previous gaol sentence of three months. He could read and write. He was 'a converted Jew', who was now a Protestant.

Unusually, Cohen was classified as a pass holder upon his arrival in Hobart Town on 20 May 1846. On 1 December 1846, Cohen officially received his ticket of leave. On 22 August 1848 he was admonished for 'misconduct'. He had been recommended for a conditional pardon only a few weeks before. The recommendation read: 'Has committed no offence. Served 3 years and 9 months of a seven year sentence'.

Moses Cohen, aged twenty-one, married Bridget McCann (who had arrived as a convict on the *Waverley*) at Launceston on 30 July 1849. Moses and Bridget Cohen had a son, Moses Henry Cohen, on 30 April 1850.

CON 33/77; CON 14/35; CON 18/45; CON 52/3, p. 71; HO 10/61, p. 113.

COHEN, Moses

Free.
Barber.

On 9 January 1841, Moses Cohen was convicted of keeping a common gambling house in Clarence Street, Sydney. He was sentenced to two months in the Sydney prison and fined £50. In default of payment of the fine, he received a further five months in gaol. On 5 October 1842, in the *Sydney Morning Herald*, he was described as 'the notorious gambling barber admonished by the Police Court'.

Commercial Journal and Advertiser, 13 January 1841; *Sydney Morning Herald*, 5 October 1842; *Australian*, 9 January 1841.

COHEN, Nancy

b. London, 1832–1866
Brothers, 1830; Free.
7 children.

The eldest daughter of Henry Simeon Cohen and Elizabeth (qq.v). Nancy married Joseph Simmons (q.v.) in London. Joseph had travelled from Australia hoping to marry her. The young couple then migrated to Australia with her mother and her siblings when her father was sent to Australia as a convict.

Nancy Simmons died at Collingwood, Victoria, 1 April 1866.

COHEN, Nathan

Countess of Harcourt (1), 1821; Convict; Sentenced to 7 years, Surrey, 1820.
Single; Tailor; Height: 153 cm.

Dark complexion, dark hair, dark brown eyes. Tattoos AC NC. Man and woman on right arm. A Jew. Nathan Cohen was sentenced at the Surrey Assizes on 17 July 1820.

In 1825 Nathan Cohen was a servant to the Rev. Mansfield and about to proceed from Hobart Town to Sydney, and it was asked that all claims against Cohen should be lodged immediately. On 3 March 1827 it was reported that Nathan Cohen had been charged with being out late at night after curfew. He claimed 'he had been fitting a coat in Rosemary Lane'. He was doing farm work following his colonial sentence.

Hobart Town Gazette, 20 May 1825; CON 23/1, no. 387; *Sydney Gazette*, 3 March 1827.

COHEN, Nathan

b. Port Macquarie, 1842–1910
7 children.

The grandson of Henry and Elizabeth Cohen (qqv.) and son of Abraham and Sophia Cohen (qq.v.) of Port Macquarie. He was born at Port Macquarie on 10 July 1842 and came to Tamworth at the age of sixteen, and lived there for the next fifty years, becoming its best-known Jewish resident and a 'founding father'of the town. He was first employed by his uncle, William Cohen (q.v.). After the death of his uncle, Nathan managed the business on behalf of his aunt, but in 1872 established his own business as auctioneer and agent. Nathan Cohen married two sisters in succession, Esther (born in 1846, and died in childbirth in December 1880) and Deborah; they were the daughters of Solomon Solomon (q.v.) of Eden. The Municipal Council of Tamworth was formed in 1876 and Cohen was an elected member. He was twice mayor of Tamworth, in 1882 and 1883. High Holyday services were held in his home at 'Brighton', 98 Carthage Street, from the 1870s.

Cohen was active in many local companies. He was chairman of the Tamworth Gas and Coke Co. He was on the Board of the Centenary Coal and Coke Co., and the Green Mount Land and Quarry Co. He helped in the creation of the Tamworth Hospital, was president of the Cricket Club and a trustee of the Jockey Club. From 1875 to 1895, Nathan Cohen was in a business partnership with David Nathan, who had married Abraham Cohen's daughter Sierlah, and who was probably the son of Asher (Arthur) Isaac Nathan and Caroline née Cohen (qq.v.). From 1895 to 1908 Cohen operated the business on his own. The dairy industry in the Peel Valley was founded by Nathan Cohen, who introduced Jersey cattle into the district and operated a butter factory.

Cohen died on 15 August 1910 and was buried in the Jewish section of Rookwood Cemetery next to his first wife. His second wife, Deborah (his first wife's sister) and seven children survived him. He was described as 'one of the old Patriarchs of his own noble race'. Deborah died, aged ninety-nine, on 19 February 1942, 'wife of late Nathan Cohen of Tamworth, stone erected by Eliot and Alice'.

Nathan's children with Esther were Ida (1867–1970), who married her first cousin Victor Isaac Cohen, the son of George Cohen (q.v.) and his wife Elizabeth, Alice (1860–1955), Percy (1870–1954), and Cora Rose (1873–1957), who married (Harry) David Cohen of Eden. Deborah had one son, Eliot Tamworth Cohen, who was born in 1883 and died unmarried at Tamworth on 6 October 1971.

I. Porush, 'The Jews of Tamworth', *AJJHS*, vol. 3, no. 4 (1950), p. 193f; W. Newman and L. Green, *Tamworth: A Pictorial History*, pp. 33, 74, 232.

COHEN, Philip

b. London, 1825–1898
Brothers, 1833; Free.
13 children.

Philip Cohen was the third son of Henry and Elizabeth Cohen (qq.v.), and arrived in New South Wales with his mother and nine siblings in December 1833. His father was at Port Macquarie as an assigned convict servant.

Philip Cohen set up a business in Armidale, New South Wales. The *Maitland Mercury* advertised the sale of a thoroughbred horse, 'Alhambro', owned by Cohen. He was listed as a seat holder in the Sydney Synagogue in 1845. On 5 February 1851, Miss Jessie Solomon, the daughter of the late Henry L. Solomon of Hobart Town, married Philip Cohen of Armidale, New South Wales, at the home of David Benjamin, Eastern Hill, Melbourne. It was Victoria's tenth Jewish wedding. Jessie (c. 1833–1916) was nineteen years old.

Philip Cohen was the first licensee of the Pier Hotel, Manly, and held the licence from 1856 to 1860. From 1861 to 1878 the family lived in Launceston and in Melbourne. From 1880 to 1884 Cohen was the licensee of the Steyne Hotel, Manly. Philip had evidently worked with his brother, Edward Aaron Cohen (q.v.), from 1864 to 1877, returning to New South Wales following Edward's death. He had an interest in anthropology and ichthyology and published a study, *The Marine Fish and Fisheries of New South Wales, Past and Present, in their Commercial Aspect* (1892), and *Early Day Aborigines* (1894).

Philip and Jessie had thirteen children: Fanny (c. 1852), Esther (1854), Sarah (1856–1930), Benjamin Henry (1858–1899), Joseph (c. 1859–1921), Arthur (1862), Elizabeth Annie (1862), Amy (1864–1885), Flora Sophia (1866–1926), Nathan Edward (1868–1868), Ernest (1870–1876), William (1871–1923), and Albert (1877–1878). Philip died at Manly on 6 February 1898 at 73 years of age and was buried at Rookwood. He was described as a 'retired oyster merchant'. Jessie died on 15 July 1916 at the age of eighty-two and is buried in the Jewish section at Rookwood.

Hobart Town Chronicle, 26 February 1851; Archives of the Australian Jewish Historical Society, Sydney.

COHEN, Phillip Joseph

b. Cambridge, 1802–1864
Alexander Henry, 1828; Free.
Single; Dealer; 13 children.

The stepbrother of Simeon Joseph Cohen (q.v.) and brother of Henry Joseph Cohen (q.v.), P. J. Cohen was born in Cambridge, the son of a Jewish pedlar. Before he left England he spent some months at the office of the *Beth Din* and took with him a certificate from Chief Rabbi Solomon Herschell, which allowed him to conduct marriages and grant Jewish divorces. He arrived on 17 May 1828 on the brig *Alexander Henry*, with Lawrence Joseph Spyer (q.v.).

The *Sydney Gazette* (19 May 1828) said it was believed that P. J. Cohen had travelled to Australia under the 'auspices' of Messrs Rothschild. Cohen promptly denied the rumour. At the end of July the firm of Cohen and Spyer had taken over 'extensive premises next to the Custom House, George St', at the corner of what is now Martin Place. In September, P. J. Cohen visited Hobart Town on business, returning to Sydney in November 1828. By January 1829, 'Cohen and Spyers' were advertising that they were opening goods 'received from their friends in England'.

Cohen officiated at the Passover services held in Sydney at 'one of his large rooms as a temporary synagogue' and earned his place in the history of Australian Jewry by his pioneer effort. However, his business was not prospering. On 24 July 1830 Cohen sold his newly purchased shares in the Bank of New South Wales to Joseph Barrow Montefiore (q.v.).

P. J. Cohen then settled in Maitland and, in 1831, asked the government for five assigned convicts. He was given two. The following year he asked for three and received two. In 1833 he was assigned one convict. In that year he asked for a grant of land adjoining the grant of Joseph Barrow Montefiore. On 27 February 1829 he had written confirming that he had capital amounting to £2552 in partnership with Mr Spyers: 'They are both merchants and retail dealers and they have stock worth £8000'. Michael Phillips (q.v.) attested to this: 'The goods are mostly paid for. Cohen has no intention of leaving business and has engaged a free man and his wife to reside at his property'. However, the Cohen and Spyer partnership was dissolved on 31 March 1831; Horatio Samuel (q.v.) and Michael Phillips witnessed the document. On 1 March 1831 'Cohen and Spyer' had been listed as insolvent, and all claims were to be directed to the 'acting trustee', Michael Phillips. On 15 May 1832 Phillips published a notice in the *Sydney Gazette* addressed to Phillip Joseph Cohen demanding rent for the space he had taken in his warehouse for over a year.

Cohen married Annette Abigail Levien on 9 October 1833. It was Sydney's fourth Jewish marriage, and Michael Phillips officiated. Annette was seventeen. She was the daughter of Solomon and Harriet Levien (qq.v.), and a granddaughter of the Anglo-Jewish banking family, the Goldsmids. Cohen had officiated at the first Jewish marriage, but chose not to officiate at the second wedding because it involved a convert to Judaism.

Cohen opened a soap factory in Maitland in 1833 and by October 1835 had become deputy postmaster at Maitland, as his brother-in-law, Alfred Levien (q.v.), had resigned to accept a situation in private employment that took him from the district. In 1839 Cohen gave £20 to the York Street building fund. In 1840 he was accused of 'chicanery', having attempted to change the time of mail departures for the Hunter area after signing a contract for the year of 1841. In April 1842 Cohen was listed as the publican of the Rose Inn in West Maitland. In July 1843 he was judged to be insolvent, with debts of £4178, and was discharged from bankruptcy on 24 December 1843. Cohen then left Maitland to become the publican of the commodious Saracen's Head Hotel, at the corner of Sussex and King streets, which advertised daily that 'Turtle Soup' would be available.

Cohen donated a Torah pointer to the York Street Synagogue and, together with Michael Phillips and J. B. Montefiore, became a trustee of the 'Jewish Burial Ground' (in Devonshire Street).

He was a member of the Synagogue Committee in 1837 and again from 1845. When the congregation split in 1859, he became the second president of the Macquarie Street congregation. The York Street congregation rescinded the resolution of 12 October 1835 that made Cohen 'a perpetual member of all committees of the York St Synagogue'. Towards the end of his life Cohen became the general manager of the Hunter River Steam Navigation Co.

Phillip Joseph Cohen died on 13 November 1864, and was buried in the Devonshire Street Jewish Cemetery; his grave is now to be found at Rookwood Cemetery. Annette died in Sydney on 2 January 1867. Their children were: Catherine (10 December 1834), born at West Maitland, married Philip J. Solomon of Goulburn, and died 21 February 1910; Harriet (10 October 1836 to 1921); Henrietta (15 July 1838), born West Maitland, married her first cousin, Robert Levien, and died at Nelson, New Zealand, in 1909; David (8 April 1840), at Maitland, died at Camden Park in 1886; Sydney (27 March 1842 to 20 April 1904), born at West Maitland; Frank (Francis) (1844–1922), married Esther Phillips in Auckland, New Zealand; Phoebe (1846 to 12 October 1848); Fanny (1848), born in Sydney; Edith Esther (February 1848), died in infancy; Janet (1850), married Harry Rouse in 1880, and was buried as a member of the Church of England in 1919; Victor (1851–1941), married Deborah Levey in 1878; Matilda Rebecca (born on the 'eve of Passover' 1854), who married twice, and was baptised in New Zealand; and Edward (1861), who married Minnie Rosenthal Raphael in 1887.

When the time came to publish the first history of the Jewish community of New South Wales in the *Report of the Committee of the York St Synagogue of 1845*, P. J. Cohen boasted that he had inaugurated Jewish worship in Australia, a claim that glossed over the efforts of many others. He said that his ambition had been to set 'himself to work he consummated the hope of his life, by drawing together the Jewish residents for Holy Worship and thus founded the nucleus of the first Hebrew congregation in the Antipodes'.

2/7827, 7 February 1833; CS 35/6942, 24 August 1835; 4/2512.2, 40/13045; 4/2295-35/6942, 24 August 1835; *Sydney Gazette*, 19 May 1828, 19 August 1828, 3 December 1828, 8 April 1830, 24 July 1830, 31 March 1831, 15 May 1832, 10 September 1833; *Sydney Morning Herald*, 8 April 1830, 27 April 1842, 8 July 1844, 10 September 1844, 15 July 1845; *Australian*, 8 July 1831, 13 January 1833, 24 May 1833, 27 October 1833, 31 December 1836, 14 July 1838; G. F. J. Bergman, 'Philip Joseph Cohen', *AJJHS*, vol. 8, no. 2 (1975), p. 48f; *AG*, pp. 151–2, 155–6, 159, 174–6, 178, 306–7.

COHEN, Rachael

b. London, 1819–1864
Free.
Single; 7 children.

Rachael was the eldest daughter of Samuel Cohen and Hannah (the daughter of Samuel Moss Solomon). Rachael (Rachel) Cohen married her first cousin, Judah

Moss Solomon (q.v.), the son of Moss and Betsey Solomon, in 1842. Rachael died on 9 January 1864 at her residence in Franklin Street, Adelaide, at the age of forty-four. She was survived by her husband, the Hon. Judah Moss Solomon, and her seven children.

Observer, 16 January 1864.

COHEN, Rachael

1833; Free.
Married; 3 children.

Rachael Cohen, with her husband, Lewis Cohen (q.v), and children Sarah, Sophia and Fanny, had migrated to Van Diemen's Land, arriving in Hobart Town on 5 December 1833. After a very short time, Lewis was charged with obtaining goods under false pretences and sent to Port Arthur. During his imprisonment, Rachael fell in love with a musician named Rolfe, moved to Sydney and formally married her lover! When her husband Lewis Cohen received his certificate of freedom in 1841 and discovered her actions, he charged her with bigamy.

Australasian Chronicle, 22 July 1843.

COHEN, Raphael

b. London, 1814
Australasian Packet, 1839; Free.

Raphael was one of the sons of Emanuel Hyman Cohen, who was the founder of the Jewish congregation in Brighton, England. He was the brother of Abraham Cohen (q.v.), Levy Cohen, and Nathan Cohen. Raphael was a cabin class passenger, and arrived on 22 October 1839. All the other passengers were French priests on their way to New Zealand. 'Ralph' Cohen was listed in the 1841 Census of New South Wales, living at Port Macquarie. He did not marry. He went into the newspaper business, as did his brothers, Levy and Nathan Cohen, who were editors of the *Brighton Guardian*.

COHEN, Robert (Abraham Robert)

b. Newington, Surrey, 1804–1886
Grenada (2), 1821; Convict; Sentenced to 14 years, London, 1821.
Single; Watchmaker, baker; Height: 157.5 cm; 4 children.

Dark complexion, brown hair, black eyes. Robert Cohen was found in possession of a forged banknote. He was the son of Lawrence Cohen, the 'Bill Broker'. Robert Cohen was sentenced at the London Gaol Delivery on 10 January 1821.

Robert Cohen was on the list of prisoners transported from Sydney to Port Macquarie on the *Lady Nelson* on 17 March 1824. He appeared in the 1828 Census as a member of 'No. 4 Iron Gang' with no religion noted. On 27 August 1832 Cohen petitioned the authorities, asking for a ticket of leave. In his petition, dated 21 July 1832, Cohen wrote that he had been assigned to the service of Mr William Crow of Appin. He had an 'unblemished character'. It had been five years since he had been in the employ of the government, during which time he had been 'unfortunately sentenced to work in Irons for six months for having absented himself for 10 days from his government work'. It had been eleven years since his arrival, and 'except for the slight offence he has never been visited with any punishment'. Cohen asked for a ticket of leave so 'that Your Excellencies may be entitled by the time of his becoming Free namely, two years and six months hence, to acquire sufficient to liquidate the expenses of his passage to England'. A certificate of freedom was issued on 10 January 1835.

Robert Cohen married Margaret Kidd (a bounty migrant) on 10 December 1849 at Scots Church in Sydney. Cohen described himself at that time as a widower. They settled in Mudgee where he became a hairdresser in Church Street. His children were Laurence (1851), Rachel (1853), Jessie (1856), and George (1859).

Robert Cohen died on 15 February 1886. A Jewish funeral service was read by his son Laurence. His tomb is still the only Jewish grave in Mudgee.

OBSP, 1820–21, case 241, p. 70; Ship Indent 4/4007, p. 389; 4/3864, pp. 117, 470–1; CF 35/0007, 4/4326; Biographical notes from P. Halpin of Lilli Pilli, NSW.

COHEN, Rosie

1822
Free.
Single.

Rosie Cohen, aged nineteen, the sister of Robert and Moses Cohen, married Abraham Phillips (q.v.) in Launceston in 1841. It was Launceston's second Jewish wedding.

COHEN, Samuel

b. London, 1796
Ocean I, 1816; Convict; Sentenced to 7 years, Old Bailey, 1815.
Single; Ironmonger; Height: 157 cm.

Dark ruddy complexion, black hair, brown eyes. Samuel Cohen was seen and caught after picking a pocket in the Strand, and sentenced at Middlesex on 5 April 1815.

Samuel Cohen was on the list of prisoners disembarked and forwarded to Parramatta for distribution. In 1819 Samuel Cohen petitioned the Colonial Secretary for a ticket of leave, which was granted. He had been assigned to George Best, yeoman of Toongabbie, who testified on 29 November 1819 that Cohen was a 'man of industrious habit'. A ticket of leave was granted on 31 January 1820 because he was 'free by servitude'. Cohen appeared on the General Muster List for 1825 as a government servant working on the Turnpike Windsor Road. Cohen was officially reported to have left Sydney for England in 1826.

OBSP, 1815, case 436, p. 211; Ship Indent 4/4005; HO 16/1; CO 201/118, p. 280; CS 4/3494, p. 337; Book of Petitions, 4/1857, p. 69; 1825 Muster, 10/19.

COHEN, Samuel

b. 1799
Guildford (6), 1824; Convict; Sentenced to 7 years.
Dealer.

Samuel Cohen arrived on 5 March 1824. He received a colonial prison sentence and was recorded in the 1828 Census as a Jew who was 'Free by Servitude', and working as a 'dealer' in Clarence Street, Sydney. The voters' list published in the *Sydney Morning Herald* on 26 April 1842 shows him to be the owner of a house in Pitt Street. William Williams (q.v.), a confectioner, was living at the same address with Samuel Cohen in Clarence Terrace. Samuel Cohen was a member of the Sydney Synagogue in 1845.

Ship Indent 4/4009; Muster 2/8262, p. 437.

COHEN, Samuel

b. London, 1812–1861
Resource, 1834; Free.
Single; Dealer; 7 children.

Samuel was the second son of Barent Cohen and Sierlah (Sarah) (née Levy) of London, and brother of Lewis (q.v.), Henry (q.v.), David (q.v.), George (q.v.), Solomon (q.v.), Abraham (q.v.), and Morris (q.v.), who also came to Australia. Two siblings, Charles and Jane, remained in England.

Samuel arrived on 19 April 1834 at Port Jackson on the *Resource*, travelling steerage. He worked with Cooper and Levey at the Waterloo Stores, Market Street, in Sydney, until 1836. On 23 August 1837, Samuel married Rachel Nathan (q.v.), the sister of Louis Nathan (q.v.) of Hobart Town, and of Rosetta Joseph (Nathan, q.v.), wife of Moses Joseph (q.v.), of Sydney. The ceremony was conducted by Henry Wineberg (q.v.) at Port Macquarie. Rachel was the daughter of Nathan Lyon Nathan (q.v.) and Sarah Nathan. Another sister was Julia Nathan (q.v.), who married David Cohen (q.v.).

In 1836, Cohen opened Lambeth House in Maitland. On 26 August 1837, the *Sydney Times* reported that Samuel Cohen had entered into partnership with his brother Lewis at Maitland. In April 1839 a branch of the store, the London Stores, was opened in Campbelltown. The partnership with Lewis was dissolved in November 1839, and David Cohen took over his debts. 'Mr Samuel Cohen of Maitland' gave £5 to the Sydney Synagogue building appeal in September 1839.

With the onset of the depression, he moved to Sydney and in December 1842 he was to be found in Bridge Street, trying to rent his premises in High Street, West Maitland. On 3 August 1843 he filed a schedule for bankruptcy and in March 1844 he was discharged from his insolvency. He returned to Maitland and was working there when, in 1845, he and his first cousin, Lewis Wolfe Levy (q.v.), helped to found the firm of David Cohen & Co, which established extensive mercantile interests in the Hunter River and New England districts. In 1843, he reported to the Sydney Synagogue that fifteen people had attended religious services at his residence in Maitland. In 1849 he bought land at Armidale and Merriwa.

Samuel Cohen was the Member of the Legislative Assembly for Morpeth in 1860, losing the seat several months later for having failed to vote on the second reading of the Robertson Land Bill because it took place on a Saturday: 'If the carrying of the Land Bill depended on his vote on the Sabbath he would not record it. Since he had been in NSW he had protected their [the electors'] Sabbath and he would protect his own even if they did not help him!' He served as a Justice of the Peace. From 1855 to 1859 he sat on the Board of the York Street Synagogue, and was a founder and first president of the secessionist Macquarie Street Synagogue.

Cohen died suddenly on 4 November 1861 at his home in Spring Street. He was forty-nine. On 5 April 1862, administration of his estate, sworn at £70 000, was granted to his widow. In October 1863, Mrs Rachel Cohen, widow of Samuel Cohen, gave three Torah mantles for the scrolls of the Macquarie Street Synagogue. Rachel died in London, aged eighty, on 26 October 1893. The seven children of Rachel and Samuel Cohen were Sarah (1839–1894), born West Maitland; George Judah (q.v.) (27 April 1842 to 1937), born Maitland; Charlotte (1844–1929), Louis (1846), born in Sydney; Hannah (1848), born West Maitland; Nathan (Norman) Samuel (1850–1917), born Tamworth; Bernard (Beresford) Samuel (1855–1905).

Lionel E. Fredman, 'David Cohen & Co; The Family and the Firm, An Anglo-Jewish Story', *AJJHS*, vol. 9, no. 8 (1985).

COHEN, Samuel

b. London, 1816
Mangles, 1835; Convict; Sentenced to 14 years, Central Criminal Court, 1834.
Single; Bread baker; Height: 163 cm.

'A Jew.' Samuel Cohen's father was Moses Cohen at Butler's Buildings, Botolph, in the heart of the East End of London. He had two brothers, Daniel Lipman, a traveller, who lived at Newington, and Philip, a baker. Samuel last lived at Whitechapel. He was sentenced on 24 November 1834, and transported for stealing a bundle of clothing from a woman. He could read and write. His hulk report was 'very bad'. The surgeon on board the transport ship wrote that he was 'troublesome'.

Samuel Cohen arrived in Van Diemen's Land on 1 August 1835, and violently rebelled against the system. On 17 February 1836 he was sentenced to one month's hard labour in a chain gang for 'feigning sickness to avoid labour'. After a brief and difficult time with a road party, he was sent as an assigned servant and was promptly returned by his master for neglect of duty, insolence and disobedience.

On 14 September 1836 he received twenty-five lashes. On 20 September, Cohen absconded from his work and it was decreed that 'on no account was he to be employed in any other way than at hard labour for six months at Grass Tree Hill'. On 26 October he refused to work and threatened to knock down his overseer at the chain gang, for which he received twenty-five lashes. On 5 December, while still a member of the chain gang, his time of hard labour in chains was extended for a month. Two days later he struck his overseer and was given fifty lashes. On 21 September 1837 he was convicted of insolence and placed in the cells for seven days.

On 11 January 1838 Cohen received twenty-five lashes for neglect of duty. The following month it was decided that his sentence of transportation was to be extended by twelve months and he was not to be assigned as a convict servant again. On 26 July 1838 he was judged insolent and disobedient and sent to solitary confinement for fourteen days. On 13 October Cohen attempted to escape once again and his sentence was extended by a period of three years, with six months in hard labour in chains. This was found to be 'illegal' as he was already serving a sentence. However, on 25 October, after another attempted escape, the Lieutenant Governor confirmed that the length of his sentence should be extended. On 11 March 1839 Cohen was working with the road party when he received six weeks hard labour for gambling. On 6 November Cohen was reported for idleness and obscene language while serving as a member of the Campbell Town Road Party. A ticket of leave was issued on 14 October 1841 and a conditional pardon on 23 September 1845, as he was 'four years clear of offence and will be free by servitude in ten months'.

CON 32/2, Supplementary Volume, p. 380: CON 31/7, no. 1862; CON 14/4, no. 1862; CON 18/6; HO 10/58, p. 312; *Hobart Town Courier*, 2 March 1838; CP 380.

COHEN, Samuel Henry

b. London, 1821–1899
Brothers, 1833; Free.
Single; 8 children.

The eldest son of Henry Simeon Cohen and Elizabeth Cohen (qq.v.) of Port Macquarie and Sydney, Samuel Henry Cohen was born in London and came out on the *Brothers* with his mother and siblings, arriving on 21 December 1833. The family had followed their father, who was an assigned convict, to Port Macquarie. Samuel Henry Cohen married Eliza Hyams, the daughter of Joseph Hyams (q.v.), on 8 April 1840 in Sydney. Cohen worked briefly as an auctioneer at Bridge Street, but on 4 January 1842 the *Sydney Free Press and Commercial Journal* reported that the auctioneer, Samuel Henry Cohen of Campbell-town, had moved to Port Macquarie and was declared bankrupt and had been forced to surrender properties in Port Macquarie, Mudgee and Scone. His debts amounted to £778 and his assets £709. The *Sydney Morning Herald* reported on 1 May 1855 that claims of £2703 12s 7d had been presented against his estate.

The Sydney Synagogue Birth Book registered that Agnes was named on 9 June 1849 (parents living at Port Macquarie) and Rosetta was named on 1 June 1851.

Samuel Cohen began work with the family-owned intracolonial trading vessel *Demi*, which he renamed the *Elizabeth Cohen*, and later the schooner *Eliza* (named in honour of his wife). Samuel Henry Cohen moved to Melbourne, where he became one of the official assignees of the Insolvency Court and in the 1880s served as a Justice of the Peace.

The children of Samuel Henry and Eliza were Frances (1841–1917), born at Port Macquarie, married Joseph Katzenstein; Charlotte (1843), born at Port Macquarie, married her first cousin, Adolphus Marks (q.v.); Sophia (1845–1905); Sarah (1847), at Port Macquarie; Agnes (Anne) (1849), at Port Macquarie, married Simeon Frankel (son of Jacob Frankel and Miriam, née Moses) in 1863; Agnes-Rebecca (1849–1892), married the Rev. Elias Blaubaum of St Kilda Hebrew Congregation in 1877; Rosetta (1851), married David Braham; and Henry (1865), born in Sydney.

Sydney Morning Herald, 8 April 1840, 10 May 1842; *Sydney Free Press and Commercial Journal*, 4 January 1842; *Australian*, 29 September 1844.

COHEN, Sarah de Abraham Torres

b. London, 1806–1857
1841; Free.
Married; 5 children.

Sarah was born on 8 March 1806, the daughter of Abraham and Esther Torres, and was the eldest of six children. She married Benjamin Cohen (q.v.), in 1825. Her husband arrived in Van Diemen's Land as a convict on the *Lord Lyndoch* (2) in 1836.

Benjamin and Sarah had five children. They were Hanoch (4 February 1827, who remained in England), Abraham (q.v.) (9 December 1828), Isaac (q.v.) (11 December 1830), Judith (12 January 1833, who died eighteen months later), and Jacob (13 December 1834). Sarah Cohen set sail for Van Diemen's Land and Hobart Town with her children Abraham, Isaac and Jacob in 1840, arriving in May 1841. Her husband was brought to Launceston to meet with her. However, before their meeting could take place, he committed suicide, as he was convinced that he was about to be burned at the stake.

In the 1848 Census, Sarah Cohen was listed as a shopkeeper of Liverpool Street, Hobart Town. She was listed as having three sons, Jacob, Isaac and Abraham. After Benjamin's arrest in London, Sarah had managed the family's confectionary shop at 8 Hackney Road. Her shop in Collins Street, Hobart Town was also a confectionary shop. Sarah was a member of the Hobart Synagogue, and when she died, aged fifty-one, on 12 July 1857, she was buried in the Jewish cemetery at Harrington Street.

There is a note in the Synagogue's Minute Book (of 24 April 1848) concerning a 'Mrs Widow Cohen'. The Rev. Maurice Cohen (no relation):

> complained that a member of the congregation had publicly and wilfully violated the precepts of our holy religion by keeping open shop on the last holy days. It was

resolved to inform her that any person wilfully violating the mosaic ordinances shall have no claim to be entitled to any benefit or priviliges of the congregation and that Mrs Cohen particularly receive notice to that effect.

Minute Book, 1848 Hobart Hebrew Congregation; Family history by Pam Zopf, Pam Zopf and Geoff Court, *From Iberia to Van Diemen's Land, A Cohen Family Odyssey*, Privately Printed 2008.

COHEN, Simeon Joseph

1811–1887

Persian, 1829; Free. Stockman; 2 children.

Simeon Joseph Cohen was the half-brother of Phillip Joseph Cohen (q.v.) and Henry Joseph Cohen (q.v.). In a case heard before the Supreme Court concerning his brother Henry and the auctioneer Abraham Polack (q.v.) 'Mr Simon Joseph' explained in the witness box: 'I have taken the name of Cohen in consequence of my brother having taken the name of Cohen prior to my arrival; my mother was first married to a person named Cohen: the plaintiff is my brother by both parents, and is named Joseph'.

In September 1839, 'Mr Simeon J. Cohen of Black Creek' donated £20 to the Sydney Synagogue appeal. By 1841 he had moved to Maitland, where he was a commission agent in partnership with Alfred Levien (q.v.). The firm traded as commission agents and dealers and also conducted a wholesale wine and spirits business. In January 1843 the business was declared to be insolvent with debts of £2458 and assets of £196. Cohen was reduced to paying three pennies in the pound. Alfred Levien was asked to carry on the business in the interests of the creditors. Twelve months later, Cohen was discharged from bankruptcy and began to work again as a commission agent.

Cohen had used the dining room of the Rose Inn as a theatre. He had helped to organise an amateur theatrical company to benefit the Maitland Benevolent Society. In August 1843, at the Northumberland Hotel in West Maitland, the performance included the ballad *Billy Barlow in Australia*, which had been written 'expressly for the occasion by a gentleman in Maitland'.

Cohen moved to Sydney (together with his half brother, Phillip Joseph Cohen). He announced that he would work as a commission agent, and then opened a wholesale and retail tobacconist shop at 99 King Street; his advertisements began to appear in the press written in verse. It would later be thought that he may have been the author of a number of bush ballads. From 1844 to 1846 S. J. Cohen managed the Saracen's Head at King and Sussex streets, where his half brother P. J. Cohen held the licence. Simeon Cohen was buried on 18 March 1887.

No. 385/54, 4/4823; Colin Roderick (ed.), *Jemmy Green in Australia*; *Sydney Morning Herald*, 17 December 1842, 30 December 1842, 5 January 1843, 23 February 1844, 23 July 1844, 30 July 1844, 12 January 1846; *Sydney Record*, 24 January 1844; *Examiner*, 27 September 1845; *Australian*, 16 March 1838, 30 July 1844. An engraving of Alfred Solomon Matinet of Middle Row Holborn alias Jemmy Green (nd) was published and circulated in Australia.

COHEN, Simon

b. 1809
Parkfield, 1839; Convict; Sentenced to 15 years, Lancaster Quarter Session, 1839.

Simon Cohen was sentenced on 28 June 1839.

Simon Cohen arrived on 1 September 1839, and received his ticket of leave in 1845.

Governors' Despatches, 1846, ML, A1239, p. 646; TL 45/704.

COHEN, Solomon

b. London, 1817
Parkfield, 1839; Convict; Sentenced to 10 years, Hertford Court, 1838.
Single, Pencil-maker; Height: 160 cm.

Dark sallow complexion, slightly pock-pitted. Black hair, dark chestnut eyes, heavily tattooed. Solomon Cohen was sentenced at Hertford on 2 July 1838 to ten years transportation for 'stealing a reticule'. No previous convictions. Can read. 'Jew.' Tattoos: Bottle two glasses, MB on upper chest, woman's bust, heart pierced by two darts on lower right arm, heart encircled by two darts on lower right arm, heart encircled by two thistles, five dots on back of right hand. 'C woman I heart. Love D.C.' on lower left arm.

Solomon Cohen arrived on 1 September 1839 and was granted a ticket of leave in 1842, and in 1846, and in 1848, and in 1853. The multiple issues of his ticket of leave must be testimony to a difficult servitude. A certificate of freedom had been granted on 17 May 1849 and must have been forfeited.

Parkfield Printed Indent, no. 39–6848; Governors' Despatches, 1846, A1239, p. 646; TL 42/328, 43/3218, 46/1479, 48/328, 53/83, in 4/4216; CF 49/276.

COHEN, Solomon

b. London, 1823–1903
Free.
Single; Dealer; 9 children.

The seventh child of Barent and Sierlah Cohen of London and the brother of Lewis (q.v.), Samuel (q.v.), Henry (q.v.), David (q.v.), George (q.v.), Abraham (q.v.), and Morris (q.v.), Solomon Cohen married Julia Hannah Cohen (who was no relation) at the home of Mrs Lewis Wolfe Levy in West Maitland on 27 February 1857. Julia was the third daughter of J. J. Cohen (q.v.) of George Street, Sydney. They had five sons and four daughters. They were Barnet, an infant, Sarah, Martha, Samuel, Francis Henry, Lionel, Charlotte Rachel, Hannah (Nance).

Solomon Cohen died at Melbourne 13 June 1903.

COHEN, Sophia

b. London
Brothers, 1833; Free.
Single; 12 children.

Sophia Cohen was a daughter of Henry and Elizabeth Cohen (qq.v.). She came to New South Wales with her mother in December 1833. She married Abraham Hyam Cohen (q.v.) in Sydney on 27 July 1836. They had twelve children. Sophia died in Sydney and was buried at the Jewish section of Lidcombe's cemetery on 26 December 1882.

COHEN, William

London
1840; Free.
Single.

William Cohen was a pioneer Jewish settler in Melbourne. In 1841 he was a clerk in the Union Bank in Queen Street. He was a founding member of the Australia Felix Lodge of Freemasons and became its second secretary.

William Kerr, *Kerr's Melbourne Almanac and Port Phillip Directory for 1841*; Land Purchase 2/7827.

COHEN, William

b. London, c. 1832–1871
Brothers, 1833; Free.
11 children.

The sixth son of Henry Simeon Cohen and Elizabeth Cohen (qq.v.) of Port Macquarie, William arrived with his mother and nine siblings as a babe in arms. In 1851 William Cohen owned the Commercial Store at Nemingah on the western side of the river at Tamworth, and in 1852, at twenty-one years old, had begun to invest money in land, purchasing town lots. (Lewis Wolfe Levy, q.v., had Tamworth's second store on the eastern side of the river.) The post office was at 'Mr Cohen's store' and William Cohen was said to be one of Tamworth's most prominent citizens in the 1850s.

On 7 September 1853 Cohen married Sarah Solomon (1835–1918), the sixth daughter of Samuel Solomon and Rebecca (née Levy), and the young couple settled in Tamworth. Sarah was the younger sister of Julia Solomon (q.v.), who married Lewis Wolfe Levy. William Cohen's store expanded and, together with Lewis Wolfe Levy, he bought two of the three large flour mills in Tamworth.

The *Australian Israelite* (20 October 1871) described its 'feelings of deepest regret' at the 'sudden and unexpected death of one of our most respected residents—Mr William Cohen, one of the firm of William Cohen and Co., storekeepers and millers of Tamworth'. Cohen had died, aged thirty-nine, at his residence Gothic Cottage, Tamworth on 2 October 1871 and was buried at Rookwood Cemetery in Sydney. Sarah died, aged eighty-three, on 10 July 1918.

Their children were Frances (Fanny) (1854), two daughters born in 1855 and 1856, Elizabeth (1857), Hannah (11 July 1858), Henry (1860–1862), Edward 1863, Rebecca (c. 1865), Violet (1867), Maud (1868), and Anne.

2/7827; *Maitland Mercury*, 10 October 1871, Philip Charles Cohen, *Henry Cohen (1790–1867)*, 1996, privately printed, p. 431f.

COLEMAN, Solomon

b. St Luke's, London, 1805–1880
Persian, 1830; Convict; Sentenced to 7 years, Old Bailey, 1830.
Single; Tailor and scourer; Height: 155 cm.

Dark complexion, black hair, brown eyes, Roman nose. Solomon Coleman was transported for stealing sixteen reams of paper. Gaol report: 'Known to the Police'. Eight years before, Coleman had been charged with stealing wearing apparel and discharged.

Coleman was assigned to the Survey Department in Van Diemen's Land and on 14 May 1831 in New Norfolk was reprimanded for being absent for a week from the road party. On 6 February 1831 he was an assigned servant to Mr Fraser, was 'found drinking at the Albion Inn' and was reprimanded. The following year he was 'absent without leave'. He was found at the house of Philip Phillips (q.v.), recaptured, and reprimanded. On 21 April 1832, still an assigned servant to Mr Fraser, he was convicted of 'laziness' and given twenty-four lashes. On 28 September in 1833 he was absent from muster and church for several Sundays, and was reprimanded. In October he was admonished for being out after hours. By 23 May 1835 Coleman held a ticket of leave when he was reprimanded for playing cards 'on the Sabbath'.

Solomon Coleman settled in Melbourne in 1838 and established a drapery store. On 14 June 1842 the *Port Phillip Herald* reported that while Coleman and his family were at the theatre watching a performance by John Davies (q.v.), his home in Bourke Lane had been ransacked.

'S. Coleman' was a founding member of the Melbourne Hebrew Congregation in 1844 and fell behind in his membership payments by April of the following year. His name appeared on the list of 'Old Colonists' on an 'Address of Loyalty' to the Duke of Edinburgh. He gave the year of his arrival in Victoria as 1838. He died on 1 May 1880 aged eighty and was buried by his wife Christina. He was 'of London'.

CON 31/7, p. 51; CON 18/2.

COLLINS, Abraham

b. London, 1823–1884
1841; Free.
Single; 11 children.

Abraham Collins was the son of Woolf Collins and Priscilla (née Marks). According to the details on his death certificate, he arrived in Sydney in 1841. He married Amelia Davis at the York Street Synagogue on 1 July that year. They had eleven children: Phoebe, Priscilla, William, Mark, Daniel, John, Dinah, Fanny, Elice, Sarah, and Julia. Abraham Collins was buried in Sydney on 4 June 1884.

Family history from Alan Collins, Melbourne.

COLLINS, David

Free.
Single; 4 children.

On 26 October 1842, in Sydney, David Collins was found to be insolvent. On 7 August 1844 Collins was an unsuccessful applicant for the job as 'keeper of the Jews' Burial Ground'. He was a seat holder in the Sydney Synagogue in 1845. In 1846 David Collins was listed as having had a son, named Abraham Samuel born 7 January 1846. Hannah was born in August 1847, Abraham born December 1850, Amelia born 2 December 1855. The fact that in the York Street Birth Register the children's mother's name (Catherine) is absent suggests that she was probably not Jewish, although the children were registered at birth as 'Hebrew'.

David Collis (sic) died at Sofala 20 March 1866, aged 51.

Sydney York Street Synagogue Minute Book, p. 145, 7 August 1844. SMH 27 March 1866.

COLLINS, Joseph (Moses SOLOMON, Moses SOLOMONS)

b. London, 1805–1898
Marquis of Wellington, 1815; Convict; Sentenced to life, Old Bailey, 1814.
Single; Messenger boy; Height: 147 cm; 15 children.

Fair pale complexion, dark brown hair, blue eyes. Was originally tried and sentenced at the London Gaol Delivery on 16 February 1814, under the name Moses Solomons. He was nine years old and he was tried and sentenced together with another nine year old, John Morris, who was described as a 'quill winder'. Solomons, with two other boys, had stolen a pair of shoes from a bootmaker's shop in Holborn and was sentenced to death. The children's sentence was commuted 'on account of their youth'. There was a group of eight or nine Jewish prisoners in the Marquis of Wellington *and one of them was Samuel Lyons (q.v.), who would attempt to abscond from Australia with John Morris.*

Following his arrival in Sydney on 27 January 1815, Collins' initial assignment was as a servant to a Mr G. Dowling. Moses Solomon was listed as a crewman on the colonial brig *Governor Macquarie* in July 1817. He was described as 'Moses Solomon, a convict Jew boy, per *Wellington*, assigned servant to the Captain (Thomas Reiby) by the Governor'. The ship was bound for Van Diemen's Land and Moses (inspired by Lyons and Morris) escaped from Van Diemen's Land on the brig *Harriet*. The *Hobart Town Gazette* of 20 June 1818 told the story: 'A boy was among the 15 convicts who had secreted themselves on the ship *Harriet*, which had left for the Cape. They were brought back on the *Neptune* and sentenced to 100 lashes each and sentenced to work in the gaol gang for twelve months.

It would not be the final escape attempt of Moses Solomon. The *Sydney Gazette*, on 20 February 1819, reported that he had escaped from the colony again by the brig *Elizabeth Henrietta* and had been brought back to Australia in 1821 on the *Medway*, having been tried on 13 October 1820, at Newgate in the name of 'Joseph Collins', who was described as a 'fruiterer'.

'Joseph Collins' was sent on to Van Diemen's Land, arriving on 13 March 1821. In Sydney, on 28 June 1826, it was reported that he was to receive an eighteen-month sentence of imprisonment in a penal settlement for stealing. 'Moses Solomon' returned to Sydney in 1832 to be assigned as 'an indoor servant'.

Ship Indent 4/4005, p. 32; CON 31/6; CON 23/1; CSO 1/169/4039, p. 25; HO 10/1; *Sydney Gazette*, 15 November 1817, 16 May 1818, 30 January 1819, 27 February 1819, 29 November 1832.

COLLINS, Joseph

b. London, 1822–1902
1841; Free.
Single; Dealer; 15 children.

The son of Mark and Annie Collins of London, Joseph Collins was listed as a Commission Agent. On 7 October 1847 'Joseph Collins of Goulburn married Lydia (Leah) Marks (q.v.) in Sydney. Lydia was the 22-year-old daughter of Mark and Juliet Marks. Joseph and Lydia had eight children: Juliet (6 September 1848), Charles (12 May 1850), Phoebe (7 September 1852), Priscilla (15 August 1854), Dinah (23 August 1856), Wolf (1857), Mark (1858), and Fanny (12 November 1859). Lydia died on 15 March 1862, aged thirty-seven, and was buried in the Jewish cemetery at Goulburn.

Joseph then married a first cousin, Priscilla Israel, and had seven more children: Henry, Albert Ernest, Ethel, Lilian, Adelaide, Mark and Amelia. In 1849 Collins became a licensed publican in Holborn on the goldfields and was elected an alderman.

Collins brought a Torah scroll to Goulburn and built an ark for a synagogue. On 3 August 1862, when the Lachlan Forbes Synagogue on the goldfields asked the York Street Synagogue for the use of a Torah scroll, they had been told to borrow one from Joseph Collins.

Joseph's son Charles was a member of the Legislative Assembly for the electorate of Naomi in 1885, 1890 and 1891, and then member for Narrabri in 1894, and from 1895 until his death. Another son, Albert Ernest, was a member for the

Narrabri electorate in 1901, 1904 and 1907, and was described as one of the founders of the community and one of the most prominent of its members.

Joseph Collins died on 7 September 1902.

M. Rosenbaum, 'Genealogy of an Australian Family', *AJJHS*, vol. 3, no. 4 (1950), p. 187f; vol. 4, no. 1 (1954), p. 16.

COLLIS, Joseph Abraham

d. 1842

Joseph Abraham Collis was the son of David and Catherine. He died in Sydney in March 1842.

COLLISON, Thomas

b. London
Strathfieldsay (2), 1836; Convict; Sentenced to life, Shropshire, 1836.
Single; Umbrella-maker.

Thomas Collison was also listed by the name 'Colocrynth', which means 'bitter apple', and may have been a translation of a name bestowed upon him by a European official. He was sentenced for 'Highway Robbery'. The ship's indent stated that he was Protestant. However, records at the Hyde Park Barracks and the office of the Colonial Secretary (2/8285) both state that he was a Jew.

Collison arrived in New South Wales on 15 June 1836 and was transferred to the Hyde Park Barracks. In the Parramatta Gaol Book for 1839 it was recorded that he was admitted on 5 December 1839 at Liverpool and sent on to the Hyde Park Barracks in Sydney. He was said to be 'lazy and useless'. He was granted his first ticket of leave in April 1840. He appeared in the Newcastle Gaol Entrance and Description Book for 1845, where he appeared at the Maitland Bench at Brisbane Waters, and was again sent on to Sydney, on 19 February 1845. His behaviour, by this time, was 'orderly'. Collison received a ticket of leave in 1846.

Ship Indent 4/6533, no. 2420; *The Cornwell Chronicle*, 18 April 1840, Newcastle Gaol Entrance and Description Book, 1841–45, 2/2008, no. 87; TL 46/825.

COOK, George

b. London, d. 1831
1829; Free; Sentenced to 7 years, Supreme Court of NSW, 1830.
Labourer.

George Cook came free to Australia. He was listed as a Jew when convicted in Sydney on 25 September 1830, and sentenced to seven years colonial transportation for robbery. He was sent to Moreton Bay Penal Settlement on January 1831 on the *Governor Phillip.* Cook escaped from the prison settlement in that year and died in the bush.

Chronological Register of Convicts at Moreton Bay, no. 2207.

CORDOZA, Isaac

b. London, 1801–1840
Shipley (4), 1822; Convict; Sentenced to 7 years, Old Bailey, 1821.
Single; Shoemaker and pickpocket; Height: 161 cm.

Slender build, sallow complexion, light brown hair, blue eyes. The initials I CAR and J CAR were tattooed on his right arm. Cordoza was a porter, employed to carry new hats made by Phineas Isaacs to the Staging Coach Inn in London. Instead, he sold the hats and pocketed the proceeds.

Originally assigned as a servant in Sydney, Cordoza received a colonial sentence of transportation for the remainder of his original servitude for attempting to escape from the colony. Accordingly, on 27 January 1823, he was sentenced to be transported to Port Macquarie for the remainder of his time. He was listed in the 1828 Census as 'Cadoza', a Catholic and a labourer, in Sydney. He received a ticket of leave on 5 August 1828 and a certificate of freedom on 24 November 1830. He was arrested on 22 March 1831 and charged with stealing. The charge was dismissed owing to insufficient proof. In January 1834 Cordoza was given one month in the Sydney Gaol for not obeying a subpoena.

Isaac Cordoza was buried as a Jew at the Devonshire Street Cemetery on 21 July 1840.

OBSP, 1820–21, case 932, p. 355; Ship Indent 4/4008, Recognition Book, 4/6298, no. 284; TL 28/747; CF 30/844; CF, 4/4225, 4/4304, and 4/4294. *Sydney Morning Herald, 1 February 1834.*

CORONEL, Henry Senor Aaron

b. London, 1824–1886
1849; Free.
Single; Dealer; 8 children.

'Henry' Coronel, the son of Abraham Coronel, wrote to his former employer, the London *Jewish Chronicle* describing the High Holyday Services in Adelaide. He had been elected the honorary secretary of the Adelaide Hebrew Congregation on 14 November 1850: 'I am happy to say that we enjoy every privilege without any barrier or distinction in this country; in a word we enjoy civil and religious liberty'.

Coronel married Mary Anne (Marianne) Cohen, the daughter of Mark Cohen of London, a merchant, on 26 March 1851 in Adelaide. Mary Anne had only arrived in South Australia thirty-three days before the wedding. Coronel described himself variously as a 'compositor, tobacconist and Hebrew teacher'.

In August 1855 he was described as a 'general dealer' of Hindley Street and in January 1856 he was declared to be insolvent and was described as a 'tobacconist'.

Henry and Mary Anne's children were Sarah Abigail (Hains) (28 December 1851–1929), Julia Louise (1853–1934), Jacob (John) (16 January 1854), Rosetta (22 October 1856–1921), Myer (Mark) (1856), Henrietta (1861), and Albert (1862). Henry Senor Coronel died in Adelaide on 27 August 1886, aged sixty-two. The local press wrote 'The deceased, who was of the Jewish race, came of an aristocratic

Portuguese Jewish family. He learned his trade in London, worked for some time (in England) with a well known Hebrew printer-tried his hand at the Bendigo diggings and returned to Adelaide. He leaves a wife, three sons and five daughters'. His wife Mary Anne Coronel died on 22 November 1892, aged sixty-four.

Pritchard Index. *South Australian Register*, 24 August 1855, 2 January 1855, 6 September 1866.

COTTRELL, Frances (née SOLOMON)

b. London, 1814–1860
1834; Free.
Single.

Frances Solomon was a child of Joseph and Harriet Solomon (q.v.), and niece of Judah Solomon (q.v.). Frances married Anthony Cottrell at the Church of England, Longford, on 21 January 1835. Cottrell (or Cotterill) was a member of the Port Phillip Association and a colleague of John Batman in his attempt to round up the indigenous inhabitants of Van Diemen's Land. The Solomons were financial supporters of the establishment of the colony of Melbourne and Cottrell had a butcher's shop in William's Town.

Frances returned to Tasmania and on 4 May 1860 was buried there as a Jew.

CRABB, Elizabeth (CRABBE)

b. London, 1830–1910
Enchantress, 1833; Free.
Single. 12 children.

The third child of Emanuel and Frances (née Davis) Crabb (qq.v.), Elizabeth arrived in Sydney at the age of three. She married Raphael Tolano (q.v.) at the York Street Synagogue in Sydney on 9 August 1848. Their twelve children were born in Bathurst, Sydney, and Brisbane.

When Elizabeth died, on 15 May 1910, the Sydney press reported: The death of Mrs Elizabeth Tolano removes another of the few remaining links in connection with the old Jewish families of Sydney. The husband of the departed lady, Mr Raphael Tolano, was well known as the lessee of the old Victoria and Prince of Wales Theatres; his son Mr Joe Tolano, the proprietor of the Eastern Market Hotel, is well remembered under the regime of Messrs Bland Holt and George Rignold by old Sydney playgoers, while the well known Mr Ray Phillips (scenic artist), the brothers Phillips and Mr Nat Phillips (Phillips and Merritt of the London Colosseum) are grandchildren. Two sisters of the late Mrs Tolano, Miss Mary Crabb and Mrs L. Solomon are still living at Moore Park. Nat (Phillip Nathan) Phillips was the seventh child of Louis and Rebecca Phillips and, in partnership with Roy Rene, 'Mo', took the stage name of 'Stiffy'.

Family research in Kim Phillips, 'One Family's Story', ms, Sydney, 1997.

CRABB, Emanuel (CRABBE)

b. London, 1791–1878
Enchantress, 1833; Free.
Married; Dealer; 10 children.

Emanuel Crabb and Frances Davis (Crabb, q.v.) were married at the Great Synagogue in Duke's Place on 17 November 1824. Emanuel arrived in New South Wales on 24 April 1833 as a free settler with his wife and four children: Philip Emanuel (1827–1850), Miriam (Maria) (1828–1914), Elizabeth (q.v.) (1830–1910), and Israel (1832–1833). Crabb's father, Phillip, was the 'inventor of manufacturing pencils by machinery in England' and followed the family to Australia. Crabb became the first paid secretary of the Sydney Synagogue in 1839 and in 1842 was appointed sexton or 'Shamash'. Crabb officiated at a number of Australia's early Jewish marriages. In 1845 he was the owner of the Golden Fleece Hotel in Castlereagh Street, and then lived at Elizabeth Street, below Goulburn Street. He was the father-in-law of Raphael Tolano (q.v.), who married Elizabeth.

In Sydney the family grew, with the births of Catherine (1 May 1834–1923), David (18 December 1835 to 22 December 1896), Lewis (1 February 1838, died 16 March 1838), George (11 March 1839–1924), May (1848), and Jacob (John) (3 August 1842 to 7 June 1848).

Emanuel's wife Frances died on 10 December 1846 and was buried at the Devonshire Street Jewish Cemetery. Emanuel died on 22 March 1878, at the age of eighty-seven, and was buried at Rookwood Cemetery.

Family research in Kim Phillips, 'One Family's Story', ms. Sydney, 1997; *Enchantress* Indent 4/5204; *Sydney Morning Herald*, 8 July 1844, 2 May 1845, 13 September 1851.

CRABB, Frances (CRABBE) (née DAVIS)

d. 1846
Enchantress, 1833; Free.
Married. 10 children.

Frances was the wife of Emanuel Crabb (q.v.), and arrived in Sydney with her husband and four children. Frances and Emanuel had six more children in Australia. Frances died on 10 December 1846 and was buried at the Devonshire Street Jewish Cemetery and later transferred to Raphael's Ground cemetery.

CRABB, Philip Emanuel

b. London, 1827–1850
Free.
Single.

Philip Emanuel was the eldest son of Emanuel and Frances Crabb (qq.v.), and died in Adelaide at the age of twenty-three. He was buried in the West Terrace Jewish Cemetery on 15 July 1850.

CRABB, Phillip (CRABBE)

Free.
Married.

Phillip Crabb followed his son, Emanuel Crabb (q.v.), to Australia. His daughter, Frances, married Joseph Jewell (q.v.) in Sydney in 1841.

CZARNICOW, Lewis Frankel

1838; Free.
Single; Trader.

'Lewis Frankel Czarnicow' established himself in the general grocery business at King Street East, next door to the corner of Pitt Street.
Australian, 16 March 1838.

D

DA COSTA, Benjamin Mendes

b. London, 1803–1868
Fairlie, 1840; Free.
Merchant.

Benjamin Da Costa and his sister Louisa (q.v.) appeared in the South Australian Census of 1841. He lived at Kermode Street in Adelaide. He was also listed as a merchant of Hindley Street in the 1841 *South Australian Almanack*. In 1843 he had moved to Grenfell Street. He gave three guineas to the building fund of the Trinity Church and kept his distance from the Jewish community. Da Costa left South Australia in 1848 and lived in London until his death on 26 November 1868. He left a large bequest to St Peter's College in Adelaide.

South Australian Gazette and Colonial Register, 4 January 1845.

DA COSTA, Louisa

Fairlie, 1840; Free.
Single.

The sister of Benjamin Mendes Da Costa (q.v.), Louisa appeared with her brother in the 1841 South Australian Census. Louisa da Costa died in England in February 1898 leaving £7624 to the Adelaide Public Hospital.

DANIELS, Daniel

b. 1761
Scarborough, 1788; Convict; Sentenced to 7 years, Old Bailey, 1784.
Single; 2 children.

Daniel Daniels stole a copper pot, a pewter dish and a pair of shoes from Joseph Solomon. He was chased by a watchman, dropped the goods in an alley and was only picked up by the police and identified six days later. He remained in custody on the Censor hulk until rounded up and sent on the First Fleet.

Daniels was sent on the *Sirius* to Norfolk Island, arriving on 13 March 1790 and remaining there until 1796. He was sentenced to thirty-two lashes in May 1791 for stealing flour from Mary Limamon (Lammerman). By 21 April 1792 he was 'off stores' and working for settlers on the island. In May 1794 he was hired for a twelve-month contract by Owen Cavenaugh. Daniels was at Norfolk Island in 1796, after which the official records have no more information. There is, however, a curious English record of Daniels' presence in Sydney in the year following the arrival of the First Fleet. A Gloucester newspaper of 1789 reported that a Mr Ephraim Daniel, a Jew, of Mile End, had received a letter from a friend in Holland concerning 'your unfortunate relation who left you with the transports for Botany Bay', informing him that his relation

> was well in February last. He has settled at Port Jackson and has leave to teach the children of some of your nation to read and write Hebrew, your nephew has two children and says all that are born there are very healthy and more born than are buried or hanged of grown people if there were enough of your people they might have a place for themselves. Norfolk Isle is so thinly inhabited that it is not worth a stranger's while to settle there'.

In 2008 the distinguished historian Geoffey Blainey published an account of the exploration of the Pacific and may have solved the mystery of Daniel Daniels' 'leave' to teach 'the children of some of your nation to read and write Hebrew' when there was only one Jewish child in the colony. Blainey explains there was a widely believed myth that somewhere in the Pacific was a continent of lost Jews who spoke Hebrew. It was reasoned that in the absence of a large landmass in the Southern Hemisphere the world itself would topple over.

OBSP, 1783–84, case 556, p. 765; HO 10/6; M. Gillen, *The Founders of Australia,* p. 94; Ruth Campbell, *RAHS Journal.* vol. 68, no. 3, p. 1697; Morris Forbes, 'The First Fleet Convict—Daniel Daniels', *Great Synagogue Journal* (Sydney), December 1987, quoting *Gloucester Journal,* 14 December 1789, Geoffrey Blainey, *Sea of Dangers, Captain Cook and his Rivals,* Viking an imprint of Penguin Books, Australia, 2008.

DANIELS, John

b. Gibraltar, 1794
Fame, 1817; Convict; Sentenced to life, Middlesex, 1816.
Confectioner; Height: 161 cm.

Dark complexion, black hair, black eyes. A pickpocket. Jew. John Daniels had been a member of a gang of three boys who stole a watch in the Strand.

On 14 March 1817, on disembarkation, Daniels was sent on to Liverpool. Following bad behaviour Daniels was sent to Newcastle on 11 May 1819. On 18 May 1822 Daniels, a servant to John Butcher, who was a district constable in Sydney, was returned to government employ. In the 1822 General Muster of New South Wales John Daniels was an assigned convict servant to his co-religionist Aaron Barnett (q.v.) of Sydney, but was officially noted as absent from employment from September 1823 to January 1825, and probably escaped from Australia.

Ship Indent 4/4005, p. 246; *Sydney Gazette,* 13 January 1825.

DANIELS, Joseph

b. Aldgate, 1825
Cressy, 1843; Convict; Sentenced to 10 years, Central Criminal Court, 1842.
Costermonger; Height: 160 cm.

Fair complexion, very dark brown hair, large nose, large dimpled chin. The Letters CB and a dot were tattooed on his right arm. He had a scar over his left eye.

Joseph Daniels arrived in Hobart Town on 20 August 1843 and was released from road-gang work on 13 November 1845. He received his ticket of leave on 28 November 1848. His certificate of freedom was issued on 23 August 1852.
CON 33/40.

DANIELS, Moses

b. London, 1797–1867
Glory, 1818; Convict; Sentenced to life, Old Bailey, 1818.
Single; Smith and groom; Height: 175 cm.

Pale sallow dark complexion, brown hair, hazel eyes. Jew. Moses Daniels and John Smith (both aged twenty) stole bedclothes and clothes from a London lodging house. Information was laid against them and they were caught in possession of the goods on the same day (24 December 1817). On 18 February 1818 they were both sentenced to death.

The convict transport ship *Glory* arrived in Port Jackson on 14 September 1818. Daniels was sent to the prison settlement at Newcastle and punished with twenty-five lashes in February 1820 'For entering the dwelling place of John Ladone during government hours with intent to steal'. On 22 September 1822 Moses Daniels was sent as an assigned convict servant to Windsor. The *Sydney Gazette* announced on 17 March 1825 that there was a letter waiting for him at the General Post Office. The 1828 Census erroneously recorded that he was thirty-four years old and working as a labourer at John Blaxland's, Newington. His mother, 'Catharine Daniels' of 2 Midford Place, Tottenham Court Road, wrote (in January 1824) to the Governor of New South Wales asking for mercy on behalf of her son:

> Your Petitioner's only son Moses Daniels 5 years under your Jurisdiction has in his letter whom your Petitioner very lately received expressed his utmost satisfaction from the humane and beneficent treatment he has received for which he is deeply thankful to beg your Honour would graciously mitigate his sentence and thereby to alleviate her various feeling for an only child.

The petition had little effect. Daniels was given a ticket of leave in 1833 for the Parramatta District, and a conditional pardon on 1 August 1840. He was listed in Parramatta on the General Returns of Convicts in 1837, aged thirty-six (he was actually forty). On 10 October 1838, the Rev. Dickinson at the Hill of Mars officiated at his marriage to Eleanor Gunn, aged forty-five, who had come to the colony as a convict on the *Fanny* (2) in 1833. His death was registered in 1867 at Parramatta.

OBSP, 1817–18, case 177, p. 69; Ship Indent 4/4006; CS 4/1872, p. 36; Newcastle, Monthly Return of Punishments, 1810–1825, 4/1718, no. 1394; Prisons Department, Parramatta Gaol Entrance Books, 1836–1838, 4/6532; Permission to Marry Book 4/4510; TL 33/84, 39/433; CP 41/154, 4/4127 (April 1839); HO 10/52.

DAVIES, David

b. London, 1823–1836
1832; Free.

The son of Michael John Davies and his wife Hannah (qq.v.), David came to Australia with his mother and siblings. He was the brother of Edward Davis (q.v.), the bushranger, and John Davies (q.v.) of Hobart Town. David was thirteen years old when he died. Strangely, the boy's tombstone at Port Macquarie, which is dated 1836, reads in Hebrew: 'The youth David the son of Meir'. Yet the first name in Hebrew carved on the tombstone of Michael John Davies is 'Michael'.

Sidney Schultz, 'Early Jewish Settlers in Port Macquarie', *AJJHS*, vol. 3, no. 8 (1953), p. 345.

DAVIES, George Louis Asher

b. Melbourne, 1834

The son of Michael John and Hannah Davies (qq.v.), George Davies briefly occupied seat no. 65 in the Hobart Synagogue in 1845. He became the publisher of a newspaper in Windsor, New South Wales, called the *Australian*. He married Arabella Mills in Sydney in 1856.

DAVIES, Hannah

1832; Free.
Married; 8 children.

The wife of Michael John Davies (q.v.), Hannah came to Australia in 1832, following her convict husband, who had been transported in 1830. Her English-born children were Ann, John (q.v), Edward (Davis, q.v.), Frances, and David (q.v.). George Louis Asher (q.v.), Jane and Sophia were born in Australia.

DAVIES, John

b. London Free.
Married; 3 children.

John and his wife, Katherine Sarah (née Salom) Davies (q.v.), came to Van Diemen's Land as free settlers in 1840 and settled in Broadmarsh, where they had a 'small well stocked farm'. On 11 July 1844, a writ was served against Davies by a Thomas

Christian for £41 4s 1d and a levy was imposed next day on three horses, seven bullocks and some furniture at his farm, called the Glebe, at New Norfolk. The property was to be sold but on the day before the sale, Reuben Joseph (q.v.) appeared and said the property belonged to him. The sheriff wrote that there was 'great suspicion' attached to the claim. The two men claimed to be brothers-in-law and had used the same manoeuvre on 'other occasions' in the past. The sheriff felt that Reuben Joseph was 'unkennelling fraud' on his office. Joseph commenced an action of trespass in the Supreme Court, causing financial risk to the sheriff and 'heavy expense'. In the end, Joseph was forced to pay £132 4s 1d.

The Davies family then moved to live in High Street in the town of New Norfolk, where John was listed as a shopkeeper in the 1848 Census. John and Sarah's children were Maurice Coleman (q.v.), born in London in 1835, Dinah and Benjamin. John paid one guinea to the Hobart Synagogue in 1845 and remained a seat holder for three years. He was then written off as a member for his failure to pay his dues.

CO 22/144/3060; AOT query 1963/257; CS 21 July 1843, Sheriff's Office A698.

DAVIES, John (DAVIS)

b. London, 1813–1872
Argyle, 1831; Convict; Sentenced to 7 years, Old Bailey, 1830.
Single; Second-class clerk; Height: 163 cm; 8 children.

Dark brown hair, oval face, grey eyes, no whiskers, long nose, large jutting out mouth, small chin. He was 'orderly' on board ship. Could read and write. Jew. John Davies was convicted, on 6 December 1830, on the charge of 'False Pretences by ordering goods without authorisation'. His father was Michael John Davies (q.v.), managing clerk in an attorney's office in Fenchurch Street, who had been transported to New South Wales on the Florentia in 1830. His two brothers, Edward Davis (q.v.) and David Davies (q.v.), were at home. One sister, Ann, lived with her husband, Thomas Jones, a fruiterer, at Covent Garden. Three sisters lived with their father and mother.

John Davies arrived in Van Diemen's Land on 5 August 1831. He was one of the very few emancipists in Van Diemen's Land who gained sufficient influence to have his convict record torn from the 'Black Books' and destroyed. According to the slightly inaccurate 'personal note' in the Allport Collection, John Davies had been tried at the Clerkenwell Sessions and sentenced to seven years transportation for stealing a money order. His shipboard report from the surgeon, Dr Brock RN, gave the description: 'incorrigible prisoner, uses bad language, employed on board as a barber'. Upon his arrival in Hobart Town he was assigned to the Commissariat Department, where he worked until January 1832. He was then assigned as a clerk to Francis Stephens Esq. of Sydney, and was taken to New South Wales in his service. His service had come to an abrupt conclusion when he briefly absconded with the wife of a ticket of leave holder who lived at Snug.

On 28 November 1832 John Davies arrived in Sydney from Port Macquarie as a prisoner to be sent to the *Phoenix* hulk to give evidence in a trial. He was then sent to the Hyde Park Prisoners' Barracks, 'to be detained until the Governor's pleasure'. His behaviour was said to be 'good' and he was subsequently sent on to Port Macquarie to join his family, returning to Hobart Town to claim his ticket of leave. Davies wrote that his assignment was 'contrary to the wishes of your petitioner. Your petitioner is quite a youth only now twenty years of age and he is necessitated to mix and associate with characters most depraved'. He asked that the Governor be 'graciously pleased to [let him] be forwarded back to Van Diemen's Land to fulfil the remained [*sic*] of his sentence'.

Davies then began a career as a journalist and as an amateur actor. Records indicate that he arrived in Melbourne from Hobart on the *Adelaide* in October 1837, and he was frequently mentioned in theatrical performances—often with Michael Cashmore (q.v.). He briefly ran a fairly disreputable little establishment called the Imperial Hotel, but journalism and the theatre were his main passions. On 20 June 1842 he starred in the amateur theatrical production of *The Queer Subject*, in which he took the horrific role of 'Bill Mattock—a notorious bone merchant'. Davies was described as 'a chubby, red necked dark headed, unmistakably Jewish visaged personage; he had a whole family of brass in his face and was not only self assertive and cheeky'. He also began an odd job as a reporter for the *Port Phillip Gazette.* On 1 November 1840 Davies applied to become constable at Penrith at the salary of £80.

Davies resigned on 9 March 1841 and returned to Melbourne where he became well known for his many stage appearances. On 11 May 1842 he wrote about himself: 'Mr Davis, reporter to the *Port Phillip Gazette* has as we are informed become the successful applicant for the appointment of Chief Constable of Portland Bay'. It was not to be; the report was false. In 1842 he wrote from the office of the *Port Phillip Gazette* to the Sydney office of the Colonial Secretary asking for a post in the Department of the Water Police. He was refused. He staged a benefit night for himself in June 1842. The *Port Phillip Herald* (14 June) thought that it must have been 'highly remunerative' but professed to be horrified when Davies ad libbed 'in an unpardonable piece of "gagging" and imitated the blustering manner of a local magistrate'.

On 28 September 1842 the *Port Phillip Gazette* wrote:

> Mr Davies, at present a reporter to this office, having engaged the Theatre for Thursday night next, will take a benefit on bidding farewell to the Melbourne stage. Mr Davies has been deservedly a favourite from his talents as an actor; and if his faults behind the curtain have involved him in censure, submission has expiated fully the failings which are common to human temper and human judgment.

The farewell was a great success. Davies made some £50 and played 'with remarkable spirit'. More benefits and farewell performances followed. On 24 April 1843 the *Port Phillip Patriot* reported that he had attracted a 'tolerably full house', and that Davies, 'despite his size, shuffled and snuffled very respectably as Sir Hector Homespun'. He returned to Melbourne with the amateur theatre company of Launceston for 'An Unprecedented Theatrical Attraction', to present yet another benefit involving the Melbourne and Tasmanian actors. The season that followed was successful and in August 1845 he asked for permission to reopen the Pavilion Theatre. The suggestion was bitterly opposed by the press and was compared to opening a brothel. Davies demanded an apology, which was readily given. However, he then traduced the wife of William Kerr, the publisher of the *Port Phillip Herald*, for a 'false, foul and malicious attack'. He was found guilty of the offence, apologised profusely, was fined £15 and left for Hobart Town.

On 30 January 1847 John Davies was appointed chief constable of Wellington, New South Wales. He was constantly in trouble. Shortly after his appointment he was accused of 'clandestinely obtaining a pair of trousers in Sydney'. He produced an 'acceptable excuse', and on 30 March 1847 he became 'Inspector of Slaughter Houses' and 'Inspector of Weights and Measures' for the towns of Montefiores and Wellington. As 'Inspector of Distilleries' on 8 April 1847, it was said that he had extorted a sum of money from John Smith before allowing Ann Melanger to be bailed out from prison. On 17 February 1848 the *Sydney Chronicle* reported that Chief Constable John Davies of Wellington had managed his own defence at the Sydney Police Court when he was charged with the assault and false imprisonment of Mrs Eleanor Richardson. He had been committed for trial and obliged to post two sureties of £40 each. Davies successfully pursued a libel case against the publisher Benjamin Isaacs (q.v.), who was fined and sent to prison for one month. The *Melbourne Morning Herald* commented (10 October 1849): 'To parties here who know Davis's [*sic*] real character this sentence will excite more than mere surprise'. At the end of 1850 the *Bathurst Free Press* wrote, with heavy irony, about 'the indefatigable, intelligent and praiseworthy late Chief Constable Mr Davies, who with his family, have left for the metropolis—gone absolutely gone!' Davies, however, was not bound for Sydney. He returned to Van Diemen's Land, as Benjamin Isaacs, then editor of the *Bathurst Free Press and Mining Journal*, reported (1 October 1851):'the pompous, impudent, bloated and unprincipled bully who formerly did the dirty work of the Bathurst Police Force is now luxuriating as emigration clerk at Launceston on 30 shillings a week, the inhabitants of which place are wonderfully surprised with the versatility of his genius'.

John Davies had married a non-Jewish woman on 16 December 1840, and on 24 February 1851, he wrote to the Board of the Hobart Hebrew Congregation from his home at 34 Patrick Street:

> Sirs, I take leave at your desire, to forward this, my application to you, as 'president' of the Hebrew Congregation there to have my name registered as one of its members and also for apportioning to my use a seat in the Synagogue for the occupation of which I am prepared to subscribe the sum of £2 12s yearly by equal monthly payment. In making this formal application, I most emphatically protest against the right of the office bearers of the congregation … Although I most freely admit that whilst a Mr Jones, one of the persons holding office in the Synagogue gave me to understand I could not become one of its members because I had impinged the 39th law

> of the congregation but, at the same time, gravely informed me that I should not be turned out of the Synagogue when I chose to visit it!! And one which you, Sir, and the officers of the congregation should be pretty proud of!

Davies called the ruling a 'gratuitous insult' and then wrote:

> I now come to the point of disqualification which I at once deny and for this very obvious reason, my marriage 'contrary to the Judaical rites' took place on 16 December 1840 whilst the laws of the congregation only came into operation on 30 June 1844 and therefore, as a matter of course, cannot in the slightest degree deny my undoubted right to become a member of the congregation for, I take it, these laws do not take a retrospective view.

As a consequence the Hobart congregation unanimously resolved on 2 March 1851 that 'seat no. 156 [a place in the corner in the back row] be appropriated for the use of Mr John Davies whenever he be present in the Synagogue, but that the Committee decline any payment or pecuniary remuneration for the same'. Davies wrote an almost identical letter to the congregation on 25 May 1855, in which he stated 'I am desirous of paying the highest amount usually subscribed'. He received no reply and evidently broke his links with the Jewish community.

Davies became the licensee of the Waterloo Hotel and Tap on the corner of Murray and Davey streets, Hobart, in 1852. Together with George Auber Jones, he then became the publisher of the *Hobarton Guardian*, which, in turn was incorporated in the *Mercury* on 5 July 1854. By September 1854 he had become the sole owner of the newspaper. He was elected to the House of Assembly as a member for Hobart in 1861, and then had to resign 'through technical ineligibility'. He was returned to the House of Assembly as the member for Devon in 1862, and later briefly represented the electorate of Franklin. In October 1871 he retired from the *Mercury*. He died on 11 June 1872. The following day, the *Mercury* poetically commented that 'a gloom overspread the city'. Davies, it was claimed, was 'much misunderstood' and 'whatever he thought he said'. The Anglican funeral service was held in the pouring rain on 14 June 1872.

A far less sympathetic portrait of Davies is to be found in Peter Bolger's book, *Hobart Town*: 'His reputation as emancipist, as Jew, as former publican and as actor was against him. His low class unpleasantly grating accent compromised his position in society'. Bolger adds that he was 'more British than the Governor, more Anglican than the Bishop and more patriotically conservative than either'.

Davies had eight children; two of his sons, George and Charles Ellis, became leading citizens of Tasmania and both were knighted.

CON 14/2; Allport Collection, Letter from Alfred Nicholas; *Argyle* Indent, A1059.6, p. 353; Greater London Record Office, ref. MJ/SR 4240, ind. 4 & 5; *Phoenix* (hulk) Entrance Book 4/6282, no. 538; CS 4/2218, 33/4319; *Port Phillip Gazette*, 8 May 1841, 11 May 1842, 28 September 1842, 5 October 1842, 22 October 1845; ADB vol 4, pp27/8. Calder Papers, SLV, p. 399; CSO 22/2/342, SLV, 42/2302; 4/3851, 30 January 1847, 26 October 1847; *Daily News*, 5 October 1852, 28 June 1855, 5 July 1855; *Hobart Town Advertiser*, 16 June 1860, 23 July 1860; *AG*, pp. 126, 130, 244, 252–7, 283, 300, 303; Peter F. Bolger, *Hobart Town*, pp. 90, 91.

DAVIES, Katherine Sarah (née SALOM)

1840; Free.
Married; 3 children.

Katherine Sarah was the wife of John Davies (q.v.) and came with him to Van Diemen's Land in 1840. They had three children, Maurice Coleman (q.v.), Dinah and Benjamin.

DAVIES, Maurice Coleman

b. London, 1835–1913
1840; Free.
Single; 9 children.

Maurice Coleman Davies was born on 24 September 1835, the son of John and Katherine Davies (qq.v.). He was four years old when he arrived in Van Diemen's Land with his parents. He left the family farm at Broadmarsh in 1851 for the Blackwood goldfields in Victoria. After working as a merchant in Melbourne, he went to Adelaide in 1866 and was involved in large infrastructure works with the railways, water supply, wharves and docks. He was a general commission agent and merchant in Gilbert Place, and, by 1877, ran a business in Grenfell Street, Adelaide.

In 1875 M. C. Davies left his family in Adelaide and became a shareholder in several small milling companies in the southwest of Western Australia, and in 1877 took over a fifty-year lease to cut timber on 70 000 acres in the southwest. An additional lease of 46 000 acres expanded his 'empire'. The family established itself at Karridale. At the height of his prosperity, Davies employed three hundred workers and was the dominant commercial force in the region, printing his own bank notes, which could be cashed at any bank in the colony of Western Australia. The timber blocks he exported were used to pave the roads of London and Melbourne. His firm was the contractor for the rebuilding of Princes Bridge in Melbourne, the Cape Leeuwin lighthouse and the railway from Adelaide to Melbourne. He acquired large pastoral holdings in the district of Katanning and, in 1881, expanded his holdings to the Kimberley region in the northwest of the colony.

On 24 March 1858 at the age of twenty-three, Davies had married Sarah Salom. Their children were Leama 'Robert' Judah (1 May 1859), Esther Hannah, who died at the age of six months in Adelaide on 11 June 1861, Katherine (Levi), (8 May 1864), Herbert (21 June 1865), Walter David 'Karri' (14 June 1867), Arthur Louis (6 December 1869), Miriam Florence (27 September 1872), Philip Vivian (22 February 1874), and Frank Benjamin (8 March 1875). Notable among his children was 'Karri' Davis, who settled in Natal Province in South Africa and became a (British) hero in the Boer War. He was captured at the siege of Mafeking, and later refused a knighthood and the Victoria Cross on the grounds that he was simply 'doing his duty'.

M. C. Davies died at his home on St George Terrace, Perth, Western Australia, on 10 May 1913 at the age of seventy-seven. His sister was Dinah Tartakover of Sydney.

B. F. Hamling, *Maurice Coleman Davies of Karridale and Liveringa, Pioneer Builder and Pastoralist 1835–1913*; 'M. C. Davies—Timber Tycoon', *Landscape*, vol. 2, no. 1 (1967), pp. 10–15; Material held by the Augusta Museum (WA).

DAVIES, Michael John (DAVIS)

b. London, 1788–1873
Florentia (2), 1830; Convict; Sentenced to 7 years, Kent Quarter Sessions, 1830.
Married; Attorney's clerk; Height: 164.5 cm; 8 children.

Ruddy complexion. Dark brown to grey hair (bald). Hazel grey eyes. Mole on right cheek. Small scar on right side of forehead. Literate. Michael Davies was the son of Isaac Davis, and at twenty-two had married Hannah (née Benjamin) (q.v.). He worked in a lawyer's office in Fenchurch Street, London. He was sentenced at Maidstone on 15 July 1830 to seven years transportation for obtaining goods under false pretences. He was the father of Ann (1810), who married Thomas Jones, a fruiterer at Covent Garden, John (q.v.) (1813), Edward (Davis, q.v.) (1814), Frances (1820), David (q.v.) (1823), George Louis Asher (q.v.) (1834), Jane and Sophia.

Michael John Davies arrived in New South Wales on 15 December 1830 and worked as an assigned servant to Mr Richard Smith in Sydney until he 'misbehaved' and was sent to the *Phoenix* hulk. He was among fifty-nine 'invalids and idiots' sent on to Port Macquarie in 1832, though Davies is described as 'a special'.

He was moved to Port Macquarie and soon set up in business for himself. His wife, Hannah Davies, and four of their children came out from England in 1832 and were able to join him at Port Macquarie. Their son David died there in 1836.

By 1838 Davies had begun to buy land at Port Macquarie and Newcastle. He held a publican's licence at Currabella in the District of Liverpool Plains, and applied for a publican's licence in Sydney. The Sydney licence, for the Family Hotel in George Street, was granted in 1839 and was transferred to a house in Pitt Street when his lease expired. A daughter of Michael John Davies and Hannah died on 16 June 1839 and was buried in the Devonshire Street Jewish Cemetery, Section D.

Davies moved to Newcastle and established a retail store at the corner of Watt and Scott streets. He 'bought' the *Victoria*, a steamer, with a promissory note worth £15, and in December 1840 was fined when Davies hit the owner of the ship when it was repossessed. Davies was in constant trouble—a great deal of which was self-inflicted. His application for a female assigned servant was refused by the magistrate, the Rev. C. P. N. Wilson, 'on the grounds of morality and public decency and propriety'. He lodged a complaint about the quality of the flour supplied to convict workers by a commercial rival. George W. Jackson wrote to the police magistrate in Newcastle, defending himself, and charging that Davies:

> is a trebly convicted scoundrel, who was turned out of Port Macquarie for repeated bad conduct—his son is the notorious Bush-Ranger lately captured by Mr Day, and it

> is more than suspected that Davis's house was a fence for those depredators—his house is also a Brothel by which he gains some support by the prostitution of his own daughters—is also a sly grog shop to the annoyance of many families here besides myself.

The accusations were unsubstantiated and the authorities took no action. It was certainly true that a man named Henry Denny, a business associate of Michael John Davies, was charged with having harboured the gang and that Denny was sent to Norfolk Island for fourteen years. However, Davies had been the Newcastle correspondent of Sydney's *Commercial Journal*, and on 31 October 1840 he had sent an article praising the bushranging gang just three weeks before his own son had joined the outlaws. Davies wrote: 'The "gentlemen"conducted themselves in the most courteous manner possible—one rebuking another on passing any indecent observations, particularly in the hearing of females'.

On 19 February 1841,'M. D. of Sydney' wrote to the *Sydney Gazette* advocating clemency for the six convicted bushrangers. The publication of the letter was delayed until 11 March 1841. Davies cleverly described the behaviour of the judge as 'beyond all praise'. He wrote:

> I was present this evening in the crowded court house when the awful sentence of death was passed upon the six convicted bushrangers, whose depredations on the Hunter have been so alarming and notorious. There are redeeming circumstances in the career of these men; they carefully in all their desperate proceedings, abstained from personal violence; their object was plunder. The Chief Justice, Sir James Dowling, whose general character and conduct is beyond all praise, and is approved of by the whole colony, will not be offended at the petition of humanity, which cries out against the commission of six more murders as a useless retribution for one. The wholesale execution of these men will be a disgrace to our society; it would certainly not take place in London.

Following the public execution of his son, Davies moved to Melbourne and later to Hobart Town. Davies became an original member of the Melbourne Hebrew Congregation, joining in April 1845 but failed to pay his dues. He was listed as a 'clothier' of Elizabeth Street in 1845, and worked for Michael Cashmore (q.v.). On 22 October 1845 Mr J. Davies informed 'the settlers of Port Phillip that he has fitted up the "Union Hotel" near the wharf at Campbell St, Hobart Town'. In that first year of the Hobart Synagogue's life, Mr M. J. Davies rented seat no. 47. He pledged fourteen shillings, which he failed to pay.

That year, Davies moved back to Melbourne and became the licensee of the Shakespeare Hotel in Collins Street, providing it was run as a family hotel. On 25 August 1847 forty members of the Jewish community of Melbourne held a festive dinner at the hotel to celebrate the laying of the synagogue's foundation stone. Business in general was poor and by the end of the year he was in continual financial trouble. He was arrested as he attempted to leave the colony for Hobart Town while still owing a Mr E. M. Lord £38 10s. He returned to Sydney in 1847 n 1853 became the owner of a shop at 181 Pitt Street, which sold china and glass.

In 1859, *Bell's Life in Sydney and Sporting Reviewer* described him as 'The celebrated patriot and orator and crockery dealer'.

Davies is said to have published *Devotions for Children and Private Jewish Families* (Greville and Co., Bridge Street, 1867). The only recorded copy of this book is listed in the Mitchell Library, but appears to have been misplaced. Davies retired in 1883 and in 1888 purchased the *Australian* newspaper of Windsor, New South Wales, and appointed his son George to be editor. Hannah died in Sydney on 15 April 1866, 'after a long and painful illness' (*Hobart Mercury*, 25 May 1866). Michael John Davies, whose profession was given as 'newspaper proprietor', died at Windsor at the home of his son George. He was buried at the Devonshire Street Jewish Cemetery by the Rev. A. B. Davies on 27 December 1873, and his tombstone, 'erected by his affectionate daughter Fanny Wright', is now to be found at the Rookwood Cemetery. His Hebrew name was *Michael ben Ya'akov*. He was survived by three children, Frances Hannah Wright of Wright's Wharf, Sydney, Mrs Sophia Palmer of the Royal Standard Hotel, Grafton Wharf, Sydney, and George Davies of the *Australian* office, Windsor. Five of his children had predeceased him.

Florentia (2) Indent 4/4016, 30-2239; Prisoners to Port Macquarie 4/3897, p. 418; CP 45/372, in 2/7839; AOT 67/75, 68/95, 4/3897, p. 418; *Commercial Journal*, 31 October 1840; CSO 20/3/88, 27 October 1845; CS Out Letters 40/9662; CS In Letters 40/12928, 41/259; *Sydney Morning Herald*, 4 January 1859, 29 December 1873; *Australasian Chronicle*, 8 December 1840; *Bell's Life in Sydney and Sporting Reviewer*, 28 March 1856, 8 January 1859, 8 August 1859; Supreme Court of New South Wales, Probate Office Register, series 2, no. 1217; *Sydney Gazette*, 14 March 1839; *Mercury*, 6 January 1874; *Sydney Morning Herald*, 5 September 1843; Information on the early connections with the bushranger gang from research by Colin John Roope, Newcastle; AG, ch. 18, p. 242f.

DAVIS, Aaron

b. Wales, 1760–1814
Alexander; 1788; Convict; Sentenced to 7 years, Bristol, 1785.
Single; Height: 163 cm; 5 children.

Aaron Davis arrived on the First Fleet. He was transported for stealing watches and rings from James Cunning.

Mollie Gillen suggests that this may be the same Aaron Davis who was charged in London on 4 December 1802 for stealing a bundle from a cart. His plea to the court was: 'I am a young lad and come out of Wales to buy beasts for my mother and father'. If this is the same person, Aaron Davis was certainly not Jewish.

On 4 March 1790 Davis was sent to Norfolk Island, where he cleared some land near Sydney Bay and was soon supporting three people. Mary Walker had three children by Davis. They were Rebecca (1791), Ann (1793), and Mary (c. 1796). Davis prospered on Norfolk Island. In 1794 he employed the Jewish convict Peter Opley (q.v.) as a labourer on his land. Davis became an importer and exporter and in 1805 was 'victualled'as a 'collector of dutys'. He left Norfolk Island in 1805 and returned to England. He applied to return to New South Wales in 1813 where members of his family lived. He was now aged fifty and had 'suffered severe losses'. He died before he could leave for Australia. There was a son, Francis, born to Davis by Elizabeth Hosier in 1804, and another son born to Mary Walker. Only his daughters Ann and Mary were mentioned in his will.

M. Gillen, *The Founders of Australia*, p. 96f.; J. Cobley, *The Crimes of the First Fleet Convicts*, p. 70; HO 10/6, 10/7; Norfolk Island Victualling List, A1958; *Sydney Gazette*, 9 September 1804, 27 March 1813.

DAVIS, Abraham (Henry WILLIAMS)

b. Commercial Road, London, 1801–1864
Coromandel, 1820; Convict; Sentenced to life, Middlesex, 1819.
Single; Butcher; Height: 165 cm.

Abraham Davis was transported twice. He was tried in London on 15 September 1819 and again at London on 12 February 1826. In 1819 he was arrested for being found with three stolen watches hidden in his clothes. Davis was part of a gang of pickpockets, who tried to rescue him when he was arrested, making the officer feel that his life was 'in great danger'. Dark, pock-pitted complexion, dark brown hair, light blue eyes. He escaped by the Leviathan in 1822.

Abraham Davis arrived in New South Wales on 4 April 1820 and on 10 April was forwarded to Windsor. He appeared on the Colonial Secretary's records on 8 September 1821 as a labourer 'victualled by Government'. On 6 March 1822 he was listed as a member of the clearing party on Mr Terry's estate. On 8 November 1823 he was discharged from Emu Plains and sent to Penrith, where he remained on the list of prisoners to be assigned to work for the government. In a petition to Governor Darling, Davis told the story of his deportation, escape and second deportation: 'After a short stay [in New South Wales] returned again to Europe'. Davis was captured in London staying with his sisters in Spitalfields. He claimed to be a Henry Williams. He was tried a second time and sentenced to life imprisonment on Norfolk Island and was returned to Hobart Town on the *Earl St Vincent* (4). He was transhipped on the *Portland* for Sydney, put on board the hulk, and in August 1827 was sent to Norfolk Island, where for three years he served as convict overseer and constable. In 1831 he asked for a mitigation of sentence and was firmly refused.

The commandant at Norfolk Island wrote: 'has acted as constable with tolerable skill'. The station at Norfolk Island was closed down and its convicts sent to the mainland where Davis received a ticket of leave. He was given permission to marry Catherine Elizabeth Solomon (q.v.) on 22 July 1835. It was Sydney's twelfth Jewish wedding. In Sydney he began a career as a dealer and as a professional pugilist and was known as 'the Australian Belasco'. A long account of a famous barehanded boxing match with Jackson, a baker, on 3 September 1832, is to be found in *Bell's Life in Australia*:

> The Israelite walked steadily into the ring, and although in his proportions as the man of dough, exhibited an iron bark trunk which seemed to put all the baker's elements at defiance. The match had been circulated as one of great interest, the tribe of Israel

> looking forward to their countryman, as the national prop. There were 25 rounds and at the 26th Davis 'sent doughey to doss' with as fine a beating as a man would wish to receive. The Jews hoisted their clansman on their shoulders and with clamorous hurras, bore him away from the ring.

The triumph was short-lived. On the way back to Sydney the victory went to the Jewish spectators' heads. As the newspaper report continued:'The more lucky Israelites challenged all whom they chanced to meet at the various public houses on the Parramatta Rd ... Mr McC—placed a hundred in the Bank of N. S. W., the fruit of his industrious earnings on this occasion'.

On 21 March 1836 the *Sydney Gazette* reported that Abraham Davis, 'check-taker of the theatre', and his wife Catherine had accused innkeeper Abraham Myers (q.v.) of assault. The case was dismissed as it turned out that 'Catherine had the best of it'.

Davis received a conditional pardon on 20 November 1837 although two offences were noted in his dossier. On 30 October 1837 he was admonished for having been found in a public house and in 1838 he was reprimanded for striking a woman in the street. Davis was granted an absolute pardon in 1843. He gave £14 to the synagogue in 1845. Davis appeared in the *Registry of Flash Men*, where it was alleged that he was part of an underworld gang, with Nathan Jacobs (q.v.), John Jacobs (q.v.), Sol Reubens (q.v. Solomon Reuben), Francis Cohen (q.v.), and Barnett Davis. Abraham Davis died in Sydney on 20 May 1864 and was buried in the Devonshire Street Cemetery. Catherine died on 27 August 1877 and was buried at Rookwood.

OBSP, 1819, case 1280, p. 452, 1825–26, case 212, p. 92; Petitions to Governor Darling, 29/8549, in 4/2051; CON 21/33, no. 302; TL no. 722, 4/4062; CP Register 6, 39/39; A1289 p. 169; *Bell's Life in Australia and Weekly Retrospect of All Events of Importance*, 7 September 1832; HO 10/53; W. A. Miles, *Registry of Flash Men*, p. 114; *Sydney Gazette*, 21 March 1836.

DAVIS, Charles

1849; Free.
Married; 2 children.

Charles and Julia Davis of Auckland had their first child registered in the Sydney Birth register in 1849. A second son, Adolphus, was born in Sydney in 1854.

DAVIS, Coleman

1822–1904
Free.

The son of Mordecai (Mark) and Hannah Davis of London, Coleman Davis was born on 23 January 1822. Coleman (Colonymous) Davis gave ten shillings and sixpence to the Sydney Synagogue building appeal in 1845. He was buried in the

Jewish section of the Rookwood Cemetery on 30 October 1904, 'beloved father of Fanny (Francesca), Phoebe, Maude and J. E. Davis'.

Sydney Morning Herald, 29 October 1904.

DAVIS, David

b. London, 1806
Agamemnon, 1819; Convict; Sentenced to life, Old Bailey, 1818.
Single; Shoemaker.

Fair pockmarked complexion, brown hair, hazel eyes. Jew. Davis was twelve years of age when he was sentenced on 17 June 1818 at the Old Bailey for a crime committed on 25 March 1817. The boy had jumped onto a moving open carriage and stolen a purse with notes to the value of £11. He had one previous conviction of eighteen months.

A conditional pardon was issued in 1848 (48/52).

DAVIS, David

b. London
Palambam, 1833; Free.
Single; Quill manufacturer.

Davis arrived in Sydney on 10 January 1833 as a free settler on the *Palambam*. He was listed as a 'quill manufacturer'. Davis was mentioned in the *Registry of Flash Men* as the owner of a small jeweller's shop in King Street, with the claim that he would 'buy anything with no troublesome questions'.

Palambam Indent 4/5204; *Sydney Morning Herald*, 28 June 1844, 19 December 1844; W. A. Miles, *Registry of Flash Men*, p. 69.

DAVIS, David

b. London, 1822–1901
1843; Free.
Single; Dealer; 13 children (6 in England).

David Davis was the first born son of Mark (Mordecai) Davis and Hannah (née Nathan) who migrated to England from Posen in 1815. Their seven children were born in Fishmonger Alley in Southwark, East London. David's brothers Coleman (q.v.) and Samuel (q.v.) also came to Australia.

David Davis was a jeweller and clockmaker (one of the first clockmakers in Australia). He married Eleanor Ellis (q.v.), the daughter of Elias and Rebecca Ellis (qq.v.), on 18 December 1844. It was Jewish marriage no. 67 in Sydney. He was a seat holder in the Sydney Synagogue from 1845 to 1848. Davis established a jewellery business at 103 King Street and then 475 King Street. On 10 March 1846 he announced in the *Australian* that he had commenced business as an 'auctioneer, appraiser and furniture broker', at the 'Furniture Mart, 518 George St, Sydney'.

David and Eleanor had seven children in Australia. They were Fanny (1845), Morris (1847), Samuel (1849 in Queanbeyan), Mark (1851), Rebecca (1852), Elias (1854), and Hannah (1856). Having made a fortune, the family returned to England and settled at 59 Gordon Square—where another six children were born.

Sydney Morning Herald, 7 February 1845, 2 September 1845, 10 March 1846; AJHS Archives, Sydney.

DAVIS, Edward (George WILKINSON)

b. Gravesend, 1814–1843
Camden (2), 1833; Convict; Sentenced to 7 years, London, 1832.
Single; Stable boy.

Dark, ruddy, much freckled complexion. Dark brown, nearly black hair. Hazel eyes. Large nose. Scar over left eyebrow. MJDBN tattooed inside lower left arm. EDHDM, 'love', and an anchor on left arm. Five blue dots between thumb and forefinger of left hand. Can read and write. A Jew. Edward Davis (or Davies) was tried for stealing, on 28 February 1832, one wooden till, valued at two shillings, and 5 shillings in copper money from a shop. He was described as 'late of Ealing a labourer' and was sentenced under the alias 'George Wilkinson'. (In that dossier he said he had been born in Sheerness.) Davis had one previous conviction with a sentence of seven days. His father, Michael John Davies (q.v.), had arrived in the colony in 1830, and his mother, Hannah (q.v.), in 1832.

The convict transport ship *Camden* arrived in Sydney on 18 February 1833. On 23 December 1833 Davis escaped from the Hyde Park Barracks in Sydney, was caught and sentenced to twelve months 'deportation'. He was sent to the *Phoenix* hulk, described as a 'shoemaker' and dispatched to the Parramatta Iron Gang and then on to Penrith. On 1 December 1835 he absconded, was caught again and sentenced to a further twelve months in gaol. On 10 January 1837, Davis absconded again and two more years were added to his original sentence. On 21 July 1838 he was again 'absent from the Gaol Gang'. Another two years were added to his sentence, but this time he remained at large.

Davis became head of a gang of bushrangers who had been operating in the region of the Lower Hunter River around the town of Maitland. The gang had been formed by five convicts who had escaped from the Hyde Park Barracks in August 1840. Edward Davis only became a member of the gang during its last desperate weeks of action. Amazement at this bizarre recruit caused the entire group to be dubbed 'The Jewboy Gang'. The gang wore 'broad rimmed Manilla hats, turned up at the front with an abundance of braid pink ribbons, satin neck cloth, splendid brooches all of them had rings and watches'. Davis wore no fewer than five rings.

Davis was reputed to have flogged a squatter at the public triangle at Wollombi and 'rounded up' the chief constable of the district and robbed him. On 1 December 1840 he entered and robbed the public house of Henry Joseph Cohen (q.v.) at Black

Creek, Maitland, situated on 'one of the most frequented roads of the colony'. At the end of December, Davis and his gang were captured at Scone, following an ambush and gunfight, and on 24 February 1841 the gang was committed for trial at the Supreme Court in Sydney. In the account of the trial in the *Australasian Chronicle*, on 25 February 1841, Edward's name is spelled 'Davies'—which was his father's surname. On 16 March 1843, 'Jewboy Davis' was hanged, 'attended by Mr [Jacob] Isaacs [q.v.], the Jewish Rabbi'. Davis set 'a keen penetrating glance upon the crowd [and] with firm step, mounted the ladder' and met his death. We now know that his father was standing in the crowd. Davis was buried in a corner of the Devonshire Street Jewish Cemetery later that same day.

Australasian Chronicle, 25 February 1841, 18 March 1841; *Phoenix* (hulk) Entrance Book, 1834, 4/6286, no. 1150; Parramatta Gaol Record Book, no. 1397, 4/6350; Mr Forde,'Old Sydney', *Truth*, 20 September 1908; William Joy and Tom Prior, *The Bushrangers*, Shakespeare Head Press, Sydney, 1963, pp. 19–20; G. F. J. Bergman,'Edward Davis: Life and Death of an Australian Bushranger', *AJJHS*, vol. 4, no. 5 (1956); *Mercury*, 25 May 1866; J. M. H. Abbott, *Castle Vane: A Romance of Bushranging on the Upper Hunter in the Olden Days*, Angus & Robertson, Sydney, 1920. C. Roope and P. Gregson, *An Organised Banditti: The Story behind the 'Jewboy' Bushranger Gang; AG, pp. 67, 205, 242–55.*

DAVIS, Elias

b. London, 1776–1806
Hillsborough, 1798; Convict; Sentenced to 7 years, Old Bailey, 1796.
Single.

Elias Davis was convicted of breaking and entering the house of a blacksmith in Whitechapel in the forenoon and stealing clothes. He was chased and caught trying to escape.

At the Criminal Court of New South Wales, the Court of Capital Jurisdiction, on 29 August 1806, Elias Davis was convicted and 'put to the bar and indicted capitally' for having stolen meat, wheat and sugar from the house of Robert Broughton, near Parramatta. He had been seen breaking the door lock and was arrested inside the house. On 31 August, it was reported that the Judge Advocate had asked him to recall 'a very recent similar act of atrocious outrage from which he had been permitted to escape under a hope of his contrition and amendment. He was now upon the very brink of eternity and the work of his own salvation became his only duty'. The end came quickly.' On Thursday, Elias Davis was executed in pursuance of his sentence-at 8 in the morning he was taken to the place of atonement, and being of the Israelite profession was attended at his own request by a friend of the same Religion. Since the stern necessity of example required so awful an atonment from the unhappy sufferer it is much to be hoped that from his dreadful fate some may be disposed to forsake the paths which lead to ignomony and remorse of conscience in the hour of death.'

It is not known who accompanied Elias Davis to the gallows, but it was probably Joseph Marcus (q.v.), who, at that time, was employed as a constable.

OBSP, 1796–97, case 332, p. 318; *Sydney Gazette*, 31 August 1806, 7 September 1806; Criminal Court of New South Wales, 7/31, ML, 1149.

DAVIS, Elizabeth (RUSSELL, née LEVY)

b. Sheerness, 1805–1875
1822; Free.
Single; 2 children.

Elizabeth was the daughter of Philip and Catherine Russell and sister of Henry Davis (q.v.), Henry Russell (q.v.), and George Russell (q.v.). Her parents, whose surname had been Levy, evidently adopted Russell, the name of one of the principal streets in Sheerness, and made it their own. Some of their children followed their example while others chose the surname 'Davis'.

Elizabeth may have come to Van Diemen's Land with Henry Davis in 1822. Henry had some highly unprofitable experiences in Launceston and Elizabeth's sister's former brother-in-law Joseph Solomon (q.v.) had built a substantial home in Evandale. On 12 February 1838 Elizabeth Russell married Thomas Fall of Evandale at the local Anglican Church. They would have lived at Tallentine, which was one of the homes of Thomas Fall, or at the Hollies, which is now known as Franklin House. By 1847 Thomas Fall had built the Clarendon Hotel, a large building in the centre of Evandale. He was granted a licence for the hotel in 1857 and in 1860 acquired the mansion called Prosperous House, which he renamed Fallgrove House.

The Falls had two daughters, Elizabeth (1839–1939) and Catherine (1842–1935). In 1888, Catherine married William Hartnoll, the member for South Launceston in the Tasmanian Parliament. When Elizabeth's brother, Henry Davis, and his wife died, Elizabeth took in their orphaned son, Philip Davis (1837–1893), who had been born in Launceston.

Elizabeth's daughters became the guardian angels of the Launceston Synagogue, preventing its sale in 1912, and leaving £500 to the Launceston and Hobart synagogues, the interest to be used for the services of a minister. Elizabeth Fall died in October 1875 and Thomas Fall in September 1888. The disposition of their estates shows that Elizabeth and her two daughters had maintained close ties with their Jewish heritage and their Jewish relatives in England. There is mention of an uncle, Michael John Russell of Woollahra, and a bequest to Sara Louisa, Lady Samuels, of London.

Research by Joanne Acton and Peter Elias, Hobart.

DAVIS, Elizabeth

b. Hobart Town, 1827–1891
Free.

Elizabeth Davis was the daughter of Henry Davis (q.v.) and Hannah Howell. Hannah was the sister of Judah Solomon's (q.v.) common-law wife Elizabeth.

On 10 February 1848 Judah Solomon applied to the Committee of the Hobart Synagogue for permission to allow the marriage of his illegitimate son Joseph Solomon (q.v.) to Joseph's first cousin Elizabeth Davis, 'having consideration that the fathers of each were Jews and that the parties had also been brought up as Jews'. Neither Joseph Solomon nor Elizabeth Davis had Jewish mothers, and both were converted. At that time Elizabeth's sister Catherine was also converted to Judaism.

Elizabeth Davis and Joseph Solomon (the son of Judah Solomon and Elizabeth Howell) were married on 14 November 1849 at Temple House in Hobart. They were twenty-two and twenty-seven years of age respectively.

DAVIS, Elizabeth

1835–1901
1839; Free.
Single.

Elizabeth Davis came to Australia with her parents, John and Louisa (qq.v.), when she was three years of age. She was a grandchild of Judah Solomon (q.v.) of Hobart Town. On 14 February 1855 she married Louis Abrahams, a draper, aged twenty-four, in Hobart Town. He had arrived as a free settler in Van Diemen's Land in 1853. His shop was at the corner of Liverpool and Murray streets. At the time of her marriage, Elizabeth lived with her parents at Brighton.

DAVIS, Folk

Folk Davis was a seat holder in the Sydney Synagogue in 1845.

DAVIS, George

b. London, 1810
John, 1832; Convict; Sentenced to 7 years, Old Bailey, 1831.
Married; Dealer; Height: 161 cm.

Very dark sallow complexion, black hair, chestnut coloured eyes, large nose. Thick set, in appearance, a Jew. No education. No children. George Davis was convicted at London on 1 December 1831 for dealing in stolen goods.

The *John* arrived in Sydney on 8 June 1832. On 2 October 1836 the *Hobart Town Courier* carried a notice warning the public about George Davis and offering a £10 reward for his capture. Davis had been an agent at the Parramatta store that belonged to Lawrence and Stephen Spyer (qq.v.). He had absconded with 'various sums of money and other effects'.

John Printed Indent, 1832, no. 32, 1236, p. 67.

DAVIS, George (George BURNETT)

b. Aldgate, 1797
Guildford (6), 1824; Convict; Sentenced to life, Middlesex, 1823.
Single; Tailor; Height: 161 cm.

Dark sallow complexion, brown hair, hazel eyes. George Davis was sentenced on 19 February 1823.

George Davis arrived in New South Wales on 5 March 1824. A police note reads 'Ran' from the colony in June 1825—he was then transported again as 'George Burnett' by the *Waterloo* in August 1833, with a seven-year sentence. He received a ticket of leave in 1844. On 5 August 1844 he was sent to Cockatoo Island for two years. Davis was punished for trying to obtain a certificate of freedom by using the date of his first conviction to show that his time had expired. He was discharged from the Maitland Stockade on 12 May 1845 and three years later was given a second ticket of leave. Davis received a conditional pardon in 1852.

Records at Hyde Park Barracks and written into *Guildford* (6) Indent, 1824, 4/5721; TL 44/8305, 48/286; CP 52/104.

DAVIS, Henry (né LEVY)

b. 1797 at Sheerness, d. 1843
1822; Free.
Single; Dealer; 7 children.

Brother of John Davis (q.v.), Henry Davis was the first free male Jewish settler to Van Diemen's Land. He was born in Sheerness. His father, whose surname was Levy, had been a shopkeeper in Sheerness but had moved to London and worked as a baker in Drury Lane. Henry Davis was said to be a relative of John Davies (q.v.), son of Michael John Davies (q.v.), who certainly had spent some time in Sheerness during his English career.

Davis wrote to Lord Bathurst before leaving England stating that he had £500 and asked for 'the usual grant allowed by the government'. The petition was signed by his brother, Phillip Russell (né Levy). By the middle of June 1822, Davis was working as an auctioneer and dealer in Liverpool Street in Hobart Town. He had imported drapery, jewellery, cash and china worth £2882 on the *Tiger* and *Denmark Hill*. He also brought out money collected by the Jews of Sheerness for Judah Solomon and his brother Joseph Solomon (qq.v.).

Henry Davis married the 20-year-old Hannah Howell at St John's Church, Launceston, on 19 August 1823. Hannah was the sister of Judah Solomon's de facto wife Elizabeth. In October 1824 Henry Davis became a licensed publican at the Commercial Tavern in Launceston and received valuable rural and urban land grants. In 1828 he fled to Sydney in order to escape his creditors, leaving his property in the possession of George Russell and Abraham Aaron (q.v.). The police intervened and Davis was put in prison in Sydney. In Ocober 1827 the Commercial Tavern burned down and Aaron suspected that John Fawkner, an associate of Judah Solomon, of arson. Aaron challenged Fawkner to a duel which does not seem to have been fought. Aaron was able to return to England in 1829.

By 1831 Davis was back in Launceston, where he claimed to have spent more than £1200 on a two-storey brick house known as the British Hotel. He applied for a grant of land to establish a 'bark bruisery'. In September 1832, following the death of an infant child, he asked for a grant of land for a Jewish cemetery. Lieutenant Governor Arthur refused the request, and the baby was buried in 'private ground' rather than in a Christian cemetery. Davis was listed as insolvent in Launceston in 1836. On 24 October 1836, 'Henry Davis and Hannah his wife' organised the gift of a plot of land at Cataract Hill, Launceston, for a Jewish cemetery. The land measured 49 feet by 10 feet and adjoined a block already owned by Davis. According to the text of the memorial addressed to the government, Davis made the gift 'In consideration of the Love and Affection which the said Henry Davis hath and beareth towards the People called Jews and of the sum of Ten shillings to the said Henry Davis in hand paid by them the said Moses Phillips [q.v.], Moses Josephs [q.v.], Samuel Hyams [q.v.], John Jacobs [q.v.], Samuel Levy [q.v.], David Solomon [q.v.], John Lyons and Isaac Abrahams [q.v.]'.

Following his discharge from insolvency, Davis moved to Oatlands, where he gained a licence to work as an auctioneer. Business was slow and Davis travelled across Bass Strait to join the new colony at Port Phillip.

In the four-year-old ramshackle village of Melbourne, in November 1839, Henry Davis opened a 'new' sales and storeroom in Collins Street and began to advertise extensively. His stock consisted of ale, port, wine, tea, coffee, cider and slop clothing, at 'very low prices'. He then imported forty-nine 'Timor Ponies'. John Pascoe Fawkner fumed at such 'folly', and wrote in his *Port Phillip Patriot*: 'We find by a notice from the importer of these RATS, half starved and useless as they are that we have incurred the high displeasure of the mighty Solomon. Can this be Solomon the wise man—oh, no no—it is only Solomon the speculator'. Davis had auction rooms in Collins Street in 1840. Always optimistic, the *Port Phillip Herald* of 29 May 1840 reported: 'Mr Davis, the auctioneer, has taken the "Victoria Tavern" in Collins St and intends building in front of it a commodious hotel and Masonic lodge'.

Davis, the auctioneer, failed and he became the hotel keeper of the Royal Exchange Hotel in Collins Street in September 1841, only to face bankruptcy proceedings again on 31 March 1842. His remaining Victorian property was compulsorily sequestered on 13 June of that year.

A daughter of Henry Davis died in 1840. Her funeral was the first Jewish burial in the new colony and created great technical difficulties. In the first place, the building in which her body lay prior to burial caught fire and the 'watchers' were forced to carry the body across the road. Second, the ground near Merri Creek in Northcote, chosen for the Jews' burial place, consisted almost entirely of solid rock. Her body was later exhumed and shipped to Hobart Town.

The children of Henry Davis and Hannah were Henry Davis jnr (1823–1899); the daughter who died in Melbourne and was born in Hobart Town

(1824–1840) Philip (1834–1893); and three daughters, Elizabeth (1827) (q.v), Catherine (1833–1856), and Sarah, (1825). Catherine and Sarah were officially converted to Judaism in Hobart Town in February 1848, at the request of their uncle, Judah Solomon. Elizabeth married Joseph Solomon (q.v.), the illegitimate son of Judah Solomon, and, confusingly, Sarah married another Joseph Solomon, the son of Samuel Solomon (q.v.). Catherine died aged twenty-three, and was buried at the Hobart Jewish Cemetery on 1 October 1856.

When Henry Davis snr died in Van Diemen's Land, 'penniless and broken', in 1847, Elizabeth (now Fall), his sister, was asked to care for his two sons, Philip and Henry jnr. There is an official reference to a 'Henry Davis of Launceston', who was the designated administrator of the estate of his father, who died in 1847. On 12 May 1852 the legal representatives of Mr Joseph Solomon of Macquarie Street in Hobart Town wrote to the authorities regarding his brother-in-law, Mr Henry Davis of Launceston, who was 'labouring under severe mental derangement'. Mr Solomon, they wrote, would pay any costs required for his upkeep.

Henry Davis (jnr) (*Zvi ben Shmuel*) died on 9 December 1899, aged seventy-eight. He was described as a solicitor of Evandale. Philip Davis died on 24 February 1893, aged fifty-seven. Both men were buried beside their aunt, Elizabeth, in Hobart's Jewish Cemetery in Cornelian Bay.

CO 201/106, 6 November 1821; CSO 1/224/5447, 11 February 1828; CSO 1/153/3700; CSO 24/156/5434; CSO 1/6, pp. 8–9; CSO 24/156/5434, 12 May 1852; Application for Land, LSD, 1/73/74 (April 1823); LSD 1/82/252; *Port Phillip Patriot*, 2, 4, 18 November 1839; *Port Phillip Gazette*, 8 May 1841, 11 September 1841, 15 December 1841; *Port Phillip Herald*, 29 May 1840.

DAVIS, Isaac

b. London, 1796–1856
Sir William Bensley, 1817; Convict; Sentenced to life, London, 1815.
Single; Labourer; Height: 161 cm.

Longish nose, ring in his left ear, black hair, dark complexion, hazel eyes. He lived with his father in Whitechapel. Isaac Davis (aged twenty) and Moss Jacobs (q.v.) (aged eighteen) were both sentenced to death. Davis picked up a woman and was taking her to a wine vault near Duke's Place. As they walked towards Petticoat Lane, they were joined by Moss Jacobs, and the two men tried to rob the woman of her shawl and her money. At the time of the offence, Davis was described as wearing a dark coat, a light waistcoat, and bright pantaloons. Both Davis and Jacobs were sent out to Australia on the same transport.

Isaac Davis appeared before the Sydney Court of Quarter Sessions on 23 April 1827 accused of receiving stolen property (clothes), together with Samuel Levy (q.v.). They were found not guilty. On 15 March 1834 he was described as having no trade or calling and was placed by the Parramatta Bench in the iron gang for twelve months. In the General Return of Convicts in New South Wales of 1830 he was listed as thirty-five years of age and working as an assigned convict servant for Thomas Hall of Windsor. Davis received a ticket of leave on 11 September 1838.

Two weeks before the confirmation of his new status, Davis wrote from the District of Windsor asking to be allowed to go to Sydney for 'the purpose of being supported by the Jews' Philanthropic Institution'. A conditional pardon was granted to Davis on 1 June 1848. He was buried by the Sydney Synagogue in 1856.

OBSP, 1815–16, case 3, p. 5; Ship Indent 4/4005, p. 294; CS 4/4122, 28 August 1838, recording TL 38/1472, and CP 48/970; Parramatta Gaol Record Book, 1834, 4/6530; Governors' Despatches, 1827, A1200, 23 April 1827.

DAVIS, Isaac

1812–1845
Free.
Single; Dealer; 2 children.

Isaac Davis married the 18-year-old Esther Hart on 8 September 1841 at the Bridge Street Sydney Synagogue. Their child, Elizabeth, was born in Sydney on 5 September 1842 and her birth was registered at the synagogue. In 1845, Isaac Davis gave £10 to the Sydney Synagogue's building appeal.

On Friday night, 7 February 1845, the home and store of Isaac Davis at Boorowa, some 25 miles north of Yass, was attacked by a group of eight armed and mounted bushrangers. The family was 'bailed up' and the store plundered. Isaac Davis fought back, was shot and wounded; he died from the effect of his wounds on 9 February 1845. Davis was working as the agent of Isaac Levey (q.v.) of Berrima, and Levey offered a reward of £20 for the recovery of his stolen property. Friends of the deceased collected together £10 as a reward for information on the bush-rangers. The government offered £80 reward or a conditional pardon for information received. The funeral of Isaac Davis 'of Boorowa' was the first Jewish funeral in the Jewish cemetery at Goulburn. He left two children, Elizabeth (1842) and Amelia (1844). His widow Esther married Moss Marks (q.v.) in 1854. She died in Sydney in 1914.

Sentinel, 19 February 1845.

DAVIS, Isaac (Hyam)

b. London, 1813–1876
Lady Feversham, 1830; Convict; Sentenced to 14 years, Old Bailey, 1829.
Single; Errand boy; Height: 148 cm; 8 children.

Ruddy fair freckled complexion. Light brown hair, hazel eyes. 'I. D.' tattooed on left arm. Isaac Davis was a pickpocket, aged sixteen, who stole a handkerchief and veils at St Paul's Churchyard. No previous conviction. Could not read or write. He was sentenced on 29 October 1829.

Isaac Davis arrived at Port Jackson on 29 July 1830 and was sent to the Carter's Barracks for Boys. On 24 September 1833 he was sentenced for disobedience and neglect of duty for fighting with the housekeeper. Isaac was placed in the cells on bread and water and then returned to assigned service. He was in the district of Cassilis in 1839, and received a ticket of leave in 1840 for the Liverpool Plains District. On 6 July 1840 he was absent from the muster, his ticket of leave was cancelled, and he was to be placed in a probationary work gang. On 22 November 1842, Isaac Davis was permitted to proceed to the Liverpool Plains as an assigned servant to Edward Hamilton for the following twelve months. A certificate of freedom was granted on 8 January 1844. (His physical description at that time shows that his mature height was 158.5 cm.)

Davis married Rachel Morrow at Scots Church, Sydney, on 18 January 1847. He lived at 394 Kent Street, near Liverpool Street, and became a dealer and fruiterer at the George Street Market. He died on 28 July 1876, aged 'sixty-six', and was buried at Rookwood Cemetery's Old Jewish Section, in grave no. 276.

Isaac's children were Abraham (1847–1904), James Benjamin (1849–1904), Elizabeth (1852–1928), Isaac (1855–1878), Solomon (1857–1890), Rachel (1859), Mary (1862–1918), and John (1865–1950). All were brought up as Christians.

OBSP, 1829–30, case 69, p. 30; Printed Indent, 1830, p. 63, also 4/4144; TL 39/1558; TL 40/2276; CF 44/0025; CP 44/25, issued 8 January 1844, 4/4247; 22 November 1842, 42/1034; *Sydney Morning Herald*, 29 July 1876.

DAVIS, Isaac

b. London
1848; Free.
Watchmaker and jeweller.

Isaac Davis and Samuel Alexander (q.v.) commenced business opposite Mr Dinwoodie's Saddlery, at 1 Collins Street, Melbourne, on 27 April 1848. They were watchmakers and jewellers and their stock included watches, silver, and musical boxes. They also bought old gold. Davis moved to Ballarat at the time of the gold rush, was active in the Jewish community and remained there for thirty years before moving back to Melbourne in his old age.

Port Phillip Herald, 27 April 1848.

DAVIS, John

b. Bishopsgate Street, London, 1785–1867
Elizabeth, 1816; Convict; Sentenced to life, Middlesex, 1815.
Single; Dealer; Height: 163 cm.

Ruddy complexion, black to grey hair, dark brown eyes, long nose. Slightly pock-pitted. A Jew. Can neither read nor write. John Davis was sentenced for receiving a pocket book with £75 in it.

John Davis had a long and grim career as a convict. After his arrival in Sydney, Davis was sent to Windsor. On 25 February 1822 he was sentenced to be transported for life for attempting to escape from the prison settlement. On 25 March he was transported to Port Macquarie and, on 28 November, was sent on to Hobart Town on the *Elizabeth Hewitt*. Davis absconded from the notorious prison at Macquarie Harbour on the island's west coast in January 1823, only twenty-four days after arriving there, and was listed in the official return of runaways as 'having perished in the woods'.

Davis, however, survived and, five years later, on 19 April 1828, was sent to Moreton Bay Penal Colony for repeatedly absconding and for being 'otherwise incorrigible'. On 1 December 1829, he was sentenced to fifty lashes for indolence and for being mutinous. On 13 October 1830 he received seven days on the treadmill for having been absent for seven days. On 30 October he was sentenced to a further seven days on bread and water for being absent from his work detail. On 24 May 1834 he received a sentence of twelve months in the iron gang for absconding and having robbed a fellow prisoner. On 17 December 1835 he was sentenced to twenty-five lashes for insolence. On 4 September 1837, he received a further fifty lashes for 'striking a light after curfew'.

In the Parramatta Gaol Record Book for 1839 Davis was recorded as having been committed at the Liverpool Supreme Court and sent to the Sydney Gaol. He had been a 'house keeper' for Mr G. Stuart at Goulburn. Davis was arraigned before the Campbelltown Quarter Sessions on 18 February 1840 'for being at large with firearms'. He stated: 'I was sentenced for bush ranging. I had no arms'. He had been absent from the road gang for two months. Davis received his third life sentence, and was sent to Norfolk Island, arriving there on 1 March 1840. During the next two years he received three severe punishments for gambling and for absence from his work gang. His name appears on the list of nine Norfolk Island Jewish convicts who wrote to the Sydney Synagogue for prayer books so that they might observe the Sabbath.

Davis was sent back to Van Diemen's Land on the *Lady Franklin*, arriving in Hobart Town on 26 November 1845, and was sent to the Cascades Prison Factory. On 1 December he was given fourteen days in solitary confinement for giving a pair of new government-issue boots from the stores directly to a fellow prisoner. November 1846 saw him at New Norfolk in the road gang. Despite minor breaches of discipline, he was issued with a ticket of leave on 1 August 1848. This came to an end in Hobart Town on 14 November 1848, when he was convicted of burglary and stealing an item valued at less than £5. He was sent to Port Arthur for eighteen months imprisonment and hard labour. A ticket of leave was reissued on 20 January 1852. On 19 April he was in trouble again for gambling and falsely pretending that he had a certificate of freedom. On 22 September 1853 he was sentenced in Hobart Town to eighteen months hard labour for theft and larceny. The ticket of leave was reissued on 19 June 1855. It was revoked again on 29 May 1857 as he had been found gambling. A conditional pardon was granted on 30 June 1857. It was revoked when Davis stole again, was issued once more in October, revoked in 1858 and again in February 1859 for being absent from the Muster. In 1860 he was admitted to the Prisoners' Barracks in Hobart Town as an invalid, and in 1863 he was moved to Port Arthur. He died there on 25 November 1867.

In *Chain Letters: Narrating Convict Lives,* the distinct possibility that Davis wrote an imaginative autobiography while at Norfolk Island is explored.

CON 33/71 no 17045; Parramatta Gaol Book 4/6533 no. 2142 for 1839; Norfolk Island Papers 4/2698.1. prisoner no. 181; Davis Narrative, in Evans Norfolk Island Convict Papers, ms. Q168, c. 1842, ML; Lucy Frost and Hamish Maxwell-Stewart (eds), *Chain Letters: Narrating Convict Lives,* MUP, Carlton, 2001, p. 49f.

DAVIS, John

b. 1803
Guildford (5), 1822; Convict; Sentenced to life, Kent Assizes, 1821.
Pedlar.

John Davis was sentenced at the Kent Assizes on 13 June 1821.

John Davis received a colonial conviction in Sydney on 3 February 1827 for sheep stealing, and was sentenced to fourteen years with hard labour in chains. He arrived at Moreton Bay on 30 April 1827 on the *Alligator*, and returned to Sydney on 5 August 1836. While described as a 'Jew' in the Chronological Register of Convicts at Moreton Bay (no. 510), Davis was listed in the 1828 Census with no religion noted.

DAVIS, John

b. London, 1804–1860
Juliet, 1839; Free.
Married; Hotel keeper; 12 children.

The son of Benjamin Davis and brother of Henry Davis (q.v.), John Davis was married on 26 March 1826, at London's Great Synagogue, to the 14-year-old Louisa (née Solomon) (q.v). When John and Louisa arrived in Van Diemen's Land, Louisa's father, Judah Solomon (q.v.), gave John Davis the lease of the Castle Inn in Brighton, twenty miles from Hobart Town and the main military post in Van Diemen's Land. Judah Solomon had financed the hotel when it was established in 1830 and when Louisa and John arrived he called in the debt. The name was changed to the Castle Inn and Brighton Hotel. Davis also became the proprietor of the Regulator Coach Service in Brighton in 1841. Within a few years Davis had acquired a number of properties in the district. When Judah Solomon died in 1856 the inn was left to his illegitimate son Joseph, though Davis retained the licence until he died.

John and Louisa Davis had twelve children. They were Benjamin (born in England), Hannah (1829), Esther (1831–1905), who married Lewis Solomon (q.v.) in Brighton in 1847, Judah (1833), Cecilia (1834), who married Godfrey Jacobs of Dunedin, Elizabeth (q.v.) (1835–1901), who married Lewis (later, Louis) Abrahams, Sarah (1839), who married Joseph Benjamin, Mary Louise (1841–1894), who married Montagu M. Lee, Rebecca (1843), who married Moss Rosenfield, Samuel (1844), Isaac Archibald (1846–1911), who married Mary Sheenan, and Joseph (1848), who married Sarah Benjamin in Victoria.

John Davis died on 26 November 1860 and was buried in the old Hobart Jewish Cemetery, at Harrington Street. Louisa died on 8 December 1885 and was buried at the Melbourne General Cemetery.

DAVIS, John

b. Whitechapel, 1813
David Lyon, 1830; Convict; Sentenced to 7 years, Middlesex, 1829. Single; House servant; Height: 165 cm.

Curly dark brown hair, black eyes. Heavily tattooed. WHRHEH, anchor, Mermaid, John Davis, on right arm. JTH on left arm with five dots between finger and thumb on the left hand.

John Davis arrived in Van Diemen's Land on 18 August 1830. He absconded from government service while assigned to Jocelyn Thomas Esq., on 22 October 1831. A reward of £2 was offered for his recapture.

Hobart Town Courier, 29 October 1831.

DAVIS, Joseph

1848; Free.
Single; 2 children.

Joseph Davis married Harriet Jacobs (q.v.) in a Jewish ceremony in Sydney on 21 November 1849. They had twins Max and John, in 1850, who were registered as 'Hebrew'. David was born 1852 and Samuel was born in 1854 in Sydney.

York St Synagogue Birth Register

DAVIS, Judah

Free.
4 children

On 31 December 1848 Lewis Solomon (q.v.) put 'a young man', Judah Davis, in charge of his shop. Davis discovered that the 'shopman', E. A. Watts, was stealing articles from the shop and notified the police.

Launceston Examiner, 7 February 1849.

DAVIS, Judah Phillip

Free.
Married; Dealer.

Judah Phillip Davis was married to Maria Harris in a Jewish ceremony on 8 March 1843. Their child Joshua, born in Sydney in 1846, was registered as a 'Hebrew'. Judah Phillip Davis was listed as a commission agent in Kent Street in *Low's Directory of City and District of Sydney* of 1847.

DAVIS, Lewis (Louis)

1844; Free.
Married; 2 children.

Lewis Davis married Rosa Lazarus, the sister of Henry Lewis, Moses, and Cashmore Lazarus (qq.v.). Davis was a founding member of the Melbourne Hebrew Congregation. He had been a widower when he married Rosa Lazarus in Melbourne on 12 November 1845 and the ceremony was Melbourne's second Jewish wedding. In a letter to the Melbourne Hebrew Congregation (letter 9), dated 9 April 1844, Lewis explained that he had 'fallen behind' in his membership payments. He wondered whether 'in these bad times' he could join the congregation anew. He also enrolled Alfred Harris (q.v.), his nephew, as a member. His financial plight continued in the next year. His name, however, appeared on the list of 'British Jews' at Port Phillip who signed an address congratulating Chief Rabbi Nathan Adler on his election as Chief Rabbi of the United Congregations of Jews in the British Empire. Lewis and Rosa had a son, Moses, born on 29 October 1846, and a daughter, Phoebe, in 1852 (by which time his first name was spelt 'Louis'—an indication of his rise in social status).

Melbourne Hebrew Congregation, Birth Book.

DAVIS, Louisa (née SOLOMON)

b. Sheerness, 1812–1885
Juliet, 1839; Free.
Married; 12 children.

Louisa Davis was the daughter of Judah and Esther Solomon (qq.v.). Louisa married John Davis (q.v.), her maternal uncle, at the Great Synagogue in Duke's Place, London, on 26 March 1826. John Davis was named in Judah Solomon's will as living in Pontville, Brighton, Tasmania. John and Louisa Davis had twelve children. Louisa Davis died in Fitzroy, a suburb of Melbourne, on 8 December 1885, and was buried at the Melbourne General Cemetery.

DAVIS, Maria

1775–1848
Hercules, 1835; Free.
Married.

Maria Davis arrived in New South Wales with her son-in-law Isaac Levey (q.v.) and daughter Dinah. She died in Sydney at the age of seventy-three on 9 May 1848 and was buried in the Jewish section of the Devonshire Street Cemetery. Her grave was later relocated to the Botany Pioneer Memorial Park.

DAVIS, Michael S.

Free.
Dealer.

Michael Davis was a clothier of Elizabeth Street, Melbourne, in 1841. He was a founding member of the Melbourne Hebrew Congregation in 1843.

DAVIS, Moses (John)

b. Whitechapel, 1786–1816
Guildford, 1812; Convict; Sentenced to life, Surrey Quarter Sessions, 1811.
Height: 165 cm.

Curly dark brown hair, black eyes. Moses Davis was convicted in Surrey on 27 March 1811.

Moses Davis arrived in New South Wales on 18 January 1812 and was sent on to Van Diemen's Land. John Davis, or Moses Davis, was listed in a proclamation in the *Sydney Gazette* among the 'list of profligate and disorderly persons who have fled into the woods to lead a life of idleness and profligacy'. The notice first appeared on 14 May 1814. Moses Davis was still absent in December, described as an 'outlaw', and was offered an amnesty providing that he surrendered. In 1816 it was officially noted in his dossier that he had 'absconded'. His death and burial were recorded in the Parish Book of St Matthews, Windsor. He was said to have 'Drowned on Sunday' 22 December 1816, and to have been thirty years of age.

CON 13/1, p. 19; *HRA*, series 1, vol. 8, p. 264; *Van Diemen's Land Gazette*, 4 June 1814; *Sydney Gazette*, 14 May 1814, 16 July 1814, 8 July 1815, 15 June 1816.

DAVIS, Moses

Perseus and Coromandel, 1802
Convict, 7 years

Moses and Milly Davis (née Jacobs) were married at the Great Synagogue, London, on 23 September 1795. On 3 December 1800 Moses Davis appeared at the Old Bailey as a witness for the presecution of two men suspected of theft. He told the Court, 'I keep a clothes shop in Grey's Inn Lane … I keep an open shop'. Davis, together with John Moore, was found guilty of theft at the Surrey Quarter Sessions of 1799/1800. They were accused of stealing two silver table spoons valued at fifteen shillings and one silver pepper box valued at fifteen shillings, the property of Abel Clifton. Davis was sentenced to seven years transportation.

Moses Davis arrived in Sydney in June or August 1802. There is a reference to an unclaimed letter waiting for him in Sydney on 12 April 1807, however on 19 March 1807 in London the same Moses Davis appeared before the London Rabbinical Court to formally divorce his wife. The Court recorded 'during the time he was away from here, his wife had fornicated with others and had given birth to two *mamzerot* (illegitimate girls). The first was named Miriam (Maria in English) and the second Hendel (Hannah). At the time Milly was again pregnant and the Rabbinical Court agreed to issue a religious divorce. The matter of the girls' status was still being sorted out in 1839.

Jeremy I. Pfeffer, *From One End of the Earth to the Other*, Sussex Academic Press (2008), p. 205f.

DAVIS, Noson, (variously spelled Narson, Nosson, Noisson).

b. Warsaw, 1778–1865
Manlius, 1830 Convict.
Married; Innkeeper; 7 children.

Davis was aged fifty-two when he was sentenced at Westminster on 27 November 1828 for obtaining goods by false pretences. He had been born in Poland and had served in the British Army. He was a 'Cook and Mess-man'. He claimed to be married to Mary Ann Davis and had two children. The Manlius *(2) arrived in Hobart Town on 12 August 1830. He was described as 171 cm, dark hair to grey, high receding forehead, dark eyes, medium long nose, wide thick under-lip.*

The record of his convict service in Van Diemen's Land is brief. He was assigned to the service of Mr Farrell. On 30 December 1830 he was accused of 'neglect of duty' and was reprimanded. On 5 August 1831 he was again reprimanded for 'laziness'. Davis arrived in New South Wales in 1838. He was aged sixty-two and a widower when, at St Andrew's Church in Sydney, he married a 16-year-old Scot named Henrietta Greenlaw. They had five children: William (1839), Esther (1840), Janet H. (1841), Amelia (1844) and Elizabeth (1856). The family lived in and around the area of Orange, Sofala and Bathurst.

Noson Davis suffered a series of insolvencies. In the *Sydney Morning Herald*, 18 December 1848, he is described as a cook living in Bourke Street, Sydney with bad debts of £54/9/- and personal property of 30 shillings. The *Maitland Mercury*, 23 February 1860 described Davis as a labourer and innkeeper of Sofala who had been declared insolvent.

Davis's death certificate states that he died at the Club House Hotel in Bathurst at the age of eighty-nine. He was buried in the Jewish section of Orange Cemetery on 14 July 1865. The funeral was conducted by Hyam Phillips (q.v.) and the witnesses were Henry Cohen and Simeon Moses.

CON 31-1-10, CON 23-1-1 CON 18-1-15. Family information supplied by Mary Caine and Karen Dixon.

DAVIS, Oscar (Anszel DAVIDOWICZ)

b. Prussia, 1777–1835
Fanny, 1816; Convict; Sentenced to 14 years, Chester, 1815.
Single; Pedlar; Height: 163 cm; 9 children.

Dark sallow complexion, black hair, black eyes. The prison keeper at Chester Castle recorded that he 'behaves well in gaol'. He was transported for having forged currency in his possession. He was arrested in Macclesfield. He sold buttons at the fairs in Manchester, Macclesfield and Chester and used the mould for making buttons to forge florins. He pleaded guilty and was sentenced on 30 March 1815 to transportation for fourteen years. His Hebrew (first) name was Asher.

Davis was transported to New South Wales, arriving on 18 January 1816, and was then sent on to Hobart Town on the brig *Emu*. On 11 March 1817 Davis married Jane Elizabeth Forbes in Hobart Town. He was thirty-five years old and Jane was twenty-one. According to Government Orders of 20 September 1817, Davis was appointed a constable for the District of Hobart Town. He was listed in the *Hobart Town Gazette* (9 January 1819) as a 'dealer'who supplied £13 13s worth of candles to the district watch house. He travelled to Sydney as part of a police escort on the *Prince Leopold*, arriving on 30 August 1819 at the trial of a convict called Henry Morgan. Upon his return to Van Diemen's Land he was granted a conditional pardon on 31 January 1820.

Davis was listed in February 1820 on government rations with a wife and one child. On 9 May 1821 he was paid £16 8s for candles that he supplied to the Hobart Town Gaol before he commenced work as a constable. On 10 August 1820, as a constable, he was fined forty shillings for 'neglect of duty'. Perhaps his second job as a dealer occupied his energies. On 31 August 1825 Davis petitioned the government for land. The Hobart Town police recommended a grant of 200 acres, stating that Davis was 'active, intelligent, useful'. On 20 January 1827 he was reported for having accepted a bribe and on 19 October he was suspended from the police force. Davis prepared to open an inn in New Norfolk. The inn still stands, opposite the township of New Norfolk.

Davis's name appeared on a petition, dated 6 February 1829, 'on behalf of the Jewish residents of Van Diemen's Land', asking for recognition. He was fined for retailing rum without a licence on 3 August 1829 and during the next two years he was convicted of several counts of harbouring convicts and allowing them to drink in his house. There were complaints to the Colonial Secretary about Oscar Davis in his double capacity of pound keeper and Messenger of the Court of Requests. One job 'requires his constant attendance at home and the other his almost constant absence from it'. Davis was dismissed from the job of pound keeper in favour of 'some more respectable character'. He was landlord of the King's Arms (1821–28), the King of Prussia (1829–34) and the Belmont Inn (1835).

Oscar and Jane had nine children, all of whom were born and baptised in New Norfolk. They were Sarah (6 December 1817 to 19 August 1839), William (28 February 1820 to 9 August 1885), Deborah (6 February 1823 to 27 March 1903), Ann (4 September 1825 to 10 October 1830), Phoebe (11 December 1827 to 26 May 1864), Mary Ann (16 November 1830 to 16 May 1838), Elizabeth (31 January 1833 to 5 August 1888), and twins, Ossa (11 March 1835 to 23 May 1916) and Jane (11 March 1835 to 30 March 1915). Oscar Davis was listed as having subscribed five guineas to the New Town Church (*Colonial Times*, 24 September 1830). After Oscar died, on 1 November 1835, Deborah, Phoebe, Elizabeth and their mother settled in New Zealand. Jane Elizabeth Davis died on 8 August 1858.

In 1846 Governor Sir Charles A. Fitzroy consulted Phineas Moss (q.v.) about the death of a Polish Jew named Anszel Davidowicz, who was said to have had the name of 'Dewis' and had been 'possessed of some property in one of the Australian Colonies'. Moss correctly identified Oscar Davis and wrote the 'name Anzell Davidocz [*sic*] appears to be Polish and may probably be in English, Ansell Davis. About twelve or fourteen years earlier, a Polish Jew had died at New Norfolk and the European Jewish name may have been changed from Ansell, or as it is often pronounced in Hebrew, Anshell to Oscar'. Upon investigation, the widow of Oscar Davis denied that her husband was the object of the search: 'he had no trade and died in indigent circumstances leaving a wife and many children who maintain themselves by labour'. Jane Davis most likely was protecting herself against a claim upon the estate from a member of her husband's family.

Macclesfield Courier, 14 January 1815, 8 April 1815; *Hobart Town Gazette*, 10 April 1819, 10 September 1819, 18 September 1819, 9 May 1821; *Colonial Times*, 24 September 1830; CO 201/118, A 1352; HO 10/1; CP 1331; CSO 1/269/649; CSO 1/334/7622, 31 August 1825; CSO 1/496/10864, April 1834; *HRA*, series 3, vol. 3, p. 597; J. Richard Davis, *Oscar Davis and his Direct Descendants* (privately printed, 1991).

DAVIS, Philip

d. 1893
Clyde, 1833; Free.
Single; Stable keeper; 3 children.

Philip Davis was a cousin of Joseph Solomon (q.v.), the illegitimate son of Judah Solomon (q.v.). Philip arrived in the colony on the *Clyde* on 18 January 1833. Philip Davis married Rebecca Hyams, aged 17, on 13 July 1859 at the Hobart Hebrew Congregation. They had three children, Louisa Anna (7 September 1860) at Spring Bay, Tasmania, Esther (8 August 1862) at Deloraine, and Kate (18 December 1868) in Longford.

On 24 February 1893 a Philip Davis, a stable keeper of Launceston, died and left property, valued at £1500, to Joseph Solomon. When Joseph Solomon jnr died, he left his property to Samuel Benjamin (son of Judah Benjamin) of Cincinnati, and to Kate Davis, a daughter of Philip Davis of Invermay near Launceston.

CUS 30, p. 188, AOT.

DAVIS, Phillip Joseph

Ann; Free.
Single; 2 children.

Phillip Davis (who had arrived on the *Ann*) married Maria Harris in the Sydney Synagogue on 8 March 1843. A daughter, Betsy, was born in Sydney in 1844, and another, Hannah, was born in 1848.

DAVIS, Samuel

b. 1796
Hibernia, 1819; Convict; Sentenced to life, London, 1818.
Married; 2 children (in England).

Davis picked a pocket and stole a purse containing £4 10s. The prisoner pleaded for mercy on behalf of his wife and two children. Gaol report: 'bad character'. Samuel Davis was sentenced on 9 September 1818, and was transported for theft.

A conditional pardon was issued on 3 October 1837 and a free pardon on 29 October 1839.

OBSP, 1817–18, case 1090, p. 346; CON 31/9, no. 87; 4/4006, p. 293; CP 531; Free Pardon no. 490.

DAVIS, Samuel

b. Southwark, 1813–1892
Georgiana (2), 1831; Convict; Sentenced to 7 years, London, 1831.
Single; Hawker; Height: 153.5 cm.

Ruddy complexion, brown hair, hazel grey eyes. Scar inside left eyebrow, scar on top of nose and on the back of his right hand. No previous conviction. Can read and write. Samuel Davis and Edmund Simmons stole the silver from the ark of the Ashkenazi Synagogue in Duke's Place (valued at £33). Davis and his nephew Sol recruited Simmons and Wilkinson (two sailors) to help them break into the building. Davis and Simmons did the actual stealing. Davis was seventeen at the time of the trial and on 6 January 1831 received a sentence of seven years. Simmons was twenty-four and was sentenced to fourteen years transportation.

There were two men named Samuel Davis in Goulburn and the community did not forget that this particular Samuel Davis had been sent out for robbing a synagogue. He was therefore nicknamed 'Thieving Davis' and, on 23 November 1844, this Samuel was charged with having false weights in his possession.

Samuel Davis was the youngest son in a family of twelve children. His father was Jacob (John) Davis, a hatter, and his mother Maria Davis (q.v.) (née Joel). His mother and eldest sister Dinah, with her husband Isaac Levey (q.v.) arrived in Sydney on the *Hercules* in 1835.

Samuel Davis was assigned to R. M. Campbell of Argyle and received a ticket of leave on 19 April 1836. He had been in the District of Goulburn from November 1835. Samuel Davis was listed in the General Return of Convicts in New South Wales as holding both a ticket of leave and a certificate of freedom, which had been issued in 1838. Samuel Davis settled in Sydney and married Frances Burnett on 26 February 1842. He died on 26 December 1892 at the home of his niece, Sarah Solomon, daughter of his sister Caroline.

OBSP, 1830–31, case 414, p. 202f.; Printed Indent, p. 65; TL 4/4103, 36/784; CF 38/460; Indent 4/4016, 31/1157; CS 38/0460, p. 132.

DAVIS, Samuel

b. Southwark, 1828–1903
1845; Free.
Dealer; 10 children.

Born on 12 May 1828 at Fishmonger Alley in the southeast of London, Samuel Davis was the son of Mordecai (Mark) Davis and Hannah (née Nathan). Mordecai had been born in Posen and was a cigar-maker. The family arrived in London in 1815, where seven children were born. Samuel was the third son and fourth child. Samuel Davis's older brother, David Davis (q.v.), arrived in Sydney in 1843, and his sister Annie (who married into the Brodziak family) and brother Coleman (q.v.) also migrated to Australia.

Samuel Davis emigrated to Australia in 1845, and set about opening a small jewellery store in George Street, only to have his store burgled on the eve of its opening. Samuel joined his older brother David in business but soon moved to Goulburn. In 1849 Davis was advertising in the *Goulburn Herald* as a watchmaker and jeweller at both the Australian Store in Auburn Street and at 475 George Street, Sydney.

On 20 May 1850 Samuel Davis married Sarah Phillips at the home of Samuel Benjamin (q.v.) in Goulburn. It was the town's first Jewish marriage. The bride was the second daughter of Barnett Aaron Phillips and his wife Clara (qq.v.). Samuel and Sarah had two children in Goulburn, Frances (Fanny) (1851), and Phillip Cecil (1852), and two children at 191 George Street, Sydney, Hannah and Gustavus Alexander (1856). Mark (September, 1856) was born at 360 George Street, Sydney.

The family moved to Brisbane where Samuel was part of the small Jewish community. In 1862 Samuel Davis built a mansion at North Quay in Brisbane called Rosalie Villa. Five more children of Samuel and Sarah were born in Brisbane. They were Clara (1861), Adelina Rebecca (1864), Kate Victoria (1866), Maurice Alfred (1868), and Raphael Lewin (1870).

In 1883 Samuel and Sarah returned to Sydney and built a mansion named Saraville at 29 Challis Avenue, Potts Point. Samuel died at this residence on 11 August 1903 and was buried at Rookwood. Sarah died on 27 January 1906, aged seventy-six.

AJJHS, vol. 14, no. 2 (1998), p. 362; *Sydney Morning Herald*, 15 May 1843, 7 October 1844; Family history from Alison Davis OAM, Sydney.

DAVIS, Solomon

b. London, 1781–1861
Providence (1), 1811; Convict; Sentenced to 7 years, Dublin City, 1809.
Single; 1 child.

The *Providence* arrived on 2 July 1811. By 1814 Solomon Davis was listed in the Muster as a convict servant living at Windsor, off rations, and assigned to Mr John Brennan. He became a dealer in Sydney. On 28 November 1828 the *Sydney Gazette* reported that Solomon Davis had been in court and had been indicted for the fraudulent sale of tea to Joseph Raphael (q.v.). Judge Field scornfully commented that the transaction was 'a mere juggle between two Jews to save as much as possible of Davis' property from the hand of his creditors'. On 19 December 1818 Davis was in court again, convicted of assault, and imprisoned for six months.

Davis, described as a dealer and aged thirty-five, married Elizabeth Robinson, aged twenty-eight, at St Philip's on 1 June 1821. A daughter, named Margaret, was born in 1823.

On 25 August 1821 Davis had been indicted for stealing £9. The prisoner was found not guilty of the robbery but was, in the words of the judge, 'proved to be a notorious gambler cool and deliberate perjurer a proper object of execration'. He was given a sentence of seven years colonial transportation, which he served for the following three years before returning to Sydney. The General Muster of 1822 showed him to be a convict employed by the government in Newcastle, and on 28 May 1822 his wife was permitted to proceed there to join him. On 25 September 1823 he was removed from Newcastle to Port Macquarie. Davis was issued with a certificate of freedom on 26 August 1828. In the 1828 Census he was listed as a 'Protestant' who worked as a carrier at John Weller's, Philip Street, Sydney. In that same year, on 10 October 1828, the *Sydney Gazette* published the warning, that 'Mr James Elder, owner of the house no. 11 Pitt St, lately occupied by one Solomon Davis, hereby gives notice that the said Solomon Davis has no legal interest in the said house whatsoever'.

Davis became a dealer with a shop in East Market Street. In 1832 he applied for an assigned convict servant and obtained one. He was permitted to take out an auctioneer's licence in June 1834. In 1839 he was listed as a 'dealer' of Druitt Street and by 1834 he had moved to Liverpool Street. Davis donated £5 to the York Street Synagogue building fund. In 1842 he was listed as the owner of a shop in Kent Street and therefore eligible to be on the first voters' list for the Sydney Municipal Council elections. On 2 June 1842, a victim of the economic depression, he was listed as insolvent. He was buried in Sydney as a Jew on 13 May 1861, aged eighty.

1814 Muster, A1225; CF 4/4425, no. 188, and 28/0779; CS 4/3505, p. 343; *Sydney Gazette*, 10 October 1818, 25 November 1818, 19 December 1818, 25 August 1821, 5 June 1834.

DAVISON, Rebecca (DAVIDSON)

c. 1764–1805
Lady Penrhyn, 1788; Convict; Sentenced to 7 years, Old Bailey, 1786.
Married; Needle-worker.

Rebecca was placed on board the Lady Penrhyn on 6 January 1787. The documents that acompanied her to the ship stated that she was the wife of a Robert Davidson. There is circumstantial evidence that she was Jewish. Rebecca was tried at the Old Bailey at the sessions that began on 25 October 1786, together with fellow prostitute Sarah Burdo (q.v.) for having stolen £3 13s 6d from a man they had taken to the Jewish-owned Jerusalem Tavern in the East End.

John Nicol, a steward on another ship of the First Fleet, tells a story about 'a number of Jewesses', led by a woman called Sarah, who tricked the inhabitants of Tenerife into giving them food by brandishing a cruxifix at them. They may well have used their knowledge of the Spanish-Jewish dialect to communicate with the people on shore.

At Sydney Cove a literate 'Rebecka Davison' married William Holmes on 17 February 1788. On 14 February 1789 both husband and wife were sent to Norfolk Island where she earned her living by dressmaking. Holmes left the island for the mainland in May 1792 and Davison left for Port Jackson on 7 November 1794. A fellow convict married Rebecca in 1801 and her death was reported by the *Sydney Gazette* on 12 February 1805.

OBSP, 1785–86, case 811, p. 1270; M. Gillen, *The Founders of Australia*, p. 100f.

De METZ, Andrew Louis

1762–1852
Sir Joseph Banks, 1833; Free.
Married; Broker; 6 children.

Andrew De Metz arrived with his family on the brig *Sir Joseph Banks* on 15 December 1833 (cabin class). He was sixty-one, his wife Ann (q.v.) was fifty-six, and his six daughters were Esther, aged twenty-two, Julia, aged twenty, Angelina, aged nineteen, Matilda, aged seventeen, Isabella, aged sixteen and Rosetta, aged fourteen. De Metz was a broker, who established Cleveland House—a Seminary for Young Ladies, which was announced on 30 December 1833 and opened on 12 February 1834. Terms were £60 per annum. Day boarders could be accepted. Cleveland House was close to the Devonshire Street Jewish burial ground.

In 1843 W. C. Wentworth put to the Legislative Council a bill that attempted to limit the rate of interest. In so doing, Wentworth uncharacteristically denounced the 'Jews and Companies of Usurers [who] had poured into the Colony from all parts of the world'. Andrew De Metz wrote to the *Sydney Herald*: 'I was in hope in these enlightened days such inappropriate allusions would not have escaped the lips of a senator of such high standing as a whole community to be held up in these days in a Legislative Assembly to derision and scorn! Look at the conduct of the Jews wherever they reside, both as to the moral and religious conduct'. Later that same year Andrew Louis De Metz was declared 'insolvent' (4 November 1843), with debts of £6555 and personal assets of £47.

Of Andrew and Ann's children, Matilda married Moses Brown (q.v.) on 23 July 1834, Julia married Lawrence Spyer (q.v.) on 30 December 1835, Rosetta married Stephen Spyer (q.v.) on 8 January 1840, and Isabella died on 30 March 1844. Andrew De Metz died in Sydney on 8 February 1852; his wife Ann died in 1860. Andrew, Ann and Isabella were buried at the Devonshire Street cemetery and subsequently transferred to Raphael's Ground cemetery.

Ship Indent 4/5205; *Australasian Chronicle*, 4 November 1833; *Sydney Record*, 24 January 1844; M. Z. Forbes, 'The Saga of the Cohens', *AJJHS*, vol. 10, no. 3 (1988), p. 183.

De METZ, Ann

b. London, 1777–1860
Sir Joseph Banks, 1833; Free.
Married; 6 children.

Ann came to Australia with her husband, Andrew De Metz (q.v.), and their children. She died in Sydney in 1860, aged eighty-three.

DIAS, Julia

b. London, 1808–1841
Roslin Castle (2), 1830; Convict; Sentenced to 14 years, Middlesex, 1829.
Single; Kitchen maid; Height: 152 cm.

Dark sallow complexion, dark brown eyes, dark hair. Could neither read nor write. SL\E tattooed on left arm. Jewess. Julia Dias was working as a prostitute. A female accomplice stole a client's trousers and his money. She was sentenced on 3 December 1829.

Julia Dias arrived in New South Wales on 29 June 1830 and was assigned to Agnes Simmons, George Street, Sydney. On 21 March 1831 she was found to be absent without leave while in the service of Moses Joseph (q.v.). She was sentenced to spend a month in the cells at the Female Factory and then returned to service.

On 23 May 1831, while working for Mrs Bushell, she was punished for being 'insolent and absconding', and returned to the government to be sent to the Female Factory for three months. She was married on 27 August 1831, by the Rev. Richard Hills of Sydney, to Thomas Francis, aged forty-seven, who came as a convict on the *Isabella* with a life sentence, and who had a ticket of leave. Julia received a ticket of leave in April 1839. This was cancelled when 'Julia Dyas' was admitted to the Darlinghurst Gaol in December 1840 and sent to spend three months at the Female Factory in Parramatta for 'Drunkenness'. She was described as a 'servant' and was released in September 1840. Julia Dias died at the Parramatta Hospital on 3 February 1841.

OBSP, 1829–30, case 228, p. 83; Printed Indent, 1830, p. 177, no. 30, 28430–88; X824, 23 May 1831; Permission to Marry Book, 4/4512, no. 236; TL 39/695, 4/4127; Parramatta Gaol Record Book 4/6543, no. 2449; Convict Death Register, COD 16.

DIAS, Rebecca

b. London, 1794–1857
Northampton, 1815; Convict; Sentenced to 7 years, Old Bailey, 1814.
Single; Servant; Height: 146 cm.

Dark sallow complexion, dark hair, dark eyes. Rebecca was a servant of Hyam Lewis. On 4 June 1814 she stole a quantity of her master's clothes and attempted to dispose of them in the Horse and Leaping Bar in Whitechapel. She was sentenced to transportation at the London Gaol Delivery, on 6 July 1814, for seven years. Rebecca was sentenced (and deported) together with Catherine Ruben (q.v.).

Rebecca Dias arrived on 18 June 1815 and on 23 June was sent on to the Female Factory at Parramatta. She worked as an assigned servant to S. Pugh. A ticket of leave was granted in 1817 and a certificate of freedom on 3 November 1825. Dias married William Wells on 21 July 1817, as 'Dryas', at St Luke's, Liverpool. Their children were William (1816), Susannah (1820), Joseph (1821), and Ester (1824), who was admitted to the Orphan School on 24 July 1828. Wells was murdered on 22 September 1823 at the age of fifty-five, and Rebecca gave evidence at the trial of the three men accused of the crime. A certificate of freedom was authorised on 24 November 1830.

Rebecca married David Rigby in Sydney in 1831. The Rev. Richard Hill officiated. Rigby had come to New South Wales as a convict on the *Admiral Gambier* with a life sentence. Rebecca was buried as a Jew in Sydney in 1857.

OBSP, 1815–16, case 565, p. 306f.; Ship Indent 4/4005; Permission to Marry Books 4/4508, no. 301, and 4/3496, p. 225; CF, TL, 4/4303; HO 10/9; CF 017/4589: CF 30/0843.

DIAS, Solomon

b. London, 1803–1872
Royal Charlotte, 1825; Convict; Sentenced to 7 years, London, 1824.
Single; Pencil-maker; Height: 164 cm.

Dark sallow and pock-pitted complexion. Black hair, hazel eyes. Barnett Lyons (Bennett Lyon, q.v.) and Solomon Dias of Houndsditch stole a basket of laundry. One spoke to the laundryman while the other stole from his barrow. They were 'well known' to the police but two weeks passed before they were caught.

Dias was initially sent to the District of Hawkesbury as an assigned servant at Wilberforce to Robert Farlow, where he was counted in the 1828 Census. Dias was granted a ticket of leave in 1829 and a certificate of freedom on 27 September 1831.

Solomon Dias died at Berrima in 1872.

OBSP, 1823–24, case 1200, p. 437; Bigge Appendix, A2130, p. 95; 4/4073, TL 29/930; 4/4010, p. 101; CF 31/0923; *Sydney Herald*, 3 October 1831.

DYTE, Edward

b. London, 1809–1887
Brothers, 1833; Free.
Single; Pen and quill manufacturer.

Edward Dyte was the grandson of David Moses Dyte and Hannah (née Lazarus) and brother of Charles. On 15 May 1800, George III went to the Drury Lane Theatre. David Moses Dyte was said to have pulled down on the arm of a would-be assassin (Hadfield), and two bullets missed their mark. (A number of others claimed credit for the same act.) Nevertheless, after 1802, he was listed in the Imperial Calendar as 'Purveyor of Pen and Quills to the Royal Household'.

Edward Dyte became postmaster at Maitland. On 23 September 1843 he was placed in gaol and committed for trial. He was discharged from the gaol on 18 March 1844. The Newcastle Gaol Entrance and Description Book 1841–1845 records that he was imprisoned during this period. Edward Dyte went to the Victorian goldfields, where he became a commission agent and the town crier, being known as 'Billy Lungs'. In the earliest years of the St Kilda Hebrew Congregation he became assistant to the minister and was subsequently appointed sexton. Edward Dyte died at St Kilda in 1887.

Edward Dyte's brother, Charles, arrived in Ballarat during the gold rush and became one of the best-known characters in the city. An auctioneer, enthusiastic mason, secretary of the fire brigade, and president, and often lay minister, of the Ballarat Hebrew Congregation, Charles Dyte represented Ballarat East in the Victorian Legislative Assembly from 1864 to 1871.

Newcastle Gaol Entrance and Description Book, 1841–1845, no. 682, 2/2008; *Maitland Mercury*, 14 October 1843.

E

EDEN, Joseph

b. London, 1808
Minerva I (4), 1824; Convict; Sentenced to 7 years, Old Bailey, 1824.
Costermonger; Height: 162.5 cm.

Brown complexion, brown hair, dark hazel eyes. 162.5 cm. Tattoos: EL and anchor on upper right arm; EF and anchor on upper left arm. Ears pierced for rings. Hairy mark on left cheek. Eden snatched a woman's reticule. He was wearing a brown coat and velvet collar, which he abandoned in a house of ill fame. The police caught him on the basis of the woman's description. He was aged sixteen, a Jew, and was sentenced in London on 14 January 1824.

Joseph Eden arrived in New South Wales on 19 November 1824 and was assigned to Mr Blaxland. He was listed in the *Phoenix* (hulk) Entrance Book as a Jew and a labourer, having absconded from gaol from 26 December 1833 to 20 August 1834. His behaviour on board the hulk was 'bad'. He was not listed in the 1828 Census. On 6 January 1834, Eden escaped from Goat Island. He had been shackled and was working at the quarry on the northern end of the island when he escaped (together with another prisoner). Eden was seen swimming naked across Sydney Harbour, 'a distance of about half a mile when he should have been at work'. His escape was blamed on the 'negligence of the Corporal on duty'. A detailed enquiry followed. Eden was recaptured and given an additional sentence of twelve months by the Sydney Bench, and imprisoned on the hulk.

OBSP, 1823–24, case 376, p. 131; Ship Indent 4/4009a, p. 123; Ship Indent 4/4010, p. 26; *Phoenix* (hulk) Entrance Book 4/6282, no. 691; CS 4/2253-34, p. 118.

ELIAS, Abraham

b. London, 1789–1856
Shipley (1), 1817; Convict; Sentenced to 14 years, Plymouth-Devon Assizes, 1816.
Single; Shopkeeper; Height: 165 cm.

Dark sallow complexion, dark hair, balding, brown full eyes. The son of Mordecai Elias, formerly of Adams Court, Aldgate, Abraham was sentenced at Plymouth Quarter Sessions, Devon, on 5 August 1816. He was sent out to Australia for fourteen years, bracketed in the ship's indent with Simeon Lear (q.v.).

Abraham Elias disembarked in Sydney on 2 May 1817 and was sent to Windsor as an assigned convict labourer. He remained dependent on the government stores for his first year in the district, and received a ticket of leave on 4 July 1820. Elias married Harriet Robinson (Elias, q.v.), aged twenty-two, who was born in the colony, at St Matthew's Church of England in Windsor on 27 August 1823. Elias was described in the marriage certificate as a 'merchant'. The witness at the marriage was Joseph Solomon (q.v.). (Solomon died in May 1824 and left his entire estate to Abraham Elias.) By the end of 1824 Elias advertised in the *Australian* that he was able to supply wheat to the inhabitants of Sydney and Windsor. Elias was closely associated with Uriah Moses (q.v.) from 1827 to 1832, who, on 12 April 1827, was accused of selling spirits without a licence, but, 'in consideration of the correct moral character of Mr Elias', the case was dismissed. Uriah Moses and Abraham Elias were listed as 'merchants of Windsor', and during that time constantly appeared in the records of the Windsor Court of Requests, trying to collect money owed to them.

Elias was listed in the 1828 Census as a Jew, a shopkeeper in Windsor who held a ticket of leave, and as owning thirty acres of cleared and cultivated land carrying four horses and twenty horned cattle. Elias moved to Sydney in 1831 and in August bought the licence to the Hen and Chickens Hotel in George Street. Elias received a certificate of freedom on 28 December 1830.

On 4 October 1833 he moved from George Street and took over the British Flag in Elizabeth Street, only to return to the Hen and Chickens on 29 June 1838. At the same time he remained in business in Windsor, delivering 200 bushels of wheat and maize and 2000 pounds of meat to the commissariat in 1824. On 11 January 1831 he received a conditional pardon and on 15 March he thanked 'all classes at the Hawkesbury of their liberal patronage and intends to move to Sydney'. However, he did not sever all links with Windsor and the Hawkesbury.

Elias was one of those who left the Sydney Synagogue in late 1838 through 1839 on the issue of emancipist participation in the synagogue, and founded a separate Jewish congregation. As soon as the quarrel was resolved Elias returned to the York Street congregation. He was treasurer of Sydney's synagogue in 1831, 1837, 1843, 1844, and 1847. In 1839 he gave £50 to the synagogue's building appeal and was one of the three guarantors of the loan to the congregation from the Bank of New South Wales in 1841. On 11 July 1840 he announced that 'having retired from business he cannot attend to any commission forwarded to him'. Elias was a member of the Sydney Fire Insurance Company and requested the directors to hold a meeting (*Sydney Morning Herald*, 20 June 1845). Abraham Elias replaced his certificate of freedom in 1847. The *Sydney Morning Herald* noted, on 2 September 1854, that 'A. Elias of Bathurst St has become the Sydney Collector for the Jerusalem Fund which supported the Jewish community in the Holy City'.

Abraham Elias died 'at his residence', at Bathurst Street west on 15 August 1856. He was an 'old and much respected colonist'. His gravestone states that he was 'one of the original founders of our Ancient Holy Faith in this city'. He was buried at the Devonshire Street Cemetery and his grave was later moved to the Jewish section of the Rookwood Cemetery. Permission for the move was given by the Mandelson family of 200 Pitt Street, Sydney.

CS 4/3509, p. 131; Register 4/4303, dated 28 December 1830, with TL 360/2389, and CF 30/904; Governors' Despatches 1832, p. 201, ML, A1210; 4/3509, p. 131; HO 11/2; Bigge Appendix, CO 201/118, p. 285; Windsor Court of Requests, 4/5689, 4/5658; Windsor Government Stores, A803, pp. 246, 271, 325; TL 2389, CF 30/0904–CF 47/4768; *Sydney Gazette*, 20 May 1824, 23 December 1824, 24 June 1824, 5 July 1826, 12 April 1827, 11 January 1831, 15 March 1831, 3 October 1833; *Sydney Monitor*, 9 April 1830, 20 June 1845; *Australian*, 15 July 1829, 5 August 1831, 4 October 1833, 23 December 1834, 29 June 1838, 23 September 1842, 11 July 1849; *Monitor*, 9 April 1830; *Sydney Morning Herald*, 15 September 1842, 2 September 1854.

ELIAS, Esther

Burrell (2), 1832; Convict; Sentenced to life, London, 1831.

On 30 July 1831 Esther Elias was indicted for stealing 35 sovereigns, eight half crowns, eight shillings, two thimbles, one watch, one pen knife, two sixpences, one ring and one box from the home of a widow, Charlotte Davey, at St Paul, Shadwell. Esther was twenty-three and had been a lodger in the house. Esther claimed that another woman had committed the robbery and that 'my senses were gone from me'. She was sentenced to death on 20 October 1831. The sentence was commuted, and she arrived in New South Wales on 20 May 1832.

OBSP, 1831, case 1963.

ELIAS, Harriet (née ROBINSON)

b. Windsor, New South Wales, 1801–1877
Free.
Single.

Harriet Robinson, the daughter of Edward Robinson of Windsor, was born in the colony of New South Wales. She married Abraham Elias (q.v.) at St Matthew's Church of England, Windsor, in 1823. Abraham became deeply involved in the life of the Jewish community in Sydney and Harriet's involvement is reflected in her autograph, dated 20 May 1850, on the five volumes of the Anglo-Jewish *Voice of Jacob* newspaper, published in London and held by the Mitchell Library.

She died on 3 February 1877 at Freeman's Reach, Windsor. She was said to be eighty-three years old.

Register, St Matthew's, Windsor.

ELIAS, Hyam

1796–1856
Caroline, 1834; Free.
Single; Dealer.

Hyam Elias came to Australia 'steerage', arriving on 11 July 1834. He established a general store in Parramatta, where he lived. He gave £15 to the Sydney Synagogue in 1845 and was a seat holder. He also sent to the synagogue building fund £3 donated by his (non-Jewish) 'friends'. *Low's Directory of the City and District of Sydney* for 1847 lists him as living at 153 Pitt Street. Hyam Elias married Sarah Joseph, the daughter of Joseph and Amelia (Minkey) Joseph (qq.v.), in a Jewish ceremony at Port Macquarie in 1838. He was listed as a 'resident of Parramatta' in October 1849. He died at his home in Elizabeth Street, Sydney, 'late of Parramatta', on 29 January 1856. The Mandelson family took care that he would be reburied at Rookwood in 1901.

Ship Indent 4/5207; *Sydney Morning Herald*, 9 October 1849, 30 January 1856.

ELLIS, Amelia

b. Melbourne, 1847–1912

Amelia was the thirteenth child of Rebecca and Elias Ellis (qq.v.). She was born on 5 March 1847 in Melbourne. Amelia's father died when she was nineteen. Nine years later, she moved into the house in Fitzroy Street, St Kilda, where her widowed sister Deborah Folk (Ellis, q.v.), her sister Esther and brothers Samuel and Barnett lived. Like most of the rest of the household she followed Deborah to England. There she married Allen Schofield Caine. She died in Brighton on 18 October 1912.

M. Chapman, *The Humanist Jew*.

ELLIS, Angel

b. Sydney, 1831–1916
15 children.

The third child of Elias and Rebecca Ellis (qq.v.), Angel was born in Sydney on 8 April 1831. Angel Ellis probably came to Melbourne with his parents and brothers in November 1846. Shortly after he arrived he became 'lost in the bush' for some hours in the vicinity of what is now Walsh Street, South Yarra, and only found his way back to the settlement of Melbourne when he caught the gleam through the trees of a lamp in the window of the hotel that became Young & Jackson's.

Elias Ellis and his 16-year-old-son Angel joined the Melbourne Hebrew Congregation on 27 June 1847. In 1849, at the age of eighteen, Angel was elected secretary of the Melbourne Jewish Philanthropic Society. He held that position for eight years. He was the first honorary secretary of the Melbourne Hebrew Congregation, and together with his father and brothers, Maurice (q.v.) and Lewis (q.v.), was active in the synagogue's affairs. Angel Ellis, together with his father, attempted to establish a Jewish School in Melbourne in the 1850s. He was involved in the petition to the government for state aid to the 'Hebrew persuasion' and helped collect the gold to be made into a cup for the Chief Rabbi in London. By 1856 he was listed as a 'merchant' living at 61 Cardigan Street, Carlton, and owning a house in Bouverie Street.

By 1860 Ellis was working as a clerk with the Melbourne Gas and Coke Company. Angel Ellis married Hannah Phillips at the Macquarie Street Synagogue in Sydney on 24 May 1864. He was thirty-three years old and she was eighteen, and the sister of his sister-in-law Lydia. They had fifteen children.

The Angel Ellis family moved to St Kilda and became involved in the foundation of the St Kilda Hebrew Congregation. Angel was a leading Freemason. He became the manager of the Collectors Staff of the Melbourne Gas Company. He retired from the company after forty-two years of service at the end of 1902. Angel Ellis died at the home of his daughter Ray and son-in-law M. M. Phillips on 1 June 1916. Hannah died on 27 July 1920.

Family papers supplied by the late Dr Archie Ellis of Subiaco, Western Australia.

ELLIS, Asher

b. Sydney, 1839–1911

Asher Ellis was the ninth child of Rebecca and Elias Ellis (qq.v.), and was born in Sydney on 8 September 1839. He joined the postal department and became the first postmaster in the town of Kerang. Asher Ellis lived at 49 Fawkner Street in St Kilda, and died on 19 October 1911. His estate was valued at £8161 4s 1d. While he never married, he left all his property to his landlady, Ada Jane Cole.

ELLIS, Barnett

b. Sydney, 1837–1912
3 children.

Named after his uncle, Barnett Levey (q.v.), who had died the year he was born, Barnett Ellis was the eighth child of Rebecca and Elias Ellis (qq.v.). Family tradition recalls that Barnett rejected his father's suggestion that he become a rabbi and that he left home to become a law clerk. He eventually worked for the auctioneering firm of Alfred Cooper of North Melbourne.

Barnett married Mrs Sarah Nash, who had two daughters from a previous marriage. They were married by a Methodist minister in the home of Barnett's older brother, Maurice Ellis (q.v.), in Emerald Hill. He and Sarah had three children before Sarah died in 1888. Barnett continued to work as an auctioneer until the end of his life.

ELLIS, Deborah

b. Sydney, 1842–1921
1 child.

Deborah Ellis was born on 8 September 1842, the eleventh child of Rebecca and Elias Ellis (q.v.). She married Isaac Folk on 10 November 1867. Isaac had been born in London in 1828 and was the son of Samuel and Amelia (née Simmons) Folk (qq.v.).

After the marriage, both sets of parents moved from Sydney to Melbourne. Deborah and Isaac lived in Alexander Terrace, Victoria Parade. They had a son, Samuel Mark Folk. After Isaac died on 18 November 1868, Deborah Folk sold her home to her brother, Maurice Ellis (q.v.), and moved to Cardigan Street, Carlton, to the house next door to her mother and sisters. Deborah, her son and her brother Maurice moved to England after 1882. She died in England on 15 April 1921.

ELLIS, Eleanor

b. London, 1827–1889
Surrey, 1829; Free.
Single.

Eleanor was the eldest child of Rebecca (née Levey) and Elias Ellis (qq.v.). She was married, at the age of fifteen, to David Davis (q.v.) at the York Street Synagogue, on 18 December 1844. Eleanor and her husband returned to England shortly after the marriage.

ELLIS, Elias (ELIAS)

b. London, 1796–1866
Surrey, 1829; Free.
Married; Dealer; 14 children.

The son of a merchant, Angel (Asher) Ellis, and his wife Amelia, Elias became a brother-in-law of Solomon Levey (q.v.), Barnett Levey (q.v.), Isaac Levey (q.v.), Philip Levey (q.v.) He came with his wife Rebecca (née Levey) and one child, Eleanor (q.v.).

Solomon Levey was in London in 1826, and the evident success of his Australian achievements must have encouraged Elias and Rebecca to emigrate. They arrived in Sydney on 29 January 1829. A son, Morris (Maurice Elias, q.v.), was born in Sydney in 1830. An infant daughter, Frances, was buried in the Devonshire Street Jewish Cemetery on 25 December 1832.

Elias Ellis worked as a merchant and dealer in Sydney throughout the 1830s and became a licensed victualler in 1833, trading from premises, the Freemason's Arms, at the corner of Pitt and King streets. He purchased three cottages in Essex Street for £138 on 7 February 1834. In September 1839 he gave £21 to the Sydney Synagogue building fund but was unable to pay his synagogue subscription. Nevertheless in September 1840 he stood for election to the committee of the Sydney Synagogue. On 23 April 1841 the family buried a son, Isaac Octavius, in Sydney's Jewish cemetery.

In May 1843 there was 'a destructive fire in the premises of Mr Elias Ellis with debts estimated at £2000 but everything was insured in the Mutual Insurance Office.

The fire was supposed to have originated by gas having been carelessly turned on and a candle burning on the counter'. Ellis was declared insolvent in 1845 with debts of £3377 and assets of £2500. The family settled in Melbourne, travelling on the *Shamrock* and arriving on 6 November 1846. Ellis began a business as a draper and tailor in rented premises on the corner of Collins and Market streets. From 1848 to 1856 Ellis owned a hotel on the corner of Elizabeth and Flinders streets, and also managed a drapery shop. He was on the committee of the Melbourne Hebrew Congregation when the foundation stone of the synagogue was laid on 23 August 1847. In 1853 Ellis gave £31 to the Melbourne Hebrew Congregation's building appeal. He was a member of the provisional committee that investigated the establishment of a Jewish school, and in 1859 was president of the Melbourne Hebrew Congregation. During 1853 and 1854 Ellis traded as a draper at 2 Great Bourke Street West, opposite the now transformed General Post Office building, and owned the freehold of 61 Cardigan Street, Carlton. Elias Ellis died in Melbourne on 21 February 1866 at Cardigan Street. Rebecca died on 4 September 1871, aged sixty-six.

Their fourteen children were Eleanor (born 1827, in London), Maurice (Morris) (19 January 1830), Angel (q.v.) (8 April 1831, in Sydney), Frances (Fanny) (15 May 1832 to 25 December 1832), Lewis (q.v.) (3 August 1833), Solomon (q.v.) (9 June 1834), Samuel (q.v.) (12 July 1836), Barnett (q.v.) (1837), Asher (8 September 1839), Isaac Octavius (died within weeks of his birth on 22 April 1841), Deborah (1842), Esther (1844), Amelia (Melbourne, 5 March 1847), and Hyman (1848, died in infancy).

The executors of the will of Elias Ellis were the Rev. Moses Rintel and Angel Ellis. He left his property to all his children with the exception of Maurice, whose children were raised as Catholics, with the proviso that if other children were to marry non-Jews, then grandson Elias Morris, the son of Angel Ellis, would inherit their part of the estate.

Morning Chronicle, 30 May 1843; *Sydney Chronicle*, 3 May 1845; *Sydney Morning Herald*, 4 February 1846;

ELLIS, Esther

b. Sydney, 1844–1897
2 children.

Esther was the twelfth child of Rebecca and Elias Ellis (qq.v.) and was born on 11 April 1844. She married Alexander John Miller, a wealthy farmer, on 5 March 1878, at Kyneton. She had two daughters, but died in Melbourne when they were both teenagers.

ELLIS, Lewis (Louis)

b. Sydney, 1833–1917
6 children.

The fifth child of Elias and Rebecca Ellis (qq.v.), Lewis was born on 3 August 1833. 'Lou' Ellis was educated at the Normal Institute on Elizabeth Street in

Sydney, and arrived in Melbourne with his family in 1846. Very soon after his arrival he began to work as an office boy in a firm of solicitors in Collins Street. Shortly after his nineteenth birthday he became a junior clerk in the sheriff's office. Two years later, in 1854, he was appointed deputy sheriff of Victoria and he remained working in the sheriff's office for the next forty-three years. On 9 April 1856 Lou Ellis married Lydia Phillips, the 19-year-old second daughter of Solomon and Rebecca Phillips. Her younger sister Hannah married her brotherin-law Angel in 1864. Lewis and Lydia were to live at 44 Drummond Street for many years, before moving to St Kilda. They had six children. Lou Ellis was a member of the first intercolonial chess team and was a keen cricketer. He was active in Jewish communal affairs.

Ellis took many years to attain his ambition to become sheriff. Political appointments had denied him the post until 1892 and then he was able to serve three years in that post. Among his duties must have been to witness the execution of the bushranger Ned Kelly in November 1880. Ellis was said to have been 'easy, genial and courteous'. However, he quarrelled bitterly with his family and was relegated to a room at the back of the family home. He died on 12 May 1917. Lydia died on 18 August 1913.

A. S. Ellis, *Elias and Rebecca Ellis*.

ELLIS, Maurice (Morris)

b. Sydney, 1830–1887
7 children.

Born in Sydney on 14 January 1830, Maurice's parents were Rebecca (née Levey) and Elias Ellis (qq.v.). Maurice Ellis became an articled law clerk and then a solicitor in Sydney in 1859. In that year he married Annie Acres. The couple moved to Hobart and lived there until 1866, when they moved to Melbourne. They had seven children who were brought up as Catholics.

ELLIS, Rebecca (née LEVEY)

b. London, 1804–1871
Surrey, 1829; Free.
Married; 14 children.

Rebecca was the last child of Moses and Deborah Levey. Rebecca was the sister of Solomon Levey (q.v.), Barnett Levey (q.v.), Isaac Levey (q.v.), Philip Levey (q.v.). Rebecca Levey, aged twenty-two, married Elias Ellis (q.v.), formerly Elias Elias, in London.

Rebecca and Elias Ellis travelled out to Australia as steerage passengers, arriving in Sydney on 29 January 1829. Rebecca Ellis died in Melbourne, aged sixty-six, on 4 September 1871. In Rebecca's will, the portrait of her brother Solomon Levey was left to her son Angel Ellis, the portrait of her husband's mother to her daughter

Amelia, and, to her niece Rebecca Moss, she left the portrait of her sister Susan. Grandson Philip was left his grandfather's gold watch.

ELLIS, Samuel

b. Sydney, 1836–1920

The seventh child of Rebecca and Elias Ellis (qq.v.), Samuel was born on 12 July 1836. Following the discovery of gold in Victoria in 1851, the young Samuel Ellis set off for the goldfields. By 1866 he owned a hotel in Sandhurst, Victoria, which he named the Supreme Court, in a cheeky response to his father's heartfelt wish that he should become a lawyer. When Elias Ellis died, Samuel returned to New South Wales to look after his mother and his sister Deborah, after the death of her young husband. He was back in the hotel business from 1869 until 1871, when his mother died, and both Deborah and Samuel joined their sister Amelia in London. He remained a bachelor and died in London on 25 April 1920.

ELLIS, Solomon

b. Sydney, 1834–1898
10 children.

The sixth child of Rebecca and Elias Ellis (qq.v.), Solomon Ellis was born in Sydney on 9 June 1834. Ellis became a general dealer in Sydney. In 1863 he married the 23-year-old Lucretia Lee (daughter of Morris and Rebecca Lee) in Melbourne and from 1874 to 1877 worked as a general dealer with premises at 279 Elizabeth Street, Melbourne. The family then moved to Sydney. Lucretia died in 1889 after giving birth to her tenth child. Solomon Ellis died in Sydney on 11 June 1898.

EMANUEL, Abraham

Psyche, 1841; Free.
Married; Piano teacher; 6 children.

The brother of Jacob (John) Emanuel (q.v.), Abraham Emanuel arrived cabin class with his wife Elizabeth Emanuel and their two children on the *Psyche* at Port Jackson on 11 June 1841. Emanuel was described as a 'Professor of Pianoforte' (*Australian*, 29 June 1841). He lived at 4 Bridge Street, Sydney, in the early 1840s. The Misses Emanuel and Hartnelle opened a seminary for young ladies at 4 Bridge Street on 27 February 1844, where Abraham acted as 'superintendent of music'.

Low's *City of Sydney Directory* records that Abraham Emanuel was a 'Professor of Music' at 23 Princes Street. Abraham and Elizabeth had four children in Australia: Elizabeth (in Sydney, 1842), Benjamin (1846, died in Richmond, Queensland, in 1919), Isabella (1843), and Caroline (1849).

Emanuel was a seat holder at the York Street Synagogue from 1845 to 1848.

Ship Indent 4/5219; *Sydney Morning Herald*, 12 June 1841, 28 April 1842, 15 September 1842, 27 February 1844, 20 March 1844; C. H. Bertie, *Old Sydney by Old Chum*, vol. 1.

EMANUEL, Barnet (Bernard ELY)

b. London, 1798–1843
Asia I (2), 1822; Convict; Sentenced to life, Westminster, 1821.
Single; Pedlar; Height: 178 cm; 2 children.

Fair, florid complexion, brown hair, grey eyes. Barnet Emanuel was well known to the police. 'He belongs to a desperate gang', the police testimony claimed. His alibi was that he 'was sick with venereal disease and not able to put one foot before the other'. The police testified that Barnet Emanuel, together with two other men in Brick Lane, Whitechapel, did 'rush' a man and his child and steal his watch. It was not his first appearance at the Old Bailey (12 April 1820). Emanuel was sentenced on 18 July 1821.

Barnet Emanuel arrived in New South Wales on 24 July 1822 and was imprisoned in the Hyde Park Barracks. According to the superintendent's report, he was there for 'upwards of five years where he worked as tradesman, cook and messenger respectively'. His behaviour was 'generally good'. In September 1826 Barnet Emanuel married Mary Jones (Julia Emanuel, q.v.) at St John's Parramatta. She was the niece of Esther Johnston and had come out to Australia on the *Grenada* (3) in January 1825 with a sentence of seven years. Consent was given for the marriage on 19 September 1826.

In the 1828 Census Barnet Emanuel was recorded as Bernard Ely, 'Jew', and listed as an assigned government servant in 'No. 5 Iron Gang', working in the Baulkham Hills. His nine-month-old son, David Ely (David Emanuel, q.v.), was also listed as Jewish and as an inmate of the Female Factory in Parramatta.

Emanuel remained in government service and the *Sydney Gazette* noted that he had absconded from his place of employment on 7 July 1828. He was working in Sydney as an assigned servant of Jacob Isaacs (q.v.) of Parramatta Road and was listed in the Sydney Gaol Recognition Book for September 1831. On 2 June 1829 'Julia Emanuel Mary Jones' was charged with stealing, and sentenced for three months to the '3rd Class of the Female Factory'. Her change of name indicates that she had by then become Jewish (by self-definition). On 1 September 1831, 'Julia Emanuel Mary Jones' of the *Grenada* (3), free by servitude, petitioned the Governor for a ticket of exemption for her husband so that he could support her as she was 'very near her confinement with a second child'. The child, Lewis Frederick (q.v.) was born to Barnet and 'Jane' (*sic*) on 17 September 1831, just sixteen days later.

Barnet Emanuel was listed in the 1837 General Return of Convicts in New South Wales as assigned to Terry Samuel in Bathurst. He received a ticket of leave for the District of Bathurst in 1839.

Barnet Emanuel died at Bathurst on 28 February 1843 and was buried in the Devonshire Street Jewish Cemetery in Sydney on 5 March 1843. A will exists, dated 22 July 1842 and written in Bathurst. In it, Barnet left £100: David was to receive £80, Julia was to receive £10 and the Sydney Synagogue was to receive £10. Lewis was not mentioned. 'Julia' Emanuel married Folk Barnett (q.v.) at the Sydney Synagogue on 12 March 1844.

OBSP, 1820–21, case 910, p. 346; Ship Indent 2/8242, p. 21; Parramatta Gaol Record Book 4/6296, no. 2251; 4/4130, TL 39/1101; Family research by Henry Emanuel Brown, Epping, NSW.

EMANUEL, David

b. Sydney, 1828

David was born on 22 January 1828, and appeared in the 1828 Census when he was nine months old, referred to as David Ely. He was listed as being at the Female Factory in Parramatta; his religion was given as Jewish. David was the son of Barnet Emanuel (q.v.) and Mary Jones (Julia Emanuel, q.v.). David had a brother, Lewis Frederick (q.v.). David married Elizabeth Cawley at Bathurst in 1847.

EMANUEL, Dinah (née Cohen)

b. Leicester, 1810–1878
1834; Free.
Married; 8 children.

Dinah was the wife of Samuel Moses Emanuel (q.v.), the daughter of Jacob Levy Cohen of Leicester, and sister of Samuel Cohen (q.v.) and Phoebe Mandelson (wife of Nathan Mandelson, q.v.). Dinah, Phoebe and Samuel were cousins of Lady Judith Montefiore and their aunt was the Baroness Rothschild.

Dinah married Samuel Moses Emanuel on 27 February 1833 at the Great Synagogue in London, and remained in England while her husband travelled to Australia. Her child, Solomon (q.v.), was born in England on 4 December 1833, after which she and her son set sail for Australia with her sister Phoebe. Her first Australian-born child was appropriately named Sydney Levy Emanuel (q.v.). He was followed by Moses (15 September 1836), Rachael (3 October 1837), Rosa (Rosetta) (q.v.) (28 October 1840), Phoebe (q.v.) (5 August 1843), Jacob (Goulburn c. 1845), and Nathaniel (Goulburn, 1846).

Dinah died at her residence, at 156 Alberto Terrace, Darlinghurst Road, 'relict of the late Samuel Emanuel of Goulburn and Sydney'. She was buried at the Devonshire Street Cemetery on 18 February 1878, and the grave was moved to Rookwood's Jewish section in 1901.

EMANUEL, Emanuel

b. 1778
Lord Lyndoch (1), 1831; Convict; Sentenced to 7 years, Kent, 1831.
Married; Tailor; Height: 165 cm; 4 children (in England).

Brown complexion, dark brown to grey hair and whiskers, long narrow head, hazel eyes, long nose with point drooping, broad jutting chin. A Jew. Hulk report 'good'. Emanuel Emanuel was transported for receiving stolen goods. His wife, Mary Emanuel, lived at Canterbury with their four children. His offence was 'Stealing china'. Emanuel was sentenced on 28 June 1831.

Emanuel Emanuel arrived in Van Diemen's Land on 18 November 1831. 'Manley' Emanuel performed the first Jewish marriage in the colony of Van Diemen's Land on 13 December 1833, in Hobart Town, between Hannah Marks (q.v.) and Mark Solomons (Solomon, q.v.). There are no entries in Emanuel's convict dossier. The *Hobart Town Courier* advertised, on 8 June 1838, that 'Manley' Emanuel, who had come on the *Lord Lyndoch*, may apply for a certificate of freedom as his sentence had expired. It may be assumed that he returned to England.

CON 18/12.

EMANUEL, Jacob (John)

1816–1882
Bencoolen, 1842; Free.
Single; Dentist; 5 children.

The brother of Abraham Emanuel (q.v.), 'Mr Emanuel' arrived cabin class from London on 12 May 1842, and advertised in the *Sydney Morning Herald* and the *Australian* (11 June 1842) that he was a dentist, who had just arrived 'from Paris'. He would practise surgical and mechanical dentistry as performed by the most eminent dentists in Europe. Emanuel had obtained his diploma as a dentist at Leyden in 1836: '*Dentist brevette du Roi d'Hollande*'. He announced that an artificial tooth would cost £2 2s, a tooth stopped with gold, 10s 6, and capped with gold leaf, 15 shillings. His rooms were in George Street North, opposite Bridge Street.

Emanuel married Caroline Abrahams in Sydney on 26 April 1843. It was Jewish wedding no. 58 and he was a seat holder in the Sydney Synagogue in 1845. Julia was born in 1844 and Fanny in 1845. Caroline died in 1846 in childbirth at the age of twenty-nine, and the child was named Caroline in her memory. 'J. Emanuel was listed as a 'Surgeon Dentist' living at 345 Castlereagh Street in *Low's Directory of the City and District of Sydney*, 1847. Emanuel appears to have remarried quickly. His new wife was called Rachel. Abraham was born in 1846 and, in 1848, the arrival of Sarah was recorded in the synagogue's Birth Register. In 1850 Emanuel and his family lived and worked in Hobart Town, and he visited Launceston to give 'professional aid'. 'John' Emanuel, with his son Abraham, returned to New South Wales in 1850 and he continued to work in his profession until 1869. Dr John Emanuel died on 6 July 1882 at his residence at 205 Albon Street, Surry Hills; he was buried in the Jewish section of the Rookwood Cemetery, described as a dentist and 'an honest man'.

Ship Indent 4/5221; *Sydney Morning Herald*, 15 September, 9 December 1842; 17 April 1845; *Australian*, 21 June 1842, 25 May 1844; *Launceston Examiner*, 2 March 1850.

EMANUEL, Julia (née Mary JONES)

b. London, 1810
Grenada (3), 1825; Convict; Sentenced to 7 years, Newgate, 1824.
Single; Housemaid; Height: 146 cm; 2 children.

Sallow complexion, black hair, hazel eyes, 'Jew'. 'Very well behaved' on board ship. It is noted in the indent that Mary Jones was a 'Niece to Mrs Colonel Johnston' (Esther Abrahams, q.v.). Esther often claimed to be Esther Julian and the surnames Jones and Julian may be connected.

Mary Jones was sentenced on 3 June 1824 and arrived in New South Wales on 23 January 1825. She married Barnet Emanuel (q.v.) at Parramatta in September 1826. In the course of the next few years she changed her first name from 'Mary' to the more acceptable (to the Jewish community) name of 'Julia'. She had two children, David and Lewis (qq.v.).

On 27 August 1828, Julia Emanuel, a prisoner, was noted to be 'at large her husband being at an Iron Gang'. The 1828 Police Report of Prisoners noted that she was therefore 'Sent to first class Factory being of a good character'. Julia was charged at the Sydney police office with theft on 2 June 1829: 'Though the legal proof of the offence was not sufficient and the male Prisoner [Barnet Emanuel?] in consequence was discharged yet there could be no doubt of the Female prisoner's Knowledge of the articles'. The prisoner was sent to the lowly '3rd Class of the Female Factory' in Parramatta. Julia had been arrested following a complaint laid by Mrs Sarah Solomon of George Street, the wife of John Solomon (q.v.), who had identified two pieces of check cloth and a piece of print that had been found in Julia's house in Kent Street. The cloth had been stolen by 'someone' entering the back door of the George Street shop, and had been made into a gown, which was valued at £6 3s. Julia had been seen with the gown 'on her back'. Julia Emanuel's ticket of leave was suspended. By 1830 Mary Myers asked for the assignment of Julia from her service with Jacob Isaacs. Isaacs had consented to the transfer. Mary Jones, 'wife of Barnet Emanuel', received a certificate of freedom on 3 June 1831.

Julia's husband Barnet died in 1843, and on 12 March 1844 she married Folk Barnett at the Sydney Synagogue. The witness was Moses Joseph and the officiating minister was Jacob Isaacs.

There is a final clue in the saga of the surname 'Julian', and Julia's relationship to Esther Abrahams. When Julia's second son, Lewis, married for the third time, it was stated on the marriage document: 'Father's name: John Emanuel. Father's occupation: Storekeeper. Mother's name and maiden surname 'Julia Ann Julien'.

Family research by Henry Emanuel Brown, Epping, NSW; State Archives, CS 29/4329, 3 June 1829; Principal Superintendent of Convicts Office, 24 August 1830; Ship Indent 4/4009a; CF 31/0537.

EMANUEL, Lewis Frederick

b. Sydney, 1831–1903

The child of Barnet (q.v.) and Julia Emanuel (née Mary Jones) (q.v.), and brother of David Emanuel (q.v.), Lewis married three times. He married Mary Ellen Balfe in 1855. His second marriage was to Alice Orchard, a widow, at St Barnabas in George Street West. His third marriage was to Mary Wheeler Wilding. Lewis died at Redfern, Sydney, on 17 April 1903.

EMANUEL, Moses

b. Portsmouth, 1772–1858
1849; Free.
Married; Watchmaker; 4 children.

Moses Emanuel's occupation on arrival in New South Wales (with his wife Rosetta) was 'watchmaker and gentleman'. He was eighty-six years old when he died on 23 October 1858, his death certificate describing him as a 'watchmaker' living at 404 Castlereagh Street. Emanuel was buried by the Sydney Synagogue. The congregation listed his children as Samuel Isaac Emanuel, Lizzy, Betty, and Julia. His grave was at the Devonshire Street Cemetery until it was moved to Rookwood.
Family research.

EMANUEL, Phoebe

b. Goulburn, 1843
6 children.

Phoebe, the sixth child of Samuel Moses and Dinah Emanuel (née Cohen) (qq.v.), was born on 5 August 1843. She grew up in Goulburn and married Julius Raphael Litten (who dropped his Germanic surname during World War I). Their six children were Ina, Stella, Violet, Alfred, Aimée and Norman.

EMANUEL, Rosa (Rosetta)

b. Goulburn, 1840–1909
8 children.

Rosa was the fifth child of Samuel Moses and Dinah Emanuel (née Cohen) (qq.v.). She was born in Goulburn on 28 October 1840, and married Frederick Cohen (son of Abraham and Sophia Cohen, qq.v.) on 17 January 1866. Their children were Abraham (1866), Mabel (1867), Adele (1869), Edith (1870), Samuel (1871), Estelle (1873), Vera (1884), and Sydney (1885).

EMANUEL, Samuel Moses

b. Portsmouth, 1803–1868
Children, 1833; Free.
Married; Glass cutter; 8 children.

Samuel was the eldest child in the family of Moses (q.v.) and Rosetta Emanuel (née Jacob) of Portsmouth. On 27 February 1833, at the Great Synagogue in London,

Samuel Moses Emanuel married Dinah (q.v.), the 21-year-old daughter of Jacob Levy Cohen of Leicester, and sister of Samuel Cohen (q.v.) and Phoebe Mandelson. Samuel Emanuel travelled steerage class to Australia on the *Children*, arriving at Port Jackson on 31 August 1833, while Dinah waited in England because she was pregnant. Dinah therefore came out in 1834 with Solomon (q.v.), her first child.

Samuel Moses Emanuel was on the same ship as his brother-in-law Nathan Mandelson (q.v.). Emanuel established a business, Manchester House, at 382 George Street, Sydney, which sold beaver hats and eau de cologne. He generously gave £35 to the Sydney Synagogue building appeal in September 1839, and was asked to collect money for the appeal. He failed 'to do his duty' and was replaced. He stood for election to the committee in September 1840 after which he resigned from the congregation.

Facing severe economic difficulties due to the depression, the family moved to Goulburn, where Nathan Mandelson was an innkeeper. In 1843 the Sydney Synagogue appointed him, together with Solomon Moses (q.v.), to be a 'representative' of the congregation in Goulburn. In 1845 Emanuel opened the Beehive Store in Auburn Street, which rapidly became one of the most significant businesses in the town. The *Sydney Morning Herald* announced each year that the shop would be closed for the Jewish High Holydays. The firm was renamed S. Emanuel and Son in 1857, the 'son' being Solomon.

The family was involved in financing and organising the Sydney Gold Escort some months before the discovery of gold. 'Was it intuition or were they in the know?' asked Mary Durack in *Kings in Grass Castles*. Durack described Emanuel and Son as 'gold buyers, bankers, shareholders in the Gold Escort, proprietors of the Steam Flour Mills, the Beehive Store and the Beehive Hotel'. The sign outside the hotel read: 'In this house we're all alive. Good liquor makes us funny. If you are dry, come on and try The virtue of our honey'.

In 1850 Samuel Emanuel and Nathan Mandelson set up a private bank at No. 8 Mandelson Buildings, which provided the capital for the Durack family to establish their 'empire' in the Kimberley region. Samuel and Nathan were gold buyers who bought direct from the miners at Braidwood and Turon.

Samuel and Dinah (also known as Diana) had eight children: Solomon who was born in England (4 December 1833), Sydney Levy (18 April 1834, born in Sydney), Moses (15 September 1836), Rachael (3 October 1837), Rosa (Rosetta) (28 October 1840), Phoebe (q.v.) (5 August 1843), Jacob (c. 1845, born in Goulburn), and Nathaniel (1846, also born in Goulburn).

Emanuel acquired large tracts of land in the area and lived there until 1857. He represented the electorate of Argyle in the New South Wales Parliament from 30 October 1862 to 10 November 1864. He was one of the eighty-one shareholders in a company named the Sydney Gold Escort. It is said that he discovered opals in the Abercrombie Ranges in 1862.

Samuel Emanuel 'of Goulburn and Sydney' died at the 'Fig Tree Cottage', 157 Liverpool Street, Sydney, on 11 July 1868, leaving an estate valued at £13 100. According to the tombstone inscription, he was 'a pillar of reliance to those who sought his aid'.

Ship Indent 4/5305; *Sydney Gazette*, 27 August 1833; *Sydney Morning Herald*, 13 September 1842, 15 September 1842, 29 September 1845, 13 July 1868; Audrey van Hattem, *Time Was*, privately printed, Perth, 1998; Family research by Mrs Val Silberberg, Melbourne.

EMANUEL, Solomon

Solomon Emanuel signed the petition to establish a synagogue in Launceston on 20 May 1843.

EMANUEL, Solomon

b. London, 1833–1895
1834; Free.
6 children.

The son of Samuel Moses and Dinah Emanuel (qq.v.), Solomon was born in England on 4 December 1833. His father had travelled to Australia and arrived in Sydney in August 1833. He and his mother followed in 1834.

Solomon grew up in Goulburn and married Sara, the daughter of Israel Myers, on 10 March 1858. They had six children: Isadore (Issey) Samuel (4 February 1860), Sydney Phillip (1861), born in Goulburn, Florence Marion (28 February 1869), Maud, Alfred, and Maurice.

Solomon joined his father in business in Goulburn in 1857. In 1879 he became a member of the New South Wales Parliament and in 1880 joined with the Durack family in applying for land in the Ord River region. He is said to have financed the Duracks' private exploration of the Kimberley region in Australia's north west.

Solomon Emanuel's sons Isadore and Sydney were West Kimberley region pioneers. During their heyday, the brothers held a significant part of the rights to twenty thousand square miles of pastoral land in the Kimberley district of north-western Australia and the Northern Territory.

Solomon Emanuel died on 4 October 1895 and was buried in Rookwood's Jewish cemetery.

CO 280/157.

EMANUEL, Sydney Levy

b. Sydney, 1834–1863
2 children.

The second child of Samuel Moses and Dinah (née Cohen) Emanuel (qq.v.), Sydney grew up in Goulburn, and married Caroline Moses, the daughter of Solomon Moses and Deborah (née Hart). Sydney Emanuel became an alderman and Justice of the Peace in Goulburn. He died on 9 May 1863 in Goulburn and was buried at the Devonshire Street Jewish Cemetery in Sydney six days later. His wife died on 2 November 1921 in Melbourne. Their children were Rosetta Ida (22 November 1861) and Julia Gertrude (25 December 1862).

F

FISCHELL, Saul

b. Danzig, 1822
Mt Stuart Elphinstone, 1845; Convict; Sentenced to 7 years, Central Criminal Court, 1844.
Single; Tailor; Height: 166 cm.

Fair complexion, black hair, large nose and chin, black whiskers. A stout man. Jew. Could read and write German. Saul Fischell was sentenced to seven years transportation for stealing ten watches. His employer, Adolphus Liepman, had employed Fischell twelve days before the theft. Liepman was 'an outfitter' at 81 Parson's Street, East Smithfield, who had known Fischell for two years. At five thirty in the morning he heard Fischell leave the house. 'I got out of bed, went into the kitchen, and he was gone. I had given him a new suit of clothes the day before. I examined my stock and missed a gold watch, nine silver watches and two German silver guards and other articles worth £25'. The police arrested Fischell the same afternoon. He had already sold two of the watches in Petticoat Lane. Surgeon's report 'fair'.

Fischell's initial period of labour was for twelve months at Port Cygnet in Van Diemen's Land. He received his ticket of leave on 1 May 1849. On 28 September 1849 he received a six-month sentence of imprisonment and hard labour for absconding from assigned service in Launceston. In 1850 he was reprimanded for being in Campbelltown without a pass. On 31 May 1851 he was sentenced at Hobart Town to six months imprisonment with hard labour, after he 'failed to return' the three coats which he had in his possession so that they could be altered. A certificate of freedom was granted on 7 October 1851.

OBSP, 16 September 1844, case 2222. CON 33/66, no. 15641.

FISHER, Henry

Free.
Single; Dealer.

Henry Fisher had a store in Argyle Street, Sydney, in 1842, and a home in Pitt Street. He was listed as a voter in the first municipal election. By August 1843 he was listed in the newspapers as a wine and spirit merchant with premises opposite the old gaol. In 1845 he gave one guinea to the Sydney Synagogue appeal.

Sydney Morning Herald, 13 September, 16 September 1842, 3 August 1843.

FOLK, Amelia

1796–1880
Indiana, 1832; Free.
Married; 6 children.

The wife of Samuel Folk (q.v.), and the 'daughter of Isaac', Amelia was buried in the Jewish section of the Rookwood Cemetery. She died at her residence, at 16 Oxford Street, Sydney, on 26 June 1880, aged eighty-four years, the 'relict of the late Samuel Folk'. Her children were Maria (q.v.), Mark, Isaac, Susie, Henry (b. 1832) and Julia (q.v.) (b. 1837).

FOLK, Julia

b. Sydney, 1837

Julia Folk was the youngest child of Samuel and his wife Amelia. In 1857 she married David Moss at the York Street Synagogue, Sydney. Her sister Maria had married Isaac Moss (q.v.) in 1842.

FOLK, Maria

b. 1821
Indiana, 1832; Free.
Single.

Maria arrived in New South Wales with her parents, Samuel and Amelia Folk (qq.v.), in 1832, when she was eleven years old. She was married in a Jewish ceremony to Isaac Moss (Moses) (q.v.) in Sydney on 19 October 1842.

FOLK, Samuel

b. Berlin, 1798–1860
Indiana, 1832; Free.
Married; Tailor; 6 children.

Samuel Folk, (aged thirty-four) his wife Amelia (forty), and children Mark Folk (six), Maria (eleven) (q.v.), Isaac (four) and Susie (nine months) travelled steerage from England as free migrants. They arrived in Sydney on 15 October 1833, and Samuel opened a shop in George Street. A child, Henry, was born in Sydney in the year of the family's arrival, and Julia (q.v.) was born in 1837. Folk joined the Sydney Synagogue in 1837 and in 1839 gave £10 to the Sydney Synagogue's building fund. Mrs Folk gave £5. By this time Folk was 'a general merchant'. In September 1840 he stood for election to the committee of the Sydney Synagogue.

He was obviously feeling 'at home'. In the 1840s Folk was one of the four Jewish ship owners in the colony, with the *Young Queen*.

In an application for naturalisation, Folk told his life story. Born in Berlin, he served in the Prussian army and fought at the Battle of Waterloo. He lived for fourteen years in England and after emigrating to Sydney, carried on a business as a tailor and draper in George Street. He was 'anxious to be placed in an equal footing' with his own children. Ten magistrates signed Folk's petition.

On 19 October 1842 his daughter Maria married Isaac Moss (q.v.) in Sydney. Samuel's shop and home were at 564 Lower George Street when he appeared on the Sydney Synagogue subscription list in 1845 with a gift of £15. He was a seat holder in the synagogue. On 20 June 1844 the *Sydney Morning Herald* listed him as one of the four Jewish owners of the intercolonial vessel the *Young Queen*, and in 1845 he advertised that he was an agent for colonial vessels, particularly those trading with Newcastle. Sydney's *Shipping Gazette* announced that on 6 December 1845 Samuel Folk had received eleven cases of merchandise from London. On 4 October 1845 he had received one trunk and, on 19 January 1846, eight cases arrived from London.

Folk died at his home, at 28 William Street, Woolloomooloo, on 26 June 1860, and was buried at the Devonshire Street Jewish Cemetery. In 1901, his remains were removed to the Jewish section of the Rookwood Cemetery. Amelia died on 26 June 1880 and was also buried at Rookwood.

Ship Indent 4/5205; Fitzroy Correspondence, 67/1847, in A1242, p. 5f., re Naturalisation; *Sydney Gazette*, 10 December 1836; *Sydney Morning Herald*, 15 September 1842, 9 July 1845.

FONSECA, Henry (Henry FONSEED)

b. London, 1767

Neptune, 1790; Convict; Sentenced to 7 years, Old Bailey, 1788.

Henry Fonseca was sentenced to transportation at the Old Bailey May Sessions of 1788 for stealing a pattern book containing twenty-four metal buttons. A tailor gave evidence that he was threatened by one of a group of men as he walked along Petticoat Lane. Fonseca, who carried a knife, refused to hand the buttons back after the tailor had surrendered them, saying, according to the tailor, 'Blast me I'll run you through! Damn your eyes you're nothing but a tailor with nothing but buttons in your pocket'. The tailor told the court that he had known Fonseca for nine or ten years but had never been molested by him before. Fonseca's coat was torn in half by an angry crowd. Fonseca had no witnesses appearing for him, and claimed this was because he had been expecting to come before the court on the following day.

After spending a year in Newgate Prison, Henry Fonseca was sent to the *Dunkirk* hulk. In November 1789 he embarked on the *Neptune*, which arrived at Port Jackson on 28 June 1790. There is no record of his time in New South Wales and many of those who sailed on the *Neptune* died during the voyage.

Michael Flynn, *The Second Fleet*, p. 668.

FONSECA, Isaac (FONSAKER)

1839; Free.
Single.

Isaac Fonseca was a member of the first committee of the Jewish Congregational Society in Melbourne in 1841, and in 1843 was listed as a member of the committee formed to approach the government regarding a grant for a synagogue. Fonseca had donated £5 to the Sydney Synagogue building fund in September 1839, and a further ten shillings in 1845.'I. Fonsaker' was a storekeeper in Port Adelaide in 1850.

Isaac may have married in the early 1850s and then died, because in January 1854 Mary Ann Fonsaker,'widow', was charged and convicted for threatening to split a neighbour's head open.

South Australian Gazette and Colonial Register, 11 January 1854.

FONSECA, John

b. London, 1803
Charles Kerr, 1837; Convict; Sentenced to 14 years, Old Bailey, 1836.
Single; Indoor servant; Height: 166 cm.

Dark ruddy and freckled complexion, black hair, brown eyes, Roman nose. Could read and write. Jew. Three scars over left eyebrow, three large scars on the back of the neck, four small moles over right cheek bone. Fonseca was a 24-year-old pickpocket in Houndsditch, and was transported for stealing a handkerchief. He was sentenced on 28 November 1836. The ship's printed indent mistakenly listed him as Fronseca.

John Fonseca arrived in Sydney on 9 October 1837 and was sent to the Hyde Park Barracks. On his arrival, John told the authorities that his brother, Moses Fonseca (q.v.), had arrived in Sydney in 1819 as a free settler on the *Bengal Merchant*. (Moses, in fact, had been transported on the *Mangles*.) Fonseca received a certificate of freedom in 1857.

OBSP, 1836–37, case 54, p. 42; *Charles Kerr* Printed Indent, p. 153: CF 57/63.

FONSECA, Moses

b. London, 1802–1848
Mangles (1), 1820; Convict; Sentenced to life, London, 1819.
Single; Chimney sweep; Height: 159 cm; 6 children.

Florid complexion, dark brown hair, hazel eyes. Tattoos of A.H.M.T., a heart with two arrows, and a compass on right arm; A.H.M.T., a man and a woman on left arm. Pearl on left eye. Jew. On 9 November 1819 Moses Fonseca was arrested as he stole a handkerchief (value three shillings) from a spectator who was watching the Lord Mayor's procession. There were two other pickpockets with him but both escaped. Fonseca had been in court before. At the Old Bailey, July Session 1818, he had been acquitted, even though it was noted that he had been in gaol before. In the July Session of 1819 he had been charged with 'larceny from the person' but was freed when the prosecutor failed to appear. Fonseca was dubbed an 'old offender' and sentenced on 1 December 1819. His brother, John Fonseca (q.v.), was also transported, and arrived in 1837.

The convict transport ship arrived on 7 August 1820, and Moses Fonseca was assigned to the Parramatta District, then sent on to Sydney Gaol on 23 January 1821. The 1822 Muster recorded him as employed by James Vincent, a settler with twenty-five acres of land at Windsor. In 1823 he was employed as an assigned convict servant by Samuel Craft at Richmond. In 1824, Fonseca was listed by the Colonial Secretary as a convict employed by Mr Archibald Bell, a landholder and a Justice of the Peace at Windsor. On 13 July 1825 he was sent, as a convict, to Port Macquarie on the *Elizabeth Henrietta*. He returned to Sydney on 4 October 1828 and was sent to work for Richard Donohue at Castle Hill.

The *New South Wales Government Gazette* of 19 June 1833 reported that Fonseca was an absconder from an 'Invalid Gang'. An application to marry the 19-yearold Esther Heaken [*sic*] Aiken was refused on the grounds that Fonseca did not hold a ticket of leave. Despite this, a baby girl, Frances, was born on 28 March 1836 (she died on 29 July 1843). A ticket of leave was issued in 1839 and on 1 April 1840 Moses Fonseca (aged forty) finally married Esther Acan (sic) a native of the colony, the Rev. H. H. Bobart officiating, in Parramatta. The couple's second child, Jane, was born on 8 January 1839. She was followed by Moses (8 January 1841 to 1848), Matilda (8 February 1843), Maria (5 October 1844), and Elizabeth (14 August 1846).

The family lived in the Castle Hill/Dooral District and Fonseca was described as a sawyer. Moses Fonseca was granted a conditional pardon on 30 January 1847. He died on 7 April 1848 and was buried at St John's, Parramatta. A baby boy, named George, who was born to Esther in early 1849, died on 11 May 1850. Esther Fonseca married Roger Hurst and had another child, Alice.

OBSP, 1819–20, case 85, p. 48; Ship Indent 4/4006, p. 165, 4/4019; Parramatta Gaol 1835/6, no. 1288, in 4/6531; Permission to Marry Book 1835, 4/4505; Convict Register 4/4130; TL 39/1128; CP 47/121; CS 4/1781, p. 395b; 4/3864, p. 526f.

FONSECA, Moses Joseph

b. London, 1813–1850
Free.
Single; Dealer.

Moses Joseph Fonseca died, aged thirty-seven, at Port Adelaide, on 3 May 1850, 'after a short illness'. He was described as a storekeeper.

Pritchard Index; *Adelaide Times*, 4 May 1850.

FORESTER, James

b. Holland, 1826
Lady Kennaway (2), 1851; Convict; Sentenced to 7 years, Clerkenwell, 1848.
Single; French polisher; Height: 150 cm.

Fresh complexion, brown hair, dark hazel eyes, medium nose. Twice convicted before: 'Very bad. A confirmed thief and gambler. Very insolent when detected. A Jew. Can read and write a little'. James Forester, born in Holland, was brought up in St Giles, London. He was transported for picking pockets in the Edgware Road.

James Forester arrived in Van Diemen's Land on 28 May 1851, was given an 18 month period of probation and sent to the Cascades. On 6 November 1852, he was absent without leave from the Cascades and placed in solitary confinement for ten days. He was sent to the Tasman Peninsula on 26 August 1852. He was to have been sent to Norfolk Island, but remained in Van Diemen's Land 'on account of his youth'. On 11 August 1853 he was under assignment to Mr King when he was found in a public house. On 9 December 1853 he was committed for trial at Launceston for larceny under £5. It appears that he absconded. His ticket of leave was officially revoked on 3 January 1854 and his convict records abruptly ceased.

CON 33/102, no. 24136.

FOX, Hannah (née LEVY)

b. London, 1802
Princess Charlotte (2), 1827; Convict; Sentenced to 7 years, Old Bailey, 1826.
Married; Prostitute; Height: 147 cm.

Fair complexion, brown hair, brown eyes. Can read and write. Jewess. Together with Ann McCoy, Hannah Fox stole a client's watch from his trousers. She was sentenced on 7 December 1826. Her husband, Thomas Fox, remained in England. She was the sister of Abraham and Barnet Levy.

Hannah Fox was assigned, on arrival, to be a servant in Parramatta. Her brother Barnett was in Sydney at the time of her arrival. She was listed as 'Catholic' at the Female Factory, Parramatta, in 1828. Hannah Fox received a certificate of freedom on 10 December 1833.

OBSP, 1826–27, case 139, p. 64; Indent 4/4012, p. 134, 4/3499 p. 175; CF 33/1325, in 4/44319.

FRANCES, Sarah

b. New South Wales
3 children.

'Sarah Frances', the daughter of Benjamin Frances (Francis, q.v.), was made a *Geyoureth* on 18 January 1833, by Messrs Michael Phillips and J. B. Montefiore, according to the records of the Sydney Synagogue that note the marriage of Sarah to John Barnett (q.v.). It was the second Jewish marriage in Australia. A son, Lewis, was born on 2 December 1833, and died on 26 April 1841. A daughter, Jane, was born in Sydney on 10 October 1836 and Emily born 10 January 1846

York Street Synagogue Birth Register

FRANCIS, Benjamin (FRANCES)

b. London, 1796–1873
Recovery, 1819; Convict; Sentenced to life, Somerset Assizes, 1819.
Single; Dealer; Height: 168 cm; 1 child.

Dark complexion, black hair, dark eyes. Francis was in Bath when he was caught paying for 'a gold watch with appendages' with a counterfeit cheque for £48. The 'Times' of London (21 September 1818) reported that he was 'a Jew, from London' who possessed 'a large cane with a sword in it, several flints and the duplicates of several watches'. On the 22 June 1819 the Bet Din travelled from London to Woolwich to grant a Get to his wife Clara, the daughter of Yeshayahu (Isaiah), and Benjamin Francis. The convict transport left England on 31 July 1819.

The son of Moses and Sarah Francis of London, Benjamin arrived in New South Wales on 18 December 1819. Francis worked as a convict labourer and as overseer at the hospital in Parramatta, and on 29 April 1820, according to the *Sydney Gazette*, opened a store in Parramatta. He then abruptly asked to be transferred to Port Macquarie. A Justice of the Peace wrote to the Colonial Secretary (9 April 1822). 'The reasons which caused him to make the application are creditable to him', as he wanted 'to become a clerk to the Acting Engineer Lt Wilton of the 48th Regiment to the Military'. In his petition to Governor Brisbane, he asked for 'the indulgence of a pardon granted to the whole of the volunteers at that station'. His ticket of leave was delayed because 'Francis was sent to the gaol gang on 9 July 1821 for decoying Mr Robert's wife from her home. He finally volunteered to be sent to Port Macquarie to break the connexion that there subsisted between himself and Robert's wife'. The ticket of leave was eventually granted on 26 November 1825 and a conditional pardon was recommended on 5 August 1834.

Francis was a dealer in Parramatta in 1826 and on 27 January 1827 announced to his customers that the Kings' Head in Penrith was to be extended. On 19 July, he became the lessee of the Royal Hotel in George Street, opposite Market Place, and on 29 May 1835 announced that he intended to operate the King's Head Inn at Penrith, which would be known as the White Hart. The inn belonged to John Moses (q.v.) and the Colonial Secretary objected to Francis being in charge of the hotel, as he was still a prisoner. After briefly working as an auctioneer, he returned to Sydney in the second half of 1836 and was a haberdasher and silk mercer in Hunter Street. On 1 October 1836, from 'opposite the Bank of Australasia, George St', Francis wrote to the Colonial Secretary asking for permission to travel by way of Launceston, as 'I intend to proceed to Port Phillip in a speculative trip and being anxious to return to my wife and family as early as possible'. The Colonial Secretary noted that he held a conditional pardon and permitted the journey. Abraham Polack (q.v.) announced that he would sell Francis's remaining stock, and Francis left Sydney for Launceston, followed by a visit to Hobart Town.

Benjamin Francis had married Elizabeth Solomons in Sydney on 20 July 1836, and the move could have been for family reasons. He became a member of the Hobart Town Hebrew Congregation in 1842, was a leader of the Jewish congregation in Launceston in the years 1842–47, and became trustee for the new Launceston Cemetery. Francis was a prominent auctioneer in Launceston during those years and owned the Cataract Mills and Water Tanks Company, which he sold in February 1845, advertising the mill as the 'El Dorado of Launceston'.

On 12 July 1848 the *Launceston Examiner* announced that Francis was about to leave for Hobart after twelve years in business in Launceston. He transferred to Hobart in partnership with Mr Pyle at Stracey's Mart. On 17 February 1847 Francis was wounded when a burglar assailed him at his home. The *Examiner* wrote that 'his residence is at fashionable Battery Point', and mentioned his wife and infant child Sarah, 'who were unharmed'. On 2 March 1850 the *Examiner* announced that he had 'removed to Melbourne', where, in April 1850, he became an auctioneer in partnership with Edward Aaron Cohen (q.v.). He continued his involvement in Jewish life and the firm of Francis and Cohen donated the very large sum of £200 to the building fund of the Melbourne Synagogue. However, the Melbourne Hebrew Congregation was not as tolerant towards former convicts as were the congregations in Hobart Town, Launceston and Sydney, and Francis was put on 'probationary membership'. In the first letter book of the Melbourne Hebrew Congregation there is a communication from the president to Francis dated 16 April 1850, which tactfully explains:

> the regulation may be unpleasing to a respectable man like yourself, so well known among us. The law was made to guard respectable men against the encroachment of blackguards. Anticipating at no distant date the name of Benjamin Francis as a colleague in the direction of the Institution which, as a Jew, you feel interested in.

In 1854 Francis left Melbourne for Sydney and lived in semi-retirement. He took a leading role in the Sydney Jewish Sabbath School and the Society for the Diffusion of Religious Knowledge, and he served a term as treasurer of the York Street Synagogue. He died in Sydney, at his residence, Melton House, Myles Buildings, Cumberland Street, on 18 May 1873. Elizabeth died in 1877. The *Australian Israelite* described him as 'an old and esteemed colonist'.

The elaborate memorial inscription on his tombstone at Rookwood Cemetery states: 'After enjoying a life of 78 years, passed in domestic devotion and worldly integrity, leaving a name honoured in the community, a memory of peerless worth to his dearly loved widow and foster family ... a trusted man, respected honest and dear'.

Jeremy I. Pfeffer, *From One End of the Earth to the Other*, Sussex Academic Press (2008), p. 198f; Ship Indent 4/4006, p. 455; Police Correspondence for 1829, p. 308, in 4/3828; CS 4/1752; Petition to Governor Brisbane, 4/1872, no. 44a, 44b, 20 July 1836; CS 4/1873, no. 77; CS 4/2309, 1 October 1836; Governors' Despatches 1834, p. 219f., 4/1873, no 77; CSO 11/18423; *Port Phillip Patriot*, 14 February 1845; Melbourne Hebrew Congregation Letter Book, 16 April 1850; *Sydney Gazette*, 29 April 1820, 26 August 1820, 20 February 1834, 28 November 1825, 22 December 1825, 27 January 1827, 10 July 1827; *Hobart Town Gazette*, 11 April 1839, 8 July 1848, 12 July 1848; *Launceston Examiner*, 29 June 1844, 17 February 1847, 29 July 1847, 27 February 1850; *Sydney Morning Herald*, 25 March 1845; *Australian Israelite*, 20 May 1873; *AG*, pp. 290, 293.

FRANKEL, Jacob

b. Breslau, 1812–1899
Calcutta, 1842; Free.
Married; 5 children.

Jacob Frankel was born in Breslau and was apprenticed to work in his uncle's linen and drapery factory at the age of thirteen. By eighteen he was a commercial traveller, and arrived in London as a young man. The authorities of the Great Synagogue in Duke's Place took him under their wing and he studied to become a minister, serving a small London congregation for three years before returning to the world of commerce. In 1834, at Greenwich, he married Miriam Sarah Moses (Miriam Frankel, q.v.), the sister of Elias Moses (q.v.). Elias visited England in 1841 and persuaded his new brother-in-law to migrate to Australia. Jacob, Miriam, and three very young children arrived in Hobart Town in October 1842. Another child was born in Van Diemen's Land and the family consisted of Mary (1836), Simeon (1840–1937), Walter and Pauline.

Frankel was one of those who helped found the Hobart Hebrew Congregation. He ran a drapery shop called the Cheap Shop. Frankel shared the prayers with Henry Jones (q.v.) on the High Holydays in Hobart in 1845. Miriam Frankel died in 1847 and Jacob's sister-in-law, Rebecca Julia, wife of Elias Moses, travelled from Sydney to Tasmania to care for the children and to take them to New South Wales. One of those children, Simeon, was later to become the long-serving secretary of Sydney's Great Synagogue. In 1849 Jacob Frankel sailed for San Francisco and was the minister of the congregation *Shearith Israel*. After three years he returned to Australia, established a business in Melbourne and worked as an assistant to the Rev. Moses Rintel (q.v.) of the Melbourne Hebrew Congregation.

On 18 February 1857, in Melbourne, Frankel, aged forty-five, married Miss Mary Marks, who was twenty-four. They left Melbourne in 1861 and moved to Dunedin until 1864. He then served as minister of the Hebrew Congregation in Wellington. Jacob Frankel died on 30 August 1899 in Wellington. Mary Frankel died in Wellington on 14 December 1899. Jacob and Mary had one son, Philip, born in 1863.

'The Life of Jacob Frankel', *AJJHS*, vol. 13, no. 3 (1996), p. 395f.

FRANKEL, Miriam Sarah (née MOSES)

d. 1847
Calcutta, 1842; Free.
Married; 4 children.

'Sarah, the beloved wife of Jacob Frankel (q.v.) of Hobart Town, Van Diemen's Land', died on 27 August 1847, at the age of forty-seven. She was buried in Sydney and her grave is now at the Rookwood Cemetery. Simeon Frankel, her son, of 94 Pitt Street, Sydney, authorised the transfer of her grave from the Devonshire Street Cemetery in 1901.

FRANKLAND, Levy

b. Bradford, 1815–1847
Marion (2), 1845; Convict; Sentenced to 7 years, Fredericktown, New Brunswick, 1844.
Single; Soldier; Height: 173 cm.

Fresh complexion, brown hair, brown whiskers, brown eyes, large nose, large mouth and chin'. Stout made. The letter D tattooed on left side and ME rather faint on left arm below elbow. Levy Frankland had worked as a blacksmith for three years before enlisting in the 33rd regiment. He served for seven years and eleven months before his arrest for 'desertion' in Newfoundland. He explained that he had been only 'absent from his post for one hour'.

Frankland was assigned to the Cascades in Van Diemen's Land for one year's initial servitude and he emerged from the work gang on 16 September 1846. He then became a constable at Port Arthur. One year later, he was sent to Impression Bay on the Tasman Peninsula, where he died on 31 October 1847.

CON 33/70, per *Ratcliffe*, 30 August 1845, no. 16406.

FRANKLIN, Mark

Calcutta, 1844; Free.
Married.

Mark Franklin travelled steerage on the *Calcutta* with his wife and family. He rented seat no. 75 in the Hobart Synagogue in 1845. He was one of the four applicants for the post of sexton in July 1845, though he was not selected. On 31 July he was given £4 by the synagogue for 'services'. In the Hobart Synagogue ledger, the word 'Left' is written after his name in 1846.

CSO 92/11/F 123; OB 7/10, p. 30.

FRANKS, Elias

Eliza (3), 1827; Convict.

Elias Franks arrived in Sydney on 10 November 1827. The List of Convicts in New South Wales of November 1828 describes Franks as a 'Jew' on government service at Melville Island. The 1828 Census placed him on Norfolk Island.

HO 10/28.

FRANKS, Gabriel

d. 1834
Free.

Gabriel Franks was buried on 13 July 1834 at the Devonshire Street Jewish Cemetery. According to the synagogue records he died 'Suddenly in Parramatta'.

FRANKS, Hyam (Himey, known as Joseph)

b. Holland, 1796–1859
Surrey I (1), 1814; Convict; Sentenced to life, Old Bailey, 1813.
Jeweller; Height: 163 cm.

Dark sallow complexion, black to grey hair, black eyes. In 1812 Hyam Franks was tried at the Old Bailey for having stolen a quantity of hats. Within the year, Franks was back in court; he and two others had attacked and robbed a baker in a street in Whitechapel at night. He was caught in the act by a night watchman, who came to the assistance of the baker. He claimed to have an aged father and mother whom he supported by his 'honest industry'. He was sentenced to death on 13 January 1813, the sentence subsequently commuted to transportation for life.

Hyam Franks arrived on 28 July 1814, and was assigned for seven years to Dr Townsend, and for one year to John Burke, the overseer of Mr Dickson of Sydney. He appeared on a list of 'servants and labourers who are absent from employment' on 23 August 1817. Franks was sent to the Newcastle Penal Settlement. The punishment book recorded that, on 21 December 1821, 'Hymey' Franks received fifty lashes for helping to cut the chains of two runaways while working at the lime burners. In 1822 he wrote to the government: 'The Humble memorial of Joseph Franks a Foreigner … pray pardon the intrusion of a poor foreigner who had faithfully served more than eight years in the colony'. Franks asked for a ticket of leave. In March 1824, still at Newcastle, he was given twenty-five lashes 'for having a shirt in his possession belonging to a fellow prisoner for which he could not account'. On 24 May he ran away, and received twenty-five lashes when he was returned. On 18 March 1825 he received fifty lashes and fourteen days in irons for 'disorderly conduct'. On 24 August he was given fifty lashes and twenty-eight days in irons for gambling. On 1 March 1826 he stole a pair of boots from a soldier and sold them to a settler's man for seven pennies and one halfpence and a gill of rum. He was sentenced to three years at a penal settlement and sent to Norfolk Island.

The 1828 Census listed him with the 'No. 4 Chain Gang' in Sydney, and in 1829 a public notice described him as 'a notorious runaway'. On 21 October 1831, he was sent to the Road Department for 'gambling on the Saboth'. In May 1832 he unsuccessfully petitioned for a ticket of leave. He wrote that ever since he had arrived he had 'experienced the most unprecedented privations' and was

> not guilty of any flagrant crime that invited his attendance in the Supreme Court or Quarter Sessions, although he much deplores having incurred Magisterial displeasure for which he has suffered by working in an Iron Gang (now here 18 years) endured by the impaired state of his health at present owing to the fatigues and hardships … which to spare Your Excellency's feelings he shall forebear to recite … amelioration of his destitute condition.

In the 1837 General Return of Convicts, 'Henry' Franks was listed as an assigned government servant in Berrima. On 31 July 1839 Emanuel Phillips (q.v.) of George Street, Sydney, wrote to the government on Franks' behalf. Phillips had arrived free in New South Wales twelve years before and had known Hyam Franks from childhood. Franks had asked two or three times for a ticket of leave and had been refused, 'though his offences were of a minor character'. Phillips advised that he was sure that were Franks to get a ticket of leave, he would respond with good behaviour: 'a great portion of the punishments this man has received have been occasioned by a mistaken idea on his part that it would be almost impossible ever to obtain the Indulgence and not from any radically bad principle'. Franks was working at Circular Wharf at the time, and had been told he must wait until October 1842 before applying for a ticket of leave 'because of the untruths with regard to punishments written in [his] 1837 petition'. Franks received his ticket of leave in 1841. He was buried by the Sydney Synagogue on 22 October 1859. He was sixty-five years old.

OBSP, 1813, case 259, p. 155, and case 279, p. 166; 4/1680, Petition 68, 4/1865, p. 68; *Sydney Gazette*, 23 August 1817, 17 March 1829; CS Newcastle, Monthly Return of Punishments, 1810–1825; 4/1718 4/2457.4, letter 39/8520; Ship Indent 4/4004; Petition 4/1267, p. 132; 4/1865, no. 5; 4/6531, Parramatta Gaol Record Book; TL 41/1975.

FRANKS, Sarah

b. London, 1791
Maria I (1); 1818; Convict; Sentenced to life, Old Bailey, 1817.
Single; Servant.

Sarah Franks was arrested for pawning stolen articles from the house in which she worked, and was sentenced on 3 December 1817.

Sarah Franks arrived in New South Wales on 17 September 1818. She was assigned in the colony to be a convict servant and housekeeper. However, on 26 September 1818, she was sent to Hobart Town on the *Elizabeth Henrietta*. On 13 July 1822, Sarah was sent to Port Macquarie on the *Lady Nelson*.

OBSP, 1817–18, case 17, p. 9; Ship Indent 4/4006, p. 107; CS 4/3864, pp. 364–5.

FRIEDEBERG, Jacob

b. Poland, 1820
William Jardine, 1850; Convict; Sentenced to 10 years, Central Criminal Court, 1848.
Married; Furrier; Height: 159 cm.

Fresh complexion, dark brown hair, reddish whiskers, blue eyes. A Jew. Can read and write. Jacob Friedeberg's birthplace was recorded as 'Courland Russia'. He was transported for forging Russian bank notes.

Jacob Friedeberg arrived in Van Diemen's Land on 14 November 1850. No offences were recorded in his dossier. In March 1851 he was assigned to Emanuel Karney (q.v.) of Murray Street, Hobart Town, and in August 1851 he was assigned to work for Simeon Levi (Levy) in Murray Street.

CON 33/98, no. 22974.

FRIEDLANDER, Samuel William (GERSHON)

b. Germany, 1797–1869
Bengal Merchant (3), 1838; Convict; Sentenced to 7 years, Central Criminal Court, 1837.
Single; Music teacher and servant; Height: 167 cm.

Dark sallow complexion; dark hair with grey, brown eyes; lame right leg; lower front teeth irregular. Roman nose. Friedlander had a counting house in Lime Street and took three watches as samples from a watch manufacturer. He then pawned them and could not redeem them. On a previous occasion he had given the manufacturers a forged bill. He was sentenced on 23 October 1837 for the theft of the watches, but was acquitted on the second charge of passing forged notes.

'William' Friedlander arrived in Sydney on 21 July 1838. A ticket of leave was issued for the Port Macquarie District in August 1842, and a certificate of freedom on 23 October 1844. The official records of births, marriages and deaths of New

South Wales recorded that, in 1869, Samuel William Friedlander died at Sydney at the age of seventy-two.
TL 42/1914; CF 44/1554.

FRIEDMAN, Isaac

b. Hungary, 1805–1875
Enchantress, 1833; Free.
Married; Dealer; 11 children.

Isaac Friedman, son of Judah, arrived in Sydney travelling steerage on the *Enchantress* on 24 April 1833. He was probably Australia's first Hungarian-born free immigrant. With him was Rebecca (q.v.), his wife, and a seven-month-old daughter, Frances (1832–5 January 1876). Friedman had an intensive Jewish education, growing up in an orthodox Jewish environment. He set up as a general dealer in Clarence Street, Sydney, and within six months had an assigned convict tailor allotted to him. A second infant died on 24 June 1835 and his wife Rebecca died on 26 August 1835. Both were buried in the Devonshire Street Jewish Cemetery. Friedman moved his business to George Street in August and, four months later, married Maria Nathan, on 23 December 1835. In 1836, he bought some land in Appin, where he opened a branch general store, with a stock 'too numerous to mention' but for sale 'at the Sydney Prices, allowing freight and carriage'.

By 1840 he had taken his wife to Hobart Town. There the Jewish community recorded the birth of four sons: Moses Joseph (27 June 1840), Solomon David (3 September 1842), Louis (26 August 1844), and Elias (27 January 1848). Friedman's other children were Ellen (1848 to 24 January 1856), Hellan (sic) (who died as an infant in 1838 and was buried in the Hobart Town Jewish Cemetery), Rebecca (28 March 1850), Ann (15 May 1852), Henry (15 September 1855–1858), and Abraham (2 April 1858).

In 1838 Friedman was licensed to be a hawker. In 1841 he became the publican of the Kensington Sun on the corner of Argyle and Bathurst streets (opposite the synagogue) and held that licence until 1849.

The first meeting of the Hobart Hebrew Congregation was held in the home of Mr I. Friedman on 16 January 1842, and resulted in the decision to build a synagogue in Hobart Town. Friedman was a committee member of the Hobart Synagogue from 1842 to 1844. In 1845 Friedman rented seat no. 8 in the Hobart Synagogue and donated £6 in his name and in the name of his children; he was elected a member of the congregation's Board of Management. Friedman worked with Phineas Moss (q.v.) and Philip Levy (q.v.) on arranging the service for the dedication of the synagogue and translating the Hebrew text. He also promised to lend the Synagogue £10 for the building costs. At the second meeting of the congregation, on 13 February 1842, Friedman complained that Philip Levy had alleged that 'Mr Friedman's house is the worst conducted in Hobart Town. Mrs Friedman was standing with brothel people and common girls at the door of her house and insulted you as you passed'. Levy then denied to the synagogue committee that he had said such a thing. A special congregational committee cleared Friedman's name. However, in 1850, the Hobart Synagogue Minutes recorded that Friedman had gone to live in New South Wales.

On 20 June 1851 Friedman was naturalised and had settled in Maitland, working as an innkeeper and general dealer. He quickly moved on Loders Station, Liverpool Plains, near Quirindi, where he leased 160 acres and opened an inn. In 1854, he returned to Hobart and, at 112 Argyle Street, near the synagogue, he opened a butcher's shop. Business was poor, and he then became a pawnbroker. Due to a shortage of coins, Friedman issued penny tokens in his own name: 'I Friedman Pawnbroker, Argyle Street' on one side of the coin and the figure of Justicia and the words 'Tasmania 1857' on the other.

In 1858 Friedman moved to the goldfield town of Sandhurst in Victoria and was elected *chazan* and *schochet* of the community; he served as its minister for ten years. He then moved to Melbourne in 1868, becoming a collector for charities in Palestine, while his wife taught in the Jewish Sabbath School. Friedman died in Melbourne on 13 June 1875.

Ship Indent 4/5204; A1214, p. 693; Egon F. Kunz,'The Rev Isaac Friedman: A Colonial Career', *AJJHS*, vol. 6, no. 5 (1968), p. 279f; *Port Phillip Patriot*, 26 July 1845; Land Correspondence 2/7862; Biographical notes from the late Dr Peter Elias, Hobart. Beverley Davis,'To Right a Historical Wrong' *AJJHS*, vol. 15, part 3 (2000).

FRIEDMAN, Rebecca

Enchantress, 1833; Free.
Married; 1 child.

Rebecca Friedman (née Nieto and sister of Rachel Nieto (q.v.)) was the first wife of Isaac Friedman (q.v.). She arrived in Van Diemen's Land with her husband and their seven-month-old daughter, Frances. She died on 26 August 1835.

Frances married Joseph Matthews in the Victorian town of Sandhurst (Bendigo) on 24 May 1864. They were to have seven children in Bendigo.

FURTADO, David Rebeiro

b. London *Jupiter*, 1829; Free.
Married; Merchant.

David Furtado arrived in New South Wales, travelling cabin class on the *Jupiter*, on 22 February 1829. With him were his wife, Sarah, Joseph Barrow Montefiore (q.v.) and Rebecca Montefiore (q.v.), and George Mocatta (q.v.).

David Rebeiro Furtado was active commercially from 1831 to 1845 in both New South Wales and Van Diemen's Land. Furtado's first visit to Hobart Town appears to have taken place in 1829, after which he travelled back 'from the Derwent' as a cabin passenger on the *Flora*, arriving on 8 November. Many members of his family in England had left the Sephardic community and converted to

Christianity, but Furtado was closely associated with J. B. Montefiore and with the Jewish community. On 14 December 1834 he was elected to be a director of both the Bank of Van Diemen's Land and the Bank of Australasia, and in July 1836 visited Sydney on business. At that time he was listed as a 'merchant' at 13 Macquarie Street, Hobart Town, and, in 1837, the *Tasmanian Almanac* described him as 'Dr Furtado' at the same address. On 9 August 1833 a convict servant had been assigned to him.

The *Atlas* of 7 December and the *Register* of 21 December 1844 reported that Furtado had become bankrupt. He and Thomas Breillat, partners in the firm of Jacob Montefiore (q.v.) and Joseph Montefiore, trading under the name of Montefiore Breillat and Co., Sydney, had incurred a 'deficiency' of £1115. At the time he was also a manager of the Van Diemen's Land Company. Furtado was present at the dedication of the Hobart Town Synagogue in 1845 but did not become a member or seat holder. Furtado was back in business by early 1847 exporting seventy bales of wool to England. He gave £15 to the Sydney Synagogue building appeal in 1845.

In April 1848 David Ribeiro Furtado was listed as an elector and house owner in Melbourne, with a 'Counting House' in Flinders Lane. On 8 December 1852 Furtado was elected the Melbourne City auditor and was then fined £25 when he refused to take up the job. In 1853 he served as the manager of the Commercial Bank in Melbourne.

Ship Indent 4/4823, and 401/70; 4/5211, 17 July 1836; Ship Indent 4/5200; *Argus*, 16 December 1852, 8 January 1853; *Hobart Town Courier*, 1 August 1834, 29 January 1836, 30 August 1837; *Colonial Times* (Hobart Town), 14 December 1832; *South Australian Gazette and Colonial Register*, 21 December 1844; *Atlas*, 7 December 1844. *Sydney Morning Herald*, 6 March 1847

FURTADO, Joseph David

b. London
1836; Free.
Single.

According to the *Sydney Gazette* of 17 December 1837, J. D. Furtado joined David R. Furtado (q.v.) in Hobart Town in 1836. He was one of the directors of the Bank of Australasia in Hobart Town.

G

GABEY, Raphael (GABBAI)

b. Amsterdam, 1811
Camden (2), 1833; Convict; Sentenced to life, Chester, 1832.
Single; Tobacconist; Height: 162 cm.

Ruddy complexion, light brown hair, grey eyes. Raphael Gabey was sentenced on 3 August 1832 for having picked pockets at Chester.

Raphael Gabey arrived in New South Wales on 17 February 1833 and was assigned to Mr James Adair, Paterson's River. A ticket of leave was issued for the District of Paterson in May 1844, and was altered to the District of Maitland on 18 February 1847. A certificate of freedom was issued on 5 May 1849.

Camden Printed Indent, p. 23; TL 44/2310, in 4/4193; CF 4/4412-49/0199.

GABRIEL, Michael

In 1845 Michael Gabriel gave £1 to the Sydney Synagogue and was (briefly) a subscriber.

GAINSBOROUGH, Aaron Hillel (GINZBERG, GAINSBOURG)

b. Koona, Poland, 1805–1882
Lady Harewood, 1832; Convict; Sentenced to 7 years, Lancaster, 1831.
Married; Jeweller; Height: 170 cm; 3 children.

Dark sallow complexion, brown and grey hair, brown eyes. Large whiskers. Lower arms hairy. Could read and write Hebrew. Aaron Gainsborough was married to Rachel Derret, and they had two sons and one daughter in England. He was convicted of buying stolen silver and sentenced at the Lancaster Quarter Sessions on 4 July 1831.

On 7 February 1832 the *Sydney Gazette* reported that Aaron 'Gainsborg' had been assigned to George Bowen, Merton/Windsor. He was still listed as an assigned convict servant to Bowen in the 1837 General Return of Convicts in New South Wales.

Gainsborough was admitted to the Newcastle Gaol on 14 January 1840 and was issued with a certificate of freedom three days later. He claimed that his imprisonment was the result of an ongoing disagreement with 'a person named Wineberg' (q.v.). Gainsborough applied for membership of the Sydney Synagogue on 28 August 1840 and offered to appear before the committee, warning the synagogue 'my business calls me a long distance'. His application was refused. When the Sydney Synagogue refused to grant permission to bury his infant son in the Jewish cemetery, a friend purchased space in the *Sydney Herald* of 29 March 1842, writing a letter that claimed that 'Mr Gainsberg is unable to speak the English Language'.

On 23 August 1844 Gainsborough applied for naturalisation. In order to buy property, he otherwise had to purchase it in the name of his wife, Rachel, who was in the colony. He wrote: 'I was born at Koona in Russia in Europe of Jewish parents in the year of our Lord one thousand eight hundred and five'. He had spent 'five years on extensive business as a jeweller and goldsmith, a month ago obtained a licence at the City Inn 336 George St, Sydney, purchased land extensively, married an English woman. I have one child. Aaron. It is not my intention to quit this colony where my only resources are'. The chief of police reported Gainsborough 'has been under my surveillance' and that while 'I have no record of any offence I have not a favourable opinion of his character. He was accused, but acquitted, on a charge of assault and robbery proffered by a person name Wineberg and gross perjury was committed by one or both of the parties. He does not hold a publican's licence and he is an applicant for a Hawker's Licence'. His partnership with Henry Wineberg was officially dissolved on 7 August 1844 (*Sydney Morning Herald*). Gainsborough transferred the licence of his City Inn to Alexander Eliot (*Sydney Gazette*, 8 March 1845). On 19 April 1845 the *Cumberland Times* reported that Gainsborough had been charged with assault and theft by his former business partner: 'Wineberg has his head shaved and encased in some six yards of calico being about to be sworn, on the merits and demerits of the English and Hebrew version of the Old Testament, which ended in Gainsborough offering to swear that Wineberg did not believe anything'. The case was dismissed as the evidence was contradictory. However, a quantity of stolen jewellery was later found in Wineberg's home.

In the *Registry of Flash Men* there was a report of a Gainsborough of King Street who, together with the pawnbroker Birnstang (Birstingl, q.v.) of King Street, 'sends silver to Europe'. He travelled through 'the country with a Box of trinkets jewellery etc. Is the brother-in-law of Derret—married Derret's sister'.

In the week that gold was discovered in the District of Bathurst in 1849, the *Bathurst Advocate* announced that 'Mr A. Gainsbourg sells out by auction his furniture clocks jewellery etc after four years in Bathurst because he had come to a determination of leaving the colony'. He also wished to sell twenty-seven allotments of land in Bathurst and the lease of his premises in George Street. He wisely changed his mind. Aaron 'Gainsborg' of Bathurst became a naturalised British subject on 28 August 1849. Aaron Gainsbourg died at St Kilda in 1882.

Printed Indent, no. 32-1506-33; CF 40/0164; Governors' Despatches for 1845, A1237, p. 819f., 23 August, p. 1240, 8 March 1846, p. 273; Land Correspondence 2/7863; Newcastle Gaol Entrance and Description Book 1840, no. 45, 2/2007; Sydney Synagogue Minute Book, p. 53, 28 August 1840; W. A. Miles, *Registry of Flash Men*, p. 66; *Bathurst Advocate*, 12 May 1849.

GAINSBOROUGH, Rachel Harriet (GAINSBOURG) (née DERRET)

b. London, 1819–1891
1832; Free.
Married; 3 children.

Rachel was the wife of the convict Aaron Gainsborough (q.v.), who arrived in the colony in 1832. At the time of her arrival they had 'two male children and one female'. Rachel had converted to Judaism in London. Because she had been born in England she was able to own the land that her husband began to buy in 1844. In 1845 Aaron applied for naturalisation. However, she remained listed as the sole owner to 1848. Her grave is to be found at the Jewish section of the Rookwood Cemetery. She died on 22 March 1891.

Land Correspondence, 2/7863.

GARCIA, Daniel

b. London, 1794–1867
Morley (1), 1817; Convict; Sentenced to life, Middlesex, 1816.
Married; Fruiterer; Height: 162 cm.

Dark complexion, black hair, black eyes. A pickpocket. Daniel was the brother of the convict William Garcia (q.v.) and son of Abraham Garcia. He was tried at Middlesex in September 1816.

Both Daniel and William were descended from Daniel and Abigail Garcia who arrived in London as refugees from Portugal in 1728. In Amsterdsam they were business associates with the Marrano merchant families Capadose, Cortisos and Mendes da Costa. Abraham Haim Garcia was a son of David de Daniel Garcia and his wife Esther de Abraham Mendes de Leon.

Daniel Garcia's transport arrived in Sydney in April 1817 and he was sent as an assigned convict labourer to Liverpool. On 2 September 1818 he was sent on to Newcastle's Prison Settlement. Garcia did not 'behave' and, in September 1819, he was despatched on the *Cockburn* (2) to Hobart Town. His first entry in the Van Diemen's Land police record occurred on 12 June 1820 when he was convicted of being disorderly at 'Church Parade' and sentenced to 'work for the Government and to be confined during this time'. He was charged, along with David Myers (q.v.), with stealing, on 21 June, from the premises of Mr Bethune in Macquarie Street, Hobart Town, nine beaver skin hats, and was sentenced on 3 July 1821 to be returned to New South Wales to the penal settlement at Newcastle for the remainder of his sentence. Myers claimed that Garcia was the thief.

Daniel Garcia married Sarah Farrell, aged twenty-four, in Hobart Town on 23 July 1821. On 4 August 1821 the Provost Marshall wrote to the Colonial Secretary: 'I have given the necessary orders for the Gaoler to receive into his keeping the seven prisoners per ship *Midas* from Van Diemen's Land'. These prisoners included David Myers, Daniel Garcia, and Sarah Garcia, who accompanied her husband. On 5 September 1823 Garcia appeared on the list of convicts received from Newcastle to Port Macquarie.

Daniel Garcia was sent on to Norfolk Island where his colonial sentence eventually expired. In 1830 he applied for a ticket of exemption from government labour. This was refused. On 6 July 1832 Daniel Garcia was in court once again. At the Magistrate's Court in Penrith he stood accused of stealing and embezzling government property and was sentenced to three more years at Norfolk Island. He was sent to the *Phoenix* hulk and on to Norfolk Island on 28 December 1832, returning to the hulk from Norfolk Island on 20 May 1835. He was then sent on to the Hyde Park Prisoners' Barracks. In 1841 Garcia was granted his ticket of leave.

On 25 July 1842 the police office in Hartley in the Castlereagh area submitted a report on Daniel Garcia. He was a 'general dealer' whose goods would be sold to pay his debtors. Nothing would be paid to the two constables who apprehended him as he paid them £5 each not to take him into custody. The sitting magistrates allowed them to keep £2 each. His ticket of leave and his property, household goods, clothes and furniture, were all auctioned on 8 July 1842, and he was sent to the Hyde Park Barracks. The police sent with their official report a batch of IOUs, one of which was to Mr A. J. Levy for £7 2s 6d.

Garcia remained in Sydney after his release and was subsequently sentenced to three days in Darlinghurst Gaol on 21 April 1843. At the time he was listed as 'bad' and 'a labourer'. He received his second ticket of leave in December 1843 for the District of Penrith. Following a communication from the Surveyor of Bridges, this permit was altered to Carcoar on 11 March 1844. He received a conditional pardon in September 1848.

Daniel Garcia died in Sydney on 6 September 1867 at the age of 82 and was granted a 'free burial' by the York Street Synagogue. His gravestone is to be found at Rookwood.

CON 31/5, no. 215; *Morley* Indent 4/4005, p. 267; *Hobart Town Gazette*, 7 July 1821; TL 41/222, and 43/4307: *Phoenix* (hulk) Entrance Book, 4/6286, p. 54; CP 993; CS 4/2585.7, dated 25 July 1842; re Convicts Out Petition for Ticket of Exemption, in 4/3669, p. 435; CS 4/3864, pp. 422–3; Darlinghurst Gaol Records, Admittance Book, 4/6534, no. 463. Family history provided by Mark Bridge of London.

GARCIA, William (William KANGAROO)

b. London, 1794
Atlas (3), 1816; Convict; Sentenced to life, Old Bailey, 1815.
Single; Fruit seller; Height: 165 cm.

Dark pale complexion, black hair, black eyes. William was the younger brother of Daniel Garcia (q.v.). He was sentenced on 10 May 1815.

In 1817, William Garcia was sent to Van Diemen's Land on the brig *Kangaroo* (hence his nickname). Between July 1818 and October 1820 he received 100 lashes for four counts of neglect of work, absence and drunkenness. In the 1821 Convict Muster Garcia was listed as living at Clarence Plains. On 3 June 1822, while an assigned servant to Mr Coward in Hobart Town, he was found aboard the whaler *Kent* without a pass and was sentenced to fifty lashes for attempting to escape. He was returned to the Public Works Department. Within three weeks (19 June) he received a further twenty-five lashes for neglect of duty. On 6 May 1824 Garcia escaped from the Prisoners' Barracks in Hobart; he was caught in Launceston on 11 March 1825. He was sentenced to three months in the gaol gang, manacled with double irons. On 2 November 1825, while at the Prisoners' Barracks, he was charged with assault and sentenced to twenty-five lashes and imprisonment on Maria Island. On 31 March 1826, while in the gaol, he was convicted by the turn-key of improper language and received twenty-five lashes. In May he received fifty lashes for absence from his work gang and for insolence. In July he absconded from the road party at Black Snake Pass and was at large in the bush for five days before he was recaptured. His punishment was twenty-five lashes. While it was recorded in his dossier that he assaulted Samuel Hyams (q.v.) in October 1824, as Garcia was at large at the time and, as the entry occurs at the end of his record, it should probably read '1826'. Hyams failed to turn up to give evidence against him at the trial, so that Garcia was discharged. The last entries in his dossier occurred on 8 August 1827, when he was sentenced to twenty-five lashes and three months in the chain gang for neglect of duty and disobedience, and on 23 August, when he was admonished for 'feigning illness and refusing to work'.

CON 31/15, no. 215; *Atlas* (3) Indent 4/4005, p. 181.

GERSHON, Henry

b. London, 1817–1898
Asia V (3), 1837; Convict; Sentenced to 7 years, London, 1837.
Single; Carter; Height: 161 cm; 5 children.

Ruddy freckled complexion, brown hair, hazel eyes, red circle around pupils of both eyes. Brown mark left jaw. Henry Gershon persuaded Joel Jewell to buy £40 worth of scrap metal and then diverted him into a hotel. His father and mother, who were waiting outside, drove away the cart with the metal. His father was sentenced to twelve months in gaol. Henry was sentenced on 27 February 1837 to seven years transportation.

The *Asia* arrived in New South Wales on 3 December 1837. Gershon's name appeared in the Newcastle Gaol Entrance Book after he was convicted in Maitland for an unspecified offence. He was sent on to Sydney and the Hyde Park Prisoners' Barracks on 17 November 1843. Gershon was issued with his Certificate of Freedom on 12 March 1844. He became a 'dealer' of Lower Campbell Street, and was a member of the Sydney Synagogue in 1848. In 1846, in Sydney, he married Rachel Moss, the sister of George Moss (q.v.), who had arrived on the *Siren* in 1836. A daughter, Catherine, was born in 1847, followed by Emanuel, who was born later that same year, and Julia in 1848. There were two other children, Elijah and Rachel.

Henry Gershon died in Sydney on 15 August 1898. His grave is to be found at Rookwood.

OBSP, 1836–37, case 737, p. 708; *Asia* (5) Printed Indent, 1837, p. 189; Newcastle Gaol Entrance Book, 1841–45, 2/2008; CF 4/4389–44/0381.

GIDEON, Jonas (James)

b. Plymouth, 1813
Surrey I (8), 1834; Convict; Sentenced to 7 years, Plymouth, 1834.
Single; Shop man; Height: 161 cm.

Ruddy freckled complexion, brown hair, blueish eyes. Nose rather small. A Jew. Transported for stealing clothes. Jonas Gideon had been in gaol for six months for a previous offence, and was sentenced at Plymouth on 17 February 1834.

Jonas Gideon arrived on 17 August 1834. His name is not to be found on the 1837 General Return of Convicts in New South Wales. However, Jonas or 'James' Gideon was issued a certificate of freedom on 19 March 1841.

Surrey Printed Indent, 1834, p. 99; CF 41/0371.

GODFREY, Thomas

b. London, 1797
America (1), 1829; Convict; Sentenced to 7 years, Bristol Quarter Sessions, 1828.
Married; Hackney coach keeper; Height: 158 cm; 1 child (in London).

Sallow complexion, brown hair, hazel eyes 'not assignable—wants both legs from the knees', scar over right eye, mole on right cheek. No education. Jew. Married, one child. Thomas Godfrey was sentenced on 14 October 1828 and transported for having stolen a parcel. He had been convicted twice before.

The *America* arrived in Sydney Harbour on 18 August 1829. On 3 July 1832 Godfrey wrote to the Colonial Secretary asking for a mitigation of his sentence. He said he was 'an invalid' and was working as a pastry cook and baker. He was 'quite capable of getting an honest livelihood but of no service to the Government, having two wooden legs and wishing to further his life by honest industry by carrying on the said Trade as also retailing of other ships' goods begs this appeal to your Excellency'. The Commandant at Port Macquarie wrote that he had 'behaved well and although with two wooden legs is active and able by his trade to obtain his own maintenance at Port Macquarie'.

On 4 September 1832 Thomas Godfrey again petitioned the Colonial Secretary, asking for a ticket of leave. He wrote that he had been sent to Port Macquarie after his arrival. He believed he could 'obtain a good livelihood by carrying on the trade of baking and selling shop goods. He having the mean of selling'. The police noted that he had no local criminal record and a ticket of leave was approved on 7 September 1832. However, this was cancelled later that year, after he was found with stolen property in his possession. He was sentenced to be a prisoner for seven years and his certificate of freedom was cancelled. In the 1837 General Return of Convicts in New South Wales Godfrey was listed as working for the government at Port Macquarie with a ticket of leave. A Thomas Godfrey died at Goulburn in 1876 aged 'eighty years'.

Ship Indent 4/4014, p. 205, no. 1456-15; CS Petition, no. 32/5666; TL 32/1017, in 4/4086; CF 4/4382-36/1159.

GOLDER, John

b. London, 1795–1866
Phoenix I (1), 1822; Convict; Sentenced to 7 years, Surrey, 1821.
Single; Journeyman, wheelwright.

John Golder was transported for felony. His hulk report was 'orderly'. He had broken into a house in Horsemonger Lane. He had served a previous sentence of twelve months for housebreaking. He lived with his father and mother at Bermondsey.

The *Phoenix* arrived in Van Diemen's Land on 2 May 1822. In 1825 John Golder was assigned to the shoemaker and tanner Samuel Horton of Launceston. At the end of 1826 he was arrested at Campbell Town and taken from Horton's service for seducing the maidservant of the local innkeeper. He was sentenced to fifty lashes and six months gaol. A lengthy correspondence ensued. Horton did not want to lose his assistant and wrote to the Colonial Secretary: 'I have always found him Honest, steady and extremely industrious until his acquaintances with this infamous woman'. The sentence was upheld. Golder had been previously tried for stealing a pair of boots. In June 1827 Horton asked for him to be returned to his service and a letter from Golder, written from the Launceston Gaol Camp, showed him to be both literate and articulate.

Golder was licensed as a hawker in Oatlands in May 1838 and, on 9 August 1839, Golder was listed as buying one acre at Oatlands. He was registered as a member of the Hobart Town Hebrew Congregation in 1842 and gave £5 5s to the synagogue in 1845.

John Golder, the son of Frederick and Susan, died at Tamworth, New South Wales, in 1866.

CON 31/15, no. 285; CSO 1/3/47; CSO 1/96/2283, p. 39; *Hobart Town Courier*, 25 May 1825.

GOLDSMITH, Clara

1803–1886
1849; *Rattler* Free.
2 children.

The daughter of Rheuben Rheuben of London and sister of Abraham Rheuben (q.v.) of Hobart Town, Clara was married to Emanuel Goldsmith, who traded in crockery and mahogany. They went from London to Honduras in the late 1830s, but after an outbreak of the plague took the lives of Emanuel and their daughter, Clara and her surviving child Daniel returned to London. Clara set sail for

Australia in 1850, encouraged by her brother Abraham's description of life in Van Diemen's Land. Shortly after arriving in Hobart Town, Clara married the emancipist Emanuel Karney (q.v.). On the marriage documents she stated her age as thirty-five, although she was actually two or three years older. Clara Karney died in Adelaide on 6 June 1886, at which time her age was given as eighty-three. The 13 year old Daniel Goldsmith sailed to Australia in 1851 on the Cornhill. He married Rachel Morris in Hobart and then settled in Adelaide

Family information from Daniel Goldsmith, Melbourne. (The record of Clara's marriage to Emanuel Kaney is not in the York Street Synagogue Register but is on a loose piece of paper).

GOLDSTEIN, Moses

d. 1878
Free.
Single; Dealer.

Moses Goldstein was a pioneer member of the early settlement of Port Phillip and was present at the Jewish community's first High Holyday services. He was one of the most traditional members of the early Melbourne Jewish community and was sometimes referred to as 'the Rev.' Moses Goldstein in tribute to his lay readership at the synagogue. In the 1860s Goldstein ran a jewellery store in Bourke Street and prospered. He strongly supported the establishment and maintenance of a Jewish school in Melbourne and became an honorary reader at the Bourke Street Synagogue. When the East Melbourne Synagogue began, he assisted in the conduct of its funerals. Goldstein was one of the instigators of the Sabbath Observance Committee in 1872. When it failed to influence the community, Goldstein wrote to the London *Jewish Chronicle* predicting the eclipse of Jewish life in Australia. He was a strong supporter of the need to provide the community with kosher meat. In 1878 his uninsured jewellery store in Bourke Street was robbed and he was reduced to penury. This, together with the death of his wife, evidently hastened his own death.

The Rev. A. S. Goldstein, the brother of Moses Goldstein, served as minister to the Auckland Hebrew Congregation.

GOLLIN, Bezalel

b. London, 1821–1874
1848; Free.
Single; Dealer; 7 children.

Bezalel Gollin ran a general store in the copper-mining town of Burra Burra. He married Eliza Barnard on 17 August 1853 at the home of the bride's father, George Barnard, at Grenfell Street, Adelaide. Bezalel died on 6 December 1874, aged fifty-three, and was buried in Adelaide's Jewish cemetery. He and Eliza had seven children: Walter Josephson (1854), George (1860–1946, who died in London),

Victoria (1862), Eugenie (1864), Eva Sarah (1868), Louis Elkin (1871), and Lillian Francis (born and died 1873).

Pritchard Index; *Observer*, 20 August 1853; *Adelaide Advertiser*, 2 January 1875.

GOODMAN, George Barron

b. London *Eden*, 1842;
Free.
Single; Photographer, daguerreotype-maker; 2 children.

George Barron Goodman, with his photographic equipment, arrived in Sydney from London on 4 November 1842. He had opened a daguerreotype gallery at the Royal Hotel by 13 December 1842. He left for Hobart Town on 21 March 1843, returning to Sydney on 3 August 1843. Goodman was the first professional photographer in Australia. He married Sarah, the daughter of Abraham Polack (q.v.), in a Jewish ceremony in Sydney on 4 January 1843. The synagogue's governing body questioned the bride's Jewish status, as only her father was Jewish, before they married.

Goodman returned to Hobart Town in January 1844 and was praised 'for some beautifully executed daguerreotype views of our rising metropolis'. The *Sydney Morning Herald* announced on 2 January 1845 that 'G. B. Goodman, 49 Hunter St', had just received permission to use a new process, 'colouring' the daguerreotype portraits. 'On account of the depression of the times the price will be limited to one guinea specimens to be seen at Mr Isaac Levey's Drapery, George St'. In August 1845 'Mr Goodman from Sydney' hired a shop in Little Flinders Street (Melbourne), and announced that he could execute a perfect likeness in the course of a few seconds. Samples of his work could be seen at Michael Cashmore's store, which was nearby. In December that year the *Port Phillip Patriot* noted critically that 'Mr Goodman has cleared out for Adelaide after four months in Melbourne during which time he took £870 in fees. He contributed not one farthing to any of the charitable or public institutions'.

G. B. Goodman's sister, Minna Cecilia Goodman, married John Levey-Roberts (Levey, q.v.) (son of Solomon Levey, q.v.) at St George's, Hanover Square, in London, on 29 June 1842. George and Sarah Goodman had two children, both born in Sydney. Their first, Hannah, born in 1844, was registered as 'Hebrew'. Minna Rebecca was born in 1847.

Sydney Synagogue Minute Book, p. 91; *Sydney Morning Herald*, 5 November 1842, 13 December 1842, 5 June 1843, 3 August 1843, 30 March 1844; *Hobart Town Courier*, 26 January 1844; *Port Phillip Patriot*, 1 August 1845; *AG*, pp. 110, 152, 273.

GOODMAN, Temple Benjamin

Nancy, 1830, Free.
Single; Pedlar.

A Benjamin Goodman is listed as a passenger on the *Nancy* on 20 March 1830. A hawker's licence was granted to 'Temple Goodman' on 17 September 1841 (*Hobart Town Courier*).

GRAVEUR, David Aaron

b. Amsterdam, 1817
Bengal Merchant (3), 1836; Convict; Sentenced to 7 years, Glamorgan Assizes, 1836.
Single; Copperplate lithographic printer; Height: 159 cm.

Dark sallow complexion, brown hair and brown eyes. Fingernails very short, dark mole on side of cheek. Jew. Could read and write. David Graveur was transported for stealing a watch, having been sentenced at the Glamorgan Assizes on 1 March 1836.

Graveur was listed as an assigned servant to Mr J. G. Austin of Sydney in the 1837 General Return of Convicts in New South Wales. He was 'free' on 1 September 1843, after having been issued with a certificate of freedom on 23 May. Graveur moved to Victoria during the gold rush and in 1860 at Inglewood took care of the Jewish burial of his 'friend', the cabbalist, gold prospector and impoverished scholar Rabbi Dr David Hailperin.

Bengal Merchant Printed Indent, arrived 9 December 1836, p. 175, no. 36-2689-90; CF 43/0823.

H

HADFIELD, Daniel (HATFIELD)

b. Russia (Poland), 1795
Parmelia (1), 1832; Convict; Sentenced to 7 years, Lancaster, 1831.
Soldier, hawker; Height: 140 cm.

Dark sallow complexion, black hair mixed with grey, chestnut eyes. Nose flat from a blow. Could read. Jew. No previous convictions. Daniel's age was recorded as thirty-seven when he was sentenced on 24 October 1831 for 'false pledging'.

Daniel Hadfield arrived in New South Wales on 16 November 1832. He was granted a ticket of leave, followed by a certificate of freedom on 8 May 1839. On 15 September 1842, in the *Sydney Morning Herald*, Hadfield appeared on the voters' list with a house in George Street. The *Sydney Record* of 20 January 1844 listed Daniel Hatfield as insolvent. The *Australasian Chronicle* of 26 August 1843 had already reported that there was a 'financial deficiency' of £187. In 1845 he appeared as a seat holder at the Sydney Synagogue and subscribed £3 to the synagogue.

Parmelia (1) Printed Indent, 1832, p. 155, no. 2743-68; CP, in 39/692, in 4/4348; letter written to the Colonial Secretary, 16 November 1838, re Pardon; TL 2743, CF 39/0692; *Sydney Morning Herald*, 9 May 1843, 15 September 1842; *Sydney Record*, 20 January 1844; CF 4/4348.

HADFIELD, Joseph (HATFIELD)

b. Poland, 1799
Camden (1), 1831; Convict; Sentenced to 7 years, Knutsford (Cheshire), 1830.

Joseph Hadfield, brother of Daniel Hadfield (q.v.), received a certificate of freedom on 11 May 1838 and was listed as a voter in the first municipal elections of Sydney in 1842 with a house in Bathurst Street.

Camden (1) Printed Indent 4/4017, p. 126; *Sydney Morning Herald*, 15 September 1842; CF 4/4342-38/0411.

HAINES, Elizabeth

b. London, 1809–1883
David Scott, 1834; Free.
Single; 9 children.

Elizabeth Haines, the daughter of London shopkeeper, arrived in New South Wales on 25 October 1834 on a 'Female Emigration Ship', having paid £5 for her passage. In 1839 her mother arrived on the *Mary*, followed by all but one of her family.

Elizabeth Haines married Mordecai Solomon (q.v.) in Sydney in 1835. Mordecai is said to have come down to the wharf when she arrived from England and 'carried her off' to live at Dapto. She died on 2 November 1852. She had nine children, although two died when they were infants. The children were Sarah (1836–1890), Myer (1837–1906), Jane (1838–1880), Vaiben (1839), Henry (1840–1900), Ellen (1842), Joseph (1844), Lewis (1848–1857), and a daughter, name unknown.

The Hain(e)s family history has been gathered by Mrs Catherine M. Anderson, Adelaide, Mrs Barbara Dickens of Canberra and Mrs Ballantyne Russell, Sydney., The spelling of the Haines surname varied and this may indicate a non-English-speaking background. In addition, the names chosen for the children (using the names of living relatives) and the choice of a career connected with the sea and stevedoring suggest that the family originated from Thessalonika. The Haines parents lived at 1 Robin Hood Lane, Poplar, Middlesex.

HAINES, Isaac (HAINS)

b. London, 1807–1874
Troubadour; Free.
Single; 5 children.

The son of Hyam and Kate Hains of London, and brother of Elizabeth Haines (q.v.), Isaac Haines married Rosetta Nathan (q.v.), the daughter of Edward Nathan (q.v.) on 2 April 1840 at Five Islands, Shoalhaven. It was Jewish wedding no. 27 and Michael Hyam (q.v.) officiated. A son, Edward, was born on 28 July 1842, and the birth was registered at the Sydney Synagogue. Edward married Adelaide Sarah. He died on 26 May 1880. Catherine was born in Sydney on 16 November 1845. She married Henry Lewis Gordon, and died in 1892. Hyam was born in 1848. Eleanor, born in 1850, married Abraham Pyke on 11 June 1884. She died on 10 August 1897. Annie was born in 1852 and married Lazarus Levy on 11 June 1884.

Isaac was a seat holder at the Synagogue in 1848. Isaac Haines 'commission agent' died on 10 April 1874 at 51 Brisbane Street, Surry Hills (Sydney).

HAINES, John

Free.
Single; 7 children.

John Haines arrived in Port Adelaide before 1849. He was known as 'John the Whaler', and is not to be confused with John Hains, known as 'John the Carrier', son of Philip Hains and Esther Hains (qq.v.). John Haines married Ann Harriet Davey on 26 November 1849. He was a whaler, sailor, stevedore, ship owner (with Philip Hains) of the ketch *Four Brothers* and the ketch *Alexander* in 1858. The names of four of his seven children are known. They were Henry Hyam (28 October 1849 to 26 November 1916), who married Sarah Abigail Coronel; Jacob (1851 to 26 November 1922), who married Annie Hepzibah; Lewis (8 Ocober 1853 to 2 May 1927); and Edward Joseph (1867), who died as an infant.

HAINES, Joseph

b. London
Free.

Joseph Haines arrived in Adelaide with his older brother Philip (Hains, q.v.) and Philip's family and his sister Jane. Joseph returned to England to marry, on 7 June 1853, Julia Delevante, the daughter of Moses and Esther Delevante. Julia and Joseph had three daughters: Rebecca (1854–1920), Catherine (1855) and Esther (c. 1856–1921). Joseph's listed occupations included ship's steward, storekeeper, stevedore and farmer.

HAINES, Lewis

b. London, 1810
1834; Free.
Single; 1 child.

Lewis Haines arrived in New South Wales in 1834 and stayed very briefly. In 1851 he returned and, on 23 December, at the Sydney Synagogue married Catherine (Kitty) Zadock, who had been recently widowed. Catherine signed the marriage certificate with a mark. They settled in South Australia, where Lewis worked as a storekeeper and printer in Lipson Street, Port Adelaide. A daughter, Caroline, was born in 1857.

HAINS, Charles

b. London 1821.
1839; Free.

Charles Hains arrived in South Australia, at Holdfast Bay (Glenelg), as a crew member of the *Buckinghamshire*. He returned to the sea for the next fourteen years, before settling in Port Adelaide permanently with his wife Hannah and two children, to join his brother Philip (q.v.) as storekeeper. One of the children was named Joseph.

HAINS, Esther (née MYERS)

b. London, 1824–1898
Troubadour, 1850; Free.
Married; 11 children.

Esther was the daughter of George and Abigail (née Martin) Myers, who married on 3 June 1819 at the Great Synagogue in London. George was a convert to Judaism. Abigail was the daughter of Jacob Nunes Martines. Esther married Philip Hains (q.v.) in 1844. Mrs Esther Hains arrived in South Australia with her husband in 1850. Esther Hains died on 11 January 1898 at the age of seventy-four, and was buried at the West Terrace Jewish Cemetery in Adelaide.

Pritchard Index; *South Australian Advertiser*, 12 January 1898; *Observer*, 15 January 1898.

HAINS, Philip

b. London, 1818–1887
Troubadour, 1850; Free.
Married; Dealer; 11 children.

Philip Hains married Esther Myers (Hains, q.v.) at the Great Synagogue, London, on 10 January 1844. He arrived on 1 April 1850 with his wife Esther, their three children, his sister Jane, and his younger brother Joseph. Philip had served as a bosun in the British Navy. In South Australia he became part-owner of the ketch *Four Brothers*. He was a stevedore and rigger and in 1862 opened a general store in Port Adelaide. From 1864 to 1877 he owned the licence for two hotels in the town. Hains was actively involved with the Freemasons and the Order of Oddfellows. He died on 2 December 1887 and was buried at the West Terrace Jewish Cemetery in Adelaide.

HAINES, Rachel

b. London
Lord Nelson, 1827, Free.
Single; 4 children.

Rachel Haines arrived in Sydney in 1827. She was fourteen years old when she married Abraham Abrahams (q.v.) on 12 September 1841 at Sarah Valley (Five Islands), Illawarra. The authorised celebrant was Michael Hyam (q.v.).

HALLENBURGH, Gustavus (HALLINBOURG)

b. Germany, 1818
Moffatt (2), 1836; Convict; Sentenced to 7 years, Central Criminal Court, 1836.
Single; Tradesman's clerk; Height: 156 cm; 6 children.

Dark ruddy complexion, dark brown hair, chestnut eyes. Three moles under left jaw. No previous convictions. Transported for stealing a watch. Jew. Could read but not write. Hallenburgh had a brother who kept a foreign-language bookshop in King William Street (in London). He spoke French and German and was out of work. A customer at his brother's bookshop offered to give him a character reference. Gustavus went to his home with him and stole his watch!

'Gustavus Hallenbourg' (also known as 'George') was brought before the Bench of Magistrates sitting at the Hyde Park Barracks on 28 November 1836 for 'neglect of work' and for being absent from his work gang. At the barracks it was noted: 'Although this man's occupation is given as tradesman's clerk it is not recorded that he could write'. He was placed in solitary confinement in the cells for ten days on bread and water. In the General Return of Convicts in New South Wales in 1837 Gustavus Hallenburgh appeared as a prisoner at the Hyde Park Barracks. He received a ticket of leave in 1841 and a certificate of freedom on 16 February 1844. George Hallinbourg (as he was now known) married Elizabeth Levy in Sydney in 1854. They had six children: Abraham (1855), Miriam, Clara, Julia, Louis and Michael.

Abraham Halinbourg married Susan Crystal Meriga on 11 December 1878 at the 'cottage rear of synagogue' Bourke Street, Melbourne. They had six children, Elizabeth married Julius Rosenfeld, Amelia married Harry Freadman, Estella who married Henry Freadman, Viola, Leonore married Frank Drexler and Beryle who married John Boothey.

OBSP, 1835–36, case 1020, p. 1034; *Moffatt* (2) Printed Index, p. 103; Bench of Magistrates, HPB X 707; TL 41/2262; CF 44/0216; Family information from Professor Ann Freadman (Vic).

HANDCOCK, Samuel

b. London
John, 1829; Convict.

In 1834 Samuel Handcock, 'a Jew', was admitted to the Parramatta Gaol. He was listed as having no trade or calling. He had been sent on 9 December, from Windsor, to the Hyde Park Barracks, arriving on 10 December. The only 'Samuel' listed on the transport ship *John* was 'Samuel Booth'. He received a certificate of freedom on 11 April 1835.

Parramatta Gaol Record 1834, no. 1569, in 4/6530; 4/4327; CF 35/0318.

HARRIS, Alfred

Free.

Alfred Harris was a founding member of the Melbourne Hebrew Congregation. His uncle, Lewis Davis (q.v.), enrolled him as a member of the congregation paying a reduced rate. In the late 1840s Alfred Harris worked as a shop assistant at Michael Cashmore's Collins Street shop. By 1855 Mr Alfred Harris was one of the members of the Melbourne Hebrew Congregation who joined a committee to raise funds for the distressed Jews of the Holy Land.

HARRIS, Deborah

b. Sydney, 1847–1926
8 children.

Deborah Harris was the second child of Elizabeth (née Levey, q.v.) and Samuel Henry Harris (q.v.), and granddaughter of Isaac Levey (q.v.) and his wife Dinah. She married Montague Marks on 3 August 1869 at the Macquarie Street Synagogue in Sydney. Montague was the son of Moses Marks and Rosetta (née Levy). At the time of their marriage, Montague was a squatter with a station in New England. He had also been a storekeeper at Tumut. They had seven or eight children.

Deborah died in Sydney on 28 March 1926.

HARRIS, Henry

d. 1843
Free.
Single; Dealer.

Henry Harris arrived in Sydney from Hobart Town on the *James* on 12 August 1839. He had a shop in Brickfield Hill and on 14 April 1840 was reportedly offered a forged cheque. He had also employed as a 'shopman' Israel Cantor (q.v.), who was accused of obtaining money and clothing through a fictitious order. On 25 February 1841 Harris, described as a 'general dealer', had his estate assigned as a prelude to an insolvency hearing. The estate was reportedly wound up on 2 April 1842 with debts of £930 and assets of £65 and a John Morris was nominated as trustee of the estate. Henry Harris died on 30 September 1843 and was buried by the Sydney Synagogue at the Devonshire Street Cemetery.

Australian, 18 May, 20 May 1840.

HARRIS, Henry (HURST)

b. Peterborough, 1805–1844
Emma Eugenia, 1838; Convict; Sentenced to 7 years, Central Criminal Court, 1837.
Married; Labourer; Height: 175 cm; 1 child.

Dark, sallow, pock-pitted complexion. Dark brown hair, brown eyes inflamed, lost the lashes. Breast hairy. Nose inclined a little to the left side. Tattoos: a woman and initials B.H. inside lower right arm. Henry Harris had served six years of a previous sentence in Bermuda. Henry Harris, alias Hurst, was a member of a group of pickpockets who surrounded and jostled a clergyman, the Rev. McLeod, and stole a watch worth £30. He was caught near Covent Garden and sentenced on 14 August 1837.

Harris arrived in New South Wales on 9 February 1838. He received a ticket of leave in 1843 and a certificate of freedom on 4 September 1844.

Emma Eugenia Printed Indent, p. 42; TL 408; CF 4/4393, 44/1307.

HARRIS, Isaac

b. Portsmouth, 1813
Bussorah Merchant, 1830; Convict; Sentenced to life, Old Bailey, 1826.
Single; Errand boy; Height: 142 cm.

Pale complexion, brown hair, long face, high forehead, hazel eyes, medium long nose. Can neither read nor write. A Jew. Harris was the youngest member of a teenage gang of four in London who intimidated a watch seller and then stole a watch from his shop. The 13-year-old Harris was sentenced to death, but this was commuted to transportation for life. He had been acquitted of a previous charge of stealing. In the hulk he was placed on bread and water once and on short rations five times. He was also punished on the Bussorah Merchant.

Isaac Harris's long police record in Van Diemen's Land began on 12 December 1833, when he received twenty-five lashes for neglect of duty while an assigned servant to Mr Archer. On 9 December 1834 he was put on bread and water and in solitary confinement for being abusive to a constable. On 26 December 1834 he was sentenced to fifty lashes for being drunk and absent from his assigned work. His assignment concluded in March 1835 and, for insolence and neglect of duty, he was transferred to the chain gang. In 1836 and 1837 he was returned to assigned service. It was not a success and he was sent to Bridgewater for three months hard labour in chains for ill-treating the bullocks of his mistress, Mrs Davis.

On 1 October 1838 Harris was ordered to leave the District of Hobart Town for being involved in a plot to rob his master's house. By 1838 he was a holder of a ticket of leave, which was 'removed' on 20 March 1839, and he was sent to Port Arthur for hard labour in chains for 'absconding and disorderly conduct'. His ticket of leave was restored in March 1843 and he was employed as a constable until he was dismissed for obscene and threatening language and received a further nine months hard labour. In June 1844 Isaac Harris was refused permission to marry Sarah Bailey, who came out as a convict on the *Rajah*. A conditional pardon was approved on 25 February 1846.

On 22 October 1849 Harris was sentenced for feloniously assaulting Mr Charles Davidson, 'putting him in fear of his life and stealing one pound and ten shillings from him' in Murray Street. The crime was counted as 'Highway Robbery'. This second colonial dossier notes that he was married.

He was sent to Port Arthur. By 1857 he was again in assigned service and on 6 December 1857 he was sentenced to one month hard labour for 'threatening and asking a watchman to fight'. By 9 March 1858 he had absconded and was still missing in 1862.

OBSP, 1826–27, case 47, p. 32; CON 31/19, no. 1028; CON 18/1; Van Diemen's Land Papers, MLA, 1059-5, p. 421.

HARRIS, John

b. 1759
Scarborough (1), 1788; Convict; Sentenced to 14 years, Old Bailey, 1783.
Single; Wax chandler; 4 children.

John Harris was tried for stealing eight silver table spoons, valued at three shillings and one penny, from the house of Peter Livius, Chief Justice of Quebec, who was temporarily living in London. Harris was caught in the act by one of the servants. His death sentence was commuted to fourteen years transportation to America. Harris was sent to the hulks and escaped in the course of a mutiny. He was again sentenced to death for 'feloniously returning from transportation', and his sentence commuted to transportation for life. He was sent out on the First Fleet.

David Collins, the former Judge Advocate, recorded:

> after frequent commissioned offences in the settlement and these deprivations continuing, a convict of the name of Harris presented to the Judge Advocate, a proposal for establishing a night watch, to be selected from the convicts. This proposal being submitted to the Governor and thoroughly digested and matured, the first attempt toward a police in the settlement commenced on Saturday 8 August 1789.

On 15 August 1789 in the proceedings of the Bench of Magistrates, John Harris testified: 'as he was going on his duty of the watch he had arrested two drunk men as they tried to climb through the window of Mrs Sarah Bellamy'. Harris, it was noted, had been sworn in on the Old Testament.

On 23 August 1793 Harris was appointed a constable on Norfolk Island and put in charge of the police at Sydney Vale, Arthur's Vale and Granville villages. Harris was granted an absolute pardon in 1795 after he had sent a number of petitions to Lieutenant Governor King. His warrant was not issued until 13 September 1796 'in consideration of good services as principal of the night watch at Norfolk Island'. Harris returned to Sydney in February 1796 with a First Fleeter named Matilda Green. Mary had been sustained by Harris, and had a son, John, in 1790, a daughter, Elizabeth (Underwood, q.v.), in June 1794, and a daughter, Susannah (later known as Hannah) (Hannah Ritchie, q.v.), in 1797.

On 1 January 1798 Harris received a grant of six and a half acres on land that he had already occupied at Windsor. There he built an inn and was licensed in the first list of victuallers. In 1800 he lost that licence: 'John Harris, a licensed victualler and retailer of spirituous liquors, having given spirits to two convicts [in exchange] for their week's rations of salt meat from the public stores, is deprived of his licence and the government has directed all his liquor to be staved'.

Governor King complained to the Under Secretary (whose surname was also King) that John Macarthur was the principal and Harris only his agent. He wrote 'A dealer, or rather the agent of a dealer, is gone to England with an intention of prosecuting me for ordering about two hundred gallons of liquor to be staved'. Harris claimed to have been victimised for refusing to become head of a newly constituted police force. His tavern was destroyed by the Governor in January 1801 and he left Sydney with his young son George. The ship foundered in Fiji and ended up in the Spanish port of Guam, which at that time was enemy territory. His two daughters, Elizabeth and Hannah, were left in the care of his friend James Larra (q.v.), who adopted them as his nieces. Harris finally reached London in October 1803, 'in great penury and distress', and petitioned the Secretary of State for some relief. His son returned to Australia in 1833.

OBSP, 1785, no. 576, *OBSP*, 1785, no. 532; David Collins, *An Account of the English Colony in New South Wales*, T. Cadell, W. Davies, London, 1802, p. 77; G. F. J. Bergman, 'John Harris, the First Australian Policeman', *AJJHS*, vol. 5, no. 2 (1959), p. 49f, and Bergman, 'John Harris', in *ADB*, vol. 1, p. 517f.; *HRA*, vol. 5, p. 274f.; M. Gillen, *The Founders of Australia*, p. 161f.; *AG*, p. 40f.; *HRNSW*, vol. IV, Government Orders of Governor King, 31 December 1800; King Papers, p. 428; CO 201/1, Corrrespondence NSW, p. 279.

HARRIS, John

b. London, 1778
General Stewart, 1818; Convict; Sentenced to life, Old Bailey, 1818.
Single; Waterman; Height: 174 cm.

Dark sallow complexion, black hair, dark eyes. Harris snatched a watch from a sailor in Duke's Place, beside the Great Synagogue, at the time of the Purim Fair. He was sentenced on 1 April 1818.

The *General Stewart* arrived in Sydney Cove on 31 December 1818. The *Sydney Gazette* of 11 November 1826 reported that 'Constable' John Harris had absconded from the service of Mr G. Druitt. However, he must have been caught and returned to his master because Harris was listed in the 1828 Census as a 'Protestant', gardener to George Druitt, at Mount Druitt. The 1837 General Return of Convicts in New South Wales reported that he was a member of the iron gang at Newcastle.

In December 1842 it was reported that a band of three 'ruffians' broke into the home of John Harris in Liverpool Street and robbed the 'aged man'. The three were caught and charged by the police.

Ship Indent 4/4005, p. 217; L. L. Robson, *The Convict Settlers of Australia*, pp. 31, 220; *Sydney Morning Herald*, 24 December 1844.

HARRIS, John

b. London, 1809–1849
Theresa (1), 1839; Convict; Sentenced to 10 years, Old Bailey, 1838.
Labourer.

John Harris, who had a previous conviction, snatched a pair of boots from a woman passerby. The police recognised Harris from her description and arrested him at a lodging house. A Jew.

Harris arrived in New South Wales on 31 January 1839 and was sent to Newcastle from Sydney by order of the Bench on 7 August 1840. He was sentenced to twelve months in the iron gang in the Maitland District on 12 August that year. On 14 January 1842 he was sent down from Maitland to spend fourteen days in the cells at the Newcastle Gaol. On 13 May he was sentenced at Maitland to two months gaol and the treadmill. He was sent on to the Prisoners' Barracks at Hyde Park in Sydney on 16 May 1846. He died, a prisoner, on 8 November 1849, at Cockatoo Island (in Sydney Harbour), and was buried by the charitable fund of the York Street Synagogue's Burial Society.

OBSP, 1838–39, case 1229, p. 985; Newcastle Gaol Entrance and Description Book, 1840, 2/2007, 2/2008, 2/2009.

HARRIS, John

b. Portsmouth, 1810–1848
Adrian, 1830; Convict; Sentenced to life, London, 1830.
Single; Pedlar; Height: 160 cm.

Dark ruddy complexion, dark brown to grey hair, dark eyes. Jew. Scar on right wrist and over left little finger and corner left eye. He was able to read. Harris was seen with a group of men when he rushed out of a London tavern and stole a watch, only to be caught. He 'danced about like an eel', trying to escape. He was convicted on 18 February 1830. He had a previous conviction with a 14-day sentence.

Harris arrived in New South Wales on 20 August 1830 and was assigned to R. W. Loane, Sydney. He then became an assigned convict servant in the District of Parramatta. In the 1837 General Return of Convicts in New South Wales he was listed as being at the hospital in Sydney and in 1838 he was 'allowed to live in Sydney so long as he continues to be in Sydney Police'.

A ticket of leave was issued in 1838 and he received a conditional pardon, dated 1 October 1842. John Harris gave one guinea to the synagogue in Sydney in 1845. He died in 1848 and was buried by the Sydney Synagogue.

OBSP, 1829–30, case 648, p. 279; Ship Indent 4/4015, p. 124, 30-1304; TL Register, 38/1653; CP 43/364.

HARRIS, John

b. Hampshire, 1813
Susan, 1834; Convict; Sentenced to 7 years, Middlesex, 1833.
Single; Shopkeeper; Height: 169 cm.

Ruddy freckled complexion, brown hair, blue eyes (inflamed). Lost part of a front tooth. Could read and write. Jew. John Harris was transported for stealing a coat. He had been convicted for a previous offence for which he had received a one-year gaol sentence.

John Harris arrived in New South Wales on 9 July 1834. He was listed as a convict servant working for the government in Port Macquarie. John Harris received a certificate of freedom dated 27 November 1840. A John Harris of Moreton Bay was a shopkeeper. The *Colonial Observer* reported, on 26 August 1843, that he was insolvent with a 'financial deficiency' of £40 6s.

Susan Printed Indent, p. 87; CF 40/1947, 27 November 1840, in 4/4363.

HARRIS, Joseph

b. London, 1802
Arab, 1822; Convict; Sentenced to life, Old Bailey, 1822.
Single.

Joseph Harris was a pickpocket, who stole a handkerchief from a passerby in Henrietta Street, Marylebone. He was sentenced on 20 February 1822.

Harris arrived in Van Diemen's Land in July 1822. His police dossier is blank.

OBSP, 1821–22, case 430, p. 205; HO 11/4.

HARRIS, Raphael

b. Hungary, 1784–1832
York, 1829; Convict; Sentenced to 7 years, Exeter-Devon, 1828.
Married; Hawker; Height: 155 cm; 2 children (in England).

Long head, grey hair, no whiskers, dark hazel eyes, medium long nose, thick lips. Can read and write. Writes Hebrew. Understands distilling in all its branches. Ralph Harris was tried at the City of Exeter on 14 October 1828, and transported for stealing a watch. He brought 11 shillings and sixpence with him on the transport ship. His wife and two children lived at 7 Partridge Court, Gravel Lane, London.

The convict transport ship arrived in Van Diemen's Land on 28 August 1829. Harris may well have been the first Hungarian to arrive in Australia. On 23 September 1829

Harris, who had been assigned to Mr Hackett in Hobart Town, was arraigned on a charge of having seven silk handkerchiefs, twenty-eight cotton handkerchiefs and ten pairs of worsted stockings in his possession, which were supposedly stolen. The charge was dismissed, but because of the 'circumstances' surrounding the trial he was convicted of being disorderly and sentenced to seven days on the treadmill: 'It appears that he was improperly allowed to sell goods in town by his master—he is to be returned to the government'. On 6 March 1830 Harris was accused of receiving stolen clothes; he was acquitted in the Supreme Court on 17 March 1830. He was sent to work on the Black Snake Road Party. In the following year he was placed on the list of invalids and in May 1831 he was given ten lashes for 'cutting up and destroying his blanket'. On 13 May he refused to join his working party and received twelve lashes. By August 1832 he was attached to the Road Party at Deep Gully. On 24 December 1832 Harris drowned at New Norfolk.
CON 31/19, no. 954; CON 18/1, no. 954; VDL Papers, ML, A1095/5, p. 43, no. 954.

HARRIS, Samuel

b. London, 1800
Marquis of Wellington, 1815; Convict; Sentenced to life, Newgate, 1811.
Single; Tailor; Height: 161 cm.

Dark brown complexion, brown hair, hazel eyes. Samuel Harris was sentenced on 14 September 1811. His deportation, on January 1815, had been delayed because of his age. Harris was said to have behaved 'very well' on board ship.

The *Marquis of Wellington* arrived in New South Wales on 27 January 1815 and Harris was initially assigned to Port Macquarie. He escaped from the colony on the *General Stewart* in early 1819 'with Jones and Bolting Billy' and was returned to Australia by the *Norfolk* in August 1825. He was listed in the 1828 Census as having arrived on the *Norfolk*. At that time Harris worked as a government servant at Port Stephens with the Australian Agricultural Company. He was described as a Jew and a labourer, with a life sentence.

Harris was granted a conditional pardon in 1844, dated July 1843. It was noted that he had two gunpowder marks on the right side of his face.
Ship Indent 4/4010, p. 107; CO 207/2.

HARRIS, Samuel Henry

b. London, 1813–1867
Asia (10), 1833; Convict; Sentenced to 7 years, London, 1832.
Single; Clerk and warehouseman; 10 children.

Sallow brown complexion, brown hair, hazel eyes, large nose, scar on chin. Could read and write. Jew. Harris was transported for stealing coins and bank notes worth more than £100 from his employers, Elias Moses and Isaac Moses, on 5 July 1832. Harris admitted to the court that he was guilty. He was the son of Henry Harris and Elizabeth (née Solomon) of London.

Harris was admitted to the *Phoenix* prison hulk in Sydney after being sent there from the Hyde Park Barracks on 17 July 1833 and was despatched to Port Macquarie on 3 September 1833. His behaviour in prison was said to be 'good'. A ticket of leave was granted in 1833. Harris was permitted to live in the District of Port Phillip from 17 June 1839. A donation of £5 was made to the Sydney Synagogue building appeal in 1845 by a 'Henry Harris'. Samuel Harris's successful rehabilitation led to the emigration of his sister Hannah Marks and brother-in-law Mark Marks (q.v.), and Rachael and Emanuel Ackman (qq.v.).

Harris was one of the four readers at the first High Holydays services in Melbourne in 1840. He had a drapery store with Jacob Marks (q.v.). Harris and Marks ran the London Mart in Queens Street and the Liverpool Mart at Collins and Elizabeth streets opposite Michael Cashmore (q.v.). On 24 April 1840 the firm advertised in the *Port Phillip Herald* regarding the London Mart in Queens Street: 'Return their sincere thanks to the public for their very flattering patronage since their commencement of business. Their stock is selected by their friends in London'. The business grew at the Elizabeth Street site. Harris and Marks began to build 'The most splendid building in the province in the course of erection', with a frontage of 37 feet, 'two storeys and forty-one feet high'. It was finished just in time for the worst of the economic depression of 1843. The 'whole of the rich and extensive stocks' were sold at an 'enormous sacrifice' and the partnership was dissolved.

Harris signed a petition to the deputy sheriff that a public meeting be called to express indignation at the calumnies against Mr Justice Willis. Harris was an original member of the Melbourne Hebrew Congregation in 1844 and president of the Melbourne Jewish Philanthropic Society in 1849. He gave £2 to the Sydney Synagogue building fund in 1845 and £100 to the Melbourne Synagogue appeal in 1853. Harris belonged to the Victorian Industrial Society in 1850. On 8 June 1853 he bought five allotments in the City of Sydney for £4102.

Samuel Henry Harris 'of Sydney' married Elizabeth Levey (q.v.) at the Sydney Synagogue on 26 March 1845. Elizabeth was the eldest child of Isaac Levey (q.v.) and his wife Dinah. By February 1846 Harris had returned to Melbourne and his name appeared on the Jewish community's formal address sent to the Chief Rabbi on his appointment. The Birth Book of the Melbourne Hebrew Congregation records the following children born to Elizabeth and Samuel Henry Harris: Elizabeth, born 22 December 1845 (who married twice—Levy and Hanochsberg); Deborah, 10 January 1847 (who married Montague Marks); Abraham and Elsie, born 16 March 1848 (who both died nine months later, on 19 and 20 December); Amelia, 9 October 1849 (who married Henry Harris); Frances, or Fanny, 1853, in Melbourne (married Sydney Cohen); Dinah, 1856, at Sydney (who married Alfred Isaacs); Henry, 1858 (who married Hannah Solomon); Isaac, 1859; and Isabella, 15 May 1861 (who married Lesser Jacobs).

Samuel died at 1 Wynyard Square, Sydney, on 28 September 1867 and was buried at the Haslam's Creek (Rookwood) Cemetery. His estate was valued at £48 000.

His lengthy tombstone inscription declares 'His was a life of honorable industry, crowned with affluence but for many years marred by a cruel malady which even though it broke his frame was powerless to shake his resignation or dim the light of his intellect. His world was in his home. His joy in the happiness of his wife and children, whose smile was a balm his sufferings, and when called from their midst by his Master, he obeyed as became a Son of Israel, with his last yearning for his family, his trust in God'. Elizabeth died on 23 January 1892 and was buried at Rookwood.

Asia Printed Indent, p. 73; *OBSP*, 1832, case 1915, p. 796f.; *Phoenix* (hulk) Entrance Book 4/6282, no. 566; ML, A1220; TL list 1838, p. 355, 38/251; 19 February 4/41464, and 4/4110, p. 107; *Port Phillip Herald*, 24 April 1840, 28 August 1843. *Sydney Morning Herald*, 30 September 1867.

HARRIS, Thomas (real name HERSCHT)

b. Cracow, 1771–1843
Moffatt (2), 1836; Convict; Sentenced to life, Old Bailey, 1835.
Married; Tailor; Height: 163 cm; 10 children (in England).

Very dark sallow complexion, pock-pitted, dark brown hair mixed with grey, dark eyes, crown of head bald. Could read. Harris was tried with Marcus Warschauer (q.v.) on 18 December 1835 for their mutual involvement in a complex scheme to forge Polish bank notes. Harris vigorously defended himself at the Old Bailey trial:

> *I have very little to say. I was molested by a parcel of foreign snakes and conspirators who laid a plan to take me. I can only say, my Lord and gentlemen, I am as innocent as a newborn child, of any knowledge of doing wrong. I say, as I said before, I never knew anything, or had any knowledge that I was guilty of doing anything wrong. The witness presented himself as a banker, and the first merchant in the country he came from, he now turns out to be a desperate character. I leave it entirely to your good sense and judgment.*

Thomas Harris arrived in Sydney on 31 August 1836. He was listed at the Hyde Park Barracks in the 1837 General Return of Convicts in New South Wales. Harris was the subject of an inquiry made by the Principal Superintendent of Convicts to the Colonial Secretary. Mr B. A. Phillips (q.v.) of George Street had asked for the assignment of Harris as tutor to his children. Harris was 'of the Jewish persuasion and only lettered in the languages of his nation'. He was sixty-six years old and 'unequal to much manual labour'. Mr Phillips was a 'free settler of very good character with a large family', and the assignment was recommended. However, the Colonial Secretary disapproved of convicts teaching children and decreed that if Harris was unfit for assignment in the ordinary way, he should be removed to the invalid (road) gang at Port Macquarie. His name, however, does not appear on the lists of convicts sent to Port Macquarie. In February 1842, aged seventy-two, he was recommended for a conditional pardon.

Thomas Harris died on 30 September 1843.

C. Pelham, *The Chronicles of Crime*, p. 404; *Moffatt* Printed Indent, p. 99; CS 37/7165, 21 September 1836; CS Letters 4/3682, p. 336, G. F. J. Bergman, 'The Bizarre Life Story of Mordecai Moses', *AJJHS*, vol. 8, no. 3 (1977), p. 100f.

HARRIS, William

Layton, 1827; Convict; Sentenced to 7 years, London, 1826.
Single; Broker; 6 children.

Wiliam Harris was transported for larceny. Acording to the surgeon's report he was 'Known as a pilferer but quiet and orderly'. He had stolen a bedstead. Harris lived at Red Lion's Court, Spitalfields, where he 'kept a broker's shop'. He was married with six children. He was convicted on 16 February 1826.

The *Layton* arrived on 9 October 1827. Harris spent his first five years in Van Diemen's Land attached to the Public Works Department at Brighton. On 11 July 1834 he was accused and acquitted of a charge of embezzling one shilling and three pence worth of goods. On 15 April 1835 he was convicted of feloniously receiving twelve yards of canvas and other goods and was sent to Port Arthur. During the next four years he was convicted of various minor offences at Port Arthur and, on 11 June 1838, he was reprimanded for 'disgraceful conduct in Church namely sitting down during the singing'. In 1840 Harris was granted a ticket of leave as a reward for his help in the capture of a gang of armed bush-rangers. By 9 March 1841 he was back in Hobart Town when he was sentenced to five days solitary confinement for being found in a disorderly house. On 14 April 1842, in Hobart, his ticket of leave was suspended for 'misconduct' and he was sentenced to four months hard labour with the Town Surveyor's Gang. On 20 August 1842 his ticket of leave was again suspended for misconduct and he was sent to the dreaded Macquarie Harbour for six months hard labour, and there his dossier ends.

CON 31/19; ID vol. 50, pp. 101–2, 1840, vol. 33, p. 54.

HART, Abraham

b. Canterbury, 1790
Lady Castlereagh, 1818; Convict; Sentenced to 7 years, Old Bailey, 1816.
Single; Glass cutter; Height: 175 cm.

Dark sallow complexion, dark eyes, brown hair. Moses Jacobs suspected that his stock was being stolen and marked some decanters 'in consequence of information' he had received. The four marked decanters were offered for sale by Abraham Hart who was therefore 'caught in the act'.

Appointed constable at Port Dalrymple in 1820, Abraham Hart was granted a ticket of leave in 1823, and a certificate of freedom in 1824. On 9 August 1823 Hart was bound over to keep the peace for a period of three months after assaulting Matilda Walker. By 3 January 1824 he was free by servitude and was put on trial for stealing a quantity of cloth. He was acquitted. One year later, in January 1825, he was found guilty of grand larceny in a trial at the Supreme Court, Hobart Town, and sentenced to seven years transportation. He was sent to the penal station on Maria Island. On 26 March 1828 he wrote to the Colonial Secretary asking for 'favourable consideration'. He had been acting as a constable and, for the previous six months, as a gaoler. His conduct had been orderly and correct. By 1828, in return for 'orderly and correct behaviour', he was allowed to become an assigned servant in the interior of the island. On 13 February 1833 he was again free by servitude when he was fined £10 for selling half a pint of gin without a licence.

OBSP, 1816, case 881, p. 418; Ship Indent 4/4006; CON 13/1, p. 191; HO 11/2; *Hobart Town Gazette*, 19 March 1824; Government Orders, ML, A1352, p. 337; CSO 1/234/5653.

HART, Abraham

Free.
Married; 5 children.

Abraham Hart 'in Windsor' was listed in the *Sydney Morning Herald* on 9 April 1840. He was a member of the new York Street Synagogue in 1845. A daughter, Deborah, married Solomon Moses (q.v.) in Sydney in 1835. Abraham Hart was listed as 'of George St'. Hart and his wife sailed from Sydney for San Francisco by the barque *Victoria* on 9 November 1849.

Mutch Index, 7/135.

HART, Alfred David

b. Adelaide, 1850–1928
Single; Merchant; 4 children.

Alfred was a son of Samuel and Harriet Hart (qq.v.) of South Australia. Hart's father was a prosperous wholesale merchant in the Province of South Australia and a pioneer of the Jewish community in Adelaide. Alfred Hart married Elizabeth Cohen at Melbourne on 14 August 1878. She was his first cousin once removed and a granddaughter of Henry and Elizabeth Cohen (qq.v.). Alfred and Elizabeth had four children: Gladys (1879–1944), Rupert (1880–1945), Elma (1882–1946) and Nola (1885–1956).

Alfred David Hart was a tobacco merchant and brewer in Melbourne and is said to have left an estate of more than £200 000 when he died in 1928. Hart's home and large garden in Charnwood Grove, St Kilda, was subdivided and became the site for the St Kilda Hebrew Congregation.

HART, Asher

b. London, 1786–1853
1841; Free.
Married; Dealer; 10 children.

Asher Hart married Phoebe Moses (Hart, q.v.) in London in 1808. Asher was the son of Lewis and Rachel Hart of London and Phoebe was the daughter of Joseph Moses and Deborah (née Barnett).

Asher and Phoebe Hart, and their large family, arrived on the *Hastings* on 4 February 1841 and settled in Sydney. Their children were Lazarus (1810–1851) (q.v.), Goodman (1812–1874) (q.v.), Henry (1814–1884) (q.v.), Deborah (1816–1884), Elizabeth (Bessie) (1818–1891) (q.v.), Rachel (1820–1889) (q.v.), Julia, Mary, Sarah and Rebecca, born 1838.

The *Sydney Morning Herald*, on 15 September 1842, listed Asher Hart with a shop and dwelling place in George Street. He was a seat holder in the York Street Synagogue from 1845 to 1847.

The *Cumberland Times* of 23 September 1845 told of a street brawl involving Asher Hart and his son, Lazarus, who assaulted Mr James Butler for being overly friendly with Rachel. The Harts, it was said, had 'promised to knock [Butler] into next Christmas and commenced the abbreviation of the intervening period by taking at least a week's growth out of him by the violence of their behaviour. Her respected parent and big brother defended the Honour of the family and the assaults complained of were committed, but which the Bench dismissed'.

Asher Hart died on 12 May 1853 and was buried by the Sydney Synagogue at the Devonshire Street Cemetery. Phoebe died at the age of seventy-four and was buried on 2 March 1864 in the Devonshire Street Cemetery. (Later transferred to Raphael's Ground.)

Of their children, Deborah married Solomon Moses (q.v.) at the Sydney Synagogue on 28 January 1835, Julia married Abraham Meyer (q.v.) at the Sydney Synagogue on 5 November 1845, Sarah married Abraham Leopold Levy on 30 March 1853, Goodman married Ellen (Eleanor Addison) in 1858, Henry married Hannah Levey on 20 March 1844, Elizabeth married Joseph Jones on 16 February 1842, Rachel married Abraham Solomon, son of Elias Solomon (q.v.) and his wife Fanny, on 16 June 1852, and Mary married Joseph Cohen in 1850.

Commercial Journal and Advertiser, 31 October 1840, 30 January 1841. Family information Jeannette Tsoulos, Sydney.

HART, Asher Hyman

d. 1842
Mermaid, 1828; Free.
Married; Dealer; 5 children.

The *Mermaid* arrived in Sydney on 21 August 1828. Hart settled in New South Wales with his wife Rachael and five children. He was buried as a Jew at the Devonshire Street Cemetery on 15 October 1842.

HART, Asher Hymen

b. London, 1813–1871
1840; Free.
Single; Merchant; 9 children.

The son of Hyam (1770–1828) and Elizabeth (1770–1848) Hart of London. His siblings were Lewis (1803–1843) (q.v.); Mirim Louisa (1805–1849); Henry Hyam (1816–1871); Rebecca (1840); Edward (1818–1854) (q.v.); and Isaac

(1820–1899) (q.v.). Asher Hymen Hart arrived in Sydney in January 1840 and on 5 February married Rachel Joseph, the youngest daughter of Joseph and Amelia Joseph (qq.v.), in the Bridge Street Synagogue. 'Mr A. H. Hart of Windsor' gave £10 to the building appeal of the Sydney Synagogue in 1839. He advertised that he was working in Windsor as an auctioneer. On 30 January 1841 the *Commercial Journal and Advertiser* announced that Asher Hart had disposed of his store and moved to the new settlement of Melbourne and brought his two brothers, Edward and Isaac, to Port Phillip. On 12 September 1841 he called the tiny Jewish community together in order to form a Jewish Congregational Society. After those first High Holydays he became the honorary reader to the Congregational Society and its second president. Hart set up business in Melbourne as a draper but became an auctioneer after fire destroyed his Collins Street shop and residence on 8 November 1842. As the fire took hold, looters stole his property, and the flames destroyed his extensive library of Judaica.

In 1844 Asher Hymen Hart became the president of the Melbourne Hebrew Congregation. He was the acknowledged religious leader of the Melbourne Jewish community through its first decade, with an excellent knowledge of Hebrew and of the liturgy of the synagogue. In 1843, as the leader of the community, he applied to the authorities in Sydney for land for a cemetery, and Sir George Gipps immediately granted one acre in trust to Michael Cashmore (q.v.), Solomon Benjamin (q.v.) and Asher Hymen Hart. No sooner had the grant been made than his brother Lewis died and became the cemetery's first occupant. On 19 November 1848 he was elected the first chairman of the Melbourne Jewish Philanthropic Society.

Asher's children were Rebecca, born in 1841, Hyam, 2 March 1842 (who was registered at the Sydney Synagogue, and died on 15 October of the same year), Lewis, 10 October 1843, Maurice, 26 May 1845 (born in Melbourne, who died, 'after a few hours illness', aged seven months), Rosetta, 19 September 1846, Rachel, 8 April 1848 (who died aged six), Hyam, 24 September 1849 (in Melbourne), Joseph, 15 February 1851 (who died aged three), and Israel, 1853.

Asher Hymen Hart gave three guineas to the Hobart Synagogue building appeal in 1845. In the first week of November 1845, Asher Hymen Hart became the first Jew in Australia to contest an election for public office when, as a result of a last-minute decision, he contested the Lonsdale Ward in the Melbourne municipal elections. He lost narrowly to his Irish opponent. As the *Port Phillip Patriot* wrote, 'Irish interest was again triumphant'. On 1 November 1851 Hart began to advertise in the Melbourne newspapers that he would pay the highest price for gold brought to his store in Collins Street, 'next to the Melbourne Club'. His purchases of gold proved to be highly successful and when the banks stepped in to be the approved bullion buyers, Hart left Melbourne to retire in London in 1854. He lived at 7 Clifton Gardens. Asher Hymen Hart died in 1871 and was buried at the West Ham Jewish Cemetery. His estate in Victoria was given as £600. Rachel died, aged sixty-one, in 1881.

Rebecca Hart, the eldest child, married Hyam Jonas and their first child married David Nathan of Wellington, New Zealand, in 1886.

First Minute Book of the Melbourne Hebrew Congregation; First Letter Book of the Melbourne Hebrew Congregation; *Port Phillip Patriot*, 3 November 1845; *Sydney Morning Herald*, 21 October 1844; *AG*, pp. 278, 285–95, 320.

HART, Benjamin

b. London, 1790
Somersetshire (1), 1814; Convict; Sentenced to life, Old Bailey, 1812.
Single; Glass cutter; Height: 164 cm.

Dark pale complexion, black hair, brown eyes. In February 1812 Benjamin Hart was convicted at the Old Bailey for breaking into a house and stealing two bolts of linen valued at £9. His death sentence was commuted to transportation for life.

Benjamin Hart arrived in New South Wales on 16 October 1814. On 25 October 1814 he was sent to Windsor as an assigned government worker. In the 1818 Muster of Convicts he was listed as a servant.

OBSP, 1813, case 382, p. 226; Ship Indent 4/4005; CS 4/3493, p. 346.

HART, David

b. London
Free.
Single; Dealer; 1 child.

David Hart was a seat holder in the Sydney Synagogue in 1845. The *Sydney Morning Herald* of 16 October 1845 listed 'David Hart & Co' opposite the Barrack Gate at 480 George Street, 'Wholesale Stores'. David Hart was married to Sarah, the daughter of James Simmons (q.v.). In 1845 in Sydney they had a son, John.

When Sarah died in Sydney in 1890, at the age of fifty-eight, her estate was estimated to be worth £234 495.

Sydney Morning Herald, 10 October 1845.

HART, Edward

b. London, 1818–1854
Pero, 1838; Free.
Single; Dealer; 6 children.

The son of Hyam and Elizabeth Hart of London, brother of Asher Hymen Hart (q.v.), and Lewis Hart (q.v.), and brother of Isaac Hart (q.v.) and first cousin of Henri Judah Hart (q.v.), Edward Hart arrived at Port Jackson from Calcutta on 8 June 1838.

'I & E Hart' established 'Waterloo House', a drapery business in Collins Street, Melbourne, and offered 'a choice selection of goods for cash'.

Edward served as the cantor at the 1840 High Holyday services in Melbourne and was an original member of the Melbourne Hebrew Congregation in 1844. In letter no. 3 in the Melbourne Hebrew Congregation files, Edward Hart applied to marry Miss Isabella Hart, who was his first cousin. It was Melbourne's first Jewish wedding. The *Ketuvah* (marriage document) was sent from Sydney and they were married on 27 March 1844, with Michael Cashmore (q.v.) and Solomon Benjamin (q.v.) as witnesses. Edward was described at that time as a 'draper'. Their six children were: Rebecca (born 9 January 1845), Hyam (30 May 1846), Lewis (10 July 1847, who died one year later), Isabella (15 January 1849), Morris (8 December 1850), and Elizabeth (1852). He became First Treasurer of the Melbourne Jewish Philanthropic Society in November 1848.

Edward Hart died in Melbourne on 18 March 1854. He was thirty-six years old. Isabella Hart, 'daughter of Isaac', was buried by the York St Synagogue on 7 February 1866.

Ship Indent 4/5213; First Letter Book of the Melbourne Hebrew Congregation; *Port Phillip Gazette*, 27 June 1842; *AG*, pp. 283, 285–6, 293.

HART, Elias

Free.

Elias Hart signed the petition to establish the Launceston Synagogue on 20 May 1843.

CO 280/157.

HART, Elizabeth

1818–1891
1840; Free.

The daughter of Asher and Phoebe Hart (qq.v.), Elizabeth married the emancipist Joseph Jones (q.v.) on 16 February 1842. She died in Sydney on 24 August 1891, aged seventy-three, 'in good old age'. She was buried in the Jewish section of the Rookwood Cemetery.

HART, Frances

b. 1751
Friendship and *Charlotte*, 1788; Convict; Sentenced to 14 years, Old Bailey, 1783.
Widowed; Mantua maker.

Frances Hart was sentenced at the Old Bailey for receiving two pairs of stolen leather boots and a pair of red morocco leather pumps. Her husband was David Hart, who was executed after attempting to escape from the transport Swift.

Hart was involved in a mutiny on the convict hulk *Helena* and was sent to the *Dunkirk* hulk, where she behaved 'better than formerly'. She sailed with the First Fleet on the *Friendship*, but at Rio de Janeiro was placed on the *Charlotte*, and according to one of the naval officers was one of 'the Six Very Best Women we have in the Ship'. On arrival in New South Wales she married one of the sailors on the First Fleet, William Robinson. It was the tenth wedding in New South Wales.

On Friday 7 November 1788 she gave evidence at the Court of Criminal Jurisdiction at the trial of John Thomas, who had robbed Mary Hill of some soap.

Frances Robinson was sworn in on the Old Testament as she was 'a Jewess'. On 17 February 1789 she and Robinson were sent to Norfolk Island on the *Supply*, arriving on 2 March 1789. Frances left Norfolk Island on 21 September 1792 on the *Atlantic*, having been on stores for 264 days in 1792. Robinson would have found no difficulty in finding work on a returning ship and there is no further record of his wife Frances.

OBSP, 1782–83, case 632, p. 840; M. Gillen, *The Founders of Australia*, p. 164; Mutch Index; J. Cobley, *The Crimes of the First Fleet Convicts*, p. 120; Cobley, *Sydney Cove*, pp. 75, 247.

HART, Goodman

b. Portsmouth, 1812–1874
Emperor Alexander, 1833; Free.
Single; Dealer; 2 children.

Goodman Hart was born at Portsea, Harts. His father, mother and sister lived in London. Goodman Hart from Hobart Town visited Sydney on 3 April 1834 on the *Eldon*. A Hebrew Prayer Book exists with his signature and an inscription, 'The Freemason's Tavern, Launceston, Van Diemen's Land 1834', and it is signed in Hebrew script, 'Tuviah ben Asher'. On 18 June 1836 Hart asked permission to marry Isabella McClure at Launceston, and in July a convict servant was assigned to work for him. In early 1839 he opened the Mitre Tavern at Longford but on 2 October 1839 disaster struck when he was sentenced at the Launceston Quarter Sessions for 'larceny'. The sentence was two years imprisonment and hard labour, and he was sent to the Cleveland Road Party. Hart was described in the police records as being 'a chemist and druggist' who had six children. The Lieutenant Governor remitted the remainder of his sentence in October 1839.

Upon his release, Hart and his family left Van Diemen's Land. His name appears on the voters' list for the Sydney Council in 1842 as he had a house in George Street. In 1846 he served as a steward at the Goulburn Races. In April 1848 it was announced that Goodman Hart of Marulan, Goulburn, was insolvent. Isaac Levey (q.v.) was appointed the official assignee. The majority of his debts included his co-religionists, Abraham Hart (£124) Michael John Davies (£102), Maurice Alexander (£110), Nathan Mandelson (£49), David Davis (£108), Joseph G. Raphael (£38), and John Moses (£150). Hart had been the owner of the Freemasons' Tavern at Marulan. On 4 November 1848 he was indicted at Sydney's Central Criminal Court for fraudulent insolvency and was sentenced to three years hard labour on Cockatoo Island.

The *Launceston Examiner* reported on 1 November 1848, 'Goodman Hart of Sydney, well known in this town, appeared before the Police Court to answer a charge of fraudulent insolvency having entered his schedule false and misleading claims making Lewis Barnett (q.v.) a creditor for £300'. The *Port Phillip Herald*, quoting Sydney newspaper reports, commented by punning on the Yiddish word *shofel* (being brought low): 'If parties who have filled their "shovels" in this district were dealt with according to their just desserts we should have a very respectable road gang to repair our streets'.

Goodman Hart moved to Adelaide, and on 15 December 1858 married Eleanor (Ellen) Addison. They had a daughter, Julia Adelaide Hart. In October 1859 Goodman John Hart was born.

Goodman Hart, aged sixty-three, died in Adelaide on 2 April 1874. His wife, Ellen, died on 25 June 1904 at Parkside, Adelaide, aged eighty-seven.

Eldon 4/5206; CON 16/1, p. 120; CON 31/1/22 p. 123. *Sydney Morning Herald*, 10 September 1842, 10 February 1846, 6 November 1848; *Sydney Chronicle*, 8, 29 April 1848; *Hobart Town Courier*, 15 February 1839; Permission to Marry Book CSO, 1/6, p. 144; *Launceston Examiner*, 1 November 1848; CON 31/22, no. 2603; Family research, Jeanette Tsoulos, Sydney.

HART, Harriet (née BENJAMIN)

b. London, 1812–1878
1848; Free.
Married; 6 children.

Harriet Benjamin, daughter of Lyon Benjamin (1779–1862) and Miriam (née Moses), married Samuel Hart (q.v.) at 64 Holywell Lane, Shoreditch, on 8 April 1840. Harriet Hart and Samuel arrived in Adelaide in 1848. Their children were Rachel (1840–1911), Benjamin (1842–1906), Caroline 1845–1940), Lewis (Louis) Henry (1849–1884), and Alfred David (1850–1928). Edward was born in July 1852 and died in Adelaide four months later.

Harriet died in Melbourne on 20 August 1878.

HART, Henri Judah (Henri John)

b. New York, 1820–1884
Barossa, 1839; Free.
Single; Jeweller and watchmaker; 4 children.

Henri Judah Hart was the son of John Hart (born 13 February 1789 and died 22 January 1864, in Melbourne), an Anglo-Jewish veteran of the battle of Trafalgar, who had migrated to the United States in 1815. Hart's mother, Isabella Levy, was a descendant of an American Revolutionary War hero. Henri Judah Hart was born on 7 May 1820 in New York, and was educated at Columbia College, so as to become a lawyer. However, he left his family and travelled to England in 1837, before migrating to New South Wales in 1839. Elvina, a sister of Henri J. Hart, married Melbourne's first Jewish 'minister', Moses Rintel (q.v.), and Edward Hart (q.v.), his cousin, married Isabella Hart in Melbourne in 1844.

Henri Hart set up in business in Sydney as a jeweller and watchmaker, only to fall victim to the recession. He was discharged from insolvency on 12 February 1844 and subsequently prospered. He became an original member of the Melbourne Hebrew Congregation and was the cousin of Isaac Hart (q.v.), whose wedding certificate he signed as a witness on 30 May 1849. He was a first cousin of Asher Hymen. Hart and worked as a jeweller and watchmaker. He was elected treasurer of the sixteen-member Gold Committee that offered a reward of £220 to the discoverer of gold within 200 miles of Melbourne. With the discovery of gold in California, a sample nugget was put on display in the window of Hart's store. Hart became a British subject and was granted naturalisation on 5 April 1852. Hart returned to the United States and married Sara Jane Rowland in Philadelphia on 21 September 1854. Sara Jane died in Melbourne at the age of twenty-seven in 1863.

On 30 March 1855 the London *Jewish Chronicle* incorrectly reported that 'The Chief Justice of Victoria has appointed Henry J. Hart a Commissioner of the Supreme Court of the Colony of Victoria—the first legal appointment of a Jew in that distant part of the world'. Henri J. Hart was appointed the second honorary consul of the United States in Victoria. He died at St Kilda on 29 April 1884.

There were four children: Isabella Hart, born in Melbourne on 16 September 1855; Abigail Sara Hart, born at 20 Woburn Place, Tavistock Square, London, on 20 December 1856; Ada Rowland Hart, born at 4 Lansdowne Terrrace, Dalgety Street, St Kilda, on 31 August 1859 (died 1939), and Edward John Hart, born in Philadelphia on 30 August 1861.

Moses Rintel, Registry of Births, Marriages and Deaths of the Families of Henri J. Hart and Sara Jane his wife, Melbourne, copy held by author; *Sydney Morning Herald*, 12 February 1844; *Government Gazette*, 5 January 1855.

HART, Henry

b. London, 1781–1818
Royal Admiral I (2), 1800; Convict; Sentenced to 7 years, Old Bailey, 1799.
Single; Labourer.

Henry Hart stole a barrel of butter from outside a shop in the West End. He was nineteen years old. He was sentenced in April 1799.

Henry Hart was assigned to work in Sydney. On 5 August 1804 the *Sydney Gazette* reported: 'On Monday Henry Hart received a corporal punishment and was ordered to work in the gaol gang for presuming to go from Sydney to Parramatta without a Pass in defiance of repeated orders'. Later that month he was listed as one of five men who stole corn out of a boat. For this he received corporal punishment with hard labour at Castle Hill.

Henry Hart died at Sydney on 1 July 1818.

OBSP, 1798–99, case 215, p. 224; *Sydney Gazette*, 5 August, 19 August 1804; Bigge Appendix; Returns of Births, Deaths and Marriages, MLA, 2130, p. 61.

HART, Henry

b. Westminster, 1803
Countess of Harcourt (1), 1821; Convict; Sentenced to 7 years, Old Bailey, 1818.
Watch and cane gilder; Height: 147 cm.

Henry Hart was transported for stealing two shillings and sixpence from a fellow prisoner in the lockup. Hart had attempted to conceal the money in his mouth. He was convicted on

9 September 1818. The hulk report reads: 'A quiet steady boy works well with the needle'. He was fifteen years old.

Henry Hart arrived on 27 July 1821. He had received his certificate of freedom by 7 December 1825. By 18 October 1828 Hart was working as a labourer and living in the Launceston District. His criminal record is sparse even though he was arrested for being drunk and disorderly in 1828, 1829 and 1833. The early Hobart Synagogue ledger records a debt of five shillings against his name.

OBSP, 1817–18, case 1301, p. 415; CON 31/18, no. 327; Ship Indent 4/4007, p. 370; *Hobart Town Gazette*, 7 December 1825.

HART, Henry

b. Portsmouth, 1814–1884
1841; Free.
Single; Dealer; 12 children.

One of the twelve children of Asher and Phoebe Hart (qq.v.), Henry Hart was managing a general store in Goulburn next door to the Royal Hotel by July 1841. Henry Hart married Hannah Levey, the fourth child of Philip and Leah Levey (qq.v.), of George Street, on 20 March 1844 at the Royal Hotel under the aegis of the Sydney Synagogue. Soon after their marriage they joined Phoebe's brother, Moses Moses (q.v.), in Yass where he owned the Argyle Store. The young men managed the Rose Inn and then later the Royal Hotel in Goulburn. (On 3 April 1844 the *Morning Chronicle* reported that Hart had taken over the licence of the Rose Inn at Yass.)

Henry Hart's name appeared on the petition to establish a Jews' burial ground at Yass, 20 December 1844. He was a seat holder in the Sydney Synagogue in 1845. In 1848 Henry Hart of the Rose Inn was charged with selling a bottle of rum on a Sunday. The charge was dismissed because there was 'insufficient evidence'.

In 1849 Henry Hart built the Royal Hotel in Yass and in 1858 he opened four adjoining shops known as Hart's Row. The Royal Hotel was built of brick and, after a flood washed away the original settlement of Yass in 1850, the new town was built around the hotel. The first telegraph 'apparatus' between Yass, Goulburn and Sydney was installed in Hart's hotel in 1858.

Henry and Hannah Hart had twelve children, all of whom were born in Yass and nine of whom married Jews. They were: Rachael (21 May 1845 to 6 July 1929), who married Barnett Aaron Moses; Deborah Emilie (29 August 1846–1927), who married (first) Lewis Benjamin on 14 May 1865 (second) David Bernston, and (third) Jonathan Wainwright on 6 March 1886; Joseph (1848 to 29 November 1900), who married Rosina Hawke on 11 October 1898; Mark Henry (1850–1929); Lewis (24 February 1852 to 28 October 1891); Sarah (10 March 1854–c. 1922); Abraham Meyer (15 March 1857 to 15 December 1930); John Moses (13 June 1859 to 2 March 1935); Asher H. (25 January 1862 to 10 February 1937); Phoebe Fanny (18 June 1864 to 1901); Phillip (31 March 1866–c. 1933); and Leah Julia (14 September 1868 to 5 September 1945).

The Rev. A. B. Davis of the Sydney Synagogue travelled to Yass to perform the marriage of Rachel Hart to Barnett, son of the late Mr Moses of Yass, on 14 September 1864. On 14 May 1865 Deborah Hart was married to Lewis Benjamin, formerly of London, in Yass.

The general store, the Beehive Stores, was owned by 'Hart & Benjamin' and concerts and theatrical events were performed in the 'magnificent ballroom' at Hart's Royal Hotel. The 'Benjamin' was Mrs Sarah Benjamin, the newly widowed wife of John Benjamin (q.v), who had joined the Hart family in Yass and had a commercial store in Cooma Street that sold wines and spirits.

Henry and Hannah Hart left Yass for Sydney on 15 February 1878. The *Yass Courier* wrote of 'the deepest regret generally expressed at the circumstances under which they had taken their departure. The Royal Hotel built and so long occupied by Mr Hart has been closed for the past day or two'. Hart had apparently invested in a failed copper mine at Cunningham Plains and the family moved to a house in Bourke Street, Surry Hills, in Sydney. Henry Hart died on 8 February 1884 and was buried at the Haslem Creek Cemetery. Hannah Hart died on 20 May 1892.

Yass Burial Ground Petition, 20 December 1844, 4/2650.4; *Morning Chronicle*, 3 April 1844; *Sydney Morning Herald*, 21 March 1844, 11 July 1844; Steve Hart, 'The Life and Times of Some Jewish Pioneers of Yass Township', *AJJHS*, vol. 16, no. 2 (2002), p. 174f. (Steve Hart notes at the end of the article that his genealogical database of the Hart–Moses family now numbers 2000 individuals).

HART, Hyam

d. 1842
Free.

Hyam Hart was buried by the Sydney Synagogue in the Devonshire Street Cemetery on 5 February 1842.

HART, Isaac

b. London
Pero, 1838; Free.
Single; Dealer; 3 children.

The son of Hyam and Elizatbeth Hart and a cousin of Henri Judah Hart (q.v.) and Edward Hart (qq.v.), and a brother of Asher Hymen Hart (q.v.) and Lewis Hart (q.v.), Isaac Hart arrived in Port Jackson with his brother Edward on 8 June 1838 and settled first in Goulburn. In September 1839 'Mr Isaac Hart of Goulburn' gave £5 to the Sydney Synagogue building fund.

In partnership with Edward he established the drapery store Waterloo House in Collins Street, Melbourne. On 2 February 1841 Isaac was one of the shopkeepers who announced that they would close their businesses regularly at 8 p.m. (with the exception of Saturday). The 'Jewish Congregational Society' of Melbourne began in the shared home of Edward and Isaac Hart on 12 September 1841. Isaac remained intensely involved in the newly created congregation, and in 1854 was the acting president when Asher Hymen Hart returned to England. Isaac Hart and Rachel Benjamin, the daughter of Moses Benjamin (q.v.), married in Melbourne on 30 May 1849. Their children were Elizabeth (born 1850), Hyam (1851), and Mary (1853).

HART, John

1740–1795
Scarborough, 1788; Convict; Sentenced to 7 years, Old Bailey, 1785.
Single; Porter.

Hart claimed to have been working as a porter after having been a sergeant in the army. He was accused of stealing a package from the Stratford coach as it stood in Whitechapel. He was sentenced to serve seven years transportation. He was sent from Newgate Prison to the Ceres hulk on 5 April 1785, at the age of forty-four and sent to Australia on the First Fleet.

Hart married Flora Larah (q.v.) on 13 February 1788, barely a fortnight after the landing of the convicts. He was literate. She made a mark in place of a signature. This was the first marriage between two Jewish people in Australia and the authorities did not take the marriage seriously. He was sent to Norfolk Island in February 1789 and she was only permitted to follow him to the remote settlement in November. He was dead, at Norfolk Island, by 3 January 1795.

M. Gillen, *The Founders of Australia*, p. 164; *OBSP*, 1784–85, case 248, p. 286.

HART, John

b. London, 1803–1877
Elizabeth, 1830; Free.
Married; Tailor; 3 children.

John Hart arrived in Sydney on the *Elizabeth* on 15 April 1830 with his wife Louisa, infant daughter Elvina, and Henry Marks (q.v.). He had a house in Darling Harbour and was a voter in the 1842 Sydney municipal election. He was listed as insolvent on 12 February 1844 and the family moved to Melbourne, where he worked successfully as a tailor and draper in Collins Street. He was one of the original members of the Melbourne Hebrew Congregation in 1844 and signed the letter of congratulations to Chief Rabbi Nathan Adler upon his appointment on 3 February 1846.

John Hart and his wife Louisa lost a stillborn male in January 1844, and were listed in the Melbourne Hebrew Congregation's Birth Register with Elizabeth (born 26 December 1844) and Mary (4 October 1846). Louisa Hart died on 18 February 1849 at the age of forty-four and was buried in Melbourne's first Jewish cemetery. John Hart died in Sydney on 2 January 1877, listed as a 'clothier'.

Ship Indent 4/5201; *Sydney Morning Herald*, 12 February 1844; *Melbourne Morning Herald*, 3 July 1849.

HART, John

b. London, 1805
Sarah (1), 1829; Convict; Sentenced to 7 years, Old Bailey, 1829.
Married; Tailor and dealer; Height: 157.5 cm.

Dark ruddy complexion. Dark brown hair. Dark hazel eyes. Scar on right forehead. Mole on centre of forehead and on left. Could read and write. Jew. John Hart's wife was Sarah. He was convicted on 11 June 1829 for 'stealing fruit', and had no previous convictions.

John Hart arrived in New South Wales on 6 December 1829. He was listed as a 'tailor and dealer' and assigned to Major William Bradley on the Goulburn Plains in 1832. He received a certificate of freedom in 1836.

AO, Indent Reel 398, 2900–125; *Sydney Gazette*, 21 June 1832; CF 36/524.

HART, Joseph

b. Whitechapel
Marmion, 1828; Convict; Sentenced to 14 years, Essex, 1827.
Married; Hatter.

Joseph Hart was transported for receiving stolen goods. His parents lived in Goulston Street, Whitechapel, where his father was a 'Master Hatter'. Joseph worked with his father. He brought ten shillings with him on the ship.

The *Marmion* arrived in Van Diemen's Land on 6 March 1828. Hart's dossier records no misdemeanours. He was granted a conditional pardon on 22 June 1838 and a certificate of freedom on 31 August 1852. Hart lived at Jericho near Hobart Town and gave two donations of £1 to the synagogue, in 1844 and 1845. He remained on the synagogue's membership list until 1848, when he was written off as 'bad' and a non-contributor. He worked as a hawker during the 1840s.

CON 31/19, no. 821; *Hobart Town Courier*, 6 September 1843; CP 1743.

HART, Lazarus

b. Portsmouth, 1810–1851
York (1), 1831; Convict; Sentenced to life, Old Bailey, 1830.
Single; Hat finisher; Height: 155 cm.

Ruddy fair freckled complexion, fair hair, blue eyes. Small scar in centre of forehead. 'Hebrew'. Tattoos included a cross (!), the letters RL repeated twice, a flower pot and sun, an anchor, heart and darts. Hart was transported for burglary. He broke into the house of Lewis Cohen at night and stole some cloth which was valued at six shillings. Cohen had known him since he was a child. The son of Asher Hart (q.v.), Lazarus said he was one of eleven children and there was no room in the family house for him. Hart claimed he was 'misled by two strangers'. He was sentenced to death on 27 May 1830, though this was commuted to transportation for life. He had no previous convictions.

The *York* arrived in Sydney on 7 February 1831. Isaac Simmons (q.v.) took Lazarus Hart in hand and in November 1832 he was assigned to Simmons. The 1837 General

Return of Convicts in New South Wales recorded that he was assigned to Joseph Moses (q.v.) in Sydney. He was working in Campbelltown in 1838 when his ticket of leave was granted. It was altered for the District of Yass in June 1839 and for Sydney in August 1841, 'for so long as he remains in the service of Mr Moses (who was his grandfather). A conditional pardon was granted on 1 July 1843. By this time he had a home and jeweller's shop in George Street and appeared on the voters' list for the Sydney Council elections. He was a seat holder in the Sydney Synagogue in 1845.

Lazarus Hart drowned while attempting to cross the Murrumbidgee River in November 1851.

OBSP, 1829–30, case 1038, p. 456f.; Governors' Despatches, 1840, p. 556, and 1844, p. 157; Ship Indent 4/4103, p. 59, no. 31-116-117; TL 39/771, in 4/4128; CP 44/241; 4/4128; *Sydney Free Press and Commercial Journal*, 25 January 1842; HO 10/53.

HART, Lazarus

b. Dover, 1830
Lady Montagu, 1852; Convict; Sentenced to 15 years, Maidstone, 1849.

Fresh complexion, brown hair, long face, high forehead, brown eyebrows, blue eyes, long nose. Jew. Can read and write. A full rigged ship in red and blue tattooed on breast. Ring on middle finger of left hand. Lazarus Hart had a previous conviction for 'vagrancy'. This conviction was for 'House breaking and larceny'.

Lazarus Hart arrived in Hobart on 9 December 1852 as the process of transportation to Van Diemen's Land was ending. An initial period of probation of three years and six months at the Prisoners' Barracks in Hobart Town was altered to twelve months hard labour when he absconded on 24 February 1853, less than two months after his arrival. At the same time he was convicted of larceny for an 'offence under £5' and his sentence was extended by eighteen months. On 3 May of that year his existing sentence of hard labour was extended by two months for disobedience of orders. On 22 October 1855 he received seven days hard labour for insolence. On 3 March 1856 he received fourteen days hard labour for being drunk. He was sent to Port Arthur on 11 March 1856 and received eighteen months hard labour for attempting to abscond. In Hobart Town on 30 October 1858 he received a further twelve months hard labour for absconding. A ticket of leave was issued on 16 May 1859. On 18 June 1860, in Launceston, he was sentenced to six months hard labour for misconduct. A conditional pardon was approved on 17 July 1860.

CON 14/43, no. 6513.

HART, Lewis (Louis)

b. London, 1803–1843
Free. Married; Draper.

A brother of Asher Hymen Hart (q.v.), and a clothier in Collins Street, Melbourne, Lewis Hart died on 15 August 1843. His was the first Jewish burial in Melbourne's

Old Cemetery and an eye witness account of the funeral was recorded by the visiting missionary the Rev. Dr James Allen, who 'thanked the Lord for giving me such a testimony of the truth of the Bible'.
AG, p. 288.

HART, Lewis

b. London, d. 1841
1840; Free.
Single; Dealer.

On 18 November 1841 'a young man of Jewish persuasion named Lewis Hart, who was employed as a shopman to Mr [Barnett] Levey, at the corner of George and Market Streets was found suspended from the Stairs—since his arrival in the colony he had often been heard to threaten suicide'.
Sydney Gazette, 20 November 1841.

HART, Maria (Mary)

b. London, d. 1844
John Craig, 1834; Free.
Single; 2 children.

'Miss Mary Hart' migrated to Australia as a steerage passenger on the *John Craig*, arriving in Port Jackson on 12 December 1834. With her were Martha Moses (q.v.) and Rachel Nathan (q.v.). Maria Hart married Moses Barnett (q.v.) on 17 March 1841 at the Sydney Synagogue. There had been some discussion about her Jewish status by the Synagogue's board and the vote was eight for and two against the marriage taking place. Their children were Hannah (born 25 December 1841) and Samuel (9 September 1843). 'Margaret', the wife of 'Moss Barnett' was buried at the Jewish section of the Devonshire Street cemetery on 1 January 1844 and removed to Raphael's Ground, Lidcombe in 1901.
Ship Indent 4/5207.

HART, Mary

b. Whitechapel, 1805
Mary Anne (1), 1822; Convict; Sentenced to life, London Gaol Delivery, 1821.
Single; Servant; Height: 155 cm.

Dark hair, dark brown eyes, cannot write. Born Castle Street in Whitechapel. Mary Hart was transported for stealing forty yards of lace. Her mother lived at Golden Lane, Cripplegate, and was a charwoman. The ship's surgeon reported that Mary Hart was a 'reprobate and a loose girl'. There is only circumstantial evidence of a Jewish origin.

Mary Hart arrived in Hobart Town on 2 May 1822 and on 17 June she was found to have absented herself from her master's premises for four days and was sentenced to one week in gaol on bread and water and to sit in the stocks for two hours on two consecutive days. On 2 July 1822 she was convicted of stealing sugar, tea and food from the house of her master, Mr Heywood, and was handed over to be kept in gaol for six months, the first fourteen days to be on bread and water, and to sit in the stocks for three hours on three consecutive days. In 1823 she was listed in the Muster as being the servant to Mrs Heywood.

On 15 December 1823 she married Adam Dillon, a convict who had arrived in Hobart Town on the *Lady Castlereagh*. On 16 January she was officially reprimanded for cohabiting with Thomas Reynolds. The following day she was charged with having taken from her husband's home her bedding and clothing. She remained in the Female Factory for three weeks, after which the Lieutenant Governor intervened and remitted her sentence. A conditional pardon was approved on 18 July 1834 and a free pardon was recommended in 1838 and approved on 9 December 1842.
CON 40/5.

HART, Moses (Moss)

b. London, 1815
Aurora, 1835; Convict; Sentenced to life, Surrey, 1834.
Single; Pen cutter and labourer; Height: 160 cm.

Convicted for housebreaking and burglary, Moses Hart was tried with two others. 'A Jew'.

There is no police record for Moses (Moss) Hart. He was assigned to the Van Diemen's Land Company at Circular Head. A ticket of leave was approved on 24 November 1843 and a conditional pardon granted on 8 December 1846.
CON 31/21, no. 1989.

HART, Philip

b. Mitre Street, Aldgate, 1823
Candahar, 1842; Convict; Sentenced to 7 years, Central Criminal Court, 1841.
Single; Baker and groom; Height: 163 cm.

Fresh complexion, black hair, no whiskers, high forehead, brown eyes, large nose. Long fingers, slightly freckled, carries an inoculation scar. A Jew. He could read and write a 'very little Hebrew' (according to Hart). Philip Hart was sentenced for 'Stealing a watch from a person with whom I lodged and several other articles'.

Hart was discharged from the initial period of probation on 21 July 1844. He received a ticket of leave on 19 March 1846. During 1845 and 1846 he was twice charged with 'felony', on both occasions escaping conviction. However, he was found guilty on six separate charges of 'disturbing the peace' and was fined five shillings for each offence.

Hart was sentenced in Hobart Town on 29 August 1850 to transportation for seven years for 'stealing £65 from a man in his cab'. The man was Michael Hogan.

Hart was sent to Port Arthur for an initial probationary period of fifteen months. By 7 January 1852 he was an assigned servant in Hobart and was caught 'absconding' on the *Pilot*, bound for Port Phillip. He was sentenced to eighteen months hard labour in chains. By March 1853 he had returned to assigned service and made an application for a ticket of leave. This was granted on 19 September 1854. On 6 September 1855 he was fined five shillings in Hobart for 'disturbing the peace'. A conditional pardon was approved on 30 October 1855.

CON 33/23; CON 37/6, p. 1950; CON 18/31; CON 16/4, p. 128.

HART, Phillip

1833; Free.
Single; Dealer.

Phillip Hart married Esther Abrahams (q.v.) on 9 May 1834. It was the sixth Jewish wedding performed in New South Wales and the only one at which Isaac Friedman (q.v) officiated. In February 1839 Mr and Mrs Phillip Hart gave £10 to the Sydney Synagogue building appeal. In 1845 he gave £30.

Hart had a draper's shop in King Street, Sydney, and on 25 April 1842 took over the licence for the Jew's Harp Hotel on the Liverpool Rd, Parramatta (*Sydney Morning Herald*). The voters' list for 15 September 1842 recorded that he had a shop and dwelling house in George Street. Hart bought land in Braidwood, Hartley and Mudgee during the 1840s and land worth more than £3700 in Sydney between 1851 and 1853. Phillip Hart 'of George St' became the Sydney collector for the Jerusalem Fund on 2 September 1854.

Land Correspondence 2/7875; *Sydney Morning Herald*, 2 September 1840, 25 April 1842, 15 September 1842, 17 September 1842, 2 September 1854.

HART, Phoebe (née MOSES)

b. London, 1789–1864
1841; Free.
Married; 10 children.

Phoebe Moses married Asher Hart (q.v.) in London in 1808. Her siblings were Isaac Moses (q.v.), Moses Moses (q.v.), John (Jacob) Moses (q.v.), Catherine Moses, Susannah Moses and Abraham Moses (q.v.). All but Catherine and Susannah came to Australia. Phoebe was the mother of Lazarus (q.v.), Goodman (q.v.), Henry (q.v.), Rachel (q.v.), Deborah, Elizabeth (q.v.), Julia, Sarah, Mary and Rebecca.

When Phoebe Hart died she had been living at 243 Castlereagh Street, Sydney. Her death certificate recorded that four of her children had predeceased her and that two sons and six daughters were still living. She was buried at the Devonshire Street Jewish Cemetery on 2 March 1864.

Sydney Synagogue Records.

HART, Rachel

b. London, 1820–1889
1841; Free.
6 children.

A daughter of Asher and Phoebe Hart (qq.v.), Rachel arrived in Sydney with her parents and siblings. Rachel Hart married Abraham Solomon in Sydney on 16 June 1852. Her children were Sarah, Lewis, Priscilla, Julia, Asher and Eve.

HART, Robert

b. London, 1813
George III, 1835; Convict; Sentenced to life, London, 1834.
Single; Cigar and tobacco manufacturer; Height: 177 cm.

Could read and write. Black hair, brown eyes, small mouth, large Roman nose. On 1 May 1834 a 'colonial produce broker' was returning from Lloyds when 'I was suddenly hustled by five or six well dressed men—the prisoner was nearest to me … I passed my hand down, felt my watch slipping from me. I grasped it in the prisoner's hand'. Hart ran fifty yards pursued by the broker, who caught him. Hart told the court: 'I being a Jew am not permitted to work on Passover. I was merely taking a walk through the City, and going through the market I heard the cry of "Stop thief!"' Robert Hart told the truth about Passover. The first day of May 1834 was the eighth and final day of the festival of Passover. However, the court believed that Hart was guilty and he was sentenced on 15 May 1834.

The Surgeon on board the *George III* reported that Hart had been his assistant in the hospital and that he had been 'uniformly kind and attentive to the sick and had charge of spirits at all times without once abusing his trust'. The ship foundered and burnt when it was near Hobart Town. Hart's conduct in extinguishing the fire was 'practically above all praise, and during the wreck, equally so'. Hart was assigned to be a hospital attendant, but was almost immediately granted a pass: 'Because of his good conduct upon the occasion of the fire on board the *George III*—to be freed from all penal coercion'.

Hart became deeply involved in the affairs of the Jewish community. He was described as a 'dealer' when he married Hannah Solomon (née Marks, q.v.), a widow, formerly the wife of Mark Solomon (q.v.), at the home of Abraham Rheuben (q.v.) on 12 June 1840. It was Van Diemen's Land's third Jewish marriage. Robert Hart was granted a hawker's licence in 1841. He became secretary to the Hobart Town Congregation in January 1842 and rented seat no. 17 in the Hobart Synagogue in 1845. He contributed to the building fund. His wife was a seat holder and Hart was one of the founders of the Tasmanian Hebrew Benevolent Society in 1847.

A conditional pardon was granted on 23 August 1843 and in May 1846 permission was extended for him to travel to all the Australian colonies. The *Hobart Town Courier* of 3 February 1843 had carried the advertisement that Hart had 'taken premises in Liverpool Street opposite John James Spirit store as Tobacconist having served apprenticeship in the extensive manufactory of Messrs Lindyfoot and Co. Vine Street, Minories and at Essex Bridge, Dublin'. The *Hobart Town Directory* of 1847 listed him as a billiard table keeper in Collins Street. In September 1848 Hart wrote to the government stating that he had a conditional pardon and, as he had spent thirteen and a half years without offence, he requested an absolute pardon. This was granted on 2 October 1849. The Hobart Synagogue's ledger records that Hart 'left the colony' in 1865.

OBSP, case 749, 1834. p. 442; CON 31/21, no. 192; CON 18/8, no. 1912; *George III* Indent; Allport Collection, Schedule Conditional Pardons, p. 303, vol. 47 (1844); *Hobart Town Courier*, 3 February 1843; Minute Book of the Hobart Synagogue.

HART, Samuel

1803–1827
Castle Forbes (1), 1820; Convict; Sentenced to 7 years, Donegal County, 1819.
Labourer.

Samuel Hart arrived in Sydney on 27 January 1820 and, evidently, was soon sent to Newcastle. On 28 April 1821 the Colonial Secretary recorded that he had arrived back in Sydney under sentence of transportation from Newcastle. He was sent, on 25 September 1823, from Newcastle to Port Macquarie. On 2 February 1825 he was returned to Newcastle on the *Mars* to be kept at hard labour in double irons. Following another attempt to escape, Hart was convicted at the Sydney Criminal Court on 22 April 1826 and given a seven-year colonial sentence. He was sent to Moreton Bay on 2 June 1826. Samuel Lewis (who was not Jewish) and Samuel Hart are both recorded as having absconded from the penal station on 25 August 1826. Hart drowned at Moreton Bay on 29 December 1827. Though described as 'a Jew' it seems doubtful that he was, as he was described in the original official convict indent as a 'farm boy' from County Donegal.

Chronological Register of Convicts at Moreton Bay (Oxley), no. 769; Ship Indent 4/4007; CS 4/3505, and 4/3513, pp. 361–2 Newcastle; *Sydney Gazette*, 12 May 1825, 26 April 1826.

HART, Samuel

b. Chester
Lucy Ann, 1845; Free.
Labourer.

Samuel Hart was sentenced in Sydney in 1847 to twelve calendar months gaol or to find securities for a bail. He was described as 'Jewish'. He was released from the Newcastle Gaol on 28 January 1850.

Darlinghurst Gaol Entrance and Description Book, 1847, no. 157, 2/2009.

HART, Samuel

b. London, 1813–1867
1848; Free.
Married; Dealer; 6 children.

The 1834 edition of the *Post Office Directory of London* lists a Samuel Hart, tailor, at 83 Berwick Street, Soho. He was married on 8 April 1840 at 64 Holywell Lane, Shoreditch, to Harriet Benjamin (Harriet Hart, q.v.), by the congregation of the New Synagogue, 'according to the rites and ceremonies of the German and Polish Jews'. At the time of his marriage (and when his first two children were born), his address was given as 3 Barbican, which was the address of his business as 'clothier'.

Samuel Hart was the treasurer of the Adelaide Hebrew Congregation from the time of its foundation in 1848. He was remembered as among those involved in the first High Holyday services in Adelaide. On 24 December 1848 he was appointed a trustee for the purchase of land on which a synagogue would be built, and became a member of the congregation's committee—his Hebrew name was listed as *Shmuel ben Avraham*. His name appears in the 1848 directory of the colony as a merchant in Rundle Street. In October 1850 the *South Australian Register* carried large public notices that he was 'relinquishing the retail business and was turning to wholesale with the arrival of 600 packages from 13 English ships'.

Samuel Hart died at Hindley Street West in Adelaide, aged fifty-four, on 19 April 1867. Harriet died at Melbourne, aged sixty-six, on 20 August 1878. They had six children: Rachel (1840–1911), who married Isaac Feldheim in 1861, Benjamin (1842–1906), Caroline (1845–1940), Lewis (Louis) Henry (1849–1884), who married Dinah Levy, Alfred David (1850–1928), who married Elizabeth Cohen (1852–1926), and Edward, who was born in July 1852 and died four months later.

South Australian Gazette and Colonial Register, 24 January 1848, 11 October 1850; *Jewish Chronicle* (London), 30 May 1851.

HARTNELL, Mary (née MYERS)

b. Germany, 1817
John Renwick (1), 1838; Convict; Sentenced to 7 years, Central Criminal Court, 1837.
Married; Nursery maid and governess; Height: 145 cm; 2 children (in England).

Mary Hartnell could read and write. She had a fair ruddy complexion, brown hair and grey eyes. She was the sister of Edward Myers (q.v.) and 'Fishmonger' Moses Myers (q.v.). She was the mother of two male children in London. She was listed on the indent of the John Renwick *as 'Mary Hartwell'.*

Mary Hartnell arrived in Sydney on 27 August 1838. According to the *Registry of Flash Men*, the 'celebrated' Mary Hartnell behaved so badly on board the convict transport ship that the Governor had her sent to the Female Factory as soon as she arrived in Sydney. She was well known in Sydney during the 1840s as a prostitute.

She held a conditional pardon in 1844 (no. 1536).

Printed Ship Indent; W. A. Miles, *Registry of Flash Men*, pp. 105–6.

HASSAN, Samuel (SILVER)

b. London, 1813–1850
Albion (3), 1828; Convict; Sentenced to life, London, 1828.
Single; Butcher and fishmonger; Height: 169 cm.

Olive complexion, black hair, black eyes. Scar right corner right eye. Could read and write. His name was also spelled Samuel Hassam and Hassen. Hassan was convicted of highway robbery after he attacked a man late at night. He was identified as one of a band of three. Hassan stole a watch, was pursued and was captured. In court he declared: 'I am a Jew. It is our holidays and my friends were at Synagogue'. The prosecutor, claimed the accused, was quite intoxicated. Hassan said he had been at the Cobourg Theatre that night. He was sentenced on 21 February 1828.

Samuel Hassan arrived in Sydney on 3 November 1828 and was listed in the 1828 Census as aged twenty-one and in government service. The census stated that he came on the *Dolphin*. He was listed as a Jew. As a butcher he was assigned to Richard Mutton in George Street, Sydney. The 1837 General Return of Convicts in New South Wales listed him as being in Sydney's House of Correction. A ticket of leave was issued on 24 March 1842. On 10 June 1844 Samuel Hassan, alias Silver, aged thirty-eight, married Jane Russell, aged thirty, who had come as a convict on the *Margaret* (1) with a seven-year sentence, and was now free. They were married by the Rev. James of Windsor. Hassen received a conditional pardon in 1846.

Samuel Hassen died in Sydney in 1850. His funeral was conducted by a Church of England clergyman in the Parish of Clydesdale.

OBSP, 1827–28, case 533, p. 288; Ship Indent 4/4013, p. 145; Permission to Marry Book, 1844, p. 62, in 4/4514; Ship Indent 4/4514, p. 145; Governors' Despatches, 1846, A1241 p. 154; TL 42/884: *Australian*, 24 March 1842.

HATCHELL, Jane (Sarah ELIAS)

b. 1774
Northampton, 1815; Convict; Sentenced to 14 years, Devon Assizes, 1814.
Single.

Jane Hatchell was transported for receiving stolen goods. Her maiden name was Elias and it is possible that she was related to Abraham Elias (q.v.).

The Marriage Register at St John's, Parramatta, recorded that 'Sarah Elias' married Alex Hewitt of Richmond on 16 April 1816. On 19 June 1826 'Jane Hatchell' married John Smith at St John's. Hatchell was listed in the 1828 Census as fifty-four years of age.

HAYES, Elisha

Palambam, 1833; Free.
Married; Dyer.

Elisha Hayes was a bond migrant who arrived on 10 January 1833 on the *Palambam* with his wife Elizabeth, travelling steerage. Also with them was Mary Anne (or Marianne)

Hayes, who was twenty-eight years of age. Despite the fact that so many of the passengers on the *Palambam* were Jewish, the Hayes family may have been Christian.
Ship Indent 4/5204.

HAYES, Henry

1840; Free.
Tailor.

On 27 August 1840 Henry Hayes, tailor and clothier of 72 George Street, Sydney, opened a Melbourne branch in Elizabeth Street, located between Collins and Flinders streets. He advertised 'Tartans and Tweeds, Buckskins and Doeskins, Cashmere'. In June 1841 the Melbourne shop was sold. In February 1842 Hayes sold his hat and cap business. The *Sydney Morning Herald* informed the public on 16 September 1842 that Hayes had a house in Kent Street where he sold ready-made clothing. On 19 October 1842 in Sydney he advertised that he was a 'free immigrant', whose shop was at 72 George Street. On 30 August 1843, an illicit still was found on his premises. Hayes was prosecuted and reprimanded while his shop continued in business: 'Henry Hayes, tailor and draper, near the Royal Hotel his tailoring business has always been the most extensive in the colony and with the effects of the depression gradually disappearing a desire for "genuine economy" is now beginning to manifest itself within the last few months [orders] have increased more than one half'. Hayes was a member of the Sydney Synagogue in 1845.
Port Phillip Patriot, 10 September 1840; *Port Phillip Gazette*, 16 September 1840; *Sydney Free Press and Commercial Journal*, 19 October 1841; *Sydney Morning Herald*, 7 January 1842, 4 February 1842, 1 June 1842, 16 September 1842, 30 August 1843, 8 January 1845.

HECKSHER, David Meyer

b. Århus, Denmark, 1805–1891
1833; Free.
Single; Watchmaker and jeweller; 1 child.

David Hecksher began business as a 'dealer' in Elizabeth Street, Hobart Town, shortly after his arrival on 27 April 1833. In April 1834 his tender was accepted for the regulation of St David's clocks at £15 per annum. On 24 January 1836 Hecksher wrote to the Colonial Secretary requesting naturalisation. In his petition he stated that he had acquired real estate and landed property but realised that, as an alien, he could not transfer the latter. The colonial government responded on 27 June 1836, stating that he needed seven years residence or a permit from the Secretary of State in the United Kingdom before embarkation for Australia. In 1839 Hecksher asked for the oath of allegiance to be rephrased so that he could make the oath as a Jew.

He was a witness at the marriage of Michael Solomon (q.v.) and Sarah Solomon in 1840—the first Jewish marriage in Van Diemen's Land. David Hecksher had married Susannah Benjamin, the daughter of Benjamin and Rosetta Benjamin. On 31 July 1838 the three-year-old Myer Hecksher was buried at the Harrington Street Hobart Town Jewish Cemetery. That year, Hecksher travelled to San Francisco in order to sell Tasmanian timber to the gold miners. Once in California it was discovered that the wood was too hard to be used for building and it was burnt on the Californian beach. In Hobart Town once again in 1842 he advertised his work as a jeweller in Elizabeth Street. Hecksher donated £20 to the Hobart Synagogue in 1843.

In 1845 David Hecksher was appointed the official 'collector' for the Hobart congregation. The *Launceston Examiner*, on 4 November 1848, listed 'D. Hecksher, Director of the Tasmanian Fire and Life Insurance Co'. Two years after the establishment of the settlement in Melbourne, 'D. Hecksher' was listed as the proprietor of sheep at Port Phillip.

David Hecksher died in Melbourne on 31 March 1891, aged eighty-six. Susannah Hecksher had died on 21 May 1882. Both were buried in the Jewish section of the Melbourne General Cemetery. Their son Philip (born 1841) married Esther Adele Solomon in 1884 in Melbourne.

Hobart Town Courier, 27 April 1833, 13 September 1839; ML, A1267-14, p. 1733, Letter to Sir A. Bourke of 12 November 1836.

HECKSCHER, Edward

c. 1840; Free.
Single; Dealer.

References to Edward Heckscher in Van Diemen's Land are limited to two years. In June 1840 he sent a consignment of potatoes to South Australia from Hobart Town and, in 1840 and 1842, advertised in Hobart Town for free emigrants to work for him.

Colonial Times, 9 June 1840, 1 September 1840; *Hobart Town Courier*, 5 August 1842.

HENDRICKS, John Herman

b. London, 1822–1859
1843; Free.
Single; Dealer.

A licence to operate a stage coach was issued to John Hendricks on 12 April 1844 (*Sydney Morning Herald*). In 1845–57 he was a seat holder at the Sydney Synagogue and in 1853 gave five guineas to the Melbourne Hebrew Congregation's building appeal. He married Jane Solomon in 1855. He was described as 'the son of the late Aaron and Ann Hendricks of London, for many years a respected resident of Braidwood, New South Wales'. His large stone warehouse still stands at Braidwood near 'Jews' Bridge'. He died on 17 November 1859 and was buried at Devonshire Street and moved to Raphael's Ground in 1901.

HENRIQUES, Joseph Augustus

b. Jamaica, West Indies, d. 1875
1842; Free.
Married; Merchant; 16 children.

Joseph Augustus Henriques married Judith Georgina Barrow Montefiore, the daughter of Joseph Barrow Montefiore and his wife Rebecca (qq.v.). Joseph and Judith Henriques stayed in the colony of South Australia for a few years in the 1840s and then moved to Melbourne. He was listed as a voter in the Melbourne municipal elections of 1849, as the owner of a house in Bourke Street.

There were sixteen children, all of whom had the names 'Barrow Montefiore' included before their surnames. The first four daughters remained unmarried. They were Sarah Evalina, Augusta, Marion, and Helen. The fifth daughter, Justina, married her cousin Joseph Barrow Levi Montefiore in 1863. Edith married David Nathan in 1878. Judith Georgina married Joseph Henriques in 1851. Herbert did not marry. Emily married Moses Benjamin Henriques in 1856. George Frederick, born in Melbourne in 1853, married Dorothy Frances Fuller in 1880. Josephine married Leopold Oppenheim in 1870. Esther Hannah married Eliezer Levi Montefiore (q.v.) in 1848. Ada married Saul Joshua in 1867. Horace married Edith Lucy Thompson in 1881. In 1849 a son, Isaac Lopez Henriques, was born, but died within four months. Josephine Augusta was born in 1852 and lived for four weeks.

In Melbourne, J. A. Henriques served as the first Consul of the United States in the colony of Victoria, and was succeeded by Henri J. Hart (q.v.). In Sydney, Henriques set up a flour and grain business, which prospered. In the *Melbourne Morning Herald* of 17 September 1851, (Benjamin) Francis and (Edward) Cohen advertised a 'Clearing Out Sale' for the haberdashery stock of J. A. Henriques of Market Square. Henriques died in 1875, leaving three daughters and two sons.

Family information from David and Jill Stevenson, Sydney.

HENRIQUES, Nathaniel

b. Kingston, Jamaica, 1827–1851
Free.
Single.

Nathaniel Henriques was born in Jamaica on 18 July 1827 and died in Adelaide on 2 January 1851, aged twenty-three. Henriques had been thrown from a horse on 25 December 1850, and died as a result of his injuries.

West Terrace Cemetery, Adelaide.

HENRY, Abraham

b. Aldgate, 1804
Ocean II (2), 1823; Convict; Sentenced to life, London, 1821.
Single; Height: 164 cm.

Sallow complexion, brown hair, hazel eyes. Abraham Henry was a pickpocket in the East End.

Abraham Henry arrived in New South Wales on 27 August 1823. He received a ticket of leave in 1829 and a conditional pardon.

Ocean Indent, p. 60; TL 29/637; CP 784.

HENRY, Benjamin

b. London, 1797–1861
Dromedary, 1820; Convict; Sentenced to 14 years, Middlesex, 1819.
Married.

Benjamin Henry was sentenced on 21 April 1819 for feloniously receiving twenty-three tablecloths stolen from an Oxford Street hotel. He was a cousin of Lewis Henry (q.v.), who came to New South Wales as a convict on the Exmouth in July 1831.

On 6 November 1822 Benjamin Henry was reprimanded for being absent from the muster and from church. On 2 April 1824 he was discovered as a stowaway on board the brig *Woodlark* and sentenced to fifty lashes. The *Hobart Town Gazette* announced on 3 December 1825 that he had opened a parchment manufacturing business at the corner of Elizabeth and Melville streets and sent out a notice to the legal fraternity. By 11 April 1826 Rachael Henry (q.v.), his wife, had arrived free and Henry was assigned to her. On 20 September of that year he was again absent from the muster and from church and on 16 June 1828 he was fined five shillings for 'carrying on his calling on the Sabbath'.

On 17 May 1830, while still officially assigned to his wife, he was 'severely reprimanded' for illegally harbouring the convict Joseph Benjamin (q.v.). On 5 January 1831 he was again reprimanded for being absent from the church parade. He was listed as a merchant in Hobart in 1832. Henry received a conditional pardon (no. 381). On 21 August 1832 he was recorded as holding a 'certificate of emancipation' and having threatened to assault and beat Lewis Henry Lazarus (Henry Lewis Lazarus, q.v.). He was bound over to keep the peace. On 16 March 1839 Henry was listed in the *Hobart Town Gazette* as a general dealer who had become insolvent. He quickly recovered. In 1841 he received a liquor licence for Hobart Town. The 1842 Census shows that he owned a brick hotel in Liverpool Street, where he lived with his 'wife and children'. He was able to give £10 to the synagogue building appeal in 1843, being the tenth-highest donor in a list of forty names. He promised to pay another £10 in 1845 but does not appear to have fulfilled his pledge.

In the wake of the gold rush the Benjamin family moved to Victoria. On 24 April 1861 the Hobart *Mercury* reported that Benjamin Henry 'formerly of this city' had died at Lockwood, Victoria!

OBSP, 1819, case 685, p. 268; CON 31/18; CSO 1/403/9098; Ship Indent 4/4007, p. 65; *Hobart Town Gazette*, 3 December 1825, 27 May 1826, 19 October 1832, 16 March 1839, 18 June 1841; *Colonial Times*, 4 May 1849.

HENRY, John

b. Copenhagen, 1815
Asia (5), 1840; Convict; Sentenced to 15 years, Central Criminal Court, 1839.
Single; Clerk and shop assistant; Height: 165 cm.

Fair complexion, dark brown hair and whiskers, blue eyes, medium nose. John Henry's behaviour on board ship was 'indifferent'. He had been sentenced for stealing a watch. A Jew. Could read and write.

John Henry's initial period of two years on probation was to be spent at Port Arthur. This time was extended by four months in 1842 for a number of offences, the major one being the theft of a book from the prison library. His behaviour reports range from 'bad', 'idle' and 'lazy' to 'good', until, on 28 December 1842, he was appointed a constable. He worked at Pontville and Green Ponds and was dismissed from the force in June 1844 for 'trafficking with a man confined in the watch house and general bad conduct'. In February 1845, as an assigned servant at Launceston, he was sentenced to three months in prison for insolence in 'refusing wages to the amount of £9 per annum'. On 8 February 1848 he received his ticket of leave. Two charges of obtaining money on false pretences were dismissed in Hobart Town in May 1849 and he received his conditional pardon on 5 February 1850.
CON 33/2.

HENRY, John Solomon

Free.

I. S. Henry was listed as a member of the committee of the Adelaide Hebrew Congregation in September 1850. In 1855 Mr J. Solomon Henry of Adelaide married a daughter of Mr Charles Marks of Plymouth (England).
Jewish Chronicle, 30 November 1855.

HENRY, Lewis (Louis)

b. London, 1808
Exmouth, 1831; Convict; Sentenced to 14 years, London, 1830.
Single; Ornamental painter; Height: 156 cm.

Pale freckled complexion, sandy haired, dark brown eyes—weak eyes. Scar right side of forehead. He could read and write. Lewis Henry was a cousin of Benjamin Henry (q.v.), who came to Van Diemen's Land in 1820. Henry was tried twice. The first offence was theft of a gun by trickery. He asked the storekeeper to wait outside a building in Duke's Place while his employer would approve the purchase. Henry left the shop and immediately tried to pawn the gun. The second offence involved the same kind of trick. However, this time he attempted to steal six pairs of boots. The offences took place on Christmas Eve and he was caught in April. He was sentenced on 15 April 1830.

Lewis Henry arrived in Van Diemen's Land on 28 July 1831. He was then despatched to the Hyde Park Barracks in Sydney where he spent a month before being assigned to Mr P. Colletts, Mt York. In the 1837 General Return of Convicts in New South Wales, Henry Lewis is listed as a convict assigned to 'J. Colletts' of Bathurst.

OBSP, 1829–30, case 1002, case 1003, p. 434; *Exmouth* Printed Indent, 1831, no. 31/1381.

HILL, Henry

b. Lambeth, 1828
Sir Robert Peel, 1844; Convict; Sentenced to 10 years, Old Bailey, 1844.
Single; Pickpocket; Height: 150 cm.

Fresh freckled complexion, black hair, long thin face, blue eyes, long nose, large chin. Jew. He had the letters HD tattooed on his right arm and MHV on his left arm. A pickpocket, Henry Hill stole a silk handkerchief in Greenwich Hill, and had previously been in prison eighteen times. He had four sentences of three months, one sentence of two months and the other sentences were of one month each. He had lived 'stealing two years besides the time in prison'. The surgeon on board ship reported that he was 'lazy and dirty'. Hill could neither read nor write. (He was aged sixteen at the time of his arrival).

From 1845 to 1848 Henry Hill was at Point Puer. In this time, he spent four and a half months in solitary confinement on four charges of being absent without leave. In February 1849 he was transferred to the Cascades in Hobart and remained there for four years, with three periods at Port Arthur. In March 1851 he received his eighth sentence for being absent without leave or for absconding, and was sent back to the Tasman Peninsula in order to 'undergo six months strict separate treatment in the new cells at Port Arthur'. He was returned to the Cascades Prison in Hobart with the recommendation that he be worked in 'heavy irons'. For sundry offences he received a total of seventy-two lashes and more than two years of hard labour was added to his sentence. On 7 November 1853 he was listed as having absconded and after he was recaptured, on 8 March 1854 he was given an additional twelve months hard labour. Hill was classified as a pass holder on 27 March 1854 and by 7 December 1854 held a certificate of freedom.

CON 33/63, no. 15029.

HIRSCH, Moses

1778–1853
Free.

According to the Hobart Synagogue Minute Book, Moses Hirsch was 'An old and infirm person' who applied for relief to the synagogue. He was said to be in the care of Mr Joseph Lyons (q.v.). Moses Hirsch was buried by the Hobart Hebrew Congregation on 8 April 1853. He was seventy-five years old.

Hobart Synagogue Minute Book, 19 September 1848.

HOFFNUNG, Sigmond

b. Exeter, d. 1904
1831; Free.
1 child.

Hoffnung was born at Exeter, the son of the small Jewish community's cantor. He started in business in Wynyard Lane, Sydney, as 'S. Hoffnung & Co' with a partner in England—Mr Henry Nathan. In 1852 he established S. Hoffnung & Co., a public joint stock company, which grew to 'gigantic proportions' and he boasted that it was one of the largest in the Southern Hemisphere. Hoffnung served as president of the York Street Synagogue. In 1874–76 he was one of the directors of the (Jewish) Philanthropic and Orphan Society. In 1858 he married Elizabeth Marks, the sister of his business partner, Benjamin Francis Marks (q.v.).

In 1876 Hoffnung returned to England, where his only son, Sidney (Solomon) Francis Hoffnung, married Violet, the daughter of Sir Julian Goldsmid, in 1889. Sidney adopted his father-in-law's surname as his own.

Hoffnung returned to Sydney in 1890 as a visitor.

Jewish Herald (Australia), 23 September 1904.

HOROWITZ, Henry

b. Prussia.
Free.
Single.

Henry Horowitz was a member of the Hobart Hebrew Congregation in 1842 and in 1843 was given £6 by the Hobart Jewish Philanthropic Society. He, in turn, was able to give £2 to the synagogue building fund on 11 April 1843. He rented seat no. 39 in the synagogue at the time of its dedication in 1845. In July of that year he applied for the post of sexton at the synagogue and received 17 votes—Moses Solomon (q.v.) won with 20 votes. In 1845 Horowitz and Abraham Wolff (q.v.) were clothiers, general dealers and partners who were to be found living at the corner of Harrington and Liverpool streets with a seven-year lease at £50 per annum. In the same year they were involved in a law case involving an unregistered solicitor. Horowitz donated his personal Torah scroll to the Hobart congregation prior to his departure for England on 2 March 1851.

Horowitz was in Melbourne in the 1860s and recruited a member of the Melbourne community to go to the congregation at Hobart Town to be minister in 1864.

Hobart Town Courier, 29 May 1845.

HORT, Abraham

b. London, d. 1869
Free.
Married; Merchant; 5 children.

Abraham Hort snr arrived in Wellington, New Zealand, on the *Prince of Wales* on 3 January 1843. He was accompanied by his wife, five daughters, one of whom, Anne, was with her husband, Solomon Mocatta (q.v.), and David M. Isaacs, who was qualified to act as cantor, *shochet* and *mohel*. Abraham snr's son Abraham Hort jnr had arrived in New Zealand in 1840. Hort snr, together with his friend Sir Isaac Lyon Goldsmid, actively encouraged the poorer Jews of England to settle in the colonies. Immediately following his arrival in Wellington, Hort commenced holding religious services in his home, and ten days after he arrived he wrote to the Governor asking for land for a synagogue and a cemetery.

Abraham Hort snr left New Zealand in 1853 to settle in Hobart Town after he saw his children marry non-Jews—his daughter Margaret not only married 'out' (to Dillon Bell), but decided to raise her first child as a Christian. Hort was welcomed as a member of the Hobart Town Synagogue by Phineas Moss (q.v.) who saw his arrival as a reinforcement of the congregation's Jewish orthodoxy. Hort's daughter Julia married Morrice R. Cohen (q.v.), aged twenty-nine, the Hobart Synagogue's reader and cantor, on 29 August 1849. It was the first wedding ceremony in the Hobart Synagogue 'and many strangers were induced in consequence to witness it'. While in Hobart Town Hort wrote a number of enthusiastic articles about Van Diemen's Land and its Jewish community for London's *Jewish Chronicle*.

Hort went back briefly to New Zealand in 1858 and then returned to Great Britain in May 1859.

Jewish Chronicle, 21 October 1850, 28 May 1852.

HORT, Abraham (jnr)

1820–1862
1840; Free.

Abraham Hort was the son of the pioneer of Jewish life in Wellington, New Zealand, Abraham Hort snr. His name bears testimony to the fact that the family was Sephardic (as does the identity of his brother-in-law Solomon Mocatta (q.v.). After a brief stay in New Zealand the son moved to New South Wales. He died at Ovalau in the Fiji islands on 7 June 1862. The elaborate tombstone inscription, which was undoubtedly composed by his father, reads that his son's

> mortal remains were conveyed to this place where they now repose, so that like his namesake the Patriarch he was gathered to his people. Not less beloved in life than lamented in death. The affectionate remembrance of those who knew him is his widow's best consolation, the only one left to her except the hope of rejoining him hereafter.

The memorial was placed in the Devonshire Street Cemetery and in 1901 was moved to Rockwood.

HOWARD, James

b. London, 1799
Mary II, 1822; Convict; Sentenced to 7 years, Old Bailey, 1819.
Single; Copying clerk; Height: 155 cm.

Dark pale complexion, dark hair, hazel eyes.

James Howard was listed in the 1828 Census as a Jew, and a clerk to Mr Mark Forster in Castlereagh Street. A certificate of freedom was granted on 13 July 1826. James Howard held a licence to operate a public house in Kelso in 1844 and in May of that year provided hot-air balloons to ascend from his hotel in honour of the Queen's Birthday. Later that year he acquired the licence to run the Bee Hive Inn. A. Gainsbourg (Gainsborough, q.v.) issued a public caution against purchasing goods from Howard, and his estate was declared to be insolvent on 6 January 1845.

Ship Indent 4/4008, p. 46; CF 054/5442; *Sydney Gazette*, 19 July 1826, p. 1, 8 May, 14 May 1844, 11 September 1844, 14 October 1844, 30 November 1844, 6 January 1845.

HUMPHREYS, Henry Jacob (HUMPHRIES)

1840; Free.
9 children.

Henry Jacob Humphreys' Hebrew name was Asher, son of Mordecai. He married Sophia Cohen (Tsifira, daughter of Tzvi Hirsh Hacohen) at the Great Synagogue in Duke's Place, London, on 23 September 1840.

'Henry J. Humphries' and Sophia had a son, Henry, in Sydney in 1841. The child was registered as a 'Hebrew'. A daughter, Rosetta, was born in 1843 and also registered as a Jew. Saul was born in Sydney in 1844, Mordecai in 1846, and Deborah in 1848. Four more children were born between 1841 and 1855.

Sydney Synagogue Records.

HUTCHINSON, Abraham (né FONSECA)

1742–1822
Barwell, 1798; Convict; Sentenced to 14 years, Surrey, 1794.
Single.

Abraham Fonseca anglicised his (Sephardi) surname. He was convicted in March 1794. Illiterate.

The *Barwell* arrived in Sydney Cove on 18 May 1798. Hutchinson appeared in the General Muster of 1800–1801, off rations and living on land that he was able to lease. The Muster of 1806 listed him as an emancipated convict, as did the Muster of 1811, which stated that he lived in Sydney. The *Sydney Gazette* of 15 April 1815 reported that he had been appointed superintendent of the Government (Grain) Mill. On 25 August 1815 he brought a case against Edward Howe, a milker, who had stolen a bag of corn and hidden it down the street with Hannah Barnett. Hutchinson remained in charge of the mill until 1821. In the Bigge Report in 1820 he was listed as one of the former convicts who was unmarried and living on his own property in Sydney and working for the government. Hutchinson (Fonseca) died in Sydney on 8 March 1822 at the age of eighty.

Bigge Report, Appendix B.T., Box 25, p. 5314; *Sydney Gazette*, 21 January 1810, 15 April 1815, 5 August 1815, 10 November 1821, 10 May 1822.

HYAM, Michael

b. London, 1799–1878
George Canning, 1828; Free.
Single; Shoe and boot maker; 8 children.

Michael Hyam was the son of David Hyam, a painter, and Sarah (née Shannon) of London. His first cousin, Samuel Shannon (q.v.), had arrived in Australia as a convict in 1822. Hyam arrived in New South Wales bringing with him goods worth £1559 bought on order for Walter Levi (q.v.). Levi died while Hyam was on the high seas. Hyam therefore sold the goods himself and with the capital established a shoemaker's shop in Sydney and applied for a land grant. After all, he had come free to the colony and he had brought considerable capital with him. He had also secured a strong recommendation for a 'First Class Land Grant'. Governor Darling furiously called him 'a perfect Jew' for this entrepreneurial manoeuvre. The Governor was scornful of a shoemaker who wanted to become a landowner even though Hyam stated that he had £1000 capital and two servants. Hyam, however, was persistent and received a grant of 1280 acres eight miles from Kiama at Illawarra on land covered by Australian cedar. Michael Hyam made Jewish history when he officiated at the first Australian Jewish religious circumcision. The story is told in the *Sydney Gazette* 20 June 1829 which corrected an account published in the *Australian* that had confused the ceremony with the observance of the Sabbath. 'There was a circumcision and Mr Hyam is duly authorised to perform the rite. The respectable Jews of the Colony are anxious to form a congregation, that they may observe the solemnities of their own Sabbath, but many difficulties are in their way'.

Hyam remained in Sydney conducting his shoemaking and retail business in George Street and, by 1832, was in financial difficulty, claiming to the court that he had been robbed. He had entered into speculation by purchasing the shop of Mr Moses in George Street and then failed to keep any books and went bankrupt. He was listed as insolvent with debts of £2742 and assets of £949. Hyam was sent to prison on 7 April 1832. Hyam was married in Sydney on 8 February 1835 to Charlotte Broughton, who converted to Judaism, and acquired the additional Jewish name of 'Rebecca'. He arrived at Jamberoo (Illawarra) a few months later and began to clear his land. He sent cedar to Sydney, built a store, public house, a racecourse and a tannery. In 1847 he moved to Shoalhaven and then to Greenhill and, in both places, worked as a trader and as a publican.

Charlotte died on 12 April 1849 aged fifty-eight. On 9 May 1853 Hyam married, Deborah Moses, the niece of Michael Hyam and the daughter of John Moses (q.v.). She died at Shoalhaven on 21 March 1865.

Hyam took an active part in the Jewish community. The *Australian* announced that he was 'licensed to circumcise by the High Priest of London' (19 January 1829), and in October of that year he circumcised the son of Joseph Aarons (q.v.). In 1836 he circumcised his own son, David, and, in 1837, his second child, Solomon Herbert Hyam (q.v.). In 1839 'Mr Michael Hyams of Woolongong' gave £10 to the Sydney Synagogue building fund.

Michael Hyam died at Nowra on 3 September 1878. He was survived by five sons and two daughters. His children with Charlotte (Rebecca) were David (1836–1923), Solomon Herbert (1837–1901), Moses (1839–1887), Sarah Zorilda (1839), who married her step-uncle Henry Moses, Esther (1842–1862), born at Illawarra, who married Lewis Aarons (the son of Joseph and Rachel Aarons) at Shoalhaven in 1862. His children with Deborah were Isaac Mark (1853–1931), Joseph, and Rebecca (1855–1928).

Petition 32/6184, in 42153; *HRA*, series I, vol. 14, p. 2, p. 618; Petition 33/1039, in 4/2160.2; 41/7285, in 4/2535.4; I. McCaffrey, *The History of Illawarra and its Pioneers*, Sydney, 1922, p. 112f.; G. F. J. Bergman, 'Michael Hyam', *AJJHS*, vol. 8, no. 4 (1977), p. 167; 4/3262.4.-37/6208; *Sydney Gazette*, 25 September 1830; 4/2153, letter 32/6184; 4/2014, letter 29/509; Petition 29/504, in 4/2014; *AG*, pp. 152–4, 176–9, 304.

HYAM, Rachael

Free.
Single; 5 children.

Rachael Hyam married Alexander Moses (Moss) (q.v.) in Sydney on 28 February 1841.

HYAM, Richard

Ocean II (2), 1823; Convict; Sentenced to 7 years.

'R. Hyam' is to be found mentioned in the Newcastle Magistrate's Book, which recorded that, on 7 January 1828, 'Richard' Hyam, who had arrived on the *Ocean*, was punished with twenty-four lashes and solitary confinement for refusing to work at the mines. He was housed at the Barracks in the penal settlement at Newcastle.

List of Convicts in New South Wales in November 1828, HO 10/28.

HYAM, Solomon Herbert

b. Jamberoo, NSW, 1837–1901

The son of Michael Hyam (q.v.) and his first wife, Rebecca (née Charlotte Broughton), Hyam was Mayor of Balmain from 1874 to 1879 and Member of the New South Wales Legislative Assembly from 1885 to 1887. He was a Member of the Legislative Council from 1892 to 1901. He was president of the Balmain Rowing Club and a keen yachtsman. He took no part in Jewish life and his wife was non-Jewish.

Sydney Morning Herald, 9 November 1901.

HYAMS, Elizabeth

b. London, 1816
David Scott, 1834; Free.
Single; Servant of all work.

Elizabeth Hyams was a bounty immigrant. She was first employed in Sydney, where she worked for Mr Kingsmill of Pitt Street. Two and a half years later she was working for Mr J. Moore at the distant settlement of Limestone Plains.

Information provided in Elizabeth Rushen, *Single and Free*, p. 122.

HYAMS, Esther (Mary GOODALL)

b. Scotland, 1801–1859
1845; Free.
Single; 8 children.

Born Mary Goodall, Esther Hyams converted to Judaism in Hobart Town in 1835. She had married Israel Hyams sometime before that, though no record exists of their marriage. Esther Hyams and her eight children were all registered in the Birth Book of the Hobart Synagogue. The children were Sarah Alicia (born 27 February 1835), Rachel (3 July 1838), Henry (29 April 1840), Rebecca (18 September 1841), Abraham (9 March 1843–1851), Rosina (23 October 1845), Louis (5 April 1848), and Julia (Clara) (2 August 1850). At the time of Henry's birth, Israel's profession was described as 'tanner' and he lived in Macquarie Street. The five subsequent children were born in Elizabeth Street and, by then, Israel Hyams had become a 'licensed victualler'.

Esther Hyams was buried in the Hobart Town Jewish Cemetery in Harrington Street on 18 April 1859 and reinterred at the Cornelian Bay Cemetery on 28 April 1878, six months after the death of her husband.

Family research by Nigel Isaacs, New Zealand.

HYAMS, Henry (Harry)

b. London, 1758
Matilda, 1791; Convict; Sentenced to 7 years, London, 1787.
Butcher.

Henry Hyams was a burglar who stole a quantity of clothes valued at 39 shillings from the private quarters of a hotel. He had been in court on three occasions during the previous eighteen months. He claimed to have the clothes in his possession as payment for work he had done in his master's butcher's shop. He was sentenced on 20 April 1787.

Hyams arrived in Sydney in August 1791. On 18 March 1793 Hyams gave evidence at the Criminal Court in Sydney concerning the trial of William Ashford, who had been accused of stealing a handkerchief valued at one shilling and sixpence and a new hat, valued at three shillings, 'with force of arms'. Hyams became a labourer who lived at Toongabbie and the accused man lived in the same hut. On 3 December 1793 Harris again gave evidence in a Criminal Court case. He had noticed 'suspicious movements' and found stolen property, identifying the thieves as fellow labourers at Toongabbie. Hyams' sentence expired in 1794 and on 19 November of that year his name appeared on a list of grants and leases of land. A certificate of freedom was issued on 25 February 1811.

By 1816 the records show that Hyams owned 30 acres of land at Mulgrave Place near Sydney. On 16 November that year the Colonial Secretary described him as 'of the Hawkesbury'. Hyams seemed to be in trouble with the law. He was on a list of persons who had arrived as convicts and who, at the previous muster, claimed to be free. The *Sydney Gazette* reported that he had been at the muster but could not show that he had a ticket of leave or a certificate of freedom. If no proof could be provided, observed the *Gazette*, he was to be considered an impostor. Jonas Mordecai (Joseph Mordecai, q.v.) and Daniel Phillips (q.v.), the latter of whom had also come out on the *Matilda*, were in the same situation. Matters were obviously sorted out because, in the 1819 Census of the colony, Hyams appeared with the date of his pardon and was listed as a carpenter. In the 1828 Census he appeared as a 'Protestant', working as a gardener to Archibald Bell, Windsor.

OBSP, 1786–87, case 333, p. 473; HO 10/8, 11/1; CSO 9/27331, p. 30; *Sydney Gazette*, 16 November 1816; Register of Pardons, 4/4427, p. 565; Criminal Court Sydney, ML 11 47, 18 March 1793.

HYAMS, Henry

b. London, 1807
Mangles, 1835; Convict; Sentenced, Devon Quarter Sessions, 1834.
Married; Labourer and glass cutter; Height: 160 cm.

Pock-pitted arms and face, pale complexion, dark brown hair, long nose, wide mouth. Could read and write. Jew. Henry Hyam's wife, Elizabeth Hyams, lived at Bath with her mother, Elizabeth Spackman. His two brothers, Joseph Hyams and Michael Hyams, were living in Houndsditch and were dealers, while Joseph's most recent address was Bristol. Hyams was transported for housebreaking and stealing a clock. He was sentenced on 20 October 1834.

Henry Hyams was appointed a constable at Swansea in Van Diemen's Land on 20 August 1841.

CON 14/4, no. 1926; CSO 22/4/25; CON 18/16.

HYAMS, Henry

b. Minories, London, 1823
Barossa (1), 1842; Convict; Sentenced to 10 years, Central Criminal Court, 1841.
Single; Watch finisher; Height: 164 cm.

Sallow complexion, dark brown hair, black eyebrows, black eyes, large nose, long chin. Henry Hyams was a pickpocket who stole a purse containing £4 3s. He had served three months in gaol before. On the prison hulk he was put in irons for quarrelling.

Arriving in Van Diemen's Land on 13 January 1842, Hyams was sent to Impression Bay for eighteen months to serve his initial period of probation. On 22 November that year he was sentenced to one month hard labour in chains for trafficking in tobacco. By August 1843 he was in Launceston, where he was found to be absent without leave and received one month's hard labour. Just over a month later, on 4 September, he was sentenced to fourteen days hard labour for insolence, after falsely misrepresenting himself as a cook (which would have allowed him to be on the streets at the time of the night curfew). On 11 October 1845, while still at Launceston and at the Prisoners' Barracks, he was given one month of hard labour with a recommendation to spend time on the treadmill for refusing to work. He became an assigned servant to a Mr Carter. On 17 July 1846 he was convicted of feloniously receiving stolen property under the value of £5 and served four months hard labour. After a brief period in Deloraine he was back in Launceston by 1847 and repeatedly sentenced for insolence and for absence without leave.

As late as 22 January 1850 Hyams was still a prisoner at Port Arthur.

CON 33/16, no. 3651.

HYAMS, Israel

b. London, 1797–1877
Countess of Harcourt (1), 1821; Convict; Sentenced to 7 years, Old Bailey, 1820.
Single; Ladies' shoemaker; Height: 165 cm; 9 children.

Dark brown hair, dark brown eyes. Israel Hyams was convicted for stealing a gold watch from a man in Whitehall. He pretended to have found the watch when caught and said 'Here it is I have just picked it up'. He was sentenced at the London Gaol Delivery on 13 September 1820. His mother lived at Friar Street, Blackfriars Road. He had a brother, Samuel, and a sister, Mary (Hart). Israel Hyams spent six months on board a hulk before embarking by the Countess of Harcourt for Van Diemen's Land.

The *Countess of Harcourt* arrived in Van Diemen's Land on 27 July 1821. Israel Hyams worked in Hobart Town as an assigned servant while, at the same time, he was evidently building up a business of his own in the manner of Judah and Joseph Solomon (qq.v.). He married Mary Susan Richardson at St David's on 15 December 1823. She had come to Van Diemen's Land as a prisoner on the *Providence* and was twenty-four years old. On 31 May 1825, while assigned to Mr Clift, Hyams was officially reprimanded for 'keeping a disorderly house in Liverpool Street and harbouring convicts there between 9 and 10 last night'. On 25 January 1827 officialdom caught up with him. While he was still assigned to Mr Clift he was found to be working on his own and illegally paying his 'master' five shillings a week. He was returned to the Department of Public Works.

Israel Hyams received his ticket of leave on 3 January 1831. A conditional pardon was issued on 21 August 1833 and a free pardon on 21 November 1836. Hyams married a second time, to Mary Goodall (who took on the Hebrew name of Esther) (Esther Hyams, q.v.), in 1834 and they had eight children between 1835 and 1850.

Esther was converted to Judaism. Israel Hyams rented seat no. 19 in the newly consecrated synagogue. The pair were listed as members of the Hobart Synagogue in 1842 and donated £15 to the congregation's building fund. On 29 April 1851, Abraham, the eight-year-old son of Israel and Esther Hyams, was buried by the Hobart Town congregation.

In 1837 Hyams owned a tannery store in Elizabeth Street, which sold leather, flax and books. He owned a brick building at 115 Liverpool Street from 1838 to 1840 and a licence for the Rose and Crown Inn in New Town from 1838 to at least 1870 (his son Louis was registered as the owner of the licence in 1878).

The *Sydney Gazette* reported on 15 February 1840 that Israel Hyams and Charles Barkenshaw had been picked up 'being drunk and gambling between 3 and 4 o'clock in Park Street. A mob had collected around them and Hyam accused the constable of stealing money from him'.

Hyams returned to Hobart Town. He donated £10 to the Hobart Town Synagogue in 1845 (and £5 from Mrs Israel Hyams). He appeared in the 1852 *Hobart Town Directory and General Guide* of householders qualified to vote for the Legislative Council. Esther was buried on 18 April 1859 at the Hobart Town Jewish Cemetery in Harrington Street. Hyams' third relationship was with a Margaret Collins. On 7 August 1862, Israel and Margaret had a son who was not registered as a Jew. The child was registered officially by Margaret and not by Israel. On 31 December at the Rose and Crown the 65-year-old Israel Hyams married the 31-year-old Esther Moss in a Jewish ceremony conducted by the Rev. L. M. Goldreich.

Hyams died on 9 November 1877 at Elizabeth Street and was buried at the Cornelian Bay Jewish Cemetery. He was described as a 'licensed victualler', who had died of age and infirmity. He had nine children and fifty grandchildren.

The children of Israel and Esther (Goodall) were registered in the Hobart Hebrew Congregation's Birth Book. Sarah Alicia (27 February 1835) was born in Hobart Town and married Alexander Davies in Hobart in a Jewish marriage ceremony in February 1855. She died at Dunedin in December 1911. Rachel (born 3 July 1838) married Henry Phillips on 7 February 1855 in Tasmania. Henry (29 April 1840) was born in Hobart Town and died in Hobart on 12 October 1881. Rebecca (18 September 1841) married Philip Davis at the Hobart Synagogue on 13 July 1859. Abraham (9 March 1843–1851). Rosina (23 October 1845) married Jacob Showman in Victoria in 1863. Louis was born on 5 April 1848, and Julia (Clara) on 2 August 1850.

OBSP, 1819–20, case 1030, p. 564; CON 31/8, no. 5651; *Hobart Town Courier*, 12 October 1838, 7 June 1839, 5 May 1843, 10 November 1843; *Colonial Times*, 25 April 1834, 21 February 1837, 28 February 1837, 29 August 1837, 25 May 1838; *Sydney Gazette*, 15 February 1840; Family notes and research, Nigel Isaacs, New Zealand.

HYAMS, John (Groggy)

1755–1838
Active, 1791; Convict; Sentenced to 14 years, Old Bailey, 1790.
Dealer.

John Hyams, thirty-five years old, was convicted at the Old Bailey for receiving stolen goods brought to him by three women. He claimed 'I am an innocent. I have not got a friend in the world but God above and the mercy of the court; I went for some drink, and while I was gone, they put it [a watch] in the dust hole'. Hyams was sentenced at the Old Bailey on 13 January 1790.

By 15 April 1795 John Hyams owned a small house and barn at the Field of Mars (between Lane Cove and the Parramatta River) when he was accused, with five other men, of rape. He was described as a labourer. In reality Hyams had simply been a witness of a drunken brawl and was found to be not guilty. However, the following week, on 22 April, he was tried for assault over the same incident. He claimed to have been drunk and denied the assault. He was found guilty and sentenced to 300 lashes on his bare back with a cat-o'-nine tails. Hyams' sentence of transportation had expired by 1804. In 1814 he was at Sydney working as a tanner and 'off rations'. Hyams worked as a sailor. On 13 October 1805, in the *Sydney Gazette*, he advertised that he was leaving on the *Governor King* and on 23 October 1808 on the *Star* and on 9 June 1809 he was 'about to leave the colony'. On 12 December 1816 the Sydney Gazette reported that he had appeared in the Court of Criminal Jurisdiction, together with Mary Horner, charged with stealing a watch. They were both acquitted. Later, in the *Sydney Gazette* of 25 April 1818, Hyams announced again that he was leaving the colony 'at the early opportunity'. He may have worked as a sailor on a whaling ship but he remained in New South Wales and in the 1822 General Muster he was in 'government employment' at the Carter's Barracks in Sydney. The 1828 Census listed him as a 73-year-old ticket of leave servant to a Mr Barrie, landholder of Petersham. Hyams was buried in the Jewish

Cemetery at Devonshire Street, Sydney, on 17 August 1838 under the name 'John Hyams or Groggy'.

OBSP, 1789–90, case 205, p. 210; Criminal Court Sydney, 15 April, 22 April 1795, ML, 1147; 1814 Muster, p. 234, ML, A1942/2; *Sydney Gazette*, 4 January 1809.

HYAMS, John J.

Free.

John Hyams obtained the licence for the Rising Sun Hotel on South Head Road on 2 May 1839, as reported in the *Australian*. According to the 1839 *New South Wales and Port Phillip General Post Office Directory*, J. J. Hyams ran a general store in Berrima.

HYAMS, Joseph (Hoppy My Hearty)

b. London, 1790–1844
Somersetshire (1), 1814; Convict; Sentenced to life, Old Bailey, 1813.
Single; Corn cutter and dentist; Height: 153 cm.

Fair pale complexion, black hair, brown eyes. A Jew. Joseph Hyams broke into a house and shop on 23 February 1813 and stole two bolts of linen valued at £9. He was chased and caught and sentenced to death on 27 October 1813 (which was later commuted).

Hyams arrived in Sydney in October 1814 and almost immediately began to work as a dentist at 34 Pitt Street, 'scaling, cleaning and drawing the tooth, when necessary, without causing pain and supplying the vacancy with others of pure Ivory—also corns extracted with ease and safety. Attendance at home or abroad'. In the following weeks the words 'and charges very moderate' were added. In 1820 the Medical Board forbade Hyams (and Simeon Lear, q.v.) from working as physicians and surgeons. His ticket of leave was withdrawn on 26 May 1820 for receiving stolen goods. A conditional pardon was issued on 28 November 1825 and he was given permission to marry at Parramatta. Hyams was convicted at the General Sessions at Sydney on 6 July 1827 for private felony and was sent to Moreton Bay that October. Hyams was listed in the 1828 Census and in the List of Convicts in New South Wales of November 1828, where he was serving a two-year colonial sentence at Moreton Bay.

Hyams returned to Sydney in 1834, only to find his wife Catherine (who came on the *Brothers* with a seven-year sentence in 1824) had been sent to Moreton Bay with a seven-year sentence. He was appointed ranger of the Race Course in Hyde Park. The appointment was recommended by the architect, who suggested he should receive eight pence a day gratuity to care for the new trees planted in Hyde Park. Hyams had already been a watchman there for some years.

Hyams believed life had treated him badly. In a petition for a ticket of leave in 1833 he recalled that he had previously held a ticket of leave for fourteen years 'without blemish'. He complained that he had been convicted on suspicion of a robbery and it was 'found afterwards not to have been committed by petitioner'. He had spent three years as a messenger at Iron Cove. He was lame, disabled and had a six-year-old child. The petition was accepted and his ticket of leave was restored on 6 July 1837. Hyams then asked for a conditional pardon, stating that he would have received one had it not been for the sudden departure of Governor Brisbane. This request was refused.

On 19 July 1837 Joseph Hyams wrote a petition on behalf of his wife. Catherine had been convicted at the Criminal Court in Sydney in August 1832. Hyams wrote that the prosecutor had now stated 'from facts that have come to my knowledge since then I declare my belief that she is innocent'. She had been in Moreton Bay for four years. He claimed that the commandant of the penal settlement at Moreton Bay 'concurs' with the petition. He once again added that he had children and that he was ill and needed help. A conditional pardon was granted her on 20 November 1837. Hyams received some unwelcome public notice in the *Sydney Monitor* on 25 February 1839 'Joseph Hyam, alias Hopping-my-hearty, and a women named Margaret Clark were charged with stealing a quantity of shawls and carpeting'. As the items could not be clearly identified the charges were dismissed.

Hyams gave £5 to the Sydney Synagogue building fund in September 1839. In the first voters' list for the Sydney Council election on 15 September 1842 Hyams was listed as having a house in Goulburn Street.

At the Sydney Quarter Sessions of 1 August 1843, Hyams was despatched to Van Diemen's Land for fourteen years. The *Registry of Flash Men* has a long entry about Joseph Hyams, described as '"Hyams a Jew" or "Hoppy My Hearty" who is now (12 September 1842) in custody on suspicion of being concerned in a robbery at Dr Kearney's, Campbell Town. Acquitted'. On 3 August 1843 he was sentenced to seven years transportation. The *Registry of Flash Men*'s author, William Augustus Miles, wrote triumphantly: 'I have long had my eye upon this rascal. Had him taken up but baffled me. Have him now'.

That punishment of colonial transportation was his death sentence. Hyams was sent from Sydney on 7 August 1843 and died at Port Arthur within the year.

Ship Indent, 1814–18, 4/4005; *OBSP*, case 382, p. 226; HO 10/28; W. A. Miles, *Registry of Flash Men*, pp. 56, 61, 2/673; 37/7495, on 11 August 1837, in 4/2347.2; 4/4523; Petition 33/3138, in 4/2180.2 and 37/6607; 19 July 1837, in 4/2362.4; 4/4436, p. 105; 4/1160, in Chronological Register of Convicts at Moreton Bay; *Sydney Gazette*, 24 December 1814, 29 July 1820, 28 November 1825; CP 37/10445 and 39/065.

HYAMS, Mrs

Royal George, 1835;
Free. 3 children.

'Mrs Hyams and three daughters' arrived in Hobart Town from London on 8 March 1835.

AOT, MB2/39/2, p. 244.

HYAMS, Samuel (Samuel Henry)

b. London, 1791–1858
Indian, 1810; Convict; Sentenced to 14 years, Old Bailey, 1808.
Single; Labourer.

On 17 October 1808 Hyams picked a pocket in a crowded gallery at the Drury Lane Theatre. He unbuttoned the victim's waistcoat, after pushing against him, and stole more than £7 in cash. The victim did not protest or complain because 'there was a parcel of Jews there'. It was only after he left the theatre that the victim felt safe enough to call a constable. Hyams explained 'My Lord and gentlemen of the jury—with respect to the charge that is now proffered against me I am totally ignorant and innocent of the circumstances altogether; and however plausible the story may be, I feel inward satisfaction that my fate is to be decided by a British jury; I shall now therefore throw myself on the mercy of the court'. He was aged seventeen and the jury sent him to New South Wales. He was sentenced on 26 October 1808.

The *Indian* arrived in Port Jackson on 16 December 1810. The *Hobart Town Gazette* advertised on 20 November 1819 that a letter was waiting for Samuel Hyams at the postal office.

Hyams appeared in the Van Diemen's Land records on 18 April 1822 as the holder of a ticket of leave, having arrived in the colony on the *Ruby*. On 2 July that year Hyams was reprimanded for keeping a disorderly house. On 28 August 1823 he was involved in the theft of cloth and on 6 September his record shows that he was free by servitude and was fined £30 for retailing spirits without a licence. Over the following seven years he appears a number of times in the police records for dealing with stolen goods, harbouring runaway convicts and illegally retailing spirits.

In September 1827 Samuel Hyams wrote to the Lieutenant Governor from the Launceston gaol. He had been imprisoned in September 1826 for 'illicitly disposing of spirituous liquors, harbouring a crown servant and purchasing a pair of military trousers'. He had been fined £150 plus court expenses and had been imprisoned because he was unable to pay the fine. He was 'destitute of a single friend' and had 'suffered much'. The police reported 'I believe he is as poor as he represents. The memorialist is much distressed, at the same time it is my duty to state his character is of the worst description'. After two more petitions in December and then January 1828 his fine was finally remitted.

Samuel Hyams was in Melbourne during its earliest years (1834–36) as a servant to John Batman and is said to have been the person who cleaned up William Buckley, 'the wild white man', who had escaped during the attempt in 1803 to settle the district and lived for thirty years with the Aborigines. Hyams claimed that the haircut alone had spoiled a pair of sheep shears and a set of razors, and he was paid a bottle of brandy for his trouble.

He was back in Launceston by October 1836, when he supported the donation of a block of land by Henry Davis at Cataract Hill for a Jewish cemetery. In 1837 Hyams appeared in the Police Correspondence. He was 'a general dealer' and the keeper of a boarding house. He had seven pigs on the property, one of which he had killed. He had then bought another smaller pig, which turned out to be stolen. Hyams was committed for trial and subsequently discharged. His pork was seized but because it had been stored with some meat that had not been properly cured it had spoiled. Hyams repeatedly asked for £5 14s 3d compensation. The Magistrate denied his request and the police report added 'This man is neither entitled to nor deserves any compensation'.

On 12 May 1843 Hyams ended up in gaol for not being able to pay a fine of £10 for having sold a gill of rum without a licence. He spent six months there until released by the government. Samuel Hyams' name appeared on the petition to the government for the establishment of a synagogue in Launceston. However, his enthusiasm for Judaism soon vanished and he found a new career path. Hyams became the subject of a conversionist tract entitled *Darkness Made Light or The Story of Old Sam, the Christian Jew*, by the Rev. A. Stackhouse (1859), published by the Tasmanian Auxiliary of the London Society for Promoting Christianity Amongst the Jews.

As the book described him, Samuel Hyams, or 'Old Sam', lived in a little shop at the King's Meadows two miles along the main road from Launceston: 'He is one of the lowest and most depraved "old hands" and is very strict in his religious duties as a Jew. He could not read English at all and could read Hebrew but not understand it'. He was visited by the Rev. Stackhouse and refused to believe that Jesus ever existed. He was married to a non-Jewish woman called Flora who began to read to him stories from the New Testament, which he mistakenly thought were stories from the Old Testament. Stackhouse wrote that Hyams had 'strange notions about certain dreams and visions'. The visits bore fruit. Hyams was baptised on 15 September 1850 and was then paid £5 annually for acting as a church sexton. He was provided with a hawker's licence and was able to 'collect widely' for the Missionary Society. Hyams died in December 1858.

CON 31/18, no, 15; *OBSP*, 1807–08, case 688, p. 459f.; Petition CSO 1/272/6560, 5 June 1824; Petition Launceston 22/24/1299–1300, 6 June 1828; CSO 5/69/1503, 14 September 1837; CSO 1/195/4163; CS 4/70151a, pp. 20–3.

I

ISAAC, Colin (Colman) (ISAACS)

b. London, 1811
Moffatt (1), 1834; Convict; Sentenced to 7 years, Plymouth, Devon, 1832.
Single; Shoemaker.

Dark complexion, black hair, long pointed nose, small mouth and chin. A tomb tattooed on his right arm. Colin Isaac was convicted on 3 July 1832 and transported for stealing a watch from a person. His gaol report described him as 'idle'.

The *Moffatt* arrived in Hobart Town on 9 May 1834. On 1 October 1836 Colin Isaacs was reported by Mr Harrison, his 'Master', for refusing to obey his orders and committing other 'misconducts'. He was returned to the service of the Crown and given three months hard labour. He was then assigned to the Spring Hill Road Party. On 14 November 1837 he was an assigned convict servant to Mr Lamb of Hobart Town when he was found guilty of 'insolence'. On 5 April 1838 Isaacs was still an assigned convict servant when he was given thirty-five lashes for 'disobedience and using obscene language'. Two days later he was found guilty of neglect of duty and disobedience and placed in the cells for fourteen days on bread and water. He was then assigned to a Mr Beveridge. On 30 July 1838 he was found guilty of neglect of duty and sentenced to twenty-five lashes. Isaacs completed his sentence in 1839 and received a pardon.

Though an original member of the Melbourne Hebrew Congregation in 1844, Isaacs quickly fell behind in his payments. He married Jane Wallis at Old St James Cathedral in Melbourne in 1847. In 1852 Colin Isaacs appeared in a newspaper report as 'a clothier in Elizabeth St'.

CON 31/24, no. 92; CON 18/15; *Melbourne Morning Herald*, 20 March 1852.

ISAACS, Aaron

b. London, 1802–1866
Guildford (5), 1822; convict; Sentenced to life, Old Bailey, 1821.
Single; Pedlar; Height: 164 cm; 12 children.

Pale complexion, dark hair, hazel eyes. The son of Solomon and Sarah Isaacs of London. Aaron Isaacs was a pickpocket who was caught as he snatched at a man's watch chain and seal with the total value of four shillings. Isaacs' father subsequently attempted to menace the prosecutor and was reprimanded by the court. Isaacs was sentenced on 5 December 1821.

The *Guildford* (5) arrived in New South Wales on 15 July 1822. According to the 1822 General Muster of New South Wales Aaron Isaacs was a convict assigned to John McArthur in Parramatta. In 1825 Isaacs was assigned to J. Pennington of Newcastle after working with the Road Party in Parramatta. Isaacs was listed on the 1828 Census, aged thirty, a 'hut keeper' working for Best and Williams at Goulburn Plains. His religion was recorded as 'Protestant'. Isaacs was granted a ticket of leave for the District of Goulburn Plains on 22 September 1831. He was acquitted at the Supreme Court in Sydney on 13 November 1834 of a charge of cattle stealing. His ticket of leave was altered for the Yass District in 1837. The General Return of Convicts in New South Wales of that year lists 'Avron Isaacs' in Yass with a ticket of leave. A conditional pardon was issued on 19 July 1838. He received an absolute pardon on 1 February 1840. His name appears on the petition to establish a Jewish burial ground in Yass in 1844.

Isaacs settled at Paterson and opened the Victoria Store in 1840. His brother, Barnett S. Isaacs (q.v.), arrived at the same time and joined him at the store in Paterson. Isaacs took an active role in an association to import Indian labourers or 'coolies' to New South Wales in 1842. Aaron married Hinda (Catherine Moss, q.v.), the daughter of Marcus Warschauer (q.v.), in a Jewish ceremony at the Bridge Street Synagogue in Sydney, on 11 May 1842.

Twins Solomon and Amos were born at Paterson on 25 April 1843. George (11 June 1844) was also born at Paterson. Michael Joseph (1845) was born in Sydney, Hinda (1847) in West Maitland, Rose (1848) in Sydney, Sarah (1849) in Queanbeyan, and Raphael (Ralph) (1851) in Sydney. Their other children were Mendel (1852), Rachel (1852), Solomon (1853) and Louis (1857).

Aaron Isaacs gave £5 to the Sydney Synagogue in 1845. Aaron Isaacs of the Victoria Store, Paterson, advertised in the *Sydney Morning Herald* of 2 March 1846, that he was selling out and removing to another part of the colony. He established a business in Maitland and then moved to Sydney, where he was 'a commission agent'. Aaron Isaacs 'of the Hebrew Mutual Benefit Society' died at his residence at 69 Campbell Street, Haymarket, Sydney, on 26 October 1866. He was buried at the Devonshire Street Cemetery and his grave is now at Rookwood.

Of his children, Amos married Elizabeth Sinclair and died on 23 December 1912; Michael Joseph married Catherine Gershon on 16 December 1868, and died on 16 August 1923; Sarah married, to become Sarah Reuben, and died on 22 January 1883; Mendel married Leah Solomon on 3 June 1888; Rachel married Charles Lester; and Louis married Mary Ann Daniels on 1 February 1878.

OBSP, 1821–22, case 2, p. 3; Ship Indent 4/4008, p. 142; Governors' Despatches, MLA, 1210, p. 1070; 4/4080, TL 31/746; CP 39/376; Petition 20 December 1844, 4/2650.4; CS 4/3687-40/104, AP 40/104; General Muster List 1825; HO 10/19.

ISAACS, Abraham

b. London, 1797
Guildford (5), 1822; Convict; Sentenced to life, Old Bailey, 1821.
Single; Labourer.

Abraham Isaacs was convicted of breaking and entering a haberdasher's shop in Mile End Road, Stepney. He stole £45 worth of goods. He was with another man, who escaped. He was originally sentenced, on 5 December 1821, to death. The official records sometimes list him as 'Isaac Aaron'.

On 24 July 1824 Abraham Isaacs was sent as a convict worker to Windsor in New South Wales. In that same year he and Mary Healey had a son, Walter Healey. At the age of seven, on 7 April 1831, Walter was admitted to the Male Orphan School. By 29 July the boy was dead. Both the List of Convicts in New South Wales in November 1828 and the 1828 Census recorded that Isaacs was at the Prisoners' Barracks in Newcastle. On 9 June 1828 Isaacs appeared before the Bench of Magistrates in Newcastle accused of theft and was acquitted. On 20 April 1830 Isaacs was sent to Port Macquarie on the *Mary Elizabeth*, and on 6 August 1830 he appeared before the Bench of Magistrates. He had been attached to the surveyor's road gang. Isaacs had venereal disease and was very ill and permitted to stay in his tent, but his rations were greatly diminished. The overseer reasoned that unless this was done all his prisoners would claim that they were ill. Isaacs refused to accept his reduced rations and demanded to see a doctor. He was found guilty of insubordination and admonished.

On 1 December 1831 Abraham Isaacs, who was still under the surveyor's jurisdiction, was accused of disobedience and continual gambling. The surveyor was reported to have said to Isaacs, 'I wish you were in [the service of the] government for you are no use to me'. Isaacs sneeringly retorted, 'No use to you ain't I?' He was placed in the iron gang for two months. On 14 December 1833 Isaacs was accused of molesting a fellow prisoner and sentenced by the Port Macquarie Bench to twelve months in irons.

Abraham Isaacs married Catherine Wilcox in 1840 at Richmond and received a conditional pardon in 17 February 1840.

OBSP, 1820–21, case 508, p. 169; List of Assignments 4/4522, on 4 November 1825; CS re Convicts Out 4/3669, 20 April 1830, p. 452; Port Macquarie Bench 1830–1832, 4/5637, pp. 34, 249f.; CS In, 4/5638, vol. 2, pp. 228, 305; Male Orphan School 4/352, no. 11; HO 10/55.

ISAACS, Abraham

b. London, 1808–1848
Florentia (1), 1828; Convict; Sentenced to 14 years, Old Bailey, 1827.
Single; Hawker, labourer; Height: 173 cm.

Dark sallow complexion. Black hair. Dark brown eyes. Jew. Tattoos AM & AB inside large heart on upper left arm. Abraham Isaacs, Abraham Moses (aged twenty), with David Moses (q.v.) (aged sixteen) and Samuel Barnett (aged fourteen), stole a pocket book from a man in Whitechapel. Their crime was watched by two Bow Street patrolmen who arrested them on the spot. Isaacs received fourteen years, and the other three received seven years transportation on 12 July 1827.

Abraham Isaacs arrived in New South Wales on 3 January 1828. He was listed in the 1828 Census as being a labourer in Richmond of the Protestant faith. Isaacs was assigned as a servant to Mr W. Bannister at Richmond in the District of Windsor. On the recommendation of the Windsor Bench he received a ticket of leave on 22 July 1834. He was listed in the 1837 General Return of Convicts in New South Wales as being in Richmond with a ticket of leave. Isaacs received permission to marry in 1840 and he married Catherine Johnson, aged thirty-six, who had been transported to Australia on the *Andromeda* (4), at the Church of England, at Richmond. He was granted a certificate of freedom on 25 May 1842. Abraham Isaacs appeared in the records of the Hawkesbury Benevolent Society list of January to May 1848. He died from 'congestion of the lungs' after two months in the Windsor Hospital. The Parish Register of St Matthew's, Windsor, noted that there was 'no religious burial service man being a Jew'.

OBSP, 1826–27, case 1584 p. 592; Ship Indent 4/4013, p. 20; CS Register 4/4094; TL 34/632; CF 42/0754; Hawkesbury Benevolent Society, A 625, p. 49b; HO 10/28; Death Book (of Convicts) 4/4549.

ISAACS, Alexander

Surrey I (3), 1819; Convict; Sentenced to 7 years, Surrey, 1818.
Dealer.

Alexander Isaacs was sentenced on 4 April 1818.

Alexander Isaacs arrived in Hobart Town on 18 March 1819. Between December 1819 and July 1821 Alexander Isaacs' convict record shows seven offences, four of which involved having been 'disorderly at Church' or having missed the Sunday Muster. Isaacs obviously hated having to attend Christian worship. The penalties for this disobedience involved extra work for the government in his own time. He was acquitted of a charge of stealing some clothes on 6 March 1820 and, on 24 January 1821, was sentenced to twenty-five lashes for 'neglect of duty'. His record ends on 4 July 1821, when he was sentenced to seven nights at the watch house for being out after the hours of the evening curfew. His police dossier concludes at this date, and Isaacs evidently received a ticket of leave. An advertisement of 29 September 1821 in the *Hobart Town Gazette* boasted 'A Isaacs and Clarke, Hatters, are about to open a shop in Bathurst St—Clarke lately arrived from England with a perfect knowledge of manufacturing hats'.

CON 31/23, no. 8; CON 13/1, p. 278; CON 31/21.

ISAACS, Amelia

Andromeda, 1839; Free.
Single.

Amelia Isaacs married Thomas Commons at St Andrew's Presbyterian Church in Sydney, in 1840.

ISAACS, Barnett S.

b. London
Free.
Dealer.

The son of Sarah and Solomon Isaacs of London and the younger brother of Aaron Isaacs (q.v.), Barnett S. Isaacs worked in partnership with Aaron as owner of the Victoria Store in Paterson, New South Wales, from 1840. In March 1846 he announced that he was 'selling out' and 'removing to another part of the colony'.

Australian, 31 August 1842; *Sydney Morning Herald*, 2 March 1846.

ISAACS, Benjamin

b. Whitechapel, London, 1795–1881
Lady Nugent, 1830; Free.
Married; Printer; 6 children.

Isaacs was an assisted immigrant who arrived in Sydney on 27 November 1830. He reported that he had been born in Whitechapel and that his parents were Jacob and Esther Isaacs (qq.v.). His father was a 'hatter'. Benjamin was married to Anne (née Woods) and their religion was 'Episcopalian'. He was the brother of Esther Dinah Isaacs (q.v.). Following the transportation of his father Benjamin was raised by the London Society for Promoting Christianity amongst the Jews and became one of the Society's most celebrated 'successes'. Family tradition states that Benjamin Isaacs arrived in Australia in 1830 and that he had left Anne and their children behind in London. In 1832 he briefly returned to England after receiving the news that his wife and some of their children had died.

Isaacs was initially employed by the *Monitor* newspaper in Sydney. He became the publisher and editor of the *Australian* newspaper in Bathurst and newspapers in Windsor and Parramatta. Isaacs regularly published items of Jewish interest despite the absence of Jewish readers in the Bathurst district. In October 1848 he echoed Deuteronomy when he wrote about Australia:

> That our colonial territories is to be forever considered as it hereto has been, a mere pastoral country, may suit the purposes of some short-sighted men, but can never benefit the colony. But this character of the country is not true. It is a land of corn and wine and oil, it is a land of iron, copper, lead and coals. It is a land adapted to the production of silk, cotton, flax and hemp and that which is required in the investment of capital and the introduction of labourers.

On 10 October 1849 the *Melbourne Morning Herald* noted 'Mr Benjamin Isaacs has been convicted of libelling John Davis [Davies, q.v.], formerly of Melbourne, and disgracefully employed by some of our local journals. Isaacs has received £20 fine and a month's imprisonment. To parties here [in Melbourne] who know Davis's real character this sentence will excite more than mere surprise'.

From the Bathurst Gaol, Isaacs petitioned for his release. He had received a two-month sentence. He was fifty-seven years old with a wife and family and his health, he claimed, had been seriously affected 'by his time in prison'. By September 1850 he was listed as the proprietor of the *Windsor Telegraph*.

Isaacs wrote to the Sydney Synagogue on 9 September 1855 enquiring about the possibility of a Jewish funeral in Bathurst. He was referred on to Mr Saul Samuel MLC, who lived in the area.

Isaacs married three times. The first marriage took place in London to Anne Woods. Their children were John (1821–1891), Elizabeth (born in 1826 and died in Australia in 1912), Maria (baptised on 30 September 1827 at Stepney), Emma Maria (baptised on 19 July 1829 and died in 1908), and Benjamin (1831–1916). His second marriage was to Elizabeth Huggard at St Philip's, Sydney, in 1833. Their son Richard was born in 1834. His third marriage was to Elizabeth Bourke in Windsor in 1872.

Family information from Kris Jacobsen, Canberra and *A Land of Promise. An account of Jacob Isaacs, Jewish Convict and Benjamin Isaacs, Christian Printer and Publisher* (self published, Canberra (2009) reviewed in AJJHS vol. 19 part 4 by Helen Besten; *Australian*, 14 January 1840, 23 January 1840, 25 January 1840; CS 4/714.1-49/10217.

ISAACS, Blouma

1840; Free.
Married; 5 children.

Blouma Isaacs was the wife of Jacob Myer Isaacs (q.v.) and arrived in Sydney with him. They had five children: Michael (1839–1852), Rebecca (1840), Maria (1842) in Sydney, Lewis (1844) and Nathaniel (1846).

ISAACS, Charlotte

b. 1806
Surrey I (9), 1836; Convict; Sentenced to 7 years, Surrey, 1830.
Single.

Charlotte Isaacs, thirty-one, was given permission to marry William Perkins, thirty-five. Charlotte (who seems to have understated her age by five years) was still serving her sentence. Perkins came free to New South Wales on the *North Briton*. The marriage was to be conducted by the Rev. Rigney of Wollongong on 21 August 1841.

ISAACS, Clara

b. London, 1828
Free

Clara Isaacs arrived in Melbourne in 1849. She was the daughter of Henry and Elizabeth Isaacs (née Barnett). She had two daughters, and brother Barnett Isaacs arrived in 1856. No husband listed.

ISAACS, Edward

b. London, 1821
1842; Free.
Single; Draper.

In the *Australian Israelite* of 1872 Edward Isaacs recalled his arrival in Van Diemen's Land:

> In the year 1842 I arrived in Hobart Town in company with a number of young Jewish men (the majority under twenty years of age) and all having been brought up rather orthodox. We were very much surprised on discovering there was no place of worship in connection with our faith. (Service was held on New Year at the 'Rose and Crown Hotel' [owned by Israel Hyams (q.v.) in New Town] for want of better accommodation.)—Shortly after my arrival I was requested to call a meeting of all the Jewish young residents which I did and the meeting was held at the house of Mr I. Freedman (sic). Subsequently Mr Nathan convened a meeting which was attended by, I believe, every Jew in town. He told them what the boys had done and what they should do.

Isaacs married Dinah Joseph (aged nineteen) on 29 December 1847 at 58 Liverpool Street, Hobart Town. It was the synagogue's nineteenth marriage ceremony. Edward Isaacs gave his profession as 'draper' and Dinah was living with her mother. Isaacs was a member of the congregation in 1842–45, renting seat no. 72 when the building was dedicated in 1845. In 1843 he gave £3 to the building fund, and he served as a chorister at the consecration of the synagogue.

In 1872 he was living at Auckland, New Zealand.

ISAACS, Elizabeth

b. 1797
William Bryan, 1833; Convict; Sentenced to 7 years, Old Bailey, 1833.
Widow; Height: 164 cm; 2 children.

Fresh complexion, brown hair, grey eyes, small nose. A widow. Elizabeth Isaacs was convicted of 'robbing a gentleman of half a crown'. She had been in prison before and was 'well behaved'. She had two children in England. She may not have been Jewish.

From 1834 to 1836 a number of charges were brought against Elizabeth Isaacs. She was assigned to at least eight different households during those two years. She was 'insolent', 'drunk', 'disobedient', and 'very impertinent'. She stole a gown, for which crime she was sent to the Female Factory. She refused to return to work for one master 'for no reason'. She was put to work at the wash tub for one month for 'impertinence'. Her record of offences appears to end on 15 September 1836 and she received her ticket of freedom (no. 211) in Van Diemen's Land in 1841.
CON 40/5; CON 18/25.

ISAACS, Esther

b. London, 1781–1856
Mary Anne I (1), 1816; Free.
Ostrich feather maker; 2 children.

Esther Isaacs travelled to Australia as a passenger on the *Mary Anne*, which was a convict transport ship. She appears to have been the second free Jewish immigrant to Australia. Her husband was Jacob Isaacs (q.v.), who had arrived on the *Baring* in 1815. Their young son Benjamin Isaacs (q.v.) was left behind in London to be raised by the London Society for promoting Christianity amongst the Jews and migrated to New South Wales as an adult.

Esther was listed as one of the persons waiting to receive an assigned convict in 1822. The General Muster of 1825 listed 'Hesther Isaacs', wife of Jacob Isaacs and mother of Rachel (q.v.), who had been born in the colony in 1817. The *Sydney Gazette* of 11 August 1825 described Esther as a 'feather maker' who ran the Tea Gardens on the Parramatta Road.

Jacob Isaacs died in 1836 and the following year Esther wrote to the Colonial Secretary saying that she had 'formed an acquaintance' with Samuel Levy (q.v.), who had come out on the *Admiral Gambier* in 1808. He had recently obtained a ticket of leave for the District of Patrick's Plains and she asked for permission to marry 'according to the rites and ceremonies of the Jewish religion of which persuasion both parties are'. The request was signed by 'Estar Isaacs'. Simeon Lear (q.v.) testified that he had known the memorialist for twenty years.

The petition caused interdepartmental confusion, and a note on the document reads 'this appears to be the first application for the marriage of Jewish prisoner. Among Christians it is customary for the Clergyman who is to perform the ceremony to make application through the Principal Superintendent of Convicts. I am not sufficiently acquainted with Jewish customs to be aware whether there is anything to prevent a similar course'. It was suggested that it be done through 'the Rabbi'. Governor Bourke noted that the application had to be made through the Colonial Office, and the marriage took place in 1837.

Esther Isaacs died at the Benevolent Asylum, Sydney, on 9 June 1856 and was buried by the Sydney Synagogue at the Devonshire Street Cemetery on 9 June 1856.
CS 4/4570D; HO 10/19; Petition 37/4256 in 4/2352, 37/3404 with 37/4256, dated 25 March 1837.

ISAACS, Esther Dinah

b. London, 1816–1855
Strathfieldsay, 1834; Free.
Single; Servant; 7 children.

The sister of Benjamin Isaacs (q.v.) and daughter of Jacob and Esther Jacobs (q.v). Esther Isaacs was a bounty migrant. She claimed to have 'friends' in Australia. Esther

Isaacs arrived in Van Diemen's Land on 11 August 1834 on the *Strathfieldsay*. After a short stay in Hobart Town she travelled to Port Jackson on the *Britomart*, arriving on 1 February 1835. She was nineteen years of age.

The *Sydney Herald*, on 27 October 1837, reported on the marriage (on 25 October 1837) of Daniel Cohen (Edward Daniel Cohen, q.v.), 'lately of Liverpool', to Miss E. D. Isaacs, 'only daughter of widow Isaacs of Olie St, London', at Port Macquarie, 'according to the rites of the Jews'. Their children were Frances (1837), a daughter buried on 22 November 1838, Lewis (1839), Moses (1841), and Eleazer Keeba (1844).

On 11 April 1848, Esther Cohen, then a widow, married George Brockstein (q.v.) (later known as Brockstayne) at the Sydney Synagogue. A son, Alfred, was born in 1849, Isaac c. 1852, and Lawrence in 1855 (died 11 February 1882). Esther appears to have died following the birth of Lawrence.

CSO 1/742/16027; 4/5208; *Australian*, 3 February 1833.

ISAACS, Fanny

b. London, 1822–1913
Alfred, 1841; Free.
Single.

Fanny Isaacs came to Sydney on the *Alfred* in 1841. She returned to England in the midst of the economic depression and migrated to South Australia on the *Sultana* in 1851. She was the founder and first president of the Adelaide Jewish Ladies Benevolent Society. She died on 28 March 1913 after having been 'in the colony 72 years'.

South Australian Observer, 29 March 1913.

ISAACS, Frances (Fanny)

1816–1856
Lady, 1841; Free.
Married; Parasol-maker; 4 children.

Fanny Isaacs was a bounty migrant and the wife of Leon Lewis Isaacs (q.v.). Her father, Wolf Abraham, was a hawker. She was a 'parasol and umbrella maker'. Frances had four children: Sarah (born 1842), Julia (1845), Judah (1846–1847), and Kitty (1850). Fanny Isaacs died in Sydney on 5 March 1856. In 1901 her grave was moved from the Devonshire Street Cemetery to the Jewish section at Rookwood, where her husband was buried.

ISAACS, Henry

1793–1818
General Hewart, 1814; Convict; Sentenced to life, Old Bailey, 1813.
Shoemaker.

Dark ruddy complexion, black hair, hazel eyes. On 6 March 1813 Henry Isaacs was seen hurrying out of a bankruptcy hearing at the Guildhall. He was followed and stopped by a police officer. The prisoner testified that: 'Saturday being a leisure day I went to Guildhall to hear the trials. I came out of the Guildhall and picked up this pocket book on the steps'. He was sent to the Portland *hulk and then embarked on one of the worst convict transport voyages on record: one in eight prisoners died.*

Henry Isaacs arrived in New South Wales on 7 February 1814. In the 1814 Muster he was listed as a convict servant in Windsor. He was first assigned as a shoemaker to Mr Hutchinson and then sent to Windsor to Thomas Jones. On 24 June 1815 the *Sydney Gazette* announced that there was a letter waiting for him at the post office. Henry Isaacs died on 6 June 1818 aged twenty-five, classified as a 'lunatic', and was buried at Parramatta.

OBSP, case 396, p. 233; CO 201/119, p. 49; HO 11/2; 1814 Muster, A1942/1, p. 37; Ship Indent 4/4001, p. 503; Governors' Despatches, 1813–1816, A1190, p. 256; Bigge Appendix, A 2130, p. 151.

ISAACS, Henry (ADLAM) (AUBURN)

b. London
Lady Harewood, 1829; Convict; Sentenced to 7 years, Old Bailey, 1828.
Single; Dealer; Height: 171 cm.

Dark complexion, dark brown hair, hazel eyes, long nose, thick lips, dimple in chin. Henry Isaacs was transported for receiving stolen goods. He stated that this was his first offence. He was sentenced on 21 February 1828.

On 30 January 1830, assigned to a Mr Maddox, Isaacs quarrelled with a fellow convict, called him an informer and assaulted him. He was severely reprimanded. On 5 December 1831 he was found to be absent from his assigned work as a clerk with the Commissioner of Accounts and was sent to the Hobart Town Prisoners' Barracks. On 2 September 1833 he was sentenced to seventy lashes for falsely imprisoning a man and extorting rum from him while serving as a police constable at Ross. He was free by servitude by 22 August 1835, when he was arrested for feloniously stealing three bottles containing port wine and two bottles of champagne and one bottle containing whisky, knowing them to have been stolen. He was sentenced at the Hobart Town Quarter Sessions of 2 October 1835 to seven years gaol with two years assigned to the Grass Tree Hill Chain Gang. The next three years record a series of offences in various chain gangs. In the latter part of 1838 he was working as an assigned servant but was returned to the Crown for being drunk and behaving in an 'outrageous' manner. On 31 January 1839, while assigned to the Public Works Department, he was sentenced to six weeks hard labour in chains for 'disorderly conduct'. On 31 January 1839, while working with the government at Launceston, Isaacs was sentenced to six weeks hard labour in chains for 'disorderly conduct'. As a member of the chain gang, on 9 February 1839, he was found guilty of insolence towards the overseer and was sent for six months to the Campbell Town Chain Gang. During 1840 Isaacs worked as a port's messenger. Four charges of drunkenness culminated in an eight-month sentence with hard labour in chains and he was sent to the Perth Bridge Road Party. Two charges of drunkenness in April 1841 and January 1842 bring Isaacs' dossier to an end.

A certificate of freedom was granted on 7 October 1842.

OBSP, 1813, case 396, p. 233; CON 31/23, no. 53; CON 32/2; CON 18/12; Governors' Despatches, 1813–16, A1190, p. 256; *Launceston Advertiser*, 5 February 1835.

ISAACS, Isaac

b. Belgium, 1804–1891
Katherine Stewart Forbes, 1832; Convict; Sentenced to life, Old Bailey, 1831.
Married; Labourer; Height: 163 cm; 2 children (in England).

Florid complexion, dark brown hair, long pointed drooping nose, rather large mouth, short chin. Isaac Isaacs was transported for stealing two Amsterdam bank notes from Michael Hart, who had recently arrived in London from Amsterdam. One bank note was valued at 300 guilders and the other at 200 guilders (worth £41 12s 5d). He asked Hart to show him the notes: 'I took them out of my pocket intending to show them to him—I held them in my own hand; the prisoner took them out of my hand with one hand and gave me a blow with his other hand, he went down the stairs—returned in the afternoon drunk and no bank notes'. He was sentenced to transportation for life on 20 October 1831. Isaacs, his wife Rachael, and their two children lived in Whitechapel.

Isaac Isaacs arrived in Hobart Town on 16 July 1832 and was assigned to Mr Michael Phillips (q.v.) in Launceston. On 23 October 1834 he was sentenced to three years imprisonment, hard labour and severe discipline at Port Arthur for 'gross, indecent conduct exposing his person to his master's female child'. On 8 July 1835, at Port Arthur, he was sentenced to three weeks in the chain gang for talking at muster. On 14 October 1835 he was put in irons for six weeks for having tobacco improperly in his possession and on 14 November he was placed in solitary confinement for three days for having a knife in his possession while confined to the gaol. On 9 February 1836 he was put in solitary confinement for five days on bread and water for refusing to work.

On 11 July 1836 he was again placed in solitary confinement on bread and water for 'idleness'. The same offence, and punishment, was decreed on 3 September 1836. On 24 January 1838 he went back into solitary confinement on bread and water for 'making use of improper language'. On 22 February 1838 he was put in solitary confinement for forty-eight hours for 'idleness' and on 28 January 1839 he 'disobeyed orders' and was placed in the cells for seven days. By the end of 1839 he had been released from Port Arthur and was assigned to the Public Works Department. On 3 December 1840, while assigned to a Mr Davis, he was convicted of stealing a small quantity of brandy together with two pounds and two shillings and sixpence, for which 'he could not account'. He was given twelve months hard labour on the roads around Ross.

A ticket of leave was issued on 6 January 1843 and in May 1843 he signed a petition asking the Lieutenant Governor to grant land for a synagogue in Launceston. On 29 June 1844 he gave 30 shillings to the synagogue building appeal. His ticket of leave was broadened on 26 May 1845 to allow him to travel between the Australian colonies. He was well known to the police and on 7 May 1844 he was discharged from an accusation of feloniously receiving stolen property. A conditional pardon 'for the Australian Colonies' was approved on 4 August 1846 as he had been 'shown worthy of higher indulgence'.

On 15 August 1848 Isaac Isaacs wrote to the Hobart Hebrew Congregation and asked for help:'Gentlemen: It is with the Deepest Regret that I am forced to make this application to you but Really gentlemen it is the Last Effort it is True. I have a Licence and Also some spectacles to get a Living but I find it Impossible to get a living solely by them'. Isaacs asked for a few pounds.

Isaac Isaacs died at Hobart on 29 July 1891. He was thought to be eighty-two years old.

OBSP, 1831, case 2105; CON 31/24, no. 75; CON 78/2, p. 166; CO 280/157; CON 34/3, no. 465; HO 10/59; *Launceston Examiner*, 29 June 1844.

ISAACS, Isaac (James STEADMAN)

b. London, 1810–1891
Asia (2), 1827; Convict; Sentenced to life, Old Bailey, 1824.
Single; Old clothes man.

Isaacs was observed by a police officer on 10 July 1824 stealing two half crowns from the pocket of a woman who was watching a military review in Hyde Park. Isaacs was said to have been twelve years of age. He was with two 'bigger boys' who tried to shield him as he stole the money. He had been tried at least four times before and had been convicted for assault and for picking pockets. He had already spent time on the hulks. He described himself at the trial as 'an Old Clothes' Man at Goodman's Yard, Alie St'. He was sentenced to transportation for life on 15 July 1824.

Isaacs arrived in Hobart Town three years after his trial in London, on 29 November 1827. He was was classified as being 'sick' with 'inflamed eyes'. It was noted that 'no confession' had been taken when he was brought up on deck on his ship's arrival in Van Diemen's Land. Isaacs' sentence began with a period at Point Puer and at the Port Arthur Penitentiary. On 9 October 1828 Isaacs was found drinking in a public house and was sentenced to the treadmill for seven days while assigned to the Prisoners' Barracks in Hobart Town. On 31 October 1831, while assigned to Mr I. Foster, he was sentenced to the treadmill for ten days for 'insolence and disobedience'. In January 1832 (still assigned to Mr Foster) he was sentenced to hard labour for four months in the north of the island of Tasmania for helping to hide two convicts who had absconded from the hulk's chain gang on his master's farm at Glenorchy. On 22 May 1832 he was sent to the treadmill for six days for having been drunk 'yesterday'. On 5 December 1834 he appeared in the Launceston Police Book, assigned to Mr John Bonney, who quickly returned him to the government as he was 'disinclined' to keep him in his service. Eight years later, on 18 January 1840, Isaacs received a conditional pardon. However, on 2 September 1843, he was charged with larceny.

Isaacs married in Launceston, and lost a child named 'Joseph' on 26 January 1851. Mary Ann Isaacs, the wife of Isaac Isaacs, died at Hobart Town on 7 December 1853. Isaac Isaacs died on 29 July 1891, aged eighty-one.

OBSP, 1824, case 1124, p. 414; CON 31/23, no. 40; CSO, p. 19, 1/215/5176; CON 78/2; Launceston Police Book, CON 78/2, p. 166; CP 2277; CON 14/50; MM 33/1; MM 33/5.

ISAACS, Jacob

b. London, 1768–1836
Baring (1), 1815; Convict; Sentenced to 14 years, Old Bailey, 1814.
Married; Hatter; Height: 171 cm; 2 child.

Dark pale complexion, black hair, brown eyes, large nose. Jacob Isaacs was charged with forging a Bank of England note valued at £500. When he admitted that he had been in possession of the note, two other charges of forgery were dropped. He was sentenced on 26 October 1814.

Jacob Isaacs arrived in New South Wales on 7 September 1815. He was joined, in 1816, by his wife Esther Isaacs (q.v.), who followed him to Australia and, therefore, became one of the first free Jewish immigrants to Australia. He lived at Petersham on the Parramatta Road, working as a farmer and then as a publican 'at the sign of the Bagnisze Wells Tea Garden', and he appeared as a supplier of pins to the post office on 8 January 1820. Isaacs had a ticket of leave by 1823. He appeared as a key witness in support of Esther Abrahams (Johnston) (q.v.) in her trial in 1829. Esther had turned to him 'craving protection' when her relationship with her children deteriorated following the death of her husband. He 'kept the Court in long continued laughter by his very precise but comical manner of delivering himself'. Isaacs appeared in the 1828 Census as a Jew who owned 50 acres of cleared land. A certificate of freedom was issued on 6 November 1828. Isaacs was granted one assigned convict servant in 1829.

He was buried in the Devonshire Street Jewish Cemetery on 8 July 1836. He was the father of Benjamin Isaacs (q.v.) and his daughter Rachel (q.v.), who was born in 1817, and who appears to have been the first child of two Jewish parents to be born in Australia. Following her husband's death Esther Isaacs applied, in March 1837, for permission to marry Samuel Levy (q.v.). Levy was about seventy years of age at the time. Official permission was granted.

OBSP, 1814, cases 96, 97, 98, p. 226; Ship Indent 2/8243, p. 168; 4/2352, 37/4256, 37/3404; HO 10/1, p. 198; *Sydney Gazette*, 8 January 1820, 11 August 1825, 10 October 1825; Governors' Despatches, A1206, p. 350; *Australian*, 20 March 1829.

ISAACS, Jacob

b. 1775
Royal Admiral I (2), 1800; Convict; Sentenced to 7 years, Old Bailey, 1799.

Jacob Isaacs was convicted in February 1799 for stealing three hides of tanned leather from a factory. His companion, David Blanco, was acquitted because he was not seen carrying the stolen hides.

Jacob Isaacs was listed as a 'person off stores' in the Muster Book c. 1801. By the Muster of 1806 Isaacs was 'free by servitude' and working as a self-employed labourer. Isaacs worked as a seaman, possibly a whaler, and the *Sydney Gazette* notified the public that he wished to leave the colony on the *Argo* in December 1806, the *Lucy* in March 1807, and the *Fox* in June 1808.

In July 1808 Isaacs was charged with stealing a pound of tea from a warehouse owned by Robert Campbell and was sentenced to seven years transportation. He was punished by being sent to become an assigned government servant on the Hawkesbury in June and July 1809. His name appears on a town map of Sydney published in 1810 with a house in Back Row East. (He was therefore the first Jew in Sydney to be a landowner.) In June 1810 it was reported that five game fowls had been stolen from the house of Jacob Isaacs and £5 reward was offered for their return.

On 24 July 1819 Isaacs appeared before the Bench of Magistrates for having light weights and measures in his possession. Isaacs received permission to leave the colony on the *Star* on 22 September 1822.

OBSP, 1798–99, case 221, p. 226; HO 11/1; *Sydney Gazette*, 3 August 1806, 28 December 1806, 29 March 1807, 10 July 1808, 31 July 1808, 22 September 1810; Bench of Magistrates, Reel 659, p. 165.

ISAACS, Jacob Myer

b. London, d. 1866
1840; Free.
Married; Reader of the synagogue; 5 children.

Jacob Isaacs was the brother of John Isaacs (q.v.), who arrived in 1833. His wife was Blouma Isaacs (q.v.). His sister Rosa Isaacs (q.v.) lived in Sydney as part of the family. Jacob Isaacs, his wife Blouma and infant son, Michael (Myer), arrived in Sydney in 1840. In that same year, on 10 May, a daughter, Rebecca, was born. Isaacs had been the treasurer of the Duke's Place Ashkenazi Synagogue in London 'for many years'. He came to Australia partly in response to the Sydney congregation's appeal to the Chief Rabbi in London for a minister. George Moss (q.v.) considered him to be capable of filling the functional position of *Mohel* and reader of the service. Isaacs wrote: 'prior to my arrival in the colony I was led to suppose that a person competent to undertake the situation of *Mohel* and *Shochet* and *Hazzan* were required and as such that was one of my inducements of coming to this colony to exert myself to forward the cause of Judaism'. The synagogue wrote that they 'could not afford except £100 a year working part-time' Isaacs responded that his brother informed him that the proposed salary was 'quite inadequate'. His application was finally accepted at the salary of £208 per annum. However, he was told that the committee of the synagogue 'could not consistently with the present state of their funds engage him in these capacities at a salary sufficient to maintain him without entering into business'. The Rev. Jacob Isaacs was unable to preach and the English addresses given from the pulpit were assigned to George Moss and P. J. Cohen (q.v.).

At the time of his application to the synagogue Isaacs was listed on the *Sydney General Trade List* as involved in the importation of corn, beef and lard from New Zealand (4 July 1840). His dwelling place was given as York Street and in 1845 he gave six guineas to the synagogue's building fund. In that year he exported one case of bullion to London.

Isaacs was still the reader of the synagogue in 1847 although his salary appears to have been reduced to £100. Isaacs was forced to go into business to augment his salary. *Low's Directory of the City and District of Sydney*, 1847, listed him as a slop seller at 576 George Street. Ford's 1851 *Sydney Commercial Directory* listed him as the 'Reader of the Jews' Synagogue' and living in Goulburn Street.

Isaacs remained active in the community as a minister until 1856. He returned to England with his wife and a small pension, which later became the cause of great dissension in the congregation. The pension ceased when he died in 1866.

Isaac's son Michael died on 13 March 1852 at the age of thirteen. His funeral is recorded as 'son of the reader of the York St Synagogue'. As well as Michael and Rebecca, Isaacs had three other children: Maria (1842), born in Sydney, Lewis (1844) and Nathaniel (1846).

Sydney Synagogue Minutes, 6 May 1840, p. 41; Shipping Register, 17 May 1845; G. F. J. Bergman, 'Jacob Myer Isaacs: Sydney Synagogue's Second Minister and his Family', *AJJHS*, vol. 9, no. 4 (1982), p. 239f. Bridge Street Synagogue Minute Book, 26 April 1840, 15 May 1840.

ISAACS, Jane

1836; Free.
3 children.

Jane Isaacs married Lazarus Jacobs (q.v.) on 1 February 1837. It was Jewish wedding no. 19 under the auspices of the Sydney Synagogue. Jane adopted the Hebrew name of Rebecca Sarah. She had two sons and a daughter. She died 29 December 1847 and was buried at the Devonshire Street Cemetery and later removed to the Botany Pioneers' Cemetery in 1901.

ISAACS, John (ISAAC)

b. Newcastle-on-Tyne, 1789–1804
Calcutta, 1804; Convict; Sentenced to life, Middlesex, 1802.
Single; Height: 152 cm.

Fair complexion. A Jew. John Isaacs was thirteen years old when he was found guilty of theft. He stole a silver watch, a gold chain and a gold seal, a jacket, trousers and a silk handkerchief, worth 35 shillings in all, from several victims who were sleeping on board the Commercial Treaty at the Leith and Berwick Wharf. Isaacs was caught when he tried to sell the stolen articles, which he claimed he had won in a raffle. When the constable came to arrest the boy it was reported to the court that he was weeping. Isaacs was sent to Newgate Prison and then to the Prudentia hulk.

Isaacs served as a sailor on the voyage out to Australia, and arrived in Sydney on 7 May 1804. He was then part of the ill-fated expedition to Sullivan's Cove. Isaacs died of scurvy at the River Derwent (Hobart Town) settlement on 2 October 1804. The fifteen-year-old convict sailor was the first Jew to be buried in Van Diemen's Land.

OBSP, 1801–02, case 373, p. 280; Ship Indent 4/4004, p. 184; CON 32/2, no. 53.

ISAACS, John

b. London, 1793–1835
Lady Castlereagh, 1818; Convict; Sentenced to life, Central Criminal Court, 1817.
Single.

Isaacs arrived in Sydney on 30 April 1818, and the convict cargo was then transhipped to Hobart Town. Isaacs had a long and tragic life as a prisoner in Van Diemen's Land. On 14 June 1819 he was sentenced to three days in a solitary cell on bread and water for assault and disobedience of orders. On 2 August 1819 he was found guilty of stealing in the house of Mr Howe and received twenty-five lashes and three months in the chain gang. On 19 August 1820 he was caught stealing spirits in the bedroom of his master, Mr George Guest. He was discharged when Mr Guest did not appear in court. On 30 April 1822 he was insolent to his master and 'neglected his duty'. He received fifty lashes and was returned to government service. He was in the Hobart Town prison on 23 October 1822 when he was seen to 'break over the wall' and sentenced to fifty lashes. He was reassigned to work for Mr Gunn, and on 4 May 1824 he was returned to the government for being drunk and disorderly. Isaacs was then assigned to work with the government boats at New Norfolk. On 3 July 1828 he was again drunk and used abusive language to Constable Kennedy in a public house and was sentenced to seven days on the treadmill.

On 12 September 1828 he was arrested for harbouring Elizabeth Healey, who was a runaway convict. The accusation against Isaacs was discharged. On 15 November he was sent to the treadmill for fourteen days for having been drunk. By 29 December he was acting as a convict overseer and was severely reprimanded for being drunk. In August 1829 a recommendation for a ticket of leave was withdrawn, as Isaacs had again been found intoxicated. On 11 October 1831 he was charged with being frequently absent from his post as convict overseer and 'going into a Public House contrary to positive orders'. He was sentenced to one week in prison and 'to be kept at Bridgewater as an overseer after the expiration of his Sentence'. On 13 April 1832 it was found that he had employed several members of his work gang to erect a fence for Mr Dean 'for his private gain and using the government bullocks for the same purpose'. The charge was dismissed.

During the remainder of 1832 and 1833 he was returned to the service of the government and was repeatedly admonished for being drunk and for being out after hours. On 30 December 1833, even though he had been reinstated as an overseer, he was found to be drunk and absent from his duty and was sentenced to 'two month's hard labour in chains'. A charge of drunkenness on 18 March 1835 caused him to be sent to Port Arthur Penitentiary, where he died on 16 November 1835 at the age of forty-two.

CON 14/5, no. 53750; CON 18/2; CON 27/8; CON 31/23; CON 13/1, p. 173.

ISAACS, John

b. America, 1798
Richmond, 1822; Convict; Sentenced to 7 years, Old Bailey, 1821.
Single; Hawker, watch finisher; Height: 159 cm.

John Isaacs was sentenced, on 12 September 1821, for stealing lead. 'A Jew'.

Isaacs arrived in Sydney on 30 April 1822 and received fifty-nine lashes on 2 July 1823 for neglecting government stock and one hundred lashes on 24 December 1824 for having two shirts and one pair of trousers for which he could not give account. He was then sent to Macquarie Harbour and remained there until 1828, when he completed the term of his initial sentence. On 28 September 1827 he stole a piece of beef and received fifty lashes and on 15 July 1828 a further twenty-five lashes for neglect of duty. On his return to Hobart Town, Isaacs was involved in a series of brutal assaults. He was told to keep the peace for six months after beating Arabella Dakers. On 15 November 1830 he assaulted Constable Rhonda in the course of his duties. In August 1831 he was 'charged with assaulting Mary Roadie and 'threatening to take the life of Ann Elizabeth Ashton' (the words 'his wife' are crossed out of the record).

In Hobart Town on 1 October 1833 Isaacs was given a life sentence for stealing from the person of John Ward two promissory notes worth £5 each and other money. He spent the next two years in Port Arthur. On 24 January 1834 he made use of improper and very unbecoming language in the presence and hearing of the men of his chain gang and his sentence was extended for two months.

He returned to Hobart Town. In 1842 Isaacs, who was serving as a constable, became involved in a fight when his friend and fellow constable Joseph Barnett (q.v.) who arrived on the *John* in 1831, was the subject of anti-Semitic remarks and both men retaliated.

A ticket of leave was issued on 16 December 1842 and Isaacs was recommended for a conditional pardon on 23 December 1843. In 1845 Isaacs was granted a 'Second Class Pardon'. The official entry regarding the pardon stated: 'A long servitude being completed. The last two and a half years give good evidence of permanent reformation'. Isaacs received permission to marry Ann Donaway in June 1846 and by 1848 he held a certificate of freedom.

CON 31/23, no. 17; MM 31/1; HO 10/59; CON 52/2, p. 244; Ship Indent 4/4008, p. 102; *Hobart Town Courier*, 30 December 1842; CSO 1/336/7715; CSO 22/35/1148.

ISAACS, John (ISAAC)

b. Lumsky, Poland, 1804–1893
Enchantress, 1833; Free.
Married; Dealer; 1 child.

John Isaacs was the brother of Jacob Myer Isaacs (q.v.), who served as the reader of the Sydney Synagogue, 1840–55. John and Rosa Isaacs (q.v.) arrived in Sydney on the *Enchantress* on 24 April 1833. He opened a shop in George Street, Sydney, where he and his family lived. In 1839 Isaac Simmons (q.v.) sold the schooner *Susannah* for £1300 to John Isaacs of the 'South Sea Warehouse'.

John Isaacs was on the Sydney Synagogue Building Fund Committee in 1839 and gave £41 to the building fund. In 1845 he donated a further £45 for the new building. He became a trustee and guarantor of the land on which the York Street Synagogue stood and was the congregation's first honorary treasurer. Through his wife's English birth he owned a house and the South Sea Warehouse in Lower George Street. In October 1842, Isaacs was asked to stand as a candidate for the Bourke Ward at the first municipal election. He was a keen Freemason and in 1842 when a Freemasons' dinner was announced, it was in his shop that tickets were available. In April 1843 he took over the Blue Post Inn in George Street and in July 1843 was permitted to operate the hotel at night. On 2 August 1849 John Isaacs, a 'General Dealer'in Sydney, was naturalised. In 1868 and 1869 he was president of the Sydney Hebrew School and in 1868 served as a member of Sydney's first *Shechitah* Committee. Rosa Isaacs had died on 18 October 1854. John died on 24 April 1893. Their daughter married Elias Cohen in Sydney in 1869.

Ship Indent 4/5204; G. F. J. Bergman,' Jacob Myer Isaacs: Sydney Synagogue's Second Minister and his Family', *AJJHS*, vol. 9, no. 4 (1982), p. 243f; *Australasian Chronicle*, 23 August 1839.

ISAACS, John

b. London
Stakesby, 1833; Convict; Sentenced to 7 years, Surrey Assizes, 1833.
Single; Gentleman's servant; Height: 174 cm.

Dark complexion, dark brown hair. Tattoo 'D. B'. A Jew. John Isaacs was convicted on 25 March 1833 and transported for stealing a watch from a passerby. He said 'I am not married. I live with a woman named Elizabeth Harris'. Gaol report: 'Bad character'. Hulk report: 'Good'.

John Isaacs arrived in Hobart Town on 4 September 1833 and was initially assigned to be a servant to a Mr Weston. On 1 March 1834 he was admonished for disobeying the orders of a magistrate when called on 'to preserve the Peace'. On 27 January 1834 he was sentenced to six months hard labour and imprisonment for 'disobedience of orders'. On 2 October 1834 while working with the Public Works he was 'severely reprimanded for using threatening and provoking language towards his fellow prisoners'. By 29 December 1834 he was classified as a 'watchman' and received two years imprisonment for 'Gross neglect of duty, leaving his post as watchman and found sleeping in one of the Huts'. It was recommended that he be attached to one of the chain gangs. He was attached to the chain gang at Green Hill with his behaviour to be reviewed at the end of twelve months. On 27 June 1836 he was found guilty of having been 'disorderly in Church' and sentenced to the treadmill for seven days. On 16 August 1836 he was found guilty of negligently driving a cart by riding on its shafts. On 7 December he repeated the driving offence and was sentenced to twenty-five lashes. Isaacs was granted a certificate of freedom in 1840 (no. 263).

CON 31/24; CON 18/20; CON 23/2; CON 27/6, no. 39097.

ISAACS, John

d. 1867
1847; Free.
Single.

John F. Isaacs married Jane Lee at the Sydney Synagogue in 1850. Isaacs, of 139 Pitt Street, died on 8 August 1867 and was buried in the Jewish section of Rookwood cemetery. It was said 'he was mourned by his wife Jane and his daughter'.

Sydney Morning Herald, 9 August 1867.

ISAACS, Lazarus

Free.

Lazarus Isaacs travelled steerage to Sydney, arriving on 3 February 1842 on the brig *William* from Launceston. A letter was waiting for him at the Sydney Post Office on 6 January 1843 (*Sydney Morning Herald*).

4/5221.

ISAACS, Leon Lewis

b. London, 1813–1876
Lady, 1841; Free.
Married; Carpenter; 4 children.

Leon and his wife Frances (Fanny) (q.v.) Isaacs were bounty migrants—among the few who were listed as Jewish. They arrived in Sydney on 13 October 1841. Leon was a carpenter—the son of Lewis Isaacs, a broker. Fanny was a parasol and umbrella maker, aged twenty-six, the daughter of Wolf Abraham, a hawker. The 1847 edition of *Low's Directory of the City and District of Sydney* listed Leon Lewis Isaacs as a 'clothes broker' of Kent Street. In 1842 they had a daughter, Sarah, who was registered as a 'Hebrew'. Julia was born in Sydney in 1845 and Judah in 1846 (he was buried by the Sydney Synagogue on 4 December 1847). Kitty was born in Sydney in 1850.

Leon Lewis Isaacs died on 1 March 1876 and was buried at Rookwood Cemetery. In the newspaper memorial notice two of his daughters were mentioned: Mrs Sarah de Groen and Mrs Vandenberg of Forbes.

Sydney Morning Herald, 2 March 1876.

ISAACS, Levy

b. Hobart Town, 1824–1849
Free.

Levy Isaacs, who had been born in Van Diemen's Land, and was aged twenty-five, a prisoner, died at Cockatoo Island prison, having been sent there from Van Diemen's Land. He was buried by the Sydney Synagogue on 18 February 1849.

The ex-soldier and convict Michael Isaacs (q.v.) appears to be the only possible person who could have been the father of Levy Isaacs.

ISAACS, Lewis

b. London, 1782–1857
Marquis of Hastings (4), 1839; Convict.
Labourer.

The transport ship arrived in Hobart Town on 23 July 1839. The *Sydney Gazette* of March 1842 contains a reference about Isaacs:

> A hint to young men! A young man named Lewis Isaacs brought before the Sydney Police Bench, charged with being idle and a disorderly character, having no visible means of gaining a livelihood and continually in the company of loose women—If our police officers are going to proceed against all those [like him] Sydney will soon be cleared out!

He was listed in the *Registry of Flash Men* as living in Brougham Place in Sydney and as being the 'bully' or pimp of Rachel Nathan (q.v.).

Isaacs was on the voters' list, with a shop in York Street, but was committed to Newcastle Gaol on 14 April 1843 by the Maitland Court and sent to Sydney for trial. On 29 May 1847 the *Sydney Chronicle* reported that Lewis Isaacs, 'dealer, of Kent St', was bankrupt. Lewis Isaacs was arraigned at the Bathurst Circuit Court on 26 September 1848 on a charge of 'uttering' a forged cheque. He had paid for a pair of boots with the cheque and was sentenced to three years hard labour at the Bathurst Gaol. On 7 September 1850 Isaacs submitted a petition for mitigation of sentence which seems to have been effective. A ticket of leave was issued on the condition that he leave Bathurst within twenty-four hours.

During the gold rush, Isaacs and Joseph Jewel (q.v.) were in charge of gold-buying for a Mr Hentin at Turon when a bag of gold sovereigns and £600 in notes were stolen from their tent.

Lewis Isaacs died at Shoalhaven on 10 May 1857 at the age of seventy-five and was buried in Sydney's Jewish cemetery.

Newcastle Gaol Entrance Book 1841–1845, 2/2008; W. A. Miles, *Registry of Flash Men*, 2/673, p. 41; *Sydney Morning Herald*, 15 September 1842, 2 October 1848; *Sydney Chronicle*, 29 May 1847; *Sydney Gazette*, 29 March 1842; CS 50/7845.

ISAACS, Mark

b. London
1843; Free.
Single; Baker.

On 28 January 1844 Mark Isaacs was chosen to bake 'the Passover Cakes' for the approaching festival. He had a bakery in Liverpool Street. Isaacs was a seat holder in the new Sydney Synagogue in 1845. He married Rachel Lea in a Jewish ceremony in Sydney on 16 November 1848. Sadly, in May of that same year, he was declared to be insolvent. Rachel and Mark had two sons, Alexander and Jacob. Mark died on 31 May 1906.

Sydney Synagogue Minute Book, 28 January 1844, p. 133; *Sydney Morning Herald*, 18 September 1848.

ISAACS, Michael

b. London, 1798–1833
Hibernia, 1819; Convict; Sentenced to life, Surrey Assizes, 1818.
Single; Soldier.

Michael Isaacs was transported for 'horse stealing'. He was the youngest child of an upholsterer, and that trade was listed in his convict dossier. He had enlisted as a soldier at the age of fifteen. He was caught robbing the dead on the Salamanca battlefield at the age of sixteen. In May 1814 he sailed for New Orleans, returning to Europe to fight against Napoleon, and his unit arrived on the scene a few days after the Battle of Waterloo. Isaacs spent 1814 as a soldier and a thief in the British war against the Americans 'near the town of New Orleans on the banks of the Mississipi'. He was returned to England and then France and was ultimately sentenced at the Surrey Assizes on 6 August 1818 for horse stealing. The surgeon on board ship believed that Isaacs possessed a 'good character'.

The *Hibernia* arrived in Hobart Town on 11 May 1819 and Isaacs was initially assigned to Elizabeth River, where he was stock keeper and servant to Lt Governor Sorrell. His supervisor was Thomas Scott who asked Isaacs to dictate the story of his life of crime which he did, with some glee, beginning with his confession that he had robbed his own father of £75 before he joined the army. He was assigned to the Public Works Department at Port Dalrymple. On 24 September 1822 he was reprimanded for being absent from his duty. On 19 March 1824 he received fifty lashes for 'disobedience'. On 22 November 1824 he was tried at the Hobart

Town Supreme Court for forging a money order worth £5 7s 6d. Found guilty on 8 January, his existing sentence was extended. Isaacs was sent to Macquarie Harbour where, on 11 April 1827, he was sentenced to twenty-five lashes for 'exhibiting repeated instances of ill temper in the discharge of his duty'. Back from Van Diemen's Land's west coast, on 13 June 1831 he was sent to the treadmill for 'being absent the whole night without leave'. From December 1830 to July 1832 he worked on the government brig *Tamar*, and was reported for 'fighting'. He was merely admonished after the chief mate stated that Isaacs had promised 'to be good'. He died in February 1833.

Michael Isaacs's unpublished hand written biography is in Sydney's Mitchell Library.

The Life of a Convict Named 'Isaacs', a Jew in Van Diemen's Land, taken down from his own dictation in 1821 by T. Scott ms, ML; CY reel 1793 B41. CON 31/23, no. 12; 4/4006, p. 297; CON 13/1, pp. 279, 303; HO 11/3; HO 10/43.

ISAACS, Michael

b. Whitechapel, 1799–1848
Anson (1), 1844; Convict; Sentenced to 15 years, Old Bailey, 1843.
Married; Watch finisher and dealer; Height: 168 cm; 2 children (in England).

Fresh complexion, dark brown hair and whiskers. Dark brown eyes, medium nose. Arms and breast hairy. Scar outside of chin. Scar on elbow on left arm. A Jew. Michael Isaacs was sentenced on 3 April 1843 for breaking and entering a warehouse and stealing rags to the value of £25. He had been tried once before and acquitted on a charge of receiving stolen goods. He was married and had two children. He could read and write.

Michael Isaacs arrived in Hobart Town on 4 February 1844 and emerged from his initial probationary period of labour of twenty-two months at Impression Bay (on the Tasman Peninsula) on 4 December 1845. By 1846 he was employed as a constable in Hobart Town when he received a sentence of ten days solitary confinement 'for neglect of duty in not traversing his beat'. From May to October 1847 he was in the service of Mr A. Solomons (sic) of Launceston and was admonished for disobedience of orders on 7 October. On 10 April 1848 he was a constable once again when he was fined 10 shillings for being absent from his beat. He died in the Hospital in Launceston on 22 September 1848.

CON 33/49; CON 63/2, no. 11576; CON 18/41.

ISAACS, Moses

b. Poland, 1821–1842
Eden (2), 1842; Convict; Sentenced, Exeter City, Devon, 1839.
Single; Clerk and hawker; Height: 161 cm.

Fair complexion. Dark brown hair, round face, dark hazel eyes, large nose, scar over left eye, large chin and mouth. Can read and write. Protestant. A converted Jew. Moses Isaacs was transported for receiving stolen silver plate valued at £20. His hulk report stated that he was four times ironed and four times whipped. The surgeon noted: 'A bad fellow. In the box four times for quarrelling. Twelve hours each time. General conduct very bad'. He was tried on 1 July 1839.

Isaacs arrived at Hobart Town on 5 July 1842 and died in the Hospital there, on 31 July.

CON 33/22, no. 5268; CON 63/1; CON 14/12.

ISAACS, Moses

b. Spitalfields, 1824–1907.
Palmyra, 1846; Convict; Sentenced to 10 years, Old Bailey, 1845.
Single; Cab driver; Height: 160 cm.

Fresh complexion, dark brown hair, brown whiskers, blue eyes, long nose, long chin. Face pimpled. Jew. Can neither read nor write. Moses was charged with having stolen 'a handkerchief from the person'. He had been convicted of a similar offence and served twelve months in gaol. His father's name was Joseph Isaacs and his mother was Leah. His brothers and sisters were Simon, Abraham, Sarah, Esther and Julia. The surgeon's report from the ship stated that he was 'indifferent'.

The *Palmyra* arrived in Van Diemen's Land on 22 August 1846. Isaacs was given an eighteen-month preliminary period of labour with the Rocky Hills Road Gang. By May 1847 he was an assigned servant in town and was sentenced for 'neglect of duty' and 'disobedience of orders', culminating on 3 July 1847 with three days in solitary confinement for 'disobedience'. From October 1848 to September 1850, Isaacs was assigned to Joseph Solomon in Launceston. Minor offences brought him periods of hard labour. He received his ticket of leave on 3 December 1850 but continued to attract the attention of the police. In August 1851 in Launceston he was found guilty of larceny and misconduct for being absent from his authorised residence. Moses Isaacs married Mary Sweeney, who had arrived as a prisoner on the *Arabia*, on 4 February 1851. She had been transported for setting fire to a hayrick. On 8 November 1852 Isaacs was fined five shillings for disturbing the peace. He held a ticket of leave but this was revoked following his conviction for misconduct in assaulting a constable. The ticket of leave was restored on 4 July 1854. A conditional pardon was granted on 6 February 1855 and a certificate of freedom on 28 January 1856.

A daughter, Sarah, was born in Hobart. There were two other children, Esther and Samuel (1855–1950). The family is known to have visited London in 1866 and then lived in Little Bourke Street, Melbourne.

Isaacs returned to England and married a second time (Mary Ann Richards). He died in 1907 at the age of 87.

CON 14/36, no. 18834; CON 18/47; HO 11/15; CON 52/1, p. 87; CON 33/78. Family information Mrs Eva Dench of Surrey (UK).

ISAACS, Rachel

b. Sydney, 1817

Rachel Isaacs was the first child to be born in Australia of two Jewish parents. She was born in the colony of New South Wales, at Petersham, in 1817, to Jacob

Isaacs (who had arrived on the *Baring* in 1815) and Esther Isaacs (qq.v.), who had followed her husband out to Australia in 1816.

In 1836, while she was in the service of a Mr Morris of the Australian Inn, Market Street, Sydney, she was accused of stealing £17. She was nineteen, and the Recognition Book of the Sydney Gaol described her as of slender build, 159 cm tall, with pale complexion, black hair and hazel eyes. She was discharged for lack of evidence. On 19 October 1837, she was charged with assaulting the wife of the man she was living with. On 17 December 1838 she was remanded for stealing two sovereigns and two half crowns. She was living with a man who said that he had left the money out for her. Rachael Isaacs married William Aulberry at St Lawrence's Church of England in Sydney in 1842. She was listed as holding a ticket of leave in 1845.

Sydney Gaol Recognition Book 1837–1838, 4/6300, no. 1531; *Sydney Gazette*, 5 May 1836, 19 October 1837, 17 February 1838; *Commercial Journal and Advertiser*, 17 February 1838.

ISAACS, Rachel

b. 1823
Free.
Single.

Rachel Isaacs came to New South Wales as a free immigrant. In 1845, aged twenty-two, she was granted permission to marry Patrick Fitzpatrick, aged thirty-three, who held a ticket of leave. Fitzpatrick had come to Australia as a convict on the *Parmelia* (2) with a life sentence. They were married by the Rev. W. J. Gore of Muswellbrook on 10 July 1845.

Permission to Marry Book 1845, p. 97, 4/4514.

ISAACS, Rosa

1810–1854
Enchantress, 1833; Free.
Married; 1 child.

Rosa arrived with her husband, John Isaacs (q.v.). Her daughter married Elias Cohen in 1869. Rosa died on 18 October 1854, aged forty-four, in Sydney.

Rosetta's death was reported in London's *Jewish Chronicle* on 2 March 1855. She was the sister of Jacob Isaacs (q.v.), the reader of the York Street Synagogue. She was also the sister of D. M. Isaacs of Liverpool, and S. M. Isaacs of New York. 'There was no Charity in Sydney of which she was not a member. She was the Directress of the Jewish burial ground [in Sydney] for a long term of years.'

ISAACS, Samuel

b. London
Active, 1791; Convict; Sentenced to 7 years, Old Bailey, 1790.
Old clothes man.

Samuel Isaacs was transported for stealing two men's hats. He was caught running down the street with them and was seen, with a companion, actually stealing them. Prisoner's defence: 'I deal in old clothes'. He was sentenced on 14 April 1790.

Samuel Isaacs was listed at Norfolk Island on 23 April 1793, after which he returned to the mainland and was described as a vagrant when apprehended in Sydney on 13 July 1799. On 27 July he appeared before the Bench of Magistrates on suspicion of having stolen a quantity of live poultry from John Palmer esquire. He was 'delivered' to the assigned service of Alexander McDonald to work as a tailor. On the 1806 Muster for New South Wales he was listed as a prisoner assigned to John Colcroft.

OBSP, 1789–90, case 378, p. 431; Proceedings of the Bench of Magistrates 1798–1800, p. 94, ML, 1/298.

ISAACS, Samuel

b. London, 1812–1896
Isabella, 1833; Convict; Sentenced to 7 years, Westminster Quarter Sessions, 1832.
Single; Pastry cook; Height: 155 cm; 4 children.

Could read and write 'a little'. Hulk report 'Orderly'. Surgeon's report 'Indifferent'. Samuel Isaacs was sentenced on 28 June 1832 for stealing a handkerchief valued at one shilling from William Campbell Robertson, surgeon, of Fleet Street, London. A 'John Smith' was an accomplice in the theft. Isaacs was the son of Michael and Elizabeth Isaacs.

Isaacs (who, despite his name, may not have been Jewish) had a brief police record. On 7 June 1836 he was admonished for neglect of duty and on 18 December 1837 he was admonished for being absent without leave. He was listed as a labourer in 1832, a pastry cook in the same year, a dealer in 1855, and a baker and pastry cook in 1863. He received permission to marry the bounty migrant Binney Smith, who had come free to the colony on the *William Metcalfe* on 24 January 1837, and they married in St David's Church of England Cathedral in Hobart Town on 20 January 1838. Their children were Elizabeth (born 1843), James (1848), Henry and Helen. Samuel Isaacs was listed as a Protestant in his convict dossier and his wife and children were Christians.

Isaacs received his certificate of freedom (no. 447) in 1846.

CON 31/24, no. 87; CON 52/1, p. 87; VDL Papers, ML, A1059-7, p. 277.

ISAACS, Samuel

d. 1896
1846; Free.
Single.

In 1847 the Melbourne Hebrew Congregation appointed Samuel Isaacs to be the *Shamash* (sexton) and to read the Torah, having been recommended to the congregation by Mr Rintel (q.v.), who at that time was the schoolmaster of the Sydney Synagogue. Isaacs, wrote Rintel, was 'a useful man in any capacity the school might require him'. When the Melbourne congregation appointed Walter Lindenthal (q.v.) to be their minister, Isaacs was paid £10 extra (deducted from Lindenthal's salary) to read the Torah.

Isaacs was soon called before the congregation's committee concerning a scandalous report and 'having no defence he was forthwith dismissed'. In 1848 he opened a school for boys and girls at 'the Eastern End of Great Latrobe St'. The school, which was under Methodist auspices, flourished, and Lindenthal taught religious instruction to its Jewish students. Isaacs moved to Geelong and served as the local congregation's honorary minister in the 1880s. Isaacs was buried in the Jewish section of the Melbourne General Cemetery on 23 June 1896.

ISAACS, Sarah

b. London, 1815
David Scott, 1834; Free.
Single; Servant.

Sarah Isaacs was a bounty migrant who arrived in Sydney on 25 October 1834. She was to be employed by John Solomon (q.v.), better known as 'Jacky the Jew', who was in the process of establishing himself as a hotel owner.

ISAACS, Simon (Cymon)

b. 1736
Coromandel (2), 1804; Convict; Sentenced to life, Kingston, Surrey, 1802.
Married; Labourer and fruitseller; Height: 169 cm.

Fair complexion, hazel eyes, dark hair. Simon Isaacs was sentenced at the Kingston Gaol Delivery on 22 March 1802.

Isaacs was granted a ticket of leave in June 1810 for the District of Sydney. On 27 April 1811 Isaacs was the key witness in a trial concerning two soldiers who were charged with assault. He testified:

> Simon Isaacs, a Jew, being first sworn according to the Jewish ritual, says I was going along on Thursday afternoon with my basket of fruit through George Street, passing the Sentry at the Store opposite Thomas's another sentry called me back and asked what fruit I had to sell—I told him I had nothing to sell. He was drunk and staggered

a good deal and had his firelock in a charging position. I was frightened and glad to get away it was getting dark.

The 1814 Muster stated that he was 'off rations' and had a ticket of leave while still working at his old 'profession' of 'Fruitman'. In the 1822 General Muster of New South Wales an Abraham Isaacs who came on the *Coromandel* was listed in Sydney. He was described as having had a life sentence.

Simon Isaacs mislaid his ticket of leave and the Colonial Secretary authorised a new document to be issued on 23 June 1823. On 9 October 1825 he applied for a return passage to England 'to his family'. He continued to agitate for a pardon, and on 23 November 1825 requested an absolute pardon. He wrote 'the heart felt satisfaction to State that from his Arrival in the Colony to the Present Period the general tenor of his Conduct has been such to Merit the good opinion of the Public at large. That Memorialist has several Children in England some of them possessed of considerable property makes him to wish to return to them and his native Country'.

The chaplain, the Rev. William Cowper, added 'the memorialist is a very aged man he is in his ninetieth year and if a Pardon from his Earthly Sovereign or from his Excellency would tend to prepare the poor old man the better to appear before his Heavenly Sovereign I should not withhold my Signature'. Isaacs was granted an absolute pardon in 1827 and presumably left Australia for England.

Register of Pardons 4/4427, p. 471; Petition to Sir Thomas Brisbane 4/1871, pp. 4–6; Register of Conditional Pardons 4/4430; Proceedings of the Bench of Magistrates, ML, 1/303, 27 April 1811; Governors' Despatches 1831, p. 37, ML, A1209.

ISAACS, Solomon

Active, 1791; Convict; Sentenced to 7 years, Old Bailey, 1789.
Labourer.

Solomon Isaacs stole a watch worth £1 from a shop: 'I went to Billingsgate market early in the morning. I could earn nothing. I went to my sister to borrow a shilling and she gave me a half penny to get a farthings worth of sand for her. I had my apron on'. (The watch was found in his apron pocket.) Isaacs was sentenced at the Old Bailey on 9 December 1789.

Solomon Isaacs arrived in New South Wales on 26 September 1791 as part of the Third Fleet. The *Active* lost twenty-one convicts during the journey, which took 183 days, leaving its 'cargo' in a 'feeble and emaciated state'. Isaacs does not appear to have survived.

OBSP, 1789–90, case 33, p. 49; Charles Bateson, *The Convict Ships*, p. 135.

ISAACS, Solomon

b. London
Southworth I, 1830; Convict; Sentenced to 7 years, Bristol, 1829.
Single; Hawker; Height: 169.5 cm.

Isaacs was transported for stealing a portmanteau with wearing apparel in it. His transport ship noted that he was 'well known in London' and of bad character, though he 'denied any other offence'. The hulk report stated 'orderly and behaved well'. He was convicted at Bristol City Quarter Sessions on 19 October 1829. Dark complexion, black hair, black whiskers, hazel eyes, roman nose, large projecting lips. 'A Jew'.

Solomon Isaacs' police dossier in Van Dieman's Land shows only one entry. On 7 April 1830 he was reprimanded for neglect of duty and disobedience while the assigned servant of Mr Clayton.

CON 31/24, no. 60; VDL papers, ML, A1059–60, p. 217. Con 18-1-21. No. 1407.

ISAACS, Stephen

b. Bishopsgate, 1796–1860
Asia (5), 1840; Convict; Sentenced to 25 years, Central Criminal Court, 1839.
Tailor; Height: 170 cm.

Dark complexioned, black hair and whiskers, dark eyes. Stephen Isaacs had a number of initials tattooed on his right arm. Literate. He was described as 'Jew and Protestant'. He was transported for stealing a horse, gig and saddle. Isaacs had been tried twice before for refusing to work on the hulk before transportation. His behaviour was noted as having been 'very bad and wanton mischievous'.

Isaacs' extensive dossier covers two large pages. His original period of probation was to be for two years at Sandy Bay but this was doubled in length owing to eight separate extensions for bad behaviour. In less than a year he was sent to Port Arthur after being especially reported for disobedience. Among his nineteen convictions recorded between April 1841 and the end of the first stage of probation in November 1844 were four punishments resulting in a total of 122 lashes for disobedience and insolence. On 5 March 1846, at the Prisoners' Barracks in Launceston, he was given eighteen months hard labour in chains for obtaining goods under the value of £5 by false pretences. On 20 April 1848 at Oatlands he was given a further six months for absconding. In March 1849 at Launceston a further nine-month sentence was recorded for assault. This sentence was extended by three months, and he was sent to Port Arthur to be kept separate from the other prisoners. Three attempts to abscond, in December 1852 at Launceston, July 1854 at Hobart Town, and June 1855 at Oatlands, further extended his initial sentence by eighteen months, nine months, and twelve months with hard labour. On 30 August 1855 a charge of petty larceny lengthened his sentence by eighteen months. He received his ticket of leave on 27 October 1857, only to have it revoked in May 1858 when he was found guilty of theft. The ticket of leave was restored on 22 November 1859 and he died in Hobart's General Hospital on 13 September 1860.

CON 33/2.

ISRAEL, Cashmore (John Cashman)

b. London, 1799–1872
Neptune (2), 1818; Convict; Sentenced to life, Old Bailey, 1817.
Baker and jeweller; Height: 166 cm; 7 children.

Fair pale complexion, dark brown hair, hazel eyes. Cashmore Israel was one of ten children. At the time of his arrest he was not living at home. His father, Isaiah Israel, was a general dealer in Houndsditch who, in December 1817, prosecuted his son for having broken into his house and stolen jewellery worth £10 and cloth. 'Nothing but the greatest necessity could induce me to come forward and prosecute him'. To what must have been his father's horror, the eighteen-year-old was sentenced to death, which was later commuted to transportation for life.

The *Neptune* arrived in New South Wales in September 1818. Cashmore Israel was listed as a 'settler's man' in the General Muster of that year and a 'government labourer' in the colony in 1820. Israel was transferred to Van Diemen's Land on the *Prince Leopold* in 1822 and until 1827 was assigned to the Public Works Department in Launceston. On 23 November 1831 Abraham Alexander (q.v.), a convict free by servitude, was bound over to keep the peace after insulting Cashmore Israel. Israel received his ticket of leave on 19 June 1830. On 6 February 1832 he, in turn, was bound over to keep the peace after assaulting Marianne Rogers. On 4 June 1832 he was found hidden aboard the barque *Augusta* and was therefore deprived of his ticket of leave. He was returned to the government with a certificate from the surgeon that stated he was unfit for physical labour. On 15 January 1835 Israel's ticket of leave was returned on condition that he live in the interior of the island.

A conditional pardon was granted on 21 August 1837 and a free pardon issued on 18 August 1841, which would have permitted him to return to England. Israel's name appeared on the petition to establish a synagogue in Launceston on 23 May 1843. In the 1843 Census of Van Diemen's Land, 'John Cashman Israel' was listed as a shopkeeper in Brisbane Street, Launceston. He was the tenant of a wooden house. He was single and lived alone. On 15 April 1848 Benjamin Francis (q.v.) sold at auction a long list of unredeemed pledges, by order of J. C. Israel, licensed pawnbroker. A second auction occurred on 30 June 1849. John Cashman Israel died in Launceston on 29 May 1872 and was buried as a Jew in the old Jewish Cemetery in Invermay, Launceston. He had seven children.

Israel Cashmore was the father of John William Israel (1850–1926), who served as the first Auditor-General of the Commonwealth of Australia.

OBSP, 1817–18, case 98, p. 41; Ship Indent 4/4006, p. 72 (also on the *Glory*'s list, arriving Sept. 1818); HO 10/1; CON 31/23, no. 10; Launceston Police Book, CON 78/2, p. 162; *Launceston Examiner*, 15 April 1848; *Hobart Town Courier*, 22 June 1832, 27 July 1838, 19 April 1839, 25 November 1842; *Australian Israelite*, 7 June 1872; CP no. 1372, Free Pardon no. 760; L. M. Goldman, 'Morris Joseph and the Launceston Community', *AJJHS*, vol. 3, no. 3 (1950), p. 126; *ADB*, vol. 9, p. 450.

ISRAEL, Esther

b. London, 1836
Travencore, 1853; Free.
Single; 2 children.

The sister of Brina Israel Esther Israel married Elias Lapidus (q.v.) in Sydney in 1853. Their children were Nathan and Rachel.

First Families 2001 (website); information by Frederick Ralph Cohen.

ISRAEL, Maria

1771–1849
Lady Juliana, 1790; Convict; Sentenced to 7 years, Old Bailey, 1789.
Single; 8 children.

Maria Israel arrived on the Second Fleet to Port Jackson. She had been sentenced to transportation for seven years for stealing two pieces of muslin valued at £3 from the shop of John Goldwell.

On 1 August 1790, two months after her arrival in Sydney, Maria Israel was sent to Norfolk Island. Within a year she had begun to live with Thomas Chaffey, who would become an overseer, constable and farmer on the island. She lived in Hobart Town at the time of the 1811 Muster. Her children were Elizabeth (born 1791), Maria (born and died 1793), Lydia (1795), Anne (1799), Zachariah (1801), Hannah (1803), George (1805) and William (1808). Her first five children were born at Norfolk Island; three were born in Van Diemen's Land. All were baptised and appear on the Register of St Philip's in Sydney. Thomas Chaffey obtained a land grant at Wrest Point and the gibbet was moved from offshore at the Derwent to 'Chaffey's Point' so that the bodies could be more easily removed once they were hanged. Despite her surname, Maria Israel may not have been Jewish. She was buried in an Anglican cemetery on 19 October 1849.

Michael Flynn, *The Second Fleet*, p. 359; *OBSP*, 1788–89, case 354, p. 431; HO 11/1; St Philip's Register, 134/261.

ISRAEL, Samuel

Convict.
3 children.

Samuel Israel was listed as an emancipated convict on Norfolk Island from July 1797 to August 1801. Three children were born on the island to Samuel Israel and Elizabeth Smith: Sarah (born 30 December 1797), Mary (2 July 1799), and Susanna (25 July 1801). The children were baptised on 24 August 1801. The *Sydney Gazette* stated that Emanuel (*sic*) Israel had permission to leave the colony on the *Fortuna* on 3 August 1806, and the family presumably left for England.

St Philip's Register 129/258.

J

JACOB, Levy (JACOBS) (Levi)

1776–1839
William Glen Anderson, 1831; Convict; Sentenced to 7 years, Old Bailey, 1831.
Married; Labourer; Height: 159 cm; 10 children (in England).

Sallow complexion, round head bald on top, grey hair, grey whiskers, short pointed nose, projecting chin. Tattoo 'EFBJ' four dots on left arm. Levy Jacob claimed to be aged sixty-seven at the time of his trial. He was, however, fifty-five. He could read and write. He was listed as 'Protestant' in the ship's indent. His wife was Elizabeth Jacob of London and they had seven sons and three daughters. Jacob was sentenced to transportation on 17 February 1831 for stealing a box from a passing cart near the London docks. He denied he was able to lift the box as he had just come out of hospital following an operation.

Levy Jacob was transferred on the *Larkins* bound for Van Diemen's Land almost immediately after his initial arrival in Sydney. Jacob was assigned to become a wardsman in the Hobart Town Hospital. On 2 October 1832 he was sent 'to be worked' in the Bridgewater Road Gang, even though he was not to be placed in irons due to his age and was to sleep in a cell at night. He had been found guilty of 'indecent familiarities with one of the Hospital patients'. The remaining part of his sentence was ultimately remitted and he received a ticket of leave on 29 March 1836. Levy Jacob was listed as a licensed hawker in the *Hobart Town Courier* of 25 May 1838.

Levy Jacobs died at Launceston on 6 June 1839 at the age of sixty-three.

OBSP, 1830–31, case 502, p. 274; CON 14/2, no. 545; CON 18/1/21; CON 31/24; MM 33/2; MM 32/6; VDL papers, ML, A 1059-6, p. 385; CON 27/5; *Van Diemen's Land Colonial Times*, 29 March 1836.

JACOBS, Abraham

b. about 1771
Scarborough (2), 1790; Convict; Sentenced to life, Middlesex, 1789.
Labourer.

Jacobs was one of the survivors of the Second Fleet. Jacobs was sentenced to death for the theft of three sheep and a lamb. Abraham Jacobs was actually seen driving the sheep past the Shoreditch Turnpike in the early morning in order to sell them to a butcher. He was described as 'a lad' who had sometimes worked as a butcher in Whitechapel. The butcher was convicted of receiving stolen property and sentenced to fourteen years transportation and Jacobs was eventually reprieved from the death sentence.

In the mid-1790s Jacobs appears to have worked as a sailor in Sydney Harbour and along the Parramatta River. He appeared in the Criminal Court in Sydney on 3 March 1797 as a witness. He was employed on the long boat bringing wheat from Parramatta to Sydney when it was robbed. He may have been on Norfolk Island by 1802 and was marked as no longer reliant on government stores by the end of 1807.

Michael Flynn, *The Second Fleet*, p. 360; *OBSP*, 1788–89, case 457, p. 558f.; Proceedings of the Criminal Court, ML5/1147 B; Ship Indent, p. 55.

JACOBS, Abraham (Jacob ABRAHAMS)

b. 1777
Hillsborough, 1799; Convict; Sentenced to 14 years, Surrey, 1798.

The *Hillsborough* was known as 'the Fever Ship', and 95 of the 300 prisoners on board died on the voyage or upon arrival. Abram Jacobs was listed in the 1806 Muster on Norfolk Island with the note 'Bull [Bullock] Carriage'. He received permission to leave Australia on the *Southwark* on 18 August 1805.

HO 11/1, and CO 207/(343.4); *Sydney Gazette*, 18 August 1805.

JACOBS, Abraham

b. Norwich, 1796–1861
Maria (2), 1820; Convict; Sentenced to 7 years, Old Bailey, 1820.
Hawker and labourer.

Abraham Jacobs was convicted at the Old Bailey on 12 April 1820 at the age of twenty-four. On April 6 Jacobs stole a trunk from the back of a cart, ran down the Old Change and hired a porter to carry it for him to Whitechapel. A constable stopped the porter in Botolph lane and arrested Jacobs and an accomplice Lazarus Lazarus who was found to be carrying counterfeit money. 'Phaehas Jacobs aged twenty-six was found guilty' (as was Lazarus).

During Abraham Jacobs' first year in Van Diemen's Land he was sentenced on 28 June 1821 to fifty lashes for 'stealing sundry articles of wearing apparel'. On 9 July 1821 he was sentenced to twenty-five lashes for neglect of duty and on 10 August 1821 he received fifty lashes for the same offence. In 1821 he was employed in a road gang building the public highway to Port Dalrymple.

On 15 July 1824 it was discovered that he was not actually being employed by the master to whom he had been assigned and he was returned to the Hobart Town Prisoners' Barracks. In October 1824 he was assigned to the road gang at Brighton. Jacobs received his ticket of leave on 21 April 1827. By 1828 he was free by servitude and on 11 August 1828 he was tried for 'having in his possession well knowing the same to have been feloniously stolen a silver watch the property of Mr Makepeace in New Town Rd'. Jacobs was eventually acquitted (on 21 March 1829). On 14 January 1834 he was found guilty of 'disorderly conduct and insulting Constable Wright in the execution of his Duty'. Jacobs was drunk and was fined five shillings.

Abraham Jacobs died at Hobart Town on 25 July 1861.

CON 31/23, no. 113; Ship Indent 4/4007, p. 20; HO 10/43; *Hobart Town Gazette*, 21 April 1827; *Tasmanian*, 15 August 1828.

JACOBS, Abraham

b. Prussia, 1812
Hercules (4), 1832; Convict; Sentenced to 14 years, Lancaster, 1831.
Single; Travelling Jeweller; Height: 156 cm.

Sallow and pock-pitted complexion, dark brown hair, hazel eyes, scar on bridge of nose. Could read and write German. Jew. Abraham Jacobs was sentenced for dealing in stolen goods. He had no previous conviction.

In the 1837 General Return of Convicts Abraham Jacobs was listed as an assigned servant to Mr Robert McInto of Lane Cove. He received a ticket of leave in 1839 for the District of Campbelltown. In March 1840 Abraham Jacobs, aged twenty-eight, received permission to marry Eliza Pearce, aged seventeen, a native of the colony. The ceremony was to be conducted on 11 March 1840 by Rev. H. H. Bobart of St John's Church of England, Parramatta. Abraham Jacobs, a dealer at Campbelltown, was declared insolvent on 16 March 1842 with debts of £35 and assets of £96 and more claims not yet presented. The authorities seem to have given him a chance to resume work because on 8 July 1842 he was granted a passport to attend the Sydney Market, bringing produce to and from Sydney and Campbelltown. On 24 August it was 'torn up' for not following the occupation for which he had obtained it.

A certificate of freedom was issued on 19 September 1845.

Hercules Printed Indent, p. 129; Permission to Marry Book 4/4513, p. 144. Governors' Despatches, A1222; TL 39/858, in 4/4129; Passport, 8 July 1842; CF 45/1245, in 4/4401; *Sydney Free Press and Commercial Observer*, 19 March 1842.

JACOBS, Abraham

b. London, 1815
Surrey I (8), 1834; Convict; Sentenced, London, 1834.
Single; Pot boy (labourer); Height: 168 cm.

Dark sallow complexion, black hair, dark brown eyes. Tattoos: 'woman rather illegible inside lower right arm, glass bottle and two tobacco pipes inside lower left arm. Abraham Jacobs' brother Joseph (q.v.) had been sent to the colony in 1825. Abraham was caught picking pockets in Aldgate on 19 February 1834, and was sentenced, on 20 February 1834 to transportation.

A ticket of leave was granted to Abraham Jacobs in 1840 for the District of Queanbeyan and a certificate of freedom on 15 October 1841. The description of Jacobs six years after he arrived stated that his height was 178 cm.

OBSP, 1833–34, case 519, p. 309; Printed Indent *Surrey*, p. 101; TL 40/410, in 4/4137; Governors' Despatches 1841, ML, A1225, p. 34; CF 4/4369-41/1420.

JACOBS, Benjamin (Jacob ABRAHAMS)

b. 1745
Royal Admiral I (2), 1800; Convict; Sentenced to 14 years, Old Bailey, 1798.

Benjamin Jacobs, alias Jacob Abrahams, was living with a prostitute in the East End. He stole a watch from a client who was sleeping with his de facto wife and was arrested when he pawned the watch. He was aged fifty-two and was sentenced in September 1798.

In the General Muster of 1806 Jacobs was listed as a prisoner working for the government in Parramatta. Benjamin Jacobs converted to Christianity and in the General Muster of 1813 was listed as 'free'. He was given salaried work as 'a pew opener in Parramatta Church'. Jacobs was permitted to return to England on the brig *Kangaroo*. The Colonial Secretary wrote, on 29 March 1817, that he was now free by servitude and was to be victualled on the colonial brig *Kangaroo* at the expense of the Crown. He left in April 1817. On board the ship was the Rev. Thomas Hassall, who wrote: 'It is a difficult voyage. "Old Ben" with tears tells me he wishes he had taken Mr [Samuel] Marsden's advice and rested his old bones in the sun'.

OBSP, 1797–98, case 511, p. 547; HO 10/1; HO 11/1; CO 201/84; *HRA*, series 1, vol. 9, p. 373; CS in Letters 1817, 4/1737; Hassall's Papers, MLA, 860, p. 158; CS 3 April, 8 April 1817, 4/1737, pp. 273, 279, 282.

JACOBS, Benjamin

b. London, 1819
Barossa (1), 1839; Convict; Sentenced to 10 years, Central Criminal Court, 1838.
Single; Labourer; Height: 165.5 cm.

Ruddy freckled complexion, brown hair, bluish eyes. Jew. Could read and write. Jacobs was heavily tattooed: a woman on right breast, naval arms and Britannia on left; crown, two flags and liberty, anchor, woman LOVE K on upper chest; bird and two twigs, KK IL and flower pot; B S on lower right arm; Mermaid and SARAH on upper left arm; 15 blue dots; KEEFE BBC Solomon FEFE on right arm. Scars on breast, knuckle, arm, left leg. Benjamin Jacobs was sentenced on 26 November 1838 for burglary.

The *Barossa* arrived in New South Wales on 8 December 1839. Benjamin Jacobs was issued with a ticket of leave in 1845.

Ship Indent 2/8243, p. 217, and 1839-1259-36; TL 45/1180; Governors' Despatches 1846, A1239.

JACOBS, Charles

b. Clerkenwell, London, 1803–1896
Phoenix (2), 1824; Convict; Sentenced to life, Old Bailey, 1820.
Single; Bookbinder; 12 children.

Charles Jacobs was transported for stealing two watch cases, valued at £3, from a boy. The prosecutor was Andrew Goswell. Jacobs had been in custody once before for breaking a window. His brother lived in White Lyon Street in Goodman's Fields. He was described as a Jew. 'I lived last with my Mother'. He was sentenced on 13 September 1820.

Charles Jacobs spent three years on a prison hulk before being sent to Australia. The *Phoenix* arrived in Van Diemen's Land on 21 July 1824 and Jacobs was assigned to a Mr Ruffey. The normal police dossier has no remarks on it because, evidently,

Jacobs was sent to New South Wales to be imprisoned at the Carter's Barracks, where the 1828 Census places him. Jacobs was returned to Van Diemen's Land and a ticket of leave was issued on 12 October 1832. Charles Jacobs received permission to marry Mary Ann Thyer, who had come free to the colony, on 16 March 1836. Jacobs lived at Pretty Plains as a farmer in Lymington. A conditional pardon was granted on 9 March 1837 (no. 1287) and a free pardon (no. 137) on 3 November 1842.

Charles and Mary Ann Jacobs had twelve children: Charles Edward, born 18 March 1838; John George, born 23 May 1839; Amelia Ann, born 12 August 1841; Thomas, born 11 February 1844; Elizabeth, born 4 April 1846; Mary Ann, born 26 February 1848; Samuel, born 28 November 1849; Henry, born 7 December 1851; James, born 19 June 1853; George, born 1 May 1855; Eliza, born 17 May 1857; and Frederick William, born 12 November 1858.

Charles Jacobs was buried in the Church of England section of the cemetery in Lymington in April 1896.

CON 31/23, no. 251; CON 52/1, p. 86; Family information from Elizabeth Law, Melbourne.

JACOBS, Charles

b. London, 1818–1886
1846; Free.
Single; Storekeeper; 11 children.

The son of Nathaniel Jacobs and Elizabeth (née Solomon) of London, according to family tradition Charles Jacobs was a ward in chancery who was to have inherited the land on which the London Hospital now stands, but proof of ownership was lost in a fire in a church. Jacobs arrived in South Australia on the brig *Emma* on 27 April 1846.

The first Jewish wedding in South Australia took place on 28 May 1846 when Charles Jacobs married the 17-year-old Elizabeth Joshua (q.v.) in the private house of her father, Michael Joshua (q.v.), in Hindley Street. The bride had arrived on board the *Dorset* from Sydney on 5 April 1846.

Their children were: Nathaniel, born 30 June 1847; Michael Charles, 19 May 1850; Elizabeth, 27 February 1851, at Gawler Town; Samuel Joshua, 28 March 1853; Moss, 22 July 1855 (who lived only a few months); John, 12 September 1858, at Kent Town; Alfred Edward, 18 December 1862; Sarah Adelaide, 21 February 1865; Edith Marion, 30 September 1866; Susan Alice, 23 November 1869; and Frederick William, 3 December 1871.

Jacobs gave £10 to the Sydney Synagogue in 1845. Jacobs commenced business as a general merchant in Gawler Town in 1846. His firm, Charles Jacobs and Sons, grew to be the largest importer of sugar into Australia and also dealt in tea and coffee.

Charles Jacobs died in Melbourne on 31 July 1886. Elizabeth died in Melbourne in 1905.

Pritchard Index; Family information.

JACOBS, Daniel

b. Canterbury
Prince Regent, 1839; Free.
Tailor.

Daniel Jacobs, a free immigrant, was admitted to the Liverpool Prisoners' Barracks on 2 August 1839 to serve a colonial prison sentence, and was sent to work on the Campbelltown Road Party. He was described as a 'Jew'.

Parramatta Gaol Book, August 1839, no. 1572, 4/6533.

JACOBS, David

1759–1802
Scarborough, 1788; Convict; Sentenced to 7 years, Old Bailey, 1784.
Fruitseller.

On 19 October 1784 Jacobs stole two livery coats, valued at £2, from the side of a coach at the bottom of Thames Street. On the day after his arrest Jacobs stood in the dock at the Old Bailey and defended himself with the statement: 'I sell lemons. I was never behind the carriage'.

Jacobs spent two years on the *Ceres* hulk and was sent to Portsmouth to be put on the *Scarborough* in February 1787. He therefore came to Australia on the First Fleet. He was sent from Port Jackson to Norfolk Island on the *Sirius* on 4 March 1790. He spent two years on Norfolk Island and was off the government stores by January 1792. He returned to Sydney on 9 March 1793 on the *Kitty* and was off the government rations by 24 October 1795. David Jacobs was buried on 5 July 1802 by St John's Church of England in Parramatta.

OBSP, 1784–85, case 1024, p. 1367; HO 10/6; Norfolk Island Victualling Book 1792–94. ML A1958; M. Gillen, *The Founders of Australia*, p. 190; Mutch Index.

JACOBS, David

b. London, 1773–1831
Dromedary, 1820; Convict; Sentenced to life, Kent Assizes, 1819.
Single; Butcher; Height: 165 cm.

Dark complexion, dark brown hair, grey eyes. Jacobs was sentenced at the Kent Assizes on 15 March 1819. His father kept a shop at Chatham. Despite or, perhaps, because of the surgeon's negative report, Jacobs became a member of a small experimental school established on board the convict transport ship. David Jacobs and Moses Cohen (q.v.) both attended the classes and Jacobs was reported to be 'very orderly and attentive'.

David Jacobs was an assigned convict servant between 1820 and 1825. He was reprimanded upon the complaint of his master, Mr T. Archer, on 6 October 1824 for insolence and disobedience of orders, and on 24 March 1825 for having been absent from the Muster and Divine Service on the previous Sunday. He was granted a ticket of leave on 13 September 1828. The *Hobart Town Gazette* reported, on 26 March 1831, quoting the newly published *Launceston Advertiser*, 'On Tuesday last—Jacobs residing at Mrs Hill's in Perth put a period to his existence by cutting his throat with a razor—he lost his money betting on a fight'.

Ship Indent 2/8241, p. 138; CON 21/33, no. 77; *Hobart Town Courier*, 13 September 1828; CSO 1/403/9098.

JACOBS, David

b. Whitechapel, 1802
Arab I (1), 1822; Convict; Sentenced to life, Berks Assizes, 1822.
Single; Porter; Height: 163 cm.

Brown hair, blue eyes, pock-pitted. 'A Jew'. David Jacobs was sentenced at the Berks Assizes on 4 March 1822, and transported for privately stealing. His behaviour on board ship was 'Bad'.

David Jacobs arrived in Van Diemen's Land on 6 November 1822. On 14 April 1823 Jacobs was working at the government stores when he was convicted of 'stealing four pounds weight of meat the property of His Majesty'. The magistrate, Rev. Knopwood, sentenced him to fifty lashes. Two years later Jacobs escaped from Van Diemen's Land. The *Hobart Town Gazette* listed him as absent from his usual place of residence on 25 February 1825 and a reward of £2 was posted by the police. His dossier ends with the word 'RUN' and he was officially struck off the colonial lists in December 1853.

CON 3/23, no. 199; CON 34/1; 4/4008 Indent; 4/1753, p. 198f.; *Hobart Town Gazette*, 6 May 1825.

JACOBS, David (Levy)

b. Dockstead, London, 1824
Hindostan (3), 1841; Convict; Sentenced to 10 years, Central Criminal Court, 1840.
Single; Labourer; Height: 155 cm.

Rather dark complexion, dark brown hair, blue eyes, oval face with a large scar on his left cheek and smaller scars on his forehead and other cheek. Jacobs was convicted for picking pockets and stealing a purse containing three sovereigns. He had previously been in gaol for stealing oranges. He was aged sixteen at the time of his trial. He could read but not write.

David Jacobs arrived in Hobart Town on 19 January 1841. His initial period of probation was to last two years, and was extended by five months for three separate offences. During this time he was reported as 'idle, dirty and indifferent and insolent', and received forty-five lashes for absence from work. His term of probation expired on 9 September 1843.

In the following six years he appeared before the courts twenty-one times—in Perth (1844), Oatlands (1845), Launceston (1847), Port Arthur (1848) and St Peter's Pass (1848–49). One notable charge of 'misconduct' was for 'not treating the Lieutenant Governor with proper respect', for which his existing term of imprisonment and hard labour was extended by three months. He received his certificate of freedom on 16 May 1850.

CON 33/4; CON 32/2.

JACOBS, Edward

b. London, 1808
Captain Cook (2), 1833; Convict; Sentenced to 7 years, Middlesex, 1833.
Single; Dealer; Height: 163 cm.

Sallow complexion, dark brown hair, hazel eyes. Large featured nose—lost nearly all front teeth in upper jaw. Can read and write. A Jew. Edward Jacobs had one previous conviction with a six-month sentence. However, the police told the court that he was a habitual criminal, 'a dreadful character', who attempted to steal a barrel from a cart in Whitechapel. He was arrested in Petticoat Lane.

Edward Jacobs arrived in Sydney on 26 August 1833. He was listed in the Parramatta Gaol Entrance Book of 1835–36 as a 'jeweller'. On 2 March 1836 he was sent to Penrith for sentencing. A certificate of freedom was issued on 17 January 1840. Jacobs married Sarah Pain at Scots Church in Sydney in 1840.

OBSP, 1832–33, case 307, p. 146; Printed Indent *Captain Cook* (2), p. 101; Parramatta Gaol Entrance Book, 1835–36, no. 266, 4/6531; CF 45/0158.

JACOBS, Elias

b. London, 1813
Moffatt (2), 1836; Convict; Sentenced to 7 years, Central Criminal Court, 1835.
Furrier's clerk; Height: 161 cm.

Dark ruddy complexion, dark brown hair, hazel eyes. Nearly bald on top of head. A scar in the centre of his forehead. Jacobs was working for his aunt's husband, George Simons, a furrier in Commercial Road. He had forged an order for a hat in the name of his uncle. He was sentenced at the Old Bailey on 26 October 1835. He was listed as a Jew in the Hyde Park Barracks.

The convict transport ship arrived in Sydney Harbour on 31 August 1836. Elias Jacobs received a ticket of leave in June 1840 for the District of Berrima, and a certificate of freedom on 3 February 1845. On 20 January 1842 Elias Jacobs, aged twenty-nine, with a ticket of leave, married Harriet Bryant, twenty, who had arrived free. The ceremony was performed by the Rev. George Vidal of Sutton Forest.

OBSP, 1835–36, case 2203, p. 1026; Printed Indent *Moffatt* (2), p. 99; Permission to Marry Book 1842, p. 275, 4/4513; TL 40/2101; CF 45/0162, in 4/4355.

JACOBS, Ephraim

d. 1837
Free.
Married; 1 child.

Ephraim Jacobs died on 29 July 1837 and was buried in the Devonshire Street Jewish Cemetery (tombstone was removed to the Pioneers Cemetery at Botany in 1901). On 29 March 1843 Ephraim Jacobs' son died and was buried by the synagogue.

JACOBS, Fred (Frederick)

Convict.

Fred Jacobs advertised in the *Sydney Gazette* that any claims should be presented as he was leaving New South Wales on 29 April 1804.

JACOBS, Harriet

Free.
Single; 4 children.

Harriet Jacobs married Joseph Davis (q.v.) in a Jewish ceremony in Sydney in 1849. Her children were John and Max (1850), David (1852) and Samuel (1853).

JACOBS, Hart

Free.

Hart Jacobs was listed as the donor of £1 to the Launceston Synagogue building appeal.

Launceston Examiner, 29 June 1844.

JACOBS, Henry

Free.
Single; Dealer.

The Hobart Town Synagogue Minute Book of 11 April 1843 recorded that Henry Jacobs gave £1 for the building fund. In 1844 his contribution was ten shillings and sixpence. Jacobs was given bail following a magistrate's hearing on a charge of robbing Nathan, Moses & Co. He absconded from bail and stowed away on board an American whaler. He was brought back from the Isle de France on the *Dawson* because it was suspected that he was an escaped convict (for whom a reward would be paid).

CON 31/23, no. 6; MM 33/2; MM 33/5; CON 18/10; CSO 6/26/587; *Hobart Town Courier*, 27 January 1844.

JACOBS, Hyam

b. Whitechapel, 1809
Manlius (1), 1828; Convict; Sentenced to 7 years, Old Bailey, 1828.
Single; Hawker; Height: 170 cm.

Pale complexion, flaxen whiskers, brown eyes, oval head, tattooed P. L. under right arm. S. J. C. inside left arm. Jacobs was sentenced to transportation for stealing a cheese. He had been in custody before. His mother and brother lived in St Martins Court, Essex Street, Whitechapel. His older brother looked after his mother, Rosa Jacobs. Hyam had been hawking curry combs prior to his arrest. His behaviour on board the transport was 'orderly'.

Jacobs arrived in Van Diemen's Land on 9 November 1828. On 26 February 1829 Jacobs received twenty-five lashes, while assigned to Mr D. Gray, for neglect of duty and falsely stating to the police that his master had already whipped him. On 5 December 1833 he received a further twenty-five lashes for neglect of work while employed by the Public Works Department as a sawyer. His record appears both in the Hobart Town and Launceston police books.

'Mr Hyam Jacobs' moved to Sydney and gave £5 to the Sydney Synagogue building appeal in September 1839 and another £5 in 1845. In 1842 he married Mary A. Furlong at Scots Church in Sydney. Jacobs evidently remembered his friends in Hobart Town and in 1843 is recorded as having sent £1 to the Hobart Synagogue's building appeal.

CON 18/15, no. 383; CON 78/2, p. 190; CON 31/23.

JACOBS, Isaac

b. 1779
Bengal Merchant (3), 1836; Convict; Sentenced to 7 years, Surrey Assizes, 1836.

Isaac Jacobs was sentenced with John Jacobs (q.v.) on 28 March 1836.

Isaac Jacobs received a ticket of leave dated 5 March 1841 for the District of Parramatta. A conditional pardon was extended on 7 March 1842 and a certificate of freedom issued on 8 August 1843. Isaac Jacobs married Margaret Campbell in 1848.

Ship Indent 2/8224, p. 50; Register 4/4148; TL 41/484; CF 43/1265, 4/4384.

JACOBS, Isaac

b. London
Alexander, 1835; Free.
Merchant.

Isaac Jacobs came from London to Sydney travelling cabin class, arriving on 30 August 1835.

Ship Indent 4/5209.

JACOBS, Isaac

John Renwick, 1837; Free.
Married; Trader; 2 children.

Isaac and Elizabeth Jacobs arrived in South Australia on 10 February 1837 and were among the earliest Jewish settlers in that colony. Jacobs appeared on the list of jurors in the province in 1839. In the census of the colony of South Australia in 1841, Isaac and Elizabeth Jacobs were both listed as being under the age of thirty-five, and their two children, Henry and Isaac, as under the age of seven. At the time they lived in 'B. District', and were therefore out of Adelaide itself.

Pritchard Index; Wilfred Oldham, *The Land Policy of South Australia.*

JACOBS, Isaac

b. London, 1810
Marquis of Hastings (3), 1828; Convict; Sentenced to 7 years, Old Bailey, 1827.
Single; Pencil-maker, clothes scourer and tailors' boy; Height: 155 cm.

Ruddy freckled complexion, dark brown hair, brown eyes. Small scar between eyes. Could read and write. Jew. Jacobs was in Whitechapel at 9:30 at night and ran past a woman, stealing a handkerchief from her open basket. He was immediately caught. The handkerchief was valued at two shillings. He was sentenced on 4 April 1827. He had one prior conviction.

Isaac Jacobs arrived in New South Wales on 12 October 1828 and was originally assigned to Mr David Smith in Sydney. He was listed on the 1828 Census as a prisoner at the Hyde Park Barracks, his religion given as 'Jew'. He was assigned to George Bowman of Richmond.

OBSP, 1826–27, case 1251, p. 479; Ship Indent 4/4013, p. 134.

JACOBS, Isaac (JACOB)

b. Lynn, 1815
Atlas (4), 1833; Convict; Sentenced to 7 years, Derby Quarter Sessions, 1832.
Single; Watchmaker; Height: 162.5 cm.

Dark complexion, brown eyes, large full lips, medium size nose. A Jew. Isaac Jacobs was a pickpocket who was transported for stealing two watches. He had previously served a sentence of three years. The surgeon's report was: 'Behaved well'.

Isaac Jacobs arrived in Hobart Town on 24 August 1833 and worked in government work parties in the District of Launceston for the first two years of his time of probation. In 1836 he was assigned to Mr Reid. On 12 August 1836 he was put in the stocks for four hours for having been found in a public house. The next day he was sentenced to three months hard labour with the Reiby's Ford Road Party for neglect of work and then, because of continued 'misbehaviour', was sent on to the Launceston Chain Gang. In October 1836 he was put in irons for a month because he had 'feigned illness' while a patient at the Colonial Hospital.

In March 1839 Jacobs possessed a ticket of leave when he was put in the cells on bread and water for fourteen days for 'misconduct'. A subsequent charge of misconduct brought about the suspension of his ticket of leave in order 'to work on the roads on probation for six months. If well behaved to be allowed to return to the Campbell Town District'.

He received a certificate of freedom (no. 101) on 2 November 1839 and was licensed as a hawker on 13 March 1840. On 20 August 1841 the *Hobart Town Courier* reported that Isaac Jacob, formerly of Campbell Town, now Hobart Town, a licensed hawker, was insolvent. On 13 July 1842 Jacobs was fined £5 for having assaulted Mr L. H. Solomon (q.v.). On 3 December 1842 Jacobs placed a notice in the *Launceston Advertiser*: 'If Lewis Cohen, tailor, does not fetch away his boxes and pay the amount due for board and lodgings, they will be sold'. Jacobs was on the brink of financial disaster. His name appeared on the petition for the establishment of the synagogue in Launceston (he signed the petition 'Isaac Jacob').

On 19 September 1843 Elizabeth Jacobs, 'a young woman', petitioned for the release of her husband from custody. She was in Perth and her husband was insolvent. She had 'a tender infant now at the breast and asks for her husband's release'. The report from the Commissioner of Insolvents was unfavourable. Jacobs had obtained goods fraudulently with no intention of paying for them. In 1842 he had moved his business from Launceston to Lincoln. That year he had exported £50 worth of apples and claimed not to have been paid for them by the man who took them to Sydney. In August 1843 Jacobs was placed in gaol and in January 1844 Jacobs appealed for mercy as he had eight more months to serve. He received a stern reply: 'The Government will not have mercy'. Isaac Jacobs pledged ten shillings to the Hobart Town Synagogue in 1845 but failed to pay. In 1851 he pledged seven shillings and again did not fulfil his pledge.

CON 31/24, no. 87; Launceston Police Book, CON 78/2, p. 181; CSO 22/24/1300, petition dated 19 September 1843; CSO 22/99/2082; CO 280/157; CON 18/3; *Hobart Town Courier*, 13 March 1840, 20 August 1841, 10 April 1844, 29 June 1844.

JACOBS, Jacob

Convict.

In L. M. Goldman's *The Jews of Victoria in the Nineteenth Century* (p. 52), there is an anecdote about an otherwise unknown Jacob Jacobs, who escaped from the Melbourne Gaol: 'Jacobs is supposed to be a prisoner of the Crown, escaped from Van Diemen's Land and the fellow who some time ago arrived in one of our colonial traders packed up in a box labelled "Glass—With Care, Keep this side up"'.

JACOBS, Jacob (John) Lewis (Wizard JACOBS)

b. Canterbury, 1813–1897
Free. Single;
Wizard, dancing teacher.

There were two 'Wizard Jacobs', both pursuing stage careers and both approximately the same age: Jacob 'John' Lewis Jacobs, and an English actor, Joseph Jacob.

The latter 'Wizard' appeared on stage in London in 1835, in Brighton in 1839, and at the Strand Theatre, London, in 1841.

Jacob 'John' Lewis Jacobs started his Australian career in March 1834, with performances of *Blackeyed Susan* and *The Cabin Boy*. He then appeared at the Hobart Town Theatre as 'a variety of the most admired Ancient Statues as performed by Mr Ducknow, with unended applause, at all London theatres'. Jacobs staged some of Launceston's earliest theatrical evenings. He called himself 'Professor' and was usually known as 'John'. He boasted that he came from the stage in London and Liverpool. On 13 June 1839 he was engaged by John Lazar to appear at Sydney's Royal Theatre, and worked there for two years. On 13 June 1839 a 'benefit' evening was staged at the Royal Victoria Theatre in which Joseph Simmons (q.v.) also acted. Wizard Jacobs was soon on tour combining feats of memory, dancing, singing and appearing in Jewish character sketches. He frequently appeared in Melbourne on the stage at the Pavilion and the Queen's Theatre Royal with Michael Cashmore (q.v.) and John Davies (q.v.). At the Queen's Theatre Royal on 21 April 1845 John Lewis Jacobs took part in yet another 'spectacular benefit' to farewell the emancipist actor John Davies on his way to Van Diemen's Land. 'Jacobs. J' is recorded as returning to Launceston on 20 December 1841 on the *Corsair*, and his signature appeared on the petition to establish a synagogue in Launceston in May 1843.

In 1848 Jacob 'John' Lewis Jacobs became manager of Adelaide's Royal Victoria Theatre and a dancing teacher. On 20 November 1850, as a result of professional jealousy, Jacobs took John Lazar to court on a charge of lewdness. Fortunately for the accused, Lazar was able to prove that he was not on stage on the night of the alleged offence and Jacobs hurriedly left Australia to continue his career in New Zealand, England and America before he could be charged with perjury.

In 1854 Jacobs, 'improvisator and ventriloquist', was back in Sydney and in January 1855 had been engaged by Mr Coppin for the Royal Victoria Theatre 'after he had performed his tricks for some weeks at the Royal Hotel'. Jacobs was in Melbourne in the 1860s and in June 1865 performed at the Royal Victoria Theatre in Sydney. *Bell's Life in Australia* wrote that, 'After an absence of seven years, Wizard Jacobs was back and we enjoyed the society of the Great Magician who has added to his former catalogue of delusions others of more modern inventions and still more wondrous amazing the public again as a ventriloquist with his puppet and as improvisator, extemporising a song on any subject'.

John Lewis Jacobs died in Melbourne at the age of eighty-four, a well-respected and pious member of the Jewish community. His gravestone records he was 'a brother of David Jacobs, Ranelagh St, Liverpool, and Solomon Jacobs, Gray's Inn Road London, left England for Port Philip 1834'.

Hobart Town Courier, 1 March 1834; *Launceston Advertiser*, 23 December 1841; Petition, CO 280/157; *South Australian Gazette and Colonial Register*, 5 January, 8 January 1848, 20 November 1850; *Sydney Morning Herald*, 1 January 1855, 3 April 1855, 24 June 1858; Alfred Rubens, 'Jews and the English Stage 1667–1850', *JJSE*, vol. 24 (1975).

JACOBS, James

b. London
Phoenix (2), 1824; Convict; Sentenced to life, Old Bailey, 1823.
Married; Fruit hawker; 2 children (in England).

James Jacobs was sentenced on 31 July 1823. His gaol report read: 'Bad, in custody before and connected with a notorious character in passing altered Bank Notes'. He had been previously sentenced to death for 'cutting dead wood'. He was transported for 'uttering a forged £10 note and two counterfeit sovereigns'. At the time of his trial he lived at John Street on the Old Kent Road. His wife's name was Sarah. He had a daughter aged twenty and a son aged sixteen.

On 13 October 1828, while assigned to Mr Shookbridge, James Jacobs was sentenced to the treadmill for seven days for using abusive language to his master. Three years later he was tried for insubordination but, as this was only the second charge in his six years with this master, he was merely 'severely reprimanded'.

CON 31/23, no. 253.

JACOBS, John

b. London, 1766
Scarborough, 1788; Convict; Sentenced to 7 years, Old Bailey, 1784.
Single.

Jacobs was probably Jewish. He was charged with highway robbery on the passage from Kensington to the Gravel Pits, London. In the pursuit down Park Lane, Jacobs ran from a police patrol, dropping a pistol as he ran. Jacobs and his two companions were caught and searched and a stolen watch was found. He claimed that he had found two pistols and the watch and a handkerchief the day before. At the Old Bailey Jacobs was sentenced on 10 December 1784. All three were sentenced to death and Jacobs' sentence was later reduced to transportation for seven years. He was housed on the Censor hulk until despatched.

Jacobs arrived with the First Fleet. On 13 June 1791 he appeared as a witness in a trial. He left the colony on the *Kitty* in June 1793 and was reported as an ex-convict and a seaman on board the ship when it called at Cork on its way home. Mollie Gillen suggests he may have returned to Australia on the brig *Reliance*, which arrived in Sydney in September 1796. A John Jacobs was in the crew when the ship sailed to Norfolk Island on 20 June 1798 and discharged at Port Jackson on 27 July 1798.

M. Gillen, *The Founders of Australia*, p. 190.

JACOBS, John

b. London, 1790
Agamemnon, 1820; Convict; Sentenced to 7 years, Old Bailey, 1820.
Married; Tobacco manufacturer; Height: 161 cm; 2 children.

Dark ruddy pock-pitted complexion, black to grey hair, light brown eyes. Could read. John Jacobs stole a harness from a warehouse. 'I was greatly distressed,' he said. He was sentenced on 14 January 1820. He was twice transported—the second time on the Adrian.

On 22 September 1820, the day the convict ship *Agamemnon* berthed in Port Jackson, James Hall, the Surgeon Superintendent on board the ship, proudly wrote to the Colonial Secretary: 'I beg leave to report to your Excellency that John Jacobs a Jew convict has embraced the Christian faith and on Sunday, August 20th at Divine service he publicly rehearsed the Belief, and is now desirous of being Baptised'.

Jacobs was sent to Parramatta and was on the 1825 General Muster List in government employment, working as a cooper in Parramatta. A ticket of leave was granted on 3 March 1827 and a certificate of freedom was issued on 17 February 1828.

Jacobs then returned to England on the *Coronal*, only to be transported again, after being sentenced for burglary to another seven years transportation on 18 February 1830 at the Old Bailey. He returned on the *Adrian*, which arrived on 20 August 1830. He was listed as 'Jewish', aged fifty, with two male children. He described himself as a cook. The trial at the Old Bailey described the adventures of a professional thief. He was seen during daytime to walk into a house, gather up a bundle of goods, and walk out. He was chased but escaped. Three weeks afterwards a constable, who had watched him go into five houses, identified him and arrested him.

Jacob's wife, Rachel, followed him to Australia on the *Prince Regent*, arriving in Sydney on 20 June 1830. In 1832 Jacobs was assigned to Michael Phillips (q.v.). He received his second certificate of freedom on 15 February 1837. The 1842 Sydney City Council listed him with a 'dwelling' in Elizabeth Street. On 10 January 1843 Jacobs placed an advertisement in the *Sydney Morning Herald* stating that his wife had left him 'in a manner which completely absolves him from her support'.

On 10 July 1844 Mr and Mrs John Jacobs (despite his previous baptism) applied to the Sydney Synagogue for a divorce. He wrote: 'We have been apart seven years. We shall never again be united'. He promised the synagogue that he would 'defray all expense'. Jacobs gave £15 to the Sydney Synagogue building appeal in 1845.

The *Sydney Morning Herald* of 30 December 1845 announced that a John Jacobs had sailed for London on 29 December. His wife, Rachel Jacobs, then promptly advertised that she had not accompanied her husband.

OBSP, 1819–20, case 361, p. 159; *OBSP*, 1829–30, case 615, p. 265; Ship Indent 4/4007, p. 214; Register of Prisoners, 4/6572, p. 137; CS Correspondence 4/1747, pp. 158–9; *Sydney Gazette*, 3 March 1827; AO Reel 398, 30, 1328/77; Sydney Synagogue Correspondence, 10 July 1844; Bridge Street Letter Book, 5 August 1844; CF 4/4337, and 4/4424.

JACOBS, John (JACOB)

b. London, 1791
Sir William Bensley, 1817; Convict; Sentenced to 7 years, Old Bailey, 1816.
Watchmaker; Height: 165 cm.

Sallow complexion, black hair, hazel eyes. Jacobs was convicted in January 1816 for being part of a confidence trick in which sailors were duped into paying money or trading their watches for an almost valueless replacement.

John Jacobs arrived in Sydney in March 1817 and was sent to Parramatta. The 1818 General Muster listed him as being in the 'Government Employ'. On 5 March 1819 he was despatched to Van Diemen's Land on the *Prince Leopold*. On 4 September Jacobs was sent on to join a chain gang and given fifty lashes for receiving stolen watches. On 13 December he received a further fifty lashes for helping a destitute ex-convict sleep inside the gaol. His final punishment as a prisoner occurred when, as a member of a gaol work detail, he was sentenced to twenty-five lashes for 'neglect of duty'.

A certificate of freedom was granted on 22 February 1823. In June 1824 he was brought before the Bench in Launceston on suspicion of felony. There was insufficient proof of this charge but he was fined £15 for retailing spirits without a licence. On 7 July 1824 he was bound over to keep the peace for keeping a disorderly house. On 20 September 1826 he was reprimanded for having been absent from muster and church on the previous Sunday. A ticket of leave was granted on 24 April 1830. On 16 June 1830, while holding a ticket of leave, he was arrested for being on board the schooner *Active* but, as he had no intention to escape, he was 'only admonished'. On 8 February 1827 he was fined for harbouring six convicts on his premises. He was ordered to pay £10 for each convict so harboured. Nine days later a charge of retailing wine and brandy without a licence was dismissed.

OBSP, 1816–17, case 193, p. 56; Ship Indent 4/4005, p. 288; CON 31/24, no. 57; HO 10/1; HO 11/2; *Hobart Town Gazette*, 22 February 1823; Launceston Police Book, 78/2, p. 177; Governors' Despatches, ML, A1206, p. 350, ML, A1210, p. 218.

JACOBS, John

b. Whitechapel, d. 1868
Lord Hungerford, 1821; Convict; Sentenced to life, Old Bailey, 1821.
Single.

John Jacobs was transported for stealing a gold watch and chain from a merchant who lived in Duke Street, Aldgate. Jacobs had four other men protecting him. Jacob's defence 'I was returning home, saw a mob collected and crossed over—a gentleman laid hold of me'. Jacobs had been sentenced before in 1810 and received seven years on board the hulks Retribution and Justitia. His gaol report read 'Bad character has been transported before'. His father lived in Whitechapel and he had a brother who was a tailor and who supported his father.

John Jacobs arrived in Van Diemen's Land on 26 December 1821, and by 1822 had been sent to Macquarie Harbour on the West Coast of the island. On 30 October 1822 he was found to be absent from work without leave and sentenced to fifty lashes. Punishment followed punishment. Twenty-five lashes were decreed on 23 April 23 for 'not assisting to apprehend 7 persons in act of absconding' and a further twenty-five lashes on 1 July 1823 for being absent without leave. On 4 February 1824 he was again absent from work and sentenced to twenty-five lashes. Only ten were inflicted before the surgeon intervened and stopped the punishment. His final punishment at Port Macquarie was on 9 August 1832 when he was sentenced to thirty-five lashes and to work in irons 'at the pleasure of the commandant'. Jacobs received a conditional pardon (no. 681) on 24 February 1835.

On 4 November 1867 he was admitted to the Cascades Depot in Hobart as a pauper and died on 19 December 1868.

OBSP, 6 June 1821, case 708. CON 31/23, no 161; 4/4009.28; *Hobart Town Courier*, 24 April 1830.

JACOBS, John

Andromeda (2), 1840; Convict; Sentenced to 7 years, Old Bailey 1832.

John Jacob(s) had married Rachel Lee at London's Great Synagogue on 26 January 1831. One year later Jacobs, aged twenty-seven, was tried at the Old Bailey for stealing some clothes from John Cox. Jacobs had been invited by Cox into his house to buy 'old articles of clothing'. After some bargaining it was agreed that Jacobs would pay £5. Jacobs then offered Cox an obviously forged banknote for £10 and then failed to entice the seller he paid him five half crown coins as a deposit while he went to a nearby public house to get change. As he left the house the wife of Cox called out 'the Jew has taken the clothes'. Jacobs was arrested at the Public Clothes Market attempting to dispose of the loot.

The trial was dramatic. Mr Cox failed to appear even though it was known that he was in the vicinity of the court. When he was found he confessed that he had been paid £5 not to appear to give evidence. Cox apologised to the judge and Jacobs was sentenced to transportation for seven years. An appeal against the sentence was made on the grounds of his 'unimpeachable character and also having a wife and child and aged mother.'

John Jacob(s) arrived in Sydney on 27 August 1840. He received his Certificate of Freedom in 1848 and returned to the United Kingdom. He formally divorced his wife in a religious ceremony in London that same year.

The Times, 22 September 1832; Jeremy I. Pfeffer, *From One End of the Earth to the Other,* Sussex Academic Press (2008), p. 202f.

JACOBS, John

1804–1859
Lucy Davidson, 1829; Free.
Married; Watchmaker and jeweller.

John Jacobs 'of Parramatta' obtained an assigned convict servant in 1833. On 29 July 1835 John Jacobs and his wife Rebecca Julia Jacobs applied to adopt 'a little boy and girl, brother and sister'. Jacobs was a watchmaker and jeweller and he and his wife lived in George Street, Parramatta, and had 'ample means'. John Jacobs submitted a 'Humble Memorial' to the Female Orphan School. He

> 'respectfully sheweth that Memorialist is Married, and not having any family is desirous of having a female about 4 or 5 years of age, placed under him and his wife's care, as an apprentice or in any way conformable to the Rules and regulations of Your Excellency's most valuable Establishment, The Female Orphan School. Your memorialist would prefer an orphan; as in the event of his and his Wife's decease that the child may be put under protection and may enjoy what property your Memorialist may have at his death'.

It was noted that the Jacobs had previously 'obtained an orphan from the Female Factory with the intention of adopting him but that premature death thwarted Memorialist laudable intention'. The child to be adopted was Adelaide Cook, whose brother was Alfred Cook and whose mother had died on board the *Lucy Davidson* during the voyage out to Australia.

By 1845, John Jacobs was a member of the Sydney Synagogue and was living in Lower George Street in Sydney and working as a hardware merchant. Jacobs became a generous supporter of the Sydney Synagogue. In 1839 'Mr John Jacobs and daughter' gave £30 to the York Street Synagogue. He was listed as insolvent on 22 April 1842 but had recovered financially two years later, advertising glass for sale, snuff despatched, pitch tar for sale and paint oils available.

In 1845, together with his (non-Jewish) 'friends', he gave the Sydney Synagogue eight guineas. He was the owner of the Hope Tavern on the west side of York Street. In 1847, Samuel, the four-year-old son of John Jacobs, was buried in the Devonshire Street Jewish Cemetery. John Jacobs died 22 September 1859 and his grave was subsequently moved to Raphael's Ground in 1901.

Governors' Despatches 1835, A1214, p. 710; Female Orphan School Papers 4/2289-5/2941; 4/2283.5, 35/5402; *Sydney Morning Herald*, 22 April 1842, 29 April 1844, 24 October 1844, 4 January 1845, 1 May 1845, 30 December 1845.

JACOBS, John

b. London, 1804–1885, arrived 1837; Free.
Widower; Dealer and publican; 10 children.

John Jacobs was the son of Rebecca and Samuel Jacobs. He married twice, the first time in London. The second marriage took place in Sydney to Sarah Myers (q.v.).

He owned a house in Elizabeth Street, Sydney, in 1842. On 4 October 1845 it was noted in the *Shipping Gazette* that he had exported 312 hides to London. He managed a small business in Elizabeth Street and later in Redfern. Jacobs was an active member of the York Street Synagogue. He became the licensee of the Post Office Hotel 1863 to 1874 after which he opened a business in Elizabeth Street and later in Redfern.

John and Sarah had ten children. The second child, Joseph Jacobs, became an internationally famed Jewish scholar and historian and edited the monumental *Jewish Encyclopaedia* (Chicago, 1901).

In 1863 John Jacobs was licensee of the Post Office Hotel in York Street and remained there until 1874. He died on 7 February 1885, aged eighty-one. Sarah 'his beloved wife' died 16 May 1865 at the age of forty-five. Her grave is at Rookwood.

JACOBS, John

b. Moorfields, 1805
Enchantress, 1833; Convict; Sentenced to 7 years, Old Bailey, 1832.
Married; Old clothes man.

Dark brown hair, long face, hazel eyes, aquiline nose. A Jew. John Jacobs was arrested after stealing a wardrobe of second-hand clothes. He offered the vendor a £10 note which was rejected: 'I suspected it was not a good one from a man of his appearance'. Jacobs made off with the clothes while his victim searched for some change, and was arrested in a nearby gateway with the stolen clothes already spread out for sale on the ground. Jacobs had a wife, Rachael, at Houndsditch, and a child. His behaviour on board the hulk in England was 'orderly'.

On 3 September 1833 John Jacobs was accused of stealing stones while with the Public Works Department. He was sentenced to two months and hard labour in the Launceston Chain Gang.

John Jacobs of Launceston, 'labourer', joined Henry Davis (q.v.) in supporting the donation of a block of land for a Jewish cemetery.

In the absence of further punishments the Lieutenant Governor allowed a remission of his sentence of transportation in March 1839 and on 4 October 1839 the *Hobart Town Courier* announced that he might apply for a Certificate of Freedom. In April 1844 the Hobart Town Hebrew Congregation recorded that he had made a pledge of one shilling in April 1844. He failed to pay the pledge. He had moved to Sydney.

John Jacobs was convicted at the Sydney Quarter Sessions on 11 August 1852 and sentenced to one year on the road gang. He was discharged from custody on 5 May 1853 with the locale listed as Moreton Bay.

OBSP, 1832, case 2284, p. 937; CON 31/24, no. 73, p. 89; Convict Description Book, CON 18/6.

JACOBS, John

Bengal Merchant (3), 1836; Convict; Sentenced to 7 years, Surrey Assizes, 1836.

John Jacobs and Isaac Jacobs (q.v.) were sentenced together at the Surrey Assizes on 28 March 1836.

John Jacobs received his ticket of leave in 1841 and a certificate of freedom on 25 February 1846.

TL 41/94; CF 46/0227, in 4/4403.

JACOBS, John

b. Aldgate, 1814–1859

Lord William Bentinck (2), 1838; Convict; Sentenced to 7 years, Central Criminal Court, 1837.

Single; Labourer and hawker; Height: 168 cm; 1 child.

Sallow complexion, black hair, long face, brown eyes, long nose and wide mouth. John Jacobs and Thomas Jones diverted the attention of a carter delivering laundry at night in Whitechapel and stole a bundle of clothes. There was a fight and Jacobs was seized by the carter. Jones tried to rescue Jacobs but both were arrested. Jacobs was sentenced on 14 August 1837. His father was a carcass butcher and his mother's name was Catherine.

Jacobs arrived in Hobart Town on 26 August 1838. After having served his initial period of servitude to Mr Thomas Gee of Launceston, Jacobs received a ticket of leave on 4 May 1843. He had been working as a hawker. According to the *Hobart Town Courier* of 17 November 1843 his licence as a hawker and carrier expired that month.

In Hobart Town on 31 May 1844 Jacobs was sentenced, at the Hobart Quarter Sessions, to fourteen years colonial transportation for receiving twelve stolen handkerchiefs, the property of Mr Louis Nathan (q.v.). He was sent to Port Arthur.

On 22 March 1848 his 'meritorious conduct in extinguishing a fire at Port Arthur' was recorded. As a consequence he was transferred to the Prisoners' Barracks in Hobart and in August 1850 was permitted to work for Mr Levi of Murray Street. In December 1850 he was assigned to the service of Mr Nathan Solomon. A ticket of leave was granted on 20 May 1851 (following a number of applications). His application for a conditional pardon was refused in March 1852 and finally approved on 24 May 1853.

John Jacobs, 'a dealer', married Julia Lyons in Launceston on 4 August 1852. Julia had come free to the colony and acquired the Jewish name 'Rebecca' before her marriage, which was the eighth Jewish wedding ceremony to be held in Launceston.

John and Julia Jacobs went to Sydney where their only child Abraham was born on 25 November 1853 in George Street, and circumcised a year later at the York Street Synagogue, on 3 Dececember 1854. Rebecca Julia Jacobs died on 26 October 1858, aged 40. Jacobs married Hannah Menser on 5 July 1859 and he died on 22 September 1859.

OBSP, 1837, no. 1860, p. 485; CON 31/25; CON 18/14; CON 34/8; VDL papers, MLA 1059-9, p. 341: CSO 19/7; CON 52/3, p. 245; CON 52/5; *Hobart Town Courier*, 12 May 1843, 17 November 1843.

JACOBS, Joseph

Andromeda, 1827; Convict; Sentenced to life, Old Bailey, 1826.
Single; Hawker.

Joseph Jacobs had been 'convicted before and imprisoned as a vagrant, once imprisoned for eight months for hawking without a licence'. Jacobs stole a purse containing one six penny piece and a few pennies and half pennies from a twelve year old boy who was redeeming a spencer from a pawn shop in Shoreditch. He was sentenced on 17 July 1826. He was nineteen years old.

The *Andromeda* arrived in Van Diemen's Land on 23 February 1827. From his arrival until April 1829 Jacobs worked in the chain gang at St Peter's Pass. On 15 July 1827 he was accused of 'disobedience and abusive language'. On 27 January 1828 he was charged by the overseer with insolence and was reprimanded. On 5 June he was sentenced to two months in the chain gang for disobedience of orders and gross neglect of duty. On 17 November he disobeyed the overseer's orders and returned to his hut instead of going to church and was given fourteen days in the chain gang. On 31 January 1829 he was sentenced to one month in the chain gang at St Peter's Pass 'for repeatedly throwing away the stones that he was ordered to break in order to save himself the trouble of breaking them'. On 24 April he threw away a hammer, 'the property of the Crown', and behaved insolently to the overseer, and another month was added to his existing sentence.

On 26 October he was accused of robbing John Mundy of £2 17s. The charge was dismissed. By 10 November he had left the chain gang and was working as an assigned servant for Dr Desailley. He was given fifty lashes for repeated disobedience of orders, insolence and general bad conduct. Several counts of bad conduct followed but, on 2 November 1830, he was accused of being repeatedly absent from his master's house on Sundays and given fifty lashes. On 3 January 1831, having been absent from his master's house on New Year's Day and the day after without leave, he was sentenced to ten days on the treadmill. On 13 February Dr Desailley complained that Jacobs had been absent one night and accordingly he received twenty-five lashes.

On 2 September 1836 notice of a ticket of leave was published. On 17 August 1837 he was sentenced to the treadmill for four days for being out after hours. A conditional pardon (no. 2244) was issued on 31 December 1839 and extended to the Australian colonies on 15 July 1845. On 12 September 1848 the *Port Phillip Herald* reported that Joseph Jacobs had been charged with larceny in Geelong and was to stand trial. He was convicted of stealing from a person on 14 September 1848 and sentenced to prison and hard labour for twelve months.

CON 31/24, no. 316; OBSP 16 February 1826, case 365. *Hobart Town Courier*, 2 September 1836, 20 July 1841.

JACOBS, Joseph

b. Whitechapel, d. 1838
Earl St Vincent (4), 1826; Convict; Sentenced to 7 years, Old Bailey, 1825.
Single.

Joseph Jacobs was transported for stealing one shilling and two pence from a boy. He had been before a magistrate once before. He lived at 10 Commercial Road in the East End. A Jew. His conduct on board both the hulk and the transport ship was 'good'. He was convicted on 27 October 1825. His brother Abraham Jacobs (q.v.) was transported in 1824.

Jacobs arrived on 13 August 1826. By January 1837 he held a ticket of leave and during this year was reprimanded twice: once, on 30 October, for being in a public house, and again, for 'disorderly conduct in striking a woman in a public street'. Joseph Jacobs died at the Hobart Town Hospital on 2 March 1838.

CON 31/23, convict no. 39440; MM 33/1; MM 33/5.

JACOBS, Joseph

b. London, 1814
Asia I (7), 1833; Convict; Sentenced to life, Middlesex, 1832.

On 10 February 1832 a man in charge of a coal barge was waylaid by Joseph Jacobs, who offered to guide him to his destination in the city. On the way Jacobs took him to five or six gin shops and then stole his watch. 'I ran after him and caught him some 30 or 40 yards off.' A fight ensued, ending with the arrival of a policeman, who seized Jacobs with the watch in his pocket. Convicted at the Old Bailey on 16 February 1832, Jacobs was initially sentenced to death.

Joseph Jacobs arrived in New South Wales on 27 June 1833. He received a ticket of leave in 1842 and was permitted to travel between Maitland and Liverpool Plains in the service of Mr How for twelve months. In 1845 this internal passport was changed so that he could travel between the Muckoi River and Morpeth in the service of Reynolds and Parnell. This permission was cancelled in January 1847 for being out of the district and for being drunk. It was restored later that year.

OBSP, case 651, p. 242; 4/017; 4/4159; TL 42/336; 42/652; 47/440; HO 10/53.

JACOBS, Lazarus (Laurence)

b. London, 1807–1855
Phoenix I (2), 1828; Convict; Sentenced to 7 years, Old Bailey, 1827.
Single; Fruit man; Height: 163 cm; 3 children.

Lazarus Jacobs (aged twenty) and David Moses (q.v.) (aged eighteen) ran past a woman in Petticoat Lane and stole her purse. Jacobs could neither read nor write. He had a pale complexion, brown hair, very bald, hazel eyes. 'Jew'.

Lazarus Jacobs arrived at Sydney Cove on 13 July 1828 and was assigned to William Hathaway at Seven Mile Creek. Jacobs was listed in the 1828 Census at the Hyde Park Barracks. No religion was noted.

Lazarus Jacobs was issued with a certificate of freedom on 8 April 1834. He married Jane Isaacs (q.v.) on 1 February 1837. It was the nineteenth Jewish wedding ceremony in New South Wales. On 19 February 1840 a Lazarus Jacobs submitted a bid to the Sydney Synagogue for baking *matzah* for Passover.

In 1841 and 1843 sons were born to Lazarus and Jane (who adopted the Hebrew name of Sarah). Jacobs was listed as a voter in the first Sydney election in 1842 and as living in Castlereagh Street. He applied for and was elected to the position of Keeper of the Burial Ground on 7 August 1844. In 1844 he was working as a grocer in Sussex Street and again unsucessfully applied for the task of baking the Passover *matzah*. On 13 February 1845 Hannah, the daughter of Lazarus and Sarah Jacobs, was buried in the Devonshire Street Jewish Cemetery. Lazarus Jacobs married Rebecca Joel in Sydney in August 1851. Rebecca signed the marriage registry with a mark. Jacobs died on 31 August 1855 and his tombstone at the Devonshire Street Cemetery was erected by the Hebrew Mutual Benefit Society.

OBSP, 1826–27, case 479, p. 1251; CF 34/0354; *Sydney Morning Herald*, 15 September 1842, 1 October 1855; York Street Synagogue Minute Book, 19 February 1840, p. 36, 7 August, p. 145, 28 January 1844, p. 133.

JACOBS, Leah

Free.
Single.

In 1849 Leah Jacobs married John Bradley at St James' Anglican Church in Sydney.

JACOBS, Michael

b. London, 1799–1853
Hebe, 1820; Convict; Sentenced to life, Middlesex, 1820.
Single; Fruiterer; Height: 164.5 cm.

Dark ruddy complexion, black hair, dark eyes. Michael Jacobs was one of a gang of three or four young men in Whitechapel who jostled a man, pushed him over and stole his watch. Jacobs was dressed in a blue jacket, a striped waistcoat and blue trousers. He tried to disguise himself by wearing a large brown great coat. He was sentenced on 17 May 1820.

The *Hebe* arrived in Port Jackson on 31 December 1820 and Jacobs was assigned to 'Bennet's Road Party'. On 16 April 1821 in Sydney Michael Jacobs was sentenced to a year's gaol for having absconded from his work as a water carrier and was sent to the convict settlement at Newcastle on the *Elizabeth Henrietta.*

On 27 September 1823 he was discharged from government service at Emu Plains and sent as a convict to Port Macquarie. Back in Sydney three years later, on 5 September 1826 Jacobs was convicted at the General Sessions for having robbed a drunken man. He was imprisoned on the *Phoenix* hulk and sent on the *Alligator* to Moreton Bay. Jacobs arrived back in Sydney on 24 September 1829 and was included in the General Return of Convicts of 1837 as an assigned servant to Mr J. W. Romer. He received a ticket of leave in that year for the District of Berrima, and a conditional pardon followed on 11 October 1844. The *Sydney Morning Herald* recorded on 10 July 1841 that a Michael Jacob subscribed to a fund to build a church at West Bargo. Jacobs was buried as a Jew in Sydney on 9 December 1853.

OBSP, 1819–20, case 667, p. 413; Ship Indent 2/8262, p. 74; 4/4007, p. 290; 4/3794, p. 11; *Phoenix* (hulk) Entrance Book 4/6281, p. 17; Chronological Register of Convicts at Moreton Bay, 4/3503, 16 April 1821, no. 903; QSA 110/30; CS Convicts Out 4/3669, p. 80; TL 37/1079; Governors' Despatches, ML, A1234, p. 11; *Sydney Gazette*, 24 May 1822, 9 September 1826; *Sydney Morning Herald*, 10 July 1841; CS 50/9210.

JACOBS, Moss

b. London, 1786–1853
Canada (5), 1819; Convict; Sentenced to 7 years, Surrey Quarter Sessions, 1818.
Watchmaker; Height: 167.5 cm.

Fair ruddy complexion, brown hair, hazel eyes. Moss Jacobs was convicted on 20 October 1818.

Moss Jacobs arrived on 1 September 1819 and, within ten days, was sent to Liverpool on assignment. He was issued with a ticket of leave on 14 April 1825. Moss Jacobs died, aged sixty-seven, on 12 December 1853, and was buried at the Devonshire Street Jewish Cemetery.

HO 10/1; Ship Indent 4/4006, p. 360.

JACOBS, Moss (Moses)

b. London, 1797
Sir William Bensley, 1817; Convict; Sentenced to life, London, 1815.
Single; Labourer; Height: 164 cm.

Dark ruddy complexion, black hair, hazel eyes. Moss Jacobs was transported for highway robbery with Isaac Davis (q.v.). Isaac Davis encountered Margaret Quinland by the Aldgate Churchyard and persuaded her to have a glass of gin' I told him I knew my way (home) and thanked him, but he would not leave me. We walked near Petticoat Lane. He stopped at a door to get the key of his apartment, which he said was there. I then saw the other prisoner (Moss Jacobs), he was standing at the corner. I don't know where he came from. He called out "Is that Isaac?" The prisoner, who was with me, answered that it was. Then the other prisoner asked him what he had got and he said it was all prime.

He was leading me by my arm and undoing my shawl and the other prisoner ran off with it, then he held me against the wall and rifled my pocket. I found his hand in my pocket and I called out "Watch! Watch! Stop thief!". Moss Jacobs called out "Stamp her bloody guts out!" I held the shawl that was round my neck as long as I ever could.' Both Davis and Jacobs were sentenced to death and sent to Australia on the same transport. Jacobs was eighteen years old. There is a note, 'Says his name is Moses but that he was convicted in the name of Moss', written in the trial notes for Isaac Davis in September 1827.

On 21 March 1817, Jacobs was forwarded to Windsor for assignment. In the 1818 General Muster Moses Jacobs was listed as a 'Government Labourer'. Jacobs was an assigned servant to Samuel Solomons (q.v.) at Richmond at the 1820 Muster. By 8 September 1821 the Colonial Secretary noted that he was a member of the 'Light Gang'. In 1825 he was allowed to remain in the District of Windsor and his employer, Mr T. North of Richmond, attested to his good character for a ticket of leave. A ticket of leave was granted 4 September 1827. The 1828 Census gave his age as thirty-five and stated that he was a labourer at Richmond. His religion was given as 'Protestant'. A conditional pardon was approved on 8 September 1836.

A Moss Jacobs worked as a cook in the Angel Inn in Lonsdale Street, Melbourne. On 15 March 1843 he alleged that his leg had been broken by a drunken intruder into the kitchen where he was working. The intruder was sentenced to one week with hard labour.

TL 27/587, 4/4065; 4/1716.2, pp. 251–2; CP, 8 September 1836, no. 708, Governors' Despatches, ML, A1216, p. 54; 4/4434, p. 494, and 1837, ML A1275.

JACOBS, Nathan (Natey)

Free.

In the *Registry of Flash Men*, Nathan Jacobs was listed as 'a suspicious character'. He was called 'Natey' and lodged in a room five doors down from the Globe public house in Castlereagh Street, Sydney. He and his brother John, or Jacky (possibly the John Jacobs who arrived first on the *Agamemnon*, q.v.), planned to buy stolen property from Hunt and 'Imey' Phillips (q.v.). Jacobs lived in his own house in Elizabeth Street. Both N. and J. Jacobs were said to be part of an underworld gang that met at S. Green's, George Street.

W. A. Miles, *Registry of Flash Men*, pp. 96, 114.

JACOBS, Phoebe

Stag, 1849; Free.
Married; 8 children.

Phoebe Jacobs was the wife of Samuel Jacobs (q.v.) and arrived in Melbourne with her husband and children in 1849.

JACOBS, Rachel

b. London
Prince Regent, 1830; Free.
Married; 2 children.

Rachel Jacobs migrated to Australia following the second transportation sentence of her husband John Jacobs (q.v.) (*Agamemnon*; *Adrian*). The reunion did not work, and in July 1844 the couple applied to the Sydney Synagogue for a divorce, saying that they had not lived together for seven years. Mysteriously, a religious divorce was granted without rabbinical sanction and John Jacobs returned to England while Rachel advertised that she had not accompanied him.

JACOBS, Ralph

b. London, 1796
Almorah (1), 1817; Convict; Sentenced to life, Old Bailey, 1816.
Single; Watchmaker and fishmonger; Height: 151 cm.

Dark yellow complexion, very bald, brown eyes. 'Very well behaved' on board ship. Ralph Jacobs was convicted in London on 30 October 1816.

Jacobs arrived in New South Wales on 31 August 1817. On 21 July 1818 he was punished for being out after hours and escaping from a constable, for which he received twenty-five lashes and fourteen days hard labour in a gaol gang. On 7 April 1819 he was sentenced to fifty lashes and ten months in the gaol gang for stealing salt meat from the premises of his employer, Mr (Eleazar) Lazarus (q.v.). On 19 October he assaulted and beat Constable Bernard Canning and received another fifty lashes. On 29 October he received three months in the gaol gang for neglect of duty. On 21 March 1820, while employed in Public Works, he was found guilty of stealing wearing apparel from a dwelling place and was sentenced to a further twelve months in the gaol gang. Jacobs was issued with a ticket of leave on 15 May 1818. In the 1818 Muster he was listed as a 'Settler's Man'. While he was assigned as a servant he was brought before the Magistrates Bench (on 27 October 1821) and found guilty of stealing sheep from his master's flock.

On 8 July 1829 the list of the Civil Establishment in the Colony of Van Diemen's Land showed that Ralph Jacobs was employed as the executioner in Launceston. His salary was £15 per annum, which was £5 less than his counterpart in Hobart Town. Judging by his subsequent behaviour his employment must have caused deep trauma. By 25 January 1839 he was a member of the Port Arthur Chain Gang. His conduct was to be reported and he was 'not to be placed in any position of trust'.

CON 13/1, no. 22, p. 1213; CON 32/2, p. 182; HO 10/1; Ship Indent 4/4005, p. 342; HO 10/43; *Hobart Town Gazette*, 27 October 1821.

JACOBS, Rebecca Julia

b. Spitalfields, 1818–1858 Free.

Julia Lyons took the name Rebecca when she married John Jacobs (q.v.) in 1852. She was the daughter of Jonas and Deborah Lyons, and sister of Joshua Lyons (q.v.). Rebecca Julia Jacobs was buried by the Sydney Synagogue at the Devonshire Street cemetery on 26 October 1858. She was forty years of age. Her remains were transferred to Raphael's Ground in 1901.

Governors' Despatches 1833, A1214, p. 710.

JACOBS, Samuel

1782–1841
Calcutta, 1803; Convict; Sentenced to 7 years, Old Bailey, 1800.
Single; Tailor; Height: 150 cm.

In the official record of his trial Jacobs was said to be 'of Norwich'. He was a Jew, of dark complexion, dark brown hair, hazel eyes. He was sentenced to transportation for a robbery in London. Jacobs had attempted to hide in a shoe shop at Tower Hill at closing time. He was seen and tried to escape with a pair of shoes valued at two shillings and ten pence. In his escape he knocked over the owner, Ann Maddocks. He was aged eighteen at the time of his trial.

Jacobs was part of the Collins Expedition that attempted to settle in Port Phillip Bay before proceeding to Van Diemen's Land. His name fails to appear in subsequent muster rolls in Van Diemen's Land. An 'S. Jacobs' was buried at the Devonshire Street Jewish Cemetery in Sydney on 22 September 1841.

OBSP, 1799–1800, case 710, p. 579; HO 11/1; Ship Indent 4/4004, p. 160; 2/8249, p. 91.

JACOBS, Samuel (Henry)

b. Poland, 1797–1867
Heroine, 1833; Convict; Sentenced to 14 years, York, 1832.
Married; Hawker; Height: 155 cm; 5 children (in England).

Dark sallow complexion, dark brown hair, brown eyes, whiskers meeting under chin. Jew. Can read. Samuel Jacobs was sentenced at the York (Leeds) Quarter Sessions on 31 December 1832 for 'stealing cloth'. He had no previous convictions. He had two sons and three daughters.

Jacobs arrived in New South Wales on 19 September 1833. He was initially assigned to the Goulburn District. On 8 April 1835 the Bench sentenced him to twenty-five lashes, on 14 April to fifty lashes for 'pilfering', and on 16 July to 100 lashes for 'insolence and disobedience'. In the General Return of Convicts of 1837, 'Henry' Jacobs was assigned to Thomas Foster of Hunters Hill. A ticket of leave was issued in 1840. However, a full certificate of freedom was withheld on 19 September 1842 because of his past colonial record. It was noted that 'in consideration of his good conduct for the past four years' he would be permitted to apply again in six months. The certificate of freedom was finally granted on 20 April 1847.

On 7 December 1843 the *Sydney Morning Herald* reported that he had declared that his business in Goulburn had failed, with debts in excess of £2000. He was permitted to travel as a carrier between Goulburn and the River Murray for twelve months. In 1847 a description attached to his new certificate of freedom described his whiskers as having turned grey. He owned the Goulburn Stores in 1848.

On 8 May 1852 Jacobs was granted naturalisation and became a British subject. Samuel Jacobs was buried at the Goulburn Jewish cemetery on 22 November 1867. He was seventy years of age.

Heroine Printed Indent, 33-2058-229, p. 121; Letters, A 664, pp. 230, 245; TL 40/2208, 20 October 1840, in 4/4414; Permission to Travel 4/4252, 11 January 1844, pp. 44/51; CF 47/0399; *Australasian Chronicle*, 22 November 1843; *Sydney Morning Herald*, 7 December 1843.

JACOBS, Samuel

b. Oxford Street, London, 1815 *Southworth* (2), 1834; Convict; Sentenced to 7 years, Old Bailey, 1833. Single; Labourer; Height: 151 cm.

Fair complexion, brown hair, dark brown eyes. Pickpocket. Samuel Jacobs was sentenced on 17 June 1833 for stealing a handkerchief. He had been in custody before.

Samuel Jacobs arrived in Van Diemen's Land on 14 January 1834. Jacobs had a long police record and a large portion of this history is to be found in the Launceston Police Book. On 7 October 1834 his master in Launceston, Mr J. Tailor, returned him to government service. He was assigned to the Launceston Chain Gang and was then moved to Perth. In the Launceston Police Book there is a note dated 8 April 1835 stating that he was an assigned convict servant suspected of pilfering and returned to the government. On 22 December 1835, while a member of a road party, he received twenty-five lashes for disobedience. On 6 July and 14 July 1836 he was sentenced to eighty-six lashes for being absent in 'very suspicious circumstances' and for being insolent. On 31 January 1837 his term of transportation was extended by three years for pilfering from his master. During the rest of the year he was a member of the Reiby's Ford Road Party. On 9 May 1838 he was found guilty of stealing a package worth less than £5 while working as a messenger for the post office in Launceston. His sentence was extended by a further two years and he was not to be assigned in town again. He was returned to the roads and in 1839 was working with the Cleveland Road Party. On 18 November 1839 Jacobs was sentenced for felony and sent to Port Arthur for a term of twelve months, six months of which was to be served in chains.

On 28 March 1843 Jacobs was fined for having 'a quantity of apples improperly in his possession' and sentenced to twelve months in chains at Port Arthur. On 18 October 1843, for having stolen a quantity of raisins, he was given fourteen days in solitary confinement, and on 5 December 1843 he received thirty days in solitary confinement for stealing twelve kangaroo skins and a quantity of hemp. On 25 July 1844, having been found to have articles in his possession for which he could not satisfactorily account, he was sentenced to six months hard labour in chains and recommended to be kept in Port Arthur for two years from that date for 'being an incorrigible thief'. On 26 July 1844 he was found to be absent without leave and sentenced to seven days solitary confinement. On 9 August 1844 he assaulted John Thompson and was sentenced to one month solitary confinement, and on 8 October 1844 he received twenty-five lashes for 'misconduct'. A certificate of freedom (no. 555) was issued in 1845.

CON 31/24; MM 33/2; MM 33/6; CON 18/20; CON 23/2; CON 78/2, p. 191.

JACOBS, Samuel

Stag, 1849; Free.
Married; Dealer; 8 children.

The arrival of Samuel Jacobs, his wife Phoebe (q.v.), and their children Harriet, Richard, Julia, Hannah, Alice, Frances, Amelia and Maria was listed in the *Melbourne Morning Herald* of 11 February 1849. In May 1849 'S. Jacobs' of the Victoria Bazaar in Collins Street advertised that he had 'recently arrived from the Lowther Arcade in the Strand, London'. His store, opposite the Melbourne Club, was described as 'Fancy' and sold oil paintings, writing desks and medical instruments.

In September 1849 'The Misses Jacobs' advertised that they were milliners and dressmakers who had learned their trade in Regent Street and were newly located at the Victoria Bazaar while their permanent premises were being rebuilt. They also taught crocheting in six lessons.

Jacobs had renamed his store the Victoria Promenade Bazaar by the end of 1851 and advertised tables, copies of 'Old Master Paintings', rings, hoops and furniture. In mid-1852, Samuel Jacobs advertised that he was a gold buyer.

Melbourne Morning Herald, 6 September 1849, 2 December 1851, 19 May 1852.

JACOBS, Samuel

b. Shoreditch, 1821–1893
Asia (6), 1841; Convict; Sentenced to 10 years, Central Criminal Court, 1839.
Single; Bricklayer, labourer, sawyer; Height: 161 cm; 7 children.

Dark brown hair, smooth shaven face, grey eyes, oval face and large nose and chin. Could read and write. Samuel Jacobs was a pickpocket who stole a gold watch chain, watch-key and two seals valued at £12 5s from the waistcoat pocket of a Mr Sutton, who had been confronted by two men, arm in arm, who stood before him while Jacobs attempted to steal his watch. When arrested, Jacobs confessed 'I took it'. In giving evidence the city police constable said he had seen Jacobs 'very busily engaged in trying different people's pockets'. Jacobs was sentenced on 15 November 1839. Jacobs' behaviour on board ship was 'good'. Jacobs had a mother, Sarah Jacobs, and five sisters, Sarah, Mary, Betsy, Anne and Rachel, all living in Shoreditch.

Samuel Jacobs arrived in Van Diemen's Land on 23 August 1841. Jacobs' period of fifteen months probation was extended four times for a total of ten months additional service. On 19 September 1842 he was found guilty of 'misconduct' for gambling and his existing period of probation was extended by three months and he was to be sent to the Tasman Peninsula. On 7 October 1842, on board the *Isabella* en route to Port Arthur, he was again found guilty of 'misconduct' in having tobacco in his possession after a robbery. He was sentenced to three months hard labour in chains. On 5 April he was sentenced to thirty-six lashes on his back for 'insolence and disobedience to orders'. On 21 September 1843 his extended period of probation expired.

On 8 February 1845 he was sentenced to six months hard labour in chains over a charge involving theft of less than £5. While in the chain gang, on 4 August 1845, his term was extended by four months for 'gross misconduct when baker in tampering with and altering the scales thereby defrauding the men and also having damper and fat in his possession'.

Jacobs received his ticket of leave on 11 May 1847 and his conditional pardon on 3 July 1849. He may have been the Samuel Jacobs who was a subscriber to the Tasmanian Hebrew Benevolent Institute in 1847. His certificate of freedom was issued on 29 November 1849. On 24 October 1848 Jacobs received permission to marry Ann Williams, who was free and residing in Hobart Town. The ceremony took place on 6 November 1848 at St George's Anglican Church. His profession was listed as 'waterman'.

They had seven children: Samuel Thomas (born 1851), William (1854), Sarah (1856), George (1858), John (1861), Susan (1864), and Lydia (1866). Samuel Jacobs died at his home, at 16 South Street, Battery Point, Hobart, on 25 April 1893. Ann Jacobs died in 1892, aged sixty-four.

OBSP, 26 November 1839; CON 33/9, no. 2083; CON 52/3, p. 235; CON 52/4; *Hobart Town Gazette*, 24 October 1848; Information from the Sonenberg family, Melbourne.

JACOBS, Sarah

1781–1825 Convict.

Sarah Jacobs died at Hobart Town on 18 April 1825. She was forty-four years old.

JACOBS, Sarah

b. East End, London, 1803
Mermaid, 1828; Convict; Sentenced to 14 years, Old Bailey, 1827.
Single; Prostitute, 'a needlewoman'; Height: 150 cm.

Fresh complexion, black hair, dark full eyebrows, light grey eyes, long straight nose, small mouth, full lips, pock-pitted, one large mole under right eye. Jew. Can neither read nor write. Sarah Jacobs was a prostitute who, with the help of four male associates, had stolen money 'from the person of John Thomson, a seafaring man', who 'lived last in Blue Coat Fields, Ratcliffe Highway'. Surgeon's Report: 'Impudent, but not disorderly'.

Sarah Jacobs worked as an assigned servant in a large number of different households between 1829 and 1837. During this time she was frequently disciplined for being absent all night from her quarters and for being drunk and for theft. She married William Wood, who had come free to Van Diemen's Land, in January 1830. In October 1833, because of her misbehaviour she was sent from Hobart to Launceston. By July 1834 she was pregnant and returned to the Launceston Female Factory. There is no record of the child being born but, in March 1835, while assigned to Mr Lewis Henry Lazarus (Henry Lewis Lazarus, q.v.) of Launceston, she was committed on a suspicion of felony and later discharged.

After being assigned once again in Launceston, and being returned to the laundry of the House of Correction for 'disobedience', she was assigned to a Mr Myers.

On 16 December 1835 she was sentenced to eight days solitary confinement for absconding and three months in prison for disorderly conduct. In 1837 her initial term of imprisonment was extended by two years for a crime involving larceny of an object valued at less than £2. At the end of 1837 she again absconded and a further sentence of six months was added. On 6 May 1838 at the House of Correction she 'forcibly, violently and in a turbulent manner' refused to obey a command and received a sentence of three months hard labour. In October an additional twelve months was added to her sentence for having been illegally at large for six weeks. On 28 December 1838 she was found to have made 'use of the most obscene language in the street' and was sent to prison for six months with fourteen days in solitary confinement on bread and water. In March 1840 she was convicted for stealing a chemise valued at six shillings and her term of transportation was extended by twelve months. She was to spend six months in the House of Correction and then be assigned in the Interior. On the day after Christmas 1840 she was found to have a pair of stockings and a shilling in her possession for which she could not account, and another three months hard labour in the House of Correction was decreed. In October 1841 she 'misbehaved' during Divine Service and was sentenced to six months hard labour. Finally in October 1843 another charge of absconding brought her a further sentence of twelve months with hard labour.

A ticket of leave was granted on 22 April 1845. Two convictions for misconduct were recorded in May and September 1845, both for being found in bed with a man, and, for each offence, she was imprisoned for two months with hard labour. On 6 April 1846 she applied to marry Daniel Newman. Her request was approved. Her name appears in both the 1846 and 1849 Musters. In 1846 she held a ticket of leave and in 1849 she was 'free'.

CON 40/5, no. 49; CON 32/2 (supplement); CON 32/5, p. 98; CON 45/1; CON 52/3, p. 244; *Hobart Town Courier*, 3 April 1840, 20 May 1844; Launceston Police Book, CON 78/2, p. 197.

JACOBSON, Nisson

b. Libau, 1794–1857
Lady Castlereagh, 1818; Convict; Sentenced to 14 years, Old Bailey, 1817.
Single; Cigar manufacturer; Height: 169 cm.

Dark ruddy complexion, black hair, hazel eyes. Transported for knowingly having a forged Bank of England note in his possession. Jacobson was 'very well behaved' on board the transport ship. He was sentenced in London on 16 April 1817.

During 1821 Nisson Jacobson was charged with repeated instances of insolence to his mistress Mrs Humphrey and was reprimanded. During November and December 1823 he was charged in the Supreme Court, Hobart Town, with five counts of insolence towards his mistress Mrs Humphrey and found not guilty on each count. *Van Diemen's Land Pocket Almanack for the Year of Our Lord*, 1825, listed Jacobson as a 'Retail Dealer' in Goulburn Street. A ticket of leave was issued on 18 November 1826 and a conditional pardon on 7 September 1829. A certificate of freedom was issued on 16 April 1831. Nisson Jacobson, a farmer of New Norfolk, at the River Dee, was listed in Ross's *Van Diemen's Land Annual*, 1837. He was buried at Sorrell as an Anglican on 19 April 1857.

OBSP, 1816–17, case 588, p. 225; CON 31/23, no. 34; CON 13/1; HO 11/2; Ship Indent 4/4006, p. 39; HO 10/1; HO 11/2; *Hobart Town Gazette*, 18 November 1826, 16 April 1831; *Hobart Town Courier*, 7 September 1829.

JEWELL, Harris

Free.
Married; 1 child.

Harris M. Jewell and Isabel had a son in 1857 who was registered as a 'Hebrew' and named in honour of their son's birthplace, Sydney.

JEWELL, Joseph (also known as Joseph Joel)

1817–1863
Free.
Single.

Joseph Jewell married Frances Crabb, the daughter of Phillip Crabb (q.v.), in the Sydney Synagogue on 10 October 1841. On 25 February 1844 he elected 'beadle' at the Sydney Synagogue and in 1846 their son Lewis was born in Sydney and registered as 'Hebrew'. Joseph died at Bathurst in 1863.

JOEL, Elijah

b. Birmingham, 1808–1849
John II, 1837; Convict; Sentenced to 7 years, Central Criminal Court, 1836.
Single; Errand boy; Height: 154 cm; 1 child.

Dark and pock-pitted complexion, brown hair, hazel eyes, scars on right cheek, left jaw, left side of neck. Jew. Tattoo: Man ECA TAJ—heart pierced by two darts. RVI, heart and two anchors lower right arm. Woman inside left arm. C upper part of left arm. Scar outside right leg. Scrofula marks upper chest. Elijah Joel stole a handkerchief in Cheapside. He had a previous conviction for a similar offence in 1834.

Elijah Joel arrived in New South Wales on 7 February 1837 and was sent to the Hyde Park Barracks. Elijah Joel received his certificate of freedom on 25 May 1843. He married Rebecca Myers (q.v.) in Sydney on 14 June1848. A son, Moss Joel, was born in Queanbeyan in 1849. On 21 February 1849 Elijah Joel died and was buried by the York Street Synagogue in the Devonshire Street cemetery. The New South Wales Burial Register noted that he was forty years old.

OBSP, 1837, case 145, p. 421, and 4 September 1834, case 146; *John II* Printed Indent, p. 23; CF 43/0833.

JOEL, Mark

b. Whitechapel, 1769–1834
Clyde, 1830; Convict; Sentenced to life, Middlesex, 1829.
Married; Labourer; Height: 170 cm; 3 children (in England).

Swarthy complexion, grey hair and whiskers, grey eyes. Medium large nose. Right arm fractured and shrunk. Joel Mark was sentenced to transportation for breaking and entering a dwelling house. His hulk report was 'good'. He was married with three children. His wife Amelia Joel lived at Sandy's Row, Spitalfields. He was sixty-one.

Mark Joel had no colonial police record. He died at Hobart Town on 12 March 1834.

CON 31/24, no. 40029; MM 33/2; CON 18/2; CSO 1/482/10711.

JOEL, S.

1789; Convict.

In his notes, the historian 'Old Forde' recalled having seen a tombstone to 'S. Joel 1820—a resident of the colony of 31 years' in the very old cemetery adjoining the Anglican Church in Belmore Road, Sydney. (N. B. No convict transports arrived in New South Wales in 1789 and three ships of the 'Second Fleet' followed in 1790-but with no convict with the surname 'Joel').

See C. Bertie, *Old Sydney by Old Chum* [J. M. Forde].

JOHNSON, Samuel (SIMMONS)

b. Spitalfields, 1828
Marion (2), 1845; Convict; Sentenced to 7 years, Clerkenwell, 1845.
Single; Labourer; Height: 144 cm.

Fresh complexion, brown hair, blue eyes, long nose, large mouth, long chin. Can read and write. Samuel Johnson was transported for stealing a coat. He had been in gaol for three months previously for 'stealing a gown'. 'Proper name Samuel Simmons'. The surgeon reported that he had been well behaved in gaol and that he was a Jew.

Samuel Johnson arrived in Van Diemen's Land on 10 September 1845 and his initial period of probation was fifteen months, to be spent at Darlington. This period concluded on 12 April 1847. On 20 December 1847 he was punished with a month's imprisonment for 'making away with a pair of government trousers'. His sentence was extended twice for 'absconding'. On 21 July 1849 his application for

a ticket of leave was refused. He was finally issued with one on 16 July 1850, and a certificate of freedom was granted on 28 January 1852.
CON 33/70, no. 16454.

JOHNSON, William (Samuel Simmons)

b. Essex, 1814
Mangles (8), 1837; Convict; Sentenced to 7 years, Central Criminal Court, 1836.
Single; Labourer; Height: 160.5 cm.

Dark ruddy freckled complexion. Dark brown hair. Dark brown eyes. Eyebrows partially meeting. Scar on upper lip. William Johnson was sentenced on 29 February 1836 for stealing from a wagon. He had no previous convictions. At sentence he gave his religion as 'none' but he was listed in the records at the Hyde Park Barracks as a Jew

William Johnson arrived on 10 July 1837. He received a ticket of leave in 1842 and a certificate of freedom on 9 September 1843.
Printed Indent *Mangles* (8), 1837, no. 1032; TL 42/211; CF 43/1490.

JONAS, David

b. 1765
Coromandel, 1804; Convict; Sentenced, Middlesex, 1802.
Labourer.

Jonas was convicted for stealing lead from an unfinished house and, when attempting to escape, stabbing the watchman. He was sentenced at the Old Bailey on 15 September 1802. His name may indicate that he was Jewish.

There are no existing colonial records for David Jonas.
OBSP, 1801–02, case 833, p. 529; Ship Indent 2/8258.

JONAS, Isaac

b. London, 1801
Morley (1), 1817; Convict; Sentenced to life, Old Bailey, 1816.
Single; Labourer; Height: 161 cm.

Dark swarthy complexion, brown hair, grey eyes. On 17 May 1816 Isaac Jonas, Hyam and Simon Solomons (q.v.) befriended a drunken merchant who was carrying £100 in notes near St Paul's Churchyard. They took him to a public house and afterwards struck him down and stole his money and his watch, valued at £20. Jonas was described by a witness as 'That little man'. Both Jonas and Solomons were sentenced to death on 29 May 1816. The sentences were subsequently commuted.

Jonas arrived in Sydney on 10 April 1817. The *Monitor* of 25 August 1826 reported that Isaac Jonas and Solomon Solomons (q.v.) had been found gambling in a 'House of Ill Fame' and both had their tickets of leave cancelled. Jonas's ticket of leave was restored on 10 December 1829 for the District of Wallis Plains and altered for Parramatta on 19 July 1836. He applied for a conditional pardon on

12 December 1835, his application supported with a brief from the Rev. Samuel Marsden. A conditional pardon was eventually approved on 31 December 1836.

OBSP, 1816–17, case 503, p. 255; Register 4/4478, p. 56; *Morley* Indent 4/4005; Governors' Despatches, ML, A1206, p. 523; *Monitor*, 25 August 1826; 4/4073, 10 December 1829; TL 29/1018; CS 4/2296-35/10518, 26 December 1835; CP 1826, Register, 4/4478, no. 801, p. 56.

JONAS, Jacob (Old Yankiff)

1762–1833
Earl Cornwallis, 1801; Convict; Sentenced to 7 years, London, 1798.
Single; Dealer.

James Smith, a broker in Lombard Street, was walking home at nine o'clock in the evening, going thro' Jewry Street Aldgate when he saw Jacon Jonas 'he immediately made a bow to me and seeing that I was lame, he snatched the watch from my pocket'. He was caught as he ran away. Jonas tried to 'chuck' the watch away as he was 'caught by his collar'. Jonas was forty years old at the time of his trial.

Jacob Jonas arrived in New South Wales on 12 June 1801. He was listed in the Muster of August 1806 as free by servitude and working as a self-employed 'dealer'. On 16 December 1816 Jacob Jonas, aged fifty-four, married Mary Harris, aged thirty-six, at St John's Church of England, Parramatta. Jonas was included in the General Return of New South Wales in 1822 as free by servitude and living in Parramatta. The Colonial Secretary recorded that in 1824 Jacob Jonas was a convict employed by Mr Archibald Bell. The *Sydney Gazette* reported that 'Jacob Jonas—commonly called Old Yankiff' was charged with suspicion of stealing a pocket handkerchief. The paper explained that he was a former resident of Parramatta and was at Windsor playing cards with the accuser. In the 1828 Census he was described as a 'lodger' in Parramatta, aged sixty-eight, and a 'Protestant'. He died at Parramatta and was buried in Sydney's Devonshire Street Jewish Cemetery on 25 May 1833. A Julia Jonas married Moses Moss at the Sydney Synagogue in 1854.

OBSP 4 July 1798, case 425. Indent 4/4004, p. 21; *Sydney Gazette*, 13 October 1827; Bigge Appendix A2139, p. 125.

JONES, Benjamin

b. London, 1809
Sir Charles Forbes (3), 1830; Convict; Sentenced to 7 years, Devon, 1829.
Single; Labourer, baker; Height: 168 cm.

A pickpocket. Could read but not write. Jew. Shipboard character 'good'. Benjamin Jones stole two gold and two silver watches. He was twenty years old.

Benjamin Jones arrived in Van Diemen's Land on 27 July 1830 and was initially assigned to Mr Gaughren. On 21 March 1831 he was reprimanded for 'neglect of duty'. On 26 September, for the same offence, he was put in a cell with bread and water for one week. On 12 October he lost his master's cattle in the bush and was reprimanded. On 13 October he was caught being 'out after hours' and sentenced to the treadmill for seven days. On 28 October he was found guilty of neglect of duty and 'insolence' and received twelve lashes. On 8 November he was charged again with neglect of duty for refusing 'to go out with the cattle'. The surgeon reported that Jones had been ill but that he now was able to go back to work. On 21 March 1832 Mr Gaughren again accused Jones of neglect of duty. In a most unusual decision the complaint was dismissed as 'frivolous' and he was returned to the Public Works Department and assigned to Mr Stewart. On 4 June 1833 Jones was 'absent' and received twelve lashes as a punishment. On 23 July he 'mislays' some money that his master had asked him to pay and was sentenced to twelve months in the Richmond Chain Gang. By 9 August he had been moved to the Hulk Chain Gang and was found to have rum in his possession. He was sentenced to twenty-five lashes. On 5 November he was caught gambling and was sentenced to thirty-six lashes. On 22 June 1835 at the Prisoners' Barracks he received fifty lashes for gambling, and on 3 November, for 'idleness', twenty-five lashes. On 25 February 1839 he was accused of'misconduct' and given seven days hard labour. On 2 February 1840 he was charged with felony and sent to Port Arthur for twelve months. His ticket of leave had been restored by 1843 and for the following year he worked as a constable in the Hobart Town Police Force.

OBSP, 1829–30, case 1014, p. 440; CON 37/6/1911; VDL papers, ML, 1059-6, p. 181.

JONES, George

b. Leominster, Herts, 1808
Blundell, 1844; Convict; Sentenced to 7 years, Central Criminal Court, 1843.
Single; Coach driver and groom; Height: 168 cm.

Sallow dark complexion, brown hair, long face, hazel eyes, large nose. Jew. Can read and write. George Jones was transported for a burglary at Kensington and sentenced to fifteen years transportation, which was later commuted to a sentence of seven years.

George Jones was sent from England directly to Norfolk Island, arriving on 12 July 1844 (together with William Jones, q.v., who was also Jewish). On 11 April 1845, while still on Norfolk Island, George Jones was sentenced to twenty-five lashes for 'disobedience'.

He arrived in Van Diemen's Land on 30 December 1846 and soon afterwards was sentenced to eight days in solitary confinement for 'misconduct', having been found in a public house on a Sunday evening. He received his ticket of leave on 23 May 1848.

CON 33/78, no. 18176.

JONES, Henry

b. London
Isabella, 1837; Free.
Married; Dealer.

Mr and Mrs Henry Jones arrived in Hobart Town on the *Isabella* on 4 January 1837 and immediately became involved in the life of the Jewish community. Jones signed the petition asking for a grant to build the Launceston Synagogue on 20 May 1843. In May 1844 he became the reader, or minister, of the Hobart Hebrew Congregation at £12 a week and 10 per cent of any money he collected on behalf of the congregation. In 1845 his salary was increased to £20 and, together with Jacob

Frankel (q.v.), he shared the task of reading the High Holyday services. In March 1846 he was asked to conduct the services at the dedication of the synagogue in Launceston. In November 1846 Jones wrote to the committee of the Hobart Synagogue telling them that he intended to establish a *mikveh* (a ritual bath) in his home. Mr and Mrs Jones were subscribers to the Hebrew Benevolent Institution in Tasmania in 1847. The London *Jewish Chronicle* reported that on 1 August 1853 the incumbent Rabbi Herman Hoelzel had appointed the 'Rev. Henry Jones, the second reader of the Hobart Town Synagogue'. Jones is described as a former pupil of *Dayan* (Judge) Aaron Levy (q.v.).

Henry Jones remained in Hobart until the end of 1863 and then took up a ministerial post in New Zealand.

Launceston Advertiser, 5 January 1837; First Minute Book of the Hobart Synagogue.

JONES, Isaac

d. 1842.
Free.

Isaac Jones was buried in the Jewish section of the Devonshire Street Cemetery on 2 September 1842.

JONES, John

b. London, 1807
Lady Kennaway (2), 1836; Convict; Sentenced to life, Old Bailey, 1835.
Married; Clothes keeper; Height: 169 cm.

Dark ruddy complexion, dark brown hair, hazel eyes, breast hairy. Mark of scald on chest, arm and wrist. Could read. John Jones was caught in the act of making counterfeit half crowns. His wife Mary was with him but only he was sentenced to transportation for life. He had no previous convictions. He was sentenced at London's Central Criminal Court on 23 November 1835.

John Jones arrived in New South Wales on 12 October 1836. The reason Jones gave for his transportation was 'for stealing a breast pin'. He also claimed to be single. According to the 1837 General Return of Convicts, he was assigned to work for James Byrne of Campbelltown. He received a ticket of leave in 1841 and a certificate of freedom on 20 April 1844. John Jones gave £10 to the Sydney Synagogue in 1845.

Printed Indent *Lady Kennaway*, no. 36-2067; *OBSP*, 1835, case 211, p. 900; TL 41/119; CF 4/4390.

JONES, Joseph

b. London, 1819
Barossa (1), 1839; Convict; Sentenced to 10 years, Warwick Assizes, 1839.
Single; Wood turner; Height: 175 cm; 3 children.

Fair ruddy complexion, light brown hair, dark grey eyes, eyebrows partially meeting. Could read and write. Jew. Joseph Jones was sentenced for 'burglary' on 27 March 1839. He had no previous convictions.

The *Barossa* arrived in New South Wales on 8 December 1839. Jones appeared on the first voters' list with a shop and dwelling in George Street. He married Elizabeth Hart (q.v.), the daughter of Asher and Phoebe Hart (qq.v.) on 16 February 1842. It was Sydney's forty-ninth Jewish wedding. In 1842, in Sydney, they had a child, Matilda, who was registered as a 'Hebrew'. Rachael was born in 1844, also in Sydney. Fanny was born in Queanbeyan in 1849 and Kitty was also born in Queanbeyan in 1850.

Jones received a ticket of leave in 1844 and a certificate of freedom on 30 March 1849. In 1853 he leased the 'Royal Hotel' in Auburn Street, Goulburn, from Solomon Moses (q.v.). Jones had been at the Harp at Queanbeyan. In 1859 Moses sold the hotel and moved to Yass. Jones took over another Royal Hotel at Bungendore.

Printed Indent of *Barossa*, p. 116; R. Wyatt, *The History of Goulburn*, p. 301; *Sydney Morning Herald*, 15 September 1842; TL 44/4412; CF 40/0078.

JONES, Joseph J.

Free.
Married; Dealer; 1 child.

Joseph J. Jones was married to Sarah. Fanny, their daughter, was born in Sydney in 1849 and was registered as a 'Hebrew'.

JONES, Lewis

b. London, 1816–1891
Recovery (3), 1836; Convict; Sentenced to 7 years, Central Criminal Court, 1835.
Single; Blacklead pencil maker; Height: 159 cm.

Dark ruddy and freckled complexion. Black hair, light brown eyes, eyebrows meeting. Mole right cheek. Jew. Could read and write. Jones picked a pocket on the Holborn Bridge. John Levi of the Jerusalem Passage, and a pencil-maker, and Henry Cowan, his foreman, gave Jones a good character reference. Jones was aged nineteen when he was sentenced at the Old Bailey on 11 May 1835 for having stolen a handkerchief valued at three shillings from William Preston on the Holborn Bridge. Jones begged for clemency for 'his mother's sake' and admitted his guilt. Jones was born in Brick Lane, Bethnal Green the son of Jonah and Rebecca Jones. He was literate and worked as an apprentice pencil maker in the Jerusalem Passage, Clerkenwall. Jones was fined for disorderly behaviour at Newgate Prison. His siblings were Maria, Frances, Sarah, Isaac and Esther.

The convict transport ship *Recovery* arrived in New South Wales on 25 February 1836. Lewis Jones was at the Hyde Park Barracks when the 1837 General Return of Convicts in New South Wales was compiled. He was sent to Queanbeyan and he received his ticket of leave in 1840 and his certificate of freedom on 29 December 1842. Rosa Phillips aged 20, married Lewis Jones (q.v.), aged 36, at the York Street Synagogue in 1852. Rosa was the daughter of Barnett Aaron (q.v.) and Clara Phillips (q.v.) and the sister in law of the Goulburn watchmaker Samuel Davis and his wife Sarah (qq.v.).

Lewis and Rosa Jones took over the Salutation Hotel in 1854 and in 1857 moved to Albury leasing the Criterion Hotel in Hume Street from Morris Asher (q.v.). Jones acted as agent for the Royal Mail coaches to Yass and Beechworth and prospered. In 1859 he was elected to first Albury town council. Jones prospered. He became Mayor of Albury, a Justice of the Peace, vice- president of the Hospital Board. Trustee of the building society. He was a freemason, a strong opponent of border customs duties between the colonies and served on committees for a public school and a hospital. Lewis and Rosa Jones had six daughters and one son. An infant daughter Lydia, died in 1874 and was buried in Albury and in 1879 the family moved to Melbourne where he ran the Sabloniere Hotel in Queen Street. Finally he became a pawnbroker in Drummond Street Carlton where he died in 1891.

OBSP, 1835, case 1181, p. 70; Printed Indent *Recovery*, p. 45; TL 40/1628; CF 42/2212. Extensive historical research by Howard C. Jones of Albury, Australian Jewish Historical Society, Newsletter no. 88 (2010) 'Pickpocket to pioneer Publican'.

JONES, Thomas

b. Birmingham, 1820
Asia (6), 1841; Convict; Sentenced to 10 years, Cheshire Quarter Sessions, 1839.
Single; Coachman and groom; Height: 175 cm.

Fresh complexioned, dark brown hair, large nose, large mouth, double chin, almost bald. A Jew. Thomas Jones was a pickpocket who had stolen £3 17s 6d from a woman at Macclesfield. He had been convicted before and the report from the hulk stated that his behaviour was 'very bad'. The surgeon on board ship described him as 'insubordinate and disorderly'. He denied that he was married. His brother Joseph Myers was living with a 'Mr Cohen'. He claimed 'I have several uncles at Sydney all free'.

After arriving in Van Diemen's Land in August 1841, Thomas Jones' initial probation period of eighteen months was extended ten times for misbehaviour. He worked on the chain gangs in Bridgewater, Fingal and Launceston and when working as a cook earned the comment that he was 'artful and bad'. On 2 May 1842 at Fingal he was found to be 'insolent and disorderly' and his sentence was extended by six weeks. On 10 June his insolence earned him a month in chains. On 14 June he hit a fellow prisoner and was ordered to sleep in a cell by himself for a month. On 13 September he sold his flannel shirt and was found to have valuable articles in his possession. His existing sentence was extended by six months and he was sent to Impression Bay. On 14 October he was found guilty of gambling for tobacco and sent to solitary confinement for three days. He was punished for obtaining boots under false pretences. For feigning illness on 19 November he received twenty-four stripes on the back. A further twenty-four lashes on his back were decreed when he was found hiding under a berth on a ship. On 29 June 1843 he was given seven days solitary confinement for having been found with a bar of soap in his possession. On 2 January 1844 his probationary period of imprisonment expired. By mid-1845 he had commenced duty as a constable in Hobart Town and in June 1846 he was dismissed for being drunk while on duty. He received his ticket of leave on 4 January 1848. On 11 September 1848, in Hobart Town, he was fined five shillings for being drunk on duty in a public place. His certificate of freedom was approved on 2 July 1849. He mischievously claimed that he had been transported to New South Wales under the name of 'Lewis Myers', on the *Mangles* (7), in order to expedite a pardon. Lewis Myers (q.v.) was his brother.

CON 33/9, no. 16640; Printed Indent *Asia* (6), no. 2086.

JONES, William (Lewis Myers)

b. Hants, 1813
Exmouth, 1831; Convict; Sentenced to 14 years, Middlesex, 1830.
Single; Fishmonger; Height: 161 cm.

Dark ruddy complexion, dark brown hair, brown eyes. Could read. Diagonal scar and a horizontal scar over it above left eyebrow. Dark mole on outer part of left eye. Ring on second finger left hand. William Jones' uncle was Abraham Polack (q.v.) of the London Tavern. Jones stole a handkerchief and was transported for picking pockets. He was sentenced on 16 September 1830.

William Jones arrived in New South Wales on 28 July 1831. Jones was initially assigned to the Australian Agricultural Company at Port Stephens and was still there at the time of the 1837 General Return of Convicts in New South Wales. Jones was granted a ticket of leave in the latter part of 1837, valid for the District of Port Stephens. This was altered for Parramatta in January 1838.

Jones was working as a carrier between Sydney and Parramatta and given a passport in 1841 (no. 395) so that he could carry on his business. The passport was extended until he was issued with a conditional pardon on 23 July 1844. A certificate of freedom was issued on 24 July 1847.

Ship Indent 4/4103, p. 148; Printed Indent *Exmouth*, 31-1419-137; *OBSP*, case 1538, p. 698; TL 37/1691; CF 47/595.

JONES, William

b. Westminster, 1817
Blundell, 1844; Convict; Sentenced to 7 years, Central Criminal Court, 1843.
Single; Baker, pastry cook and cook; Height: 164 cm.

Sallow complexion, dark brown hair, black eyebrows, forehead low and contracted, long narrow face, large aquiline nose, large mouth. Can read and write. Jew. William Jones was sentenced on 2 August 1843 and transported for burglary with violence. It was his first conviction. He had stolen plate and money with two men who were also sent to Norfolk Island.

William Jones and George Jones (q.v.) were sent directly from England to Norfolk Island, arriving there on 12 July 1844. William was then sent on to Van Diemen's Land on 26 February 1847 and assigned to John Davis (q.v.) of Brighton. He was tried at Hobart Town for stealing a coat (28 November 1849) and sent to Port Arthur for seven years. His description in 1849 read: 'Trade Baker. Dark complexion, dark hair, oval head, whiskers none, long narrow face. Blue eyes, nose large aquiline. Forehead low and contracted. Large mouth'.

He could only have served three years of the sentence because in 1852 he was arrested in Launceston for trying to escape. He received a ticket of leave on 7 November 1854 and a conditional pardon on 10 February 1857.

OBSP, 1829–30, case 1074, p. 470; CON 33/78, no. 18180 (a); CON 37/6/1911.

JOSEPH, Amelia (Minkey) (née NATHAN)

b. London, 1787–1857
Brothers, 1833; Free.
Married; 12 children.

Amelia, known as Minkey, married Joseph Joseph (q.v.) in 1798. She was the daughter of Fanny and Hyam Nathan, a 'fancy tailor' of London, and sister of Sarah Nathan, Jacob Hyam Nathan and Esther Nathan. Esther married Henry Moses on16 November 1842.

Amelia was the mother of twelve children: Jacob of Wellington, New Zealand, Moses (q.v.) of Sydney, Tobias, Miriam, David, Sarah, Hyam, Israel (q.v.), Nathan, Louis, Rosetta and Rachel (q.v.). Rachel married Asher Hymen Hart (q.v.) in February 1841. Amelia was buried at the Devonshire Street Cemetery on 5 June 1857, aged seventy-six.

JOSEPH, Dinah

b. London, 1788–1844
1828; Free.
Married.

Dinah Joseph followed her husband, Reuben Joseph (q.v.), to Van Diemen's Land in 1828. She had obviously brought with her enough money to buy two allotments of land in Collins Street, Hobart Town, on which to build a home and a shop. She wrote to the Colonial Secretary on 7 January 1829 that she had employed Simon Solomons (q.v.) to be 'her manservant—to open the shutters of her shop'. A few weeks later she claimed that Solomons had stolen about £40 of goods from the shop. The Police Superintendent believed that 'the sole reason for the whole proceedings' was to get Reuben Joseph assigned to his wife.

Dinah Joseph died at New Norfolk on 4 September 1844 aged fifty-six. Her funeral was the second to be conducted by the Hobart Hebrew Congregation.

CSO 1/367/8367; CSO 1/901/19147.

JOSEPH, Henry

Dryad, 1834; Free.
Merchant.

Henry Joseph 'a merchant' was recorded as arriving on the *Dryad* from England on 2 June 1834.

Indent, ML 4/5206; *Australian*, 3 June 1834.

JOSEPH, Hyam Moses

b. Sydney, 1835–1912

Hyam Moses Joseph was the son of Moses Joseph (q.v.) and Rosetta (née Nathan, q.v.). He was the first mayor of Bombala and master of the Mountain Lodge of Freemasons 'for many years'. He died on 18 January 1912.

Hebrew Standard, 26 January 1912.

JOSEPH, Israel

1792–1833
Free.

Israel Joseph was listed in the New South Wales Register of Deaths for the year 12 March 1833. His age was given as forty-one and his religion as 'Hebrew'. It was noted that he 'died at the home of his brother Moses Joseph' (q.v.).

JOSEPH, Israel (JOSEPHS)

b. London, 1812–1853
Brothers, 1833; Free.
Dealer.

The son of Joseph and Amelia (Minkey) Joseph (qq.v.), Israel was the brother of Moses Joseph (q.v.), Jacob and Rosetta Joseph (qq.v.). Israel Joseph travelled to Australia on the same ship as the family of Henry Simeon Cohen (q.v.).

On 2 March 1838, the *Hobart Town Courier* listed Israel Joseph as the recipient of a licence to be an auctioneer. On 25 May he received an additional licence to be a hawker. 'Joseph Israel' was licensed as an auctioneer on 23 December 1834. Joseph then moved to Sydney and opened a store and auction room in George Street called the London Depot. In July 1836 he announced the opening of a general store at Maitland. It was described as Israel Joseph's Sydney Store in Maitland, a large general store, auction room and commission agency. Leaving Peter Moody in charge, Joseph went to England, returning (steerage) on the *Australasian Packet* from London on 24 October 1839.

Joseph began to develop commercial ties with New Zealand beginning in 1842. Notices in the *Sydney Morning Herald* in 1843 and 1844 stated that Israel Joseph had sailed for Port Nicholson (Auckland). His brother Jacob Joseph, of Wellington, was an early settler in New Zealand. Another brother, Moses Joseph (q.v.), had important commercial ties across the Tasman and Israel Joseph sent £10 towards the building of the Sydney Synagogue in 1845. Israel Joseph opened a store at Kororareka on the Bay of Islands and quickly moved to Auckland where he opened a tent store in Commercial Bay. He officiated at the marriage of David Nathan (q.v.) to Rosetta Aarons, the first Jewish wedding in New Zealand and for two years worked as a partner with David Nathan.

Joseph returned to Sydney in 1847. The *Sydney Morning Herald* of 29 July 1847 reported:

> Mr Israel Joseph has recently returned to this colony and has commenced the manufacture of preserved provisions on a large scale. When he was in England he paid a large premium to be allowed to work in one of the patent houses, in order to learn the mode of performing the various operations. Having mastered [the art] he purchased the requisite apparatus and materials and came to Sydney.

Backed by capital from Moses Joseph a factory was established at Camperdown — the first food processing plant in Australia.

Israel Joseph had married Rosetta Braham in Montreal. He died at 390 George Street, the residence of his brother Moses Joseph, on 12 March 1853 at the age of forty-one. He was buried at the Devonshire Street Cemetery and his grave was relocated to Rookwood. The inscription on his grave reads: 'Here lies Israel son of Joseph far away and to his relatives he was known as an honest man'. Rosetta died in Melbourne on 13 October 1899 at the age of ninety-three.

Ship Indent 4/5205; *Australasian Packet* Indent, 4/5215; *Sydney Gazette*, 30 July 1836, 16 July 1844; *Australian*, 23 December 1834, 23 January 1835, 19 May 1835, 30 July 1835, 4 March 1836, 14 June 1842; *Sydney Morning Herald*, 21 March 1843, 16 July 1844.

JOSEPH, Jacob

d. 1837
Active, 1834; Free.
Single; Dealer.

Jacob Joseph married twice, first to Catherine (Kate) Nathan, and second to Rose Joseph. He arrived in Sydney on the *Active* on 18 September 1834. Jacob Joseph was buried by the Sydney Synagogue in the Devonshire Street Cemetery on 23 January 1837.

Australian, 27 September 1834.

JOSEPH, Joel

b. London, 1789–1874
Indian, 1810; Convict; Sentenced to life, London, 1808.
Single; Height: 173 cm.

Dark ruddy complexion, black hair, dark eyes. Joel Joseph was a pickpocket who stole a purse in Fleet Street. He was sentenced at the London Gaol Delivery on 14 September 1808. He was the son of Moses and Eliza Joseph of London.

Joel Joseph arrived in New South Wales on 16 December 1810. He was listed in the 1811 General Muster in Sydney on government rations and working as a driver. On 29 June 1811 Joseph was sent to Newcastle on the *Lady Nelson* for stealing promissory notes. On 27 February 1813 the Colonial Secretary was notified that Joseph had suffered 'punishment' at the prison settlement. On 13 July the *Sydney Gazette* reported that he had been charged with 'desertion'.

Joel Joseph was called as a witness at the trial of lieutenants McNaughton and Conner who had beaten a man to death in Pitt Street. Joseph testified that he 'lives in Pitt St' and was standing at the door of his house when the murder occurred. Joseph received a conditional pardon on 31 January 1818 and a licence to sell liquor in July of that year. He described himself as 'a free man—my house being in the centre of the street—with good accommodation' and in February 1820 asked for a licence to operate a hotel and sell liquor. He was a dealer in Pitt Street from 1820–22. In the *Sydney Gazette* of 24 February 1821 Joel Joseph placed a notice declaring that he 'feels extreme sorrow for any insulting language he used toward Mr Bernard Williams as he having incautiously been at the time rather intoxicated proffers his unfeigned apology'. On 18 January 1822 the *Sydney Gazette* published a notice concerning payment of £4 5s to Joel Joseph for the supply of two reams of paper for the use of the Sydney Criminal Court. On 26 April 1833 he advertised that he had millstones for sale. Joel Joseph was granted a certificate of freedom (no. 827) later that same year.

Joel Joseph married Maria Carr in a Church of England ceremony at St Lawrence's in Sydney in 1842. In 1844 the Sydney Synagogue recorded that Joel Joseph was appointed beadle at the salary of £25 a year. He was to live on the premises of the new synagogue and was entitled to take into custody any person disturbing the service.

OBSP, 1810, case 491, p. 268f.; HO 11/2; *Sydney Gazette*, 31 July 1813; CO 201/118; 1814 Muster, A1942-2, p. 240; CP Register 4/4430, p. 105; Sydney Synagogue Minutes p. 134.

JOSEPH, Joel Moses (JOSEPHS)

b. London, 1794–1820
Admiral Gambier (2), 1811; Convict; Sentenced to life, Old Bailey, 1810.
Single; Trafficker (pedlar); Height: 171 cm; 3 children.

Dark ruddy complexion, black hair, hazel eyes. Son of Simeon and Hannah Josephs of Petticoat Lane. He is described as a 'pickpocket and noted character'. On 17 April 1810, Joel Joseph and Isaac (Ikey) Solomon (q.v.), who were both tall young men and must have been easy to notice in a crowd, stole a pocket book containing £40 in bank notes and a warrant for payment for £56. They stole the pocket book in the Palace Yard in Westminster in a crowd near Westminster Hall. A constable saw them going through the purse. Josephs attempted to stuff the bank notes in his mouth to dispose of them. In Ikey's words:

> *'On 17 April curiosity led me to go to the Westminster Meeting. I had not been in the crowd two minutes, the crowd was so great I ran out for fear of being hurt. I proceeded to Westminster Hall and I had not been there one minute before somebody caught hold of me. The five pound notes was my own property.'*

Both Ikey Solomon and Joel Joseph were sent from Newgate Prison to the convict hulk anchored in the Medway Estuary near Sheerness and from the hulk Joseph was put on board the *Admiral Gambier* to be sent to Australia. He arrived in Sydney on 29 September 1811.

On 2 January 1813 Josephs and three other prisoners escaped from the penal colony at Hunter's River. The evidence given at his trial for desertion and reported in the *Sydney Gazette* of 13 February told his story:

> On Saturday 6th instant four prisoners viz Joel Josephs, Samuel Waters, John Maxwell and Joseph Batters were taken before a Bench of Magistrates assembled at Windsor,

> charged with desertion from Hunter's River to which place they were ordered returned. Josephs left the settlement on 2 January and two days after they fell in with a party of natives who killed one of them and stripped them and left them without food or raiment to prosecute the perilous journey along the coast which they nevertheless completed to Broken Bay and gave themselves up to a boatman who took them to a constable as soon as they reached the Hawkesbury.

Josephs was sent to the Prison Station of Newcastle, where he received twenty-two lashes. Between 1816 and 1818 Josephs developed a delivery service between Sydney and Bathurst. His horses, bullocks and carriages were used on an expedition exploring the River Lachlan and in working on the roads for the government. Josephs claimed 'to have been useful to the police on several occasions'. Simeon Lord testifies that he had found him 'an honest man in his dealings'. As a consequence Joseph petitioned Governor Macquarie asking for a ticket of leave: 'Eleven years have passed he is of general good character, his length of servitude completed'.

Sofia Hanukkah Josephs (Sophia Hannah Josephs, q.v.), daughter of Joel Josephs and Ann Cooper, was born on 13 July 1817 and baptised on 10 August 1817. (She married Ambrose Wilson at St Philip's in Sydney in 1834.) A son, born on 13 June 1821 after his father's death, was named Joel Josephs and was baptised on 29 April 1822.

Josephs was buried, by special application, as a Jew on 28 August 1820 in the right-hand corner of the Christian Burial Ground in Sydney, which was 'allotted to the Hebrews'. His burial therefore was historic, as this was the first burial in a Jewish section of an Australian cemetery.

The value of his estate was £400. By the time he died he had three brothers in New South Wales. In his will, he left £25 to his brother Abraham Moses (q.v.) and, to his brother David Joseph(s) (q.v.), £25 and 'all my clothes'. To Catherine Mackenzie he left £100 and three years free tenancy of the small house next door. He gave his gold watch to his brother Moses Josephs (q.v.), and to 'his dearly beloved natural daughter, Sofia Hanukkah Josephs, my two houses situated in Pitt Street when she is 21 or married'.

OBSP, 1810, case 401, p. 267; Bigge Appendix, BT, Box 2, p. 594f., Box 21, p. 3932c, Box 25, p. 5487; *HRA*, series 1, vol. 8, p. 10f.; Wentworth Papers A764, p. 165; CP Register 4/4430, p. 135; *Sydney Gazette*, 13 February 1813, 17 May 1817, 2 September 1820, 13 December 1822; Supreme Court of New South Wales, Probate Office, no. 79-1.

JOSEPH, Joseph

b. London, 1763–1850
Brothers, 1833; Free.
Married; Dealer; 12 children.

Joseph Joseph and Amelia (Minkey) Joseph (q.v.) were the parents of twelve children. Joseph and his son Israel Joseph (q.v.) came to Australia as steerage passengers. Joseph's time in Australia did not begin well. The *Sydney Gazette* carried a public notice in August 1833: 'If Joseph Joseph does not fetch away the goods he left at my house by Saturday next they will be sold to pay for his Board and Lodging.

A. Moses. King St'. Joseph Joseph signed a petition to the Governor in 1836 asking that conditions for new settlers to the colony be eased. Joseph was struggling to maintain his family and took a loan for fourteen years on premises in that part of George Street called Brickfield Hill where, for 'a serious outlay of capital', he built a house and shop. In November 1836 Joseph complained to the Colonial Secretary: 'The Public Surveyor caused the road to be cut away so close along the front ... so that the front of the house is useless'. Eight inches of pathway were disputed and he claimed that his business would be altogether destroyed and very deeply injured. He asked for damages for himself, his wife and his numerous children. The engineer reported that 'the road is perhaps two or three feet taken over the alignment—no damages due. The house in question is a poor one and I have no doubt will be pulled down and a better one built'. In 1839 'Joseph Joseph Snr and Mrs Joseph Joseph' gave £20 and £10 respectively to the new synagogue fund in Sydney.

Most of their children migrated to Australia and constituted a powerful colonial network. They were Jacob (q.v.) Moses (q.v.), Tobias Joseph (who married Amelia Samuels), Miriam (who married Jonas Melbourne Hart), David, Sarah (who married Hyam Elias, q.v.), Hyam, Israel, Nathan, Louis (q.v.), Rosetta (q.v.), and Rachel (who married Asher Hymen Hart, q.v.).

Joseph Joseph died on 13 June 1850, aged eighty-seven, at the residence of his son Moses at 390 George Street and was buried in the Devonshire Street Jewish Cemetery. Minkey (Amelia), the wife of Joseph Joseph, died on 1 June 1857, aged seventy-six.

Brothers Indent 4/5205; Governors' Despatches 1836, ML, A1216, p. 601; CS 4/2309, 36/9237; *Sydney Gazette*, 13 August 1833.

JOSEPH, Lewis

b. London, 1801–1840 *Sarah* (1), 1829; Convict; Sentenced to 7 years, London, 1829. Married; Moulder and founder groom; Height: 157.5 cm; 2 children (in London).

Ruddy complexion, brown hair, hazel eyes. Heavily tattooed. Darts. Love. EK on right arm. Hope and anchor, sprig and heart. Below elbow LJBK, 'Love me little Love me Long' on upper part of left arm. Could read and write. Jew. Lewis Joseph was found guilty of stealing fifty yards of silk twist. Abraham Brown told him that if he would go quietly with me to the (police) office it would be some proof of his honesty. He first said he was a tailor and then a pencil maker. He went very quietly part of the way to the office. He then said 'I know where you are going to take me, but if you will go to my father's I will give you ten shillings'. I then said 'I must handle you'. He then offered me one pound and when we got to the office he offered me thirty shillings'. Lewis Joseph was sentenced on 9 April 1829. He was twenty-six years old.

Lewis Joseph arrived in New South Wales on 10 December 1829. On 31 March 1830 Lewis Joseph, an 'Assigned Servant', was transferred from Patrick Byrne to J. H. Humphrey. Lewis Joseph received his certificate of freedom on 9 April 1836.

The *Sydney Gazette* reported on 4 March 1837 that Lewis Joseph had been committed to gaol for fourteen days for 'prevarication' while giving evidence. He was fined £5 or two months gaol for an assault on Esther Shaw. Three days later the two of them were charged with keeping a brothel. On 13 April 1837 at the Central Criminal Court in Sydney, Lewis Joseph was sentenced to twelve months on the Road Iron Gang. On 14 January 1840 Joseph was sentenced to twelve months imprisonment with the treadmill and solitary confinement every fourth week. The punishment broke his body, and within weeks he was dead. He was buried at the Devonshire Street Jewish Cemetery on 1 April 1840.

Sarah (1) Indent 4/4015, p. 15; Correspondence Out, CS 4/3669; OBSP 9 April 1829, case 731. Central Criminal Court, 13 April 1837, 4/6448; House of Correction Register, 1837, 40 4/4569, p. 205; CF 36/0202; *Commercial Journal and Advertiser,* 15 January 1840.

JOSEPH, Louis (Lewis JOSEPHS)

Resource, 1837; Free.
Single; Trader.

Louis Joseph was listed on the ship's manifest as 'Lewis' Joseph. There was a former convict in Sydney with the same name who had just been convicted of being a brothel keeper, which might have caused the change in spelling. Lewis Joseph was the son of Joseph and Amelia (Minkey) Joseph (qq.v.).

Lewis Joseph arrived in Sydney on 24 June 1837 as a free settler. He gave £5 to the new Sydney Synagogue fund on 15 September 1839. He was in Adelaide in 1845 and sent a £5 donation to the Sydney Synagogue at the time of its dedication. In March 1846, in Sydney, Mr Louis Joseph of Adelaide was married to Sarah, the daughter of Lewis Barnett (q.v.) of Jamison Street, Sydney. On 20 June 1846 Joseph dissolved his partnership with Bertram Nathan (q.v.) and disposed of his linen and drapery shop in Hindley Street to Mr B. Nathan. On 5 August 1846 Emanuel Solomon (q.v.) announced the sale of Mr Louis Josephs' household furniture prior to his immediate departure for England. Joseph returned to South Australia two years later and on 30 September 1848: 'Louis Joseph informs the Aristocracy, Ladies and Settlers of South Australia that after a very great outlay of capital in erection of the new spacious premises in Hindley Street he will open them on 4 October and offer his cheap goods for sale'. Louis Joseph was a member of the Committee of the Adelaide Hebrew Congregation in 1850.

South Australian Gazette and Colonial Register, 11 March 1846, 20 June 1846, 5 August 1846, 30 September 1848, 11 September 1850; *Sydney Gazette*, 4 August 1837.

JOSEPH, Moses

b. London, 1803–1889
Albion (2), 1827; Convict; Sentenced to life, Warwick Assizes, 1826.
Single; Jeweller and pedlar; Height: 164 cm; 9 children.

Ruddy dark complexion, black hair, brown eyes, flat feet. Can read and write. Moses Joseph was transported for robbing a pedlar and stealing jewellery and was sentenced on 25 March 1826. He was the second son of Joseph and Amelia (Minkey) Joseph (q.v.) and his transportation was directly responsible for the migration to Australia and New Zealand of an entire tribe.

The *Albion* arrived in New South Wales on 14 February 1827. The prisoner, Moses Joseph, brought £10 11s 6d with him. Joseph was assigned to the firm of Cooper and Levey. On 24 January 1832 Moses Joseph petitioned the government for permission to marry Rosetta Nathan (q.v.), and to change his legal status. Rosetta was the daughter of Nathan Lyon Nathan (q.v.) and Sarah of London. Minkey was the sister of Sarah Nathan and therefore the bridal couple were first cousins. Moses Joseph wrote that Rosetta was 'a respectable and virtuous woman who lately arrived in this colony per the ship *Margaret* evincing thereby the continuance of her attachment and her determination to share the fate and misfortune of petitioner Moses Joseph. That your petitioners are of the Jewish persuasion and with your Excellency's sanction are about to be married according to the laws, rights [*sic*] and ceremonies of that religion'. They asked for permission to marry and for a ticket of leave or exemption to be granted to Joseph. The ticket of exemption (32/707) and permission to marry were issued. Their wedding on 30 January 1832 was Australia's first officially sanctioned Jewish marriage. The 'clergyman' was Phillip Joseph Cohen (q.v.), 'by authority of the Rev. Solomon Herschell Chief Rabbi of the Jews in London'.

Joseph set up a general business in George Street and by 6 January 1834 was advertising that he had 'trousers and other clothing for sale'. The business quickly prospered. He was elected to the Board of Management of the Bridge Street Synagogue in 1837 and served as its treasurer and a member of the Building Committee. From 1840 to 1848 he was president of the synagogue's Board of Management and was nominated one of the five trustees when land was purchased in York Street in 1841. As president of the York Street Synagogue he pledged £150 to its construction. In July 1833 he was permitted to proceed to Hobart Town and to Launceston on business. He is recorded as having arrived in Launceston on the *Ann* on 4 July 1833 and on the *Pickwick* on 22 August 1839. Moses Joseph was granted an absolute pardon on 1 February 1840. Joseph's family spread through Australia and New Zealand. Louis Nathan (q.v.) in Hobart was his wife's brother. Three brothers, Jacob, Isaac and Israel Joseph (q.v.), together with Rosetta's brother David Nathan (q.v.), virtually founded the Jewish community in New Zealand. Kate, the sister of Moses Joseph, married his brother-in-law Joseph Edward Nathan (1835–1912) of New Zealand.

Rosetta and Moses had nine children. They were: Caroline, born in Sydney on 7 January 1833 and married Sidney Joseph Abraham Moses Merton on 20 August 1851; Hyam Moses (q.v.), born 25 June 1835 who married Rachel Elias Moses and died 18 January 1912; Charlotte, born 20 December 1836 who married Louis Charles Lumley; Lewis, born 1842–1848; Marianne (Miriam), born 27 May 1843; Israel (Isaac Arthur), born 1 May 1845 and died in London 1916; Sarah (Stella), born 1849 and died 15 December 1926 in London and who married Jacob Edward Moss; David, born 1850 who married Rosetta; Jerrold (Joseph), 1851–1916 who married Lillian Julia Cohen and Julia, born in 1853 and who married Joseph Edward Moss.

Moses Joseph developed extensive land holdings (108 000 acres in the New England district by 1849). Deeply involved in intercolonial and trans-Tasman trade he eventually owned fourteen ships, with the barque *Rosetta Joseph* the pride of the fleet. On 21 November 1846 the *Citizen* reported: 'Moses Joseph's whaling brig *Eleanor* is wrecked. She was not insured—and we are sorry to say that the loss to her owner Mr Joseph is estimated at £4800. The ship was wrecked on Yule's Reef North West of New Guinea on 21 May 1846. The crew saved themselves'. Moses Joseph subsequently bought land in Sydney and Melbourne, and in Auckland and Wellington in New Zealand.

A conditional pardon was granted on 17 February 1840 and in 1847 Governor Fitzroy recommended to England that Joseph be granted an absolute pardon. This was granted on 22 January 1848 and Joseph left for England on 7 February 1849. When gold was discovered in California, Joseph immediately despatched the *Rosetta Joseph* to San Francisco laden with household goods, wheelbarrows and pickaxes for the miners. The ship foundered off Lord Howe Island on its return journey and it was reported that the crew and passengers had desperately jettisoned 'bags of gold dust'.

Together with his brother Israel, who provided the expertise, Moses Joseph was the founder of canned meat processing in Australia. On 27 July 1847 the *Sydney Morning Herald* advertised 'M. Joseph, Patent Preserved Meat Manufactory, Camperdown', which he guaranteed would allow fresh provisions 'to remain in a complete state of preservation in any climate for several years'. His products included turtle, beef, ducks, oysters and milk. The *Sydney Morning Herald* explained that Israel Joseph had 'paid a large premium' to learn the process and buy the 'requisite apparatus' and had then returned to Sydney.

By 1852 Moses Joseph was the largest licensed gold buyer in New South Wales, sending more than 1000 ounces to London in a single year. Moses returned to London in 1863 or 1864 to live at 17 Bedford Square, Paddington Square. Rosetta died at 47 Bedford Square on 22 January 1891 at the age of eighty. Moses died in London on 7 February 1889, leaving an estate in the United Kingdom estimated at £300 000. In Australia his estate was valued at £185 499. In the 1860s, during the American Civil War, Joseph had lost a fortune when, inspired by Judah P. Benjamin, he had invested more than £250 000 in the Confederate States.

Howard T. Nathan,' Rosetta Joseph: The Bell, Her Husband and His Money', *AJJHS*, vol. 17, no. 1 (2003), p. 5f; Ship Indent 2/8240, p. 195; Ship Indent 4/4012, p. 39; CS Letters, 32/107, 24 January 1832, in 4/2132, and 47/323, 14 December 1847; 4/3687 CP 39/379 and 40/104; Absolute Pardon, 4/3692, no. 47/323, pp. 455, 478; *Australian*, 6 January 1834, *Sydney Chronicle*, 22 January 1848; *Citizen*, 21 November 1846; Land Correspondence 2/7894, 15 August 1849.

JOSEPH, Nathan

b. London, 1815–1859
1834; Free.
Married; storekeeper; 11 children.

Nathan Joseph subscribed to the Sydney Patriotic Fund on 23 June 1835. Nathan's family settled in Singleton, New South Wales, in 1835, where Joseph was a 'store keeper'. Joseph Nathan 'of Sydney' bought land at Maitland and opened a store there in 1836. There is a reference to Nathan Joseph in a report made by the Patrick Plains Police regarding the sum of £2 10s, being 'the moiety of a fine of £5 imposed upon Nathan Joseph at this Court on the 21st ultimo, for employing a servant of Dr Bowman's and request you will have the goodness to hand it over to the Treasurer of the Benevolent Society'. As the economic crisis deepened in the 1840s, 'Joseph Nathan, merchant at Singleton, Patrick Plains', asked debtors to pay him their outstanding accounts. He advertised a horse for sale in West Maitland on 12 September 1849.

The local authorities turned to Nathan for assistance to arrange a Jewish funeral when, in 1834, William Myers (q.v.), a Jewish prisoner, was killed at Patrick Plains. The expenses of £6 15s 4d were reimbursed by the Sydney Synagogue's Benevolent Fund. Joseph Nathan was a seat holder at the Sydney Synagogue in 1845 and gave £2 2s to the building fund.

Nathan Joseph married Sarah Moses (q.v.) on 1 June 1836 at the Bridge Street Synagogue. The Sydney Synagogue Birth Book records eleven children born to Sarah and Joseph Nathan: Moses (1837), born in Singleton; Joseph (1839-1905), Caroline (1841), Frances (Fanny) (1843), Rosetta (1845), Abraham (1847-1893), Hyam (1849-1915), and Rachel (1853), born in Sydney; Israel Elias Joseph(1856-1900), born in Scone; and Jacob Samuel Joseph (1858-1926), born in Singleton. Fanny died on 2 January 1847 and an infant Abraham on 19 November 1847.

Nathan Joseph 'of Singleton' died on 23 March 1859 and was buried in the Jewish section of the Devonshire Street Cemetery, where Sarah would be buried in 1892, before being reburied at Lidcombe in 1901.

Sydney Morning Herald, 23 June 1835, 25 December 1841; *Australian*, 4 January 1842; CS 4/2420.2, 1 January 1838; Land Purchases 2/7894; *Maitland Mercury*, 12 September 1849; Mutch Index, 15/135.

JOSEPH, Norman (Nahum) (SIMONS)

Palambam, 1833; Free.
Married; Hebrew tutor and *schochet*.

Norman Joseph came to Australia on 10 January 1833 as the tutor and *schochet* for Abraham Moses (q.v.) for his large family. Joseph was incorrectly listed in the indent as 'Norman Simons' and described as a 'rabbi'. Simon Nahum acquired a licence for the British Standard in George Street on 7 April 1834. On 31 March 1835 Nahum Simons, 'of Maitland', bought land at Berrima and Bathurst, and in June advertised that he was about to open a general store in the town of Bathurst.

Ship Indent 4/5294; *Sydney Gazette*, 12 January 1833, 7 April 1834, 26 June 1835; Land Records 2/7971.

JOSEPH, Philip (JOSEPHS)

b. London, 1802
Mangles (3), 1824; Convict; Sentenced to 14 years, Surrey Special Sessions, 1823.
Single; Labourer and pedlar; Height: 166 cm; 1 child.

Dark complexion, black hair, grey eyes.

Philip Joseph was appointed turnkey at the Newcastle Gaol on 4 October 1826. In the 1828 Census he was listed as a Jew in government service and still working at the Newcastle Gaol. Joseph married Margaret Ryan at Christ Church, Newcastle, on 25 February 1830. In recognition of his service as a constable he was exempted from government labour in September 1830. He obtained a ticket of leave for his part in the capture of cart robber Felix McCans, alias Kearney, who was executed at Maitland. He was allowed to remain in Newcastle and at that time was a shopkeeper. He wrote, 'because of decreasing population' and because he had a wife and child, he requested permission to transfer to Parramatta. The Colonial Secretary believed that 'His correct object is to live in Sydney I have no doubt'. His request to move was allowed for Maitland and then for Parramatta, on 25 June 1832, where he was listed in the General Return of the Colony of 1837.

Philip Joseph gave £20 to the York Street building appeal in September 1839. The voters' list for the Sydney municipal election of 1842 shows that he had a shop and dwelling house in Castlereagh Street. In November 1842 Joseph lent the Sydney Synagogue the huge sum of £1500 for three years at 10 per cent interest because the colony's recession had brought fundraising to an abrupt stop and the synagogue was being built. Joseph was honoured by being called to the Torah as 'Bridegroom of the Beginning' (*Chatan Bereshit*) at the Festival of *Simchat Torah* in 1842. In 1845 he was a seat holder at the York Street Synagogue and donated £20 to the congregation. 'Mrs Philip Joseph' had a daughter in Sydney on 27 September 1844.

4/4073 TL 29/930; 4/4010, p. 101; *Sydney Gazette*, 4 October 1826, 27 September 1831; Petition in CS 4/2116, 2 August 1831, 31/6897; Bigge Appendix, A2130, p. 95; CS Exemption from Government Labour, Letters 4/4284, no. 30/152, and 4/2146, in 4/2146.

JOSEPH, Reuben (Rheuben)

b. London, 1794–1862
William Miles, 1828; Convict; Sentenced to 14 years, Middlesex, 1827.
Married; Tailor; Height: 165 cm.

Florid complexion, large round head, black brown hair, reddish bushy whiskers, broad square face, bushy arched eyebrows, high broad forehead, dark brown eyes, small mouth, straight nose, long pointed chin. Much pock-pitted face. Reuben Joseph was sentenced on 25 October 1827. He was described in his dossier as a 'notorious receiver of stolen property who was convicted of receiving stolen plate. His house had been searched by the police on many occasions'. He had a brother at 34 Monomeith Street who 'keeps my shop—an Old Clothes warehouse. I was taken from my house, my wife Dinah Josephs [Joseph, q.v.] is coming out Free'. Joseph brought with him on board ship a small trunk with books and wearing apparel and a small bag. He brought £2 1s 8d with him to Australia.

Reuben Joseph arrived in Van Diemen's Land on 29 July 1828. Dinah, his wife, was in Hobart Town by January 1829 with a shop in Collins Street. She had employed Simon Solomons (q.v.) to be her servant and to open the shutters of her shop. (She had a sister Mrs Sarah Joseph who was also in Hobart Town.) Dinah Joseph claimed that Solomons had stolen goods worth £40 or £50. However, the Police Superintendent suspected that the whole 'manoeuvre' was merely an attempt to get Reuben Joseph assigned to his wife in order to protect her. Joseph's convict record has only one entry. On 16 October 1832 he was alleged to have refused to pay wages due to Thomas Rippon. The case was dismissed. Joseph eventually received a ticket of leave on 1 July 1833.

On 14 October 1836 Reuben Joseph of New Norfolk advertised in the *Hobart Town Courier* that he owned 'a most beautiful Cart Horse called "Moses" for serving mares'. Reuben Joseph received a conditional pardon on 16 November 1836.

On 16 February 1838 Reuben Joseph of New Norfolk, a creditor of Henry Savery, a local farmer, had Savery declared insolvent for the £50 debt and became provisional assignee of Savery's estate. Reuben Joseph subsequently received two separate land grants of approximately '1 rood and 30 perches' each on High Street and Montagu Street, New Norfolk, in February 1833. A certificate of freedom was granted in 1841.

Joseph became a member of the Hobart Hebrew Congregation in 1842 and rented seat 45 when the building was dedicated in 1845. Mrs Dinah Joseph rented a seat in the Synagogue and it was noted that her subscription came in 'per Mr I. Solomon'. Dinah died on 4 September 1844 at the age of fifty-six and was buried by the congregation—its second funeral. According to the Minute Book of the congregation, Joseph was appointed the community's first kosher butcher on 13 September 1846. He was a founding member of the Tasmanian Hebrew Benevolent Institute in 1847.

On 18 March 1845 in the Supreme Court in Hobart a trial was held involving his 'brother-in-law' John Davies (q.v.) of New Norfolk. Reuben Joseph occupied the Glebe Farm at New Norfolk by lease. (John Davies lived in Broadmarsh.) Davies' eldest son Levi had 300 sheep. Levi moved his horses, cattle and goods to Joseph's farm to prevent them being seized for his debts. Joseph had debts of £3060 and assets totalling £475, being made up of £250 of stock in trade, forty Bank shares worth £160, two horses valued at £35 and furniture worth £30. The bailiff took property from Joseph's farm in order to pay a debt that was due to the teacher of the children of Davies. Joseph claimed that the goods belonged to him and demanded damages. The bailiff's actions were upheld, and Joseph's house and store were offered up for sale on 24 May 1844. On 4 July 1845 Reuben Joseph declared himself to be insolvent after having been arrested in February for the non-payment of £115 19s 10d to a Mr Kerr. The sheriff didn't know how to collect his fees.

Reuben Joseph had acted as the butcher supplying the Hobart congregation with kosher meat however following his financial problems the congregation was forced to terminate his appointment and in July 1849 Isaac Friedman (q.v.) took his place.

In 1856 Reuben married a widow, Rachel Levien, at the Hobart Synagogue. Reuben Joseph died on 21 November 1862 at the age of seventy-two and was buried in the Harrington Street Jewish cemetery in Hobart.

VDL Papers, ML, A1059/4, p. 7; CON 18/20, no. 359; CON 31/24; CON 21/33, no. 359; CSO 1/367/8367, 7 January 1829, 22/142/2997, 4 July 1845; CP 1158; CF 41/771; Hobart Town Synagogue Minute Book, 13 September 1846; *Hobart Town Courier*, 16 February 1833, 19 April 1839, 18 March 1845.

JOSEPH, Rosetta

b. London
1833; Free.
Single; 3 children.

The daughter of Joseph and Amelia Joseph (qq.v.) of London, and sister of Moses (q.v.) and family, Rosetta married Kauffman Samuel (q.v.) in Sydney on 10 March 1835. Their children were Deborah, born 1835, Caroline, born 1838 and Moses, born 1840 and who died as an infant.

JOSEPH, Samuel

b. London, 1803
Maria I (2), 1821; Convict; Sentenced to 7 years, Old Bailey, 1819.
Single; Shopman.

On 29 October 1819 Joseph was found with two carriage glasses in his possession. He was sentenced on 1 December 1819 and transported for seven years for 'felony'. He was not known at the gaol before and his hulk report was 'orderly'.

Samuel Joseph was listed on the ship's indent as being eighteen years old and, in 1821, was a servant to Mr Dowell at Hobart Town, as was Jonas Myers (q.v.), aged sixteen. Joseph's conduct record is blank. The 1821 Convict Muster stated that he was 'off the stores' and assigned to Mr W. McDonald. The records indicate that Jonas Myers escaped from custody and the colony. It is tempting to guess that the two Jewish teenagers, who were sentenced at the Old Bailey within months of each other, escaped together.

OBSP, 1819, case 88, p. 48; Ship Indent 4/4007, p. 21; HO 10/43; VDL Papers 4/1235, p. 104; CON 3/23.

JOSEPH, Saul

Surprize, 1790; Convict; Sentenced to 7 years, Old Bailey, 1787.

Saul Joseph stole twenty-four pairs of shoes and was caught carrying them away in the street.

A 'John Saul' was convicted of entering a dwelling house and stealing sundry articles in Sydney in 1822. He was sentenced to seven years colonial transportation.

OBSP, 1786–87, case 495. p. 701; *Surprize* Indent, p. 39; *Sydney Gazette*, 1 March 1833.

JOSEPH, Udin

b. 1788
Dromedary, 1820; Convict; Sentenced to 7 years, Old Bailey, 1819.

Udin Joseph was sentenced at the Old Bailey after breaking into a house in Harrow. He had been caught on the road carrying the stolen goods away.

Joseph arrived in Van Diemen's Land on the *Dromedary* in January 1820. There is no police record after his name. Joseph was sent on to Sydney in 1820.

OBSP, 1818–19, case 602, p. 245; 4/4007, p. 67; CON 31/23, no. 81.

JOSEPHS, David

b. London, 1797
Surrey I (1), 1814; Convict; Sentenced to life, Old Bailey, 1813.
Single; Labourer; Height: 171 cm.

Swarthy complexion, black hair, dark eyes. Aged sixteen, David was the younger brother of Joel Josephs (Joseph, q.v.) and Abraham Moses (q.v.). He was sentenced on 17 February 1813.

The *Surrey* arrived in New South Wales on 28 July 1814. On 18 August David Josephs was sent to Windsor, where he seemed unable to keep out of trouble and was sent to the prison establishment at Newcastle. He absconded from Newcastle in February 1816 and six months later the Colonial Secretary noted (7 August 1816) that he was 'continually running away'. In 1820 he was recaptured and sent, once again, to the Newcastle Penal Settlement, on 11 June 1821, to serve a sentence of imprisonment for two years. In May 1822 Josephs received fifty lashes for 'making away with his slop clothing'.

On 22 November 1822 Josephs wrote to Thomas Goulburn:

> I arrived in this Colony per ship *Surrey I* in 1813 since I have endeavoured to obtain an honest livelihood. I was plunged into trouble a short time since being extricated from which I have suffered much hardship since I have been in the Colony and am resolved to lead a New Life'.

Josephs asked for a ticket of leave 'since the death of my brother I am thrown in the wide world'.

A new petition was written, dated 27 September 1823. He had 'at length come into the possession of a small property by the death of an older brother and anxious rather to increase than diminish it which latter must necessarily be the case so long as Petitioner shall be continued in the employ of the Government'. A note written on the petition says 'Tillen the bushranger was in his company when apprehended'. Following the rejection of the petition Josephs escaped. He had been discharged from the chain gang at Emu Plains and given a pass. It was noted that he 'did not return' and was at large with a forged ticket of leave until April 1823 when he was 'apprehended' and sent to Port Macquarie for a year.

Sydney Gazette, 17 February 1816, 6 December 1822; 4/3502, 27 July 1820; Petitions, no. 20, 23 November 1822, and no. 21, 27 September 1823, 4/1866; Punishments at Newcastle, 4/1718, May 1822.

JOSEPHS, Isaac

Free.
Tailor.

The *Sydney Gazette* reported on 14 October 1834: 'Isaac Josephs, a retail trader in weaving apparel, who has a stall in the market place sought redress from a Mr Owen Byrne, a retailer, who tried to destroy his stall and who tried to expel Josephs from the market in place of the vendor of butter and other provisions. Byrne was fined twenty shillings and ordered to pay costs of 5 shillings and two pence 'for damage done'.

JOSEPHS, John

York I (1), 1829; Convict.

John Josephs arrived in Hobart Town on 28 August 1829. A ticket of leave was issued to John Joseph and was listed in the *Hobart Town Courier* on 23 September 1836. In September 1842 John Josephs, who was free by servitude, was refused permission to marry Catherine Forsyth (who had arrived on the *Atwick*) 'on account of female's conduct'.

Permission to Marry Book, CON 52/2, p. 87; CON 31/23; CON 18/1; MM 31/1; MM 33/5.

JOSEPHS, Joseph

b. London, 1785
Ocean II (1), 1818; Convict; Sentenced to 7 years, Old Bailey, 1816.
Single; Seaman; Height: 164.5 cm.

Joseph Josephs was transported for breaking a window of a clothing shop belonging to Benjamin Lyons. He was 'in company with others' and ran away carrying a pair of pantaloons valued at four shillings. He was sentenced at the Old Bailey on 18 September 1816.

On 16 January 1818 Joseph Josephs was sent to Windsor to be assigned. On 6 August 1819 he was 'a prisoner to be sent to Newcastle'. The Colonial Secretary noted, on 8 September 1821, that Joseph Josephs was a member of the Sydney Gaol Gang. On 27 December Joseph Josephs, 'a sailor', was sent to Newcastle on the *Elizabeth* to serve the remainder of his sentence. He was granted his certificate of freedom on 26 March 1824. The week before the certificate was officially granted, on 18 March 1824, he announced in the *Sydney Gazette* that he was leaving the colony on the *William Shand*. A Letter of Administration of his goods, chattels, etc. was granted to Abraham Elias (q.v.) of Windsor on 20 May 1824. According to the General Muster List for 1825, Josephs had 'cleared out' on 24 March 1825.

OBSP, 1816–17, case 894, p. 421; *Ocean II* (1) Indent, no. 1542; HO 10/1, p. 201; 4/3504a; *Sydney Gazette*, 4 July 1818, 16 October 1823, 20 May 1824; HO 10/19; CF 4/4423.

JOSEPHS, Moses

b. 1780 Free.
Single; 1 child.

Moses Josephs was sentenced in Sydney on 25 March 1819. He was the brother of Abraham Moses (q.v.), David Josephs (q.v.) and Joel Joseph (q.v.), all of whom came to Australia.

On 20 June 1820 Moses Josephs, aged forty, married Elizabeth Weir, aged eighteen, at St Philip's in Sydney. Both were free. Moses Josephs was a 'dealer'. Witnesses to the wedding were Joseph Raphael (q.v.) (who was barely literate) and Ann Raphael. On 21 October 1821 Moses Josephs wrote to the colonial administration seeking clarification of his legal rights as an emancipist.

St Philip's Register, 398/25, 1820, no. 96, and 463/108; *HRA*, series 1, vol. 4, p. 549.

JOSEPHS, Philip (Moses) (JOSEPH)

d. 1855
Caledonia (1), 1820; Convict; Sentenced to 14 years, Oxford, 1820.
Single; Labourer; 4 children.

Philip Josephs was also known to the authorities as Moses Josephs and Philip Joseph.

On 24 February 1824 one quarter of Philip Josephs' annual salary as a member of the police force was confiscated when he was found drunk on duty at the Hobart Town Gaol. On 26 March 1825 Josephs was dismissed from the force 'for neglect of duty and cowardice' when confronted by bushrangers at Jericho. He was returned to the government and began to work as an assigned servant. Phillip Josephs married Catherine Richards at Launceston. She had arrived in 1826 on the *Providence* (2) with a sentence of transportation for seven years. Catherine was continually in trouble for drunk and disorderly conduct and her police dossier lists twenty-five offences between her arrival and 1840.

On 21 October 1828 Josephs was set upon in his own home by thieves who bound him up. For his 'manifest cowardice', Josephs was returned to the government and was not to be assigned again for six months. On 11 November 1828 he was convicted for receiving a stolen canvas bag valued at ten pence, knowing that it had been stolen. His original sentence was extended by twelve months and it was ordered that he be sent to a penal settlement. During this sentence he was given twenty-five lashes for being absent from his work gang (on 3 September 1829). On 20 March 1833 he was sentenced to three days solitary confinement on bread and water for disobedience while working as a javelin man. On 19 November 1835 he was charged with having a coat valued at £2, knowing that it was stolen. The case was dismissed.

On 12 January 1837 Moses Josephs, living at the lower end of Brisbane Street in Launceston, asked for an assigned servant. The police report described him as 'a most abandoned character'. Josephs responded: 'I am a householder in

Launceston carrying on the business of a dealer and supporting a young family with respectability'. He attached a list of local merchants who were ready to attest to his 'industrious, sober life and habits'. A further official inquiry was made on 18 February 1837. The police replied by enclosing his convict record, and describing him as a 'very improper person', and noting that a stolen coat had recently been found in his possession. A district constable stated that a woman whose husband, Richard Ray, kept a public house in Hobart Town was cohabiting with Josephs as his wife. His own wife was not living with him. Another constable, a convict, testified to having heard that Josephs wanted to have a convicted forger, named Brown, assigned to him. Brown had married a daughter of a man named Josephs who lived at New Norfolk. They hoped to go into partnership together.

A hawker's licence was issued to Josephs in Launceston on 25 May 1838, and expired on 12 April 1839.

Josephs visited Sydney from Launceston on business in 1835 and 1842. His name appeared on the petition for the establishment of a Launceston synagogue in 1843. He was already a member of the Hobart Synagogue and gave two guineas to the Hobart Synagogue's building appeal in 1845 and a similar sum to the Sydney Synagogue.

On October 1846 he was finally granted a licence for the 'Sportsman's Hall' at Charles and Balfour streets—objections to his character included concern that his auction rooms were generally filled with merchandise and that he had only just married his mistress. He was involved in a bigamy hearing in August 1847 when W. Homes, the de facto husband of his first wife, came to Launceston from Melbourne in the hope of blackmailing him.

Philip Joseph died on 7 August 1855 and an inquest was held into his death. Joseph's grave is shown on the map of the old Jewish cemetery in South Street, Invermay, Launceston. It was isolated from the other burials and may indicate that he committed suicide or it may simply mean that the congregation disapproved of his bigamous relationship. His wife was Margaret, and his children were Moses, Philip Joshua, Louisa and Abraham by his first wife Catherine. He left an estate of £1700.

CSO 5/11/162; CON 31/23, no. 107; CO 280/157; Launceston Synagogue Petition, 20 May 1843; Launceston Police Book, CON 78/2, p. 227, *Tasmanian and Port Dalrymple Advertiser*, 30 March 1825; *Launceston Advertiser*, 11 November 1828, 7 September 1829; *Hobart Town Courier*, 4 February 1842, 20 May 1842; *Launceston Examiner*, 14 May 1845; CSO 5/11/162, 12 January 1837, signed with both his names: Moses and Philip Moses.

JOSEPHS, Sophia Hannah

Free.
Single.

Sophia Hannah Josephs 'of Sydney' married Ambrose William Wilson in Sydney at St Philip's on 14 February 1834.

No. 34/8, ML, A6031.

JOSEPHSON, Emma (née MOSES) (MOSS) (MENDOZA)

b. London, 1781–1868
Morley (2), 1820; Free.
Married; Umbrella-maker; 8 children.

Emma Josephson was the daughter of Emanuel and Sarah Moses of London and was born on 4 June 1781. She was baptised on 6 July 1814 at St Mary's, Whitechapel. Emma had three children from her first marriage to Henry Wilson (né Isaac Goodman): Sarah (married Barnett Levey, q.v.), Henry and Charles. Emma's second marriage was to Jacob Josephson (q.v.). When he was convicted of theft and transported, Emma travelled to New South Wales to be with her husband. She brought her children with her. Jacob and Emma's children were Joshua Frey Josephson (q.v.), christened on 26 March 1815, Lewis, born at Oxford in 1818, and Emanuel, Isaac and John, who were born in Australia.

Emma died on 6 December 1868 at Elizabeth Street, Sydney.

S. Rubinstein, *The Street Trader's Lot: London, 1851.*

JOSEPHSON, Jacob

b. Breslau, 1776–1845
Neptune I (1), 1818; Convict; Sentenced to 14 years, Oxford, 1817.
Married; Hebrew teacher; Height: 163 cm; 5 children.

Dark ruddy complexion, black hair, dark eyes. Born on 21 April 1776, Jacob Josephson was the son of Joseph Lazarus Josephson and Rachael of Breslau. Josephson was listed as a 'Hebrew teacher' in the convict transport. He was, however, a teacher of Christianity to the Hebrews. He had been employed by the London Society for Promoting Christianity among the Jews and had been caught having stolen the communion plate from the church at Stanstead.

'The Rev Mr Frey' (né Levi) was employed by the London Society at the salary of £250 per annum in 1813. Josephson was baptised at St Mary's Whitechapel on 6 July 1814, with his wife Emma (q.v.). He was ordained a 'Minister of the Gospel to the Jews' in 1815. The society's journal, *Repository*, added that he had been 'absent from his father's house for 20 years and the Lutheran Minister in his native place gives him the news of his family'. In 1817 the society abruptly lost both of its Jewish 'ministers'. One (a Mr Tepper) was found guilty of incest, and Josephson was found guilty of theft.

After receiving a conditional pardon from Governor Macquarie on 30 June 1820 'at the expiration of two years from his arrival', Josephson opened a jewellery and silver shop at 3 Pitt Street, next door to Mr Samuel Terry, where he repaired jewellery and silver, bought old gold and sold perfume. In 1821 Josephson was appointed one of the trustees of the new Wesleyan Church in Sydney and asked for government aid for the benefit of his church: 'Earnestly praying that all pious undertakings may be sanctioned with the Divine blessing and that the common cause of our Lord Jesus Christ may increasingly prosper'.

In 1822 he wrote, in a petition, that he owned a house at 49 Ridings Mart in Hamborough valued at £2000 for which rent had been held up in England. His business was faltering and he wrote to the *Sydney Gazette* asking for 'patience and I will pay you all'. He owed £20 000, and addressing his debtors he declared: 'Their late requital of the kindness of the now calumniated Jew is no honourable commentary on Christian gratitude'.

Josephson appeared before the Full Bench of Magistrates in Sydney on 10 April 1824 on a charge of 'perjury'. The newspaper noted: 'This being the second or third time so serious a charge against Mr Josephson had occupied the attention of the Bench'. The magistrates concluded that the charge was 'cruel, malicious and infamous'. On 22 April the *Sydney Gazette* continued the story. The chief witness wrote defending the man who had brought in the charge: 'It was also my advice to Mr Forbes, to ponder the difficulties of prosecuting such a man as Josephson who, by his own wealth has created many friends. [He is] a foreign Jew, whose evidence one of our Solicitors declares, to not have been worth a straw'. *The Sydney Gazette* gave the case a great deal of space and in its editorial sympathised with Josephson: 'owing to Mr Josephson speaking broken English and being so considerably perplexed he gave his testimony incoherently and confused, that, in fact, he seemed to say nothing'. The *Gazette* wrote in its editorial column: 'It is much more the honour of man to be designated "a foreign Jew" than "a colonial swindler"'. Josephson replied: 'Let Mr Hall remember that he has endeavoured (he, a Christian preacher!) to make up lies and wrong a foreign Jew'. Josephson continued:

> E. S. Hall, as a preacher, must be very ignorant, when he calls me 'a foreign Jew'. Surely he ought to know that all Jews are foreigners, and as a good Christian, it behoves him to believe a foundation stone of his religion (for I suppose that he is a Christian) that Jews are to be foreigners over the whole world, and the greatest mystery is that though Jews are foreigners and wanderers everywhere yet are they everywhere at home. For let the poor Jew arrive in a foreign town or place, he instantly begins to do something for the support of himself and his family.

With legal proceedings looming he sold his 'valuable and very large stock of plate and jewellery' in 1825 and wrote another petition asking for an absolute pardon so that he would be able 'to revisit England to recover considerable property unjustly withholden'. Sir Thomas Brisbane would not agree to his proposal and Josephson remained in Sydney.

Josephson was frequently involved in court battles and scandal and was imprisoned in 1827 for bankruptcy, claiming that he had been robbed. In the 1828 Census he was listed as the holder of a conditional pardon, aged forty-six and a 'Protestant'. The Census stated that he was married to Emma, aged forty, and their children were Joshua, fourteen, Emanuel (Manuel), seven, and Isaac or John, four, who were all 'Protestant'. Jacob Josephson became an innkeeper in Sydney, Penrith, Maitland and at Newcastle. The first hotel was the Black Horse near his home in

Philip Street. In 1832 he advertised accommodation at the Emu Ford Inn, later called the Governor Bourke.

Josephson was active in the affairs of the Theatre Royal in Sydney following the death of his son-in-law Barnett Levey (q.v.) in 1837. (Barnett Levey had married Josephson's stepdaughter Sarah Emma Wilson in 1825.)

Josephson had adopted the three children of Emma's first marriage—Charles Abraham Wilson, Henry Wilson, and Sarah Emma Wilson. His children were Joshua Frey Josephson (q.v.) Lewis, Emanuel, Isaac and John (the last three born in Australia).

Josephson was a prominent member of the Methodist Church in Sydney but he gave £10 to the new Sydney Synagogue in 1845. He died on 6 December 1845 at the age of seventy-two and was buried at St Peter's. Emma Josephson died on 6 December 1868 and was said to have been eighty-seven years old.

Ship Indent 4/4006, p. 60; Petition to Governor Brisbane, 4/1874, no. 119; Petition, 1 March 1822, in 4/1866; *HRA*, series 1, vol. 14, p. 560, vol. 24, p. 47; Bigge Appendix, BT Box 52, pp. 1135–6; *Sydney Gazette*, 3 October 1818, 20 February 1819, 20 January 1820, 13 May 1820, 6 May 1823, 15 April 1824, 29 April 1824, 29 November 1824, 9 December 1824, 10 November 1825, 26 November 1825, 27 May 1826, 19 November 1827, 13 March 1838, 12 May 1838, 3 June 1838; *Australian*, 21 October 1824, 4 November 1824, 26 November 1834; *Sydney Monitor*, 14 December 1831; *AG*, pp. 88, 97, 112, 144, 147, 186–90, Governors'Despatches, A 1267, (1830); J. Backhouse, *A Narrative of a Visit to the Australian Colonies*; G. C. Mundy, *Our Antipodes*, vol. 1, p. 96; Sailman, *The Mystery Unfolded*.

JOSEPHSON, Joshua Frey

b. London, 1815–1892
Morley (2), 1820; Free.

A son of Jacob and Emma Josephson (qq.v.), Joshua Frey Josephson was baptised at St Matthew's, Bethnal Green, on 26 March 1815. Joshua arrived in Sydney (with his mother) at the age of six. According to the *Sydney Gazette* of 31 August 1830, 'On the eve of the day that Mr [Barnett] Levey [q.v.] was to give up his theatre to the Tontine he had a concert and Master Josephson played the piano'. An advertisement on 10 July 1832 in the *Sydney Gazette* announced that: 'Mr Joshua Josephson, residing with his father at Emu Ford (Penrith) gives lessons on the Piano, Flute or Flagelot. On the retirement of Mr Josephson from Sydney to Penrith his oldest son is about to practise as a teacher of music. He is a young gentleman … his talents will ensure his success'. Joshua Frey Josephson married Miss L. J. Davies at the St Lawrence Chapel on 4 December 1838. He became mayor of Sydney in 1848, a Member of the Legislative Assembly for Braidwood, and later a judge of the Eastern District Court of New South Wales. Joshua Frey Josephson, barrister, pastoralist, company director and judge, died in 1892 leaving an estate of £169 247.

H. T. E. Holt, 'Joshua Frey Josephson', in *ADB*, vol. 4, p. 492f.

JOSHUA, Elizabeth

1829–1905
1839; Free.
Single; 11 children.

The daughter of Michael and Sarah (née Solomon) and sister of Esther Joshua (q.v.), Elizabeth married Charles Jacobs (q.v.) in South Australia's first Jewish marriage ceremony on 28 May 1846. She died in 1905 and was buried in Melbourne.

JOSHUA, Esther

b. London, 1832
1839; Free.
Single; Four children.

The second daughter of Michael Joshua (q.v.) and Sarah (née Solomon), Esther married Solomon Lyon Marks (q.v.) at the home of her parents at Holdfast Bay, Glenelg, on 13 February 1850. The ceremony was performed by the 'Rev.' Abraham Jacob Solomon, 'lately arrived from London'. The bridegroom was twenty-two years old and had been in Adelaide for three years. Their four children all died young. Pritchard notes that the couple went to Melbourne and then settled in Queensland.
Pritchard Index.

JOSHUA, Michael

b. c. 1806–1887
1839; Free.
Married; Dealer; 6 children.

Michael Joshua arrived in Sydney on 8 December 1839 with his wife Sarah (née Solomon) and their five children, Elizabeth (Eliza) (1829–1905), Michael, Esther (1832), and two whose names are not known. Michael and Sarah had married at the Great Synagogue in London on 24 August 1826. Sarah was the sister of Vaiben and Emanuel Solomon (qq.v.).

Michael Joshua first visited South Australia on the *Dorset* in 1840. The Joshua family are recorded as returning from Van Diemen's Land to Sydney on the *Sultana* on 9 September 1842. Michael and Sarah Joshua had a son, Samuel (26 June 1842 to 1918), who was born in Sydney. The Joshua family was listed as living in Bridge Street in 1842 and suffered a robbery in which £60 worth of clothes were stolen. On 8 September 1843 Michael Joshua, dealer in Lower George Street, was declared insolvent with a deficit of £628. A Certificate of Discharge was issued on 6 February 1844. The family then moved to Adelaide, where Michael's brother Moses (q.v.) lived. Michael's daughter Elizabeth (q.v.) married Charles Jacobs (q.v.) in South Australia's first Jewish wedding at Michael's house in May 1846. His daughter Esther (q.v.) married Solomon Lyon Marks (q.v.), 'of the firm of M. & S. Marks', in Adelaide on 13 February 1850.

Their children were Samuel (1842), Susan (ca. 1843), Eve (1845), John (1847) and Philip (1848).

Sydney Morning Herald, 13 September 1842, 8 September 1843, 6 February 1844.

JOSHUA, Moses

Dorset, 1840; Free.
6 children.

The brother of Michael Joshua (q.v.), Moses Joshua arrived in Adelaide on the *Dorset* from England on 5 April 1840 with his wife and six children. In the 1841 Census of the Adelaide colony he was living in Light Square. Both he and his wife were under thirty-five years of age. His name appeared on the list of people claiming the right to vote on 19 September 1840. He ran an auction room and on 16 September 1846 announced that he was to build 'a handsome erection suited for respectable business and family occupancy' on the site of Adelaide's first stockyard.

South Australian Gazette and Colonial Register, 19 September 1840, 16 September 1846.

JOSHUA, Sarah (née SOLOMON)

b. London, 1806 1839; Free.
Married; 6 children.

Sarah was the daughter of Samuel Moss Solomon (q.v.) and Betsy (née Moses), and the sister of Vaiben and Emanuel Solomon (qq.v.). She married Michael Joshua (q.v.) at the Great Synagogue, London, on 24 August 1826. She arrived in Sydney on 8 December 1839 with her husband and five children. A sixth child, Samuel, was born in Sydney in 1842.

JUDELL, Joseph

b. Prussia, 1810
Fairlie (1), 1834; Convict; Sentenced to 7 years, Middlesex, 1833.
Single; Cap-maker and fellmonger; Height: 160 cm.

Dark sallow complexion, dark brown hair, dark hazel eyes. Mole on left cheek and mole on right side of nose. Can read and write. Jew. No previous conviction. Joseph Judell was employed as a cap-maker and stole caps. Judell first said that he had 'declared them'. They were worth £20. Then he changed his story and claimed that they were stolen from him while he had a drink. Later he admitted to the constable that he had stolen them.

Joseph Judell arrived in New South Wales on 15 February 1834. A ticket of leave was granted for the District of Goulburn on 25 March 1840 and a certificate of freedom issued on 22 July 1841.

OBSP, 1832–33, case 1312, p. 743; Printed Indent *Fairlie* (1), 4/4018, p. 314; Principal Superintendent of Convicts, TL butts, 1836–37, 1840, 4/4367, and 4/4138; TL 40/674; CF 41/1004 in 4/4367.

JULIAN, Jacob (JEWLIN)

b. London, 1810–1870
Hooghly (2), 1828; Convict; Sentenced to 7 years, Old Bailey, 1825.
Single; Tailor; Height: 150 cm; 1 child.

Ruddy freckled complexion, auburn hair, brown eyes. Tattoos of two doves and branch and sun on right arm. A woman, M. S. heart, darts on left. Jew. Can read and write. Together with two other boys, William Carwarden and Samuel Falgate, Jacob Julian, aged sixteen, robbed a very young child of her mother's beads valued at two shillings. He was sentenced on 7 April 1825. He had lost his right leg from the thigh and was deemed to be 'not assignable'.

Jacob Julian was a tailor. His parents were Moses and Elizabeth Julian. Moses was a 'coach proprietor in London'. Jacob was the nephew of Ann Solomon (q.v.), the wife of Isaac (Ikey) Solomon (q.v.) and brother of Moses Julion (q.v.).

The convict transport ship *Hooghly* arrived at Port Jackson on 30 January 1828 and, according to the census of that year, Jacob Julian was a member of the Iron Cove Chain Gang. No religion was stated. He was then assigned as a servant in Parramatta and on 13 June 1831 was punished by being placed in the Parramatta Gaol for six days.

Jacob Julian obtained a certificate of freedom on 7 April 1832, which was renewed on 30 August 1834. In 1851, in Queensland, Jacob Julian bought land in Ipswich, where he lived. He had married Maria Keighon. They had a son, Jacob Julian jnr, who married Mary Maria Doyle in Mudgee on 20 September 1858. The first of their five children, a daughter Sarah, was born at Mudgee, where her father, Jacob jnr, was an innkeeper, on 1 March 1861.

Jacob Julian died on 30 December 1870 and his widow signed the death certificate with an 'X'. His granddaughter, Sarah, died at Toowong on 20 January 1932.

OBSP, 1824–25, case 709, p. 300; Ship Indent 4/4013, p. 50; Parramatta Gaol Book 4/6529, entry 752; Petition for Land 2/7895; TL 32/287.

JULION, Moses (JULIAN)

b. London, 1812
Roslin Castle (1), 1828; Convict; Sentenced to 7 years, Middlesex, 1828.
Single; Stable boy; Height: 150 cm.

Dark complexion, dark brown hair, hazel eyes, medium long nose with a scar on the bridge. 'Large scar nearly covering left hand with skin puckered at the wrist. 'The characterisation of a Jew boy.' Moses Julion was transported for larceny. His gaol report was 'Bad'. His hulk report was 'Orderly'. On arrival in Van Diemen's Land he stated that he had been transported for 'Robbing my Master Charles Batley in George Yard Whitechapel of 33 shillings and five pence'. Moses had been in gaol before for being out late at night and spent one month in the House of Correction in Cole Bath Fields. His mother and father lived in George Yard, Whitechapel. His mother, Elizabeth Julian, was Ann (Hannah) Solomon's (q.v.) sister. He believed his brother, Jacob Julian (q.v.), was transported on the Juliana: 'My sister is also transported'. In fact, his brother arrived in New South Wales on the Hooghly (2), on 24 February

1828, and reached Hobart Town on 18 December 1828. The colonial offical noted 'Ann Solomons is the wife of the notorious Ikey Solomon' (q.v). Moses Julion brought sixteen shillings and nine pence with him on the transport ship.

On 7 January 1829 Moses Julion was listed at the Prisoners' Barracks when he was charged with neglect of duty for leaving his work gang without leave and coming into the barracks intoxicated at night. He was placed on the treadmill for seven days. On 26 January 1829 he was put back on the treadmill for a week because he had been absent from the Church Muster. On 18 March 1830 he was found on the New Town Road without authority. He was given twelve lashes and returned to his duty. On 9 October 1830 he was convicted of disorderly conduct in the Prisoners' Barracks and admonished. On 16 April 1831 he was discovered to be absent from the barracks for some nights. He was sentenced to the treadmill for fourteen days and it was recommended that he be sent to the Interior. He was still in Hobart Town on 24 August 1831 and sentenced to eighteen lashes for neglect of duty. Julion was a member of the Prisoners' Barracks boat crew and had been found absent from the prison at night. He was to be imprisoned and kept to hard labour at Bridgewater and afterwards sent into the Interior. On 30 July 1832, as an assigned servant to a Mr Walker, he absconded and remained at large until being apprehended at the Clyde. Julion was sentenced to hard labour for two years and set to work at the government garden. On 14 January 1833 he was sentenced to the treadmill for six days for being drunk. On 25 October 1833 he was sentenced to twenty-five lashes for 'holding conversation with some of the crew of the Cutter *Shamrock* and with receiving some tobacco from one of the said crew in breach of the settlement's regulations'. Julion was sent to Port Arthur, where his dossier ends.

CON 31/23, p. 130, no. 388; MM 33/1; CON 18/22.

K

KARNEY, Emanuel

b. Bethnal Green, 1816
Recovery (3), 1837; Convict; Sentenced to 7 years, Norfolk Quarter Sessions, 1836.
Single; Hawker; 1 child.

Dark complexion, brown hair, grey eyes. 'A Jew'. Karney was transported for stealing a silk handkerchief 'from a gent's pocket'. His behaviour in gaol was 'bad' and the hulk report was 'Indifferent'. He had been placed in irons for swearing.

The *Recovery* arrived at Hobart Town on 8 October 1837 and Emanuel Karney was placed in assigned service. On 17 April 1838 he was sentenced to three days hard labour for 'disobedience of orders'. By June 1838, for repeated disobedience, he was returned to government service. On 24 November, at Launceston, he was charged with felony and for want of conclusive evidence was returned from assignment to Mr Reeve into the care of the government. He was severely reprimanded for insolence in February 1839. In April 1840 he had formed 'an improper connexion' in Launceston and was reassigned to the Oatlands District. On 2 November 1841 he was found to be absent from his work as a labourer and reprimanded. A ticket of leave was issued on 29 May 1842 and a certificate of freedom (no. 877) in 1843. Karney appeared in the Supreme Court on 28 January 1845 and was found to be not guilty.

The first name on the petition of 20 May 1843 to establish a synagogue in Launceston was that of Emanuel Karney. Karney rented seat no. 91 in the Hobart Town Synagogue in 1845. In 1844 he had pledged sixteen shillings and sixpence but only gave two shillings and sixpence. On 23 August 1846 the committee of the Hobart Town Synagogue suspended Karney from all congregational honours for a month for 'publicly insulting the President of the synagogue on going out of the synagogue on the Sabbath'. He was a subscriber to the Tasmanian Hebrew Benevolent Society in 1847.

On 27 January 1850 Emanuel Karney married Clara Goldsmith (q.v.). She was illiterate and a widow. He was described as a hawker, aged thirty-four years, and they were married in his house, which was in Church Street, Hobart Town.

Strangely, the marriage was also registered to have taken place in Sydney in the same year under the aegis of the Sydney Synagogue.

Karney's niece, Rachel Morris, aged twenty, who was living with the family, married Daniel Goldsmith on 5 December 1855. Daniel Goldsmith was a 23 year-old dealer. The Jewish ceremony was held at the Goldsmiths' house in Murray Street in Hobart.

Both Emanuel and Clara Karney moved to Melbourne and Clara died in 6 June 1886, aged eighty-three. Emanuel died in August 1875.

CON 31/25, no. 579, CON 18/22; CSO 5/73/1622, p. 240.

KASNER, Barnett

In 1846 Barnett Kasner was one the three initial trustees of the Maitland Jewish cemetery. He is listed as an auctioneer in the *Maitland Mercury* during 1847 and he appears to have left for Port Phillip on 2 February 1848 (*Sydney Morning Herald*). From 1854 to 1880 (Moses) Kasner and Moss advertised as opticians at 17 Collins Street, Melbourne.

Research by Gary Luke.

KEESING, Barnett

b. London, 1819–1874
Free.
Single; Trader; 12 children.

Barnett Keesing migrated from England to New Zealand and the Bay of Islands by way of Sydney in 1838. He returned to Sydney to marry Hannah Solomon (1828–1918) at the Sydney Synagogue on 18 June 1845. Hannah was the daughter of Samuel and Rebecca Solomon and signed her marriage certificate with a cross. The children of Barnett and Hannah Keesing were Sarah, born in Sydney in 1848, Rosetta, Julia, Kate, Rebecca, Thomas, Henry, Samuel, Harriet, Abraham, John, and Ralph.

KEESING, Henry

1825–1896
Free.
Single; Merchant; 11 children.

Henry Keesing was born in England 2 July 1825. He was the brother of Barnett (q.v.), visited Sydney in 1848 and married his newly acquired sister-in-law, Julia Solomon, on 14 June 1848. Julia was the daughter of Moss Solomon (q.v.) and

Betsy (née Myers). Henry Keesing's business dealings are recorded in Sydney's Shipping Register of September and November 1845, when he exported sheep, blankets and drapery to Auckland. The *South Australian Almanack* of 1849 lists 'H. Keesing—merchant' in Adelaide. Henry and Julia had a son named Henry Judah Keesing on 8 June 1849. Three of their children were born in Australia and eleven in Auckland, New Zealand. Keesing died at Auckland 29 February 1896.

Keesing Family History.

KING, Moses

b. Poland, 1799
Layton II (2), 1839; Convict; Sentenced to 14 years, Somerset Assizes, 1837.
Married; Labourer; Height: 155 cm; 5 children (in England).

Dark complexion, black hair and whiskers, hazel eyes, a long nose and an oval face. Moses King had not been in custody before. He had a wife, Ann, and five children at Bristol. He was sentenced to transportation for having received a stolen gun.

The *Layton* arrived in Van Diemen's Land on 7 December 1839. King's police dossier begins on 19 November 1841, with a classification of 'invalid', when he was placed in six days solitary confinement for neglect of duty while working as a gatekeeper. He remained with this classification through 1842. On 19 March 1844, while assigned to Mr Louis Nathan (q.v.), he was admonished for misconduct. On 19 July 1844 he was recommended for a conditional pardon, which was approved on July 1845. King applied for a job as sexton (*shamash*) of the Hobart Synagogue in July 1845. In the board meeting in which the four applications were considered, King received no votes.

On 22 October 1845 he was tried at the Hobart Town Supreme Court for receiving three yards of satin, the property of Richard Lewis. He was sentenced to a further fourteen years transportation, of which at least three years were to be served at Norfolk Island. There, despite a number of harsh punishments for minor offences (such as having his trousers on his hammock on 16 May 1847, which merited seven days hard labour in chains), he obviously received a good general report and he returned to Hobart Town to be issued with a pass. An appeal for a remission of the remainder of his sentence was refused on 14 June 1849. After a series of petitions he received a ticket of leave on 2 November 1852. Ten days after this King was found to be absent from his authorised residence and given two months hard labour, after which he was to be allowed to find employment only in the interior of the island, north of Bridgewater and south of the District of Launceston. A conditional pardon was granted on 15 August 1854. It was to be valid for 'everywhere save in the United Kingdom and New South Wales'.

CON 31/25, no. 682; *Hobart Town Courier*, 25 October 1845; Minute Book of the Hobart Synagogue, 27 July 1845.

KRAKOUER, Theodor

1817–1877
Mermaid, 1851; Convict; Sentenced 15 years, Portsmouth, 1849.

Krakouer was married to Brina Israel and was sent to Western Australia arriving on one of the first convict transports to Fremantle. He had been convicted of stealing clothes and a small amount of money. He stated that he was a 'wool shearer'. He could read and he was a 'Jew'.

A ticket of leave was granted on 12 September 1852 and a certificate of freedom on 7 February 1865. He set up a business partnership managing a livery stable with his fellow Jewish emancipist Elias Lapidus (q.v.). Krakouer died on 11 May 1877.

Fremantle Convict Database and Aviva Goldman.

L

LANGLEY, David Ottolangui

b. Aldgate, 1812–1882
David Lyon, 1830; Convict; Sentenced to life, Old Bailey, 1830.
Carter; Height: 157.5 cm; 8 children.

David Langley was born in Aldgate, the son of Amelia (Miriam) and Israel Ottolangui. David had a dark complexion, dark brown eyebrows, black eyes, sharp nose. No whiskers. 'A Jew.' He was a member of a large Sephardi family that had originated in Livorno. He was tried at the Old Bailey for having stolen, on 14 December 1829, one cheese valued at twelve shillings from Thomas Davidge, a cheesemonger who lived at 48 Minories. He had been convicted on 1 May 1829 for stealing a brass screw cap from a shop window and served three months in prison. He arrived in Van Diemen's Land on 19 August 1830. His behaviour on board the ship had been 'orderly'.

In Hobart Town on 26 December 1836, David Langley married Phillis Skinner, who had also been a convict. Their children were: Amelia (born 2 September 1837), David (1839), Sophia (5 December 1841), Sarah (31 January 1844), and another daughter (21 December 1846). On the birth registrations for these children Langley was listed as a 'bricklayer' or 'master bricklayer'.

Langley appears to have followed the Californian gold rush. He was listed in the 1860 Census in California as a 'teamster' with 'Esther' a 25-year-old English-born wife and two Californian-born children, Lewis (1854) and Amelia (1859). Celia was born in 1866. His occupation changed from stone mason in 1870 to general dealer in 1880. David Langley died in San Francisco in July 1882.

The brother of David, Moses Ottolangui, was born in London in 1808 and migrated to Melbourne with his wife Emma (née Bensabbat) in 1866. They came to Australia with their large family to join their son Jacob (John) Ottolangui and his wife Fanny (née Simmonds). Moses died in Melbourne, aged seventy-four, in 1885. Their graves are to be found in the old Jewish section of the Melbourne General Cemetery.

Family information on www.geocities.com; documentation from Ron and Liz James, Melbourne.

LAPIDUS, Elias

b. 1818
Hashemy, 1849; Convict, 14 years.
Jeweller; 3 children.

Elias Lapidus arrived in Sydney on 9 June 1849. He married Esther Israel (q.v.), aged seventeen, in Sydney. They had two children, Nathan and Rachel. A ticket of leave was granted 10 August 1851 and due to expire on 29 April 1854. Esther's sister Brina Israel married the Jewish convict Theodor Krakouer (q.v.) and followed her husband to Western Australia. Elias Lapidus eventually joined Krakouer in Perth jointly managing a livery stable. His official record shows that he travelled to Singapore in 1855. Elias had been sentenced at Monmouth, Wales for receiving stolen goods, so he had been convicted before.

First Families 2001 (website); Information by Frederick Ralph Cohen and Aviva Goldman.

LARAH, Flora

b. Whitechapel
Prince of Wales, 1788; Convict; Sentenced to 7 years, Westminster, 1787.
Single.

Flora Larah was placed in Newgate for the theft of a mahogany tea chest and a half-guinea gold coin. She was called 'Flora Sara' in the prison list and described as 'an evil disposed person and not minding to gain her livelihood by truth and honest labour but going about daily to contrive the honest subjects of our said Lord the King of their goods and Chattels and Monies for the support of her profligate way of life'. She had told Sarah Blackwall that she could magically multiply her money through a foreign bank in a place called Savadee.

On 13 February 1788, Flora married John Hart (q.v.) at Port Jackson and was sent to Norfolk Island on the *Supply* in November 1789. Hart had been in Norfolk Island since February of that year. Hart died in January 1795 and Flora remained on the island. The 1814 Muster listed her as single and living at Parramatta. Mollie Gillen notes that Laura Flora, who arrived on the *Prince of Wales* in 1796, had married at Port Jackson in 1819. Gillen suggests: 'In 1821 she is perhaps the woman marked dead as Laura Ford'.

It is possible that neither Flora Larah nor John Hart were Jewish. However, Flora's surname was a fairly common Sephardic name. She may have been a relative of James Larra (q.v.), and may have chosen to live in Parramatta to be near her family.

M. Gillen, *The Founders of Australia*, p. 213f.; *AG*, pp. 19, 24, 52.

LARRA, James

b. France, 1749–1839
Scarborough, 1790; Convict; Sentenced to life, Old Bailey, 1787.
Single; Shipbroker.

On 11 October 1787 James Larra stole a silver tankard from the Northumberland Coffee House and was caught in the act. Knowing that he would probably be hanged for the theft Larra begged for his life at the Old Bailey: 'My Lord, to deny the fact would be very horrid, I was much intoxicated'. The Judge observed: 'An honest man, if was ever so drunk, would not steal'. Larra replied: 'Very just, my Lord'. The prisoner was sentenced to death and later the penalty was commuted to transportation for life.

Larra arrived in New South Wales on the *Scarborough* in June 1790 and soon was appointed principal of the night watch, succeeding Constable John Harris (q.v.).

The two Jewish prisoners and emancipists became firm friends and Larra became the honorary uncle of Harris's two daughters Elizabeth (Underwood, q.v.) and Hannah (Ritchie, q.v.).

Larra was granted a conditional pardon in 1794. He married Mrs Suzannah Langford on 10 November 1794. In May 1797 he received a grant of fifty acres to establish a farm in the Field of Mars. The farm prospered. In Governor King's returns of 1802 Larra owned fifty acres of cleared land with forty-six acres in wheat and maze. By 1806 he had four convicts employed and three free men working for him. The holding had increased to eighty acres. The land was granted by Governor Hunter and Larra owned four horses, forty-three cattle, ten sheep, thirty-four hogs, with eight people on the property, all off government stores. In 1798 Larra received one of the first liquor licences in the colony and opened the Masons Arms in Parramatta. When François Péron, the French naturalist, visited Australia in 1802, he described Larra as a French Jew whose tavern had been recommended to him by the Lieutenant Governor, Colonel Paterson. Larra was said to have served his guests 'with an elegance and even luxury'. On 4 June 1800 he was granted a free pardon.

Larra became the holder of a number of leases and grants totalling 1800 acres, some of which were held in trust for his 'nieces'. He became sergeant major in the Military Loyal Parramatta Association. Suzannah Larra died in 1811 and Larra married again in 1813. His second wife, Phoebe Waldron, was the widow of the owner of the important Sydney public house the Duke of York. She died the following year and Larra was accused of her murder through 'improper sexual practices'. He was speedily acquitted following a sensational trial. In 1817 he married Mary Ann Clarke, an actress who remained part of the theatrical world of Sydney until the 1840s. Larra's considerable fortune was dissipated and, in May 1821, his wife left him. Larra's 'niece' Hannah Harris had left New South Wales and lived in Van Diemen's Land. James Larra was cared for by his other 'niece', Elizabeth, who had married Joseph Underwood. Larra died, at the age of ninety, on 2 February 1839 and Elizabeth arranged for him to be buried in the Jewish section of the Devonshire Street Cemetery.

OBSP, 1787–88, case 6, p. 13; ML 1147, Criminal Court, 2 February 1797; *HRA*, series 1, vol. 7, p. 305, vol. 6, 137, vol. 8, p. 203; Bigge Appendix, BT Box 12, p. 72f; Memorial no. 184, in 4/1822; Magistrates Book 1/297, September 1798; CO 201/21, p. 48; G. F. J. Bergman, 'James Larra: The Commercial Nabob of Parramatta', *AJJHS*, vol. 5, no. 3 (1960); *Sydney Gazette*, 15 June 1811, 20 June 1812, 2 October 1813, 17 September 1814, 19 April 1817, 22 November 1817, 7 November 1818, 16 January 1823, 31 March 1838; Marriage CO 201/138, 95; CO 201/16, p. 84; *AG*, pp. 24, 44, 47–61, 141.

LAURENCE, James (John LAWRENCE)

b. London, 1795–1871
Indefatigable (2), 1815; Convict; Sentenced to 7 years, Lancaster, 1814.
Single; Actor/player; Height: 166 cm.

Born in Jewry Street, Aldgate, James Laurence was the son of Henry Laurence, a diamond broker. He was sentenced at the Lancaster Quarter Sessions on 27 April 1814. He had previously been convicted of theft. Ruddy complexion, light brown hair, hazel eyes. He came to be known as 'Blind Larry'.

According to his own long and detailed (and imaginative) autobiography James Laurence (Lawrence) was sent to an academy in Crutched Friars with the Rev. James Whiffen in 1805 and left the school at the age of fourteen 'with a tolerable share of education'. He then went to Kingston, Jamaica, to become an apprentice book keeper in an uncle's export-import business, but hurriedly left Jamaica at the end of 1811 to be with his father, who had been arrested for receiving stolen property. He sang in the chorus of the Drury Lane Theatre and then went on an unsuccessful tour and ran out of money. He stole from a doctor and impersonated him to a family and was forced to leave England. Laurence was related to the prominent Hart family in Greenwich Street, New York, and stole $1000 from them. He went on tour again and bolted from Canada with the entire proceeds of a benefit night. Back in London he robbed a man of £94, had an illegitimate child, stole again and travelled around provincial England. He was arrested and sent to the hulks with a seven-year sentence for carrying out a robbery in Manchester. In October 1814 he sailed from England on the *Indefatigable*, arriving in Sydney on 26 April 1815.

Laurence was assigned to Parramatta and then Appin to be a shepherd. He received twenty-five lashes for disobedience, ran away and, when he was caught in Sydney, received a further fifty lashes. He was sent to be a stockman for Mr E. S. Hall at Surry Hills. He was punished for insolence and assigned to a clerk in a lumberyard. He then worked as a dealer and kept a stall at the Sydney Market. In November 1816 he was arrested for robbery and taken before Mr Wentworth, who sentenced him to three weeks solitary imprisonment and two years in Newcastle. He worked at the lime burners in chains: 'I was to carry lime in Launches Boats up to me neck in water, no clothing, no bedding nearly the whole time'. He claimed that in the process he received 600 lashes, and that 'At my arrival in Newcastle I met my eldest brother under the care of Baron Fields, Judge of the Supreme Court'.

Two months later James Laurence claims to have stolen £500 from Mr Oxley and stowed away on the ship *Claudine*. He was out of irons by the time the ship reached Calcutta. He robbed and almost killed a man and was sentenced to death on 15 March 1819. 'There were very few of my persuasion in Calcutta but I informed Mr Thompson that I was an Hebrew and that if I was to suffer I should die as one.' Laurence claimed that he had been reprieved at the last minute and sent back to New South Wales on the *Sir Michael Dillon*. On arrival he was described as having a dark sallow complexion, black hair, dark hazel eyes, blind in left eye. His height was 170 cms. He had been sentenced to fourteen years transportation. In Sydney's Hyde Park Barracks he received seventy lashes for singing after 8 o'clock. He claims to have escaped from Sydney again and to have reached Rio de Janeiro. The story does not make sense however we know that in Sydney he was given one hundred lashes, sent to Emu Plains and then to Port Macquarie. In 1826 he received a ticket of leave. In the *Sydney Monitor* 7 July 1826 there is an account of a riotous gathering at Nettleton's pub with 'a marvelous concatenation of Jew and Gentile'... The head of the supper table which was well laid out, was most conveniently (as I should seem) filled by our worthy promoter of the Peace Mr Israel Chapman-and Mister Lawrence, alias Blind Larry, alias Monsieur Laurent, acted as croupier.' The following week the *Monitor* carried a letter of protest from the innkeeper 'as to Larry, I consider you to have wantonly injured my house, in representing him as a conspicuous guest at my table, and cast disrespect on the very respectable persons who were present.' Lawrence's troubles were only beginning. On 2 August 1826 he was sentenced at the Sydney Quarter Sessions to seven years transportation for stealing thirty-eight yards of cloth and was sent to Moreton Bay, where he claimed to have received 1225 lashes in five years and nine months. In August 1836 Laurence was free again. He went to Hobart Town on business. He gave a concert at the Ordinance Arms in Liverpool Street though 'very few attended as just previously there had been another concert by Mr Simmons' (Joseph Simmons, q.v.). A concert in Launceston cleared £22, but Laurence was gaoled for debts and sent to St George's Sound.

He returned to Sydney and appeared on stage with Barnett Levey (q.v.). However, he was pursued by creditors and was attacked by one. After a brief interlude in Van Diemen's Land he returned to Sydney, married Sarah Shervington, a convict, on 5 May 1835. In July 1836 he was tried at the Sydney Quarter Sessions for defrauding a man and sentenced to seven years. He spent five months on the *Phoenix* hulk and was then sent on to Norfolk Island where he encountered Captain Alexander Maconochie who was 'humane, kind, religious and justice stares us in the face'. The *Description Book* of the Phoenix hulk states that Lawrence had a pock-pitted face, a large broken Roman nose, blind in one eye and with a withered arm.

On 26 December 1840 a Norfolk Island prisoner, Levi Abrahams (q.v.), wrote to the Sydney Synagogue on behalf of his fellow Jewish convicts asking for supplies to be sent to them for Passover. Abrahams wrote about his 'regret to state that one of our number [John Lawrence] has been so irregular in his religion, litigious and otherwise objectionable that he has been indispensably separated from us and the *kehillah* [congregation] will use its own pleasure in supplying him'.

On Norfolk Island Laurence initiated a performance of *Castle Andalusia* in the so-called Royal Victoria Theatre 'in honour of Her Majesty's birthday'. Laurence's name appeared at the top of the cast on the handbill that was distributed. He also incurred the wrath of the Rev. Thomas Sharpe, who wrote in his diary: 'Last Sunday a Jew of the name of Laurent, had the audacity to write out on the Sunday a Play Bill, of some performance they wished to get up for New Year's Day, in case the Commandant gave them [the convicts] a Holiday. The Bill was taken from him, but he was not punished'. The commandant gave 'a temporary place [to worship] for the Jews, there are only eight in number, no work for the Jews on Saturday—every man was treated in accordance to his conduct'. Laurence's biography, written at Norfolk Island, concludes 'now I am to return to Sydney'.

A. W. Cohen of Hastings, England, asked the Colonial Secretary to find out what had happened to 'a man named Lawrence' who might have been murdered by Aborigines at Port Phillip in 1841. Laurence's parents wanted to know. In Melbourne in 1861 (*Age*, 14 December 1861) he was acquitted in a trial for receiving a stolen watch however the following year he was charged with receiving a stolen shawl and while in prison 'Lawrence, the bleary-eyed Jew' was charged with receiving a watch chain. He was sentenced to eighteen months imprisonment and he begged for mercy in vain. 'He had lately been discharged from the Hospital, afflicted with an incurable disease, and he hoped the court would take into consideration his age and infirmities.' (*Age*, 5 February 1863).

The Melbourne Hebrew Congregation recorded that James Lawrence died in the Collingwood Prisoner Stockade on 28 September 1863, aged seventy-six.

The Historical Acount of the Life of James Lawrence. Autobiographical mss, DL MS Q168; A detailed analysis of the autobiographical manuscript appears in the *AJJHSJ, Blind Larry: the Jewish Actor as Habitual Criminal* by Robert Jordan Vol. 19, part 4 (2010) p7f f. Aaron Price, Norfolk Island History, DL MS Q249; *Indefatigable* Indent 4/4007, p. 47; Melbourne Hebrew Congregation Burial Book; Governors' Despatches A1292, p. 505f., 27 November 1843. CP no 5047, 4/6514.

LAWRENCE, John

b. London, 1812
Andromeda I (2), 1833; Convict; Sentenced to 7 years, Old Bailey, 1832.
Widower; Hatter.

Dark sallow complexion, dark brown hair, brown eyes. Two scars on outer corner of left eyebrow. John Lawrence stole a roll of carpet from a cart near Tower Hill and was caught running away with the stolen property.

John Lawrence was listed in the 1837 General Return of Convicts in New South Wales. He was the assigned servant of John Atkinson in Berrima and he held a ticket of leave. It is possible that he then tried his luck in Van Diemen's Land. A John Lawrence took out a licence to become a hawker in Hobart Town in January 1844. John Lawrence rented seat no. 62 in the Hobart Synagogue from 1845 to 1847 and gave the congregation £1 3s 4d. He was also a member of the Hebrew Hobart Benevolent Institution in 1847.

OBSP, 1832, case 2145, p. 873; *Andromeda* Printed Indent, 1833, p. 37; *Hobart Town Courier*, 19 January 1844.

LAWRENCE, Samuel

b. London, 1816–1904
1848; Free.
Married; Dealer; 13 children.

Samuel Lawrence was the son of Philip Lawrence, a paper manufacturer, of London. Samuel married Sarah (née Solomon) in London. Sarah, born in 1822, was the daughter of Samuel and Esther Solomon. Samuel Lawrence opened a store in Adelaide. According to the birth certificates of his children he worked as a draper, general clothier, auctioneer and furrier. A photograph exists of a Lawrence furrier business in a building marked Emu House. He was listed as a committee member of the Adelaide Hebrew Congregation in 1850. Sarah Lawrence died at Paddington on 20 July 1895 at the age of seventy-four. Samuel Lawrence died at Parramatta on 13 July 1904 and was buried in the Jewish section of the Rookwood Cemetery.

Their children were Elizabeth (born c. 1847), in London, Philip (6 August 1849), in Adelaide, Ellenor (27 May 1851), in Rundle Street, Katherine (7 January 1853), Reyna (21 December 1854), Morris (4 July 1856), Rachael (21 May 1858), Charles (21 August 1859), Henry (9 March 1861), Julia (24 October 1862), Jessie (23 April 1864), Alfred (12 October 1865, died March 1866), and Montagu (15 July 1867).

Information by John Richard Lawrence, Queensland, and Rick Carter-Smith, in First Families 2001 (website); Pritchard Index.

LAZAR, John (LAZARUS)

b. Edinburgh, 1804–1879
Lady MacNaghten, 1837; Free.
Married; Tailor and actor; 8 children.

John Lazarus grew up in London. His father Abraham was a 'clothier'. Julia Lazar was the daughter of Henry and Miriam, furriers in London. The *Lady MacNaghten* sailed from Cork on 5 November 1836 carrying a cargo of bounty migrants. An epidemic of scarlet fever broke out and so many passengers died that an official inquiry was held.

John Lazar and his family sailed to Australia under the surname of Lazarus. John was listed as a tailor who could read and write. His wife Julia (q.v.), who was also literate, was aged thirty. A daughter, Rachel (q.v.), who could read and write, was aged ten and was 'convalescent' when the ship arrived. Abraham, aged eight, could read and was deemed 'healthy'. Mary, aged five, died on board the ship on 7 January. Lazarus, aged one, died on 15 January, and Priscilla, aged three, died on 6 February 1837.

John Lazarus initially rented a house at 2 Malcolm Place, George Street, in Sydney. Money was obviously very scarce. Soon after the family's arrival Lazar wrote to the government to say that he had been paid only £2 3s for clothes that had been destroyed at the Quarantine Station. Their value was £5 4s 6d. His claim was rejected. The Lazar family struggled on. Twins, Sydney and Samuel, were born in January 1838. Sydney died on 28 March 1838, and was buried in the Devonshire Street Jewish Cemetery. Victoria was born in 1840.

By 1839 Lazar was listed as 'J. Lazarus, dealer, Kent St' in the Post Office Directory, but 'Mr and Mrs John Lazar' pledged £25 to the Sydney Synagogue building appeal in 1839 and in September 1840 stood for election to the committee of the Sydney Synagogue.

Lazar's abiding passion was the stage. He initially became manager and actor in the Theatre Royal of Barnett Levey (q.v.) at the considerable salary of £8 a week.

In 1845 John Lazar resumed a commercial career in Adelaide, importing hardware and clothing while advertising that he was a skilled silversmith. Lazar travelled extensively throughout the Australian colonies and returned to Adelaide. In partnership with George Coppin, he leased Queen's Theatre from Emanuel Solomon (q.v.) and returned to the stage in 1848. According to the *South Australian Register* (23 February 1848), 'our old favourite Mr Lazar, made his debut after 5 years of absence from Adelaide's boards. The new Queen's Theatre is now under the management of Mr Lazar'.

On 13 March 1848 the *Sydney Gazette* quoted Lazar's words from the stage: 'The more oftener you come to see us the better'. The report went on: 'We shall not stay to discuss the accuracy of Mr Lazar's grammar but while he persists in bringing out still more of the trashy absurdities dignified with the name of melodramas which have lately disgraced the Sydney stage'. Some of the 'entertainments' presented during 1853 and 1854 were translated from the French by Eliezer Levi Montefiore (q.v.). They included *Contradiction or a Wife Upon Sufferance* and a pantomime, *Za Ze Zi Zo Zu* (which sounds suspiciously like an exercise in Hebrew grammar).

On 12 October 1837 Rachel appeared in a Benefit. The *Gazette* wrote that her father had been 'heavily afflicted' and that she was 'his now only child' and wished her well. Benefits were profitable and Lazar put on *The Rich Man of Frankfurt* with himself in the role of Isaac ben Samuel. Rachel had 'very gracefully danced a Millenese hornpipe in which she was vociferously encored'. Lazar's stage appearances were not so favourably reviewed:

> When we saw him as the Jew, we gave him much credit for adapting his voice to the Jewish style, not supposing he was playing in his usual tone. We however found that Mr Lazar not only personates the Jew on stage, but that he is a Jew off: so that when playing the Moor he was unable to disguise his being a true son of Israel, which is a considerable drawback to his personification of such characters as Othello he invariably pronounces horse, orse, house, ouse, but this is very evident he can break himself of because he does pronounce H in many words, and in some where it should not be; for instance he calls arm, harm; of this habit Mr Lazar should break himself, for he never can play Shakespeare's characters well, till he does. But he also has another draw back—he lisps. We could not find fault with him in Shylock for this, but it is very remarkable in his Othello.

John Lazar was a founding member of the Adelaide Hebrew Congregation and he sang *Kol Nidray* at the first Day of Atonement Service in 1848. He was a member of the committee of the congregation in 1850. Lazar served as a member of the Adelaide City Council in 1851–59, in 1853 becoming an alderman for the Gawler Ward and, despite his fractured English, serving as mayor of Adelaide in 1855–57. Lazar was also a prominent Freemason. He became Provincial Deputy Grand Master of South Australia and later Provincial District Grand Master of Westland (New Zealand).

Lazar was forced to leave South Australia in 1863 owing to disastrous losses incurred by mining speculation and handed over the management of the Queen's Theatre to his son Samuel. John Lazar arrived in Dunedin in 1863 to become its town clerk, and consecrated the Dunedin Synagogue in 1864. He later served as town clerk of Hokitika on the west coast of the South Island, where he also become the provincial treasurer. Lazar died on 7 June 1879. His wife Julia died in Sydney, aged seventy-three, on 26 December 1888. He was survived by two sons and two daughters.

John Lazar had two sisters, Julia and Leah Lazarus (qq.v), who arrived in Australia as assisted migrants.

Ship Indent, ML, 1267-15, pp. 253–4; Lazar Papers, ML, A651; *Sydney Gazette*, 27 May 1837, 12 October 1837, 13 March 1838; *Commercial Journal and Advertiser*, 15 August 1840; H. Munz, *Jews in South Australia*, p. 47f.; Hand Bill in DL ADD 59, 25 June 1839; The Last Days of Pompeii, October 1844, ML 4/2653, and mss dated 30 March 1846, 4/4732; Miscellaneous Persons, CS Out 4/3548, p. 269; CS 4/4561.1, 26 July 1843; *South Australian Gazette and Colonial Register*, 23 February 1848; 37/6197, in 4/2378; *AG*, pp. 124–30, 138, 154, 272, 274–5.

LAZAR, Julia

1807–1880
Lady MacNaghton, 1837; Free.
Married; 8 children.

Julia Lazar was the wife of John Lazar (q.v.). She died in Sydney on 26 December 1888 and was buried at Rookwood.

LAZAR, Rachel

b. London, 1827
Lady MacNaghten, 1837; Free.

The daughter of John and Julia Lazar (qq.v.), Rachel was a survivor of an ill-fated voyage during which three of her younger siblings died of scarlet fever. Within a month of her arrival on 30 May 1837, the *Sydney Gazette* reported that her father had put her on the stage in Sydney to perform 'a Benefit' on behalf of her family, in which she 'gracefully' danced a 'Millenese hornpipe'. The ten-year-old prodigy played 'Little Pickle' in the farce *The Spoiled Child*, and performed the character with 'great success'. It was her debut. On 12 October 1837, with Rachel again on the stage, the *Sydney Gazette* wrote: 'her father has been heavily afflicted in the loss of nearly all his family. Circumstances like these, painful as they are, should enlist patronage to his now only child and she will receive it'. In that year, Rachel Lazar advertised (*Sydney Gazette*, 12 August 1837) that 'she will give dancing lessons so no interruption may arise from her theatrical duties'. On 13 March 1838 the *Sydney Gazette* reported: 'Miss Lazar still continues to be one of the principal if not the chief attraction in the theatre. We are glad to see that her dancing assumes more of a British character. The respectable public of Sydney is not yet sufficiently Italianised to relish the, we almost said lascivious, notions of foreign figurantes'.

Rachel Lazar performed on the stage in South Australia for several decades after her family moved and then went with her parents to live in New Zealand in 1863.

Sydney Gazette, 27 May 1837, 30 May 1837, 12 August 1837, 13 March 1838.

LAZAR, Samuel

b. Sydney, 1838

Samuel Lazar, the son of John and Julia Lazar (qq.v.), founded Lazar's Italian Opera Company in South Australia.

LAZARUS, Abraham

Free.
Dealer.

Abraham Lazarus is listed in the 1833 *New South Wales Directory* as living in George Street, Sydney. In 1864 Lazarus was chosen to be the sexton of the Macquarie Street Synagogue.

LAZARUS, Benjamin

b. London, 1809–1857
John Woodhall, 1832; Free.
Married; Watch and clockmaker; 1 child.

The *John Woodhall* arrived from London, with Benjamin Lazarus as a passenger, at Hobart Town on 17 February 1832. The *Launceston Independent* of 24 August 1833 reported 'We have much pleasure in observing that Mr Lazarus has fulfilled his pledge to the Public in the erection of a beautiful illuminated clock he must have sacrificed a considerable sum in its erection. We much commend the enterprising spirit of Mr Lazarus and consider him entitled to, in no small degree, the patronage and support of the Colonists'.

His five-year-old son Eleazar died in Sydney on 5 July 1857. Benjamin Lazarus died in Sydney on 7 October 1857. In 1901 the tombstones of Benjamin and Eleazar were moved to the Botany Pioneers' Cemetery.

Hobart Town Courier, 25 February 1832, republished in *Sydney Gazette*, 31 March 1832.

LAZARUS, Cashmore

b. London, 1807–1894
1840; Free.
Single; Dealer; 2 children.

Cashmore Lazarus was the son of Mordecai Lazarus (q.v.) and Julia (Gittel), née Cashmore. His siblings were Henry (q.v.), Moses (q.v.), and Rosa, and he was a first cousin of Michael Cashmore (q.v.).

Cashmore Lazarus opened a shop in Collins Street in early 1840 'on the wrong side of the street'. In fact in front of his shop there was a 'perpendicular fall of some six feet … was it not for the light afforded nightly in the shop of Mr Lazarus we feel sure we should ere this have had to record some dreadful accident'. Cashmore Lazarus of Elizabeth Street was accepted as a member of the Melbourne Hebrew Congregation on 21 January 1844. His application to join the congregation is letter no. 1 in the files. He married Caroline Harris on 1 January 1851 in Melbourne's ninth Jewish marriage. They were registered in the congregation's birth book as having two children, Hannah Catherine, born 18 October 1851, and Julia, born August 1852, who died three months later.

Cashmore Lazarus and Solomon Benjamin (q.v.) were the witnesses at Melbourne's second Jewish marriage, when Lewis Davis (q.v.) married Cashmore's sister Rosa on 12 November 1845. 'C. Lazarus' signed the community's address to the newly appointed Chief Rabbi Adler, written in Port Phillip in February 1846.

Lazarus was one of the five Jewish dealers fined five shillings each for exposing goods for sale on the footpath during April 1845. (A second, more severe police action, in 1853, brought about a fine of £3.) Later in 1845, Cashmore Lazarus was temporarily removed from membership in the Melbourne Hebrew Congregation for 'highly immoral conduct'—a motion proposed by Moses Benjamin (q.v.) and seconded by Edward Nathan (q.v.). Cashmore Lazarus was buried in the Jewish section of the Melbourne General Cemetery on 11 July 1894.

Port Phillip Gazette, 2 March 1840, 5 April 1845; First Minute Book of the Melbourne Hebrew Congregation.

LAZARUS, David

b. Portsmouth, 1803
Neptune I (2), 1820; Convict; Sentenced to 7 years, London, 1818.
Height: 157.5 cm.

Fair pale complexion, black hair, dark eyes. Lazarus was convicted on 31 March 1818. He was fourteen years old and described as an errand boy when he stole a microscope in a mahogany case from an optical instruments shop in Aldgate. In court the constable described the arrest: 'I met him, collared him and said he must go with me. I took him to the prosecutor. I said he was the boy—he denied it. I sent for his father. He then said he sold it to one Isaacs for 5 shillings. Isaacs denied it. At last he promised to bring it back in five minutes—but he did not'. Lazarus may be the brother of James Laurence (q.v.).

David Lazarus arrived in New South Wales on 16 July 1820 and appeared as a 'labourer on stores, 8 September 1821'. He was listed by the Colonial Secretary's office as a 'person to be assigned' on 9 May 1823. The 1825 General Muster recorded that he was a government servant assigned to Messrs Scott and Heywood at Parramatta. Lazarus, 'late of Parramatta', appeared before the Campbelltown Quarter Sessions on a charge of assaulting Constable Joseph Kerr on Christmas Day 1828.

David Lazarus was granted a certificate of freedom in Sydney on 13 July 1829. He was sentenced once again in Sydney on 1 May 1830 to life for burglary. His prison term was to be served 'in chains'. The sentence was subsequently commuted to three years and three months. He was sentenced again in the Sydney Supreme Court on 12 October 1844 and given a life sentence for 'robbing a man in company'. The conviction was listed in the *Registry of Flash Men* (p. 126), which noted that 'Joe Abrahams' was his 'colleague in the offence'. Lazarus was transported to Van Diemen's Land on the *Water Lily* in 1845 and his name appeared on the 1849 List of Miscellaneous Convicts in the colony.

On 21 September 1853 the remainder of his sentence was remitted.

Registry of Colonial Pardons 4/4494, 4/8383, p. 271; VDL HO 10/41; HO 10/13, 10/19, 10/41; CF 29/0670; Tasmanian Miscellaneous Convicts, Norfolk Island, 4/6271, 17 March 1849, 4/4523; Prisoners sent from New South Wales, February 1845 4/6271; Prisoners from Norfolk Island, 17 March 1840; CS 53/8213.

LAZARUS, Eleazar

b. London, 1775–1827
Fanny, 1816; Convict; Sentenced to 14 years, Derby Assizes, 1815.
Married; Glass cutter; Height: 157 cm.

Dark pale complexion, black hair, dark eyes, blind in right eye. Could neither read nor write. Eleazar Lazarus was sentenced at Chester on 22 March 1815. He was said to be forty-seven years old.

Lazarus arrived in New South Wales on 18 January 1816. He was assigned to the Sydney General Hospital, where he was an assistant to the Dispensary and ultimately worked as an overseer of the hospital. He testified to the Bigge Enquiry that he had 'behaved himself pretty well' and that he had been 'lately dismissed for not issuing clean linen'. Dr D'Arcy Wentworth supported his petition for a conditional pardon, which was granted on 31 January 1820. On 3 September 1821, Eleazar Lazarus, aged fifty, 'a dealer' and a widower, was permitted to marry Eliza Jarrett, alias Brooks. The witness was Elizabeth Josephs. Lazarus owned a small general store 'on the corner' at 7 York Street. He served on a jury dealing with an inquest on 17 September 1821. On 22 March 1822 he received a publican's licence for an inn in York Street.

The Governor, Sir Thomas Brisbane, authorised a land grant to Eleazar Lazarus in Sydney on 30 June 1823. On 17 March 1825 the *Sydney Gazette* reported that he had been fined four dollars and court costs for 'allowing two prisoners of the Crown, habituated as such, to sit drinking in his house after dark'. Lazarus fought the charge and, as a result, on 1 April 1825, two constables were charged with extorting money from him. In February 1826 he was elected as a member of the Licensed Victuallers' Committee of New South Wales and held a licence for a hotel in Pitt Street, Sydney. In August 1826 Lazarus was forced to caution the general public about giving credit to Eliza, his wife. On 10 August 1827 Samuel Lyons (q.v.) advertised in the *Sydney Gazette* that he would be selling 'effects and house of the late Mr E. Lazarus at auction'. Probate was granted to his estate on 12 October 1827. Property valued at £1000 was left to Elizabeth Wilson, the wife of Thomas Wilson, and to Joel Josephs, the son of E. Wilson by her former husband Joel Joseph(s) (q.v.). His wife Eliza Lazarus was left £100.

On 25 March 1828 Eliza Lazarus married Ambrose Johnson.

HO 10/3; *Sydney Gazette*, 28 July 1821, 22 March 1822, 17 March 1825, 21 April 1825, 12 August 1826, 30 August 1826, 10 August 1827; Pardons Book 4/4430, p. 141; Wentworth Papers A765, pp. 136, 147; Bigge Enquiry, BT Box 6, pp. 2363, 2366; Probate, 12 October 1827, Will no. 337.

LAZARUS, Elijah

b. London, 1808–1895
Recovery (3), 1836; Convict; Sentenced to life, Old Bailey, 1835.
Widower; Shoemaker; Height: 154 cm.

Ruddy complexion, black hair and whiskers, long face, high forehead, hazel eyes, aquiline nose and small chin. Jew. He had lost one front upper tooth and had a scar on his right eyebrow. Elijah Lazarus was sentenced on 6 April 1835 to transportation for stealing 1500 yards of silk waist-coating worth £600 from the shop of John and Sydney Smith, Wood Street, Cheapside. Lazarus protested: 'I was never in prison before'.

Lazarus arrived in Sydney on 25 February 1836 and was listed in the General Return of Convicts in New South Wales of 1837 as working for the government in Sydney. He obtained his ticket of leave on 14 May 1844 for the District of Parramatta.

His brother-in-law Philip Levy (q.v.) immediately asked that Elijah Lazarus be allowed to join him in Van Diemen's Land and in July 1845 he received permission to travel to live in Van Diemen's Land, arriving in Hobart Town on the *Water Lily* in that year. A ticket of leave was granted on 23 August 1845. He was recommended for a conditional pardon in July 1847 and received the pardon on 9 January 1849. The official note against his name reads: 'Transported to Sydney in 1836 and transferred to Van Diemen's Land in 1845. No offence against him since transportation'. He was buried in Tasmania in 1895.

CON 37/2, no. 505; 4/3691, 24 June 1845, p. 481, approved, p. 485; Tasmanian Miscellaneous Convicts, HO 10/41; HO 10/60; TL 44/1451.

LAZARUS, Hannah

Wave, 1830; Free.
Married; 6 children.

Hannah was the wife of Henry Lewis Lazarus (q.v.).

LAZARUS, Henry

b. 1785
Earl Spencer, 1813; Convict; Sentenced to 7 years, Old Bailey, 1812.
Labourer.

Henry Lazarus was tried at the Old Bailey on 8 April 1812 for having stolen a bundle of paper (two reams) from a cart being loaded at the Custom House Quay. The theft was seen by an officer of the police: 'I struck him over the legs with a stick, he fell down and rolled over two or three times, and [I] called out stop thief the whole time, I got hold of him; he got up again and said he would not be taken, he said he was an honest man'. Lazarus was twenty-seven years old.

Henry Lazarus arrived in New South Wales on 9 October 1813.

OBSP, 1812, case 322.

LAZARUS, Henry (ELLIS) (LEWIS)

b. London, 1779
Calcutta, 1803; Convict; Sentenced to 7 years, Old Bailey, 1801.
Married; Pedlar; Height: 168 cm; 1 child (in England).

Jew. Dark complexion, brown hair, grey eyes. On 17 June 1801 Lazarus stood trial for having stolen a pocket book with a £300 banknote in it, and a draft from the Bank of England for £500. The evidence at the trial was contradictory and the chief witness against him, David Belasco, committed perjury. Lazarus told the court that he lived in Gravel Lane, Houndsditch, and that his wife and child were 'in a distressed condition—our child is sleeping naked'. Lazarus was acquitted. On 20 August Lazarus stole linen worth four shillings and nine pence from a shop in Oxford Street, and on 16 September 1801 was sentenced to seven years transportation.

Lazarus was deported to Australia twice. The first time he had come as a convict with the Collins Expedition to Sorrento at Port Phillip Bay. When that experiment failed the expedition sailed south to Van Diemen's Land. During the voyage out he served as a sailor and evidently became servant to Lieutenant Governor Collins. Lazarus was listed as 'sick' at the Hobart Town Hospital on 10 November 1804. A letter to him was listed as waiting for collection in Hobart Town in August 1806. By this time Lazarus had been permitted to leave Van Diemen's Land and to travel to New South Wales in order to find the resources to return home.

He travelled to England in April 1817 and may well have discovered that his child and wife had died. They are not mentioned when he appeared at the Warwick Assizes on 30 March 1822 accused of highway robbery. He may possibly have wanted to return to Australia. At this trial he was sentenced to transportation for life and returned to Australia in chains on the *Morley* in 1823. He appeared on the Convict Musters in Van Diemen's Land of 1825 and 1830 using the name Henry Ellis. In the 1825 Muster he appeared as an assigned convict servant to Mr R. Maunder. On 10 April 1830, while an assigned servant to Mr O. Smith, he left a horse and cart he was driving unattended in the street and was fined ten shillings. He received a ticket of leave in 1833. On 4 July 1834 his driving habits once again got him into trouble when he was fined ten shillings for 'riding in his dray in Macquarie Street without anyone on foot guarding same'. He received a conditional pardon on 29 February 1836.

OBSP, 1801, cases 678, and 703; Ship Indent 4/4001, p. 162; CO 201/33, p. 242; CON 31/9; *Sydney Herald*, 5 July 1832; CP no. 836.

LAZARUS, Henry Lewis (Lewis Henry)

b. Caermarthan, 1804
Wave, 1830; Free.
Married; Watchmaker; Height: 160.5 cm; 6 children.

Henry Lazarus was the son of Mordecai and Julia (Gittel) Lazarus (qq.v.) and the brother of Moses (q.v.), Cashmore (q.v.) and Rosa. He and his wife Hannah (q.v.)

arrived on the *Wave* in 1830. They travelled cabin class with their family, arriving in Sydney on 7 August 1830. Their children were Benjamin, Lewis, Thomas, Charles, Mary Ann (q.v.) and Sarah.

Lazarus applied for two assigned convicts in 1831 and was refused. He was listed as a watchmaker in George Street, Sydney, in 1832 and then moved to Van Diemen's Land in 1833 on the *Maria Ann*. On 7 June 1833 Henry Lewis Lazarus had a convict servant assigned to him. He opened a jeweller's shop in Charles Street, Launceston, in 1834 and began to look for an apprentice. On 9 September 1836 he applied to be declared insolvent.

On 15 May 1837 Lazarus received a life sentence at the Hobart Supreme Court for an attempt to defraud Judah Solomon (q.v.) of £145. Lazarus had forged a bill for the money using the name of George Dudfield of Oatlands. Lazarus spent the following three years at Port Arthur. On 19 November 1840, as an assigned servant in Hobart Town, he was sentenced to six months hard labour for 'falsely representing himself as a solicitor'. On 28 July 1841, while with a work gang, he was sentenced to twelve months hard labour in chains at Port Arthur for pawning a watch that had been given him to take to be repaired. From August 1841 to January 1842 there were nine charges of idleness while he was at the Port Arthur Penitentiary. At the end of 1842 he was sent to road gangs in Picton and Oatlands until 3 April 1843 when he was sent back to Port Arthur for 'general idleness'. On 1 January 1844 he was sentenced to be detained at Port Arthur for twelve months for 'want of vigilance and not making a manly resistance when his station was attacked by absentees'. On 21 March 1844 Lazarus was granted a pass by the Lieutenant Governor. He returned to his family in Hobart Town and, in 1845, joined the Hobart Hebrew Congregation where, between 1845 and 1848, he was listed in the ledger as living in Argyle Street. Lewis Henry Lazarus of 46 Liverpool Street in Hobart Town complained to the authorities in January 1846 that 'the houses in my immediate vicinity were on fire and a large part of my premises were pulled down to arrest the progress of the flames and protect a vast amount of city property'. He asked for compensation.

The *Hobart Town Courier* reported on 22 January 1846, apparently inaccurately, that he had been acquitted in the Supreme Court for having a forged Bill of Exchange in his possession. He had been found guilty and was sent to prison at Port Arthur for six months. A provisional conditional pardon was granted on 10 October 1849 and a conditional pardon granted for 'outside VDL and the UK', which allowed him to go to the Australian mainland and leave Tasmania. He was listed as 'Free' in 1849 and in March 1849 he was elected the Hon Secretary of the Hobart Synagogue's plan to build a ritual bath. On 5 July 1854 the Hobart *Mercury* reported that the six-and-a-half-year lease of his business premises had been sold to Abraham Rheuben (q.v.) 'for the goodly sum of £1500'.

In 1846, Mary Ann Lazarus, one of the children of Lewis Henry Lazarus, caused a colonial crisis when she (temporarily) converted to Christianity on the advice of a zealous colonial chaplain while her father was in gaol.

Wave Indent 4/5201, 7 August 1830; CON 31/25, p. 363, no. 1064; CON 35/1, p. 363, no. 1064; CON 16/1, p. 53; HO 10/41; *Hobart Town Courier*, 7 June 1833, 9 September 1836, 22 January 1846, 17 May 1837; *Launceston Advertiser*, 22 September 1834; *Sydney Gazette*, 7 September 1830, 31 October 1831.

LAZARUS, Joseph

1838; Free.
Merchant.

Joseph Lazarus announced the opening of his Adelaide Stores in Hindley Street on 10 March 1838. He was invited to attend the 'Governor's Levee' to celebrate the anniversary of the colony on 7 December 1839. By July 1840 he had renamed his shop the Victorian Store and advertised in July that he had just received a 'large consignment' of 750 pairs of trousers. In June 1841 he wrote a letter to the editor of the *South Australian Almanack* suggesting the formation of a philanthropic society. On 18 September 1841 such a society was established, but without Lazarus.

South Australian Gazette and Colonial Register, 10 March 1838, 29 August 1839, 7 September 1839, 7 December 1839, 21 December 1839, 11 July 1840, 19 June 1841.

LAZARUS, Joseph

b. 1817
King William, 1843; Free.
Married; Carpenter.

Lazarus arrived in Van Diemen's Land a 'bounty migrant' on 28 January 1843 with his wife Rebecca (q.v.). In 1844 Joseph Lazarus paid ten shillings and sixpence to the Hobart Synagogue. He advertised that he was a 'carver and guilder' who made picture frames. In 1845 his shop was at 64 Liverpool Street (two doors from the hardware shop of Philip Levy, q.v.). In 1846 Lazarus owed the synagogue three shillings and sixpence and he continued to be listed in the ledger book of the congregation until 1848.

CSO 8/76/1706; *Colonial Times*, 8 February 1845.

LAZARUS, Julia

b. London, 1819
Boadicea, 1836; Free.
Single; Parasol-maker; 6 children.

Julia, aged eighteen, arrived in Hobart Town from London as a bounty migrant with her sister Leah (q.v.) and Elizabeth (Cohen) the wife of Moses Cohen (q.v.). On arrival, she was employed by Mrs (Samuel) Moses as a general servant at a wage of ten shillings a week. On 5 May 1840 Julia married Thomas Meyer, who was described as a 'tin man'. On 31 December 1841 they were listd as living at 5 Campbell Street, Hobart Town. They had five children. The census lists them and their children as members of the Church of England—Thomas Elijah born 26 March 1841 (died in infancy), Joseph Frederick born 2 February 1843 and his twin Henry James, Frederick Nathaniel 13 April 1847 and Eleanor born 7 February 1842. Thomas died in Hobart Town on 8 October 1849 and Leah who died in 1852 aged two.

Julia married Saul Solomons at the house of Henry Benjamin (q.v.) on 30 January 1853. Before her marriage Julia presented three of her children to be named in the Hobart Synagogue. Julia was included in the list of licencees of the Waterloo Hotel, Murray Street, Hobart 1856–58. In the 1860s Julia went to New Zealand.

Family information from Peter Dunn. CSO 1/848/17942.

LAZARUS, Leah

b. 1818
Boadicea, 1836; Free.
Single; Parasol-maker.

Leah Lazarus, an assisted female bounty migrant and sister of Julia Lazarus (q.v.) and John Lazar (q.v.), arrived in Van Diemen's Land on 2 February 1836. Leah was said to have been 'very good' on board ship but by the time she arrived in Hobart Town she was declared to be insane. She was admitted to the Queen Orphan School.

CSO 1/848/17942; Elizabeth Rushen, *Single and Free: Female Migration to Australia*, p. 134.

LAZARUS, Lewis

b. Whitechapel, 1795–1837
Grenada (2), 1821; Convict; Sentenced to life, Old Bailey, 1820.
Single; Hawker; Height: 160 cm.

Dark sallow complexion, black hair, black eyes. Lewis Lazarus was a pickpocket who stole a watch valued at £5 from a man trying to get on the Dover Coach. A witness testified: 'I saw a gang of well known pickpockets returning from Hyde Park Corner'.

Before Lazarus left England a rabbinic court was assembled at the coastal town Gosport opposite Portsmouth to arrange a religious divorce. The ceremony was held on 5 March 1821. Lazarus was identified as the son of Mordecai Etilsdorf and Rachel Jacobs, the daughter of Ya'akov the potato merchant. Lewis and Rachel had been married at London's Great Synagogue on 2 March 1814.

Lewis Lazarus arrived in New South Wales on 16 September 1821 and in December was sent on to the penal settlement at Newcastle for two years. In September 1822 Lazarus was listed on the Monthly Returns of Punishment as having received fifty lashes for disobedience to orders. On 6 June 1825 Lazarus applied for permission to marry Elizabeth Fox, who was free. He was subsequently sentenced at Parramatta on 25 June 1825 to three years colonial transportation and was sent to Moreton Bay on the *Lalla Rook*. He was able to return to Sydney on the *Lucy Ann* in July 1828. He was listed in the 1828 Census as being at Moreton Bay. No religion was specified.

Lewis Lazarus was buried by the Church of England at St Luke's, Liverpool, in 1837. His wife 'Eliza' died in 1855, aged eighty-seven.

OBSP, 1819–20, case 1257, p. 626; Ship Indent 4/4007, p. 391; Monthly Returns of Punishment at Newcastle, 1822, 4/1718; Chronological Register of Convicts at Moreton Bay, no. 725, 4/3794, p. 3; *Phoenix* (hulk) Entrance Book 1828, no. 1383, in 4/6281; *Sydney Gazette*, 9 February 1833. *AJHSJ*, vol 18, part 3, (2007), Jeremy I Pfeffer *The First Bet Din Convened in Australia*. p. 284

LAZARUS, Lewis

b. Hull, 1801
Isabella I (1), 1818; Convict; Sentenced to life, Old Bailey, 1817.
Single; Tailor; Height: 148 cm.

Florid complexion, brown hair, hazel eyes. Jew. The Old Bailey trial records contain two trials involving Lewis Lazarus. In the first he was fifteen when he was caught with another boy stealing eight brushes valued at two shillings. He was sent to gaol and whipped. In the second case he snatched a watch from a salesman as he stood on a doorstep of a house in the Minories. For this second offence he was sentenced, on 3 December 1817, to be transported for life.

Lewis Lazarus arrived in New South Wales in September 1818. On 14 June 1819 he received twenty-five lashes and six months in the gaol gang for having been involved in a robbery. In December he received a further twenty-five lashes for refusing to work. In April 1821 he was sent to Newcastle for two years for armed robbery. On 27 May 1823, while at the Barracks in Emu Plains, he received a sentence of twelve months for stealing clothes. During the following months he was given one hundred lashes and sent to Port Macquarie for running away and for having attempted to stab two men. He ran away again and was speared four times by Aborigines. His petition, written in Sydney on 8 September 1826, is reproduced here with the spelling untouched:

Jaol Sydney: To Governor Darling: Sir:

> I hope to be Exused for writen has I consider my case very hard I was apsent from my gang a few days and was sentenced one hundred lashes By Dr Wentworth and the Remainder of my Sentence to a penal Settlement which his life which I whas first sent to Port Macquarie which I Remaned ther for a wile and then Capn Wright Sent me up has I whas sent down By a magstrat and whem I caim from the cceal I whas taken to the jaol which I think hit a very good cais that I should Recive the same indulgence has my fellow priners your hunbel servant Lewis Lazarus Ship Esibelar the first.

Lazarus was committed for trial, once more, on 11 February 1833 for having stolen property in his possession. On 19 July 1833 he received a sentence of six months in the iron gang for stealing a cheese at Sydney's Hyde Park Prisoners' Barracks. During the next four years he was stationed both at the Hyde Park Barracks and the gaol at Sutton Forest. During this period he received a total of 136 lashes for assault and drunkenness, an extra year in irons for theft and, on 20 August 1836, one month in the cells for drunkenness with six weeks on the treadmill for the same offence.

After a term in hospital he was sent on to the Sydney Gaol and then on to Moreton Bay. Sixteen months later he again escaped from custody and was at large for two months, making his way down the eastern Australian coast and surrendering to police at Port Macquarie. He was able to give some information about the largely unexplored region of the 'Big River', for which he was promised 'something beneficial at the conclusion of six months at Port Macquarie'. Lazarus was sent to Sydney in order to be returned to Moreton Bay. He was given the position of assistant at the prison hospital but when the notoriously cruel commandant became lost in the bush Lazarus was promised a conditional pardon should he be able to use his bush craft to find Captain Logan. Lazarus found Logan's decomposed body and helped to bring it back to Moreton Bay. As a result he fell ill and almost died.

He was then returned to Sydney and assigned to Joseph Raphael (q.v.). After twelve months service he was charged with theft. He was sent to gaol for six months and then returned to the service of Raphael, who soon found it necessary to lodge an official complaint. Lazarus was returned to government service and made a complaint of his own about his rations and about the behaviour of the superintendent of the Hyde Park Barracks.

Lazarus was then sent to Port Macquarie, where he remained for three years. At the age of thirty-eight, after having been a prisoner for twenty-two years, Lazarus petitioned for a pardon. His petition was refused. He finally received a ticket of leave on 3 February 1843 for the District of Port Macquarie.

OBSP, 1816–17, case 868, p. 302; *OBSP*, 1817–18 case 97, p. 40; Ship Indent 4/4006, p. 89; Petition, 40/8189, 22 August 1840, 4/2513; Moreton Bay Records, 4/3794, p. 3; Chronological Register of Convicts at Moreton Bay, no. 36. 4/1917.1, and 4/3794, p. 265; ML, A1817, p. 112f., 8 September 1826; *Phoenix* (hulk) Entrance Book 4/6282, no. 556; TL 1843/427, in 4/4173; *Sydney Gazette*, 4 September 1823, 29 December 1825, 1 April 1826, 28 June 1832; TL 43/427.

LAZARUS, Mary Ann

Wave, 1830; Free.

Mary Ann, a daughter of Hannah and Lewis Henry Lazarus (Henry Lewis Lazarus, q.v.), arrived in Hobart Town as an infant. Mary Ann Lazarus's father was sent to prison and while she was being cared for in the Hobart Town Orphan Asylum the girl was baptised by the zealous chaplain. On 27 July 1846 the President of the Hobart Hebrew Congregation wrote to the Colonial Secretary:

> Inasmuch as the girl was under age, and had a father and mother in Hobart Town, the Baptising her without their knowledge and sanction, in the Lieutenant Governor's opinion is most improper, and his Excellency deeply regrets the circumstance. His Excellency deems it proper to inform the Secretary of State [in England] of this unfortunate meddling of the Chaplain, but I must say the Jewish people do not seem to be alive to the children's religious interests by leaving them in such establishments to become servants.

Louis Nathan replied with thanks and added 'the members of the Hebrew Congregation of this City, have hitherto been too limited in number to maintain generally the children of Prisoners of their own Faith, or to prevent occasionally seeking the asylum allowed by Her Majesty's Government in the orphan schools'.

On 21 March 1855 Mary Ann Lazarus married Leo Susman at his home at 22 Liverpool Street 'in accordance with the rites and ceremonies of the Jews'. The Rev. Herman Hoelzel officiated. Susman was an observant Jew who had been born in Germany and who, it is said, fell in love with Mary Ann on his first day in Hobart in 1854.

CSO 11/28/546, to President of the Hobart Hebrew Congregation, 27 July 1846; *AG*, pp. 192, 193.

LAZARUS, Mordecai

Platina, 1842; Free.
Married; Dealer; 4 children.

On 2 September 1842 M. Lazarus announced his arrival on the *Platina* and established a shop called Portland House, which was opposite the Royal Hotel in Melbourne. Mordecai and Julia (Gittel) Lazarus were the parents of Henry Lewis Lazarus (q.v.), Moses (q.v.), Cashmore (q.v.), and Rosa. An M. Lazarus (senior) was listed in the Melbourne Hebrew Congregation's membership list of 1843. Mordecai paid a subscription of one shilling and donated three shillings to the Hobart Town Synagogue in 1844. On 7 February 1847 he was accepted as a member of the Melbourne Hebrew Congregation.

At the dinner that celebrated the laying of the foundation stone of the first Melbourne synagogue in August 1847 Mr Lazarus stood up and sang—'to the greatest surprise and applause of the audience—the singer although upwards of three score and ten, delivered himself with a strength and sweetness of voice'.

Port Phillip Patriot, 24 August 1847.

LAZARUS, Moses

b. London, 1816–1865
Portsea, 1839; Free.
Single; Draper and clothier; 1 child.

The parents of Moses Lazarus were the London glass cutter Mordecai Lazarus (q.v.) and Julia (Gittel), née Cashmore. Moses was the brother of Henry Lewis Lazarus (q.v.), Cashmore (q.v.) and Rosa. Moses Lazarus and his wife Caroline (née Hart) arrived in Sydney on 18 December 1838 and then moved to the new township of Melbourne in 1839. The opening of a shop selling jewellery and clothing in Collins Street was first advertised on 2 November 1839 and followed on a letter Moses Lazarus wrote to the Colonial Secretary on 22 October 1839 telling him that he hoped to open a jeweller's shop in Collins Street early 'in the ensuing month'. He needed a skilled watchmaker and asked for the assigned service of Samuel Wolfe (q.v.), who had arrived in Hobart Town 'lately' on the *Pyramus* in December 1838. An official record attached to the petition notes that Wolfe arrived on the *Portsea*.

On 5 January 1839 Lazarus imported five crates of earthenware. His drapery and clothing shop in Collins Street West was called Portland House and High Holyday services were held there as early as 1839. He was a member of the first Melbourne (Jewish) Congregational Committee in 1841. On 1 July 1842 he witnessed the dissolution of a deed of partnership between his uncle, Michael Cashmore (q.v.), and Lewis Davis (q.v.) (who had married his sister Rosa). In the week the partnership was dissolved he announced that his business had expanded into 'more commodious and centrically situated premises and that his shop embodied 'elegance combined with economy'. The move was not a success and on 11 August 1843 the *Melbourne Times* announced that he was insolvent.

Moses Lazarus was in Hobart Town in September 1844 and was listed as one of the founding members of the Hobart Town Synagogue.

From 1841 to 1851 Lazarus was listed in the *Port Phillip GPO Directory* as living at 87 Elizabeth Street, and in 1856 he lived at 28 La Trobe Street, and was a 'gentleman'. He died on 13 December 1871.

Sydney General Trade List for 1839, 5 January 1839; *Melbourne Times*, 11 August 1843; *Port Phillip Gazette*, 29 October 1842; Jeremy I. Pfeffer, *From One End of the Earth to the Other*, Sussex Acamic Press (2008), p. 207f.

LAZARUS, Moses

Free.

Moses Lazarus was a member of the Hobart Town Synagogue in 1844 and gave £2 1s 6d as a donation to the congregation. He rented seat no. 56 in the synagogue in 1845 and his Hebrew name was recorded as *Moshe ben Mordecai*. His publican's licence for the Cornish Mount was transferred to W. Bastian in May 1846. He lived in Barrack Street, Hobart Town, from February 1844. (The *Registry of Flash Men* mentions a Moses Lazarus in Sydney, who was said to have been 'Lately free from Mr Bonney's Gang and caught with stolen goods'.)

Hobart Town Courier, 16 February 1844; W. A. Miles, *Registry of Flash Men*, p. 99.

LAZARUS, Nathan Moses

b. London, 1823–1901
Free.
Single; Carpenter; 10 children.

Nathan Moses arrived as a free migrant in the 1840s. He worked for some years at Abraham Meyer's store in Monaro Street, Queanbeyan. He then opened his own store in Macquarie Street under the banner 'Lazarus, I. X. L. Store: Grocery, Ironmongery, Hardware, Drapery, Clothing, Boots and Shoes'. He later added coffin-making as a sideline and from that followed undertaking.

In 1856 Lazarus married a widow, Harriet Grogan, whose first husband had been drowned when he had attempted to ford the Queanbeyan River at full flood. Harriet bore Nathan ten children.

In 1860 Lazarus donated a sundial to the town—its oldest public artefact. In April 1885 Nathan Lazarus became one of the nine alderman elected to the first Town council and in 1891 Nathan Moses Lazarus, JP, became mayor of the town. Before he died he requested that he be buried in 'no man's land' between the Anglican and Methodist section of the town cemetery. He died in 1901.

Hamerkaz (ACT Jewish Community Journal), April 1985.

LAZARUS, Rebecca

b. 1815
King William, 1843.
Married; Umbrella-maker.

Rebecca and her husband Joseph Lazarus (q.v.) were bounty migrants to Van Diemen's Land.

LEADER, Joseph

b. Birmingham, 1820
Barossa (1), 1839; Convict; Sentenced to 10 years, Stafford, 1839.
Single; Labourer; Height: 166 cm.

Sallow complexion, dark brown hair, brown eyes, eyebrows partially meeting. Thick nose. Joseph Leader was sentenced on 3 July 1839. His uncle was Mosely Moss Cohen (q.v.), a jeweller, in George Street, Sydney.

Joseph Leader arrived in New South Wales on 8 December 1839. He received a ticket of leave in 1844 and a certificate of freedom in 1849.

Barossa Printed Indent, p. 116; TL 44/565; CF 49/0262, in 4/4408.

LEAR, Simeon (Simon)

b. Amsterdam, 1786–1847
Shipley (1), 1817; Convict; Sentenced to 14 years, Plymouth Assizes, 1816.
Single; Dentist; Height: 166 cm.

Dark ruddy complexion, black hair, hazel eyes. Simeon Lear was sentenced at Devon on 5 August 1816. He appeared on the ship indent bracketed together with Abraham Elias (q.v.), who was also transported with a 14-year sentence. On 30 January 1812 a religious divorce was granted by Simon Lear (Shimon Ben Moshe) to Hannah (Bat Shmuel Known as Zanvil). They had been married at the Great Synagogue in London on 3 August 1803.

Simeon Lear was one of the first dentists in Australia. He was granted a ticket of leave in May 1818. On 20 July 1820 the *Sydney Gazette* printed a General Order that was dated from Government House on the same day, which announced that a medical board of three surgeons had examined five men 'who were represented as practising Surgery and Physic … at Sydney the said persons are not duly qualified either as Surgeons or Physicians being ignorant of these professions, Joseph Hyams (q.v.) and Simon Lear'. On 7 August 1823 Lear, 'an oculist', married Mrs Elizabeth Tuckwell (née Williams), 'a butcher' aged forty, at St Philip's. He was one of the early members of the Sydney Synagogue and acted as their *mohel* (ritual circumciser) until 1835.

By the 1828 Census Simon Lear held a ticket of leave, which had been renewed on 18 September 1823. He was listed as thirty-nine years of age (though he was forty-two) and working as a dentist at his home at 10 Macquarie Street. He advertised that he was 'an occulist [*sic*], dentist and corn operator'. Lear received a conditional pardon in 1830 and in 1831 successfully applied for the services of one assigned convict.

In 1836 Simon and Elizabeth Lear wrote to the Colonial Secretary complaining that alterations made to Macquarie Street had damaged their property. The Government Engineer responded 'the improvement of the street will more than compensate the owners'.

By 1837, in addition to his previous specialities, Lear had added 'exotic snuff' which could cure headaches. He contributed £10 to the synagogue building fund in 1839.

He died on 18 September 1847, aged sixty-one, leaving his property to the Sydney Synagogue and the Jewish Philanthropic Institution. His executors were Abraham Polack (q.v.), Moses Joseph (q.v.) and James Simmons (q.v.). His property consisted of the south-western corner of the intersection of Martin Place and Macquarie Street and two houses in Elizabeth Street. The bequest was subject to his wife having access to the income during her life.

Shipley (1) Indent 4/4005, p. 272; CP 30/114; *Sydney Gazette*, 29 July 1820; CO 201/118; TL 582/743, and no. 1542. Governors'Despatches 1832, A 1210; *Sydney Times*, 17 June 1837; 'Sydney B. Glass', *AJJHS*, vol. 4, no. 4 (1956), p. 163.

LEE, Benjamin (Belcher)

b. London, 1797
Marquis of Wellington, 1815; Convict; Sentenced to 7 years, Old Bailey, 1810.
Labourer.

Benjamin Lee stole a pocket book from a bystander at a public pillory at Charing Cross. He was caught immediately. He had an accomplice, Joseph Chinnery. Lee was sentenced on 19 September 1810. His age was recorded as fifteen but he may have been younger as he was not sent out to Australia until 1815. Lee was transported twice—first on the Marquis of Wellington *in 1815 as 'Benjamin Lee', and then on the* Albion *as 'Benjamin Belcher'.*

The *Marquis of Wellington* arrived in New South Wales on 27 January 1815. Lee was sent on to Windsor to be assigned work. A Benjamin Lee tried to stow away with Henry Phillips in 1823 and escape from the colony. The two were betrayed by Samuel Lyons (q.v.) who asked for a ticket of leave as a reward for their capture. There is a record stating that Benjamin Lee left Australia on the *Harriet* after the expiry of his sentence on 6 October 1817. Benjamin Lee, alias Belcher, returned to serve a second sentence and received a second certificate of freedom on 2 November 1826.

OBSP, 1810, case 721, p. 385; AOT, 22 December 1817, 012/5800; Letter 14, dated 16 April 1823, in 4/1870; 4/1870, p. 14; CF 4/4424.

LEE, Benjamin (LEVY)

b. London, 1797–1884
Mary, 1829; Free.
Married; 11 children.

Benjamin Lee arrived in Sydney on the *Mary* on 20 January 1829 travelling steerage and accompanied by his wife Rebecca (née Harris) (q.v.) and four children, one girl over the age of twelve, and one boy and two girls under twelve. Lee settled in Parramatta and in 1833 asked for, and received, one government servant. His daughter Belinda died on 25 December 1832, and was buried in the Devonshire Street Jewish Cemetery. A son, Morris, was born in Sydney in 1834, followed by Benjamin (jnr), in 1836. Henry was born on 4 September 1838, Joseph in 1840, Caroline in 1843 (at Moreton Bay), Elizabeth in 1846 (at Moreton Bay), and Miriam in 1848 (in Sydney).

In 1836 Lee moved to George Street and opened a shop dealing in general goods. In 1837 he acquired the Weatherboard Inn at Wentworth Falls in the Blue Mountains from the firm of Isaac Simmons and Co. The cost was £155. Lee obtained a licence to open the Bathurst Traveller, an inn in the District of Clwyd, 25 miles from any established town. He joined the Sydney Synagogue in 1837, and continued to be a member and supporter through the years ahead.

On 9 May 1839 the *Sydney Gazette* carried an article entitled 'Ingratitude':

> Some weeks ago a lad named Jacobs called at Mr Lee's shop in George Street and said he was just arrived and that he was destitute. Mr Lee, with that good feeling, which is remarkable among the members of the Jewish persuasion, at once received him in his house and treated him with much kindness. Lee soon missed some articles which were traced to a butcher. Jacobs then turned into an informer against the butcher. Mr Lee's loss is estimated to be £30. The culprit is yet to be identified.

In 1841 Lee became the licensee of the Flower Pot Tavern in George Street. He became an early free settler in Moreton Bay in 1843. On 13 November 1843, Lee was voted to be one of the two Jewish representatives of the Sydney Synagogue in Moreton Bay. The northern settlement struggled to survive and there were twenty cases tried in the Court of Requests for the recovery of small debts between 1844 and 1846. Lee was a licensed publican in Queens Street, North Brisbane, in 1845–46, returning to Sydney in 1847, where he remained as a general dealer.

Benjamin Lee died on 12 May 1884 and was buried in Raphael's Ground. Rebecca died 30 September 1863.

Sydney Gazette, 23 May 1837, 9 May 1839; 4/2363.1, letter 37/6076; Sydney Synagogue Minute Book p. 126.

LEE, Elizabeth (Betsy)

Tam O'Shanter, 1836; Free.
Married; 6 children.

Elizabeth 'Betsy' Lee (née Isaacs) and her husband Philip Lee (q.v.) arrived in South Australia on 20 November 1836, the first Jews in the new colony.

LEE, Edward

b. Memel, East Prussia, d. 1842
Free.
Married; Dealer; 4 children.

Mr Edward Lee and his wife Sara (née Howe) were in Sydney by 1830. In 1831 he signed a public petition for the recall of Governor Darling, who singled him out when he wrote home to England, describing Lee as 'an insolvent Jew broker'. Lee, in fact, worked as a ship's agent and was fairly successful.

Belinda Lee, the second daughter of Edward and Sara, died on 25 December 1832. Frederica Henrya Lee, their fourth daughter, was buried in the Devonshire Street Jewish Cemetery on 9 November 1834.

The *Sydney Gazette* reported on 23 July 1835 that Edward Lee had been 'severely assaulted by his drunken servant with an axe'.

Edward Lee was a member of the Sydney Synagogue Committee in 1837 and 1838 and in 1839 'Mr Edward Lee and family' gave £21 to the synagogue building appeal. Edward Lee was an active member in the Masonic Lodge of Australia.

The *Australian* reported on 18 November 1842 that Mr Lee 'late of Bligh St died at Memel' in East Prussia on 27 June 1842. Mrs Lee and her children returned to Sydney from London on 13 June 1844. She died in Sydney on 25 September 1879.

Sydney Gazette, 5 February 1835; Miscellaneous Letters, p. 120, MLA 2146, Letters 1832; *Australian*, 18 November 1842; *Sydney Morning Herald*, 1 April 1843.

LEE, Harriet

b. 1809
Royal Saxon, 1841; Free.
Married; 1 child.

Harriet and her husband John Lee (q.v.) arrived at Port Phillip on 17 July 1841 together with their 18-month-old child Morris. Both John and Harriet could read and write and were Jewish. They were 'imported' by J. B. Wise of Melbourne.

Elizabeth Rushen, *Single and Free*, p. 164; 4/4813.

LEE, Henry

b. London, 1807
Marquis of Huntley (2), 1826; Convict; Sentenced to life, Newgate, 1824.
Single; Butcher; Height: 165 cm.

Ruddy complexion, brown hair, hazel eyes. Deep scar on right temple. Jew. Could read and write. Henry Lee was convicted of stealing in a dwelling house and sentenced on 29 October 1824.

Henry Lee arrived on 13 September 1826. He was listed in the 1828 Census assigned to the 24th Iron Gang, Windsor. No religion was noted.

Ship Indent 4/4012, p. 78.

LEE, John

b. 1805
Royal Saxon, 1841; Free.
1 child.

John Lee, aged thirty-six, his wife Harriet Lee (q.v.), aged thirty-two, and Morris, their son, aged eighteen months, arrived at Port Phillip on 17 July 1841. Both adults were Jewish and could read and write. They were 'imported' by J. B. Wise of Melbourne to become 'farm servants'.

Elizabeth Rushen, *Single and Free*, p. 164; 4/4813.

LEE, Michael (Abraham)

d. 1845
Active, 1791; Convict; Sentenced to 7 years, Old Bailey, 1789.

Michael Lee stole a gentleman's trunk full of clothes. He had hidden under a moving carriage and attempted to cut away the straps that held a travelling trunk at the front of the vehicle. The robbery took place in the Seven Dials area of London. Lee had an accomplice who acted as a lookout. He was sentenced on 25 February 1789. On 22 July 1790 after 'Confinement for near two Years in a crowded Prison whereby your Petitioner's health is much affected', Lee asked to be permitted to serve the remainder of his time by joining the Royal Navy. It was reported that his behaviour had been 'orderly and quietly'. However, in the third year of his sentence Lee sailed for Australia.

Lee arrived in Sydney in September 1791 and, with thirty-one other convicts on the naval ship HMS *Gorgon*, a ship of the Third Fleet, was immediately sent to Norfolk Island on the *Queen*. By May 1792 he was listed as selling produce to the government. He had half an acre cleared and had built 'a house of two floors, shingled and boarded 23 feet by 20 feet'. Michael Lee's name is found among the actors in a primitive theatre established on Norfolk Island during the regime of Lieutenant King in 1793.

In January 1794 Lee gave evidence in the Magistrates' Court about 'a Disturbance' that had broken out backstage in Norfolk Island's makeshift theatre. It is noted that he took the oath on the Old Testament. His association with the theatre evidently persisted through his time on Norfolk Island.

On 31 March 1801 he obtained a government lease on the east side of Cascade Road for two shillings and sixpence a year, and on 20 July 1801 he bought the remainder of the lease on twelve acres. For several years Lee was listed as a seller of large amounts of pig meat and small amounts of wheat and maize. When the decision was made to transfer the Norfolk Islanders to Van Diemen's Land, Lee asked for the payment of £16 from the government for the expense of building his house. His claim also concerned half an acre of ground that belonged to the Freemasons' Society, of which he was a member. On 15 May 1808 Michael Lee's name appeared in a list of settlers embarked on the *Estramina* schooner bound for the Derwent, and which arrived on 5 June 1808. Lee's name is listed on the loyal address of welcome to Governor Bligh when he came to Van Diemen's Land on his way back to England. This political action was not welcomed by the island's Lieutenant Governor and Lee was relieved of his status as constable and briefly imprisoned in the guard house.

Lee had been granted a half-acre of land on behalf of the Freemasons' Lodge on the New Town Road. The Lodge of St John still existed in 1819 but did not flourish and in 1827 a dispute about the ownership of the land led Lee to describe himself as 'now Advanced in Years and one of the oldest Residents in the Island'. The documents he produced showed that Lee had received a grant of thirty acres of land at Clarence Plains as compensation for the loss of his house and property on Norfolk Island. The *Hobart Town Gazette* of 16 October 1819 described him as the proprietor of the Freemasons' Arms. It was a weatherboard house in Liverpool Street, near Wellington Bridge.

According to an advertisement in the *Tasmanian* of 3 October 1828 Michael Lee was the licensee of the Castle Inn in Harrington Street, Hobart Town. On 6 February 1829 Michael Lee and Oscar Davis (q.v.) wrote on behalf of the Jewish residents in Van Diemen's Land praising the authorities for granting them land for a cemetery. In 1829 the government wished to know more about a member of the Jewish community and the Colonial Secretary wrote to Davis and Lee. Lee was buried in the Jewish Cemetery in Hobart Town in 1845 and a tombstone was placed on his grave by Bernard Walford jnr (q.v.).

OBSP, February 1789, pp. 318–22; ML, A 1958, p. 35; Van Diemen's Land Convict Muster 4/1233-4; Robert Jordan, *The Convict Theatres of Early Australia*, pp. 123, 271–3; Bigge Appendix, BT Box 12, ML, p. 152; CSO 1/269/6497; *Tasmanian*, 3 October 1828; AOT LSD1/83, pp. 304–5.

LEE, Philip

b. London, d. 1861
Tam O'Shanter, 1836; Free.
Married; Dealer; 6 children.

Philip Lee and Betsy (Elizabeth Lee, q.v.) (née Isaacs), his wife, arrived in South Australia on 20 November 1836, and were the first Jews in the new colony. In 1837

Lee announced to the inhabitants of Adelaide that his wine and coffee rooms, Section 113 Currie Street, were open for the reception of gentlemen: 'Breakfast, dinners etc provided—Beds'. Mr Lee was the leader of the orchestra at the opening of Adelaide's first theatre, the Theatre Royal, and played there from time to time. In September 1838 a partnership was drawn up between Philip Lee and Thomas Davies as livery stable keepers.

The partnership was dissolved in September of 1840 and Lee carried on the business while increasing the stud 'by several excellent horses'. Lee was mentioned in the list of landowners in 1840 and in the *South Australian Almanack* of 1842 he appears as a settler at Sturt River with thirty cattle, two horses, cultivating oats, maize and potatoes. In 1846 the *Almanack* listed him as a storekeeper and in 1848 as a slops seller. Lee was a founder of the Adelaide Hebrew Congregation in September 1848 but took no part in communal life.

A daughter, Sarah Henrietta Lee, was born in 1840 and registered as a 'Hebrew' in New South Wales. She married Louis Barnard in Adelaide at the home of her father. Louis had arrived in Adelaide from Portsmouth in 1855. Two children who were born to Philip and Betsy in Adelaide, died at birth, in 1846 and 1857. A son, John Phillip, was born in January 1850 at Hindley Street, where his father was listed as a 'general clothier'. Janetta was born at Rundle Street, on 3 September 1851, and Lewis on 30 March 1854.

Philip Lee died at Glenelg on 21 January 1861.

H. Munz, *Jews in South Australia*, p. 18; *South Australian Gazette and Colonial Register*, 12 August 1837, 20 January 1838, 19 May 1838, 22 September 1838, 6 September 1838; *South Australian Almanack*, 1846, 1847.

LEE, Rebecca (née HARRIS)

1807–1879
Mary, 1829; Free.
Married; 6 children.

Rebecca Harris married Benjamin Lee (q.v.) in London's Great Synagogue on 20 May 1824. Rebecca Lee died in Sydney, aged seventy-two, in 1879.

LEFTWICH, H

James Pattison, 1838; Free.
Shoemaker.

A passenger on the *James Pattison*, which arrived in Sydney in December 1838. In June 1846 a Mr Leftwich, a boot and shoemaker, of Pitt Street, was swindled by 'a man named Israel Harvey, who represented himself to be a Jew dealer'.

Morning Chronicle, 13 June 1846.

LEIPMAN, Moses Wolffe (LIPMAN)

b. Königsberg, 1788
Ocean, 1816; Convict; Sentenced to 7 years, Old Bailey, 1814.
Furrier; Height: 169 cm.

Dark pale complexion, black hair, hazel eyes. Moses Woolfe Leipman was sentenced at the Old Bailey on 14 September 1814, having been indicted on 8 June 1814 for stealing two counterpanes, 550 seals valued at £20, and 500 cornelian stones valued at £20. Leipman defrauded the wife of Lieutenant Colonel John Stewart of 66 Cavendish Square by pretending to be impressed by two coverlids that she had made and wishing to buy her stock of semi-precious stones. He said that he was the son of a rich merchant in Paris and presented a printed card, 'M. W. Leipman, 7 Gun-square', and an absurd letter of introduction from the 'High Priest Dr Hirschell'.

Moses Wolf Leipman was listed in the 1818 General Muster on 'Government Employment' and on 14 October 1819 was on the list of convicts sent to Newcastle for three years. Leipman was among those allowed to leave the colony on the *John Barry* in December 1821.

OBSP, case 839; HO 11/2, 10/3; Convicts to Newcastle 4/3500, 14 October 1819; *Sydney Gazette*, 15 December 1821.

LEON, Lewis

b. Portsea, 1813–1877
Rubicon, 1832; Free.
Married; Trader; 5 children.

Lewis Leon married Rebecca Pollock in 1830. Both Lewis and Rebecca were seventeen years old. Mr and Mrs Lewis Leon and their two-year-old daughter Annie arrived in Port Jackson on the *Rubicon* on 24 July 1832. They established a shop, the Oil and Colour Warehouse, at 79 George Street.

In November 1832 Leon returned to Sydney from New Zealand on the *City of Edinburgh*. The *Shipping Gazette* of Sydney showed that Leon quickly established a flourishing export-import business, sending hardware to Melbourne and Adelaide, importing thirty boxes of sperm whale candles from Hobart Town, and sending a box of paintings to London. The shop expanded into an adjoining property in George Street. It dealt with sperm whale candles, window glass, hardware and paints. Mr and Mrs Leon sailed with a 'supercargo' on 22 May 1838, bound for Calcutta and London on the *Elizabeth*.

An account of the return journey on the barque *Elizabeth* is described in a typescript by Fowles, which described 'Mrs Leon, a Jewess, and her daughter' going out to Australia in search of a husband. The ship was wrecked. According to the *Australian* of 12 March 1840: 'Mrs Leon had a very narrow escape. Mr Leon has lost everything'. However, on 2 December 1839, the marooned family welcomed the birth of a child in Fremantle. Phillip Leon's name was later registered in the Birth Book of the Sydney Synagogue as the first Jewish child to have been born in Western Australia. On 3 February 1841 Lewis Samuel (q.v.) sold his business and his extensive stock in trade to Lewis Leon. The Leon family was growing with the birth of a third child, Charlotte, on 17 December that year, and a fourth, Catherine (Kate), in 1843. Little wonder that Mr Leon advertised for a cook for their George Street home in the *Sydney Morning Herald* of 4 November 1844.

In Sydney in November 1842 Leon built on the business that dealt with wax, sperm whale oil and candles and created a factory that made blacking for shoes and iron. Leon's Oil and Colour Warehouse in George Street continued in business until March 1846 when Leon retired. It sold sulphuric acid to chemists and soda-water makers, cloth for candle-makers and bluestone for builders. Leon claimed that his business was one of Sydney's oldest firms. It certainly was strong enough to survive the economic depression of the 1840s.

Lewis Leon gave the York Street Synagogue £15 in 1844 and two guineas at its consecration in 1845. 'Mr' Phillip Leon (who had been born in Fremantle in 1839) and 'Miss Leon' both gave one guinea each.

Lewis Leon was the honorary auditor of the Sydney Synagogue in 1845. However, when the congregation put him on the synagogue's board, he wrote, on 24 September 1845, saying that he was 'surprised' by the appointment and that he declined to accept it.

On 10 May 1845, at her residence at 79 George Street, Rebecca gave birth to a stillborn baby. Eight days later Rebecca also died and was buried at the Rookwood Cemetery. She was thirty-two years old.

In the *Sydney Morning Herald* of 7 March 1846 Mr Edward Salamon (q.v.) announced that he would sell the Leon's household furniture and effects: 'In consequence of that Gentleman's departure for Europe'. The business that he had established in 1830 was sold to Chapman & Co., while Leon presented his 'grateful acknowledgements for the extensive patronage he has received'. Lewis Leon and his four children left on the *Templar* for London where, at 65 Hatton Gardens, Holborn, he worked as a 'merchant and dealer in watches'. Lewis Leon prospered and moved to Tavistock Square, where he described himself as a West India merchant. He died on 28 May 1877 at the age of sixty-four. His estate exceeded £70 000.

The surviving children in London were Annie (1831–1891), Phillip Leon (1839 to 24 March 1879), who married Alice Montefiore in 1868 in London, Charlotte (1841–1893) and Kate (23 July 1843 to 18 December 1869).

Rubicon Indent 4/5216, and 4/5218; *Sydney Monitor*, 26 July 1832; *Sydney Morning Herald*, 14 March 1846, 20 March 1846; *Shipping Gazette*, 19 October 1844, 15 November, 29 November 1845, 14 March 1846, 20 March 1846, 18 October 1846; Fowles Typescript, p. 60, ML; Family history notes by Tony Martin-Jones, Archives of the AJHS (Sydney).

LE ROSS, John

b. London, 1751–1820
Neptune, 1790; Convict; Sentenced, Kingston Assizes, 1786.
Single; Jacket-maker.

John Le Ross, 'a jackhitt maker', aged thirty-four, was sentenced to death on 22 March 1786, together with William Yardley, for the burglary of the drapery shop of John Thomas in Southwark. Three weavers were acquitted of the same charge and a few days after sentencing both Le Ross and

Yardley were reprieved and sentenced to transportation for life. A note on one of the documents tendered to the court says that 'Jack Le Ross was the son of the Jew woman who applied to the Ambassador for his release from prison', indicating that the family was of foreign origin. Le Ross remained in the county gaol until 27 November 1787, and was then placed upon the hulk Justitia. *He was embarked upon the convict transport ship on 12 November 1789.*

John Le Ross received a conditional pardon about 1800, and in 1801 was recorded as an employee of Mary Newton, whose business interests included a bakery. In 1806 he was described as a self-employed baker holding an absolute pardon. In 1813 he was appointed a constable in Sydney. His burial was recorded at St Philip's, Sydney, on 23 November 1820 and the *Sydney Gazette* reported that he had arrived on the *Neptune* in 1790, that he was aged seventy-five, and that he had died in his Kent Street home. He 'has been well known in the town of Sydney for the past twenty-five years by the appellation, Jack Le Ross, the baker'.

Michael Flynn, *The Second Fleet*, p. 398; *Sydney Gazette*, 25 November 1790.

LEVEY, Ann (Hannah)

b. Sydney, 1819

In the Female School Admission Book of Sydney, (Jane) Ann Levey is listed as being admitted in September 1825. She is 'supposed to have a mother living in Sydney'. She was also listed in the orphanage's admission book on 1 January 1828.

LEVEY, Barnett

b. Whitechapel, 1797–1837
John Bull, 1821; Free.
Single; Trader; 4 children.

Barnett Levey was the brother of Solomon Levey (q.v.), Samuel Levey (q.v.), Isaac Levey (q.v.), Philip Levey (q.v.) and Frances Marks. He was the fourth child and third son of Moses Lyon Levey and Deborah. Barnett Levey paid for his passage by signing on as the captain's clerk aboard the convict ship *John Bull*, which sailed from Cork with eighty Irish convicts and twenty-two free passengers, most of whom were women and children—relatives of convicts already in Sydney. The ship arrived in Sydney on 21 December 1821.

Barnett Levey was the father of the Australian theatre and one of the first Jewish settlers to come free to Australia. Barnett Levey left England to join his spectacularly successful emancipist brother, Solomon Levey, in Sydney. Solomon soon gave his brother cause to set him up in business on his own at 72 George Street. On 26 December 1821 Samuel Levey, another brother, arrived in Van Diemen's Land on the *Lord Hungerford* and soon proved to be mentally ill. The brothers Barnett and Solomon Levey wrote to the Colonial Secretary offering to pay whatever expenses would be caused by placing him in the Castle Hill Asylum near Sydney. In 1825 Barnett married Sarah Emma Wilson (q.v.), who was the stepdaughter of Jacob Josephson (q.v.) and daughter of Emma Josephson (q.v.) (née Moses).

Barnett Levey promoted many different schemes in the course of a colourful career. He built a windmill on the top of a wheat store and flour mill behind his warehouse and hotel, the Royal Hotel. In the 1820s it was the tallest structure in Sydney. He formed a lending library. He issued Australia's only bank notes backed by Indian rupees. He attempted to build a housing project at what is now Bondi Junction.

From 1826 Barnett Levey battled with the authorities to establish Sydney's first theatre. The dream was repeatedly thwarted by Governor Darling. In December 1832, with the arrival of the new Governor Bourke, Levey succeeded in opening his Theatre Royal. Five hectic years later he was dead. He had provided Sydney with a stream of melodramas, serious plays, operas and operettas. He was impoverished by his grandiose schemes and haunted by his bad temper and his craving for alcohol. His widow and four children were left in poverty. Levey was buried as a Jew on 3 October 1837.

Barnett Levey's children were Emma Rebecca Levey (born 1826), who married Dr George Clarke on 8 April 1847, Barnett Francis Levey (22 November 1827), who became a school master, Jacob Philip Levey (10 October 1829), and Deborah Frances Levey (14 November 1831). Sarah died in Sydney on 17 November 1873, and in her will carefully changed her name to Levvy (as did her daughter Deborah).

Court of Appeals, Minutes 1810–24, 4/1773 October–December 1823, p. 54; 4/2063, letter 30/230, 7 January 1830, to hold Balls and Concerts, 4/1939, 27/6873, in 4/2196.1; application to distil liquor, 4/1934, 27/5586; application for mill, 4/2082, 30/7134; to hold an 'At Home', 34/1843, no. 466; CS In letters 4/1760, p. 217; *HRA*, series 1, vol. 13, p. 81; Add (Dixson) 159; Land Purchased 2/7906, 29 January 1825, 14 July 1825, 1 January 1827; *Royal Australian Historical Society*, vol. 49, no. 6, March 1964; Eric Irvin, 'Barnett Levey's Theatre Royal: A Reassessment', *AJJHS*, vol. 7, no. 3 (1972); Memorial for Land 1825, 4/1845; *Sydney Gazette*, 11 March 1825, 30 June 1825, 28 July 1825, 26 September 1825, 27 June 1827, 2 July 1829, 13 October 1829, 31 October 1829, 8 May 1830, 7 May 1831, 3 September 1832, 10 September 1832, 16 April 1835, 30 October 1836, 24 November 1836, 26 November 1836, 23 September 1837; Governor Darling, 21 June 1832, p. 95, and p. 120, Governors' Despatches, A2146. *AG*, pp. 82, 92, 110–23, 125, 127, 129, 138, 144, 168, 188–9, 304.

LEVEY, Benjamin

Free.
Married; 1 child.

Benjamin and Anna Levey of Sydney registered their newly born son Jacob as a 'Hebrew' in 1848.

LEVEY, Elizabeth

b. Liverpool, 1828–1892
Hercules, 1835; Free.
Single; 10 children.

The eldest child of Isaac Levey (q.v.) and Dinah (née Davis), Elizabeth married Samuel Henry Harris (q.v.), a merchant of Port Phillip, at the Sydney Synagogue on 26 March 1845.

LEVEY, Isaac

b. London, 1798–1860
Hercules, 1835; Free.
Married; Merchant; 4 children.

The fourth son of Moses Lyon Levey and Deborah, Isaac Levey was the brother of Solomon Levey (q.v.), Samuel Levey (q.v.), Barnett Levey (q.v.), Philip Levey (q.v.), and Frances Marks. Isaac Levey had married Mrs Dinah Emanuel (née Davis), a widow, in London on 4 December 1825.

The *Hercules* arrived in Sydney on 27 July 1835. Isaac Levey was accompanied by his wife Dinah, his mother-in law Maria Davis (q.v.), and four children. They travelled cabin class. The ship's agents were Cooper and Levy and the family travelled with Richard Roberts—the brother-in-law of Solomon Levey. On board ship was Isaac's nephew, the 16-year-old Jacob Marks (q.v.), who would become his son-in-law. Dinah Levey's brother was Samuel Davis (q.v.), a convict, who had arrived in Australia on the *Georgiana* in 1831.

Isaac Levey was a member of the Sydney Synagogue Committee in 1837. On 21 August 1839 the Sydney merchant H. B. Spark noted in his diary: 'Mr Isaac Levey [is] tottering in consequence of his foolish purchase of rice. He owes me about £1400'.

On the Sydney voters' list of 1842 Mr Isaac Levey was shown as owning a shop and dwelling in George Street. Levey became a bailiff for the court, which elicited a sneer: 'The person who lives at the corner of George and Market Streets has a capital name for a bailiff. It is I. Levey. He will stand a good chance for employment in that line from his landlord should he want it'.

On 26 March 1845 the *Sydney Morning Herald* announced that Elizabeth Levey (q.v.), eldest daughter of Isaac Levey of Lower York Street, had married Samuel Henry Harris (q.v.) of Melbourne.

Levey owned the Australian Drapery Warehouse at 532 George Street. In January 1845 Levey advertised that specimen photographs taken by G. B. Goodman (q.v.) could be seen at his shop. In April he advertised 'newly imported goods like manchester, muslin with shawls, gloves etc'. At the same time he began to sell real estate and advertised the Harp of Erin, a public house in rural Burrowa. Levey's involvement in land grew. The Land Purchases records show purchases of land at Hunter's Hill, Sydney, on 19 October 1836 for £75, Bungonia on 31 December 1836 for £38, and plots in Yass, Newcastle and Scone for £125 on 31 December 1836. On 15 September 1846, with his sons-in-law, Samuel Henry Harris and Jacob Marks, there were purchases of land for £14 and £30. Land was bought at Yass for £34 on 18 September 1847, at Upper Picton for £21 on 31 May 1847, at Yass for £6 on 19 January 1849, and additional property, costing £38, at Yass on 18 April 1848, and in Sydney on 1 October 1850 for £708. In January 1850 the Governor of New South Wales agreed to give a grant of land for a school house for members of the Jewish faith. Isaac Levey was one of the four trustees appointed.

In 1853 Levey was elected president of the York Street Synagogue in Sydney. George Moss (q.v.) described him as 'our esteemed and liberal president'.

Isaac Levey died on 30 May 1860, aged sixty-two, and was buried in the Jewish section of the Devonshire Street Cemetery. Dinah Levey had died on 22 May 1860, aged seventy-five, eight days earlier. Isaac Levey's estate was valued at £40 000. Their four children were: Elizabeth Levey, born in 1828 at Liverpool, England; Susannah Levey (q.v.), born in 1829; Isabella Dinah Levey (q.v.), born in 1830; and Montague Levey (q.v.), born in 1834.

Hercules Indent 4/5209; Diary of H. B. Spark 1836–1856, ML, A4869-4870, p. 179; *Omnibus and Sydney Spectator*, 11 March 1843; Land Purchases, 2/7906, between 1836 and 1850; *Sydney Morning Herald*, 18 November 1844, 2 January 1845, 28 March 1845, 15 April 1845, 10 February 1846.

LEVEY, Isaac (LEVY)

b. London, 1806
Planter (1), 1832; Convict; Sentenced to 14 years, Old Bailey, 1832.
Single; Glass cutter and pedlar; Height: 163 cm.

Dark, ruddy, pock-pitted complexion, dark brown curly hair, hazel eyes, large nose, small mouth. The 26-year-old Isaac Levey and George Sculthorpe stole a mirror and a frame from a shop and were seen in the act. They dropped the mirror and escaped to a public house where, after a scuffle, the police arrested them. Isaac Levey was sentenced on 5 April 1832. Levey had been convicted of larceny before and had served one month in prison.

Levey arrived in New South Wales on 15 October 1832. Isaac Levy was listed in the 1837 General Return of Convicts in New South Wales, working as an assigned servant to Edmund Burke at Berrima. Levy was granted a ticket of leave in 1838 for the District of Berrima. This was altered for the district of Goulburn on 27 June 1842.

OBSP, 1832, case 1094, p. 446; *Planter* Printed Indent, p. 119, 15 October 1832; Governor's Despatches for 1839, ML, A1220, p. 468; TL 38/2125.

LEVEY, Isaac

b. Gloucester, 1822
William Jardine (2), 1850; Convict; Sentenced to 7 years, Central Criminal Court, 1847.
Married; Tailor.

Isaac Levey was convicted for larceny 'from the person', for stealing a silk handkerchief at London Bridge. He had never been in prison before. His behaviour on board was 'indifferent'. Sallow complexion, pock-pitted, black hair, bald on top, black whiskers, black eyebrows, blue eyes, large nose, medium mouth, small chin. Long scar on chin. Mermaid and the initials 'E. L' tattooed on right arm. Heart and house and other figures on left. 'Jew'.

Isaac Levey arrived in Van Diemen's Land on 14 November 1850. His initial period of probation was to be two years. He was sent to Norfolk Island and on 27 December 1850 his sentence was extended by two months for disobedience.

He was returned to Van Diemen's Land and sent to the penitentiary at Port Arthur and remained there until 21 July 1853. His time at Port Arthur must have been a nightmare as he was continually in trouble.

Levey 'told a lie' on 21 July 1851 and was given seven days solitary confinement. On 28 October he was absent from his work and was sent back to the cells for a further period of ten days solitary confinement. On 10 December 1851 he received fifty lashes and six months was added to his sentence for 'disobedience and insolence'. Five days later he was found to be 'dirty' and 'absent from work'. He was punished with fourteen days on the treadwheel. On 16 February 1852 he recived fifty ashes for 'disobedience and insolence'. On 1 June 1852 he told a 'wilful lie' and was 'disobedient for which he was sentenced to two months on the treadwheel. On 19 July the sentence was repeated. His final offence at Port Arthur was 'malingering' on 6 September 1852.

A certificate of freedom was granted on 14 December 1854.

CON 18/52; CON 33/98, no. 23036; CON 14/2.

LEVEY, Isabella Dinah

b. Liverpool, 1830
Hercules, 1835; Free.
Single.

Isabella Levey was the third daughter of Isaac Levey (q.v.) and his wife Dinah, and the sister of Elizabeth (q.v.), Susannah (q.v.) and Montague Levey (q.v.). Isabella married her first cousin, Maurice (Morris) Alexander (q.v.), the son of her aunt, Susannah Alexander, on 20 October 1847.

LEVEY, John (LEVEY-ROBERTS)

b. Sydney, 1819 Free. Single.

John Levey was born in Sydney on 13 November 1819, the son of Solomon Levey (q.v.) and Ann (née Roberts). John's mother had married when she was fourteen years old. By 1821 she was pregnant with a second child by another man. Ann died in January 1824 after having given birth to a daughter, who died at the age of two. Solomon Levey accepted responsibility for his son, and took him 'Home' to London in 1826. John was brought up a Christian and, when he was twenty-one, he added his mother's surname to his own. He returned to Australia in September 1836 on an unsuccessful attempt to salvage property that remained from his father's colonial Swan River adventure with Thomas Peel. He also applied for a grant of land in the new colony of South Australia. In 1842 Levey-Roberts married Minna Cecilia Goodman, the sister of George Barron Goodman (q.v.) and Sarah (née Polack) at St George's in Spitalfields. Levey-Roberts returned once more to Australia to wind up his father's estate and was in Sydney in 1844. His son,

Charles, was born on 25 December that year, at Rose Bay. In 1851 an agreement was concluded in Perth between John and the swindler Thomas Peel of the Swan River colony, which confirmed his right to a share in the grant of the Cockburn Sound Land.

Sydney Morning Herald, 25 October 1844; *AG*, pp. 110, 168.

LEVEY, Leah (née MORDECAI)

b. London, 1800–1869
Andromeda, 1843; Free.
Married; 10 children.

Leah arrived in Sydney with her husband, Philip Levey (q.v.), and their ten children. She died in Sydney on 27 December 1869 and was buried in the Jewish section of the Rookwood Cemetery.

LEVEY, Montague

b. London, 1834
Hercules, 1835; Free.
Single; 6 children.

Montague Levey was the only son of Isaac Levey (q.v.) and Dinah, and the brother of Elizabeth (q.v.), Susannah (q.v.) and Isabella Dinah (q.v). He married his first cousin, Catherine Levey, the daughter of Philip (q.v.) and Leah (née Mordecai) (q.v.), in 1856. They had six children: Deborah (1857), Maria (1858), Sarah (1860), Isaac (1862), Leah (1864) and Phillip (1866).

LEVEY, Morris Joseph

b. London, 1822–1866
Andromeda, 1843; Free.
Single; 7 children.

Morris Levey was the eldest son of Philip Levey (q.v.) and Leah (née Mordecai) (q.v.), and came out to New South Wales with his brothers, sisters and parents in December 1843. In 1852 Morris Levey was the local postmaster and storekeeper at Ophir, the first goldfield of New South Wales. Morris remained there, and on 15 April 1856 was granted a publican's general licence for the Stage Inn at Peeper's Creek, now named Rockley. On 19 June 1856 Morris Joseph Levey married Mary Armstrong at St Michael's Church, Bathurst.

From 1858 Morris was the licensed publican of the Rockley Inn and, in 1865, was the licensee of the Farmer's Inn. After his death, his wife Mary became the licensee.

Levey died at Bathurst on 7 April 1866 and was buried there as a Jew. His estate was valued at £200. His seven children were brought up as Catholics.

LEVEY, Philip

b. London, d. 1837
Free.
Single.

Philip Levey was buried by the synagogue in the Devonshire Street Cemetery on 1 June 1837. He was described by the synagogue as the 'son of Jacob [Levy] of Whitefriars Gate'.

LEVEY, Phillip

b. Whitechapel, 1799–1862
Andromeda, 1843; Free.
Married; 10 children.

The sixth and youngest son of Moses (Lyon) and Deborah Levey, Phillip's siblings included Solomon (q.v.), Barnett (q.v.), and Isaac (q.v.). Phillip Levey married Leah Mordecai (Levey, q.v.) at the Ashkenazi Synagogue in Duke's Place on 4 July 1822. They arrived in Sydney with their children on 7 December 1843 as steerage passengers. Their children were Morris Joseph Levey (q.v.) aged twenty-one, Mrs Sarah Benjamin (q.v.), twenty, with her husband John Benjamin (q.v.) (they had married three weeks before leaving England), Fanny Abigail Levey, eighteen (who died in Sydney on 23 November 1856), Hannah (q.v.), sixteen, Rebecca (q.v.), fifteen, Mark, fourteen, Solomon (q.v.), twelve, Susan, eight, Rosetta (q.v.), six, and Catherine, five.

Phillip Levey and his family began their new life in Australia in George Street. In the *Sydney Morning Herald* of 18 November 1844 there was an advertisement for a 'furniture and foreign curiosity warehouse'. Low's *City of Sydney Directory* listed Phillip Levey as a having furniture warehouse, looking glass and artificial flower manufactory at 528 George Street.

Phillip Levey moved to 528–530 George Street next to Isaac Levey, at 532 George Street, where he had an upholstery, bedding and furniture shop. By 1855 he had moved to 135 George Street, working as an upholsterer with his brother Isaac Levey at 133 George Street. The two families were closely linked. Isaac's son Montague (q.v.) married Philip's daughter Catherine in 1856. Philip and Leah were mentioned in Isaac Levey's will. Rosetta married John Solomon in 1853, Rebecca married Morris Asher (q.v.) in 1846, and Hannah married Henry Hart (q.v.) in 1844.

Phillip died, aged sixty-three, at his residence in York Street, Sydney, and was buried at the Devonshire Street Cemetery. The grave was subsequently transferred to Rookwood, where his wife Leah was buried in 1869.

Sydney Morning Herald, 8 December 1843, 14 August 1844, 2 October 1844, 18 November 1844, 3 February 1845, 14 March 1846.

LEVEY, Rebecca

b. London, 1828–1905
Andromeda, 1843; Free.
Single; 14 children.

Rebecca Levey was the fifth child of Philip and Leah Levey (qq.v.). On 11 February 1846, in Sydney, she married Morris Asher (q.v.).

LEVEY, Rosetta

b. London, 1837–1908
Andromeda, 1843; Free.
Single; 10 children.

Rosetta Levey, the ninth child of Philip and Leah Levey (qq.v.), must have been staying with her brother, Morris Levey (q.v.), in Bathurst when she met John Solomon. They were married in 1853. His younger brother, Joseph Solomon, married Rosetta's sister Susan in 1866.

By the end of 1875, Rosetta had lost eight of her ten children and her husband, who died in 1870, at the age of forty-one. On 26 October 1882 Rosetta married Isaac Davis, the father of her son-in-law, Coleman Davis.

Rosetta died on 21 March 1908 at 'Cyrene', Bondi Road, Bondi.

LEVEY, Samuel (LEVY) (John LEE)

b. London, 1791–1872
Lord Hungerford, 1821; Convict; Sentenced to life, Old Bailey, 1821.

John Lee, alias Samuel Levy, was 'a bad character' according to the gaol report. He was transported for snatching a bundle of clothes from an elderly woman in the East End. He had been sentenced to transportation before but had served four years in the hulk Belleraphon.*At the time of his second trial he had a brother in Sydney called Solomon Levy, who was known as Solomon Levey (q.v.). Samuel's other siblings were Barnett (q.v), Isaac (q.v.), Philip (q.v.), and Frances Marks.*

Samuel Levey, Lee, or Levy, arrived in Van Diemen's Land on 26 December 1821. On 4 July 1822 his name appeared on the list of prisoners to be assigned for work. On 26 March 1823 he was a prisoner in the Sydney Gaol and considered to be insane. He was transferred to the Asylum at Castle Hill and in the 1825 Muster in New South Wales he was listed as an inmate of the Lunatic Asylum in Parramatta.

Official papers attested that: 'it appears that the unfortunate man is in a State of Insanity'. In a letter written by the Provost Marshall's Office in Sydney on 26 March 1823, J. Campbell wrote:

> It is within my own knowledge that Levy is considered by his Brothers and the Public Generally, as a madman and that he has been so considered for several month's

> past, and it is further within my knowledge that he was committed for a breach of Peace towards his brother's wife whom he had frequently disturbed and assaulted altho' she was always reluctant to his being punished under the consideration that he was insane.

On 7 November 1823 Barnett and Solomon Levey wrote to the Colonial Secretary from Barnett's home at 72 George Street offering to pay for a private apartment for their brother and saying that they would pay all his victualling, medical attendance, washing and any other charges that may be required. The next day Barnett Levey wrote that while his brother Solomon was out of Sydney he would 'most willingly pay' whatever expenses were needed. On 1 April 1824 Samuel Levy ran away from the Lunatic Asylum at Castle Hill and was 'being taken care of by his friends in Sydney'.

The family obviously continued to care for him and Samuel died on 18 August 1872 at 237 Macquarie Street, Sydney. Arrangements were taken care of by his nephew Solomon (q.v.), the son of Philip and Leah Levey (qq.v.) of 53 Lower Fort Street. The funeral was conducted by the synagogue. Samuel's will had been witnessed by Morris Asher (q.v.), the husband of his niece Rebecca (Levey, q.v.), and David Barnett, merchant, of 53 Lower Fort Street, who must have been his nephew Solomon Levey's father-in-law. His estate was valued at £4000 and was bequeathed to his nephew Solomon.

OBSP, 1820–21, case 780, p. 360; *Lord Hungerford* Indent 4/4009, p. 28; CON 31/27; HO 10/20; Provost Marshall's Office, Sydney, 26 March 1823; CS 4/4570, DD pp. 71, 73; 4/3508, p. 47; 4/3509, p. 669; 4/1777, p. 152.

LEVEY, Samuel

Free.
Married.

Samuel and Julia Levey of Maitland registered the birth of their daughter Matilda in 1848.

LEVEY, Solomon

b. Whitechapel, 1794–1833
Marquis of Wellington, 1815; Convict; Sentenced to 7 years, Old Bailey, 1813.
Single; Broker; Height: 168 cm; 1 child.

Dark pale complexion, black hair, dark hazel eyes, slender build. The brother of Barnett Levey (q.v.), Isaac Levey (q.v.), Samuel (q.v.), Philip (q.v.) and Frances Marks, Solomon Levey was sentenced to transportation for being an accessory to the theft of ninety pounds of tea and a wooden chest.

Solomon Levey's Australian career was meteoric. He arrived in Sydney on 27 January 1815 and was listed as a prisoner working in the gaol gang at Windsor. The Government Store Ration Book notes the rations he was issued. Within four years of his arrival, on 8 February 1819, he was granted an absolute pardon from Governor Macquarie after a successful business career in Sydney as a dealer. On 11 February 1819, in the presence of Edward and Elizabeth Franks, Levey married the 14-year-old Ann Roberts and received a rich dowry from her emancipist father. It was not a happy marriage, but there was a son, John Levey (q.v.), who renamed himself John Levey-Roberts. In 1819 a second child was born, named Jane Ann, who apparently was not Solomon's child. Her name appears in the February 1821 monthly return of children admitted to the colonial orphanage named the Second Public School at Sydney.

In the *Sydney Gazette* of 25 August 1823 Solomon Levey warned the public against extending his wife any financial credit. Ann Levey died on 1 September 1824 and was buried at St John's, Parramatta. However, on the basis of the newly acquired capital he had received from his father-in-law, Levey built up a vast business in Sydney, trading with the South Pacific, owning a water mill at Liverpool, a Sydney business partnership with fellow emancipist Daniel Cooper, and within three or four years the firm of Cooper and Levey was one of Sydney's most significant mercantile firms. Because of a local shortage of cash the business minted its own bank notes and defied the presence of the Bank of New South Wales by challenging the power of the new bank's cash reserves.

In 1826 Levey triumphantly returned to London. His presence undoubtedly encouraged Jewish interest in Australia and encouraged the migration of a number of free settlers, such as Michael Phillips and Joseph Barrow Montefiore (qq.v.). Levey's most spectacular venture was his almost hidden association with Thomas Peel and the settlement at Swan River in Western Australia. Peel failed to contact Levey once he reached Australia and his inability to implement the colonisation project brought about a financial catastrophe. Levey died in London on 10 October 1833 and was survived by his son, John Levey-Roberts.

John had been brought up as a Christian, but married Minna Goodman, the sister of George B. Goodman (q.v.). Their son Charles was born in Rose Bay, Sydney, on 25 December 1844.

Royal Australian Historical Society, vol. 49, no. 6; George F. J. Bergman, 'Solomon Levey', and 'Barnett Levey', *ADB*, vol. 2; *OBSP*, 1813, case 982, p. 511f.; *Marquis of Wellington* Indent 4/4004, p. 553; Windsor Government Ration Store Book, ML, A 803, p. 121; ADD 59, dated 27 August 1824, DL CO 207, no. 553.9; Register of Pardons 4/4427, 8 February 1819; Memorials for Land 1825, 4/1843, no. 467; Bigge Appendix, BT Box 20, p. 3531, and BT Box 25, p. 5354f.4; *Sydney Gazette*, 21 June 1819, 13 January 1821, 30 January 1823, 1 May 1823, 21 October 1823, 18 September 1823, 30 October 1823, 16 September 1824, 21 October 1824, 16 December 1824, 8 April 1826, 26 April 1826; Register of Pardons 1819, 4/4467, p. 67; *Colonial Times*, 30 March 1826; *AG*, pp. 91f.

LEVEY, Solomon

b. London, 1831–1872
Andromeda, 1843; Free.
Single; Clerk.

Solomon Levey, the seventh child of Philip and Leah Levey (qq.v.), married Fanny Barnett at 1 Wynyard Square (the residence of his uncle, Isaac Levey, q.v.), according to Jewish rites, on 28 June 1865. In 1872 he lived at 53 Lower Fort Street, Sydney, where he was described as a 'glass and china warehouseman' by his uncle Samuel Levey (q.v.), who left him £4000. When his mother died on 27 December 1869, Solomon appeared on her death certificate as living at 96 Lennox Street, Newtown.

LEVEY, Solomon Hyman

Louisa, 1844; Free.

Solomon Levey arrived in Hobart Town, travelling cabin class, on 13 December 1844. The publican's licence for the Caledonian Hotel of Elizabeth Street was transferred to Solomon Hiram (sic) Levey on 6 February 1845. In the Hobart Synagogue ledger, Saul Hyman Levey paid dues of £4 6s 6d in 1844. In 1845 Levey acquired the licence of 'The William the Fourth' in Liverpool Street.

CSO 92/13/F 110; *Hobart Town Courier*, 6 February 1845.

LEVEY, Susannah

b. London, 1830
Hercules, 1835; Free.
Single; 14 children.

Susannah was the daughter of Isaac Levey (q.v.) and Dinah. She arrived in Australia at the age of five, travelling with her family and her 16-year-old first cousin, Jacob Marks (q.v.). Jacob and Susannah were married in the Sydney Synagogue on 14 May 1846 and her husband was described as 'of Port Phillip'.

LEVI, Aaron Alexander

1824–1883
Free.
Single.

Aaron A. Levi married Sarah Moses, a daughter of Simon Moses, in a ceremony conducted by the Sydney Synagogue in 1850. The Rev. A. A. Levi served as an official of the Sydney Synagogue for some thirty years. Rabbi Israel Porush's history of the 'Great Synagogue' states Levi 'could scarcely be classified as a qualified spiritual leader. As well as reading the Services he acted as a conglomeration of offices, from marriage celebrant to collector, from Sexton to Beadle'. The Rev. A. A. Levi died on 3 July 1883 and was buried at Rookwood.

Israel Porush, *The House of Israel*, p. 7.

LEVI, Benjamin (Levi BENJAMIN)

b. London, 1762
Royal Admiral I (2), 1800; Convict; Sentenced to 7 years, Old Bailey, 1796.

Benjamin Levi was part of a street gang who jostled a medical student and stole his watch. At the trial Levi said: 'I am a hard working fellow. I was going to my master's. Pitt [a patrolman] laid hold of me'. He was sentenced at the London Gaol Delivery in November 1796.

After arriving in New South Wales on 20 November 1800, Benjamin Levi served his time and was permitted to leave the colony to return to England on the *Governor Macquarie* on 19 October 1811.

OBSP, 1796–97, case 50, p. 73; *Royal Admiral* Indent 4/3999, p. 377; *Sydney Gazette*, 19 October 1811 (listed as Benjamin Levite).

LEVI, Edmund

b. Surrey, 1827–1895
Juno, 1842; Free.
Single; Dealer; 4 children.

Edmund Levi was born on 6 December 1827, the son of Nathan Philip Levi (q.v.) and Sarah Levi (q.v.). He was the brother of Philip Levi (q.v.) and brother-in-law of Montague Levi Phillipson.

In 1854, together with his brother Frederick (q.v.), Edmund Levi joined the firm of Philip Levi & Co. He took an active part in droving stock overland from New South Wales and became involved in the pastoral industry. Both Frederick and Edmund returned to England in the 1860s where Edmund married his first cousin Gertrude Goldsmid in 1864. Following the financial losses incurred as a result of the American Civil War he brought his family to South Australia, where he became involved with the mining industry. Edmund was active in the Jewish community and a generous supporter of the synagogue. However, following his death in 1895, his widow and children adopted the Christian faith. There were four children, including Constance (Corrie), Frederick and Goldsmid Levi.

Pritchard Index.

LEVI, Frederick

Free.
Single; Merchant.

The son of Nathan and Sarah Levi (qq.v.) and grandson of the banker Abraham Goldsmid, Frederick worked with his brothers Edmund (q.v.) and Philip (q.v.) in the firm Philip Levi & Co, and became extremely wealthy. He returned to England to marry his cousin Cecilia, the daughter of Sampson Goldsmid of Middleburgh Square, in 1859.

South Australian Gazette and Colonial Register, 14 November 1859.

LEVI, George

b. Warsaw, 1818–1859
Duncan, 1841; Convict; Sentenced to 7 years, York West Riding, 1840.
Single; Tailor, scourer and dyer; Height: 165 cm.

Swarthy complexion, black hair, oval face, grey eyes and large nose. Could read and write Hebrew and read but not write English. George Levi's mother and father lived in Warsaw. He had a prior three-month conviction for stealing a bolt of cloth from a shop. He was transported for having stolen pocket knives from a shop in Sheffield. The English gaol report described him as 'a travelling thief'.

George Levi arrived in Hobart Town on 18 April 1841. Levi served twelve months initial probation at the Prisoners' Barracks in Hobart Town and at Perth. His period of probation was extended by one month for gambling—'having in his possession a pack of playing cards'. After assignments in Launceston, Perth and Campbell Town his term of probation expired. On 28 February 1843 he was sentenced to three months hard labour in chains for having destroyed his master's property while he was an assigned servant. A ticket of leave was issued on 24 October 1844 and a certificate of freedom on 24 June 1847.

On 1 April 1859 the *Portland Guardian* reported that 'George Levi, well known farmer and one of the oldest residents in the district', was killed after falling from his horse.

CON 33/8-1851; CON 14/5, no. 1343.

LEVI, Hannah (Frances) (Ann)

b. London, 1789
Minstrel (1), 1812; Convict; Sentenced to 7 years, Old Bailey, 1811.
Single; Prostitute; 5 children.

Sarah Wise, Hannah Levi, Elizabeth Walters, Sarah Atkins and Sarah Stone were all put on trial after Stone and Atkins picked up a man in Bishopsgate and stole his watch, gold seal and his money. The victim testified that he was set upon by a waiting ruffian who, together with five women, beat him until he began to think he would die: 'I cried out and begged for mercy'. Hannah claimed she had just met the other girls. She was aged twenty-two and the oldest of the group. The police caught her with the stolen money in a nearby gin shop. The women were sentenced on 10 July 1811.

The *Minstrel* arrived in Sydney on 25 October 1812 with Hannah Levi and Sarah Wise on board. Hannah Levy married Charles Rutherford on 8 June 1813 at St John's Church, Parramatta. In the 1814 Muster she was listed as being in Parramatta as 'Frances Levy per *Minstrel*, Convict and wife to Charles Rutherford'. The *Sydney Gazette* of 15 January 1815 listed an unclaimed letter awaiting Francis Levy. A ticket of leave was approved in 1817. In the 1817 Muster List of Female Convicts she was listed as an inmate at the Public Factory.

In the 1828 Census, Frances Rutherford was listed as a Protestant, aged forty-two, free by servitude, married to Charles Rutherford, who was aged forty-eight and had a ticket of leave, having arrived on the *Admiral Gambier* in 1807 with a sentence of transportation for life. They had five children, all born in the colony. They were Ann (1818), Charles (1820), Hannah (1822), and twins Francis and Elizabeth (1825).

OBSP, 1811, case 546, p. 308; HO 10/9; *Indefatigable*, *Emu*, and *Minstrel* Indent, May 1812; HO 11/2; Ship Indent 4/4004 p. 429; 1814 Muster A1942-1, p. 115; Family history from Patricia Macgregor, Johns River, NSW.

LEVI, Joseph

b. London, 1807
Marquis of Huntley (3), 1830; Convict; Sentenced to 14 years, Leeds (York), 1830.
Single; Dyer.

Joseph Levi was sentenced at York on 11 January 1830.

Joseph Levi was listed in the 1837 General Return of Convicts in New South Wales as assigned to John Dixon in the District of Cook. He received a ticket of leave in 1836. He was in the District of Goulburn in that year. In 1837 his ticket of leave was altered for Campbelltown. A certificate of freedom was issued on 7 February 1844.

Governors' Despatches, A1217, p. 492; TL Book 4/4108, 36/1932; CF 4/4389, 44/0166.

LEVI, L.

Craigevar, 1830; Free.
Single.

L. Levi arrived as a bounty migrant and settler.

LEVI, Mary

Convict.

Mary Levi appeared before the Supreme Court in Sydney on 3 October 1815 charged with having entered a public house in Bligh Street and stolen two glass tumblers from a table. The hotel was owned by Solomon Wiseman. Mary was sentenced to be sent to Newcastle.

LEVI, Moses (LEVY)

b. London, 1798–1857
Morley (1), 1817; Convict; Sentenced to 7 years, Old Bailey, 1816.
Single; Tailor; Height: 161 cm.

Ruddy complexion, black hair, black eyes. On 7 June 1816 Moses Levi stole a handkerchief valued at six shillings from the watchman on duty at the Bow Fair. He was sentenced on 10 July 1816 at the Quarter Sessions of the Old Bailey.

The *Morley* arrived at Port Jackson on 10 April 1817 and Moses Levy was forwarded to Liverpool for distribution. He quickly gained a bad reputation. On 14 November 1817 the Colonial Secretary noted that Levi, who was to be consigned as a prisoner at Newcastle, was 'one of the most notorious old rogues and fences in the colony'.

He was sent to the Newcastle Prison on 29 October 1817 for a period of two years. On 14 November 1817 he signed a petition protesting against the behaviour of the Commandant. He appeared on the 1818 General Muster as a 'settler's man'.

Moses Levi died at Maitland in 1857.

OBSP, 1816, case 760, p. 345; HO 16/1; *Morley* (1) Indent 4/4005, p. 266; HO 11/2; Principal Superintendent of Convicts, Butts of CF, 1844–1845, 4/3496; CS 4/1806, p. 96.

LEVI, Nathan (Nathaniel) Philip

b. London, 1794–1843
Seahorse, 1841; Free.
Married; Merchant; 7 children.

Nathan Levi was the son of Philip and Sarah Levi. Philip had founded the firm Philip Levi & Co. of George Yard, Lombard Street. Philip's father had changed his name from Pheis ben Moshe. Nathan Levi had married Sarah Goldsmid (Levi, q.v.), daughter of Abraham Goldsmid and Petty (née Sampson) Goldsmid.

Nathan Philip Levi was a brother of Moses Nathan Levi of Godmanchester, Huntingdonshire, whose daughter was the mother of Isaac Lazarus Lincoln (q.v.) of Melbourne. His wife Sarah was a first cousin of Lionel and William Samson (qq.v.). She brought with her a dowry of £2000.

Nathan was among the first holders of an occupation and depasturing licence in South Australia, which was taken out in December 1842. Nathaniel Philip Levi died, at the age of forty-nine, on 24 July 1843, just a few weeks before the arrival of his wife, who, the *West Australian Inquirer* of 16 August had noted, had arrived in Fremantle with Mr and Mrs Lionel Samson. (Mrs Samson was Fanny, q.v., Sarah's daughter.) Sarah and her two youngest daughters were proceeding to South Australia. Nathan Levi was 'much respected for his urbanity of manner, kindness of disposition and gentlemanly conduct such that his memory will long be cherished by a large circle of his friends'. His was the first Jewish funeral in South Australia and it was conducted by Emanuel Solomon (q.v.). His young son Philip Levi thanked the Lieutenant Governor 'for the facilities so readily offered by you towards obtaining a burial place for my Father and those members of the Jewish persuasion that may hereafter die in this Province'.

Nathan and Sarah Levi had three sons and four daughters. They were Caroline (1820–1889), who married her uncle, Montague Levi Phillipson (q.v.), in 1839; Philip (1822–1898), whose common-law wife was Elizabeth Symes; Fanny (1823–1888), who married Lionel Samson; Edmund (1827–1895) (q.v.), who married Gertrude Goldsmid; Frederick (q.v.), who married Cecilia Goldsmid; Adelaide (1833–1910), who married Jules Joubert; and Martha, who married Charles James Fox Campbell of Campbelltown.

South Australian Archives, 10 October 1843, GRG, 24 January 1843/247; *South Australian Gazette and Colonial Register*, 10 March 1847; A. P. Joseph and K. J. Ireland, 'The Family of Nathan ben Elijah', *AJJHS*, vol 7, no. 7 (1974), p. 513f; *Inquirer*, 16 August 1843.

LEVI, Philip (LEVY)

b. Petticoat Square, 1806–1849
Morley (4), 1823; Convict; Sentenced to life, Old Bailey, 1822.
Single; Spectacle-maker; Height 160 cm.

Brown hair, dark grey eyes, a scar on his left cheekbone. Levi stole the gold watch of Mr Aaron Joseph, a merchant in the Minories. The watch was being carried by Mrs Matilda Joseph. He had previously stolen a watch for which he had been whipped. He was sentenced on 22 May 1822.

The *Morley* arrived in Van Diemen's Land on 11 January 1823. During his first four years in Van Diemen's Land Levi experienced punishments totalling 225 lashes for 'neglect of work'. His most serious offence occurred on 10 January 1824 when he was convicted for breaking and entering a dwelling house and stealing clothes. Most of his time was spent at the Hobart Town Prisoners' Barracks and at New Norfolk.

On 27 February 1827 the *Hobart Town Gazette* reported that Levi had absconded from Public Works in Launceston ten days before. He was quickly recaptured and continued to work as a convict.

Ironically, on 2 November 1830, the authorities appointed Levi a flagellator. He found that he was unable to fulfil his duty. His ticket of leave was suspended for twelve months for abusing the Chief Constable in the execution of his duty and for 'improper and violent conduct at the Police Office'. He was put on bread and water and in solitary confinement for fifteen days. On 24 October 1834 his ticket of leave was removed entirely and he was sent to the Spring Hill Road Party for attempting to obtain eight shillings and sixpence through false pretences. It was said that he had 'induced others to become unruly' and was given two years hard labour and imprisonment in the hulk chain gang. In December 1834 the Lieutenant Governor, in view of his long police record, decided to send Levi to Port Arthur, 'there to undergo severe discipline'. On 4 February 1837 he was convicted of trafficking pieces of soap and received an extra three months at Port Arthur. In 1838 he was transferred to the Public Works Department and became part of the New Town Chain Gang and in 1839 joined the Campbell Town Gang. On 23 October 1839 he absconded from his assigned road party and was sentenced to seventy-five lashes. He was transferred to the Cleveland road party and on 15 January 1840 Levi 'absconded under particular circumstances' and was punished with two years imprisonment with hard labour in chains and ordered to be removed to Port Arthur. The 1841 Muster of Convicts listed him at the Launceston Prisoners' Barracks before he was sent to Port Arthur. Levi remained in the north of the island for two years. He was placed in solitary confinement three times and was found to have his irons broken. In 1843 he was transferred to Ross and continued to be insolent and disobedient. During his work assignments Levi received a further 150 lashes and an additional three years and three months hard labour for offences ranging from absconding, and pilfering meat, to 'stirring up trouble', stealing some sugar and 'conniving at a fellow prisoner having his irons broken'.

On 27 December 1842 he was convicted of indecent exposure and returned to work twelve months hard labour in chains. At the end of 1845 his servitude concluded and he received a ticket of leave, only to lose it on 19 November 1846 when he stole a cheese. He was sent once again to the prison at Port Arthur to serve another twelve months hard labour in chains. He was granted a conditional pardon on 30 November 1847. It is not surprising that both his spirit and body were broken. He died at the New Norfolk Lunatic Asylum on 30 September 1849.

OBSP, 1821–22, case 775, p. 321; *Morley* (4) Indent 4/4008, p. 250; CON 32/1, no. 236; CON 31/27; CON 34/1; CON 63/2, no. 236; CON 32/4, Launceston Police Book; CON 78/2, p. 330, 4/4008; HO 10/40; *Hobart Town Gazette*, 24 February 1827; *Hobart Town Courier*, 16 May 1844.

LEVI, Philip

b. Balham Hill, Surrey, 1822–1898
Eden, 1838; Free.
Single; Merchant; 12 children.

Philip Levi was the son of Nathan Philip Levi and Sarah Levi (qq.v.), and the brother of Edmund (q.v) and Frederick (q.v.), and the grandson of the banking magnate Abraham Goldsmid. Isaac Lazarus Lincoln (q.v.) was a first cousin once removed. Philip Levi arrived on the same ship as his uncle and future brother-in-law Montague Levi Phillipson (q.v.), who married his sister Caroline in 1839.

Philip Levi was sixteen years old when he arrived in South Australia and twenty-one when his father died and his mother and two sisters arrived in the colony. He initially worked as a clerk in the customs department in the new colony of South Australia. His father had obtained a licence to graze sheep and he became involved in the sheep run called Dustholes near Truro. He then developed the firm Philip Levi and Co. with his brothers Edmund and Frederick.

Philip Levi has been described as 'a merchant prince of South Australia'. At one time in the 1860s he owned 172 000 sheep and cattle and was involved in droving thousands of cattle and sheep from the eastern plains of Australia to the west. With energy and with a daring speculative spirit, together with his two brothers he fostered the import business of the colony. He expanded the boundaries of pastoral settlement and became involved in mining ventures.

His commercial interests were wide ranging. When his brothers returned to England to live off their Australian investments, Philip Levi remained the entrepreneur. He raised stock for wool. He fostered intercolonial trade. He boldly extended his business to London, Liverpool and the Orient, often bartering cargo for cargo, dealing with wool and copper, and offsetting these South Australian exports against goods and materials needed in Australia.

Ironically, Levi was one of the founders and trustees of the Adelaide Club, which would later exclude Jewish members. In 1846 Levi had a general store in Rundle Street and worked as a ship agent. He hoped to open the Murray River to steam navigation and in 1849 launched a thorough investigation into its suitability for traffic.

On 10 March 1847 the *South Australian Register* reported:

> A bold and hitherto inexplicable robbery was attempted upon the premises of Mr Levi, residing with his mother and family in South Terrace. The house is an extensive one. Mr Levi had gone to dine with Mr Campbell leaving the ladies and younger brother at home—£360 worth of jewellery was stolen and was hidden in the stable and found—the jewels were replaced by bricks and then the police waited for the robbers to return—they didn't but they pelted Mr Levi's house with stones.

In a scholarly paper, 'The Enterprise of Philip Levi', E. S. Richards wrote: 'Philip Levi, a young London Jew was the first and most successful of his people to make (and to lose) a fortune in the new colony'.

Levi encountered two parallel disasters. South Australia was gripped by severe drought, which crippled the pastoral industry. As he told one of his property managers 'This [drought] would be enough to break a Rothschild'. At the same time he backed the wrong side in the American Civil War. The *South Australian Gazette and Colonial Register* reported (on 6 September 1866): 'We regret exceedingly to have to report that Messrs P. Levi & Co., merchants, have suspended payments and have issued circulars for a meeting of their creditors'. Liabilities amounted to £217 169. The debt was cleared by 1881 with the sale of assets that realised just over half a million pounds.

Philip Levi died on 13 May 1898 without having married. He was seventy-six years old and left an estate valued at less than £200. He was said to have been 'the life and soul of social gatherings, being a good raconteur and full of reminiscence and shrewd experience'. Levi had lived with two common-law wives: Elizabeth (Symes), who bore him eleven children, and Mary Anne (Martin), who had one child. Only three of Levi's children married.

E. S. Richards, 'The Enterprise of Philip Levi', *AJJHS*, vol. 8, no. 4 (1977), p. 149f; A. P. Joseph and K. J. Ireland, 'The Family of Nathan ben Elijah', *AJJHS*, vol. 7, no. 7 (1974); H. Munz, *Jews in South Australia*, pp. 35f.

LEVI, Rebecca

b. Penzance, 1798–1876
Medway, 1827; Free.
Married; 4 children.

Rebecca was the wife of Walter Jacob Levi (q.v.) and the daughter of Leman (known as Lemon) and Mary Hart of Fenchurch Street, London. Lemon Hart was a distiller, who became one of the largest spirit merchants in Britain supplying the British navy with rum.

Walter Jacob Levi and Rebecca had four children. Rebecca was listed in the 1828 Census with the three young children—Jacob, Simon and Letitia. Following the death of her husband in 1828, she remained in Sydney and their fourth child was born there in 1829. On 26 October 1829 she wrote to the Colonial Secretary asking for a grant of land 'to build a cottage for the abode of myself and children in a retired situation'. She suggested that the land should be on South Head Road between the 'Gaol Walls' and Robert Cooper's land grant, and this suggestion was accepted. Samuel Lyons (q.v.) advertised her 'elegant household furniture' for sale in February 1831 and she evidently left Sydney shortly after the sale. She married her first cousin Frederick Jacobs in London on 25 June 1834.

CS 2/7096 Petition, 26 October 1829; *Sydney Monitor*, 2 February 1831; A. P. Joseph, 'Some Genealogical Notes on the Family of Rebecca, wife of Walter Jacob Levi', *AJJHS*, vol. 7, no. 3 (1972), p. 231f.

LEVI, Samuel

b. London, 1823
Maitland Union, 1847; Free; Colonial Sentence, Sydney, 1847.
Single; Dealer; Height: 168 cm.

Samuel Levi was tried and convicted at Sydney on 8 November 1847 for receiving stolen goods. He was described as having a ruddy complexion, dark brown hair, dark eyes, and as a Jew. He was sentenced to three years work on the roads. On 14 February 1848 he was sent from Darlinghurst Gaol (Sydney). On 9 November 1848 he was sentenced to fourteen days in the cells for refusing to work.

Transportation Register 4/6571, p. 40.

LEVI, Sarah

1799–1889
Madras, 1843; Free.
Married; 7 children.

Sarah was the daughter of the banker Abraham Goldsmid, and the wife of Nathan Philip Levi (q.v.). One of Sarah's children was Fanny Samson, wife of Lionel Samson (qq.v.). Sarah arrived in South Australia just two months after the death of her husband in Adelaide. She travelled with the Samsons and her two youngest daughters, Martha and Adelaide. She died in March 1889, 'keen and active all through life, retained her faculties until very shortly before her death and was benevolent in a quiet, unostentatious way and strict in her observance of the forms of the Hebrew religion'.

A. P. Joseph and K. J. Ireland, 'The Family of Nathan ben Elijah', *AJJHS*, vol 7, no. 7 (1974), p. 513f.

LEVI, Walter Jacob

d. 1828
Emma Kemp, 1827; Free.
Married; Merchant, investor, farmer; 4 children.

Walter Jacob Levi, brother of Isaac Levi and Solomon Levi, was one of Australia's first free Jewish settlers. On 7 November 1826 Mr Walter Levi, of 4 King Street, Finsbury Square, wrote to Earl Bathurst telling him that he had £5000 to invest in growing cotton and sugar. He asked for a grant of 5000 acres of land at Port Macquarie and hoped to buy 10 000 acres more. Levi had lived for 'many years' in the West Indies and said that at Barbados he had become 'personally known' to the Governor of that island, 'from the year 1809 to 1825'. He had been an 'extensive dealer in military clothing, land estates and owned a plantation'. He proposed 'to embrace extensively the ordinary methods of Agricultural improvements by rearing Stock and growing Corn, and that I shall be anxious to employ, in this and other objects, from 70 to 100 Crown Servants'. Levi arrived in Sydney on 22 September 1827 and quickly took a leading role in the life of Sydney's respectable social circles. His wife Rebecca (q.v.), and children Jacob (born 1821), Simon (1823) and Letitia (1825) came out on the *Medway* in 1827. Rebecca was the daughter of Leman (Lemon) Hart.

The family lived at 108 Pitt Street. Levi asked for a grant for a town house while his livestock, sheep, cattle and brood mares, were being looked after for a heavy price by others. The request was refused and he was told that he could apply for land for farming. Levi was the first to introduce cotton seeds to the colony and offered a prize for their successful cultivation. Upon the arrival of the seeds in June 1828, Levi wrote to the Colonial Secretary asking whether custom dues would be applied. The Colonial Secretary replied 'The Colonial Secretary does not think it necessary to address the government on every trifling occasion'. In reality, officialdom did not believe that Levi was serious about his agricultural ambitions and delayed granting Levi the land to which he was entitled. Levi died suddenly in Sydney on 1 August 1828 before the birth of his fourth child in 1829 and was buried in the Devonshire Street cemetery and the tombstone is now to be found in the Botany Pioneers Park. His estate exceeded £15 000.

HRA, series 1, vol. 12, p. 736f., vol. 14; 4/1963, 28/632; 4/1983, 28/4943; Land Correspondence 2/7906; *Sydney Gazette*, 12 May 1828, 9 July 1828, 14 July 1828, 4 August 1828; *AG*, pp. 150–4, 169, 176–7; G. F. S. Bergman, 'Walter Jacob Levi and Governor Ralph Darling: The Sad Story of a Gentleman Planter', *AJJHS*, vol. 6, no. 8 (1970), p. 416f.

LEVIEN, Alfred

b. London, 1813
Westmoreland, 1833; Free.
4 children.

Alfred Levien was the fourth child of Solomon and Harriet Levien (qq.v.) and arrived in Sydney with his parents and most of his nine siblings on the *Westmoreland* on 14 May 1833. Alfred Levien became postmaster in Maitland and resigned in 1835, allowing his brother-in-law P. J. Cohen (q.v.) to take over the position. He remained in Maitland as a storekeeper and was one of those 'of Maitland' who signed a petition congratulating Queen Victoria on her accession to the throne in 1838. In 1843 Alfred Levien of Singleton asked for permission from the Colonial Secretary to hold amateur theatrical performances at the local hotel. He then became a partner of Simeon J. Cohen (q.v.) of Maitland. They were dealers at High Street in West Maitland and Tamworth. They were declared insolvent on 16 December 1842 with a debt of £200 and assets of £40 and were discharged from insolvency on 23 February 1844. Alfred Levien, storekeeper of Rocky River, was again declared insolvent on 5 June 1858.

Alfred was married to Rebecca and they had a child named Alfred in 1841 and another son, Henry, in 1845.

Two children were buried at the Maitland Jewish cemetery: Myalla Levien, who died on 21 November 1850, aged four, and George Levien, who died on 28 June 1852, also aged four.

Westmoreland Indent 4/5204, 1838, A1218; *Sydney Morning Herald*, 17 December 1842, 30 December 1842, 5 January 1843, 23 February 1844; Letter 43/8993, in 4/2624, re theatrical performances; *Sydney Record*, 29 January 1844.

LEVIEN, Benjamin Goldsmid

b. London, 1806–1890
1837; Free.
Married; Merchant; 5 children.

Benjamin Levien was the grandson of the magnate Abraham Goldsmid and the cousin of John Levien (q.v.). Benjamin married Eliza (Elizabeth) Lindo in 1833. Benjamin Levien first came to the attention of the Australian public in September 1837 when he announced through the press that he had for sale a liquid that destroyed flies. His next public appearance came when the *Sydney Gazette* published an announcement (28 April 1838): 'Mr Benjamin Goldsmid Levien having broken his agreement with the undersigned in renting his House for an inn at Munimba, Patrick Plains in the new line of road to Muswellbrook, the house shall be let otherwise'. In August 1839 Levien notified the public that he had 'recently let his farm in the District of Parramatta and moved to Sydney'.

Mr B. G. Levien of Phillip Street then obtained approval to take his assigned convict servant, William Smith, with him to the new colony at Port Phillip and was one of the first settlers in Williamstown. By that time, he and Eliza had three children, Harriet Amelia, Robert and Henrietta Mathilda (q.v.). From 1840 to 1845 he owned a small hotel near Footscray, the Victoria Hotel, and handled the punt over the Salt Water River. On 20 March 1843 Levien was granted a licence for pasturing cattle and sheep in the District of Western Port. Levien wrote to the Colonial Secretary for 'permission to place a punt on the Yarra—as it is for the support of my father who, I believe, is already known to your Honour and who will undertake the management'. Levien then offered to chart the Maribyrnong River and place buoys that he had designed. Receiving no answer, he then moved to Geelong where he opened a plant nursery.

The Melbourne Hebrew Congregation recorded that Levien was 'a Geelong settler' who registered the birth of two children, Jonas Felix Australia Goldsmid

Levien (q.v.), who was born in Williamstown on 24 March 1840, and who was the first Jewish child born in Victoria, and Solomon, who was born on 12 March 1843 in Geelong. Both children were circumcised on 1 June 1848. B. G. Levien supported the establishment of a synagogue in Geelong, to the determined opposition of the already established Melbourne Hebrew Congregation, and in 1846 signed the formal address to Chief Rabbi Adler on his appointment. Benjamin Goldsmid Levien died on 24 February 1890. His wife Eliza died on 11 December 1887, aged eighty-three.

Port Phillip Patriot, 3 October 1840; CS Out 4/3687, p. 361, 21 December 1839; 39/9475 in 4/2456.5, 19 August 1839; Trustee of Geelong Synagogue, ML 2/1852; CS 42/1419, 2 August 1842, 42/1323; *Sydney Gazette*, 28 April 1838.

LEVIEN, Harriet (née SALAMONS)

1780–1862
Westmoreland, 1833; Free.
Married; 5 children.

Harriet Levien arrived in Sydney with her husband Solomon Levien (q.v.). She died aged eighty two 'at her residence, William Street in Sydney on 12 August 1862, relict of the late Solomon Levien', and was buried at the Devonshire Street Cemetery. The grave was later 'relocated' to Rookwood by the authority of Sir Edward Samuel Bart.

LEVIEN, Henrietta Mathilda

b. London, d. 1864
Free.
Single; 4 children.

Henrietta Mathilda Levien, the daughter of Benjamin Goldsmid Levien (q.v.), married Saul Samuel (q.v.) on 16 December 1857. Henrietta died on 5 June 1864.

LEVIEN, John James

b. London, 1815–1877
Surrey (2), 1833; Convict; Sentenced to life, Old Bailey, 1832.
Single; Stockbroker's assistant; Height: 161 cm; 9 children.

Dark brown hair, aquiline nose, large mouth, small chin. John Levien was the fifth child of Solomon and Harriet Levien (née Salamon) (qq.v.). On 2 August 1832 the 17-year-old Levien presented a forged cheque made out for the sum of £200 to a banking house in the Strand. He pretended to be the stockbroker for whom he worked—a Mr Watts. On being questioned about the cheque he tried to commit suicide by drinking some laudanum that he held in his hand. Two letters were found in his pocket—one written to his mother and the other to his sister in the event of his death. His employer, for whose firm he had worked for three years, testified to his 'excellent character' during the trial at Old Bailey at the Sessions of 6 September 1832. Levien (who was related to the Salamons and Goldsmids) was sentenced to transportation for life with a strong recommendation for mercy 'on account of his character and his youth'. His behaviour on board ship was said to be 'very good'.

The *Surrey* arrived at Hobart Town on 7 April 1833. The only entry in his police record in Van Diemen's Land was made on 22 January 1835 when, as an assigned servant to a Mr Butler, he was found drunk in a public house after hours and was reprimanded. He received a conditional pardon on 31 March 1836. Probably due to family influence the pardon was granted, 'extenuating circumstances having been reported'. On 4 January 1837 he received permission to proceed from Van Diemen's Land to New South Wales providing there is 'approved security' to prevent his escape by travelling on the ship *Francis Freeling*.

Levien was an early settler in the colony of Port Phillip. He began as a carcass butcher at William's Town (now known as Williamstown) on Port Phillip Bay, where Anthony Cottrell (the son-in-law of Joseph Solomon of Evandale) owned a butcher's shop. On 7 October 1839 he was included among the list of citizens welcoming Superintendent Charles Joseph La Trobe to the District of Port Phillip. On 18 May 1842 the *Port Phillip Gazette* noted that 'John Levien of Williamstown had been injured in a fall from a horse'. The following year, on 8 September 1843, he became the licensee of the British Hotel.

Levien was one of the founding members of the Melbourne Hebrew Congregation but quickly fell behind in his membership payments. In 1850 he married Miriam Saunders (born 27 November 1829 at Bristol) at the Anglican Cathedral of St James (Register 1394). He worked as a wine and spirit merchant with Edward Norman until the partnership was dissolved on 7 April 1853, and then, in 1855, became a partner in Levien and Steinmetz of 113 Flinders Lane.

Levien died on 27 December 1877 at 184 Albert Terrace, Darlinghurst. In his will he is described as 'late of Sydney, a wine and spirit merchant leaving Miriam Levien his widow'. His estate in Tasmania was transferred to New South Wales on 28 January 1878. Miriam died on 29 April 1930 at Woollahra. Of their nine children the eldest, Clara Ellen Levien (1851–1940), married Jonas Felix Australia Goldsmid Levien (q.v.), her first cousin.

OBSP, 1832, case 1885, p. 789f.; CS. Miscellaneous Persons Out Correspondence, p. 134, in 4/3683; CON 31/28, no. 712; Warrant, p. 341, Panel D. vol. 29, p. 341; VDL Papers 1059-7, p. 145; CP no. 161; *Melbourne Times*, 8 September 1843; *Port Phillip Gazette*, 18 May 1842.

LEVIEN, Jonas Felix Australia Goldsmid (Jonah)

b. Williamstown, 1840–1906

The fourth child of Benjamin Goldsmid Levien (q.v.) and Eliza (née Lindo), Jonas was born on 24 March 1840, the first Jewish child to be born in Victoria. He was named Felix Australia in honour of his birthplace. Following a basic education at Melbourne Church of England Grammar School, Levien followed pastoral pursuits. His father had a plant nursery in the Geelong area and he established a seed farm in Drysdale. He was elected to the Victorian Legislative Assembly in 1871 for the electorate of South Grant, defeating the hero of the Eureka Stockade uprising Peter Lalor. He held the seat until 1877 and again from 1880 to 1906. From 1883 he served as Minister of Mines and Agriculture. Levien was a founder of the Australian Natives' Association. He was involved in the business collapse of the 1890s and was blamed by a Royal Commission of 1896 for his part in it.

Jonas married Clara Ellen Levien, the daughter of John Levien (q.v.), on 15 March 1871.

P. Maxwell, *ADB*.

LEVIEN, Joseph Henry

b. London
Westmoreland, 1833; Free.
Single; Merchant.

Joseph Harry Levien was the third child of Solomon and Harriet Levien (qq.v.). In April 1835, he applied for a post in the Colonial Secretary's office and then withdrew his application when he was made to understand that it was not a permanent position. He had heard of the post 'from his father'.

In August 1837 Joseph Henry Levien joined with Francis Newsham and Lewis Samuel to form 'Newsham, Levien & Co'. The partnership dissolved on 1 May 1838 (*Australian*).

Levien became a merchant but was declared insolvent in March 1843. He then joined Frances Mitchell and Co as a ships' chandler and the *Shipping Gazette* recorded large consignments of goods to and from New Zealand sent in his name. On 14 December 1845 he arrived in Hobart Town on the *Sir John Byng* travelling cabin class, bound for New South Wales.

CS 29 April 1835, in 4/2283.7; *Shipping Gazette*, 19 October 1844, 14 December 1844.

LEVIEN, Solomon

b. London, 1776–1851
Westmoreland, 1833; Free.
Married; Merchant; 9 children.

Solomon Levien and his wife Harriet (née Salamons) (q.v.) came to Sydney with five of their nine children following the transportation to Australia of their fifth child, John James Levien (q.v.). (Harriet's brother, Sir David Salamons, would become the first Jewish Lord Mayor of the City of London.) The children who accompanied them were Alfred, aged twenty, Annette, aged sixteen, Henrietta, aged thirteen, Matilda, aged eleven, and George, aged ten. Alfred travelled steerage and Abigail Asser (q.v.), nursemaid, accompanied the family.

Sol Levien became deputy postmaster at Maitland on 30 December 1833 and the owner of the Rose Inn at Maitland in 1834. Levien defended Samuel Levy in 1835 when Levy was convicted in Maitland for 'exposing goods for sale without the necessary licence'. Throughout the 1830s Levien frequently applied for permission to hold concerts at his hotel. In November 1836 Levien and fellow publican John Sparke wrote to the Colonial Secretary as licensed victuallers, 'having noted that female prisoners will not be assigned in future to Public Houses or Inns we appreciate the excellent intention'. Too many female prisoners were assigned to 'the lowest order of Publicans for the most immoral purposes. But the Pulteney and Royal Hotel are filled up with accommodation of respectable families on their first arrival in the Colony or visiting Sydney from the interior'.

Levien had obtained the licence for Sydney's Pulteney Hotel in 1836 with permission to hold musical entertainments on the premises like Barnett Levey (q.v.). In 1838 he served as chairman of the Licensed Victuallers' Association. In 1837 Levien also became the lessee of the Sydney Market in George Street. It was an investment that brought him little joy. Some six years later he would write to the *Sydney Morning Herald* regarding a suggestion to open the market on Sundays. Levien said that 'as an ex-lessee of the George St Markets that he, altho' a Hebrew objected to the opening of the marker at Sunrise on Sundays. That being so why should Christians sanction it?'

Levien invested in the new colony of Victoria: 'Mr Hodgson's new premises in Flinders Street have been leased by a company at £600 opening a large family hotel to be managed by Mr Solomon Levien of the Pulteney Hotel, York Street, Sydney'. While Solomon was out of Sydney, his wife Harriet advertised that she 'was fully empowered to act on behalf of S. Levien' (*Australian*, 10 June 1840). Levien was listed as insolvent on 18 June 1842 with debts of £3557 and assets of £671, and he moved to the Hunter River District, becoming the licensee of the Hinton Hotel and the Blacksmith's Forge. The following year the Sydney Synagogue appointed him official representative of the congregation in the Hunter. In 1845 he returned to Sydney, living first at 100 Kent Street and, by 1847, on the South Head Road.

Harriett Levien died at Sydney on 12 August 1862, aged eighty-four. Solomon Levien died at Balmain on 9 November 1851, aged seventy-five, and was buried at the Devonshire Street Cemetery. In 1901 he was reinterred at Rookwood Cemetery. The inscription on his tombstone recalled his more glorious days: 'Sacred to the memory of Solomon Levien. Formerly stockbroker of the City of London'.

Sydney Times, 2 January 1835; CS 4/2296, 35/5545; 35/2069, in 4/2283.7; 4/2257, 7 January 1834; Miscellaneous Persons CS Out, 4/3549, 28 May 1835, p. 135; CS 4/2322, 36/9109; *Port Phillip Herald*, 29 May 1840; *Sydney Times*, 2 January 1835; *Australasian Chronicle*, 16 July 1847; *Sydney Morning Herald*, 27 June 1842, 2 August 1843, 2 September 1844, 10 November 1851.

LEVINE, Joseph

b. London
Brothers, 1833; Free.
Married; Merchant; 9 children.

The emigrant ship the *Brothers* arrived at Sydney on 21 December 1833. Joseph Levine travelled cabin class and described himself as a 'merchant'.

Ship Indent 4/5205.

LEVINE, Mary

b. 1799
Brothers, 1824; Convict; Sentenced to 14 years.

Mary Levine arrived on 7 May 1824 but was not to be found on the 1828 Census of New South Wales.

LEVINE, Solomon (LEVIN)

b. Goodman's Fields, 1789
Susan (4), 1842; Convict; Sentenced to 14 years, Central Criminal Court, 1841.
Widower; General agent; Height: 168 cm.

Black to grey hair, long face, high broad forehead, brown eyes, large nose inclined to the right, broad double chin. A Jew. Solomon Levine was aged fifty-three when he was deported. His left eye had scars above and under it. Levine was a widower who owned a private house in St Thomas Apostles. He was sentenced to transportation for receiving eighty pieces of calico, knowing them to have been stolen.

Solomon Levine was in Van Diemen's Land on 24 July 1842. His behaviour on board the *Susan* had been 'troublesome, litigious', and his initial period of probation was accordingly set for three years. During this time his behaviour was noted as 'quiet and harmless, orderly and good'. He emerged from the probation period and the road gang at Impression Bay on 20 October 1845. In November 1846 he found employment at Bertram Nathan's (q.v.) business in Launceston. This concluded in September 1847 when he was sentenced to one month's imprisonment and hard labour on the treadmill for 'using obscene language in a public street', after which he was not be allowed to return to Launceston. In 1847 and 1848 Levine was quartered at the Prisoners' Barracks in Hobart Town. In August 1848 he was assigned to Aaron Mendoza (q.v.) of Brisbane Street. His ticket of leave was granted on 26 June 1849 and a conditional pardon was approved on 2 October 1851.

CON 33/24, no. 5833.

LEVISON, Myer Jacob

b. Holland, 1796–1836
Asia I (8), 1836; Convict; Sentenced to life, Old Bailey, 1835.
Married; Optician.

Levison was sentenced for forgery. He claimed to have signed his name to an English letter, which he could not understand, for his cousin, having been told that by doing so it would 'cure eyes'. In actual fact it was a Bill of £85 on M. Stephens and the court did not believe his account of the events. His wife Eliza and three or four children were living in Amsterdam. The surgeon reported that he was 'very well behaved' on board the transport ship.

Myer Levison arrived in Van Diemen's Land on 21 February 1836. Levison had no police record while in the colony and he died in the Colonial Hospital in Hobart Town on 8 October 1836, eight months after his arrival.

CON 31/28, no. 961.

LEVY, Aaron

b. Poland, 1811
1830; Free. Rabbi.

Rabbi Aaron Levy, one of the *dayanim* (judges) of the Jewish Ecclesiastical Court in London, was sent out by the Chief Rabbi to organise the issuing of a *get* (religious divorce) and to bring it back to London as the official 'messenger' of a convict said to be known as 'Long (Samuel) Zanwill', who lived 'by the sea coast in the country of New South Wales', and who could be identified as Samuel Levy (q.v.) who came out on the *Admiral Gambier*. Once this mission was carried out, Levy's wife in London would no longer be 'chained' to her marriage and could marry again.

Rabbi Levy was only twenty-six years of age when he came to Sydney. During the five months of his stay he conducted services, wrote a scroll of Esther, prepared a marriage certificate and delivered sermons. He united the two factions in the community that were quarrelling about the suitability of former convicts to hold office and to take an active part in the life of the Jewish community. He made a number of conversions and he brought with him a Torah scroll and a number of prayer books. P. J. Cohen (q.v.) later recalled that, from Levy's visit 'May be dated the establishment of our religion in this colony on firm basis'. Reflecting his religious outlook, the 'laws and rules of the Sydney Synagogue adopted in 1833' were, according to Rabbi Israel Porush, 'rather strict'. They discriminated against persons married contrary to Jewish law or who had not observed the law of circumcision and excluded them from membership.

Levy's visit was probably the reason for the garbled report of the visit of a 'Jewish Priest' who had come to stay with James Simmons (q.v.) in 1830.

Tradition relates that the community put a cow on board so that he would have fresh kosher milk available on the voyage home.

I. Porush, 'The Australian Rabbinate in 200 Years of Australian History', *AJJHS*, vol. 10, no. 5 (1989), p. 386f; Cecil Roth, 'Rabbi Aaron Levy's Mission to Australia', *AJJHS*, vol. 3, no. 1 (1949), p. 1f.

LEVY, Abraham

b. London, 1766
Royal Admiral (2), 1800; Convict; Sentenced to 7 years, Old Bailey, 1799.
Married; Fruitman.

Abraham Levy was selling oranges in a basket when he attempted to steal a seven-shilling piece from a customer who had some change in the palm of his hand. Levy was chased and caught and counterfeit money found upon him. In his defence, he said: 'I am innocent. I have a very large family and have always worked very hard'. He was sentenced at Middlesex in June 1799.

Abraham Levy appeared before the Bench of Magistrates in Sydney on 11 September 1813 as a witness in a case in which John Moss was accused of having an illegal still. Levy testified that he was 'frightened' of Moss.

OBSP, 1798–99, case 431, p. 521; 2/1958, 11 September 1813.

LEVY, Abraham

b. London, 1791–1858
Fortune (2), 1813; Convict; Sentenced to life, Old Bailey, 1811.
Single; Glass cutter; Height: 170 cm; 1 child.

Dark ruddy complexion, black hair, dark eyes. A police officer observed Levy in a crowd of spectators watching the ascent of a balloon in Hackney. Levy seemed to be acting suspiciously, according to the policeman: 'I saw the prisoner in the company with a dozen more. I saw the prisoner take something out a gentleman's pocket. It contained an American passport. I was attacked by those about him. I received a violent blow in my mouth'. Levy denied the charge: 'It is all stories, every word, what he had said at Bow St'. Levy presented five character witnesses to the jury. He was found guilty and was sentenced on 16 February 1811. He was nineteen years old and said he was a glass cutter.

The *Fortune* arrived in New South Wales on 11 June 1813 and Levy was sent to be an assigned servant to Edward Fletcher, the first constable of Appin. Levy had been removed from government rations by the 1814 Muster. In his own petition to Governor Macquarie requesting a ticket of leave, Levy wrote 'since his arrival he has been employed in the Service of Mr Edward Fletcher, a District Constable of Appin honest, industrious and sober'. Fletcher attested to this with his mark. On being granted a ticket of leave in 1818, after having worked as a servant to Mr John Jones, Levy moved to Sydney where he worked as a dealer and glazier at 15 Pitt Street. When Joel Joseph (q.v.) died in 1820, Abraham Levy applied to Archdeacon Cowper for the allotment of a Jewish section of the burial ground at the end of George Street.

The *Sydney Gazette*, on 17 November 1821, reported that Abraham Levy, 'a crown prisoner was charged with purloining a hat in the public market place on Friday morning'. He was sentenced to 100 lashes, 'to be sent to Newcastle and from thence transported to Port Macquarie for the remainder of his sentence'.

A certificate of freedom was granted on 2 October 1823. On 12 November 1825 the attorney W. C. Wentworth wrote on behalf of A. Levy to the sheriff demanding 'the return of a Box containing silks, ribbons, furs and shawls which were seized by the police at his home'.

In 1825 Levy asked for a conditional pardon. He had 'enjoyed a ticket of leave since 31 January 1818. He was married to a free woman, a native of the colony'. Archdeacon Cowper attested that Levy was 'a sober, industrious and peaceable man' who lived at 15 Pitt Street, Sydney. The petition was approved by Governor Brisbane and he received a conditional pardon (102) on 17 August 1825.

Levy married twice—first, to Maria Gardner at St Philip's, on 13 July 1824, and then, after Maria's death on 14 April 1827, to Maria Allen (a convict who had arrived on the *Grenada*), on 5 November 1828. Both wives lived to the age of thirty years and six months and Levy placed both names on a tombstone in the Christian section of the Devonshire Street Cemetery. A daughter, Elizabeth Levy, was born in 1832 and was registered by Levy as a 'Hebrew'.

Levy was listed as a Jew in Sydney in the 1828 Census, working as a servant to William Cairns in King Street, Sydney. Evidently his glass-manufacturing business, which he had announced in 1824, had failed. Levy became a publican in York Street in 1832 and the owner of the Sign of the Red Cross at the corner of Kent and Druitt streets from 1834 to 1842 and of the Governor Macquarie in Pitt Street. Levy was a seat holder and member of the Sydney Synagogue from 1839, when he pledged £11 5s to the building appeal. He was included in the voters' list of 1842 as living in Druitt Street, Sydney. Levy was treasurer of the Hebrew Mutual Benefit Society for several years. He died on 13 March 1858 and a gravestone was erected at the Devonshire Street Cemetery by the Hebrew Burial Society.

OBSP, 1811, case 734, p. 390; *Fortune* (2) Indent 4/4004, p. 459; 1814 Muster A1942-2; Bench of Magistrates, ML, 2/1958; TL 18/1356; Convicts to Newcastle 4/3504a; Petition 4/1852, letter 209, Petition 4/1874, letter 129, 1825; HO 11/2; Wentworth Legal Letter Book A1440; TL 37/309; *Sydney Morning Herald*, 10 October 1834, 15 September 1842, 17 September 1842; *Sydney Gazette*, 28 April 1821, 17 November 1821, 18 January 1822, 17 April 1823, 2 October 1823, 28 May 1824.

LEVY, Abraham (Bloody Luck LEVY) (Levi Abrahams)

b. London, 1795–1858
Marquis of Wellington, 1815; Convict; Sentenced to life, Old Bailey, 1814.
Single; Fruitman; Height: 163 cm.

Pale complexion, dark brown hair, hazel eyes. Abraham Levy was sentenced to transportation for life on 16 February 1814 for stealing a watch from a visitor at the Newgate Prison.

Levy arrived in New South Wales on 27 January 1815 and was assigned to Mr George Turnbull for twelve months. As a result of bad behaviour he was sent to Newcastle on 22 October 1822 on the *Estramina* to serve a sentence of four years. He was then assigned to the Public Works Department in Sydney and sent on to Emu Plains for the following three years. He was listed as a Jew in the 1828 Census. Levy spent seven years at the Nepean River as an assigned servant to Mrs Elizabeth Field and then became the messenger for the Sheriff's Department at the Sydney Gaol, where he worked for three years. He was then sent back to work on the roads in Patrick Plains and received his ticket of leave in March 1837. His ticket of leave was cancelled on 16 March 1842 for disorderly conduct and gambling, and restored on 30 March 1842. He became a dealer at the Sydney Market, bringing goods in from Windsor. Levy moved to Penrith in 1842. He was permitted to live in Sydney in November 1843, where he was allowed to work as a servant. He received a conditional pardon in 1847. The official Government Gazette, 20 April 1852, confirmed his conditional pardon which was available 'everywhere save the United Kingdom'. Levy was buried by the York St Synagogue on 9 November 1854.

The purpose of Abraham Levy's nickname, 'Bloody Luck Levy', was to distinguish him from his brother, Abraham Joseph Levy (q.v.), who came free to Australia in 1833. Upon Abraham Levy's death, the children of A. J. Levy shared a legacy of £100.

HO 11/2; HO 10/1; HO 10/28; HO 10/54; Convicts to Newcastle 4/3504a, 4/3494; TL 37/309, in 4/4110, February 1837, 37/309, extended 4/4240-40/230, and 42/3390; CS Petition 39/11961, 5 November 1839; CP 4/4430, p. 197.

LEVY, Abraham

1840; Free.
Single; Dealer.

Abraham Levy was the first Jew in Geelong. Levy ran a draper's store in Corio Street, North Geelong, in 1841. In that year Abraham 'Levi' married Mary Baxter in a Presbyterian ceremony in Geelong. 'Mr A. Levy' served as clerk of the course at the first formal meeting of the Geelong races on 29 July 1843. By January 1844 he was holding monthly auctions of land in the Geelong District. On 19 July 1844 Abraham Levy wrote to Mr Asher Hymen Hart (q.v.) at the Melbourne Hebrew Congregation asking for advice: 'One of our body, has unfortunately married a Christian woman which he greatly regrets and therefore, if possible, to return his steps. He has had a daughter born and has applied to our committee to have her named agreeable to the Jewish custom. He has also made a second application for his wife made a *Geurister*'. The matter was discussed on 11 August 1844 and the congregation resolved that 'no application to the Jewish faith be received by this congregation or entertained in any shape'.

A. Levy served as vice-president of the Geelong Hebrew Congregation from 24 February 1848. On 1 September 1849 'A. Levy's child' died in Geelong and a disagreement broke out between the Geelong and Melbourne congregations regarding the child's status. She was buried in Geelong. On 16 September 1849 a letter to the Melbourne Hebrew Congregation from Benjamin Goldsmid Levien (q.v.) proposed the establishment of an independent Geelong congregation. In opposing the suggestion the congregation scornfully recorded that 'Mr A. Levy [has] never paid one shilling towards our establishment'.

On 5 August 1851 the *Melbourne Morning Herald* carried an announcement from 'Abraham Levy, Draper and Auctioneer of Geelong', that he would convey and assign all his estate and personal effects to his creditors, James Noble, merchant, and John Donnelly, licensed victualler.

Melbourne Hebrew Congregation Letter Book, 8 July 1844, 16 September 1849, and Minute Book, 1 August 1844.

LEVY, Abraham

b. Hobart Town, 1824–1849
Sentenced, Hobart Town.

Abraham Levy, who is described as 'a native of Hobart Town', was buried on 15 May 1849. He died at Cockatoo Island in Sydney Harbour, where he was a prisoner.

The York Street Synagogue Burial Society recorded that he was twenty-four years old, that he had 'family' at Hobart Town and the congregation took care of the burial. The description of the place of his birth may discreetly refer to his status as a convict.

Woolloomooloo Stockade, Iron Gang, 1836–1840, 7 January 1840, 4/6271; CS Out 4/3687.

LEVY, Abraham Joseph

b. London, 1800–1867
Palambam, 1833; Free.
Single; Tailor; 7 children.

Abraham Levy was the brother of Abraham 'Bloody Luck' Levy (q.v.). The *Sydney Gazette* reported on 21 July 1833 that the partnership of Dunn and Levy, tailors, had been dissolved on the previous 24 June. Abraham Joseph Levy would carry on the business alone. Levy married Catherine (Kate) Phillips, sister of Solomon Phillips (q.v.), on 13 November 1833, the fifth Jewish wedding in Sydney.

A. J. Levy served as a member of the Sydney Synagogue Committee in 1837. In June 1838 he applied for a licence to run a 'road house' and became the licensee of the Weatherboard Inn near Penrith. After a brief period as a dealer in 1839, he returned to the hotel business with the Red Cross public house in George Street, Sydney, which obtained special permission to remain open until midnight. On 5 July 1842 Levy received a permit to hold theatrical events at the Garrick's Head Hotel in Pitt Street. In 1844 he was advertising Harmonic Meetings at the hotel, which also received a licence to serve liquor at night.

In 1858 A. J. Levy was granted a publican's licence at Solomon's Temple at 72 Clarence Street at the corner of Erskine Street. He remained there until 1863, when he moved to the Wynyard Hotel. Levy held that licence until his death on 23 July 1867 at the age of sixty-nine, 'a very old and respected colonist … after a long and protracted illness'. The funeral left from the home of his son-in-law, L. Lipman, 99 York Street. Kate, his wife, died on 16 October 1887 at the age of sixty-nine.

The children of Abraham Joseph Levy and Catherine were: Elizabeth (born 19 July 1834), Phillip (30 August 1836-1 June 1837), Phoebe (19 July 1838), Joseph (13 September 1840); at Bathurst, Solomon (20 May 1842); in Sydney, Sarah Rosetta (2 January 1846), and Abraham Luck (1853).

Sydney Gazette, 21 July 1833; *Sydney Morning Herald*, 19 December 1839, 5 July 1842, 15 September 1842, 4 May 1843, 18 May 1844, 1 July 1844, 7 April 1845, 25 July 1867; Application for Licence 38/6634, in 4/2414.

LEVY, Alexander

Alexander Levy was a Sydney Synagogue seat holder in 1845. An Alexander Levy, the son of Morris and Sarah, died at Liverpool in 1883.

LEVY, Amelia (Mary)

b. London, 1768
Lady Penrhyn, 1788; Convict; Sentenced to 7 years, Surrey, 1787.
Furrier.

Amelia Levy was a convict on the First Fleet. In company with another woman, Amelia stole some silk handkerchiefs from a shop. She was sentenced on 7 January 1787.

Amelia Levy appeared constantly in the earliest records of the sittings of the first Magistrates Court to convene in Australia. On 11 November 1788 a man came into the hut Levy shared with two other women and stole some clothing. In evidence Ann Warburton said that she was in bed, saw the intruder and thought he had come to 'visit' Amelia Levy, whom she described as a 'loose girl'. It was Christmas Day and Amelia Levy and Elizabeth Fowles spent the night with Corporal Plowman and Corporal Winstead in return for the gift of a shirt each, which they were accused of stealing. On 17 January 1789 Levy acknowledged that a shift she was wearing had been missed from Ann Ward's hut some time previously. The shift was confiscated and Levy was accused of stealing a shift worth one shilling. She was sentenced to receive fifty lashes at the Cart's Tail on three successive Saturdays while the provisions were being issued and there would be a large crowd to see her humiliation. On 24 February 1789 she was brought before the magistrates again for 'theft'.

On 2 March 1789 the Judge Advocate took a deposition on oath from Amelia Levy who was sworn on the Old Testament. The deposition was marked by an illiterate Amelia with a cross. On Thursday 25 June 1789, Levy gave evidence in another trial involving the theft of shoes and clothing and again it was noted that she was sworn on the Old Testament before she gave evidence. On 14 November she was sentenced to fifty more lashes for 'uttering scandalous and abusive language to Sergeant William Clayfield'. Levy denied having used bad words and said that the members of the working party had pelted her with stones.

Levy was sent to Norfolk Island on 4 March 1790. In 1794 the records show that she was 'married' to William Knight and that she had been off the public stores for almost the whole year. Knight was a convict on the Second Fleet and was a 'useful second string actor' in Sydney's earliest theatrical performances. Amelia and William Knight returned to the mainland on the *Francis* on 26 July 1794 and they were subsequently legally married in 1814. On 7 November 1795 Amelia was cited in a trial at the Criminal Court in Sydney: 'Amelia Levy a Jewess being sworn on the Old Testament said she resided with a settler on the road to Prospect Hill, about a mile from Parramatta'. It was claimed that Amelia had been offered stolen goods for sale knowing that they were stolen. Knight owned a property in Parramatta, which was purchased by D'Arcy Wentworth in 1800.

In 1815 Mary Levy, alias Gorman, was among the list of convicts sent to the Newcastle Prison settlement for two years.

HO 10/6; HO 10/7; CO 207/1 Proceedings of the Bench of Magistrates p. 11/25, ML 1/296; Criminal Court, ML, 1147, 7 November 1795; 4/3494 List of Convicts to Newcastle, April 1815–1816; Norfolk Island Victualling Book, ML, 1958, p. 55; Biographical notes on W. Knight, in Robert Jordan, *The Convict Theatres of Early Australia*, p. 225f.

LEVY, Andrew (Asher)

b. 1759
Canada, 1801; Convict; Sentenced to 7 years, Old Bailey, 1797.
Dealer.

Andrew Levy was transported for having stolen and pawned his landlady's daughter's clothes. He was sentenced on 12 July 1797. (There is a discrepancy in the records, which also state that he was tried at Westminster on 8 April 1795 and sentenced to 7 years transportation.)

Asher Levy arrived in Sydney as a convict on the *Canada* in December 1801. Levy was brought before the court in Sydney in April 1803 described as 'a free man' and found guilty of attempting to convey liquor to a prisoner in gaol. On 17 April the *Sydney Gazette* had reported that Andrew Levy had been arrested for 'conveying spiritous liquors to a prisoner confined in gaol'. Asher Levy was sent to Norfolk Island on the *Buffalo* on 14 May 1803, where he remained until 23 December 1807. During that time he remained on government rations and held no land. He was despatched on the *Porpoise* to Van Diemen's Land, arriving 17 January 1808. He appeared in the 1811 Muster of Convicts in Hobart Town as 'Andrew Levy'. In that year he was listed as a convict who had become a settler. The *Hobart Town Gazette* of 14 December 1816 reported that 'Andrew Levy a free man' was convicted of retailing spirits without a licence and was fined £5. If unable to pay he was to serve twenty-eight days hard labour in the county gaol. He paid the fine.

In 1819 he was described as 'an aged invalid' drawing rations from the government. The 1823 Hobart Town Muster recorded that he was on 'charity'. No date of death is known.

OBSP, 1797–98, case 62, p. 67; HO 10/42; HO 11/1; *Canada* Indent 4/4004, p. 49; *Sydney Gazette*, 17 April 1803, 11 December 1803; Arthur File 4306, pp. 219–24; VDL Muster 4/1233-1234; *Hobart Town Gazette*, 14 December 1816; CSO 1/177/4306, p. 221.

LEVY, Angel

b. London
William and Anne, 1791; Convict; Sentenced to 7 years, Old Bailey, 1787.

Two brothers, Jacob Levy (q.v.) and Angel Levy, broke in and stole thirty-two pounds weight of wool valued at fifteen shillings. They were caught when Jacob tried to sell the wool. He showed his customer a sample of the wool and said that he would come back later because he must hurry as 'our Sabbath will begin soon'. When he returned next day he declared 'It is our Sabbath and I dare not touch money'. Angel pleaded that he was present at the incident only through curiosity: 'I know nothing about it'. The brothers were sentenced at the Old Bailey on 18 April 1787 for possessing stolen goods.

There is a note in the ship's indent that Angel Levy 'Left the colony in the *Indispensable* in 1794. Came in *William and Anne*'.

OBSP, 1786–87, case 410, p. 551; 4/4003; *William and Anne* Indent, 1788–1801, p. 299, no. 174/23/116/11.

LEVY, Ann

Angelina, 1844; Convict; Sentenced, Manchester, 1843.
2 children.

On her arrival at the end of 1844, Ann Levy's two children, Margaret (aged six years) and Thomas (aged two), were placed in the Hobart Town Orphanage. The children were discharged on 20 July 1850. Ann Levy was listed at that time as having a ticket of leave.

Ann Levy married John Hill (a convict who had been transported on the *William Jardine*) on 21 August 1848.

HO 10/41, Tasmanian Miscelllaneous Convicts; CON 52/3, p. 191.

LEVY, Ann (LEVI)

b. Norfolk Island 8 children.

Ann Levy, born on Norfolk Island, married John Hurley, a coxswain and emancipated convict. Hurley arrived in New South Wales on the *Eliza* on 21 January 1820. They were to have eight children.

Ann was convicted in the colony and was sent to the Female Factory in Parramatta in 1825. She escaped from the factory in May 1826 and after being brought back to prison petitioned for a remittance of her sentence. She continued to misbehave and caused a disturbance in the prison. In 1831 she asked to be assigned to Archibald McLeod of Norfolk Island. Her request was denied. John Hurley died at Bells Flat in 1853.

Information supplied by Lesley Alice Whitlam, First Familes 2001 (website); Female Factory Records, Parramatta 26/4351, in 4/1896; 267072, in 4/1906 (1826); 27/10190 in 4/1952 (1827); 31/9624, in 4/2121 (1831).

LEVY, Asher

b. 1784
Minorca, 1801; Convict; Sentenced to 7 years, Westminster, 1795.
Single.

Asher Levy was sentenced on 8 April 1795 to seven years transportation but because he was only eleven years old he remained in England until 1801.

Asher Levy arrived in New South Wales on 14 December 1801. On 28 September 1802 he appeared before the Bench of Magistrates in New South Wales charged with theft. Asher Levy left New South Wales by the brig *Maria* in December 1803.

Minorca Indent 4/4004, p. 65; *Sydney Gazette*, 11 December 1803.

LEVY, Barnett (Bernard or Baruch)

b. London, 1792–1866
Somersetshire (1), 1814; Convict; Sentenced to life, Old Bailey, 1813.
Single; Brickmaker; Height: 166 cm.

Dark complexion, black hair, brown eyes. Barnett Levy and Henry Abrahams (q.v.) violently assaulted and robbed a passerby, who recognised them because they had both grown up outside his bakery in Houndsditch. The witness said they were reputed to have been thieves. Barnett Levy's father spoke on his behalf. Barnett was one of five children. In the Old Bailey Sessions of September 1813 both young men were sentenced to death—which was later commuted to transportation for life. Abrahams came out on the same ship as Levy.

Levy arrived in Sydney on 16 October 1814 and was initially sent as an assigned servant to work with Mr Blaxland. In the 1816 Male Muster, Levy was listed as a government labourer in Parramatta. In October 1817 Bernard or 'Borach' Levy was 'capitally convicted with two accessories who broke into a store and stole three casks of wine'. He was, at the time, working at the Sydney Market. The sentence was commuted to seven years colonial transportation and he appeared on a list of convicts being sent to Newcastle on 20 October 1817. At the settlement he was given twenty-five lashes 'for having in his possession a quantity of messes of his fellow prisoners not being able to account for the same'. The *Sydney Gazette* reported that Mr Barnett Levy, 'not the musical amateur', was called upon by the police to corroborate Joseph Raphael's (q.v.) story of a brawl at the Sydney Market with Michael Naphtali (q.v.).

Levy was listed in the 1828 Census, aged fifty-one, in government service working on '15 Road Party' in Parramatta, 'Jew'. The *Sydney Gazette* noted (11 July 1833) that he had a convict assigned to him: 'To Bernard Levy a Tailor's boy'. In 1836 Levy received permission to marry Rebecca Devine at St John's Church, Wilberforce. His bride was aged fourteen years and six months.

Levy was described in the *Registry of Flash Men* as 'the most notorious thief and pocket picker which the colony has ever produced'. The 1841 Census listed Barnett Levy as head of a household that included two females aged between fourteen and twenty-one and one younger than seven. Levy was given a conditional pardon in Sydney on 5 September 1862.

Christ Church in Castlereagh has a record of 'Levy Brntt' of Emu Plains, who was buried on 21 August 1866 'aged sixty-five'.

OBSP, 1813, case 861, p. 463; *Somersetshire* (1) Indent 4/4005, p. 19; CO 201/119; *Sydney Gazette*, 25 October 1817, 20 December 1826; Prisoners Punished at Newcastle, 4/1718, September 1820; York Street Synagogue Minutes, 2 March 1862, 22 March 1862, October 1862.

LEVY, Barnett

b. London, 1823
Royal Admiral, 1843; Free. Single; Carpenter; Height: 177 cm.

The *Sydney Morning Chronicle* reported on 27 May 1846: 'A young man named Barnet Levy, rather respectably dressed, was placed in dock of the Police Office on suspicion of picking pockets—discharged'. On 7 November 1846 the short-lived *Sydney Weekly* reported 'David Barry and Barnett Levy, sent to gaol for three months for being rogues and vagabonds'. His police record described him as: sallow complexion, dark brown hair, dark hazel eyes, Jew.

Levy evidently became infamous. On 10 July 1847 the *Port Phillip Patriot* reprinted an item from the *Sydney Morning Chronicle* with the headline 'Audacious Impudence of a Sydney Pickpocket'. 'Bernard' Levy had sauntered on board the brig the *Union* as it was loading cargo bound for London. Mr Levy was shown around the ship by the captain who was given to understand that he would book a cabin for the voyage 'home' and that he would bring with him a cargo of 100 bales of wool from his station in the interior. Levy said his name was Cohen and that he was staying at the Royal Hotel. When the captain went to visit him, he found there was no Mr Cohen at the hotel. He then spied him walking along George Street 'nearly opposite the Bank of Australasia', one of Levy's haunts. Levy 'made off in the crowd'.

On 10 February 1848 the *Sentinel* wrote:

> The indefatigable and notorious Barnett Levy, who not long since was brought to the Police Office as a rogue and a vagabond, but discharged without punishment on the pledging of his word that he had been engaged as a seaman on board a whaler which was to sail next day, was on Sunday observed by Constable Ash, in the Domain, attempting to introduce his fingers into the pockets of one of the Romish priests, who had scarcely been five minutes on shore from the *St Vincent*.

Levy was sentenced to six weeks in gaol. Scarcely had he left prison than he was back in the hands of the police for stealing eight shillings in Liverpool Street at midnight. He was committed to gaol six times within six years, and was dubbed the 'celebrated scion of the house of Levi'. He was charged by Jacob Josephson with 'Highway Robbery' and was sentenced at the Sydney Court on 8 March 1848 to five years labour on the roads or public works. The first two years were to be served in irons. On 27 June he was found guilty of idleness and neglect of work and sentenced to five days in the cells. On 18 July he was given another five days in the cells for neglect of work. On 31 October he was sentenced to twenty-one days in the cells for 'insubordinate and outrageous conduct'.

On 10 May 1853 he was given ten years hard labour for larceny. *Bell's Life* noted: 'Amongst the most fashionable arrivals from Cockatoo Island was the celebrated Barent Levey [sic] esq. A gentleman of whom the [*Sydney Morning Herald*] thus graphically and ungrammatically speaks: There were burglars and highway robbers extending the list of crime through all the series of property predators up to that notorious thief and pocket picker which the colony has ever produced: Barney Levey'.

Levy was eventually pardoned, on 5 September 1862, on condition that he left the colony. The tables had been turned and Australia was now deporting its criminals back to England!

In September 1862 Maurice Alexander (q.v.) MLA for Goulburn, together with Montague Levy at Wynyard Square, tried to raise funds for his fare to Calloa in Peru. His departure was postponed. Levy was transferred from Cokatoo Island to Darlinghurst Gaol where he constantly misbehaved and enticed others to do the same. He was deported on 26 March 1863.

Transportation Register 4/6571, p. 48; Register of Colonial Pardons 4/4494, 4/3896 (Sheriff) for 16 April 1849; *Sydney Chronicle*, 9 March 1848; *Sentinel*, 10 February 1848; *Bell's Life in Australia and Weekly Retrospect of All Events of Importance*, 11 March 1848, 12 January 1861; *Citizen*, 7 November 1846; Helen Lloyd, *Exiled Colonial Prisoners Banished from NSW*, 2004.

LEVY, Benjamin

Free.
Married; Dealer; 3 children.

Benjamin and Esther Levy had a son, Emanuel, in Sydney in 1843 and registered him as a Jew. Samuel was born in Sydney in 1845, and Joseph was born in 1846. Benjamin Levy, his wife and three children sailed for San Francisco and the Californian goldfields on the barque *Victoria* on 9 November 1849.

LEVY, Bernard (Borach) (Burnett)

b. London, 1797
Morley (1), 1817; Convict; Sentenced to life, Old Bailey, 1816. Labourer; Height: 161 cm.

Sallow complexion, brown hair, grey eyes. Bernard Levy was a pickpocket who stole a watch from a visitor to the Newgate Prison, where he was promptly identified and caught. He was sentenced on 18 September 1816.

Levy was assigned to the District of Windsor in 1817 and remained there as a 'settler's man'. On 18 October 1817 'Borach' Levy was convicted of burglary and sentenced on 25 October. The 1828 List of Convicts in New South Wales stated that he was a 'Protestant' working for William Wilberforce, and that he was thirty-two years old. He received his ticket of leave in 1829. Levy worked as a dealer. On 10 May 1835 the Colonial Secretary noted that Levy was absent from his assigned district and his ticket of leave was suspended for three months: 'whether it will be renewed will depend on the prisoner's future conduct'. Later in 1835, he received permission to travel regularly from Windsor to the Sydney Market. 'Burnett Levy' was listed in the 1837 General Return of Convicts in New South Wales as living in Windsor with a ticket of leave. A conditional pardon was granted on 3 July 1838.

Morley (1) Indent 4/4005, p. 260; HO 11/2; HO 16/1; *Sydney Gazette*, 25 May 1830; Register 4/4072, with TL 29/834, and 4/4235; Passport, 19 November 1835, in 4/4076; CP 38/0979.

LEVY, Brinah

Free.
Married.

The wife of Henry Levy (q.v.), who had arrived in 1833, Brinah came out to join her husband and was in the colony by 1836.

LEVY, David Lewis

1831; Free.

David Lewis Levy fell victim to the economic recession of the 1840s and was listed as a commission agent and wool broker of George Street, Sydney, whose debts amounted to £87 6s 6d, and whose assets were 'Nil'. He appeared on the Sydney Insolvents' List of 20 January 1844.

Port Phillip Patriot, 29 January 1844.

LEVY, Eleazar

b. Bishopsgate Rd, 1824
Matilda, 1844; Free; Sentenced to 6 months, Hobart Quarter Sessions, 1845.
Single; Tailor; Height: 168 cm.

At his trial in Hobart Town on 22 February 1845, Eleazar Levy stated: 'I came free to the Colony by the *Matilda*. I paid my way'. Eleazar Levy was sentenced to six months imprisonment for stealing three books from Dr Bedford. He was described in his police file as 'Dark complexion, dark brown hair, retreating forehead, brown eyes, broad nose, large thick lips. Jew. Can read and write a little'. He was assigned to the work gang at Brown's River for six calendar months, and was discharged from his prison sentence on 23 August 1845. He appeared on the List of Miscellaneous Convicts of 1849 as 'Free'.

HO 10/41, Tasmanian Miscellaneous Convicts.

LEVY, Elias (Elijah LEVI)

b. London, 1802
Lotus, 1833; Convict; Sentenced to 14 years, Old Bailey, 1832.
Single; Boot and shoemaker; Height: 157.5 cm.

Dark complexion, round head, black whiskers, oval face. Medium large nose. A Jew. Elias Levy was found guilty of receiving eight stolen £50 notes. The notes were stolen from a bag in an iron chest in the shop of a chemist and druggist at 22 Houndsditch. His mother Rhina gave evidence that her son was 'very honest and industrious'. Moses Levy, a boot and shoemaker, and Catherine Abrahams, a cousin, gave evidence in mitigation of his sentence. He was sentenced on 29 November 1832.

Elias (Elijah) Levy arrived in Hobart Town on 16 May 1833. In 1838 a series of minor misdemeanours were recorded, principally for being out after hours and on suspicion of keeping a disorderly house. Between 1837 and 1839 his occupation was listed as post messenger in Hobart Town. Levy received a ticket of leave on 31 May 1839, a conditional pardon on 24 May 1842 and a certificate of freedom on 7 January 1847.

His signature appears on the petition of 20 May 1843 to establish a synagogue in Launceston.

In 1846 Levy was living in Oatlands when the Hobart Hebrew Congregation asked him to officiate at a marriage ceremony between Simeon Benjamin (q.v.) and the widow Elizabeth Solomon. Levy refused to perform the ceremony. He had a seat in the Hobart Synagogue from 1845 to 1848. He was listed as donating thirteen shillings to the synagogue in the year that it was built. In September 1846 he addressed to the government a petition for assistance. He was a resident of Oatlands and claimed to be 'free'. Three years previously he had been employed to plough and prepare five and a half acres of land for the district constable for which he hadn't been paid. 'I am a poor man', he claimed, adding that he wanted the £6 owing to him for the work 'for which he had hired a good ploughman'. He took the matter to court and lost, as he could only produce one witness and his statements in court were said to be 'a tissue of falsehood'.

Levy moved to Port Phillip and his luck did not change. The *Argus* reported on 26 June 1849 that Elijah Levi had been charged with absconding from the service of Mr Robert Gibson of Mount Alexander. Levi was described as 'a disreputable character who has frequently been before the carts' and was sentenced to three months imprisonment with hard labour. In July 1850 stood trial for 'Robbery and Attempt to Murder'. In fact, he was committed for trial for having stolen a pair of trousers and 'circumstances' showed the prisoner was innocent. A letter to the *Melbourne Morning Herald* from 'An Israelite' complained that in 'another paper' Levy had been described as a 'Diminutive Israelite' and stated that mention of his religion was offensive. Sadly, Elijah was indicted for the indecent assault of an eight year-old girl named Maria Ann Perkins in a lane off Bourke Street. Elijah was well known in the township of Melbourne as a cake seller. He was found guilty on 18 December 1850 and sentenced to work on the public roads for three years.

OBSP, 1832, case 150, p. 83; CON 31/28, no. 718; CON 18/15; CP 432; CSO 20/10/890, September 1846 (petition); *Melbourne Morning Herald*, 2 July, 28 July 1850.

LEVY, Elizabeth

1805–1849
Free.
Married.

Elizabeth Levy, widow of Philip Levy (q.v.), died in Hobart Town on 23 April 1849 and was buried by the Hobart Synagogue.

LEVY, Ellen

b. London, 1831–1890
Calcutta, 1844; Free.
Single; 10 children.

The sister of Philip Levy (q.v.), Samuel Levy (q.v.), and Lazarus Levy (q.v.), Ellen was born in London on 31 July 1831. She married Bertram Nathan (q.v.) on 20 October 1847 in Hobart Town at the home of her brother Philip. She died on 8 October 1890 and was buried beside her husband at the Melbourne General Cemetery.

LEVY, Emanuel

b. London, 1796
Indefatigable (1), 1812; Convict; Sentenced to life, Middlesex Quarter Sessions, 1811.
Single; Height: 163 cm.

A Jew. Large full eyes and bowlegged. Emanuel Levy together with Timothy Murphy in Hackney and in company with a third individual, robbed a nine-year-old boy and stole his watch. The boy testified: 'They crowded me up, they pushed me, they got me between one another and I was standing between them. They pushed against me and squeezed me, they crowded me up and said "Stop young fellow". Then they snatched at my watch and broke the chain'. Levy claimed to have been on an errand for his father down Hackney Road. He was sixteen years of age when he was sentenced on 30 October 1811.

Levy arrived in Hobart Town on 19 October 1812 on the ship *Ruby of Calcutta* from Sydney. On 18 December 1815 Levy was sentenced to fifty lashes for neglect of duty and disobedience of orders. On 21 June 1816 he received 100 lashes and twelve months in irons in a chain gang for burglary from the house of John Colley. On 11 July 1816 the *Hobart Town Gazette* reported that five men had broken out of the prison room of the guard house in Hobart Town and that Emanuel Levy had joined the bushranger Michael Howe and his gang of desperadoes. This story proved to be untrue, and Levy surrendered to the police on 31 August 1816. He was immediately sent back to Hobart Town. In August 1817, Levy was ordered to give one week's work in his own time for 'neglect of duty and disobedience'.

Levy was granted thirty acres of land in the district of Ormaigh in 1820. It appears to have been the first land grant to a Jew in Van Diemen's Land. On 5 June 1821 he was reprimanded for appearing dirty at church. By 21 November 1829 he held a ticket of leave and was reprimanded for breaking the night curfew. On 7 January 1832 Levy was acquitted of a charge of stealing a watch through lack of sufficient proof, and on August 1833, while holding a ticket of leave, he was fined five shillings for being found drunk.

Levy received a conditional pardon on 2 September 1836.

OBSP, 1810–11, case 849, p. 448; CON 31/27 L. 46; CON 13/1, p. 13; *HRA*, series 3, vol. 3, p. 573; TA Query no. 1964/17; Land Register VDL, vol. 3, p. 178; *Hobart Town Gazette*, 13 July 1816, 31 August 1816; CP 1026; *Hobart Town Courier*, 2 September 1836, 23 March 1838; G. F. J. Bergman, *AJJHS*, vol. 6, no. 1 (1964), p. 34, n. 15.

LEVY, George (Godfrey) Barnett

1821–1880
1841; Free.
Single; Dealer; 4 children.

George Levy of Launceston was licensed as a hawker in December 1841. His name appears on the Launceston Synagogue petition in May 1843 and in June 1844 he gave £5 to the Launceston Synagogue building fund and £4 to the Sydney Synagogue building fund. George Barnett Levy was listed in the *Launceston Examiner* as one of four creditors of the insolvent David Solomon (q.v.) on 17 March 1849. On 27 January 1847 Sarah Solomon (q.v.) of Hobart Town married Godfrey Barnett Levy, 'draper', in Jewish marriage no. 14 in Van Diemen's Land. The ceremony was held at the private residence of Sarah's father, Isaac (Ikey) Solomon (q.v.), New Town Road, in Hobart Town.

Their children were John Barnett Levy (24 October 1847), born in Launceston, Isaac (9 April 1849), Ann (3 February 1851), born in Hobart, and a daughter born on 14 July 1853. Sarah was buried at the old Harrington Street Jewish cemetery, and no date of death was recorded. Godfrey Barnett Levy died in Sydney on 12 August 1880, and was buried at Rookwood.

CO 280/157; *Hobart Town Courier*, 10 December 1841; *Launceston Examiner*, 17 March 1849.

LEVY, Gershon ('Gosher')

b. 1774
Royal Admiral I (2), 1800; Convict; Sentenced to 7 years, Old Bailey, 1798.

Gershon Levy was sentenced at the London Gaol Delivery in April 1798 to transportation for attempting to steal a bolt of linen cloth from a warehouse.

Gershon Levy was known as 'Gosher' in the colony. The *Sydney Gazette* carried his public request on 5, 12, and 18 May 1805 to leave the colony on the *Richard and Mary*.

OBSP, 1797–98, case 262, p. 296; HO 11/1; *Sydney Gazette*, 5 May 1805.

LEVY, Harriet

b. Liverpool, 1807–1847
York, 1833; Free.
Married; 6 children.

Harriet Levy was the wife of John Levy (q.v.). They arrived in Van Diemen's Land in 1833 and had moved to Melbourne by 1841. Harriet died in 1847 giving birth to her baby, who was named in her honour. Both were buried by the Melbourne Hebrew Congregation in 1847. Her surviving children were Sarah, Ann, Henry, Esther and Sophia.

LEVY, Henry

b. 1767
Barwell, 1798; Convict; Sentenced to 7 years, Old Bailey, 1796.

Levy (aged thirty-nine) was staying at a boarding house run by Mr and Mrs Lazarus Phillips. He told his landlady that his name was Thompson and that he worked at a bank. He asked permission to go off to work early. At 6 a.m. he left, but found the front door was locked; before he could leave the landlady discovered that his room had been emptied. He told the court 'I did not intend to wrong this woman. I was very much in liquor. I had some business to do … my intention was to replace [the linen]'. He was sentenced on 14 September 1796.

Levy arrived in Sydney in May 1798 and even though he was listed in the Mutch Index there appears to be no further record of his life in Australia.

OBSP, 1795–96, case 489, p. 813f.; *Barwell* Indent 2/8243, p. 249.

LEVY, Henry

Free.
Married; 2 children.

Henry Levy is listed in the census returns of South Australia of 1841. His wife was under the age of thirty-five. He was under the age of fifty. They had two children, both under the age of seven. The family lived in Hindmarsh.

LEVY, Henry (LEVI)

b. London, 1813
Mary III (4), 1833; Convict; Sentenced to 7 years, Old Bailey, 1832.
Married; Hawker; Height: 156 cm; 7 children.

Sallow and slightly pock-pitted complexion, brown hair, grey eyes. Jew. No education. Lost a front tooth in lower jawbone. Henry Levy was sentenced at the Old Bailey on 5 January 1832. He had stolen a groom's coat from an unattended cart and was seen and identified in Threadneedle Street. He had no previous conviction.

Levy arrived in New South Wales on 6 January 1833 and was immediately assigned to Richard Fitzgerald in Windsor, where he was recorded as working as a hawker. The 1837 General Return of Convicts in New South Wales listed him as still working for Fitzgerald in the District of 'Capita'.

Henry's wife Brinah (q.v.) followed him out to Australia. A child, Frances, was registered at birth in Sydney as a 'Hebrew' in 1837. Joseph, born in 1839, was registered as a 'Hebrew'. Charlotte, 1842, was born in Sydney, and Elizabeth was born later that same year. Samuel, 1843, was born in Sydney, followed by Jacob, 1846, and Esther, 1852.

A certificate of freedom was issued to Henry Levy on 4 July 1840.

In September 1846 Henry Levey, 'a prisoner', was detected stealing a copper discharge pipe from a small engine at Jacques Wharf, Sussex Street, Sydney.

OBSP, 1832, case 461, p. 214; *Mary III* Printed Indent, 6 January 1833; Prisoner no. 33-86, 81, p. 3; *Sydney Gazette*, 4 April 1833; CF 40/1065; *Citizen*, 5 September 1846.

LEVY, Isaac

b. Petticoat Lane, London, 1826
Lord Auckland (1), 1844; Convict; Sentenced to 10 years, Central Criminal Court, 1844.
Single; Labourer; Height: 160 cm.

Fresh complexion, grey eyes, dark brown hair. Illiterate. Deaf and dumb. Isaac Levy was sentenced for stealing a purse containing six half crowns and four shillings with the assistance of two adults. When Levy was stopped in his tracks by a shoemaker: 'he got hold of me by the throat and tried to trip me up. A young woman came up and said "Let the poor deaf and dumb boy go" ... When we were in the (police) station I made signs to him to know if he was a Jew. I spelt the word "Jew" with my fingers. He nodded his head first and shook it afterwards'. This was his second conviction. He was eighteen years old.

Isaac Levy was initially sent to Wedge Bay for his period of probation and was released on 2 November 1846, to be removed to a central depot, when it was noted that he could stuff birds. In October 1847 he absconded and received twelve months imprisonment with hard labour. On 7 July 1849 he appeared before the Launceston Supreme Court and was convicted for burglary, though he was judged to be incapable of pleading. He was sent to Impression Bay for the remainder of his sentence. On 21 August 1850 he was given fourteen days solitary confinement for playing two-up, described by the official dossier as 'tossing half pence with another man in the water closet during divine service'. On 11 April 1854 he received his certificate of freedom.

OBSP 8 April 1844 case 1275. CON 33/61; CON 14/30; CON 18/38.

LEVY, Isaac

b. Petticoat Lane, London, 1827
Equestrian (1), 1843; Convict; Sentenced to 10 years, Central Criminal Court, 1843.
Single; Carpenter; Height: 145 cm.

Fresh complexion, slightly freckled, dark brown hair, hazel eyes, broad nose, thick large upper lip and long chin. Isaac Levy was aged sixteen at the time of his trial. He was a pickpocket and was sentenced for stealing a handkerchief. He had been apprenticed for only nine months before his arrest.

Arriving in Hobart Town on 1 May 1843, Isaac Levy was sent to Point Puer (the boys' prison) at Port Arthur, emerging from the work gang on 12 October 1846. He was then assigned to Mr P. Levy (q.v.) of Bathurst Street for twelve months and appears to have remained as a servant working for him. Isaac Levy married Elizabeth Coombes on 29 October 1850.

His conditional pardon was approved on 25 March 1859.

CON 33/54; CON 14/25; CON 18/41; CON 52/3, p. 278.

LEVY, Israel

b. Holland, 1789–1864
Isabella I (1), 1818; Convict; Sentenced to 7 years, Old Bailey, 1817.
Married; Hatter; Height: 173 cm; 3 children.

Dark ruddy complexion, dark hair, dark eyes. Israel Levy, together with an accomplice, attacked a drunken sailor at two o'clock in the morning. When the sailor got to the watch house to report the attack, he found that Levy had already been arrested, and that he was wearing the stolen waistcoat. Levy's improbable defence was that he had been drunk and lost his way, and came upon a man 'in distress', who sold him the waistcoat for two shillings. Levy was sentenced to death and transported to New South Wales with his younger brother, Lazarus Levy (q.v.).

Levy was initially assigned to work at Liverpool and on 31 March 1823 he was employed at the Bonded Store in Sydney. He had married Mary Kelly at Liverpool in June 1822 and once he moved to Sydney asked to be assigned to his wife. Frederick McIntosh, who was Mary's employer, attested that Levy had 'the misfortune to be injured by lightning at the latter end of December [1824], which has rendered him unfit for hard labour. Mary Kelly/Levy was a free settler and a servant woman and Levy has conducted himself and behaved well'. Israel Levy worked as a dealer but appeared in court in July 1827 for embezzling goods held on commission. Levy was listed in the 1828 Census as a dealer living in Harrington Street, Sydney, with his wife.

In October 1829, Levy, together with Lazarus Levy (q.v.), was sentenced to seven years colonial transportation for receiving stolen goods and they were sent to Norfolk Island 'notwithstanding his praiseworthy conduct in the late attack upon the Hulk'. During his time on Norfolk Island the authorities intercepted a letter from his sister Jane in England and it was noted on the margin of his dossier 'A letter dated London 17 July 1831 from the scoundrel's sister was rec'd here from the Post Office giving an account of his wife at home who was then living—Levy married a woman named Kelly in this colony. He is now at Norfolk Island 27 February 1835'.

The letter from Israel Levy's sister Jane informed him that his father had died leaving each child a legacy of £20. She asked him to send over an order that his wife may receive it: 'The poor blind boy being a great tye to her and were it not for her eldest son she would actually perish'. His wife was unable to go to Australia as she had no money and three children: 'Your wife and children sends her love to you and hopes you will not be sparing of paper but let us hear from you often as your letters are the only comfort she has left. You must not mind the postage—do not neglect to write immediately enclosing the will and power (for the money)'.

From 1832 to 1835 Levy worked as a convict overseer on Norfolk Island. On 7 March 1835 Major Anderson of Norfolk Island wrote to the Colonial Secretary about Levy 'who is authorized to be returned to Sydney by your letter of 2 February 1835. [Levy] wishes to remain at Norfolk Island on a salary of 1/- per diem from this date and as I think is deserving I have sanctioned him to remain here—until I hear from you—if his request can be granted'. By 1845 he had returned to the mainland and received a ticket of leave for the District of Maitland. In 1849 a charge of larceny was dismissed for lack of evidence but his ticket of leave was suspended for twelve months. It was restored in April 1850 for the District of Bathurst. A conditional pardon was granted on 12 October 1854. Levy died on 30 March 1864 at the Benevolent Asylum, Liverpool, and was buried in the Devonshire Street Cemetery by the Sydney Synagogue.

In the 1828 Census, James Thomas Levy, aged eleven, was listed as born in the colony, and as an 'inmate' with Edward Reynolds in Wilberforce. He may well have been the son of Mary Kelly and Israel Levy.

OBSP, 1816–17, case 1178, p. 403; List of Assignments 4/4452, 26 February 1825; Correspondence Re Convicts, CS 4/3669, p. 307; *Phoenix* (hulk) Entrance Book 4/6286, p. 97; TL details 40/2278, 4/4144; Applications to Marry 1842–51, 41/1942, in 4/4154, 18 September 1841; TL 50/47; CP 12 October 1854, in 4/4222, 54/8888; Petition from Norfolk Island, 4/2245, 34/9280, and 34/9272, 22 December 1834; Colonial Secretary, Letter Received, 1835, 35/1397, in 4/2283.7.

LEVY, Israel

Constant, 1848; Free.
Single; Sailor.

Israel Levy arrived as a cabin class passenger on the barque *Constant*. He had 'served as a seaman before the mast' and, on 7 January 1849, following an arrest, wrote a petition to the Colonial Secretary asking to be released from the Darlinghurst Gaol.

LEVY, Jacob

b. London
William and Ann, 1791; Convict; Sentenced to 7 years, Old Bailey, 1787.

Jacob Levy and his brother Angel Levy (q.v.) were both tried for the theft of thirty-two pounds weight of wool, which Jacob was caught trying to sell. They were sentenced at the Old Bailey on 18 April 1787.

Jacob Levy arrived in New South Wales on 28 August 1791. Jacob Levy testified in the Sydney Criminal Court on 12 February 1794 that he had bought a silk handkerchief for one shilling. The handkerchief had been stolen.

HO 11/1; ML A1147, Sydney Criminal Court, 12 February 1794.

LEVY, Jacob

b. Poland, 1771–1860
Countess of Harcourt (3), 1824; Convict; Sentenced to 14 years, Middlesex, 1823.
Dealer in old clothes; Height: 163 cm.

Brown hair, pock-pitted, yellow complexion. Remarks: 'Very bad, a Jew'. Jacob Levy waited outside a watchmaker's house while the 17-year-old boarder at his house stole a watch from a victim, for which he was immediately paid eight shillings. Levy was fifty-three years old.

Immediately after his arrival in Sydney on 12 July 1824 Jacob Levy was sent on from the Hyde Park Barracks to Windsor 'for distribution'. On 3 April 1827 the *Sydney Gazette* recorded that he had complained of harsh treatment from his master who was 'not only a Catholic but is married to a black woman'. She refused to give him shoes and called him a 'Jew rascal and much worse'. Levy was permitted to move to Sydney.

The 1828 Census listed him as an assigned servant working for Mrs Jenkins in Parramatta, aged fifty-eight. Levy received a ticket of leave for the County of Airds on 18 December 1830. On 19 October 1831 his ticket of leave was cancelled by the Campbelltown Bench for 'gross immorality'. On 12 January 1832 it was reported that he had absconded from the colony. However, he was brought before the Bench of Magistrates for 'causing himself to be forwarded to Sydney pretending to be free'. He was returned to his road party after seven days on the tread-wheel. One year later, on 3 March 1833, the *Sydney Gazette* reported that he had been apprehended and put in the 'Invalid Gang'. The House of Correction Register recorded that he was sent to prison on 20 July 1839 for 'keeping a bawdy house'. He was sentenced to twelve months hard labour at the Sydney Quarter Sessions.

A certificate of freedom was issued on 22 July 1839. The *Registry of Flash Men* mentioned a 'Levy of O'Connell St', who was a fence for stolen goods and a brothel keeper. On 1 June 1845 he was sentenced to fourteen days imprisonment for dealing in stolen goods. On 18 October 1845 at the Sydney Criminal Court Jacob Levy and Joe Corton were indicted for assaulting and robbing Patrick Casefield. Corton were found guilty and Levy was discharged after he produced a proven alibi.

Jacob Levy was buried by the Sydney Synagogue on 21 August 1860.

OBSP, 1822–23, case 1254, p. 464; *Countess of Harcourt* (3) Indent 4/4009, p. 209, and 4/4013, p. 135; CO 207/2; House of Correction Register 4/4569, p. 168, 20 July 1839; 4/4007, 19 October 1831; TL Register, 27 December 1830, 4/4077; CF 4/4349–39/1002; *Sydney Gazette*, 3 April 1827, 18 December 1830; W.A. Miles, *Registry of Flash Men*, p. 134; *Cumberland Times and Western Advertiser*, 1 October 1836, 18 October 1845.

LEVY, John (LEVI)

b. Liverpool, 1797–1870
York, 1833; Free.
Married; Dealer; 6 children.

The son of shopkeeper Isaac Levy, and his wife, Sophia (née Barnett), of London, John Levy arrived in Van Diemen's Land with his wife Harriet (q.v.) on the *York*, on 4 January 1833. He was an early settler in Melbourne, being in the settlement by 1841. Levy was a shopkeeper who sold clothes and who had a house and shop in Little Collins Street. He gave evidence in the bankruptcy trial of James Simeon (q.v.). In January 1842 he was committed for trial for illegally holding a stolen watch. Apart from the shop Levy conducted a lodging house under the name of 'William Smith' and was said to have handed on a watch stolen from a recent immigrant to a woman in the course of a police raid on a house of ill repute where he had been playing cards. On 19 January in the course of giving evidence Constable George Nuge testified that he knew Levy and two other men 'to be connected with all the cattle stealers and housebreakers in town'. On 16 February Levy was acquitted of the charge of larceny.

In December 1845 Levy was elected to the committee of the nascent Melbourne Synagogue. John Levy signed the address of welcome to the newly appointed Chief Rabbi Adler in February 1846 and took an active role in the life of the new Jewish congregation. He was active in the establishment of the Melbourne Jewish Philanthropic Society (1849).

Harriet died in childbirth in 1847, and her infant daughter, who was also named Harriet, died within hours of her birth. The tragedy constituted Melbourne's sixth Jewish funeral. The surviving children were Sarah, Ann, Henry, Esther and Sophia. Sophia, born in Melbourne on 20 February 1846, and registered in the congregation's Birth Book, was six and a half years old when she died on 24 August 1852. She was described as the daughter of 'Mr John Levy, Collins St, Melbourne'.

John Levy was a witness at the wedding of Lewis Levy and Rebecca Salom in Collingwood on 6 December 1854. On 28 November 1855 the young Nathaniel Levi from Liverpool married Sarah Levy at the home of her father, Carlton Terrace, King William Street, Collingwood. John and Nathaniel were first cousins and Sarah was the daughter of John Levy. In the Hebrew document Sarah is 'the daughter of Yaakov' and Nathaniel is 'the son of Yosef'. John Levy married a second time in Ballarat and moved to Maryborough and opened a store with Philip Solomon (q.v.) in 1853.

Levy returned to Melbourne and in 1859 became a member of the Melbourne Benevolent Asylum. John Levy, a Justice of the Peace, was buried in the Jewish section of the Melbourne General Cemetery on 7 November 1870.

CUS 30 p. 180, AOT; VPR, Series 30P, Box 185, N.C.R 19; Levi family papers; Melbourne Hebrew Congregation Birth Book.

LEVY, John (Lawrence)

b. London, 1806–1886
Marquis of Hastings (3), 1828; Convict; Sentenced to 7 years, Old Bailey, 1827.
Single; Tailor and scourer; Height: 165 cm.

Pale freckled complexion, light brown hair, blue eyes. Could read and write. Jew. John Levy stole two saws valued at twenty-five shillings from a building site and was caught offering one of them for sale at a very low price. He had no previous conviction.

John Levy was assigned to George Rankin at Bathurst. He received a ticket of leave in 1832 and a certificate of freedom on 26 December 1834. The *Sydney Morning Herald* of 22 January 1846 carried a long list of pensioners who were due to receive a 'compassionate allowance' of four pence halfpenny a day. Levy appears to be the only Jew on the list.

Levy died in the Liverpool Asylum in 1886, where he was described as 'Lawrence Levy'.

OBSP, 1827–28, case 166, p. 85; *Marquis of Hastings* (3) Indent 4/4086, and 4/4013, p. 135; TL Register 4/4062, 32/1192; CF 34/1630; CS 4/3681, p. 384; CF 4/4326.

LEVY, John (Abraham DAVIS)

b. Whitechapel, 1817
Somersetshire, 1842; Convict; Sentenced to 7 years, Central Criminal Court, 1841.
Tailor; Height: 155 cm.

Fair complexion, black hair and whiskers, light hazel eyes and a small scar on his forehead. Jew. Could read and write. Levy told the convict supervisor who interviewed him on arrival in Hobart Town: 'I was caught in fact of housebreaking and stealing wearing apparel'. He had been sentenced to two years gaol for a previous similar offence. The convict dossier stated that his 'proper name' was 'Abraham Davis'. According to Levy 'a man named Jacobs wanted me to come to this country'. He had a mother named Amelia. His father was Benjamin Levy and he had three brothers and three sisters in London.

John Levy's initial period of probation, which was fixed at two and a half years, was spent at Southport. Levy was sentenced to five days in solitary confinement for 'idleness' on 21 October 1842. On 30 March 1843 he was reprimanded for 'retaining his old shoes for the purposes of making away with the new ones'. On 23 August he was given five days in solitary confinement for 'idleness'. He was released from this first stage of probation on 30 November 1844. He was then assigned to shopkeepers in Hobart Town and the Jewish community came to his aid so that he was assigned to one Jewish merchant after another. By 1849 Levy was listed in the Colonial Secretary's Returns of Convicts as the holder of a conditional pardon and was an 'absentee'—in other words he had escaped. Levy was struck off the list of convicts on 30 December 1853.

OBSP 1 March 1841 case 837. CON 33/21; HO 10/40; CON 14/13, no. 5048.

LEVY, Joseph

1770–1788
Scarborough, 1788; Convict; Sentenced to 7 years, Old Bailey, 1784.

Joseph Levy was sentenced to transportation for having stolen a copper kettle valued at eight shillings from its hob in a London street as its owner sold saloop in the early morning hours to labourers who were passing her house. Levy was arrested in Church Row by the Aldgate Church and tried in May 1784. Levy was sent to the Censor *hulk and embarked at Portsmouth on 27 February 1787. He arrived in Australia on the First Fleet with only half his sentence left to serve.*

On Wednesday 21 February 1788, at the second sitting of a court in Australia, Joseph 'Levi' was taken in charge by the guard and put in irons. On Thursday 22 February 1788 he was charged before Captain Collins and Mr Alt with insolence and with threatening to take away his life to an overseer William Parr, a convict. David Gordon, another convict, gave evidence. Parr said that between six and seven o'clock on Wednesday night he had met David Gordon who told him about some things he had lost that were said to be in one of the tents. He entered Levy's tent with Gordon. The culprit arrived and abused them in 'an insolent and infamous language'. Parr then reported Levy to the officer of the guard and Levy was put in irons. Levy denied abusing the overseer, was found guilty and sentenced to one hundred lashes. He was pardoned by Governor Phillip after representation by Mr Parr. The prosecutor said Levy had previously been in trouble and had escaped 'no thanks to Mr Parr'.

Levy was buried on 15 April 1788, at Sydney, according to the Burial Register of St Philip's in Sydney. He may well have carried out his threat to put an end to his own life.

The eighteen-year-old became the first Jew to be buried in Australia.

OBSP, 1783–84, case 560, p. 767; CO 207/1; HO 10/7, also HO 19/6; Magistrates Proceedings, ML, 1/296, p. 3 11/1; St Philip's Register 112/180.

LEVY, Joseph (Joshua)

b. London, 1792
Admiral Gambier (2), 1811; Convict; Sentenced to 14 years, Old Bailey, 1809.
Single; Watchmaker; Height: 154 cm; 1 child.

Sallow complexion, dark brown hair, brown eyes. Aged sixteen, Joseph Levy snatched and ran off with a watch and got away, only to be recognised by a witness a short time later. He was sentenced on 20 September 1809.

Joseph Levy was assigned to Mr Edward Reynolds of Windsor for five years and then lived with Mr James Dunn as an assigned servant. He appeared in the 1814 Muster as 'Joshua Levy, a 'convict servant'. In the Muster of 1816 he was 'off stores' and an assigned convict servant to Captain Piper. In Windsor he claimed to have conducted himself 'honestly, soberly and industriously' and asked for a ticket of leave, which was granted on 31 January 1820.

Levy was listed in the 1825 General Muster as a labourer working for Mr Wilberforce. Levy moved to Sydney and in the 1828 Census he was listed as aged thirty-six, a Jew, a watchmaker at Thos. Planks, George Street, Sydney, with a ticket of leave. A certificate of freedom was granted on 2 October 1823 and reissued on 5 January 1828.

Levy was still listed as an innkeeper at Berrima in 1861.

OBSP, 1808–09, case 702, p. 431; CO 201/118; Petition to Governor Macquarie, no. 18-119; 4/1859, *Admiral Gambier* (2) Indent 2/8240, p. 123; 4/4004, p. 382; 1814 Muster, A1942-1, p. 43; Ration Book, Windsor, A803, pp. 233, 239; TL 2038; CF 28/8; *Australian*, 27 May 1841; HO 10/8; HO 10/19; Bigge Report, CO 201/118; *Sydney Gazette*, 2 October 1823; CF 4/4291.

LEVY, Joseph

b. London, 1799–1862
Mangles (1), 1820; Convict; Sentenced to life, Surrey, 1819.
Single; Labourer; Height: 160 cm; 2 children.

Dark complexion, black hair, dark brown eyes, aquiline nose, scar on nose, some pockmarks on forehead, scar outside right elbow, scar right thumb, scar forefinger of left hand. Joseph Levy, a labourer of the Parish of St Saviour of Southwark in Surrey, was tried 'for feloniously stealing on 23 September 1819, one watch value £10, one watch chain of the value of £4, one watch key value £1 and one seal value £5 from the person of Theophilus Hearsey'.

The *Mangles* arrived in Sydney on 7 August 1820 and immediately upon arrival Levy was sent to Emu Plains, where he served as overseer for two years. Levy may have attained some degree of very dubious immortality through these years of servitude. In the convict novel *Ralph Rashleigh*, attributed to James Tucker, the hero is drafted into a work gang clearing land commanded by Joseph Levy, 'a bandy-legged chocolate cheeked Jew who delighted in oppressing his men as much as possible'.

The General Muster of New South Wales of 1825 listed him as a government servant at Emu Plains. Levy received his ticket of leave in 1827 and in the 1828 Census he was described as a labourer at 'George's Field' at Evan. The 'field' was the property of David Johnston, the son of Esther Johnston (née Abrahams, q.v.).

Levy received a ticket of leave for the District of Evan in 1827. Levy wrote to the government saying that he had a job with Lewis Solomon (q.v.) and that 'through error it has been made out for Evan'. This suggestion of a mistake was rejected and Levy was forced to remain and worked for John Moses (q.v.), who was able to take out the licence for the King's Head Inn in Penrith. The police advised against the move because Levy had once received fifty lashes and seven weeks in a gaol gang for having a forged pass in his possession. He had also been gaoled for three months for 'refusing to work'. However, the next year when John Moses moved to Sydney, Joseph Levy asked permission to go with him and this time was successful. On 6 May 1831 the *Sydney Gazette* reported: 'On Friday last, a man named Joseph Levy, was driving a cart along York Street, one of the wheels raising on the pathway tilted Levy who had taken a drop, on the ground. When he lay insensible for some moments, till recovering gradually, and pretty well sobered by his tumble, poor Moses remounted and jogged homewards, but so much indisposed as to be forced to lie up for many days in a rather dangerous plight'. This time he was allowed to move as 'he is so well recommended'. Levy wrote 'Abraham Myers [q.v.] of George Street is a relative and is willing to take him as a partner in his business'.

Levy began a new chapter in his relationship with officialdom when he married Sophia Smith (aged seventeen and born in the colony). The ceremony was performed by the Rev. Dr Lang at Sydney's Scots Church in August 1832 and a daughter, Elizabeth, was born in 1833. Only her father's name was registered in the Birth Register and she was described as a 'Hebrew' and given the Hebrew name of Rebecca. A conditional pardon was granted on 28 February 1834 and an absolute pardon on 2 June 1841, which was confirmed 9 April 1842.

Levy had moved to Berrima in 1835 and opened a general store. In 1837 he founded a small brewery. He boasted the Imperial Brewery produced 'the best colonial beer, equal to any in the Colony … [and] added to his establishment the trade of Cooperage in all branches'. Levy sold the business to Hyam Philipson in 1840 and became an auctioneer and the owner of Berrima's Queen Victoria Inn. The building still stands in the centre of the town. In Sydney he lived with Abraham Joseph Levy (q.v.), the licensee of the Sign of the Red Cross. He handed the inn over to his nephew Lewis David Levy (q.v.) in 1841 when he was granted his absolute pardon. He worked in George Street, Sydney, and in Berrima as a dealer and auctioneer. He was a member and seat holder of the Sydney Synagogue to which both he and Rebecca, his daughter, contributed £15 in September 1839.

Levy declared in the *Australian* of 30 September 1841: 'Joseph Levy, formerly of Berrima, is in no way connected with the boy Joseph Levy' (q.v.). It should be noted that the 11-year-old boy was, in reality, his great-nephew.

He was a ratepayer in Sydney in the 1840s, maintained his links with Berrima and sent a consignment of haberdashery to Melbourne in December 1844. He purchased land at Berrima (1834 and 1839), Mittagong (1852) and Sydney. The pioneer coaching firm on the great Southern Road, which linked the settlement of Port Phillip with Sydney, was run by 'Doyle and Levy'. The booking office in Goulburn was at the Argyle Store, which belonged to Benjamin and Moses. The 1841 Census of New South Wales lists Levy as living in Bong Bong Road in Berrima Town.

The *Sydney Gazette* of 3 February 1842 tells a cautionary story about Levy and his dog:

> Mr J. Levey formerly of Berrima, Hotel Keeper but now of Bathurst Street in the town of Sydney writes to warn all gentlemen, particularly settlers from up the country that having had the misfortune to take the house formerly occupied by the notorious Mother Heywood; he has also secured the services of a bulldog of the 'first water' who goes by the name of 'Boxer'—Gentlemen are therefore advised from not visiting this house, more especially the gentleman who left his name in the waistband of his breeches only few nights back, in the jam of Boxer.

In November 1860 Levy wrote to the York Street Synagogue asking for help to prosecute culprits who had injured a Jew named (Daniel) Garcia (q.v.), who lived at Berrima.

'Joseph Levy of Berrima' died at the age of sixty-three, on 25 September 1862 in Sydney and was buried by the York Street Synagogue at the Devonshire Street Cemetery. He was one of the last to be buried in the cemetery and his grave is now at Rookwood. He had two children, Joseph and Rebecca. Rebecca (Solomon) was buried in the same grave as her father.

Index of Applications for Grants of Land, 1825, Petition 4/1874, p. 130; CS In Letters 4/4561.1, 43/3310; 4/1953, 9 November 1827; *Sydney Gazette*, 14 September 1827, 6 May 1831, 13 May 1831, 5 August 1834; *Australian*, 5 January 1839, 1 May 1839, 12 October 1839, 2 June 1840, 30 September 1841, 16 September 1842, 11 April 1844; Petition 31/5979, 4 August 1831, in 4/2112; Petition 32/2598, 22 March 1832, in 4/2139; Governors' Despatches, ML, A1231, 21 October 1841; 4/4062, TL 31/377; 4/4432, p. 421; Permission to Marry 4/4508, no. 261; CP Register 4/4431, p. 422-210; HO 10/52, 10/53; AP 41/210; G. F. J. Bergman, 'A Yiddishe Ghost: Joseph Levy the Brewer of Berrima', *AJJHS*, vol. 8, no. 6 (1979), p. 363f.

LEVY, Joseph

b. Sydney, 1830
Colonial Sentence, 7 years, Berrima Supreme Court, 1841.
Height: 144 cm.

Joseph Levy was the son of Lewis David Levy (q.v.). The 11-year-old Levy was sentenced to seven years colonial transportation at the Berrima Supreme Court on 21 September 1841 for 'perjury'. He had given evidence against a man who maliciously stabbed a mare. When called upon to give evidence for the prosecution the boy denied the truth of the whole matter. The prisoner was acquitted but the boy was sentenced to seven years in Van Diemen's Land. He was described as of slender build, with a fresh complexion, brown hair, hazel eyes and a small nose. He was sent on the schooner *Marian Watson* in October 1841. The Governor directed that the boy be sent to Point Puer at Port Arthur.

On 25 January 1842 Levy was convicted of 'gross misconduct' and given twenty-five stripes on the breach. On 23 February, for misconduct, he was given eighteen stripes. On 9 March, for repeated misconduct, he received five days solitary imprisonment. On 25 April, for disorderly conduct, he received forty-eight hours solitary confinement. On 11 April 1843 he was absent without leave and was sentenced to fourteen days solitary confinement. He was repeatedly sentenced for misconduct, in May 1843 receiving twenty stripes, on 5 June twenty stripes, on 6 September fourteen days in solitary confinement and on 15 December twelve days in solitary confinement. On 24 February 1844 he was given twenty-five stripes for being absent without leave and on 7 June 1844 for misconduct he received fourteen days in solitary confinement. A certificate of freedom was granted on 21 September 1848 and he was returned to Sydney on the *May Queen* in November 1848.

CSO 16/2/58; Prisons Department, Sydney and Darlinghurst Description Books for 1843, 4/6297; CON 35/1, no. 1400; Transportation Ledger, 4/4523, p. 94.

LEVY, Joseph Henry

Free.
Married; Butcher

Joseph Henry Levy was listed as the agent for the Sydney newspaper the *Atlas* at Berrima in June 1845. He was listed as a butcher at Berrima in 1850.

Atlas, 7 June 1845.

LEVY, Lawrence

b. 1810
Captain Cook (1), 1832; Convict; Sentenced to 7 years, 1831.

Lawrence Levy arrived on 2 April 1832. He was listed in the 1837 General Return of Convicts in New South Wales as working for Mrs Underwood in Parramatta.

The Hobart Synagogue Minute Book of 11 April 1843 recorded that Lawrence Levy donated £5 to the synagogue building fund.

LEVY, Lazarus (LEVI)

b. London, 1798–1838
Isabella I (1), 1818; Convict; Sentenced to 7 years, Old Bailey, 1818.
Single; Groom; Height: 163 cm.

Dark pale complexion, brown hair, hazel eyes. Illiterate. Lazarus was the brother of Israel Levy (q.v.), who was sent out on the same boat for a different offence. In London, Lazarus, Sarah Rose, and at least one other man stole 500 pounds weight of sugar from a warehouse in Whitechapel. Lazarus Levy was caught because the sugar had left a trail leading to the room in which he was sleeping with Sarah Rose. He was sentenced on 14 January 1818. Sarah Rose was acquitted.

Lazarus Levy arrived at Sydney Cove on 14 September 1818 and was initially sent to Windsor for distribution as an assigned servant. He obviously caused trouble because he was sent on to Van Diemen's Land.

On 20 August 1820 Levy was convicted in Hobart Town of attempting to commit rape. He received 200 lashes and on 9 November 1821 was sent on the *Sally* to the penal settlement in Newcastle. On 23 September 1823 he was removed to the convict station at Port Macquarie on the *Elizabeth Henrietta.* A certificate of freedom was granted on 20 January 1825. Levy married Ann Turner (who had arrived on the *Mary Ann*) on 30 May 1825 at St John's, Parramatta. On 2 August 1825 he was remanded for ill-treating his wife and, also, under suspicion of stealing and receiving stolen goods. On 7 June 1826 he was charged by Catherine Martin for theft when he offered her a cotton gown for two dollars, accepting a dollar and handing over 'two old bags of wrapping'. She ran after him and the gown was found hidden inside his hat. A trial was held on 12 June and he was acquitted!

In August 1826 Lazarus Levy was indicted for stealing three sovereigns from the man whose house he shared. Levy was again acquitted. At Windsor in July 1827 Levy was charged by Benjamin Francis (q.v.) with stealing carpenter's stock bits and found not guilty. Described as a 'hawker' he was, however, convicted for stealing in the dwelling place of William Parks, Parramatta, on 5 March 1828 and was sentenced to death; this was later commuted to seven years hard labour in chains at Moreton Bay. The colonial sentence was again altered in October 1828. Levy, together with Israel Levy (q.v.), was sent to Norfolk Island from 1829 to 1833. By 26 December 1833 Levy was in Van Diemen's Land, where he served three years of servitude punctuated by imprisonment and hundreds of lashes for idleness, neglect of duty, stealing clothing and 'feigning illness'.

He began work as an assigned servant to a Mr Barrow and, on 27 December 1833, he was found to have in his possession thirteen shillings and threepence halfpenny 'for which he cannot satisfactorily account and strong suspicion of having stolen it from some Person while confined in the Watch House'. Levy was sentenced to be imprisoned with hard labour for six months. He spent the next year as a member of the chain gang. He was given an additional six weeks imprisonment on 7 January for 'neglect of work'. On 24 January 1834 he was sentenced to thirty-five lashes for 'neglect of work'; on 7 March, as a member of the chain gang, to a further twenty-five lashes for 'neglect of work'; on 9 April, for 'neglect of work', twenty lashes; on 17 April, for the same 'crime', twenty lashes; on 7 May, thirty lashes; on 14 May, for 'neglect of work', twenty-one days in solitary confinement on bread and water; on 8 August, in Launceston, fourteen days imprisonment and hard labour for 'neglect of work'; on 30 August, as a member of the chain gang, six extra weeks hard labour for 'pilfering stores'; on 6 September, for pilfering a pair of trousers, thirty-five lashes; and, on the same date, for feigning illness and gambling, one additional month of imprisonment and hard labour was added to his sentence. On 15 September 1834, as a member of the chain gang, he was punished with twenty lashes for improperly receiving a pair of shoes; on 20 October, for 'neglect of work', twenty-five lashes; on 27 October, for 'gambling', thirty-five lashes; on 3 December, for being 'continually idle', twenty-five lashes; on 27 October, for 'gambling', thirty-five lashes; on 17 December, for 'feigning illness', one month was added to his sentence, and it was recommended that he be sent to Port Arthur.

The nightmare of his imprisonment continued. On 23 December 1834, for 'neglect of work', he received thirty lashes. On 9 January 1835, for 'continued idleness', twenty-five lashes, and on 23 January, for 'disobedience of orders and idleness', he was placed in solitary confinement for twenty-eight days, and fed on bread and water.

Somehow he survived. Levy arrived back at the *Phoenix* hulk in Sydney on 13 September 1836, declaring himself to be a 'jeweller' and claiming to be free of his original sentence and his colonial sentence. In 1837 he was in Sydney working as a shopkeeper in Brickfield Hill. His wife had been convicted of helping with a robbery at Aaron's Tavern, George Street, in May 1826 and for being a prostitute. She had been released from the Female Factory with a ticket of leave for Sydney in August 1837, 'on the strength that this was where her husband lived'. As soon as she was released she refused to return to her husband 'of eleven years'. Levy wrote to the Colonial Secretary saying that he felt 'in danger of his life' because ten years previously he had denounced her to the police as a prostitute. The *Sydney Gazette* reported that 'Lazarus Levy, dealer in George Street, had been brought before the bench charged with having threatened to annihilate his wife who stated that he was in the habit of taking up an axe and threatening to murder her'. Levy was bound over to keep the peace. Levy left Sydney to become a servant of Abraham Moses (q.v.) and was sent by him to manage his general store at the Snowy River. In September 1837 Lazarus Levy was said to have 'absconded with a considerable amount of money' and Moses cautioned the public to beware of having contact with him.

Lazarus Levy was buried at the Devonshire Street Jewish Cemetery on 18 August 1838 at the age of forty-one.

OBSP, 1817–18, case 295, p. 112; *Isabella I* Indent 4/4006, p. 95; CON 31/27, no. 84; CON 3/28, no. 778; CON 18/13, Sydney and Darlinghurst Gaol Description Books, August 1836, 4/6297; HO 11/3; CF; *Sydney Gazette*, 20 January 1825, 11 August 1825, 7 June 1826, 12 October 1828, 15 October 1829; *Monitor*, 18 August 1826; *Australian*, 8 July 1837, 15, 17 and 20 October 1840; Supreme Court Sydney, Petition 37/7637, in 4/2376; Governors' Despatches, A/1204, p. 407; *Phoenix* (hulk) Entrance Book, 1836, p. 95; TL 29/899, CP 39/78, 4/6286.

LEVY, Lazarus (LEVI)

b. Whitechapel, 1811–1884
Lord Lyndoch, 1836; Convict; Sentenced to 7 years, Old Bailey, 1833. Single; Labourer and pencil-maker; Height: 161 cm.

Dark complexion, face freckled, dark, black eyes, black hair, large nose. A Jew. Lazarus Levy was convicted on 17 August 1835 and transported for 'housebreaking'.

Lazarus Levy arrived in Van Diemen's Land on 26 August 1836. Commonly known as 'Blackguard Levi', because he always used very bad language (according to the personal notes preserved in the Allport Collection), Levy was a big, roundfaced, dark-complexioned man, blustering and rough spoken. Levy was assigned to the service of a Mr Rowcroft and remained with him for three years. During this time he received 200 lashes for insolence and insubordination on four different charges and two years were added to his sentence when he attempted to abscond. Lazarus Levy denied the charge in a petition. He claimed to be serving his master at Norfolk Plains when he was ordered to proceed to the police station. On the way to the station he claimed he had been arrested for being at large without a pass. He was sentenced to hard labour in chains for general misconduct and for being absent from work without leave. On 2 June 1839 he was found to have a quantity of rice in his possession for which he was unable to account. He was sentenced to four days in solitary confinement on bread and water. On 27 December 1839 he was sent to Port Arthur for twelve months.

He received his ticket of leave on 26 August 1841 and his certificate of freedom in 1844.

OBSP, 1817, case 1178; CON 31/28; CON 18/13, no. 995; ML, A1059-8, p. 79; Personal Notes, Allport Collection p. 87; CF no. 66.

LEVY, Lazarus

b. Bishopsgate, 1817–1884
Isabella I (5), 1833; Convict; Sentenced to 7 years, Middlesex, 1833.
Single; Jeweller; Height: 161 cm.

Dark complexion, brown hair, hazel eyes. Surgeon's report 'Bad'. 'Jew'. Lazarus Levy was transported for stealing five pairs of boots belonging to a barrister at the Middle Temple. He was the son of Philip Levy of London, and brother of Samuel Levy (q.v.), Philip Levy (q.v.), and Ellen Levy (q.v.).

Levy was an inveterate gambler. During his initial assignment at Windsor, on 27 December 1833, Levy was found to have thirteen shillings in his possession for which he had no explanation and he was assigned to six months hard labour. Levy was sent to Van Diemen's Land for two years, returning to New South Wales on the *Queen Charlotte*, and then was sent on to the Newcastle prison settlement. Levy was 'removed' from Newcastle and sent to Port Macquarie on the *Elizabeth Henrietta*. He spent from January to May 1834 as part of a chain gang and was punished nine times for 'idleness', for which he received a total of 170 lashes. During a further four months in prison and in the Launceston Chain Gang during 1834 he received a further 200 lashes for pilfering stores, for gambling and for idleness. On 2 October 1835, while an assigned servant to Mr Lord, he struck a fellow servant and was sent to work with a road party for twelve months.

In August 1837 he was described as a 'confirmed gambler' and it was recommended that he be sent to the Interior for hard labour in chains. He was sent to the Campbelltown Gang. On 11 July 1838, an assigned servant, he was sentenced to be sent to Snake Banks Road Party because of 'insolence'. He returned to Campbelltown and to the chain gang and for 'continual misbehaviour' he received a total of fifty-seven lashes in 1839 and three extra months of hard labour. He was suspected of being an accessory to a robbery and sent for six months to the Cleveland Road Party. On 20 May 1839 he was sentenced to twenty-one lashes on the breach for misconduct. On 9 July he was sentenced to thirty-six lashes and returned to the Cleveland Road Party for being an accessory to the robbery of the house of Mr Handling. On 21 January 1840, while a member of the road party and in hospital, he was sentenced to a further thirty-six lashes for gambling in the hospital.

Lazarus Levy of Hobart Town was granted a hawker's licence on 17 September 1841 (*Hobart Town Courier*) and his name appears among those hawkers who organised a public meeting on 19 January 1844 to petition the Governor to cease issuing further licences for hawkers and therefore limit competition.

Lazarus Levy became a member of the Hobart Hebrew Congregation in 1842 and when the synagogue was built, rented seat no. 45 in 1845. The Hobart Synagogue Minutes recorded that he made 'a disgraceful disturbance in synagogue on the Festival of Simchat Torah and he was not to be called up to the Torah until Passover'.

On 21 January 1846 (*Hobart Town Courier*) he was declared to be insolvent and was placed in gaol. On 22 December 1847 he married Rebecca Harris who had been born in London in 1817, the daughter of Wolff and Rachael Harris. The Jewish marriage ceremony took place in his home in Murray Street. She was 'a servant' and he was described as a 'General Dealer'. They had seven children, who were all born in Hobart: Sarah (born 5 November 1848, died in Hobart Town, 19 May 1853), Alfred Lazarus (1851), Rachael (1852), Frederick Benjamin Woolfe (1854–1855), Woolfe Barren, who died in 1855 at the age of two and a half months, Elizabeth (1855), Sarah (1860), and Dinah (1863).

Levy settled in Hobart Town and became a member of the Hobart Synagogue only to be suspended after the High Holydays in 1845 for having 'misconducted himself'. The ban was imposed for six months.

Levy owned a shop in Liverpool Street and then moved to Murray Street next to Valentine the hairdresser. He was well known for his shop's frequent 'sales'. His brothers, Samuel Levy and Philip Levy, followed him to Van Diemen's Land. Philip, a pawnbroker, was nicknamed 'Gentleman Levi' and Samuel owned a clothing shop.

Lazarus Levy served on the Board of the Hobart Synagogue through the 1860s and still appeared in the Hobart Synagogue Ledger in 1874.

He died at the London Family Hotel in Beach Street, Port Melbourne, on 7 February 1884, and was buried at the Melbourne General Cemetery. Rebecca died on 18 June 1882.

Colonial Secretary, Copies of Letters sent within the Colony, 1814–27, 4/3499, 25 July 1818 to 27 February 1819; 4/3504a, 25 October 1821 to 8 March 1822; 4/3504, p. 31; 4/3864, pp. 424/5; CON 31/28, no. 778; CSO 16/16/26; Launceston Police Book, 78/2, p. 335; *Hobart Town Courier*, 21 January 1846, 17 September 1841, 19 January 1844; Minute Book Hobart Synagogue, 17 November 1845.

LEVY, Leah

Convict.

Leah Levy was buried by St John's Church in Parramatta on 31 May 1814.

Mutch Index.

LEVY, Leah (Mary)

Neptune, 1788; Convict; Sentenced to 7 years, Old Bailey, 1784.
Single; Hawker; Height: 170 cm.

Leah Levy was sentenced to transportion in September 1784 for receiving stolen goods. She was listed on board the Lady Penrhyn on 13 March 1787, having embarked at Woolwich. Leah Levy can be mistaken for Amelia Levy as both were known as 'Mary Levy'.

Leah Levy formed a de facto relationship with a prisoner named Gorman. She was convicted in the colony and sent to Newcastle for two years in 1815.

OBSP, 1784, case 375, p. 503; HO 10/2; 4/3494, List of Convicts sent to Newcastle, April 1815.

LEVY, Lewis

b. Aldgate, 1815
Mangles (7), 1835; Convict; Sentenced to 7 years, Old Bailey, 1834.
Single; Labourer; Height: 156 cm.

Dark complexion, hazel eyes, long nose. Could read and write 'a little'. Jew. Tattooed with the letters LL and ML above elbow of right arm. Levy (or Levi) accosted a confectioner who was carrying a load of bulk sugar in Brick Lane. Levy said to him 'You seem to have a very awkward load there', and offered to help carry the sugar with the help of a friend. The two then escaped with eight and a half pounds of sugar valued at five shillings and eight pence together with a handkerchief. Levy was sentenced on 15 December 1834. His father David Levi was a dealer in old clothes. Lewis had two brothers and two sisters.

Lewis Levy arrived in Van Diemen's Land on 1 August 1835. On 11 January 1836, while assigned to Mr Clarke, he was charged with neglect of duty and sentenced to twenty-five lashes. On 17 February 1838 at Launceston as an assigned convict servant to Mr Glover, a similar charge of neglect earned him fifty lashes. On 1 January 1840 he received a ticket of leave and on 12 April 1841 he was given ten days on the treadwheel for 'misconduct'. Later in that same year a certificate of freedom was issued in his name.

On 10 March 1842, in Launceston, he was charged with felony and was acquitted. Lewis Levy travelled from Hobart Town to Sydney on the *Marian Watson* on 7 February 1838. In 1849 Lewis Levy married Margaret Robertson at Scots Church in Sydney.

OBSP, 1834–35. case 244, p. 275; CON 18/16, no. 899; CON 31/28, no. 899; CON 78/2, Launceston Police Book, p. 347; CF 1040; *Hobart Town Courier*, 9 February 1838, 10 December 1841; CS Reports ofVessels Arrived 1838, ML 4/5213.

LEVY, Lewis

1815–1879
Free

Lewis Levy was the nephew of Joseph Levy (q.v.) of Berrima and the brother of Michael, Nathan, John (Henry), Frances (Emanuel) and Sarah. Lewis Levy married Ann Taylor at the Camden Church of England in 1840. The bride (née Armfield) was the sister of Rebecca Armfield who married Noel Chapman (q.v.).

The 1841 Census of New South Wales listed Lewis Levy as living at Yellow Street in Berrima Town and in charge of the Queen Victoria Inn which he eventually inherited from his uncle. The birth of twin daughters to Ann Levy at the Victoria Store in Berrima was announced in the *Sydney Morning Herald* on 17 December 1852. In 1855 Levy received a licence to act as an auctioneer.

Lewis Levy died on 15 October 1879 and was buried in the Jewish cemetery in Rookwood.

Family information Jeannette Tsoulis and Terry Newman.

LEVY, Lewis David

Washington Irving; Free.

Having arrived in the late 1830s, a ticket of leave was granted to Lewis D. Levy at Goulburn on 31 January 1857. He had come free to New South Wales on the *Washington Irving* and received a colonial conviction.

LEVY, Lewis Wolfe

b. London, 1815–1885
1840; Free.
Merchant; 13 children.

Lewis Wolfe Levy was the son of Martha (1787) and Benjamin Wolfe Levy (1773–1829), the nephew of Moses (Lyon) and Deborah Levey and nephew of

Sierlah and Barent Cohen. Lewis Wolfe Levy was therefore a cousin of Solomon Levey (q.v.) and his siblings, and of Lewis Cohen (q.v.) and his siblings.

Lewis Wolfe Levy spent a brief time in Maitland working with his cousins David and Samuel Cohen (qq.v.). In February 1845 he married Julia Solomon (q.v.), who had come to New South Wales with her mother, Rebecca Solomon (q.v.), and eight siblings in 1835. Her father, Samuel Solomon (q.v.), had arrived as a convict in 1833.

In 1845 Tamworth's pioneer general store belonging to Carden Terrence Williams was unable to pay its accumulated debts to David Cohen & Co. of Maitland, and Lewis Wolfe Levy arrived in the ten-year-old settlement to take over the business on behalf of his family. Levy commenced business under his own name and became one of the most important businessmen in Tamworth. In 1849 he was joined in partnership by his cousin Abraham Cohen (q.v.). In Tamworth's earliest years of settlement the other Jewish storekeeper and merchant was William Cohen (q.v.) (the son of Henry Simeon Cohen, q.v.), who married Julia Levy's younger sister Sarah in 1853. A close commercial partnership developed between the two men. During the gold rush Lewis Wolfe Levy and various members of the Cohen family became gold buyers. The firm Cohen and Levy traded in Tamworth until 1905.

In 1864 Levy returned to Maitland and became the dynamic partner in David Cohen & Co. with his cousins, David and Samuel Cohen (qq.v.). Two daughters and two sons of Lewis Wolfe Levy married sons and daughters of David Cohen. Another two daughters of Lewis Levy married sons of Samuel Cohen.

Lewis Wolfe Levy served as the Member for Maitland in the Legislative Assembly, 1871–74. While he lived in Maitland he laid the foundation stone of the local synagogue in 1879. He became a Member of the Legislative Council in 1880 and remained a member until his death. He had served on the board of the Hunter River New Steam Navigation Co., United Insurance Co., the Australian Gaslight Co., the Newcastle Wallsend Coal Co., and the Commercial Banking Co. of Sydney. He was a director of the Prince Alfred Hospital and the Indigent Blind Institution, and trustee of Wynyard Square. He died on 25 January 1885, leaving the large estate of £245 311. Levy was the second president of the secessionist Macquarie Street Synagogue in Sydney.

The children of Lewis and Julia were: May (1848–1914), who married Louis Cohen; Rebecca (1849–1933), who married George Judah Cohen (q.v.); Benn (Wolfe) (1851–1908), who married Zara Cohen; Celia (1852–1854 and buried in Maitland); Lewis (Eliot) (1854–1934), who married Annette Cohen; David (Lewis), (1856–1942), who married May Charlotte (Ray) Moses; Caroline (1857–1911), who married Norman Cohen; Rosalind (Rossi) (1859–1930), who married Neville Cohen; Henry (Harry) (1860–1918), who married Octavia Jacobs; Bertha (1862–1958), who married Burnett Cohen; Louis Tamworth (1864–1931); Herbert (1866–1951), who married Bertha Meyer; Septimus (1867–1934), who married Gwendoline Marks; and Octavius (1870–1949), who married Hannah Joseph.

M. Cohen, 'The Jews of Tamworth', *AJJHS*, vol. 3, no. 7 (1952), p. 350f.; *Australian*, 27 May 1841; *Sydney Chronicle*, 13 January 1848; *Maitland Mercury*, 20 September 1849; C. N. Connolly, 'Lewis Wolfe Levy', *ADB*, vol. 5.

LEVY, Lipman

Free.

Lipman Levy was listed as having donated five shillings to the Sydney Synagogue building fund in 1845. In May 1859 he was in Wellington, New Zealand, and signed a farewell petition in tribute to Abraham Hort snr (q.v.).

LEVY, Lyon (Levy LYONS)

b. London, 1783–1814
Anne II, 1810; Convict; Sentenced to life, Old Bailey, 1808.
Old clothes man.

In the recorded account of the case at the Old Bailey, Lyon Levy is called 'Levy Lyons'. He was found to have clothes and linen that had been reported stolen in Bethnal Green. He was an old clothes dealer who was well known to the police and it was reported that he had resisted arrest in George Street. The 'culprit' had been surrounded by a 'parcel of girls', one of whom had a knife in her hands. The rescue attempt had failed. Levy was accused of house breaking in company with a Robert Whittingham and having stolen items over the value of forty shillings. He was sentenced to death on 13 July 1808 and this was subsequently commuted to transportation for life.

Levy arrived in New South Wales on 27 February 1810. 'Lion' Levy was listed on the General Muster of 1811. On the Muster of 1812 he was listed as working as a labourer at the Hawkesbury.

'Lean Levy' was buried at St John's, Parramatta, on 31 May 1814.

OBSP, 1807–08, case 481, p. 337; HO 10/1; HO 10/3; L. L. Robson, *The Convict Settlers of Australia*, p. 223.

LEVY, Lyon

b. Leadenhall Street, London, 1805
Richmond, 1822; Convict; Sentenced to 7 years, Old Bailey, 1818.
Single; Tailor and errand boy; Height: 162.5 cm.

Fresh complexion, dark grey eyes, brown hair. Lyon Levy stole a hat and gloves belonging to an assistant at a dispensary in Bishopsgate Street. He was caught 'in the act'. He was thirteen years old and told the court 'I beg for mercy'. His parents lived in Whitechapel and his father was a hawker. The boy last lived with a Mr Cohen in Devonshire Square. He had been in custody before for stealing coats in Gillespie Street, Compton. His dossier noted 'put to many trades but does not appear to have the capacity' to learn. He was sentenced on 9 September 1818.

Lyon Levy arrived in Van Diemen's Land in May 1822 and was sent to work as an assigned servant. In March 1823 he was returned to the government. He was arrested within days and found guilty of stealing six brooches valued at six shillings. In January 1824 his master, Mr Dillon, complained about Levy's behaviour, which was described as 'insolence to his master who, it appears, did not employ him regularly. Deemed a suspicious character and sent to the Penitentiary'. On Monday 13 March 1826 Levy was found guilty in the Supreme Court in Hobart Town of stealing 338 yards of printed cotton from the window of the shop of Messrs Murray and Burns. On 27 November 1826 he was given fifty lashes for attempting to 'break the walls' of the Hobart Gaol to escape, and was sent to Macquarie Harbour. One year later (30 November 1827) he was sentenced to 100 lashes and six months in irons for 'indecently exposing his person'. During these six months he received a further 150 lashes for five different charges of refusing to work and for neglect of duty.

On 30 January 1840, after becoming free by servitude, Levy was found guilty of sodomy at the Hobart Supreme Court and was sentenced to death. This was commuted to life imprisonment with the instruction that he was to be sent to Port Arthur for ten years. The Muster of Convicts in Van Diemen's Land in 1841 listed him in Richmond, and noted that he had a conditional pardon.

On 17 October 1848 he received his ticket of leave. A pardon was granted for 'everywhere except the United Kingdom and Van Diemen's Land' on 21 October 1850. This pardon was revoked on 25 November 1851 following his conviction for larceny under £5, for which he was given eighteen months hard labour on 28 October 1851. Levy was classified as an invalid on 2 October 1852 and his pardon restored on 12 March 1853. Two months later he broke a condition of holding a pass by failing to report at the Prisoners' Barracks and he received a sentence of six months hard labour. A further three-month sentence was imposed upon him on 16 May 1854 when he was arrested for being drunk. A ticket of leave was reissued on 21 January 1855 and a free pardon on 4 February 1862. The last entry on his record reads 'Invalid, Port Arthur, Chronic Ophthamalia'.

OBSP, 1817–18, case 1080, p. 342; CON 31/27; *Hobart Town Gazette*, 22 March 1823, 24 September 1825, 18 March 1826, 9 September 1826; *Sydney Gazette*, 18 October 1826, 9 January 1827.

LEVY, Mary Ann

b. 1811
China; Free.

Mary Ann Levy, aged thirty-three, married Michael Curran, who had come to Australia on the *Neptune* (4) as a convict with a life sentence, which he was still serving when they married on 17 December 1844. The Rev. Charles Spencer officiated at Raymond Terrace.

Permission to Marry Book 4/5414.

LEVY, Moses

Rubicon, 1833; Free.
Single.

A steerage passenger from England on the *Rubicon*, Moses Levy arrived in Sydney on 15 November 1833. He was described in the indent as 'A gentleman'. In 1841 Moses Levy was listed as a lodging house keeper of Little Bourke Street. In 1853

'M. Levy' gave five guineas to the building appeal of the Melbourne Hebrew Congregation.

Rubicon Indent 4/5205.

LEVY, Philip (Phillip)

b. London, 1801–1880
Surrey I (5), 1829; Convict; Sentenced to 7 years, Surrey, 1829.
Single; Shoemaker (of women's shoes); Height: 166 cm; 11 children.

Single. Can read and write. A Jew. Philip Levy was the son of Ezekiel and Elizabeth Levy of London. He was convicted of stealing three stoves. He was later charged with receiving stolen property and then discharged. He carried thirty-four shillings with him on the transport. Philip had a sister Ellen and two brothers who came to Van Diemen's Land: Samuel Levy (q.v.), who married Sarah Caspar, and Lazarus Levy (q.v.).

Assigned on arrival in Van Diemen's Land (on 14 December 1829) to the Public Works Department, Philip was commonly known as 'Gentleman Levi', and kept a shop in Liverpool Street. He held a ticket of leave by 1834. Philip Levy married Maria (Mary) Moors, who had been transported on the *Jane* in 1833.

Levy appears to have married a second time. This Jewish marriage ceremony took place on 3 February 1842 at the home of Mrs Redgate, 83 Elizabeth Street, Hobart Town. The bride was Mary Moses (q.v.), a daughter of Emanuel 'Money' Moses (q.v.), who had been transported to Van Diemen's Land with the Caspars for his part in the great Gold Dust Robbery at Covent Garden. Philip, who described himself as a draper at the time of his marriage, was a member of the Hobart Town Hebrew Congregation in 1844 and was able to lend the congregation £20. He is credited with having helped to arrange the order of the dedication service for the congregation and his wife embroidered the curtain in front of the Ark. Philip's sister Ellen Levy (q.v.) married Bertram Nathan (q.v.) on 20 October 1847 at Philip's home.

Mary and Philip Levy had the following children: Priscilla (born 4 October 1842), Emanuel (26 October 1844), Dinah (6 January 1847), Alfred (21 August 1848), Henry Philip (9 October 1850), Montagu (1851), Rachel (13 March 1853), Sarah (6 September 1856), Samuel (11 September 1858), Rebecca Josephine (1 August 1865), and Joseph Angel (14 December 1866).

On 13 January 1869 Priscilla Levy, aged twenty-six, the daughter of Philip Levy of Bathurst Street, married Israel Morris Goldreich (aged thirty-four), who was the minister of the congregation. Levy retired to live in a cottage in Bathurst Street. He was 'a very quiet respected man. Had a large family all of whom married'. Philip Levy left Tasmania for Victoria in 1874 and was presented with a silver tea and coffee service by the Hobart Congregation. He lived in Drummond Street, Carlton, and died on 4 June 1880 and his tombstone stands in the Melbourne General Cemetery together with a memorial to his wife Mary.

VDL Papers, ML, A1059-5, pp. 184, 275; *Surrey I* (5) Appropriation List; CON 31/27; CON 18/19; CON 27/4; *Independent* (Launceston); Allport Collection, Personal Notes, p. 87.

LEVY, Philip

b. London, 1812–1865
Mary III (2), 1830; Convict; Sentenced to 7 years, Middlesex, 1829.
Single; Blacklead- and pencil-maker; Height: 159 cm; 4 children.

Fair complexion, dark brown hair, round face, Roman nose. Jew. Was convicted of stealing a bank note worth £50. Ship board character 'Lazy'.

Philip Levy arrived on 10 April 1830 and on 10 May, at the Prisoners' Barracks in Hobart Town, was charged with being absent from the Muster that preceded church. On 6 August 1830, while still at the Prisoners' Barracks, he received twelve lashes for conveying articles into the cells contrary to orders. From January to May 1831 he was assigned to Mr Ludgater and on 27 May he was sentenced to be sent to Port Arthur for two years for 'using threats of an indelicate nature towards the daughter of Mrs Ludgater'. His record shows that while he was at Port Arthur during 1831 and 1832 he received two sentences for neglect of work for which he was given forty-eight lashes. He returned to Hobart Town on 9 September 1836, and was permitted to apply for a ticket of leave. He held a hawker's licence in 1838–39, but on 16 May 1844 he was fined £2 for hawking without a licence. On 26 June 1845 the *Hobart Town Courier* announced that Philip Levy was insolvent. That same day Philip Levy of Van Diemen's Land sent a Memorial to the Colonial Secretary asking that his brother-in-law Elijah Lazarus (q.v.) be allowed to join him in Hobart Town. The request was granted as there was 'no objection'.

Philip Levy had married Leah Lazarus. Their children were Lewis (born 9 December 1839), Isaac (15 January 1842), Asher (11 August 1844), and Sarah (30 April 1845). In the Van Diemen's Land Census of 1842, Philip Levy of 68 Liverpool Street was listed as a tenant of a brick building in Liverpool Street with wife, son, daughter and two male servants. He advertised 'Tin and Hardware' and called his shop the 'Permanent Tea Kettle'. In 1843 he gave £10 to the Hobart Synagogue building appeal on behalf of himself and his family and in 1845 he rented seat no. 36 in the synagogue. Philip Levy, formerly of Liverpool Street, died in Auckland, New Zealand, on 2 November 1865. He was said to have been seventy years old.

CON 31/28, p. 503; CON 18/15; MM 33/2; VDL Papers, ML, A1059-6; *Hobart Town Courier*, 2 November 1838, 1 November 1839; *Colonial Times*, 4 March 1845; CS 46/4543.

LEVY, Phillip

b. London, 1805–1849
Convict.

The prisoner Phillip Levy, born in London on 2 May 1805, son of Lewis and Elizabeth Levy, was baptised at Norfolk Plains in Van Diemen's Land on 23 July 1831. He died on 30 September 1849 and was buried in the New Norfolk Anglican Cemetery.

LEVY, Samuel (LAZARUS) (JONES) (SAMUEL LAWRENCE) (HENRY LAWRENCE)

b. London, 1765–1849
Admiral Gambier (1), 1808; Convict; Sentenced to life, Staffordshire Assizes, 1806.
Married; Dealer; Height: 178 cm.

Sallow complexion, pock-pitted, black hair, hazel eyes. 'Thief' Samuel Levy, known as 'Long Levy', was the reason for the visit to Australia by Rabbi Aaron Levy (q.v.) in 1830, following a request from Minkie Zanwill, daughter of Judah Leib in London, for a religious divorce from Samuel, son of Mordecai, son of Meir. Levy was arrested in 1806 using the alias Henry Lawrence. He was brought before a Justice of the Peace accused of counterfeiting and passing a fake seven shilling piece at the Wolverhampton Fair on 6 July 1806. At the trial he stated that he lived with his mother at 14 Dean Street, Fetter Lane, Holborn and that he travelled around the country selling hadware and soft goods. He also stated that he had a brother, Samuel Lawrence who lived at 4 Rosa Alley, Bishopsgate Street. He stated that he had no wife. In reality he had been married at the New Synagogue in London in 1801 to Amelia (Minky) née Samuel.

Shortly after his arrival in Sydney on 22 December 1808, Samuel Levy was sent to Van Diemen's Land and on 18 November 1811 was sentenced to death for helping to steal eight sheep. The sentence was commuted to hard labour in New South Wales 'for the term of his natural life'. On 11 February 1812 Levy was sent on the *Duke of Portland* to the new prison settlement at Newcastle. He remained there until the penal station was closed and he was transferred to Port Macquarie on the *Lady Nelson* on 25 September 1823. Levy wrote that he had exhibited 'long suffering and patient endurance' and asked for a pardon. His petition was initially refused and he was assigned to Joseph Raphael (q.v.) in Sydney in 1826. In 1827 he wrote he had 'laboured under much affliction, hard labour and stress. Your petitioner is now at the advanced age of sixty-five years. He was now doing hard labour on the public roads and he was afflicted with Rheumatism and pains in his limbs'. He was in possession 'of a small principal' and was able to support himself.

In 1827 Levy asked to be assigned to Israel Chapman (q.v.) but received no answer. Joseph Raphael wrote that he had applied 'eight times to the Governor' being moved to do so 'on account of his [Levy's] age and of his being of the Jewish persuasion'. Raphael soon regretted his gesture and accused Levy of 'gross insolence and disobedience'. Raphael said Levy had refused to obey orders and even to return money for goods he had sold at the Sydney Market. Levy was ordered to be sent to a chain gang working on the roads at some distance from Sydney. In July 1828 Levy was convicted at Windsor of theft and sent to the distant prison settlement at Moreton Bay for twelve months.

Levy was then assigned to Mr William Phillips, who sent him into the interior to peddle goods.

No religious divorce had been arranged before Levy's transportation in 1808 and in 1830 Rabbi Aaron Levy (q.v.) arrived in Sydney to grant a Get to his long suffering wife Minkie. A Bet Din was convened on 27 September 1831 and 'a divorce document was written, sealed, signed to Samuel who is known as Zanvil ben Mordecai'. There were three members of the Bet Din and two witnesses (whose identity is unknown). Rabbi Aaron Levy then returned to England and the London rabbinate formally received the document. We have no idea the purpose of the elaborate, and costly, expedition. As Dr Jeremy I Pfeffer has written 'Long Levy was over sixty years of age in 1839 and Amelia was at least forty five. Moreover, he had been transported in 1808; the couple had been separated for more than twenty years. And, furthermore it is most unlikely Rabbi Aaron Levy would have undertaken the mission without knowing in advance that the husband Samuel had agreed to give the *Get*'. Pfeffer conjectures that the rabbinic journey may also have been connected with the marriage of John Moses (q.v.) to Mary Connelly.

In April 1835 Levy was arrested in Maitland for having no hawker's licence and he was sent to a prison hulk at Port Macquarie. It was noted that Levy had 'for some years been employed selling different articles privately'. He had £11 5s in his possession and a silver watch and a key with him. Solomon Levien (q.v.) then organised two petitions in Maitland and in the Hunter River District, which were successful. Levy had been placed in the *Phoenix* hulk. The Police Magistrate evidently regretted his sentence and wrote: 'I apprehended Samuel Levy exposing goods for sale in Maitland. Levy's Master did not even hold the necessary licence. [Mr William Phillips of Liverpool Street, Sydney] had previously offended before—he should be deprived of any assigned servants. Levy is an old man and has long served his Probationary Period. [I] recommend him for a ticket of leave'. Sol Levien and James Simmons (q.v.) signed a petition stating that Levy had served for twenty-seven years as a prisoner and, with the exception of a twelve-month sentence to Moreton Bay nearly eight years since, his character for twenty-five years had been 'unimpeachable'. The Colonial Secretary noted on the back of the petition that 'Levy is a very old man—and a Jew—being utterly unaccustomed to agriculture'. As a consequence a ticket of leave for the District of Patrick Plains was issued, and Levy was ordered assigned to someone in Argyle or Bathurst.

Levy married Esther Isaacs (q.v.), the widow of Jacob Isaacs (q.v.), in 1837. On 21 March 1838 'Samuel Levy of Patrick Plains' was acquitted of an accusation involving the theft of a considerable sum of money. Samuel Levy 'of Maitland' gave £10 to the new Sydney Synagogue building fund in September 1839. His ticket of leave was cancelled in June 1838 for harbouring and employing a bushranger.

On 26 September 1838 the property of 'the convict Levi', namely a horse and cart, was offered for sale by the office of the Colonial Secretary. Levy's freedom was restored on 1 November 1839. A conditional pardon was issued on 30 January 1841 and confirmed on 14 October 1847. Samuel Levy had been a prisoner for forty years. He died in Sydney on 8 April 1849 and was buried as a Jew. He was thought to be seventy-eight years old, though he was six years older.

Admiral Gambier (1) Indent 2/8240, p. 107, Ship Indent 4/4004, p. 295; Commutations of Sentence, 4/3492, 18 January 1812, Bundle M/7020; Petition to Brisbane, letter 10, 4/1870; CS In Correspondence, petition no. 73, 23 January 1824; *Sydney Gazette*, 6 November 1811, 18 January 1812, 13 December 1826; *Phoenix* (hulk) Entrance Book (1835), 4/6286 p. 51; *Sydney Gazette*, 13 December 1826; CS Letters Received 1835—Prisoners, 4/2296 petition -35/5545, 4/1953-27, 2/0405-5, 4/1870 letter 10 in 4/3681 p. 36; CS 4/3689 p. 9. 4/3692. Jeremy I Pfeffer,

The First Bet Din Convened in Australia in *AJHSJ* vol18, part 3 pp292–296. p. 425; 4/2318-32/2239; CS 39/4902; CF 40/204; HO 10/52; 4/3899, 1 September 1835, to Port Macquarie; Governors' Despatches, ML A1220, 1840, p. 534; CS 4/2296, 35/5545, 35/5318, 24 July, 27 July 1835; Chronological Register of Convicts at Moreton Bay, no. 1448.

LEVY, Samuel

b. London, 1789–1842
Surrey I (1), 1814; Convict; Sentenced to 7 years, Sussex Assizes, 1813.
Dealer in slops and jewellery; Height: 163 cm.

Dark ruddy complexion, black hair, brown eyes. Samuel Levy was sentenced to transportation for seven years on 28 March 1813.

In the 1818 General Muster Levy was listed as a convict servant assigned to Sir James Jamieson at Windsor. He received a free pardon on 8 February 1819 and left Australia later that same year.

On 6 June 1821 he was sentenced a second time, this time to transportation for life. He had stolen a gown. He arrived in Van Diemen's Land on the *Lord Hungerford*. On this second journey he was known to the authorities by the alias 'John Lee'. The police record noted, however, that he had been transported seven years before and returned to England, and that he had a brother in Sydney named Solomon Levy. The dossier also says that he had served four years on the hulk *Bellerophon*. There are no entries in his Tasmanian dossier. A note on the fly leaf of the Hobart Town Synagogue Minute Book says 'S Levy died on the last day of Passover 22 April 1842'.

Surrey I (1) Indent 4/4004, p. 553; CO 207/1, no. 553.9; HO 10/1; *Sydney Gazette*, 11 December 1819.

LEVY, Samuel

b. 1801
Sir Charles Forbes, 1824; Convict; Sentenced to 7 years, Old Bailey, 1823.
Old clothes dealer.

Levy was transported for seven years for stealing three shillings and sixpence 'from the person'. He had been in gaol before for three months, and had two boxes of possessions on board the transport ship. Samuel Levy had been caught picking the pockets of a spectator in a crowd watching a military review and was sentenced at the Old Bailey on 13 July 1824.

Levy arrived in Van Diemen's Land on 23 November 1824. On 8 August 1825, five days after Levy had been returned from assigned service to a Mr Pritchard, a sentence of twenty-five lashes was decreed for being disorderly in the street, being drunk and for having been insolent to his overseer. Levy remained in government service at the Prisoners' Barracks in Hobart Town during the next three years, and received a further twenty-five lashes for refusing to work in 1828. From March 1829 to 1834 his dossier was duplicated in the Launceston Police book as he was assigned to a number of different homes and farms in the north of the island.

For nine charges of insolence, neglect of duty and absence without permission he received a total of 275 lashes and a month in irons. It is hard to believe that Levy was able to survive this savage official assault.

Levy received his certificate of freedom on 16 July 1831 (*Hobart Town Courier*). On 30 March 1834 he was fined £5 for 'allowing W. Ellis, a convict to remain in his premises', indicating that Levy was no longer on assigned service. On 14 October 1834 he was charged with being drunk and with having assaulting constables Reed and McDonald. Levy was fined £5. On 2 October 1835 he was fined £2 for assaulting Constable Andrews 'in the execution of his duty'. No less than ten breaches of the peace and charges of being drunk were recorded against him between 1837 and 1842. Samuel Levy, 'a laborer' of Launceston, supported the petition of Henry Davis (q.v.) in October 1836 to establish a Jewish cemetery at Cataract Hill. Levy was given permission to work as a hawker on 11 August 1837. His convict record concludes with a note that he was discharged as an invalid from Impression Bay on 14 January 1850 and had been warned that the government would not support him if he was unable to find a livelihood.

OBSP, 1823–24, case 1156, p. 419; CON 31/27, no. 344; VDL Papers, ML, A1059-1, p. 33; HO 10/5; *Hobart Town Courier*, 16 July 1831, 11 August 1837.

LEVY, Samuel

Medway, 1827; Free.
Married; Dealer; 4 children.

Samuel Levy came as a free settler to Van Diemen's Land with his wife and four children in August 1827. He was the licensee of the Caledonia Hotel at 40 Elizabeth Street, Hobart Town. On 28 November 1855 the *Mercury* in Hobart Town reported that he was living in England and that a presentation had been made to him by friends prior to his departure from Australia.

Hobart Town Gazette, 20 August 1827, 13 February 1845.

LEVY, Samuel

b. Chatham, 1805
Tortoise, 1842; Convict; Sentenced to 14 years, Maidstone, Kent, 1841.
Dyer; Height: 163 cm.

Sallow complexion, dark hair and whiskers, dark eyes, large nose, broad chin. Jew. Can read and write. Samuel Levy was sentenced to transportation for stealing a handkerchief valued at two shillings and sixpence, and threepence, the property of a sailor. He was convicted on 1 July 1841. Levy had been in prison a number of times for buying supplies and goods issued to soldiers. He had been fined £24 for concealing a deserter and, unable to pay, had been imprisoned for six months.

Samuel Levy arrived in Hobart Town on 19 February 1842: his initial period of probation, served at Salt Water Creek, was completed without incident on 19 February 1844. He received his ticket of leave on 22 February 1848. On 29 November he was convicted at the Hobart Town Quarter Session for receiving a stolen writing desk and other articles knowing them to have been stolen. He was sentenced to be transported for fourteen years and to be sent to Norfolk Island for three years. At Norfolk Island he was disciplined for not answering his name when called on 25 June 1851, and on 27 September 1852 he was given seven days hard labour for 'disobedience'. Levy was returned to Tasmania in 1853 and was assigned to Mr John Lynch. On 17 December 1853 he was sentenced to nine months hard labour in chains for wilfully destroying his master's property and for having thrown a crowbar at him. Despite two 'minor' acts of disobedience at the Prisoners' Barracks, a ticket of leave was approved on 2 December 1856. A conditional pardon was granted on 6 July 1858.

CON 14/13, no. 4078.

LEVY, Samuel

b. London, 1815
Waterloo, 1835; Convict; Sentenced to 7 years, Old Bailey, 1834.
Single; Bricklayer's labourer; Height: 165 cm.

Fresh freckled complexion, black hair, grey eyes, long nose. Pickpocket. Could read and write. Hulk report 'Bad'. Surgeon's report 'Quiet and orderly'. Samuel Levy had been 'spotted' by a police constable on the Old Street Road and was followed. Within a few minutes Levy had stolen a handkerchief, valued at five shillings, from the pocket of a Mr John Williams, who was unaware that he had been robbed until he was confronted with his property and the thief. Levy was nineteen years old.

Upon arrival in Van Diemen's Land on 2 March 1835 Samuel Levy was placed on the assignment list to the Public Works Department in Ross. On 2 May 1835 he received twenty-four lashes for 'repeated idleness'. On 6 June 1835 he was sentenced to thirty-five lashes for his 'insolence to the overseer'. On 18 January 1836 he was still assigned to the Public Works Department when he was accused of stealing a shirt and subsequently discharged. He spent ten days in solitary confinement for disobedience of orders on 24 February 1837. By 15 April he was an assigned servant to Mr Dawson and was reprimanded for being in a public house. He was returned to the Survey Department, and on 7 September he was found to be absent from the Prisoners' Barracks and placed on the treadmill for six days. On 26 February 1838 he was found gambling and removed from his work as a messenger for the Colonial Secretary's Office and sentenced to three days hard labour on the roads. The offence was repeated and on 27 July he was sent to the Bagdad Road Party for three months. On 6 November 1838 he was suspected of stealing some pennies and given six months in a road chain gang. He was once again allowed to work as an assigned servant. On 9 September 1839 he was sentenced to twelve months hard labour, having accused his mistress Mrs Harrison of being drunk. He was sent to the Cleveland road party and then to Launceston. A certificate of freedom was issued in 1841. It was noted that he was 'free by servitude'.

OBSP, 1834, case 765, p. 448; CON 18/21; Allport Collection; *Waterloo* Indent, ML,VDL, 1059-7, p. 10, no. 883; also CON 31/8, no. 883; HO 10/52; CF 418.

LEVY, Samuel

b. London, 1821–1870
1843; Free.
Single; Dealer, clothier; 11 children.

Samuel, the son of Ezekiel and Elizabeth Levy (née Nathan) of London, had two brothers and a sister. They were Philip Levy (q.v.), Lazarus Levy (q.v.), and Ellen Levy (q.v.). Samuel Levy was nicknamed 'Intermediate Levy'. Samuel Levy married the 20-year-old Sarah Casper on 28 January 1846 at his residence in Murray Street, Hobart Town. It was Van Diemen's Land's eleventh Jewish marriage. Samuel was listed as a bachelor and twenty-five years old. He was a member of the Hobart Hebrew Congregation in 1843 and gave £3 3s to the building appeal. He rented seat no. 93 in the synagogue when it was dedicated in 1845. His last entry in the synagogue ledger was in 1870.

All the children of Samuel and Sarah Levy eventually settled in Victoria. They were: Alfred (born 4 December 1845), Andrew (10 March 1848), Elizabeth (Joel) (28 October 1849), George (1852), Matilda (21 November 1853), Ellis Reuben (2 April 1854), Grace (Rosenberg) (22 October 1855), Harriet Rosetta (17 May 1857), Henry (25 March 1859), Edmund (6 September 1860), and Albert Edward (9 November 1866).

Samuel Levy of Murray Street was listed in the Hobart Town Directory's list of householders who paid £10 a year on rates and who were entitled to vote for the Legislative Council. Levy died at his home in Liverpool Street, Hobart on 22 April 1870 and was buried at the Harrington Street Jewish Cemetery. Sarah died on 4 March 1907 at the age of eighty-one, and was buried at the Melbourne General Cemetery.

Many family details from the research of Mrs Joan Creighton, Melbourne.

LEVY, Samuel

b. Aldgate, 1822
Cressy, 1843; Convict; Sentenced to 7 years, Central Criminal Court, 1842.
Single; Clothes dealer; Height: 160 cm.

Fresh complexion, black hair, dark eyes, long large nose and long chin. Could read but not write. Samuel Levy was sentenced for 'stealing seventy-two pounds weight of candles from Mr Burrow's confectioner's shop in Houndsditch'.

Samuel Levy's initial period of labour was for eighteen months and he was assigned to the road gang at Bucklands. This first sentence was more than doubled for a series of six offences. After repeated punishments, and after having been assigned to the coal mines on the Tasman Peninsula in August 1844, he was struck off the probation records in April 1845 and sent to Port Arthur as punishment for insubordination and misconduct. There he remained through 1846 until March 1847. On 26 August 1847 he was convicted at Oatlands for receiving stolen goods under the value of £5. He was sentenced to twelve months hard labour and returned to Port Arthur. Soon after he returned to Hobart Town he was convicted of petty larceny and sent to the Cascades. Levy spent all of 1849 and 1850 in Hobart Town as an assigned servant and on 27 May 1850 he was sentenced to three months hard labour for insolence to his overseer. He received a certificate of freedom on 22 February 1851. On 31 August 1851 he was sentenced at Hobart to ten years colonial transportation for burglary and sent to Norfolk Island from Port Arthur on the *Tortoise*, arriving on 21 November. Levy stayed on Norfolk Island for thirty months. His behaviour on the island was 'tolerable'. He was returned to Tasmania in 1854, where he was 'not to enter service south of Oatlands nor in the District of Launceston'. Levy received a ticket of leave on 16 January 1855. On 7 April 1855 he was convicted of obtaining goods by false pretences and received an eighteen-month sentence, which he spent at Impression Bay Prisoners' Station on the Tasman Peninsula. He, once again, qualified for a ticket of leave on 5 May 1857 and a colonial conditional pardon was approved on 11 May 1858. It had taken him sixteen years to complete the initial sentence of seven years transportation.

CON 33/40, no. 9641; CON 37/7, no. 2187; CON 39/2; Tasmanian Papers, ML, 197, 1852.

LEVY, Samuel

1845; Free.
Dealer.

Samuel Levy, a free immigrant, was convicted in February 1846 of obtaining goods under false pretences. He was sentenced to six months in Sydney Gaol with the last week of each month to be spent in solitary confinement. The *Sydney Morning Herald* reported that Samuel Levy and David Dougherty, 'two notorious Sydney thieves', were apprehended in the possession of a stolen coat, which they had bought from the pawnbroker and dealer Abraham Davis (q.v.). Dougherty was acquitted.

Bell's Life in Australia, 7 February 1846; *Sydney Morning Herald*, 1 June 1847.

LEVY, Samuel

b. London, d. 1850
Free.
Single; Dealer.

In 1838 Samuel Levy of Launceston was granted a hawker's licence for Launceston. Samuel Levy married Rachael Moses (q.v.), a minor, on 29 June 1842. Rachael was the sister of Mary Moses, who married Philip Levy (q.v.). The celebration was the fifth Jewish marriage in Van Diemen's Land. Levy briefly owned a clothing shop in Liverpool Street before moving to the north of the island. Samuel Levy signed a petition on 19 September 1843 for the release of the debtor Isaac Jacobs (q.v.), who was in debtors'prison in Launceston. In June 1844 he gave £5 to the Launceston Synagogue building fund and was one of the trustees of the Launceston Synagogue at its dedication in 1846.

Samuel Levy died in Launceston on 16 September 1850.

CO 280/157; *Launceston Examiner*, 29 June 1844; *Hobart Town Courier*, 25 May 1838.

LEVY, Samuel Michael

Free.
Married; Dealer; 4 children.

Samuel Michael Levy was listed as a 'paint manufacturer'on his daughter Miriam's death certificate. He was married to Sarah, née Simmons (1790–1883), who had two children, Julia and Alexander, from her previous marriage to Barnett Barnard (in London). Samuel Michael Levy and Sarah had four children: John, Michael Samuel (c. 1831–1894), Miriam (c. 1834–1911), and Samuel. The family preserved the tradition that Samuel Michael Levy had served at the Battle of Trafalgar. Miriam became the wife of George (Godfrey) Alexander (q.v.) in 1850.

Samuel Levy died on 19 October 1851 and his monument is the oldest Jewish gravestone in the Geelong Jewish Cemetery. Sarah died on 15 January 1883. Her residence was the Provincial Hotel at 301 Brunswick Street, Fitzroy. Sarah was buried in the Jewish section of the Melbourne General Cemetery.

LEVY, Saul Hyman

Free.
Married; Merchant.

Levy opened a shop in Sydney in early 1843 and advertised that he would 'buy phosphorus in any quantity', presumably to make matches. On 27 March 1843 the *Sydney Morning Herald* announced that Mrs S. H. Levy of 33 Castlereagh Street had died in childbirth. Levy sailed from Sydney on the *Shamrock* on 24 April 1844.

Subsequently, Saul Levy, a 'merchant', applied to the Hobart Hebrew Congregation for permission to marry Mrs Nancy Redgate (q.v.), a shopkeeper and widow of Liverpool Street, on 21 July 1844. The committee decided that Mrs Redgate must 'ask permission'—which was apparently granted. The wedding, which was Van Diemen's Land's eighth Jewish marriage ceremony, took place on 20 August 1844. Saul H. Levy rented seat no. 31 when the synagogue opened in 1845.

'Solomon' Hyman Levy announced in a large advertisement on 18 February 1845 that he held the licence for the Caledonian Hotel in Elizabeth Street, Hobart Town.

Sydney Morning Herald, 3 March 1843, 27 September 1843, 24 April 1844; *Hobart Town Courier*, 6 February 1845.

LEVY, Sizer de

b. 1812
Surrey (3), 1833; Convict; Sentenced to life, Middlesex, 1832.
Married; Butcher; Height: 170 cm.

Dark complexion, black hair, oval face, long visage, retreating forehead, black eyebrows, brown eyes, aquiline nose, wide mouth, lips projecting, short chin. A Jew. A 'Mahometan' [sic] *sailor, unable to speak English, was picked up by a prostitute who herself was not able to speak very much English. She took him to a brothel in Essex Street, Whitechapel. The sailor gave the girl three shillings—after which Sizer de Levi, with two other men, burst in and robbed the sailor of his remaining money. The police intervened as the argument continued outside in the street. Sizer denied the episode. He said that he worked very hard as a butcher for the sake of his mother and father. He was condemned to death on 5 July 1832 and the sentence was commuted to transportation for life. He had a wife, Ellen, who lived in Northampton.*

Sizer de Levy had a ticket of leave in October 1844 and received permission to marry Ann Summerfield who had come as a convict to Van Diemen's Land on the *Navarino*. He received a conditional pardon in 1849. The official comment on his application for mercy was: 'Has served nearly 15 years—clear of offence for 18 months'.

OBSP 1832–33, case 1420, p. 592; CON 18/20; Description Book, CON 31/39, no. 1617; Permission to Marry Book, CON 52/2, p. 428; HO 10/60, p. 440.

LEVY, Walter

b. London, 1799–1829
Neptune I (1), 1818; Convict; Sentenced to life, Old Bailey, 1817.
Single; Slop seller; Height: 164 cm.

Dark ruddy freckled complexion, brown hair, hazel eyes. Walter Levy was transported for having stolen a watch and chain from a pedestrian in a London street. After the theft, he had run straight into the arms of a passing watchman. He had also been noticed in the company of another pickpocket. He was sentenced on 29 October 1817.

Levy arrived in Sydney in May 1818 and was assigned to the service of Mr D'Arcy Wentworth. On 8 September 1821 he was employed at the New Lumber Yard and victualled from 'H. M. Magazines'. The Colonial Secretary's records show that in April 1824 Levy was an assigned convict working as a carpenter. On 26 April 1826 the *Sydney Gazette* reported that he had been sent to work in irons for three months for burglary. In October 1827 he was sent on the *Lucy Anne* from Sydney under Lieutenant Taylor's command as one of eight 'trusty' prisoners to prepare the way for the establishment of a new settlement at Western Port in Victoria. He was described as a carpenter. Within a year he was back in Sydney and on 15 September 1829 Walter Levy, 'a carpenter' and a convict, died at the hospital in Sydney. He was buried by the parish of St James, Sydney.

OBSP, 1816–17, case 1525, p. 502; *Neptune I* (1) Indent 4/4006, p. 58f.; HO 1 May 1818; CS 4/5781, p. 86; Deaths' Book 4/4549; 4/7032 (Western Port Bundle) 1826–1827; *Sydney Gazette*, 26 April 1826, 15 September 1829.

LEWIN, James

b. London, 1794–1854
Clyde I (2), 1832; Convict; Sentenced to 7 years, Surrey, 1830.
Single; Attorney's clerk; Height: 161 cm.

Dark complexion, dark brown hair, balding, chestnut eyes. Jew. Could read and write. Described on the ship's indent as 'A London attorney's clerk' who was transported for embezzlement, James Lewin was sentenced at the Surrey Quarter Sessions on 25 October 1830.

James Lewin arrived in New South Wales on 27 August 1832. He was sent from the Hyde Park Barracks to the *Phoenix* hulk. His behaviour on board the hulk was described as 'good'. Lewin was sent to Moreton Bay on the *Isabella* on 26 December 1832 and by 1836 he was the holder of a ticket of leave. In the 1837 General Return of Convicts in New South Wales he was listed as a government servant at Port Macquarie. He received his certificate of freedom on 10 April 1838.

An 'I.' Lewin was appointed the representative of the Sydney Synagogue in the town of Windsor on 13 November 1843. James Lewin was a member of the Hobart Synagogue in 1844 and a subscriber to the Tasmanian Hebrew Benevolent Institute in 1847.

James Lewin, aged sixty, was buried in Hobart Town by the synagogue on 20 July 1854.

Clyde Printed Indent, p. 101, no. 32-1818-144, 4/6282; TL 36/1615; Sydney Synagogue Minute Book, p. 126, 13 November 1843; *Australian*, 10 April 1838.

LEWIS, Abraham (Judah or Hugh NATHAN)

b. London, 1820–1896
Fairlie (1), 1834; Convict; Sentenced to 7 years, Middlesex, 1833.
Single; Barber; Height: 161 cm.

Sallow complexion, brown eyes, brown hair. No education. Heavily tattooed: two flags; death's head and bones; Crown of Glory on upper hand, J. N. inside lower right arm. A cripple. Transported for stealing a silk handkerchief in a shop. Lewis said that he had hoped to buy secondhand shoes so that he could walk more easily. He had a previous conviction for theft, with a fourteen-day sentence.

Abraham Lewis arrived in Port Jackson on 15 February 1834 and on 19 March was sent to the *Phoenix* hulk from the Hyde Park Barracks. He was classified as an invalid and was to be sent to Port Macquarie on 19 May. His conduct was 'tolerable'. The 1837 General Return of Convicts in New South Wales listed him as a government servant at Port Macquarie. Lewis was subsequently sent on the *Governor Phillip* to Moreton Bay. A certificate of freedom was issued on 9 January 1844.

On 23 August 1849 Lewis appeared before the Supreme Court in Sydney having stolen thirty silver watches from the shop of a watchmaker in George Street and melted them down together with a quantity of watch cases. When arrested, he declared 'it would be the ruin of me and my family'. He was sentenced to seven years hard labour on the roads.

His final story was told in the *Australian Hebrew* of 17 January 1896:

Judah Nathan alias Abraham Lewis committed suicide by jumping from Holsworthy Bridge into the George River because he was not re-admitted in Sydney's Monte fiore Home. He had been expelled in May 1890 for drunkenness. He had been transported to New South Wales at the age of fourteen and after sixty years in the colony was admitted to the Montefiore Home in 1889. He was identified as Hugh Nathan known as 'Louis the Barber' in Liverpool where he carried on his business.

OBSP, 1832–33, case 1044, p. 569; *Fairlie* Printed Indent, p. 21; Ships to Moreton Bay 4/3899, p. 86; *Phoenix* (hulk) Entrance Book 1834, p. 24, 4/6286; *Phoenix* (hulk) Return 4/4534; Corrective Services, Calendars of Prisoners Tried on Criminal Charges, 1847–1856, Supreme Court 4/6449; CF 44/0026; *Australian Hebrew*, 17 January 1896; CF 4/4388.

LEWIS, David (LOUIS)

b. London, 1813
Lady MacNaghten, 1835; Convict; Sentenced, King's County, Ireland, 1834.
Single; Soldier; Height: 175 cm.

Sallow complexion. Brown hair. Dark grey eyes. No previous convictions. Listed as 'Protestant' at the time of his conviction, but as a Jew in colonial records, Lewis was convicted on 23 June 1834 for stealing a watch. He could read and write.

David Lewis arrived in Sydney on 30 October 1835. He was brought to Sydney on 19 March 1841 from Liverpool and sent on to the Hyde Park Barracks. A certificate of freedom was issued on 22 September 1842.

Darlinghurst Gaol Admission Book 4/6534, no. 491; *Lady MacNaghten* Printed Indent, 35-2415-33; CF 4/4377, 42/1699.

LEWIS, George

Free.
Labourer.

"In November 1840, at the Windsor Police Court, George Lewis, a diminutive Jew, appeared before their worships to answer the complaint of another of the tribe of Israel and ornamented with a pair of whiskers and specks that could not disgrace the phiz of a Bond Street lounger, for absenting himself from his hired service. 'Poor little Mo' in a most emphatic manner, denied the charge, but the Bench believing otherwise, he was sentenced to four years imprisonment."

Commercial Journal and Advertiser, 7 November 1840.

LEWIS, Isaac

b. London
William, 1842; Free.
Single; Refiner.

Isaac Lewis, a 'Jew', was committed for trial on 25 July 1842 for larceny at Parramatta. He was sent to the Hyde Park Barracks and then to the Darlinghurst Gaol.

Darlinghurst Gaol Entrance Book 1842, no. 952, 4/6534.

LEWIS, Levy (Lewis)

b. London, 1808
Lady Kennaway (2), 1836; Convict; Sentenced to 7 years, Central Criminal Court, 1835.
Single; Clothes keeper; Height: 166 cm.

Dark ruddy complexion, dark hair, hazel eyes. Slender. Breast hairy, mark of severe scald on chest. Large scar under left wrist. Convicted for stealing a breast pin. Levy Lewis was convicted on 23 November 1835.

A ticket of leave was granted to Levy Lewis in January 1841.

Lady Kennaway (2) Printed Indent, p. 137, no. 36-2067; Description Book 4/6299, no. 1080; TL 41/11.

LINCOLN, Isaac Lazarus

b. Lincoln, d. 1850
1834; Free.
Married; Clothier; 8 children.

The son of Jonas and Rosceia Lazarus of Lincoln, Isaac Lazarus Lincoln was a grand nephew of Nathan Philip Levi (q.v.) of Adelaide. Lincoln and his wife Nancy (née Levi) first settled in New South Wales. The Sydney Synagogue's Birth Book records Jonas, born in Sydney on 6 April 1835; Solomon, born in Penrith on 3 April 1837; and Michael, born in Illawarra on 2 December 1839; after which the family moved to the new settlement of Port Phillip. Lincoln became a draper in Collins Street and then an auctioneer and commission agent. Further children recorded in the Melbourne Hebrew Congregation's Birth Book were Ellen (born 9 July 1841, the first Jewish child to be born in Melbourne), Edward (26 May 1843), Moses (2 May 1845), Asher (15 June 1847), and Rosa (3 July 1849).

On 5 April 1845 the *Port Phillip Gazette* reported that Lincoln was one of five Jewish dealers who had been fined five shillings for exposing goods on the public footpath in front of their shops. Lincoln's drapery store did not flourish. On 21 February 1842 he was fined twenty shillings and costs for not showing a light in front of his hotel, the Builders' Arms. In April 1842 his application for a licence for the Edinburgh Hotel in Collins Street was refused. Lincoln moved to Seymour and once more applied for a licence, only to be refused again.

Isaac's brother, David Lazarus Lincoln, married his cousin Ann Levi (or Levy), both of Maryborough, on 20 February 1856. Ann Levy was illiterate and was the daughter of Joseph Levy.

Lincoln was willing to circumcise the sons of non-Jewish women who were married to Jews so that the children would not be lost to the Jewish community and this caused a confrontation between him and elements in the Melbourne Hebrew Congregation (including the Rev. Rintel, q.v.) who disapproved. Lincoln was also the first in Australia to use chloroform at circumcisions.

Lincoln faced insolvency proceedings due to non-existent book-keeping practices, extravagance and gambling debts, and was formally discharged from bankruptcy on 12 February 1849, paying six shillings and twopence farthing in the pound. Lincoln left Melbourne with his family for California, and he and his family were drowned, save for his first-born son Jonas, when they were shipwrecked on the voyage home.

Melbourne Morning Herald, 12 February 1849, 27 October 1849.

LINCOLN, Nancy (née LEVI)

b. Liverpool, d. 1850
1834; Free. Married; 8 children.

Nancy was the wife of Isaac Lazarus Lincoln (q.v.) and cousin of John Levi (Levy, q.v.)

LINDENTHAL, Walter L.

b. London 1847; Free.
Single; 'Professor' of German and Hebrew.

Lindenthal's father served as a reader in the London New Synagogue. Lindenthal was in Australia between 1847 and 1849. He advertised in the *Sydney Morning Herald* of 11 September 1847 that he was 'from London', and working as a professor of Hebrew and German at 224 Elizabeth Street North, King Street. He had 'practiced [*sic*] with satisfaction for many years in London'. The German version of his advertisement included a number of elementary spelling errors. At the conclusion of the High Holydays he was permitted to give an 'able discourse' at the York Street Synagogue. In November it appears he attempted to establish an elementary school for Jewish children in Sydney. The ambitious project was rejected at a meeting of the community and on 27 November he wrote:

> The long impolitic and rude controversy, as well as the great noise and confusion which prevailed at the public meeting on Wednesday last, having prevented Mr Walter L. Lindenthal claiming a hearing, he begs by these means to resign being a candidate for the mastership of the long proposed school now spoken of by a few persons as likely to be carried out.

Three days later he wrote an apology for his words as 'somewhat rash and unwarranted'.

Lindenthal was invited to Melbourne. On 21 December 1847, 'The Committee of the Melbourne Congregation having heard of your leaving Sydney for Goulburn' offered him the job of cantor and headmaster of a soon to be established Jewish school. The president Asher Hymen Hart (q.v.) wrote: 'In order that there may be no mistake I wish you to understand that a commercial not a classical education is required among our members who being engaged in business wish their children to be educated accordingly'. In January 1848, he was appointed cantor at the salary of £65 a year with the understanding that he would establish a congregational school. He relinquished an extra £10 a year rather than be compelled to read the Torah scroll during the service. The president of the Melbourne

Congregation wrote to the Chief Rabbi in London about 'a young man, son of Mr Lindenthal, of the New Synagogue to teach Hebrew and English to the children who are mostly very young'. In September 1848, Lindenthal's employment was terminated. The school was not a success and his knowledge of Hebrew was too limited. In September 1848 the congregational officers were horrified to learn that Lindenthal had been summoned to the Court of Requests by his manservant for non-payment of his salary. It was deemed 'a disgraceful position in which he had placed himself', and on 15 October 1848 Lindenthal was told to vacate the premises of the synagogue.

Lindenthal moved to Van Diemen's Land and on 5 January 1849 the *Melbourne Morning Herald* noted that he was due to deliver a series of lectures at the Hobart Town Synagogue. The *Hobart Town Advertiser* wrote of his 'high character' and 'attainments'. The *Melbourne Morning Herald* of 5 January 1849 commented:

'We could not help laughing outright when we read this notice about this erratic gentleman'.

On 28 February 1849 Lindenthal published a series of four lectures (sixty pages) on the origin and progress of the English language 'by kind permission of his Excellency Sir W.T. Denison Kt', the Lieutenant Governor, who was thanked effusively in the preface.

Lindenthal evidently returned to England.

M. H. Kellerman, 'Walter L. Lindenthal', *AJJHS*, vol. 3, no. 3 (1950), p. 109f.

LINDO, Alexander

b. London, d. 1838
Thomas Lawry, 1837; Free.
Married; Attorney; 3 children.

Alexander Lindo was the son of David Alexander Lindo and Matilda (née Salomons). His wife was Clara, née Brandon (q.v.), whose mother, Matilda Salom died just after Alexander's arrival in Sydney with his wife and two children on 3 April 1837. An infant daughter, Mathilda Lindo, aged two, was buried at the Devonshire Street Jewish Cemetery on 4 April 1837. A son, Solomon, was born on 12 April 1837, and registered as a 'Hebrew'. On 9 June Lindo gave notice that he was applying for admittance as an attorney. The following month he was admitted to the Supreme Court. On 6 March 1838 the family moved to Regent Terrace in Hunter Street.

On 1 April 1838 the *Sydney Gazette* reported that Mr Lindo had drowned when his leisure craft *The Pet* sank on Sydney Harbour in a squall. (The boat was later raised and was found to be undamaged.) The following year, Clara Lindo wrote to the Colonial Secretary about an unfinished project prepared by her husband. He had written the first Digest of New South Wales Law. She wanted to know if she had it finished whether the government would purchase a minimum number of copies. She described herself as a widow with children to support. The answer was affirmative and, if published, the colonial administration would take thirty copies at two guineas each. On 23 October 1839 Clara Lindo applied to the Colonial Secretary to go to Moreton Bay. One of her children, Alexander J. Lindo, died at Ipswich in 1859. Solomon Lindo died at Sydney on 26 October 1884 at the age of forty-seven.

Ship Indent 4/5212; Correspondence, 39/5317, CS Letters Received 1839, 39/11557, in 4/2456.5

LINDO, Clara

Thomas Lawry, 1837; Free.
Married; 2 children.

Clara, her husband Alexander (q.v.), and their two children arrived in Sydney on 3 April 1837. Her daughter Mathilda was buried at the Devonshire Street Jewish Cemetery on 4 April 1837. On 1 April 1838, Clara's husband was reported to have drowned in Sydney Harbour.

Ship Indent 4/5212; *Sydney Gazette*, 1 April 1838.

LINDSEY

Free.

A mysterious entry in the *Registry of Flash Men* for 1844 described: 'Lindsey, Kent Street, near Erskine Street, a receiver advertising in dealings with Simon Hart. This man tho' is a Jew.—Daniels suspected him and spoke to him in Hebrew and the fellow answered immediately. So much for Mr Lindsey. The man had several of Beaumont's [stolen] watches'.

W. A. Miles, *Registry of Flash Men* for 1844, p. 96.

LIPMAN, Lewis (Louis)

b. London, 1823–1894
William Turner, 1841; Free.
Single; Storekeeper; 18 children.

The son of Rachel and Joseph Lipman of London and originally named Lipman Lipman. The nineteen year old migrant Lewis came to Australia sponsored by Alan Campbell Esq. to assist him at Patrick Plains near Muswellbrook. In the ship's log he is listed as a 'farm servant'. He was literate and claimed to be able to speak and write Hebrew. His future father-in-law Abraham Moses (q.v.) had a brother Isaac. Sarah Moses, his future wife, had arrived on 17 March 1840 with her family. Sarah was 16 years old at the time of her arrival.

Lewis Lipman was active in intercolonial trade and travelled from Sydney to Van Diemen's Land and Port Phillip in 1843 and 1844. He gave £10 to the Sydney Synagogue building appeal in 1845. While still living in Muswellbrook, Lipman married Sarah (Moss) Moses (q.v.) at the Sydney Synagogue on 23 June 1847. Sarah signed her marriage certificate with a mark. Lipman gained an auctioneer's licence in Sydney in 1848. The children of Lewis and Sarah Lipman were Phillip (born at Patrick Plains 10 June 1848 and who died in 1855); Abraham (31 December 1849); Joseph (10 April 1853), born at 58 Phillip Street, Sydney; Albert (26 August 1856), born at 26 O'Connell Street, Sydney; Rachel (31 March 1858); and Joshua (1860), at 199 York Street. Sarah Lipman died in April 1865 and was buried at the Devonshire Street cemetery.

Lewis Lipman's second marriage was to Sarah Rosetta Levy, the daughter of A. J. Levy and Catherine (née Phillips) on 3 May 1866. They were to have thirteen children, although many of them would die in infancy. Philip Joseph, the second of Lewis's children to bear that name, was born on 18 May 1867 at the family home at 199 York Street, Sydney. Julia Kate Lipman was born on 27 September 1868 and lived for eleven months. David was born on 7 February 1870, Albert Lipman on 14 May 1872, Edward in 1873 (died in infancy), Rosetta in 1875, Julia [Juliette] in 1876 (died 2 November 1897), Alice in 1879 (died that same year), Rebecca in 1880, Ruby in 1881, Montefiore in 1882, Ethel in 1884, and Percy in 1885 (died the same year).

From 1876 Lipman lived at 125 Elizabeth Street. He worked for Samuel Cohen, the manager of the London Loan and Mortgage Co. From 1879 to 1881 the family lived at 109–125 Elizabeth Street, where Lipman was described as an accountant. From 1884 to 1890 they lived at 437 Riley Street, where Lipman was variously described as an 'accountant', 'clerk', 'financier'and 'pawnbroker'. In 1894 Lipman lived at 422 Elizabeth Street.

Lipman was deeply involved in congregational life and served as president of the Hebrew Mutual Benefit Society (*the Chevra Kadisha*) and secretary of the Jewish Denominational School.

Lipman was one of the stalwarts of the breakaway Macquarie Street congregation in 1859 and became its first honorary secretary and, in 1863, its paid secretary. When Lipman retired from this post in 1872 the committee paid tribute to him, 'not only for his years of work as a paid official, but for past services performed for the congregation for years previous to his receipt of the salary now drawn by him and extra services performed by him beyond his duty as secretary'. He remained a member of the secessionist congregation until its closure in 1877.

Lewis Lipman, who was a Justice of the Peace, died at his residence at 422 Elizabeth Street, near Devonshire Street, on 8 July 1894 and was buried at the Rookwood Cemetery. His sons Abraham, Joseph, Joshua, Philip, David and Albert and wife Sarah were mentioned in the *Sydney Morning Herald*'s funeral notice. Lipman had fathered 21 children, of whom at least 10 had predeceased him.

Sydney Morning Herald, 14 September 1843, 16 January 1844; *Sydney Chronicle*, 13 January 1848; *Maitland Mercury*, 18 December 1847; Col Choat, A Leaf on our Tree—a brief biography of Lewis Lipman, family history, held by Col Choat, Mt Colah, NSW and published in AJHSJ vol 17part 4 p. 463 ff.

LISSOUR, Caro

b. Breslau, 1791
Lady Castlereagh, 1818; Convict; Sentenced to 7 years, Portsmouth, 1817.
Single; Servant and teacher; Height: 157 cm.

Fair, pale, pock-pitted complexion, brown hair, hazel eyes. Caro Lissour was sentenced at Portsmouth on 9 October 1817.

Caro Lissour arrived in New South Wales on 1 May 1818. Evidence was tendered at the Bigge Commission about Caro Lissour,'a convict lately employed as an overseer and dismissed for theft'. Lissour brought charges against the Deputy Assistant Commissioner Cordeaux of pilfering stores and accepting poor-quality wheat into government stores. In response Cordeaux said Lissour stole liquor and because of this he was returned to the convict barracks and there was a formal court martial because of the charges. On 4 February 1820 Lissour brought charges against Mr W. Harvey, the confidential clerk of Mr Cordeaux, who Lissour alleged had perpetrated the frauds. Lissour's evidence was proved to be correct and he was permitted to transmit to the authorities his 'long list of charges', which he had written while he was incarcerated at the Prisoners' Barracks after his dismissal.

Before the formal hearing could he held the Governor and the Commissioner discovered that Lissour had 'disappeared' from the colony by quietly leaving on the *Claudine*.

Lady Castlereagh Indent 4/4006, p. 47; Bigge Appendix, BT Box 10, pp. 4120, 4218, Box 20, p. 3506, Box 21, p. 2924, Box 22, pp. 4256–7.

LOW, James (Jemmy the Jew)

1850; Free.
Single.

James Low alias 'Jemmy the Jew' was accused of stealing two horses from the stable of the Royal Oak Inn in Queens Street, Melbourne, according to the *Melbourne Morning Herald* of 17 September 1851.

LUBLIN, John

1840; Free.
Single; Cloth cap maker.

On 2 May 1840 Sydney's *Commercial Journal and Advertiser* wrote that John Lublin had 'just arrived from England to establish himself as 'Military, Naval and Fancy Cap maker and Furrier at 32 Cumberland St'. Lublin manufactured bathing caps in oiled cloth for ladies and gentlemen. This must have been Australia's first beach wear. On 30 November 1842 he offered a reward for a lost marriage certificate, which he had mislaid in the street near his shop. In the *Sydney Gazette* of 30 April 1842,'John Lublin cloth cap maker' was declared to be insolvent. He had debts of £66 and assets of £41. He was discharged from insolvency on 12 October 1842. In September he was advertising 'Wholesale Naval Military, Naval and Fancy Cloth Cap manufacturer has opened a shop in Hunter St'. He claimed to be the 'only real cloth cap manufacturer in Sydney'. The *Sydney Morning Herald* listed him as a cloth cap maker in George Street on 11 January 1845.

Sydney Gazette, 4 January 1842; *Australasian Chronicle*, 20 September 1842; *Sydney Morning Herald*, 15 April 1842, 26 April 1842, 14 May 1842, 12 October 1842, 13 October 1842, 30 November 1842.

LYON, Bennett (Barnett)

b. London, 1801
Royal Charlotte, 1825; Convict; Sentenced to 7 years, Old Bailey, 1824.
Single; Fruit man; Height: 160 cm.

Dark complexion, dark brown hair, chestnut eyes. Barnett Lyons was convicted with Solomon Dias (q.v.) for stealing a basket of laundry in Houndsditch and was sentenced on 15 July 1824.

Bennett Lyon arrived in Sydney on 29 April 1825 and was assigned to the District of Evan. He was sentenced to eighteen months colonial transportation at Sydney on 3 May 1826 and sent to Moreton Bay on the *Amity* on 29 August 1826.

Royal Charlotte Indent 4/4010, p. 101; 4/3794; *Sydney Gazette*, 6 May 1826.

LYON, Isaac Leo (LYONS)

b. Portsmouth, 1787–1850
Aeolus, 1809; Free.
Married; School teacher.

Lyon's father, the Rev. Solomon Lyon, ran a small boarding school in Cambridge, the first Jewish boarding school in England. The musician Isaac Nathan (q.v.) attended Lyon's school in 1805.

Isaac Leo Lyon married Maria Worland at St Martin in the Fields on 16 March 1808, and they set sail for New South Wales in early July. Maria died on the voyage and Lyon arrived in Sydney on 26 January 1809. Lyon thought he would be teaching at a school for orphaned boys but the school had not been built. Lyon was summoned to serve on a jury at an inquest at Kissing Point in October 1809 and was therefore the first Jew to serve on a jury in Australia. Lyon found employment at a school run by Thomas Pascoe Crook in Parramatta and remained teaching there for ten months, until he was suspended by government order on 27 October 1809: 'Isaac Lyons having, from negligence and incapability, proved himself totally unfit for the Situation of School Master at Parramatta, he is suspended from this day'. The Rev. Samuel Marsden informed the Archbishop of Canterbury:

> One of the schoolmasters of the name of Lyons who was to have attended to the Orphan boys turned out a bad character he has been discharged. The sum of £60 per annum which was allotted him by the Government is too small a sum to induce a man of character and Education to come to this country.

Lyons found employment in Sydney working with a merchant, Robert Jenkins, and in early December 1812 returned to England on the *Minstrel*, working his passage as a clerk to the captain.

Lyons also returned to the Jewish community and, in 1822 in London, married Anna Levi. They had three children, Solomon, Rachel and Julia. Lyons published an edition of the Prayer Book in Hebrew and English, was active in communal affairs and in teaching poorer members of the community. He died at his home in Whitechapel on 24 December 1850, aged sixty-three.

Naomi Cream, 'Isaac Leo Lyon: The First Free Jewish Migrant to Australia?', *AJJHS*, vol. 12, no. 1 (1993); CS Reports of Coroner's Inquests 1809–1822, 4/1819, pp. 503, 505; SZ993, p. 185.

LYONS, Abraham

b. London, 1782–1857
Brothers, 1832; Free.
Single; Dealer.

The son of Levi and Hannah Lyons of London and the older brother of Saul Lyons (q.v.) and Samuel Lyons (q.v.) and Mrs Lydia Samuel (q.v.), Abraham arrived in Sydney with his widowed sister Lydia and her son Saul (q.v.). Lydia's second son Lewis Samuel (q.v.), had been in Sydney since August 1829.

Abraham Lyons arrived in Sydney on 25 August 1832. He was listed in the New South Wales Directory as a wine and spirit merchant in Reiby's Buildings, Castlereagh Street. In the same year Abraham and Saul Lyons purchased the Rose Inn at Maitland for £775. They also had a store in Pitt Street, selling cigars, beef, sugar, stout ale and even a billiard table. 'A & S Lyons' became one of the most important Jewish-owned firms in Sydney in the mid-1830s. They were ship agents and importers. Lyons acted as the agent for the brig *Louisa*, which sailed between Port Phillip and Sydney, and purchased the *Water Lily* for £2200. They sold wine and spirits and exported wool to Van Diemen's Land. The business grew and in 1835 they asked for six assigned convicts and received two. On 22 March 1839 Abraham Lyons returned, with his brother Samuel Lyons, for a visit to England. In September 1839 he donated £25 to the Sydney Synagogue building fund. The firm of A & S Lyons at 9 Pitt Street in Sydney was declared bankrupt in the depression of the 1840s. Abraham Lyons died on 7 May 1857 and was buried by the Sydney Synagogue. He was not married and appears to have died interstate.

Governors' Despatches 1835, ML, A1214, p. 715; CS Reports of Vessels Arrived 1839, 4/5214, 22 March 1839; *Sydney Gazette*, 12 March 1833, 9 April 1833; *AG*, pp. 84, 86, 123, 156, 301.

LYONS, Emanuel

b. Houndsditch, 1799
Countess of Harcourt, 1821; Convict; Sentenced to life, Old Bailey, 1820.
Hawker, fruit seller; Height: 172 cm.

Dark complexion, dark brown hair, hazel eyes. Emanuel Lyons and his sister Sarah Myers (q.v.) were tried together. Myers had picked up a man and taken him to a brothel run by her sister. Lyons was apparently waiting there. He was well known to the police. Lyons stole a pocket book containing £1 19s. Lyons had a previous conviction for assault. His father, a hatter, and his mother lived in Houndsditch. Lyons was sentenced on 6 December 1820.

Lyons arrived in Van Diemen's Land on 27 July 1821. He was convicted on 14 July 1822 of being disorderly in the Prisoners' Barracks and received twenty-five lashes. On 20 February 1823 he received a further fifty lashes for abusing his overseer at the barracks. On 13 January 1825 he was sentenced to another fifty lashes for 'neglect of duty'. His ticket of leave was suspended for six months in 1830 for 'making a false statement designed to shield a ticket of leave man in his employ so that the man's absence would not be discovered'. Lyons then volunteered to join the expedition against the Aborigines in order to regain his own suspended ticket of leave. His offer was not accepted. On 5 December 1833 he was admonished for being absent from the muster and from church. Lyons received a conditional pardon on 23 March 1838.

OBSP, 1820–21, case 144, p. 50; *Countess of Harcourt* Indent 2/8254, and 4/4007; CON 31/27; Dixson Library ADD 84; HO 11/4; *Hobart Town Courier*, 23 March 1839.

LYONS, Isaac

b. London, 1801–1870
Adamant, 1821; Convict; Sentenced to life, Old Bailey, 1820.
Single; Labourer; Height: 160 cm.

Dark swarthy complexion, black hair, dark eyes. Isaac Lyons, the son of Solomon Lyons of London, was a pickpocket. He 'fell' heavily against a man in Whitechapel Street and attempted to steal his watch. He was sentenced on 6 December 1820.

The *Adamant* arrived in New South Wales on 8 September 1821 and four days later Lyons was sent on assignment to Windsor. Lyons was assigned as a labourer to the Australian Agricultural Company at Port Stephens. He is listed as such in the 1828 Census. He was also on the List of Convicts in New South Wales in November 1828. On 30 October 1829 he was sent as a convict to Port Macquarie on the *Sally*. He was returned to Sydney and in 1835–36 was listed as a prisoner on the convict hulk *Phoenix* with a twelve-month colonial sentence. His behaviour was 'tolerable'. He was then returned to Port Macquarie. On 8 July 1837 he was placed in the cells for seven days for having been found gambling.

He was granted a ticket of leave for the District of Port Macquarie in 1841. This was altered for Windsor in the same year and then reverted to Port Macquarie. On 6 April 1844 his pass was extended to allow him to travel between Windsor, where he lived, and Sydney 'in consideration of his being blind and also to attend the Jews' Synagogue'.

Lyons was granted a conditional pardon in June 1846. He died at 266 Castlereagh Street, Sydney, on 6 January 1870, at which time he was described as a 'dealer'.

OBSP, 1820–21, case 33, p. 15: *Adamant* Indent 4/4007, p. 382; 4/3854, p. 87; Register of Pardons 4/4150; *Phoenix* (hulk) Entrance Book 4/6286, p. 50; Port Macquarie Bench Book, 1836–37, 4/5639, p. 444; TL 41/797.

LYONS, Joseph

b. Whitechapel, 1811
Candahar, 1842; Convict; Sentenced to 10 years, Central Criminal Court, 1841.
Married; Fishmonger; Height: 157 cm; 7 children.

Fair complexion, black hair, brown eyes, clean shaven, large nose, small mouth and small dimpled chin. A Jew. Can read and write. Stated this offence: he stole three brass weights, the property of Mr Warner of Irving Crescent. Joseph Lyons' wife was Rosetta (née Simons).

Joseph, the son of Mordecai and Betsy Lewis, had two brothers Moses and Saul. In the 1841 census he was listed as living in Petticoat Lane with two children Hannah aged two and Samuel aged ten months. Hannah was dead by July 1845 when her mother and younger brother left for Australia. Joseph's trade was listed as 'dealer'.

Lyons arrived in Van Diemen's Land on 21 July 1842. Joseph Lyons' initial period of probation was for two years. After a period on the roads, stationed at Jerusalem (Colebrook) he was assigned to a Joshua Lyons at Launceston from 25 September 1844 to 3 September 1846. The reports of his behaviour as a prisoner read 'good' and 'very good'. On 25 September 1844 it was noted that his conduct was 'meritorious' at a fire in Launceston, where he 'exerted himself helping to remove a quantity of gunpowder'. There is only one offence noted in his police dossier and that is 'insolence to the storekeeper', for which he received seven days in solitary confinement. In September 1846 Lyons was removed from Launceston and returned to his initial period of imprisonment in Jerusalem because he was under suspicion of having received stolen property. A ticket of leave was issued on 14 September 1847 and a conditional pardon on 15 May 1849.

There was a 'J. Lyons' on the committee that helped establish the Launceston Synagogue in 1845–46.

Rosetta and her son Samuel followed her husband out to Van Diemen's Land on the *Jane* arriving in Launceston on 6 November 1845. Samuel died on 9 July 1856 in Melbourne at the age of fifteen. They had five more children, four of whom were born in Van Diemen's Land. Isaac born 15 August 1846, Mordecai born 1848, Sarah born 1849, Simeon born 1852 and Jane born 1855. The family left Tasmania for Sydney on 24 August 1854 and two years later, in December 1856, Joseph and Rosetta and their children left Melbourne for London and the East End on the *Mermaid*. Only Simeon would return to Melbourne where he married Elizabeth Gertrude O'Brien in 1879. One of their five children was Eileen Lyons, a noted singer.

CON 33/23; Terry Lyons, *The Launceston Lyons*, privately printed, Townsville, Qld, 2004.

LYONS, Joshua

b. London, 1808–1884
1836; Free.
Single; Dealer, publican; 13 children.

Joshua Lyons was the son of Jonas and Deborah Lyons who had been born in Poland. His sister, Julia, took the name Rebecca when she married John Jacobs (q.v.) in Launceston in 1852. Joshua Lyons came to Australia as an unassisted free migrant, arriving in Van Diemen's Land in 1836. In October of that year, 'John Lyons of Perth, a dealer', was named by Henry Davis (q.v) as a supporter of his proposal to use a block of land in Launceston for a Jewish cemetery.

Lyons married Priscilla Sutton at St John's in Launceston on 26 April 1837. Priscilla was aged nineteen and was a 'nursemaid' who had arrived in Launceston as a bounty migrant on the *Amelia Thompson* with 300 other young single women.

Joshua and Priscilla had eleven children: Samuel Jones Lyons, (born 1838, the only child to have been baptised), Jona (John) (1840–1850), Solomon (1842), Deborah (1843–1932), Henry Saul (1844–1918), Abraham Arthur (1847–1927), Alfred Aaron (1848–1931), Charlotte Miriam (1849–1889), Henry Moses (1854–1931), Rachel Rebekhah (1858–1944), and John James (1861, who died the same year). Priscilla died the week after the birth of John James Lyons, at the age of forty-two, and was buried in the Anglican burial ground in Launceston on 26 January 1861.

On 13 January 1862 Joshua Lyons married Esther Brody (née Nathan). The marriage was performed on 30 January 1862—in the District of Port Sorrell where, at the time, Lyons was the licensee of the Commercial Inn at Tarleton. The 'Minister' was Elias Levy (q.v.) and the witnesses were Moses Judah Solomon and Maurice Nathan (q.v.), the brother of the bride. Esther and Joshua had two children, Mary Ann Elizabeth, born 1862, and Eliza, 1864–1933.

Lyons was variously listed on the birth certificates of his many children as 'shop keeper', 'merchant', 'licensed victualler', 'publican'and 'inn keeper' in and around Launceston, Port Sorell, Torquay and Devonport.

In 1842 Joshua Lyons was the licensee of the Sir William Wallace Inn at Franklin Village, south of Launceston and, by September 1843, was declared to be bankrupt. In June 1844 Joshua Lyons gave £10 to the Launceston Synagogue building appeal and in 1846 he was listed as a member of the committee of the synagogue in St John's Street, Launceston.

In the early 1850s Joshua owned a general store in the coal mining town of Tarleton and in 1856 moved to the west side of the River Mersey (now Devonport). The Torquay Hotel became known as Lyons' Hotel. Joshua Lyons was its landlord until the time of his death. He was buried in the old Jewish cemetery in Launceston on 17 September 1884, the 'beloved husband of Esther'.

Remarkably, while three of the daughters (none of whom had married) were buried as Jews, the rest of the family lost their Jewish identity—in spite of their names. Deborah Lyons died on 6 August 1932 at the age of eighty-nine, and the burial was at the Melbourne General Cemetery in Fawkner, with the ceremony performed by Rabbi Israel Brodie. Deborah's sister Rachel Rebekhah died in December 1944 and was buried beside her sister at the Fawkner Cemetery. Charlotte seems to have followed Esther, her stepmother, to Melbourne two years after Joshua Lyons died. Charlotte died on 8 September 1889 at the age of forty, and was buried in the Jewish section of the St Kilda Cemetery.

Terry Lyons, *The Launceston Lyons*, privately printed, Townsville, Qld, 2004; *Launceston Examiner*, 12 March 1842, 29 June 1844.

LYONS, Lewis ('Little Mo')

b. Whitechapel, 1800
General Stewart, 1818; Convict; Sentenced to life, Surrey Assizes, 1818.
Single; Watch finisher; Height: 151 cm; 4 children.

Dark ruddy complexion, black hair, dark eyes, nose broad and rather flat. On 2 September 1817 in Whitechapel, Lewis Lyons tried to pawn some silver, which was found to have been stolen the night before. The booty amounted to thirty-six silver table forks, fifteen table spoons and other articles of plate valued at £50, stolen from the home of George Hibbert Esq. of Clapham Common. Lyons claimed to have found the silver hidden on Clapham Common and that he was as 'innocent as a child unborn'. He could not call on any witnesses for his defence. On 30 March 1818 he was sentenced to death and that sentence was later commuted to transportation for life.

Lyons arrived in Sydney on 31 December 1818 after a long journey of more than six months. The ship had stayed at St Helena on the way. When the *General Stewart* berthed at Port Jackson the surgeon officially complained that the ship's captain had starved the convicts and that they were 'frequently abused, threatened, harshly treated and beaten'.

Lyons was sent to work in a convict gang in the township of Windsor, where the convict architect Francis H. Greenway had designed a new St Matthew's Church and was rewarded with extra rations when it was finished. Lyons worked in the Windsor Town Gang during the latter part of 1822 and was listed in the 1825 Muster serving at the Hyde Park Barracks. Lyons appears in the 1828 Census as a Jew, a dealer, living at Mary Larkins' home in Kent Street, Sydney. Mary Larkins had six tenants of whom four were Jews: Lewis Lyons, Mordecai Abrahams (q.v.), Isaac Moses (q.v.) and Solomon Simpson (q.v.)

Lyons received a ticket of leave on 17 June 1827 and a conditional pardon on 15 June 1835. On October 1836 at St John's Cathedral in Parramatta, Lyons married Sarah Jane Crane, who had arrived in the colony as a bounty migrant on the *David Scott* on 25 October 1834. They had four children, all of whom were baptised: Esther Jane, Hannah (Ann) Elizabeth (born 1839), Margaret Rebecca Charlotte (1842), and Dinah Anne (1847). In June 1838 Lyons applied for and obtained the licence of the Pilgrim Inn on Lapstone Hill in the Blue Mountains on the road to Bathurst. In 1844 it was described as a 'small way-side public house, where slovenly slipshod women, dirty floors and a powerful odour of stale tobacco-smoke prevailed'. By mid-1840, Lyons had returned to Sydney and opened a general store in Sussex Street.

The *Sydney Record* noted on 4 October 1843 that 'Lewis Lyons, dealer', was listed as insolvent with a deficiency of £59 7s 6d. In 1844 he worked as a labourer in Sydney. However, he was once again listed as a 'dealer' in Sussex Street in *Low's Directory of the City and District of Sydney*, 1847.

General Stewart Indent 4/4064, 4/4005, p. 228; 4/4077, 6 January 1831; Court of Appeals, Minutes 1822, 4/1756, p. 108; Eric Riddler, 'Lewis Lyons: A Jewish Emancipist', *AJJHS*, vol. 14, no. 4 (1999), p. 572f.; 4/3681, 35/312; TL 27/414; CP 542.

LYONS, Lewis

b. London, 1808–1842
Lord Lyndoch (1), 1831; Convict; Sentenced to 7 years, Old Bailey, 1831.
Single; Hatter; Height: 155 cm.

Brown complexion, dark brown hair, low wrinkled forehead, brown eyes, long nose, round chin. A Jew. Lewis Lyons was reported to have been 'Quiet and orderly' on board the transport ship. He had stolen a 21-pound-weight cheese from a cart parked in Aldgate and was caught in the act by a passing constable. He was sentenced on 7 April 1831.

The *Lord Lyndoch* arrived in Van Diemen's Land on 18 November 1831. Lyons' police dossier records only that on 7 April 1836, as a ticket of leave holder, he was admonished for being 'disorderly and out after hours in the streets'. Lewis Lyons applied for permission to marry Catherine Cunningham who had come out as a convict on the *Frances Charlotte* in August 1837. The marriage was permitted. The *Hobart Town Courier* advertised that Lyons may apply for a certificate of freedom on 6 April 1838. The newspaper notice described him as an 'itinerant fish vendor' (12 February 1841). The Hobart Synagogue's Philanthropic Society recorded that it paid £3 2s 6d for funeral expenses for burying Lewis Lyons in February 1842.

OBSP, 1830–31, case 719, p. 386; CON 31/28, no. 644; VDL Papers, ML, A1059-7, p. 172; Petition to Marry CON 52/1; Description Book CON 18/12.

LYONS, Samuel

b. London, 1791–1851
Marquis of Wellington, 1815; Convict; Sentenced to life, Old Bailey, 1814.
Single; Tailor; Height: 165 cm; 4 children.

Dark pale complexion, thin, brown hair, hazel eyes. Samuel Lyons was transported for stealing a handkerchief valued at under five shillings. He was a member of a juvenile gang 'well known to the Police' who had them under surveillance at the time of their arrest on London Bridge. He was sentenced on 16 February 1814. He was the son of Levi and Hannah Lyons of London and the brother of Abraham and Saul Lyons (qq.v).

Lyons was assigned as a servant to Mrs Armytage and together with the twelve year old Jewish convict John Morris (q.v.) attempted to escape from Sydney in April 1815. The two were discovered by the captain of the ship, offloaded, and brought back to Sydney, where Lyons was whipped and reassigned as a convict. In August 1816 he was sent to Hobart Town on the brig *Kangaroo* where, together with John Morris, he once again attempted to escape by hatching a plot with the ship's Lieutenant Captain Jeffreys. Lyons promised to produce 2000 gallons of rum to be smuggled into Van Diemen's Land as payment for a passage back to England. Lyons, together with four other fellow convicts were discovered before the ship sailed for home.

During 1817 he participated in public boxing matches, together with his fellow shipmate Moses Moses (q.v.) and began a business as a tailor and general dealer. The *Hobart Town Gazette* wrote on 4 October 1817: 'The third and last battle was between another Hibernian and Lyons, a tailor of the Jewish persuasion. Both stood well to each other for a long time, but the tailor's seams were completely flattened'.

Lyons' business career was interrupted when he was charged, together with John Morris, John Pascoe Fawkner and John Fawkner, with robbing the government stores in July 1819. He was sentenced to receive 200 lashes and four years at the dreaded coal mines at Newcastle Prison Station. As Colonel Godfrey Charles Mundy, the acidic contemporary observer of colonial society, wrote 'Perhaps the devil was whipped out of him. Perhaps reflection cast the foul fiend out'. By early 1822, Lyons was the assigned servant of Joel Joseph (q.v.) of Pitt Street, Sydney and on 28 May 1822 he married Mary Murphy, who had been born in the colony, with the rites of the Roman Catholic Church.

Lyons wrote to Governor Brisbane on 16 April 1823 claiming to have 'rendered great Services to the Police Officers, and by Indefatigable Exertions has been Instrumental in the discoveries of various offenders Benjamin Lee [q.v.] and Henry Phillips for stowing away and eight others for different crimes'. His petition was supported by the signatures of no less than six Justices of the Peace. He 'prays to be restored to that rank in society from which he has been so long excluded'.

Lyons opened a store in Pitt Street and in June 1827 received a ticket of leave. He was then able to receive an auctioneer's licence and appeared as such in the 1828 Census. His career as an auctioneer was spectacular. On 14 July 1828 the *Sydney Gazette* wrote: 'As a man of integrity Mr Lyons deserves what he is acquiring by his extraordinary application to trade'. He was granted an absolute pardon in October 1832. At the time he was living at the corner of George Street and Charlotte Place.

In 1834, of the £117 537 worth of land sales conducted in Sydney, Lyons transacted £61 872. In 1835 Lyons averaged a turnover of £12 000 a month. On 20 June 1836 the *Sydney Herald* criticised the system of auctioneering. It claimed 'it is to enrich low disreputable persons at the expense of the British exporters and the respectable colonists, with few exceptions. Auction Rooms may well be designated as dens of Thieves'. On 23 June the *Herald* continued the campaign: 'Thus the property of the British capitalist, and of resident colonists is parcelled out among a band of transported felons'. Lyons accepted the challenge and sued and, in response, the paper claimed that Lyons was the 'foster father' of a pamphlet *Extracts from Humanitas* that accused the press of corruption, cruelty and monopolistic practices. The paper was unable to prove its case in court and the *Sydney Herald* was fined £200.

Lyons travelled to England in 1836 and returned to Australia in 1840. It was during his absence that the auctioneer Abraham Polack (q.v.) flourished. Lyons resumed his career as auctioneer, financier and money lender. On 4 November 1845 the *Port Phillip Patriot* reported 'During examination of Mr Samuel Lyons of Sydney before the Select Committee on the Auctioneers' Licensing Bill it was revealed that between 15 October 1839 and 31 July 1845 Mr Lyons had disposed by public auction of property amounting to £1 420 089 and three shillings'.

Lyons was an enthusiastic advocate of steam navigation and the building of railways throughout New South Wales. He was active in politics and gave generously to local charities. He was noticeably active in the political campaign in 1850 to abolish the transportation of convicts to Australia. Lyons brought out to Australia his brother Saul Lyons (q.v.) in 1827, his nephew Lewis Samuel (q.v.) in 1829 and his older brother Abraham (q.v.) and his aunt Lydia Samuel (q.v.) and her son (later Sir) Saul Samuel (q.v.). His generosity was compromised when, in 1833, he began legal proceedings against his brothers demanding payment for the cost of their passage to Australia and other costs.

Lyons joined the Sydney Synagogue in 1832 and gave the building fund £150 and a silver pointer (*yad*) for the Torah between 1839 and 1845. He was a major shareholder at the establishment of the Bank of New South Wales in 1828. Colonel Mundy wrote of Lyons in his book *Our Antipodes* about the economic depression of the 1840s: 'At the time of the general money quake he fell like the rest and by a strong effort he succeeded in paying 20 shillings in the pound and having thus reduced himself to beggary he recommenced life undismayed and with resolute energy'. In fact, the Bank of Australia claimed debts of £230 000 against him. Lyons was the only Jew listed among the bank's shareholders.

Mary Lyons died in March 1832 and Lyons quickly renewed a relationship that dated back to Hobart Town with 'Ann'. Ann was brought to Sydney and a daughter Mary was named and baptised on 27 February 1834. Lyons sent his three (legitimate) children to England, George Joseph Lyons born 4 April 1823, Hannah Lyons born 10 October 1824, Samuel Lyons Jnr 9 June 1826. All his children were brought up as members of the Church of England.

George became a barrister in England. Samuel took over his father's business and became a Member of the Parliament of New South Wales.

Samuel Lyons died on 3 August 1851 and even though, by this time, he was not a member of the synagogue, he was buried as a Jew. His funeral cortege 'consisted of a hearse, nine mourning coaches, sixty private and hired carriages and ten gigs, altogether eighty vehicles'.

OBSP, 1814, case 251, p. 151; *Marquis of Wellington* Indent 4/4005, p. 32; P. E. Le Roy, 'Samuel Lyons', *ADB*, vol. 2, p. 141f.; *HRA*, series 1, vol. 14, p. 560, and series 3, vol. 2; petition 58, 13 May 1822, in 4/1866; Letter, 10 April 1823, and petition, 16 April 1823 (letter 14), in 4/1870; TL 27/108; AP 92; *Hobart Town Gazette*, 4 October 1817, 9 January 1819, 12 June 1819, 24 July 1819, 31 July 1819; *Sydney Gazette*, 2 May 1827, 14 July 1828, 16 June 1829, 18 October 1832; *Sydney Herald*, 2 December 1833, 3 March 1834, 20 June 1836; *Australian*, 7 March 1834; *Colonist*, 1 October 1836, 3 November 1836; CS 4/1870, 23/3234, CS 4/1864, December 1832; Colonel Mundy, *Our Antipodes* Dixson Library, Add 151, no. 86; *AG*, pp. 78–90, 123, 144–5, 146–7, 174, 183–4, 300, 309, 314. *AJHSJ*, Nick Dyrenfurth: *The Complex Colonial: The Case of Samuel Lyons*. Vol 17, part 2 (2004) p164 f

LYONS, Sarah

b. London, 1769–1837
Lady Juliana, 1790; Convict; Sentenced to 7 years, Old Bailey, 1788.
Single; 2 children.

Sarah Lyons stole seven yards of silk from a haberdasher's shop in the City of London. She made some small deposits on various articles but was stopped and searched as she left the shop and the silk fell to the ground. At the Old Bailey she said 'I was very willing to be searched as I knew I was innocent'. She claimed that her sister would call in with the balance for the materials she wished to purchase and that her sister was 'a small black girl'. She was sentenced in July 1788.

Sarah Lyons arrived in Sydney on the Second Fleet. Eight weeks later she was sent on to Norfolk Island, arriving there on 7 August 1790. From August 1790 to March 1793 Lyons was at Norfolk Island. On 26 March 1791 she was sentenced to receive twenty-five lashes for having attacked a fellow female prisoner. Lieutenant Ralph Clark wrote in his diary 'The woman is a D[amn] B[itch]'. On 6 June 1791 Clark sentenced her to fifty lashes for abusing D'Arcy Wentworth who, in his official capacity, watched the punishment and stopped the flogging after she had received sixteen strokes. On 14 July Clark sentenced her to twenty-five lashes for entering the island's main town without permission. She became the partner of a marine, William Tunks, and probably married him in 1791. The couple moved to Sydney in March 1793, and a son, John, was born in March 1795, and was baptised at Parramatta in June. Another son, Charles, was born in 1802.

Tunks was granted 140 acres at Evan on the Nepean River only to lose his farm as a consequence of floods. In November 1795 Sarah lived at the back row of the houses at Parramatta and was approached to buy stolen clothes. Amelia Levy (q.v.), who had visited her, knew the name of the thief and did not want to buy the garments. It was noted that Sarah was a Jewess. In September 1795 Sarah Lyons 'a Jewess' gave evidence in a trial and was sworn in on the Old Testament. Her evidence was supported by Amelia Levy. In the Rev. Samuel Marsden's Female Muster of 1806 she was listed as 'a concubine with two male illegitimate children'.

The family moved to Sydney and Sarah Lyons was listed in the 1811 Muster. Tunks died in Sydney on 6 August 1821. Sarah Tunks was probably living with her married son John, a publican in Parramatta, when she died on 27 July 1837. She was buried at St John's cemetery.

M. Flynn, *The Second Fleet*, p. 411; *OBSP*, 1787–88, case 406, p. 537; HO 11/1, HO 10/2; Female Convict no. 122, in Norfolk Island Victualling Book, A1958; Criminal Court Proceedings, ML, 1147, 7 November 1795; Samuel Marsden, 1806 Female Muster, ML, ms. 18.

LYONS, Saul

b. London, 1799–1878
Harvey, 1827; Free.
Single; Dealer.

Saul Lyons was the son of Levi and Hannah Lyons of London and brother of Samuel Lyons (q.v.), Abraham Lyons (q.v.), and Mrs Lydia Samuel (q.v.). In the 1828 Census Saul Lyons declared himself to be a Protestant. However, once the synagogue was consecrated in 1845, he became a member and a seat holder and a contributor to its building fund.

Lyons married Mrs Esther Nettleton (aged twenty) at St Philip's Church on 30 October 1828, the service being conducted by the Rev. William Cowper. The bride, 'of Parramatta', had been the first child christened in that church nineteen years before. They were to have no children.

In 1828 Lyons owned the hotel with the memorable name, At the Sign of the Leather Bottle. This was replaced by the hotel Governor Macquarie at 9 Pitt Street and in November 1832 the licence was transferred to his nephew, Lewis Samuel (q.v.). Saul Lyons became involved in a dispute about the cost of bringing his sister, nephews and brother Abraham to Sydney, and the matter ended inconclusively, and with great bitterness, in the Supreme Court in the second half of 1833.

Lyons owned the Rose Inn and the Stony Creek Farm near Maitland in 1834 and had built 'a spacious dwelling and warehouse in George Street, corner of Charlotte Place'. Saul joined his brother Abraham Lyons conducting 'a wholesale business under the firm of Abraham and Saul Lyons at 9 Pitt St'. They sold sugar, pig iron, wine and spirits and exported wool from New South Wales and Van Diemen's Land to England. In the 1830s they employed the architect John Verge to build some houses in Pitt Street near the site of today's Martin Place where Saul had received a grant measuring 'thirty-six perches'. On 7 January 1835 the *Sydney Gazette* wrote that the design appeared to be 'very unique' and the *Sydney Times* wrote that 'the building is to present an appearance worthy of the metropolis of Great Britain rather than of her remotest colony'. Joseph Fowles noted, in *Sydney in 1848*, that Gill's Hotel, built by Saul Lyons, was 'one of the best houses in Sydney'. In 1842 Lyons advertised for a coachman who 'must be single' and another man 'to wait on table'. Mrs Lyons advertised for a cook and a housemaid.

Saul Lyons pledged £25 to the Sydney Synagogue building appeal in 1839 and £5 to the Launceston Synagogue building appeal in 1844. Though the partnership of Abraham and Saul Lyons in Pitt Street was declared insolvent in the depression of the 1840s with a deficiency of £3525, the firm had recovered its position by the gold rush era and was one of the most important Jewish merchant businesses in Sydney. On 21 September 1844 Saul Lyons charged P.J. Cohen (q.v.) with libel.

They were quarrelling about the tenancy of the Rose Inn at Maitland and Cohen had written 'a malicious article' about him in the *Sydney Morning Herald* of 9 September 1844.

Abraham Lyons died in May 1857 and Saul seems to have retired from business. His home was at 16 Elizabeth Street and he moved to 201 Macquarie Street where he lived until his death on 6 February 1878 at the age of seventy-nine. His wife had predeceased him. He left an estate of £30 000 to the children of his nephew, Sir Saul Samuel.

Sydney Gazette, 31 October 1828, 12 March 1833, 9 April 1833, 7 January 1834; *Sydney Monitor*, 17 November 1832, 14 June 1833, 2 November 1833; *Sydney Herald*, 13 June 1833; *Morning Chronicle*, 21 September 1844; Governors' Despatches 1832, A1210, p. 223, 1833, A1211, p. 663, 1835, A1214, p. 713; *Launceston Examiner*, 29 June 1844; *Sydney Morning Herald*, 15 April 1842, 26 May 1842, 26 October 1842, 14 February 1843, 19 March 1844, 30 July 1844; 2/3267, State Records of New South Wales, p. 75; *AG*, pp. 82, 84, 301.

LYONS, Solomon

d. 1849
China, 1846
Convict; Sentenced to 15 years, Central Criminal Court, 1845.

Solomon Lyons arrived at Norfolk Island on 16 May 1846. In the 1849 Return of Convicts in Van Diemen's Land, Lyons was listed as having been buried by J. Jackson, presumably on Norfolk Island.

HO 10/49.

LYONS, Solomon

b. London, 1802–1878
Tottenham, 1818; Convict; Sentenced to life, Old Bailey, 1817.
Single; Basket boy, weaver; Height: 152 cm.

Dark pale complexion, brown hair, hazel eyes, club feet. Solomon Lyons was a 15-year-old pick-pocket who was caught stealing a woman's purse at the Newgate Market. He was sentenced on 17 September 1817.

Solomon Lyons arrived at Port Jackson on 14 October 1818. He settled at Parramatta, where he was first assigned as a convict servant. He married Phoebe Benjamin (q.v.) at St John's Church in Parramatta in July 1826. The officiant was the Rev. Samuel Marsden and, following the marriage of John Hart to Flora Larah (qq.v.) on 13 February 1788, it was the second marriage in Australia between two Jews. A ticket of leave was issued to Solomon Lyons in June 1827, followed by a conditional pardon.

Solomon Lyons was listed in the 1828 Census as a Protestant living in Parramatta. In 1835 Lyons was arrested in Parramatta and sent to Sydney for trial. Evidently, he was acquitted because his conditional pardon was valid in August 1835. He was then listed as a dealer. The Description Book adds that, by this time, he was 'nearly bald'.

Solomon Lyons was buried at Parramatta in 1878. He was said to be eighty-three years old, although he was seventy-six.

OBSP, 1816–17, case 1283, p. 433; *Tottenham* Indent 4/4006, p. 123; TL Register 4/4064, 27/359 (27 June 1827); CP 452; Parramatta Gaol Entrance Book 1835–36, 4/6531, no. 664; Description Book 1836, 4/6299, no. 1124.

M

MAGNUS, Edward

b. Königsberg, Prussia, 1800–1855
Waterloo (2), 1835; Convict; Sentenced to life, Sussex, 1834.
Married; Linen draper; Height: 170 cm; 1 child.

Pale complexion, large round head, black hair and whiskers, blue eyes, large nose, full lips, wide mouth. Edward Magnus had an anchor and wreath and the letters E. M. tattooed in red on his right arm. He was described as 'a travelling Jew'. He was sentenced at the Sussex Quarter Sessions on 16 October 1834 to be transported for life for stealing a gold watch. His wife Sophia was in London and they had one child. Magnus must have arranged a religious divorce before embarking for Van Diemen's Land.

Magnus was sent to the Risdon Assignable Gang, after serving four days on the treadmill, because he had been absent from his initial assigned service with Mr R. Lewis of Hobart Town, who had discovered that Magnus was 'unqualified for the trade of draper which he represented himself to be'. In November 1836 he was sentenced to two years hard labour, of which one was to be worked in chains. He had been a constable and was found guilty of the theft of a rug and some other household articles. One month later, on 19 December, he was absent from the Town Surveyor's Chain Gang's muster and was sent to Bridgewater with an extra three months hard labour. By 1838 he was working as a convict in Picton and in July he was removed from his post as clerk of the Picton Road Party Station for stealing tea and sugar. Magnus then began to work as a constable in Campbell Town. On 8 October 1838 he spent ten days in solitary confinement on bread and water for misconduct while on duty. On 3 April 1839 he was charged with accepting a bribe and on 6 August he was charged with receiving stolen property.

On 28 December 1840, while still a member of the Campbell Town Police, he 'burst open the door of a female assigned servant and attempted to take indecent liberties with her'. Magnus was given two years imprisonment and hard labour and was dismissed from the police. He was sent to the Jordan's Creek Road Party and then to the Launceston Prisoners' Barracks. By the first week of January 1841, 'from a doubt that has arisen in favour of Magnus on account of a discrepancy in the evidence', the Lieutenant Governor ordered that his sentence be remitted and Magnus be returned to duty in the police force, although in another district.

One year later, on 8 April 1842, Magnus was sentenced to twelve months hard labour for trying to obtain money under false pretences while a member of the police force. The 1842 Van Diemen's Land Census reported that Edward Magnus, a Jew, was living at Green Ponds as a tenant in a wooden house and was married to a member of the Church of England. His 1842 conviction concluded in December 1842. On 25 July 1843 he received a further three months hard labour for insolence while working in the Commissariat Department. A ticket of leave was granted on 10 October 1843. In September 1845 in Hobart Town a further three-month sentence was imposed on Magnus for assaulting Jane Chillmore.

This led Ann Magnus, the wife of Edward, to petition the Lieutenant Governor Sir John E. Wilmot and ask for help. Ann explained that her husband had been charged with the assault of a girl employed by Mr Henry Jones (q.v.) of Elizabeth Street and that the charge had been 'maliciously exaggerated' by information put to the police by Michael John Davies (q.v.), innkeeper of Campbell Street. Her husband had received a sentence of three months hard labour for 'this paltry occurrence'. Because of the prison sentence, the little business was going to ruin. She lived at Albion Cottage, New Town Road. Magnus was a member of the Hobart Synagogue between 1842 and 1845, renting seat no. 44, and was thanked for 'the trouble' he had taken to make the candles for the dedication of the synagogue in 1845. However, in November 1845, when Magnus was allowed out of prison he overstepped the rules of the congregation by independently writing out a traditional Jewish Marriage Certificate for the marriage of Simeon Benjamin (q.v.) and Elizabeth Solomon. He subsequently apologised to the synagogue. In the Synagogue Minutes of 6 September 1846 the following note from Edward Magnus appears: 'Finding little happiness has attended the wrong step I have taken which has led me astray from the Rites of our Holy religion which my Forefathers professed the woman with whom I am connected has expressed a wish to be admitted to the faith which is mine'. The request was accepted on the casting vote of the president (Louis Nathan, q.v.).

A conditional pardon for Edward Magnus was approved on 23 November 1847. A certificate of naturalisation, dated 7 February 1849, exists in the hands of a private collector. Magnus was described on it as a shopkeeper residing at Tanunda in the Barossa Valley, South Australia. In 1854 he is listed as carrying on a business in King William Street, Adelaide. Edward Magnus was buried in Adelaide as a Jew on 6 August 1855, 'Born Konigsberg, Prussia'.

CON 34/5, no. 1295; CSO 20/3/88; Ship Indent List, ML, A1059-7, p. 26; Certificate of Naturalisation (South Australia), 7 February 1849.

MAGNUS, Maurice Moses

b. Aldgate, 1809–1874
Asia (9), 1832; Convict; Sentenced to 7 years, Old Bailey, 1831.
Single; Salesman; Height: 168 cm; 4 children.

Dark ruddy complexion, dark brown hair, dark eyes. Large scar under left jaw. Could read. A Jew. On 30 June 1831 Maurice Magnus was sentenced to be transported for stealing a bundle from a carriage in the West End. He was seen in the act and identified and arrested a little later. He was the son of Henry Morris Magnus and Fanny (Solomons).

Magnus arrived in New South Wales on 13 February 1832. He was granted a ticket of leave in 1837 that was valid for the District of Goulburn and a certificate of freedom on 22 September 1838. He married the 23-year-old free immigrant Catherine Adolphus. Magnus was employed as a barman by Henry Robert Reuben (q.v.), and gave evidence at a trial in Sydney on 13 July 1841. He was listed in the *New South Wales Almanack and Remembrancer of 1848* as an 'agent and dealer' living in Pitt Street.

Maurice and Catherine Magnus had four children: Henry (born 1841), who died in infancy, Philip (1843), Lazarus (1846), and Esther (1849).

According to the *Sydney Morning Herald* of 22 January 1874 Maurice Magnus died at his home, at 35 Wexford Street, East Sydney. He was 'an old and respected colonist, aged 64 years, leaving an affectionate wife and three children to mourn their loss'. He was buried as a Jew. Catherine Magnus died, aged sixty-six, on 24 October 1882 and was buried as an Anglican.

Asia (9) Printed Indent, p. 17, no. 32–269; TL 37/547; Principal Superintendent of Convicts, Butts of CF 1838, no. 38/850, 4/4344; A1531-4, p. 617; family history notes from Mrs Jane Ives, Sydney.

MANDELSON, Nathan (MENDELSOHN)

b. Warsaw, 1804–1867
Children, 1833; Free.
Married; Baker; 6 children.

Nathan Mandelson arrived in New South Wales travelling steerage with his wife Phoebe (q.v.) on the *Children* on 31 August 1833. Samuel Moses Emanuel (q.v.), Phoebe's brother-in-law, was on the same ship. Nathan's surname was sometimes spelled Mendelson or Mendelsohn. Nathan was the son of Naphtali and Rachel.

After three years operating a business in George Street, Sydney, Nathan Mandelson opened a business in Bungonia some miles east of the Goulburn Plains where, between July 1836 and 1839, he held the licence of the Hit and Miss Inn.

He advertised: 'The travellers up and down the Maneroo will find good stabling and feed for horses; also four hundred acres of rich lands divided into paddocks, well secured for cattle'. As the land opened up the traffic moved eastwards and in 1839 Mandelson moved to Goulburn where, in May 1840, he purchased the Goulburn Inn from Isaac Moses (q.v.) for £1750 and moved to Sloane Street in Goulburn. Mandelson applied for naturalisation in 1843 (which would have enabled him to own land). He wrote that he had carried on business in Sydney and as a licensed victualler in Goulburn. He was actually at Bungonia, some miles east of the Goulburn Plains. A Letter of Denization was issued on 2 November 1844.

On 4 April 1843 the *Sydney Morning Herald* reported that 'Jacob Mandelson, an infant died after circumcision—death caused by composing a draught of opium'.

Mandelson bought two adjoining properties in the centre of Goulburn and, in 1846, built Mandelson's Hotel. The building remained a landmark in the town for the next hundred years and Mandelson became one of Goulburn's best-known identities. The Sydney Synagogue had appointed Mandelson its official representative in the district on 13 November 1843 and he was authorised to perform circumcisions.

The family moved to Sydney, where he advertised that he was a general commission agent and purveyor of wine and spirits. In June 1851 Mandelson advertised in the *Bathurst Free Press* offering twenty-two guineas to the first party who would find a goldfield in the Police District of Goulburn. The gold fields at Braidwood were soon discovered and Mandelson put on a coach service from Goulburn to the new goldfields. Mandelson was a staunch member of the Jewish community and in 1862 was elected president of Sydney's York Street Synagogue. He briefly returned to Goulburn, where he died on 3 July 1867 'from an attack of apoplexy'. He was sixty-three years old. His elaborate tombstone now stands in the Jewish section of Rookwood cemetery. Phoebe had died in 1856.

The first child of Nathan and Phoebe Mandelson was named in honour of Phoebe's family: Levy Mandelson was born on 4 July 1833 in Sydney. They had five more children: Naphtali (born 1834), in Sydney; Leah (1835), who married Abraham Cohen (q.v.) in 1856; Betsy (1838), born in Goulburn; Jacob Solomon (3 April 1843, died 18 September 1843), whose body was taken to Sydney for a Jewish burial in the Devonshire Street Cemetery; and Judah Joseph (9 August 1844), in Goulburn.

A brother, Naphtali Mandelson, joined the family at the time of the gold rush, and married Caroline Samuels in Sydney in 1857.

Children Indent 4/5805; Governors' Despatches, A1232, for 1843, p. 215f.; Sydney B. Glass, 'The Jews of Goulburn', *AJJHS*, vol. 1, no. 8 (1942), p. 282f.; *Sydney Morning Herald*, 29 December 1836, 9 September 1846, 6 July 1867; *Australasian Chronicle*, 10 September 1839; Sydney Synagogue Minute Book, p. 126; *Bathurst Free Press*, 7 June 1851.

MANDELSON, Phoebe (LEVY)

b. Leicester, 1806–1856
Children, 1833; Free.
Married; 6 children.

Phoebe was the wife of Nathan Mandelson (q.v.), and the daughter of Jacob Levy Cohen of Leicester. Her sister Dinah was the wife of Samuel Emanuel (q.v.). Phoebe had married Nathan in 1830.

Phoebe Mandelson was buried at the Devonshire Street cemetery on 1 September 1856 and re-interred at Rookwood in 1901.

MARCUS, Abraham

b. Hamburg, 1810
Clyde, 1832; Convict; Sentenced to 14 years, Liverpool, 1831.
Single; Tailor ('good'); Height: 168 cm; 4 children.

Sallow complexion, a little pock-pitted, brown hair, grey eyes. Could read and write. Abraham Marcus was transported for stealing a watch and was sentenced at Liverpool Quarter Sessions on 24 October 1831.

The convict transport ship *Clyde* arrived in New South Wales on 27 August 1832 and in January 1833 Marcus was assigned to Mr McQuade in Windsor. He was granted a ticket of leave for the District of Campbelltown in May 1838. The ticket of leave was cancelled in February 1842 following a letter from Mr Joshua Jones to the Colonial Secretary claiming that Marcus owed him the large sum of £70, which he 'had failed to liquidate'.

The background to the whole story was exposed in the *Sydney Gazette* on 22 June 1839 under the heading 'Convict Discipline':

> Abraham Marcus, formerly an assigned servant of Mr McQuade of Campbelltown, now a ticket of leave holder acted as shopkeeper, whilst still an assigned servant to Mr McQuade in his shop in Sydney and transacted business in every respect as a free man whilst his Master, residing in Campbelltown, could not have control over him. Now Marcus is residing in Campbelltown and has succeeded to the business of Mr McQuade!

In 1842 the cancelled ticket of leave was restored and it was altered for Sydney on 16 February 1843. A conditional pardon was authorised in October 1843.

Marcus received a certificate of freedom on 23 October 1845 and was subsequently allowed a conditional pardon. In 1845 he was listed as a seat holder in the new York Street Sydney Synagogue. He was insolvent in 1847 and discharged as bankrupt on 19 May 1847. Marcus was granted a publican's licence for a house in Bathurst Street West on 23 September 1848.

Sarah, daughter of Abraham and Mary Ann, was born in 1839, Lavinia was born in 1851, Eleanor, or Ellen, in 1851, and died in 1856, and 'Jane Marcus—an infant' was buried as a Jew in 1848.

Governors' Despatches 1839, A1220; TL 38/1631, 26 February 1838, 4/4123, restored 42/1687; CP recommended, A1295, p. 55; *Sydney Gazette*, 28 February 1833, 22 June 1839; *Sydney Morning Herald*, 23 September 1848; *Sydney Chronicle*, 19 May 1847.

MARCUS, Joseph

b. Mannheim, 1758–1828
William Pitt, 1792; Convict; Sentenced to 7 years, Staffordshire Lent Assizes, 1791.
Single; Hawker.

Marcus claimed to have studied at yeshivot (rabbinical colleges) in Poland and in Jerusalem. He was sentenced to death on 9 March 1791 for having entered the house of Michael Dainty of Leck and stealing five spoons, two salt holders, a mustard pot, four salt spoons, two pairs of sugar tongs, one wine strainer, a cup and two linen shirts. His sentence was later commuted to transportation for seven years.

Joseph Marcus arrived in New South Wales on 17 February 1792 and on 18 September 1795 he stowed away on board the supply ship *Endeavour* (not to be confused with Captain James Cook's ship). On board were fifty emancipists and almost as many convicts whose time had not expired. Bad weather and the leaky condition of the ship forced the captain to scuttle his vessel at Dusky Sound on the bleak southern most corner of New Zealand. In 1797 the American ship the *Mercury* found the starving survivors and took them to Norfolk Island. As Governor Hunter informed London they were 'unfortunate people whose deplorable situation for so long a time had given me much concern'. Marcus was returned to the Australian mainland in April 1804. He had been ship wrecked for twenty months. Marcus was employed in Sydney as a constable from 1806 to 1808 and may well have accompanied the doomed Elias Davis (q.v.) to the gallows in 1806. In March 1806 and March 1807 Marcus applied for permission to leave the colony possibly working as a whaler. Marcus became a servant in the household of Simeon Lord and on 5 April 1807 was caught as he 'entered his master's house through a window during the night, with a suspicious design'.

On 21 October 1809, fifteen Aborigines or 'native bandits' attacked his home on the Parramatta Road, and wounded his de facto wife with a spear, and stole two muskets and some artefacts from his farm. Marcus then rented a farm on the George River and on 14 July 1810 was sentenced for fraudulently obtaining seed wheat from government stores. He was charged with having supplied his seed wheat for next season's food supply to a baker. He was sentenced to three months hard labour for his 'turpitude'. On the basis of having been in the colony for nineteen years, Marcus wrote to Governor Macquarie asking for a grant of land. Macquarie refused, writing on his petition: 'Not to have any grants, not being a good character'. The Governor was probably referring to the fact that Marcus was not married and so, in November 1811 Marcus married Dorcas Jane Broughton at St John's Church in Parramatta. His marriage did not solve his financial predicament and he was weighed down with debt.

On 10 July 1811 the Colonial Secretary noted that Marcus could receive land in the new Districts of Airds and Appin. Grateful for 'official beneficence' Marcus gave a donation to the building of a new courthouse in Sydney. On 27 December 1813 the Provost Marshall announced that he would sell the four acres of land that belonged to Marcus together with its crop of potatoes. The land was finally transferred to Solomon Levey (q.v.) in 1819. In 1820, 'Jane Marcus … a most profligate character was charged with the cruel treatment to her husband a palsied and infirm old man'. She was sentenced to six months hard labour. Marcus was granted John James, 'a government servant', and the arrangement worked well because in September 1824 Marcus recommended John James for a ticket of leave. In the 1828 Census he was listed as a householder, aged seventy, living in George Street, Sydney. Marcus died on 26 November of that year. The death of 'Jane' Marcus, aged fifty, occurred in the same year. Marcus was buried in the old Jewish cemetery in Sydney. A copy of his gravestone was later moved to the Pioneers' Cemetery at Botany Bay. The Jewish community must have arranged for the headstone to be purchased and on it is carved, in Hebrew, the final verse of the medieval hymn *Adon Olam*.

The colony's Anglican chaplain, the Rev. William Cowper, had a long relationship with Marcus. Cowper hoped to convert Marcus to Christianity and described his conversations in some detail to the London Society for Promoting Christianity Amongst the Jews. Marcus obviously enjoyed the discussions about the Bible and the meaning of Hebrew phrases and Cowper imported some Hebrew books for Marcus to study. According to Cowper, Marcus had officiated at Sydney's first Jewish funeral services between 1817 and 1825. Marcus must be remembered as Australia's first 'rabbi'.

William Pitt Indent, p. 272; www.tasfamily.net.a/~schafferi/Survivors of the Endeavour, HRASeries 1, vol. 2 p. 115 *Governor Hunter to the Duke of Portland* 10 January 1790. *Sydney Gazette*, 14 July 1805, 19, 23 March 1806, 29 March 1807, 5 April 1807, 21 September 1809, 24 September 1809, 10 July 1810, 14 July 1810, 22 February 1812, September 1820; Petition to Governor Macquarie, 15 January 1811, Memorial no. 204, in 4/1822; 4/1866, p. 13. Piper Papers, V. 1.387, A254; London Society for Promoting Christianity Among the Jews, *Annual Reports*, 1818–1827; John S. Levi, *The Tale of Australia's First "Rabbi"—Joseph Marcus AJJHS*, vol. 8, no. 2 (1975), p. 29f.

MARCUS, Samuel

b. Germany, 1801
America (1), 1829; Convict; Sentenced to 7 years, Bristol, 1828.
Widower; Fustian dealer; Height: 156 cm.

Dark ruddy complexion, brown hair, hazel eyes. Jew. Could read and write. Widower. No children. Samuel Marcus was transported for 'stealing money'.

Samuel Marcus arrived in New South Wales on 18 August 1829. He was assigned on arrival to Andrew Brown at Toongabbie and was entered in the Campbell-town Punishments Books as a member of 'No. 33 Road Gang'. On 21 April 1830 he was found to have been insolent to a constable and was placed on the treadmill for three days. On 9 April 1832 he was accused of insolence and given twenty-five lashes, and was to be returned to the road gang. On 16 April 1832 he was reprimanded for being absent without leave. Two days later he was convicted of having accused the overseer falsely and was given six months in irons in the road gang. A conditional pardon was granted in 1838 and on 30 October Marcus was granted a certificate of freedom.

America (1) Indent 4/4014, p. 207; CP 38/930; Campbelltown Punishments Book, ML, F47, 9 April 1832, 16 April 1832, 18 April 1832; CF 4/4344, 38/0930.

MARGERSON, George (MAGERRISON)

1813–1858
Isabella I (4), 1832; Convict; Sentenced to 7 years, Derby, 1831.
Single.

George Margerson arrived in Sydney on 15 March 1832 and was assigned to the Hyde Park Barracks, where he was listed as a Jew. On 26 May 1846 he was discharged from the barracks and sent to Cockatoo Island in Sydney Harbour for punishment lasting one month. He died in the District of Wellington in 1858 and was not buried as a Jew.

ML 2/8285.

MARKS, Abraham

1850; Free.
Single.

Abraham Marks married Rebecca Abraham at Hobart Town on 24 July 1850. Abraham Marks became the honorary treasurer of the Hobart Synagogue in the 1860s.

MARKS, Adolphus

b. Sydney, 1837–1882

The firstborn son of Solomon Marks (q.v.) and Hannah (née Ann Cohen, q.v.) Marks, Adolphus married his first cousin, Charlotte Cohen, the daughter of Samuel Henry Cohen (q.v.), in Melbourne in 1860.

MARKS, Benjamin Francis

b. Sydney, 1846
5 children.

Benjamin Marks was the second child of Solomon Marks (q.v.) and Hannah (née Ann Cohen, q.v.). In 1876 Benjamin Francis Marks married his first cousin Jane (Jenny) Matilda Cohen (1849–1930), the daughter of Abraham and Sophia Cohen (qq.v.). They settled in Brisbane. One of their five children, Gladys Marks (1883–1970), was the first woman to be appointed an acting university professor in New South Wales.

MARKS, Blanche

b. Austria, 1798–1846
1838; Free.
Married.

The wife of Blucher Marks (q.v.), Blanche followed her husband out to New South Wales. Blanche Marks was buried in Sydney on 21 July 1846. She was forty-eight years old, 'a native of Austria', and a member of the York Street Synagogue.

MARKS, Blucher (Mark BLUCHER)

b. Austria, 1801–1846
Dunvegan Castle, 1830; Convict; Sentenced to 7 years, Nottingham, 1829.
Married; Indoor servant and jeweller; Height: 158 cm.

Ruddy freckled and pock-pitted complexion. Brown hair. Hazel eyes. Scar on forepart of left leg. Could read. A 'Hebrew'. Blucher Marks was transported for stealing a quantity of lace at Nottingham. He was sentenced on 14 January 1829. He had no previous conviction. Blucher Marks seems to have reversed his name at some time following his arrival, causing some official confusion. He was married to Blanche Marks (q.v.).

'Mark Blucher' arrived in New South Wales on 30 March 1830. It was noted that the government would retain the £6 that he had brought out on the convict transport until he received his pardon. He was counted in the convict muster at the Hyde Park Barracks on 1 April 1830. He was granted a ticket of leave in 1836 and a certificate of freedom on 14 January 1843. At the conclusion of his sentence, Marks was issued with the £6 that had been held for him in the Savings Bank while he was still a convict. In 1838 he was joined in Australia by his wife Blanche, a 'native of Austria', who came free. Blucher Marks was licensed as the publican of the Steam Packet Hotel at Market Wharf in Sydney on 21 July 1837. He was a member of the Sydney Synagogue. Blucher died intestate in Sydney, on 20 July 1846, and left an estate of £38.

Dunvegan Castle, Printed Indent, 1830, A1217, no. 30–522, p. 463; Governors' Despatches 1838, A1218, p. 493, and 1847; Principal Superintendent of Convicts, Butts of CF, 1842–43, 4/4379, p. 499; TL 36/1120 and 36/1217; CF 43/0073; *Sydney Morning Herald*, 21 July 1837.

MARKS, Caspar (Casper)

b. Pest, Hungary, c. 1793–1879
Achilles, 1841; Free.
Married; Dealer; 7 children.

Casper Marks was born, probably in 1793, in Pest. By the year 1838 he was in New York, married to his wife Julia, and already the father of a number of children. The family moved to Manila in the Philippines and arrived in Sydney on 12 July 1841. He brought to Australia '28 Packages, one cask, one bundle, two chests and three trunks amounting to cash, jewellery and goods to the value of £600'.

The Marks family could not have arrived at a worse time due to the economic depression. As he stated before the Chief Commissioner of Insolvent Estates:

> In almost every transaction, since I had been in the colony, I have lost money by the goods I purchased; on the 10th of this present month I had been twelve months in this colony … I have bought most goods by auction … I had a shop to sell the goods I bought … I can recollect every article I had in my shop that was marked; although I kept no books, I can recollect what loss I have had by distinct transactions; I swear I never told anyone that I keep books. I can figure a very little.

As a consequence of this inability to keep clear accounts, on 26 June 1842, Casper Marks, 'a dealer in Bridge St', was summoned to the Supreme Court in Sydney to be declared insolvent. The description of the hearing was savage as he successfully contested a charge of fraudulent insolvency. Marks was described as a dealer who maintained a linen drapery store in Bridge Street. His debts amounted to £2011 and his assets £1001. He was described as 'an Austrian who cannot write, neither can his shopman write or count'. He gave his trustees 'all that he had', £252, and his insolvency was discharged on 2 January 1845 with the payment of 8s 6d in the pound. On 7 October 1842, Casper Marks was charged with 'fraudulent' insolvency because he had concealed two sovereigns prior to his departure for Bombay with a bag of gold. He was found 'not guilty' and discharged from insolvency on 3 January 1845.

On 6 January 1843 Marks had applied for a passport so that he could go to Van Diemen's Land on business. He gave his address as Brickfield Hill, George Street, Sydney. He and his wife Julia had six children still living at home. They were: Nancy, Henry, Janette, Alexander, Rachel and Maria. A daughter Ann was married to a Mr Whitefield. Ann died on 10 December 1846 at the age of nineteen. Her husband was 'at sea' at the time and she was buried in the Jewish cemetery.

Mr and Mrs Marks and their six children went to Manila in January 1843 on the *Giraffe*, returning again in June 1844. He faced a charge of fraud by John Joel Cohen (q.v.) that he had misled the court and that he possessed a bag of gold while he claimed to be bereft of funds.

Marks was listed in *Low's Directory of the City and District of Sydney* in 1847 as a 'slop seller' with a shop at 673 George Street, Sydney. Marks gave a donation of £6 to the synagogue in 1845 and was a seat holder. The family travelled to San Francisco and to the Californian gold rush and then returned to Australia. It was at his business address in Sydney that the 'marriage of Mr Julius Rosenthal of Melbourne, son of the Reverend Moses Jacob Rosenthal, Chief Rabbi of the Province of Wartzburgh, to Jeanette, eldest daughter of Mr Casper Marks', took place. By the 1850s the Marks sons, Alexander and Henry, lived in Melbourne. In 1847 'Mr and Mrs Marks' moved to Melbourne and, in April 1847, asked for a reduced membership fee in order to join the synagogue. Casper Marks joined the Melbourne Hebrew Congregation on 28 September 1853 and remained in Melbourne as a 'merchant'.

In 1858 Alexander and Henry Marks set out for China and Japan and became merchants in Hong Kong and Yokohama.

Julia Marks of Drummond Street, Carlton, died on 13 January 1874. Casper Marks died on 20 May 1879 at the age of eighty-six. Both were buried in the Melbourne General Cemetery.

Egon Kunz, *Blood and Gold: Hungarians in Australia*, p. 25f.; *Sydney Gazette*, 2 June 1842; *Sydney Morning Herald*, 15 October 1842, 2 January 1845; *Sydney Free Press*, 26 June 1842; Melbourne Hebrew Congregation Minute Book, 28 September 1853.

MARKS, Charles

b. Fleet Street, London, 1821
London (1), 1844; Convict; Sentenced to 7 years, Central Criminal Court, 1843.
Single; Tailor; Height: 152 cm.

Fresh complexion, dark brown hair and whiskers, large nose, prominent mouth and chin. Literate. Scar on second finger left hand. Small scar on forehead. A Jew. Charles Marks obtained umbrellas and stockings by false pretences using the name of a Mr Nathan. He had been convicted six months before for a similar offence.

Charles Marks arrived in Van Diemen's Land on 9 July 1844. He emerged from his initial time of service at Broadmarsh on 11 October 1845 and began a six-year period of assigned service in Oatlands (1846), Green Ponds (1846), Hobart Town (1847), Richmond (1847), and Launceston and the surrounding district (1848–50). In January 1851 his period of service was extended with six months hard labour and he was to be kept on probation for having absconded from assignment in Hobart Town.

CON 33/56, no. 13271.

MARKS, Edward

b. London, 1826
1848; Free.
Single; Dealer.

Edward Marks was a brother of Morris Marks (q.v.) and, through the Levey family, a cousin of Jacob Marks (q.v.). In 1849 Edward Marks lived on the premises of the store of Philip Phillips (q.v.) and was employed by Jacob Marks to keep an eye on the business of Philip Phillips of Geelong.

MARKS, Ellen

b. 1805
Free.

Ellen Marks, aged thirty-nine, married George Rose, aged thirty, on 1 April 1844 in Hobart Town.

MARKS, George

d. 1871
Free.

In the 1842 Census in Van Diemen's Land, David and Solomon Benjamin (qq.v.) and George Marks were listed as shopkeepers who lived in Elizabeth Street, Launceston. All three were single. George Marks signed the May 1843 Launceston Synagogue petition. On 7 June 1843 George Marks, insolvent, asked for a discharge from bankruptcy but was refused as fees had not been paid. A George Marks died at George Town on 6 January 1871, at the age of forty-three.

Launceston Examiner, 7 June 1843; CO 280/157.

MARKS, Hannah

1818–1904.

The third daughter of Henry and Elizabeth Cohen (qqv.). Married Solomon Marks (q.v.), a school master in Sydney on 3 August 1836. Their children were Adolphus (1837–1882), Benjamin Francis (1846), Esther (1850), Elizabeth, Frank Samuel (c1865-1893).

Hannah died in Sydney at the age of eighty-six on 14 February 1904 and was buried at Rookwood.

MARKS, Hannah (Anna)

1818–1876, Whitechapel
Grenada, Free.

Arrived with her mother and siblings in 1827.The daughter of Philip and Sarah Marks (qqv.) Hannah 'of the New Town Road' married Mark Solomons (Solomon, q.v.) in the first Jewish marriage in Van Diemen's Land on 13 December 1833 (*Hobart Town Courier*). Mark Solomon died on 25 June 1837. On 12 June 1840, Hannah married Robert Hart (q.v.). When Hannah married Mark she became the stepmother to his young daughters, Hannah aged 10 and Rachel aged 8. Although both girls had been baptised. Hannah seems to have raised them as Jews and they both married the Anderson (q.v.) men and are buried in the Jewish section of the Rookwood cemetery. Hannah Solomon had evidently managed the King William IV Hotel in Liverpool Street, Hobart Town, together with her husband and in 1839 she was granted the licence in her own name. Mark and Hannah had one child, Simon, who was born in 1835 and died 9 August 1894. Hannah Solomon died at Melbourne 25 February 1876.
Family information Susan Groenhout and Gerry Whitmont.

MARKS, Henry

Elizabeth, 1830; Free.
Married; Tailor.

Henry Marks arrived in Sydney on 15 April 1830, on the same ship as John Hart (q.v.). Both were tailors.

MARKS, Hyam (Hoppy My Hearty)

b. Whitechapel, 1823
1840; Free; Sentenced to 7 years, Sydney Quarter Sessions, 1843.
Single; Dealer; Height: 170 cm.

Hyam Marks came to Sydney, probably in 1840, as a free, young man. He was a dealer in Prince Street, Sydney. His business collapsed in July 1843 and he was sent to gaol. On 13 September 1843 he was sentenced in Sydney to seven years transportation for stealing a cash box containing £33 from Mr Hayden of King Street. Marks had a dark complexion, brown hair, long face, long nose and small chin and mouth. He had a large scar on the top of his forehead. He was described as a labourer and draper and a Jew. He could read and write. His mother was Phoebe Marks of Church Lane in London. He had a brother and five sisters who were in London, and Hannah (q.v.), who lived in Van Diemen's Land. At the time of his trial, Marks was only twenty years of age. He was sent to Van Diemen's Land on the *Sir John Byng* for the crime of 'stealing from a dwelling'.

His initial period of probation lasted for fifteen months, which he completed on 29 January 1845. He then served for several months as a constable in Hobart Town, until he was accused of making the improper arrest of Mr G. Harrison. Marks was sentenced to four months hard labour and was dismissed from the police. He received his ticket of leave on 22 February 1848. In 1849 he was given two sentences of a month in solitary confinement in Hobart Town—one for making a false statement and one for common assault. His conditional pardon was recommended on 4 December 1848 and approved on 1 January 1850. Joseph Lewis Marks, son of Hyam Marks, was buried by the Sydney Synagogue on 21 February 1859, aged eighteen months.

'Humphrey Marks' was listed as renting seat no. 67 in the Hobart Synagogue in 1845.

CON 31, no. 245; CON 16/1/2; CON 38/1/1; CON 37/1/1, p. 245; HO 10/61, p. 96; *Sydney Morning Herald*, 21 June 1843, 2 August 1843, 19 September 1843.

MARKS, Isaac

Free.

Isaac Marks was a member of the Hobart Synagogue from 1842 to 1845. He gave a donation of ten shillings in April 1843 and ten shillings in 1844. The synagogue ledger recorded: 'Left the colony 4 January 1845'.

MARKS, Jacob

b. London, 1819–1896
Hercules, 1835; Free.
Single; Dealer; 14 children.

Jacob Marks was the fifth child of Lyon Marks and Frances (née Levey), known as Fanny, who was the favourite sister of Solomon Levey (q.v.). Five of Jacob's siblings also settled in Australia. Jacob Marks travelled steerage on the *Hercules*, arriving in Sydney on 27 July 1835, with his uncle, Isaac Levey (q.v.), and described as a 'settler'. Jacob followed his uncle Isaac to the Yass District, where he bought land and opened a store at Curryong Creek. In a petition to Governor Gipps dated 11 June 1839, and written at Mr (Isaac) Levey's Australia House, George Street, Sydney, Marks wrote that he was a storekeeper at Curryong Creek (not his own store) when three armed bushrangers held up the store at a time when the bushrangers Hall and Mayne had just been executed. In defending the store Marks received gunshot wounds, one in his cheek, which broke his jawbone and the rest in his head and body, which 'rendered him incapable of gaining his livelihood.' Marks asked for a grant of a small portion of land 'for the purpose of turning his attention to agricultural pursuits, affording him the means of subsistence'. Governor Gipps replied, 'I have no power to grant land to anybody'.

Marks moved to the colony of Melbourne in 1840 and went into business as a shopkeeper. 'Harris and Marks' formed one of the most effective drapery partnerships in early Melbourne and the partners built a two-storey store. However, no sooner was it completed than economic depression forced the dissolution of the partnership and a 'sacrificial sale' of their 'rich and extensive stock'.

On 14 May 1846 'Jacob Marks of Port Phillip' married his 16-year-old first cousin Susannah (Susan) Levey (q.v.), the daughter of Isaac Levey and his wife Dinah, at the Sydney Synagogue. Susannah was ten years younger than the groom and had arrived in Australia on the same ship. Jacob Marks was a signatory to the 1846 address of the 'British Jews resident in Port Phillip', which congratulated Chief Rabbi Nathan Adler on his appointment as chief rabbi.

In the Melbourne Hebrew Congregation's Birth Register, Jacob Marks was listed as a 'draper' when, in 1847, a daughter, Selina, was born.

In 1840 Marks had begun to buy property scattered through Victoria in Warrnambool, Geelong, and North Melbourne. He was involved in a 'scam' with Philip Phillips (q.v.) of Geelong, who attempted to save part of his stock in bankruptcy proceedings by holding a fake auction at Colac. By 1850 Marks had moved to Sydney and the records show three significant purchases of land in the Sydney area costing more than £3000.

In February 1860 the Sydney City Council resolved to lease from Jacob Marks a building at 6 Carrington Street that had been the home of the Union Club. The council remained there as his tenant for eight years. When the Union Club later moved to Bligh Street, Jacob's house became the Town Hall and then the Imperial Hotel and finally the site of Australia House.

Jacob and Susannah travelled extensively in his latter years. They had fourteen surviving children. Jacob died in Brighton, England, on 3 March 1896, and Susannah in 1904.

Their children were Selina (5 August 1847), born at Collins Street in Melbourne; Leon (Lyon) (13 November 1848), at Swanston Street in Melbourne; Deborah (1850), at Scone, New South Wales; Maria (2 December 1851), in Sydney; Frances (22 May 1853); Montague (1854); John (1856); Dinah (1860); Alice (1861);

Alfred (1862); Isabella (1863); Harold (1865); Arnold (1868); and Septimus (1872). The last seven children were born in London.

Petition, 11 June 1839, 39/6555, in 2/7914, Land Correspondence; *Port Phillip Herald*, 28 August 1843; *Sydney Morning Herald*, 2 September 1854.

MARKS, John

b. London, 1809
Florentia (1), 1828; Convict; Sentenced to 14 years, Old Bailey, 1827.
Single; Dyer's boy; Height: 161 cm.

Dark sallow complexion, black hair, dark brown eyes. Could read. A Jew. John Marks was a pick-pocket who stole a watch. At Tower Hill he accidentally fell over a bundle of clothes and the watch was revealed. Marks resisted arrest. Though the court records note that he was nineteen, according to the 1837 General Muster of Convicts in New South Wales, he was twelve years of age at the time of his trial.

John Marks was the assigned servant of William Pothers, Cook's River. A ticket of leave was issued for the District of Liverpool. In the latter part of 1837 it was cancelled as he was found to be absent from muster, drunk and disorderly. A certificate of freedom was granted on 19 August 1841. On 18 June 1845 Marks was sent to the Maitland Stockade for trial where he was sentenced to twelve calendar months imprisonment in the Maitland Stockade. His behaviour was 'orderly'.

OBSP, 1826–27, case 1208, p. 469; 4/4094 lists TL 34/747; *Florentia* (1) Indent 4/4013, p. 21; Newcastle Gaol Entrance and Description Book, 1841–1845, 2/2008; CF 4/4368, 41/1113.

MARKS, Joshua

1816–1891
Grenada, 1827; Free.
Single; Dealer; 6 children.

Joshua Marks paid £1 to the Hobart Synagogue building appeal in 1843 and rented seat no. 6 in the synagogue. He married his first cousin Esther Marks, the daughter of 'Leon the Hatter', on 12 September 1844. It was Van Diemen's Land's ninth Jewish wedding. Their children were Elizabeth (Betsy) (born 27 May 1845, married Isaac Lazarus 2 August 1876 and died in Melbourne 9 April 1911), Rosetta Sarah (27 May 1846 married John Jacob Davis 6 August 1873. Died 20 August 1906), Lewis (21 July 1847 married Catherine Emden 24 February 1875. Died 19 July 1917), Solomon (24 April 1849 married Minnie Bauman 1885. Died Victoria 1921), and Catherine (22 November 1850, who died three and a half months later). Philip was born in Hobart in ca 1854 and died Melbourne 6 November 1913. He married Hamer Maria (Hannah) Cottren on 24 January 1876. The Hobart Synagogue Ledger noted that the family 'left the colony' in 1870.

Hobart Town Courier, 9 June 1843.

MARKS, Julia

d. 1874
Achilles, 1844; Free.
Married; 7 children.

Julia was the wife of Casper Marks (q.v.). She died on 13 January 1874.

MARKS, Leah (Lydia)

b. London, 1811–1875
Penyard Park, 1850; Free.
Widow; 8 children.

The daughter of Frances Levey (1783–1857) and Lyon Marks (1780–1842), Leah Marks married Lewis Harris in London in 1829. Leah was the granddaughter of Moses Lyon Levey and Deborah. She was therefore the niece of Barnett Levey (q.v.), Solomon Levey (q.v.), Isaac Levey (q.v.), and Rebecca Ellis (q.v.). She arrived in Australia on the *Penyard Park* on 2 March 1850 with five of her eight children. She died in Sydney on 8 July 1875.

Leah and Lewis's children were Elizabeth Harris (born 1830), Henry Harris Marks (1831), Maurice Harris Marks (1833), Frances (Fanny) Harris (1837), Ailsie Harris (1840), Susan Harris (1842), Emanuel Victor Harris (1847), and Lionel Harris (1849).

Elizabeth married Henry Cohen, who settled first in Melbourne in 1853, and then Sydney in 1855, with his Monster Clothing Store at 402 George Street. They had thirteen children. Henry settled in New York. Maurice married Elizabeth Phillips, the daughter of Emanuel and Hannah Phillips, on 14 September 1853. They lived at Southridge, Christchurch, New Zealand. Frances married Alexander Conway, and lived in Sydney. They had seven children. Ailsie married Lewis Conway in 1859. They had eight children, and lived in rural New South Wales and Adelaide, where Conway took the surname Jacobs. Susan married Moses Moss on 7 May 1863 in Sydney (Moss was born Moses but was known as Montague). Emanuel had been living in Scone before his marriage on 28 August 1878 to Kate Moss in Adelaide. They had four children. Lionel married Leah Phillips on 17 March 1875, and they lived in Christchurch, New Zealand.

Archives of the Australian Jewish Historical Society, Sydney.

MARKS, Lewis

Free.
Single.

Lewis Marks married Eve Solomon in a Jewish ceremony in Sydney on 20 March 1850. Eve was the daughter of Elias Solomon (q.v.) and his wife Fanny.

MARKS, Lydia (Leah)

1825–1863; Free.
8 children.

Lydia, the daughter of Mark and Juliet Marks of Sydney, married Joseph Collins (q.v.) of Goulburn at the Sydney Synagogue on 7 October 1847. Lydia had eight children and died on 15 March 1863. She was buried at the Jewish cemetery at Goulburn.

MARKS, Mark

b. London 1801
Anson, 1844; Convict; Sentenced to 10 years, Central Criminal Court, 1843.
Married; Gold and silver refiner; Height: 163 cm.

Fresh complexion, hair and whiskers reddish, light brown eyes, medium mouth, nose and chin. A Jew. Could read and write 'a little'. Mark Marks bought gold rings knowing them to be stolen. Marks had been tried once before for a similar charge and acquitted.

Marks arrived in Hobart Town on 4 February 1844. His initial period of probation was set at twenty months and Marks was sent to Seven Mile Creek. He emerged from the road gang in October 1845. During the following years of assigned service his record showed that the Jews of Van Diemen's Land attempted to look after him and, in quick succession, he was assigned to Bertram Nathan (q.v.), Moses Phillips (q.v.), Solomon Nathan (q.v.), and Louis Nathan (q.v.). Louis Nathan refused to put up with any nonsense and reported Marks to the authorities for insolence and for being absent without leave on 23 September 1846, one day after the festival of the Jewish New Year. He was sentenced to three weeks imprisonment and hard labour. On 17 November 1846 in Deloraine he was charged with misconduct for having in his possession a quantity of tea and sugar for which he could not give a satisfactory account. He was sentenced to seven days solitary confinement. A ticket of leave was granted on 29 May 1849. On 5 July 1850 he was fined ten shillings for a breach of the Police Act while working for Mr Nathan in Launceston and a conditional pardon was approved on 19 August 1851.

CON 33/50, no. 11624.

MARKS, Mark

1845; Free.
Married.

Mark Marks arrived in Sydney in 1845 with his wife Hannah, the sister of Rachael Ackman (q.v.) and Samuel Henry Harris (q.v.).

MARKS, Mordecai

b. 1768
Ganges, 1797; Convict; Sentenced to life, Kent Assizes, 1794.
Height: 163 cm.

Mordecai Marks was sentenced at the Kent Assizes on 17 March 1794.

In the General Muster of 1806 Mordecai Marks had a ticket of leave and lived at Parramatta. In October 1809 Marks received official permission to leave Australia for England on the *Boyd*. However, Mordecai remained in New South Wales and, in the 1814 Muster, was listed as free with a ticket of leave and working as a constable. An absolute pardon was granted and Marks returned then to England.

Ganges Indent 2/8261, p. 3; New South Wales Muster, 12 August 1806; *Sydney Gazette*, 15 October 1809, 22 October 1809; Convict Indent COD/9.

MARKS, Morris

Free.
Single; Dealer; 2 children.

Morris Marks was a cousin of Jacob Marks (q.v.) and a brother of Edward Marks (q.v.). In the *Sydney Morning Herald* of 16 April 1842, 'Morris Marks, Merchant, Maitland', was listed as insolvent. In 1845 he was a Sydney Synagogue seat holder. On 22 September 1845 his store was in George Street at the former site of the Bank of Australia. He was the sole agent for 'Electro-Galvanic Rings: for use for gout, rheumatism, cough, scurvy, ring worm', which were manufactured in London by D. Marks & Co. In the 1847 edition of *Low's Directory of the City and District of Sydney*, Morris Marks was listed as a bookseller and stationer at 99 Kings Street.

Morris Marks married Rebecca Moses (q.v.) (who was a minor) in Hobart Town on 30 June 1847. Morris Marks and Rebecca were listed as early members of the Melbourne Hebrew Congregation. A licence was granted to Morris Marks to manage the Rainbow Inn, King Street, providing that his house on the premises could be completed by 30 June 1848. In Geelong, on 1 April 1848, a son, Moses, was born, but lived for only one month and nine days. A daughter, Elizabeth, was born on 23 February 1849; her father's occupation was listed as 'publican'.

Port Phillip Herald, 9 May 1848; *Melbourne Morning Herald*, 9, 15 February, 17 April 1849; *Sydney Morning Herald*, 22 September 1845.

MARKS, Morris Lyon

b. Liverpool, 1824–1893
Abberton, 1846; Free.
Single; Dealer; 13 children.

Morris Lyon Marks was the sixth child of Frances and Lyon Marks. He was born on 7 September 1824 and arrived in Australia aboard the *Abberton* on 13 December 1846.

Morris Marks moved to Adelaide and, on 3 March 1847, M & S Marks was listed as one of the thirty-one principal shops in a poll on early closing (7 p.m.). On 16 February 1848 Marks advertised that he was looking for more employees. Morris Marks and his brother, Solomon Lyon Marks (q.v.), sold their store at the copper mining town of Burra Burra on 8 July 1848, and advertised a stocktaking sale on Saturday 27 July 1848. The partners called their Hindley Street store Burra Burra House. The business prospered and on 7 March 1849 they announced that they were 'selling off prior to moving to more capacious premises in Adelaide'. On 12 May 1849 it was reported that 'Hindley Street will soon be additionally enhanced by the opening of Messrs M. and S. Marks' handsome new drapery and silk store. The Messrs Marks have already acquired considerable eminence in Adelaide and the renowned Burra Burra store and we have no doubt their funds will follow them'.

Morris Marks became the honorary treasurer of the Adelaide Hebrew Congregation in 1850. The *South Australian Register* reported on 31 January 1850 that Morris Marks of the Liverpool Mart in Adelaide had married Leah Solomon (q.v.), sister of Judah Moss Solomon (q.v.). They were married by Mr Abraham Solomon (q.v.), who was 'a Jewish rabbi lately arrived from London'. Morris and Leah had two sons in Adelaide (Lyon Solomon Marks and Moss Phillip Marks). Before sailing for London aboard the *Australian* on 15 February 1854, Lyon died in Adelaide at the age of twenty months. On the voyage to London, Moss also died. A daughter, Elizabeth, was born in London in 1855. Between 1856 and 1860 three more sons were born in Adelaide. Morris also adopted his niece, Caroline Phillips, the daughter of his sister Susan Marks (Phillips, q.v.). The family moved to Melbourne (where a son was born in 1861), before moving to Wellington, where another six children were born, making nine sons and four daughters. Morris Lyon Marks died in Melbourne on 4 March 1893 and Leah died on 4 August 1905.

Their surviving children were Elizabeth, Morris (born 1856), Sidney (1858), Frederick (1859), Albert (1861), Marcus (1863), in Nelson (New Zealand), Louis (1865), Lionel (1867), Fanny (1869), and Leah (1870) in Wellington, New Zealand.

South Australian Gazette and Colonial Register, 31 January 1850; Pritchard Index.

MARKS, Moses Abraham

d. 1848

Moses Abraham Marks was buried in the Jewish section of the Old Melbourne Cemetery on 5 September 1848 and reinterred in Fawkner in 1923.

MARKS, Moss (Moses)

1815–1869
British Sovereign, 1834; Free.
Single; Butcher; 5 children.

Moses and Solomon Marks (q.v.) were passengers on board the *British Sovereign*, and arrived in Sydney on 18 September 1834. The *Sydney Morning Herald* of 16 April

1842 listed the insolvency of Moss Marks of West Maitland with debts of £1378 and assets of £1113. Marks was a butcher. His trustees were Alexander Dodds of East Maitland and Samuel Cohen (q.v.) of West Maitland.

Moss Marks married Esther Davis (née Hart) and they made their home in Adelaide. Esther had two children from her first marriage and five from the second. They were: Elizabeth (born 1842), Amelia (1844), Alice (1855), Kate (1856), Amy (1858), Maria (1861), and Charlotte (1863). Moss Marks died 5 August 1869 at the age of fifty-three. He had been the Honorary Secretary of the committee formed to organise the building of a chapel in the Goulburn Jewish burial ground.

Esther Marks died in 1914.

Sydney Morning Herald, 16 April, 22 April 1842.

MARKS, Mr

Hartley, 1837; Free.
Married; 1 child.

A family of three with the last name Marks arrived in Adelaide on the *Hartley* on 28 October 1837. In the 1842 census in South Australia both husband and wife were listed as under thirty-five years of age, with one male child under the age of seven.

MARKS, Philip

b. Houndsditch, ca 1770–1864
Transported twice: the *Alexander* in 1806 and *Asia II* (2) in 1824; Convict; Sentenced to life, Old Bailey, 1822.
Married; Hat-maker; 3 children.

Philip Marks first appeared at the Old Bailey on 24 October 1801, at the age of twenty, Marks together with Thomas Williams, a thirteen-year-old friend, were sentenced to seven years transportation for 'larceny'.

Philip Mark (sic) was sent out to New South Wales on the convict transport *Alexander* arriving in New South Wales on 2 August 1806 by which time he had already served most of his sentence. He obviously returned to London as soon as he could and subsequently married Sarah Solomon at the Great Synagogue on 9 December 1818. They had three children. There is a family tradition that one child was given to his brother Lyon in England.

Marks was convicted at the Old Bailey for a second time on 4 December 1822 for stealing a gold watch from the person of George Cotton who was 'hustled' as he stood on the front step of a London public house near Pall Mall. At the time of his arrest on 11 November 1822 he brazenly protested 'I was only standing at the door and am as innocent as my five babies at home'. Marks together with his nineteen–year-old accomplice John Ryan, were sentenced to transportation for life for larceny. After a chase through the streets of London, Marks was found to have in his possession a gold watch, a gold chain, two gold seals and a gold key, eleven guineas in gold, a pocket-book containing three one pound notes, a silk handkerchief a dollar and a new, unopened umbrella. Sarah, Philip's wife, fought a valiant battle to save her husband from deportation.

His convict dossier in Van Diemen's Land shows that Philip Marks spent most of his period of servitude frantically trying to escape. On 2 April 1824, while assigned to Mr Thornton, he was found to have secreted himself on board the *Woodlark* with intent to escape from the colony. He was given fifty lashes and returned to the Hobart Town Prisoners' Barracks. On 24 February 1825 he was charged with having absconded from the colony on the *Prince Regent* in October 1824. He was brought back to Van Diemen's Land from Mauritius per the *Philip Dundas* and was sentenced to another fifty lashes. In October 1825, while working as a baker on a chain gang, he was sentenced to fifty lashes for going aboard the schooner *Sally* with intent to escape to New Zealand. In July 1826 he received twenty-five lashes for being absent from the chain gang. On 21 October he received fifty lashes for 'defacing his leg irons'. On 3 November he escaped from the chain gang and remained at large for two weeks. When recaptured he was sentenced to a further fifty lashes and was to be sent to Macquarie Harbour. On 27 November, while waiting to be sent to the West Coast, he 'breaks the walls of H. M. Gaol' and was captured while trying to escape.

Marks served his time at Macquarie Harbour and in 1830 he returned to Hobart Town, where his wife was waiting for him. On 5 January 1831, while assigned to his wife Sarah Marks (q.v.), he was 'admonished' for being absent from muster at church. On 20 May 1834 Marks held a ticket of leave and was reprimanded for being in the Green Gate public house after hours. A conditional pardon was granted on 10 October 1836 and a free pardon was approved on 21 May 1840.

Marks worked as a fishmonger on stall no. 25 in the new Hobart Town market in 1834. On 2 June 1837 Philip Marks of the New Town Road was considered to be respectable enough to have had the Jewish convict George Moss (q.v.) assigned to him. The arrangement did not last long and Moss was soon imprisoned at Port Arthur. By 11 August 1837 Marks was licensed as a hawker and he retained his licence until 1841. His home was at 131 Elizabeth Street in Hobart Town. In January 1852 Marks, aged 72, travelled on the *Sacramento* to Melbourne. His occupation was given as 'English Grocer' who lived at 131 Elizabeth Street, Hobart Town.

He was a member of the Hobart Synagogue, donating £2 9s 6d in 1844 and rented seat no. 19 in 1845. The synagogue records that Joshua died in Melbourne in September 1891. Rosetta (q.v.), and Anna (Hannah) died in Hobart.

Despite having received 250 lashes for his escape efforts Phillip Marks died aged eighty-six in Hobart on 31 March 1864. He was buried in Hobart's Harrington Street Cemetery and re-interred in 2002 in the Jewish section of the Cornelian Bay Cemetery with his wife Sarah Marks (q.v.).

He left his estate to his son Joshua Marks.

CON 31/29, no. 464; HO 10/56; CP no. 1085; FP no. 560. OBSP 24 October 1804 case 569 and OBSP 4 December 1822 case 102. Family information from Susan Grounhout and Gerry Whitmont; vide: Sarah Marks at OBSP 9 April 1823, case 645.

MARKS, Rosetta

b. Whitechapel, d.1865
Grenada, 1827; Free
Single, 10 Children.

The daughter of Philip Marks (q.v.) and Hannah Marks (q.v.). Rosetta arrived with her siblings and mother while her father was serving a life sentence and she was educated while living in Argyle Street. She was reunited with her father when he was assigned to her mother in 1832. Rosetta married Abraham Rheuben (q.v.) in 1837 and bore ten children, four daughters and six sons. She began her married life in Newtown Road and later moved to Elizabeth Street. (Her husband owned more than thirty properties throughout his life.)

The circumcision of Moses, her first son, on 2 January 1843, was considered worthy of newspaper coverage. Rosetta managed the house and family and frequently advertised for domestic servants. She was able to send some of her children to the prestigious Hutchins and Oldfield schools. She opened her home for the marriages of her siblings and her daughter and cared for her parents in their old age. Rosetta died at Elizabeth Street on 29 January 1865 and was buried at the Harrington Street cemetery and reinterred in 2002 in the Jewish Section of the Cornelian Bay cemetery.

AOT. ADM 1010/30 reel 3196. Family information Gerry Whitmont and Susan Groenhout.

MARKS, Samuel

Free.
Tailor.

Samuel Marks was said to be the brother of Henry Valentine (q.v.). In 1834 the *Sydney Gazette* wrote: 'A man was charged with stealing a coat from a Mr Bayliss' and the case rested on the testimony of Samuel Marks, 'who so grossly prevaricated in giving evidence that the Bench order him to stand committed'. In the *Registry of Flash Men* it is noted: 'Marks [no initial] was arrested for helping rob a cash box at Heydon's Auction Rooms on 3 August 1843. S. Marks, his brother, is involved in an illegal still'. Samuel Marks was listed as a tailor in George Street and, according to the *Registry of Flash Men*, was a police informer.

Sydney Gazette, 25 January 1834; W. A. Miles, *Registry of Flash Men*, 14 September 1843, p. 68 (2/673).

MARKS, Sarah

1828–1858
Grenada, 1827; Free.
Married; 6 (?) children.

The wife of Philip Marks (q.v.)., on 9 April 1823 Sarah Marks of no. 3 Petticoat–place accused Abraham Samuel alias Romaine, George Taylor, Thomas Harris and William

Allensby of conspiring to swindle her in the hope of being able to free her husband from Newgate. She had seen Samuel in Petticoat Lane who said 'Mrs Marks, I understand your husband is in trouble. I know the officers who have taken him and if you have got any money I could settle it'. The bribe required was twenty pounds. She sold her bed, bedstead, drawers, two tables and stove. Mary Ryan, the sister of John Ryan, who had helped the pickpocket Marks, raised four pounds. It was all in vain. The court released Harris and Allensby, the police constables, and sentenced Samuel and Taylor to two years imprisonment.

Sarah arrived in Hobart Town on 9 January 1827. Travelling with her were her children Joshua (ten), Anna (nine), and Rosetta (eight). Her husband was a prisoner at the notorious convict settlement at Macquarie Harbour at the time of her arrival.

She died at the age of sixty-nine years in 1858 and was buried in the Harrington Street cemetery.

AOT, ADM 101/30, reel 3196. OBSP 9 April 1823 no. 645. Family history Gerry Whitmont.

MARKS, Solomon

1775–1817
Active, 1791; Convict; Sentenced to 7 years, Old Bailey, 1790.
Single.

The 15-year-old Solomon Marks was convicted for entering the house of Levy Goldsmith, 117 Gravel Lane, Houndsditch, about ten in the night of 24 April 1790 and stealing clothes and bedding valued at thirty-nine shillings. He had then attempted to sell them to Solomon Israel, who refused to have anything to do with him. Marks had then offered them to Mrs Jacob Phillips for two shillings and sixpence. Shortly before this episode, Marks had stolen two pewter pots from a public house in Whitechapel, valued at two shillings, for which he was 'privately whipped'. Marks was sentenced on 26 May 1790.

Solomon Marks was a convict on the Third Fleet, arriving at Sydney on 26 September 1791. On 21 July 1798 he was sentenced to fifty lashes for assaulting a soldier. He appeared on the list of 'vagrants and vagabonds' apprehended in Sydney on 13 July 1799. He was said to be a convict who had absconded from his service and was sentenced to a further fifty lashes and to work in the gaol gang. On 2 February 1802 he was again charged with vagrancy.

The General Muster of 1806 listed him as a prisoner assigned to Mr P. Blaxcell (as was Philip Marks, who had also come on the same ship). The *Sydney Gazette* noted, on 10 August 1806: 'Wednesday Solomon Marks was detected breaking into the dwelling house of James Buttersworth at Parramatta who pursued and overtaking him knocked him down with a hoe and afterwards beat him so as to prevent his escape and to render it necessary he should be received at the hospital'.

On 12 June 1808 the *Sydney Gazette* reported that Solomon Marks had been found guilty of stealing a shirt and was sentenced to seven years transportation. He was sent, as a convict labourer, to the Hawkesbury District and was maintained on the government stores during the first half of 1809. He was listed in the 1811 General Muster and appeared in the 1814 Muster in Sydney as a 'convict servant'. A little later that same year he was on government rations as 'a sick man'. Marks died at the hospital at Parramatta, aged forty-five, on 17 October 1817 (and was buried the same day).

OBSP, 1789–90, case 491, p. 542, case 255, p. 276; Minutes of the Bench of Magistrates, 1/297, 1/298; 1814 Muster, ML, A1255, A1942-2; Bigge Appendix; Returns of Births, Deaths and Marriages, ML, A2130, p. 41.

MARKS, Solomon

1816–1852
British Sovereign, 1834; Free.
Single; Dealer, school master; 6 children.

Solomon Marks was on the *British Sovereign*, which arrived at Port Jackson on 18 September 1834. On the same ship was his brother Moses Marks (Moss Marks, q.v.). Solomon Marks 'of Bungadore' married Ann (Hannah) Cohen (q.v.) at the Sydney Synagogue on 3 August 1836. The marriage was performed by Michael Rose (q.v.). Marks was granted an auctioneer's licence on 15 October 1836. Joseph Simmons (q.v.) and Marks were in business as auctioneers in King Street from January 1836 to 3 October 1837. The *Sydney General Trade List* of 20 March 1836 reported that Solomon & Marks had imported four cases of glass, three cases of lamps and two cases of whiting (paint) from London. On 29 June 1837 Marks purchased the business of Samuel Onions in King Street. He assured the public that he would continue as an ironmonger, and 'from the knowledge acquired in this business in England will give satisfaction'.

Solomon Marks was declared insolvent on 19 February 1842 and George Moss (q.v.) was authorised to settle accounts for the late firm S. Marks & Co. On 10 March 1841 'Joseph Simmons and Solomon Marks bankrupts' were able to pay one shilling in the pound in addition to the five shillings paid previously. Marks's debts totalled £356 and his assets £20. He had a home in Sussex Street.

Solomon Marks died, aged thirty-six, on 18 October 1852, and was buried by the Sydney Synagogue at the Devonshire Street Cemetery. The grave was later transferred to Rookwood.

The children of Solomon and Hannah Marks were Adolphus (q.v.) (2 June 1837 to 1882), born in Sydney, Benjamin Francis (q.v.) (born 1846), Esther (1850), Elizabeth, who married Sigmond Hoffnung (q.v.) in 1858, and died in England in 1914, Sarah Miriam, who died in infancy and was buried on 29 April 1850 in the Devonshire Street Cemetery, and Frank Samuel (c. 1852–1893).

Sydney Gazette, 15 October 1836, 12 January 1837, 29 June 1837, 10 March 1841, 16 April 1842, 15 September 1842; *Australian*, 3 August 1836, 6 October 1837; Land Correspondence 2/7914, 20 September 1836; *Sydney General Trade List*, 5 December 1835, 19 December 1835, 20 February 1836, 29 June 1837.

MARKS, Solomon

Free.
Hawker.

Solomon Marks was granted a hawker's licence for Launceston in July 1843. In May 1843 he signed the petition for the establishment of the Launceston Synagogue and on 19 September signed the petition for the release of the debtor Isaac Jacobs (q.v.) from the Launceston Gaol.

CO 280/157; *Hobart Town Courier*, 14 July, 19 September 1843.

MARKS, Solomon Lyon

b. London, 1827–1875
1846; Free.
Single.

The seventh child of Frances (née Levey) and Lyon Marks, Solomon Lyon Marks was born on 4 April 1827 and arrived in Australia in 1846, entering into partnership at the Liverpool Mart, Hindley Street, Adelaide, with his brother Morris Lyon Marks (q.v.). On 13 February 1850 he married Esther Joshua (q.v.), the second daughter of Michael Joshua (q.v.) and Sarah (née Solomon) of Glenelg, South Australia. They had four children, all of whom died young. Lyon Morris Marks (1851), born at Port Adelaide, died in Melbourne in 1860. Sarah Frances Marks (1855), born in Melbourne, died there in 1860. Herbert Leicester Marks (1857) and Florence Mary (1859) were also born in Melbourne. Florence died at the age of two.

The grave of Solomon Lyon Marks is in the Cooktown Cemetery, Queensland, and is the only grave there with a Hebrew inscription. Marks died in 1875. He had been a successful merchant in Cooktown and donated a large portion of the costs of the town's first public hall.

Pritchard Index.

MARTIN, Abraham

Free.

Abraham Martin signed the petition for the Launceston Synagogue on 20 May 1843. He donated £2 to the Launceston Synagogue building appeal in 1844. Martin married Caroline Barnett (née Phillips) in Victoria on 3 December 1870 however they appear to have been living as husband and wife by 1857.

CO 280/157; *Launceston Examiner*, 29 June 1844.

MARTIN, David

b. Mile End, 1814
Lady Nugent, 1836; Convict; Sentenced to life, Central Criminal Court, 1836.
Single; Height: 163 cm.

Dark complexion, black hair, dark brown eyes, long nose, large chin, wide mouth. S.M. D.M. E.L. tattooed on arms. Martin was transported for burglary and was sentenced on 9 May 1836.

The prosecutor was Mrs Hart of Gravel Lane. His fellow thieves Aaron Moses (q.v.) and Joseph Aaron (q.v.) were also on board. The transport ship's surgeon reported that Martin's behaviour was 'orderly'.

The *Lady Nugent* arrived in Hobart Town on 12 November 1836 and Martin was first sent out to work as an assigned servant. By the end of July 1837, after a series of minor complaints and rebukes, he was forced to work on the roads. On 7 August 1837 he was sentenced to receive twenty lashes for 'idleness' and was assigned to the Campbell Town Chain Gang. In February 1839 he was punished for absconding and was sentenced to six months hard labour in chains. He was sent to the Perth Chain Gang and then on to Launceston. At Perth he received thirty-five lashes for 'idleness and disobedience'. By September 1841 Martin was an assigned convict servant in Launceston. A separate record book shows that during his time in Launceston he was punished a number of times by the lash and by solitary confinement for 'insolence' and 'general misconduct'. By mid-1844 he was placed in the Invalid Party and was admitted to the hospital in Launceston as a patient. He received a ticket of leave in December 1844 and a conditional pardon on 17 November 1846.

CON 18/16, no. 1448; CON 32/4, p. 86; CON 31/31; CON 18/14, no. 1448.

MAYERS, Frederick

b. London
Fairlie, 1837; Free.
Married; Clergyman (Christian); 7 children.

The Rev. Frederick Mayers arrived in Van Diemen's Land on the *Fairlie* from London with his wife and seven children to take up an appointment as (Anglican) Chaplain at Hamilton. Mayers was a Jewish convert to Christianity and the *Courier* described his first preaching assignment at Trinity Church in Hobart Town:

> We had the pleasure of hearing the Rev. Mr Mayers on Tuesday last, at Trinity Church and was [*sic*] highly gratified with the ease of his delivery and perspicacity of his discourse. Gratification is experienced in listening to arguments in favour of Christianity from the mouth of a converted member of the Jewish faith, combating against his own national prejudices and convinced of the Truth of the evidences in favour of the Gospel.

On 7 January 1838 the *Courier* noted that a son had been born to the Rev. and Mrs Mayers. Mayers was the author of *The Guardian—a Useful Miscellany*. On 13 March 1839 he received a grant of two acres in Hamilton. However, on 17 February 1840, he was 'forced to resign owing to ill health and small stipend' and returned to England.

Hobart Town Courier, 20 January 1837, 6 January 1837, 7 January 1838, 13 March 1839, 17 February 1840; ID, 1838, vol. 42, pp. 95, 102, 1840, vol. 34, p. 56.

MEERS, Sarah

b. Yorkshire, 1823
Surrey I (10), 1840; Convict; Sentenced to 10 years, Old Bailey, 1840.
Single; Child's maid; Height: 153 cm.

Ruddy freckled complexion, brown hair, chestnut eyes, broad nose, scar on left cheek. Another scar on right cheek bone, two large inoculation scars on upper left arm. Blue dot tattoo on back of left hand. Jewess. No education. Sarah Meers was sentenced on 3 February 1840 and transported for robbery of three shillings, two pennies and a farthing from a 17-year-old boy client (she was also seventeen years old). She had three previous brief sentences.

Sarah Meers arrived in New South Wales on 14 July 1840 and first was sent to the Newcastle Gaol and then, on 30 July, to be a nursemaid for Mrs Crummer. She was returned to the prison in November and reassigned to Dr Walton. She was sent back to the gaol one week later. On 27 February 1842 she was assigned to be a servant for John Callanan, only to be returned within the month. On 28 March 1842 she was sent to John Champain in Maitland and on 2 June 1841 to the Rev. Mr Smith in Maitland. Her work record was disastrous until on 30 November she was assigned to Mrs Rae in Maitland where, it seems, her wanderings ceased. A certificate of freedom was issued to her on 25 March 1850.

OBSP, 1840, case 682, p. 478; *Surrey* Indent 1840–42, p. 202; Prisons Department, Newcastle Gaol Entrance Books, 1840, 2/2007, no. 853, no. 1201, no. 1379, and 1841–45, 2/2008, no. 1379; CF 4/4414–50/0171.

MENDEL, Moritz

Free.
Merchant.

Moritz Mendel was listed as a guest at the levee held to mark the departure of Lt Governor Grey from South Australia on 29 October 1845. The *South Australian Gazette and Colonial Register* stated that 'Moritz Mendel, merchant', had returned to Adelaide from Sydney on 7 July 1847.

South Australian Gazette and Colonial Register, 29 October 1845, 7 July 1847.

MENDES, Daniel (Mendez)

1775–1857
Fanny and Kangaroo, 1814; Convict.
Venetian blind maker.

On 12 October 1816 Daniel Mendes advertised in the *Hobart Town Gazette* that black lead pencils and Venetian blinds could be made by application to Mendes, whose residence was on the Pottery Hill. On 8 April 1817 Mendes was fined five shillings for being drunk. On 14 August 1817 he received fifty lashes for 'assault'. On 3 October 1817 he was 'absent from his lodging' and was sentenced to twenty-five lashes and fourteen days extra labour. A Daniel Mendez was recorded as having been sent to New South Wales on the *Fanny* and returned to Van Diemen's Land on the *Emu* on 27 January 1818. On 17 February 1818 he was acquitted on a charge of having stolen property from the home of Ralph Jacobs (q.v.). By 1 June 1825 he was free by servitude, but was subsequently bound over for six months because he kept a disorderly house. Mendes was a resident of Launceston when he died on 11 May 1857.

CON 31/29, no. 4; *Hobart Town Gazette*, vol. 1, no. 20, 12 October 1816.

MENDOZA, Aaron

Active, 1791; Convict; Sentenced to 7 years, Middlesex, 1788.
Tailor.

Aaron Mendoza, together with a soldier, accompanied an Italian seaman to a bank on Lombard Street where the various foreign banknotes the sailor had accumulated were transferred into English currency. Mendoza then went to a Houndsditch pawnbroker, who knew Mendoza 'well' and redeemed his coat and waistcoat. One of the notes had been marked by the suspicious teller and both men were sentenced to transportation.

Mendoza worked as a tailor in Parramatta and, on 9 January 1792, gave evidence at the trial of John Thompson, who was accused of stealing a coat.

OBSP, 1878–88, case 591, p. 739f.; HO 11/1; J. Cobley, *Sydney Cove*, p. 208; Convict Indents COD/9; HO 11/1.

MENDOZA, Aaron

b. Commercial Rd, East London, 1826
Duncan, 1841; Convict; Sentenced to 7 years, Central Criminal Court, 1840.
Single; Tinman, tailor and brazier; Height: 165 cm; 1 child.

Dark complexion, black hair and whiskers, large nose, hazel eyes, long chin, low forehead. His right leg had been amputated. 'Jew'. Could read and write. Mendoza was convicted for stealing four brushes valued at two shillings and sixpence. He claimed to have found a customer who would buy the brushes and left the shopkeeper's wife standing outside a public house for an hour while he disappeared, only to be found later in Petticoat Lane.

Mendoza arrived in Van Diemen's Land on 18 April 1841 and was put on probation for twelve months. On 19 July 1841 he was reprimanded for having 'feigned illness'. On 12 October 1842 he absented himself from the Bridgewater Station without leave and was found to have two flannel shirts in his possession, for which he was sentenced to hard labour in chains and in the coal mines. His overseers reported that he was a 'very bad, cunning, suspected thief'. On 12 November 1843 in the Hobart Town Prisoners' Barracks, Aaron Mendoza was sentenced to ten days solitary confinement for fighting in the ward. On 12 April 1844 his term of probation expired and a ticket of leave was issued on 24 October 1844.

By 1845 Mendoza was in Launceston, where he was twice admonished for 'misconduct'. He was free by servitude by 17 August 1847. Aaron Mendoza married

Ann Stewart on 10 September 1854. On the marriage documents he was described as a 'dealer' and she was illiterate. Saul Solomons and Michael Levy witnessed the wedding, which was registered as Jewish marriage no. 28 in Van Diemen's Land.

Mendoza remained involved in the affairs of the congregation through the next twenty years. On 10 June 1872 he wrote to the Hobart Synagogue from Sydney, where he lived, in need of a copy of his marriage certificate. Mendoza was living in Castlereagh Street near the Haymarket. On 26 July 1874 he was appointed the official congregational 'collector' and on 1 November 1874 he resigned from his position of *shamash*. He was thanked for the manner in which he had performed his services and the congregation wished him and his family success. In Sydney in 1865 an Aaron Mendoza and Christina Beckman had a child named Frederick and, in 1873, Aaron married Christina.

CON 33/8, no. 1853; CON 14/5; CON 18/27; CON 27/8. OBSP 17 August 1840 case 2103.

MENDOZA, Abraham

b. London, 1790–1839
Morley (1), 1817; Convict; Sentenced to life, Old Bailey, 1816.
Shoemaker; Height: 157 cm.

On 7 April 1816 the twenty-two year old Mendoza was found guilty of 'felonious assault' having stolen a watch, two seals and a key chain from a drunken man in Petticoat Lane. The victim admitted in the court that he had been 'the worse for liquor'. Mendoza had violently pushed and robbed his victim and within minutes had been caught by a vigilant watchman. Almost immediately, Mendoza declared 'I am totally innocent. There was a cry of "stop thief" and I was running with the others and there was a man near where the property was found.' The court sentenced Mendoza to death which was subsequently commuted to transportation.

Abraham Mendoza arrived in Port Jackson on 10 April 1817. According to the assignment list, Mendoza was forwarded to Liverpool the following week, on 18 April 1817. Mendoza was initially assigned to John Moulds, the overseer of carpenters and then, for three years, worked as a servant to the overseer Henry Hadcock. The 1818 General Muster describes him as a 'settler's man'. In 1819 Mendoza petitioned for a mitigation of his sentence. He asked that Governor Macquarie should 'in your great goodness to grant the petitioner a ticket of leave. His further conduct may be depended upon … so great be made of Your Excellency's favour'. The ticket of leave was granted on 31 January 1820 for the District of Sydney and was renewed in 1831, 1834 and 1837.

The 1822 General Muster of New South Wales listed Mendoza as a convict working with the Parramatta Road Party. Mendoza was included in the 1828 Census as 'Ambrose Mendoza, shoemaker, employed at Bakers, Cumberland Street, Sydney. Religion Jew'. The 1837 General Return of Convicts reported that he was living in Sydney and had a ticket of leave. Mendoza died at the Sydney Hospital on 19 December 1839 and was buried by the Sydney Synagogue at the Devonshire Street Cemetery.

OBSP, 1816–17, case 591, p. 739; *Morley* (1) Indent 4/4005, p. 260; Petition 4/1859, p. 44; Bigge Appendix, p. 283, CO 201/118; TL Register, 4/4069, 29/113, and 4/4078, 31/118; Principal Superintendent of Convicts: Death Register 4/4549.

MENDOZA, Isaac (John JONES)

b. London, 1809
John (2), 1833; Convict; Sentenced to 7 years, Old Bailey, 1833.
Single; Height: 159 cm.

Dark sallow complexion, dark brown whiskers, low forehead, dark brown eyes, medium long nose, long fleshy chin. Isaac Mendoza was convicted at the Old Bailey on 4 July 1833 for stealing a handkerchief. He had served a previous sentence for breaking a window (in an attempted robbery). He was the second-youngest child of 'the noted pugilist' Daniel Mendoza, and brother of Sophia Mendoza (q.v.). His accuser testified: 'On 13 June I was trying to get through St Paul's Churchyard. I could not get on and was forced to stand still—I felt a hand in my pocket. I turned and saw the prisoner giving my handkerchief to another person. I took it from his hand and took him into custody'. Mendoza had a different story. 'I had taken some work home for my master and was going through the crowd when this gentleman took hold of me'.

Mendoza arrived in Hobart Town on 1 December 1833 and eleven days later was sent to the treadwheel for six days for being absent from the muster at the Prisoners' Barracks. Mendoza was then sent to work with various road gangs during 1834. On 29 December 1834 he received thirty lashes for feigning sickness. One year later, on 3 December 1835, he was found to have in his possession a silk handkerchief and a waistcoat for which he could not give a satisfactory account, and was sent to Reiby's Ford Road Party for six months. In January he received fifty lashes for idleness, an offence that one year later, as an assigned servant, caused his sentence to be extended three months. He was returned to government service. On 9 May 1839, as an assigned servant, he received thirty-six lashes for neglect of duty and on 4 April 1840 he was sentenced to six weeks imprisonment and hard labour for feigning illness while a member of the Red Hill Road Party. A certificate of freedom was issued in 1840.

Mendoza crossed Bass Strait and turned up in the Police Court in Melbourne on 11 March 1843. He was charged by Mr Elms of the Geelong district of having absconded from his service after signing himself up for twelve months and drawing sundries on account. The prisoner, who claimed to be partially deaf, passed himself off as John Jones. He was sentenced to spend one month in prison on the treadmill.

Mendoza remained in the district and the *Port Phillip Patriot* of 1 November 1845 noted that he had arrived at Port Phillip on the schooner *Ellen and Elizabeth* from Portland. On 11 August 1847 the *Port Philip Patriot* noted: 'An Israelite, named Isaac Mendoza, was yesterday brought before the bench of magistrates charged with appropriating a watch valued £4 belonging to a brewer named Mr McDonald'. Mendoza was caught in the act by Mrs McDonald who 'surrounded' him until her husband returned home. The evidence given in court was so contradictory and the McDonalds, it was noted, 'do not bear the very best of characters', that the case was dismissed. On 17 March 1849 the *Melbourne Morning Herald* reported 'Isaac Mendoza, a pugilist of some former ability, was charged with stealing a breast of mutton valued at sixpence. Mendoza claimed that it had been given to him by the butcher's assistant. On 17 April 1849 he was found guilty and imprisoned for two months. The *Melbourne Morning Herald* reported that Mendoza was back in court on 18 July 1850 for having stolen a waistcoat from a private house and pawned it for three shillings. This time he was imprisoned for four months with hard labour for his 'paltry offence'. In August 1854 the Melbourne Jewish Philanthropic Society voted to pay for his passage to Launceston where 'his sister could take care of him'.

CON 18/11, no. 1156; CON 31/31; CF 496; *Melbourne Times*, 11 March 1843; *Melbourne Morning Herald*, 17 April 1849.

MENDOZA, Sophia

b. London, 1792
Harmony, 1829; Convict; Sentenced to 7 years, Old Bailey, 1828.
Single; Servant-maid of all work; Height: 155 cm; 3 children.

Dark complexion, dark brown hair, high cheek bones, forehead high and narrow, eyebrows brown, eyes, dark brown. Lost one front tooth. 'Jewish countenance'. Sophia Mendoza was one of ten children, and the third child of the Jewish pugilist Daniel Mendoza, 'the noted bruiser', and sister of Isaac Mendoza (q.v.). At trial she said that 'I was last with Mr Shepherd, Mile End Rd as a servant of all work', and that she was a 'Protestant'. She was transported for 'larceny'.

During her first six years in Van Diemen's Land Sophia Mendoza was assigned to eighteen different masters and was in court twenty-one times for such crimes as 'gross improper conduct', 'drunkenness', 'disobedience', and 'making use of gross and beastly language'. On 27 January 1835 she was given an additional three years servitude for 'absconding'. From 1832 to 1845 she was under the jurisdiction of the Launceston Police. On 19 May 1835, while assigned to a Mr Wellman, she was convicted of being repeatedly absent without leave and sentenced to six months in the Female House of Correction with an additional three weeks in solitary confinement on bread and water and was not to be assigned for two years.

She was granted a ticket of leave on 15 September 1843. Mendoza received permission to marry Daniel Denyer, who came free, on 12 January 1844, and at the end of the year (20 December 1844) applied to marry John Wilson. They were actually married at Launceston on 26 March 1845. Despite a charge of felony in March 1844 Sophia Mendoza appeared to settle down. On 13 April 1847 it was noted that she had served twelve years of a fourteen-year sentence and had been free from offence for two and a half years. On 9 January 1849, a conditional pardon for all countries (except Great Britain and Ireland) was granted. On 23 August 1853 she was issued with a certificate of freedom.

CON 40/7; CON 32/4; VDL Papers, ML, A1059.2, p. 207, and 1059.5, p. 114; Launceston Police Book, vol. 2, p. 434; CON 72/2; ML, A1059-5, p. 114; CON 52/2, p. 234; HO 10/60, p. 579; *Hobart Town Courier*, 15 September 1843.

MEYER, Abraham (MYERS)

d. 1857
Single; Dealer; 6 children.

Abraham was the brother of Solomon Meyer (Meyers) (q.v.), and Benjamin Meyer (Meyers) (q.v.). On 4 September 1833 the Cross Keys public house in Goulburn South was transferred to Abraham Myers. As a young man he had joined the firm of Benjamin and Moses at Goulburn and managed their Argyle Steam Boiling Works. On 21 April 1844 he sent to Sydney the sum of £17 12s, which he had collected from his Goulburn 'friends' for the building of the Sydney Synagogue. He was a seat holder in the synagogue in 1845 and then became the manager of the Queanbeyan branch of Benjamin and Moses. He then established himself in his own business.

He married Julia, the daughter of Asher and Phoebe Hart (qq.v.), at the York Street Synagogue on 5 November 1845 and their first child, Hannah, was born in Goulburn in 1849.

He sold out in 1854 and with his wife and six children went on a voyage to England. He and his family were drowned on their way back to Australia in the wreck of the *Dunbar* 20 August 1857.

Sydney Gazette, 4 September 1833; Errol Lea-Scarlett, *Queanbeyan, District and People.*

MEYER, Benjamin (MEYERS)

d. 1860
Free.

Benjamin was the brother of Solomon Meyer (Meyers) (q.v.) and Abraham Meyer (Myers) (q.v.). In 1860 Benjamin Meyer of King's Plains was riding to Carcoar to attend court when his horse bolted and he was killed: 'The deceased being a member of the Jewish persuasion, he was buried in accordance with the rites of the Church, in consequence of which Mr S [Solomon] Meyer read the Burial Service, and while reading it, was so overcome, that at times he could not proceed'.

Sydney Morning Herald, 2 November 1860.

MEYER, Solomon (MEYERS)

b. London, 1823–1902
Ageaoria, 1841; Free.

The brother of Abraham Meyer (Myers) (q.v.) and Benjamin Meyer (Meyers) (q.v.), and the son of Jacob Meyers, a silk manufacturer, Solomon arrived in Hobart Town on 21 December 1841. Solomon Meyers gave £10 to the Hobart Synagogue building fund in 1843. Meyers held the wine and spirit licence for the Derwent Hotel, Murray Street, Hobart Town, which was sold to Frederick Seville in November 1844. The Hobart Synagogue listed an additional donation of £5 in 1845.

Solomon Meyer married in Launceston in 1844.

In 1849 Meyer bought the store of Joseph Simmons (q.v.) at Carcoar and was therefore involved in the wealth of the gold rush. The *Sydney Morning Herald* described his store as 'most commodious'. It was 'literally like a bee hive, from the ingress and egress of customers, and the numerous calls on the worthy proprietor to see what this [gold nugget] will weigh'. Meyer was arrested for 'sly grog selling of liquor on a large scale and in the most impudent manner'. Meyer moved to Sydney to develop his business there. However, 'unfortunate speculations' sent him back to Carcoar, where he managed and owned a flour mill. He became a magistrate and represented Carcoar in the colony's parliament from 1874 to 1876. He rebuilt his business in Sydney and, surprisingly, was elected to the Board of the Macquarie Street Synagogue in 1873. Meyer moved to Goulburn and the Australian Stores, served as an alderman and president of the local hospital and was a leading freemason. When Meyer died in 1902 his funeral was held at the Anglican Cathedral in Goulburn. In the eulogy the celebrant said: 'We rejoice that a Jew who had lived such an honourable and useful life in our midst could be held up as an example for others to follow'.

CSO 92/7/F83; *Van Diemen's Land Courier*, 19 November 1844; *Sydney Morning Herald*, 16 June, 17 June 1851; G. C. Mundy, *Our Antipodes*, vol. 3, p. 348f.; M. Z. Forbes, 'The Jews of NSW and the Gold Rushes', *AJJHS*, vol. 12, no. 2 (1994), p. 288f.

MICHAELS, Michael

Neptune, 1790; Convict; Sentenced to 7 years, Old Bailey, 1788.

A convict on the Second Fleet, Michael Michaels was convicted for stealing 100 pounds weight of lead, valued at fifteen shillings, on 15 May 1788. He was caught with the stolen material in his possession. He was sentenced on 25 June 1788. His name indicates he may have been Jewish.

OBSP, 1787–88, case 479, p. 597; CS 4/4427 Principal Superintendent of Convicts, Register of CF, 1810–14, vol. 1, p. 274.

MICHAELS, Michael

b. Liverpool, 1776–1824

Calcutta, 1803; Convict; Sentenced to life, Old Bailey, 1802.

Single; Brickmaker; Height: 170 cm.

Michael Michaels, son of Jonas Michaels and Rebecca (née Russell) and cousin of Esther Solomon (q.v.), was part of the Jewish community at the Thames Estuary port of Sheerness and was transported on two counts. The first was making and uttering seven counterfeit shillings. The second was trying to sell a watch to Captain Lucas, master of a coastal vessel. The transaction took place near Tower Hill in London. Michaels offered the sailor a watch for a bargain price and then pretended to change his mind. Michaels had received two seven-shilling pieces from the captain, but returned him two forged coins. In court he was described as 'the Jew', with a 'dark complexion'. He had already served a year in the County Gaol in Surrey and had been convicted in Guilford on 15 July 1800 for a similar crime. He was sentenced to death, but this was commuted to transportation for life.

Michaels had three brothers (David and Jonas were two of them). When David visited Michaels at Newgate Prison to give him a guinea, Michaels, furious at not having been rescued by his family, ripped his brother's stomach open with a knife. David was taken to St Bartholomew's Hospital and survived the attack.

Michaels was sent out to Australia on the *Calcutta* which, under Lieutenant Colonel David Collins, first attempted to start a colony at Sorrento in Port Phillip before proceeding to the River Derwent. Soon after arrival in Van Diemen's Land Michaels became an overseer of the convicts. Subsequent surveys of the colony's livestock and housing showed Michaels' increasing wealth and power. He was one of the first 'general dealers' in the colony. The Rev. Knopwood noted in his diary that: 'at 4 A.M. on 3 January 1805 the home of Joseph [*sic*] Michael, a Jew, caught fire and was consumed'. He received a free pardon on 10 October 1810 and owned a farm of sixty acres at Cornelian Bay. Michaels also owned a pawnbroking and money-lending shop in Elizabeth Street. Michaels returned to England in 1812 and sold his 30-acre farm at Risden to William Mann. Michaels appointed Dr Bowden as his agent to collect notes of hand to the value of £1333. This task in turn was taken over by Thomas Newby who, on 5 June 1819, advertised in the *Hobart Town Gazette*: 'In consequence of the total disregard that has been paid by the whole of the persons to the several notes May 10 and onwards including printed handbills distributed requesting payment to Michael Michaels late Elizabeth Street, Hobart Town, merchant'.

The colony's chaplain the Rev. Robert Knopwood had inherited the task. Michaels, who lived at 2 Swan Street, East Smithfield, in London, died in 1824 and his wife's nephew, Abraham Aaron (q.v.), took up the challenge to recover the fortune. Aaron travelled to Australia on what would be a futile mission, as the Rev. Knopwood denied all knowledge of the money.

The family's links with Australia continued to multiply. Jonas Michaels, his brother, was a dealer in marine wares and pawnbroker. Hannah, his sister, married Isaac Tobias in Scotland, where Isaac was a lay reader of the Jewish community and a theatrical entrepreneur. Hannah and Isaac Tobias had seven children: Janet (born 1835), Julius (1837), Reuben (1839), Jonah (1843), Rachel (1848), Tobias (1849), and Sarah (1852). In 1853 Isaac sailed for Australia on the *Anna Maria* with his three oldest children and they were shipwrecked on Kangaroo Island. Upon arrival in Melbourne, Julius and Reuben went to the goldfields, where Isaac died of dysentery. Janet stayed in Melbourne. Julius was at the goldfields near Stawell, where he met Harriet Sarah Tucker. He not only changed his name to William Julius Thompson, but also converted to Christianity and lied to his new family about his parents and his origins. Hannah Tobias and her four remaining children came out to Australia in 1866 to join Reuben, who had settled in Queenscliff, Victoria. Hannah was buried in the Jewish section of the Ballarat Cemetery, 'a native of Sheerness'.

OBSP, 1802, case 262, p. 188; HO 11/1; CSO 1/242/5844; CS, Musters of Van Diemen's Land, 1811–22, 4/1233, 4/1234; *Hobart Town Gazette*, 28 March 1817, 11 April 1817, 10 May 1817, 5 June 1819; Returns of Livestock, CO 201/35; 4/433, p. 29; CS 4/4427; Marjorie Tipping, *Convicts Unbound*, p. 295.

MILLINGEN, Phillip David (VAN MILLINGEN)

b. Holland, 1819–1890
Sesostus, 1839; Free.
Single; Dealer; 13 children.

The son of Joseph van Millingen, a Dutch diamond merchant, Phillip Millingen married Rachel Abrahams (q.v.), the daughter of Abraham and Elizabeth Abrahams (qq.v.). The marriage was celebrated in Sydney on 15 November 1843. The bride was fifteen years old. Mr P. D. Van Millingen gave £5 to the Sydney Synagogue's building appeal on 15 September 1839. Phillip and Rachel moved to Port Phillip. Phillip was accepted as a new member of the Melbourne Hebrew Congregation on 7 February 1847. They settled in Geelong, where Phillip initially worked as a watchmaker and then as an auctioneer. Thirteen children were born (at least two of whom died in infancy) during the next eighteen years, and Rachel died in 1861 at the age of thirty-four.

The children were: Joseph (1844), born in Sydney; Elizabeth (1845), Charles Samuel (1847), in Melbourne; Kate (1848), Sarah (1850), Henry (1852), Hannah (Annie) (1854), Phillip, James (1856), Caroline (1859), Louisa, Grace, and John.

Family information from Tony Ingram, Melbourne.

MITCHELL, John

b. Stepney, 1812–1880
St Vincent (3), 1853; Convict; Sentenced to 10 years, Central Criminal Court, 1849.
Tailor; Height: 157 cm.

Dark complexion, black hair, grey eyes, medium nose, large mouth. Jew. Can read and write. Previous conviction in Gibraltar. John Mitchell's prison report stated that this was his second conviction, though he denied it Documents were produced showing that he had been tried in 1841 under the name of Abraham Davis and sentenced to be confined for two years. On 29 January 1849 Mitchell was found in a private house having forced a locked drawer, stolen its contents, attempted to escape only to fall at the bottom of a flight of stairs into the arms of a constable. Mitchell was transported for housebreaking and larceny. Mitchell claimed to have a brother in Hobart Town. His claim seems to be correct. In 1836, a case was heard that involved a nineteen- year- old thief named Solomon Hyams, who was also known throughout the East End as 'Mitchell'.

Mitchell came out on the last convict transport to Van Diemen's Land, arriving on 26 May 1853. By 15 December he had a ticket of leave. On 11 May 1854 he was arrested on suspicion of sacrilege in the Hobart Synagogue. The prisoner was discharged without a conviction because the damage (theft?) had not occurred in a church but rather in a Jewish place of worship. On 3 January 1855 in Hobart Town he was convicted of playing skittles (on Sunday?). He was admonished. A conditional pardon was issued on 14 May 1855. Michael Mitchell, age 6, the son of John and Sarah, was buried by the synagogue in 1863. 'Residence Woolloomoloo'.

John Mitchell died in Sydney on 20 August 1880 and was buried as a Jew in the Rookwood Cemetery. He was said to be sixty-eight years old.
CON 33/115, no. 54581; OBSP, 9 May 1836, case 1134. CON37/9, p. 2954; CON 14/47; CON 18/59.

MITCHELL, Joseph

1801–1847
Canada (5), 1819; Convict; Sentenced to 7 years, Surrey, 1819.

Joseph Mitchell arrived in New South Wales on 1 September 1819. He was issued with a certificate of freedom on 2 March 1826. Joseph Mitchell was buried as a Jew in Sydney on 26 May 1847. The synagogue recorded that he was forty-two years old and that he was a member of Sydney's Jewish Philanthropic Society.
Ship Indent 4/4006, no. 4990, p. 362; CF 018/4990.

MOCATTA, George Gershon

b. London, 1815–1893
Jupiter, 1829; Free.
Single; 4 children.

Born on 21 March 1815, George was the fifth of eight children of Daniel Mocatta and Anne, née Goldsmid. Daniel Mocatta was the tenth son of Abraham Lumbrozo de Mattos and had taken his mother's surname. George Mocatta's brother-in-law was Joseph Barrow Montefiore (q.v.). George was fourteen years old when he arrived in Sydney with his sister and family on 22 February 1829.

George Mocatta spent four years in Sydney and was listed in the *New South Wales Calendar and General Post Office Directory* as living in O'Connell Street. In 1835 he was in Mudgee, and then moved to Wellington Valley where, in 1837, despite his youth, he became manager of J. B. Montefiore's properties. At the time this region was the Australian frontier and in 1836 he asked the government to provide more soldiers for the district. In 1839 he was granted a number of pastoral leases totalling 18000 acres in the counties of Bathurst, Westmorland and Georgina and 3200 acres in the Brisbane Valley. When the transportation of convicts to New South Wales ceased, Mocatta was forced to engage immigrants. On 13 June 1840 he advertised in the *Australian* and offered £10 for information leading to the apprehension of two hired migrants who had absconded. On 17 April 1841 Mocatta advertised in the *Australian* that he was leaving the district, but in December 1842 he was still in Blacktown. Mocatta bought 'Dalbey' in the Darling Downs and took 1600 head of cattle in a pioneering three-month journey overland from Sydney to Moreton Bay. The stock belonged to Messrs Suter, Mocatta and Lee.

In May 1848 he was present at Adelaide's first Jewish marriage, when his cousin Esther Hannah Montefiore (q.v.) married Eliezer Levi Montefiore (q.v.).

In 1848 George Mocatta of Myall Creek Station was running 4000 sheep on Crown lands near Gwydir. Mocatta was listed in 1849 as holding a run of 20 000 acres in the Darling Downs District. There was Johngboon of 16 000 acres, Malmaison of 24 000 acres, Wigton of 16 000 acres and a further 16 000 acres near Gayndah. A mountain on the Great Dividing Range bears his name. There is a family tradition that George Mocatta was the last white man to see the explorer Leichhardt alive.

Mocatta moved to Sydney and opened a grain store on Circular Quay in July 1857 and in 1858 married Mrs Lydia Harries Hankin, née Voss, at the Registry Office at Balmain. Mocatta became a merchant, opening 'exclusive stores at Circular Quay' in connection with their stores in Liverpool. In 1858 and 1859 he was listed as a 'produce merchant'. Mocatta was a member of the Sydney Synagogue until 1843 and continued to contribute to the congregation even after he moved to Darling Downs. Following his marriage, he became an Anglican.

After many years in Europe, Mocatta went to New Zealand, where he owned the Tauranga Station, returning to Sydney to retire. He died at 248 Liverpool Street in 1893, one day after his seventy-eighth birthday. His death certificate listed him as a 'shipbroker'. He was buried at the Gore Hill cemetery (near Artamon) in the Congregational section, and his four children were not brought up as Jews. His death certificate noted 'no minister present'.

George Voss Mocatta was born at Camden in 1860. William Hugh Mocatta was born at Balmain on 17 November 1861 and was appointed Judge of the District Court in New South Wales in 1922. Houlton Walters Mocatta was born in Wales on 28 September 1863. Brenda was born in 1865.

Ship Indent 4/4823; G. F. J. Bergman, 'George Mocatta: A Notable Pioneer Squatter', *AJJHS*, vol. 8, no. 1 (1975), p. 62f; CS Letters Received 1848, Attorney-General, 4/2823; CS letters Received 1849, Miscellaneous B-G, 4/286.1, 36/4930; *Sydney Gazette*, 24 August 1842; Commissioner of Crown Land, A1764.1, no. 56; family history research by Chris Robson, Kalinga, Queensland.

MOCATTA, Jonathan Brandon

b. Altona, Germany, 1800–1852
Free. Single; Teacher.

Jonathan Mocatta was from Altona, near Hamburg, which had a small but significant Sephardi community. He was a remittance man sent out to the colonies by his distinguished family. His father was Aaron Mocatta who, at the time of his son's death, was living at 112 Kings Road, Brighton, England. Soon after Jonathan arrived in Van Diemen's Land the *Colonial Times* carried the following warning: 'Caution to the Public!—Whereas Jonathan Brandon Mocatta has left my service as a Teacher without any reasonable cause—This is to give notice that any person or persons harbouring him after this date will be dealt with according to Law—23 February 1838 sgd Richard Lucas'.

Mocatta moved to Launceston and on 9 January 1840 announced in the *Launceston Advertiser* that he had established a 'Commercial and Classical Academy':

> Mr J. B. Mocatta begs leave to apprize the Public of Launceston generally, that he is about opening an Establishment in Wellington Street, two doors from the Colonial Hospital for the instruction of Young Gentlemen. Mr Mocatta's experience in the Scholastic profession in England, and on the continent of Europe to blend into one the excellence of the British and continental system of education. Wednesdays and Saturday afternoons private tuition is available.

At the Jewish New Year in September 1843 Mocatta gave £2 to the synagogue building fund. He died in Hobart Town on 8 May 1852 of 'delirium tremens' in the Hobart Hospital. In the hospital's record book was written: 'Free to the colony—object of charity but considerable property depends on his correct age [written] on proper death certificate'. Mocatta was buried by the congregation at the Harrington Street Jewish cemetery.

Launceston Advertiser, 9 January 1840; *Colonial Times*, 6 March 1838.

MOCATTA, Solomon

b. London, 1818–1862
1828; Free.
Single; Merchant.

Solomon Mocatta, the seventh child of Daniel Mocatta of London, and three years younger than his brother, George Mocatta (q.v.), arrived in Sydney in 1828, then and returned to England where he married Anne Hort, daughter of Abraham Hort (q.v.), in London on 21 January 1835. He returned to Sydney on the *Hope* on 17 October 1838 with Eliezer Levi Montefiore (q.v.). In 1843 Solomon Mocatta and his wife settled in New Zealand with his father-in-law, Abraham Hort. In 1849 Solomon and his wife moved to Port Adelaide in South Australia. According to the *South Australian Almanack* in 1849 he was a ship broker and merchant. He served as the appointed lay minister to the Adelaide Hebrew Congregation in 1857. Solomon Mocatta died in Adelaide on 7 February 1862 and was buried in the Jewish section of the West Terrace Cemetery. His wife Anne died in Adelaide on 9 February 1857 at the age of forty-two.

Ship Indent 4/5213.

MONTEFIORE, Eliezer Levi

b. Barbados, 1820–1894
Hope, 1838; Free.
Married; Merchant; 13 children.

Born at Barbados on 24 June 1820, Eliezer was the second son of Isaac Levi and Esther Hannah (née Montefiore, the sister of Jacob and Joseph Barrow Montefiore, qq.v.).

He arrived in Sydney on 17 October 1838 with Mr and Mrs Mocatta (Solomon Mocatta, q.v.). Eliezer's elder brother was Jacob Levi Montefiore (q.v.). Both Jacob and Eliezer took on their mother's maiden name in order to please their eminent uncle, Joseph Barrow Montefiore.

Eliezer arrived in South Australia in 1843 and set up business as a shipping agent and importer. On 20 September 1843, E. L. Montefiore was appointed trustee of the Jewish part of the Adelaide Cemetery. The *South Australian Gazette and Colonial Register* recorded on 16 June 1843 that E. L. Montefiore ran a General Store in Hindley Street that sold 'everything from coffee to whaling gear'. He was agent for the Australasian Colonial and General Life Assurance Company of London and Sydney and Jacob Montefiore was one of the directors (12 July 1843). The *Sydney Morning Herald* carried the same announcement in a similar advertisement that added he was 'agent' for Adelaide. On 3 February 1844, E. L. Montefiore announced he was agent for the *Clipper*, taking cargo to Sydney. In 1845 Montefiore moved his store to King William Street and on 18 January 1845 proclaimed that he was a strong opponent of sending convicts to South Australia.

Eliezer married his 19-year-old first cousin Esther Hannah Barrow Montefiore (q.v.) at the home of the bride's father, Joseph Barrow Montefiore, at St John's Street (now called East Terrace), on 3 May 1848. The ceremony was performed by Burnett Nathan (q.v.). Their first son, Arthur Augustus, was born on 6 May 1849 (died in 1883). Frederick was born on 12 March 1852 (died at the age of three months).

The Montefiore family left Adelaide in mid-1852 and visited Jacob Levi Montefiore in Sydney. Five months later they settled in Melbourne. Jacob Levi Montefiore was born in 1853 in Collingwood, Victoria. An infant son, George Jacob, aged three months, died on 1 February 1855, 'of Richmond'. More children followed: Caroline (1856–1932), Frank Albert (1857–1858), Amy (1859), Eliza Jessie (1861), Mary (2 May 1863), Esther Lilian (7 July 1866), Ethel Octavia (1868–1873), Ella Hortense (1871), and Alice (1873, died the same year).

The firm of Montefiore and Graham, which Eliezer managed in Victoria, was to be found in William Street from 1854 to 1859. Montefiore's sketch books of his travels and of early Melbourne and Adelaide are now held by the La Trobe Library. The Art Gallery of New South Wales also holds a portfolio of sketches and etchings. Montefiore exhibited black and white sketches and etchings in a number of exhibitions. In February 1871 the *Argus* announced: 'The Public will be glad to learn that Mr E. L. Montefiore, the late secretary of the Australasian Insurance Company, who will shortly leave Melbourne to fill the post of Secretary of the Pacific Insurance Company in Sydney, has consented to not wholly withdraw himself from the conduct of the affairs of the [Victorian] Public Library, Museum and National Gallery'. Montefiore had served as a trustee of both the Victorian National Gallery and the Melbourne Public Library.

Montefiore moved to Sydney in 1871 and lived in Balmain at the 'Hampton Villa'. In 1884 the insurance industry in Sydney formed the Insurance Institute of New South Wales and, even though Montefiore was overseas at the time, his colleagues elected him to become the first president of the institute. He was actively involved with the founding of the New South Wales Academy of Art. Upon retiring from business at the age of seventy-two, in 1892, he was appointed the first full-time director of the Art Gallery of New South Wales. He was a prolific author and an accomplished artist. He organised the first exchange exhibition of pictures between the Sydney Gallery and the galleries in Melbourne and South Australia.

Eliezer Levi Montefiore died in Sydney on 22 October 1894 and was buried at the Rookwood Cemetery. His wife had predeceased him in 1882. His surviving children were Caroline, Amy, Jessie, Mary, Lily and Ella. Mary married Amos Henriques Iffla on 13 March 1889 at the Great Synagogue in Sydney.

Nicholas Draffin, 'An Enthusiastic Amateur of the Arts: Eliezer Levi Montefiore in Melbourne, 1853–1871', *AJJHS*, vol. 13, no. 4 (1997), p. 687f; Ruth Faerber, 'Eliezer Levi Montefiore', *AJJHS*, vol. 8, no. 4 (1977), p. 185f; Rodney Benjamin, 'Eliezer Montefiore, 1820 to 1894: Artist, Gallery Director and Insurance Pioneer: The First Significant Australian Jewish Artist', *AJJHS*, 2004; ML 4/5213; *Sydney Morning Herald*, 11 January 1845; *South Australian Gazette and Colonial Register*, 14 June 1843, 12 July 1843, 3 February 1844; SA Archives, GRG, 24 January 1843, no. 226 (20 September 1843).

MONTEFIORE, Esther Hannah Barrow

1829–1882
1846; Free.
Single; 13 children.

Esther married her first cousin, Eliezer Levi Montefiore (q.v.), in Adelaide on 3 May 1848. She died in Sydney on 10 July 1882, and was buried in the Rookwood Cemetery.

MONTEFIORE, Frederick Barrow Levi

Free.
Single; Merchant.

Frederick B. Levi Montefiore was in business in Moreton Bay on 8 April 1848. 'Fred Montefiore' was listed on the electoral roll for Brisbane in 1848: only eighty-three (male) property owners were eligible to vote. He appears to have left the colony in 1849.

MONTEFIORE, Jacob Barrow

b. Jamaica, 1801–1895
Medway, 1846; Free.
Married; Stockbroker; 11 children.

Jacob Montefiore was born in Bridgetown, Barbados, and was the eldest of three children. His father was a merchant and owned a sugar plantation. Jacob grew up in England. He became a member of the Committee of the Royal Colonial Institute and a Fellow of the Royal Geographical Society and a partner of Montefiore Brothers, which developed extensive land holdings in New South Wales.

Through the influence of his illustrious cousin Sir Moses Montefiore he became one of the eleven commissioners appointed by King William IV to plan and supervise the colonisation of the new colony of South Australia. Prior to this appointment he had been a commissioner with the Colonial Produce Trade.

Jacob was the older brother of Joseph Barrow Montefiore (q.v.), and uncle of Eliezer Levi Montefiore, and had visited Australia in 1837, 1840 and 1842. In 1837 he had visited Adelaide in May before travelling on to Sydney on the *Lord William Bentinck*, arriving on 10 October. The *Sydney Morning Herald* reported on 23 February 1840 that 'our old and esteemed colonist' returned on the *Hope* 'after an absence of four years'. On 17 April 1841 he was described as a Director of the Australian Colonial and General Life Assurance Co. He arrived in Adelaide again on 29 July 1846, on the brig *Medway*. The party included Mr and Mrs Joseph Barrow Montefiore and their children, Misses Esther, Emily, (Sarah) Evelina, Justina, Augusta, Josephina, Marion and Edith, Master Horace Montefiore, another Miss Montefiore, and two female servants.

In 1852 Montefiore came to Victoria as an agent for the Rothschilds. In Victoria he went into business as the gold rush transformed the colony's economy and a number of newspapers carried his appeals to buy 'drays' (wagons), which were in very short supply because of the need to transport supplies to the goldfields.

J. Montefiore & Co was located at Market Square in Melbourne. Jacob Montefiore and his wife, Justina Lydia (née Gompertz), had a Melbourne-born child named Victoria Violet (whose birthplace was recorded as Collingwood) in 1853.

CS Letters Received 1837, Miscellaneous, 4/2363.2, letter 37/9105, 4/2240.5, letter 34/7994, ML; *Sydney Morning Herald*, 19 December 1844, 10 January 1845; *Melbourne Morning Herald*, 20 March 1852; H. Munz, *Jews in South Australia*, p. 11f.; *Australian*, 24 June 1841; *South Australian Gazette and Colonial Register*, 1 July 1848, 25 May 1850; SA Archives, GRG, 24/1/1845/5.

MONTEFIORE, Jacob Levi

b. Barbados, 1819–1885
Prince Regent, 1839; Free.
Married; Merchant.

The son of Isaac Levi and Esther Hannah (née Montefiore, sister of Jacob Barrow Montefiore, q.v., and first cousin of Sir Moses Montefiore), Jacob Levi took on his mother's surname. He was born in Bridgetown, Barbados, in the West Indies. Four of Jacob Levi Montefiore's siblings settled in the Antipodes: Eliezer Levi Montefiore (q.v.), who married Esther Hannah Barrow Montefiore), Joseph Barrow Levi Montefiore, who married Justina Barrow Montefiore, Octavius Montefiore (q.v.), and Frederick Barrow Levi Montefiore (q.v.).

Jacob Levi Montefiore arrived in Sydney on 19 August 1839 to join the firm of Jacob Barrow Montefiore. He soon went into partnership with Moses Joseph (q.v.) and from 1846 was in partnership with the Scot, Robert Graham. Montefiore, Graham & Co. soon opened branches in Brisbane and Melbourne. The Melbourne branch was managed by his brother Eliezer. He was a director of the Bank of

Australasia by 1855 and president of Sydney's Chamber of Commerce in the 1860s. He was associated closely with George Mocatta (q.v.) and his squatting ventures in New South Wales and Queensland from the 1850s.

The Mitchell Library preserves a letter written by Jacob Levi Montefiore from Sydney of 6 November 1846 to T. Cohen, in which he discussed the Governor's refusal to approve a grant to the Sydney Synagogue: 'I am willing to believe that in respectability our community is approaching a higher stand although they are still very far from what they might be'.

Montefiore was a lifelong friend of Henry Parkes and a Member of the Legislative Council in New South Wales from 1856 to 1860 and 1874 to 1876. Parkes recalled: 'In 1852 I began to take an active part in the constitutional discussion outside the Legislature. The Gentlemen who took part with one in those agitations were certainly not demagogues or men wanting in social influence. Among them … Mr J. L. Montefiore'. Montefiore represented merchant interests against 'landed interests' and published two substantial pamphlets about Free Trade, *A Catechism of the Rudiments of Political Economy*, and *A Few Words upon the Finance of New South Wales. Addressed to the Members of its First Parliament by One of Themselves* (1856). He was one of the first to write about economic theory in Australia, and he also wrote the librettos for French light operas and comedies. He composed the Jewish historical libretto for Isaac Nathan's (q.v.) opera, *Don John of Austria*. He wrote the text for *The Duel, A Drama in Two Acts*, first produced in Sydney in 1843, and in 1847 *Marguerite or He Might Do Worse—A Comedy in Three Acts*.

Montefiore was an active member of the Jewish community. He married Caroline Antonine Geradine Louyet in London in 1851. He became a magistrate in 1857 and was chairman of the Chamber of Commerce, 1866–69 and 1874–75. In 1863 he became the Belgian Consul in Sydney. (One of his brothers, George Levi Montefiore, was a member of the Belgian Senate.) Montefiore left Australia in 1876, resigning from the Legislative Council, and settled in England. He was Fellow of the Royal Colonial Institute from 1877, and in 1880 served on the London Commission for the Sydney International Exhibition. He was a director of the Queensland National Bank and the Queensland Investment Company. Jacob Levi Montefiore died in England on 24 January 1885.

Martha Rutledge, 'Jacob Levi Montefiore', in *ADB*, vol. 5; Libretto and Plays 4/474, 43/5494, in 4/4561.1; 47/3785, in 4/2771.1; H. Parkes, *Fifty Years in the Making of Australian History*; Montefiore family research by David and Jill Stevenson, Turramarra.

MONTEFIORE, John Israel (John Julius)

b. London, 1809–1898
Prince Regent, 1829; Free.
Married; Merchant.

John Israel was sometimes called John Julius Montefiore. He was a cousin of Joseph Barrow Montefiore (q.v.) and of Jacob Montefiore (q.v.). J. J. Montefiore, Mrs Montefiore and Master Montefiore arrived in New South Wales on

19 August 1829. After two years in business in Sydney, Montefiore went on to New Zealand. In Sydney in 1831, together with some businessmen, he had become involved in plans to purchase land in New Zealand when the site for the capital city had been chosen. Montefiore arrived in the Bay of Islands in 1831 and opened a store trading with the Maori. He returned to Sydney in 1837–39 and then went back to New Zealand. He established a business in Auckland as a trader and land agent at 3 Lower Queens Street. He died at Portsea, in England, in 1898.

Prince Regent Indent 4/5200; 4/4823, no. 643/312; *Sydney Gazette*, 13 October 1831.

MONTEFIORE, Joseph Barrow

b. London, 1803–1893
Jupiter, 1829; Free.
Married; Merchant; 13 children.

Joseph Barrow Montefiore was born in London on 24 June 1803, the son of Eliezer Montefiore, a merchant of London and Barbados, and his wife Judith (née Barrow), and the cousin of Sir Moses Montefiore. He was educated at Hurwitz's school in Highgate and Garcia's Academy at Peckham, and had a strong Jewish background. He was nineteen years of age when he entered the London Stock Exchange in 1826 and became one of the twelve 'Jew Brokers' at the price of £1500. At the same time he obviously began to dream of Australia. Like Lionel Samson (q.v.), Montefiore was inspired by the return to London of the emancipist Solomon Levey (q.v.).

Joseph Barrow Montefiore arrived in Australia in 1829 with glowing testimonials paving his way. Mr G. R. Brown wrote to Sir George Murray on 19 June 1828 that Montefiore was 'a most respectable gentleman. Mr Montefiore's means are most ample, his character excellent and his exertions being founded on practice and experience, will I should think, render him a most valuable acquisition to the colony'. Montefiore wrote from Finsbury Square on 1 June 1828:

> I am now desirous of removing there with my family to establish myself as an agriculturalist I respectfully solicit a grant of five thousand acres of land my means are entirely adequate I propose taking with me an experienced agriculturalist in all its branches and as I have resided many years in the West Indies I anticipate being able to develop the cultivation of drugs, marino [*sic*] sheep, breeding of horses and horned cattle.

Joseph arrived in New South Wales on 22 February 1829 with his wife Rebecca (née Mocatta) (q.v.) and two daughters, Judith Georgina and Esther Hannah Barrow Montefiore, accompanied by George Mocatta (q.v.) and David Ribeiro Furtado (q.v.) and his wife. The *Sydney Gazette* reported: 'It is said that Mr Montefiore, who arrived the other day by the *Jupiter*, is connected with the highly respectable house of that name in London and that he has brought out a capital of £20 000. He has found us at an unfortunate crisis but we hope he will not ultimately be disappointed'. By July, Montefiore was inadvertently and unfairly involved in the Sudds Thompson Affair. The *Monitor* commented on 18 July 1829: 'We will be glad to know that Montefiore, and Mr Poole, signed the address [of protest to the Governor] for seeing they are hardly fixed in the Colony. What can these gentlemen know of Sudds and Thompson, as indeed of any other of the subjects of the address?'

The Montefiore family moved into 'the residence of the late Mr W. Balcombe Esq. in O'Connell Street by Mr Montefiore, the merchant'. His firm was called Montefiore Brothers and the brother was Jacob Montefiore (q.v.) of London. He served as the first president of the Jewish congregation of Sydney from 1832 to 1835 and helped secure land for the Jewish cemetery in 1835. He was determined to have the Jewish community of the colony treated as political equals in matters of state aid. However, when the emancipist Abraham Polack (q.v.) became president in 1836 he severed his relationship with the congregation and even refused to pay his annual dues.

Montefiore negotiated the matter of a land grant and satisfied the Land Board that he had almost £5000 capital to invest and access to additional capital. He was granted 5000 acres at Wellington at the confluence of the Bell and Macquarie rivers. He told the board that he had 'no intention to leave mercantile pursuits but hoped to put profits into development of land'. Between 1834 and 1839 he bought more than 4000 acres adjoining his original grant in the Wellington District. On 23 December 1840 he purchased land at Portland in the Port Phillip District.

During the 1830s he had travelled extensively, usually taking Horatio Samuel (q.v.) with him. He went to New Zealand in 1831, having taken the time and trouble to hire two Maori in Sydney to teach him the language. He chartered a barque in August 1830 and stayed four months. He later stated that New Zealand was 'a perfect paradise. I think so highly of the country that, although when I went out to New South Wales, His Majesty George IV granted me 5000 acres of land, I would readily have changed it for 1000 in New Zealand'. Montefiore was in London in 1837–38, 1840 and 1843. He gave evidence to the Select Committee of the House of Lords that was set up to investigate the viability of a colony in New Zealand.

In partnership with his brother Jacob Montefiore, who was a member of the South Australian Colonisation Commission in London, he made a fortune in real estate, helped found the Bank of Australasia and was one of those responsible for the importation of English capital into New South Wales. On 25 July 1840 Montefiore arrived in the new district of Port Phillip on the barque *Andromache* and on 17 August paid the highest prices for allotments in the Melbourne and Geelong land sales. In Melbourne, where only 3000 people lived at the time, he bought block no. 1 in allotment no. 9 for £440. In Geelong he bought a block for £420 before proceeding to Sydney. In 1841, to the shock of the entire business community, the Montefiore firm of Sydney and London went bankrupt and Joseph returned to England.

On 29 July 1846 Montefiore returned to Australia with his wife, nine daughters, two sons, two servants, a harp, a piano, 300 packages, and capital newly raised through family connections. He and his nephew Eliezer Levi Montefiore (q.v.) set up in business in Adelaide as importers and shipping agents.

Montefiore found a friendly and supportive city. He invested heavily in mining ventures, was a member of the Stock Exchange, a committee member of the Adelaide Chamber of Commerce and a founding trustee of the Savings Bank. In December 1848 he was appointed a magistrate in the Province of South Australia, the first Jew to sit on the Bench in any Australian colony. His 19-year-old daughter, Esther Hannah Barrow Montefiore (q.v.), married her first cousin Eliezer Levi Montefiore on 3 May 1848. It was South Australia's second Jewish wedding.

He stood for election to the Legislative Council in 1851 and was defeated. He returned to England in 1860 and in retirement was one of the active members of the West London Synagogue of British Jews, the first Reform Synagogue in the United Kingdom.

He died in Brighton, England, on 4 September 1893 leaving ten daughters and three sons! They were: Judith Georgina Barrow Montefiore (Mrs Henriques), Esther Hannah Barrow Montefiore (Mrs Levi Montefiore), Emily Barrow Montefiore (Mrs Henriques), Sarah Evelina Barrow Montefiore (7 June 1832), born in Sydney, Justina (29 September 1835), born in Sydney, Augusta Barrow Montefiore (1836), born in Sydney, Josephina, Herbert Barrow Montefiore (10 April 1839), born in London, Marion Barrow Montefiore (May 1842), born in London, Horace Barrow Montefiore, Edith Barrow Montefiore, George Barrow Montefiore, and Helen Barrow Montefiore (14 February 1855), born in Adelaide.

Ship Indent, ML, 4/5200; *HRA*, series 1, vol. 14, pp. 243–5, vol. 18, p. 8f.; ML 2/7930, Land Correspondence, 4 September 1830; *Lord William Bentinck* Indent 4.5212; *Hope* Indent 4/5216, *St George* Indent 4/5223, ML; *Sydney Gazette*, 26 February 1829, 4 June 1829, 13 October 1829, 25 November 1830, 9 July 1831, 15 December 1831, 22 July 1834, 8 October 1836; *Monitor*, 18 July 1829; *Port Phillip Herald*, 28 December 1848; *Port Phillip Patriot*, 10 October 1840; Montefiore family research by David and Jill Stevenson, Turramarra.

MONTEFIORE, Octavius

b. London, 1835–1893
Single; Merchant.

Octavius was the younger brother of Jacob Levi Montefiore and Eliezer Levi Montefiore (qq.v.). He died in Sydney in 1893 and was buried at Rookwood Cemetery.

MONTEFIORE, Rebecca (née MOCATTA)

b. London
Jupiter, 1829; Free.
Married; 13 children.

Rebecca Montefiore arrived in New South Wales on 22 February 1829 with her husband, Jacob Barrow Montefiore (q.v.), two daughters, and her brother, George Mocatta (q.v.).

MORDECAI, Joseph

b. London, d. 1818
Salamander, 1791; Convict; Sentenced to 7 years, Old Bailey, 1789.

Mordecai was caught with forty shillings worth of lead stolen and hidden in a yard in Houndsditch. He was charged together with Thomas Homer: 'We were very much in liquor and coming along we saw the gates open and we went in and that there gentleman came and knocked at the gates and he said thieves and we were afraid and we run away'. Mordecai called four witnesses to testify in his defence, but was sentenced at the Old Bailey on 25 February 1789.

The *Salamander* arrived in New South Wales on 21 August 1791. Mordecai was permitted to leave Sydney to settle in Norfolk Island in May 1806. He was then sent on to New Norfolk in Van Diemen's Land on the brig *Estramina* in 1803. Mordecai's sentence had expired in 1796 and a certificate of freedom was issued on 6 March 1811. By 1814, Mordecai had returned to the mainland as a labourer at Windsor. In November 1816 he was in the Hawkesbury District on a list of convicts who had no ticket of leave yet who were 'free' and could therefore be officially considered 'impostors'. In the General Musters of New South Wales of 1816 and 1818 he was listed as 'Free' and a labourer.

On 24 February 1818 Joseph Mordecai was found drowned at the water's edge of the farm of Thomas Ardell Esq. He had been working as a member of the crew of a small boat collecting grain from farmers. His job had been to weigh the quantities of wheat. An inquest was held on 28 February 1818.

OBSP, 1789, case 206, p. 268f.; CS Copies of Conditional Pardons, May–August 1849, 4/4467 p. 294–5; HO 10/8; *Sydney Gazette*, 25 May 1806, 16 November 1816; Bigge Appendix, BT Box 12, p. 152; Arthur File, 4/4306, p. 224, Inquest, 28 February 1818, pp. 235–40.

MORRIS, Aaron

b. London, 1816
Arab (2), 1834; Convict; Sentenced to 7 years, Old Bailey, 1833.
Single; Labourer; Height: 165 cm; 2 children.

Dark complexion, low forehead, brown eyes, brown hair, medium large nose, small chin. One mole back of neck. A Jew. Aaron Morris was transported for larceny, for 'stealing a hat'. He had previously been in prison three times for picking pockets. His hulk report was 'very bad'. Surgeon's report: 'careless, thoughtless, no application to his lessons though somewhat improved'.

The convict transport ship arrived in Van Diemen's Land on 30 June 1834. Morris was assigned to the Public Works Department. On 18 April 1835 he was placed in solitary confinement on bread and water for ten days for 'feigning sickness and refusing to go to work when ordered'. On 20 May 1835, for 'repeated idleness', he received twenty-five lashes on the back. The convict overseer charged Morris with insolence and refusing to work and he was sentenced to a further fifty lashes. He was assigned to a road party in March 1836 for refusing to work and for gross disobedience. By 30 September 1839 he was working as a constable and was fined five shillings for 'misconduct'. He held a ticket of leave, and was dismissed from the Police Force and sent to the interior of the island. Aaron Morris received his certificate of freedom in 1840.

An Aaron Morris married Rachel Hart on 14 June 1843 in the Bridge Street Synagogue. In 1845 he was listed as a seat holder in the newly dedicated York Street Synagogue. Aaron and Rachel had a son, Joseph, in Sydney in 1845. Another son (not named in the official records) was born in 1848.

CON 31/31, no. 1213; CON 18/3; CF 723.

MORRIS, John

b. London, 1793
Almorah (1), 1817; Convict; Sentenced to 14 years, Middlesex, 1816.
Single; Watch motion maker; Height: 166 cm.

Very dark complexion, black hair, brown eyes. 'Well behaved' on the Almorah. John Morris was sentenced at the Old Bailey on 18 September 1816.

Morris arrived in New South Wales on 29 August 1817 and was sent on to Van Diemen's Land. In Hobart Town on 30 October 1818 he was arrested for being drunk and disorderly and spent seven nights in gaol. He was absent from the Muster on 17 May 1819 and spent another seven nights in gaol. On 20 July 1819 he was found to have entered the government stores and stolen crown property. He was sentenced to 200 lashes, which he evidently survived, and was sent to Newcastle for four years. By the time of the 1828 Census he was listed as aged thirty, a Jew, free by servitude, and a dealer. Elizabeth, his wife (alias Gill), twenty-four years of age, in government service, had arrived in 1824 on the *Grenada*.

A certificate of freedom was issued for John Morris on 2 March 1826. The *Hobart Town Courier* recorded that on 11 August 1837 he was licensed to be a hawker in Van Diemen's Land. The Van Diemen's Land convict records state that he came on the *Almorah* and the *Pilot*.

CON 21/39, no. 55; CON 13/1, p. 125; CF 4/4423–159/2749.

MORRISHESKY, Moses

Ocean (1), 1816; Convict; Sentenced to 7 years, Portsmouth, 1815.
Musician.

Morrishesky arrived in New South Wales on 30 January 1816. He was on the list of convicts disembarked and sent on to Windsor for assigned work. He was listed as 'Moroseholy' with a life sentence. On the list of prisoners to be sent to Newcastle on 10 June his name is recorded as 'Henry Die Mozesky'. In June 1818 his name appeared on the list of prisoners who were punished at Newcastle. 'Merrishesky' was tried at the Sydney Criminal Court in 1820 for stealing various articles in the dwelling house of Mary Burrows of Sydney. He was found guilty and sentenced 'to be transported back to Newcastle for the term of his natural life'. On 25 February 1825 he was removed from Newcastle on the *Mermaid* to Port Macquarie. Henry Mosesky was listed in the *Sydney Gazette* as an absconded prisoner on 31 May 1817. The 1822 General Muster of New South Wales listed Henry Moseshesky as a convict in Newcastle serving a seven-year sentence.

Reports of Prisoners tried in the Courts of Criminal Jurisdiction 1820–24, 4/3503, 4/7021, X820, p. 21; CS Copies of Letters Sent 29 March 1815 to 19 June 1816, 4/3494, p. 337; Principal Superintendent of Convicts, Butts of CF, 24 December 1844 to 18 February 1845, 4/3496, p. 178; 4/1718 p. 65; CS Copies of Letters to Port Macquarie 1822–25, 4/3864, pp. 393–4.

MOSES, Aaron

b. Spitalfields, 1815–1858
Lady Nugent, 1836; Convict; Sentenced to life, Central Criminal Court, 1836.
Single; Labourer; Height: 173 cm.

Fresh freckled complexion, reddish hair, dark brown whiskers, long face, grey eyes, a broad nose. The letters RM AM were tattooed inside his left arm and EH inside his right arm. Aaron Moses was sentenced for burglary at the Old Bailey on 9 May 1836, and transported along with fellow culprits, David Martin (q.v.), Solomon Hyams and Joseph Aaron (q.v.). All four young men were sentenced to death with a recommendation for mercy by the Prosecutor 'on account of their youth'. The ship's surgeon reported that Aaron Moses was 'Ironed and handcuffed on board for thieving and threatening the Chief Constable that he would "do" for him'.

Aaron Moses' 'bad conduct' on the passage to Van Diemen's Land led him to be sent immediately to Deep Gully to work on the roads in the chain gang. He remained at Deep Gully for a year. On 10 October 1837 he received thirty-five lashes for being absent without leave 'under very aggravated circumstances'. On 21 March 1838 he was found guilty of pilfering and given twelve months hard labour. He was sent to the Perth Chain Gang and on 16 July 1838 received fifty lashes for disobedience. He remained in the chain gang for the remainder of 1838 through to May 1839. On 23 October 1839 he was sentenced to twelve months hard labour in chains and was sent to the Hulk Chain Gang at New Town Bay. On 20 January 1840 he received thirty-six lashes for having apples in his possession for which he could not account. On 17 August 1840 Moses was given two years hard labour in chains for having absconded from government service and for having stolen four pounds weight of pork from Mr John Fox.

In March 1842 Aaron Moses, a prisoner in the Penitentiary, wrote to the Hobart Town Synagogue Committee and asked that Mr Reuben Joseph of New Norfolk be 'caused to pay the balance of an allowance due to him the nonpayment of which he would place Joseph in gaol'. The synagogue took no action. A ticket of leave was granted to Aaron Moses on 15 October 1844. On 1 April 1845 Moses received a second-class pardon.

Aaron Moses, son of Charles and Frederica Moses, died in Sydney in 1858.

OBSP 9 May 1836, case 1134, CON 31/31, no. 1449; CON 32/4, p. 86; CON 31/31, no. 1449; CON 34/6; VDL Papers, ML, A1059–8, p. 471.

MOSES, Abigail (née BARNETT)

1789–1841
1836; Free.
Married.

Abigail Moses was the wife of Marcus Warschauer (q.v.), alias Mordecai Moses. She had followed her husband out to Australia following his conviction.

She was the stepmother of George Moss (q.v.). According to the inscription on her tomb, Abigail was 'the wife of Mordecai Moses, 'an officer of the Sydney Synagogue and sexton of this ground', the Devonshire Street Jewish Cemetery. Abigail died on 6 July 1841. Her grave was transferred to the Rookwood Cemetery in 1901.

MOSES, Abraham

Free.

There were a number of public notices in the *Sydney Gazette* regarding the departure of Abraham Moses from the colony (12 October 1806, 12 June 1808), indicating that he was working as a sailor.

Sydney Gazette, 12 October 1806, 12 June 1808.

MOSES, Abraham

b. London, 1791–1858
Dora, 1840; Free.
Married; Dealer; 2 children.

The son of Harry Moses and Ann (née Lazarus) and brother of Isaac Moses (q.v.). Abraham Moses arrived in New South Wales on 17 March 1840 and settled Muswellbrook. Abraham Moses had married Rebecca Davis (in London in 1824. They had two children, Sarah (Moss) Moses (1824), who married Lewis Lipman (q.v.) in 1847, and Isaac Moses. Abraham Moses died at Sydney in 1858.

MOSES, Abraham (Jacob JOSEPHS)

b. London, 1792–1837
Surrey I (1), 1814; Convict; Sentenced to life, Old Bailey, 1813.
Single; Watch finisher, dealer; Height: 171 cm.

Dark sallow complexion, black hair, brown eyes, large nose. On 25 January 1813 Moses was seen entering the home of Mr Judah Cohen in Whitechapel and stealing some silver candlesticks. He was caught when he tried to sell the candlesticks to a pawnbroker. He was convicted at the Middlesex Gaol Delivery on 17 February 1813 and sentenced to death, though this was later commuted to transportation for life. He was the brother of Joel Joseph (q.v.) and David Josephs (q.v.).

Moses arrived in New South Wales on 28 July 1814 and was sent to Parramatta and assigned to Mr Faultless. He was listed in the 1816 Male Muster as a 'Government Labourer' in Parramatta. On 3 February 1816 the *Sydney Gazette* reported that Moses had stolen two silver spoons, the property of James Wright of Parramatta, and the following week he was sentenced to seven years hard labour in the gaol gang at Newcastle. In the 1818 General Muster he was listed as a government labourer.

In October 1820 Moses sent a petition to Governor Macquarie stating that he had spent five years at Newcastle and that his brother Joel Joseph, 'lately deceased', had left him some property. A few days before his death he had 'expressed his earnest wish to see his brother'. Moses wrote that he hoped Governor Macquarie 'will be humanely pleased to dispense with the unexpired part of his Sentence by ordering his return to Sydney "because the offence he had committed was not of an atrocious Nature"'. Macquarie responded: 'The remaining portion of his sentence at Coal River is to be remitted and he is to be permitted to come to Sydney' (14 October 1820). The prayers, which were held for a week following the death of Joseph, are the first recorded Jewish services held in Australia.

On 11 June 1821 his name appeared on the list of prisoners transported to Newcastle on the *Governor Bligh*. He was listed as 'Abraham Moses or Jacob Josephs'. The 1822 General Muster of Convicts in New South Wales listed Moses as a prisoner serving his sentence in Newcastle.

In 1825 Moses wrote again to the Governor begging for a ticket of leave. He had been in the employ of the government for twelve years, three of which on the estate of the late Secretary Mr Campbell, until called to join the party of (the explorer) Major Ovens. His present employment was in the government boat that served the hulk *Phoenix* in Sydney Harbour.

Moses eventually received a ticket of leave, dated 8 November 1830, for the District of Sydney. On 2 November 1836 he asked for 'a reward for his uniform good conduct'. He claimed his character would bear 'the strictest scrutiny', and was recommended for a conditional pardon on 14 December 1836. He died in Sydney on 23 January 1837.

OBSP, 1813, case 281, p. 168; Convicts sent to Newcastle 4/3494; Petition to Governor Macquarie, October 1820, Letter 24, 4/1861; Petition 161, 24 October 1825, for Mitigation of Sentence 4/1784; TL 30/791; CS Letters Received 1836, Convicts, Petitions, 36/9610, in 4/2309; *Sydney Gazette*, 3 February 1816, 10 February 1816; 4/3516, p. 66.

MOSES, Abraham

b. London, 1798–1873
Palambam, 1832; Free.
Married; Dealer; 4 children.

Abraham Moses was the son of Joseph Moses and Deborah Moses (née Barnett), and the brother of Phoebe Hart (q.v.), Moses Moses (q.v.), Isaac Moses (q.v.) and John (Jacob) Moses (q.v.). He arrived on the *Palambam* in 1832 in Van Diemen's

Land with his wife Leah (née Moses) and children. Leah was the sister of Samuel Shannon (q.v.), which is probably the reason that Samuel employed Moses prior to their falling out over a 'lost' cheque in 1842. Moses was a bonded migrant. A John Barnett (q.v.), a 'Cooper', was on the same ship.

Abraham Moses arrived in New South Wales on 10 January 1833 as a free settler, travelling with his family. With them was 'Norman Simon, a rabbi', who was Norman (Nahum) Joseph (q.v.). Abraham Moses' wife had an infant in arms. The children listed included Sarah (who married Nathan Joseph, q.v., on 1 June 1836), Julia (who married Elias Moses, q.v., in 1840), Moses and Jacob, who was born in Australia in 1834.

In 1833 Abraham Moses was the owner of the Joiners' Arms in King Street, Sydney, and, in the same year, was the proprietor of the Red Cross Hotel in King Street. In March 1837 he went into business at the Monaro Plains. He had a consignment of new stock in his store in Monaro by 9 March 1838 and became the agent of the *Australian* newspaper. In November 1838 he advertised that his store was for sale and on 1 January 1839 the *Australian* reported that he was about to travel to England. Mr and Mrs Abraham Moses gave £30 to the Sydney Synagogue building appeal with additional pledges of £5 in the name of Jacob and Julia. Abraham Moses returned a year later and opened the Squatters Arms at Dr Reid's Flat. In 1839 he wrote in a petition that he was living at Bangery or Dr Reid's Flat: 'For the past year he has run the mail from Queanbeyan to the Snowy River, a distance of 100 miles. Owing to the drought he has suffered a great financial loss. There is no hotel to be found within 40 miles of Maneroo [*sic*] where the petitioner resided. He asked for ten acres at Bangery or Doctor Reid's Flat for a hotel for travellers to Cooma, the Snowy River, Nimatabell, Twofold Bay and Biger' [*sic*]. He politely wrote that he was visiting Sydney because his licence to run a licensed public house 'seems to have been delayed'.

During 1840–41 Abraham Moses managed the White Hart Hotel in Yass. In March 1840 his store 'on the road to the Snowy River, Port Phillip and South Australia', which had been there for the past two years, was declared to be trespassing on ground given to a cattle man. There was, claimed Moses, no other store within 27 miles of Woolwoi Creek. He had built a house, a store, and a stockyard and fenced in a small paddock. The petition to set aside the ruling was refused. The official wrote that he 'regrets very much' that Moses must move. The newspapers were filled with numerous appeals to debtors to pay him during the depression of March to October 1841 and, in 1842, he moved to Sydney.

By September he had a house and store in Bridge Street, had purchased extensive land in Sydney and was active in supporting candidates in the first municipal election in 1842. Moses rented two rooms in his Bridge Street residence for the Sydney Jewish community to use as a temporary synagogue. His property in Bridge Street was described as 'a forge and store'. However, he used it as a liquor store and, in February 1844, charged four women and a man with stealing a dozen bottles of wine. In 1844 he purchased the schooner *Mumford* and in 1845 advertised that he sold the 'only genuine sperm candles in the colony' from his store in Bridge Street.

Moses donated £60 to the building fund of the synagogue in 1839 and was a seat holder in 1845. He served on many congregational committees and was particularly concerned about a proper supply of kosher meat. In August 1848 he was an unsuccessful candidate for the post of president of the synagogue. The Land Correspondence files show that Abraham Moses made some substantial purchases in Sydney totalling more than £50 000 in the years 1849 to 1852. In 1837 he had become the first Jew to receive a licence to pasture stock beyond the established boundaries of settlement in the colony. In the 1840s he acquired the leasehold of nearly 50 000 hectares along the Murrumbidgee.

In 1852 he was listed as an original shareholder in the Australian Joint Stock Bank and owned a Bond Store in Argyle Place. Abraham Moses left Australia for London in 1859. When he died in London at his residence at 68 Russell Square, on 27 February 1873, his estate was said to have been in the vicinity of £650 000. Abraham Moses Esq., 'late of Sydney, was in the 75th year of his life'.

His son Moses married Caroline Joseph, daughter of Moses and Rosetta Joseph (q.v.) in Sydney in 1851. They moved to London in the 1850s. Moses changed his name to Sydney Merton and died in 1880.

Palambam Indent 4/5204; *Sydney Gazette*, 13 August 1833; *Sydney Morning Herald*, 13 September 1842, 7 February 1844, 9 February 1844, 23 May 1844; *Australian Israelite*, 9 May 1873; CS 39/13050, dated 5 December 1839, in 4/2457.1; Land Correspondence, 2/7933, for urban property purchases, 1849–1851, Petition 'Upper Pitt St', 25 February 1839; Errol Lea-Scarlett, *Queanbeyan District and People*.

MOSES, Abraham

b. London, 1799
Lady Castlereagh, 1818; Convict; Sentenced to 7 years, London, 1817.
Single; Fruiterer; Height: 167.5 cm.

Dark ruddy complexion, hazel eyes, dark brown hair. On 14 June 1817 Abraham Moses stole one watch valued at £1, a seal, chain and key from a passerby in Crooked Lane near the Monument. He was sentenced on 2 July 1817, and was 'Well behaved' on the ship.

Moses arrived in New South Wales on the *Lady Castlereagh* in May 1818 and was then sent on to Van Diemen's Land. Abraham Moses was off the government rations in 1821. On 12 June 1822 he received fifty lashes for 'discharging firearms, refusing to give up same, assaulting a constable', and in November 1822 was reprimanded for having been absent from church. The *Hobart Town Gazette* advertised on 31 August 1822 that he had a sale at his house in Elizabeth Street of 'clothing, knives and forks, crockery, tomahawks, Bengal soap etc etc'. In December 1823 he was returned to the Public Works Department for 'harbouring a female named Prince'.

Moses received his certificate of freedom on 17 September 1824. By 1824 he was free by servitude. He appeared in the Launceston Police Book in 1825 for 'abusing and challenging H. Bateman to a fight' and was bound over to keep the peace for six months.

OBSP, 1816–17, case 949, p. 327; Ship Indent 4/4006, p. 37; CON 31/29, no. 90; Launceston Police Book, CON 78/2; CON 13/1; *Hobart Town Gazette*, 31 August 1822, 17 September 1824; HO 10/43.

MOSES, Abraham

b. Houndsditch, 1808
Isabella I (6), 1842; Convict; Sentenced to 7 years, Central Criminal Court, 1841.
Single; Shell dealer; Height: 163 cm.

Dark complexion, black hair, hazel eyes, medium nose, high retreating forehead. Breast hairy. A Jew. Could read and write. Abraham Moses stole a basket containing clothes from a shop. He had been imprisoned once before for assault, and previously fined 20 shillings and £2 for similar offences. Abraham Moses had married the Sephardi woman Hannah Martinis at London's Great Synagogue on 25 March 1828.

Moses arrived in Van Diemen's Land on 19 May 1842 and was allotted eighteen months initial period of probation and sent to Flinders Bay on the Tasman Peninsula to work as a baker. By 9 September 1842 Moses was at Impression Bay. During that year his file recorded frequent complaints that he was dirty and impudent. He was charged with misconduct when he permitted a prisoner to enter the cook house but was found not guilty of the charge. His original term of probation expired on 21 November 1843. He was moved to the Prisoners' Barracks in Bridgewater and on 8 April 1844 he was charged with feloniously receiving stolen goods, under the value of £5, and his existing sentence of transportation was extended by nine months. In 1846 and 1847 he was at the Prisoners' Barracks in Launceston. Abraham Moses received a ticket of leave on 8 February 1848 and a certificate of freedom on 2 November 1848. A curious footnote has been discovered in the records of the London rabbinical court dated 19 December 1850 when Hannah bat Yaacov Nunis Martinus came before the rabbis to confess that she had been living illicitly with one Joseph Hart of 7 Buckle Street, Whitechapel for three years'. Her husband had been transported to Sydney ten years before 'and has not been heard from since'. Hannah obviously hoped that, in the prolonged absence of her husband, she would be permitted to marry a second time.

CON 33/20, no. 4817. Jeremy I Pfeffer 'From One End of the Earth to the Other' (2008), p. 208.

MOSES, Alexander (MOSS)

b. London, d. 1850
1836; Free.
Single; 5 children.

Alexander Moses was the son of Marcus (Moses) Warschauer (q.v) and the brother of George Moss (q.v), Catherine Moss (q.v.) and Rosetta Moss (q.v.). He arrived in Australia in 1836 with his sisters and stepmother, Abigail Moses (q.v.). Moses was the first Jew to apply for a licence for depasturing stock beyond the boundaries of the colony (*New South Wales Gazette*, 18 January 1837). His place of residence was in Sydney and he applied for licence no. 47 for the Monaro. Alexander Moss (Abraham Moses) married Rachael Hyam (q.v.) at the Sydney Synagogue on 28 February 1841. Two children were registered in the synagogue's birth book,

Moses (Morris) (15 January 1842) and Abigail (11 May 1843). Alexander Moss (as he was now known) returned with his family to England, where he died, in London, in 1850. His poverty-stricken wife was sent back to Australia on the *Ann* in 1853 with her five children. The fare was paid by the Jewish Emigration Loan Society. Moses (Morris) married Elizabeth, daughter of Michael Joseph Russell (q.v.), on 10 May 1868. They lived in Maitland.

Family history by Lea Woolf and Lynn Samuel, Melbourne.

MOSES, Benjamin

b. London, 1797–1876
Free.

Benjamin Moses was the son of Elijah Moses. A publican's licence was granted on 13 October 1843 to Benjamin Moses, for the public house Labour in Vain on Campbell Street, Hobart Town. The licence was transferred on 6 February 1845 following the announcement of his insolvency on 10 December 1844. On 5 December 1844 Benjamin Moses 'late of Campbell St in Hobart Town was confined to gaol for debts'.

Hobart Town Courier, 13 October 1843, 17 December 1844, 6 February 1845; *Hobart Town Advertiser*, 10 December 1844.

MOSES, Daniel

Convict.

Daniel Moses was issued with a certificate of freedom on 19 October 1842.

Australian, 20 October 1842.

MOSES, David

b. London, 1795–1870
Duckenfield, 1831; Free.
Married; Dealer.

David Moses was the son of Moses and Elizabeth Moses of London, and the brother of Rachel Moses (q.v.) (who married Samuel Benjamin, q.v.) and Elias Moses (q.v.). He was the uncle of Michael Simeon (q.v.), James Simeon (q.v.) and David Simeon (q.v.) of Victoria. David Moses and his wife Sophia (q.v.) came to Sydney in 1831 and arrived in Hobart Town on the *Duckenfield* on 17 August 1831. Having seen the local conditions, he travelled to London in 1833, returning to Hobart Town on 6 December 1834 on the *Margaret*. He then commissioned J.C. Clark to build the London Mart in Liverpool Street, which opened in late 1836. The business prospered and he moved to a new shop in the same street in 1840.

The *Hobart Town Courier* on 30 March 1838 graphically recorded a fight between David Moses and John Moses (q.v.): 'It appeared David was trying to force himself into the pit of the theatre and, prevented by John, who succeeded in pushing him into the street; half an hour later he returned and asked for John who, the moment he appeared, was knocked down by a huge piece of paling which struck him on the head. He was fined forty shillings or two months in the House of Correction'. David paid the fine!

David Moses was one of those involved in founding the Hobart Town Synagogue and became a member of the first committee and eventually rented seat no. 2. He donated £20 to the congregation in 1844 and £25 in 1845. The *Hobart Town Courier* reported, on 7 January 1842, that Moses exported a case of china and clothing apparel on the *Flying Squirrel* to Port Phillip and on 4 February imported two cases of British goods. The Van Diemen's Land Census of 1842 recorded that he was married to a Jewish woman, that they were both 'aged between 21 and 45', that they had arrived free, and owned their own home in Liverpool Street. David Moses was listed as a member of the committee of the Tasmanian Masonic Benevolent Society (*Hobart Town Courier*, February 1846). The *Tasmanian Colonist* on 1 December 1853 announced his 'departure from this colony' and recorded that he was presented with a silver snuff box. He had been a resident of Tasmania for twenty years. His departure had been delayed by Sophia's illness. On 6 May 1853, she died at their residence at Liverpool Street at the age of fifty-seven, and was buried in the Harrington Street Cemetery.

David Moses had already established links with the Jewish community in Sydney and was listed as having given £50 to the Sydney Synagogue in 1843 and £10 in 1845. Upon his arrival in New South Wales he became the licensee of the Barley Mow Inn in Castlereagh Street. He died there on 26 July 1870, aged seventy-five. David and Sophia Moses had no children.

Tasmanian Times, 13 August 1870; Wayne Index; *Hobart Town Courier*, 30 March 1838, 7 January 1842, 18 November 1842; *Tasmanian Colonist*, 1 December 1853; Ship Indent 4/5213.

MOSES, David

b. London, 1809
Asia I (4), 1828; Convict; Sentenced to 7 years, Old Bailey, 1827.
Married; Glass cutter; Height: 161 cm.

Fair ruddy complexion, brown hair, hazel eyes. Tattoos: DN upper part, doves, heart and anchor on under part of left arm. D N, heart and A C on right arm. David Moses, together with Lazarus Jacobs (q.v.) (aged twenty) struck a woman in Petticoat Lane and stole her purse. He was sentenced on 12 July 1827, and had two former convictions.

David Moses arrived in New South Wales on 13 March 1828 and was initially assigned, briefly, to Susannah Fletcher, Lower Minto. Moses appeared on the 1828 Census twice and was listed as 'Protestant' and as a member of the No. 14 Road Party and also in the town gang of Parramatta. Moses was still in Parramatta in 1834 when he appeared in the gaol record, having been admitted on 12 May 1834 and sent on to Sydney on 19 May 1834. His trade was listed as 'none'. At the Bathurst General Sessions on 26 June 1829 he was convicted for stealing and sentenced to three years colonial transportation. He was sent to Moreton Bay in August 1829 on the *Waterloo*. He was returned to Sydney from Moreton Bay on 4 February 1833, and was granted a certificate of freedom on 17 January 1842.

On 10 October 1846 the *Citizen* told the story of a man named David Moses who was committed for trial upon a charge of stealing four one-pound notes from a sailor. Moses 'snatched the notes from his bosom' but when apprehended denied the charge. By the time of his arrest he only had six shillings and sixpence left. Fortunately for the accused, in January 1847, Moses was discharged because the principal witness in the case had 'gone to sea'.

OBSP, 1826–27, case 953, p. 360; Ship Indent 4/4013, p. 68; CON 18/16, no. 899; Launceston Police Book, CON 78/2, p. 347; Prison Department, Parramatta Gaol Entrance Books, 1833–34, no. 646, 4/6530; Chronological Register of Convicts at Moreton Bay, no. 1856; *Citizen*, 10 October 1846, 2 January 1847; CF 42/0076.

MOSES, David

b. London, 1811
Marmion, 1828; Convict; Sentenced to 7 years, Old Bailey, 1827.
Single; Fishmonger; Height: 161 cm.

Dark complexion, bushy brown hair, dark grey eyes, long oval face, large nose broad bridge, narrow thick lips. A Jew. Born Winfield Street London. David Moses (aged sixteen), Samuel Barnett (aged fourteen) and Abraham Isaacs (q.v.) (aged twenty) stole a pocket book from a man in Whitechapel. They were watched by two of the Bow Street Patrol, who arrested them immediately. David Moses was tried on 5 April 1827 and sentenced on 31 May. Moses was detected stealing on board a convict transport and was described as a 'lazy, impudent fellow' who was 'a Jew', 'bad', and a 'regular thief'. His father lived in Bell Lane, Spitalfields. 'I was last employed by Davis the fishmonger in Houndsditch'. He brought fifteen shillings and five pence with him on board the Marmion.

David Moses arrived in Van Diemen's Land on 6 March 1828 and on 24 December 1828 was sentenced to three months in irons and six months in a road party for insolence and neglect of duty. On 3 January 1829 he was sentenced to two additional weeks in the chain gang for having surreptitiously removed his irons. Twelve days later he received twenty-five lashes for insolence. During the year he worked with the road parties in New Norfolk, Bell Mountain and Black Snake. At the latter he received twenty-five lashes for three absences. He remained with the chain gangs through to December 1833 (although, on 12 April 1833, he was listed as having 'absconded').

On 8 July 1835 Moses was free by servitude and was charged with 'burglariously breaking and entering the dwelling place of John Johnstone and stealing thirty-five pieces of silk handkerchief'. Moses was acquitted. On 19 October 1836 he was charged with having assaulted Deputy Constable Benjamin Watkins who declined to prosecute. Finally, on 24 August 1838, he was sentenced to two years at Port Arthur for stealing a pound and half of English salmon.

During 1841 and 1842 Moses was the assigned servant of Mr Cawthorn and for a number of 'minor' offences involving absence without leave, neglect of duty and insolence he received twenty-three days in solitary confinement and three weeks in irons. His convict record concluded on 26 December 1842 and a ticket of leave was granted on 6 October 1843.

OBSP, 1826–27, case 1584, p. 592; CON 34/2, no. 620; CON 31/29; CON 32/1, no. 620; CON 18/15 (Description Book with first name 'Daniel'); HO 10/51; VDL Papers, p. 107, ML, A1059–4; *Hobart Town Courier*, 12 April 1833, 31 August 1838, 6 October 1843.

MOSES, David Lionel

b. London, 1827–1845
1842; Free.
Single.

David Lionel Moses was the fourth son of Henry Moses, merchant of London, and the brother-in-law of Louis Nathan (q.v.). He joined the synagogue in Hobart Town as soon as he arrived in 1842 and on 11 April 1843 gave £25 to its building appeal. He rented seat no. 70 in the synagogue's first year. He died on 27 September 1845 at the home of his sister and brother-in-law in Murray Street. He was eighteen years old. His funeral was the fourth to be carried out by the synagogue. In December 1854 his brother, Hyam Leopold Moses (q.v.), gave £200 to the Hobart Town congregation so that a protective wall could be built around the Harrington Street Jewish cemetery.

Hobart Town Courier, 8 October 1845.

MOSES, Elias

b. London, 1812–1874
Ann, 1833; Free.
Single; 12 children.

Elias Moses was the son of Moses and Elizabeth Moses of London, five of whose children came to Australia. Elias's siblings were Samuel, David (q.v.), Catherine, who married Moses Benjamin (q.v.), Rachel (q.v.), who married Samuel Benjamin (q.v.), and Miriam (Frankel, q.v.), who married Jacob Frankel (q.v.).

The log book, or shipboard diary kept by Elias Moses, and now held by a private collector in Sydney, begins with his embarkation on 1 May 1833 and concludes when the barque *Ann* arrived in Port Jackson. Moses finished his diary with the words: 'They say experience makes fools wise. Strive for the next voyage. I hope I shall be able to keep a better log. Arrived Sydney (Thank God) November 13, 1833'.

Elias Moses founded the firm of Benjamin and Moses in Goulburn in the year he arrived in Australia. He also became the owner of Sydney House in George Street, Sydney, and the London Stores, George Street, Windsor. Elias married

Julia Moses (q.v.) on 15 April 1840. She was the daughter of Abraham Moses (q.v.) of Monaro and who had travelled to New South Wales on the Palambam. Elias and Julia had a daughter, Rachael, in Goulburn in 1841. Deborah (1843 [born in London]), Elizabeth Julia born 3 January 1845 at Goulburn, Fanny born 1850, Moses born 1852, Joseph born in Sydney in 1854, Samuel Benjamin Moses born 23 December 1855 and died in 1931, Catherine born Melbourne in 1856, Sophia 1859–1946, Amelia born 1861, Louisa 1863, and Florence in 1866.

Elias was an activist within the Sydney Jewish community and the linchpin of an important Australian Jewish colonial family. He was a seat holder in the new York Street Synagogue in 1845 when he gave the congregation ten guineas and was listed as living in Goulburn. The first High Holyday services in Goulburn were held at his home in Auburn Street in 1844. The Argyle Store in Goulburn established by Moses and (Samuel) Benjamin in Goulburn's earliest years became one of the leading businesses of pre-gold rush Goulburn. Both Elias and Solomon Moses (q.v.) lived in Auburn Street and were listed in the 1841 Census. Elias was one of the trustees of the Goulburn Hospital (*Sydney Morning Herald*, 26 April 1845). In 1845 Samuel Benjamin and Elias Moses owned the Argyle Steam Boiling Establishment, which bought surplus sheep from farmers and boiled them down for fat. He was one of the four trustees to be responsible for the land granted by the governor to the community, on 8 April 1850, to build a Jewish school in Sydney, and he was one of the instigators of the Macquarie Street secession when the Sydney community split into two. During the early 1850s the records of the New South Wales Government showed that he purchased land at Goulburn (for £20), Sydney (for £247), Wynyard Square in Sydney (£996) and Sydney (£1604). Elias died in Sydney at his residence, 582 Bourke Street, and was buried on 14 June 1874. He was sixty-two years old and described on his tombstone, in the old Jewish section of Rookwood Cemetery, as 'an honest man' who was 'buried with great respect'.

Ship Indent 4/5205; Land Purchased 2/7933; *Sydney Morning Herald*, 15 November 1833, 26 April 1845; *Voice of Jacob*, 6 June 1845.

MOSES, Emanuel (Money Moses)

b. Peterboro, 1780–1841
Lord Lyndoch (2), 1841; Convict; Sentenced to 14 years, Central Criminal Court, 1839.
Married; Publican and fence; Height: 173 cm; 3 children.

Florid complexion, black to grey hair, round face, high forehead, light brown eyes, prominent nose. He could read and write 'a little'. Emanuel Moses was involved in the case of the great gold dust robbery by the Caspar family (Ellis Casper, Lewin Casper, qq.v.). His daughter Alice Abrahams, aged thirty-three, was arraigned in the same case. His conduct on board the transport ship was 'good'. Emanuel's wife, Sarah (q.v.), and their children, Mary (q.v.), Rachel (q.v.) and Rebecca (q.v.), travelled out to the colony on the Mayflower.

Griffiths, in *The Chronicles of Newgate*, tells the story of the fate of Emanuel Moses, more generally known as 'Money Moses'. Moses was tried with his daughter, Mrs Alice Abrahams, who, it was said, helped him melt down the stolen gold dust:

> he was the most daring and successful of fences ... Such an event as the conviction of 'Money Moses' almost the father of his particular line of trade, produced an amazing consternation among his fellows. Originally exhibiting upon his person all the signs of indulgent living, his confinement reduced him to the shadow of his former self and there were to be heard among his friends apprehensions that a voyage to Australia would complete the work which the air of [Newgate] prison had commenced.

His friends were correct! Moses disembarked at Hobart Town on 5 February 1841 and was sent straight to the hospital at New Norfolk, where he died on 5 July 1841. Griffiths added that 'Money Moses', who was very well known in the vicinity of Covent Garden, 'was a direct descendant of [Isaac] Ikey Solomon' (q.v.). While he was ostensibly the publican of the Black Lion in Vinegar Yard, Drury Lane, there 'secretly he did business as one of the most daring and successful fencers ever known in the metropolis'.

CON 35/5, no. 1046; CON 31/32, no. 1944; CON 63/1; A. Griffiths, *The Chronicles of Newgate*, pp. 474, 480; 'The Life of Elias moses' by Chris George in *AJHSJ*, vol. 20, part 4, June 2012, p. 501f.

MOSES, Hannah

Convict.
Prostitute.

The *Sydney Gazette* of 5 August 1820 recorded that there had been a burglary from the home of Hannah Moses. On 18 March 1826 the paper reported that she had been sentenced to three months gaol as a 'notorious prostitute'.

MOSES, Hannah (AARONS)

b. London, 1819
Free.

Hannah Moses was one of the daughters of Joseph and Rachel Aarons (qq.v.). She married Isaac Moses (q.v.) on 28 February 1839. On 16 June 1846 the Colonial Secretary replied to Mrs Hannah Moses of Elizabeth Street North (Sydney) regarding her plea on behalf of her father, who was in Parramatta Gaol for a period of two years. She was told that the government could not interfere. On 22 September she wrote again and the rest of the sentence was remitted. Hannah also intervened on behalf of her mother, Rachel Aarons, who, she said, was in 'bad health' while she remained in the Darlinghurst Gaol. Her plea for mercy was granted on 6 November 1845.

CS Correspondence Miscellaneous Out, 4/3550, p. 87; CS Copies of Letters Sent Re Convicts, 1845–48, 4/3692, p. 14.

MOSES, Henry

1809–1859
Free.
Married; Dealer.

Henry Moses was one of the thirteen Jewish men in Yass who signed a petition for the establishment of a Jewish cemetery in Yass. In May 1847 Henry Moses, in Yass, wrote to the Colonial Secretary stating that he would like to buy two acres of crown land at Binalong. There was no store within 23 miles. He promised to establish a store and a tannery with a properly qualified person in charge. He would sell all kinds of merchandise at the lowest possible prices, taking colonial produce in exchange.

Henry Moses died at Parramatta in 1859, aged fifty.

Colonial Secretary, Letters rec'd: Land for Churches, Schools, Parsonage and Cemeteries 1825–54, 4/2650.4, 20 December 1844.

MOSES, (Moss) Henry

Free

A 'currency lad' born in Sydney in 1831. The second child of Mary Connolly, who became Rebecca Moses (q.v.).

On 7 September 1848 the 17 year-old Henry Moses was convicted, with his father John (q.v.), at the Goulburn Circuit Court on 7 September 1848, for perjury and given a seven-year sentence and sent to Sydney.

On 2 June 1851 Moses, a prisoner on Cockatoo Island, saved a soldier from drowning. As a reward a year of his probation period was remitted and a pardon was granted on 31 August 1853.

Moses was not permitted to return to the Yass district and settled in the area of Shoalhaven and worked for some time with Michael Hyam (q.v.), an old friend of his father. In 1862 Henry married Michael Hyam's daughter, Sarah Zorilda Hyam.

He built a hotel, the Shoalhaven Central Hotel, in Greenhills. By that time he had changed his name to Henry Moss. He became mayor of Shoalhaven for a year and then became the first mayor of Nowra. He was re-elected mayor six times and served on the council for the rest of his life. He was honorary secretary of the Shoalhaven Turf Club. One of his hobbies was prospecting and a volume of his poetry was published.

Inspector-General of Police, Convict Branch, Register of Colonial Pardons 4/4494; CS 51/4862, 53/7568. Alan Clark: 'He had a Vision for Nowra' in *JAJHS* vol X!, part 4, p. 643.

MOSES, Hyam

b. London, 1809
Lady Feversham, 1830; Convict; Sentenced to 14 years, Old Bailey, 1829.
Single; Dealer; Height: 161 cm.

Dark ruddy freckled complexion, black hair, dark brown eyes. BW tattooed on right arm. No education. Jew. Hyam Moses stole twelve handkerchiefs that he grabbed from the front of a hosier's shop on 15 September 1828. Two days later he was caught in Whitechapel after trying to snatch six veils from a shop. He was sentenced on 29 October 1829 to be transported for seven years for each offence.

Hyam Moses arrived on 29 July 1830 and was sent to the Hyde Park Barracks. Moses was first assigned to Col. Allen of the 53rd Regiment and then to W. Smith at Wiseman's Point. He ran away and was apprehended on 31 March 1832. When he was recaptured, he was sent to the treadmill for twenty-one days and then to work with the Twenty-Third Road Gang. In 1837 he was assigned to Mr C. Roberts of Sydney. He married Louisa Nixon in 1841 at St James' Church of England in Sydney. He was granted a certificate of freedom on 4 January 1844.

OBSP, 1827–28, p. 917; *Lady Feversham* Printed Indent, no. 30-1304; CF 4/4388, 44/12; Indent 4/4013, p. 116; *Sydney Gazette*, 31 March 1832; Mutch Index 116/25.

MOSES, Hyam Leopold

b. London
Calcutta, 1842; Free.
Married; Merchant; 2 children.

Hyam Leopold Moses arrived in Hobart Town on the *Calcutta*, travelling cabin class from London, on 17 October 1842. He was the third son of Henry Moses of London and a brother of David Lionel Moses (q.v.) and Samuel Moses. He donated £5 to the synagogue in 1844. In 1845, together with Henry Samuel Benjamin (q.v.), he served the congregation as its honorary auditor, and was assigned seat no. 7 in the synagogue. He also gave £5 to the Sydney Synagogue and twelve shillings and sixpence to the newly formed Melbourne Hebrew Congregation at the High Holydays of 1844. Hyam Leopold Moses returned to England to find a wife and, on 2 June 1847, the Chief Rabbi, the Rev. Dr Adler, married Hyam Leopold Moses Esq. of Hobart Town to Rosetta Bloom, eldest daughter of Lawrence Phillips Esq. of the Strand. On 10 March 1848 the birth of a son was reported in the *Hobart Town Courier*. In 1854 Hyam Leopold Moses gave £200 to build a wall around the cemetery in which his younger brother, David, was buried. The family left Hobart Town in August 1854 and returned to London. Moses changed his family name to 'Beddington' in 1868.

Angela Shire (ed.), *Great Synagogue Marriage Registers, 1791–1850*; *Hobart Town Courier*, 29 December 1843; *The Times*, 5 June 1847; family research by Stephen Hanford, Melbourne.

MOSES, Isaac (MOYSE)

b. London, 1766
Royal Admiral, 1792; Convict; Sentenced to 7 years, Old Bailey, 1792.
Single.

Isaac Moses picked a servant's inside coat pocket, in which there was an empty leather pocket book valued at sixpence. At the Old Bailey in June 1792 he was sentenced to seven years transportation. Isaac Moyse, aged twenty-seven, had been sentenced to death at Bury Street, Edmonds, on 25 March 1789. He was subsequently pardoned, but was reported to be on the Royal Admiral *in 1792.*

It appears that Moses was the only Jew on board the transport (although there was a Nathan Harris, aged twenty-five, who was a porter.) The Home Office records contain the following letter, written by the convict James Lacey from False Bay at the Cape of Good Hope:

> Y'r Honour,
>
> We are now arrived at this Place, after a very prosperous and healthy voyage so far. Soon after leaving the land, our confinement, which before was particularly severe, was in great measure abated, our treatment in every respect far superior to what we from the outset were led to expect, until a Jew convict, who from his former bad conduct to his associates met with continual taunts, and not having any other mode of revenge, informed Cap'n Bond that there had been a plan concocted on board of the *hulks* for the convicts to gain possession the vessel and in consequence eight men intrely [*sic*] innocent of that crime suffered a very severe punishment, but in very short time he was detected and in turn the Jew underwent a discipline in itself very severe, yet not in any away adequate to his deserts [*sic*]; the Jew has formerly been admitted on evidence and on his depositions several weer [*sic*] transported, when his dread of meeting on the settlement, as is supposed, and the aforementioned desire of revenge actuated to make the report of a fictitious meeting.

Isaac Moses' sentence had expired by 1811 and he was permitted to leave the colony in June 1818. He travelled to England on the *Lynx* in that month.

HRNSW, vol. 2, p. 479f.; HO 10/1; *Sydney Gazette*, 30 May 1818, 27 June 1818.

MOSES, Isaac

b. London, 1795–1846
Surrey I (4), 1823; Convict; Sentenced to 14 years, Surrey Quarter Sessions, 1822.
Single; Servant; Height: 168 cm; 4 children.

Sallow slightly pock-pitted, dark brown and curly hair, grey eyes, large nose, inclined to right. Scar over right eyebrow.

Isaac Moses was the brother of Phoebe Hart (q.v.), John (Jacob) Moses (q.v.), 'pastry cook, who came to the colony free and lived in George Street', Moses Moses (q.v.), of Yass, Catherine Moses, Susannah Moses, and Abraham Moses (q.v.). All but Catherine and Susannah came to Australia. He arrived in New South Wales on 4 March 1823 and was initially assigned to the District of Sydney. On 17 March 1823 he was sent to Port Macquarie to serve the initial part of his sentence. Moses was listed in the 1828 Census as a 34 year-old dealer living in Sydney at the house of Mary Larkins in Kent Street.

Larkins had six tenants and four of them were Jews: Isaac Moses, Lewis Lyons (q.v.), Mordecai Abrahams (q.v.), and Solomon Simpson (q.v.). Moses was listed as owning two horses and six head of cattle. An exemption from government labour was issued on 2 January 1830 and on 20 March 1830 the *Sydney Gazette* reported that Isaac Moses had been charged with having imposed upon the Deputy Sheriff by pretending to be free and having £30 worth of property and to reside with his brother in George Street. He was let off with a warning and was told that when he was able to prove that he did indeed hold a certificate of exemption he would be able to conduct a business and to sue and be sued. A ticket of leave was issued in Sydney on 24 April 1830. Moses received a ticket of leave on 1 May 1830 and was given exemption from government labour and allowed 'to reside with his brother John Moses in George St'. In 1831 Isaac Moses received permission to marry Mary (Maria) Bellamy (aged twenty-three), who came free to the colony. Two years later, in 1833, the Rev. Dr Lang officiated at the marriage of the widower Isaac Moses to Hannah Thrum, aged sixteen, at Scots Church.

The *Sydney Gazette* reported, on 16 March 1833, that Mr Isaac Moses had been struck by a man who had an umbrella after Moses had followed him after seeing him stealing a pair of trousers from Mr Isaac Simmons' auction rooms. On 13 September 1834 his ticket of leave was changed to allow him to reside in the Parramatta District. The Colonial Secretary received an angry letter from a James Maguire who complained that Isaac Moses had caused him serious injury 'riding him down on the Sydney racecourse'. A jury had found in favour of Maguire and Moses was ordered to pay Maguire £15 and costs totalling £40 9s 3d. Maguire was still waiting for his money and he believed 'Isaac Moses had plenty of property at Parramatta'. Maguire alleged that Moses had entered into 'a collusive agreement' with his father-in-law and his brother, who said his goods belonged to him.

Moses was issued with a certificate of freedom on 18 August 1836.

Moses bought two blocks of land at the first Yass land sales on 31 July 1837. On 25 January 1838 Moses bought additional blocks of land at Berrima, Muswellbrook, Gosford (in 1840) and Goulburn (1839) for a total cost of £167. I. & M. Moses of the Argyle Store, Yass, gave 'grateful thanks for encouragement' since they had opened their store in the town. Isaac Moses built the Rose Inn, on Comur Street, Yass, in 1837. In 1839 when it was sold at auction it was described as containing eleven rooms, three of which were eighteen feet by eleven feet, a cellar, a stone-built kitchen outside and a ten-stall stable. The Rose was sold 'solely on account of ill health of the proprietor' on 21 January 1839 to James Middleton, who subsequently leased the hotel to Isaac's nephew Henry Hart (q.v.).

Hannah Moses died in 1838 at the age of twenty-one, and was buried as a Jew in the Parramatta. Isaac Moses married a third time, on 28 February 1839. This time the marriage was conducted by the York Street Synagogue. His wife was Hannah Aarons 'of Castlereagh St', and it was Jewish marriage no. 23. The children of Isaac and Hannah Moses were Abraham (27 June 1840), born in Sydney, Aaron (2 December 1841), and Barnett (11 May 1843).

John and Isaac Moses both signed a petition for a Jews' burial ground in Yass on 20 December 1844. Moses supported the establishment of the synagogue in Sydney, contributing £25 for the 1839 building appeal and renting a seat in the synagogue in 1845.

An attack on Isaac Moses was published in the *Omnibus and Sydney Spectator* (25 March 1843) for 'carrying on a roaring game' with the cattle of Dr W. Evans.

Isaac Moses died on 20 May 1846 at the Tarban Creek Asylum and was buried at the Devonshire Street Jewish cemetery and in 1901 was reburied at Raphael's Ground in 1901.

Petition 4/2650.4, 20 December 1844; CS 4/4081, 24 November 1831, with TL 31/926, and TL 30/2204; Exemption from Labour 4/4283, 2 January 1830; Permission to Marry Book 4/4512, p. 29, no. 339; Petition for Jews Burial Ground, Yass, 4/2650.4, on 20 December 1844; 4/2284.6, 9 January 1835, in 35/239; *Sydney Monitor*, 28 April 1830; *Sydney Gazette*, 24 April 1830, 5 April 1832, 16 March 1833; Steve Hart, 'The Life and Times of Some Jewish Pioneers of Yass Township', *AJJHS*, vol. 16, no. 2 (2002), p. 174.

MOSES, John (Jacob)

b. London, 1800–1883
Asia I (1), 1820; Convict; Sentenced to 7 years, Westminster, 1820.
Single; Fruit dealer; Height: 163 cm; 8 children.

Ruddy complexion, brown hair, hazel eyes. John (Jacob) Moses had pretended to be drunk and then suddenly snatched at a man's watch. At the trial he wept and said 'I beg for mercy'. He was convicted and sentenced on 28 June 1820. He was the son of Joseph Moses and Deborah (née Barnett), and the brother of Moses Moses (q.v.), Isaac Moses (q.v.) and Abraham Moses (q.v.) and Phoebe Hart (q.v.).

John Moses arrived in New South Wales on 28 December 1820 and on 9 November 1821 was sent on the *Caledonia* to be 'Cook and Confectioner' to Government House in Hobart Town.

On 13 January 1824 Moses was fined ten shillings for riding in a cart without reins. By 7 August 1824 he held a ticket of leave and was reprimanded when he was found to be absent from the muster and from church. The Rev Knopwood found him to have been absent from church on 20 September 1826 and he was again 'reprimanded'. On 3 January 1828 he was bound over to keep the peace for three months following a public dispute with Robert Southey. In Hobart Town, on 5 December 1826, Moses married Mary, the daughter of Mr Charles Connolly. Mary was aged sixteen when she married, having arrived as a convict on the *Lord Sidmouth* in 1823. In late 1828 John Moses advertised the opening of a general store in Hobart Town at the corner of Elizabeth and Liverpool streets. He wanted to purchase gooseberries, raspberries, kangaroo and seal skins, wheat barley, butter and cheese. He had also imported confectionery from Sydney. It was apparently a very brief colonial attempt to set up a business in Hobart Town. Moses moved back to Sydney and before leaving asked for his assigned servant Lewis Barnett (q.v.) to go with him and help set up in business as a confectioner in George Street. Permission for Barnett to leave for Sydney was denied because of his 'bad record'. Moses, however, eventually returned to Sydney, opened a shop in George Street, and boasted to potential customers that he had supplied His Excellency the Governor with confectionery.

A Jewish marriage ceremony was performed on 10 July 1831 in Sydney and the traditional *ketuvah*, or marriage document, still exists. The bridegroom was 'Jacob the son of Joseph', and the bride was 'Rebecca the daughter of Abraham our Father', indicating that Mary had converted to Judaism. The traditional text was written in Aramaic by an expert and the personal details and Hebrew date appear to have been written by the Rabbi Aaron Levy (q.v.). The witnesses to the marriage were the twenty-five year old Phillip Joseph Cohen (q.v.), who officiated (as Levy had left the colony), Philip Solomon (q.v.), and Moses Brown (q.v.).

In 1829 Moses became the owner of the licence of the King's Head Inn at Penrith. The *Sydney Gazette*, on 28 September 1830, reported his 'excellent, first rate accommodation, said to be provided by Mr Moses, the proprietor of the King's Head Inn, Penrith', and asked the Colonial Secretary to allow him to put Benjamin Frances (q.v.) in charge of the business while he remained in Sydney. The request was refused as Frances was still a prisoner of the Crown. On 1 April 1830 the *Sydney Gazette* reported that 'Mr Moses, the late pastry cook, has been in town the last few days—the only person in the colony who knows … the art' of making *Matzot*. 'John Moses of Nepean, merchant, frequently appeared in the lists of the Windsor Court of Requests during 1829 to 1831, collecting debts owing to him. He returned to England and then came back to Australia, with his family, on the *Palambam* in 1832, 'accompanied by an entire Colony of the same [Jewish] nation the money lending tribe'. John and Sarah Moses, with six children, visited Sydney from Van Diemen's Land in 1833. He had established the London Mart in Hobart Town by 1836. In 1839–40 he acted as a shipping agent for the *Maria*. He was reported to have travelled to Port Phillip and returned to Hobart Town with a cargo of sheep. The *Maria* plied the Hobart Town to Port Phillip route. In December 1840 Moses sold the ship to a Captain Smith and the *Hobart Town Courier* reported that there was a dispute about the value of the cargo. The paper noted that John Moses and a servant returned from Sydney on 19 July 1841 on the *Sisters*.

Moses opened a restaurant and confectionery shop in King and Elizabeth Street, Sydney, in the vicinity of the Supreme Court House. Moses returned to Hobart Town and in 1838 was listed as the licensee of the St John's Tavern at the corner of Murray and Collins streets in Hobart Town.

In February 1839 the *Sydney Commercial Journal and Advertiser* reported that 'Mr Moses, formerly a confectioner of Sydney, now a boniface at Hobart has purchased the Hobart Town Theatre for the small sum of £2025 and will open it as soon as he gets the corps dramatique together'. The Hobart Town Catholics wanted to try to buy the theatre to convert it into a chapel, but could not come to the required terms. Moses found that the theatre was not profitable, although he certainly did his best. The Sydney press, quoting the Hobart Town *Colonial Times*, said that Mr John Moses intended to issue annual tickets for the boxes in the theatre to 'assure a respectable audience'. When David Moses (q.v.) tried to force his way into the theatre to claim some money back John was assaulted by 'a huge piece of paling' (*Hobart Town Courier*, 30 March 1838). He then proposed building a theatre at the back of the Colonial Bank. The *Hobart Town Courier* said that he had fraudulently left Hobart Town owing £2000 and on 26 November his assigned estate was put up for sale. Moses had left for New South Wales and avoided being seen in Sydney. On 1 February 1842 John Moses was listed on the Insolvency Index.

In 1844 John Moses was described as a publican at the brand new township of Yass, with his brother Isaac Moses. In November 1844 two of his daughters, Sarah and Hannah, died in an accident and their burials preceded the consecration of the Jewish cemetery in Goulburn. A month later, Moses organised a (successful) petition for the establishment of a Jewish burial ground at Yass. In 1848 John Moses and his son Harry were sentenced to seven years transportation for perjury following a fire that burned down the stables of his inn near Yass. The Governor commuted the sentence to five years. 'Rebecca, the wife of John Moses', was buried at Goulburn on 8 January 1854, aged forty-six. The children of their marriage were Deborah (1827–1865), who married her uncle, Michael Hyam (q.v.), in 1853, Henry (Harry) (1828–1887), who changed his name to 'Moss' and married Sarah Zorilda Hyam on 25 December 1862, Hannah (1830–1844), and Sarah (1832–1844).

Six years after Rebecca's death, on 23 October 1860, John Moses married a second time, at the Registry Office in Sydney. His new wife was a 23-year-old Irish woman, Mary Ann Shea. He was sixty years old, although on the marriage certificate (no. 686) his age is recorded as 'fifty'. John and Mary Ann's children were Rebecca (1858–1901), Jacob (Jack) (1860–1945), Joseph (born 1864), and Abraham (1870–1899).

John Moses died on 29 November 1883 leaving an estate of £425. He was buried in the Jewish section of the Rookwood Cemetery in Sydney. Jack Moses was a friend of Henry Lawson and became a popular colonial poet himself. He was the author of the ballad 'Nine Miles from Gundagai'.

OBSP, 1819–20, case 819, p. 481; Ship Indent 4/4007, p. 272; CON 31/29, no. 413; Petition 36, 4/1863; Petition no. 104, 4/1866, in 1822; 4/3507, p. 98; CS 1829, 4/3828, p. 308, and 4/5689; 4/1760, p. 136; 4/1760, p. 136, 9 November 1821; *Hobart Town Gazette*, 14 May 1824; *Tasmanian*, 4 January 1828, 1 April 1830, 28 September 1830; *Tasmanian and Austral-Asiatic Review*, 4 January 1828, 14 December 1832; *Sydney Gazette*, 15 August 1835; *Hobart Town Courier*, 7 April 1837, 30 March 1838, 13 December 1839, 24 January 1840, 11 December 1840, 18 July 1841; *Sydney Gazette*, 20 February 1839; *Colonial Times*, 16 April 1840, 10 November 1840, 20 August 1841; CSO 5/243/6338. *Sydney Morning Herald*, 7 January 1840, 25 March 1845, 12 October 1848; I. Porush, 'The Earliest Australian Jewish Marriage Document, 1831', *AJJHS*, vol. 8, no. 7 (1979), p. 404f; G. F. J. Bergman, 'John Moses and Mary Connolly: The First Jewish Marriage in Australia', *AJJHS*, vol. 8. no. 7 (1979), p. 410f; Register of Colonial Pardons 4/4494; *Sydney Morning Herald*, 12 September 1848; *Bell's Life*, 28 July 1849, Rabbi Raymond Apple, *Religion and Politics-Mary Connolly Revisited, AAJS Conference February 2011. Family information from Vivien Solo.*

MOSES, John

b. London (Bishopsgate), 1825
Duchess of Northumberland (1), 1843; Convict; Sentenced to 7 years, Central Criminal Court, 1842.
Single; Errand boy; Height: 157 cm.

Dark complexion, black hair, no whiskers, oval face, high forehead, hazel eyes, large nose, small mouth. A Jew. Can read. John Moses was transported for stealing. It was his second offence. He was 'idle and disorderly' on board ship.

John Moses began his sentence in Van Diemen's Land with a two-year period of probation and was sent to Fingal. On 26 July 1843 he was absent from work and found attending a boxing match. He was punished with ten days solitary confinement. On 8 December 1843 he was given twenty-five lashes for having in his possession a fellow prisoner's trousers. His first stage of probation concluded on 14 April 1845 and he was assigned to service in Launceston. On 19 February 1846, at the Prisoners' Barracks, he was sentenced to six weeks hard labour for gambling. On 13 July 1846 he committed 'gross disorderly conduct on the Sabbath day' and was demoted. On 2 June 1847 he was found to be out after hours and strongly suspected of having committed a burglary for which he received six months imprisonment and hard labour. On 26 February 1848 in Avoca he was convicted of insolence and neglect of duty and sentenced to a further two months imprisonment and hard labour. On 8 July 1848 in Launceston he was found gambling and given two days solitary confinement and on 6 December 1848 he was given a further two months imprisonment and hard labour for being drunk. A certificate of freedom was approved on 19 May 1849.

Prisoner no. 8771; *Launceston Examiner*, 2 June 1847.

MOSES, Joseph (ANDERSON)

b. York, 1771–1835
Elizabeth I (1), 1816; Convict; Sentenced to 7 years, York City, 1815.
Hawker and pedlar; Height: 162.5 cm.

Dark ruddy complexion, black hair, hazel eyes. Joseph Moses was sentenced at York City Quarter Sessions on 13 January 1815.

Joseph Moses, alias Anderson, arrived in New South Wales on 5 October 1816 and was sent to Windsor for assignment. He was listed by the Colonial Secretary as 'Moses alias McRobinson'! He was sent to Newcastle Prison Station 'until further notice' on 11 February 1817 on the *Lady Nelson*. He was recommended for emancipation in 1821.

Joseph Moses was buried by St Phillips, Sydney in 1835.

Ship Indent 4/4005, p. 199; 11 February 1817, in 4/3495, p. 183; ML, A1214, p. 728, 1835.

Moses, Joseph

d. 1845
Palamban, 1833, Free.
7 children.

Joseph Moses, a widower, was the father of Moses (q.v.), Isaac (q,v,) John (q.v.) and Abraham (q.v.) and Catherine and Susannah Moses and Phoebe Hart (q.v.). He arrived with some members of his family, and in Sydney in 1833 Joseph Moses applied for one assigned convict servant. His grandson Lazarus Hart (q.v.) was assigned to him in 1837. Joseph Moses took over the license of the Red Cross Hotel, on the corner of King and York Streets in 1834. On the list of donors to the Sydney Synagogue in 1839 he was listed as 'Joseph Moses Snr' and donated £5 to the building fund. Joseph Moses was named as a publican at Patrick Plains, Darlington. In 1843 a Joseph Moses was a draper in George Street who had stock to be sold in private because of the demolition of his house. He was a seat holder in the new synagogue in 1845 and was buried in the Jewish section of the Devonshire Street Cemetery in 1845. His occupation on his death certificate is given as 'rabbi'. The subsequent death certificates of his children describe his occupation as 'dealer'. In 1901 Rebecca Hart (Asher Hart's daughter) applied in 1901 to transfer Joseph Moses' tombstone to Raphael's Ground Lidcombe.

ML A1214, p. 728, 1835, *Sydney Morning Herald*, 5 January 1843; *Sydney Gazette*, 5 January 1843. Information by Jeannette Tsoulos.

MOSES, Julia

b. London, 1822–1904
Palambam, 1833; Free.
Single; 12 children.

Julia, the daughter of Abraham Moses (q.v.) and Leah Moses, married Elias Moses (q.v.), on 15 April 1840 at the Bridge Street Synagogue. They had twelve children: Rachel (1841); Deborah (1843); Elizabeth Julia (1845); Fanny (London 1850); Moses, later known as Merton (1852); Joseph (1854); Samuel (1855); Catherine (Melbourne 1856); Sophia (1859); Amelia (1861); Louisa (1863); and Florence (1866). Julia Moses died in Sydney on 27 May 1904 and was buried at the Rookwood Cemetery.

'One son, seven daughters, 47 grandchildren and 32 great-grandchildren mourned her death', *Sydney morning Herald*, 30 May 1904.

MOSES, Martha

John Craig, 1834; Free.
Single.

Martha Moses came out from England travelling steerage with Maria (Mary) Hart (q.v.) and Rachel Nathan (q.v.), arriving at Port Jackson on 12 October 1834.

MOSES, Mary (Maria)

b. London
Mayflower, 1841; Free.
Single; 11 children.

Mary Moses arrived in Hobart Town in March 1841, having travelled steerage with her mother Sarah (q.v.) and sisters Rachael (q.v.) and Rebecca (Ellen) (q.v.). Mary Moses was a daughter of Emanuel 'Money' Moses (q.v.) who, at the age of sixty, was transported to Van Diemen's Land for his part in the great gold dust robbery at Covent Garden.

Mary Moses was also the sister of Angel Moses, who reversed his name to Moses Angel and was the headmaster of the Jews' Free School in London. She married Philip Levy (q.v.), aged thirty-six, in Hobart Town on 3 February 1842. The Minute

Book of the congregation recorded that in 1845 Mrs Philip Levy had embroidered the *parochet* (curtain) for the Ark.
CSO 92/6, p. 65; CON 52/1, p. 107.

MOSES, Michael

1830; Free.

On 9 February 1851 the committee of the Hobart Synagogue received an application for financial assistance for Michael Moses. He was described as 'a poor man'. It was decided to give him six shillings a week.

MOSES, Moses (MOSS)

b. London, 1791–1858
Marquis of Wellington, 1815; Convict; Sentenced to life, Old Bailey, 1813.
Single; Glass cutter; Height: 164 cm; 14 children.

Dark complexion, dark brown hair, dark eyes. He was the son of Joseph and Deborah (née Barnett) Moses, and brother of John Moses (q.v.), Isaac Moses (q.v.), Abraham Moses (q.v.) and Phoebe Hart (q.v.), the wife of Asher Hart (q.v.). Moses was transported for stealing a pocket book containing £7. He was one of four males who hustled a passerby and stole two pocket books from the victim. He was sentenced on 14 July 1813.

Moses arrived in Sydney in January 1815 and was assigned to the farm of Mr Hovell, from which he absconded in July. He was then assigned to work at the Brickfields. On 7 May 1817 Moses Moses and Samuel Lyons (q.v.) were discovered stowed away on board a ship that was about to leave the colony and were sentenced to work on the roads for one month. In the words of a witness, when Lyons and Moses were found aboard the ship the captain asked them how long they had been on board. Samuel Lyons said 'three days', to which Captain Jeffreys thoughtfully replied, 'I thought you were a long time making me a pair of pantaloons'.

Moses was sent to Van Diemen's Land on the *Kangaroo* in 1817. On 6 January 1818 Moses tried to escape again, but was found concealed on the *Pilot* and received six months in the gaol gang. Two months later he received fifty lashes for being repeatedly disorderly in the chain gang. On 1 September 1819 he received fifty lashes for disobeying the orders of his master Mr T. Florence. Moses married Sarah Brown on 18 June 1821 and set up shop in Hobart Town selling bread and confectionery. Sarah, aged twenty-seven at the time of her marriage, had arrived in Van Diemen's Land on the *Morley* in 1820. Moses stated at the wedding that he was twenty-eight, two years younger than he was.

In August 1821 Moses was charged with receiving stolen property, but was released from custody when the Public Prosecutor failed to turn up in court. Moses Moses owned a baker's shop in Collins Street in Hobart Town. In 1824 he was brought before the court for overcharging for bread. The case was dismissed.

On 15 July 1825 he held a ticket of leave and was found to have in his possession an illegal weight. He was fined £1 10s for attempting to sell bread that was short of its legal weight. On 20 September 1826 Moses was reprimanded for being absent from church and on 1 November 1827 he was fined £1 for 'travelling with a cart on the Lord's Day'. Moses was also one of the semi-professional Jewish pugilists in Hobart Town. A conditional pardon was issued on 25 July 1834 (*Hobart Town Gazette*).

Meanwhile, the marriage of Moses to Sarah had deteriorated. The 1823 Van Diemen's Land Muster recorded that they were married but her convict dossier shows that it was not a happy marriage. On 23 August 1826 she absconded and went to New Norfolk without a pass. She was 'remanded and returned to her family' on 4 September. On 12 April 1831 Sarah was sent to gaol for thirty-six hours of solitary confinement on bread and water for 'very disorderly conduct and making use of violent and obscene language'. She was free by servitude by 14 August 1833.

Following the granting of his conditional pardon in 1834, Moses travelled from New South Wales to Van Diemen's Land and ran into a bureaucratic tangle when it was revealed that his pardon did not have 'Royal Approval' and that its conditions differed from the form of approval used in New South Wales. Moses was forced to consult a lawyer for permission to proceed to Sydney on the ship *Gulmare*. Moses returned to New South Wales and settled in the new town of Yass. He was appointed the Keeper of the Pound in 1837 and in 1840 he opened the Yass Hotel in Conner Street, which, he said, was 'the best hotel out of Sydney'. The following year the 47-year-old Sarah died 'of a broken heart from peculiar family trials' and she was buried at St John's Cemetery in Parramatta on 1 April 1841. The 'peculiar' trial may have arisen from the 'marriage' of Moses to Hannah Dray in Sydney at Scots Church in 1840. The grave stone inscription reads: 'Peace to her soul. May the Divine creator receive her soul into everlasting rest—and pardon her former unnatural oppressors'.

In 1842 Moses, single-handed, seized the bushranger Massey in the dining room of his hotel and handed him over to the police (from whom he quickly escaped). For his bravery the citizens of Yass presented Moses with an inscribed silver medallion 'for his gallant conduct in endeavouring to capture the bush-ranger Massey and in which he failed only in not being supported by the constable present, and upon whose assistance he naturally calculated'. The policeman had allowed the bushranger to escape the moment he had left the hotel.

Moses became a member of the first Yass Town Council in 1843 and a trustee of the Yass Hospital. The hotel prospered and he built a 47-room semi-Gothic mansion called Old Linton. He organised the consecration of a corner of the Yass Cemetery for Jewish burials in 1844. He was a contributor to and seat holder of the Sydney Synagogue in 1845. On 27 February 1846 he transferred his publican's licence from the White Hart Inn to the Yass Inn. Moses died at Yass on 11 July 1858 and was buried in Yass. The funeral service was read by Mr Moritz Michaelis of Burrowa and the inscription on his tombstone reads: 'He was one of the oldest inhabitants of the Town of Yass. He was much respected by all who knew him'. The inscription stated that he was sixty-eight years old.

Even though Moses was a generous supporter of the Sydney Synagogue, local tradition held that the daughters of his first marriage were baptised in the same year so that they might be able to find a suitable husband to marry. However, this appears to be a myth. A daughter, Sarah Tabitha (born 1 May 1827), died in Yass on 2 February 1843 (aged fifteen), and was buried as a Jew. Another daughter, Maria (15 February 1823), married J. G. Raphael (q.v.) in Sydney on 30 December 1840. Moses and Sarah (née Brown) had four other children: William (12 October 1821), Phoebe (7 May 1825 married Daniel Murray in 1846 and died in 1863. She was buried as a Jew and her remains were transferred to Bunnerong from Devonshire Street in 1901), Joseph William (9 October 1829), and Abraham (8 November 1831).

Moses and Hannah (née Dray) had eight children: Barnett Aaron (born 1841), Jacob (1843), Deborah (Ellen) (25 October 1845), Sophia (16 July 1847), Elizabeth (14 June 1849), Caroline (21 June 1851), Jesse (11 June 1853), and Hannah (8 February 1856).

OBSP, 1813, case 738, p. 404; CON 31/29, no. 10; CON 13/1, p. 59; *HRA*, series 3, vol. 2, p. 255; Ship Indent 4/4005, p. 34; Petition 4/2650.4; *Hobart Town Gazette*, 8 September 1821, 15 June 1822, 15 August 1822, 28 May 1824; CP 377; *Sydney Gazette*, 17 April 1823; *Sydney Morning Herald*, 17 March 1845, 28 January 1846, 27 February 1846; William A. Bayley, *Yass Municipal Centenary History*; Steve Hart, 'The Life and Times of Some Jewish Pioneers of Yass Township', *AJJHS*, vol. 16, no. 2 (2002), p. 174f; 4/2218, 33/2158; *Australian*, 31 December 1840, 6 June 1998.

MOSES, Moses (MOSS)

b. London, 1819–1883
Free.
Single; Merchant.

The son of Jacob Moses and Clara (Jonas) of London, Moses Moses was the younger brother of Samuel Jacob Moses (q.v.) of Hobart Town. Moses Moses married Esther Nathan (q.v.) at the Bridge Street synagogue in Sydney on 16 November 1842. Esther was his cousin, and a sister of Rosetta Joseph (Nathan, q.v.) of Sydney. The young couple made their home in Launceston and Moses Moses was a member of the organising committee that built the Launceston Synagogue. At the time of the gold rush on the mainland Moses and Esther Moss moved to Sydney, where he founded M. Moss and Co., which became one of the most important wine and spirit merchants of New South Wales. He served as president of the York Street Synagogue from 1869 to 1875.

MOSES, Nelson (Nisson)

Convict.
Single.

Nelson (Nisson) Moses married Mary McCarthy on 2 November 1812 at St Matthew's, Windsor. Both were 'free'. Mary signed the marriage certificate with her mark.

MOSES, Phoebe

b. Aldgate, 1811
City of Edinburgh, 1837; Free.

A bounty migrant, aged twenty-six, Phoebe Moses arrived in Sydney on 31 August 1837. It was recorded that she had 'A good character, good health. Jewess. Brother in the country'.
Mutch Index 381/31.

MOSES, Rachael

Mayflower, 1841; Free.
Single.

Rachael was the daughter of Emanuel 'Money' Moses (q.v.) and Sarah Moses (q.v.). Her sisters were Mary (Maria) Moses (q.v.), who married Philip Levy (q.v.), and Rebecca (Ellen) (q.v.) Moses. Rachael Moses married Samuel Levy (q.v.) in Hobart Town on 29 June 1842.

MOSES, Rachel

b. London, 1811
Free.
Single; 11 children.

The sister of Elias Moses (q.v.), Rachel married her brother's business partner, Samuel Benjamin (q.v.), in 1835.

MOSES, Rebecca (née DAVIS)

Dora, 1840; Free.
Married; 2 children.

Rebecca Moses came to Australia with her husband, Abraham Moses (q.v.).

MOSES, Rebecca (Ellen)

Mayflower, 1841; Free.
Single; 2 children.

The daughter of the convict Emanuel 'Money' Moses (q.v.) and Sarah Moses (q.v), Rebecca arrived with her mother and her two sisters, Mary (q.v.) and Rachael (q.v.), on the *Mayflower*. Rebecca Moses married Morris Marks (q.v.) in Hobart Town on 30 June 1847.

MOSES, Rosetta

Convict.

Rosetta Moses, the holder of a conditional pardon, was listed as a tenant of Mr Edward Churchill at the Hawkesbury in October 1820. On 30 June 1823 she was granted thirty acres of land in the township of Howick, New South Wales, 'by Government Order of 31 March 1821'.

Bigge Appendix, BT Box 24, p. 5174.

MOSES, Rosetta Blanche

Piscata, 1841; Free.
Married; 11 children.

Rosetta Blanche Moses married Samuel Jacob Moses (q.v.) in 1836.

MOSES, Samuel

b. London, 1806–1844
Phoenix (3), 1828; Convict; Sentenced to 7 years, Old Bailey, 1827.
Single; Fishmonger; Height: 161 cm; 2 children.

Sallow complexion, brown hair, hazel eyes. Could read. Jew. Samuel put his hand through a broken shop window and attempted to steal five handkerchiefs (valued at ten shillings). Samuel Moses was caught in the act despite 'a desperate effort to escape'. He had two previous convictions, and was sentenced on 31 May 1827.

Samuel Moses was assigned as a labourer to Sydney Water Works. He was listed in the 1828 Census as attached to the Mineral Surveyor's Department. No religion was noted. A ticket of leave was granted on 11 March 1833, valid for the District of Sydney. Samuel Moses married Emma Hooper at St James' Church, Sydney, in 1830. Moses Samuel was buried in the Jewish section of the Devonshire Street Cemetery on 12 July 1844, and an inquest into his death was held on 3 December 1844.

The children of Samuel and Emma Moses were William (1839) and Louisa (1843).

OBSP, 1826–27, case 1237, p. 476; Ship Indent 4/4013, p. 101; 4/4087; TL 33/118; *Sydney Gazette*, 17 February 1833; *Sydney Morning Herald*, 3 December 1844.

MOSES, Samuel Jacob

b. London, 1807–1873
Piscata, 1841; Free.
Married; Dealer, merchant; 11 children.

In 1836 Samuel Jacob Moses married Rosetta Blanche Moses (q.v.) the daughter of Henry Moses and Esther (née Nathan). Samuel was both brother-in-law and first cousin of Rosetta's older sister, Harriette Nathan (q.v.), and the brother-in-law of Louis Nathan (q.v.). He arrived with his wife Rosetta, their two children, Clara (born 1837), and Alfred (1839), and two servants. The family spent some time in Sydney in 1840, where their baby daughter, Henrietta Rachael, was born and registered as a 'Hebrew'. Samuel Moses moved to Hobart Town on 17 February 1841, with his wife, three children and two servants. He was to represent Henry E. and M. Moses of Cannon Street, London. His father-in-law, Henry Moses, had given Louis Nathan and Samuel Moses the sum of £100 each with which to begin business in the colonies.

The Moses family stayed with the Nathan family for those first years and the two men shared the same highly successful business in Hobart Town. Their grand home was called Derwent Park. Moses travelled a great deal, frequently visiting Sydney and returning with the family to the United Kingdom in 1843 and 1846. His family and his fortune grew rapidly. The *Hobart Town Courier* of 29 December 1843 announced that Mrs Moses had given birth to a son (Lewis Frederick) at the family home in Victoria Place, Macquarie Street. Henrietta Rachael Moses died in Hobart Town on 17 February 1853 at the age of thirteen and was buried at the Harrington Street cemetery. A baby boy, Samuel, born 9 August 1849, died within five days of his birth. Their other children were Edward Hyam (1847), Charlotte (1848), Henry (1851), Laurence (Lawrence) Hyam (June 1852), Lionel David (1854), and Howard Joseph (March 1855).

Moses was active in the life of the Jewish community and undoubtedly helped to give the community some respectability. He was trained as a *mohel* (ritual circumciser) and brought out with him, handwritten on vellum, an 'Order of Service for a Circumcision'. He served as the synagogue's first secretary in 1842 and was a trustee of the congregation. He gave £25 to its building fund in 1843 and £10 to the Sydney Synagogue in 1845. He rented seat no. 6 in the synagogue.

On 5 January 1845 Samuel Moses was presented with a 'beautiful piece of plate' by members of the Hebrew community of Hobart Town, as 'a token of respect and esteem'. A testimonial was presented to Moses by the congregation, which declared that he was 'an upright and enterprising citizen ... We rejoice in the hope that the separation between us will only be temporary and we shall hail with feelings of pleasure your re-appearance amongst us'. Moses was about to visit England by the *Calcutta* and, according to the newspaper report 'was well known ... had been eminently successful. His firm was said to be one the largest importing and exporting houses in Van Diemen's Land'. In 1854 the firm of Nathan & Moses advertised frequently that they were interested in purchases of wool, oil and gold dust. Samuel Moses was the first Jew to be appointed a Justice of the Peace in Tasmania.

In 1857 the Governor attended a 'sumptuous ball' held at his home, Boa Vista, in New Town. The family returned to England in early 1859. Samuel Moses continued to support the congregation from London, sending cheques to repair the old burial ground and funds to the synagogue itself. He bought a mansion at 100 Lancaster Gate and died in London on 2 October 1873. Alfred stayed behind for some years to look after the business in Tasmania. All the children subsequently

changed their surnames to Walford. The *Mohel* Book was taken back to England by Moses and is in the possession of his descendants.
Jewish Chronicle, 16 May 1845, 25 December 1853; CSO 92/16 F78; *Hobart Town Courier*, 10 July 1857.

MOSES, Sarah

1817–1892
Palambam, 1833; Free.
Single; 10 children.

Sarah was the eldest child of Abraham Moses (q.v.) and Leah, and was aged fifteen when she arrived in Sydney with her family. On 1 June 1836 she married Nathan Joseph (q.v.) in Sydney, and their family grew up in Singleton, New South Wales.

Sarah died 'at her residence', at 66 Botany Street, Moore Park, in 1892, and was buried in the Jewish section of the Devonshire Street Cemetery. Sarah was said to be the 'relict' of Nathan Joseph and mother of Mrs E. Mandelson, Potts Point, Mrs Jacob Joseph and Mrs Coleman Phillips, of Wellington, New Zealand, and Jacob Nathan Joseph of Sydney. Her reburial would be at Lidcombe in 1901.
Sydney Morning Herald, 11 April 1892. Family information Jeannette Tsoukos.

MOSES, Sarah (MOSS)

1824–1865
Dora, 1840; Free.
Single; 6 children.

The daughter of Abraham Moses (q.v.), Sarah Moses arrived in Sydney with her parents on 17 March 1840. Sarah married Lewis Lipman (q.v.) of Muswellbrook at the Sydney Synagogue on 23 June 1847. Phillip was born on 10 June 1848 at Patrick Plains, and died, aged seven, in 1855. Abraham was born on 31 December 1849. Lewis and Sarah moved to Sydney in 1850. On 10 April 1853 their third child, Joseph, was born at 58 Phillip Street. Albert was born on 26 August 1856 at 26 O'Connell Street, Sydney, and died in 1860. Rachel was born on 31 March 1858. Joshua was born at the family's home at 199 York Street, a few houses from the York Street Synagogue.

Sarah Lipman died on 8 April 1865. She had borne six children, of whom three predeceased her.

MOSES, Sarah

Mayflower, 1775–1864. Arrived 1841; Free.
Married.

Sarah Moses brought her three daughters Rachael (q.v.), Mary (q.v.) and Rebecca Ellen (q.v.) to Hobart Town, arriving on 26 March 1841. She was the wife of convict Emanuel 'Money' Moses (q.v.), who died at the hospital at New Norfolk on 5 July 1841. She gave £10 to the synagogue building appeal in 1843 and paid £2 9s to the Hobart Synagogue in 1844–45. In 1845 the Hobart Synagogue Ledger described her as 'widow'. Sarah remained in Van Diemen's Land and lived at the corner of Harrington Street and Collins Street. On 27 April 1855 the *Hobarton Mercury* reported that Mrs Sarah Moses had been involved in 'a serious confrontation' with her maid Susan McMahon, an Irish immigrant 'dressed in a crepe frock and a handsome shawl'. Sarah Moses accused her maid of stealing grapes from 'an old and valuable vine' in her garden. Her mistress told her that she was a liar and an Irish bitch and that if she could she would drink her blood and then threw an old carving knife at her. Sarah Moses denied Susan McMahon's charge that she was an 'unnatural woman' because, she said, she was the mother of sixteen (sic.) children and thirty grandchildren. The case, which lasted an hour in the Police Court, was dismissed.

Sarah Moses died in Hobart 'after a long and painful illness' on 31 May 1864 in her eighty-ninth year.

Hobart Town Courier, 30 March 1841. *Mercury*, 27 April 1855, 1 June 1864. Family information from Phil Lipshut of Melbourne.

MOSES, Solomon

b. Sheerness, 1800–1875
Arundel, 1832; Free.
Single; Dealer; 12 children.

Solomon Moses, son of Simeon and Caroline Moses of Sheerness, arrived in Port Jackson on 10 September 1832. Moses was elected a member of the first Sydney Synagogue committee in September 1833. On 8 February 1834 the *Sydney Gazette* reported: 'Solomon Moses, a dealer, who keeps a stall in the market place was robbed of some black silken handkerchiefs'.

Moses married Deborah Hart (q.v.) on 28 January 1835. Deborah was the child of Asher and Phoebe Hart (qq.v.). It was Sydney's seventh Jewish wedding, and they arrived in Goulburn in 1835. In 1837 their first child, Lewis, was born in 'Bungonia, Goulburn', the first Jewish child to have been born in the district. On 1 July 1836 Moses opened the Travellers' Home Inn, Goulburn Plains. He later built a new hotel and transferred his licence to it in 1841, calling it the Royal Hotel. It cost £9000 to build and he borrowed £1500 from John Isaacs (q.v.). On 10 July 1838 the *Sydney Gazette* reported: 'Mr Solomon Moses, formerly of Sydney, lately of Goulburn, was forwarded to Sydney last week on suspicion to be implicated in the robbery of the Maneroo Mail'. Malicious information had been laid against him concerning the purchase of stolen goods. Bail was set at £400. On 24 July the *Sydney Gazette* reported that 'after interrogation Moses was discharged as he was shown not to have been implicated in the Mail Robbery'.

The Royal Hotel became the social centre of Goulburn. The *Sydney Morning Herald* of 3 September 1845 described the 'great bachelor ball, with great supper and excellent band of music'.

Solomon Moses of Goulburn was appointed the local official representative of the Sydney Synagogue on 13 November 1843. He was a seat holder in the new Sydney Synagogue of 1845 and in that year gave £100 to its building appeal. His children were registered at the Sydney Synagogue. They were: Abraham (born 25 December 1835, at Goulburn), who died in June 1896 (in Auckland); Lewis (Eleazar) (2 September 1837, in Goulburn), who married Minni Phillips, and died on 11 April 1903 (in Auckland); Caroline Deborah (27 September 1840 to 2 November 1921), who married Sydney Levi Emanuel; Simeon Simon (18 September 1842), who married Mattie Jones; Morris (30 July 1844 to 28 March 1909), who married Emily Taylor; Joseph (20 June 1846 to 13 February 1933), who married Caroline Phillips; Moses (4 December 1848); Leah (13 October 1850, at Bathurst); Rebecca (22 May 1853), at Sydney; Fanny (1855 to 8 September 1927); Rachel (14 November 1856, at South Lambeth, England), who died on 8 February 1938; and Jacob Israel (18 November 1858, born at Cumberland Street, Sydney).

Solomon Moses died at Bishopthorpe Terrace, Glebe Road, Sydney, on 7 October 1875. His widow Deborah died on 7 December 1884 at Dunedin.

Mutch Index 7/135; Errol Lea-Scarlett, *Queanbeyan District and People*; Cecil Roth, *The Rise of Provincial Jewry*, p. 96; *Sydney Gazette*, 8 February 1834, 19 July 1836, 10 July 1838; *Sydney Morning Herald*, 19 April 1844, 3 September 1845; 4/5218, 2 November 1840; family research by Nigel Meinrath, Phillip Moses and Mrs Mim Segal.

MOSES, Solomon (Moses SOLOMON)

b. 1805; Convict.
Single.

At the Old Bailey on 16 February 1814 a nine year old 'Moses Solomon', together with two other boys, John Morris (q.v.) and Joseph Burrell, was sentenced to death for breaking and entering a shop in Holborn and stealing some oranges, nuts and a pair of shoes. The prisoners were recommended to mercy on account of their youth'.

On 20 June 1818 the *Hobart Town Gazette* reported that a boy was among the convicts who had secreted themselves on the ship *Harriet*, which had left Van Diemen's Land for the Cape of Good Hope. They were discovered and brought back to Hobart Town in the *Neptune* and sentenced to 100 lashes each. They were to work in a gaol gang for twelve months. In February 1819 Solomon Moses escaped from the brig *Elizabeth Henrietta*.

On 28 June 1826 Moses received an eighteen-month sentence with colonial transportation for stealing.

OBSP, 16 February 1814, case 208., Hobart Town Gazette, 20 June 1818; *Sydney Gazette*, 16 May 1818, 20 February 1819, 28 June 1826.

MOSES, Solomon

d. 1860 Free.
Single; 2 children.

Solomon Moses had one of the first stores in Queanbeyan and remained there until September 1851, when he moved to Bungendore to open the Victoria Stores. Shortly after the store opened it was flooded out. On 5 November 1856 Solomon Moses married Phoebe Levy, the daughter of Abraham Joseph Levy (q.v.) and Catherine (née Phillips). Their two children born in 1858 and 1860 both died in infancy. In 1853 he founded the Beehive Stores in Bungendore, which was barely profitable until he opened the Beehive Hotel next to the original store at the corner of Gibraltar and Molonglo streets. Moses drowned in Deep Creek, Queanbeyan, on 27 October 1860 and was buried in the Goulburn Jewish Cemetery. He left an insolvent estate.

Errol Lea-Scarlett, *Queanbeyan District and People.*

MOSES, Sophia

b. London, 1796–1853
Duckenfield, 1831; Free.
Married.

Sophia Moses came to Van Diemen's Land in 1831 with her husband David Moses (q.v.). She died in Hobart Town on 6 May 1853 and was buried in the Harrington Street Jewish Cemetery.

MOSES, Uriah

b. Whitechapel, 1778–1847
Royal Admiral I (2), 1800; Convict; Sentenced to life, Middlesex, 1798.
Single; Glass cutter; 9 children.

Uriah Moses entered a house in Whitechapel on 8 December 1796. Moses stole linen, lace and silk (valued at £5) from the display window of a draper's shop in Whitechapel by using a diamond cutter to cut the glass from the window. His father lived in Petticoat Lane and, as Uriah had cut his hand on the glass, his father took him to Guy's Hospital, where Uriah was arrested. At the same trial his landlady, Mrs Hannah Benjamin, was implicated and was found guilty of theft. Moses was sentenced to death on 10 January 1798, though this was later commuted to transportation for life. Mrs Ann Benjamin was sentenced to fourteen years transportation but her name fails to appear on the lists of those sent to Australia.

Moses arrived in New South Wales in November 1800. In the 1806 General Muster Moses was listed as living in Sydney. A ticket of leave was granted on 1 January 1812. The latter was reaffirmed on 22 January 1812 while Moses was living in the Hawkesbury District. The 1814 General Muster listed him as a 'landholder'. By 1818 he was shown as renting three acres of wheat, seven acres of maize, fourteen hogs and as the owner of three bushels of wheat. In 1819 his holding had increased to twelve acres. By 1820, together with Abraham Elias (q.v.) and John Moses 'of Nepean' (q.v.), he had begun to supply significant quantities of wheat to the government. A conditional pardon was issued to Uriah Moses on 25 October 1821.

In 1823 Moses sold 300 bushels of wheat to the commissariat at seven shillings and sixpence per bushel and a further 1000 bushels on 18 December 1823. In the 1828 Census Moses was listed as a baker in Windsor and the holder of a conditional pardon. In 1832 the convict William Poulston, a 'baker's boy', was assigned to him. By 1832, now described as a 'merchant', he had begun to make frequent appearances in the Windsor Court of Requests collecting debts owed to him by the small farmers.

On 9 March 1830 Uriah Moses married Ann Daley at St Matthew's Church in Windsor. According to the 1828 Census, Ann was the former assigned servant of Abraham Elias of Windsor. In the *General Post Office Directory* of 1835–36, Uriah Moses was listed as a 'dealer' living in George Street, Windsor.

Moses donated £10 to the Sydney Synagogue in 1845, the year of its dedication. However, in December 1847, Uriah Moses lay on his deathbed and asked the local vicar in Windsor for baptism. Bishop Stiles of Sydney was asked by the local vicar whether this could be done without proper instruction in the catechism. Stiles answered: 'Yes, should our fallible judgement after our best efforts to discuss the truth be misled, we may humbly hope that He will not lay it to our charge'. The episcopal answer came just in time. Uriah Moses died on 5 December 1847. The Parish Register of St Matthew's proudly described him as a shopkeeper who was a 'converted Jew'. His will had been witnessed by Abraham and Harriet Elias (qq.v.).

Nine of the twelve children of Ann and Uriah Moses survived infancy. Ann Moses remarried on 4 March 1869 (when aged fifty-nine) to James Powell, a 'gentleman', at Randwick. Uriah's second child, Henry Moses, born 6 November 1832, and baptised on 2 December 1832, became a leader in commerce in New South Wales. He was a director of the Perpetual Trustees Company, the Commercial Bank, the Commercial Union Assurance and the owner of many rural and metropolitan properties. Henry Moses died in June 1926.

OBSP, 1797–98, case 73, p. 87; Principal Superintendent of Convicts, Registers of CF 1810–14, 4/4427, p. 464; Bench of Magistrates, Singleton, Letters Sent, 1836–37, 4/5658-9; Correspondence of the Rev. Stiles, ML, A269, p. 77; Governors' Despatches, 1833, p. 669, ML, A1211; *Sydney Gazette*, 27 February 1823, 18 December 1823, 16 August 1832.

MOSS, Abraham *see* TAYLOR, Thomas

MOSS, Abraham Alfred

d. 1843
Free.

Abraham Alfred Moss was buried in the Jewish section of the Devonshire Street Cemetery in Sydney on 25 October 1843, and the grave was moved to Rookwood in 1901. The exhumation permit was signed by Montefiore Moss.

MOSS, Catherine (Hinda)

b. London, 1807–1885
1836; Free.
Single; 12 children.

A daughter of Marcus Warschauer (alias Mordecai Moss) (q.v.), and stepdaughter of Abigail Moses (q.v.) (née Barnett), Catherine was known as 'Hinda'. Catherine Moss married Aaron Isaacs (q.v.) in Sydney on 11 May 1842. They had nine children: Solomon and Amos (twins) (born 1843), George (1844), Michael Joseph (5 October 1845), at Paterson in New South Wales, Hinda (1847), Rose (1848), Sarah (1849), Raphael (Ralph) (1851), Mendel (1852), Rachel (1852), Solomon (1853), and Louis (1857).

Aaron Isaacs died in 1866. Catherine died on 17 November 1885 and her death certificate noted that her father was 'Mordecai Moss, Jewish Rabbi' [*sic*].

MOSS, Emily (née GOLDING MORGAN)

1817–1902

On 17 August 1841 Emily Golding Morgan married Phineas Moss (q.v.), who would become the honorary secretary of the Hobart Synagogue. She had been converted to Judaism before the marriage. She was aged twenty-four and he was forty-six years old. Moss died in 1866, leaving Emily in financial distress.

The Hobart Synagogue granted Emily the sum of ten guineas 'in recognition of the services rendered by the late Mr Moss' in May 1866. In 1894 the congregation began to pay her a monthly allowance as she was obviously living in poverty. Part of her rent was paid in February 1902. The synagogue paid the doctor's account in April and her funeral expenses on 23 May 1902. She was buried in the Hobart Jewish Cemetery on 27 January 1902.

MOSS, Gabriel (Hopping Moss)

b. London, 1813
Mary III (4), 1833; Convict; Sentenced to 14 years, Middlesex, 1832.
Single; Hawker; Height: 166 cm.

Ruddy dark complexion, dark hazel eyes, large nose, scar corner left eye. Jew. Could read and write. No previous convictions. Moss was a member of a group of six pickpockets who worked a crowd in a London street. A witness testified: 'He put one of his arms up to his throat and took the watch with his other hand'. The victim said: 'The prisoner struggled me about'.

Gabriel Moss arrived on 6 January 1833 and was assigned as a hawker to J. T. Bayles of Sydney. In 1837 Moss was arrested on George Street with no pass in his possession and seven shillings and ten pence. At the time the constable was also taking a woman into custody. Moss interfered and the woman escaped. Moss was then sentenced to a year in prison (16 October 1837). In 1838 he petitioned the Colonial Secretary for a pardon from the Woolloomooloo Iron Gang and his plea was rejected. He was given permission to marry in 1839 while he was still on assigned service. His wife-to-be was Sarah Ann Davies, aged twenty-one, who had come to the colony as a free settler. The officiant was the Rev. W. H. Walsh and the official document included the note that: 'The usual engagement having been entered into by the assignee of Moss to keep both partners in his service'. In the *Registry of Flash Men* he was described as 'Hopping Moss having returned from the Iron Gang, dresses well, smokes his Havana and is a friend of Hyams'.

OBSP, case 1014, p. 422; *Mary III* (4) Printed Indent, p. 5; *Sydney Gazette*, 28 February 1833; Principal Superintendent of Convicts, Register of Convicts' Applications to Marry 1839, 4/4513, p. 97; CS Letters Received 1838, Police, Sydney, 38/1501, in 4/2421.2; W. A. Miles, *Registry of Flash Men*, 2/673.

MOSS, George (MOSES)

London, 1809–1854
1832; Free.
Single; 5 children.

George's father was Marcus Warschauer (Mordecai Moses) (q.v.), who was transported to Sydney in 1836. His mother was Amelia (née Cohen). His siblings who came to Australia were Alexander (Moses, q.v.), Catherine Moss (q.v.) and Rosetta Moss (q.v.). George Moss was elected secretary of the Sydney Synagogue at the first General Meeting of the Jews of Sydney in 1833. Moss was a newspaper man who wrote regular contributions from Sydney for the *Jewish Chronicle* in London. On 15 October 1833 in the *Sydney Gazette*, 'George Moss informed the gentlemen of the Hunter that he has taken over the Rose Inn at Maitland'. In January 1834 Solomon Levien (q.v.) became the inn's owner and Moss moved to Sydney, where he served on the Sydney Synagogue Committee from 1833 to 1838.

By 1835 the 26-year-old Moss had acquired a 15-year-old non-Jewish common-law wife, Louisa Wilkes. In 1836, their daughter Maria (Miriam) was born in Sydney and registered as a Jew. George jnr was born in 1837, and Rosetta was born in 1838. Three children must have been too difficult for the congregation to ignore and, following Rosetta's birth, George Moss resigned as a member of the committee of the congregation and ceased to be its honorary secretary. On 2 November 1839 Moss wrote to the president of the congregation stating that he wished to be married 'agreeably to the rites and customs of the Hebrew nation'. He 'sincerely trusted that the person in question [his de facto wife] would become a *Geyoureth* and his marriage be solemnised according to our religious tenets … To prevent any misrepresentation he would attend the Committee any time to answer all that may be required'. The letter concluded 'with the profound respect for the religion of our forefathers'. The marriage (and conversion) was authorised and took place on 23 March 1840 'according to the Jewish Mosaic tenets'. Louisa Wilkes became 'Leah Abrahams', and the marriage was performed by Moss's father,

Mordecai Moses (q.v.), who, at the time, was the *shamash* of the synagogue. Three more children were subsequently born, Abraham (1842, who died a year later), Montague (3 May 1844), who called himself 'Montefiore' M. Moss, and Lewis (April 1846). Their mother, Leah (Louisa), died on 8 May 1851 at the age of thirty-one.

On 4 July 1837 the *Australian* newspaper announced that Moss had been appointed 'collector' on behalf of the newspaper and, on 31 March 1839, George Robert Nichols, the proprietor of the *Australian*, announced that without Moss's signature no receipt for money for the newspaper would be valid. Moss gave £15 to the Sydney Synagogue building appeal in September 1839, and was a seat holder in the new synagogue in 1845. He founded the short-lived Sydney Jewish Library in 1846 and was the editor of Australia's first Jewish newspaper, *Voice of Jacob*, which briefly appeared in the early 1840s. He served as secretary of the York Street Synagogue and became the regular Australian correspondent of the London weekly edition of *Voice of Jacob*.

Moss was listed as having a house at Bridge Street and a house in Kent Street (*Sydney Gazette*, 9 September, 19 September 1842). When Nichols ceased to be involved in the *Australian*, Moss became a proprietor in partnership with the Rev. W. M. Hesketh, and on 12 July 1843 that partnership was dissolved. Moss held a licence for the City Hotel in George Street near Hunter Street (18 January 1844) and a night licence was granted on 1 July 1844. In December the licence was transferred to George Howell. On 27 October 1845 Moss was appointed collector for the Sydney City Council. His sureties were Moses Joseph (q.v.) and Lewis Leon (q.v.).

A few weeks before Moss's 17-year-old daughter Miriam died, on 14 March 1854, Moss had unwisely written an article for the *Sydney Morning Herald* called 'Jewish Intelligence' that made fun of the Sydney Synagogue for failing to have found a rabbi. It is possible that the letter was a Purim joke or that it was written at a time of great stress. The synagogue's committee was not amused and believed that Moss had published an article that reflected poorly on the Jewish community. Moss was suspended. He apologised but the committee was adamant. A Special Meeting of the congregation approved an annuity of £100. However, this was disallowed, and a grant of £50 a year was approved for a single year and was to be subject to confirmation each successive year. The dispute broke both his heart and his mind. George Moss died on 19 November 1854 at the Tarban Creek Lunatic Asylum at the age of forty-four. His tombstone, commissioned by the congregation at the cost of £4 10s, reads that he had been 'Secretary of the York Street Synagogue until infirmity overtook him'.

On 24 August 1856 Moses Moss asked the York Street Synagogue's Board of Management what was to happen to the children of George Moss. They had been in the care of the Rev. Jacob Isaacs, who had decided to return to England. Almost a year passed until, at the meeting of the board on 9 August 1857, it was reported that 'the children were not properly provided for', although the two boys were costing the synagogue £50 per annum. One of them was now 'old enough to be apprenticed to a good trade so as to be capable of obtaining his own living'.

Two weeks later, it was resolved that the children be handed over to the Jewish Orphan Society and that £50 be given to the society for their upkeep. In August 1859 that sum was halved, as the older boy had 'been placed in a position to obtain his own livelihood'.

Siren Indent 4/5211; *Sydney Morning Herald*, 15 September 1839, 23 March 1840, 15 September 1842, 12 March 1846; *Sydney Gazette*, 15 October 1833, 12 August 1841; *Australian*, 4 July 1837, 31 March 1839, 18 January 1844, 1 July 1844, 11 December 1844, 27 October 1845; G. F. J. Bergman, 'George Moss, An Early Worker of the Sydney Jewish Community', *AJJHS*, vol. 9, no. 2 (1981), p. 77f.

MOSS, George

b. Old Gravel Lane, 1810–1842
Argyle, 1831; Convict; Sentenced to life, Middlesex, 1830.
Single; Labourer; Height: 163 cm.

Dark complexion, dark brown hair, brown eyes. He had a tattoo 'MM' on his right arm and 'SM & DM on his left arm. He could read and write. Moss was transported for stealing a watch. He had served a previous seven-year prison sentence, on the hulks at Chatham and Sheerness, for stealing a purse. His father was David Moss, a chiropodist in Aldgate. He said that his brother, Martin (aka Morton) Moss (q.v.), had been transported to Australia in 1825.

Moss began life in Van Diemen's Land as a convict servant on 5 August 1831 and, on 2 June 1837, Philip Marks (q.v.) of the New Town Road had George Moss assigned to him. Moss was repeatedly charged with disobedience and neglect of duty. On 23 June 1837 he was found guilty of stealing a large case of tobacco and was sentenced to three years at Port Arthur to work in the chain gang. On 13 February 1839 Moss was one of the eight prisoners who stole the Commandant's Whale Boat. The *Sydney Gazette* of 1 June 1839 reported about the 'Port Arthur Runaways' and told the story of 'seven' men who had been captured at Twofold Bay in New South Wales. They were to be returned to Van Diemen's Land, where Moss was sentenced to be imprisoned at Norfolk Island. Moss was shot and killed at Norfolk Island when a group of convicts tried to capture the brig *Governor Phillip* in an attempt to escape.

CON 14/2; *Sydney Gazette*, 1 June 1839; *Hobart Town Courier*, 19 July 1842; Aaron Price ms., Norfolk Island History (Dixson 249); I. Brand, *Escape from Port Arthur*.

MOSS, George

Siren, 1836; Free.
Married; 2 children.

The *Siren* arrived in New South Wales on 14 October 1836. George Moss married Leah Abrahams (q.v.) in Sydney in 1840 and their children were Abraham (1842) and Lewis (1846). Both children were registered by their parents as 'Hebrew'. Rachel Moss, a sister of George, married Henry Gershon (q.v.) in Sydney in 1846.

MOSS, Isaac

Married; 2 children.

Isaac Moss may not have been Jewish even though the listed names of his family would indicate that he was. His wife was Lydia.

Nearly all the references to Isaac Moss involve his intention to leave New South Wales. He had been 'about to leave' on the schooner *Brothers* on 7 December 1811 and on the *Governor Macquarie* on 26 June 1813. Lydia Moss and daughter were to travel on the *Seringapatum* on 10 September 1814 and sailed on 8 October 1815. He was 'shortly to depart' on the brig *Governor Macquarie* on 11 March 1815 and on 8 November 1815 (with Francis Silver).

Moss was granted a licence for the Cherry Tree Inn at Sydney on 19 April 1817. Finally, on 13 September 1817, Isaac Moss, Lydia Moss, Susannah Jane Moss and Joseph Moss were to leave Sydney 'at the earliest opportunity' and all claims were to be directed to 18 Castlereagh Street in Sydney, where Moss lived, as he was 'about to leave' on the *Admiral Cockburn* on 22 January 1820.

Notices in *Sydney Gazette* for dates cited.

MOSS, Isaac (MOSES)

Free.
Married; 4 children.

Isaac Moss had a house and shop in George Street, and married Miss Maria Folk (q.v.), daughter of Samuel and Amelia Folk (qq.v.), at the Sydney Synagogue on 19 October 1842. Rosette and Elizabeth (twins) were born on 11 May 1843. The last issue of the *Omnibus and Sydney Spectator* of 1 April 1843 mocked the pregnant Maria, 'Mrs Folk, your daughter, dear lady, is no doubt a beautiful creature, and as to the swelling, it merely reminds one of a Moss Rose'. Moses was born in Sydney in 1845. Deborah was born in 1849 and died on 26 October 1851. Isaac Moss gave £5 to the York Street Synagogue in 1845 and was a seat holder in the synagogue.

Marriage 2685/74, in Mutch Index; *Sydney Gazette*, 5 January 1837.

MOSS, John

b. London, 1810
Waterloo (5), 1838; Convict; Sentenced to 7 years, Central Criminal Court, 1837.
Single; Skin dyer; Height: 165 cm.

Dark ruddy complexion, brown hair, hazel eyes. Two small scars over right eyebrow. Two small moles on lower part of throat. Breast hairy, brown natural mark beneath left breast. Could not read or write. John Moss was sentenced on 8 May 1837, and transported for stealing the harness of a horse as it stood at the corner of a London street after midnight. Moss had been stopped and questioned by a policeman.

The *Waterloo* arrived in Sydney on 8 January 1838. The Newcastle Gaol Entrance and Description Book recorded that he was bound over in 1843 and sentenced at

Maitland to fourteen days in the cells. He was sent back into government service on 30 September 1843. He was listed as 'Jewish' and a 'labourer'. A certificate of freedom was issued on 15 June 1844.

Waterloo (5) Printed Indent, no. 227, p. 30; Newcastle Gaol Entrance and Description Book, 1841–45, 2/2008, no. 658; CF 4/4392-44/0925.

MOSS, Lewis

Free.

Lewis Moss was listed as a seat holder in the Sydney Synagogue in 1845.

MOSS, Moses (MOSES) (Morris MOSS)

c. 1840; Free.
Married.

The son of Henry Moses of London and first cousin of Louis Nathan's (q.v.) and Moses Joseph's (q.v.) families, Moses Moss married Esther Nathan (q.v.), sister of Arthur Isaac Nathan (Asher Isaac Nathan, q.v.), in Sydney on 16 November 1842. Moss was an active member of the Launceston Jewish community. In September 1843 he supported the petition to free Isaac Jacobs (q.v.) from debtor's prison. His name appeared on the 1843 petition for the establishment of a synagogue in Launceston and he gave £2 9s 6d to the Hobart Town Synagogue in 1844 and a further donation of 'offerings' adding up to £7 16s. He gave £50 to the Launceston Synagogue building appeal in June 1844 and a £25 donation from his father 'Henry Moses of London per Moses Moses of Hobart Town'. Moses Moss was the honorary treasurer of the Launceston Synagogue at the time of its dedication in March 1846. Moses Moss represented Nathan, Moses and Company of Hobart Town during the 1840s. Launceston's second Jewish cemetery was acquired on 16 April 1847 and Benjamin Francis (q.v.) and Morris Moss, 'gentleman', were named as trustees. In 1847 the *Launceston Examiner* reported that Moss had taken over 'new and extensive premises at the corner of Charles and York Streets'. Apart from the presence of Joseph Solomon (q.v.) in Evandale, who left the Jewish community, his business was the only 'Jewish' firm of any significance in Launceston.

Launceston Examiner, 29 June 1844, 11 May 1857; CSO 8/169/2350.

MOSS, Martin (Morton)

b. London 1803.
Convict, Transported twice. *Medway* (2) 1825, 7 years and *Lotus* 1833, 7 years.
Single.

Fair complexion, black hair, hazel eyes, black whiskers meeting under the chin, aquiline nose. 174cm. 'A Jew'. Indicted for stealing two bags of seeds valued at eight shillings from a cart in the yard of the White Horse Inn, Cripplegate on 26 December 1824. He was tried at the Old Bailey two days later and arrived in Van Diemen's Land 14 December 1825. His ill- fated brother George Moss (q.v.) was transported in 1831.

After serving his period of probation Moss became a servant working for Mr Marshall at Macquarie Plains in February 1828 when he absconded from his master and was found to be in Hobart Town. His term of imprisonment was extended by two months and he was returned to his master. On 11 September 1828 he was charged with neglect of duty and disobedience and was sentenced to work in irons for one month in the New Norfolk road gang. On 22 September 1828 his sentence was extended by fourteen days for neglect of duty. He continued to work for the government at New Norfolk and on 24 November 1828 was sentenced to one month in irons for neglect of duty and disobedience. On 30 March 1829 he was sentenced to fifty lashes for stealing potatoes from the field of Mr Thomas Able. On 19 April 1829 he absconded from his road gang and was at large for ten days before being captured and placed in irons for one month. His sentence expired and he returned to London where he married 'Ann'. On 29 November 1832 at the Old Bailey he was found guilty of stealing from the back of a cart.

The *Lotus* arrived in Hobart Town on 16 May 1833. On 7 November 1835 Martin Moss was serving his initial period of probation with the government when he was convicted of being drunk and neglecting his work and was returned to the service of the Crown. On 21 September 1836 he was sentenced to hard labour one month for being drunk. On 8 September 1836 he was sent to the cells for ten days for 'gambling in the Colonial Hospital'. On 2 February 1837 he was 'out after hours'. On 8 August 1837 he was said to be in possession of a stolen pencil case and was sentenced to six months hard labour and sent to the Snake Banks road party. On 11 August 1837 he was again found to be drunk. On 2 July 1838 he was found to have 'various article in his possession for which he cannot satisfactorily account' and he was returned to the government. On 6 November 1838 he was again found to be drunk and sentenced to seven days solitary confinement on bread and water. He received a certificate of freedom in 1839 and presumably, once again, returned to England.

OBSP 1827 case 503, CON 31/1/30, CON 18/1/13 p. 69.

MOSS, Nathan

1839; Free.
Dealer.

Nathan Moss was one of the earliest Jewish arrivals in Melbourne and signed the address of loyalty to the Duke of Edinburgh.

L. M. Goldman, *The Jews in Victoria in the Nineteenth Century*, p. 235.

MOSS, Phineas

b. Hampshire, 1795–1866
1835; Free.
Single; Clerk.

Phineas Moss was born in Portsea, Hampshire, in 1795 and received a fine secular and traditional Jewish education. He described himself as a 'gentleman' on the manifesto of the ship that brought him to Australia in 1835 and his first job was as clerk at the police station in the remote Tasmanian town of Bothwell at an initial annual salary of £80.

On 30 April 1840 Moss resigned. He had done his duty to the best of his ability but he had been subjected to a 'system of tyranny, oppression and contumely on the part of the Assistant Police Magistrate [in Bothwell] which has more recently developed itself in attacks on my fair name in quarters where it is impossible for me to vindicate myself, and where indeed he forbade me the opportunity of exposing his misrepresentations. With the resignation of my office I depart from a Colony where I had hoped to share the advantages which it might have offered'.

The Bothwell community published a public testimonial to Moss for his 'unremitting exertions' on behalf of the Bothwell Literary Society. In Hobart Town it became his task to keep all the convict dossiers up to date and, in 1842, he received an extra £10 'for preparing returns of offences committed by convicts at Probation Stations with their punishments from July 1841 to June 1842'. He was also obliged to be a storekeeper and supplier of books and stationery in the department and to keep and deliver all books to all schools at the different penal stations. On 22 October 1842 he asked for an increase in pay. He detailed his duties and explained that he also had to arrange for the interchange of all books from the central library in Hobart Town. His request was refused because his superior 'has not seen him working beyond office hours'. Moss became a popular lecturer at the Mechanics Institutes of both Hobart Town and Launceston, lecturing on scientific subjects such as 'pneumatics', astronomy and mathematics.

On 17 August 1841 Phineas Moss married Emily Golding Morgan (Emily Moss, q.v.) (a proselyte) in Hobart Town. It was the island's sixth Jewish wedding and was conducted by Rheuben Joseph (Reuben Joseph, q.v.) at 55 Brisbane Street, Hobart Town. The witnesses were Robert Hart (q.v.) and Louis Nathan (q.v.). Moss became the honorary secretary of the Hobart Town congregation in 1842 and was assigned seat no. 22 in the newly built synagogue in 1845. Moss was a fine calligrapher in both English and Hebrew and the early minute books and convict dossiers reflect his skill.

In 1842 Moss became a chief clerk in the Principal Superintendent's Department. He was promoted to the Comptroller General's Department in 1843 and then remained in the Convict Department until 1865 at a salary of £180.

In 1846, when the colonial administration needed to find the whereabouts of Anszel Davidowicz Davis, it turned to Moss for information. He replied: 'very few foreign Jews retain their common Judaic or surnames on their arrival in England', but identified him as Oscar Davis (q.v.), formerly of New Norfolk.

The 1857 *Hobart Town Directory* recorded that Moss lived at 29 Murray Street and was a 'bookseller and stationer'. In 1853 he arranged to have printed in London, and published in Hobart Town, the first Jewish calendar for Australia in the Hebrew and English languages, dedicated 'To the honourable and pious matrons of the House of Israel in this island, and in other lands of the Southern Hemisphere. Anno Mundi 5612'. In 1859 he published a paper with the Royal Society of Tasmania, *The Science of Astronomy Among the Ancient Jews.* He died in Hobart on 13 April 1866, aged seventy-one and was buried in the Harrington Street cemetery. His widow died on 26 January 1902. The synagogue in Hobart owns a colonial portrait of Phineas Moss, attributed to William Dowling.

CSO/50/16, in 1835; G. F. J. Bergman, 'Phineas Moss', *AJJHS*, vol. 6, no. 5 (1968), p. 267f; CSO 19/1, p. 254; CSO 22/52.304, 22 October 1842; CSO 22/41/13, 10 September 1842; CSO 20/29/681, 1846; Peter Elias and Ann Elias (eds), *A Few from Afar*, p. 41f.

MOSS, Rosetta

1836; Free.
Single.

The daughter of Marcus and Abigail Warschauer (q.v.), Rosetta Moss married Woolf Lewis Pyke (q.v.) on 8 August 1844.

MOSS, Sarah

1820–1845
Free.
Single.

Sarah Moss married Laurence Phillips (q.v.) at the Sydney Synagogue on 24 January 1844. Sarah died, aged twenty-five, on 21 June 1844, and was buried at the Devonshire Street Jewish Cemetery.

MURRAY, Joseph

b. Edinburgh, 1815
Agincourt, 1844; Convict; Sentenced to life, Central Criminal Court, 1844.
Single; Upholsterer; Height: 157 cm.

Fair complexion, curly light hair, grey eyes, medium nose and mouth. Jew. Can read and write. Joseph Murray was transported for housebreaking. It was his second sentence of transportation, as he had been previously transported. He was tried with James Davis and they were sentenced on 4 March 1844.

Joseph Murray was immediately sent to Norfolk Island on the *Agincourt* for the initial three years of his sentence, arriving there on 9 November 1844. On Norfolk Island he was sentenced to three weeks in chains for having made a false statement (25 June 1846), six days in solitary for insolence (9 July 1846), one month hard labour in chains for idleness, six weeks hard labour in chains for having a pipe in his possession, and, for having two figs of tobacco in his possession, he was punished with six days in solitary confinement (11 January 1847). On 9 April 1849 he arrived in Van Diemen's Land on the *Pestonjee Bomanjee* and for six months was the assigned servant of Aaron Mendoza (q.v.) of Bathurst Street. He was then transferred to New Norfolk and on 6 November 1849 he was charged with having been in the cell of an insane patient at the asylum and strongly suspected of having beaten him. He was sentenced to six months hard labour. Murray absconded from Australia and between June 1857 and 10 November 1857 he was officially gazetted as 'missing'.

CON 33/83, no. 19314.

MYERS, Abraham

b. London, 1801–1881
Guildford (5), 1822; Convict; Sentenced to 7 years, Old Bailey, 1821.
Single; Pedlar; Height: 174 cm.

Pale complexion, brown hair, blue eyes. On 27 October 1821, together with accomplice Robert Day, Myers stole two parcels from a cart in which were twenty-eight pieces of calico worth £22 and four hearth rugs valued at £4. The cart had been parked at the Saracen's Head Inn at Aldgate. The arrest was made by a watchman who testified: 'I went up and collared Myers—he begged of me to stash it, which means say nothing of it. He offered me £2 to let the property go'. Myers was a relative of Joseph Levy (q.v.), who had been transported on the Mangles *in 1820. Myers was sentenced at Middlesex on 5 December 1821.*

Abraham Myers arrived in New South Wales on 15 July 1822. Myers was listed in the 1828 Census as a government servant. He was described as a Jew who was employed as a labourer working for James Grono in Pitt Town. A certificate of freedom was issued on 2 March 1829. On 1 February 1830 Myers married Sarah Hobbs at Pitt Town's Church of England. He was admonished and discharged from the Police Court for street fighting with Andrew Fitzsimmons on 7 April 1831.

Myers had a business in George Street in Sydney in 1832 when Joseph Levy (q.v.) asked permission to join him. On 21 March 1836 Mr and Mrs Abraham Myers found themselves charged with serious and aggravated assault by Catherine Davis (Catherine Solomon, q.v.), who had been thrown out of their hotel for insulting other clients in the hotel. The case was dismissed.

In 1845 Abraham Myers was listed as a seat holder in the York Street Synagogue and donated £10 to its building appeal. 'Myers and Alexander' advertised their 'Yass Store' in December 1845 under the bold headline 'Advance Australia', and announced that they were 'real estate agents'.

Myers was designated the collector for the York Street Synagogue for the District of Goulburn. Myers died, aged eighty, on 17 June 1881 and was buried at the Old Jewish Section, Rookwood Cemetery.

OBSP, 1821, First Session, case 94, p. 65; Ship Indent 4/4008, and 2/8261, p. 429; CF 4/4296; Great Synagogue Burial Register; *Sydney Gazette*, 9 April 1829; *Sydney Monitor*, 31 December 1835; *Sydney Morning Herald*, 9 December 1845.

MYERS, Abraham

b. London, 1812
David Malcolm, 1845; Convict; Sentenced to 15 years, Central Criminal Court, 1844.
Glass cutter; Height: 159 cm.

Fair complexion, freckled, brown hair, grey eyes, medium nose. Jew. Can read and write. Abraham Myers was tried for 'feloniously assaulting, Robert Clayards, and stabbing, cutting and wounding him in and upon the left side of his chest and right hand with intent to murder him or to maim and disable him'. Clayard testified 'I believe he keeps an open house in North Alley. I believe he did keep some wine rooms in Windmill Street but he keeps a house of ill fame'. Myers attacked Robert Clayard with a knife and stabbed him in the chest after an exchange of 'vile words' in a public bar.

Myers was sent directly from England to Norfolk Island on the convict transport ship *David Malcolm*, which arrived on 25 August 1845. On 14 November 1846 he was admonished for 'misconduct'. In May 1847 he was sent by the *Tory* to Van Diemen's Land and to Port Arthur where he remained until 7 August 1847 when he was assigned to Lazarus Levy (q.v.), of Murray Street, Hobart Town. He received a ticket of leave on 9 March 1852. A conditional pardon was granted in 1854 after which his ticket of leave was revoked and cancelled on 19 August 1859.

OBSP 21 October 1844, case 2429. CON 33/80, no. 18604-b.

MYERS, Abraham

d. 1893 Free.
Tailor.

Myers was one of the first Jewish settlers in Western Australia. He was naturalised in 1849. He was said to have been a tailor in Fremantle.

David J. Benjamin, 'Western Australian Jewry', *AJJHS*, vol. 2, no. 5 (1946), p. 238.

MYERS, Charles

b. Whitechapel, 1813
Augusta Jessie (1), 1835; Convict; Sentenced to life, London, 1834.
Single; Labourer; Height: 168 cm.

Dark complexion, brown hair, dark brown eyes, sharp pointed nose. Stout. Mark under right eye. A Jew. Transported for stealing in a dwelling house. Hulk report: 'Very bad'. Charles Myers had been found guilty of breaking into the house of Solomon Aaron in Duke Street, Aldgate. He had already served an 18-month sentence 'for stealing from my Master'. Surgeon's report: 'Good'.

The *Augusta Jessie* arrived in Hobart Town on 7 January 1835. At the end of the year Myers was placed in a chain gang for 'disorderly conduct and disobedience of orders'. On 12 March 1836 he absconded and when caught was sentenced to six months hard labour in irons. In August 1836 a further charge was brought against him, while he was in No. 2 Chain Gang and he was sent to the hulk chain gang. On the hulk he received two separate sentences of fifty lashes, one for striking an overseer and one for refusing to go to work.

From June to August 1837 Myers worked in the Hobart Town Gaol and in December was sent to Port Arthur for two years for striking the overseer of the chain gang in which he was working. In November 1838 his sentence of hard labour at Port Arthur was extended by a further three years for insubordination to his overseer. In December 1840 Myers attempted to escape from the coal mines of the Tasman Peninsula and received an additional two years hard labour as punishment. Twenty-four further charges followed in the ten years of his servitude, including two charges of assault, four of refusing to work and 'disobedience', six for being 'absent without leave', four for 'insubordination', three for 'theft', and three for 'misconduct'. Finally, in June 1853, Myers received a ticket of leave and, although this was revoked twice in 1854, his conditional pardon was approved on 17 July 1855.

CON 34/5; CON 18/3, no. 1264.

MYERS, David

b. London, 1790
Almorah (1), 1817; Convict; Sentenced to 14 years, Old Bailey, 1816.
Married; Watchmaker; Height: 164.5 cm.

Fair ruddy complexion, hazel eyes, sandy hair. Illiterate. David Myers was convicted of receiving stolen property from a prostitute and sentenced on 18 September 1816. He was 'very well behaved' on the convict transport.

Myers arrived in Port Jackson on the *Almorah* on 31 August 1817 and was immediately sent on to Van Diemen's Land on the *Pilot*, where he was first assigned to Barnard Walford (q.v.). By February 1818 he held a ticket of leave and found employment in the police force in Hobart Town. On 5 June 1819 his ticket of leave was forfeited as he had been insolent to three military officers as he passed them on the street. On 4 April 1821 a temporary ticket of leave was confiscated for 'fraudulently removing three silver ornaments from a liquor stand and other-ways defacing it. The said stand being given to him to repair'. On 3 July 1821 Myers and Daniel Garcia (q.v.) were found guilty of stealing nine hats from the premises of A. Bethune, and Myers was sent to Newcastle to serve the remainder of his sentence. He was returned on the *Midas* (with the prisoners Daniel Garcia and Farrel Garcia).

In May 1822 he received twenty-five lashes at Newcastle for 'holding intercourse, trafficking and quarrelling with a soldier'. In 1826 Vaiben Solomon (q.v.) applied for David Myers to be sent down from Port Macquarie to be his assigned servant. Solomon claimed that Myers was a relative and that he could help him run his shop. The petition was refused. Solomon was a pencil-maker not a watchmaker and it was doubted that they were related. They had, however, both been at Port Macquarie as prisoners.

In August 1828 Myers petitioned the Governor to grant him a ticket of leave. He claimed to have acted as an overseer for Lieutenant Governor Sorrell who 'had granted a ticket of leave which he held for four years when he was suddenly ordered to Newcastle by W H. Humphreys, Police Magistrate'. In fact, Myers served two and a half years as an overseer and then worked as constable in the Newcastle prison settlement. When the settlement was cleared of convicts he was transferred to Port Macquarie where he was constable under the four successive commandants. He had been allowed to come to Sydney as an assigned servant to Mr Robertson, the Government Watchmaker. His petition was refused as the documents showed that he had been sent to Newcastle by the Deputy Judge Advocate. This Myers denied.

The 1828 Census shows Myers to be working for James Robertson in George Street and the List of Convicts in New South Wales in November 1828 stated that he was a Jew and that he was thirty-six years old. A ticket of leave was issued on 24 August 1829. After having worked for Robertson for three and a half years he set himself up in business on his own. Only six months later the *Sydney Gazette* reported (17 April 1830) that there was, in the Supreme Court, 'a man named David Myers, Prisoner of the Crown for fourteen years, holding a ticket of leave, charged with having in his possession a stolen watch valued at £20. The prisoner said he had it to repair and mentioned a man's name from whom he said he had received it'. P. J. Cohen (q.v.) went to court and gave him 'a good character'. The court, however, sentenced Myers to seven years colonial transportation and on 21 May 1830 Myers was exiled to Norfolk Island. By 1837 Myers was back in Sydney and working as an assigned servant to Mr R. Broad, when he was sentenced to two months at the Hyde Park Barracks for 'disorderly conduct', after which he was returned to assigned service. Myers was granted a certificate of freedom on 22 November 1837.

OBSP, case 938, p. 430; *Almorah* Indent 4/4005, p. 346, and 2/8240, p. 226; 4/3504, pp. 198–9; 4/1718, p. 148, Petition 109; *Hobart Town Gazette*, 10 April 1819, 7 July 1821; *Sydney Gazette*, 17 April 1830; HO 10/43; CON 21/39, p. 125; CON 13/11; CS In Correspondence 4/1750, p. 20; Petition 109, in 4/1817; Petitions A2167, pet. 99, dated August 1828; Governors' Despatches, A1206, p. 486; House of Correction Register 4/4569, 1 September 1837, p. 23.

MYERS, Edward

b. London, 1819

Free. Single; Teacher of languages and music; Height: 145 cm.

Edward Myers was the brother of Moses Myers (q.v.) and Mary Hartnell (q.v.). Edward first settled in Adelaide, South Australia where, on 9 March 1840, he was convicted of 'obtaining money under false pretences' when he forged a note for £15. He was sentenced to seven years. The description recorded of him read: 'Pale complexion, brown hair, blue eyes, medium nose and chin. Jew. Can read and write. Large scar inside right hand. A cripple who uses crutches'.

Myers came to New South Wales on the *Mary Ridgeway*, arriving on 20 April 1840. After obtaining his ticket of leave, Myers lived in Bridge Street, Sydney, where he taught languages. He was also well known to the police and was written up in the *Registry of Flash Men*: 'Edward Myers, brother of (Moses) Myers the fishmonger. The most arrant little rogue. He wrote a novel *Frederick or the Reclaimed* opening a subscription in 1844. He declared himself to be a teacher of music, drawing and language'.

Myers was sentenced at Maitland in December 1844 for claiming to have a valid ticket of leave for the district. He was gaoled for fraud, and recommended for imprisonment on Cockatoo Island or Port Macquarie. According to the *Registry of Flash Men*, 'his sister is the celebrated Miss Hartnell, a prostitute … The fellow has gone to Maitland without giving notice to the Police. In for it again'. On 1 March 1845 he appeared in the Newcastle Gaol Entrance Book, having been committed at Maitland to be sent to the gaol at Port Macquarie and then forwarded to Sydney. His behaviour was 'orderly'. His initial period of probation in Van Diemen's Land was thirty months and, in July 1852, he was sent to Port Arthur.

On 26 May 1853, having been returned to Hobart Town, he was convicted of misconduct for (again) falsely representing to the senior clerk that he had received a ticket of leave. He was sentenced to three months hard labour. On 4 July 1853 he was found guilty of a second charge of misconduct for 'preparing a false return by which William Ryder (by the *London, 2*), was discharged from the Prisoners Barracks before completing his sentence.' His existing sentence of hard labour was extended by six months. On 19 November 1854, while still at the Prisoners' Barracks in Hobart, he was sentenced to an additional three months hard labour for being absent without leave. Another ticket of leave was issued on 16 January 1855 and a conditional pardon 24 August 1856.

Union Indent, 1851, no. 2125; Printed Indent, 40–859; W. A. Miles, *Registry of Flash Men*, p. 105, 2/673; Newcastle Gaol Entrance and Description Book, 1841–45, 2/2008, no. 108.

MYERS, Elizabeth

d. 1834
Mary, 1829; Free.
Married; 3 children.

Elizabeth and her husband, Joseph Myers (q.v.) of Parramatta, arrived as free settlers on 20 January 1829. Elizabeth Myers was buried in the Jewish section of the Devonshire Street Cemetery on 27 May 1834.

MYERS, Emanuel (Monkey Myers)

b. London, 1795–1855
John Barry (1), 1819; Convict; Sentenced to life at the Old Bailey, 1819.
Single; Tailor; Height: 162.5 cm; 4 children.

Fair pale complexion, dark brown hair, dark chestnut eyes. A taylor, Myers was one in a gang of thieves who surrounded and jostled a man at an election meeting in the vicinity of Covent Garden and was sentenced to transportation for life on 17 February 1819. Myers declared at the trial, 'the evidence is false'.

Myers arrived in New South Wales on 26 September 1819 and was assigned to William Pendray, a merchant tailor and draper in Sydney. He was listed as a tailor in George Street in the 1828 Census. He was refused a ticket of leave in 1828 because of offences he had committed in 1825 and 1826 when he absented himself from work and for which he had been given twenty-five lashes. Myers was charged with having harboured the runaway Susan Courtney in his house and was sentenced to the treadmill for ten days. On 17 March 1828 he had received twenty-five lashes for being absent without leave and on 31 May 1828 he was put in the gaol for five days for drunkenness and absence from work.

Greg McCarry, a descendant of Emanuel Myers, has published a detailed biography of his ancestor. In 1827 Myers applied for permission to marry Lydia Shaw, who was aged twenty-two. She had come to Australia as a convict and approval was refused 'Being both prisoners of the Cown'. The next year he applied for permission to marry Charlotte Byfield. This application was approved but the marriage did not eventuate and, within a few months, Emanual Myers married Mary Anne Burnsides on 4 March 1829 at St James in Sydney. Six months later, Emanuel applied on 24 September 1829 for an exemption from 'Government labor' so that he would be able 'to reside with his wife Mary Ann (sic), formerly Burnsides, born in the colony'. Marry Anne had been working as a servant in Windsor and was one of the children of a soldier, Ambrose Burnsides. A ticket of leave was granted on 11 September 1833 (33/573) for the district of Sydney on 27 October 1836 requiring Myers to remain in the Windsor district. The ticket was issued 'In lieu of No 3/573 dated 10 September 1833 returned mutilated and cancelled'. On 8 September 1836 Myers received a conditional pardon. The *Sydney Times* (25 March 1837) advertised that he had just 'opened a general store next door to the sign of the Bull's Head opposite the Market Place, George St'. An absolute pardon was granted on 10 June 1843 and, in that year, Myers was shown to have a shop in King Street, Sydney.

In the list of 'Bridge St members 1835–42' Emanuel registered his first three children. Benjamin born 9 July 1830, Joseph born 19 October 1833 and Hannah born 24 July 1836. The first two children were born in Sydney and Hannah in Windsor. Hannah appears to have died as a young child and Priscilla was born between 1841 and 1843. By this time Mary Anne had become 'Rebecca'. A son, Henry, was born on 7 July 1839, Priscilla was born 19 December 1841 and Abraham on 5 December 1843. On 10 August 1840 Emanuel (re)married his wife in a Jewish religious ceremony. Mary Anne, or Rebecca, had been accepted as a convert by Isaac Simmons (q.v.) and the officiating minister at the ceremony was Jacob Isaacs (q.v.). The marriage had not happened without drama within the congregation with a special committee meting of the synagogue in May 1840 followed by a second debate in August.

By this time Myers was known as an 'auctioneer and dealer' who lived at Castlereagh Street and for a brief time was a partner of Abraham Moses (q.v.). On 2 January 1845 the 34-year-old Rebecca Myers, 'the wife of a dealer in Castlereagh Street' died 'in her sleep' and her funeral was held immediately after her death in accordance with Jewish custom. It was reported that 'certain suspicions' were 'caused by the extraordinary haste with which she was interred' (*The Australian*, 6 January 1845). However no inquest appears to have been held and on 19 June 1845 Emanuel married Abigail Barnett (q.v.) at the York Street synagogue. Abigail signed the marriage certificate with a mark and within six months her marriage appears to have collapsed, 'Emanuel Myers, better known as "Monkey Myers" was charged by his better half "Abigail" with thrashing her repeatedly where she could not show her marks—the case was settled out of court' (*Bell's Life in Sydney and Sporting Reviewer*, 3 January 1846). By 1847 Myers was living in York Street. In 1855 the three young children of Mary Anne (Rebecca), 'Henry, Priscilla and Abraham Myers, three juveniles, taken into custody for protection, were forwarded to the Asylum' (the New South Wales Benevolent Asylum), from which they 'absconded'. In June 1856 'Emanuel Myers, of York Street, dealer' charged Abigail with having threatened to take his life'. Later it was stated that Emanuel thought that his wife was made and unless restrained would do him 'some serious bodily harm'. Indeed, it appears that Abigail was placed in prison. Reunited, Abigail and Emanuel continued to haunt the courts with mutual accusations of violence while apparently various customers stole objects from Emanuel's shop.

Emanuel Myers died on 3 September 1855 aged 'about 60 years old' and, seemingly abandoned by his family, was buried in the 'Jews' Burial Ground.

OBSP, 1818–19, case 437, p. 181; Ship Indent 4/4006, p. 387; CS 29/7573, in 4/2047; 4/6671, p. 85; Principal Superintendent of Convicts, Register of Convicts' Applications to Marry, Permission Granted 1826–33, 4/4508; TL Register 4/4089, TL 38/573; CF/721; HO 10/53; Exemption from Government Labour, no. 30/16, 4/4283; *Sydney Morning Herald*, 2 August 1832, 2 December 1841, 24 January 1842, 15 September 1842, 23 June 1843, 26 April 1844, 24 August 1844; August 1853; 2 March 1855; 25 June 1856; *Sydney Times*, 25 March 1837. 'The Myers Line, Emanuel and Joseph: a Limp on a Branch of the McCarry–Brother Family Tree', in *AJHSJ*, June 2012, vol. 20, part 4, p. 534.

MYERS, Emanuel Moses (Emanuel Myer MYERS)

London, 1827
1845; Free.
Single; Trader; 6 children.

The son of Moses and Sarah Myers of Great Poultney Street, Golden Lane in London's East End, Emanuel Myers was born on 19 June 1827, and named at the Great Synagogue in Duke's Place.

Emanuel Moses Myers must have been in Hobart Town in 1845 when the synagogue in Argyle Street was built. Myers painted the *trompe l'oeil* depicting the Ten Commandments above the Ark on the synagogue's eastern wall. In January 1848 the Melbourne Hebrew Congregation voted to pay Emanuel Myers of Swanston Street the large sum of £11 for 'so much labour and expense' for painting a canvas of the Ten Commandments to be placed above the Ark in the new synagogue building. Myers subsequently failed to join the congregation and, on 8 November 1848, the president wrote a 'reminder' to him that if he failed to join as a founding member he would have to pay twenty-six shillings in addition to the membership fee when he finally decided to affiliate.

Emanuel Moses Myers married Matilda Caspar (Casper, q.v.), the daughter of Ellis and Elizabeth Casper (qq.v.), in a Jewish ceremony in Hobart Town on 26 May 1853. The Rev. Emanuel Myers was minister of the Melbourne Hebrew Congregation from 1857 to 1864 and presided over the consecration of Melbourne's completed Bourke Street Synagogue in 1858. The famed Jewish traveler Rabbi Saphir wrote 'There are about 1000 Jews in Melbourne, the majority English, a minority Polish. There are two synagogues-the larger, more beautiful 'Shairith Yisroel' where the English Jews worship ... They have a cantor, a reader who sometimes preaches and teaches, a wise and respected man, the Rev E. M. Myers'. He was said to be a relative of the Hon Nathaniel Levi and in October 1860 was charged with burying the child of Nathaniel Levi without permission of the congregation's president and consecrating a tombstone with 'a peculiar expression on it.' (There is no evidence of a strange phrase on the stone as it now still stands).

Bankrupt and ill, Myers and his family moved to Montreal Canada in 1864. His book *The Jews, Their Customs and Ceremonies* was published in Brooklyn, New York, in 1880. The Myers eventually moved to Waco, Texas, where Matilda died in 1895.

Their children were: Dinah (born 1854), who died in infancy, a son (1855), who also died in infancy, Andrew (1856), Miriam (1858), Henry (1860), and Elizabeth (27 September 1862).

Family information from Simon Marks-Isaacs, Sydney.

MYERS, Esther (née SOLOMON)

b. London, 1809–1869
Palambam, 1833; Free.
Married; 8 children.

Esther Solomon was a daughter of Samuel Moss Solomon (q.v.) and Elizabeth (Betsy). Esther, 'the daughter of Sh'muel', married Israel Myers (q.v.), son of Asher, at the Great Synagogue, Duke's Place, London on 27 June 1832. In 1833 Esther and Israel Myers arrived in Sydney. Esther Myers died in Sydney on 3 December 1869, and was buried at the Rookwood Cemetery. Her children were Samuel Israel, Anne, John, Phillip, Sarah, Eve, David, and Julia.

MYERS, Esther

1845; Free.
Married; 1 child.

Esther Myers was married to Isaac Myers (q.v.) and came out to Australia with him in 1845.

MYERS, Felix

b. Düsseldorf, Prussia, 1810
Neptune II, 1838; Convict; Sentenced to 7 years, Leicester Quarter Sessions, 1837.
Single; Musician and professor of languages.

Felix Myers was sentenced for receiving stolen silver spoons. Gaol report 'good'. Hulk report 'Good'. The surgeon on the transport wrote that Myers acted as a school master on board and that he had behaved 'very well'.

The *Neptune* arrived in Hobart Town on 2 January 1838. Myers acted as 'Sub Overseer' of the Bagdad Road Party until he was found guilty of overstaying his pass and representing himself to be free on 11 September 1838. He was sentenced to hard labour on the treadmill for fourteen days before being returned to his road party. A charge of 'misconduct' on 22 August 1839 earned him three months hard labour. He was sent to Green Ponds to work on the roads. On 2 December 1839 he was admonished for 'refusing to work on the plea of inability'. On 24 October 1840 he was working as a post office messenger when his repeated absence from duty earned him five days in the House of Correction. On 21 October 1840 he repeated this behaviour and was sentenced to five days on the treadmill. On 16 November 'neglect of duty' put him in the cells on bread and water for six days and on 18 December 1840 he was placed back in the cells on bread and water for three days for 'misconduct in attempting to avoid his duty' at the Post Office.

A conditional pardon was granted on 31 May 1843 and a certificate of freedom in 1844 (no. 592). 'George Meyers' gave £2 to the Hobart Synagogue building fund on 9 June 1843 (*Hobart Town Courier*).

CON 31/32, no. 1602.

MYERS, Gabriel

1787–1841
Fanny I, 1816; Convict; Sentenced to 7 years, Middlesex, 1814.

Gabriel Myers was tried for attempting to steal a piece of cotton netting from a stocking shop in the East End. His friend John Abrahams stood by the door as Myers put the cloth into his pocket.

Myers arrived in Sydney by the *Fanny* on 18 January 1816 and was quickly sent on to Hobart Town on the *Emu*. Myers was free by servitude by 8 December 1821, according to the *Hobart Town Gazette*, when he advertised that all claims against him should be presented so that he could leave Van Diemen's Land 'by an early opportunity'. Myers settled in Sydney and worked as a trader. He was recorded as arriving in Sydney on the *Dorset* from Port Phillip on 11 March 1840 (he travelled steerage). Gabriel Myers married Clara Hayter at St Lawrence's in Sydney in 1840 and was listed as a voter in the first Sydney council election, with a house in

Parramatta Street. Fate intervened and he was buried in the Jewish section of the Devonshire Street Cemetery in April 1841.

OBSP, 1814, case 69, p. 47; CON 21/39; CON 13/1; ML 4/5216; *Sydney Morning Herald*, 15 September 1842.

MYERS, George (MARKS)

Vittoria, 1829; Convict; Sentenced 1828.

George Myers arrived in New South Wales on 17 January 1829. He was sent on to Port Macquarie on 19 June 1830 on the *Isabella*. George Myers may be the 'crown prisoner residing at Port Macquarie', who was referred to as 'Myers or Miers' when he was sentenced to twelve months transportation for receiving stolen goods (*Sydney Morning Herald*, 3 February 1844).

Prisoners to Port Macquarie, 19 June 1830, 4/3505.

MYERS, Godfrey

Emma, 1842; Free.

Godfrey Myers arrived in Hobart Town from Sydney on 5 November 1842 He was a young activist in the Hobart Hebrew Congregation. He gave £2 on 11 April 1843 to the synagogue building fund. Myers officiated at Jewish wedding no. 4 in Launceston and was an official witness at a number of other weddings, where he signed his name with the title 'Registrar'.

A 'Mr Myers from Hobart Town' started a Jewish school in Melbourne in 1856 after having tried his luck at the goldfields at Sandhurst.

CSO 92/9, p. 94; AOT, CB 7/10, p. 18.

MYERS, Henry

b. England, 1815–1856
1849

Sadly nothing is known about Henry Myers apart from his year of arrival, his age and his place of birth. He died on 2 May 1856 and is buried in an unmarked grave in the West Maitland Jewish cemetery.

Maitland Court Register of Deaths. Information from Gary Luke.

MYERS, Isaac

Troubadour, 1845; Free.
Married; 1 child.

Isaac and Esther Myers (q.v.) had a child named Israel John Myers on 10 May 1845, and the child was registered at the Sydney Synagogue.

MYERS, Israel

Hashemy, 1849; Convict; Sentenced to 7 years, Central Criminal Court, 1847.

Israel Myers was convicted for picking pockets and stealing a handkerchief on 5 April 1847. He had been previously convicted at Clerkenwell in February 1846. The City Police Constable reported that Myers was 'very violent, and asked what we wanted to do with him. There was an attempt made to rescue him'. A witness testified "I have known him since he came out (of prison) and a long time before. When I have seen him he has always been in the company of thieves'.

The *Hashemy* arrived in New South Wales on 9 June 1849 and was the fourth last convict transport ship to New South Wales. The transportation system in New South Wales was in its last stages and a ticket of leave was issued to Israel Myers four months after he arrived in October 1849! He was hired by R. Fitzgerald Esq. in Mudgee for twelve months, paying the government £12 a year. He was transferred to Cassilis on 14 January 1850.

OBSP 5 April 1847, case 926. 4/4526; TL 49/113; CS 49/4180.

MYERS, Israel John

b. London, 1806–1890
Palambam, 1833; Free.
Married; Dealer; 9 children.

Israel Myers arrived steerage on the *Palambam* with his wife Esther (née Solomon) (q.v.) on 10 January 1833. No trade was indicated. Esther Myers was a daughter of Samuel Moss Solomon (q.v.) and a sister of Vaiben and Emanuel Solomon (qq.v.). Israel and Esther married in London's Great Synagogue on 27 June 1832.

In July 1833 he acquired the licence for the British Standard Inn in George Street. The children of Israel and Esther Myers were Samuel Israel Myers (1833), born in Sydney, who married Elizabeth (Lizzie) Dorsetta, the daughter of his uncle Emanuel Solomon in Adelaide, on 24 November 1858, Anne (1835), John Michael (1837), Phillip George. (1839), Sarah (1841), born in Sydney, Eve (1842), David Moss. (1845), and Julia (1847).

In September 1839 the *Post Office Directory* listed him as a butcher in York Street. The voters' list for 5 September 1842 showed that Israel Myers had a shop and house in George Street. In the 1840s, according to the *Shipping Gazette*, Myers exported and imported cases to New Zealand of such items as kauri gum, slops, and spades. Myers gave £20 to the York Street Synagogue building fund in 1839 and was a seat holder in the synagogue. In September 1840 he stood for election to the Sydney Synagogue's committee. 'Myers and (Abraham) Moses' established sales rooms in King Street advertising second–hand clothes and crockery during 1842 and 1843. Israel John Myers was buried at the Rookwood cemetery on 21 May 1890, aged eighty-four. Esther died in Sydney in 1869.

Sydney Morning Herald, 26 June 1843. Family history notes by Ian Nicol.

MYERS, Jacob

b. London, 1810–1880
Marquis of Huntley (1), 1826; Convict; Sentenced to life, London, 1825.
Single; House servant; Height: 162.5 cm; 15 children.

Ruddy, freckled complexion, dark brown hair, black eyes. Jacob Myers was fifteen years old. He was a Jew. He could read but not write. He was sentenced to transportation for using violence in order to steal a silver hunting watch from a seventeen year old. The prisoner told the court 'I throw myself entirely on the protecton of your Lordship'. Sentenced to death. Jacob Myers was listed as Jacob Meyer on the ship's indent.

Myers arrived in Sydney on 13 September 1826. He received a colonial conviction at the General Sessions in Bringelli on 10 June 1830 for absconding from his master's service for a second time. He was sentenced to three years colonial servitude and sent on the *Governor Phillip* on August 1830 to Moreton Bay. He was returned to Sydney on 22 October 1833.

In 1834 Jacob Myers received permission to marry Caroline Thomas, aged thirty-nine, who came on the *Princess Royal* with a seven-year sentence. They were married by Rev. Cartwright at St Luke's, Liverpool, in 1835. Caroline was still classified as 'bond', as was Myers, who received a ticket of leave in 1837 for the District of Liverpool. The 1837 General Return of Convicts in New South Wales noted that he was an assigned servant to Mr Frederick Westmacott of Liverpool. Caroline died on 30 June 1837 and was buried at Liverpool. Jacob married a second time, to Ann Clegg, who was born in the colony and was seventeen years of age, at Liverpool's St Luke's Church on 20 November 1837.

By 1839 Jacob was listed (on a son's birth certificate) as a grocer at Liverpool. Jacob's ticket of leave was altered to Campbelltown on 12 April 1840.

Jacob Myers 'of Yass' bought land at Gundagai for £14 on 17 September 1841. Myers signed the petition for a Jewish burial ground in Yass. A conditional pardon (no. 178) was issued on 1 February 1845. In Noel Chapman's (q.v.) letters of administration, his widow Rebecca was noted as living at Yass and working as a housekeeper for Jacob Myers, following her husband's death in 1849.

The Myers family conducted a general store in Yass from the latter part of 1843 where Jacob seems to have been in partnership with Jacob Alexander (q.v.) of Goulburn. In 1851 Jacob Myers owned an Inn on the Bathurst to Sydney, road eight miles from Bathurst. In April 1853 Myers was issued with a licence for the White Horse Cellar in George Street, Sydney, where he offered accommodation to 'settlers, up country gentlemen and gold diggers'. His career as a publican prospered. However, on 31 July 1857, Ann, 'formerly of Yass' and thirty-five years of age, died after giving birth to her eleventh child, named Leah (Lucy) Ann. Her tombstone at St Stephen's Church in Camperdown bears the Hebrew and civil date and the child Leah was named at the Sydney Synagogue.

Jacob Myers' third wife was Caroline Jane Dunlop (née Solomon), who had been born in Sydney 'about 1832'and was the daughter of John Solomon (q.v.).

She married Jacob on 30 May 1858, and they had four children. The family moved back to Yass and Jacob conducted business at the nearby goldfields. In November 1872 he was in business with Maurice Lazarus in Gulgong at the Capitol Cordial Company.

Jacob Myers died in Sydney on 5 June 1880 and was buried in the Jewish section of the Rookwood Cemetery. His widow Caroline died on 13 August 1914 at her daughter Anna's house in Arncliffe.

Ann and Jacob Myers' children were William (born 1838), Henry, Sarah, Joseph, Alexander, Abraham, Edward, Charles, Lewis, Frederick and Leah (Lucy) Ann. Jacob and Caroline's children were Emily (1860), Alfred (1861), Ewan (1864), and Anna (1866).

OBSP 13 January 1825, case 924. Ship Indent 4/4111, with TL 37/734, and 4/4011; Chronological Register of Convicts at Moreton Bay, no. 2141; Permission to Marry Book, 1834, 4/4512, p. 156, entry 422, and 4/4509, p. 139; Governors' Despatches, A1295, p. 55; CP 178, Land Purchase 2/7936; HO 10/53, series 1, no. 2078, New South Wales Office In, Letters of Administration; family information from Peter Meyer, Sydney, and Julie Skellern, New Zealand.

MYERS, John

b. London, 1802
Hercules II (1), 1825; Convict; Sentenced to 7 years, Old Bailey, 1824.
Single; Chair-maker; Height: 156 cm.

Pale complexion, little pock-pitted, dark brown hair, hazel eyes, stout. Together with Thomas Jones, a 20-year-old accomplice, Myers stripped an empty house of its lead and copper and was caught in the act. He had taken 200 pounds (weight) of lead and 200 pounds of copper. Myers told the court: 'It was a very wet night and I had no place to go and seeing this empty house and all the windows broken, we went in for shelter'. He was sentenced at London on 7 April 1824. He was 'Very well behaved' on board the transport.

The *Hercules* arrived in New South Wales on 7 May 1825 and Myers was assigned to the District of Evan. He was registered in the 1828 Census as a member of No. 4 Iron Gang. On 11 March 1833 Myers was still a prisoner at the Hyde Park Barracks working as a member of the 'Garden Gang' when he was found to have escaped from the group. He was captured and given ten days on the treadmill.

John Myers, aged forty-five and a holder of a ticket of leave, married June Young, alias Forbes, on 24 December 1844, the marriage conducted by the Rev. John Dufus of Liverpool. He received a certificate of freedom on 30 June 1843. Despite his surname, Myers may not have been Jewish.

OBSP, 1823–24, case 668, p. 244; Ship Indent 2/8262, and 4/4010, p. 120; Description Book 4/6299, no. 1391; Principal Superintendent of Convicts, Register of Convicts' Applications to Marry, 1842–51, 4/4514, p. 81; TL 43/1038; CF 4/4383, X 825, 11 March 1833.

MYERS, John

Earl Grey, 1838; Convict.

A certificate of freedom was issued for John Myers on 13 May 1854.

CF 4/4416, 54/0045.

MYERS, John

b. London
Glenelg, 1849; Free.
Married; Dealer; 1 child.

John and Rachel Myers arrived in South Australia in 1849 with their five-year-old son Alfred. John Myers was listed as a member of the committee of the Adelaide Hebrew Congregation in September 1850. The family settled in Kooringa and at Wallaroo, which were copper-mining towns in the mid-north of South Australia.

Jewish Chronicle (London), 30 May 1851; family information from Mrs Margot Bailey, Adelaide.

MYERS, Jonas

b. London, 1805
Maria I (2), 1820; Convict; Sentenced to life, Middlesex, 1820.
Pen-cutter; Height: 163 cm.

Brown hair, brown eyes. A Jew. Jonas Myers was outside Covent Garden and deliberately ran against a passerby and stole his watch. On the way to the watch house a crowd attacked the accuser and his jaw was broken. Jonas explained: 'I went to the play with my sister and lost her coming out, heard the cry "Stop Thief!" and ran. The gentleman stopped me. I never saw his watch!' He was aged fifteen, and had been in custody before. He was sentenced on 12 April 1820. Hulk report: 'indifferent'.

Myers arrived in Van Diemen's Land on 1 December 1820. The List of Convicts in Van Diemen's Land (1820) recorded that he was 'Now servant of Mr Dowell of Hobart Town' where Samuel Joseph (q.v.) was also assigned. On 28 March 1821 Myers was sentenced, for 'neglect of duty', to labour the same hours as the gaol chain gang for one week. His convict dossier then has the word 'RUN' written over it. Myers escaped from custody before any further misdemeanours were recorded and a reward of £2 was offered for his recapture. In the 1841 Muster of Convicts in Van Diemen's Land it was recorded that he had 'absconded'. He was struck off the list of convicts in December 1853.

Samuel Joseph's dossier is also blank and it is possible that the two teenagers escaped from the colony together.

OBSP, 1819–20, case 411, p. 299; Ship Indent 4/4007, p. 21; CON 31/29, no. 255; HO 10/43, 10/49.

MYERS, Jonas (MYER)

1824–1909
1909; Free.
Single.

Jonas Myers married Sarah Benjamin on 7 December 1853. She was aged twenty-five, and the marriage took place at the home of Samuel Hart, at Franklin Street, Adelaide. Sarah was the youngest child of Lyon Benjamin and his third wife Rachel. Sarah and Jonas had eight children. Henry Jonas (1856–1876), infant (1858), Rachel Ada (1859–after 1926), Lionel Benjamin Myers (1861–1862), Rebecca Judith (1862–1939),

Edward Myer (1864–1926), Rosetta (1866–1867), Florence (1868–1943). Jonas died in Brisbane 8 January 1909. Sarah died in Brisbane 20 January 1899. The inscription of his tombstone reads: 'This stone is erected by the members of the Jewish Community in Brisbane, in deepest reverence and devotion to the memory of heir late minister, teacher and friend who served them faithfully for 45 years'.

MYERS, Joseph (MEYERS) (MEERS)

1777–1814
Calcutta, 1803; Convict; Sentenced to 7 years, Shropshire, 1802.
Pedlar.

Joseph Myers was transported for felony. Despite his name and his occupation, Myers may not have been Jewish.

Myers was a member of the initial attempt to settle Port Phillip Bay as part of the Collins Expedition, which then moved to the Derwent. In the General Orders Book of Lieutenant Governor Collins, 1803–1808, there is an entry dated 21 December 1803 dealing with the embarkation of the men to Van Diemen's Land: 'The Superintendent will select two able groups of fifteen men each under the overseers Joseph Meyers and John Whitehead who will attend every day at the store and assist in the moving of the provisions to the boats'. On 17 May 1807 the *Hobart Town Gazette* announced that Joseph Meyers had absconded from the Van Diemen's Land settlement: 'Any person who shall be found to have any communication with [him] shall be deprived of all Indulgences from the Crown'. The Rev. Knopwood noted in his diary of 15 August 1807 that Joseph Myers, 'a bushranger', was still at large and that he had 'plenty of dogs'. Joseph Meyers gave evidence before the Bench of Magistrates in December 1813 in the case of Denis McCarty. He was buried in Hobart Town on 6 October 1814, aged thirty-seven.

HRA, series 3, vol. 1, p. 555; CS Muster of Hobart Town, Port Dalrymple and Norfolk Island, 1811, 4/1233-4; ML, A341, General and Garrison Orders—Lieutenant David Collins 1803–1804, AOT; CSO 201/33.

MYERS, Joseph

Mary, 1829; Free.
Married; Dealer; 3 children.

Joseph Myers was listed in the *New South Wales Calendar and Post Office Directory* for 1832, living in Campbell Street, Parramatta. Joseph and Elizabeth Myers (q.v.) had a daughter, Charlotte, in 1834, whose birth was registered at St John's Church of England, Parramatta. Elizabeth Myers, wife of Joseph Myers, died on 27 May 1834 and was buried at the Devonshire Street Jewish Cemetery.

MYERS, Judith

Free.
Married; 3 children.

The wife of Michael Myers (q.v.), Judith came out to New South Wales with three children in order to join her husband, and was sent on to Van Diemen's Land.

MYERS, Lewis

b. London, 1812
Lord Lyndoch (1), 1831; Convict; Sentenced to 7 years, Old Bailey, 1831.
Single; Labourer; Height: 166 cm.

Dark complexion, oval face, sloping forehead, straight nose, thin lips, broad chin, stout. A Jew. The surgeon reported that on the journey out to Australia he was 'quiet and orderly'. Lewis Myers was transported for stealing a silver soup ladle worth £3 from his brother Henry Myers who was a stationer and rag merchant. His brother had spent £100 to send Lewis overseas but he had left the boat and come home. His sisters and mother lived with Henry.

Lewis Myers arrived in Van Diemen's Land on 18 November 1831. By May 1833 Myers was working as a constable in Hobart Town but, in November 1833, was sentenced to twelve months in prison and dismissal from the police force for allowing two prisoners to escape from his custody. On 25 November the Launceston Police Book recorded that he was a member of a road party who rendered assistance to the police in the recapture of some escaped prisoners. It was recommended that, for his own safety, he be moved to another part of the island colony. On 23 April 1834 he was sentenced to fifty lashes for absconding from his road party. By 1836 he was working as an assigned servant and on 30 June that year he was returned to the Public Works Department for 'idleness, neglect and filthiness'. He was not to be assigned again as 'his head was so full of vermin'. He was sent to the Surveyor's Gang at Hobart Town. During 1837 Myers was charged twice with drunkenness, once with neglect of duty, once for being dirty at church and once for refusing an order to work. He was punished with forty-nine lashes and three months hard labour in chains. A further three months hard labour was imposed on 24 August 1837 when, as an assigned servant, he offered two sheep for sale to Mr Benjamin. Later in the year he was tried at Hobart Town for breaking and entering and stealing 3000 cigars, and was sentenced to eight years incarceration at Port Arthur.

OBSP, 1830–31, case 907, p. 460; CON 31/30, no. 925; CON 78/2, p. 440; CON 18/12; CON 37/9/2967; VDL Papers, ML, A1059-7, p. 184; *Hobart Town Courier*, 22 November 1833; *Independent*, 15 September 1832.

MYERS, Lewis (William JONES)

b. Leadenhall Street, 1822
Mangles (8), 1837; Convict; Sentenced to 7 years, Central Criminal Court, 1837.
Baker; Height: 164 cm.

A fresh complexion, dark brown hair, clean shaven, hazel eyes, long nose and large chin and mouth. He had a scar under lower lip. Heavily tattooed with bottle, anchor and crown, half moon, seven stars, sun and the initials M.M. H.M.C.M. J.M. S.M. A.M. A Jew. Can read and write. Lewis Myers was sentenced on 30 January for 'Perjury. I swore falsely about a robbery that had occurred relative to an order for money'.

William Jones, alias Lewis Myers, arrived in Sydney on 10 July 1837. On 18 July he was sentenced to fifty lashes for disorderly conduct, and on 6 September 1839 to fifty lashes for absconding. On 23 March 1840 he was put in irons for one month for stealing bananas.On 25 March 1840 he received a further fifty lashes for absconding.

Following a trial at Berrima he was sent to Norfolk Island from 19 December 1840 until 1843. Returning to the mainland it seems he encountered trouble almost immediately. On 23 February 1844 he was placed in irons for one week for 'threatening to take a policeman's life named Lewis Solomon'. On 22 March 1844, 'for smoking in the barracks and insolence to the superintendent', he was sentenced to a punishment of 150 lashes. 'Only' twenty-nine lashes were inflicted before the medical officer stopped the flogging. On 19 November 1844 he was put on bread and water for assaulting his overseer. Seven days later a further sentence was imposed for obscene language. On 3 April 1845 he was sentenced to seven days in irons for giving tobacco to a gaol gang. Myers was sent to Van Diemen's Land on the *Lady Franklin* on 12 October 1845. On 28 July 1846 he received six months hard labour in chains for 'sleeping in another man's berth'. On 10 August 1846 at the Hobart Town Prisoners' Barracks his sentence was extended by six months for absconding. He was transferred to the Cascades Prison, where he was put in solitary confinement for twenty days as a punishment for assaulting a fellow prisoner. He was granted a certificate of freedom on 22 August 1846.

OBSP, 1836–37, case 508, p. 489; CON 33/71, no. 16640; Register of Convicts on Norfolk Island in August 1844, ML, COD 2.

MYERS, Michael (MIERS)

b. London, 1775
Surrey I (1), 1814; Convict; Sentenced to 7 years, Old Bailey, 1813.
Married; Slop seller; Height: 155 cm; 3 children.

Dark complexion, black to grey hair, black eyes. Michael Myers pulled a coat off the driving box of a chaise that was standing in Portland Place. He put the coat into a green bag that he had tucked under his arm. He was sentenced on 7 April 1813. He was thirty-eight years old.

Michael Myers arrived in New South Wales on 28 July 1814 and on 18 August was forwarded to Parramatta for assigned service. By 1821 he was free by servitude and permitted to leave the colony. On 17 March 1821 he gave notice that he would be leaving in the brig *Campbell Macquarie*. The Principal Superintendent's Office on 25 August 1821 recorded the name of Judith Myers (q.v.) (who was free) on a list of prisoners to embark on the *Campbell Macquarie* for Hobart Town: 'Judith Myers and three children, to join her husband by order of his Excellency … the Governor'. Myers remained in Hobart Town until 1827. On 21 May 1827 he was fined five shillings for misbehaviour and was listed as 'Free by Servitude'. Myers returned to Sydney and was listed (as Michael Miers) in the 1828 Census as free by servitude, a Jew, a labourer, and lodging at Patrick Conlon's in Clarence Street, Sydney. Judith and the three children were not with him.

OBSP, 1813, case 477, p. 273; *Surrey I* (1) Indent 4/4004, p. 549; *Sydney Gazette*, 17 March 1821; CS In Correspondence, 4/1750, p. 76.

MYERS, Moses

b. London
Free.
Fishmonger.

Moses Myers, known in the colony as 'Fishmonger Moses Myers', was the brother of convicts Edward Myers (q.v.) and Mary Hartnell (q.v.). William Augustus Miles, in the *Registry of Flash Men* (p. 105), wrote, in the mid-1840s, that Moses Myers was the brother of 'the most arrant little rogue in Sydney and his sister is the celebrated Mary Hartnell'.

MYERS, Phillip

b. London, 1803–1865
Free.
Married; Merchant; 2 children.

Phillip Myers was the owner of a residence in George Street, Sydney, in September 1842. On 28 October 1842 Phillip Myers, a butcher at Brickfield Hill, was listed as insolvent. A child, Eve, had been born on 15 January 1842 and registered by the Sydney Synagogue (she died on 5 July 1860, aged eighteen). A male child was also born that year. Phillip Myers was an unsuccessful applicant who applied to the Sydney Synagogue for the post of 'Keeper of the Jews' Burial Ground' on 7 August 1844.

He died on 2 October 1865, age sixty-two, and was buried in the Devonshire Street Cemetery by the Hebrew Mutual Benefit Society.

Sydney Morning Herald, 15 September 1842, 28 October 1842, 8 December 1842; *Australasian Chronicle*, 8 November 1842.

MYERS, Rebecca

Free.
Single; 1 child.

Rebecca Myers married Elijah Joel (q.v.) in Sydney in 1848. A son, Moss Joel, was born in 1849.

MYERS, Samuel

b. London, 1791–1831
Fortune (2), 1813; Convict; Sentenced to life, Old Bailey, 1812.
Single; Groom; Height: 158 cm.

Fair complexion, dark brown hair, brown eyes. Samuel Myers, Israel Saunders and Mordecai Julian robbed a sailor of his purse in which was £57. The other two men stood by as the deed was done. Saunders was found not guilty and Julian was not brought to trial. At the Middlesex Gaol Delivery of 1 July 1812 Myers was sentenced to transportation for life.

Samuel Myers was assigned as a convict servant to Captain Piper from 1813 to 1815 and sent to Newcastle for two years from March 1816. Myers volunteered for work at Moreton Bay and arrived there in 1824. On 14 April 1825 he absconded from his work detail and he was listed as a labourer who was absent from Byrne's Road Party in 1827. It was assumed by officialdom that he had been killed by the Aborigines in the bush in 1831.

OBSP, 1812, case 541, p. 348; Convicts Sent to Newcastle, 23 March 1816, in 4/3494; Chronological Register of Convicts at Moreton Bay, no. 1128; HO 11/3; 1814 Muster, A1225; *Sydney Gazette*, 14 April 1825, 24 March 1827.

MYERS, Samuel (MEYERS)

b. London, 1803–1846
Agamemnon, 1820; Convict; Sentenced to 7 years, Old Bailey, 1820.
Single; Pen-maker; Height: 152 cm.

Dark complexion, black hair, dark eyes. Samuel Myers was transported for stealing the coat of a servant while it hung on the railings outside a house. The coat was valued at seven shillings. On being confronted with the evidence, Myers, aged seventeen, declared: 'Not a word he has spoken is true!' He was sentenced to seven years transportation on 17 February 1820.

Samuel Myers arrived in New South Wales on 22 September 1820, and five days later was sent to Emu Plains for work distribution. On 31 March 1824, while serving Mr Thomas Perry, he was punished at Evans. Samuel Myers received a certificate of freedom on 19 February 1827. In 1832 he was refused permission to marry Eliza Watson, who was still serving a seven-year sentence, because, according to government records, she was already married. Myers married Mary Ann Woodbury at Scots Church in Sydney in 1834. Mary Ann had arrived as a bounty migrant on the *Bussorah Merchant*. The 1837 General Return of Convicts in New South Wales listed a 'Robert' Myers, living at Camden and holder of a ticket of leave.

On 17 July 1839 the Colonial Secretary noted that 'Samuel Myers and his wife are of intemperate habits'. They lived in George Street and were not to receive any more assigned convict servants. He was named in the first Sydney voters' list as the owner of a house in George Street. Samuel Myers 'of Chippendale' was buried in the Devonshire Street Cemetery by the Poor Fund of the Sydney Synagogue on 10 March 1846. An inquest followed his death and the verdict was that he 'died after visitation of God'.

OBSP, 1819–20, case 481, p. 201f.; *Agamemnon* Indent 4/4007, p. 219; 4/6671, p. 68; CF 047/6055; Principal Superintendent of Convicts, Register of Convicts' Applications to Marry, 1831–37, 4/4512, p. 13; Convict File from CS Out, 4/3687, p. 53; *Atlas*, 14 March 1846.

MYERS, Sarah

b. London, 1803–1832
Providence II (1), 1821; Convict; Sentenced to life, London, 1820.
Single; Prostitute; Height: 150 cm; 2 children.

Sarah Myers' first offence occurred when she was aged seventeen and, together with Edith Waterhouse, aged fifteen, she stole a necklace of beads from a 15-month-old baby. The second, much more serious, offence concerned the assault, intimidation and theft of a man enticed into a house of ill repute. Sarah was tried and sentenced for felony with Emanuel Lyons (q.v.), who was her brother. Her gaol report was 'very bad'.

Sarah Myers arrived in Van Diemen's Land on 18 December 1821. On 22 October 1823 she was accused of 'neglect of duty' while working as an assigned convict servant to Mr F. Barnes and sent by the magistrate, the Rev. Knopwood, to the Female Factory. The following year her master James Neill accused her of insolence and she was returned to the Female Factory. On 5 June 1826 she absconded from the service of Mr Munday; she was apprehended fourteen days later at Kangaroo Point and returned to the factory.

Thomas Arnott, a watchmaker in Hobart Town, married Sarah in 1827. Arnott had come to Van Diemen's Land on the *Calcutta* in 1803 and was therefore one of the first Europeans in the colony. At the time they married, Thomas Arnott was described as a turner and chair-maker. Sarah and Thomas had two daughters. Hannah was born in 1830 and Priscilla in 1831. Sarah died 'of fits' in November 1832. The *Hobart Town Courier* of 30 November 1832 noted: 'An inquest was held on Wednesday on the death of Sarah Arnett [*sic*], a Jewess, the wife of a chair maker at Kangaroo Point, who being subject to fits, was found dead in bed. Mr Row who attended was prevented by the form of the Jewish religion from opening the body, in order to give evidence as to the immediate cause of her death, until the Coroner decided that it should be so'. We are left wondering who tried to prevent the post mortem. It may well have been her brother. The Jewish cemetery in Hobart Town had been newly established and this brief newspaper paragraph indicates that the community had begun to establish its own profile of observance.

Sarah's daughters were placed in the Queen's Orphanage in Hobart Town, until Thomas remarried in 1834. His new wife, Sarah Ainsworth, died in 1839, and the two girls were sent back to the orphanage.

CON 40/7; HO 10/41; *Hobart Town Gazette*, 28 October 1826; historical research by Julie M Skellern, Auckland, New Zealand, who reported (in 2004) that she had located 529 descendants of Sarah Myers.

MYERS, William

1787–1834
Surrey I (1), 1814; Convict; Sentenced to life, Chambley Court Martial, 1813.
Soldier; Height: 169 cm.

Sallow complexion, dark brown hair, brown eyes. A soldier in the 100th Regiment, William Myers was tried at Court Martial and initially sentenced to death.

William Myers arrived on 28 July 1814. Myers was granted a ticket of leave in 1829, and a certificate of freedom in 1832. In the General Return of Convicts in New South Wales, William Myers, aged fifty, was listed at Patrick Plains holding a ticket of leave.

In 1834 Joseph Nathan of Singleton and Maitland arranged the Jewish funeral of a William Myers, a prisoner at Patrick Plains. Nathan was reimbursed by the Sydney Synagogue £6 15s 4d for the funeral expenses incurred. Myers had died when a cart ran over him, and his few personal effects—clothes, shoe horn and cigar box—were sold by the police to help defray the cost of the funeral.

CS 39/4902; TL 29/857; CF 32/484.

N

NAPHTALI, Michael

b. Whitechapel, London, 1785 (?)–1847
Glory, 1818; Convict; Sentenced to 7 years, Old Bailey, 1818.
Single; Glasscutter; Height: 173 cm; 11 children.

Dark ruddy complexion, pock-pitted, dark brown hair, dark eyes, 'blind of left eye'. Naphtali was a member of a gang that stole four baskets of glass lamps valued at £30. He was caught trying to sell the lamps. When arrested he was found playing shuttles with a crowd of 'fellow thieves'.

Naphtali arrived in New South Wales on 14 September 1818 and on 22 September was sent to be given work on assignment in the Windsor area. He may well have been assigned to James Dunn, who had been a convict on the Third Fleet and owned a farm at Sackville. On 31 October 1821 Michael Naphtali asked for permission to marry at Windsor and on 17 December 1821, at Windsor, he married Frances (Fanny) Dunn (who had been born in the colony). One year later, in the 1822 Muster, Michael was listed as the owner of a flourishing 30-acre farm, which he had purchased from his father-in-law. By September 1826 Naphtali was in a position to own a general store in York Street from which Sudds and Thompson stole a quantity of cloth in order to obtain a discharge from the army and remain in Australia. He also managed a stall at the market and in December 1826 was reported to have sold it to Joseph Raphael (q.v.) in exchange for Raphael's coat, worth fifteen shillings.

Naphtali was listed in the 1828 Census as 'Free by Servitude', living as a shopkeeper in Pitt Street together with his wife Frances, aged twenty-two, and children Catherine, aged seven, Joseph, aged four, and James, aged two. Catherine was baptised in 1822 and Joseph on 14 November 1824. Michael Naphtali appeared on the published list of licensed publicans on 6 March 1829. His hotel was the Shamrock, Rose and Thistle. In 1830 he held the licence for the Bunch of Grapes in Pitt Street. In 1833 he moved from the Captain Piper in George Street to the Ropemaker's Arms, Market Street. In March 1833 Michael Naphtali was declared to be insolvent and in April he was thrown in prison. He owed the crown £90 and was unable to pay following the loss of a bond from a man called Spicer, who had absconded from the colony. The sheriff freely admitted that Naphtali had been 'left in the lurch'. Naphtali testified that he had 'a large family' and was of 'industrious character'. Naphtali wrote from Market

Street on 5 January 1835 that he had a hard struggle to pay his debt. He had suffered 'recent losses in trade', and had 'six young children and a wife who has been ill'. However, by 3 April 1835, he had paid the court £10 'more'. In 1839 he held the licence for the Bald Faced Stag and was granted permission to allow the public house to stay open after hours. He held the licence until 1845. Both he and his wife were seat holders of the York Street Synagogue when it was dedicated. On 17 March 1847 he was, once again, reported to be bankrupt. Naphtali died on 21 July 1847 and was buried in the Devonshire Street Jewish Cemetery in Sydney.

On 5 October 1849, Frances Naphtali, a widow and pauper, filed for bankruptcy: 'I beg to state that the greater part of my debts were contracted 18 month or 2 years ago when I kept a public house in George Street Sydney which did not answer the rent being too high'.

Their children were Catherine (1822), born at Windsor, Joseph (1824) at Windsor, James (1826), at York Street, Mary Ann (1829–1879), at Pitt Street, Eliza (1831), Benjamin (1833), Henry (1835), Ellen (1838), Maurice (1841), and Alfred (1843), Albert Augustus (1846).

Frances Naphtali married William Everingham in 1850. Her third marriage was to Roger Caine in 1862. She died 2 September 1872 and was buried at Haslem's Creek (Rookwood).

OBSP, 1817–18, case 512, p. 174; Ship Indent 4/4006, p. 77; 4/3504a, p. 47; HO 11/3; Petitions and Memorials, 1827–1832, 14 July 1829, ML, A 2167; *Sydney Gazette*, 16 December 1826, 3 October 1833; *Sydney Morning Herald*, 5 July 1842, 16 September 1843, 7 April 1845; *Sydney Chronicle*, 17 March 1847; CS 4/2298, in 35/2370; family research by Jan and Neil Reid, Greystanes, NSW.

NATANSON, Berthold

Black Swan, 1840; Free.

Berthold Natanson arrived in Launceston on 17 July 1840. He was convicted in the Launceston Quarter Sessions, on 16 August 1854, for stealing two watches and two chains, the property of Mr H. Patching. He was sentenced to be imprisoned in the Launceston Gaol for two years. The remainder of his sentence was remitted by the Lieutenant Governor on 7 March 1855.

Black Swan Indent, CON 37/8, no. 57150, p. 2519.

NATHAN, Abraham (Solomon)

b. Houndsditch, 1785
Chapman (1), 1824; Convict; Sentenced to life, Newgate, 1824.
Labourer and dealer; Height: 162 cm.

Fresh complexion, brown whiskers, long narrow visage, light grey eyes, long nose, large mouth, small chin. A Jew. Scar on right cheek. Abraham Nathan was sentenced for stealing handkerchiefs from a shop. The gaol report noted 'bad connexions'.

Nathan had a long, sad and depressing record. He was initially assigned to J. Jacobs but on 28 November 1825 was returned to the Public Works Department as his master had no means to support himself. On 9 June 1826 he absconded from his work at the punt across the River Derwent and was sentenced to fifty lashes and twelve months in irons. The lashes were held over but on 2 September he received twenty lashes for neglect of duty and for gambling. Three days later he was convicted of insolence to Constable Henderson and sent to Maria Island for three months. On 29 September 1826, while a member of the chain gang on the island, he received fifty lashes for threatening to strike the overseer of the penitentiary and 'abusing' his fellow prisoners. On 17 March 1827 he abused Constable Henry Perry and received a further fifty lashes. On 27 October he was given fifty lashes for 'barking trees' and on 30 May 1828 a further fifty lashes for being drunk, absent from his work party and insolent to a police officer.

In April 1835 Nathan spent two hours in the stocks for being 'out after hours'. In November 1835, while working with the Public Works, he refused to assist Commissioner Allwort, using indecent language to do so, and was sentenced to twelve months with the Second Road Party at Westbury. On 11 January 1837 his insolence, while an assigned servant to Mr Kent, earned him a sentence of two months hard labour in chains at Reibey's Ford. On 11 March 1837 he was found in Launceston without a pass and his sentence was extended by three months. Part of this punishment was due to his 'disorderly and violent conduct before the Police Magistrate'. On 24 October 1837 he was found drunk and sent to join the Oatlands Chain Gang. On 26 October, while a watchman with the Public Works Department, he was charged with stealing a valise. The case was unproven but he was dismissed and returned to the road party.

Nathan received his ticket of leave on 9 September 1840 and a conditional pardon on 27 September 1843, 'having shown definite proof of reformation' according to the official list of Conditional Pardons in 1844. Sadly, on 30 January 1844 he was charged in Launceston with larceny and acquitted on a technicality. A third-class pardon was granted on 19 January 1847. Abraham Nathan's name appeared on the Launceston Synagogue petition of 20 May 1843.

CON 31/29; CON 32/1; *Hobart Town Courier*, 11 September 1840, 6 October 1843; Launceston Police Book, CON 78/2; CON 18/3, no. 338; CP 730; HO 10/58, p. 296.

NATHAN, Asher Isaac (Arthur Isaac)

b. London, 1814–1863
1842; Free.
Single; 7 children.

The son of Nathan Lyon Nathan (q.v.) and Sarah Nathan, Asher Isaac was the twin brother of Rachel Nathan (q.v.), who married Samuel Cohen (q.v.), and brother of Louis Nathan (q.v.), David Nathan (q.v.), and Mrs Rosetta Joseph (Rosetta Nathan, q.v.).

Arthur Isaac Nathan signed the petition for the establishment of a Launceston Synagogue on 20 May 1843. In September he also signed a petition asking for the release from gaol of Isaac Jacobs (q.v.). On 29 June 1844 he donated £50 to the Launceston Synagogue building appeal. In 1845 he officiated at the wedding of John Aaron and in 1853 at the last Jewish wedding in Launceston. Though he was based in Launceston he was one of the members of the Hobart-based Tasmanian Hebrew Benevolent Society at its founding in 1847. On 23 August 1843, at the synagogue in Sydney, Arthur Isaac Nathan married Caroline Cohen (q.v.) of Melbourne, the daughter of Henry Simeon Cohen (q.v.) of Port Macquarie.

Arthur and Caroline Nathan were the parents of Lewis Arthur (30 May 1844–1909), born in Launceston, who would marry his cousin Stella, the daughter of Moses Joseph and his wife Rosetta of Sydney.

Lewis was active in the firm of L. D. Nathan & Co., founded by his uncle David. Walter Isaac Nathan was born in Launceston, went to Wellington, New Zealand, where he joined his cousin Jacob Joseph's business. Their other children were Arthur Hyam Nathan (born 2 May 1847), David (15 May 1849), Edward (25 January 1851), Sarah (29 May 1853), and Sidney Jacob Nathan, the sixth son, who was born in Sydney in 1860 and married Frances Baume.

Arthur Isaac Nathan, 'late of Launceston Tasmania', died in England aged forty-nine on 7 August 1863. He had lived at 28 Tavistock Square, and was buried at the West Ham Jewish Cemetery in London. Caroline died in England in March 1881.

NATHAN, Benjamin (WILLARD)

b. London
Isabella I (1), 1818; Convict; Sentenced to 7 years, London, 1817.
Married; Artist and dentist; Height: 147 cm.

Sickly pale complexion, brown hair, brown eyes. Benjamin Willard alias Nathan was convicted for stealing three beds and their bolsters, three quarts of ale and one cask from a public house at Tower Hill. Willard and his wife lived next door and he was said to own a 'medicine shop'. He was sentenced at Middlesex on 3 December 1817.

Benjamin Nathan arrived in New South Wales on 14 September 1818. The Colonial Secretary's office accepted Nathan's alias of 'Willard' as his surname. On 22 September 1818 he was among the list of prisoners sent to be assigned in Parramatta. On 1 February 1819 it was decided to send him to the penal settlement at Newcastle and, in March 1820, he was punished at Newcastle. On 4 January 1821 he petitioned for a mitigation of his sentence. He was 'of Windsor' and wrote: 'The undersigned humbly begs leave to remind your Excellency of the promises you were pleased to make to me of granting my Liberty through the medium of Mr Cox J. P. I have applied to that gentleman and he refuses to comply'. On 6 February 1822 he was transported to Newcastle again (on the

Elizabeth Henrietta). On 15 February 1823 Willard was removed from Newcastle and sent to Port Macquarie on the *Sally*. A certificate of freedom was issued on 3 December 1824.

OBSP, 1817, case 153; CS 4/1718, p. 100; 4/1863, p. 110; CS Copies of Letters Sent Within the Colony, 1821, 4/3504, p. 403; Principal Superintendent of Convicts, Registers of Certificates of Freedom, 1823–25, 003/2952, in 4/4423; CS Copies of Letters Sent Within the Colony, 1818–19, 4/3499, pp. 57, 295; CS Copies of Letters to Port Macquarie, June–October 1825, 4/3864, p. 503.

NATHAN, Bertram (Burnett)

b. London, 1815–1871
Caroline, 1832; Free.
Single; Dealer; 10 children.

Bertram Nathan arrived in Hobart Town on 12 December 1832. He was the son of Nathaniel Nathan, merchant of London, and Elizabeth (née Levy). His full legal name was 'Isaacar Bertram Nathan'.

Bertram Nathan was seventeen years old when he arrived in New South Wales as a migrant on 2 January 1832. He was listed as giving £5 to the building fund of the Sydney Synagogue in 1839. Nathan, 'who came free to this colony', was sentenced at the Sydney Quarter Sessions of 4 January 1840 for receiving stolen goods. He was convicted of having purchased 100 stolen waistcoats knowing them to have been stolen. He was ordered to spend six months of the seven-year sentence working on the roads. Nathan was transported by the *Abercrombie* to Hobart Town on 12 February 1840.

On 22 June 1840 Nathan became a member of the field police. On 21 July 1840 he was admonished for neglect of duty. On 2 June 1841 he was fined for having made use of indecent language. On 3 December he was sentenced to seven days in solitary confinement for 'misconduct'. On 9 May 1842 he was sent back to work on the roads for six months for having associated with the prisoners and gambled on a Sunday while he held the post of constable. His sentence concluded in October 1842 and he received a ticket of leave on 16 February 1844. On 20 March 1845 he was 'admonished' for being absent from the Sunday morning muster. A conditional pardon, valid in the Australian colonies, was approved on 16 December 1845 for 'having behaved with propriety'.

Nathan left Van Diemen's Land as quickly as he could and by 3 December 1845 he had set up shop in Currie Street in Adelaide. He became a shipping agent for goods bound for Launceston and imported haberdashery from Tasmania. On 20 June 1846 the *South Australian Register* advertised an auction by Emanuel Solomon (q.v.) at B. Nathan's Currie Street premises in consequence of the dissolution of the partnership between Messrs B. Nathan and L. Joseph (Louis Joseph, q.v.). The whole of the stock was to be sold. Nathan finally bought up the other part of the business and announced that 'his wholesale and agency business will be closed on Saturday and on all Jewish holidays'. On 6 August 1846 (in the

South Australian Register) 'Burnett' Nathan proudly advertised 'stock ex *Medway*' as 'the largest and latest assorted stock of fancy goods ever imported into this colony'.

On 17 June 1846 'Isaacher' B. Nathan (aged twenty-nine) married Phoebe Solomons (q.v.), the 16-year-old daughter of Aaron Solomons (q.v.), in Launceston. Phoebe died seven months later, on 6 January 1847, and, on 20 October 1847, Nathan married Ellen Levy (a minor) at the home of her brother, Philip Levy (q.v.) ('Gentleman Levy'), in Bathurst Street in Hobart Town. Ellen Levy had been born in London on 31 July 1831 and had arrived on the *Calcutta* in 1844. Nathan was described as a widower whose profession was 'draper'. They were to have ten children: Elizabeth (27 September 1849 to 29 May 1850), Esther (born 14 October 1850), Priscilla Elizabeth (25 December 1851), Sarah (16 March 1853), Rosetta (1856), Nathaniel (1857), Elizabeth (1858), Alfred (1861), Maurice (1862), and Phillip (1866). The first six children were born in Launceston and the 'first' infant Elizabeth was buried in the Launceston Jewish burial ground. On 31 December 1855 vandals destroyed Elizabeth's gravestone (together with memorials to the children of George Robinson (q.v) and Joshua Lyons). The bereaved parents offered a reward of £25 for information that 'may lead to the conviction of the parties who committed so vile an act'. There was no response from the general public. The family moved to Melbourne in 1858, where Bertram Nathan conducted a business at 59 Latrobe Street. Bertram Nathan died on 10 January 1871, aged fifty-six, and was buried at the Melbourne General Cemetery. Ellen died on 8 October 1890 and was buried beside her husband.

CON 31/32, no. 503; Prisoners Sent from New South Wales to Van Diemen's Land, 4/4523; *South Australian Gazette and Colonial Register*, 3 December 1845, 7 January 1846, 6 August 1846; The Launceston Exaniner, 1, 3, 8 January, 1856. Death Certificate 175859; HO 10/59.

NATHAN, Betsy

b. 1801
Undaunted, 1835; Free.
Single.

Betsy Nathan was a bounty migrant who arrived from England travelling steerage on 3 February 1835. Her full name was Elizabeth Nathan (q.v.).

Ship Indent 4/5208.

NATHAN, Burnett (Baruch)

b. London, 1817–1865
1833; Free.
Merchant; 7 children.

Burnett Baruch Nathan was the last of the sons of Nathan Lyon Nathan (q.v.) and Sarah Nathan of 13 New Quebec Street, London, to reach Australia.

On 10 June 1833 the *Launceston Independent* carried the announcement that the 16-year-old 'Burnett Nathan begs to intimate to the Public generally that he has just arrived in Launceston where he intends to carry on the business of French Polisher'. With the establishment of the township of Adelaide, Nathan moved to South Australia, leaving his original occupation behind him. He briefly returned to London to marry MaryAnne Collins (Nathan, q.v.) (daughter of Hyman Collins, né Kalisch) at her parents' home at 29 Orchard Street, Marylebone, on 12 March 1845.

On 14 March 1846 the *South Australian Gazette and Colonial Register* announced that Mr Burnett Nathan was a ships' agent for goods to and from Western Australia and Manila. The *Launceston Examiner* published the advertisement that 'Burnett Nathan, General Importer and Commission Agent, Adelaide begs to intimate to merchants and others in Van Diemen's Land that he is prepared to receive consignments'.

Burnett Nathan was a staunch supporter of the local Jewish congregation and became its first president. He gave the new Adelaide Hebrew congregation an Ark. The *Register* did not fully understand its purpose and wrote that Nathan had presented to the congregants a most splendid repository for the voluntary offerings of his fellow worshippers whose contributions will, it is hoped, now enable the children of Israel to erect a Temple to their God in Adelaide. The cabinet is somewhat of a sarcophagus form made from the finest variegated Australian cedar. It is a superb example of colonial workmanship. Its inscription reads '*Kall* [*sic*] *Nidchi Israel* (All the dispersed of Israel) Presented by Mr Burnett Nathan to the congregation of Adelaide on Wednesday 27 May 1846'.

One day after the presentation, Elizabeth Joshua (q.v.) of Hindley Street was married to Mr Charles Jacobs (q.v.) of Sydney by Burnett Nathan, who acted 'under authority from Sydney'. On 16 September, under the headline 'Local Improvements', it was reported that 'Mr Burnett Nathan (one of our many fortunate newcomers) is occupying some of the site of the late Southern Cross Hotel by nine cottage residences'. On 14 April 1848 Nathan advertised that he was 'the agent for the ship *Harriet Nathan* sailing for Hobart Town'.

Burnett Nathan was again elected president of the congregation in 1849, and in 1859. He later returned to live in England. On his death he was buried in the Jewish Cemetery at West Ham. The tombstone inscription reads 'Late of Adelaide, South Australia. Died 30 June 1865, age 48'. His wife MaryAnne died in London on 13 August 1868, aged forty-three.

Their children, born in Adelaide, were: Caroline (11 November 1848, who died seven months later), Sarah (28 December 1845, who died three and a half years later), Charlotte (11 March 1847), Nathaniel (7 October 1851), Mary (4 January 1854), Julia (27 September 1855), and Hyam (27 September 1855).

Independent (Launceston), 1 June 1833; *Launceston Examiner*, 7 October 1846; *South Australian Gazette and Colonial Register*, 14 March 1846, 24 May 1846, 30 May 1846, 16 September 1846, 15 April 1848; Pritchard Index.

NATHAN, David

b. London, 1816–1886
Orient, 1839; Free.
Single; Merchant; 4 children.

A son of Nathan Lyon Nathan (q.v.) and Sarah Nathan of London, David Nathan arrived in Sydney travelling steerage on the barque *Orient* on 8 December 1839. Nathan had intended to settle in Adelaide but because of the colonial depression he sailed by the *Achilles* for New Zealand and the trading settlement of Kororareka, arriving there on 21 February 1840, just two weeks after New Zealand had been proclaimed a British colony. Nathan set up his store on the beach front, stocked with goods he had bought in London from the capital of £100 given to him by his uncle, Henry Moses. Moses Joseph (q.v.) came to Auckland and bought land at the first land sale on 19 April 1841 which he then leased to David Nathan and to his brother Israel Joseph (q.v.).

David Nathan established the 'Commercial House' in Auckland in 1841. The business was closed on the Sabbath and Holydays and the first Jewish religious services were held in his home. In October 1841 David Nathan and Israel Joseph travelled northwards to Kororareka at the Bay of Islands to welcome Rosetta Aarons, a young widow from Hobart Town. Her first husband, Michael Aarons, had been a sea captain who had been lost at sea while travelling to Australia. Rosetta arrived with her Hebrew marriage certificate, which was copied for her second *ketuvah*.

The first Jewish marriage in New Zealand, between David and Rosetta, therefore took place at Kororareka on 31 October 1841. Israel Joseph performed the ceremony and the marriage was witnessed by George Russell (q.v.), a 'hotel keeper'.

The *Shipping Gazette of New South Wales* reported that David Nathan had exported 10 bales of 'slops' (ready-made clothes) to Auckland on 22 and 29 November 1845. Nathan founded the oldest surviving, and very successful, mercantile business in New Zealand. Moses Joseph had bought land in Auckland in order to establish his brother Israel and his first cousin and brother-in-law David and his blind brother Jacob Joseph in Wellington. The two-acre allotment was on the corner of Shortland Crescent and High Street and the first 'Nathan and Joseph' store opened for business on 14 August 1841. On 10 January 1843 David and Rosetta's eldest daughter, Sarah, was born. In 1846 their son Laurence David was born in Auckland; the child was circumcised in Sydney in the following year. The circumcision was performed by Samuel Moses (q.v.) of Hobart Town. In 1848 David and Rosetta celebrated the arrival of a daughter, Elizabeth. A son, Nathan, was born in 1850.

Nathan was president of the newly formed Auckland Hebrew Congregation in 1854, in 1860, and from 1878 to 1883. (He was elected to the first Auckland Borough Council but did not serve.) He was one of the commissioners set up to operate the Port of Auckland Board. He was president of the Chamber of

Commerce and was appointed trustee of the Auckland Savings Bank in 1864, and served until 1885.

L. M. Goldman, *The History of the Jews of New Zealand*; Howard T. Nathan, 'Rosetta Joseph: The Bell, Her Husband and the Money', *AJJHS*, vol. 17 (2003), no. 1, p. 11; Lawrence D. Nathan, *As Old as Auckland*.

NATHAN, Edward

b. London, 1779–1861
Margaret, 1835; Free.
Married; Shoemaker.

Edward Nathan arrived steerage at Hobart Town with his wife Hannah, son Michael (q.v.) aged twenty-eight and his daughter Fanny (Frances) (q.v.), and granddaughters Maria, aged eighteen, and Rosetta (q.v.), aged twenty. He became the licensee of a public house, the Talbot Inn, on Melville Street. On 2 September 1842 a new licence for his public house was refused. He was a member of the Hobart Synagogue in 1842 and in April 1843 gave £1 to the building fund. The Nathan family left Hobart Town in 1845 and went to Melbourne, where Edward opened a clothing shop in Elizabeth Street.

In January 1845 Edward Nathan gave his first donation to the Melbourne Hebrew Congregation. On 18 July 1845 he was among the group who petitioned the board 'to consider the propriety of making guerists'. He was also one of five general dealers who were fined five shillings for exposing their goods for sale on the footpath in front of their shops. 'Edmund' Nathan's name was on the list of the Jews in Port Phillip who signed an address congratulating new Chief Rabbi Nathan Adler on his appointment. Edward Nathan died, 'at the bar of his hotel'-the Royal Hotel- in Orange in 1861 and his death is reported in some detail in the Western Examiner mentioning his nephew Asher Nelson and nephew Harris Levy Nelson MLA.

Margaret Indent 4/5208; *Hobart Town Courier*, 2 September 1842; *Port Phillip Gazette*, 5 April 1845.

NATHAN, Elias

b. 1768
Barwell, 1798; Convict; Sentenced to 7 years, Old Bailey, 1797.
Dealer.

Elias Nathan (who lived in Piccadilly) owed a woman £80. He had, in his possession, a stolen Bill of Exchange valued at £19 13s 6d. Nathan owned a sale shop in Swallow Street and asked the woman to cash the stolen cheque on his behalf, 'as it was his Sabbath'. He was sentenced on 11 January 1797.

The *Barwell* arrived in New South Wales on 18 May 1798. In the Settlers' Muster Book of 1800 (List 4) he was listed as a person 'off stores'. In Sydney, on Saturday 1 January 1802, Elias Nathan was charged with having sold a quantity of black calico to Elizabeth Bennet that had been stolen from Simeon Lord's warehouse.

Nathan claimed to have bought it from a sailor who had 'gone southward' on a whaling expedition. He was to be bound over on bail until the sailor returned.
OBSP, 1796–97, case 98, p. 139; 4/4003, p. 345; Minutes of Bench of Magistrates, 1 January 1802, 12/35, ML, 1/299.

NATHAN, Elizabeth

Undaunted, 1835; Free.
Single; Servant.

On 1 April 1835 Elizabeth Nathan of Pitt Street in Sydney sent a 'humble petition' to the Colonial Secretary's office in Sydney concerning 'the theft of her meagre possessions', which a Mr Bryant, a fellow passenger in steerage, had persuaded her to place in his trust. When the migrant ship arrived in Australia in February 1835 Mr Bryant 'forgot' to return her property and used it to pay for his passage. The ship's agent then impounded Elizabeth's bedding and clothes. She had been to the police, who failed to take her complaint seriously, leaving her 'destitute without a second change of clothes'. The official response was that it was too early to take action.
CS Letters Received, 1825, Miscellaneous, 35/2378, in 4/2284.2.

NATHAN, Esther

b. London
Orient, 1839; Free.
Single.

Esther Nathan, the daughter of Nathan Lyon Nathan (q.v.) and Sarah Nathan (q.v.), arrived from London on the *Orient* on 10 December 1839. Esther's sister was Rosetta (Nathan, q.v.), the wife of Moses Joseph (q.v.) of Sydney. Esther married Moses Moss (Moses Moses, q.v.) on 16 November 1842 in Sydney in Jewish marriage no. 55. They lived first in Launceston and then in Sydney.

NATHAN, Frances

1808–1844
Margaret, 1835; Free.
Married; 4 children.

Frances, her husband, Michael Nathan (q.v.), and their daughter, Rosetta, arrived in Sydney in 1835. Frances had three children in New South Wales: Woolf, who was born in 1840, at Illawarra, and two other sons, both of whom seem to have died in infancy. Fanny (Frances) Nathan died on 12 August 1844, aged thirty-six.

Her funeral was the first to be arranged by the Hobart Town congregation, and her infant child was buried with her.

NATHAN, Frances

d. 1898
Free.
Single; 5 children.

Frances, the daughter of Edward and Hannah Nathan, married Benjamin Nelson (q.v.) in Hobart Town on 9 November 1842. Their son, Henry, died at the age of seven months in 1844 and was buried at the Harrington Street cemetery.

NATHAN, Gaucher Burton

b. 1817
Free.
Single.

Gaucher Burton Nathan, aged twenty-nine, married Phoebe Solomon (q.v.), aged nineteen, in Launceston on 17 June 1846.

NATHAN, Harriette (née MOSES)

b. London 1834; Free.
Married; 4 children.

Harriette was the wife of Louis Nathan (q.v.).

NATHAN, Henry

1842; Free.
Single.

Henry Nathan was a friend of Edward Isaacs (q.v.) and was part of the group of young congregational activists who helped establish a synagogue in Hobart Town. He was a member of the Hobart Synagogue in 1842–45. He sang in the choir at the consecration service and was chosen to read a psalm in Hebrew at the service. He was allocated seat no. 73 in the synagogue. On 17 September 1843 the congregational committee voted to give Henry Nathan a new suit of clothes in recognition of his poor financial situation and his enthusiastic support for the congregation. In 1844 he successfully tendered for the task of baking the congregational Passover *matzah*.

Nathan was in Sydney in the 1870s and followed the gold rush to Dunedin, New Zealand.

NATHAN, Hyam Edward

b. London, 1828–1885
1833; Free.

Hyam Edward Nathan, son of Nathan Lyon Nathan (q.v.) and Sarah Nathan (q.v.), and brother of Rosetta Nathan (q.v.), arrived from London and briefly settled in Sydney (1833) and later moved to Dunedin. His family business was to grow into the multinational business of Glaxo and Woolworths (New Zealand).

NATHAN, Isaac

b. Canterbury, 1790–1864
York, 1841; Free.
Married; Musician; 12 children.

The son of the Cantor Menahem Mona, a Polish language master, Isaac Nathan told the preposterous story that he was an illegitimate son of King Stanilaus II. In 1814, at his suggestion, Lord Byron wrote a series of poems on Jewish themes and Nathan set them to music, making use of melodies from his father's synagogue. Nathan's life in England was 'colourful'. He gambled heavily, eloped twice with his pupils, was prosecuted for assaulting an Irish peer and fought a duel for the honour of Lady Caroline Lamb. Isaac Nathan's musical career in England came to an abrupt end in 1838 when Lord Melbourne refused to pay him £2000 for a mysterious (and imaginative) mission to Europe. By that time he had six children to support, and a second wife. To avoid further confrontation, he set sail for Australia. (His second wife would also bear him six children.)

The *Port Philip Patriot* of 8 February 1841 reported that Isaac Nathan had arrived in Australia by the *York*. He was described as 'an eminent scholar and musician and the bosom friend of Lord Byron'. The *Australasian Chronicle* of 8 April reported: 'Mr Nathan and family has arrived in Sydney. We hope that he is destined to enjoy a long and brilliant career in his adopted land, with profit to himself, and with much gratification to the community'. One week later the same newspaper announced (13 April 1841): 'We are happy to announce that this talented musician and his family have been engaged to conduct the choir at St Mary's Cathedral'. Nathan also established his Sydney Academy for the Formation, Cultivation and Management of the Human Voice and on 30 June 1841 presented a Grand Oratorio of the Sacred Music at St Mary's Cathedral, performing music by Handel and Nathan, for which 'Mr Nathan has engaged every professional musician in the colony'. In early

July 1841 it was reported that 'the whole society of Sydney attended the concert including the American Vice Consul, the Vicar General and about twenty of the clergy. Beethoven's Mass in C was sung for the first time'. On 25 December 1841 the *Australasian Chronicle* boasted 'The Choir of St Mary's under the laborious and judicious induction of Mr Nathan will soon be one of the best in the British Empire. Mozart's Mass will be presented at Christmas'.

Isaac Nathan was Australia's first serious composer. Australia's first opera, *Merry Freaks and Troubl'lous Times*, was privately presented in 1843. The libretto was written by Jacob Levi Montefiore (q.v.). 1844 was a hectic year. On 1 March Isaac Nathan, 'composer of music', was listed on the Insolvency Index. He composed an ode for the inauguration of Sydney's first municipal council titled 'Australia Wide and Free'. He wrote two choral pieces, 'Long Live Victoria' and 'Hail Star of the South'. He was in charge of the music at the dedication of the York Street Synagogue in 1844. He conducted the choir and wrote a number of compositions for the great day. In 1846 he wrote an elegy mourning the death of the explorer Leichhardt but then Leichhardt's return to civilisation forced Nathan to hurriedly write 'The Greeting Home Again'.

In May 1847 Nathan produced *Don John of Austria*, Australia's second opera, which has a strong Jewish historical theme. The *Atlas* reviewed the opera on 8 May 1847: 'Public expectations had been raised very high by reports of its great literary and musical merits—yet the music I found very heavy dull and uninteresting, the language not very select—soul-less music. It will never, in its present heavy form, at least, be a favourite with an Australian audience'. In 1849 Nathan published *The Southern Euphrosyne and Australian Miscellany*, which included the first attempt to transcribe and present Aboriginal music. The *Australasian Chronicle* wrote of 'Koorinda Braia—A Genuine Aboriginal Native Song' that 'it is destined to be preserved as a memorial of ancient Australian melody after the race of ill-fated aborigines have ceased forever to sing and hold their corroborees'.

Nathan built a large house in Randwick, which he nostalgically called Byron Lodge. He died alighting from a horsedrawn tram in Sydney on 15 January 1864 and was survived by a family of twelve children.

One of his sons, Alfred Nathan, sang as a basso in Nathan's concert in Sydney on 16 October 1847. Another son, Charles, became a prominent physician and had fifteen children of his own. Eight of Isaac Nathan's children founded families. Although he had remained a Jew, and was remembered within the family reciting his morning prayers draped in a prayer shawl, despite this recollection Isaac Nathan was buried in the Anglican cemetery at Camperdown in New South Wales.

Graham Pont, 'The Rediscovery of Isaac Nathan: Or Merry Freaks in Troub'lous Times', *AJJHS*, vol. 12, no. 1 (1993) and *Isaac Nathan's Songs; in Glenarvon and Ada Reis: Leaves from a Secret History*, AJJHS, vol. 19, part 4 (2010); *Atlas*, 27 June 1846, 8 May 1847; *Australasian Chronicle*, 8 April 1841, 13 April 1841, 6 May 1841, 19 June 1841, 3 July 1841, 6 July 1841, 25 December 1841; Catherine Mackerras, 'Isaac Nathan', in *ADB*, vol. 2, p. 279f.; *AG*, p. 132f. The Opera 'Don John of Austria' arranged by Sir Charles Mackerras is recorded by the Sydney Symphony, great, great, great grandson of Isaac Nathan (2011). ABC Classics 4764114.

NATHAN, Isaac

Free.
Married; 1 child.

Isaac and his wife Maria of Sydney had a son, Henry, in 1836 and registered him as a 'Hebrew'.

NATHAN, John

b. London, 1802–1838
Charles Kerr, 1837; Convict; Sentenced to 7 years, Old Bailey, 1837.
Widower; Old clothes man; Height: 166 cm.

Very dark sallow complexion, dark brown hair, hazel eyes. Jew. Could read. Lost two front upper teeth, marks of cupping on back of neck. John Nathan was an 'old clothes man' who stole a coat from a tailor's shop off Oxford Street. Three months later the tailor recognised him in Whitechapel and seized him. Nathan had been previously convicted for theft. He was sentenced to transportation on 2 January 1837.

John Nathan arrived in New South Wales on 9 October 1837 and was assigned to Mr G. Rouse at Penrith. At Copper Valley, William Thompson recalled: 'We have to work 14 to 18 hours sometimes up to our knees in cold water'. Following a convict uprising, he recounted: 'on Saturday July 2, 1838 we were all paraded in front of the scaffold. The nine unfortunate men were all paraded in front of the scaffold. The nine unfortunate men came on with a firm step. Among them were John Nathan, George Cox, Edward Hull from the Old Bailey. The nine men seemed to cry out with one voice "We die happy!"'

Hugh Anderson, *Farewell to Judges and Juries*, Red Rooster Press, Melbourne, 2000, p. 488; there appears to be a mistake regarding the year of the execution; *Charles Kerr* Printed Indent, p. 159, no. 37-2202, X640; General Returns of Convicts in New South Wales 1837.

NATHAN, Joseph

b. London, 1813–1866
Coromandel (3), 1838; Convict; Sentenced to 7 years, Central Criminal Court, 1832.
Married; Height: 174 cm; 3 children.

Dark complexion, round large head, black hair, black whiskers, dark brown eyes, large thick nose, broad chin, slightly pock-pitted. Joseph Nathan was sentenced on 29 January 1832 for larceny. On 29 January 1838 he was convicted for stealing two sheets and two shirts from a private house. His hulk report was 'Bad'. He had a wife, Esther (Hester), in London with two children.

Joseph Nathan arrived in Van Diemen's Land on 25 October 1838. A ticket of leave was granted on 3 November 1842. Joseph Nathan signed the Launceston Synagogue petition on 20 May 1843 and gave £3 to the Launceston Synagogue building appeal in 1844. On 9 February 1844 Joseph Nathan was bound over to keep the peace on a bond of £25 following a complaint from Aaron Solomons (q.v.).

A conditional pardon was approved on January 1845 and he was free by servitude on 29 June 1845. The *Launceston Examiner* reported on 7 July 1849 that eight yards of flannel had been stolen from Joseph Nathan's shop. The prosecution against a suspected thief fell through as 'Mr Nathan appeared particularly anxious to let the Attorney General know that he was unable to swear to the flannel'. On 17 August 1851 Joseph Nathan of Launceston wrote to the Hobart synagogue and asked that his son be circumcised. He stated that his 'wife' was 'a Christian woman'. (The response is not known as the synagogue's committee ceased to meet following its August meeting.) Joseph Nathan married Eliza McDermott, aged twenty-one, in Launceston on 23 July 1852. On 28 November 1864 Nathan was sentenced at Launceston to four years gaol for 'removing goods with intent to defraud his creditors'. Nathan died at the Port Arthur prison on 15 February 1866.

OBSP 29 January 1838, case 620. CON 37/10; CON 31/32, no. 468; CON 18/5; *Launceston Examiner*, 29 June 1844, 7 July 1849; CF 154/1845; *Hobart Town Courier*, 1 December 1843; *Launceston Examiner*, 9 February 1844, 7 July 1849.

NATHAN, Julia

b. London 1839; Free.
Single; 8 children.

Julia was the youngest child of Nathan Lyon Nathan (q.v.) and Sarah, and sister of Rosetta Joseph (Nathan, q.v.), Louis (q.v.), Asher Isaac Nathan (q.v.), Rachel (q.v.), David (q.v.), Esther (q.v.), Miriam (q.v.) and Burnett (q.v.). She married David Cohen (q.v.), a brother of Samuel Cohen (q.v.).

NATHAN, Louis

b. London, 1811–1886
1834; Free.
Married; Merchant; 4 children.

A son of Sarah and Nathaniel Lyon Nathan (q.v.), Louis Nathan was the first of Rosetta Joseph's (Nathan, q.v.) brothers to arrive in Australia. On 22 February 1834 he married Harriette, who was the granddaughter of his uncle Hyam (Henry) and Esther Nathan.

Louis and Harriette Nathan arrived in Sydney in 1834. They briefly stayed with Rosetta and Moses Joseph (q.v.), before setting sail for Hobart Town. They arrived in Van Diemen's Land with their son and three daughters. Louis opened a general warehouse in 1839 in Elizabeth Street in partnership with Samuel Jacob Moses (q.v.), his wife's cousin and brother-in-law. His firm traded extensively in China and the South Seas. By 1843 Nathan, Moses & Co. operated from Commercial House at the corner of Murray and Liverpool streets.

Nathan was elected president of the Hobart Congregation at its first meeting on 16 January 1842 and rented seat no. 5. In 1843 Nathan donated £100 to the initial

Hobart Synagogue building appeal. Mrs Nathan founded the Tasmanian Hebrew Benevolent Institution (*Nediv Yad*) in 1847. Louis Nathan was president of the synagogue for eleven years and left for England in 1848. He was the only Jewish member of the Hobart Town Jockey Club—a high social distinction! Nathan returned to the colony and lived in Launceston. The *Launceston Examiner* reported, on 29 February 1849, that Nathan, Moses & Co. were owners of the whaling brigs *Grecian*, *Marianne*, *Nimrod*, *Prince Regent* and the *Pryde*. They owned five of the thirty-eight whaling boats (in partnership with the sea captains) that were listed in Hobart Town. Louis Nathan and his wife Harriette returned to England to live in Tavistock Square. Louis Nathan died as a result of an accident on 28 May 1886. His estate was estimated at £72, 285.

Louis Nathan's generous financial support enabled his brothers and sisters to create an astonishing mercantile network in colonial Australia: it included Rosetta, the wife of Moses Joseph, of Sydney, Asher (Arthur) Isaac Nathan (q.v.), David Nathan (q.v.) of New Zealand, Burnett Nathan (q.v.) of South Australia, Miriam Benjamin (Nathan, q.v.) of Melbourne, Esther (Mrs Moses Moss) (Nathan, q.v.) of New South Wales, Rachel (Mrs Samuel Cohen) (Nathan, q.v.) of Sydney, and Julia (Mrs David Cohen of Maitland) (Nathan, q.v.).

Herbert A Wolff, 'A Century of Hobart Jewry', *AJJHS*, vol. 2, no. 1 (1944), p. 3f; *Jewish World*, London, 7 May 1886; *Hobart Town Courier*, March 1844; *Launceston Examiner*, 29 February 1849; P. Elias and A. Elias (eds), *A Few from Afar*.

NATHAN, Mark

b. London, 1814–1898
Free

Mark Nathan was born in England on 8 March 1814. On 24 May 1852, in New York, he married the seventeen year old Flora Horowitz whose brother Henry Horowitz (q.v.) arrived in Hobart Town in 1842 and remained there until 1861. In 1853 Mark and Flora followed Mark from New York to Melbourne and then to Hobart. For the next eighteen years they lived in Tasmania. Mark was the owner of a drapers' shop at 161 Liverpool Street and then became a pawnbroker at 154 Liverpool Street. He was active in the congregation until his departure for Melbourne in 1863. Flora and Mark Nathan eventually moved to Sydney where they both died within months of each other in 1898. They had seven children.

Peter and Ann Elias, 'The View from Afar', 2005, p. 90

NATHAN, MaryAnne (née COLLINS, KALISH)

b. London, 1825–1868
1847; Free.
Married; 7 children.

MaryAnne was the wife of Burnett Baruch Nathan (q.v.), who returned to England to marry her on 12 March 1845. Their first child was born in Adelaide in 1848 when MaryAnne was twenty-three years old. (Burnett Nathan had first arrived in Van Diemen's Land when he was sixteen years old, in 1833.)

NATHAN, Maurice (Morris)

b. London, 1834–1893
1849; Free.

Maurice Nathan was a free migrant who arrived in Van Diemen's Land in the late 1840s. He set up a store at Port Sorrell, 15 kilometres east of the Mersey River on the northern coast of Tasmania. He opened the Great Western Store in 1855 and a second store at Green's Creek in the early 1860s. He moved to Latrobe in 1863 and built a small wharf for the export of timber palings to the growing city of Melbourne across Bass Strait. In 1877, in partnership with Mr Henry Murray, he formed a shipping business, Nathan, Murray and Co. Nathan was also one of the founders of the North East Coast Navigation Company, which owned and operated a small steamer called the *Amy*. In 1878 Nathan and Murray became grain and general produce merchants on the northern coast of the island. Nathan died at Latrobe on 15 September 1893. His sister Esther Brody (née Nathan) had married Joshua Lyons (q.v.) of Torquay in 1862 and Maurice was a witness at the wedding. 'M. Nathan' lived at Latrobe in northern Tasmania in the 1860s, according to an undated Launceston Synagogue's membership list. The Hobart Congregation's records show that an account was sent by the synagogue to Michael Nathan in 1870.

Maurice Nathan was buried in the Jews' Burial Ground in Launceston on 16 September 1893.

Terry Lyons, *The Launceston Lyons*, privately printed, Townsville, Qld, 2004.

NATHAN, Michael (Abraham)

b. London
Margaret, 1835; Free.
Married; Dealer, shoemaker; 4 children.

Michael Nathan and his wife Frances (Fanny) (q.v.) arrived in Sydney on the *Margaret* on 10 January 1835. On 7 July 1836 the family appeared at Sydney's Central Criminal Court on a charge of assault. Michael Nathan was fined £10. Michael's wife Frances Nathan was deemed to be not guilty and discharged.

In 1840, at Illawarra, Michael and Fanny had a son and named him Woolf. Two more male children were born in 1842 and 1843 but not named on the official register and probably died in infancy.

The family moved from Sydney to Hobart Town and Frances, wife of Michael Nathan, died on 18 August 1844, aged thirty-six and it was listed as the first Jewish funeral organised by the Hobart Hebrew Congregation.

Michael Nathan remained a member of the Hobart Town Synagogue in 1842 and on 11 March 1843 gave £1 to the building fund. Nathan also gave the first donation to the Melbourne Hebrew Congregation's building appeal. His signature appears when five members wrote (on 18 July 1845) calling a meeting of 'all the Jews in Melbourne to consider the propriety of making converts'. On 20 May 1851 Michael Nathan, a widower of Melbourne, married Anne Nathan. On 4 March 1853 Michael Nathan asked the Melbourne Jewish Philanthropic Soceity for a loan of £15. His request was refused.

Ship Indent 4/5208; Sydney Criminal Court 1836, 4/6448; 18 July 1845, Melbourne Hebrew Congregation Letter Book.

NATHAN, Miriam

b. London, 1825–1882
1840; Free.
Single; 17 children.

The daughter of Nathan Lyon Nathan (q.v.) and Sarah Nathan of London, Miriam was a sister of Louis Nathan (q.v.), David Nathan (q.v.), and Mrs Rosetta Joseph (Nathan, q.v.), and therefore a sister-in-law and a cousin of Moses Joseph (q.v.). Miriam arrived in Sydney and stayed with Rosetta and Moses Joseph. Miriam married Solomon Benjamin (q.v.) in Sydney on 11 August 1841 and set up her household in Melbourne. She was the great great grandmother of the author of this book!

NATHAN, Nathan

b. Spitalfields, 1819
Lady Raffles, 1841; Convict; Sentenced to 10 years, Central Criminal Court, 1840.
Single; Hawker; Height: 164 cm.

Stout. Fresh complexioned, dark brown hair and eyes, a round face, broad nose, small mouth and a double chin. Could neither read nor write. Nathan was sentenced to transportation for picking pockets. He had a previous conviction for hawking without a licence. His behaviour on the ship was reported to be 'indifferent'. He had been sentenced in London on 17 June 1840.

Nathan arrived in Van Diemen's Land on 17 March 1841. His period of probation was fifteen months, which was extended twice by an additional eleven months. He received good reports for his work as a sawyer. However, on 21 July 1841 he was charged with misconduct, in conspiring with other men to make a false statement respecting two prisoners named Smith and Cowderoy. His sentence was extended by three months. Shortly after this he received twenty-five lashes for 'violently striking a fellow prisoner in the hut'. His time on probation finally ended on 17 May 1843.

Nathan worked as an assigned servant in Richmond and in Launceston. On 11 May 1847 he received his ticket of leave. In January 1848 he was given fourteen days hard labour for being in a public house during Divine Service and later the same year, in Launceston, he was given one month's hard labour for 'inducing a female prisoner, the wife of another man, to leave her home'. He was then not permitted to live in either Hobart Town or Launceston and was sent to Oatlands. He attempted to return to Launceston and on 7 December 1848, in Oatlands, received a six-month sentence for trying to bribe a constable so that the pass restrictions could be changed so that he could return to live in Hobart Town or Launceston.

On 2 April 1850 he received permission to marry Mary Ann Brennan, at Longford, who had come as a convict on the *Elizabeth and Henry* in 1845. Finally, on 18 June 1850, Nathan received his certificate of freedom.

CON 33/6, no. 9970; CON 52/3, p. 330.

NATHAN, Nathan (Nathaniel) Lyon (Nathaniel NEWTON)

b. London, 1784–1850
Royal Admiral I (2), 1800; Convict; Sentenced to 7 years, Old Bailey, 1799.
Single; Apprentice; 9 children (born in England).

Nathaniel, the 16-year-old son of Judah Nathan of Amsterdam, snatched a parcel away from an old woman in Cornhill. Upon being arrested he told the police that his name was Isaac Newton. He was described as an apprentice. He was sentenced on December 1799.

The *Royal Admiral* arrived in New South Wales on 20 November 1800 as part of the Third Fleet. Nathan left the colony when his sentence expired. He applied to leave in January 1807 on the *King George*, and on 14 March 1807 on the *Dart*. The *Sydney Gazette* advertised for the following three years that he had mail waiting for him at the Post Office (20 August 1809, 19 November 1809, 17 March 1810).

Nathan's full name was Nathan Lyon Nathan. Almost immediately after his return to London from Australia on 11 November 1807 he married Sarah Nathan at the Great Synagogue in Duke's Place, and with his marriage came prosperity. Their eldest daughter, Rosetta Nathan (q.v.), travelled to Sydney as a free immigrant in order to marry her first cousin and convict, Moses Joseph (q.v.). Rosetta was the niece of Henry Moses of the wholesale clothing warehouse in Monkton and Cannon streets in London.

Rosetta's aunt Esther (the sister of Sarah) had married Henry Moses who owned a wholesale clothing warehouse in Monkton and Cannon streets and who backed each member of his extended family with £100 worth of goods when they emigrated.

The Bequest Board in the Hobart Town Synagogue records that both Nathan Lyon Nathan and his wife left money to the synagogue even though they both lived in London. A son, Louis Nathan (q.v.), of Hobart Town, was the synagogue's first president.

Another son, Asher Isaac Nathan (q.v.), emigrated to Van Diemen's Land in 1842. A daughter, Rachel (q.v.) (1813), married Samuel Cohen (q.v.) in Sydney on 23 August 1837. Other children were David (q.v.), Burnett (q.v.), Esther (Moss) (q.v.), Julia (Cohen) (q.v.), and Miriam (Solomon Benjamin) (q.v.).

Nathan Lyon Nathan died in 1850 and left an estate of £800. His generosity to the young family members during his lifetime had a profound influence on the development of the Jewish community in Australia and New Zealand.

OBSP, 1799–1800, case 46, p. 28; HO 11/1, p. 263; *Sydney Gazette*, 4 January 1807, 15 March 1807, 20 August 1809, 19 November 1809, 17 March 1810; Howard T. Nathan, 'The Benefits of a Conviction', *AJJHS*, vol. 13, no. 1 (1995).

NATHAN, Nathaniel

b. London, 1799
Surrey I (6), 1831; Convict; Sentenced to 14 years, Middlesex, 1830.
Married; Cook, butcher, drover; Height: 168 cm; 4 children.

Dark ruddy complexion, black hair, brown eyes, perpendicular scar right side upper lip. Can read. A Jew. No previous conviction. Nathaniel Nathan was transported for stealing cloth. He married Edal daughter of Menachem Mendel at the New Synagogue in London on 11 June 1829. At the time of his transportation he had one daughter in England.

Nathan arrived in New South Wales on 20 November 1831 and was initially assigned to Mr H. Peppercorn, and then to Samuel Lyons (q.v.). He received a ticket of leave in 1838 for the District of Maitland. The pass was cancelled on 11 April 1839 for 'highly disorderly and immoral conduct'. His 'conduct' consisted of 'seducing a young female named Harriet Smith. Mr Poole [David Poole, q.v.] appeared for Nathan who has been the assigned servant to Abraham Elias' (q.v.). The girl had been an adopted member of the household of Elias and had become pregnant (*Sydney Gazette*, 21 March 1839). Nathan was sentenced to gaol for two months and returned to the Hyde Park Barracks in Sydney. On 4 May 1839 Nathan was given a further two months hard labour for 'trafficking' at the Barracks.

Nathan's ticket of leave was restored on 12 May 1841 on the condition that Nathan was 'to be employed at a distance from Sydney'. He was sent to Melbourne and became the messenger at the Melbourne Gaol. A certificate of freedom followed on 5 February 1845. He appeared as a founding member of the Melbourne Hebrew Congregation in 1843 and he prospered. His new wife was Louisa Darcy. The records of the congregation note the birth of his son Samuel on 19 September 1843. The child's mother's name was left unrecorded, indicating that she was not Jewish. On 3 August 1843 Nathan's son was circumcised by Isaac Lazarus Lincoln (q.v.), as it had come to be considered 'a special case'. Nathan's profession was recorded as clothier. Nathan was one of the Jewish drapers and clothiers fined five shillings for exposing goods for sale on the footpath (*Port Phillip Gazette*, 5 April 1845). Nathan's name appeared on the Melbourne Jewish community's address to Rabbi Dr Adler on his appointment as Chief Rabbi, written in early 1846.

On 18 July 1845 Nathan was one of five members in the Melbourne Hebrew Congregation who asked to call a meeting 'to consider the propriety of making converts'. In the Letter Book of the Melbourne Hebrew Congregation, no. 1, dated 21 May 1850, Nathan asked permission to have another son circumcised.

The request was refused despite the fact that his two previous sons had been accepted. A General Meeting of the congregation was then held and decided in favour of the application, but the Rev. Rintel (q.v.) was not swayed by this exercise in democracy. On 16 December 1850 the Nathans of Elizabeth Street had another son, and the synagogue's minister was firmly told by Michael Cashmore that there was 'no objection to the circumcision of Mr Nathan's child'. The Rev. Rintel again refused to officiate and the president wrote (on 19 December 1850) of 'my greatest surprise at your inconsistent conduct'.

Nathan took his whole family to England in 1853. On 18 April a sitting of the rabbinic court granted him a divorce from Edal and on the 30 January 1854 Louisa (Leah) and her five children were immersed in the ritual bath and became Jewish. At the time Samuel was aged 10, Esther aged 8, Yehudah aged 5, Chaim aged 3 and Rachel aged fourteen months. Nathan and Louisa married at London's New Synagogue on 7 February 1854 of 2 Bedford Square. He was described as a gentleman and widower (!) and signed the certificate with a mark.

Surrey I (6) Printed Indent, X634-31-1773, p. 101; Indent 4/4103; Register of TL 31/1773, 38/2152, in 4/4125; CS Copies of Letters to the Collector and Controller of Customs and the Surveyor of Distilleries, 1840–45, 41/973, in 4/3698; CF 45/176; Register of House of Correction, 1837–1840, pp. 90, 142; VDL Correspondence, 41/851; Melbourne Hebrew Congregation Letter Book, 1, 21 May 1850, 18 July 1845, 3 August 1845. Jeremy I. Pfeffer, 'From One End of the Earth to the Other' p. 317f.

NATHAN, Rachel

John Craig, 1834; Free.
Single.

Rachel Nathan arrived on the immigrant ship *John Craig* on 12 December 1834, travelling with Martha Moses (q.v.), Solomon Barnett (q.v.) and Maria (Mary) Hart (q.v.). Rachel married Joshua Lewis Barnett (q.v.) in Sydney in 1846. Rachel fell into very bad company and worked as a prostitute under the 'care' of Lewis Isaacs of Brougham Place (q.v.), who was her 'bully'.

Ship Indent 4/5207; W. A. Miles, *Registry of Flash Men*, p. 41, 2/673.

NATHAN, Rachel

b. London, 1813–1893
Free.
Single; 7 children.

A daughter of Nathan Lyon Nathan (q.v.) and Sarah Nathan, and the sister of Rosetta Joseph (Nathan, q.v.), Rachel arrived in Sydney and stayed with her sister Rosetta and brother-in-law Moses Joseph (q.v.). She married Samuel Cohen (q.v.) of Maitland at the Pulteney Hotel on Macquarie Street on 23 August 1837 and she died at 5 Clanricarde Gardens, Kensington (London), on 26 October 1893. She appears to have left Australia shortly after the death of her husband. With her, at the time of her death, was her 35-year-old daughter Charlotte, who had been born in Australia. The value of her estate at her death was £38 816 3s 9d.

Her children were Sarah (1839–1894), George Judah (1842–1937), Charlotte (1844–1929), Louis (1846), Hannah (1848), who died as an infant, Nathan (Norman) Samuel (1850–1917), and Bernard (Beresford) Samuel (1855–1905).

Family history research by Dinah Harvey, Sydney.

NATHAN, Rosetta

b. London, d. 1859
Margaret, 1831; Free.
Single; 11 children.

The eldest daughter of Nathan Lyon Nathan (q.v.) and Sarah, Rosetta Nathan was one of nine children and all of her siblings would eventually live in Australia and New Zealand. Rosetta was the niece of Frances and Michael Nathan (qq.v.).

Rosetta followed her first cousin, and convict, Moses Joseph (q.v.) to Sydney. Moses Joseph described her as 'a respectable and virtuous woman who lately arrived in this colony per the ship *Margaret* evincing thereby the continuance of her attachment and determination to share the fate and misfortune of petitioner Moses Joseph'. Their marriage on 30 January 1832 was the first officially sanctioned Jewish marriage in Australia. Their children were: Caroline (born 1833), Hyam Moses (q.v.) (1835), Charlotte (1836), Sarah (Stella) (1839), Lewis (1842), Marianne (1843), Israel (Isaac Arthur) (1845), Alice born 1848) David (1850), Joseph [Jerrold] (1851–1961) and Julia (1853).

Howard T. Nathan, 'Rosetta Joseph: The Bell, Her Husband and His Money', *AJJHS*, vol. 17, no. 1 (2003), p. 5f.

NATHAN, Rosetta

b. London
Mariat, 1835; Free.
Single; 5 children.

Rosetta Nathan was the daughter of Edward Nathan(q.v.). and arrived in Sydney with her parents in 1835. Rosetta married Isaac Haines (q.v.) in a Jewish ceremony at Five Islands on 2 April 1840. Their children were Edward (born 1842), Catherine (1845), Hyam (1848), Eleanor (1850), and Annie (1852).

NATHAN, Samuel (SMITH)

Free.

Samuel Nathan, alias Samuel Smith, was tried in Melbourne on 16 December 1849 for uttering a forged cheque. He was discharged the next day when no evidence could be found against him.

Melbourne Morning Herald, 17 December, 18 December 1849.

NATHAN, Sarah

Free. Single.

In the Hobart Town *Colonial Times* of 2 May 1837 there was a report of a Sarah Nathan having been admitted on a charge of stealing a lace cap made by (her sister?) Jane Nathan. The case was not proven. In Launceston, on 21 February 1838, Sarah Nathan married Robert Wells.

NATHAN, Solomon

b. Houndsditch London, 1808
Chapman (2), 1824; Convict; Sentenced to life, Old Bailey, 1824.
Single. Unemployed.

Transported for stealing a package containing nine handkerchiefs, valued at thirty five shillings, from a Holborn hosiery shop. He had attempted to hide the parcel under his hat. The sixteen-year-old boy 'pleaded distress'.

The *Chapman* arrived in Hobart Town on 27 July 1824. On 28 November 1825 his master (possibly John) Jacobs (q.v.) was forced to return Nathan to the government as he had 'no means to support him'. A long series of infractions followed. On 6 March 1826 he was accused of 'neglect of duty' and confined in irons for one month. On 6 May 1826 he stole a quantity of wheat from a warehouse and was sentenced to twenty-five lashes. On 9 June 1826 he received a further fifty lashes for being absent from work. He was sentenced to work in irons for the next twelve months. On 2 September 1826 he was sentenced to twenty lashes for 'neglect of duty and fifty and gambling'. On 5 September 1826 he was sentenced for being'disorderly and extremely insolent to Constable Henderson' and was sent to join the Maria Island chain gang. On 29 September 1826 as a member of the chain gang on the island he was given fifty lashes for threatening to strike the overseer. Back on the mainland on 17 March 1827 he was sentenced to a further fifty lashes for 'abusing Constable Henry Perry'. On 27 October 1827 he was part of a work party based at the penitentiary as punishment for deliberately ring-barking trees property of the Crown for which he received fifty lashes. On 30 May 1828 he was found to have been absent from his work party and insolent to his overseer and was punished with a further fifty lashes. On 30 June 1829 he was sentenced to two hours in the stocks for neglect of duty and absence from government labour. Nathan was then assigned to the 'Marine Department'. On 13 April 1835 he was found to be out after hours and was sentenced to a further two months with the chain gang. On 18 November 1836 he refused to 'assist in the line of duty and uttering indecent language' and two years in the work party followed. In 1837 he was assigned to Mr Kent but on 11 January 1837 he was found to have been insolent and sentenced to two months hard labour and discharged from private service.

Nathan finally received a ticket of leave 19 January 1847. During his time as a prisoner he had received 345 lashes, spent time in the public stocks and months shackled in irons working in the chain gang. It was a heavy price to pay for having stolen a packet of nine handkerchiefs from a shop in London.

CON 31/1/29; OBSP, 14 January 1824, pardons no. 738, 27 September 1843.

NATHAN, Solomon

b. London, 1796

Augusta Jessie (1), 1835; Convict; Sentenced to life, Old Bailey, 1834.

Married; Dealer, labourer; Height: 162 cm; 4 children.

Fresh complexion, small oval head, brown whiskers, long narrow face, high forehead, light grey eyes, long nose. A Jew. Scar on right cheek. Nathan's wife Jane lived at Commercial Road and they had four children. He was transported for stealing silk, blankets, sixty-one yards of satin and ribbons from a workshop above a coffee shop at 43 Brick Lane, Spitalfields. The materials were valued at £12. He was sentenced to transportation for life on 3 July 1834. He was forty-two years old.

The *Augusta Jessie* arrived in Hobart Town on 22 January 1835. On 5 March 1835 Solomon Nathan was convicted for disobedience of orders and forwarded to Hobart Town from the Public Works Department 'on suspicion of being a lunatic'. On 11 March 1837 he was found to be in Launceston without a pass, having absconded from his road party. He was sent to the Reiby's Ford Chain Gang for one month. On 14 March 1837 he was found guilty of violent conduct in the presence of the Police Magistrate and his existing sentence of hard labour was extended by three months. On 25 October 1835 he was sentenced to twenty-five lashes for being drunk and disorderly. On 13 March 1838 he was sentenced to two months hard labour in chains for being concealed in a disorderly house while he was assigned to the Marine Department. He was sent to the Oatlands Road Party. On 4 October 1838 he was charged with the theft of a packet of letters and some clothes. The witness for the prosecution failed to appear but Nathan was dismissed from his position as watchman. He continued to work at Oatlands through 1839, being charged with a number of instances of neglect of duty and disorderly conduct resulting in a month's solitary confinement. A ticket of leave was issued on 3 September 1840.

OBSP, 1834, case 1086, p. 603f.; CON 31/33; CON 18/3, no. 337; CSO 1/781/16664.

NATHAN, Solomon

William Metcalf, 1834; Convict.

Solomon Nathan was described on the appropriation list of his convict transport ship as a labourer, a Jew, and assigned to the Public Works Department. His name did not appear on the ship's indent, or in the list of convicts registered in Van Diemen's Land.

VDL Papers, ML, A1059-7, p. 123.

NATHAN, Solomon

Free.
Married; Dealer; 5 children.

Solomon Nathan and his wife Miriam had a son, Benjamin Albert Nathan, in Melbourne in 1845. The child was registered as a Jew. Subsequently, Leah Phillips Nathan was born in 1846, Lion in 1847, Moss in 1848, and Carol in 1851. In the elections of 1861, Abraham Nathan, the brother of Solomon Nathan, was arrested for impersonation following an attempt to swamp the number of voters at Mornington by a boatload of impostors who were hired for the occasion. Solomon protested that his other brother, John Nathan, was the real villain.

L. M. Goldman, *The Jews in Victoria in the Nineteenth Century*, p. 149.

NELSON, Benjamin (Levy)

b. Fordon, Prussia, 1813–1894
1839; Free.
Married; Dealer, Hawker; 8 children.

Benjamin Nelson was the brother of Morris Nelson (q.v.), and of Hanna, who married Harris Cohen, brother of P. J. Cohen (q.v.). Benjamin was licensed as a hawker on 26 January 1841 (*Hobart Town Courier*). Benjamin and his brother Morris shared a house in Elizabeth Street, being partners in a general business. On 9 November 1842 Benjamin Nelson married Frances (Fanny) Nathan in the seventh Jewish wedding in Van Diemen's Land. His profession was given as publican at the time of the wedding. She was the daughter of Edward and Hannah Nathan (qq.v.). Louis Nathan (q.v.) officiated at the wedding, which was held at the home of Isaac Friedman (q.v.).

Henry, their infant son, died aged seven months on 10 October 1844 and was the synagogue's third funeral. 'B. Nelson' was listed as giving £5 to the Hobart Synagogue building fund. In 1843, as a resident of Longford, he contributed two shillings and sixpence when there was an appeal for the family of a constable killed by bushrangers on 9 June that year (*Hobart Town Courier*). Nelson also had a store in Perth. In 1844 he gave two guineas to the Launceston building fund.

By 1846 Nelson had moved to Maitland and was named as one of the three founding trustees of the local Jewish cemetery. In 1847 Benjamin and Frances Nelson were living in West Maitland in 1847 where their daughter Hinda was born. Rebecca was born at Scone in 1850. Rachael was born at Sydney in 1853 and Amelia in 1857.

On 9 September 1854 Benjamin Nelson of Liverpool Plains became a naturalised British subject. Morris and Benjamin established a trading company that operated in Maitland, Sydney and Orange. Benjamin served as a magistrate in Orange for twenty-four years and was twice mayor of the town. He died in Sydney at the age of eighty-one after a marriage that lasted fifty-nine years. Frances died on 13 June 1898. Only four of their eight children survived their parents.

The children were Henry (died 1844), Hannah (married Harris Cohen), Phoebe (married Joseph Leeds), Rosetta (married Adolphe Alexander), Amanda, Reginald (married Sarah Brodziak), Edward (married Bertha Brodziak), Elizabeth Nelson.

Hobart Town Courier, 26 January 1841, 5 March 1841, 9 June 1843; *Launceston Examiner*, 29 June 1844. Family information Mrs Jane Walters and Vivien Solo,

NELSON, Caroline

1832–1911
Free.

Caroline, daughter of Raphael Benjamin was the wife of Morris Nelson (q.v.). She died in Sydney on 31 August 1911 and was buried at Rookwood Cemetery.

NELSON, John

b. London, 1801
Prince George, 1837; Convict; Sentenced to life, Central Criminal Court, 1836.
Labourer; Height: 164 cm.

Dark ruddy complexion, dark brown hair, dark brown eyes, several small moles on cheeks. Lost a front tooth. Could read and write. Jew. John Nelson was sentenced on 13 June 1836 to be transported for life for stealing a watch. No previous convictions were recorded.

John Nelson arrived in New South Wales on 8 May 1837 and was sent from the Hyde Park Barracks to work at the convict station on Goat Island in Sydney Harbour. 'Edward' Nelson, who came out as a convict on the *Prince George* in 1837, received a conditional pardon on 2 March 1846 and a certificate of freedom on 13 September 1851.

Prince George no. 37-782, Printed Indent, p. 67 (Fiche 727); 1837 Principal Superintendent of Convicts, Butts of Certificates of Freedom, 5 May 1851 to 26 February 1854, 4/4415; CF 46/241–51/0106.

NELSON, Morris

1818–1877
Free.
Shepherdess, 1840, Dealer; Married; 12 children.

In March 1841, Morris and his brother Benjamin Nelson (q.v.) were listed as sharing a house in Elizabeth Street in Hobart Town, where they had a general business. In 1844 a 'Nelson', a non member, gave ten shillings to the Melbourne Hebrew Congregation.

In June 1852 Morris married Caroline Benjamin, daughter of Raphael Benjamin (q.v.) and one year later had a daughter, Hannah, who was registered as a member of the Jewish community in Melbourne. The following month Morris Nelson was able to give a donation of £10 10s to the synagogue building appeal. In 1857 Nelson took a leading role in the establishment of the break-away East Melbourne Hebrew Congregation and served as its first honorary treasurer. In December 1859 Nelson laid the foundation stone of the Jewish School established by the East Melbourne Synagogue.

Morris Nelson died on 5 July 1877 at his home at 33 Lower Fort Street, Sydney. He was described as the former treasurer of the East Melbourne Synagogue and 'of the firm of Nelson Bros, Orange ... leaving an affectionate wife and large family to mourn their loss'.

The family consisted of Hannah (married Henry Mitchell), Joseph (married Isabelle Lesser), Rachel (married Solomon Morris). Hannah (married Henry Woolf), Solomon (married Abigail Sanders), Leah, infant daughter, Julia (married Leopold S. Benjamin), Ernest (married Adele Joseph), Elizabeth (married Henry Isaacs), Herbert (married Constance Bourke), Florence (married John Levi) and Ina Nelson.

Hobart Town Courier, 5 March 1841; *Sydney Morning Herald*, 9 July 1877. Family information Mrs Jane Walters, Melbourne.

NEWTON, David

1813–1853
Free.
Single; Dealer; 8 children.

David Newton married Hannah Phillips (q.v.), the sister of Solomon Phillips (q.v.), in Sydney at the Sydney Synagogue on 6 January 1841. A son, Solomon (Charles), was born in Sydney on 18 September 1841. Michael was born on 7 December 1842. An infant, Henry, born in 1843, was buried at the Devonshire Street Jewish Cemetery on 25 August 1843. A daughter, Eva, was born in Sydney in 1844. Isaac was born in Sydney in 1847. Julie was born in Queanbeyan in 1849. The Melbourne Hebrew Congregation's Birth Register listed Nancy, born on 22 March 1851. Newton was listed as a 'fruiterer'.

The 1842 Sydney voters' list showed that Newton was working as an auctioneer with a house and shop in George Street. He had given the Sydney Synagogue building fund £10 in 1839 and was a seat holder in the new Sydney Synagogue in 1845, however, David Newton 'a dealer' was forced to meet with his creditors on 24 February 1843.

David Newton died on 10 March 1853, having been confined 'for some time' in the Lunatic Asylum. He was forty years of age.

Sydney Morning Herald, 15 September 1839, 9 September 1842, 15 September 1842, 24 February 1843, 13 September 1843. Family information John Norris.

NIETO, Rachel (NETTO)

b. London, 1810–1898
David Scott, 1834; Free.
Single; Servant; 8 children.

Rachel's brother-in-law was Isaac Friedman (q.v.), who was married to Rebecca Friedman (q.v.) (née Nieto). They were descendants of England's first Sephardi rabbinic family. Rachel was a bounty migrant, and had arrived on 25 October 1834. She married William Quick in 1838 and settled in Maitland, where she is said to have had eight children.

Information from Dr Elizabeth Rushen.

NORTON, P. W.

c. 1843; Free.

P.W. Norton asked the Hobart Congregation for financial assistance on 23 June 1845.

O

OPLEY, Peter

b. 1768
Alexander, 1788; Convict; Sentenced to 7 years, Maidstone, Kent, 1786.
Single; Butcher.

Peter Opley, 'of the Jewish persuasion', was sentenced with a John Smith on 13 March 1786 for stealing a woman's printed cotton gown, valued at 9 shillings. Both men were described as labourers 'late of the parish of Greenwich'. Opley, aged eighteen, was sent to the Ceres *hulk on 13 June 1786, and delivered to the* Alexander *on 6 January 1787 to join the First Fleet.*

At Sydney Cove on 30 April 1788, 'Hopely' was convicted of stealing a quart tin pot, which he 'found' on a beach and sold to Mary Phillips for a handkerchief. He was punished with one hundred lashes. An accusation of cutting a tent on 21 July 1788 was dismissed for lack of evidence. On 16 January 1789 he was given another hundred lashes for having been absent from the Rose Hill camp for three days. On 15 March 1789 he received twenty-five lashes for the theft of a crust of bread. On 4 March 1790 he was sent to Norfolk Island on the *Sirius*.

Opley was off the government stores by March 1792. In early 1793 he took a lease for three years on land at Sydney Town and paid £6 to buy stock—two sows, a cock and six hens. In May 1794 he was employed by Aaron Davis (q.v.). He gave up his own land and worked as a sawyer in 1796. In June 1796, free by servitude, he returned to England on the *Marquis of Cornwallis*.

M. Gillen, *The Founders of Australia*, p. 268f.; CO 201/10, p. 100; J. Cobley, *The Crimes of the First Fleet Convicts*, p. 202f.

P

PARKER, James

b. Copenhagen, 1820
Sir Robert Peel, 1844; Convict; Sentenced to 7 years, Central Criminal Court, 1844.
Married; Ship steward; Height: 165 cm.

Fresh complexion, long head, brown hair, dark brown whiskers, hazel eyes, long nose. Jew. Can read a little. Previously James Parker had been imprisoned for six months for stealing a cloak. This similar offence was his second conviction, and was for stealing a cloak and a shawl from Mr Webb of Red Lion Street. The surgeon's report was: 'indifferent'. In his police dossier, the surgeon reported 'it appeared that a charge of murder was prepared against this man on the afternoon previous to the sailing of the ship'.

James Parker's initial period of detention in Van Diemen's Land was for fifteen months and he was sent to a work gang in Deloraine. His ship arrived on 26 December 1844 and on 1 January 1846 he was found to be absent from his work and put in solitary confinement for ten days. On 1 July 1846 he was found guilty of boiling down bones for fat (for his own profit) and posing as a washerman. His sentence was extended by two months. He gained his ticket of leave on 20 February 1849 but on 28 April 1864 at Deloraine he was found guilty of larceny and sentenced to twelve months imprisonment with hard labour.
CON 33/63, no. 5110.

PASS, Esther

Active, 1791; Free.
Married.

Mrs Esther Pass was the wife of the convict Mordecai Pass (q.v.). Esther had paid for her journey to Australia on the same convict transport ship as her husband, 'under the protection of the (ship's) master'. The colony was too young to be able to cope with someone who was neither a convict nor part of the military establishment and she was subsequently 'allowed' to leave New South Wales by Lieutenant Governor King, after he had been convinced that she was not a convict and had no place in the colony. Governor Phillip wrote (24 November 1791): 'The Master of the *Active*, Transport, having made Oath that a woman of the name of Esther Pass, who came out in that Ship, is not a convict and never was intended to remain in the Settlement, she is permitted to proceed with him'. Esther left Australia, on the *Active* for England, by way of India, in 1792. By accompanying her husband on the Third Fleet, Esther unwittingly became Australia's first free Jewish adult immigrant.

Letter by David Collins to Lt Gov. King, 5 January 1792, and Gov. Phillip to Under Secretary Nepean, 24 November 1791, in *HRA*, vol. 1, p. 316 (there is a misprint in the transcript of the letter).

PASS, Mordecai (James)

Active; 1791; Convict; Sentenced to 7 years, Old Bailey, 1790.
Married.

Mordecai Pass stole a box containing 564 pairs of shoe buckles valued at £20 from a cart and was sentenced at the Old Bailey on 7 July 1790. On board the Active (a ship of the Third Fleet) there was a reference to his wife Esther Pass (q.v.).

'Moddica Pass' was listed in the Settlers' Muster Book, List 3, as a 'Person off Stores' with a ticket of leave in 1800, and received a certificate of freedom on 9 June 1810.

James Pass, alias Mordecai, was charged with receiving stolen goods 20 January 1813 and was sentenced on 20 March 1813. On 27 July 1816 he was a sailor on a vessel that was wrecked to the north of Port Stephens. Understandably reluctant to board another ship, Pass asked the Colonial Secretary whether he could proceed overland to Sydney from Newcastle.

OBSP, 1789–90, case 538, p. 664; King's Letter Book, L187, p. 85, Letter by David Collins to King, 5 January 1792; TL 263; *Sydney Gazette*, 20 March 1813, 28 September 1816.

PERARA, Joseph

b. London, 1805–1847
Albion (1), 1827; Convict; Sentenced to 7 years, Old Bailey, 1825.
Married; Tailor; 2 children.

Fresh complexion, brown hair, hazel eyes. Could read and write. Joseph Perara, who had a wife and small child living in London, stole a bundle of six shovels from a cart on the way to a warehouse. He had no previous conviction.

In December 1825, only a few months after his marriage, Joseph de Isaac Pereira, a tailor, was convicted to transportation to Australia. Because there was no expectation that he would ever be able to return to England, his wife, Rosa, the daughter of Naphtali Bengegui, obtained a divorce through the Sephardi religious court. She also petitioned the Elders of the synagogue for assistance. In January the Mahamad, which served as the Council of the Sephardi community, satisfied of the truth of her statement granted her £5 'for once'. Due to her plight she continued to receive regular small sums of money, sacks of coal in winter and several pounds of unleavened bread every Passover. She died in 1880 and was buried at the community's cemetery at Mile End.

Perara took £1 2s with him on the convict transport ship and the money was placed in the New South Wales Bank on his arrival. In the 1828 Census he was listed as a labourer working as an assigned servant with the Australian Agricultural

Company at Port Stephens in the District of Maitland. He was granted a ticket of leave on 29 September 1831 for the District of Maitland and a certificate of freedom in 1833. Perara was free in November 1837 when he was detained at the House of Correction for 'neglect of work'.

A child was born to Joseph Perara at Lane Cove, Sydney, in 1842. Perara was found drowned on 15 December 1847 and was buried as a Jew.

OBSP, 1825–26, case 39, p. 21; *Albion* (1) Indent 4/4012, p. 43; House of Correction Register 4/4569, p. 35; The Spanish and Portuguese Synagogue Bulletin, 1988. Principal Superintendent of Convicts, Registers of Exemptions from Government Labour, 15 November 1830 to 24 September 1832, in 4/4080, TL 31/761; CF 353; no. 761, 1831, 4/4062.

PHILIPPS, Henry

Henry and Margaret Philipps had a child in Sydney in 1831 named Hyam J. Philipps.

PHILLIPS, Abraham

b. London, 1811–1853
Free.
Single; Dealer.

Abraham Phillips married Hannah Levey on 20 December 1840. It was Jewish wedding no. 38 in New South Wales. Phillips died on 2 April 1853 and was buried by the Sydney Synagogue in the Devonshire Street Cemetery.

PHILLIPS, Abraham

Free.
Single.

Abraham Phillips married Rosie Cohen, aged nineteen, at Launceston's second Jewish wedding in 1841. Robert Cohen (q.v.) and Moses Cohen (q.v.) signed the certificate as witnesses.

PHILLIPS, Alexander

d. 1832
Globe, 1819; Convict; Sentenced to 7 years, Exeter, 1818.
Single; 3 children.

The *Globe* arrived in New South Wales on 8 January 1819. Alexander Phillips appeared in the 1828 Census as 'free by servitude'. His wife was Sophia, aged twenty-three and born in the colony, and their children were Louise (born 1824), Alexander jnr (1825), and John (1827). Phillips was a publican and baker in Newcastle. His religion was listed as 'Protestant'. However, Phillips was buried as a Jew at the Devonshire Street Cemetery on 3 February 1832.

PHILLIPS, Barnett Aaron (Bernard Aaron)

b. Liverpool, 1792–1862
Westmoreland, 1833; Free.
Married; Dealer and stage carpenter; 16 children.

'Barney Aaron' Phillips and his wife Clara (née Solomons) (q.v.) arrived in Sydney on 14 May 1833 with their eight children, Charles Aaron (1823–1867), Alexander Aaron (born 1824), Anna (Hannah) (1826–1877) married David Newton (q.v.) on 6 June 1841), Michael Aaron (1827), Samuel Aaron (born 1828–26 July 1902), Sara (born 1831–1906 married Samuel Davis (q.v.) 29 May 1850), Jacob Aaron (born 18 April 1832 died 20 August 1893 married Susan Moses ca 1854), and Rosa (1833–1893 married Lewis Jonah Jones in Sydney 24 March 1852). Miss Abigail Asser (q.v.) accompanied the family.

On 23 May 1833 the *Sydney Gazette* announced: 'Mr B. A. Phillips—General Mechanist from Theatre Royal, Covent Garden and eight years foreman at Drury Lane—commenced business in George Street. Carpenter, joiner, venetian blind maker, furniture repairer, locksmith, bell hanger'. He asked for six government servants and was granted one. Phillips asked for Thomas Harris, or Herscht (Harris, q.v.), to be assigned to him from the Principal Superintendent of Convicts in order to be the Jewish teacher of his children. The request was refused. On 2 May 1834 Phillips moved to premises 'lately occupied by Isaac Simmons' (q.v.), and then moved again, on 9 December 1835, to the Malcolm Building in George Street.

Barnett Levey (q.v.) had obviously encouraged Phillips to come to New South Wales and they worked together during Levey's theatrical career. But Phillips quickly understood that he would not be able to rely on the theatrical successes of Barnett Levey and, in 1836, Phillips announced that he had imported from England 'a well built hearse and mourning coach and has commenced as Furnishing Undertaker'. The hearse was said to be for hire and, at the same time, Phillips advertised the sale of cabinets and glassware.

The B. A. Phillips children born in Sydney were Rebecca (born 24 September 1834, who died on 15 March 1837 from scalding), Nancy (born 29 October 1835), Jane (born 3 December 1836, who died on 31 June 1840), Philip (1837), Eve (born 29 August 1839), Wolff (Wellington) (born 21 November 1840, who died aged five months), Leah (born 19 April 1841 to 1862), and Isaac Aaron (born 7 January 1844).

Phillips was a freemason and actively sold tickets for masonic dinners and balls. He was employed to fit out the Bridge Street Synagogue in 1836, with its 'well arranged' 130 seats and an ark for the Torah scrolls, which can still be seen at Sydney's Great Synagogue. He became a member of the synagogue committee in 1839 and gave £15 to the building fund. He had a shop and house in George Street in 1842. He applied for a licence on 13 April 1843 for the Star in the East public house in George Street but, sadly, did not escape the depression and was declared insolvent on 21 December 1843.

B. A. Phillips died at the home of his daughter Nancy and son-in-law Asher Jude in Bourke Street, Melbourne, on 24 November 1862. Clara died on 20 June 1861, aged fifty-seven.

Westmoreland Indent 4/5204; *Sydney Gazette*, 23 May 1833; 1835 Governors' Despatches, 12 November 1836, ML 1214, p. 734; Principal Superintendent of Convicts, 37/7615, 21 September 1836; *Sydney General Trade List*, 8 August 1835; *Sydney Morning Herald*, 2 December 1836, 15 September 1842, 27 December 1843; *Sydney Gazette*, 21 May 1833; *Commercial Journal and Advertiser*, 7 February 1838.

PHILLIPS, Caroline (née SOLOMON)

1813–1904
Enchantress, 1833; Free.
Married; 14 children.

Caroline married Solomon Phillips (q.v.) in 1832 and came to Australia with him. Their children were Rosetta, Phillip David, twins Ephraim and Daniel, Lydia, Joseph, Mondle Emanuel, Elias Edward, Louis (Lewis) Samuel, Hannah, Simeon, Abraham, David Solomon, and Samuel Asher.

PHILLIPS, Charles Saul Aaron

Free.
Married; Watchmaker and jeweller; 1 child.

Charles Saul Aaron Phillips was a watchmaker and jeweller in Castlereagh Street, according to the *Sydney Morning Herald* of 17 May 1844.

PHILLIPS, Clara (née SOLOMONS)

1814–1861 *Westmoreland*, 1833; Free.
Married; 16 children.

Clara Phillips travelled to New South Wales with her husband, Barnett Aaron Phillips (q.v.), and their eight children born in England.

PHILLIPS, Daniel

Matilda, 1791; Convict; Sentenced to 7 years, Stafford, 1790.

Daniel Phillips arrived in New South Wales on 1 August 1791 and his sentence expired in 1797. He had been a labourer at Wilberforce. In May 1810 Daniel Phillips petitioned Governor Macquarie and told him that he had come on the ship *Matilda* nineteen years ago. He had served the whole of his time in the employ of the government, frequently employed by governors Hunter and King and Mr Andrew Thompson to explore the mountains and other interior parts of the colony in search of curiosities. The petition continued: 'His wife had died four years ago leaving him with a small family to provide for. He rented a few acres in 1809 and lost the total crop of wheat in the flood. Lieutenant Governor Paterson granted him seventy acres of land and he humbly implored that it may be renewed for the sake of his "infant family"'. Phillips was illiterate, and Mr A. Thompson had written the petition on his behalf. The grant of seventy acres was confirmed by Governor Macquarie. On 16 and 23 November 1816 Phillips was listed as being at the Hawkesbury, and as 'an impostor' pretending to have a pardon. Jonas Mordecai (Joseph Mordecai, q.v.) and Henry Hyams (q.v.) were accused of being involved in the same scheme. Phillips's true status was eventually confirmed. In 1821, cedar wood worth £42 was supplied by Phillips to the police.

Matilda Indent 4/4005; CS Letters Received 1810, Memorials L–Y, no. 259, in 4/1822, 20 January 1807, A85, p. 184; Bigge Appendix, BT Box 24, p. 5174; HO 10/3; Wentworth Papers, ML, 1816–1821, D. 1.

PHILLIPS, Emanuel

1806–1879
1827; Free.
Single; Merchant; 7 children.

Phillips was a storekeeper at the Reform House 336 George Street 1830 to 1839 and served on the Sydney Synagogue's committee in 1839. By 1842 he owned two shops and a home in Park Street. Emanuel Phillips married Hannah Phillips on 8 April 1835 and the bride and groom were first cousins. It was the Sydney synagogue's eleventh wedding. Their children were Elizabeth (born 1836), Phillip (1837), Rosetta (1838), Saul (1840), Sarah (1841), Abraham (1842), and Lewis (1845). All were born in Sydney.

On 31 July 1839 Emanuel Phillips wrote a petition to the Governor asking for consideration of the plight of Hyam Franks (q.v.). Phillips described himself as a storekeeper in George Street, who had arrived free in 1827. Phillips was listed in the 1833 *Post Office Directory* as a 'dealer' in York Street and was elected 'collector' for the synagogue at its first general meeting in 1833. The following year he moved to a shop in Pitt Street and then opened a general store named the Reform House, at 1 Park Street. In 1839 Mr and Mrs E. Phillips gave £25 to the York Street Synagogue building fund. In September 1840 he agreed to be nominated for the office of treasurer at the Sydney Synagogue. He was one of the eight Sydney subscribers to London's *Voice of Jacob* newspaper.

Phillips was a seat holder at the synagogue in 1845 and donated £25 to the congregational building appeal. In 1845 he opened the London Warehouse at 336 George Street. On 16 August 1845 he announced in the *Maitland Mercury* that he had moved to open a new business in the town: 'Emanuel Phillips of London Warehouse, George Street, Sydney, late "Reform House" in Park Street announces his new drapery etc business'. Phillips died at Christchurch, New Zealand, on 25 August 1879.

Letter to Governor, 31 July 1839, 4/2457.4; Land Correspondence 2/7950, 20 January 1835; *Sydney Morning Herald*, 16 September 1842, 16 July 1845; *Sydney Gazette*, 11 July 1833; *Commercial Journal and Advertiser*, 10 September 1836; *Maitland Mercury*, 16 August 1845.

PHILLIPS, Emanuel

b. London, 1807
Hercules II (1), 1825; Convict; Sentenced to 7 years, Old Bailey, 1824.
Single; Orange seller; Height: 160 cm.

Pale ruddy complexion, dark brown hair nearly bald, dark hazel eyes. Large nose. S & P and EP tattooed on left arm. Emanuel Phillips belonged to a group of three young males who stole a half-full tea chest of tea from a warehouse. He told the police that he was an orange seller and that he was hired by two men to carry the chest, not knowing that it was stolen. He was sentenced on 14 January 1824.

The *Hercules* arrived in New South Wales on 7 May 1825. Phillips was initially assigned to the Prisoners' Barracks in Sydney. On 22 August 1826 the *Australian* reported that Emanuel Phillips, a prisoner attached to the Hyde Park Barracks, was charged with stealing a loaf of bread from a cart. Phillips was with a companion who escaped from the police. He was remanded for punishment and sentenced to work in chains for three months. Emanuel Phillips appeared in the 1828 Census. No religion was noted and he was recorded as a shepherd in government service in the region of Bathurst. Phillips was granted a certificate of freedom on 14 January 1831. The *Sydney Gazette* of 5 July 1832 reported that Moses Solomon (q.v.) was assigned to Emanuel Phillips. The assignment ended abruptly when Solomon was sent to Norfolk Island for his part in a robbery.

OBSP, 1823–24, case 232, p. 84; *Hercules* (2) Indent 4/4304; Principal Superintendent of Convicts, Butts of Certificates of Freedom, 28 September 1830 to 28 March 1831, CF 31/0019; Ship Indent 2/8262, p. 350; 4/4010, p. 120; *Australian*, 22 April 1826; *Sydney Gazette*, 22 April 1826, 5 July 1832.

PHILLIPS, George

1758–1831
Earl Cornwallis, 1801; Convict; Sentenced to life, Old Bailey, 1800.
Single; Soldier.

Phillips was caught stealing in a shop by the owner's wife. Phillips was a soldier and was dressed in uniform.

The convict transport *Earl Cornwallis* arrived in Port Jackson on 12 June 1801. George Phillips was the assigned convict servant to Mr Faithfull in 1819. George Phillips was listed as a Protestant in the 1828 Census and described as a 'waterman'. He was aged seventy and 'Free by Servitude'.

Earl Cornwallis Indent, p. 26, 4/4004; *OBSP*, 1799–1800, case 440, p. 392f.

PHILLIPS, Hannah

b. London, d. 1877
Westmoreland, 1833; Free.
8 children.

The daughter of Barnard Aaron Phillips (q.v.), Hannah Phillips married David Newton (q.v.) on 6 January 1841, in the fifth Jewish wedding in New South Wales.

They had eight children: Solomon (Charles) born 1841, Michael born 1842), Eve and her twin Mary Frances born 1844, Rose born 1846, Isaac born1847, Julia born 1849, and Nancy (Anne) (1851). Hannah was born 1851. After David Newton's death in 1855 Hannah married Richard Treeve and left the Jewish community. She died 22 May 1877.

Family information from John Norris.

PHILLIPS, Henry

Warrior, 1835; Free.
Single; Merchant.

The *Warrior* arrived on 27 February 1835. Mr Henry Phillips, a merchant from England, arrived travelling cabin class. According to the list in the *Sydney Morning Herald* for the first municipal elections in 1842, Henry Phillips maintained an office in Elizabeth Street. Phillips was a Sydney Synagogue seat holder in 1845. On 9 February 1848 Henry Phillips married Rosetta Moses in Sydney.

Henry Phillips of Belfast (in Victoria-now Port Fairy) bought local land in 1849.

Henry and Rosetta moved to the Victorian goldfield at Mt Blackwood in the region of Ballarat and Daylesford. In 1855, at Golden Point, Rosetta gave birth to a son, Solomon, and a collection had to be made from the local Jewish residents to allow the Rev. Moses Rintel (q.v.) to travel from Melbourne to officiate at a *brit milah*. When the goldfield was exhausted Henry Phillips and family moved to Ballarat.

Ship Arrivals 4/5208; *Sydney Morning Herald*, 16 September 1842; Mutch Index, 82/135; Land Register, 2/7950, 1849–50.

PHILLIPS, Hyam

b. London, 1783–1829
Vittoria; Convict; Sentenced 14 years, Old Bailey, 1828.

Hyam Phillips was found at a London bank attempting to cash a £5 note that had been stolen the previous evening from the pocket of a country visitor to London. He was sentenced on 21 February 1828.

Phillips died at sea of 'chronic diarrhea' on 18 October 1829.

OBSP, 1828, case 495; Ship Indent 2/8281, p. 89f.

PHILLIPS, Hyam (Hyman)

b. London, 1797–1874
Morley (1), 1817; Convict; Sentenced to life, London, 1816.
Single; Labourer; Height: 164 cm.

Dark complexion, black hair, black eyes. Hyman Phillips was indicted for feloniously assaulting Edward Douglas in Bishopsgate Street at 10 o'clock on the night of 7 May. Douglas said: 'A woman accosted me, and took me up Alderman's Walk, which is not a thoroughfare; I remained there for the space of three or four minutes. She had just left me when I received a blow, which knocked me down. There was a violent pulling at my chain; it was a gold chain; it broke and was separated from my watch'. The victim chased Phillips, who was caught by three watchmen. Phillips declared: 'I am totally innocent', and was sentenced to death, though this was later commuted to transportation for life. On the convict ship the names of Simon Solomons (q.v.) and Isaac Jonas (q.v.) were bracketed together with Phillips'.

In the 1822 General Muster of New South Wales 'Hyman' Phillips is recorded as a convict working at the Lumber Yard at Parramatta. Hyam Phillips received thirteen lashes on 3 December 1824 for overworking a government bullock. A ticket of leave was issued to him for the District of Parramatta on 24 April 1830. Phillips then asked for a conditional pardon. He lived at Church Street, Parramatta, punctually attended musters (and church parades) and claimed to have 'apprehended two bushrangers and gave information which led to the apprehension of five runaways'. A conditional pardon was granted on 27 April 1837, followed by a certificate of freedom.

Phillips moved to Berrima. On 15 August 1842 he signed a petition with Samuel Benjamin (q.v.) and Philip Solomon (q.v.) asking that Mr William Sherwin of Berrima be made a Justice of the Peace. On 13 November 1843 he was appointed (with Joseph Levy, q.v.) to be a representative of the synagogue in Sydney in the District of Berrima. Hyam Phillips and Co. took over Joseph Levy's store and business at Argyle Street, Berrima, in November 1840. The *Australian* said that Levy would assist Phillips in the brewery business. 'Hyman' Phillips was still a resident of Berrima on 11 April 1844. From Berrima in 1845 came a donation of £25 to the Sydney Synagogue in his name. Hyam Phillips moved to George Street, Sydney, and was listed as a land agent for Israel Solomon (q.v.), who bought ten acres at Bongodong on the Murrumbidgee on 7 July 1847.

Hyam Phillips conducted the funeral for Noson Davis (q.v.) in Orange in 1865. A Hyam Phillips died at Cooma in 1874. His age was registered as eighty-two.

OBSP, 1816–17, case 530, p. 271; CS Letters Received 1840; 4/25181.1, 15 August 1842; 4/4074, 27, TL 30/186, April 1837, CP 37/0922; CS 36/5093, in 4/2309; Petition 4/2578.1, 15 August 1842; *Sydney Gazette*, 3 December 1824; CS Conditional Pardon Register, 4/4435, p. 324, 1 December 1833; 4/4492, p. 27; *Australian*, 3 November 1840, 21 November 1840.

PHILLIPS, Hyam

b. London, 1812
Mary III (4), 1833; Convict; Sentenced to 7 years, London, 1832.
Single; Butcher; Height: 156 cm.

Dark ruddy complexion, a little pock-pitted, dark nearly black hair, blue eyes. Hyam Phillips was transported for stealing a box full of books from a carrier in Houndsditch. He was sentenced on 5 January 1832.

Phillips was assigned to J. Hobbins of Sydney on 28 February 1833. A ticket of leave was issued on 4 December 1837, and a certificate of freedom on 19 October 1844. 'Imey Phillips' appeared in the *Registry of Flash Men*. He lived in the North Shore of Sydney Harbour and was 'a considerable fence who comes into Sydney every Saturday to sell his ill gotten stock'.

OBSP, 1831–32, case 390, p. 175; *Mary* Printed Indent, 6 January 1833, p. 3; TL, A1276, p. 287, 4 December 1837; *Sydney Gazette*, 28 February 1833; *Sydney Morning Herald*, 11 April 1844; Principal Superintendent of Convicts, Butts of Certificates of Freedom, January–February 1842, CF 42/91, 4/4371; W. A. Miles, *Registry of Flash Men*.

PHILLIPS, Isaac

Free.
2 children.

Isaac Phillips was a brother of Philip Phillips (q.v.). Isaac and Maria Phillips had two children, both born at Merton's Creek, Victoria. The first, Elizabeth Davis Phillips, was born in 1850 and registered as a 'Hebrew'. The second, also a girl, was born in 1851.

PHILLIPS, John

b. London, 1801
John Barry (1), 1819; Convict; Sentenced to life, Old Bailey, 1819.
Single; Butcher; Height: 160 cm.

Dark sallow complexion, black hair, dark eyes. John Phillips was sentenced with Hyam Alexander (q.v.). Phillips stole a pocket book from the Rt. Hon. Thomas Lord Foley at an election meeting at Covent Garden.

John Phillips was not listed on the 1822 General Muster of New South Wales.

OBSP, 1818–19, case 396, 17 February 1819; *John Barry* (1) Indent 4/4006, p. 387.

PHILLIPS, Laurence

Free.
Single.

Laurence Phillips married Sarah Moss (q.v.) in the Sydney Synagogue on 24 January 1844. Sarah died on 21 June 1844 and was buried at the Devonshire Street Jewish Cemetery.

PHILLIPS, Lewis

Free.
Married; Dealer; 1 child.

Lewis and Sarah Phillips had a son, John, in Sydney in 1849, and registered him as a 'Hebrew'.

PHILLIPS, Louis

b. London, 1816
John Calvin (1), 1846; Convict; Sentenced to 10 years, Central Criminal Court, 1846.
Married; Diamond dealer; Height: 173 cm; 1 child (in London).

Louis Phillips lived in Finsbury Square. He was listed as a Jew. He could read and write. His wife was Esther. He had five brothers, Moses, Isaac, David, Lawrence and Joseph, and two sisters, Sarah and Maria (who lived in America). Phillips was convicted at the Old Bailey on 23 February 1846 for having forged and presented a cheque for £280. He was 'very well behaved' on board ship. He had a fair complexion, brown hair, brown whiskers, sharp face, narrow forehead, brown eyebrows, grey eyes, long nose, medium mouth and chin.

Phillips arrived in Norfolk Island on 21 September 1846. He was sent on to Van Diemen's Land in November 1849. By 20 April 1852 Phillips had a ticket of leave and lived at Kingston, south of Hobart Town. On 30 April 1852 he was fined £30 'for having employed Mathews and Hunt and Woods, knowing them to be deserters from H. M. Brig *Fantome*'. A conditional pardon was approved on 31 May 1853. He was recommended for a conditional pardon on 16 December 1856. On 13 April 1859 at the Supreme Court in Hobart Town Phillips received a colonial sentence with hard labour for uttering a forged note of acceptance for £84. He was sent to Port Arthur where he remained until 18 June 1859. Phillips was free by September 1860.

CON 17/3, p. 8; CON 33/88; CON 37/9, p. 4070; HO 11/15.

PHILLIPS, Michael

b. London
Nimrod, 1827; Free.
Married; Merchant; 7 children.

Michael Phillips arrived in Sydney on 29 December 1827 and within days received a land grant from the colonial government. His wife (née Samuel) and six children followed him in April 1830. Phillips announced that he was a merchant and ships' agent and was granted 2560 acres of land in 1831.

Phillips had originally planned (in 1827) to settle in Western Port, in what would become Victoria, on the advice of the emancipist Solomon Levey (q.v.) in London. Writing from 108 London Wall on 4 January 1827, Phillips wrote to Earl Bathurst that it was his intention

> to fix my permanent residence in New South Wales, my wife and six children to follow. I have fixed upon that part of the Colony called Western Port, as the most desirable; the soil is congenial for the production of Grain, to which I shall mostly direct my attention; and, by having most respectable connections in the Brazils, I look forward with a prospect of ultimate success in establishing there the consumption of New South Wales wheat, as it has already a preference to the American flour. It is my intention to proceed to Sidney [*sic*] with an Investment of a considerable Amount. I humbly solicit a location of four thousand acres with further privilege of purchasing four Thousand acres more. I intend to take 30 convicts in my employ. I beg to refer your Lordship as regards my character Respectability and Means to the respectable House of Messrs Samuel and Phillips of 8 South St Finsbury.

On 28 February 1827 Bathurst replied 'The Governor of New South Wales will be directed to afford you any encouragement … but the quantity of land must depend upon the amount of capital which you may have on your arrival there'. In the Returns of 1828, Governor Darling authorised a grant of 2560 acres. However, three years later Phillips was still waiting for the grant. He asked for 5000 acres and undertook to remain in the colony for three years. Only 2560 acres were approved and on 15 September 1831, Phillips formally applied for the grant. His agricultural ambitions were never realised but had Phillips remained committed to Western Port he would have been Victoria's first settler.

On 20 January 1832 his brother-in-law, Horatio Samuel (q.v.), died, aged nineteen, at the Phillips' home in O'Connell Street. During the first quarter of 1832, four of the Phillips children also died, and were buried in the Jewish section of the Devonshire Street Cemetery. George died on 30 January, Alexander on 3 February, Sydniana on 28 February and Caroline on 5 March. Together with J. B. Montefiore (q.v.), Michael Phillips obtained a distinct grant of land for the Jews' burial ground in the Devonshire Street Cemetery. On 23 July 1832 Michael Phillips and the trustees of the Jews' burial ground offered a reward of £25 for information after 'some evil disposed person or persons have forcibly entered the Jews' Burial Ground and have wantonly removed and demolished the Tombs of my deceased children'. The *Sydney Herald* described it as 'one of the greatest violations of all that is held sacred in all climes and countries', and the *Sydney Gazette* said it was 'one of the most infamous and inhuman outrages that has ever disgraced' the colony. The culprits were never found.

In September 1832, *Currency Lad* reported: 'Mr Michael Phillips has become purchaser of the cargo of the American ship for which he is to pay in colonial produce. We rejoice to learn this may perhaps afford an introduction to an extensive trade with the American ports'. In April 1833 he advertised that he wished to rent his home and adjoining stores 'replete with every comfort and convenience', as he wished to move from his present residence. On 12 November 1832 Phillips wrote to the Colonial Secretary 'I have now arrived from New Zealand the Ship *City of Edinburgh* with a large cargo of Spars, Plank oars, scantlings and other descriptions of timber and some flax'. He noted that he faced difficulties unloading the bulky cargo and paying charges for the use of the wharf. The ship had to leave port as soon as possible and there was commercial precedent allowing him to unload at the Timber Yard adjoining George Street free of wharfage. Phillips' request was accepted by the Colonial Secretary.

On 30 September 1833 Michael Phillips was elected to the committee of the Sydney Jewish community's first general meeting. Phillips continued to take an active part in the commercial life of Sydney and left on a business trip to England on the *Enchantress* in May 1834, and in August 1835 the authorities took note that 'Michael Phillips esq. Merchant Sydney' had returned from England on the *William Harris* on 11 August 1835. On 8 June 1837 the *Sydney Gazette* reported a court case in which Michael Phillips was sued for overdue bills to the sum of £543: 'He received goods from Jones, Phillips and Co in London and there was a transaction by Phillips which his Honour deemed not honest and that it was clear that Phillips' intentions were to benefit his creditors in England at the expense of his creditors in this Colony'. While on a visit to Hobart Town in 1837 Phillips was served with a summons to pay £658 made out in promissory notes to Samuel Lyons (q.v.).

Phillips denied that he was leaving Australia but was unable to find the cash: 'being almost a stranger and unknown in this colony was unable to procure bail. [He was] extremely alarmed for the situation in which his wife then enceinte and family of five children who had come down from Sydney were likely to be placed'. On 15 March 1837 the Phillips family lost another child, named Rebekhah, who was buried by the Sydney Synagogue. Phillips remained in prison in Hobart Town for almost a year until financial guarantees could be sent from his family in England. Although he returned briefly to Sydney and rejoined the Sydney Synagogue as a member, he left for England shortly after 1845 and would never return.

Nimrod Indent 4/5198; *Sydney Gazette*, 22 May 1834, 13 August 1835, 8 June 1837; Land Grant 2/7950; *HRA*, series 1, vol. 13, p. 132f., and vol. 14, p. 672; *Sydney Herald*, 23 July 1832; *Currency Lad*, 1 September 1832; CS 32/8498, in 4/2160, 15 November 1832; *Sydney Gazette*, 31 March 1832, 6 April 1833, 17 July 1833, 8 June 1837; Petition, Hobart Town, CSO 5/77/1724; Land Correspondence 2/7950; *Hobart Town Courier*, 9 February 1838.

PHILLIPS, Morrice (Morris)

b. London, d. 1896
City of London, 1838; Free.
Single; Printer, actor, dancer.

Morrice Phillips arrived steerage on the *City of London* on 12 July 1838. On 2 August he wrote to the Colonial Secretary telling him that he had just arrived in the colony and understood that there were several situations vacant in the Colonial Department. He was staying with his brother, Michael Phillips (q.v.), at 11 O'Connell Street, Sydney.

On 13 September 1839 the *Sydney Gazette* reported that Phillips would present a Grand Historical Drama entitled *The Massacres of Jerusalem* by Mr Morris Phillips, newly arrived from London. It was to be presented at the 'Victoria Theatre … first appearance on the stage in one of the leading characters'. Two days later the *Gazette* published its review: 'A more dull, absurd and stupid mass of nonsense without plot or design. The repeated allusions to the distinguished abilities of the Jewish People are absolutely disgusting … the sooner Mr Phillips returns to his printing the better will it be'.

The *Commercial Journal and Advertiser* reported, on 30 January 1839, that Mr Morris Phillips 'is also a dancer and danced a "pas de deux" with Miss Lazar' (q.v.). On 14 January 1839 Phillips produced *Fidelio* at the Victoria Theatre. The Sydney press reported that: 'We have not room to notice particularly the new piece called Fidelio, from the pen of Mr Morrice Phillips, residing in Sydney, but for the present we cannot allow the opportunity to pass without expressing our belief that it will "take" … the scenery and dresses are admirably conceived and well executed'. In the *Australian* of 21 August 1841 Phillips announced that he would appear at the Royal Victoria Theatre to dance the favourite 'Pas Seul'.

'Morris Phillips' was buried in the Jewish section of Rookwood Cemetery. The gravestone is missing, but it was noted that he died on 3 September 1896.

City of London Indent, 4/5213; Letter to CS 38/8104, in 4/2406.4; *Sydney Gazette*, 13 September 1838, 15 September 1838; *Australian*, 21 August 1841; *Commercial Journal and Advertiser*, 30 January 1839; Eric Irvin, Jewish Personalities of the Early Sydney Stage, ms, n.d.

PHILLIPS, Moses

1875–1862
Medway (1), 1821; Convict; Sentenced to life, Surrey, 1820.
Married; 10 children.

Moses Phillips was sentenced to transportation for life, at Surrey on 3 August 1820, for house breaking. Of 'Bad character', his hulk report was 'orderly'. His height was 157.5 cms. He had brown hair, light grey eyes. He said he was a watchmaker. It was noted that he was a 'Jew'.

Moses Phillips appeared in the 1821 Convict Muster at Clarence Plains. He worked as an assigned convict servant in government service until 1827. On 22 July 1822 his convict dossier records that he was acquitted after having been accused of receiving a stolen silver spoon knowing that it had been stolen. On the 1 December 1823 his assigment to Mr Oliver Smith was terminated when it was found he was not sleeping under his master's roof at night. He was returned to the supervision of the government. He married on 16 July 1823 to Mary Ann Griffin (née Higgs). The first of their four colonial children was born later that same year but his marriage was far from successful. On 31 December 1827 he was found to be absent from his assigned task as a watchman on the Hobart Town wharf. On 20 February 1828 Phillips complained to the Colonial Secretary that his wife had been seduced by a hotel keeper named Withers. Phillips, it turned out, was in partnership with Withers, who managed a public house called the Druid, while, at the same time, he was supposed to be an assigned convict watchman at the Government Wharf. His letter of complaint brought this anomaly to the attention of officialdom. The Principal Superintendent of Police considered it to be 'improper' that Phillips should 'gain income in this way', and ordered that Withers be warned. A notice promptly appeared in the *Hobart Town Courier* on 22 March 1828 announcing the 'dissolution of partnership between Joseph Withers and Moses Phillips by mutual consent'. Together they had operated the public house, and a bakery and biscuit business in Murray Street (and briefly in Argyle Street), for which Phillips was responsible. In 1828 Moses Phillips married Mary Ann Higgs in a Jewish religious ceremony. Shortly afterwards Phillips received a ticket of leave (on 18 October 1828), moved to Launceston and became a publican again. In June 1832 he was fined £2 10s for allowing a convict to remain on his premises. On 18 July 1834 he illegally drove his cart across the footpath in a public street in Launceston and was fined five shillings.

In September 1836 he was convicted of 'disorderly conduct' for playing billiards and placed on bread and water and put in solitary confinement for twenty-four hours. Moses Phillips, 'a Carrier', joined with Henry Davis (q.v.) in the purchase of a small block of land at Cataract Hill in Launceston in October 1836 for a Jewish cemetery.

A conditional pardon No. 1211 was granted on 21 November 1836. Phillips applied for an assigned convict servant and received one on 14 June 1839 (*Hobart Town Courier*). His financial position deteriorated sharply, and in a petition dated 10 December 1840, Phillips wrote to the Colonial Secretary pleading for help. He had been in Launceston for seven years and a shoemaker for four years. Six weeks before, 'owing to heavy losses in trade', he had been declared insolvent. He claimed to have a wife and eight children, the youngest being five months old, and without assigned servants would be unable to carry on his business. The Police Magistrate had advised against the petition, but the Governor declared in favour of Phillips, as he was 'an honest man', and on 6 June 1839 he was permitted to employ two convict servants. Phillips must have traded out of his difficulties because, on 20 May 1843, he signed the Launceston Synagogue petition, and on 29 June 1844 (according to the *Launceston Examiner*) gave £4 to the Sydney Synagogue appeal.

Phillips died at the home of his daughter Caroline and his son-in-law, Abraham Martin (q.v.) at Chewton in Victoria on 7 December 1862. There were ten children. Daniel, Moses, Phillip, Sarah, Devorah, Catherine (Kate), Solomon, Priscilla and Rebecca. There were two Jewish sons-in-law. Caroline married Joseph Barnett (q.v.) in Launceston in 1841. Following the death of Barnett in 1850 she married Abraham Martin on 3 December 1870 in a civil ceremony. In 1857, she witnessed Solomon's wedding and signed her name as Caroline Martin. Sarah married George Robinson (q.v.) in March 1842.

CON 31/34; 4/1235; CSO 1/244/5904; CSO 5/270/6986; *Hobart Town Gazette*, 22 March 1828, 6 June 1839; *Hobart Town Courier*, 22 March 1828, 18 October 1828. Family information Robyn Blenheim.

PHILLIPS, Moses

Australia, 1830; Free.
Married; 6 children.

Moses Phillips came as a free settler to New South Wales with his wife and six children. The *Australia* arrived on 17 April 1830. Four of the children died in the cholera epidemic of 1832.

PHILLIPS, Nathan (Nathaniel)

b. London, 1815–1899
Hooghly (4), 1834; Convict; Sentenced to 7 years, Southwark, 1834.
Single; Stage dancer, dealer; Height: 157 cm; 7 children.

Dark complexion, a little pock-pitted, dark brown hair, chestnut eyes. H. P. tattooed inside lower right arm. Fingernails short. Jew. Could read and write. Nathan Phillips, the son of Hyam and Mary (née Cohen), was transported for picking pockets. He was sentenced at Surrey (Southwark) on 7 April 1834.

Nathan Phillips arrived in New South Wales on 18 November 1834. Phillips received a certificate of freedom on 31 July 1843. He was listed in the 1837 General Return of Convicts in New South Wales as 'Nathaniel Phillips', working as an assigned servant to Mr William Viviers at Merton. Phillips married Roseanna Elbra, a house servant, and they had seven children: Hyam, John, Mary, Sarah, Simeon, Aaron and Louis. Nathan Phillips was buried in Narromine, New South Wales, in 1899. Roseanna died in 1913 at Parkesborough (UK).

Hooghly Printed Indent, p. 165; CF in 4/4384, 43/1233.

PHILLIPS, Philip

b. Leadenhall Street, London, 1778–1858
Countess of Harcourt (1), 1821; Convict; Sentenced to 7 years, Old Bailey, 1820.
Married; Die-maker, seaman, glasscutter; Height: 152 cm; 2 children.

Ruddy complexion, black hair, broad face, hazel eyes, long nose, small mouth and chin. Could read and write. Tattooed initials PP and IP on right arm. Phillips was convicted for stealing robes, a bible, carpet and furniture from the Congregational Chapel in Cannon Street Road. The goods were discovered at his house in Rosemary Lane. Fortunately for Phillips his crime was not deemed to be sacrilege, 'as this term can only be applied to the Established Church'. This legal technicality undoubtedly saved his life. He was sentenced on 25 October 1820. His wife and two children lived at 2 Thomas Street, Church Lane, St George in the East.

Philip Phillips arrived in Hobart Town on 8 April 1821. On 12 June 1822 he was convicted for stealing provisions while assigned as a cook at the hospital, and given fifty lashes and returned to the Public Works Department. On 12 August 1823 he was sentenced to a further fifty lashes for stealing some tape and thread. On 7 June 1832 he was fined £1 for having harboured the convict Solomon Coleman (q.v.).

On 9 August 1833 the *Hobart Town Courier* reported at length about a large quantity of stolen property that was found

> in the home of a sort of pawnbroker named Phillips who kept a little store in Barrack Street near the bridge ... an immense collection of tools, wearing apparel, watches, plate jewellery, female attire etc was found. Phillips has long been a suspected character and not long since narrowly escaped conviction in the Supreme Court by some legal formality. He belonged by public profession to the notable fraternity of Hobart Town usurers, of whose exploits in that particular line, the most expert and hard headed of them had reason to be proud, his usual percentage being not 20 or 30 but 1000 per cent. Not longer than Saturday evening last a poor woman with a family of children applied to him for a loan of three shillings to buy them a dinner for Sunday when Phillips required a pledge in return of 15 shillings worth of clothes and an engagement to pay nine pennies a week until the whole was redeemed.

Phillips spent the next six years at Port Arthur serving a 14-year sentence. A ticket of leave was granted on 7 October 1840 and a conditional pardon in 1844. The official report said that he had spent ten and a half years in the colony and more than eight years with a ticket of leave. He had been 'well conducted since his second (colonial) conviction'. A certificate of freedom was issued in January 1848.

Phillips was appointed the 'collector' for the Hobart Town Synagogue at its first meeting on 16 January 1842. He lived in the same street as the synagogue and was a seat holder at the synagogue when it was built in 1845, but in November 1845

Phillips refused to be called up to the Torah and was fined 21 shillings, which he refused (or was unable) to pay. On 19 April 1849 he was sentenced at the Supreme Court in Hobart Town to seven years in prison for stealing two dozen metal files. He was, by this time, a widower and a 'very decrepit old man', and the theft may have been a manoeuvre to get back into gaol, with a guarantee of food and shelter.

Phillips served sixteen months at Port Arthur. A second ticket of leave was issued on 19 October 1852 and a certificate of freedom at Launceston on 8 April 1856 even though a surcharge of £17 14s 6d was levied against him for hospital charges made by the Colonial Government. He died at his home in Lower Brisbane Street, Launceston, on 18 August 1858 and left his total estate to the Hobart Town Synagogue. His will had been witnessed by Isaac Friedman (q.v.), Henry Horowitz (q.v.) and Louis Nathan (q.v.)

OBSP, 1819–20, cases 1258, 1259, p. 627; CON 31/34; CON 37/5, p. 1500; *Countess of Harcourt* Indent 2/8254, p. 218; HO 10/58; HO 11/4; *Hobart Town Courier*, 23 May 1829, 9 August 1833.

PHILLIPS, Phillip

d. 1850
Free.
Married; Trader; 6 children.

The brother of Solomon Phillips (q.v.), Samuel Phillips (q.v.) and Isaac Phillips (q.v.), Phillip Phillips was an innkeeper at Muston's Creek. He had married Susan (née Marks) (Susan Phillips, q.v.), the fourth child of Lyon Marks and Frances (née Levey), in England on 21 August 1839.

Phillips was an early storekeeper in Geelong and Colac, where he was one of the town's pioneers. In 1846 the Melbourne Hebrew Congregation Birth Book recorded that he was a 'storekeeper' in Geelong. The children of Phillip and Susan (Susannah) were: Elizabeth (born 1840), Jane, who died at the age of six months in Melbourne in 1844, Leah who died in 1846 aged six months, Lion (Lionel) (23 December 1846), Moss (18 October 1848), and Caroline (29 September 1850), born at Muston's Creek where Philip Phillips, like his brother-in-law Morris Marks (q.v.), owned the 'Rainbow Inn'.

In February 1846 Phillips' name appeared on the address of the 'British Jews residing in Port Phillip' congratulating Chief Rabbi Adler on his appointment. During the early part of 1849 Phillip Phillips contested a long hearing into his insolvency, which concluded with his indictment on criminal charges. Phillips had conspired to sell to Harris and Marks most of his stock at an absurdly low price by holding a 'public auction' in Colac at an early hour in the morning with little or no public announcement. On 22 May 1849 the *Melbourne Morning Herald* announced that Phillips would be able to pay twenty shillings in the pound as Samuel Henry Harris (a relative of his wife's) had come to the rescue and paid out his debt of £773 14s 3d.

Phillips was accidentally drowned in Muston's Creek and his was the first Jewish burial in Geelong, on 1 January 1851. Susan moved to Adelaide, where her brother

Morris Marks (q.v.) lived and on 17 June 1855, she married Solomon Lawrence of Hindley Street in Adelaide. Susan died in Melbourne in 1888 at the Yarra Bend Asylum, aged sixty.

Melbourne Morning Herald, 9 February, 15 February, 22 February 1849; *Geelong Advertiser*, 7 September 1848.

PHILLIPS, Phillip

b. Margate, 1822
St Vincent (3), 1853; Convict; Sentenced to 15 years, Central Criminal Court, 1847.
Single; Labourer; Height: 166 cm.

Dark complexion, black hair, brown eyes, large nose. Jew. Cannot read. Phillip Phillips was a pickpocket and had stolen a watch. He denied he had any previous convictions but the police report stated that this was his sixth. He was sent out on the final convict transport to Van Diemen's Land.

Phillips arrived in Hobart Town on 26 May 1853 and was assigned to the police. On 24 December 1853 he was reprimanded for being absent from duty. On 23 June 1856 he was arrested for being drunk and fined £5. A conditional pardon was granted on 13 October 1856.

CON 37/5; CON 33/115.

PHILLIPS, Rosetta

b. London, 1787–1844
Free.

Rosa Phillips, 'relict of Phillip Phillips of London' and 'the daughter of Sholom', died on 3 March 1844 'at Parramatta' and was buried at the Devonshire Street Jewish Cemetery. The notice in the *Sydney Morning Herald* reported: 'At her residence, Church Street, Parramatta ... of the firm of R. and S. Phillips, aged fifty-seven'. In 1901 Solomon Levy authorized the removal of her grave from the Devonshire Street cemetery to Rookwood.

PHILLIPS, Samuel

Industry, 1834; Free.
Single; 'Gentleman'; 3 children.

The *Industry* arrived in Sydney on 18 May 1834. Samuel Phillips married 'Leah' Cohen on 2 November 1842. Leah Cohen was born 'Ellen', and must have converted to Judaism. Their wedding was Jewish marriage no. 54 in New South Wales. In 1843 the official Birth Register of New South Wales records that Samuel Phillips and 'Ellen' had a newly born son called Lewis, who was listed as a 'Hebrew'. Lydia was born in Sydney in 1845. Samuel Phillips and J. Jones were listed as 'clothes brokers' in Clarence Street, Sydney, in *Low's Directory of the City and District of Sydney*, 1847. In 1848 the *New South Wales Almanack and Remembrancer* had an entry for 'Samuel Phillips, Woollen Draper, Aerial Clothing Establishment, 165 York Street South'. According to the *Sydney Morning Herald* of 6 January 1845, Phillips owned fifty acres in Bathurst. He purchased additional land at Molong and held the licence for the Travellers' Inn at Summer Hill in the District of Bathurst. Phillips was a seat holder in the York Street Synagogue in 1845.

Their three children were Lewis (1843), Lydia (1845) and Joshua (1847) who were all registered in the York Street register.

The burials of Samuel Phillips and Ellen were in the Toowong cemetery in the 1880s.

Industry Indent 4/5206; *Sydney Morning Herald*, 18 November 1844, 6 January 1845, 21 April 1845; Land Correspondence, 2/7950, 'of Molong' purchases, 1844 and 1850, Wellington Pastoral District, no. 5, 80 (1848). Additional research by Gary Luke.

PHILLIPS, Solomon

b. London, 1810–1877
Enchantress, 1833; Free.
Married; Dealer and minister; 14 children.

Solomon Phillips married Caroline (née Solomon) in 1832 when he was twenty-one years old and she was nineteen. The *Enchantress* arrived on 24 April 1833 and the family travelled steerage. Also on board were his sisters, Sarah Phillips, Julia Phillips, who married Abraham Wolff (q.v.).

Phillips took up a position as assistant minister at the newly formed synagogue in Bridge Street. His first recorded assignment was to officially name Elizabeth, the daughter of Vaiben Solomon (q.v.) and Sarah Solomon (née Smith), on 14 June 1834. He officiated at the marriage of Solomon Moses (q.v.) to Deborah Hart (28 January 1835) and Samuel Benjamin (q.v.) to Rachel Moses (q.v.) (4 February 1835) and at six other weddings between 1835 and 1840. Phillips moved to Parramatta in 1839 to open his own auctioneering premises. In September 1839 he was able to give £20 to the Sydney Synagogue building fund. He was appointed the official representative of the synagogue in Parramatta on 13 November 1843. Phillips was called upon to assist at the 1845 opening of the York Street Synagogue and donated £25 to the building appeal, together with a £1 donation to the Launceston Synagogue building fund.

Phillips moved to Parramatta and appears in the 1841 Census of New South Wales. In June 1851 George Moss (q.v.) wrote: 'He has acted as Baal Tefillah [prayer leader] during the High Holydays last four years and mohel bringing 50 infants into the covenant of Abraham. His conservative Jewish character has always been respected by Christian brethren. He has been active in the political, benevolent and literary affairs of Parramatta and was secretary and treasurer of the Road Trust and Town Council'. In 1852 Phillips and his large family moved to Melbourne, where he opened a furniture business in partnership with a Mr Bowling. The business dealt in furniture, ironmongery and pianos! Solomon Phillips and family left Melbourne in 1856 after being presented with an 'elegantly chased silver cup inscribed in Hebrew and English' and presented by a large crowd of grateful co-religionists.

In 1859 Phillips was selected by the newly formed secessionist Macquarie Street Synagogue to become its minister and remained in this post until 1874. He died in Carlton, Melbourne, on 23 February 1877, aged sixty-six. Caroline Phillips died on 15 May 1904 at the age of ninety-one.

Their children were: Sarah Rosetta (1834–1916), Phillip David (P. D.) (1836–1909), born in Parramatta, twins Ephraim and Daniel (1838), who both died in infancy and were buried at the Devonshire Street Jewish Cemetery on 6 March and 19 March 1838, Lydia (1839–1913), Joseph (1840), Mondle Emanuel (1841), Elias Edward (1843), Louis (Lewis) Samuel (1845), Hannah (1846–1920), Simeon (1847), Abraham (1849–1910), David Solomon (1850), born in Parramatta, and Samuel Asher (1852–1913).

Sarah Rosetta (Lipman) married Alexander Fox, and their son, Emanuel Phillips Fox, became a distinguished Australian artist. P. D. Phillips became a well-known solicitor and an Australian Shakespearean scholar. Simeon represented the electorate of Dubbo in the New South Wales Legislative Assembly from 1895 to 1904. He was also elected Mayor of Dubbo.

V. Cohen, 'Rev. Solomon Phillips and his Descendants', *AJJHS*, vol. 1, no. 3 (1940), p. 73f; *Empire* (Sydney), 10 June 1851; *Launceston Examiner*, 29 June 1844; A. S. Ellis, *Elias and Rebecca Ellis: The Phillips Connections and some of their Descendants*, privately printed, 1974; *Sydney Morning Herald*, 9 January 1845.

PHILLIPS, Susan (née MARKS)

b. London, 1818–1888
Free. Married; 6 children.

Susan Marks was the fourth child of Francis (née Levey) and Lyon Marks. She married Philip Phillips (q.v.) in England on 21 August 1839. They were in Melbourne by 1844. Philip Phillips drowned in 1851 and, in 1855, in Adelaide, Susan Phillips married Solomon Lawrence.

PHILLIPS, William

b. Liverpool, 1807
Mt Stewart Elphinstone (2), 1848; Convict; Sentenced to 10 years, Liverpool, 1844.
Married; Pawnbroker; Height: 160 cm; 1 child.

Jew. Can read and write. 'Very bad connexions.' William Phillips was sentenced for house breaking and stealing watches and jewellery. His father was Phillip Phillips, who lived in Liverpool and was born in Poland.

William Phillips arrived in Van Diemen's Land on 18 May 1848. Phillips was twice convicted for illegal hawking. A conditional pardon was granted on 28 December 1852. It was revoked on 8 July 1859. A conditional pardon was recommended for 'a later date'.

CON 33/89; CON 14/38; CON 18/49.

PHILLIPSON, Montague Levi (né Jonas Moses Barnet LEVI)

b. London, 1818–1879
Eden, 1838; Free.
Married; Merchant; 7 children.

The children of Moses Philip Levi (1786–1817) and Sophia (née Phillips) (1787–1845) adopted the surname 'Phillipson'. Jonas Moses Phillipson and his nephew, Philip Levi (q.v.), arrived in Adelaide on the *Eden* on 24 June 1838. Phillipson was therefore one of the early settlers in South Australia. Jonas Phillipson took 'Montague' as his first name. He was one of the original members of the 'Adelaide Club'. In 1839 he was recorded as having bought five town allotments at Port Lincoln. Montague Levi Phillipson married Caroline Levi, his niece, in London, on 31 July 1839.

Montague Phillipson's son, Nathaniel Edmund Phillipson (q.v.), who pioneered the development of the cattle industry in northern Australia, was born in Adelaide in 1844. There were six daughters, among them Ellen, Sophia (born 27 November 1847), Jeanette (21 January 1850), and Fanny (April 1854). Only one of the daughters married.

Phillipson was one of the foremost early shipping agents in South Australia. However, on 6 March 1850, in the *South Australian Register*, 'Montague Levi Phillipson, formerly of King William Street, Adelaide and now at St Mary's Village South Rd declares himself to be insolvent'.

Montague Levi Phillipson died in Adelaide on 2 January 1879. His wife Caroline died in Adelaide on 23 July 1889, at the age of sixty-nine.

South Australian Gazette and Colonial Register, 29 August 1839, 10 March 1847, 6 March 1850; Family Tree at SA Library; A. P. Joseph and K. J. Ireland, 'The Family of Nathan ben Elijah', *AJJHS*, vol. 7, no. 7 (1974), p. 513f.

PHILLIPSON, Nathaniel Edmund (Eliezer)

b. Adelaide, 1844–1898

Born in Adelaide in 1844, Nathaniel was the son of Montague Levi Phillipson (q.v.) and nephew of Philip Levi (q.v.). In 1862 he worked at Sir Thomas Elder's Umberatana Station. In the early 1870s he became joint manager of Elder, Smith and Co. He became managing director and largest share holder of the Beltana Pastoral Co., which was the northern part of Elder Smith. His career included learning the language of the Afghan camel drivers imported to develop the camel trade.

Nathaniel had married a Miss Zillah Levien in 1880, and in 1892 settled in Walkerville in Adelaide. N. E. Phillipson died on 18 August 1898.

Pritchard Index; research by Kingsley Ireland, Angaston, SA. Family notes by Owen Mace.

POLACK, Abraham

b. London, 1797–1873

Agamemnon, 1820; Convict; Sentenced to 7 years, Old Bailey, 1820.

Single; Merchant's clerk; Height: 179 cm; 3 children.

Fair ruddy complexion, dark brown hair, brown eyes. Abraham was the eldest son of the highly respected miniaturist and engraver Solomon Joel Polack and Sarah, and his family was said to have been one of the first Ashkenazi families to have settled in England. Abraham Polack accompanied a friend to an oyster shop after a night at the Drury Lane Theatre and stole the owner's watch while she was in another room with his friend. He was only arrested two months after the incident, and was sentenced on 17 February 1820. Polack's nephew, William Jones (q.v.), arrived as a convict on the Exmouth *in 1831. Joel Samuel Polack (q.v.), a younger brother of Abraham, arrived in Sydney in 1827.*

The *Agamemnon* arrived in New South Wales on 2 September 1820. In 1822 Polack wrote a petition to the Colonial Secretary asking for mercy and a mitigation of his sentence. He had been 'confined for four months on board ship by severe sickness and 25 weeks at the General Hospital subsequent to arrival. His health continues precarious'. He wrote that he was 'the son of a very respectable artist, a miniature painter in London. He served five years as an apprentice to a Mercantile House and was superintendent of a ship for two years in the Mediterranean trade with credit to himself and satisfaction to his owner Messrs Cropper Benson and Co of Liverpool. He was able to support himself without expense to the government as far as his state of health will admit'. He asked for a ticket of leave. His petition was accompanied by a medical certificate from William Bland, Surgeon, which stated that Polack had been in a bad state of health for the previous eighteen months. His request was refused.

In the 1822 General Muster of Convicts in New South Wales Abraham Polack was listed as a government servant assigned to Jacob Josephson (q.v.) in Pitt Street. His service was abruptly terminated when Polack testified to the police about Josephson's fraudulent disposal of property. Polack narrowly escaped being indicted for perjury and was saved by a technical dispute: 'There was much difficulty in coming to the conclusion as to whether Polack had been sworn as a Hebrew or as a Christian. The Chief Justice observed that an oath taken by a Jew in a Court was as equally binding and as solemn, as that of a Christian'.

Polack, 'clerk and shopman', aged twenty-five, married Hannah Bryan, aged nineteen, the daughter of James and Annie Brian, at St Philip's, Sydney, on 27 September 1824 and his religious affiliation often seemed to change. One of the witnesses to the wedding was Simeon Lear (q.v.). Sarah Polack, their daughter, was born on 27 June 1825 and baptised on 24 July 1825 at St James' Church. Solomon (1827) and Isaac (1829) were Polack's two other children. Only Sarah would marry a Jew—George Barron Goodman (q.v.). A ticket of leave was granted to Polack in October 1824. James Hall testified that 'it is our Certain belief' that Polack was 'an honest, sober and industrious character having served faithfully Mr Jacob Josephson from September 1820 to September 1824'. The following month Polack opened a grocery store at 6 Hunter Street and in 1825 he bought a sloop, *Sally*, which sailed south in an unsuccessful expedition in search of seals.

In 1826 he opened the Waterloo Shop, which Cooper and Levey assured the general public had no connection with their own Waterloo Warehouse. A certificate of freedom was issued on 17 February 1827. From 1827 to 1833 Polack held the licence of the London Tavern. In 1828 he petitioned the Governor to allow the Jews of Sydney to establish a synagogue. The petition was refused with the comment from Governor Darling: 'It is hard, if they cannot procure some other representative. Put away'. On 16 February 1833 Polack announced that he had received a licence as a 'Vendue Master' and became an auctioneer, and within a very short time became Sydney's most prominent auctioneer. He purchased extensive land holdings. When Samuel Lyons (q.v.) temporarily retired from business in 1836, Polack took his place. He became one of the first subscribers to the Commercial Bank and he sold large parts of Solomon Levey's (q.v.) enormous estate. In 1836 he was elected president of the Sydney Synagogue and in 1839 was chairman of the building appeal, generously donating £400 to the building fund in his own name, the name of his wife and his three children.

In 1837 he handed over the auctioneering side of his business to James Ablett, alias Mr T. J. Wilson, to carry on the business at 74 George Street in the premises formerly occupied by V & E Solomon. In October 1839 Wilson left New South Wales having successfully stolen at least £50 000. The newspapers wrote 'Speedy as his rise has been still more speedy was his downfall! ... Before his departure however by some means yet inexplicable he had contrived to entangle a mercantile firm. On Wilson's arrival Mr Abraham Polack, the auctioneer, a wealthy Jewish emancipist took him by the hand, and became security'. Polack had been in London when the crash came, and returned to Sydney with his brother Joel Samuel Polack (q.v.). But the damage was too extensive and in May 1848 he was declared bankrupt. His creditors allowed him to keep 'his wearing apparel'.

On 1 July 1848 he was able to renew his licence and resumed his career as auctioneer. An article in the *Illustrated Sydney Advertiser* quoted in London's *Jewish Chronicle* of 22 September 1854 credited him with being the first Australian businessman to send wheat to Valparaiso and the first individual to devise and to plan the establishment of railways in New South Wales. Sadly, tragedy awaited him. On 15 October 1860 he was charged at the Central Police Office for obtaining money under false pretences from the Sydney solicitor W. P. Moffat. Polack was convicted on 6 February 1861 for having swindled the solicitor of £140 by claiming to have been the owner of a property between George and Pitt streets. He was sentenced to three and half years hard labour on the roads. The sentence was soon changed to hard labour within the Darlinghurst Gaol 'due to Abram [sic] Polack's health'.

Polack endured the prison sentence. He died on 12 June 1873. Mrs Hannah Polack died on 11 June 1873, and was buried as a Christian at Rookwood. They were survived by their two sons and their daughter. Elizabeth Poole (q.v.), one of Abraham Polack's sisters, was the wife of David Poole (q.v.). The other sister, Rebecca, was married to John Salmon, and was the mother of Alexander Salmon (q.v.), whose daughter was the last queen of Tahiti.

OBSP, 1819–29, case 418, p. 184; *Agamemnon* Indent 4/4007, p. 219; Petition 4/1763, p. 203; CS 4/1747, 4/1867, no. 15, 9 May 1822; Petition 48, in 4/1870; 4/1716.1, p. 250; *Sydney Gazette*, 17 February 1825, 13 February 1828, 18 February 1828, 3 February 1838; *Australian*, 14 April 1824, 20 January 1825, 23 June 1825, 25 November 1824, 9 December 1824, 23 June 1825, 20 March 1830, 1 January 1833, 17 January 1833; CF 041/6019; *Sydney Chronicle*, 18 April 1848; *Port Phillip Herald*, 10 January 1840; *South Australia Gazette and Colonial Register*, 6 May 1848; *Bell's Life*, 9 March 1850; G. F. J. Bergman, 'Abraham Polack: Rise and Fall of a Jewish Emancipist', *AJJHS*, vol. 7, no. 5 (1973), p. 348f.

POLACK, Asher (POLLOCK)

d. 1834
Albermarle, 1791; Convict; Sentenced to life, Old Bailey, 1790.

Polack was convicted of 'Highway robbery'. Together with an accomplice he took a quantity of cloth away from a 13-year-old messenger boy in a Whitechapel street. Its value was approximately £4. Asher Polack was sentenced to death at the Old Bailey Sessions on 13 January 1790, though this was later commuted to transportation for life.

Polack arrived in New South Wales in October 1791. In the 1814 Muster, Asher Polack was listed as a convict servant assigned to the Parramatta District. On 23 November 1814 Asher Pollock was sent to the Newcastle Penal Settlement for three years. He was still in Newcastle during the General Muster of 1820. According to the General Muster of Convicts in New South Wales he was working as an overseer of the water carts in Sydney in 1822. An Asher Polack was named in the 1828 Census as a carpenter at the Hyde Park Barracks. He died in the General Hospital, Sydney, on 24 September 1834 and was buried in the Devonshire Street Jewish Cemetery.

OBSP, 1789–90, case 159, p. 172; *Albermarle* Indent 4/4003, p. 378; A1225; HO 10/1; HO 10/13; 1814 Muster A1225; CS Copies of Letters Sent Within the Colony, 1814–15, Convicts sent to Newcastle, 23 November 1814, 4/3493.

POLACK, Joel Samuel

b. London, 1807–1882
Elizabeth, 1827; Free.
Single; Merchant and ship's chandler.

The younger brother of Abraham Polack (q.v.) and the son of the well-known engraver and miniaturist, Solomon Joel Polack and Sarah Polack, J. S. Polack arrived in Sydney on 27 April 1827. He briefly set himself up in business, and left in November to work in Madagascar as 'Painter and Designer' to the King of Madagascar. The King died shortly after Polack's arrival and he returned to New South Wales on the *Chalcedony* in 1830. In 1831 he moved to Hokianga on the west coast of the North Island of New Zealand and became one of the earliest European traders in both New Zealand and the islands of the South Pacific.

Polack returned to England in 1837 by way of Sydney and founded J. S. Polack & Co., ships' chandlers, at 7 George Street, selling charts of 'near-by seas' and basic commodities for ships. By 1838 he was in England and appeared before the Select Committee of the House of Lords that had been set up to inquire into the state of affairs of New Zealand. He was described as 'a worthy and wandering offshoot of the tribe of Abraham' and his testimony was scornfully belittled by the London *Times* on the grounds that Polack was a Jew and therefore could not to be believed. Polack was subsequently awarded £100 damages for libel. The following year Polack published a two-volume authoritative book, *New Zealand: Being a Narrative of Travels and Adventures*, which he skilfully illustrated, and in which he frequently noted similarities between Jewish law and Maori law and custom.

Polack served as United States Vice-Consul in Auckland from 1845 to 1848. With his brother Abraham Polack, he established a store, first at Hokianga and then Kororareka (Russell) at the Bay of Islands. He was present at the first land sale at Auckland. Polack remained at Kororareka, where his store and inn became the central focus of battle in the Maori War of 1845 and Polack was seriously wounded. Polack moved to Auckland and worked as a ship's broker and buyer of flax. James Busby, the British Government's Official Resident, hated Polack, who had manufactured New Zealand's first beer and sold it to the Maori: 'He is universally detested here. The other settlers know that he is as great a rogue as the worst of them and he, forsooth, wants to play the gentleman amongst them. Confound the scamp that I should have taken up so much paper with him!'

J. S. Polack bought land in the first Melbourne land sale of 1847. His block was in Lonsdale Street, immediately behind the land set aside for a synagogue. Polack set up business in Sydney in 1849 advertising 'Coloured Daguerreotypes' at his rooms at 49 Hunter Street. Later that year Polack followed the gold rush to California and subsequently married Mrs Mary Hart in the United States. He died in San Francisco on 17 April 1882.

L. M. Goldman, *The History of the Jews in New Zealand*; G. F. J. Bergman, 'Abraham Polack: Rise and Fall of a Jewish Emancipist', *AJJHS*, vol. 7, no. 5 (1973), p. 349.

POLACK, Samuel (Solomon POLOCK)

b. London

Scarborough (2), 1790; Convict; Sentenced to life, Old Bailey, 1787.

'Solomon Polock' was indicted for stealing 60 yards of manchester cotton, which he took from the counter of a shop. A witness said that Polock had been acting suspiciously as he came out of the warehouse with the cloth. He was dressed as a porter. He was caught after a short chase through the city streets. He was sentenced to death on 10 January 1787, and held at Newgate for two and a half years before being among 100 convicts whose sentences were commuted. He was the son of the artist Solomon Joel Polack and brother of Abraham Polack (q.v.) and Joel Samuel Polack (q.v.).

Polack arrived in Sydney on 28 June 1790. He escaped from Sydney on the *Matilda* in December 1792 with a crew of twenty-eight men and boys. The ship was on the way to the Marquesas Islands and ran aground on a reef near Tahiti on 25 February 1792. Most of the crew managed to reach Tahiti in boats. Captain William Bligh on the *Providence* took the survivors on board in April. He wrote that he 'took note of sailors' names and a person who I am informed was transported for life to Port Jackson, called Samuel Pollent [*sic*], escaped in the *Matilda,* remains also on the islands, but I could get no further information about him, than that he was a Jew'. A missionary, the Rev. Dr Thomas Haweis, told a similar story from Tahiti: 'At Otahate I found several Englishmen who had been shipwrecked. They had been

there about twelve months one of them who they said was a Jew … There is also one of the convicts. He got there from Botany Bay. They seem to live at their ease!'
OBSP, 1786–87, case 176, p. 263; Rev. Dr T. Haweis, ms, ML, A1963; Wm Bligh, Log of HMS *Providence*, ML, A564.

POLACK, Sarah

b. Sydney, 1825

Sarah was the daughter of Abraham Polack (q.v.) and his wife Hannah. On 4 April 1843 the first letter book of the Sydney Synagogue recorded that Abraham Polack's application for his daughter Sarah to be married in a Jewish ceremony was 'met with entire approbation'. She married George Barron Goodman (q.v.).

POLLARD, Lewis

b. Bishopsgate, 1814
Waterloo, 1835; Convict; Sentenced to 7 years, Westminster, 1834.
Married; Labourer; Height: 166 cm; 1 child.

Pale complexion, oval full face, black hair, hazel eyes, medium long nose, high forehead. Lewis Pollard had been in prison before as the result of a 'row'. He was sentenced at Westminster, on 25 August 1834, to transportation for robbing a woman of a box at a market. Pollard was married and lived at Bishopsgate with his wife Frances and one child. The surgeon reported that his behaviour on board ship was 'quiet and orderly'.

On 6 July 1835, while working with the Public Works Department, Lewis Pollard was admonished for fighting. On 29 November 1835 he was put in irons for fourteen days for 'neglecting work'. By 10 June 1836 he was working as an assigned servant, when he was found to be drunk and spent four hours in the stocks. He remained on assigned service, with two minor misdemeanours, until 18 April 1849 when he was granted a certificate of freedom (no. 939).
CON 31/35, no. 1113; CON 18/21, Description Book.

POOLE, David

b. London, 1776–1859
Sarah, 1828; Free.
Married; Attorney and solicitor; 3 children.

David Poole was admitted to the King's Bench, Westminster, in 1795. He lived at Old Broad Street in the City of London. Poole arrived in Sydney on 31 July 1828 with his wife Elizabeth (née Polack) (q.v.), aged twenty-seven, and their children, David jnr (q.v.), aged eight, Sarah, aged four, and Amelia, aged two. Elizabeth Poole was the sister of Abraham Polack (q.v.). Poole was already fifty-two years of age when he came out to Australia. He was the only member of the legal profession in Australia who was Jewish.

Poole was admitted as a barrister, solicitor attorney and proctor of the Supreme Court of New South Wales on 15 August 1828. Five days after he was admitted,

Rebecca Levi (q.v.), the widow of Walter Jacob Levi (q.v.), asked Poole to be her proctor. In March 1829 he represented Esther Johnston (Esther Abrahams, q.v.) when she was arraigned in court by her son Robert.

The Poole family was listed on the 1828 Census as 'Protestant'. They lived in Castlereagh Street. Poole practised as a solicitor in Sydney and refused the post of Solicitor General in 1830. He was deputy chairman of the Australian Steam Conveyance Co. (1833), director of the Australian Wheat Co. (1835), and director of the Sydney Gas Co. (1836). Poole took a leading role at a meeting of the Patriotic Association in Sydney on 1 June 1835 that advocated a bicameral parliamentary system. He was a leading freemason in Sydney and agent for the new colony of Victoria in January 1840. Poole served as the honorary solicitor of the congregation in 1839 and during the years of the York Street Synagogue's construction he donated £50 to the building appeal.

In 1841 the new Sydney Synagogue's committee presented Poole with a 'handsome silver salver in gratitude for his services' to the congregation. He stood unsuccessfully for the Sydney Municipal Council in 1842. He told the electors 'I refer to what I have already accomplished for the City's advancement and prosperity, namely the introduction of steam vessels on our river and shares that useful help to our comfort and protection, the Gas Light, a company which was formed greatly with my help and protection'. In 1843 he was elected auditor for the City of Sydney's Brisbane Ward. He maintained close links with Tahiti, where his cousin-in-law Alexander Salmon (q.v.) lived. In 1845 Poole went to England. On the way home he was admitted to the Bar in Van Diemen's Land on 30 May 1845. He lived at 18 Davey Street, Hobart Town, and applied to practise as a solicitor, describing himself as 'formerly of Old Broad Street, in the City of London, gentleman, one of the attorneys of the Queen's Bench at Westminster, Solicitor of the High Court of Chancery, late of George and Castlereagh Streets, Sydney'. With his wife and two daughters he joined the new Hobart Town congregation while he was in Tasmania. He was allotted seat no. 10, paying £5 to the synagogue but refusing to be called to the Torah at *Simchat Torah*, for which he was fined one guinea. He refused to pay but in January 1846 gave the synagogue £5 in cash as a parting shot before he left the colony. Poole appeared in the *London Directory 1851* as a solicitor at 27 Albany Street, Regent's Park. Poole died in London on 31 October 1859.

G. F. J. Bergman, 'David Poole: The First Jewish Lawyer in Australia', *AJJHS*, vol. 7, no. 3 (1972), p. 239f; *Colonial Times*, 19 March 1830; *Sydney Gazette*, 30 January 1834, 5 June 1834, 10 December 1835, 16 April 1836, 2 June 1835, 12 September 1842; *Voice of Jacob* (London) 1841, p. 22; *Hobart Town Courier*, 24 May 1845.

POOLE, David jnr

b. London, 1820–1865
Sarah, 1828; Free.
Single.

David Poole jnr came to New South Wales with his siblings and parents in 1828. He grew up in Sydney. In 1839 David Poole jnr was dismissed by his employer, Mr G. Ralston of Bathurst. In a subsequent law case Ralston was fined five shillings for having assaulted Poole snr at the Royal Hotel. In 1841 Poole jnr went to live in Tahiti, where Alexander Salmon (q.v.), the son of his aunt, Rebecca (née Polack), lived. Alexander Salmon was married to a Tahitian princess. At the same time David's sisters and parents went to Hobart Town. The *Sydney Gazette* reported: 'Mr David Poole has been honoured by the Queen of Tahiti with the public and private seal. This favour has conferred to Mr Poole the office of Lord Chancellor and Lord Privy Seal of her sable Majesty'. David Poole jnr arrived in Sydney as a cabin passenger on the *Emma Prescott* from Tahiti on 17 February 1852, and left Sydney a month later. He returned to Tahiti and his name appeared on an address to the French rear admiral who began the French occupation of the islands.

Poole eventually returned to England and became a 'coffee-house keeper'. When he died, on 9 June 1865, he left assets valued at less than £200.

G. F. J. Bergman, 'David Poole: The First Jewish Lawyer in Australia', *AJJHS*, vol. 7, no. 3 (1972), p. 239f; *Sydney Gazette*, 5 July 1842.

POOLE, Elizabeth (née POLACK)

b. London
Sarah, 1828; Free.
Married.

Elizabeth was the wife of David Poole (q.v.), and the sister of Abraham Polack (q.v.).

PYKE, Woolf Lewis (Ze'ev)

Free.
Single; Dealer; 6 children.

Woolf Lewis Pyke, the son of Eliezer Pyke of London, married Rosetta (Rosa) Moss (q.v.), the daughter of Marcus and Abigail Warschauer (q.v.) and sister of George Moss (q.v.), on 8 August 1844. A child was born in Sydney on 11 October 1845. Pyke was a seat holder in the new York Street Synagogue in 1845. He went bankrupt during the first half of that year. The *Sydney Chronicle* wrote: 'The insolvent attributes his insolvency to dullness in trade and losses sustained in his business'. He was listed in *Low's Directory of the City and District of Sydney*, 1847, as a tailor and cap-maker at 80 York Street.

Pyke apparently left his wife and family in the 1850s and went to live in New Zealand. Rosetta, known as Rosa, died aged ninety-seven on 5 March 1914. Woolf and Rosa had six children: Charlotte (1845), born in Sydney, Abraham (1847), Alexander (1849), born in Queanbeyan, and Lewis and twins, Amelia and George (1857), who were born in Bathurst.

Sydney Chronicle, 17 June 1848.

R

RAPHAEL, Henry

1825–1894
1842; Free.
Married; Dealer; 13 children.

The brother of Ralph Raphael (q.v.) and Joseph (John) George Raphael (q.v.), Henry Raphael was listed as a founding member of the Melbourne Hebrew Congregation in 1843 and, almost at once, embarked upon a congregational career as heckler and trouble maker. On 26 November 1843 he was fined five shillings for 'being repeatedly called to order' at the Annual General Meeting of the congregation. An apology was demanded from him at a general meeting on 7 January 1844. Cashmore Lazarus (q.v.) and James Simeon (q.v.) were on Raphael's side. They lost the debate and the vote, and consequently the three dissidents resigned. Somehow, Raphael was back on the committee two weeks later (21 January 1844). Raphael left Melbourne to find a wife. On 4 June 1851, at the Great Synagogue, London, he married Caroline Simmons, the third daughter of S. Simmons of Edgware Road, London.

In 1854 Henry Raphael was accused by David and Moses Benjamin (qq.v.) of having called the officers of the synagogue 'a set of thieves'. The quarrel continued a few days later on Rosh Hashanah in the synagogue and as a consequence he was fined £10 10s and his membership was cancelled from 1 January 1854.

Raphael became involved in the creation of the East Melbourne Synagogue in the 1870s. Raphael was, by this time, an estate agent in Collins Street, and an unsuccessful candidate for the Melbourne City Council in 1870. Raphael became a supporter of the Jewish religious Reform Movement in the early 1880s and, while on a European tour, investigated the latest trends in religious reform.

Henry Raphael served as Sergeant Instructor in Military Drill at the Melbourne Hebrew School until the school closed in 1886. He died on 3 May 1894. His wife Caroline died on 3 March 1896, aged sixty-two.

Their children were : Katherine (1852), Philippe (1854), Rachael (1855), Isaac (1860), Henrietta (1861), Joseph George (1861?), Alexander (1863), Harry (1865), Frederick (1866), Elias (1868), Louis (1869), Charles (1872) Beaconsfield (1879).

Melbourne Hebrew Congregation Letter Book, no. 1, 16 October 1853. Research by Dr Rodney Eisfelder of Melbourne.

RAPHAEL, Joseph (RAPHELL)

b. Stepney, London, 1785–1853
Calcutta, 1803; Convict; Sentenced to life, Middlesex, 1802.
Single; Orange seller; Height: 155 cm; 2 children.

Dark complexion, black hair, black eyes. Could read and write. Jew. Lived near the corner of Flower Street and Dean Street, Spitalfields. Joseph Raphael was convicted of 'Highway Robbery'. Together with three other men Raphael had attacked Peter Theodary, a drunken Portuguese sailor, on his way from Wapping to Whitechapel. The gang had stolen Theodary's silver watch and clothes. Raphael was described by witnesses as 'the little one'. He was sentenced to death at the Old Bailey on 20 April 1802, and this was subsequently commuted to transportation for life.

Joseph Raphael was an involuntary participant in the pioneering attempt to establish and outpost at Sorrento on Port Phillip Bay and then settled at the Derwent. He was involved in an attempt to escape from Van Diemen's Land in 1807 and on 20 March 1811 was sent to Newcastle and was listed in the Muster of 1811 in New South Wales. The records show that Raphael was a disobedient and unruly prisoner who was frequently punished. On 28 June 1812 he was listed as a 'runaway' under the name of 'Rayfield'.

On 1 December 1817 Raphael wrote a petition from Newcastle to Governor Macquarie asking for a pardon and claiming to be incapacitated: 'That from Petitioner's incapability to Labour was sent from Hobart Town to this Station. He has made it his study to do credit by entering into an extended Line of Business, and he has never been guilty of or accused of a wrong action'. Archdeacon Cowper added 'I believe the petitioner to be a sober and industrious man'. As a result he was issued with a conditional pardon. However, Raphael continued to attract trouble and only a few weeks later his pardon was cancelled.

Raphael moved to Sydney and in September 1818 he wrote another plea for a pardon. He praised the Governor's

> gracious clemency by being permitted to return from Newcastle to Sydney. [Raphael] presumes to say that his future life and conduct shall not only make atonement for his past Errors but prove himself not untrustworthy. Your Excellency was pleased to insert Petitioner's name for a conditional pardon in January last but your Petitioner was so unfortunate as to involve himself in a Dilemma he shall ever deplore before he had the benefit of that Emancipation has lately been married by Your Excellency's special licence at Newcastle.

Raphael was twenty-eight and had married Ann Clements (aged twenty-two), who had come to Australia on the *Mary Anne*. Ann had a daughter Jane and an adopted son.

In 1819 Raphael was fined £40 by the Magistrate, Hannibal Macarthur, for displaying goods for sale without a hawker's licence. In 1824 a visitor to Sydney described him as among those Jews 'who were rich, keeping a handsome Tilbury rather stout and not too tall'.

Raphael opened a shop at 11 Pitt Street where he sold calico, vinegar and tea. On 10 June 1823 he made a deposition about some stolen cloth and escaped a trial.

Raphael was ever enterprising. In December 1826 he appeared in court charged with having destroyed a stall at the market. The *Sydney Gazette* reported that he 'conducted the case in a stream of unrivalled eloquence'. Evidently Raphael had given Michael Naphtali (q.v.) a coat he was wearing, and in return Naphtali had allowed Raphael to 'eliminate' his rival at the market. He appeared at the Supreme Court in Sydney on 28 November 1828 in an action to recover six chests of tea, a cart, a mare and harness. Judge Field called it 'a mere juggle between two Jews' and dismissed the case. Raphael's fury about the verdict was evident and, on 9 December 1830, Raphael assaulted the Magistrate, Captain Brabyn, in Pitt Street and was find £10 and sentenced to three months in gaol.

Raphael had moved his shop to 92 George Street by October 1827 but still did business from 'a sort of Moveable shop' (*Sydney Gazette,* 21 June 1826). The *Australian* (2 September 1826) tells how Raphael had arrived in Newcastle, selling his goods by auction: 'He treated his customers with such potent libation of peppermint and brandy during the sale that more than one half of the bidders became subject to its powerful influence; and were covered at mid day to their respective habitations unconscious of the piteous exhibition they were making to their more sober neighbours'.

In September 1826 Raphael brought his adopted son to study at the Parramatta Commercial Academy. The principal was then confronted by Mrs Joseph Aaron, Mrs Josephson and Mr Harper, who withdrew their children in protest. However, the boy was admitted.

On 26 June 1830 Raphael told the *Sydney Gazette* that he was about to open the Manchester Arms in the mansion built by Mr Daniel Cooper on the site of the 'old' Manchester Arms in George Street at the north corner of Park Street: 'The alteration would be sedulous and respectful'. The role of innkeeper did not suit Raphael, and in December 1830 he was insolvent; David Poole (q.v.) was the solicitor for the estate. Raphael returned to the Sydney market and Ann Clements, alias Raphael, who had received a conditional pardon on 26 November 1825, absconded. Raphael wrote in the *Sydney Gazette* of 8 December 1831 that she had left him 'without any just cause or provocation', and he disclaimed her debts. On 25 November 1833 the *Australian* announced that Joseph Raphael would be 'leaving the colony having succeeded to a fortune'. Sadly, Raphael did not leave Sydney and would be declared insolvent in 1832, 1837 and 1843.

The *Sydney Gazette* of 31 October 1835 described yet another court case:

> Mr Joseph Raphael of facetious notoriety was charged at the Police Office on Thursday last, with having indecently exposed his person in the public market place on the Friday previous. Honest Joe and a fair dame y'clept Ann Jones occupy stalls in the market place opposite each other and that they are rival butter merchants. Raphael is selling for one shilling and six pence and she for two shillings. By way of rejoinder to a most inoffensive expression of the fair lady the defendant committed the act of public indecency. The humorous Joseph (not the Joseph of Holy Writ) talked of his large family of orphan children and his long decent and respectable career of 34 years in this colony.

He was fined £5.

Joseph Raphael received an absolute pardon on 18 August 1842, though he still refused to 'behave'. The *Sydney Chronicle* on 6 April 1848 reported 'Joseph Raphael, a gentleman well known in Sydney, preferred a complaint against Henry Lord, a tailor for assault'. Raphael had bought a suit of clothing for £3 5s and paid only £2. Consequently the tailor and his apprentices 'have been in the habit of giving Raphael "a salute" on the subject every time he passed their premises. "Imagine, Your Worships", said Raphael, "what would be the consequence if every gentleman who owed on his clothes was to be so served"'. The case was dismissed. Joseph Raphael died on 26 September 1853 and was buried by the Rev. J. Eggleston of the Methodist Church. The tombstone of Raphael (aged seventy-two) and his wife Ann (aged fifty-seven) still stands at the Pioneers' Park in Botany Bay.

Marjorie Tipping, *Convicts Unbound*, p. 303; *OBSP*, 20 April 1802, 4/3491, p. 286; Petition no. 274, 1 December 1817, 4/1852; Petition no. 3, 4/1860, p. 219f., Petition for Mitigation of Sentence 1818, 4/1856, p. 219f.; Bigge Appendix, BT Box 19, p. 2920, 18 September 1819; Court of Criminal Jurisdiction, X820, p. 31; HO 10/53; Letter, 16 January 1824, G. T. Boyes, from Sydney, ML, Q/9911b,; *Sydney Gazette*, 28 November 1818, 31 July 1819, 18 March 1820, 9 December 1820, 21 June 1826, 23 August 1826, 2 September 1826, 16 December 1826, 20 December 1826, 16 July 1827, 10 October 1828, 28 November 1828, 26 June 1830, 8 December 1831, 25 July 1837, 4 October 1838; *Australian*, 18 November 1824, 2 September 1826, 6 September 1826, 9 July 1830, 6 August 1831, 24 February 1832, 31 October 1835; *Sydney Chronicle*, 6 April 1848.

RAPHAEL, Joseph George (John)

b. London, 1818–1879
1839; Free.
Single; Merchant; 7 children.

Born on 16 February 1818, the son of Phillip and Grace Raphael of London, and the brother of Henry Raphael (q.v.) and Ralph Raphael (q.v.), J. G. Raphael arrived in Sydney in 1839. His first job was in a draper's shop selling ribbons. The 22-year-old Joseph George Raphael married Maria Moses, the eldest daughter of Moses Moses (q.v.), on 30 December 1840 at the Bridge Street synagogue. In 1842 he began a business in partnership with James Simeon (q.v.), as a general dealer, and later, with John Barnett (q.v.), in Lower George Street. 'Raphael & Co' was well known for its locally produced household furniture. In the *Sydney Morning Herald* of 10 June 1844 Raphael announced that he had taken over the 'old established Seaman's Shipping and Registry Office in Lower George Street'. In Fowles' *Sydney in 1848* there is a picture of his shop, where he was a 'Clothier and Draper'. Raphael fell victim to the economic slump and on 10 November 1843 was declared to be insolvent with debts of £502 and assets of £32.

Raphael served as a member of the York Street Synagogue Committee and as its honorary treasurer. In 1859 he supported the establishment of the Macquarie Street Congregation and remained on the committee until 1867. On 15 December 1859 he was elected an auditor of the Sydney City Council. It was his second attempt to be elected, the first being in 1857. On 1 December 1860 he was elected an alderman for the Bourke Ward. He stood three times for election as mayor of the City of Sydney and failed each time—1865, 1870 and 1871. In January 1872 he was elected to the Legislative Assembly as a member for West Sydney. Raphael served for one term in the Assembly. In October 1873 he proposed a bill to give the vote for mayor to the general population instead of to the aldermen. Not surprisingly the bill failed to enlist the support of his fellow aldermen. Raphael's health was failing and in November 1878 the council presented him with a sterling silver cruet and kettle. The Lieutenant Governor wrote: 'I am sorry, for the sake of the religious community to which you belong, that you are retiring from the important office'. Raphael was a well-known supporter of charitable causes. He died on 2 February 1879. His wife Maria died on 24 October 1899.

Raphael was instrumental in establishing a Jewish cemetery in Lidcombe, which was popularly known as 'Raphael's Cemetery'. Four daughters were living when J. G. Raphael died. Of their children, their daughter Caroline was born in 1841 in Sydney; Rosetta, born in 1843, became the wife of Woolf Benjamin Lee of Sydney; Elizabeth Dinah, born in 1844, became the wife of Meyer Mandel, jeweller and watchmaker of Armidale; Deborah was born in 1846; and Esther Matilda, born in 1847, became the wife of Jacob Samuel Rosenthal of Lower Fort Street, an oculist and aurist.

E. S. Marks, 'Joseph G. Raphael', *AJJHS*, vol. 1 (1943), no. 10, p. 368f; Dennis Bluth, 'Jews on the Council of the City of Sydney', *AJJHS*, vol. 11, no. 6 (1993), p. 872f; CS Miscellaneous Persons, Out, 4/3550.

RAPHAEL, Ralph

b. London, 1823–1890
Free.
Single; Dealer; 4 children.

The brother of Joseph (John) George Raphael (q.v.) and Henry Raphael (q.v.), Raphael was in Melbourne in 1841 and was described as a 'shopman' of Elizabeth Street who had charge of Michael Cashmore's (q.v.) 'branch establishment opposite Victoria House'.

Ralph Raphael moved to Adelaide in 1849. The *South Australian Register* reported that he had married Esther Simmons, the daughter of S. Simmons of Edgware Road, London, on 17 November 1849. When his brother Henry Raphael left the colony in 1851, Ralph was authorised to look after any of his unfinished business. Ralph Raphael was listed as a member of the committee of the Adelaide Hebrew Congregation in 1850.

The children of Ralph and Esther Raphael were Philip (born 10 July 1850), Simeon (7 September 1851), Henry Joseph (13 March 1855), and Samuel Phillip (6 June 1859). The family lived at North Terrace.

Ralph Raphael died on 29 October 1890 at the age of sixty-seven. Esther had died on 28 September 1879 at the age of fifty.

South Australia Gazette and Colonial Register, 4 February 1850, 7 September 1850.

REDGATE, Nancy

Mayflower, 1841; Free.

A 'widow' Nancy arrived in Hobart Town on 26 March 1841. She accompanied her grandchildren and her daughter Sarah Moses (q.v.) who was married to Emanuel 'Money' Moses (q.v.).

'Mrs Redgate' lived at 83 Elizabeth Street, Hobart Town, where the Jewish marriage of Philip Levy (q.v.) to Mary Moses took place on 3 February 1842. On 20 August 1844, following a dispute with the congregational authorities about a financial settlement, she was permitted to marry Saul Hyman Levy (q.v.) in a ceremony sanctioned by the Hobart Synagogue.

Minutes of the Hobart Synagogue and the congregational Marriage Register; *Hobart Town Courier*, 30 March 1841.

REICHENBERG, Joseph

b. Naples, 1792–1851
1824; Free.

Joseph Reichenberg was the Roman Catholic band master who arrived in Australia with the 40th Regiment in 1824. Born in the Kingdom of Naples, he joined the British Army as a drummer boy, and in 1828, he left the army and became a 'Professor' of music in Van Diemen's Land. Reichenberg was a friend of Henry Russell (q.v.), who organised an 'instrumental group' that held a concert in Hobart Town in July 1833.

Reichenberg became 'Director of Music' at the Hobart Theatre in early March 1834 and worked closely with John Lewis Jacobs (Jacob Lewis Jacobs, q.v.) in the presentation of *Black Eyed Susan*, and *The Cabin Boy*, and regularly presented musical interludes at the theatre. Reichenberg arranged the Jewish liturgical music provided by John Henry Anderson (q.v.) and conducted the choir for the dedication of the Hobart Synagogue in 1845. On 9 September 1845 it was resolved by the Board of the Hobart Synagogue to ask him to teach the choir the extra tunes for the High Holydays. On 30 July 1845 Reichenberg had advertised in the *Hobart Town Courier* that he had compiled a collection of Hebrew melodies, which he hoped to publish 'if sufficient money' was to be subscribed. The music was published: *Shirot V'Zimrot—Ancient Hebrew Melodies—sung at the consecration of the Syngagogue, Argyle Street, Hobart Town V. D. L. dedicated to Mrs Louis Nathan. Harmonized and Arranged for the Pianoforte by J. Reichenberg*, Thomas Browne, 54 Liverpool Street, price 6 shillings.

Reichenberg had three daughters, one of whom served as organist for St Joseph's Church in Hobart from the 1870s to 1929.

Hobart Town Courier, 26 July 1833.

REUBEN, George

Canada, 1842; Free.
Single.

George Reuben came to Van Diemen's Land from London on the *Canada*, travelling steerage and without government assistance. Reuben was a member of the Hobart Town Synagogue in 1845. He paid ten shillings and owed twenty-six shillings. He couldn't pay, and it was still listed as a debt when in 1848 he offered three shillings as his donation.

CSO 671/8F0/107; *Hobart Town Courier*, 29 April 1842.

REUBEN, Henry (Hyam) Robert

1811–1897
1829; Free.
Single; Dealer; 5 children.

The brother of Solomon Reuben (q.v.), Henry Reuben was appointed official collector for the *Australian* and was the only person authorised to receive money on behalf of the newspaper, according to the *Australian* of 7 March 1834. In the same issue it was also reported that Samuel Lyons had sold 593 pounds of wool to Mr Reuben. The *Sydney General Trade List* of 7 February 1835 included one bale of 'slops' (ready-made clothes) imported by Reuben from London. On 10 October 1835 the *Sydney Gazette* noted that the store of Mr Reuben in Lower George Street had been broken into. In 1837 Reuben became a member of the Sydney Synagogue Committee and 'Hyme' Reuben married Emma Solomon (q.v.) in Sydney on 8 August 1838 (Jewish marriage no. 22). He signed a petition of good wishes to Queen Victoria from a list of Maitland residents on her accession to the throne. Reuben was listed as one of the applicants for additional publican's licences on 18 September 1840 and became the innkeeper of the Black Swan in George Street, Sydney. In September 1842 he moved to the Dove Inn, Brickfield Hill, and held the licence until he was declared insolvent on 15 December 1843 (*Sydney Morning Herald*). He was discharged from insolvency on 18 March 1844. Reuben was able to donate £4 to the synagogue at its dedication ceremony in 1845. He was one of the three initial trustees of Maitland's Jewish cemetery in 1846.

The Maitland Mercury of 19 February 1848 advertised 'H. R. Reuben of West Maitland' as a manufacturer of 'Ginger Beer, Lemonade and Soda Water since 1844'.

Two children were registered in the Sydney Synagogue's Birth Book, Deborah (11 June 1839) and Esther (9 November 1840). Their other children were Morris (1848), born in Sydney, Elizabeth (1850), born in Paterson, Scone, and Henry (1855), born in West Maitland. Deborah married Morris Cohen, the son of Barnett and Sierlah in Sydney in 1856.

The *Hebrew Standard* of 3 September 1897 noted Reuben's death at the age of eighty-six, reporting that he 'came to the colony in 1829 and in 1838 married Emma Solomon'.

Sydney Morning Herald, 12 February 1839, 16 September 1842, 13 August 1843, 6 December 1843, 10 March 1844; *Sydney Gazette*, 10 October 1835, 14 May 1840; *Australian*, 12 February 1834, 7 March 1834; Petition A1218, p. 274.

REUBEN, Solomon (Sol REUBENS)

b. London, 1807–1849
Georgiana I (2), 1831; Convict; Sentenced to life, Old Bailey, 1831.
Married; Salesman; Height: 156 cm.

Dark complexion, ruddy, pock-pitted, dark brown hair, and dark eyes. Can read and write. A Jew. Solomon Reuben and William Rowley were members of a gang who attempted to rob a drunken man on Saturday night, 1 January 1831. The trial took place five days later. Reuben claimed to have been running for a doctor for his pregnant wife, having lost a child a day or two before the incident, and his wife was expecting another baby. He was sentenced on 6 January 1831. Reuben was listed as 'single' in the ship's indent.

On arrival in Sydney, Reuben was assigned to service with Chief Justice Forbes. Reuben was mentioned as a witness in a case involving Michael Abrahams (q.v.), who was convicted of swindling. At the time 'Sol Reubens' was an assigned servant of Mr Isaac D. Nichols, the son of Rosanna (née Abrahams or Julian) (qq.v.) and Isaac Nichols. He received a ticket of leave in 1839 for the district of Sydney 'so long as he is employed by Mr G. Nichols'. A conditional pardon was granted on 1 April 1841. Solomon Reuben married Elizabeth Turner in 1844. He gave £5 to the Sydney Synagogue at its dedication in 1845.

Solomon Reuben was a professional pugilist. The *Omnibus and Sydney Spectator* reported on 1 April 1843: 'Considerable interest is excited in the sporting circles in the forthcoming fight between John White and the light weight Solly Reuben'.

Reuben was a witness in an assault case in Maitland on 14 January 1846 (*Maitland Mercury*) and he was mentioned in the *Registry of Flash Men*: 'He is the brother of Reubens of the "Black Swan". He is a suspicious character from Sydney. He was one of the ring in England' and 'alleged to be part of a fancy gang'. Reuben was buried by the Sydney Synagogue on 22 August 1849. He was said to be forty years of age.

OBSP, 1830–31, case 418, p. 208f., *Georgiana* Printed Indent 4/4103, p. 67; TL 39/2409, in Governors' Despatches 1841, A1224, p. 1203; CP 42/99; Principal Superintendent of Convicts, TL Butts, 12 December 1839 to 20 January 1840, 4/4135; Conditional Pardon Registry, 4/4440, p. 239f. no. 31, 1213, and 41/1487; *Sydney Gazette*, 14 January 1836; W. A. Miles, *Registry of Flash Men*, pp. 15, 114, 2/673; *Omnibus and Sydney Spectator*, 1 April 1843; *Maitland Mercury*, 14 January 1846.

RHEUBEN, Abraham (REUBEN)

b. Whitechapel, 1810–1876
Bengal Merchant, 1828; Convict; Sentenced to 7 years, Old Bailey, 1827.
Single; Tailor's boy; Height: 161 cm; 11 children.

Fair complexion, dark brown hair, grey to hazel eyes, forefinger of right hand broken. Abraham Rheuben was born at 65 Whitechapel Road, where his parents lived at the time of his trial. His father, Reuben

Rheuben, kept a broker's shop. Abraham had been apprenticed to a Mr Myers, a tailor on Bermondsey Street. He was sentenced to transportation for stealing a sovereign and a half crown from a woman who was 'looking at a new linen-draper's shop in Whitechapel'. A policeman had observed him in the crowd, 'very active at the baskets and reticules', and followed him along Essex Street: 'I followed him and collared him and said "I know you have got it, tip it up!" He said "I have done nothing. I picked it up". I said "Give it to me and he gave me this [stolen] purse"'. Rheuben was sentenced at the Old Bailey on 31 May 1827. He was sixteen years old and he brought eighteen shillings and one penny with him to Australia. Rheuben was listed as a Protestant in the ship's papers.

Abraham Rheuben arrived in Hobart Town on 10 August 1828. His only colonial offence, which earned him twenty-five lashes, was to be 'insolent and neglectful of his duty to the master G. C. Clark'. By 1835 he had served his sentence and in 1837 he married Rosetta Marks. Rheuben opened a corn store and prospered. By 1842 he was advertising in the *Hobart Town Courier* as a carrier. The business prospered. In 1852 he was listed in the *Hobart Town Directory and General Guide* as a 'corn merchant' living on his own freehold property in Elizabeth Street. Rheuben became a dealer in land and produce (hay, grain, timber, coal, beef, tea). He lent money, was an investor in the Tasmanian Steamship Navigation Company and part owner of the Port Arthur coal mines from 1858. He was ship owner, magistrate and Justice of the Peace!

By June 1854 he advertised that he had completed 'his large and commodious' Franklin Stores at New Wharf and on 5 July he purchased the lease of H. Lazarus (Henry Lewis Lazarus, q.v.) in Liverpool Street for £1500. Rheuben became well known as a keen gardener who won many awards and introduced many new varieties to Tasmania.

Rheuben and Rosetta had ten children. They were: Esther (born 30 June 1838), Louisa (13 August 1840 to 25 July 1925), Moses (Albert Maurice) (26 December 1842 to 27 June 1917), Phillip (4 October 1844 to 7 July 1930), Reuben (28 December 1846 died 'Richard' 18 January 1896), Elizabeth (2 December 1848 to 21 October 1877) Solomon (18 October 1850, died in Hobart in 1914), Samuel Amos (6 November 1852 to 11 July 1915), Edward Frank (2 December 1855, died in Waverley on 7 September 1938) and Fanny (1863). Five of the ten children married Jews. Esther married Edward Franck, Louisa married Gustavus Gabriel, Samuel who married Phoebe Davis and Dinah Richards (Bahr), Edward married Charlotte Janet Lee and Frances (Fanny) married Louis Solomon. One of the children of Moses (Albert Maurice) converted back to Judaism.

Rheuben applied to the administration for his first land grant and on 12 June 1839 he received enough land to build a house. On 12 June 1840, at the home of Abraham Rheuben on the New Town Road, the marriage of Robert Hart (q.v.) and his sister in law Hannah Solomon (née Marks, q.v.) took place. Louis Nathan (q.v.) officiated at the marriage in his role as president of the congregation.

Rheuben was a founding member of the Hobart synagogue in 1842 and an active member of the Jewish community. In September 1845 he was elected a member of the Hobart congregation's board of management. In 1850 Rheuben brought from London his widowed sister Clara (Gola) Goldsmith (q.v.) and her 13-yearold son Daniel. Rheuben successfully applied for further land grants throughout the 1850's and purchased Crown lands in 1863.

Rosetta died on 29 January 1865 and was buried in the Harrington Street cemetery. On 24 January 1866 Rheuben married for a second time. His wife, said to be his housekeeper, was the 38-year-old Miss Sarah Abrahams. There was one daughter from this marriage. In June 1854 Rheuben opened his 'large and commodious'emporium'. In 1872 he became an alderman of the Hobart Council only resigning one week before his death, which occurred on 25 September 1876. Abraham Rheuben was buried in the Hobart Jewish Cemetery in Cornelian Bay where his elaborate tomstone still stands. The value of his estate was £720.

According to personal notes in Hobart's Allport Collection Rheuben was a nephew of Isaac (Ikey) Solomon (q.v.). Ikey was the son of Fanny Rheuben (née Solomon).

OBSP, 1827, case 1195; CON 31/4, CON 18/1, CON 23/3; MM 33/1; Allport Collection, Personal Notes; VDL Papers, ML, A1059-4, p. 175; *Hobart Town Courier*, 4 March 1842; *Hobarton Guardian or True Friend of Tasmania*, 28 June 1854, p. 3; ATO 26/2764, 2/165; *Hobart Town Directory and General Guide*, 1852; family notes by Scott Whitmont, Gerry Whitmont and Susan Groenhout of Sydney and Daniel Goldsmith, Melbourne.

RINTEL, Moses

b. Edinburgh, 1823–1880
1844; Free.
Single; Minister; 8 children.

The Rev. Moses Rintel grew up in Edinburgh and London. His father was a scholar and worked as the Edinburgh community's first *schochet* and teacher. Moses arrived in Sydney in 1844 and established the Sydney Hebrew Academy of which he was the principal. He functioned as a teacher at the Hebrew school attached to the Sydney congregation and was a certified *schochet*.

George Moss (q.v.) wrote to the London Jewish newspaper *Voice of Jacob*: 'Our respected shammas, with Mr Rintel, recently proceeded to the Paterson and Hunter, to initiate some Hebrew children in the Abrahamic covenant. This was a labour of love. Mr Rintel's Hebrew School progresses, next year he hopes to have a public examination of his pupils'.

On 29 January 1849 he was 'called' to become the Melbourne Hebrew Congregation's first permanent minister and on 22 August 1849 married Elvina, the daughter of John Hart (q.v.). Asher Hymen Hart (q.v.) officiated at the marriage.

Following a quarrel with the Melbourne Hebrew Congregation his employment was terminated on 1 April 1857 and he formed a breakaway congregation called *Mikveh Israel* (the Hope of Israel), which later became the East Melbourne Hebrew Congregation in Albert Street. He was ill-prepared to serve as an independent preacher of a breakaway congregation and was fortunate to have his first sermons 'ghost written' by a scholarly Congregational minister the Rev. Alexander Morison of the Collins Street Independent Church.

In 1864 Rintel established the first *Beth Din* (religious court) in the British Empire outside London and in 1868, to the consternation of the Melbourne Hebrew

Congregation, the Chief Rabbi named him the Senior Rabbi of the Melbourne Jewish community. Rintel had an independent source of income from his marriage into the Hart family, which enabled him to build up a second Melbourne congregation despite its small numbers during its first decade. His career was marked by endless quarrels with his community about proselytes and the children of mixed marriages. He was very active in communal and philanthropic affairs. Rintel was a well-known member of the wider Melbourne community and a distinguished Freemason.

Moses Rintel died on 9 May 1880. He was survived by his wife and seven of their eight children, Henri John Rintel (born in 1850 and died in infancy), Isabella (born 1851), Myer (1853), Henri (1856), Simeon (1858), Edward (1859), Adelaide (1862), and Sara (1867). Moses Rintel left an estate valued at £3831.

J. S. Levi, 'Moses Rintel', in *ADB*, vol. 6, p. 31; *Voice of Jacob* (London), 22 May 1846; *Jewish Herald* (Melbourne), 21 May 1880.

RITCHIE, Hannah (née HARRIS)

b. Sydney, 1797–1899
Free.
Single.

Hannah Ritchie was the daughter of John Harris (q.v.) and Mary Green, the sister of Elizabeth Underwood (q.v.) and John Harris (jnr), and the adopted 'niece' of James Larra (q.v.). On 9 November 1818, John Clears stated to the Rev. Mr Shepherd:

> That he knew Hannah Harris at Sideny where she lived latterly with her sister—the widow of a Mr Lang (afterwards married to Mr Joseph Underwood) previous to which she lived with her uncle Mr Larra—who is a man of considerable property and has one of the best Houses and largest farms at Parramatta—that her sister [after her husband's death] had lived with her uncle—but after he had married a second wife they both went to live at Sydney. That he [Clears] was on board the brig *Greyhound* commanded by Capt Ritchie—that previous to her sailing, two women came on board, with a detachment of soldiers, dressed in women's clothes. That after the captain had weighed anchor, a sailor came on board with the above named Hannah Harris, who immediately went down to the Captain's Cabin. That he did not see any Box or bundle of clothes brought on board with her. That for a month or more she remained in the Captain's Cabin without coming on Deck when she did she wanted to return and offered a sailor £100 if he would get her back—the Captain then turns her among the men—Captain sets her ashore at Tricommalie— at Timor she follows the boat 'up to her middle in water' and goes to see the Governor's lady who considers her a little deranged.

Clears believed 'her mental malady to have risen from ill usage'.

The *Sydney Gazette* on 11 September 1819 told a slightly different story. In the case of the *Government versus Thomas Ritchie* in the Supreme Court, evidence was heard that Hannah had been on very bad terms with her sister, with whom she had lived in Sydney. She was determined to quit the colony and offered Ritchie £50.

The ship was going out the Heads when she laid hold of a rope and got up the ship's side. She was landed at Ceylon for reasons of bad health and Ritchie eventually brought her back. Ritchie was fined £1000.

Hannah Ritchie died in Hobart on 15 December 1899.

John Clears to the Rev. Shepherd, 9 November 1818, 4/1741, p. 92; Ritchie's reply, CS In Letters 4/1752, 181722, p. 52; *Sydney Gazette*, 11 September 1819; *Launceston Examiner*, 15 December 1899; *AG*, pp. 50, 51.

ROBERTS, Joseph (John REUBEN)

b. 1814
Bengal Merchant (3), 1836; Convict; Sentenced to 7 years, Nottingham Quarter Sessions, 1836.
Single; Hawker.

Ruddy, a little pock-pitted. Light brown hair, blue to grey-coloured eyes. Joseph Roberts had no previous convictions. He was sentenced on 11 January 1836.

Joseph Roberts, or John Reuben, arrived in New South Wales on 9 December 1836 and was listed in the indent as 'Joseph Roberts'. John Roberts was a convict at Norfolk Island on 29 May 1840, when he signed the letter to the Sydney Synagogue asking for Jewish prayer books and prayer shawls. Roberts received a ticket of leave in 1841.

On 28 March 1842 a John Reuben was arrested for being illegally at large at Birdwood, carrying £20 worth of money orders for which he could not account. He was sentenced to six months in the iron gang. He regained his ticket of leave and in 1844 was granted a certificate of freedom.

CS Copies of Letters Sent Re Convicts, 23 January 1841 to 30 December 1842, 4/3689, 26 March 1842, p. 355; *Bengal Merchant* Indent, X638-9, no. 36-2788-190; TL 41/1263; CF 44/217.

ROBINSON, George

Canada, 1842; Free.
Single; Dealer; 10 children.

George Robinson travelled as a migrant in steerage without government assistance. He married Sarah Phillips on 1 April 1842. It was the third Jewish marriage performed in Launceston, and Morris Whyle (q.v.) officiated. Sarah was one of the ten children of Moses Phillips (q.v.) of Launceston. Robinson was a 'dealer', who pledged £10 to the Launceston Synagogue building appeal on 29 June 1844. He rented seat no. 98 in the Hobart Synagogue in 1845 and was then unable to pay his dues. He paid ten shillings and owed 26 shillings. He was still listed on the synagogue's ledger in 1848. He offered to pay three shillings, which he then couldn't pay. George and Sarah had a son, Phillip, on 22 May 1846. On 6 January 1847 George and Sarah Robinson were accepted as new members of the Melbourne Hebrew Congregation and Phillip was circumcised under the aegis of the congregation on 11 April 1847. They were listed in the Melbourne Hebrew Congregation's Birth Book as living at Fingal in Van Diemen's Land. In December 1855 vandals destroyed the gravestone of a child who belonged to the Robinson family and was buried in the newly established Launceston Jewish cemetery. Robinson, together with Bertram Nathan (q.v.) and Joshua Lyons (q.v.), offered a reward for information regarding the culprits. No one was forthcoming.

The eleven children of George and Sarah Robinson were Elizabeth, Phillip, Joseph, Samuel, William, Kate, Hart, David, Henry, and Esther.

Hobart Town Courier, 29 April 1842; *Launceston Examiner*, 29 June 1844, 1, 3, 8 January 1856.

ROCKOTZ, Moses (ROCKETTE) (ROCHCHATS)

b. Poland, 1788–1841
Baring (1), 1815; Convict; Sentenced to life, Old Bailey, 1814.
Single; 'Jew Merchant'; Height: 166 cm.

Dark ruddy complexion, black hair, brown eyes. Moses Rockotz (also known as Moses Rochetrid, Moses Rockette and Moses Rochotz), together with Joachim Boaz (q.v.), was a newcomer to England and unable to speak English. They successfully stole twelve yards of cambric valued at thirty shillings at one store and £15 worth of cambric lace at a London warehouse. On the second attempt on the same afternoon their nervousness and their inexperience caused them to be caught. They were sentenced to death on 6 July 1814, their sentences later commuted to transportation for life.

Rockotz arrived in Sydney on 7 September 1815 and was sent as an assigned convict servant to William Cox jnr of Richmond, remaining with him until 1819. In that year he wrote a petition asking for a pardon and stating that he had 'conducted himself soberly, honestly and industriously'. Three Justices of the Peace and an assistant chaplain signed the petition, which was successful. In the 1828 Census Moses Rockette was listed as a farmer with a ticket of leave and thirty-three acres of land. No religion was listed. Moses Rochotz (aged thirty-eight) obtained permission to marry Ellen Grenville (aged twenty-five) in January 1827. The ceremony was conducted by the Rev. J. Cross of Richmond. He married a second time in Windsor in December 1837, to Ann Warr. A conditional pardon was granted on 9 January 1835. In September 1839 Mr Moses Rochats of Windsor gave £10 to the Sydney synagogue building appeal. Moses died intestate at Bathurst with an estate of £18 13s to be apportioned by the court. He was buried as a Jew in Sydney's Devonshire Street Jewish Cemetery on 16 January 1841 and reinterred at the Botany Pioneer Memorial Park in 1901.

OBSP, 1814, cases 585, 586, p. 315f.; *Baring* Indent 4/4005; Register 4/4432, p. 444; CO 201/118, p. 273; CS 27/562; Petition 4/1860, no. 14, in the year 1819; 2/8243, p. 163.

ROSE, Michael

b. London
Mary, 1835; Free.
Married; Dealer and minister.

Michael Rose came to Sydney with his wife Mary on 25 September 1835 on the barque *Mary*. He was described as a 'dealer'. He brought with him credentials from the Chief Rabbi in London, which enabled him to be employed by the Sydney congregation as reader, *schochet* and *mohel*. Rose briefly served as minister of the synagogue, conducting six weddings, with the express permission of the congregation's president, Abraham Polack (q.v.). In 1838 Rose was employed as the official collector for the synagogue. On 6 March 1838, Isaac Simmons advertised in the *Australian* that he would be selling at auction 'a variety of household goods at the residence of Mr M. E. Rose, Fort Street, because Mr Rose is leaving for India'. On 10 March 1838 Mr and Mrs Rose sailed on the *Waterloo* for Madras.

G. F. J. Bergman, 'A Note on the Reverend Michael E. Rose', *AJJHS*, vol. 6, no. 5 (1968), p. 287f.

ROSENBERG, Harris

b. Poland, 1798–1857
Duchess of Northumberland, 1843; Convict; Sentenced to life, Aberdeen, 1842.
Married; Silversmith; Height: 171 cm; 2 children.

Dark complexion, dark brown curly hair, brown eyes, medium nose. A Pole. Literate. Aged forty-five. Harris Rosenberg was convicted for having deliberately set fire to his dwelling place in which was his jewellery and furrier's shop. His wife's name was Aledia. His behaviour on board the transport ship was 'orderly and quiet'.

Rosenberg arrived in Hobart Town on 18 January 1843 and was assigned to an initial three years probation on government service and sent to the Cascades Prison in Hobart. He emerged from the work gang on 18 January 1846 and received his ticket of leave on 11 June 1850. The Jewish community took pity on him. He was an assigned servant to Mr David Moses (q.v.) of Liverpool Street, Hobart Town, in 1846, Moses Solomon (q.v.) of Elizabeth Street in 1847, Mr (Reuben?) Joseph of Liverpool Street in 1847, Lazarus Levy (q.v.) and Jacob Frankel (q.v.) in 1848, and Joseph Solomon (q.v.) in 1849.

On 15 November 1846 Rosenberg wrote to the Hobart Hebrew Congregation asking for help from the synagogue 'to obtain the migration of his two children who were under the guardianship of a Mr Joseph of Chester'.

He received his conditional pardon in 1853. However, in January 1855 he was back in court for having allowed firewood to remain on a public road. On 5 September 1855 Rosenberg was arraigned in Hobart Town for 'common assault upon Julius Harris' and was sentenced 'to be imprisoned in Her Majesty's Gaol Hobart Town for twelve months'. A conditional pardon was issued on 24 September 1857. He died in the Hobart Town Government Hospital on 24 September 1857 at the age of fifty-nine. Following a post mortem he was buried the next day by the Hobart Hebrew Congregation.

CON 33/36, no. 2764; CON 18/34; CON 37/8, p. 2764.

ROSENZWEIG, Aaron Lazarus

b. Warsaw 1840; Free.
Single; 6 children.

Rosenzweig was born in Poland and migrated to Scotland when he was in his early teens. He arrived in Melbourne in 1840 and opened a pawnbroker's shop. In 1852 he married Louisa Cohen in Adelaide (she had been born in London). They came back to Melbourne, and Aaron tried his luck as a trader on the goldfields. It was not a great success and Rosenzweig eventually became an agent for Gillespie's Flour Mill. Aaron and Louisa had six children. The last child was Abigail, who was born in Brisbane, and she was the only child of her generation to marry.

Information supplied by family.

RUBEN, Catherine (Ruby)

b. London, 1794
Northampton, 1815; Convict; Sentenced to 7 years, Middlesex Gaol Delivery, 1814.
Single; Straw bonnet maker.

Catherine Ruben (also known as Reuben) and Hannah Giddes were indicted for stealing one hundred yards of ribbon from a crowded haberdashery shop. The women were seen hiding the stolen property in an umbrella. The 16-year-old Giddes was sentenced to one year in the House of Correction. Ruby Ruben was fifteen years old when she was convicted in London for 'larceny'. She had already spent time in Newgate Prison. She was sentenced at the London Gaol Delivery on 6 July 1814, together with Rebecca Dias (q.v.).

The *Northhampton* arrived in Port Jackson on 18 June 1815 and on 23 June Catherine Ruben was sent to the factory at Parramatta. On 22 August 1820 she was sent as a convict on the *Princess Charlotte* to Van Diemen's Land. In September Ruby was sent on the *Emerald* from New South Wales to Van Diemen's Land. The 1820 Muster showed that she was the holder of a ticket of leave and that she was a servant to the Governor in Chief, Hobart Town. However, the Bigge Report referred to Catherine Ruby being sentenced in Hobart Town to serve the remainder of her sentence for attempting to abscond from the colony.

There are many newspaper notices, both in the *Sydney Gazette* and in the *Hobart Town Gazette* (11 August 1820, 15 June 1822), that announced that she was about to leave Hobart Town as 'Miss Catherine Ruby'. In 1821 a certificate of freedom was issued. She had served her time and, presumably, she returned to England.

OBSP, 1814, case 567, p. 307; Ship Indent 4/4005; CS In Letters 4/1732; PRO R 109, 29 January 1820; TL 1531; Bigge Report 4/3502, p. 217.

RUSSELL, Elizabeth

b. London 1804
Strathfieldsay, 1834; Free.

Elizabeth, who was the sister of Henry Davis (q.v.), arrived in Van Diemen's Land on 13 August 1834 on board the 'Strathfieldsay'. She married Thomas Fall at Evandale in 1839 and they had two daughters Elizabeth (1838–1901) and Catherine (1842–1935). She also cared for Henry's two sons, Henry (jnr) and Philip. She died 21 October 1874 and left the Hobart Synagogue the large legacy of £1500. Her daughters assumed responsibility for the unused synagogue building in Launceston on St John's Street and the neglected Jewish Burial Ground in Invermay (Launceston).

RUSSELL, Esther (née MOSES)

b. Southwark, 1814
George Hibbert, 1834; Convict; Sentenced to 7 years, Old Bailey, 1834.
Single; Cook and nursemaid; Height: 150 cm.

Fair, ruddy complexion, a little freckled, brown hair, chestnut eyes. Lost a front tooth. Mole on left cheek. It was stated that Esther Russell had a brother and sister who were publicans in Sydney with the surname of Moses. She had no previous convictions. She was transported for having robbed a man, and was sentenced on 17 April 1834. In the records of the Old Bailey 'Rosa' Russell is found to have stolen clothes from the house of Mr and Mrs Abraham Cardoza. Two weeks prior to this she had evidently stolen some jewellery from the top of a chest of drawers. She was said to be fifteen years old. Mr Aaron Isaacs of Goulston Square and Mr Samuels gave the prisoner 'good character'.

In the 1837 General Return of Convicts in the Colony of New South Wales, Esther Russell, aged twenty-three, was shown as an assigned convict servant to Mr J. C. Phillips of Sydney. Esther assumed the alias of 'Quirk' and became the wife of William Cooper, who had arrived as a convict on the *Katherine Stewart Forbes* in 1830. Esther received a ticket of leave on 23 August 1841.

OBSP, 1833–34, case 1996, p. 566; *George Hibbert* Printed Indent, arrived Port Jackson 1 December 1834, 4/4019, and X636; CF 4/4368.

RUSSELL, George (né LEVY)

b. Sheerness, 1800–1867
Hope, 1824; Free.
Single; Dealer; 5 children.

George Russell arrived in Hobart Town on 10 April 1824. He was the son of Philip and Catherine Russell and brother of Elizabeth Davis (q.v.), Michael Joseph Russell (q.v.) and Esther Solomon, wife of Judah Solomon (q.v.). On 28 January 1828 George Russell wrote to the administration: 'I am residing on my land and have done so for some time—the property is called New Plain. Mr Abraham Aaron [q.v.] has 649 sheep on my property. Aaron had not been able to make improvements on the land even though he had been there for two years owing to the lack of an official survey'. Russell had spent twelve months at New Plain and now he felt he was obliged to move owing to the lack of government action.

The Colonial Secretary took the complaint very seriously and wrote:

> Mr Russell is the brother of Mr Henry Davis who was some time a woollen draper in Hobart Town afterwards kept a public house in Launceston and subsequently went to Sydney (in order to avoid his creditors) where he is now imprisoned. When Mr Russell arrived in the colony as a steerage passenger, he had not money to pay his passage which was, at length, paid by Mr Davis. He and Abraham Aaron acted rather

as servants than the partners of Mr Davis. The sheep owned by Russell and Aaron are most of them supposed to be the property of Davis the three men are Jews and were born at Sheerness, the father of Davis and Russell kept a sort of clothes shop there and removed to Drury Lane where he kept a Baker's shop.

Russell went on to Auckland, New Zealand, and became one of New Zealand's earliest European settlers. In 1841 he established one of the eight seafront hotels at the Bay of Islands and named it after himself. Subsequently, this pioneer European New Zealand trading post and township of Kororareka was renamed Russell.

The Maori War devastated the European settlement at the Bay of Islands and on 30 April 1845 the committee of the Hobart Synagogue received a plea for help from Russell: 'All his property had been destroyed in New Zealand'. The community sent him a generous gift of £10. Russell moved to Auckland and in May 1845 advertised that he was an 'agent for Mr David Nathan [q.v.] under power of attorney'. He built a hotel on vacant land owned by Joel Samuel Polack (q.v.), much to the anger of the Maori, who were acutely aware of the social impact of the availability of liquor. Russell allowed Nathan to build a warehouse and auction room next to his public house.

In 1850 George Russell returned to London where he married Rebecca Leman at the 'New Synagogue' on 30 April 1850. He described himself as a 'merchant' and his father as a 'dealer'. His brother Henry had accompanied him back to England and was a witness to the ceremony. George returned to Sydney, where Rebecca gave birth to their first child Leon Lionel in 1853. A daughter was born at Auckland on 11 April 1855 and a son, Philip, on 6 June 1856. In 1857 they had moved to Melbourne and lived in Stephen Street, where his son Philip died and a daughter, Leonora, was born (and died in infancy). His occupation was listed as confectioner.

In 1859, Samuel, a fifth child, was born in Goulburn. George and his family returned to London some time around 1860. He died in England at 74 Boslover Street, Marlybone in 1867.

Hobart Town Gazette, 16 April 1824; LSD 1/1/75, dated Launceston, 28 January 1828; CSO 1/224/5447, 11 February 1828; *Port Phillip Herald*, 21 January 1841; Cecil Roth, *The Rise of Provincial Jewry*, p. 98; Joanne Acton, The Fall Family, ms, Hobart, 2002, *New Zealander*, 17 May 1845, 2 February 1853, 13 April 1855, 7 June 1856, 1 February 1860; Family tree, supplied by Mr Eric Cohen OAM; Russell family history researched by Dan Russell, Woodford, Queensland.

RUSSELL, George

b. Swartsburgh, Germany, 1808
Asia V (2), 1831; Convict; Sentenced to 7 years, Waterford City, Ireland, 1831.
Single; Jeweller and musical box maker; Height: 164 cm.

Ruddy, much freckled and pock-pitted complexion, light brown hair, grey eyes, nose flattened, scar in centre of forehead and under right eyebrow. Could read and write. Jew. George Russell had a previous conviction, and had been flogged. He was transported for stealing jewellery, having been sentenced at Waterford City on 14 January 1831.

George Russell arrived in New South Wales on 2 December 1831.
Asia Printed Indent, no. 31-2058.

RUSSELL, Henry (né LEVY)

b. Sheerness, 1812–1898
Lady East, 1833; Free.
Single; Musician; 3 children.

Henry Russell was born on 12 December 1812, and arrived in Van Diemen's Land on 28 October 1833. He was the son of Philip and Catherine Russell of London and the brother of Michael Joseph Russell (q.v.), Mark Russell (q.v.), George Russell (q.v.), Henry Davis (q.v.), and Elizabeth Davis (q.v). He was a nephew of Judah and Esther Solomon (qq.v.).

Also, Henry Russell appears to have been the first cousin of the well-known musician of the same name (1813–1900), who was also born in Sheerness, sang with the Children's Opera Co, studied music with Rossini and wrote a number of popular music hall songs, including 'Cheer Boys Cheer' and 'A Life on the Ocean Wave'.

The antipodean Henry Russell appeared in the *Hobart Town Courier* of 26 July 1833 as the 'leader of an instrumental group' that held a concert organised by Mr Reichenberg (q.v.), the band master. Henry Russell became the proprietor of the Music Hall in Collins Street and on 4 January 1845 announced that he would be exhibiting a performance of camera obscura (*Hobart Town Courier*). Russell was described as 'a well known composer and singer of song'. Henry Russell was an active member of the Hobart congregation in the year of its dedication and served on its committee of management.

Henry worked with his brother George Russell (q.v.) in Auckland and accompanied him back to England in 1850, where he was a witness at his brother's wedding. He then returned to New Zealand and married Catherine Elias on 1 May 1853. Their first son, Philip, was born in Auckland on 1 May 1853, and David was born there on 7 February 1857. Elizabeth was born in Sydney in 1862. Henry Russell became a furniture dealer on the Old South Head Road and later at Liverpool Street, Sydney. His sons Philip and David were listed as 'music teachers' during the 1880s.

Russell died in Sydney on 11 February 1898, aged eighty-six.

CS 30, p. 31; *Launceston Examiner*, 11 September 1888; 'Transactions of the Jewish Historical Society of England: Isaac Nathan', *JJHSE*, vol. 34, 1994–96, p. 229; *JJHSE*, vol. 24, 1975, p. 162f.

RUSSELL, Mark

b. Sheerness 1808–1883
Free.

A son of Philip and Catherine Russell. Died 6 May 1883 in Sydney and buried at the Haslam's Creek Cemetery. The 'late beloved brother of Michael Russell, 108 Goulburn Street, Sydney' (*Sydney Morning Herald*, 7 May 1883).

RUSSELL, Michael

b. London, 1812
Marquis of Hastings (3), 1828; Convict; Sentenced to life, London, 1827.
Single; Broker's boy; Height: 160 cm.

Dark ruddy complexion, dark brown hair, brown eyes. Jew. Can read and write. The 16-year-old Michael Russell had appeared at the Old Bailey twice. The first time he was accused of stealing one seal and three watch keys and was released when the prosecutors failed to appear. The second time he was sentenced to death for stealing a piece of cloth worth ten shillings from a shop in Drury Lane. The shopkeeper's wife was sitting in the shop reading a newspaper when he committed the theft. When caught, he told her: 'I am an orphan and in distress'. The woman replied: 'You seem not to want for victuals and you have a good coat on your back'. He was sentenced on 10 December 1827.

Russell arrived in Sydney on 12 October 1828 and was assigned to the Carter's Barracks for Boys. He was listed in the 1837 General Return of Convicts in New South Wales working as an assigned convict servant of the Australian Agricultural Company at Port Stephens. He received a ticket of leave on 12 December 1843 and was allowed to remain at Port Stephens. In August 1843 he was permitted to move to Maitland. He received a conditional pardon on 1 November 1848.

OBSP, 1826–27, case 2226, p. 852, and 1827–28, case 246, p. 111; Ship Indent 4/4013, p. 137; 4/4183; TL 42/2935, and 43/2935; CP 48/2054.

RUSSELL, Michael Joseph (John)

b. London, 1798–1889
1839; Free.
Married; Dealer; 5 children.

The son of Philip and Catherine Russell, Michael was the brother of Henry Russell (q.v.), Henry Davis (q.v.), and George Russell (q.v.), Elizabeth Russell (q.v.). Michael Russell married Catherine Lee (1805-1874) in 1838 at the Great Synagogue in London. He was described at the time as a glass chandelier fitter. Following his marriage and the birth of his first child (Adelaide) the family traveled to New Zealand where his brother George (q.v.) had opened a store at the Bay of Islands. His brother George Russell had arrived there from Van Diemen's Land in 1839. Following the Maori War Michael Russell migrated to Hobart Town and in 1845 he rented seat no. 55 in the Hobart Synagogue. In 1846 he gave sixty glass ornaments to the synagogue in Hobart Town for its chandelier. At the end of the next financial year he owed the synagogue eighteen shillings, and the debt was written off as 'bad'. Russell moved to Sydney and, in 1849, opened a general store, near the Rocks. He was listed as insolvent on 2 May 1856. From 1861 to 1880 he had an electroplating business with his brother Mark.

His children were Adelaide born in London in 1839, Albert Aaron, born in 1843 at the Bay of Islands, New Zealand, Elizabeth born in Van Diemen's Land in 1845, Jane (1849), Joseph, born in 1851 in Sydney.

At the time of his death 30 August 1889, Michael Joseph Russell was described as having lived at 149 Campbell Street, Sydney, the home of his son-in-law Henry Solomon (q.v.), and having been a 'crockery dealer'. The grave of M. J. Russell's eldest daughter Adelaide is at Rookwood. She died at the residence of her parents

112 Stanley Street, Woolloomooloo of consumption at the age of twenty-nine years and six months. Her tombstone was 'erected as a mark of esteem to the deceased by her fellow teachers and the children of the Sydney Jewish Sabbatical School'.
Information researched by Barbara Joffe, Sydney. *Sydney Morning Herald*, 4 September 1868.

RUSSELL, Reuben Thomas (alias John Williams)

b. Sheerness 1817–1909
Hashemy, 1849; Convict

Born on 11 December 1817, Son of Catherine and Samuel Russell. Tried at Faversham 19 April 1847. Given 10 years transportation for stealing from a dwelling house.

Arrived on the Hashemy arriving at Port Phillip in May 1849. A number of the convicts disembarked at Sydney. The remainder were sent to Moreton Bay.

Reuben was initially assigned to the Maitland District and by 1854 was in Goulburn On 14 June 1849 his ticket of leave was withheld during the pleasure of his Excellency due to 'misconduct during the voyage'. A ticket of leave was issued for the District of Maitland on 1 October 1849 and subsequently cancelled when Russell was found to be in Sydney without permission. He was placed on eight months probation and a pass to proceed to a road gang was issued.

On 26 Juy 1853 he was arrested for being in Sydey (again) and sent to work at the shipyards on Cockatoo Island. A ticket of leave was issued for the Goulburn district on 25 March 1854 and a conditional pardon was granted in March 1854.

Reuben Russell married Marion Allison in the Presbyterian Church in Goulburn 26 June 1856.

Reuben worked as a butcher and Marion became a midwife. They were residents of Queanbeyan from 1860 to 1862. Reuben returned to Goulburn where he had a butcher's shop in Auburn Street in the 1870's.

Reuben died aged 92 at 1 Mary Street Newtown in Sydney on 22 August 1909 and was buried by a Church of Christ minister at the Rookwood cemetery.

RUSSELL, Samuel

b. Sheerness, 1804–1851
Albion (3), 1828; Convict; Sentenced to 7 years, London, 1826.
Broker; Height: 164 cm.

Dark ruddy complexion, brown hair, brown eyes. Large nose. Jew. The firstborn son of Moses Russell and Sarah (née Levin), Samuel Russel was a brother of John, Mark (q.v.), Israel, Anne, and Elizabeth (q.v.). He was convicted of stealing a large quantity of carpenter's tools from a building at 15 Lincoln's Inn Fields on 20 February 1826, and was sentenced on 6 April 1826.

Samuel Russell was assigned in New South Wales to the Carter's Barracks and arrived in Van Diemen's Land on the *Freeling* on 6 April 1836. He gave a small donation to the Hobart congregation in 1844 and rented seat no. 59 in 1845. There was no further mention of him in the synagogue ledger book.

Russell died in Bendigo, Victoria, in 1851 from 'the effects of alcohol'.
OBSP, 1826, case 809; CSO 92/2, p. 38, reel 398.

S

SADLING, John

b. Prussia, 1814–1870
Recovery (3), 1836; Convict; Sentenced to life, Old Bailey, 1835.
Married; Clerk and shopman; Height: 168 cm.

Sadling could read and write. He was sentenced at the Old Bailey on 15 June 1835. He was described as having a dark ruddy complexion, dark brown hair, dark chestnut eyes, large nose with a front upper tooth gone and a brown patch under right jaw. A Jew. Sadling was said to be a member of a street gang. He had no previous convictions. He was convicted of 'cutting and maiming' a horse.

The *Recovery* arrived in Sydney on 25 February 1836. On 18 May 1836, while working on a street gang in Sydney and housed at the Hyde Park Barracks, Sadling was 'absent from his work gang' and placed on bread and water for six days. In the 1837 General Return of Convicts in New South Wales John Sadling was listed as a prisoner at the Hyde Park Barracks in Sydney and subsequently sent to the Road Department.

Sadling received a ticket of leave in 1843 and a conditional pardon in 1847. He was buried 'a native of Konigsberg' as a Jew in 1870, aged 66.

Recovery Printed Indent, p. 45; AO NSW, CS, Monthly Returns of Summary Trials of Convicts Before Benches of Magistrates, August 1832 to December 1836, X707; TL 43/2131; CP 47/337.

SALAMON, Edward

b. London, 1810–1860
1832; Free.
Married; Merchant; 5 children.

Edward Salamon was the son of Sir David Salamon of London and a nephew of Mrs Harriet Levien (q.v.). Edward Salamon arrived in Sydney in January 1832 with a recommendation for a land grant from the Home Secretary. He was 'summoned to the Colonial Office' but, 'unacquainted with the procedure', entrusted his representation there to his agent and cousin Michael Phillips (q.v.), with whom his capital was invested. Salamon explained in a petition to the Colonial Secretary in Sydney on 20 December 1837 that the money he had invested with Phillips had vanished 'because of [Phillips'] personal calamities and neglected his duties and in consequence he [Salamon] was deprived of the grant'. In 1838 he wrote again. Obviously his previous appeal had yielded no response. It was only in 1853 that Salamon had enough capital to buy land in Sydney.

Salamon went into business at 3 Colonnade, Bridge Street, as a wine merchant and general trader. He sold cut glass, Devonshire cider, stout, brandy and wine. The *Sydney General Trade List* recorded the importation of thirteen cases of clocks and toys on 7 February 1835. In 1836 he returned to England, gathered together some capital and stock and on 13 September 1837 announced in the *Commercial Journal and Advertiser* that he had returned to the colony by the *Ellen* and reopened his shop in Bridge Street, which sold china, jewellery, haberdashery and liqueurs.

Edward Salamon married his first cousin, Henrietta Levien, the daughter of Solomon Levien (q.v.), on 9 October 1839 under the auspices of the Sydney Synagogue. In 1845 he was a seat holder at the York Street Synagogue and donated ten guineas towards the new building.

Salamon boasted that he had a 'large' auction room in George Street. In October 1842 he announced that he was a wine merchant in George Street and in High Street, West Maitland, but on 26 August 1843 a meeting of creditors was called. On 30 November 1843 an arrangement was signed and the claim of insolvency was withdrawn. On 20 December he applied for an auctioneer's licence, gave up his Sydney premises and moved to West Maitland. On 23 August 1845 the *Morning Chronicle* reported that the storekeeper Edward Salamon of West Maitland was suing Joseph Cashmore (q.v.), who had once been an employee, and who was owed £52 in salary and some stock. Their battle was referred to Messrs L. Spyer (q.v.) and P. J. Cohen (q.v.) for adjudication. The Jewish conciliators found in favour of Salamon, and Cashmore then took the matter to the civil court.

On 27 April 1844 Salamon imported two cases of general goods from London and on 16 May 1846 exported thirty-four cases of gum. The *Sydney Chronicle* of 13 January 1848 described him as one of the three Jewish auctioneers in the city and he was still active as an auctioneer in the 1850s.

A daughter, Harriett, was born in Sydney in 1842. Personal tragedy overtook the family when three of Edward and Henrietta's children died. Francis Edward Salamon, aged six years and six months, died on 25 September 1850, and in the same week a daughter, Florence Matilda, aged one year and seven months, Montague Edward, who had been born in Sydney in 1846 died as an infant. John Benson Salamon, their third son, died aged two, on 21 March 1859.

Edward Salamon died 'immediately after a visit to Melbourne' on 27 October 1860, aged forty-nine, leaving an estate valued at £20 000. He was buried at the Devonshire Street cemetery and the grave was transferred to Rookwood in 1901 by the request of Sir Edward Samuel Bart.

Land Correspondence, 2/7965, 20 December 1837; *Sydney Morning Herald*, 18 October 1842, 26 August 1843, 30 November 1843, 28 October 1844, 20 December 1843, 21 August 1845, 29 October 1860; *Maitland Mercury*, 2 September 1843; *Morning Chronicle*, 23 August 1845; *Commercial Journal and Advertiser*, 13 September 1837; *Shipping Gazette*, 27 April 1844, 16 May 1846.

SALMON, Alexander

b. Hastings, Sussex, 1820
Hope, 1839; Free.
Single; Merchant.

Alexander Salmon was the son of John Salmon and Rebecca (née Polack). Rebecca was the sister of Abraham Polack (q.v.), Joel S. Polack (q.v.), and Elizabeth Poole (q.v.). In 1839 New South Wales was faced with a severe shortage of wheat and Abraham Polack chartered the vessel *Hope* to procure wheat from Valparaiso, Chile. Alexander Salmon, Polack's nephew, sailed in the ship as Polack's representative and ship's officer. The ship left Chile in June 1839 and visited Tahiti in July, arriving in Sydney in September.

Salmon returned to Tahiti, and in 1843 married Tahitian Princess Arii-taimai, whose daughter became the wife of King Pomare V and was therefore the last queen of Tahiti. The young David Poole (q.v.), who was a first cousin of the Queen, represented Tahiti overseas.

Family history from James L. Sanderson, Sydney; ML Q659/P.

SALOM, Mark (MAYNARD)

b. Mile End Road, 1808
Elphinstone (4), 1842; Convict; Sentenced to 7 years, Central Criminal Court, 1841.
Single; Sailor, hawker; Height: 163 cm; 2 children.

Black hair, grey eyes, long chin, large nose. He could read and write. His dossier stated that he was a Protestant. Mark Salom had not been in prison before. After his conviction he remained in England for almost a year before embarking for Hobart Town. He behaved so well on board ship that he served as a supervisor of the convicts.

Salom originally came to Australia in 1829 working as a fourth mate on the *Lord William Bentinck*. He spent six months in Sydney. He then moved to Hobart Town and was briefly in business with 'A. Solomon'. His reputation was not enhanced when, in 1834, at the theatre at the corner of St John Street and Brisbane Street in Launceston, one Mark Salom, alias Maynard, gave an entertainment 'Maynard at Home', with tickets at 7s 6d. Mark was his own money taker and when the hall was full he began to sing 'Bath bricks a penny a lump'. The audience walked out in disgust and he pocketed the takings. The *Hobart Town Courier* noted that Salom was a resident of Launceston and had received a licence as a hawker on 5 October 1838. His behaviour aroused the suspicion of the police. The Perth police report of 27 July 1838 was printed in the *Hobart Town Courier*: 'John Davis and Mark Salom, alias Maynard, who left Hobart Town under very peculiar circumstances, were apprehended at Perth and taken before the Police Magistrate at Campbell Town on suspicion of being runaway convicts and discharged'. Mark Salom was granted a hawker's licence for the District of Launceston 2 October 1839.

Having earned enough money to return to England he quickly fell foul of the law, and in February 1841 was arrested and sentenced to seven years transportation for having cashed a cheque for £6 which he had promised to take to Boulogne.

Salom arrived back in Van Diemen's Land, on the *Elphinstone* (4), arriving in Hobart Town on 28 July 1842. In September 1843, his second initial period of probation ended and he was sent to be an assigned servant in Launceston. He then moved to Hobart Town, became a constable, and rented seat no. 100 in the back of the synagogue for the year 1845. He was soon in trouble once again and, in the early part of 1845, was expelled from the police force in Hobart Town and given six months hard labour for falsely claiming a reward for the recovery of a missing boat and for having expropriated a five-shilling fine. On 7 May 1846 the Hobart Synagogue refused an appeal for financial aid and Salom subsequently abandoned the Jewish faith. Salom was granted a ticket of leave on 27 February 1846 'for having exerted himself at the hazard of his life in extinguishing a fire in Launceston'. In October 1846 he resigned from the post of overseeing the Launceston Town Surveyors' Department. In November 1846 he married Mary Marr, who had come free to the colony. In 1846 and 1847 Salom petitioned the Lieutenant Governor for permission to live in Sydney. His request was refused.

Salom was involved in an acrimonious court case in which he accused Solomon Levien (q.v.) of 'indecent language'. Salom testified 'I was passing the shop of Bertram Nathan (q.v.) in Charles Street, Launceston, when the prisoner Solomon Levien was standing at the door. He said: "You bloody Bugger. I suppose you are looking after more shofel pitchers", meaning passers of bad money and alluding, as I understood to a case which I was lately a witness'. Bertram Nathan testified that Salom was 'an apostate Jew, a ticket of leave holder, a man notorious for his vindictive feelings towards certain members of the Jewish persuasion and especially towards Levien and myself (Nathan)'. Levien had worked as an assigned servant for Nathan, and Salom had abused Levien on a previous occasion. Several character witnesses testified on oath that Levien was a 'well conducted, harmless, inoffensive man'. The magistrate was not convinced, and commented: 'Mark Salom had rendered himself obnoxious to the lower members of the Jewish persuasion. [Bertram] Nathan's servant, or rather partner, is of the same creed—no time is lost of taunting and reviling Salom in public as he passes along the streets in his capacity of hawker, a course of proceedings which I have good reason to believe that Levien has been particularly active in'. The magistrate upheld the complaint and Levien was reprimanded.

Salom was granted a conditional pardon in 1846. The official note stated 'Information had been given to the police which led to his conviction of receiving stolen property. He has completed six years of a seven years sentence and held a ticket of leave for fourteen months' (sic). The pardon was approved and Salom was free by February 1848 when his sentence of transportation officially expired.

Mark Salom had a son, Maurice, and a daughter, Sarah, who married Maurice Coleman Davis (q.v.).

CON 33/25, no. 6161; CON 14/16; CSO 24/28/750, 14 September 1847; CSO 20/38/888; Permission to Marry Books CON 52/2, p. 437; HO 10/60, p. 363; *Hobart Town Courier*, 5 October 1838; Hobart Synagogue Minute Book, 7 May 1845.

SALOM, Maurice

1832–1903
Free.
Single; 4 children.

Maurice Salom married Kate Solomon (q.v.), the daughter of the late Moss Solomon (q.v.) of Sydney, at the bride's mother's home in Hindley Street, Adelaide, on 27 April 1856. Abraham Moss Salom was born on 16 July 1857. Rebecca was born on 2 June 1860. On 18 July 1863 their four-year-old daughter Leah Rachel died. Elias Salom, son of Maurice and Kate Salom, died at Glenelg on 16 February 1885 at the age of twenty-one.

Maurice Salom died on 12 October 1903, aged seventy-one. Kate Salom died on 7 June 1928, aged ninety-one.

Pritchard Index.

SAMSON, Fanny (née LEVI)

b. Brighton, 1824–1888
1845; Free.
Married; 6 children.

Fanny Levi was the granddaughter of the Anglo-Jewish banker Abraham Goldsmid. Family tradition relates that young Lionel Samson (q.v.) fell in love with his first cousin, Sarah, who was Fanny's mother, and the wife of Nathan (Nathaniel) Philip Levi (q.v.). In the spirit of the biblical Naomi she rebuffed him by saying that she was too old and that one day he would marry her daughter. That day would come in 1841. When they met again Fanny was seventeen and Lionel was forty-two years old. Both were visiting the Goldsmid estate in Surrey. Lionel returned to Western Australia and then travelled back to England to marry Fanny, whose uncle and family were in the throes of emigrating to the new colony in South Australia. In Perth, on 16 August 1843, the *Inquirer* newspaper reported that Lionel Samson with his new wife, his mother-in-law and her two younger daughters had arrived and were on their way to Adelaide.

In Fremantle, Fanny Samson was totally isolated. Her relatives remained in England and Adelaide. Her brother-in-law William Samson (q.v.) sailed for South Australia in 1846. In 1855 an Order of French nuns arrived in Western Australia and Fanny was the only person in the colony with sufficient education to be able to speak with them. She interpreted for them and ultimately taught them English.

Fanny's children were Michael (1844) (q.v.), Caroline (1845), Adelaide (1847), Louis (1849), Elizabeth Mary (1850) and William Frederick (1855). Fanny died on 6 May 1888 and was buried in the Jewish section of the cemetery in Fremantle.
AG, p. 261f.

SAMSON, Horace

b. London, d. 1910
Sterling, 1841; Free.
Single.

Horace Samson came to Western Australia with his uncle, Lionel Samson (q.v.), in 1841. Horace Samson became a draftsman and lithographer in the Survey Department. He designed and printed the first postage stamps of Western Australia, including the famous black swan stamp. His watercolours and sketches of the colony of Western Australia are important historical records of the settlement's earliest years. Horace Samson moved to Victoria and became Registrar of Titles. He died in England in 1910.
Inquirer, 17 March 1841.

SAMSON, Lionel

b. London, 1799–1878
Calista, 1829; Free.
Single; 6 children.

Lionel Samson inherited his father's seat on the London Stock Exchange. It was one of the twelve places set aside for Jews. Apparently inspired by the emigration of Michael Phillips (q.v.) and the stories of Solomon Levey (q.v.), Lionel Samson of 5 Broad Street Buildings wrote to Under Secretary Twiss on 27 January 1829 stating that it was the intention of his (younger) brother (William Samson, q.v.) and himself to emigrate to the new settlement at Swan River and to invest £1000 in the venture. He wanted to be told 'what is required to be done to gain the advantages offered by the Government'.

Samson was the only Jewish migrant to Australia to receive a regal farewell from England. A few days before his departure, Lionel was a guest of King George IV at a grouse shoot. When the royal hunter accidently knocked and cracked his signet ring he took it off and gave it to Samson as a token of good luck. The ring still belongs to the Samson family.

Lionel Samson arrived in Fremantle on 5 August 1829 on the *Calista*, the second immigrant ship to Western Australia. In the colony's first muster, on 30 January 1830, he was listed as thirty years old, born in London, and 'a merchant'. His brother William was listed as an 'assistant'. The general muster also recorded the people who had claimed land and described their families, servants and property imported into the colony. Lionel Samson was listed with his brother, four servants and £352 5s 4d, applicable to the improvement of land, and £130 13s 5d, which was defined as working capital.

Samson established a general business in Fremantle and he and his brother became the first official auctioneers at the Swan River settlement. Lionel Samson was also the first merchant in the colony to be granted a liquor licence to deal in wine and spirits. Samson's name appeared on the colony's first grant of rural land on 29 September 1829 when he was allocated 4696 acres at Swan River. He was the colony's first postmaster and acted in an honorary capacity. Samson became one of the founding directors of the Bank of Western Australia in 1837. On 27 July 1837 he was a partner in the foundation of the Western Australian Whaling Co., and was active as ships' agent and estate agent. In 1842 Samson travelled to England and married his cousin, the 18-year-old Fanny Levi (Samson, q.v.), at Brighton, on 19 October 1842. Samson remained in England until 1844 and lived at 11 Warnford Court, Throgmorton. During his time in England he lobbied Lord Stanley about the poor postal communications between the United Kingdom and its Western Australia colony. Lionel and Fanny Samson had six children: Michael (q.v.), Caroline, Adelaide, Louis, Elizabeth Mary, and William Frederick.

In 1847 the Samsons' role in Western Australian society was described in a book published in London: 'And now let us get on towards Mr Samson's which is that large building apparently without chimneys and seemingly but half finished. Messrs Samsons are the largest merchants in the colony and are deservedly liked and esteemed for their constant exertions to merit the confidence of their connexion'.

Samson built one of Perth's most elegant houses on the northwest corner of St Georges Terrace and Barrack Street. Lionel Samson served as a member of the Legislative Council in 1849–56 and 1859–68. He died on 15 March 1878 and was buried in the small Jewish section of the Fremantle cemetery. Fanny Samson died on 6 May 1888.

David Mosseson, 'Lionel Samson', in *ADB*, vol. 2, pp. 417–18; *HRA*, series 3, vol. 6, pp. 622, 625; *Western Australia Historical Society Journal and Proceedings*, vol. 1, no. 1; *Perth Gazette and Western Australian Journal*, 26 April 1834, 17 May 1834, 25 October 1834, 16 May 1835; *Inquirer*, 17 March 1841, 16 August 1843; CO 18/6, 27 January 1829; *Swan River News and Western Australian Chronicle* (London), no. 39, 1 March 1847, by G. J. Webb, Deputy Assistant Commissioner General; Governors' Despatches, August 1844, ML, A 1274, p. 365; *South Australian Gazette and Colonial Register*, 29 June 1839; *Perth Gazette*, 20 May 1837, 22 July 1837; *Enquirer* (WA), 7 May 1845; George Seddon and Barbara Haddy, *Looking at an Old Suburb: A Walking Guide to Four Blocks of Fremantle*, University of Western Australia Press, 2000; *AG*, p. 260f.

SAMSON, Michael

b. Fremantle, 1844–1907
Free.
Single; 3 children.

The eldest child of Lionel and Fanny Samson (qq.v.), Michael was the first of six siblings. He was educated at St Peter's College in Adelaide and at the newly founded Catholic Brothers College in Fremantle. He initially worked with his father and uncle at the family business in Fremantle and was employed at the office of the Convict Department in Fremantle. Having fallen out with his family, he travelled to China where he worked as an exporter. When he returned to Western Australia and to Fremantle he became a customs inspector. Michael Samson married Mary Murphy in the old St Patrick's Church in Fremantle in 1889. They had three children: William Frederick (born 1892), Kathleen (1894) and Adelaide Rita (1896). Michael Samson became Mayor of Fremantle in 1905 and died two years later. His son, William Frederick Samson, was mayor for twenty-one years and was known as 'Mr Fremantle'. The home built by Michael and Mary Samson in 1889 is now cared for by the Western Australian Museum.

SAMSON, William

b. London, 1801–1880
Calista, 1829; Free.
Single; 4 children.

William arrived with his older brother, Lionel Samson (q.v.), on the *Calista* on 5 August 1829. He was listed as his brother's 'assistant'. He was licensed to sell goods by auction on 12 March 1831. At the end of 1834 William Samson had been appointed Government Auctioneer. Samson married Elizabeth Mary Pace on 18 June 1840. Her father was a sea captain and her mother ran a general store and hotel in Fremantle. In 1841 William Samson was appointed a Justice of the Peace in Western Australia and was listed as one of the seven directors of the Swan Boat Co. He became a member of the Governor's Executive Council in 1844. He was one of the directors of the Perth branch of the Bank of Australasia (of which Jacob Montefiore (q.v.) was a London director). The partnership between Lionel and William Samson was dissolved on 2 December 1846 and William moved to Adelaide the following year. The *Swan River News* of 1 March 1847 described him as one of 'the largest merchants to the colony', and he became an auctioneer, taking over the business of Emanuel Solomon (q.v.). The *South Australian Gazette and Colonial Register* reported on 4 October 1848 that Samson Wickstead & Co. had bought out Mr J. B. Neales, the largest auctioneering firm in South Australia, after which his business was one of the foremost in the colony. Samson retired from business in 1855 and worked as a broker until his death in June 1880. A Christian minister, the Rev. Frank Coghlan, conducted his funeral and said: 'He leaves behind him a tolerably large family'. His children were Elizabeth Jessy, born 17 April 1841, Walter Louis, born 4 March 1843, and Jane Maria, born 22 January 1845.

Enquirer, 24 November 1841, 23 June 1880; *HRA*, series 3, vol. 6, p. 625; *Perth Gazette*, 20 June 1840; *Swan River News*, 1 February 1844, 1 March 1847; *Western Australia Chronicle and Perth Gazette*, 12 March 1831; *South Australian Almanack*, 1847; *South Australian Gazette and Colonial Register*, 10 February 1847, 20 November 1847, 1 October 1842; *Inquirer*, 23 June 1880, p. 26.

SAMUEL, Barnett

b. London, 1821
Anson (1), 1844; Convict; Sentenced to 10 years, Central Criminal Court, 1843.
Single; Labourer; Height: 173 cm.

Dark complexion, dark brown hair, dark brown eyes, large nose, large mouth. Jew. Can read and write. Barnett Samuel was transported for picking a lady's pocket of two shillings and six pence and one penny and some half pence. He had previously been in gaol for one month for picking pockets. Gaol report: 'Bad character and connections. Sullen'.

Barnett Samuel's initial period of probation in Van Diemen's Land was for eighteen months and he was released on 4 August 1845. He was sent to the north of the island for assigned service. On 8 December 1845 he received one month's hard labour for selling his master's victuals without permission. On 27 July 1846 he was in prison in Launceston when he was found to be gambling on the Sabbath day and was given six weeks with hard labour and the treadmill. He was still in the Prisoners' Barracks in Launceston when he was found to be drunk and was sentenced to two months hard labour. On 24 April 1848 in Launceston he spent a night sleeping out of the depot and was sentenced to two months hard labour, after which he was sent to Oatlands 'in the interior'. A ticket of leave was issued on 24 September 1849 and he was recommended for a conditional pardon on 12 August 1851.

CON 33/50, no. 14732.

SAMUEL, Horatio

b. London, 1813–1832
Australia, 1830; Free.
Single.

Horatio Samuel arrived in Sydney on 18 April 1830. Horatio was the brother-in-law of Michael Phillips (q.v.), and travelled with the Phillips family. The family settled in Sydney, while Michael Phillips attempted to gain a large grant of land. Samuel was a witness of the conclusion of the partnership between P. J. Cohen (q.v.) and Lawrence J. Spyer (q.v.).

Horatio Samuel died at the home of his brother-in-law in O'Connell Street on 20 January 1832, and was buried in the Devonshire Street Cemetery before the Sabbath began. It was the third burial in the Jewish cemetery. On Monday 23 January 1832 the *Sydney Herald* carried the death notice: 'death on Friday last, after a few days illness, at the residence of Mr Michael Phillips O'Connell St. Horatio Samuel esq. of London age nineteen years. Deeply deplored by a numerous circle of acquaintances'.

Sydney Gazette, 31 March 1831; *Sydney Herald*, 23 January 1832.

SAMUEL, Joseph (Joseph the Jew) (Horne Tooke)

b. London, 1760
Royal Admiral (2), 1800; Convict; Sentenced to 14 years, Old Bailey, 1797.
Dealer.

Samuel was convicted of receiving stolen property. According to evidence at the Old Bailey trial a thief had been told to fetch Joseph the Jew, he called him Horne Tooke. Question: 'Was there anything said about there [sic] not being stolen?' Answer: 'No, because he did not care whether they were or not; I asked him where they were got, for "got" in their language is just the same as stolen I knew that if I did not turn upon Haines [the other thief in the case] the Jew would have turned upon me and hung us both'.

Samuel was sentenced at the Middlesex Gaol Delivery on 12 July 1797.

Joseph Samuel was listed in Governor King's Settlers' Muster Book (no. 907). He was not to be found in the 1805–06 Muster, nor in any subsequent record.

OBSP, 1796–97, case 439, p. 433; *Royal Admiral* Indent 4/3999.

SAMUEL, Kauffman

b. Germany, 1807–1851
Coronet, 1828; Free.
Single; Clerk; 3 children.

Kauffman Samuel began life as 'Samuel Kauffman' but reversed the order when he married. Samuel Kauffman appeared in the 1828 Census as a clerk working for Cohen and Spyers, George Street, Sydney. In 1831 he went into partnership with Lewis Cohen (q.v.), and on 10 January 1832 the partnership was dissolved and he went into business on his own at 2 Denmark Place, George Street, almost opposite the office of the *Sydney Gazette*. In 1833 his request for an assigned government convict was refused.

On 10 March 1835 Kauffman Samuel married Rosetta Joseph (q.v.), a sister of Moses Joseph (q.v.), under the auspices of the Sydney Synagogue. Their children were Deborah (24 December 1835 to 14 February 1850), Caroline (born 26 April 1838), and Moses (2 August 1841). On 3 March 1841 Samuel 'of Lower George St' acquired an allotment in Sydney and wrote to the Lands Department and asked, 'being a German Jew', that the Deed of Grant be made out in the name of his wife Rosetta.

Kauffman Samuel sailed for Wellington on the *Exporter* in July 1842, where he became a partner in the establishment of the mercantile firm of Samuel and Joseph, which became one of the largest importers of goods into colonial New Zealand. According to the obituary notice that appeared in London's *Jewish Chronicle*:

> In the infancy of New Zealand Messrs Samuel and Joseph were extensively connected with the whale fisheries and were the largest exporters of oil and bone and were most zealous in encouraging the flax trade. As a warm and zealous advocate of free institutions he never flinched from bearing his part in the struggle which, in

regard to these institutions, has so long been waged between the colonists and the Governor in Chief.

It was from Wellington, New Zealand, that Samuel sent £15 as a donation to the York Street Synagogue in 1845. He was listed as one of the three trustees to the Wellington Hebrew Congregation in 1843. He died on 29 July 1851.

Sydney Gazette, 24 January 1824, 12 November 1828; CS Letters Relating to Land, 2/7965, dated 8 September 1840, 3 March 1841; Governors' Despatches, ML, A1211, p. 695 (1833); *Jewish Chronicle*, 30 July 1851.

SAMUEL, Lewis

b. London, d. 1867
Patience, 1829; Free.
Single; Merchant.

A cabin class passenger on the ship *Patience*, Lewis Samuel came from England 'to join his parents'. He was the nephew of Saul Lyons and Samuel Lyons (qq.v.), and the brother of Abraham Samuel and Saul Samuel (q.v.). His widowed mother was Lydia Samuel (q.v.). The *Patience* arrived in Sydney on 19 August 1829. In 1832 Lewis Samuel applied for an assigned servant and his request was refused. He applied the following year and was assigned one servant. In November 1832 a newspaper identified him as the nephew of Saul Lyons who, together with his brother Abraham, had been given the licence for the Governor Macquarie Hotel in Pitt Street.

On 9 August 1834 the *Sydney Gazette* mentioned that Lewis Samuel was living at the Governor Macquarie Inn, Pitt Street, but would apply for a reward for the apprehension of burglars of the Rose Inn, Maitland. Samuel's name began to appear in the *Sydney General Trade List* by 1835 as an exporter of fruit and vegetables to Launceston and importer of haberdashery from Liverpool. In 1836 he was the contractor for lighting public lamps in the town of Sydney and in April 1837 was forced to offer a reward for those caught vandalising the new street lights that he had installed. At the end of the year he terminated his partnership with Wright Thomas Burrons and took over the general store at 79 George Street.

The business in George Street expanded to include 80 George Street and in 1840 Samuel advertised paints, oils, lamps and mats. In February 1841 Samuel sold his business to Lewis Leon (q.v.) and, together with Saul Samuel, bought a property at Wellington in New South Wales. In 1845 he announced that he was looking for a horse-breaker to proceed to Wellington. Two mares were to be sold from his station in January 1846 and in February he advertised for a 'good overseer to care for his sheep station'. Lewis Samuel was appointed a Justice of the Peace in 1846. He was a member of the Sydney Synagogue and helped to organise a Jewish Library.

Lewis 'retired' to London, where he died on 17 February 1867.

Ship Indent 4/5200; *Sydney Gazette*, 18 February 1836, 5 July 1836; CS 4/23023, 36/7013; *Sydney Monitor*, 17 November 1832; *Sydney General Trade List*, 4 July 1835, 8 December 1838; *Sydney Morning Herald*, 9 August 1834, 9 July 1845, 2 January 1846, 16 February 1846; *Sentinel*, 29 April 1847; *Australian*, 17 January 1836, 18 April 1837, 1 August 1839, 4 February 1843.

SAMUEL, Lydia

b. London
Brothers, 1832; Free.
Widow; 2 children.

The daughter of Levi and Hannah Lyons of London and widow of Sampson Samuel, Lydia Samuel arrived in Australia with her younger son Saul Samuel (q.v.), and her brothers Abraham Lyons (q.v.) and Saul Lyons (q.v.), to join their prosperous emancipist brother Samuel Lyons (q.v.). A bitter family dispute broke out shortly after her arrival, when the hot tempered Samuel Lyons refused to keep his promise and pay for the passage of the family to New South Wales.

SAMUEL, Michael (SAMUELS)

Alexander, 1835; Free.
Single; Tailor; 1 child.

Michael Samuel came steerage on the *Alexander*, arriving in Sydney on 30 August 1835. He travelled with Raphael Alexander (q.v.). They were both tailors. In 1849 Michael and his wife Sarah registered the birth of a daughter, Sophia, in Queanbeyan.

Ship Indent 4/5209.

SAMUEL, Saul (Sir)

b. London, 1820–1900
Brothers, 1832; Free.
Single; Merchant; 6 children.

Saul Samuel's father, Sampson Samuel, had died before Saul's birth. Saul was the brother (and business partner) of Lewis Samuel (q.v.), and nephew of Samuel Lyons (q.v.) and Saul Lyons (q.v.). He came to Sydney with his mother, Lydia Samuel, née Lyons (q.v.), on 25 August 1832. At the age of seventeen he was sent by his family to observe the first official land sale in Melbourne on 1 June 1837. He was not impressed by the village and decided not to buy anything. On 16 December 1859 Saul married Henrietta (Harriet) Mathilda Levien (q.v.) (who died on 5 June 1864). Through this marriage he became the son-in-law of Benjamin Goldsmid Levien (q.v.), the twice-related nephew of Mr and Mrs Saul Lyons, and brother-in-law of Phillip Joseph Cohen (q.v.). Saul Samuel was a committed Jew and was a seat holder in the Sydney Synagogue in 1845.

In 1837 he joined the counting house of his uncles, A. & S. Lyons, and then, with his brother Lewis, formed the firm of L. & S. Samuel with a store at Bathurst. Samuel amassed pastoral licences beyond the official boundaries of settlement, amounting to tens of thousands of acres. Saul Samuel Esq. of Wellington was appointed to the Bench in 1846, becoming the first Jewish magistrate in New South Wales.

Following the discovery of gold Samuel became a leading merchant in Bathurst, with interests in the mining industry, consigning wool and gold to Sydney and London. He diversified his business in Bathurst while the firm of L. & S. Samuel in Sydney bought gold. He became a director of the Bathurst Copper Mining Co. and a director of the Ophir Copper Mining Co. Samuel stood for Parliament. He opposed a 'bunyip aristocracy' that would rule through an unelected upper house. He described himself as a free trader. He favoured a national system of education. He was elected unopposed to the New South Wales Legislative Assembly in 1854. It was his first public office in a long and distinguished political career, during which he would serve as cabinet minister in a series of governments. At his election, Samuel felt obliged to issue a statement regarding his status: 'A report has been circulated that because he was of the Jewish faith, he would not conform to the oath required by law, prior to his taking a seat in the House. In New South Wales, he was happy to say, that such was not the fact'.

Saul Samuel was a member of the board of the York Street Synagogue, trustee of the Jewish section of the Devonshire Street Cemetery and, from 1871, chairman of the Sydney Hebrew Denominational Board. On 26 January 1875 he laid the foundation stone of the Great Synagogue and later served as the congregation's president. He was a member of the Royal Society of New South Wales and the New South Wales Academy of Arts.

Samuel became a London director of the Mercantile Bank of Sydney. He joined the council of Jews' College, which trained clergy for the Anglo-Jewish ministry. He was a member of the council of the Royal Colonial Institute and was a vice-president of the Society of Arts. In 1880 his public career was crowned with his appointment as Agent-General for the colony of New South Wales in London. Samuel was appointed KCMG in 1882, CB in 1886, and was created a Baronet in 1898.

He died in London on 29 August 1900, his estate valued for probate at £17 000. The children of Saul and Henrietta Samuel were Lydia (born 1858), Florence (1859), Lewis (1860), Edward (1862), and Henri (1864). Following Henrietta's death, at the age of twenty-six, on 5 June 1864, Saul Samuel married Sarah Louisa (née Isaacs), on 31 October 1877. They had one son.

4/5214; CS Correspondence Out 4/3550, 18 December 1846; *Sydney Morning Herald*, 7 January 1837, 15 September 1842; G. F. J. Bergman, ' Sir Saul Samuel', in *ADB*, vol. 6; M. Z. Forbes, 'The Jews of New South Wales and the Gold Rushes', *AJJHS*, vol. 12, no. 2 (1994), p. 292f; *Empire*, 24 October 1854; Jeremy I. Pfeffer, From One End of the Earth to the Other, Sussex Academic Press (2008), p. 201f.

SAMUELS, Abraham (SAMUEL)

b. Poland, 1794–1846
Manlius (1), 1827; Convict; Sentenced to 14 years, Manchester, 1827.
Married; Pedlar; Height: 165 cm; 4 children (in England).

Ruddy pockmarked complexion, dark brown to black hair, dark hazel eyes. Could read and write. A Jew. Scar on nose. Abraham Samuels was transported for purchasing stolen goods in Manchester. He was sentenced on 15 January 1827. He had four children in England. Before being deported a Jewish religious divorce was arranged. The rabbinical court traversed to Woolwich on 19 March 1827. He was identified as Abraham, son of Moses of Warsaw and his wife was Reina, daughter of Ari known as

Zoeb. Reina refused to accept the divorce document and she waited until Samuels returned to London in July 1843 and paid her £50.

Abraham Samuels arrived in New South Wales on 11 August 1827. In the 1828 Census Samuels was listed as a labourer working in government service with Samuel Dawson, blacksmith, and classified as an 'Israelite'. He lived at South Creek in the district of Melville. Dawson (or Daws) was constable of the Penrith Police. Samuels worked for Daws for two years and four months. He captured two bushrangers and was 'opposed by an axe' and claimed to have been promised a reward by the Bench. He also claimed to have helped capture six bushrangers in a previous attempt.

A ticket of leave was issued on 2 May 1831 at Evans. On 30 March 1832 Samuels lost the ticket of leave for playing at cards and it was restored on 20 August 1833. He was appointed to be a constable in Penrith and on 1 January 1836 was promoted to be a district constable. One of the local Justices of the Peace testified that he was 'the best constable at Penrith'. This praise was 'noted' and in September 1837 Samuels was told that it was too early for the administration to issue a conditional pardon. The pardon was issued on 1 November 1838 and an absolute pardon was listed on 1 February 1840.

Samuels was a member of the Sydney Synagogue Committee and, in 1845, he gave the synagogue £5 5s. The *Shipping Register for New South Wales* for 13 December 1845 and 1 March 1846 showed that Abraham Samuels sent bales of wool to London and brought nine cases of merchandise from London. Abraham Samuels died at Sydney on 29 December 1846, aged fifty-two.

Ship Indent 4/4012, p. 176; *Sydney Herald*, 2 May 1831, 30 May 1833; TL 33/459; CF 4/4264; CP 41/121, 39415; AP 40/104; Petition 4/2376, 37/8189, and Petition, 4/2076, 30/4501, in 4/4087; CF 4/4364.

SAMUELS, Abraham

b. London
Georgiana, 1830; Convict; Sentenced to 7 years.
Labourer.

A ticket of leave was granted to Samuels on 25 March 1836. He entered the Newcastle House of Correction in June 1837. He was sent there for 'insolence and neglect of work', having been assigned to Mr W. Sparke. He was put in gaol for two months. Samuels was then sent on to the Hyde Park Prisoners' Barracks in Sydney to be placed on the treadmill for fourteen days. A conditional pardon was issued in 1840.

Principal Superintendent of Convicts, Register of Convicts—House of Correction, Carters Barrack, 29 April 1837–24 February 1841, 4/4569 p. 7, June 1837; Newcastle Gaol Entrance and Description Book, 2/2005, no. 566; CP 40/104.

SAMUELS, Abraham

b. London, 1805
Susan (1), 1834; Convict; Sentenced to 7 years, Old Bailey, 1833.
Single; Tailor and stableman; Height: 162.5 cm.

Dark sallow and freckled complexion. Black hair. Chestnut eyes. Scar over left eyebrow, eyebrows meeting, scar on right eyebrow, mark of a burn on the left cheek, small dark mole on back of right wrist. Could read and write. Jew. Samuels stole a watch worth twenty shillings from a ship broker in Crutched-friars Lane. Samuels was part of a gang and was seized by his victim and delivered to the police. In court Samuels said: 'My mother was ill in bed. She desired me to go to my aunt's in London Rd. I was running across Gracechurch Street and two or three persons came and said I was a thief. I was struck in the mouth several times. I can assure you I have maintained my mother for six years, ever since the death of my father. I get my living in an honest way. I know nothing of the mob they speak of'. He was sentenced at the London Gaol Delivery on 5 September 1833.

Samuels arrived in New South Wales on 8 July 1834. By 14 March 1836 he was a 'free man' and was appointed district constable at Penrith, only to be dismissed one month later. Samuels was listed in the 1837 General Return of Convicts in New South Wales as assigned to Mr E. S. Hall of Inverary. On 27 November 1837 he was sentenced to six days on the treadmill for 'disobedience'. On 23 March 1840 he was reprimanded for tippling in a public house. He received his ticket of leave on 1 December 1843 and a certificate of freedom on 23 November 1844 because his behaviour 'proved that a thorough reformation had taken place'.

OBSP, 1833, case 1295, p. 720; *Susan* Printed Indent, X 636, p. 83, no. 34-1327-118; *New South Wales Government Gazette*, 16 March 1836; HO 10/40; HO 10/59, p. 222; CF 4/4372, 42/642.

SAMUELS, Henry (SAMUEL)

b. London, 1803
Prince of Orange (1), 1821; Convict; Sentenced to 7 years, Middlesex, 1819.
Single; Errand boy; Height: 164.5 cm.

Dark ruddy complexion, brown hair, grey eyes. Henry Samuels was sentenced on 1 December 1819. He had stolen two sheets valued at seven shillings. He had been arrested at 6 a.m. on Edgware Road with a bundle under his arm. A policeman looked him 'full in the face' and he immediately threw the bundle down and ran off.

The *Prince of Orange* arrived at Port Jackson on 12 February 1821. Samuels received a ticket of leave on 11 June 1825 and a certificate of freedom on 28 November 1832, which replaced a certificate issued on 10 May 1827. Henry Samuels married Hannah Beson in Sydney in 1836. 'Samuel Solomons', who had arrived on the *Prince of Orange*, received an absolute pardon on 19 May 1840.

OBSP, case 151; CF 4/4313, and 4/4289; CS 4/3688, 40/300; TL 25/297; CF 32/1052.

SAMUELS, Israel

1826–1860
Free.
Single; Hawker.

'Israel Samuels, a young man of not more than twenty years, was committed to take his trial in Sydney for embezzlement. He took stock from a dealer to hawk through the city and was to be paid two shillings and sixpence a day.' Apparently Samuels disappeared with the stock and it was revealed that he had been before the police court on a similar previous charge. A 'Samuel Israel Samuels' was buried as a Jew in the Melbourne General Cemetery on 15 November 1860.

Morning Chronicle (Sydney), 22 August 1846.

SAMUELS, Joseph

b. London, 1781–1806
Canada (1), 1801; Convict; Sentenced to 14 years, Old Bailey, 1795.
Single; Apprentice.

Joseph Samuels was tried at Middlesex on 20 May 1795 for stealing bed and table linen cloth, and two silver tablespoons valued at seventy-five shillings. At the trial there was mention of an older accomplice. Samuels was arrested in Petticoat Lane. He was fourteen years of age.

On 28 August 1803, Constable Joseph Luker, a convict, was found, 'a breathless corpse, shockingly mangled and with the guard of his cutlass buried in his brain'. A witness had seen the corpse being lowered into a grave by men associated with the night watch. The only clue was the bloodstained wheel of a barrow and the barrow without a wheel was soon found at the home of Sarah Laurence, where Isaac Simmons (q.v.) lived. A witness then identified Joseph Samuels at the scene of the crime. The two men were promptly arrested and were together in the same cell. Under interrogation Samuels confessed to the robbery but denied all knowledge of the murder. He cried 'I didn't even know Luker was dead. I didn't see him. I only took his money'. Simmons and two of his cronies had to attempt to explain how a bloodstained shirt and three blood-spattered handkerchiefs had been found in his room. He declared that he had suffered a nosebleed. His friend explained away the blood on his clothes by claiming it was the result of slaughtering a pig. The trial was swift. Only Samuels was found to be guilty, and the sentence of death was decreed on 18 September 1803.

The execution was to be long remembered. The grim ceremony began at half past nine on the morning of Monday, 26 September 1803—which happened to be the Jewish Day of Atonement. The doomed man was accompanied to the place of execution 'by a person of his own profession'. In an impassioned speech Samuels told that he had exchanged an 'oath of secrecy in the Hebrew tongue' with Simmons, who knew where the stolen money was hidden. Simmons, who stood among the crowd, calmly interjected during Samuels' denunciation and persuaded the crowd that Samuels was lying, and 'at length the signal was given and the cart drove from under him, but by the concussion, the suspending cord was separated at the centre, and the corpse fell to the ground on which he remained motionless with face downwards'. Samuels was hoisted back and, again, the rope unravelled. The third time, the hangman's rope broke and pandemonium ensued. Governor King was immediately notified, and wisely granted Samuels a reprieve, saying 'It would seem there has been Divine Intervention'.

Samuels was despatched to the new and distant penal settlement at Risdon Cove in Van Diemen's Land. When this settlement failed he was returned to New South Wales and sent on to King's Town (Newcastle). On 16 May 1805 he was suspected of plotting to escape in a boat to Timor and was sent 'up river' to gather cedar by the overseer who had forestalled the attempt. On 18 August 1805 Samuels was convicted of theft and whipped. In December 1805 there was a robbery in King's Town and Joseph Samuels was arrested. He eventually confessed to having been involved in the theft (with another prisoner, whom he incriminated). The stolen property could not be found but the accused was whipped. Samuels absconded from the Public Works Department in King's Town with seven other convicts on 1 April 1806 and drowned in the attempt to escape.

Story of Two Jewish Convicts', *AJJHS*, vol. 5, no. 7 (1963); *OBSP*, 1794–95, case 283, p. 759; Tardif, *John Bowen's Hobart*, p. 213; *Sydney Gazette*, 2 October 1803 (an account of the 'execution') and 22 December 1805; King Papers, 1799–1829, ML, A 1976, p. 103f. (Samuels is listed as 'John' Samuels); *Sydney Gazette*, 28 August 1803, 4 September 1803, 2 October 1803, 15 August 1805, 22 December 1805, 1 April 1806; *AG*, ch. 6.

SAMUELS, Ralph

b. Bristol, 1817
Susan (3), 1837; Convict; Sentenced to 14 years, Old Bailey, 1837.
Single; Labourer; Height: 171 cm; 3 children.

Sallow complexion, black eyes, black hair, medium nose. Ralph Samuels was sentenced at the Central Criminal Court on 8 May 1837 for stealing a coat, valued at £2, from Mr Davenport on 5 May. The coat had been on a carriage seat. He had previously been convicted for a similar theft. Mr Davenport was disturbed by the severity of the sentence and the effect it would have on a young man's life. In Samuels' own words, 'He tried to get me off (the transport ship). Came on board to see me'.

The *Susan* arrived in Hobart Town on 21 November 1837. On 27 November 1837 Samuels was sentenced to six days on the treadmill for 'disobedience'. On 25 March 1840, as an assigned convict to a Mr Pike, Samuels was admonished for having been seen 'tippling' in a public house. He received his ticket of leave on 1 December 1843 and a conditional pardon was recommended on 27 May 1845, and officially approved on 22 May 1846.

OBSP, 1837, case 1177, p. 27; CON 18/19; CON 31/41.

SAMUELS, Samuel

Free.

Samuel Samuels arrived in Sydney from Launceston on 9 March 1839. On 30 May 1853 it was reported to Sydney that Samuel Samuels, having been charged with felony, had escaped from custody at Gundagai 'near Albury' and had 'made off on his horse'.

Colonial Secretary's Office, Letters rec'd 1853, 4/3200, 53/4749.

SAUNDERS, Alexander

1788–1851
Free.

Alexander Saunders rented seat no. 65 in the Hobart Synagogue in 1845. His death, at the age of sixty-three, was recorded by the Colonial Hospital on 23 November 1851. He was buried by the Hobart Synagogue on the same day.

SAUNDERS, Daniel

Free.

Daniel Saunders paid three shillings and sixpence to the synagogue in 1845 and remained on the Hobart congregation's lists for two more years. He declined to pay the synagogue any more money.

SAUNDERS, Herbert

b. Dulwich, d. 1839 Free.

Herbert Saunders, 'of Dulwich', was buried on 21 July 1839 in Sydney's Devonshire Street Jewish Cemetery. The birth register of the colony recorded that Hannah Saunders, a 'Hebrew', the daughter of 'Hannah', with no father specified, was born in 1839.

SAUNDERS, John

b. Holland, 1813
Waterloo (6), 1838; Convict; Sentenced to 7 years, Old Bailey, 1837.
Single; Labourer; Height: 171 cm.

Dark sallow complexion, dark brown hair, hazel eyes. Lost a front upper tooth. J and S tattoo inside lower right arm, scar under left eyebrow. On 23 May 1837 John Saunders picked a pocket and stole a handkerchief in Fleet Street. He had been convicted once before for a similar offence. He was sentenced at the Central Criminal Court on 12 June 1837.

The *Waterloo* arrived in New South Wales on 8 January 1838. A ticket of leave was issued to Saunders in 1844 and a certificate of freedom followed on 22 June 1844.

OBSP, 1837, case 1432, p. 191; 1838 *Waterloo* (6) Printed Indent, no. 236; CF 4/4392, 44/0953.

SHANNON, Esther

b. London, 1807–1848
Free

Esther was the sister of Lawrence and Samuel Shannon (qqv). She was a witness at Lawrence's wedding to Sarah Tucker at St James' Church in 1839. She was the wife (de facto?) of Alfred Cooper, a non-Jewish emancipist. Two months before her death she gave birth to a son, George Alfred Cooper who was baptised after her death. She was buried in the Devonshire Street cemetery. When the cemetery was uprooted for the construction of the Central Railway Station, no remains were found.

Family information: John Stanhope, Epping, NSW.

SHANNON, Lawrence Israel (Lewis)

b. London, 1815–1861
Surrey I (8), 1834; Convict; Sentenced to 7 years, Old Bailey, 1831.
Single; Shoemaker; Height: 160 cm; 5 children.

Born London. Fair ruddy complexion, sandy brown hair, eyebrows partially meeting, mole right cheek, another mole on side of chin. Could read and write. Jew. Lawrence Shannon was transported for stealing clothes. At the Old Bailey trial he was described as a slipper-maker and 'shoe makers' boy', who stole property to the value of ten shillings from the man with whom he shared a room in a boarding house at Mile End Road. He was sentenced on 12 May 1831. The son of Jacob and Fanny and brother of Samuel Shannon (q.v.) and Esther Shannon (q.v.).

Shannon received a certificate of freedom on 29 May 1838 at the end of his seven-year sentence. He was listed as a member of the Sydney Synagogue in 1848. On 28 January 1848 he wrote a letter from Sydney to the Chief Rabbi in England. In the letter he described himself as 'Israel Shannon'. He wrote that he came to Sydney as a prisoner of the Crown in 1833 or 1834 as a very young man and was assigned to a settler 'in a distant part of the colony'. In 1838 his good behaviour permitted him to marry 'to a Christian girl in a Church' (Sarah Tucker) and he was then assigned to his wife and allowed to work on his own behalf in his trade as a shoemaker. By 1848 they had five children. He wanted his wife to be converted to Judaism. He wrote that he had observed Jewish tradition strictly, attended the synagogue, and did not eat forbidden food. On 14 June 1848, Chief Rabbi Adler in London replied that Shannon's wife (and children) could not convert to Judaism as there was no *Beth Din* (Rabbinic court) in Sydney and no *mikveh* (ritual bath). The family of seven surviving children and their parents moved to Cooma in 1858.

Lewis (Israel) Shannon died at Cooma in December 1893 and was buried in the grounds of Samuel Shannon's house 'The Wren's Nest'. His brother was buried beside him. The Jewish community, however, had lost a family. Sarah died on 9 June 1896 and is buried in the Mittagong Roman Catholic cemetery in Cooma.

Surrey Printed Indent, arriving 17 August 1834, p. 101; *OBSP*, 1830–31, case 1134, p. 567; CF 4/4342, 38/0458.

SHANNON, Leah

Leah was the sister of Esther, Lawrence and Samuel Shannon (qq.v). She married Abraham Shannon (q.v.) in London c. 1815. She arrived in Sydney on 10 January 1833 on board the *Palambam* with four children.

SHANNON, Samuel

b. London, 1802–1868
Richmond, 1822; Convict; Sentenced to 14 years, Kent Assizes, 1821.
Single; Merchant's clerk; Height: 161 cm; 8 children.

Samuel Shannon had a fair complexion, dark brown eyes and hair. He was the son of Jacob Shannon, who was a confectioner at Cannal Place, Kent Road, London. Samuel Shannon was born in

Bishopsgate Street in London. Samuel was convicted for having and forging bank notes. He was imprisoned on the hulk Retribution *at Sheerness for three months and then transferred to the transport ship* Richmond. *Gaol Report 'good', Hulk Report 'orderly'.*

Shannon arrived in Van Diemen's Land on 30 April 1822 and was assigned to work for James Cox near Hobart Town. In the 1828 Census Samuel was listed as aged twenty-eight (though he was twenty-six), working on the Cox family farm in Evandale as a labourer for George Cox, the brother of James. Shannon was listed as Protestant and as having arrived on the *Mariner* in 1821. On 10 March 1823 Shannon received 25 lashes for 'disobedience of orders'. It was his only offence listed on his record. Shannon was issued a certificate of freedom on 28 August 1835. His certificate of freedom stated that he had a dark complexion, dark brown hair and eyes and scarred hands and that he was a carpenter. Since his arrival he had grown half an inch in height.

Shannon was a cousin of Michael Hyam (q.v.), whose mother had been Sarah Shannon of London. Samuel Shannon moved to New South Wales and married Emilia Abrahams (q.v.) in a Jewish ceremony in Sydney on 10 February 1841. Shannon became a pioneer of the Monaro district. His brother-in-law Solomon Solomon (q.v.) transferred the licence of the Squatters' Arms Inn to him on 19 December 1842. (The hotel had been established by Abraham Moses in 1838.) Shannon established a store at Reid's Flat (which was nicknamed Jews' Flat, owing to the presence in the little township of members of the interrelated families of Abraham Moses (q.v.), Solomon Solomon, and Shannon). Solomon had married Emilia Shannon's sister, Rachel, in 1840. In 1843 Shannon was appointed the official representative of the Sydney Synagogue at 'Menero' (Monaro).

Rebecca Shannon was born some time in 1841 or early 1842, followed by Abraham (1843-1925), John Ernest (1845), Esther, who died aged one year, on 3 June 1849, Isaac Albert (1848-1922), John Frederick (1850), and Eli Augustus (1854).

On 23 November 1850 Samuel Shannon 'of Mowles Gully' (about ten miles from Cooma) bought land in the township of Cooma and established a store on the corner of Sharp and Bombala streets, and in 1854 he was granted a spirit merchant's licence. In January 1856 he sold his property to Abraham Levy (q.v.). In December 1857 he was the owner of a licence for the Victoria Hotel in Cooma.

The *Goulburn Herald* reported: 'Good news—five ounces of gold brought from Numeralla—a beautiful sample—bought by Mr Shannon', in 1858. In 1859 he rebuilt his Bombala Street store and the *Illawarra Mercury* reported (11 September 1859) that: 'another building worth mentioning is Mr Shannon's new store. It is about forty feet by twenty feet, and consists of a ground store and a large room above it of the same size. This is the only building with a second storey in Cooma, and a dwelling house is about to be joined to it'.

During 1860 Shannon was recorded as having built two cottages, a bakery and a new store for Solomon and Harry Solomon.

On 21 May 1860 Shannon's daughter Rebecca married Robert Barr, a carpenter from Scotland. Only Eli Shannon, who married Emily Cohen in 1892, married a Jew. Samuel Shannon died on 16 May 1868 and was buried by his brother-in-law and friend, Charles Solomon JP (q.v.). When Emilia Shannon died in 1891, Charles Solomon performed the burial ceremony, which took place on land adjacent to the Anglican cemetery.

AOT CON 31-1-38 p. 136 no. 406. Land Correspondence, 2/7969, 23 November 1850; CF 35/0914; HO 27/21; John Stanhope, 'Samuel Shannon: Cooma Businessman, 1802–1868', *AJJHS*, vol. 11, no. 2 (1991), p. 269f.

SILKMAN, Elijah

b. Algiers, 1804
Bengal Merchant (4), 1838; Convict; Sentenced to 14 years, Old Bailey, 1837.
Married; Barber; Height: 163 cm; 5 children.

Very dark sallow complexion, pock-pitted, black hair with grey, dark chestnut eyes. Bald. Mole on right side of nose. Two large scars on left arm. Can read and write. No previous convictions. Silkman was tried on 28 October 1837. He kept a lodging house, was married, and had been on the synagogue's poor lists for two years. He had blackmailed a 13-year-old boy, Manley Abrahams, who worked for a Jewish wholesale dealer, John Davis, into stealing goods worth more than £20. Silkman was found with the stolen goods at his home.

Elijah and Sophia Silkman's daughter Annie was born in Goulburn in 1860. Esther was born 1863, Miriam died on 6 May 1865 aged four and a half years, and was buried by the York Street Synagogue in Sydney. Jacob Charles born 1865, Fanny born 1867.

Bengal Merchant (4) Printed Indent, arrived Sydney, 21 July 1838, p. 90; *OBSP*, 1837, case 2331, p. 928f.

SIMEON, David

1837; Free.
Dealer.

The nephew of David Moses (q.v.) of Hobart Town and the older brother of James and Michael Simeon (qq.v.), David Simeon was the son of Peter Simeon and Sarah (née Rees) 'of Exeter'. Peter Simeon had migrated to England from Prussia with the original name of Simeon Cohen. Sarah's sister, Sophia (q.v.), was the wife of David Moses. By October 1828, the family was living in London and, in a court case involving the alleged theft of a bundle of clothes from young David, Peter Simeon, a tailor, testified: 'I live in Market Street, Finsbury Newmarket'.

David appears to have arrived in Melbourne in 1837 with a cargo of cattle belonging to Solomon Benjamin (q.v.). On 12 December 1842 the *Port Phillip Gazette* reported 'David Simeon, a draper in Collins Street, claimed to have been robbed of a roll of ten £5 notes. He had a brother with a shop in Collins Street and went to it while a customer waited for extra shirts'. When he returned the notes were gone. As he had not told the bank of the theft, the court did not believe the story and the case was dismissed. Ten days later the *Gazette* described him as 'the

Bolter Simeon'. He had 'fled' via Hobart Town to Sydney, leaving his debts behind, and 'with silks, satins etc. hidden by his brother'. He claimed later that he had been solvent at the time. However, there was a claim against him from David Moses for a payment of £74 4s 4d. In the investigation that took place in Melbourne in March 1843, Simeon asserted that there had been a meeting of creditors before he left Melbourne and a schedule was drawn up that could not be conducted properly as he had not taken stock.

OBSP, 1828, case 2105, 23 October 1828; history of the Simeon family, researched by Stephen Hanford, Melbourne.

SIMEON, James

b. London, 1815–1874
1837; Free.
Single; Dealer; 10 children.

James Simeon, the nephew of Sophia Moses and David Moses (q.v.) of Hobart Town, and brother of David and Michael Simeon (qq.v.), gave evidence on 20 October 1831 at the Old Bailey at the trial of a thief who had stolen a handkerchief. Simeon described himself as 'a shop lad, at a sale-shop in Holywell Street'. The 18-year-old thief was sentenced to be transported for life.

Mr James Simeon pledged £6 to the Sydney Synagogue building fund on 15 September 1839. In 1840 he joined in a brief business partnership with Joseph G. Raphael (q.v.). He then moved to Melbourne and opened a clothing store in Collins Street in 1841. On 1 March 1842 the *Port Phillip Herald* reported that he had taken legal steps against 'his servant maid for having forsaken his lawful flea trap. Shylock was not more resolved upon his bond than his countryman'. Simeon was obviously quick to anger. On 8 April 1842, the *Port Phillip Gazette* reported that 'Simeon, a clothier in Collins Street had been involved in a fight after he had made a sarcastic remark about a fish being carried by a passer-by. The fish ended up all over Simeon's clothes'.

In October 1842 Simeon opened the Emporium of Fashion in Collins Street. On 18 May 1843 the *Port Phillip Patriot* carried a report about the involuntary sequestration of James Simeon's assets. Asher Hymen Hart (q.v.) and John Levy (q.v.) testified that Simeon had intended to recover his capital by asking his uncle in Hobart Town to make his debt larger than it really was and therefore keep the money in the family. Hart said he remembered a conversation with Simeon in his home, where he spoke of declaring that his debt was £500 or £600 in place of £70. John Levy testified in court 'I am a clothier (in Collins St) and I know the defendant. In passing my door he said "what do you think of my *Pockle*?"—it means a hump', by which Levy implied he was carrying his cash in a hidden purse on his back. A discussion then ensued on whether Simeon's testimony on oath was valid because he had been sworn on a Bible containing both the Old and New Testaments. Hart stood up and declared that an oath was equally binding whether it was sworn with a hat on his head or on the Bible, as the Ten Commandments forbade false witness.

Simeon was always in trouble. On 15 February 1844 the *Port Phillip Patriot* carried a story from the Magistrates Court headlined 'An Honest Tradesman'. It concerned a customer of Simeon's: 'While she was paying the money, Simeon wrapped up what purported to be her purchase in paper. However, upon opening and inspecting the trousers [she had bought] she found that this honest man had "rung the changes"'.

Simeon married Eleanor Haidee Saunders at St David's in Hobart Town in March 1843. Eleanor was the daughter of John Saunders and Mary Ann Howell and may therefore have been the niece of both Judah Solomon's (q.v.) de facto wife (Elizabeth Howell) and Hannah Davis, the wife of Henry Davis (q.v.). Simeon became a founding member of the Melbourne Hebrew Congregation in 1844. On 16 July 1845 Moses Benjamin (q.v.) and Samuel Henry Harris (q.v.) called for a congregational meeting in order to register the birth of the son of James and Ellen Simeon. This was followed two days later by a call from five men for a meeting 'to consider the propriety of making *guerists*' (converts to Judaism).

His Jewish marriage to Eleanor, who was now called 'Sarah', was reported in the first issue of the *Age* newspaper on 17 October 1854, only three days after the family had returned from an extended visit to Europe (where four of his children and his wife Eleanor were converted to Judaism). The conversion ceremony was conducted at the Hague and registered by the rabbinate in London on 24 April 1854.

James Simeon died, aged fifty-nine, on 20 August 1874 and was buried as a Jew. He had lived at 397 Albert Road, Emerald Hill. Eleanor died in Kew, Melbourne, on 11 June 1910 and was not buried as a Jew. On her grave is a plaque which reads 'In Memory of Eleanor Haidee beloved wife of James Simeon. One of the first colonists of Melbourne. A true wife and devoted mother of the first Jewish (sic) born in Victoria. Erected by her son Marcus'.

OBSP, case 2046, 20 October 1831; Melbourne Hebrew Congregation Letter Book, 16 July 1845; VPR, series 30P, Box 2-1-21-5; Michael Cannon *Old Melbourne Town*, p. 66; *Port Phillip Gazette*, 20 February 1841, 27 August 1842, 12 October 1842, 17 May 1843, 19 October 1844. Jeremy I. Pfeffer, 'From One End of the Earth to the Other' p. 319.

SIMEON, Michael

b. 1824
Flying Squirrel, 1843; Free.
Married; Dealer; 1 child.

On 22 October 1843 Michael and Sarah Simeon arrived on the *Flying Squirrel*, cabin class, with their son. Michael Simeon was the younger brother of David and James Simeon (qq.v.) and a nephew of David Moses (q.v.) and Sophia Moses of Hobart Town. He was one of the founders of the Hobart Town Synagogue in September 1844, and eventually rented seat no. 71 in the synagogue. Sarah Simeon rented seat no. 2 in the Ladies' Gallery. He was a chorister at the consecration service of the synagogue in 1845 and the *Hobart Town Courier* reported that he 'possesses a falsetto voice of good quality rarely met with'. He donated £2 2s 6d to the synagogue in its first year and was asked to assist Isaac Solomon (q.v.) in arranging the music for the dedication of the synagogue building. Sarah Simeon was listed in the 1847 *Hobart Town Directory and General Guide* as a hosier in Liverpool Street.

Michael Simeon returned to England in the early 1850s and, in 1863, married Augusta Bloom Phillips in London.

CSO 92/11, p. 103.

SIMMONDS, Jacob

b. London, 1819
Enchantress, 1833; Convict; Sentenced to 7 years, London, 1831.
Single; Pastry cook and baker; Height: 160 cm.

Dark complexion, dark brown eyes, long nose, large mouth. A Jew. Jacob Simmonds was a brother of Solomon Simmonds (q.v.). Simmonds stole a watch valued at twenty shillings. A shopkeeper saw him come out of a room at the back of her shop. Simmonds said that he had come in to buy a penny's worth of apples. She took hold of him. He gave her a blow on the face. His gaol report was 'Not known'. His hulk report was 'Good'. His surgeon's report was 'Orderly'.

Jacob Simmonds arrived in Hobart Town on 31 July 1833. On 4 December 1833, while assigned to the Public Works Department, he was reprimanded for 'neglect of work'. A second reprimand followed on 11 February 1834. On 11 April 1835, as an assigned servant to Mr Underwood, he was placed in solitary confinement on bread and water for insolence and neglect of duty. On 15 September 1835 his master Mr Wilman found that Simmonds was absent from his premises during the night, for which he was severely reprimanded. On 4 March 1836 he was absent without leave and insolent and was given seven days solitary confinement on bread and water. Simmonds received permission to marry Jane Goodwin on 20 January 1838. He received a licence as a hawker in Launceston on 24 July 1840. Simmonds, with his wife and child, travelled steerage from Launceston to Port Jackson by the *William*, arriving on 1 February 1841.

CON 31/40; CON 18/6; CON 52/1; *William* Indent 4/5219; Permission to Marry Book, 1834–40; Shipping records 4/5219; CON 31/40; *Hobart Town Courier*, 24 July 1840.

SIMMONDS, Michael

b. Shoreditch, 1810
Augusta Jessie (1), 1835; Convict; Sentenced to 7 years, London, 1834.
Single; Labourer; Height: 153 cm.

Fresh complexion, small oval head, dark brown hair and whiskers, eyebrows meeting, brown eyes, straight nose, large full lips. A Jew. Blue mark on right cheek. Michael Simmonds was transported for stealing from the person. He stated this offence: 'Stealing linen'. His gaol report noted that he had been 'Imprisoned and transported before in 1826'. His previous sentence, of seven years, was for stealing pocket books. He had served the whole time at Chatham on board the hulk Cumberland. *His hulk report was 'Good'. He had also served a 14-day sentence for vagrancy. The surgeon's report was 'Good though once flogged'.*

Michael Simmonds arrived in Van Diemen's Land on 22 January 1835. His probation period was not a success and he was ordered by the Secretary of State to be worked in the 2nd Class Chain Gang. On 2 February 1836, while assigned to Mr Cleary and Mr Davis, Simmonds was admonished for disobedience of orders. On 31 October 1836 he was admonished a second time for being out after hours. On 9 February 1837 he was again found to be out after hours and guilty of using obscene language, and given thirty-six lashes. On 4 July 1837 he was found to be 'insolent' and sentenced to the treadmill for forty-eight hours and 'returned to the Government for a period of punishment'. By 24 August 1839 Simmonds was serving as a constable when he was ordered to refund the poundage fees out of his wages for illegally impounding a cow, the property of Mr Lucas. He was also to be kept in prison with hard labour on the treadmill for one month. On 13 January 1840 Simmonds, holding a ticket of leave, was again sent to the treadmill for forty-eight hours for 'misconduct'. On 26 February 1840 he was still listed as a constable when he was found guilty of misconduct for being out after hours and for making use of indecent language in a public house. He remained a constable and, on 8 February 1841, was accused of assaulting Alfred Williams. The case was dismissed. However, on 6 May 1841 he was fined ten shillings for neglect of duty when he failed to come to the office to prove the service of some summonses. A certificate of freedom was granted in 1841.

CON 18/3, no. 1944; CON 31/40; CF 467.

SIMMONDS, Ralph

b. London, 1818

Mangles (8), 1840; Convict; Sentenced to life, Central Criminal Court, 1839.

Married; Salesman; Height: 152 cm.

Fresh complexion, dark brown hair, oval face, blue eyes, long nose, large mouth, eyebrows partially meeting. A Jew. Could read and write. The letters R. S. were tattooed on his lower left arm. He was sentenced for having broken into a house using stolen keys and taking linen and a number of clocks from a clockmaker's shop. He had served a previous sentence of fourteen days for having stolen a violin. He was convicted on 21 October 1839.

Simmonds' wife died during the early part of his sentence in Australia and they had no children. Simmonds arrived in New South Wales on 27 April 1840 and was then sent on to Norfolk Island on the same ship in May 1840. Several days later his name was included in a list of nine Jewish convicts who wrote to the Sydney Synagogue asking for a set of prayer books. The words 'lately arrived' appear next to his name—the letter being dated 29 May 1840.

Simmonds was at Norfolk Island when an experimental individual 'mark system' was in force. He earned 6111 'good' marks and was fined 159 marks for the following: careless field labour; selling a shirt, and pilfering clothes at Government House, for which he was given two months in gaol and sent to field labour.

Two minor offences completed his record on the island. He arrived in Hobart Town on the *Maitland* in 1844 and was placed on assigned service. A brief period as a constable came to an end on 4 January 1845. He was acquitted of a charge of petty larceny but was dismissed from the police force and sent to Bridgewater. On 9 March 1847 he received his first ticket of leave. He was again allowed to join the police force. In January 1848 he was found guilty of larceny under £5 and sentenced to eighteen months imprisonment and hard labour in chains. Simmonds was condemned to be sent to Port Arthur and remained there a year. A second ticket of leave was approved in August 1850 and he was permitted to live in the district of New Norfolk. On 17 February 1852 he was reprimanded for misconduct for being absent from the district. A conditional pardon was approved on 28 October 1853.

CON 33/51 no 12143; *Mangles* Printed Indent 40-932, p. 96; CON 14/26; CON 18/42; Return of the English Prisoners under sentence of Transportation for Life, ML, A 1228, p. 701.

SIMMONDS, Solomon

Free.

The brother of Jacob Simmonds (q.v.), Solomon Simmonds was licensed as a hawker at Hobart Town in July 1840. On 20 June 1847 the Hobart Synagogue voted that 'Solly [Solomon] Simmons—a poor man' be granted three shillings a week from the charitable funds held by the congregation.

Hobart Town Courier, 24 July 1840.

SIMMONS, C.

Free.

'C. Simmons' lived in Portland, Port Phillip District, in 1841. On 14 April 1841 he applied for membership in the Melbourne Hebrew Congregation and in 1844 he is recorded as donating 11 shillings.

SIMMONS, Henry

b. London, d. 1850
Palambam, 1833; Free.
Married; Bricklayer; 2 children.

Henry Simmons, with his wife Sarah (q.v.) and their children, John, aged two, and Ann, 'an infant', arrived on the *Palambam*. They may have been bounty migrants.

A Henry Simmons died in Sydney on the same day and was buried by the synagogue as a pauper in the Devonshire Street Cemetery on 25 September 1850.

SIMMONS, Isaac (Ikey BULL) (Hikey BULL)

b. London, 1765–1833
Glatton, 1803; Convict; Sentenced to life, Old Bailey, 1799.
Single; Labourer.

The Old Bailey trial described a robbery that happened in Gracechurch Street. Simmons and another man followed a victim from a shop where he had changed a £30 bank note. Simmons, who was illiterate, declared 'I am as innocent as the child unborn'. He was sentenced to death, though this was commuted to transportation for life. Ikey Bull appeared in the records of the Old Bailey in 1802, when he was cited as a witness in the trial of Levi Cohen and Ephraim Jacobs, who were accused of forgery. In Newgate Gaol, Ikey Bull 'always has money' and was a turnkey in the prison. Martha Graves was his de facto wife and went by the name of Simmons. His sentence was handed down at the London Gaol Delivery on 15 February 1799.

The *Glatton* arrived in New South Wales on 11 March 1803. Simmons was obviously a big man, and his nickname 'Bull' was written on his Indent page (on which his surname was recorded as Simmonds). He was appointed a constable very soon after he landed in New South Wales. The Court of Magistrates was told on 7 May 1803 of the following confrontation between Simmons and one James Oram. On Thursday night, between 10 and 11 p.m., Simmons accosted Oram and asked 'Who comes there?' 'A friend!' came the answer. Simmons replied 'Damm your eyes why don't you go home?', and hit Oram upon the head with a staff of office. Witnesses testified that Oram was drunk and that Simmons was brutal. The constable was advised for the future to be careful not to beat prisoners but to offer assistance and to conduct them, when disorderly, to prison and report them.

Simmons was soon implicated in the brutal murder of Constable Joseph Luker on 28 August 1803. The *Sydney Gazette* reported that the body of Luker had been seen being lowered into a grave by persons belonging to the Watch, 'one of whom is at present in confinement on suspicion of his murder'. At the trial Simmons declared that he was innocent, even though he had to explain why he had bloodstains on his clothing: 'He said that his nose had long been habituated to bleed, whereby his handkerchiefs had become stained, and the spot of blood on the shirt must have proceeded from a fish he had cleaned, or a duck stolen by Samuels which he had killed. The Court cleared and in few minutes returned with a verdict—Not Guilty'. The abortive execution of Joseph Samuels (q.v.) followed the trial of Simmons. Nobody really believed that Simmons was innocent. The *Sydney Gazette* of 9 October 1803 wrote: 'Yesterday Isaac Simmons was brought from the Battery at George's Head, and punished with fifty lashes in front of the gaol, for disorderly conduct, neglect of work and for being refractory. In the evening he was returned to the Battery, there to remain till further Orders'.

On Joseph Luker's tombstone this poem, with its pointed reference to Jehovah, was carved:

My midnight vigils are no more,
Cold Sleep and Peace succeed;
The pangs of Death are past and o'er,
My wounds no longer bleed.
But when murderers appear
Before Jehovah's Throne,
Mine will it be to vanquish thee
And theirs to endure alone.

Isaac 'Simmonds' was listed in the 1811 General Muster. He was transferred to the Newcastle Penal Station and on 8 December 1817 he petitioned Governor Macquarie for a remission of his sentence. The Rev. William Cowper testified with the usual phrase that he was 'an industrious, honest and sober man', and a pardon was issued on 31 January 1818. He was not listed in the 1828 Census. Simmons died on 13 October 1833 and was buried in the Devonshire Street Jewish Cemetery.

OBSP, 1796–97, case 160, p. 241, 1802, case 206, p. 155; Bench of Magistrates, County of Cumberland, Minutes of Procedures, 24 March 1800 to 29 November 1805, 1/299, 7 May 1803, 12/39, Deposition, 23 July 1803 12/42; Petition 299, 1817, 4/1852; HO 10/1/1819, listed as an emancipated Government labourer; G. F. J. Bergman, 'Two Jewish Convicts', *AJJHS*, vol. 5, no. 7 (1963), p. 320f; *Sydney Gazette*, 4 September 1801, 4 September 1803, 8 September 1803, 9 October 1803.

SIMMONS, Isaac

b. London, 1805–1872
1829; Free.
Married; Dealer; 12 children.

Isaac Simmons, the brother of James Simmons (q.v.), arrived in Sydney with his wife Matilda (q.v.) in 1829. That year, Isaac and Matilda Simmons had a son, born in Sydney, who was registered as 'Hebrew'. The child was named James in honour of Isaac's brother, who had died in Sydney a few months previously. In 1832 Simmons asked for and received two assigned government servants. One of the convict servants was Lazarus Hart (q.v.).

Simmons opened the London General Warehouse at 60 George Street opposite the police station on 25 September 1832. By 25 May 1833 the store was called the London House and Simmons advertised dresses that had all been imported from England. The business prospered and in April 1834 he announced that he was moving from his London House to the Jerusalem Warehouse, which had been 'lately occupied by his brother James Simmons'. On 23 May 1837 Isaac Simmons and Co. advertised it carried a 'large stock of painting and engravings'. On that same day Simmons disposed of the Weatherboard Inn at Wentworth Falls in the Blue Mountains at £155 to Benjamin Lee (q.v.).

Simmons announced that he was a ship's agent for the brig *Alice* sailing between Sydney, Port Phillip and South Australia. On 16 July 1839 the *Sydney Gazette* reported that Simmons had launched a new brig built for his South Australian trade and that he had named the ship the *Jewess*. This ship became a significant participant in Melbourne's early intercolonial trade. In July 1839 Isaac Simmons of Sydney spent some weeks in Melbourne conducting stock auctions of sheep and horses that had been brought overland from Sydney. The records of the *Shipping Gazette* testify that he easily survived the economic depression of the 1840s with cargoes being despatched to Auckland, London and Tahiti. In December 1842 Simmons opened new rooms in George Street, which were opposite the Barrack's Wall and became the City Auction Mart. In April 1844 his bid of £250 for the cutter *Ranger* was accepted by the colonial government. In September 1844 Simmons purchased the brig *Caroline*.

While honorary treasurer of the synagogue building appeal of 1839, Simmons donated £145 in his name and in the name of his wife and two sons James and Barnett. Isaac Simmons was intensely proud of his Jewish heritage and flaunted it. He served as president of the Sydney Synagogue in 1838–40. He was treasurer of the building committee and a trustee of the synagogue's land. In 1840 Simmons spent over £600 buying land in rural towns with a major purchase in Maitland. In September 1844 Simmons stood as an unsuccessful candidate for the Brisbane Ward in the municipal elections.

Matilda and Isaac Simmons had twelve children. They were James, born in Sydney (1829); Sarah (1831); David (5 March 1833, died on 20 May 1836 and was buried at the Devonshire Street Jewish Cemetery); Barnett (born 18 February 1835); Fanny (27 August 1836); Julia (10 April 1838); Solomon (20 October 1840); Morris (John) (1841); Joseph (1844); Samuel (1846); Moses (20 October 1847); and Henry (1848, died on 12 November 1852).

Simmons was a seat holder at the York Street Synagogue in 1845 and gave £25 to the building fund. The records of the synagogue in Hobart Town in 1845 show that he rented seat no. 75 in 1845 and his name was crossed off the list in the subsequent year. He was evidently 'only visiting'.

Simmons died on 16 April 1872 on board the ship *Strathdon*, returning to Sydney from a visit to England. A memorial stone was later placed in the Rookwood Jewish Cemetery. Matilda Simmons died 15 October 1867 at the age of fifty-seven and was buried at Rookwood.

CS Miscellaneous Persons 4/3548, p. 156; CS, Letters Relating to Land, 2/7971, 22 July 1840, 10 October 1840; *Port Phillip Patriot*, 18 July 1839; *Sydney Gazette*, 25 September 1832, 29 November 1832, 25 May 1833, 17 April 1834, 23 May 1837, 5 January 1839, 16 July 1839; *Shipping Gazette*, 1 January 1844, 11 May 1844, 22 February 1845, 11 October 1845, 3 January 1846; *Sydney Morning Herald*, 12 January 1842, 4 February 1842, 12 December 1842, 29 April 1843, 31 August 1844, 17 September 1844.

SIMMONS, James (SIMONS)

b. London, 1795–1849
Marquis of Wellington, 1815; Convict; Sentenced to life, Old Bailey, 1813.
Single; Calico glazier; Height: 160 cm; 7 children.

Dark ruddy complexion, light brown hair, dark hazel eyes. James Simmons was the young assistant of Joseph Richardson, an escaped convict. A group of at least four individuals broke into the home of the

Dowager Marchioness of Downshire in Hanover Square and stole watches, silver and money to the value of £1500. On 2 June 1813 Simmons was sentenced to death, later commuted to transportation for life.

An accomplice, James Simons, aged fifty, was sentenced to transportation for fourteen years for his part in the robbery. The Old Bailey records described him as the father of the 16-year old boy (the boy being Simmons). Sarah Simons, Simmons' mother, and James Frankel, the father of Sarah, were found not guilty. Simons does not appear to have reached Australia.

James Simmons had five siblings. Elizabeth (who married Henry Cohen (q.v.), Samuel, Ann who married Henry Israel. Isaac Simmons (q.v.), (an auctioneer who came to Australia as a free migrant in 1829). Another brother, Joseph Simmons (q.v.), was also a free settler and well known Sydney actor, theatre manager and entrepeneur.

James Simmons was assigned as a servant to the architect Francis H. Greenway in 1816 and then assigned to Mr William Small in Richmond in 1819. He married Miss Agnes Thorley at St Peter's, Richmond, on 14 November 1821 and in 1822 Simmons received a beer licence for Richmond. In 1823, having sold his house and land in Richmond for £484 14s, he became the owner of the Emu Inn at Richmond. He was granted a conditional pardon on 17 August 1825. In 1827 he moved to George Street, Sydney, and opened a store named Emu House. In 1828 he opened an auction room and general business, which he boldly called the Jerusalem Warehouse.

The *Sydney Gazette* of 1 April 1830 reported:

> It is not generally known that there is in Sydney a Jewish priest of the name of Sebbet who arrived here four months ago, a native of Germany. He came out under the auspices of the London High Priest. Mr Simmons has hospitably provided him with a home and has made a very liberal offer of a piece of ground for the erection of a synagogue. But we believe no decisive step has been taken by his brother Israelites for the accomplishment of this object. Mr Sebbet is said to be of most exemplary character and of eminent achievements as a scholar.

The 'Jewish priest' must have been Rabbi Aaron Levy (q.v.), who stayed in Sydney for almost half a year. Simmons became involved in a breakaway Jewish congregation in 1829–30 that consisted of emancipists and old colonists. He began to charter whole ships of cargo to bring from England to Australia and he visited England in 1833, 1838 and 1842. After his first journey, the *Sydney Gazette* of 11 September 1834 advertised: 'James Simmons (late of the Jerusalem Warehouse) informs friends and the public that he has just returned from England and Adelaide—has rented stores in King Street and has a general assortment of merchandise'.

Simmons was granted an absolute pardon on 29 March 1833. In 1848 Simmons became the first Jewish alderman of the City of Sydney. He briefly participated in the affairs of the council from 1 November 1848 to 29 January 1849, when ill health intervened. He died on 2 May 1849.

The children of James and Agnes were: Sarah (subsequently Mrs David Hart), Joseph (born in England and married his first cousin Sarah Simmons);

Sarah (1832–1890), who married David Hart (q.v.); Frances (see below), Agnes (married her cousin James Simmons), David (1833–1850) born at Tamworth; Isaac (1836–1857); Elizabeth (1835–1925) and Edward. His will specified that his children were to be disinherited if they married outside the Jewish faith and his estate was estimated at £150 000. After his death his eldest son Joseph (named in honour of his uncle) remained in Australia to look after his father's business while most of the family returned to England.

Frances 'Fanny' eloped and married Edmund Minto Gibbes and was therefore disinherited by her father. Edmund was the third son of Colonel John Gibbes MLC, the Collector of Customs. Frances subsequently inherited a fortune from her mother. Her first marriage ended tragically as she lost her two young children in infancy and her husband from TB. In 1854, in London, Frances married a second time to Roger Gadsen, a barrister, and had four children.

On 21 August 1857 the *Dunbar* was wrecked on South Head with the loss of 121 people. One of these was Isaac Simmons who was, according to the *Sydney Morning Herald*, returning to Australia 'to take possession of his share of the property of his father'.

OBSP, 1813, case 574, p. 313f.; Ship Indent 4/4005, p. 34; CS Miscellaneous Persons, Out 4/3682, 14 November 1836; *Monitor,* 10 April 1830; *Australian*, 6 January 1842; *Sydney Morning Herald*, 25 September, 2 November 1848; *Sydney Gazette*, 9 January 1823, 30 January 1823, 18 December 1823, 23 April 1827, 3 February 1827, 9 July 1828, 5 September 1828, 13 October 1828, 1 April 1830, 30 June 1831, 26 January 1833, 18 September 1834; TL no. 241, see no. 27, in 4/1860, CS Letters Received 1819, Petitions for Mitigation of Sentence. Family information from Stephen Gibbes also *Murray of Yarralumla* by Gwendoline Wilson (OUP 1968) and *A Colonial Woman* by Patricia Clarke. (Allen & Unwin 1986).

SIMMONS, Joseph

b. London, 1810–1893
Arab, 1830; Free.
Married; Dealer, theatrical producer; 9 children.

Joseph Simmons was the son of Nathan and Sarah Simmons of London, and the younger brother of the emancipist James Simmons (q.v.) and the free settler Isaac Simmons (q.v.). Joseph Simmons first appeared on the stage in London when he was twelve years old and at the age of twenty he set sail for Sydney to join his emancipist brother. In June 1831 Simmons took out an auctioneer's licence and entered into a commercial partnership with his brother James at the Jerusalem Warehouse in George Street. On the voyage home he stopped in Van Diemen's Land and held popular pioneer theatrical evenings in both Hobart Town and Launceston. He returned to England in 1832 where he married Nancy Cohen (Simmons, q.v.), the daughter of the London broker Henry Simeon Cohen (q.v.) and his wife Elizabeth Cohen (q.v.).

Simmons packed up all the family and returned to New South Wales in 1833 together with his mother-in-law and her large family when Henry Cohen had been convicted of trading counterfeit bank cheques. The *Sydney Gazette* of 21 January 1834 announced: 'Mr Joseph Simmons, lately arrived from England, has opened a new warehouse which he designated "The Paddington House" in Underwood's Building, George St'. He boasted that he was selling fancy and other goods unequalled in Sydney for variety, quality and cheapness. Simmons embarked upon a parallel theatrical career, working for Barnett Levey (q.v.) at the Theatre Royal as stage manager and actor. In 1835 a son, James, was born to Joseph and 'Hannah' Simmons in Sydney. In May 1843 a seven-week-old daughter Sarah was buried in the Devonshire Street Jewish Cemetery. In 1847 (a second) Sarah was born to Joseph and Nancy Simmons in Bathurst. The 15-year-old James married his first cousin Agnes in a Jewish ceremony in Sydney in 1850.

On 10 March 1836 the *Sydney Gazette* reported that Simmons was considering going to Calcutta in order to take on the lease of the Dum Dum Theatre. He remained in Australia and later in 1836 it was reported that he had 'abandoned all thoughts of theatrical glory and taken himself to the more lucrative employment of auctioneer. We will have a little peace and quietness in theatrical matters'. The report was overly optimistic. Simmons visited Van Diemen's Land in 1836 where he performed and sang 'very successfully' at several 'At Homes'. In 1839 Mr Joseph Simmons pledged £20 to the Sydney Synagogue building appeal. In 1840 Simmons took over Sydney's Royal Victoria Theatre and produced a drama and comedy in three acts called *The Duellist*, which he said was 'the first truly original drama ever produced in the Colony'. His evening 'entertainments' were regularly held. They consisted of a 'choice collection of glees, duets, solos, serious and comic and a weekly budget of Extemporaneous drollery such as "George Street Courtship" or "The Strictest Propriety" presented by Mr Simmons'. On 31 June 1842 Simmons played Iago in *Othello* in the Royal City Theatre. On 1 July 1842 Joseph Simmons, 'actor and manager', filed a schedule for bankruptcy; he was discharged from insolvency on 12 February 1844. Simmons took over the Tavistock Hotel in September 1844 and, at his Simmons' Salon, held Concert Nights.

By 1848 Simmons had begun a new career in Bathurst as the owner of the Cheap General Stores. In 1849 he was active as a director in the Bathurst Copper Mining Co. He became the proprietor of Simmons Store at Bathurst and Carcoar. On 23 February 1850 Simmons moved back to Sydney, leaving his Bathurst Beehive to be managed by Raphael Tolano (q.v.), formerly of Canowindra, while his store at Carcoar was managed by Mr R. Copen. Simmons was very unlucky. Immediately after his move to Sydney the gold rush began. The Bathurst store was bought by S. Solomon and Co. and his Carcoar store by Raphael Tolano, both whom were among the first Australian gold buyers. In 1859 Simmons served as the president of the Sydney Synagogue.

Simmons settled in Melbourne, where he worked as an 'elocutionist'. He died at the age of eighty-four on 9 August 1893 at 33 Upper William Street, Darlinghurst, at the hotel owned by his nephew George Cohen. His death certificate described him as an 'elocutionist' and he was buried at Rookwood. His estate was valued at £44.

Joseph Simmons had eight children: James (born 1835), Edward (1840), Isaac (1842), Sarah (1843), Walter (1844), Sophia (1845), Sarah (1847-1904), Jane (1851).

Sydney Gazette, 30 June 1831, 21 January 1834, 10 March 1836, 30 October 1836; *Sydney Morning Herald*, 14 February 1843, 31 June 1842, 1 July 1843, 12 February 1844, 24 April 1844, 4 September 1844, 14 September 1844; 4/2655 *The Duellist*; *Bathurst Free Press*, 9 February 1850; *The Bee of Australia*, 2 November 1844; CS (Mss of Plays) 4/2655; Miscellaneous Persons 4/3548; H. L. Oppenheim, 'James Simmons', in *ADB*, vol. 2, p. 445f.

SIMMONS, Joshua

b. Spitalfields, 1801
St Vincent (3), 1853; Convict; Sentenced to 10 years, Central Criminal Court, 1849.
Married; Dealer; Height: 160 cm.

Fair complexion, dark brown hair, light brown eyebrows, blue eyes, large nose. Jew. Can read and write. Joshua Simmons was transported for receiving stolen property. He had kept a second-hand clothes shop in Field Lane and was 'well known' to the police. The police noticed him carrying a bag along Holborn Hill. When questioned he claimed it contained trousering stuff bought from a stranger in Oxford Street. He then attempted to bribe the police officers and was promptly arrested. He broke free and was chased and, before being caught, managed to poke one of his pursuers in the eye with his umbrella. A Judah Solomons gave evidence in support of the prisoner, saying that he had been offered a piece of similar material. Fifteen witnesses gave evidence of good character but only one even knew where Simmons actually lived. On 20 August 1849 the jury took four and a half hours to come to its verdict of guilty. The police then testified that Simmons' house was 'a den of thieves and criminals who had returned from transportation'.

Simmons was sent out on the last convict transport to Van Diemen's Land, and arrived on 26 May 1853. He was initially assigned to Louis Nathan (q.v.) in Murray Street, but was soon sent on to the penitentiary in Hobart Town and then to Port Arthur to serve a two-year sentence. The system treated him leniently and he was issued with a ticket of leave on 13 December 1853. On 23 March 1855 he was tried for assaulting a constable and was fined £1. A conditional pardon was issued on 28 August 1855.

CON 33/115; CON 14/47; CON 18/59; *The Times*, 24 August, 25 August 1849, and quoted in L. L. Robson, *The Convict Settlers of Australia*, p. 227f.

SIMMONS, Lipman

b. London
Waterloo, 1849; Free.
Single.

'I arrived in Sydney by the ship *Waterloo* in November 1849 and was welcomed by some of my relatives here. My cousin Mr J. G. Raphael [q.v.], who is a respected person here (Draper, George St) stated I shall always find a welcome home among his family. Please give my sincere love to my brother Joseph Simmons, now in your school [the Jews' Orphan Asylum in London] and inform him, if I do any good, he and my sister shall partake in it. Sydney 26 November 1849'.

Jewish Chronicle (London), 5 July 1850.

SIMMONS, Matilda

b. London, 1810–1897
1829; Free.
Married; 12 children.

Matilda was the wife of Isaac Simmons (q.v.). James, her first child, was born in Sydney in 1829, and was followed by Sarah (born 1831), David (1833–1836), Barnett (1835), Fanny (1836), Julia (1838), Solomon (1840), Morris (John) (1841), Joseph (1844), Samuel (1846), Moses (1841), and Henry (1848–1852).

Matilda died on 26 October 1897 and was buried at Rookwood. She died at her home at 166 Alberto Terrace, Macleay Street, aged eighty-seven.

Sydney Morning Herald, 19 October 1867.

SIMMONS, Moore

b. Poland, 1817
Asia (5), 1840; Convict; Sentenced to 10 years, Edinburgh, 1840.
Single; Gentleman's servant; Height: 155 cm.

Dark complexion, dark brown hair and whiskers, dark hazel-coloured eyes, large nose. M. S. and a heart tattooed on his right arm. A Jew. Could read but not write. Moore Simmons was tried at the Edinburgh Court on 10 January 1840, and transported for theft. His general behaviour on board ship was 'good'.

Simmons arrived in Van Diemen's Land on 6 August 1840. He received his ticket of leave on 6 September 1845 after having served his initial period of probation at Sandy Bay by the Derwent River near Hobart Town. A copy of a letter from the Superintendent Mr R. Hills certified 'that he found this man, whilst employed in the capacity of a servant, of very good disposition, industrious, civil and obliging'. In 1846 Simmons was sentenced to three months hard labour for being found in bed with the wife of a man named Hull. A further three-month sentence was imposed in September 1846 at Deloraine when he 'falsely accused a fellow prisoner of forging his name'. His ticket of leave was restored on 24 October 1847 and a conditional pardon was granted on 27 November 1849. A certificate of freedom was approved on 22 March 1850.

CON 32/2; CON 27/8.

SIMMONS, Samuel (JOHNSON)

b. Spitalfields, 1828
Ratcliffe, 1845; Convict; Sentenced to 7 years, Clerkenwell General Sessions, 1845.
Single; Labourer; Height: 142 cm.

Fresh complexion, blue eyes, long nose, large mouth and chin. A Jew. Could read and write. Samuel Simmons was seventeen at the time of his trial. He had stolen a coat. He had a previous three-month gaol sentence for stealing a gown.

Samuel Simmons was transported to Van Diemen's Land under his alias Samuel Johnson. His initial period of probation was for fifteen months and concluded on 12 April 1847. On 15 February 1848 and 19 July 1848 he was sentenced to imprisonment and hard labour for two separate charges of absconding. The first punishment was for twelve months and the second for six months.

On 16 July 1850 he gained his ticket of leave, and a certificate of freedom was granted on 28 January 1852.

CON 33/70.

SIMMONS, Sarah

Palambam, 1833; Free.
Married; 2 children.

Sarah Simmons arrived in New South Wales with her husband Henry Simmons (q.v.) and two children.

SIMONS, Asher (SIMON)

b. Hamburg, 1805
Isabella I (5), 1833; Convict; Sentenced to 14 years, Liverpool, 1833.
Hawker; Height: 172.5 cm.

Both Asher Simons and Morris Whyle (q.v.) were German Jews and hawkers. They were convicted of receiving three stolen watches at Liverpool on 7 January 1833.

Asher Simons arrived in Hobart Town on 14 November 1833.

Ship Indent, ML, A1059-7, p. 273; MM 33/2; CON 31/40; CON 27/6.

SIMONS, John

b. London, 1808
Royal Admiral (2), 1830; Convict; Sentenced to life, Bermuda Island—Court of Assize, 1830.
Single; Carter; Height: 158 cm.

Pale pock-pitted complexion, brown eyes and brown hair, blue spots tattooed forefinger and thumb on right hand. He could read and write. A Jew. John Simons had already served two and a half years of a seven-year sentence in Bermuda, having been sentenced on 4 May 1830. Simons was transported for assault with intent to murder.

John Simons arrived in New South Wales on 9 November 1830 and was assigned to Mr James Dunstand in Wilberforce.

Royal Admiral (2) Printed Indent, 1830, no. 30-2210, 4/4016, p. 53, and 4/4103, p. 52.

SIMONS, Samuel

b. 1774
Ganges, 1797; Convict; Sentenced to life, Old Bailey, 1796.
Dealer.

Samuel Simons was a dealer in hardware and tobacco. He was dressed in black with no hat and appeared to be an immigrant priest. To complete the disguise he was wearing spectacles with no glass in them. Simons offered to mind a sailor's bags while the sailor called a coach. The sailor assumed that Simons was a shop owner, and Simons took the bags into a shop. The shopkeeper suspected that something was wrong and called a constable. Simons became confused and offered the sailor ten shillings and sixpence if he would drop the charge. Simons explained: 'I am subject to fits. I fell in one and lost my hat. I put his portmanteau in the shop till he returned'. Simons was described as 'a Jew'. He was condemned to death on 13 January 1796 and the sentence was later commuted to transportation for life.

Samuel Simons arrived in the colony on 2 June 1797. In the 1805 Muster of New South Wales and Norfolk Island, Samuel Simons was described as free by servitude and a 'self employed labourer'. He does not appear in any subsequent official record.

Ship Indent 4/4004, p. 380.

SIMONS, Solomon (SYMONS)

b. Germany, 1794
Atlas III, 1816; Convict; Sentenced, Old Bailey, 1815.
Watchmaker, Hawker; Height: 153 cm.

Ruddy complexion, brown curly hair, grey to blue eyes, eyebrows meeting. Nose thick. Small raised scar below right side of underlip. On 23 April 1815 Solomon Simons and Thomas Smith were found guilty of stealing a watch valued at 30 shillings in 'an assault on the King's Highway'. The two ambushed a passerby, who was stunned and fell to the ground. When he recovered his composure he returned to the scene of the attack and identified his assailants: 'I knew his person immediately. He looks very much like a Jew'. Simons went by the nickname 'Old Solly'. On 10 May 1815 Simons, aged twenty, and Smith, aged thirty-two, were sentenced to death.

The *Atlas* arrived in New South Wales on 22 July 1816. Simons received a ticket of leave in October 1837 for the district of Merton. A certificate of freedom was granted in 1839. The *Sydney Gazette* carried a report in 1831 that a Benjamin Simon, 'a German Jew', had been charged with committing a violent assault upon Charlotte Clarke and was committed for trial. In the dossier of Maria Benjamin (q.v.) it was noted that she was the sister of Solomon Simons (Symons) in Australia.

OBSP, 1815, case 594, p. 272; Ship Indent 4/4017, p. 67; TL 37/1372, in 4/4115; CF 39/150, in 4/4348; HO 10/8; *Sydney Gazette*, 28 May 1831.

SIMPSON, Solomon

b. London, 1801
Tottenham, 1818; Convict; Sentenced to 7 years, Old Bailey, 1817.
Single; Butcher; Height: 173 cm.

Pale complexion, black hair, dark eyes. Solomon Simpson, a Jew, aged nineteen, snatched a shawl from a servant opposite Whitechapel Church at 11 o'clock at night.

Solomon Simpson arrived in New South Wales on 14 October 1818. He received a ticket of leave on 23 September 1824. In the 1828 Census Simpson was listed as a 'dealer' living at the boarding house of Mrs Mary Larkins, Kent Street, Sydney. Simpson received his certificate of freedom on 27 November 1828. Mrs Larkins had six tenants, of whom four were Jews: Lewis Lyons (q.v.), Mordecai Abrahams (q.v.), Isaac Moses (q.v.) and Simpson.

OBSP, 1816–17, case 1275, p. 431; HO 10/1; Ship Indent 4/4005, p. 124; CF 28/0991.

SISE, William (William Kangaroo)

b. Dover, USA, 1813
Marquis of Huntley (1), 1835; Convict; Sentenced to 14 years, Worcester Quarter Sessions, 1834.
Single; Compositor; Height: 161 cm.

Dark complexion, brown hair, grey eyes, long face, large nose, scar on each eyebrow, small scar in centre of forehead and on chin. Powder marks on lid of right eye. Jew. Born Dover, New Hampshire. William Sise was transported for 'demanding money'.

William Sise arrived on 5 July 1835. He was granted a ticket of leave in 1847. On 22 February 1847 he was in the District of Port Phillip, known as 'Size' (Seixas?). A certificate of freedom was issued to him in 1850.

Marquis of Huntley Printed Indent, p. 94, also Indent 4/4019, in Fiche 713, with details of Pardons; TL 47/254; CF 250, in Principal superintendent of Convicts, CF butts, 22 February 1850 to 5 May 1851, 4/4414.

SLOMAN, R. B.

1837; Free.
Dealer.

R. B. Sloman signed the petition for a Jewish burial ground in Yass on 20 December 1844. He was one of the first settlers in Port Phillip in 1837.

L. M. Goldman recounts the story of Sloman suing an auctioneer in Melbourne in the 1850s. Sloman had instructed the auctioneer in writing to sell straw hats at twelve shillings each. They were sold at twelve shillings a dozen and the auctioneer had to pay Sloman £50.

Petition 4/2650.4; L. M. Goldman, *The Jews in Victoria in the Nineteenth Century*, p. 118.

SMITH, John

b. London, 1806
Mangles (3), 1824; Convict; Sentenced to life, London, 1823.
Single; Porter; Height: 161 cm.

Freckled complexion, red hair, hazel eyes. Aged seventeen, 'John Smith' was sentenced to transportation for life on 10 September 1823. He was caught in company with another young thief as they picked a pocket, and was seized as he stole a handkerchief, valued at one shilling.

On 30 October 1824, immediately after his arrival in New South Wales, Smith was sent to work as an assigned convict servant in Windsor. In the 1837 General Return of Convicts in New South Wales he was listed as an assigned servant at the Lunatic Asylum in Liverpool. Smith received a ticket of leave for the Windsor District on 11 September 1838. He appeared in the 1841 Newcastle Gaol Entrance and Description Book and was described as 'a Jewish labourer'. He was tried on 18 June 1841 at the Maitland District Quarter Sessions and placed in the stockade for two months. Smith was granted a certificate of freedom on 11 November 1843. A conditional pardon was confirmed on 8 November 1847.

OBSP, 1822–23, case 1018, p. 379; Ship Indent 4/4010, p. 26; CO 207/2; Newcastle Gaol Entrance and Description Book 1841–45, 2/2008, no. 255; CF 4/4387, 43/1936.

SMITH, William

b. London, 1810
Lady Kennaway (2), 1836; Convict; Sentenced to 7 years, Middlesex, 1835.
Single; Carter; Height: 157.5 cm.

Dark ruddy complexion and a little pock-pitted. Dark brown hair. Brown eyes. Lost two front upper teeth. No education. A Jew. William Smith was transported for picking pockets. He was tried at Westminster and sentenced at Middlesex on 20 August 1835. He had served a previous prison sentence of one month.

Smith arrived in New South Wales on 12 October 1836. He was listed in the 1837 General Return of Convicts in New South Wales, aged fifty-two (though he was twenty-seven!), working on Goat Island in Sydney Harbour. He received his ticket of leave in 1840, a certificate of freedom in 1843 and a conditional pardon in 1848.

Lady Kennaway Printed Indent, no. 36-2227; TL 40/2462; CF 4/4381, 43/404; CP 48/1250.

SMITH, William

b. London, 1817
Equestrian (1), 1844; Convict; Sentenced to 7 years, Clerkenwell, Middlesex, 1843.
Single; Tailor; Height: 155 cm.

Ruddy, deeply pock-pitted complexion, brown hair, blue eyes, long nose, large chin. A Jew. 'William Smith' was sentenced for larceny. It was his second conviction. He had previously stolen a twist of wool at Oxford Street. His previous sentence was for three months. He could read Hebrew and had an imperfect reading knowledge of English.

William Smith arrived in Van Diemen's Land on 1 May 1844 and was given an initial period of probation of fifteen months at the convict station at Seven Mile Creek. This period of his punishment concluded on 1 August 1845. He received his ticket of leave on 16 November 1847 at Launceston after being housed in the Prisoners' Barracks. In August 1848 he was arrested for being drunk and out after hours in Hobart Town and was sentenced to fourteen days solitary confinement. In Launceston, on 23 October 1849, he was again found guilty of being out after hours and sentenced to one month's imprisonment with hard labour.

A similar offence occurred in Launceston on 28 December 1849 and brought him three weeks imprisonment and hard labour at the Prisoners' Barracks. On 1 January 1850 he received fourteen days solitary for 'idleness'. His ticket of leave was restored on 18 March 1850 and a certificate of freedom was authorised on 22 November 1850.

CON 33/54, no. 12911.

SMITHERMAN, John (Thomas)

Sir William Bensley, 1817; Free.
Single; Cook.

John Smitherman was a 'converted Jew'. His mother was named Sarah and his sister Betsy. A 'Thomas Smitherman' came to Van Diemen's Land on the *Admiral Cockburn* in 1819. The record in the Tasmanian Archives states that Smitherman was fifty-five years old 'at time of offence', presumably occurring in New South Wales.

CON 31/38, p. 57; CON 35/1, p. 507; CON 16/3, p. 492; CON 13/1, p. 338; CON 13/2, p. 535.

SOLOMON, Aaron

b. London, 1793–1872
Indefatigable (1), 1812; Convict; Sentenced to life, Old Bailey, 1811.
Single; Labourer; Height: 157 cm; 9 children.

Fair complexion, brown hair, grey eyes. Jew. Aaron Solomon's father was Isaac Solomon and his mother was Hannah. With two other young men, Solomon held up and attempted to rob a stonemason's labourer in Brick Lane, Whitechapel. They were chased and Solomon was caught. He told the judge at the Old Bailey: 'I am as innocent as a new born child. I was coming down the street. I went down that court. There was no thoroughfare. The watchman catched hold of me, and the prosecutor said that I was the man some yards before he came nigh to me'. Solomon was sentenced to death on 29 May 1811 and the sentence was later commuted to transportation for life.

Aaron Solomon arrived in Van Diemen's Land on 19 October 1812. He was sent to Sydney to give evidence in a trial concerning sheep stealing in 1818 and returned to Van Diemen's Land on 21 October 1819 by the *Hibernia*. He had been a witness in the case of the King versus Slater, and was sent back to Van Diemen's Land by the *Prince Leopold*. Evidently he was rewarded for his cooperative attitude with a ticket of leave. He appears to have been reincarcerated and on 21 February 1821 was sent back to Sydney and, on 4 March 1821, was sentenced to be despatched to the Newcastle Penal Settlement for three years on the *Elizabeth Henrietta*. The 1822 General Muster noted that he was a prisoner in 'government employ' in Newcastle.

Solomon was sentenced to fifty lashes in March 1825 for attempting to escape. On 27 February 1826 he appeared before the Bench of Magistrates in

Newcastle for having been seen by the Chief Constable attempting to hide a stolen shirt that he had received. He was sentenced to three months in the chain gang. On 25 March 1826 he 'threw his frock over a keg of spirits and attempted to steal it whilst at his usual work of wheeling coals'. Solomon was listed in the 1828 Census as a convict at the Prisoners' Barracks in Newcastle. His religion was not stated. A ticket of leave was granted in July 1834 for the district of Newcastle and altered for Parramatta in 1834. A conditional pardon was granted on 1 April 1841.

Aaron Solomon married Margaret Ewings in Parramatta in October 1835. The officiating minister was the Rev. Samuel Marsden. Ewings was said to be a direct descendant of Oliver Cromwell and had been transported for embezzling £231 9s. The children of Aaron and Margaret Solomon were: Aaron (born 1836), Hannah (1838), Margaret (1840), Oliver (1843), Abraham (1845), Phoebe (1848), Louisa (1851), Maria (1854), and Alice (1857).

On December 1841 the *Sydney Free Press and Commercial Journal* mentioned that Solomon was 'a general dealer' with a shop in George Street. Aaron Solomon died in Sydney on 7 August 1872.

OBSP, 1810, case 464, p. 277; Ship Indent 4/4004, p. 418; CON 31/38, no. 51; CON 23/1, p. 347; 4/3500, p. 311; HO 10/53; Monthly Return of Corporal Punishments inflicted at Newcastle, Newcastle Police Court, ML, F 49, p. 34; 4/1718, p. 201. Pardons, Governors' Despatches, A1231, CP 42/104, p. 284; Permission to Marry Book, 4/4512, p. 190; *Australian*, 9 April 1842.

SOLOMON, Abraham

b. Frankfurt, 1811–1869
Lady Kennaway (2), 1836; Convict; Sentenced to life, Liverpool Quarter Sessions, 1836.
Single; Butcher; Height: 161 cm; 5 children.

Dark sallow freckled complexion, black hair, brown eyes. Scar on cheek. Could read and write. Abraham Solomon was transported for house breaking and sentenced at Liverpool on 18 January 1836.

Abraham Solomon arrived in New South Wales on 12 October 1836. The 1837 General Return of Convicts in New South Wales reported that he was working as an assigned convict for Mr Alexander Smith at Blackwattle Swamp. In the Parramatta Gaol Register for 1839, 'Irvin Solomon' was said to have been born in Berlin and was a watchmaker. He was sent, with five others, in January 1839, to the Supreme Court in Sydney for a trial concerning a felony at Bathurst. Abraham Solomon was listed in the 1841 Census of New South Wales, living in Dapto in the District of Illawarra. He received his ticket of leave in 1844 and a conditional pardon in 1848. Solomon married the 17-year-old Mary Ann Munson in 1851 and had five children. Mary Ann died on 16 March 1861 and later that same year Abraham Solomon married a second time, to Eliza Jane Nancarrow. Abraham Solomon died on 12 December 1869 at Bundarra.

Lady Kennaway (2) Printed Indent, 1836, 2189-25 (X638-9); Parramatta Gaol Register for 1839, 4/6533, TL 44/678; CP 48/2250; family information from Maggie Wilde West.

SOLOMON, Abraham Jacob

b. London, 1826–1889
Constant, 1849; Free.
Married; Dealer, minister; 14 children.

Abraham Jacob Solomon was the grandson of the 'world renowned matzah baker' of London of the same name. On 4 July 1849 the 23-year-old Abraham Jacob Solomon of Cutler Street, Aldgate, married Julia Isaacs (Solomon, q.v.) of Harrow Alley, Aldgate, in the New Synagogue in London. Chief Rabbi Adler officiated. They arrived, travelling steerage, in Adelaide on the barque *Constant* on 23 December 1849. The small Adelaide congregation quickly appointed him as the Reader for a salary of £52 a year. Solomon conducted the consecration of the new synagogue building on 5 September 1850. An economic depression in South Australia brought the congregation's agreement to pay Solomon to an abrupt end. There were fewer than 150 Jews in South Australia, and Solomon offered to continue as synagogue reader in an honorary capacity.

In June 1852 Solomon was appointed Reader at the Melbourne Hebrew Congregation for six months, and then returned to Adelaide. On 27 October 1853 he wrote to the Adelaide Hebrew Congregation: 'Being compelled through unforeseen circumstances to leave for Melbourne Port Phillip I am obliged to forgo the position I hold in your congregation as officiating Minister. Believe me Gentlemen it grieves me much that I have to do so after receiving such kind treatment from you all since my return from Melbourne'.

Armed with a cheque for £10 for 'past services', Solomon, his wife and three children set sail for the Victorian goldfields at Carisbrook (near Maryborough). By 1855 Solomon, his wife and three young children had returned to Adelaide, where he became the lessee and manager of the Queen's Theatre in Gilles Arcade, which, in turn, was named the Theatre Inn. He was the licensed victualler on the premises in Hindley Street. He subsequently became a hotel 'valuator and broker' in the name of A. J. Solomon and Son, Licensed Valuator and Brokers in the Exchange Building, Pirie Street, Adelaide, and officiated at many of the services at the Adelaide synagogue.

Solomon was always ready to travel throughout rural South Australia and New South Wales to perform circumcisions. By 1876 his 'Brit Book' listed 176 babies he had named.

A. J. Solomon and his wife Julia had fourteen children, five of whom died as young children (one of these was Ellis, born in 1869). Abraham died on 10 January 1889 and was buried in Adelaide's West Terrace Jewish Cemetery. Julia Solomon died on 30 December 1895. Their nine surviving children were: Miriam (born 30 October 1850), Judah Abraham (1852), Sarah (1855), Rachel (1858), Henry (1861), Rebecca (1863), Sophia (1865), Leah (1866), and Julia Blanche (1870). Three daughters remained in Adelaide: Miriam married Joseph Solomon; Rachel married John Barnet Saunders; and Rebecca married James Slater. Those who moved to the eastern states were Judah Abraham, who married Martha Townsend, Sarah, who married Jacob Neustadt, Henry, who married Hannah Phillips, Sophia, who married John Elsner, and Julia Blanche, who married Manny Bloom.

Helen Tversky-Steiner, *Abraham Jacob and Julia Solomon (née Isaacs)*, privately published, Adelaide, 2012.

SOLOMON, Ann (née JULIAN)

b. London, 1791–1877
Mermaid (1), 1828; Convict; Sentenced to 14 years, Old Bailey, 1827.
Married; Dressmaker; Height: 154 cm; 6 children.

Dark fresh coloured complexion, small head, dark brown hair, narrow oval-shaped face, dark arched eyebrows. Dark brown eyes, small mouth, sharp pointed chin. A Jewess. Aged thirty-five. Gaol report: 'A notorious receiver of stolen goods'. Ann Solomon gave the Hobart Town officials a sanitised version of her offence and background: 'Receiving stolen goods—a watch'. The prosecutor was a captain or master of a vessel. She had lived off Commercial Road (Bell Lane) in Spitalfields, and had two girls, Anne (Nancy) (q.v.), aged seven, and Sarah (q.v.), aged five, and two boys, David, aged nine, and Mark, three years old. 'My husband I believe has gone to America. I have two children gone to Sydney. John [q.v.], aged twenty-one, and Moses [q.v.], aged eighteen, as gentlemen to settle. My father is a coach master named Moses Julian who lives in Aldgate. My husband was a jeweller and lived in Bell Lane.' Ann had been sentenced on 13 September 1827. In 1828 two of her nephews were sent to Australia. They were Moses Julion (q.v.), who arrived in Hobart Town on the Roslin Castle, and Jacob Julian (q.v.), who came out to New South Wales on the Hooghly (2).

Ann (Hannah) Solomon was married to the notorious Isaac (Ikey) Solomon (q.v.). She arrived in Hobart Town (with her four younger children) on 27 June 1828 and was assigned as a convict servant to police officer Newman. She was soon joined in Hobart Town by her two adult sons, John and Moses, and then by her husband. Her older sons had hoped to have their mother assigned to them but their petition was denied.

During Ikey's subsequent deportation and trial in England, Ann became estranged from him and formed a liaison with the emancipist George Madden. Ikey Solomon was returned to Van Diemen's Land to serve a sentence of imprisonment. On 20 July 1835 Ann was charged with 'disorderly conduct in using opprobrious epithets to her husband and otherwise ill treating him. Disturbance having continued in the family ever since the warning given them on 3 July and appearing to arise from a combination between the mother and the children against the father'. Ann Solomon was returned to the Female Factory for the disposal of the Principal Superintendent J. Mason. Ann spent some months in prison before a ticket of leave was issued in September 1835 followed by a conditional pardon in 1840.

Ann Solomon was very much in the public eye. The *Age* in England published the following report, which was republished and ridiculed in the *Hobart Town Courier* of 3 May 1833:

> New Jew Colony 'our peoplesh' are about to establish a Jewish colony in Van Diemen's Land under the patronage of Mrs Ikey Solomons. (This we presume will be news to

Mrs Solomons herself, as well as all the rest of the Jewish 'peoplesh'. The *Age* is very inventive in a small way.)

In 1877, 'Hannah Solomon relict of Isaac Solomon of Hobart Town died aged eighty-seven'.

CON 40/9, no. 129; *Hobart Town Courier*, 5 June 1840, supplement, A 1059/1, p. 429; 40; CP (Government Notice) no. 2396, 27 May 1840; CON 18/24; CSO 1/295/7163; *Launceston Examiner*, 22 December 1877.

SOLOMON, Anne (Nancy)

b. London, 1820
Mermaid (1), 1828; Free.
Single.

The fourth child of Hannah (Ann Solomon, q.v.) and Isaac (Ikey) Solomon (q.v.), Anne was the sister of John (q.v.), Moses (q.v.), David (q.v.), Sarah (q.v.), and Mark (q.v.) Anne came to Australia with her younger siblings on the *Mermaid*, the ship on which her mother was transported as a convict.

Anne Solomon married John Shakespeare at Campbell Town (Van Diemen's Land) on 23 April 1847. The Marriage Register also lists an Anne Solomon who married John Wilson at Oatlands on 4 May 1840, and Ann Solomon, aged twenty-two, who married William Wilson, aged twenty-six, in Hobart Town on 22 November 1841.

SOLOMON, Barnett (alias Youner Barnett (q.v))

d. 1835
1823; Free.

Barnett Solomon was buried in the Devonshire Street Jewish Cemetery in Sydney on 18 February 1835. He had not been listed in the 1828 Census.

SOLOMON, Benjamin

1810–1851
Lonach, 1833; Free.
Married; 5 children.

Benjamin Solomon migrated to Australia, arriving on 25 October 1833 with his wife, Jane, and children, Sarah, Louisa, Esther, Henry and Jessie. A publican's licence was issued to a 'Mr Solomon' for the Roseneath Inn, Main Road, Austin's Ferry, in 1834. Solomon was listed as a steerage passenger on the *Marian Watson* from Hobart Town to Port Jackson, arriving in Sydney on 16 August 1838.

Benjamin Solomon was buried as a Jew on 30 March 1851. A few weeks later, on 20 May 1851, Louisa Solomon, aged seventeen, married Moses Abrahams 'of full age' at 'the private residence' of Mr (Simeon) Benjamin (q.v.), Liverpool Street, Hobart Town'. The bride was described as 'living with her mother'. The Hobart synagogue records that a daughter of Louisa and Moses died 17 May 1854.

CUS 30, pp. 307, 65, AOT.

SOLOMON, Benjamin (Lewis Solomon)

b. London, 1810–1857
Vittoria, 1829; Convict; Sentenced to 7 years, Old Bailey, 1828.
Single; Errand boy; Height: 160 cm.

Dark ruddy complexion. Dark brown hair. Hazel eyes. 'ZR' tattooed on right side of left arm. A small scar under chin. No education. No previous convictions. Jew. Benjamin Solomon was transported for 'picking pockets' with another young accomplice. They were 'caught in the act' by a constable in Whitechapel. Solomon was sentenced on 21 April 1828.

Benjamin Solomon arrived in New South Wales on 17 January 1829 and was promptly assigned to Mr W. Macarthur's farm at Camden. In February 1832 he was listed as a 'stable man' who had absconded from Road Gang no. 25, and who was described as being 165 cm tall. In November 1842 Benjamin Solomons, 'a prisoner' attached to the bullock team working from the stockade at Maitland, was found to be absent from his post when his water carrier bullock team forced a valuable horse into the creek and drowned it. Solomon received fifty lashes and his sentence was extended by twelve months. Solomon received a ticket of leave in 1844 and a conditional pardon, dated 15 November 1848.

Benjamin Solomon married Sarah Chitty Rotton in East Maitland's Church of England on 29 June 1847. Benjamin Solomon died in 1857.

HO 10/20; *Vittoria* Indent 4/4014, p. 130; CS 4/2578, 2 November 1842, 42/8693; Petition 48/2251, dated 1848; 4/4267, 47/753.7; TL 44/939; CP 48/2251.

SOLOMON, Benjamin

b. Brisbane, 1844–1922

Benjamin Solomon was born in Brisbane in November 1844 and grew up in Adelaide, South Australia. He was the son of Judah Moss Solomon (q.v.) (who became Mayor of Adelaide), and brother of Vaiben Louis Solomon (briefly Premier of South Australia), and Moss Judah Solomon (q.v.), who was president of the South Australian Hebrew Congregation for thirty-five years. Benjamin began a general agency and auctioneering business and then joined the public service as an officer of the Adelaide Local Court. He joined the land tax department and became assessor and valuer for the probate department, and government auctioneer. He retired in 1915. He served as vice-president of the Civil Service Association, a founder of the Public Service Provident Fund and president of the Public Service Federal Council. In 1860 Benjamin Solomon had joined a Battery of the Adelaide Field Artillery and in 1878 became a captain. In 1897 he was appointed

lieutenant colonel and retired in 1905 from the army with the rank of colonel. During World War I, he was appointed Chief Censor in South Australia.
Colonial Secretary, Copies of Letters sent within the Colony, 4/3505, 8 March 1822–28, June 1822.

SOLOMON, Caroline

d. 1842
Free.

Caroline Solomon was buried at the Devonshire Street Jewish Cemetery on 11 July 1842.

SOLOMON, Catherine

1804–1833
Elizabeth I (2), 1818; Convict.

Catherine Solomon arrived in New South Wales on 19 November 1818. She received official permission to marry at Parramatta on 7 July 1823. She died at Hobart Town on 25 September 1833.
Reel 6010, 4/3508, p. 642.

SOLOMON, Catherine Elizabeth

b. Bethnal Green, 1804–1877
Mermaid, 1828; Convict; Sentenced to 7 years, Old Bailey, 1828.
Single; Fruit hawker, Height: 160 cm.

Bloated, much pock-pitted complexion, dark brown hair, high and narrow forehead, eyes light grey, broad long nose, large mouth, lips full and projecting, sharp chin. Can neither read nor write. Jewess. Catherine Elizabeth Solomon stole calico prints from a shop in the Minories. When arrested she had 33 shillings in her possession. Her father was Jacob Solomon, a hawker. Her brother was Simon Solomon (Solomons, q.v.), who was already in Van Diemen's Land. Catherine claimed: 'I used to hawk fruit in the city'. Her gaol report listed her as a 'prostitute'. Surgeon: 'Idle disposition but orderly'.

Catherine Solomon was an assigned servant in Hobart Town during the latter half of 1828 and 1829. On 3 February 1829 she was noted as having been absent from her master's house (T. Dixon) for two hours. She was reprimanded. On 13 May 1829 she was absent from her master's house under false pretences. She was sent to the House of Correction on 8 November 1829. For 'general disorderly conduct in the service of Dr Ross' she was returned to the House of Correction and, upon her release, was to be assigned to the Interior (6 December 1831). Catherine received a certificate of freedom on 10 January 1835, and was permitted to travel to New South Wales.

Catherine Elizabeth Solomon married Abraham Davis (q.v.) in Sydney on 22 July 1835. Her new husband was a pugilist and a butcher who had escaped from New South Wales, was arrested in London and returned to Hobart Town and afterwards sent to Norfolk Island before being released from servitude in Sydney. Six months after her marriage, on 26 December 1835, Catherine Davis was involved in an altercation in the public house belonging to Abraham Myers (q.v.). She was described as a 'buxom lady possessing symmetry and muscle', and 'like a bullock'. Her complaint was dismissed on the grounds that in the brawl she had 'got the best of it'.

Catherine died on 27 August 1877 and was buried in the Jewish section of Rookwood Cemetery in New South Wales.

CON 18/24; CON 40/9; *Sydney Monitor*, 31 December 1835.

SOLOMON, Charles

b. London, 1833–1915
Britomart, 1835; Free.
8 children.

Charles Solomon was a son of Samuel and Rebecca Solomon (qq.v.). He arrived with his mother, his five sisters and two brothers in Sydney on 1 February 1835. He was aged two. The family grew up at Jews' Flat where his father owned a hotel and a general store. As a very young man he rode 'many a horse to victory' in local horse races. He then became a cattle dealer and drover, being one of the first to take a mob of cattle south to Gippsland over uncharted mountains. In 1861 he came to live in Cooma and together with a fellow drover began a general business known as the Big Drum, in a stone building owned by Samuel Shannon (q.v.) at the corner of Sharp and Bombala streets. In 1862 he joined the gold rush at Kiandra. Together with David Moses, he had a store and hotel at Jindabyne and a store at Buckley's Crossing. In 1862 Solomon built the Cooma Hotel at the corner of Massie and Vale streets. Moses and Solomon established a general store in Cooma in 1865.

Charles Solomon married Selina Cohen. He was the first mayor of Cooma. He was president of the Monaro Jockey Club, a member of the school board, a foundation member of the Masonic Lodge, president of the School of Fine Arts and member of the Hospital Board.

He died at Cooma on 15 November 1915. His son, Lewis Samuel Solomon, carried on the business in Cooma and a second son, Henry Hyam Solomon, a solicitor, served as clerk of the Monaro Shire.

Felix F. Mitchell, *Back to Cooma Celebrations* (1926), quoted by G. F. J. Bergman in *AJJHS*, vol. 6, no. 8 (1970), p. 539f.

SOLOMON, Coleman (KALMAN)

Free.
Single.

Coleman Solomon married Catherine Leaton at Old St James (Anglican) Cathedral, Melbourne, in 1849.

Register no. 1215.

SOLOMON, David

b. London, 1792–1839
Arab, 1822; Convict; Sentenced to life, Old Bailey, 1822.
Married; Old clothes man; Height: 168 cm; 3 children.

Brown hair, hazel eyes. 'Jew hawker'. David Solomon was 'shabbily dressed' and was well known to the police who arrested him on the basis of a description given by a victim whose watch he had snatched. He had no previous convictions. At his trial he said that his children were being looked after in Spitalfields, 'with Solomon who keeps a clothes shop. I used to go about Mary le Bone and Oxford Street as an old clothes man'. He was sentenced on 20 February 1822.

David Solomon had no criminal record in Van Diemen's Land (apart from a fine of forty shillings for a breach of his license conditions). He first worked as a constable in Launceston. He was listed as a 'Sheriff's Officer' with a salary of £40 a year in 1829. On 19 December 1831 he requested a grant for an allotment of land in Launceston to build a weatherboard house. He had received a conditional pardon on 17 July 1830. He was already in possession of one allotment of land by purchase in Paterson Street. On his petition it is noted: 'This applicant is a Conditional Emancipist. He has some property and a good house in Launceston. He was latterly a Sheriff 's Officer'. On 27 April 1832 he received a grant of land on High Street and Windmill Street on condition that he built a house worth £500 within the next 18 months.

On 9 August 1833 Solomon received a further grant of thirty perches on Paterson Street in Launceston. In 1834 he ran the Blue Anchor Tavern at Campbell Town. The next year he took up the licence for the White Hart Inn of Antill Ponds, Oatlands, which he held until 1838, and he also received two convict servants to work his farm there. On 8 October 1835 Solomon wrote to the Colonial Secretary from Campbell Town claiming to have discovered, within a mile of the town, 'limestone of good quality'. He asked the Colonial Secretary 'to grant me for my children an allotment of ground on this township'. This petition was granted on 22 July 1837 and an acre of land was set aside. (On 1 November 1845 Solomon was warned that his grant would be cancelled if it was not paid for.)

'David Solomon of Campbell Town, Licensed Victualler', supported the memorial of Henry Davis (q.v.) of 24 October 1836 to use a block of land at Cataract Hill, Launceston, for a Jewish cemetery.

A free pardon was granted on 25 September 1837. Solomon died on 5 June 1839, having made his will one month before his death. His witnesses were Moses Phillips (q.v.) and Joshua Lyons (q.v.) Solomon had taken some time to marry the mother of his children. His marriage to Ann Anderson became official in Launceston on 26 October 1830. Elisa Solomon, daughter of David and Ann, died in Launceston on 3 January 1841. His other daughters were Esther Rebecca (q.v.) (1826) and Leah (q.v.).

On 13 October 1839 Ann Solomon was granted 100 acres in trust for her daughter Hester (Esther) Rebecca Solomon, for her 'intrepid conduct when her father's house was attacked and plundered by a gang of armed bushrangers'. The incident had occurred in 1835, when: 'most awful to relate, my daughter was alarmed by her father being put on his knees to lose his life, when my daughter from her innocence stepped forward and craved the life of her father, who is since dead never having overcome the shock leaving behind a widow and two orphan girls to deplore his loss'.

CON 31/38, no. 464; *OBSP*, 1821–22, case 441, p. 209; Ship Indent 2/8241; HO 11/4; *Hobart Town Gazette*, 13 October 1837; *Hobart Town Courier*, 9 July 1831, 16 February 1838, 12 October 1838; CSO 1/830/17607, 8 October 1835; CSO 5/16/278, 12 October 1838; Land Grant LSD, 1/82/501-2, and 1/76, p. 19; *Launceston Examiner*, 15 January 1848, 3 January 1849, 17 February 1849, 28 November 1849; *Independent*, 9 July 1831.

SOLOMON, David

b. London, 1819–1860
Mermaid, 1828; Free.

David Solomon was the third child of Ann and Isaac (Ikey) Solomon (qq.v.). His siblings were John (q.v.), Moses (q.v.), Anne (q.v.), Sarah (q.v.), and Mark (q.v.). David spent time in an orphanage in Hobart Town after arriving with his mother, who was a convict. On 19 October 1835 he took up the cudgels on behalf of his mother when his father attempted to assert his authority over her household in New Norfolk after his release from prison. The teenage David had taken over running the house and collecting the rent and saw his position usurped. David called his father 'an old vagabond and a nasty stinking wretch', and on 19 October 1835 wrote to his father from Hobart Town, ordering him to send his possessions to him:

Mr Solomon,
Unless you send me my things down by the fust coveyance I shall emediately go to Capt Forster about them. You have got a bed and being, a box of Tules a gun and rod, fiddle, dressing table and two Boxes of Closes and a box of Sunderies and dining table of Mying.
DSollomon

A neighbour in New Norfolk delivered the letter to the office of the Colonial Secretary in Hobart Town with a note: 'The letter sent from the son to his father is a precious morceau, and I hope Mr Solomon's case is well looked into. He has been used ill'.

David Solomon married Sophia Christinia Raynor at New Norfolk on 7 October 1837. David Solomon, 'of Longford', died on 21 August 1860.

CSO 1/849/17494; CSO 1/820/17494; *Mercury*, 21 September 1860.

SOLOMON, David

b. Sheerness
Free.

David Solomon was the son of Joseph Solomon (q.v.) of Evandale and his first wife Harriet, who had remained in England. The first references to David Solomon occur in relation to New South Wales and Parramatta. A coach licence was granted to him on 13 November 1843, at which time his address was Parramatta Road. He was insolvent by 15 March 1844 and was confined to the Parramatta Gaol. In July 1844 he applied for a certificate of discharge from insolvency, which must have been granted. He then moved to Van Diemen's Land. The *Hobart Town Courier* reported that there was a letter waiting for him at the Launceston Post Office that carried insufficient postage and would require extra payment.

David Solomon (of Evandale) ran two coaches, the Hero and the Wonder. The Hero travelled from Launceston to Perth and the Wonder from Launceston to Evandale. David Solomon's coach was still running from Perth and Longford when the Wonder had disappeared. It does not seem to have belonged to Solomon in the first place. The *Launceston Examiner* then reported that Solomon's business had failed. Four major creditors were listed, and one was Godfrey Barnett Levy (George Levy, q.v.). On 28 November 1849 it was reported that David Solomon was the owner of the Longford Stage Coach, Teaser.

David Solomon was allowed bail on a charge of having, during his insolvency, concealed the ownership of a coach. The case failed. On 9 February 1850 the *Examiner* announced that 'Solomon's Coach' was running from Longford to Launceston.

Sydney Morning Herald, 14 July 1843, 13 November 1843, 18 March 1844, 30 April 1844, 4 May 1844, 23 July 1844; *Hobart Town Courier*, 17 May 1844; *Launceston Examiner*, 15 January 1848, 3 January 1849.

SOLOMON, Edward

Free.
Married; Dealer; 2 children.

Edward and Henrietta Solomon had two children registered with the Sydney Synagogue. They were Harriett, born 21 July 1842, and Francis Edward, born 18 March 1845. The Mutual Fire Insurance Company reported that Edward Solomon had insurance cover for £500 in October 1842. The *Maitland Mercury* of 9 December 1843 reported that Edward Solomon 'of Maitland', a wine and spirit merchant, had been declared insolvent and would pay seven shillings and sixpence in the pound.

SOLOMON, Elias

b. London, 1789–1863
1850; Free.
Married; Dealer; 12 children.

Elias Solomon and Fanny (née Simmons) were the parents of twelve children, six of whom remained in England. They evidently arrived in Sydney in time for the marriage of their daughter Eve to Lewis Marks (q.v.).

Their (adult) children who migrated to Australia were Saul (q.v.), Abraham, Priscilla, John, Eve and Mark. Elias Solomon died at Bathurst Street on 6 January 1863. Fanny died in Sydney on 31 January 1874.

SOLOMON, Elias

b. London, 1839–1909
Alfred, 1841; Free.
Manager.

Elias Solomon was born in London on 2 September 1839 and arrived in Adelaide with his parents, Moss (Moses) Solomon (q.v.) and Leah (née Myers), at the age of one. Moss was the older brother of Vaiben and Emanuel Solomon (qq.v.). The family arrived in Sydney on 19 January 1841. On 3 March 1841 the family set sail for Adelaide on the *Dorset*, a brig owned jointly by Emanuel and Vaiben Solomon.

South Australia was in the midst of a severe depression and the family returned to Sydney, where Moss died in 1849. His widow and family subsequently returned to Adelaide.

Solomon went to Western Australia in 1868 in the brig *Eliza Blanche* and commenced business with two of his nephews as an auctioneer at 'E. Solomon & Co' in Hindley Street. The business was short lived and he was employed to be a supervisor on the French barque *Cora* to make a substantial purchase of sugar in Mauritius for the Australian market. He joined Lionel Samson (q.v.) and, working closely with William Frederick Samson (q.v.), soon became the general manager of the business. Elias Solomon was Mayor of Fremantle for several terms in the latter part of the nineteenth century. He served in the State Parliament from 1892 to 1900. He became a member of the first Commonwealth Parliament, representing the Fremantle electorate. He was consular agent for Italy, a member of the Technical School Board, and chairman of the Fremantle Tramways Board. Elias married twice, first to Agnes Elizabeth Buckley and a second time, in 1887, to Elizabeth Stokes. He died on 23 May 1909 and was buried in the Jewish section of the Fremantle Cemetery.

Table Talk, 27 May 1909.

SOLOMON, Elizabeth

b. London
Brothers, 1833; Free.
Single; Servant.

Elizabeth Solomon arrived on 21 December 1833, travelling steerage. She came out as a child with the family of Elizabeth (Betsy) Cohen (q.v.) and her ten children. Elizabeth Solomon was their maid servant.

Elizabeth Solomon married Elias Watson at the Church of England in Castlereagh in 1839.

Ship Indent 4/5205.

SOLOMON, Elizabeth

b. Bath, 1820–1854
Britomart, 1835; Free.

Elizabeth Solomon was a child of Samuel and Rebecca Solomon (qq.v.). She arrived with her mother and her seven siblings on the *Britomart* in 1835. Her father had been sent out as a convict on the *Mangles* in 1833. Elizabeth married Colman Zadock (q.v.) in 1840. She died 'at the residence of her father and mother, Elizabeth Street', Sydney, on Monday, 16 October 1854, after 'a severe and protracted illness. Mrs E. Zadock the eldest daughter of Mr Samuel Solomon deeply regretted by all who knew her'.

Sydney Morning Herald, 18 October 1854.

SOLOMON, Elizabeth

b. London, 1821–1898
Enchantress, 1833; Free.
Single; 10 children.

The daughter of Samuel Moss Solomon (q.v.) and his second wife Esther (née Davis) (q.v.), Elizabeth married Michael Cashmore (q.v.), a pioneer of the Melbourne Jewish community.

SOLOMON, Elizabeth

Free.

Elizabeth Solomon married Robert Watts in 1843 at the Presbyterian Church in Parramatta.

HO 18/191.

SOLOMON, Emanuel

b. Spitalfields, 1800–1873
Lady Castlereagh, 1818; Convict; Sentenced to 7 years, County Durham, 1817.
Single; Lead pencil maker; Height: 164 cm; 9 children.

Dark complexion, black hair, dark eyes. Emanuel Solomon was the son of Samuel Moss Solomon (q.v.) and Betsy (Moses) of Wentworth Street, Spitalfields, pencil-maker. He was charged on 4 August 1817 with his older brother, Vaiben Solomon (q.v.), with breaking into the farmhouse of Thomas Prest in Heighington and stealing coats and other clothes. The brothers were imprisoned in the Durham Gaol for ten months until being sentenced on 5 August 1817. They were sentenced to death for being in possession of stolen goods (and found not guilty of housebreaking). The boys invoked an ancient Benefit of Clergy ruling allowing people who were able to read Psalm 81 to have their death sentences commuted.

Emanuel and Vaiben Solomon arrived in Port Jackson on the *Lady Castlereagh* on 30 April 1818 and were immediately sent on to Hobart Town. On 9 October 1818 Emanuel Solomon was sentenced to work for the government in his own time for fourteen days and to be confined at night for 'neglect of duty'. On 8 January 1820 he absconded from George Town and was found going out in the woods, for which he received fifty lashes and six months in the gaol gang. On 9 March 1820, for 'repeated irregularities neglect of duty and disobedience of orders', he was sentenced to twenty-five lashes. On 17 August 1820 he was found to have been absent from the muster at church, for which he was sentenced to three days work for the government and three nights in gaol. On 7 October 1820 he was found to have an iron pick in his possession, the property of the Crown, for which he received fifty lashes. On 17 January 1821 he was suspected of robbery in the house of Mr Newby. The trial was aborted when Mr Newby failed to prosecute. On 3 March 1821 Vaiben and Emanuel were found guilty of stealing the wearing apparel of Mr William Copperwheat and both brothers were sentenced to three years servitude at the Prison Settlement in Newcastle, New South Wales.

The harsh conditions at Newcastle seem to have made a profound impact on both young men. After Newcastle they were free by servitude and avoided the penal system. Both must be numbered among Australia's most successful emancipists. Emanuel Solomon was granted a certificate of freedom on 5 August 1824.

Emanuel married Mary Ann Wilson on 6 November 1826 at St Philip's in Sydney. Mary had been transported to Australia on the *Midas* in 1825 with a life sentence. She was described as having a brown complexion, and dark brown eyes. Mary Ann Solomon (whom Emanuel named 'Rachel') appears to have died around 1830. The Solomon brothers opened the Cheap Wholesale and Retail Warehouse at 74 George Street in 1829 sewing ready-made clothes. In 1831, after having left the fraternal business, Emanuel attempted to claim that he was insolvent: 'The applicant stated that he had been in partnership with his brother, as general dealers, in George Street, but that some time back, he withdrew from the firm, receiving a bonus of £1250 for his share in the concern, with which he set up in business, but had been unsuccessful in his ordinary calling, as well as a speculative trip to Van Diemen's Land'. The court's assessors refused to believe Emanuel was insolvent and he escaped from the court pursued by the bailiffs.

In 1838 Emanuel moved from Sydney to Adelaide. With Emanuel was Celia Smith, a native of Ireland who became his second wife. Emanuel and Vaiben Solomon built up a flourishing intercolonial trade based on their ownership of the *Dorset*. A Business Letter Book is preserved in the State Library of South Australia. A descendant of Emanuel Solomon, Trevor Cohen of Melbourne, quotes the South Australian Archivist: 'In his letters Solomon unwittingly paints his own portrait, and though one recoils from a certain ruthless and choleric vindictiveness towards his rivals, it is clear that he possessed in good measure the experience, vigour and decision necessary for success'. His business, reinforced by a liquor licence, flourished. On 11 July 1841 he opened Australia's first purpose-built theatre on mainland Australia, the Queen's Theatre. The structure of that theatre still stands. It cost £10 000 and was closed the following year due to the economic depression. It reopened in 1850 with a new facade and was renamed the Old Victoria Theatre with 180 seats. The complex included the Gilles Arcade and a tavern and associated shops.

Emanuel Solomon had married Celia Smith at Scots Church in Sydney on 12 April 1844 because, to his chagrin as noted in the Sydney Synagogue Minutes of 28 February 1844, his application to be married 'agreeable to Jewish rites' was refused. Their children were Elizabeth Dorsetta (1839–1914), Samuel (born 23 March 1841–1856), Rosetta (1842-1901, Julia (1844-1881), Joseph Samuel 1846-1940) and Catherine Leah (15 June 1848-1897).

Emanuel Solomon worked as an auctioneer in Adelaide from 1843 to 1847. The two brothers dissolved their partnership in 1844. In 1863 he was elected the Member for West Adelaide in the Legislative Assembly and became a Member of the Legislative Council in 1867.

Celia Solomon died in 1852, and four months later Emanuel married Catherine Abrahams (born in Portsmouth) in Adelaide in 1852; the children of their marriage were Abigail (18 January 1853 to 15 April 1854), Vaiben Joel (27 November 1854 to 27 January 1936), and Judah Moss (8 October 1857 to 27 February 1925). Judah changed his surname to 'Senior'.

Emanuel Solomon won his place in the history of the Australian Catholic Church when he took Sister Mary Helen McKillop under his protective wing. (Perhaps she reminded him of his Irish-born wife Celia.) When Sister Mary was excommunicated by the Catholic Bishop of Adelaide in September 1871, Emanuel Solomon set aside two of his houses in Flinders Street to accommodate the twenty homeless nuns who had followed their inspired and irrepressible leader into temporary exile.

Emanuel Solomon died on 3 October 1873 and was buried in the Jewish cemetery in Adelaide. Solomon had made provision in his will for land in Port Pirie to be made available 'to the first religious body which might desire a church there on'. The Bible Christians 'took advantage' of the offer.

HO 10/1; HO 11/2; CON 31/38, no. 92; Ship Indent 4/4006, p. 34; CF 4423; E. S. Richards, 'The Fall and Rise of the Solomon Brothers', *AJJHS*, vol. 8, no. 2 (1975); *Sydney Monitor*, 10 July 1830; Convicts to Newcastle, 4 August 1817, in 4/3504; *Sydney Gazette*, 1 August 1831, 4 August 1831, 6 August 1831, 23 June 1832, 18 October 1832, 23 April 1833, 27 August 1833, 27 November 1838, 6 August 1839; *South Australian Gazette*, 14 December 1839, 10 March 1847; *South Australian Gazette and Colonial Register*, 10 January 1845, 6 February 1847, 25 July 1849, 28 July 1849; *South Australian Almanack*, 1843; *Australian*, 22 June 1830, 25 March 1831, 10 January 1834, 12 September 1834, 9 January 1835, 5 June 1835, 23 June 1835, 25 October 1836; *Sydney Morning Herald*, 3 April 1844, 29 April 1844, 21 May 1844, 4 June 1844; Rodney Cockburn, *Nomenclature of South Australia* (1908); Family history from John David Johnston of Blackheath, NSW. *AG*, pp. 127, 128, 153, 177, 184, 272, 273, 309, 313; Trevor Cohen, 'Emanuel Solomon and Mary McKillop', *AJJHS*, vol. 18, part 2, p. 1608 (2006).

SOLOMON, Emma

b. 1824
Britomart, 1835; Free.
Single.

Emma Solomon arrived in New South Wales at the age of eleven with her mother Rebecca (q.v.) and her eight siblings. Her father, Samuel Solomon (q.v.), had been sent to Australia as a convict. Emma Solomon married Henry (Hyam) Robert Reuben (q.v.) in 1838.

SOLOMON, Esther (née DAVIS)

b. Hammersmith, 1775–1875
Enchantress, 1833; Free.
Married; 2 children.

Born in Hammersmith (London) on 1 January 1775, Esther was the daughter of Isaac Davis. She was the second wife of Samuel Moss Solomon (q.v.), her first cousin, who is credited with the invention of a method of mass producing lead pencils. Her stepchildren included Vaiben and Emanuel Solomon (qq.v.), and her children were Isaac Solomon (q.v.) and Elizabeth (Betsy) Solomon (q.v.). Esther came out to Australia with her husband, bringing her son Isaac, and her stepgrandson Judah Moss Solomon (q.v.). Samuel Moss died in Sydney in 1842. Esther moved to Adelaide where her stepson Emanuel and her son Isaac lived. She died in Adelaide on 13 July 1875, aged 100 years and six months.

Observer, 9 January 1875, 17 July 1875.

SOLOMON, Esther (RUSSELL née LEVY)

b. Sheerness, 1775–1861
Palambam, 1832; Free.
Married; 8 children.

Esther (née Levy, renamed Russell), widow of the son of Abraham Abrahams, and mother of Hannah (born 1802), married Judah Solomon (q.v.) in London on 6 January 1805. She was the aunt of the Russell brothers (q.v.) and Elizabeth Davis (q.v.). Judah and Esther had seven children in England: Rachel (born 1811 died 2 December 1869), Louisa (Davis, q.v.) (born 1812 died 8 December 1885), Lydia (Benjamin, q.v.) (born 1813 died 21 January 1880), Isaac (q.v.) (1814 died 7 September 1897), Michael (q.v.) (born 1815 died 30 December 1899), Rebecca (q.v.) (born 1818 died 24 March 1875), and Sarah (q.v.) (born 1819 died 20 March 1881).

The *Palambam* arrived in Hobart Town on 12 December 1832. Esther was accompanied by her two single daughters, Rebecca and Sarah, and her married daughter Lydia Benjamin, who was travelling with her husband, Henry Samuel Benjamin (q.v.), and their two children, Henry and Esther.

> Among the passengers on the *Palambam* is Mrs (Esther) Solomon, the wife of Mr Judah Solomon, merchant of this town. We understand that this lady has proceeded to the Colony to join her husband, after many years separation, with her two lovely daughters. Report states that her arrival has produced some little embarrass of a delicate nature.

Judah, her convict husband, had taken a common-law wife, and refused to return to Esther. He vacated Temple House, which he had built in Argyle Street. Esther fought long and hard to prevent Judah gaining his emancipation while he 'lived in sin'. On 27 January 1845 Esther wrote to the Lieutenant Governor:

> Although my husband was one of the highest in the colony as regards mere wealth he was and is one of the very lowest in morals. He has openly for many years and lives up to this moment in the same state with his Paramour and her spurious offspring within a few yards of His Excellency's residence. He left me with ten young children the youngest then unborn. To ameliorate their condition in a foreign land a subscription was necessary made amongst their brethren (in Sheerness) which subscription formed the basis of their present wealth.

The battle between Judah and his wife was painful and apparently endless. In March 1835 she complained to the Colonial Secretary that her husband had 'threatened to dash her brains out'. On 21 June 1837 Judah wrote to the authorities imaginatively alleging that Esther had been living 'a most abandoned life' and, referring to his Argyle Street house, claiming that 'she has made away with property valued at £1700'. On 29 January 1845 Judah presented a petition for an absolute pardon that had been signed by twelve Justices of the Peace. Esther blocked its acceptance. On 28 May 1846 she asked for information regarding Judah Solomon's free pardon, adding 'address your answer at my daughter's Mrs Abrahams in Liverpool St'. She was told that a free pardon could not be granted.

Esther Solomon, 'relict of the late Judah', died on 24 September 1861, aged eighty-six, at her residence, New Town, 'Deeply respected by a large circle of friends'. The official death certificate mistakenly recorded that she was ninety years old. She was buried in Hobart's Jewish cemetery at Harrington Street.

CSO 20/30/710; *Colonial Times*, 18 December 1832, p. 2; CSO 20. 30/710; *Hobart Town Gazette*, 30 September 1861.

SOLOMON, Esther

Deveron, 1829; Free.
Single.

Esther Solomon married David Benjamin (q.v.) in Hobart Town on 15 December 1840. Esther was the second daughter of Henry Solomon (q.v.).

Hobart Town Courier, 15 December 1840.

SOLOMON, Esther

b. Hobart Town, 1840–1894
Free. Single; 7 children.

Esther Solomon married Richard James Edwards, tobacconist, in Hobart Town.

SOLOMON, Esther Rebecca

b. 1826 Free. Single.

On 13 October 1839 Esther Rebecca Solomon of Antill Ponds, received a grant of 100 acres for having saved the life of her father. She had asked for a grant of 1000 acres of land. The land was granted due to her bravery when the family home was attacked, and her father, David Solomon (q.v.), had his life threatened. It would have been held in trust by her mother, Ann Solomon (q.v.), until Esther either married or turned twenty-one. Esther Rebecca Solomon, aged seventeen, married Benjamin Dowling, aged twenty-one, at Avoca on 29 April 1843.
CSO 8/5/104; LSD 1/23/380–385.

SOLOMON, Eva Sarah

d. 1901
1848; Free.
Married; 12 children.

Eva was the wife of Nathaniel Solomon (q.v.).

SOLOMON, Frances (vide: Frances Cottrell)

b. London, 1814–1860
1834; Free.
Single.

SOLOMON, Francis (Frederick)

b. London, d. 1806
Fortune (1), 1806; Convict; Sentenced to 7 years, Old Bailey, 1805.
Single.

Solomon stole fifty pounds weight of lead from the house of a butcher in Spitalfields. Solomon claimed that it was sold to him by a man in the street who asked him: '"Jew, do you know where to sell any lead?" I told him I did not know where to sell it. I came from Bristol where I had lived twenty-one years. I have got an old father and mother in London. They are very old. My father is ninety-two and my mother is seventy-two'. He was convicted on 24 April 1805.

Francis Solomon arrived in Sydney on 20 August 1806 and died shortly after arrival.
OBSP, 1804–05, case 243, p. 220; HO 11/1; Ship Indent 4/4004, p. 231; 2/8257, p. 295.

SOLOMON, Frederick

Surrey I (1), 1814; Convict; Sentenced to life, Old Bailey, 1813.

Frederick Solomon was listed in the 1820 General Muster of New South Wales as a 'government labourer'.

HO 10/13.

SOLOMON, Goodman

b. Whitechapel, 1807
Lady East, 1825; Convict; Sentenced to 7 years, London, 1822.
Single; A tailor's lad; Height: 157.5 cm.

Dark complexion, dark hair, scar on nose. Lost front tooth in upper jaw. A mermaid and the letters 'G.S' tattooed on right arm. Goodman Solomon, aged fifteen, and John Bailey, aged ten, went into a shop to buy a penny Jews' harp and stole a piece of a brass crimping machine. They were caught when they tried to sell it to a nearby ironmonger. Solomon was sentenced at the Old Bailey on 23 October 1822. Solomon had been in custody before and his gaol report was 'a bad lad'. Perhaps he learned from that experience because his hulk report was 'a good boy. This lad is a Jew. His general conduct on this ship have been attentive to his trade'. He was on the list of eighteen boy convicts discharged from the Hulk Belleaphoron *at Sheerness for New South Wales on 21 October 1824.*

Solomon arrived in Van Diemen's Land on 9 April 1825. He had been considered too young to send to Australia following his trial and remained in custody for three years before his transportation at the end of 1824. He was assigned to John James, a tailor. On 20 September 1826 and on 3 March 1827 he was reprimanded for absence from the muster and from church while working as an assigned servant to Mr John James. On 29 September 1827 he was returned to the government for having 'connived at immoral practices with Catherine, wife of Mark Solomon [q.v.] who has absconded and is illegally at large'. (Catherine was working as a prostitute.) On 4 February 1829 he was sentenced at Hobart Town to two months with the chain gang for having absconded from a work party at the Ross Bridge.

Unable to survive alone he had finally surrendered himself at the Prisoners' Barracks at Hobart Town. On 3 October 1829 he was sent to the chain gang at St Peter's Pass for insolence to the overseer of his work party. Twelve days later, for 'insolence and indolence', while attached to the chain gang at Oatlands, he was confined to the chain gang for the remainder of his sentence. A certificate of freedom was issued on 26 October 1829.

OBSP, 1821–22, case 1500, p. 570; CON 31/38, no. 661; VDL Papers, ML, A1059-1, p. 136; HO 11/5; *Hobart Town Courier*, 31 October 1829; CF 29/266.

SOLOMON, Hannah

b. London, 1818–1852
Enchantress, 1833; Free.
Single.

Hannah Solomon arrived with her father, Samuel Moss Solomon (q.v.), and stepmother Esther Solomon (q.v.) in April 1833. Hannah married Benjamin Samuel Cohen.

SOLOMON, Hannah

Born in the Colony, 1803–1831; Free.
Single, 6 children.

The daughter of Mark Solomon (q.v.) and Catherine Flanagen (sic.) Born 15 July 1803. Hannah Solomon married Aaron Aarons (John Henry Anderson, q.v.). Hannah had at least six children of whom three died in infancy. Catherine died at the age of 30 in 1833 at her home in Elizabeth Street, Hobart Town and Mark died in 1837.

Hobart Town Gazette, 5 October 1838, 11 October 1839.

SOLOMON, Henry

b. Sheerness, 1801–1843
Deveron, 1829; Free.
Married; Jeweller; 3 children.

Henry Solomon was a brother of Judah (q.v.), Joseph (q.v.), and Samuel Solomon (q.v.). His wife was Elizabeth. He arrived as a free settler in Hobart Town on 23 December 1829. He was listed as a cabin class passenger on the *Prince Regent* that arrived in Port Jackson 20 June 1830. He was said to have been born in England. He was a resident of Hobart Town and a dealer. The *Colonial Times* reported on 15 July 1834 that he had a shop and was a jeweller and silversmith at 14 Argyle Street in Hobart Town. By 1836 he had moved to 39 Elizabeth Street. The 1842 census showed that he was a tenant in a stone building and had three children below the age of fourteen. Henry Solomon, 'jeweller of Elizabeth St', stood surety for the notorious Isaac (Ikey) Solomon (q.v.) (who was probably a cousin) when he needed bail after Judah Solomon had been forced to withdraw his support.

Henry's daughter Sarah, 'a minor', married her cousin Michael Solomon (q.v.) at the home of her parents in Elizabeth Street, Hobart Town, on 6 June 1840. Louis Nathan (q.v.) and David Hecksher (q.v.) signed the official marriage certificate to the first Jewish marriage in Van Diemen's Land.

At Michael's insolvency hearing in August 1842 at the Supreme Court in Melbourne, the court was told of 'a person named Henry Solomon of Van Diemen's Land who was said to have accepted 700 sheep, a horse and a dray in place of a "large debt"'. The veracity of the story of the arrangement was dismissed by the judge.

Henry Solomon 'of Victoria House' in Elizabeth Street in Hobart Town died on 30 March 1843 and left an estate worth £200. In November 1845 his widow Elizabeth asked permission from the synagogue to marry Mr Simeon Benjamin (q.v.). The congregation decided to give her permission to do so providing she settled £1000 from her late husband's estate on her children. A further £25 was also demanded because she had not previously supported the congregation as a member. The couple refused to comply (and judging from the size of the estate could not comply) and on 8 January 1846 the congregation informed the registrar that the proposed marriage would not take place. On 21 January 1846 Mrs Solomon paid the congregation £18 7s 3d and the marriage was performed. Esther (q.v.), the daughter of Henry and Elizabeth Solomon, married David Benjamin (q.v.) at her parents' house 15 December 1840. On 20 May 1851 Louisa Solomon, aged seventeen, married Moses Abrahams, a draper, at her stepfather's house in Liverpool Street.

Hobart Town Courier, 23 December 1829, 15 December 1840, 10 March 1843; *Prince Regent* Indent 4/5201; CSO 5/13/3131, 10 July 1838; *Port Phillip Herald*, 23 August 1842, 17 November 1845; Hobart Synagogue meeting, 21 January 1846; *Colonial Times*, 15 July 1834.

SOLOMON, Henry (PALMER)

b. London, 1808–1854
Charles Kerr, 1837; Convict; Sentenced to life, Old Bailey, 1836.
Single; Servant.

In his trial at the Old Bailey Henry Solomon, alias Palmer, was described as a servant who used to be a baker and had done odd jobs such as cleaning windows. He was accused of stealing £80 from a fellow servant whose dying father had given her the money. He got drunk after the theft and gave himself away. He was sentenced on 19 September 1836.

Henry Solomon was listed in the 1837 General Return of Convicts in New South Wales, working as an assigned servant for Mr John Ginger in Sydney. Solomon received a ticket of leave for the district of Sydney in 1845. On 10 June 1848 *Bell's Life* reported that Henry Solomon had been sentenced to six months hard labour in Sydney for stealing a £1 note. He received a second ticket of leave on 31 December 1849 and a conditional pardon in 1851. Henry Solomon married Mary Mason at Scots Church in 1848.

The Colonial Secretary asked on 30 March 1850 why 'certain enquiries' had been made about Henry Solomon, which had caused 'unceasing trouble'.

Solomon died on 30 September 1854 but was not listed on the York Street Burial Register. It is possible, therefore, that, despite his name and given the choice of his place of marriage, Henry Solomon was not Jewish.

OBSP 1836, case 2055, p. 789f.; TL 45/2079; CS 50/3217, 30 March 1850.

SOLOMON, Henry (Harry)

b. London, 1816–1881
Free.
Single; Dealer.

Henry was the younger brother of Samuel Solomon (q.v.) who and had arrived in Australia on the *Mangles* in 1833, and his mother Rebecca (q.v.) followed, with eight of the children, in 1835. Henry stayed behind in England and migrated later.

Within ten years the fortunes of the Solomon family had improved and Samuel Solomon had established a general store at Reed's (Jews') Flat, five miles from Cooma. Harry Solomon managed the general store on behalf of the family. He married Caroline Magnusson who died 7 May 1857 in Bombala and was originally interred in the Devonshire Street cemetery. Authority for her re-interment was by her daughter Deborah Solomon who was the only child of the marriage.

Henry Solomon of Eden died on 1 May 1881 and was buried at the Rookwood Jewish Cemetery three days later. He was said to be sixty-six years old and was described in the Hebrew inscription as 'a good and honest man'.

Family information Dinah Harvey.

SOLOMON, Isaac (Ikey)

b. Houndsditch, 1783–1850
William Glen Anderson, 1831; Convict; Sentenced to 14 years, Old Bailey, 1830.
Married; Dealer; Height: 175 cm; 6 children.

Dark complexion, black hair, black whiskers, long narrow face, high forehead, brown thin eyebrows, hazel eyes, roman nose, projecting short chin. Isaac Solomon was transported for receiving stolen goods. Isaac Solomon's father Henry was sentenced at the Old Bailey in 1827 to a mere six months gaol, 'on account of his great age', for receiving stolen jewellery.

Ikey Solomon may well have been the model for Fagin in Charles Dickens' novel *Oliver Twist*. Dickens, a court reporter at the time, almost certainly used a play on the Yiddish/Hebrew word *ganef* to personify 'the Jew' who was London's most infamous fence. It should, however, be noted that a London magistrate, Fagin, whom Dickens despised, may also have provided the novelist with the name of his villain.

On 17 April 1810, together with Joel Moses Joseph (q.v.), the 21-year-old Isaac Solomon was convicted for stealing a purse containing £40 and a warrant for £56 from a man attending a political meeting at New Palace Yard in front of Westminster Hall. Both men were sentenced to be transported for the term of their natural life and sent to the convict hulk *Zealand*, anchored off Sheerness. Joseph was sent to New South Wales on the *Admiral Gambier*. In an episode that suggests that Solomon was protected by the Solomon family in Sheerness or Chatham, Ikey remained on board the hulk where he prospered, being supplied with clothes and trinkets from the shore. In 1816 he escaped from custody and, four weeks later, wisely surrendered to the authorities. In exchange for this virtuous act, on 26 October 1816 the magistrates granted him a free pardon and Isaac began to work for an uncle who lived in nearby Chatham.

Some ten years earlier, Ikey had married the 14-year-old Ann Solomon (née Julian) (q.v.), and together they established a network of organised crime throughout the metropolis of London. Presumably, with the help of friends in high places, he became a Navy Agent and was therefore able to ship stolen goods overseas. By 1825 it was said that he had established a chain of brothels in London. In May 1826 a series of brazen London robberies caused such an outcry that the police were forced to act, and a warrant was issued to search the Solomons' premises in Bell Lane, near Petticoat Lane, in Spitalfields. Ikey escaped the police raid and remained at large for almost a year. On 23 April 1827 he was brought before the Lambeth Police Court charged with the possession of five stolen watches, and on 3 May was charged with possessing stolen goods worth more than £1400. Solomon was sent to Newgate Gaol and a writ of habeas corpus caused him to be taken to the King's

Bench at Westminster. Mysteriously, Ann's father managed to take the role of the coach driver, and, even more dramatically, in the course of the brief journey across London the accused man escaped and found himself ensconced on a ship bound for Denmark. From Denmark, Ikey travelled to New York, while, in London, his wife, together with anyone who bore the surname Solomon, was confronted by the police. Ann Solomon faced trial at the Old Bailey in September 1827 and was duly sentenced to fourteen years transportation. She was sent to Van Diemen's Land, with permission to take her four youngest children with her.

When the American newspapers reported the extraordinary saga of the Solomon family's deportation, Isaac Solomon set sail for Van Diemen's Land, arriving in Hobart Town on 15 February 1829. Not surprisingly, as one of London's most notable criminals, he was immediately recognised. However, to the acute embarrassment of the authorities, he could not be arrested until his identity and his alleged crimes could be officially identified.

On 1 December 1829, Lieutenant Governor Arthur wrote to Under Secretary Twiss:

> he has been brought before the Court under a Writ of Habeas Corpus, and there is much apprehension that the Judge will discharge him, but his honour has not yet decided. If he gets off, however, I am prepared immediately to issue another Warrant, and I shall give it all the formality of proceeding from the Governor in Council—it appears to me monstrous that an offender of such notoriety should escape the hands of Justice.

After complicated legal manoeuvres Solomon was sent back to England to stand trial. Strangely, he was not tried for escaping from custody but for the original charge of receiving stolen goods.

The trial took place at the Old Bailey in July 1830. It was hardly surprising to discover the evidence had vanished, because the Solomons could not have flourished without the connivance of the Metropolitan Police. Ikey therefore escaped execution. He was sentenced to fourteen years transportation and sent back to Hobart Town! When he arrived there he attempted to exploit the system of the colonial classification of prisoners. Ikey declared that in 1810, under the alias of Moses Joseph, he had been sent out to Australia for having stolen a pocket book. He claimed to have been pardoned and that within three or four years he had been able to return to England. This information was duly entered at the top of his convict dossier.

In 1832–33, Solomon was at Richmond Gaol where he became a javelin man. It is said that this privileged form of punishment was a reward for having warned the crew of the transport ship that his fellow convicts were planning a mutiny. During his time in Richmond he was convicted twice for abusive language and tendering false and malicious charges against the administrators of the gaol. In January 1835 he was granted a ticket of leave on condition that he live at least twenty miles from Hobart Town.

His family no longer wished to live with him. On 18 February 1835 he was 'severely reprimanded for using obscene language in an argument with Reuben

Joseph [q.v.] in the presence of many respectable females'. On 3 July 1835 he received a warning about 'drunkenness and abusive behaviour towards his family—equal blame existing on the part of Solomon and his family'. Solomon remained at New Norfolk until 1838, when he moved to New Town. He received a conditional pardon in May 1840 and a certificate of freedom in 1844. His youngest daughter, Sarah (q.v.), married Godfrey B. Levy (George Levy, q.v.) under the marriage canopy on 27 January 1847 at his home on the New Town Road. Solomon became a member of the Hobart Town Synagogue and owned a small tobacconist shop in Hobart Town. Ikey Solomon died, aged sixty-six, on 3 September 1850. His was the eighth Jewish funeral to be conducted in Hobart Town. His Hebrew name was Isaac the son of Tzvi.

The children of Isaac and Ann Solomon were John (born 1807) (q.v.), Moses (1809) (q.v.), David (1819) (q.v.), Anne (Nancy) (1820), Sarah (1823), and Mark (1825) (q.v.).

OBSP, 1830, case 107, p. 57; CON 14/2; CON 18/21, no. 1407; CON 31/39.S, 1407; CON 14/2; Letter from George Arthur to the Bishop of London, 17 October 1828, Aa 75/3, at ML, OD, vol. 4, p. 661f.; *Launceston Independent*, 22 December 1832; *Launceston Advertiser*, 16 November 1829; *Colonial Times*, 8 January 1830; *Hobart Town Courier*, 30 August 1828, 28 November 1829, 20 November 1830, 25 September 1840, 19 March 1841, 26 March 1841; J. J. Tobias, *Prince of Fences*; *AG*, ch. 7, p. 217f.; Judith Sackville-O'Donnell, *The First Fagin*.

SOLOMON, Isaac

b. London, 1814–1897
1833; Free.
Married; 18 children.

Isaac Solomon was the fourth child and first son of Judah Solomon (q.v.) and Esther Solomon (q.v.) (née Levy, Russell). His first marriage was to Elizabeth Solomon (born 1817 and the daughter of Samuel Solomon) in London. Isaac and Elizabeth Solomon arrived in Van Diemen's Land in March 1833. It may have been a de facto relationship, because it was recorded that Isaac Solomon married Elizabeth Solomon in Launceston on 3 July 1834 in what was obviously a Christian marriage ceremony. Solomon was granted a licence to run the Hope and Anchor Tavern in Launceston in 1834.

On 21 December 1833 Elizabeth Solomon and a servant visited Sydney on the *Brothers*. Solomon held the licence for the Perth Inn between 1835 and 1837. Isaac Solomon became a member of the Hobart Town Synagogue in 1842 and served on its committee that year. In the 1842 census of Van Diemen's Land he was listed as a shopkeeper living in Collins Street with four children under the age of seven and two assigned convict servants. He rented seat no. 1 in the Synagogue and gave the congregation £50 in 1843 and a further £50 in 1845.

On 17 January 1845, in the *Hobart Town Advertiser*, Solomon announced that he had imported 400 000 'Segars'. They could be purchased at his shops in Elizabeth Street and Murray Street opposite the Post Office and at his store in Collins Street.

On 13 December 1846 the minutes of the synagogue tell of a confrontation between Mrs Isaac Solomon and the wife of Louis Nathan (q.v.). It was a matter of 'outrageous conduct and violent language used by Mrs Isaac Solomon towards Mrs Nathan. Mr Isaac Solomon admitted his wife had 'done wrong'. It was resolved to 'remove' Mrs Solomon from her assigned seat no. 7 in the synagogue. On 2 December 1847 the committee of the Hobart Synagogue accepted a letter of resignation from Solomon as he wrote that he would be 'shortly returning to England'. He must have changed his mind.

All twelve children were born in Hobart Town. Isaac and his half-brother Joseph Solomon (q.v.) worked as partners as wine and spirit merchants at Temple House from 1854. When Judah Solomon died in 1856, Isaac inherited the mansion, with Joseph managing the business in Hobart and Isaac in Launceston. Isaac had left Tasmania for New Zealand by the end of 1863 and the mansion was put on the market. Isaac and Elizabeth Solomon joined in the gold rush to the South Island of New Zealand, taking their large family with them. None of their children appear to have married Jews.

The children were: Samuel (born 19 May 1835, in Hobart Town), Judah (10 October 1836), Rachel (16 May 1838), Esther (17 January 1840), Sarah (8 March 1842), Hannah (22 December 1843), Michael (24 September 1845), Joseph (22 January 1848), Rebecca (1 October 1849), Dinah (10 September 1851), Miriam (13 February 1856), and Catherine (19 November 1857).

Elizabeth died in Dunedin on 1 February 1877. Samuel lived with Mary Jane Stephenson in Dunedin and they had six children. They were: Mary Hetherington (born 31 August 1883), Daisy (3 May 1885), Matthew Harold (12 February 1887), Violetta (7 December 1888), Lilian Jane (7 December 1889), and Herbert Ormond (3 September 1891).

Isaac Solomon died on 7 September 1897 at Dunedin.

Hobart Town Gazette, 9 October 1834, 8 October 1835; LSD 1/76, p. 29; *Hobart Town Advertiser*, 7 January 1845.

SOLOMON, Isaac

b. London, 1818–1901
Enchantress, 1833; Free.
Single; Dealer; 12 children.

Isaac Solomon, born on 5 April 1818, arrived in Sydney with his parents on the *Enchantress.* He was a son of Samuel Moss Solomon and Esther Solomon (qq.v.), a half-brother of Emanuel and Vaiben Solomon (qq.v.), and eight other siblings and a step-uncle of Judah Moss Solomon (q.v.). Isaac Solomon returned to London in 1837 and then came back to Australia in order to marry his 22-year-old step-niece, Isabella Solomon (q.v.), at the Sydney Synagogue on 15 June 1842.

Isaac then began business with his half-brother Emanuel Solomon. He became Queensland's first land auctioneer, conducting the first land sales on behalf of the New South Wales Government. During the years 1843–45 Isaac, with Judah M. Solomon, and alone, bought land in Brisbane, South Brisbane and Ipswich. Solomon settled in Adelaide and 'Isaac Solomon of Adelaide' gave £10 to the Sydney Synagogue building appeal in 1839. He was listed as the innkeeper of the Shakespeare Tavern in May 1841 and was active selling tickets for Emanuel Solomon's new theatre in Adelaide. In 1846 Solomon returned to Sydney and developed extensive trade links with the South Pacific. By mid-1848 Isaac Solomon was listed as the innkeeper of the Crooked Billet in Sydney. Solomon returned to Adelaide to work as an auctioneer in the new province, working together with Mark Salom (q.v.). Salom married Solomon's stepsister Elizabeth Solomon and the partnership Solomon and Salom was formed. The first meeting to form a Jewish congregation was held in their Temple Tavern in Weymouth Street, near the Court House, on 10 September 1848. The setting was far from salubrious.

On 14 March 1849 a hearing was held to investigate the granting of a 'Tap' to be kept at the inn by Abraham Lazar, the son of John Lazar (q.v.). The magistrate, Mr Green, observed: 'We hear of bad accommodation in your house!' Mr Edward Stephens, a second magistrate, said: 'The tap is also complained of. It is very noisy. I wish you would sweep around it. People cannot attend the court with clean boots while it is covered with all kinds of nastiness'. Appropriate promises were made and the licence for the public bar was granted.

Isabella died in Adelaide on 1 December 1863 at the age of forty-three. Isaac died in Melbourne at the home of his daughter, Mrs Josiah Marks (née Julia Solomon), on 27 July 1901.

Isaac and Isabella Solomon's children were: Samuel (1843) and Moss (1844), both born in Sydney, Judah Moss (18 September 1846) born in Adelaide (and later known as Judan Moss Solomon Jnr), Saul (20 June 1848), Joseph (21 August 1849, who died at the age of three months), Elizabeth (24 January 1851, who married the Rev. Abraham Tobias Boas, the 27-year-old minister of the Adelaide Hebrew Congregation, on 15 May 1873), Esther (18 April 1852), Morris (3 February 1854, who died at the age of seven weeks), Emanuel (7 October 1855), Leah (24 June 1857, who died on 4 February 1858), Julia (14 December 1858), and Kate (4 November 1862).

British Sovereign Indent, arrived Port Jackson, 22 May 1838; Land Purchases 2/7974, 18 February 1845; *Shipping Gazette*, 13 June 1846; *Sydney Chronicle*, 6 May 1848; *Australian*, 4 April 1837, 29 June 1838; *Sydney Morning Herald*, 1 April 1844, 15 November 1844; *South Australian Gazette and Colonial Register*, 8 May 1841, 18 February 1847, 10 September 1848, 14 March 1849.

SOLOMON, Isabella

b. London, 1820–1863
Free.
Single.

The eldest daughter of Samuel Moss Solomon (q.v.) and Betsy (née Myers), Isabella was born on 17 September 1820. On 15 June 1842, at the age of twenty-two, Isabella married her uncle, Isaac Solomon (q.v.), son of Samuel Moss Solomon (q.v.).

Isabella died on 1 December 1863 at her home in Norwood, South Australia, and was buried in the Jewish Cemetery at West Terrace.

Her twelve children are listed in the previous entry.

SOLOMON, Israel

b. London, 1809
Ann, 1833; Free.
Married; Book binder; 8 children.

The *Ann* arrived in Sydney on 13 November 1833 with the free emigrant Israel Solomon, twenty-four years of age. With him were his wife Sarah (q.v.), aged twenty-one, his father John Solomon (q.v.), and his mother, Sarah (q.v.).

Israel and Sarah Solomon had a daughter, Georgiana, born on 8 October 1833 during the journey to Sydney. Israel was listed as the exporter of 80 bales of wool to England in May 1842. Israel Solomon served on the synagogue committee in 1839 and 1842. He was a seat holder in the Sydney Synagogue and gave £30 to its building appeal in 1845. In 1847 he bought 10 acres of land at Bongodong on the Murrumbidgee River (near Gundagai). According to the *Shipping Gazette* of 7 April 1845, he was importing small quantities of goods from London for resale.

A second daughter, Rebecca (6 October 1835), was born in Sydney, followed by Sarah (1838), Mary (1840), Leah (1842), Rosetta (1844), Eve (1846), and Rachael (1849).

Ship Indent 4/5205; *Sydney Morning Herald*, 26 May 1842, 30 September 1843, 7 April 1845; Land Correspondence 2/7974, July 1847; *Shipping Gazette*, 14 December 1844, 29 January 1846.

SOLOMON, John (Jackey the Jew)

b. London, 1783–1853
Larkins (1), 1817; Convict; Sentenced to 14 years, Kent, 1817.
Single; Dealer; 7 children.

John Solomon was granted a ticket of leave on 10 November 1824 and a conditional pardon on 28 November 1825. He was well known around Sydney Town, having the nickname 'Jackey the Jew', according to the *Sydney Gazette* (22 December 1825). On 1 April 1830 the *Sydney Gazette* reported that:

> John Solomon, or Jackey the Jew, as he is commonly called, has been lately up before the police on two distinct charges of breach of peace. First, an assault on Saul Lyons [q.v.] in George Street at which instance Jackey was committed to take trial at Quarter Sessions. Then a complaint by Mrs Reynolds about his behaviour to her and her family and Jackey was held in sureties to be of good behaviour for the next twelve months.

By 1831 Solomons was included in the general list of licences issued for public houses in Sydney. He owned the Hole in the Wall in Pitt Street and in 1833 was the holder of a licence for the Barley Mow Inn of Castlereagh Street. He was allotted an assigned convict servant. John Solomon pledged £25 to the Sydney Synagogue building appeal in 1839. In 1841 he held the licence for the Albion Inn, which held a night licence to be open until 9 p.m.

John Solomon married Matilda Maria Hopwood at St John's, Parramatta. In 1841 the Albion Hotel in Darling Harbour burned down and Solomon appealed for financial help, saying he had seven children, had been in business for twenty years in Sydney, and was now completely ruined. A subscription list was organised by George Robert Nichols (the grandson of Esther Abrahams (q.v.) and a prominent solicitor), Moses Joseph (q.v.) and (brother-in-law) Charles Smith. Solomon was able to open a new public house called the Star in the East in 1843 in premises formerly known as the Australian Auction Company's rooms. The hotel was renamed the Albion Hotel but, by January 1844, Solomon was again insolvent. He was a member of the York Street Synagogue in 1845.

Ship Indent 4/5205; *Australian*, 20 October 1835, 20 March 1841; *Sydney Gazette*, 1 April 1830, 22 June 1837, 4 March 1841; *Monitor*, 29 October 1841; *Australasian Chronicle*, 6 March 1841; *Sydney Morning Herald*, 13 April 1843, 13 July 1843.

SOLOMON, John

b. 1783
Ann, 1833; Free.
Married; Dealer.

John Solomon, and his wife Sarah (q.v.), were reported to have arrived in Sydney on 13 November 1833 on the *Ann*, together with their son Israel Solomon (q.v.) and daughter-in-law Sarah (q.v.). John Solomon was aged fifty and his wife Sarah was forty.

In 1835 Solomon advertised that he was the ship's agent for the *Champion* bound for Hobart Town. At that time he lived on the corner of Market Street and York Street.

The *Cumberland Times*, 29 November 1845, announced that John Solomon had 'the Cheapest Wine and Spirit Store in Parramatta', located at Harris Street, near the steamer wharf.

Sydney Morning Herald, 15 November 1833.

SOLOMON, John

b. London, 1807–1889
Australia, 1828; Free.
Single; Dealer.

John Solomon was a son of Isaac (Ikey) Solomon (q.v.) and Ann Solomon (q.v.), and the brother of Moses (q.v.), Anne (Nancy) (q.v.), David (q.v.), Sarah (q.v.) and

Mark (q.v.). On 26 September 1828 John Solomon, a free settler who had arrived on the ship *Australia*, had commenced business in George Street, Sydney, as a merchant in partnership with his brother Moses Solomon. The 1828 Census listed John Wilson, aged forty-seven, as a servant to John Solomon. The Solomons wrote to the authorities about their mother, Ann Solomon, who was 'a Crown Prisoner at Hobart Town with a young and large family of Infant children, four in number exclusive of his brother and petitioner'. John said that he was about to proceed to Hobart Town 'to take his mother off government stores and hoped to get permission to bring the young family to Sydney'. The official note on the petition reads 'Cannot be done'.

Nevertheless, John and Moses Solomon moved to Hobart Town, sailing from Sydney on the same ship that had brought their mother and younger siblings to Van Diemen's Land. (The captain of the *Mermaid* had obtained permission to make a commercial journey between Sydney and Hobart Town.) In late 1829 the two brothers hired the barrister William Tice Gellibrand to prevent their father being deported to England, where it seemed he would be executed. The action delayed Ikey's deportation by some months. On 26 June 1830 they placed an advertisement in the *Hobart Town Courier* announcing that John Solomon had just landed from the schooner *Active* with 'clothes, cottons, etc and sugar'. All sorts of colonial produce would be taken in exchange. His business was being conducted in Liverpool Street opposite the White Horse Inn. By April 1831 John Solomon announced an evening sale at his Tasmanian Auction and Commission Mart in Liverpool Street. He was licensed as an auctioneer on 14 January 1832 and later that year received a licence for the William IV Hotel in Liverpool Street. On 26 April 1833 he received a government grant of '11 perches' at the corner of Goderich Street and Bathurst Street, Hobart Town. On 1 February 1834 John Solomon arrived in Port Jackson on the *Fame*. He was described as a 'dealer from Van Diemen's Land', and remained in New South Wales advertising in the *Sydney Gazette* that he had established 'a stationery warehouse and circulating library'. He also sold 'guns and pistols, violins and flutes, veterinary and surgeons instruments and Greek portraits'.

Solomon was in Bathurst when the gold rush began. 'John Solomon & Co' was able to buy 48 pounds weight of raw gold for £1800. Back in Sydney as a well-known and shrewd bullion buyer, he published the *Gold Circular*, which listed the news from the goldfields together with the price of gold in Melbourne and Sydney.

In 1871 John Solomon took a leading part in the purchase of land for the Great Synagogue in Castlereagh Street. Solomon dealt in property and built a number of the commercial buildings in the City of Sydney.

John Solomon JP of Alberto Terrace, Darlinghurst Road, 'merchant and gold bullion broker', died on 25 July 1889. His tombstone adds quaintly: 'Here lies a man who slept seven days'. His Hebrew name was Ya'akov the son of Yitzhak. He left an estate of £180 993. A fine portrait of John Solomon by the colonial artist Richard Noble is in the possession of the Jewish Museum of Australia, in Melbourne, and a companion portrait of his wife Elizabeth is owned by the Art Gallery of South Australia.

Petition CS 4/1993, 28/7647, dated 26 September 1828; CSO 1/295/7163, p. 161; *Hobart Town Courier*, 23 April 1831, 26 June 1830, 23 April 1831, 14 January 1832, 21 September 1832, 26 April 1833; M. Z. Forbes, 'The Jews of New South Wales and the Gold Rushes', *AJJHS*, vol. 12, no. 2 (1994), p. 298f.

SOLOMON, John

b. London, 1825
Victoria, 1849; Free.
Married.

An assisted migrant, John Solomon came to New South Wales with his wife Phillipa (aged twenty) in 1849.

SOLOMON, Jonas Barnett (Youner)

b. London, 1795
813; Convict; Sentenced to 7 years, Old Bailey, 1812.
Single; Apprentice.

Jonas Solomon was convicted for stealing three reams of paper, valued at £5, from a stationer's cart at Bridge Row in London. His father, Barnard Solomon, tried to protect his son when the ward beadle came to his home, by shouting out a warning 'in Dutch'. His father, aged fifty, was sentenced to seven years transportation but does not seem to have arrived in Australia.

James (Jonas) Barnett Solomon purchased an allotment of land in Hobart Town on 12 May 1824. On 9 October 1827 Youner Solomon was assigned to work as a messenger at the Colonial Secretary's office, when he was found to have a silver watch in his possession of which he was unable to give a satisfactory account. He was sentenced to be sent to a penal settlement for eight years. Six years later he held a ticket of leave and, on 22 November 1833, was appointed to be a constable in Hobart Town. On 30 March 1835 he was charged with gross neglect of duty, drunkenness and permitting a prisoner in his custody to get intoxicated. Solomon was dismissed from the police force, his ticket of leave was cancelled, and he was ordered to move to another district. He seems to have learned his lesson and was permitted to return to work for the police.

On 22 June 1838 he was granted a conditional pardon. 'His Excellency the Lieutenant Governor [was] pleased to allow this man to proceed to Sydney by the schooner *Marion Webster*', and Jonas Barnett Solomon resigned from the police on 24 August 1838. On 18 February 1851 Solomon was permitted to travel to any of the Australian colonies, but not to return to Great Britain.

OBSP, 1812, p. 172; *Hobart Town Courier*, 22 November 1833, 24 August 1838; LSD 1/73, p. 134; CP 1746.

SOLOMON, Joseph

b. London, 1780–1851
Prince Regent I (1), 1820; Convict; Sentenced to life, Kent Quarter Assizes, 1819.
Divorced; Dealer, fruit merchant; Height: 173 cm; 4 children.

Face dark, black hair, hazel eyes. The son of Isaac. Deported with his brother Judah Solomon (q.v.). Joseph Solomon was sentenced on 2 August 1819. Before leaving England, Joseph gave Harriet (née Lazarus), his wife, a religious divorce. That document states that Joseph's father was Isaac Shtakenman and his mother's name was Judith (Harriett). Joseph's Hebrew name states that he was the son of Abraham Our Forefather meaning that he was not born a Jew and that, at least at the time of his birth, his mother was not Jewish. Both Joseph and Judah and their families lived in Sheerness. There were at least three other brothers, Henry (q.v.), Samuel (q.v.) and Isaac. Joseph and Harriett/Judith had seven children of whom four would survive. Lyon Henry (q.v.), Frances (q.v.), Mary (q.v.) and Sarah (q.v.). On 21 October 1819 The Times reported that 'On Thursday last, the ceremony of divorcement, according to the Jewish custom, took place at the Fountain-inn, Sheerness, between Joseph Solomons and his wife. It was performed by the High Priest and Chief Rabbi, who arrived for the purpose in a coach and four. The husband was permitted to come ashore (from the Bellerophon hulk), under an escort, and in irons: and, after the ceremony, he returned on board to suffer that expatriation his guilt had brought upon him.'

The two brothers, Judah and Joseph, started business as general dealers very soon after they arrived in Sydney on 27 January 1820 and were sent on to Van Diemen's Land, arriving in Hobart Town on 1 March. Both had brought with them the large capital sum of £60. On 10 February 1821 the two Solomon brothers 'informed the public', in an advertisement in the *Hobart Town Gazette*, that they had for sale at their residence in Argyle Street 'all items generally to be found in a general store, jewellery and gentlemen's wearing apparel which could be made to measure at the shortest notice'. This advertisement continued to appear throughout 1821 and 1822. In 1822 the Solomon brothers received an additional injection of capital, donated to them by the Jewish community of Sheerness and brought out by Henry Davis (q.v.). In that same year Joseph opened a branch of the partnership 'J & J Solomon' in Launceston and that arrangement remained for two years.

On 9 June 1821 Joseph Solomon was charged with retailing spirits without a licence and was acquitted. On 26 August 1831 he held a ticket of leave and was accused of selling 5 gallons of rum without a valid licence. The case was dismissed. On 2 September 1831 a charge of selling five gallons of gin without having a valid licence was quashed. On the same day he was also charged 'upon five other Informations for selling Spirituous liquors in quantities above five gallons'. The case was withdrawn. On 13 September 1831 he was fined £20 plus costs for selling five gallons of gin without a licence. On 15 September 1831 the charge of selling five gallons of rum was upheld and he was fined £10 with costs and on the same day he was 'further charged' with selling five gallons of brandy and five gallons of rum without having obtained a valid licence, and was fined £20 plus costs. The *Hobart Town Courier* of 18 October 1831 commented: 'Mr Solomon is a rich man but, unlike his namesake, not a wise one'. The question of attempted coercion of the Bench arose when Mr Gilles the magistrate refused to grant the licence and Solomon indignantly took his money out of the Gilles Bank.

In 1833 Joseph Solomon wrote in a petition:

> I arrived in this colony early in the year 1820 under sentence of transportation for Life. After having been in the colony some time I received a ticket of leave which indulgence I have ever since enjoyed. I resided in Hobart Town with my brother Judah Solomon near two years which period my conduct I flatter myself was such as to meet the approval of the authorities and most respectable inhabitants ... for the last six years I have resided in the County of Cornwall, the latter four of which entirely in Launceston where I again am happy to observe my general conduct has met the approval of all.

Joseph asked for the 'high indulgence of emancipation'. The petition was written in 1833 and a conditional pardon was granted on 13 March 1833.

On 23 November 1843 the *Launceston Independent* reported that Joseph Solomon had been married by special licence at St John's Church, on 17 November, by the Rev. Dr Browne, to Mrs Eliza Backhouse, eldest daughter of Shortland Graves Esq. of the County of Waterford. On the basis of this relationship Joseph, who had joined the newly formed Hobart Synagogue in 1842, and had rented seat no. 3 in 1845, left the Jewish community. In Launceston, just before his marriage, he became a member of the Church of England and abandoned his honoured seat in the Synagogue.

Joseph's business in the north of the island expanded and branch stores were opened in Evandale and Campbell Town. During the 1830s Joseph Solomon's four children by his first wife, Lyon Henry Solomon (q.v), Mary (q.v.), Frances (Cottrell, q.v.), and Sarah (q.v.), had joined him in Launceston. On January 1834 Joseph Solomon and John Euston asked for a wholesale wine and spirits licence for the Bonding warehouse in Charles Street, Launceston.

Mary married William Roberts of Hobart Town on 5 November 1835. Despite Joseph's disapproval, Sarah married Benjamin Walford (q.v.), the son of Barnard Walford (q.v.) on 4 January 1838. Frances married Anthony Cottrell, whose interest in the settlement of Port Phillip led Joseph Solomon to become a member of the syndicate that originally settled Melbourne. Although Judah and Joseph were partners, the business was referred to as 'Mr J. Solomon of Launceston' as Judah was still technically a convict. Joseph Solomon (q.v.) jnr, a nephew of Joseph, and the son of his brother, Samuel Solomon, took a large flock of sheep to Melbourne to become one of the first three farmers in the new settlement. Joseph jnr married Sarah Davis, who was his first cousin, and the daughter of Henry Davis (q.v.). Joseph snr sold his interest in the Port Phillip Association in 1839 for £411.

Solomon became a significant land owner. He received a 100-acre land grant in Evandale and twenty acres in Longford in January 1844. He owned 1500 acres at Perth and an allotment in George Town.

In 1848 the newspapers reported that six armed men had 'visited the establishment of Joseph Solomon esq. at Evandale and demanded money. Mr S. although he is, as is well known, advanced in years, stoutly resisted the fellows, and in the affray got rather badly used. He offered them his plate but this was refused and they finally took fifteen shillings'.

Joseph Solomon 'of Evandale' died on 8 May 1851. His wife Eliza survived him in Tasmania. He bequeathed £25 to his first wife Harriet, 'which I have been in the habit of sending her'. His children Lyon, Mary, Frances and Sarah were all remembered in his will, as was his brother Samuel Solomon (q.v.). However, Sarah, the wife of Benjamin Walford, was to inherit her portion of the estate 'only after Benjamin Walford dies'. The will was signed with an X, 'the Mark of Joseph Solomon'. Joseph Solomon was buried in the Church of England graveyard in Evandale. His son Lyon Henry Solomon is buried with him. His daughter Sarah died in New South Wales on 18 January 1875 and was buried as an Anglican at Balmain.

CON 31/38, no. 217; CON 13/2, p. 19; CON 31/38, p. 73; CON 23/3; CON 13/2, p. 36; Ship Indent 4/4007, p. 83; HO 11/3; CSO 1/336/7708; LSD 1/75/252; *Hobart Town Courier*, 18 October 1831, 5 November 1835; CP no. 333, 13 March 1833; *Independent*, 23 November 1833; *Hobart Town Gazette*, 10 February 1821; *HRA*, series 3, vol. 4; Dixson 163b, 6 January 1834; Hamish Maxwell-Stewart, 'Land of Sorrow, Land of Honey', p. 13f., and David F. Solomon, 'From Convict to Colonist: Joseph Solomon of Evandale', in P. Elias and A. Elias (eds), *A Few from Afar*, p. 65f.; *Moreton Bay Courier*, 8 July 1848, quoting *Cumberland Courier*. Jeremy I Pfeffer '*From One End of the Earth to the Other*'. Chapter 8, pp 246-279.

SOLOMON, Joseph (Solomon JOSEPHS)

d. 1824
Indian, 1810; Convict; Sentenced to life, Surrey, 1808.
Divorced; 1 child.

Joseph Solomon was tried at Surrey on 14 August 1808 and sentenced to transportation for life. Joseph Solomon was frequently called 'Solomon Josephs' in colonial documents. He had been sentenced to be hanged in August 1796 for assaulting Willliam Brown 'with a certain knife, feloniously, willfully, maliciousy and unlawfully … upon the neck and throat with intent … to kill and murder the said William Brown.' On 27 November 1806 the rabbinic court had convened at Newgate Prison to grant a Get for Chaim ben Yosef and his wife Malka bat Reuben. His wife promised not to remarry during the following seven years. His wife's 'English name' was Molly Joseph and they had a son named Ralph (Reuben) whose birth was registered at London's Great Synagogue.

Listed in the 1811 General Muster as 'Solomon Josephs', having been convicted in London in August 1808, Joseph Solomon was assigned to James Mitcham for three years. He then kept the Macquarie Arms at Windsor, 1813–1818, but was only discharged from reliance on the government stores on 27 January 1816. In the 1814 Muster he was listed as a convict and an assigned servant.

Solomon subsequently wrote:

> I have held the Macquarie Arms Inn for about five years and two months (though sometimes the licence was in the name of another servant of Mr Fitzgerald who is a cripple). After I had been at the Inn for two years, I used to sell pipes and tobacco and prints and calico on my own account. Mr Wentworth would not give me a licence as long as I was a prisoner. I have always been in the house and sold for Mrs Fitzgerald some of the wheat (of Fitzgerald which goes into the store) was in my name.

On 15 December 1817, at Windsor, Solomon petitioned for a mitigation of his sentence, which was duly granted in the form of a conditional pardon on 31 January 1818. In February Solomon asked the Colonial Secretary's office for a 'renewal' of his spirit licence for Windsor. On 25 October 1819 Joseph Solomon, a servant to Mr Fitzgerald of Emu Plains, supplied the Government Commissariat with 41 bushels of wheat and received a bill of £18 9s, which he made over to John Solomon. During the next four years, Joseph Solomon of Windsor supplied the government with large quantities of pork and wheat. Governor Macquarie granted a spirit and wine licence to Solomon Joseph for the Macquarie Inn at Windsor. The magistrates objected on the grounds that it was their job to grant licences. According to the Bigge Report, the favouritism exhibited by Governor Macquarie was the result of a good meal. On 19 March 1820, 'A Joseph Solomon, Hotel Keeper, Macquarie Arms, Windsor supplied breakfast to Governor Macquarie'. In the Bigge Report it was claimed that a Mr Richard Fitzgerald, 'formerly a convict', was a friend of Governor Macquarie. He 'keeps an inn and spirit shop in the town of Windsor, called the Macquarie Arms, the management of which, although ostensibly in the hands of an emancipated Jew is controlled by Mr Fitzgerald and his wife, who occupied a house adjoining and who are in the habit of giving orders upon the Jew for the delivery of goods and spirits in payment of services performed by the convicts'. At the Bigge Commission, William Wentworth cited the case of Joseph Solomon in support of his contention that Macquarie's behaviour was arbitrary while 'some of the most respectable people did not obtain licences and those who had purchased liquor and built houses in expectation of having their licences continued have suffered very great injury'.

An inquiry was held into charges that Solomon sold liquor for food vouchers issued to the prisoners. He denied this accusation by explaining that his prices were higher than other sellers. He claimed the charge was trumped up because he had gone directly to the Governor and not waited for a licence from the local magistrates.

'Solomon Josephs' was listed in the 1822 New South Wales General Muster as a dealer at Windsor. He died in May 1824, leaving all of his estate to Abraham Elias (q.v.).

Jeremy I Pfeffer, *The First Bet Din Convened in Australia* in *AJHSJ* vol 18, part 3, (2007) p. 284f. Bigge Report Appendix, BT Box 6, p. 2637, p. 3995, Box 21, p. 3932, Box 23, pp. 4474, 4481, BT Box 2, p. 595f., on 19 November 1819, BT Box 7, pp. 3020, 3028; Macquarie Memoranda, p. 141b, A772, Petition for Clemency 4/1851, p. 196; *Sydney Gazette*, 15 March 1817, 20 June 1818, 31 July 1823, 4 December 1823, 18 December 1823.

SOLOMON, Joseph (Johnny)

b. London, 1819– 1890
Free.
Single; 13 children.

Joseph was a nephew of Judah and Joseph Solomon (qq.v.), and the son of Samuel Solomon (q.v.). He has been called 'Joseph III' to differentiate him from his cousins who had the same name, and was also known as 'Joseph Solomon jnr'. He was born in London in April 1819.

John Pascoe Fawkner noted in his diary on Saturday 19 December 1835 that 'Young Solomon had landed from the *Adelaide*'. 'Joseph Solomon Jnr' came to Port Phillip in 1835 with the first settlers of the Port Phillip Association, and established a sheep station (one of the first three) near Saltwater River (now known as the Maribyrnong River). Saltwater River lay between his station and that of his cousin-in-law, Anthony Cottrell. Cottrell had married Frances (Cottrell, q.v.), the daughter of Joseph Solomon of Evandale.

Joseph Solomon brought with him 1000 sheep from Van Diemen's Land and he promptly lost 500 of them to the Aboriginal people. He managed the property of Anthony Cottrell on the Saltwater River. The Melbourne Court Register noted that on 14 November 1837 Joseph Solomon, a settler at Cut Paw Paw, was fined fifty shillings for assaulting an employee. His name appeared together with Michael Solomon's (q.v.) in the *Port Phillip Herald* of 8 September 1840 in a list of persons entitled to depasture stock. Joseph 'Slomon' was listed in the 1841 Census of New South Wales living at 'Mereberriong, Salt Water Creek'. He bought the property that lay between that of the Cottrells and Michael Solomon, and, in October 1849, purchased 353 acres on the western side of the Saltwater River for £353 17s 6d. It was sold for £460 on 8 March 1854.

Joseph married his first cousin Sarah (q.v.), the daughter of Judah Solomon of Hobart Town and his first wife, Esther Solomon (q.v.), at St John's Church, Evandale, on 2 August 1838. They travelled to Melbourne, by the *Henry*, on 24 September 1838 from Launceston. At the second land sale at Port Phillip, Joseph Solomon bought a block of land in Bourke Street, just west of the site of the General Post Office, for £39. He also bought a parcel of 353 acres on the eastern side of the Saltwater River for £1 an acre.

Joseph and Sarah travelled to Tasmania in 1852 to manage his uncle Joseph's estate, and stayed there for ten years, returning to Victoria, and to Braybrook, in 1862. Solomon died at Moffatt Street, South Yarra, in Melbourne, on 24 April 1890 'an old colonist of 55 years'.

Solomon had little or no contact with the Jewish community. However, the first letter book of the Melbourne Hebrew Congregation included the following note to Mr J. Solomon on 13 November 1844 about the remains of the daughter of the late Mr Henry Davis: 'You are supposed by us to be the nearest relative'. The grave site was an unsuitable one, having been dug in a field of basalt rock, and the congregation asked for £5 to help remove the body to a more suitable cemetery. (The body was removed and was reburied in Hobart Town.)

Joseph and Sarah Solomon were buried in the Church of England section of the Melbourne General Cemetery. Sarah died as the result of a carriage accident in 1881 at the age of 61. There were thirteen children, six of whom were alive at the time of Joseph's death. The children were: Joseph (born 1839), Henry (born 1840), Felix (1842), Alfred (1845), Charles (1846), Louisa (1848), Jessica (1850), Francis (1851), Esther (1852), Arthur (1854), Frances (1856), Albert (1858), and Walter (1859).

Paul R. Mullaly, 'Jewish Community Involvement in the Criminal Life of Melbourne, 1835–1850', *AJJHS*, vol. 17, no. 1, p. 84f.; Pastoral licence 4/41, Deep Creek 40, VDL, 45/8b M55773; V.J.Jones, 'Solomon's Ford', *AJJHS*, vol. 9, no. 5 (1983), p. 313f; *Port Phillip Patriot*, 20 February 1839; *Port Phillip Gazette*, 8 October 1844, 27September 1845; David F.Solomon, 'From Convict to Colonist: Joseph Solomon of Evandale', in P.Elias and A. Elias (eds), *A Few from Afar*, p. 69f.

SOLOMON, Joseph

b. Hobart Town, 1826–1894
Dealer.

Joseph Solomon was the illegitimate son of Judah Solomon (q.v.) and Elizabeth Howell. On 10 February 1848 Judah Solomon wrote to the board of the Hobart Town Synagogue asking that his son Joseph Solomon be permitted to marry, at the synagogue, Elizabeth Davis, daughter of Henry Davis (q.v.) and Hannah Howell.

He asked that it 'be taken into consideration that the fathers of each were Jews and that the parties had also been brought up as Jews'. The Rev. Cohen told the committee that both would have to be formally converted to Judaism. It was also agreed that Miss Catherine Davis be admitted as a *gioret* in the same manner as her sister. Joseph Solomon married Elizabeth Davis in Hobart Town on 14 November 1849. He was twenty-three years old and she was twenty-two.

Joseph worked with his father Judah Solomon and, in 1854, became a partner with his uncle Isaac in a wine and spirit business, which operated from Temple House in Hobart and Launceston. Joseph managed the Hobart Town part of the business and lived in Temple House from 1854 to the time of his death in 1894.

Elizabeth Solomon died in 1892 at the age of fifty-four. Joseph died, aged sixty-three, on 16 June 1894. Both were buried beside Judah Solomon's grave in the Hobart Jewish Cemetery at Cornelian Bay.

Joseph Solomon gave generously in his will to his wife's family, the Hobart Synagogue, the Hobart Benevolent Society and the Hobart Hospital. Temple House was left to his nephew, Samuel Benjamin (q.v.).

P. Elias and A Elias (eds), *A Few from Afar*, p. 24f.

SOLOMON, Joseph Solomon

b. Adelaide, 1843

Joseph Solomon Solomon was born in July 1843 in Adelaide, the son of Emanuel Solomon (q.v.). His first job, after leaving school, was droving cattle for Philip Levi (q.v.) of Adelaide. He then joined his father's wholesale grocery firm and in 1894 purchased a seat on the Adelaide Stock Exchange. He married Miriam Solomon, the daughter of M. A. J. Solomons.

Sydney Morning Herald, 23 July 1845; Land Purchase 2/7974 (1850).

SOLOMON, Judah

b. London, 1781–1856
Prince Regent I (1), 1820; Convict; Sentenced to life, Kent, 1819.
Married; Dealer; Height: 173 cm; 11 children.

Judah Solomon was described as having a 'ruddy complexion, dark brown hair, hazel eyes'. He was aged thirty-nine when he arrived in Australia. He was part of the Jewish community in Sheerness and was the son of Isaac and Judith/Harriett and the brother of Joseph Solomon (q.v.), who was transported with him. The records of the London rabbinical court notes that Joseph was a convert to Judaism while Judah is described as a Jew (whose mother was therefore Jewish). Judah Solomon had married Esther Abrahams (née Levy, Russell) (Solomon, q.v.), the daughter of Philip and Catherine, on 6 January 1805 in Sheerness. The brothers were convicted for organising a team of thieves to pilfer the warehouses in the Sheerness port. Unfortunately one of the warehouses, which they robbed of seventy-eight watches and some silver, belonged to Abraham Abrahams, the former father-in-law of Judah's wife Esther. Regardless, or perhaps because, of this relationship, Abrahams prosecuted Judah and Joseph Solomon. Esther was pregnant with her eighth child when her husband was convicted. Unlike his brother, Judah did not obtain a religious divorce before he left England. Judah's other brothers were Henry Solomon (q.v.), Samuel Solomon (q.v.), and Isaac Solomon.

Judah and Joseph Solomon arrived in Sydney on the *Prince Regent* on 27 January 1820 and were sent on to Van Diemen's Land by the same ship, landing on 1 March 1820. Their emancipation came rapidly, aided by £60 capital each brought out. The Solomons were able to open a general store in Argyle Street, Hobart Town, very soon after they landed and apparently ran an illegal still at the back of their store. In 1822 Judah and Joseph Solomon received a gift of cash from the Sheerness Jewish community, brought out for them by Henry Davis (q.v.), which enabled them to build up a flourishing partnership. At the same time a change in government policy towards the purchase of wheat favoured the Solomon brothers' policy of granting credit to small farmers on the future security of their approaching harvest.

The police, however, kept a close watch on their activities, which were obviously often questionable. The first charge against them, on 9 June 1821, for selling spirits without a licence, was dismissed and Judah was acquitted of a second charge on 5 July 1823. On 25 October 1826, listed as holding a ticket of leave, his weights were confiscated for being incorrect.

In 1825 Judah Solomon built a mansion, Temple House, on the corner of Argyle and Macquarie streets. It is now one of the four surviving Georgian townhouses in Australia and cost £500 to build. It was large enough to be a residence and a business and store house. It was said that the first Jewish services were held in the mansion, giving rise to its name. In 1828 his brother Joseph moved to the north of the island to establish a branch of the business in Launceston. On 27 July 1830 Judah was found to be 'living in a state of illicit intercourse with a woman named Howell—he undertaking to send her to her mother's tomorrow'. He was admonished. On 2 September 1831 a case against him for selling more than five gallons of gin without having a valid licence was quashed. His solicitor was obviously an able man. Five 'informations' were then brought against him concerning the sale of liquor and the case was withdrawn. On 13 September the police succeeded in convincing the court and he was fined £20 plus costs. A similar charge concerning brandy brought him a fine of £10 plus costs and another £10 for selling rum. A conditional pardon was granted to him on 24 February 1832, even though the Chief Police Magistrate complained that he 'held a licence for a public house which was conducted in the most disorderly, and I may say, infamous manner. His home was the resort of most of the pickpockets in town and he defied the police in every way'. On 1 June 1833 he was fined £10 plus costs for permitting Sarah Tilling, Ellen Pitt and Joseph Josephs (q.v.) to remain in his licensed house after hours. On 25 May and 3 August 1833 he was fined £10 on each count for breaking the licensing regulations.

Judah and Joseph were among the first subscribers to the Bank of Van Diemen's Land in 1823 and their names appear among the first to be registered buying land. But Judah's marital problems were just beginning. In December 1832 Esther Solomon arrived to find Judah ensconced with Elizabeth Howell and her first (illegitimate) child Joseph (Solomon, q.v.) in his new mansion on Argyle Street. Esther's enmity, following his rejection, would never abate. She began a battle to force the Governor to return her husband and to prevent Judah from obtaining an absolute pardon (one was recommended on 5 October 1843 by the administration but was not ratified by London). Though denied public respectability, Judah became one of Hobart Town's wealthiest inhabitants with his Auction and Commission Rooms at the corner of Argyle and Liverpool streets. He became the treasurer of the synagogue and donated £200 to the building fund, together with a £250 loan, in addition to the donation of land next to his former home for the new synagogue building. The partnership with his brother Joseph was officially dissolved in 1841. Judah remained staunchly Jewish. Joseph became an Anglican.

In 1850 Judah asked for a free pardon so that he could visit England. He claimed to have obtained a conditional pardon in 1832 and a free pardon in 1843—which Esther had blocked as a consequence of a letter written on 28 May 1846.

Judah Solomon died 18 February 1856 aged seventy-eight. His children with Esther were: Hannah (born 1802 and died 1864, married Henry Abrahams); Rachel (born 1811) (Rachel Barnett, q.v.), Louisa (1812) (Davis, q.v.), Lydia (Benjamin, q.v.) (born 1813 died London 20 January 1880, Isaac (1814) (q.v.), Michael (1815) (q.v.), Rebecca (1818) (q.v.), and Sarah (1819) (q.v.). His son with Elizabeth Howell, Joseph, was born in Hobart Town in 1826.

At his death, Judah left his son Isaac his home, Temple House, at the corner of Liverpool Street and Argyle Street, next door to the synagogue. He made provision through trusts for Lydia (who had by then married a second time), wife of Lewis

Cohen, dancing master of Hobart Town, and Joseph Solomon of Church Street, Hobart Town. Solomon's station on the Saltwater River at Port Phillip was left to his son Joseph. Catherine, the fourth daughter of Henry and Hannah Davis, Joseph jnr (q.v.) and his wife Elizabeth are buried in the family plot beside Judah Solomon in the Hobart Jewish Cemetery at Cornelian Bay. Sarah, his legitimate wife, died 24 September 1861 in New Town, Tasmania.

CON 31/38, no. 216; Ship Indent 4/4007, p. 83; HO 11/3; CSO 5/13/3131, 16/6/203; CSO 20/30/710; Governors' Despatches, A1267-14, p. 1738; CO/280/258, October 1850; Hamish Maxwell-Stewart, 'Land of Sorrow, Land of Honey', and Anne Rand, 'Temple House and the Judah Solomon Family', in P. Elias and A. Elias (eds), *A Few from Afar*, pp. 13f., 21f. Jeremy I Pfeffer, 'From One End of the Earth to the Other' Chapter 8, pp. 246–279.

SOLOMON, Judah Moss

b. London, 1818–1880
Enchantress, 1833; Free.
Single; Dealer; 16 children.

Judah Moss Solomon arrived in Sydney in 1833, at the age of fifteen, aboard the *Enchantress*. He came to South Australia on the *Dorset*, which was owned by his uncles, Emanuel and Vaiben Solomon (qq.v.). He was listed as an 'auctioneer'.

On 27 October 1840 Judah Moss Solomon wrote 'on behalf of V. & E. Solomon' tendering for the transportation of convicts from Adelaide to Sydney at £10 each by the *Dorset*. The ship was a 'regular trader facilitating the communication between the Government of the two Colonys [*sic*]'.

Judah Moss Solomon married his first cousin Rachael Cohen (q.v.) at the Sydney Synagogue on 7 August 1842. Rachel was the daughter of his father's sister Hannah (née Solomon) and Samuel Cohen. He and his wife moved to the new settlement of Moreton Bay, and on 13 November 1843 Solomon and Benjamin Lee (q.v.) were appointed the official representatives of the Sydney Synagogue.

Judah and Rachael had a son named Moss Judah Solomon in 1843 (q.v). Their child was the third free non-Aboriginal baby born in Brisbane. A second son, Benjamin (q.v.) (3 November 1844), was born at Moreton Bay. There followed Elizabeth (1846), born in Sydney; Samuel (15 January 1848), born at Currie Street, Adelaide; Hannah (20 July 1849, who died 11 months later); Leah (16 June 1851); Vaiben Louis (1853), born in Adelaide; and Emanuel (7 May 1860).

When Judah and Rachael returned to Sydney, Judah established himself in business, taking over the premises of Philip Solomon (q.v.) in George Street, opposite the police station. He sent a large consignment of goods to Auckland in the *Dorset* on 22 November 1845. Solomon became a seat holder in the new York Street synagogue in 1845. Between 1843 and 1845 Judah Moss Solomon and his father's half-brother, Isaac Solomon (q.v.), bought parcels of land in Brisbane and Ipswich together. In 1846 Judah had moved to Adelaide, where he worked as an auctioneer, and where his uncle Emanuel Solomon lived. In 1867, Judah Moss Solomon married a second time, to Ada (Adela) Pulver, the daughter of Isaac Pulver.

Judah Moss Solomon served as the first president of the Adelaide Hebrew Congregation in 1851. He was elected to the Adelaide City Council in 1852 and was Mayor of Adelaide in 1869 and 1870. During 1858 he served in the House of Assembly for the City of Adelaide. From 1861 to 1866 he was a Member of the Legislative Council. From 1872 to 1874 he was a Member of Parliament for West Adelaide. His son, Vaiben Louis Solomon, would become a member of the first Commonwealth Parliament.

Judah Moss Solomon died on 29 August 1880, at his home at King William Street South, and was buried at the West Terrace Jewish Cemetery. He had sixteen children, of whom only seven survived him.

Trevor Cohen, 'The Honourable Vaiben Louis Solomon', *AJJHS*, vol 8, no. 3 (1977), p. 89f; SA Archives, GRG 24/1/1840, no. 554; *Sydney Morning Herald*, 9 August 1842, 31 March 1843, 2 April 1844, 20 May 1844, 26 July 1844, 5 August 1844, 2 July 1845; Land Purchases, 7 December 1843 to 18 February 1845, in 2/7974.

SOLOMON, Julia

b. Bath, England, 1826–1914
Britomart, 1835; Free.
Single; 15 children.

Julia was a daughter of Samuel Solomon (q.v.) and Rebecca Solomon (q.v.) (née Moss) and arrived in Australia with her mother and eight siblings. She married Lewis Wolfe Levy (q.v.) at the York Street Synagogue in Sydney in 1845. She died at 'Cahors', Macleay Street, Sydney, on 5 September 1914.

SOLOMON, Julia

b. London, 1828–1867
1841; Free.
Single.

Julia Solomon was the daughter of Moss Solomon (q.v.) and his first wife, Betsy (née Myers). Julia married Henry Keesing in Sydney on 14 June 1848 and lived in Auckland, New Zealand.

SOLOMON, Julia (née ISAACS)

b. London, 1829–1895
Constant, 1849; Free.
Married; 14 children.

Julia was the wife of Abraham Jacob Solomon (q.v.) and the youngest daughter, and seventh child, of Judah and Sarah Isaacs of Harrow Alley, Aldgate. She died on 30 December 1895.

SOLOMON, Kate

b. London, 1837–1928
1840; Free.
Single.

The youngest daughter of Moss Solomon (q.v.) and his wife Leah Solomon (q.v.), Kate was born on 19 June 1837, and arrived in Sydney with her parents and some of her siblings. The family left Sydney in 1841 and moved to Adelaide. Kate married Maurice Salom (q.v.) on 27 April 1856. She died on 7 June 1928 in Adelaide.

SOLOMON, Leah (née MYERS)

b. London, 1807–1871
Alfred, 1841; Free.
Married.

Leah was the daughter of Judah Myers of London. She married her brother-in-law, Moss Solomon (q.v.), in the early 1830s, following the death of her sister Betsy. Moss Solomon died in Sydney in 1849, and Leah Solomon settled in Adelaide. She was the mother of Samuel Moss Solomon (q.v.) (born 1835), Philip Solomon (April 1836) (q.v.), Mrs Kate Salom (19 June 1837) (Kate Solomon, q.v.), and Elias (2 September 1839) (q.v.). She lived at North Terrace, and died in Adelaide on 4 January 1871.

SOLOMON, Leah

b. 1827
Free.
Single.

Leah Solomon, aged seventeen, married Thomas Thorpe, aged thirty-two, in Campbell Town on 21 October 1844.

SOLOMON, Leah

b. London, 1830–1908
1841; Free.
Single.

The fifth child of Moss Solomon (q.v.) and his first wife Betsy, Leah married Maurice Marks (Morris Marks, q.v.), aged twenty-five, on 30 January 1850, at the home of her stepmother, Leah (née Myers) Solomon (q.v.), Currie Street, Adelaide. Leah died in New Zealand on 9 August 1908.

SOLOMON, Lewis

b. London, 1792–1868
Admiral Gambier (1), 1808; Convict; Sentenced to 14 years, London, 1806.
Single; 2 children.

Solomon smashed a shop window and attempted to steal a silver-plated milk pot. On 19 February 1806 he was sentenced to death with a recommendation for mercy 'on account of his youth'. He was aged between nine and fourteen years old (depending on which document is trusted). Confronted by the judge and jury at the Old Bailey, Solomon made his plea, and even as a youngster he was eloquent:

> When he catched hold of me, he says 'Where is that milk pot?' There was a mob came round me, and the milk pot was chucked on the ground, and the gentleman picked it up directly. I am not guilty of the crime, you may depend upon it; I do not know anything of it at all; I never did such a crime in my life; I hope you will give me hardly any punishment.

Lewis Solomon was sent from Sydney to Hobart Town in 1811 and was officially listed as 'a settler who had been a convict'. He was granted his 'certificate of emancipation' (a ticket of leave) on 1 April 1813.

On 31 March 1822 Lewis Solomon 'of Pitt St' was 'struck off the victualling list' and permitted to have an assigned convict mechanic under his care. Later that year he was listed as a carpenter and joiner at 6 Upper George Street in Sydney and had an assigned servant, James (Mordecai) Woolf (q.v.). He was granted a certificate of freedom on 25 September 1823 and moved out of Sydney. In January 1824 he was paid £206 to begin to outfit St Luke's Church in Liverpool and also St Peter's Church in Campbelltown. By 1825 he was described as a 'Carpenter, Innkeeper and Undertaker' at Liverpool and was paid a total of 3622 Spanish dollars from the 'Ecclesiastical Establishment' for fitting up the interior of the Liverpool Church and the Campbelltown Church.

The Colonial Secretary's files note that Solomon visited Van Diemen's Land and that, on 17 September 1824, his certificate of freedom was stolen by persons unknown 'from his chest' at Hobart Town. He became a general dealer and publican of the Manchester Arms at 60 George Street in September 1826. He was in and out of court, quarrelling with rivals, taking on the military and giving evidence on behalf of his friends. Solomon was tried before a jury for an alleged assault on an officer. He was acquitted but it was recorded that the verdict 'has given much offence to the military'.

In 1827 Solomon purchased the lease for the Sydney Market at £99 per annum and was officially appointed constable for the market. He complained that he could not persuade anyone to pay rent for using the market as conditions had not been adjusted since Governor Macquarie established it. Solomon could not afford to pay the rent 'as the populace is not using the official market for stock to market transactions'. The administration's unhelpful reply was that it could not 'force people to take cattle to market'. Solomon went bankrupt and was sent to prison, being released at the beginning of January 1829. He was described as the 'late lessee of the Market'. Lewis Solomon had been employed as the pound keeper during 1827 and on 14 July 1828 the *Sydney Gazette* told the story of David Hayes, who drove his cart past Solomon at the market and called out 'Look here, you Jew looking scoundrel. I've a load of pigs'. Solomon knocked Hayes down, alleging that he was driving dangerously and took him to the watch house. The prisoner was acquitted.

Solomon continued to be confronted with charges of insolvency over the following two years and was declared bankrupt in July 1831, at which time he offered to pay his creditors seven shilling and sixpence in the pound.

Lewis Solomon was listed in the 1828 Census with Mary Solomon (Linegan), who had arrived on the convict transport ship *Lord Wellington* from Ireland in 1820. They were married at St John's in Parramatta in 1830. Their child, Lewis Solomon jnr, was born on 22 June 1821 at Liverpool, and was baptised on 19 August 1821 at St Luke's. Elizabeth was born in 1823.

Mary Solomon died on 28 March 1832, aged thirty-three, and was buried at Campbelltown. Solomon was listed as the publican of the Forbes Hotel, Liverpool Road, in Campbelltown in 1828–32. In 1831 he was named as an executor of the innkeeper Thomas Collis snr, who died in May 1832 after a long illness. Three weeks after his death, Solomon married Sarah Collis of Bankstown at St Peter's, Campbelltown. Sarah had three surviving children from her second marriage and three from her first marriage. At that time Solomon owned the licences of the Hammond Inn, the Forbes Hotel and the Weavers' Inn.

On 5 May 1836 Solomon was convicted of stealing a horse at Penrith and was placed on the *Phoenix* hulk among the prisoners to be transported to a penal settlement for 'the remainder of his natural life' (with a minimum period of ten years). As the Acting Chief Justice said:

> It is much to be lamented that a person of your respectable appearance should be placed in such a situation. The Jury, however, after a careful examination of the case, have brought in a verdict of guilty. With that verdict I am perfectly satisfied. It appears that you went to the pound and took the horse, with the chance of no one coming afterwards to claim it. As a careful experienced man of the world, you ought to have closely examined the brand.

Solomon imaginatively wrote to the authorities from the hulk, arguing that he had arrived free by the *Hope* in 1813 and had left for England the same year, returning in 1818. He had been a hotel keeper for most of his time in the colony. He was sentenced to transportation for life for the serious crime of horse stealing. He denied the crime and described how he thought he was reclaiming a horse he had lost from his own yard.

On 28 June 1836 he was despatched to Norfolk Island and was one of the nine convicts who wrote to the Sydney Synagogue for prayer books and other religious items on 29 May 1840. He was listed in the General Return of Convicts in New South Wales, 'aged forty-four', in the *Phoenix* hulk in Sydney Harbour. In 1845 Solomon wrote to the authorities asking for mercy. He claimed to have had no punishment record during his time on Norfolk Island and that he was 'a steady man but old'. He was officially described as a 'rough carpenter, not strong, elderly', and fifty-four years of age. In 1845 the prison settlement on Norfolk Island was closed down, and it was decided to return Solomon to New South Wales. He had 'obtained his certificate of freedom twice' and had been punished for 'slight offences'.

In July 1845 Sarah Solomon was indicted for bigamy and was sentenced to spend two years at the Parramatta Gaol. Sarah had married Thomas Humphrey on 31 May 1837 after Solomon 'got into trouble' and had been sent away. Sarah argued that her marriage to Solomon was not valid as it had been conducted in a Church of England and Solomon was not baptised. The court disagreed!

In 1855, a Lewis Solomon was listed as a merchant at 57 Hunter Street, Sydney. The death of a Lewis Solomon was recorded as 28 December 1868 at Young in New South Wales.

OBSP, 1806, case 152; Ship Indent 4/4004, p. 288; Register of Pardons 4/4427, p. 352f.; HO 10/42; LSD 1/73/195; *Phoenix* (hulk) Entrance Book 4/7206; CS 4/1713, p. 129f.; 4/1947, 10 September 1827, 27/8882; Petition (re: Sydney Market) 4/1940, 27/7175; CS Petition 36/5633, in 4/2338.1; Central Criminal Court 4/6448, 5 May 1836; *Colonial Times* (Hobart Town), 24 February 1826; 28 September 1832; *Sydney Gazette*, 17 October 1827, 19 April 1831, 7 May 1836, 12 July 1845; *Morning Chronicle*, 12 July 1845; *Sydney Herald*, 5 May 1825, 3 October 1825, 25 June 1832; *Monitor*, 6 January 1827; *Australian*, 14 July 1825, 9 February 1826, 5 April 1826, 9 September 1826; Clare Stapleton Concord, *Lewis Solomon in Australia*, Madison, Wisconsin, 2004.

SOLOMON, Lewis

b. 1795
Marquis of Wellington, 1815; Convict; Sentenced to 7 years, London, 1814.
Single; Pedlar.

Dark sallow complexion, dark brown hair, hazel eyes.

Lewis Solomon arrived in the colony on 27 January 1815. Lewis Solomon was listed in the 1828 Census. He was aged thirty-one and free by servitude. He declared his religion to be 'Protestant'. He was a labourer working in the District of Airds. There was continual bureaucratic confusion as there were two other Lewis Solomons.

Ship Indent 4/4005, p. 32.

SOLOMON, Lewis

b. 1826–1906
Free.
Single

The son of Benjamin Solomon. Lewis Solomon, aged twenty-one, married Esther Davis, a minor, on 4 May 1847 in Brighton (Van Diemen's Land). Esther was the daughter of John Davis and his wife Louisa Solomon (q.v.) and the sister of Elizabeth Davis, who married Louis Abrahams.

Lewis Solomon died at 21 George Street, Fitzroy South (Melbourne) in 1906 age 79 and Esther died at Richmond in 1905. Their children were Alfred, John (died aged 10 months), Louis, Gertrude (Solomon), Mrs Isaac Abraham of London, Mrs David Harris of Kaniva and Mrs Abraham Gershon of London. Esther (age 22) married Philip Hecksher (age 40) in 1884. Alfred (age 21) married Rosetta Solomon (age 18) in 1875 and Lucy married David Harris.

Victorian Death Index . Research by Dr Rodney Eisfelder.

SOLOMON, Lyon (Lion) Henry (Lewis Henry)

b. London, 1809–1884
Free.
Single; 13 children.

A son of Joseph Solomon (q.v.) and his first wife Harriet, 'Lewis' Henry Solomon was initially listed as a farmer at New Norfolk in 1831. In Campbell Town in 1833 he asked the colonial authorities for a carpenter to be assigned to him. There was no answer. Complaining to the government, he wrote: 'I have continually suspended my capital in building and other improvements several of which I have completed. I have, at this time, three buildings in this Township I am anxious to complete'. This time he received the answer: 'No mechanics available'. However, in October and November, convicts were assigned to him. On 21 January 1834 he wrote to the Collector of Internal Revenue wanting a liquor licence for wholesale wine and spirits for his store in Campbell Town. Lion Henry Solomon's name appeared on the 'Loyal Address of the inhabitants of Campbell Town to Sir John Franklin', on 10 March 1837.

Lion Henry Solomon married Fanny (Frances) Symonds at St John's, Launceston, on 26 July 1833. Their three children were Joseph Henry Solomon born Campbell Town 20 July 1834; Edward Solomon born Campbell Town 28 January 1836, died Launceston 26 July 1872; and Harriet Anne Solomon born Campbell Town 10 September 1837, died at Manchester 22 February 1868.

Their other children were Robert Fookes Solomon born 22 August 1839, Henry Lawrence Solomon born 16 April 1841, Margaret Elizabeth Solomon born 26 December 1842, Frank Solomon born 17 September 1844, Mary Frances Watts Solomon born 22 June 1846, Richard John Symmonds Solomon born 20 December 1848, Alice Jane Morgan Solomon born 23 July 1851, William Fookes Solomon born 17 November 1853, and Louis Solomon born 26 January 1860 died 10 June 1861.

Lyon's name appeared on the petition for the release from the Launceston Prison of the debtor Isaac Jacobs (q.v.). This act of mercy ended in disaster when Jacobs assaulted Solomon. In 1844 Lyon Solomon gave £5 to the Launceston Synagogue appeal. In 1845 he donated fifteen shillings to the Sydney Synagogue building appeal, and in 1846 three shillings and sixpence to the Hobart Synagogue.

On 7 February 1849 the *Launceston Examiner* reported that Mr Solomon had to leave home for a short time and that 'a young man', Judah Davis (q.v.), had been placed in charge of his shop. Davis detected the shop assistant, E. A. Watts, stealing articles from the shop and a search warrant was obtained in order to find other stolen articles. In October 1849 Lewis Solomon (q.v.) and Thomas Phillips (Abraham Cohen, q.v.) were both indicted for stealing four pairs of trousers and two waistcoats belonging to Nathan Solomon. Joshua Jacobs was indicted for receiving them. When it came to the trial Nathan Solomon 'cannot identify' the stolen goods, and Lewis Solomon was therefore acquitted while Phillips was remanded because there was another case about a stolen shawl pending. He was later acquitted from that accusation.

'Lyon' Henry Solomon died on 1 May 1884 at the age of seventy-four, and was buried in the same grave as his father in the Church of England Cemetery in Evandale.

One of Henry Solomon's sons was Edward, whose son Albert Edgar Solomon became Premier of Tasmania.

Independent, 9 July 1831, 29 November 1833; Letter 17248, in CSO 1/807, dated 11 June 1835; Dixson Library, ADD 206; *Launceston Examiner*, 29 June 1844, 7 February 1849, 11 October 1849; David F. Solomon, 'From Convict to Colonist: Joseph Solomon of Evandale', in P. Elias and A. Elias (eds), *A Few from Afar*, p. 70f.

SOLOMON, Mark

b. London, 1799–1837
Lady Castlereagh, 1818; Convict; Sentenced to life, London, 1817.
Single; Fruit seller and pugilist; Height: 157 cm; 3 children.

Dark ruddy complexion, brown hair, hazel eyes. Mark Solomon was transported for picking pockets. He was one of a gang of four youths who pushed against a passerby and stole his watch and chain valued at £2 10s. He was chased and caught. Jew. Scar on right corner of upper lip and a few pockmarks on his face. He was sentenced at Middlesex on 9 July 1817.

Solomon arrived in Sydney on 30 April 1818 on the same transport as Vaiben and Emanuel Solomon (qq.v.). The three young men may have been troublesome and Mark Solomon was sent on by himself to Van Diemen's Land, where he worked first as an assigned convict servant in Hobart Town. On 19 December 1818 he was found aboard the brig *Portsea* with intent to escape and was sentenced to twenty-five lashes and three months in the gaol chain gang. Solomon was repeatedly involved in public boxing matches during the next three years of his prison service. On 29 July 1820 he was reprimanded for appearing in a 'pugilistic contest'. On 11 January 1822 he was admonished for being absent from church. On 16 December 1823 he was again involved in a fight. Solomon was listed as a 'general dealer of Elizabeth Street' in 1825 and 1826 in the *Tasmanian Almanac*. On 25 October 1826 illegal weights in his possession (for body-building exercises) were confiscated. On 2 July 1833 he was once again reprimanded after a public boxing match. Solomon had been appointed javelin man to the Sheriff in December 1828 with a salary of £10 per annum and the promise of a pardon at the end of four years. On 7 March 1829 Mark Solomon had obtained a licence to sell liquor and he opened the Imperial Wine Vaults in Elizabeth Street in Hobart Town. Mark Solomon was granted a conditional pardon on 12 September 1832.

On 2 June 1823, at Hobart Town, Mark Solomon had married Catherine Flanagan, aged nineteen, a convict who arrived on the *Mary Anne* (1). They were to have three children, Hannah (born 15 July 1823 and married Aaron Aarons [John

Henry Anderson (q.v.)] in Launceston 1840). Hannah had three children: Sarah Catherine (born 1840), a son (born 1844), Henry Aaron Anderson, and Rachel (born 15 May 1825 and died 22 December 1877). Simon, son of Hannah and Mark, was born 1834 in Hobart Town and died 9 October 1894. Simon married Janet 'Jessie' Grant 23 November 1883.

Mark's first marriage to Catherine was a disaster. In October 1827 Catherine absconded from her husband in favour of John James and was sent to gaol for fourteen days. On 5 August 1828 Catherine Solomon was charged with 'disorderly conduct towards her husband on Saturday night last' and was reprimanded. On 18 April 1833, 'Catherine, wife of Mark Solomon', was admonished for being found in a house of ill repute. On 26 July 1833 Mark Solomon was put on an official bond of good behaviour for threatening to assault and beat his wife. Catherine was buried at Hobart Town on 25 September 1833.

On 13 December 1833 Solomon married a second time: 'On Sunday last, according to the Mosaic law by Mr Manley Emanuel (q.v.), Mr Mark Solomons of Elizabeth Street to Miss Hannah Marks (q.v.) of the New Town Rd. As this was the first ceremony of the kind performed in the colony, it was attended by most of the Children of Israel on this side of the island'. In October 1834, Mrs Mark Solomon of Elizabeth Street gave birth to Simon. A free pardon for Solomon was approved on 6 October 1836.

Mark Solomon died on 25 June 1837. Mark Solomon had been a licensed victualler in partnership with his wife Hannah and ran the King William IV public house in Liverpool Street from 1835. The executors of his estate of £550 were 'my friends' Thomas Lucas, victualler and Benjamin Henry (q.v.), dealer.

OBSP, 1816–17, case 1219, p. 415; Ship Indent 4/4006, p. 43; HO 11/2; CON 13/1; CON 31/38, no. 100; Petition for a Conditional Pardon, CSO 1/611/13954, dated 21 July 1832; CP 409; Free Pardon, 214; *Hobart Town Courier*, 27 September 1833, 20 December 1833, 24 October 1834; *Hobart Town Gazette*, 10 May 1823, 11 May 1827, 10 October 1834.

SOLOMON, Mark (SALMON)

b. 1805

Dunvegan Castle (1), 1830; Convict; Sentenced to 14 years, Warwick, 1829.

Mark Solomon arrived in New South Wales on 30 March 1830. He received a ticket of leave in 1836 and a certificate of freedom on 9 August 1843.

TL 36/1030; CF 43/1271.

SOLOMON, Mark

b. London, 1825–1877

Mermaid, 1827.

The youngest child of Ann and Isaac (Ikey) Solomon (qq.v.), Mark Solomon came to Australia with his mother, on board her convict transport. Mark Solomon married Matilda Miller in Hobart Town on 13 July 1847. He died on 25 January 1877 and was buried in Hobart.

SOLOMON, Mary

Free.

The daughter of Joseph and Harriet Solomon (q.v.), Mary Solomon of Evandale married William Roberts of Hobart Town on 5 November 1835 at Longford.

AOT, Arthur File, vol. 2, pp. 482–3; *Hobart Town Gazette*, 13 November 1835.

SOLOMON, Maurice (Morris)

b. London, 1829–1873
Britomart, 1835; Free.
Single; 7 children.

The son of Samuel and Rebecca Solomon (qq.v.), Maurice Solomon arrived with his mother and seven of his siblings. He married Rebecca Levy on 1 September 1854 at the York Street Synagogue. He died at Bombala in New South Wales on 3 September 1873. Rebecca died in Sydney, aged ninety-eight, on 1 May 1931. One of their children, Mr S. H. Solomon, was the city treasurer of Sydney.

Hebrew Standard, 8 May 1931.

SOLOMON, Michael

b. Canterbury, Kent, 1815–1899
Deveron, 1829; Free; Sentenced to 15 years, Hobart Town, 1847, Colonial Sentence.
Single; Clerk; Height: 180 cm; 5 children.

Michael Solomon was the fifth child of Judah and Esther Solomon (qq.v.). He came to Australia with his uncle, Henry Solomon (q.v.), and Henry's wife Elizabeth, in December 1829. Following his 1847 colonial conviction he was described as being of 'fresh complexion, black hair, brown whiskers, dark hazel eyes, large nose, large mouth and chin'.

In 1835, at the age of twenty, Solomon crossed Bass Strait to settle in Port Phillip at Moode Yalla, Yarra Yarra. He was listed as one of the pastoral pioneers of Port Phillip, holding licences from the Crown at Keilor (1835–41) and Carrum Swamp (1837–42). He worked in partnership with his brother-in-law E. D. Ferguson. Solomon's Ford on the Saltwater River, or Maribyrnong River, was named after Michael Solomon. Michael returned to Hobart Town in order to marry his first cousin Sarah Solomon at the house of her parents, Henry and Elizabeth Solomon, on 6 June 1840. Michael was described as a farmer and Sarah as a minor living with her parents. The 1841 Census of New South Wales listed him at 'Moodi Tallo' in the District of Port Phillip.

By April 1842 Michael Solomon 'of Dandenong' was in financial trouble. Two of his workers had abandoned him and had gone to work for a money lender. They had taken with them a number of sheep in lieu of payment and Solomon tried to pursue his property through the courts. It was too late and he was declared insolvent in June 1842. In the Supreme Court in Melbourne he had claimed that he was indebted 'to a person named Henry Solomon of Van Diemen's Land and had handed over to him 700 sheep, a horse and a dray'. No contract actually existed, as Henry Solomon was in Hobart Town and the sheep were in Victoria. The judge rejected the story about the contract and the assets were sequestered.

Michael returned to Van Diemen's Land and, on 27 January 1843, wrote to the Colonial Secretary asking for a government job. He explained that he had arrived in the colony in 1829 and had worked since then as chief clerk in a mercantile firm of 'the highest respectability'. His application was refused on 20 January 1843. Solomon obviously was out of work. On 27 July 1845 he received twenty votes in a contested election for the position of *shamash* (beadle) of the Hobart Synagogue, and was elected. However, the salary was minuscule and his marriage fell apart.

In late 1846, 'after a long trial', he was convicted of stealing the silver plate from his estranged mother-in-law (who by then had married Simeon Benjamin, q.v.). According to the *Hobart Town Courier* of 23 December 1846: 'a large amount of watches and jewellery was stolen. The thief was Michael Solomon, a near relative of Mrs Benjamin, who had been in charge of Mr Barnett's public house the Rising Sun where he [Solomon] lived'. The police had taken Solomon by surprise and recovered the goods. His penalty was fifteen years transportation. After his father-in-law had bankrupted him and, after he had been convicted of the theft of his mother-in-law's property, a Jewish divorce document or *get* was issued on 29 January 1854. Sarah and Michael were divorced while Michael was a prisoner of the Crown.

Solomon's initial period of probation from 1847 lasted twenty-one months. On 20 September 1848 he was admitted as a prisoner at the Prisoners' Barracks and worked as an assigned servant in Hobart Town. It was noted that he 'gained' fifteen days remission of service for 'extra work' performed on behalf of his assigned 'master', Elias Levy (q.v.), at Oatlands. Solomon received his ticket of leave, in the District of Oatlands, on 22 July 1852. On 14 June 1854 he was fined one shilling for having assaulted Catherine Fields and on 1 August 1854 he was committed for trial for perjury. On 31 October he was sentenced to be severely admonished for 'misconduct in having an unmarried female being with him for criminal purposes'. A conditional pardon was approved on 19 December 1854.

Michael Solomon married a second time, in a Presbyterian Church at Oatlands, on 13 November 1854, to Elizabeth Salmon. He was thirty-eight and she was twenty-one. They had five children: Rosa (born 25 December 1852), Michael (23 April 1855), Joseph Haydn (11 October 1858), Mary Elizabeth (7 June 1861), Albert Henry (20 July 1864, died 16 August 1929). All the children were born in Oatlands, and they were not Jews.

On 13 July 1854 a case involving Solomon was heard ex parte (Ward [1863] 1 NSWLR 874), which questioned the verdict handed down at his trial: 'had no sufficient evidence been given irrespective of hearsay, the writ being granted, eventually on the ground that the conviction disclosed no offence'. On 12 February 1855 Michael Solomon was admonished for being out of the Oatlands District without a pass. He received a free pardon on 8 January 1856. In Finigal on 16 October 1880 Solomon was imprisoned for four months following a trial for 'Larceny'.

In November 1848 'Solomon's Ford' was officially renamed 'Braybrook', which is now a suburb of Melbourne. Michael Solomon died at Mangana, Tasmania, on 30 December 1899.

Deveron Indent, no. 842; *Port Phillip Herald*, 8 September 1840, 26 August 1846; *Hobart Town Courier*, 23 December 1846, *Launceston Examiner*, 9 January 1847; CON 52/7, p. 456; CON 37/3, no. 842; CON 16/3, p. 344; AOT, NS, 829/1.

SOLOMON, Mordecai

b. London, 1800–1883
Hercules II (1), 1825; Convict; Sentenced to life, London, 1824.
Single; Hawker; 9 children.

Fair complexion, flaxen hair. Mordecai Solomon was sentenced on 16 September 1824. His behaviour on board the transport ship was 'middling'. Mordecai was the son of Myer Solomon of London, who had married Gittle Kalisch. Myer was the 'minister of the Western Synagogue' in London. Mordecai Solomon and James Argent had appeared at the Old Bailey in 1817 where they were both found guilty of stealing ten tame rabbits in Whitechapel. They were both aged 17 and both sentenced to six months in prison.

Mordecai Solomon arrived in Sydney on 7 May 1825. Upon arrival, 'Moses Solomon' was sent as an assigned convict servant to Minto. Moses Solomon was listed in the 1828 Census as a convict assigned to a chain gang. No religion was noted. In 1883 his death certificate stated that he had been in the colony sixty-five years, though there was no 'M. Solomon' in the colony in 1818. ('Moses' Solomon of the 1828 Census seems to be the only likely candidate!) In 1835 Mordecai Solomon of Illawarra, 'a small settler', applied to George Moss (q.v.) at the Sydney Synagogue for permission from the president of the Synagogue, J. B. Montefiore (q.v.), to marry Elizabeth Haines (q.v.). Elizabeth had come out on the *David Scott* as an immigrant, paying £5 for her passage, and Mordecai went down to the ship to carry her away.

Their first three children, Sarah (1836), Myer (1837), and Jane (1838), were born in the Illawarra District. Vaiben (1839) and Henry (1840) were born in Sydney, followed by Ellen (1842), and Joseph (1844). Two other children, Lewis (1848) and an unnamed girl, died in infancy. Their son Henry subsequently took on an active leadership role in the life of the Sydney Jewish community.

Mrs Elizabeth Solomon 'a modest and sweet woman' died on 3 November 1852 aged 43 leaving eight children 'to deplore their loss'. She was buried at Haslam's Creek (Rookwood). Mordecai lived with his daughter at Eglington, Glebe

Point, where he died at the age of eighty-three. He was buried at Rookwood on 11 March 1883.

Ship Indent 4/4009a, p. 197. *Sydney Morning Herald,* 3 November, 1852.

SOLOMON, Morris

Free.
3 children.

Morris Solomon rented seat no. 64 in the Hobart Synagogue. His name was crossed out on an amended list. 'M.Solomon' was messenger of the synagogue in 1845 and paid £15. Morris Solomon and Theresa Solomon registered their three children, all born in Sydney, as 'Hebrew'. They were Henry (1850), Rebecca (1853), and Fanny (1855).

SOLOMON, Moses

b. London, 1801
Hercules II (1), 1825; Convict; Sentenced to life, Old Bailey, 1824.
Single; Hawker; Height: 180 cm.

Fair complexion, blue eyes, flaxen hair. Upper eyelids swelled. 'Very well behaved' on board the convict transport ship. Moses Solomon was sentenced on 16 September 1824 and transported for violently assaulting a man and his wife in Petticoat Lane and then attempting to rob them.

Moses Solomon arrived in Sydney on 7 May 1825 and was initially sent to be the assigned convict servant to Mr Wood of Minto. He was listed in the 1828 Census as a member of the Parramatta Iron Gang. On 1 February 1828 the Sydney police report of prisoners stated that Moses Solomon was a runaway from the Five Mile Station. He was placed on the treadmill for twenty-eight days. At the end of that period, on 28 February, Solomon was 'bound over' for 'having abused a Serjeant on duty'. He was judged to be 'incorrigible' at the Sydney General Sessions in January 1829 after he escaped from his chain gang, and sent to the prison settlement at Moreton Bay for 1829–31.

On 2 April 1830 an official complaint was lodged with the Colonial Secretary by the police when Solomon, who was a member of the Botany Bay Road Party, refused to obey the orders of an Assistant Surveyor of Roads. The matter was brought to court. Solomon seems to have learned his lesson and on 17 August 1831 the Principal Superintendent of Convicts asked the Colonial Secretary to permit him to 'sleep out of Barracks, his duty requiring that he should be employed until a late hour at night'.

In July 1832 Solomon Moses was assigned to work for Emanuel Phillips (q.v.) as a hawker. This employment abruptly concluded when Solomon was convicted at Sydney on 24 May 1833 for receiving stolen jewellery (in company with Lewis

Lazarus [q.v.], who was acquitted). Solomon was sentenced to fourteen years colonial transportation and sent to Norfolk Island.

Moses Solomon was rewarded for his part 'in the rescue of crew and passengers of the Schooner *Friendship* that was wrecked off the coast of Norfolk Island'. A ticket of leave was granted in 1843. In 1845 he was permitted to travel between Berrima and the Murrumbidgee with a bullock team belonging to George Merryman. In 1846 this permission was repeated, but as a drover in the service of Hyam Phillips (q.v.). A conditional pardon was granted to Solomon for the District of Berrima on 10 July 1848.

OBSP, 1823–24, case 1450, p. 535; CO 207/2, p. 197; Passport Register 4/4528, 45/660; CS 1829, 4/3828, p. 302; *Sydney Gazette*, 28 May 1833; Chronological Register of Convicts at Moreton Bay, no. 1719, *Phoenix* (hulk) Return, 4/4534; Principal Superintendent of Convicts, 4/2114, 31/6434; CS 4/3687, 39/847; TL 43/2050; CP 48/2050.

SOLOMON, Moses

b. London, 1809
Australia, 1828; Free.
Single; Dealer.

The second eldest child of Isaac (Ikey) Solomon and Ann Solomon (qq.v.), Moses Solomon and his brother, John Solomon (q.v.), sailed to Sydney in anticipation of their mother's arrival on a convict transport ship. Ann Solomon and her younger children were sent to Van Diemen's Land on the *Mermaid*. The brothers then wrote a joint petition, on 26 September 1828, asking for permission to bring their mother to New South Wales. Their request was refused and the two young men sailed from Sydney bound to Hobart Town on the same ship that had been used to send Ann Solomon out from England.

In 1829 John and Moses Solomon took legal steps to prevent their father being deported to England from Van Diemen's Land, hiring Joseph Tice Gellibrand to question the decree and invoke a writ of Habeas Corpus before the Chief Justice. The matter was finally decided by the Judge and the Lieutenant Governor after months of legal wrangling.

Moses Solomon married Frances Godwin (a widow) at St David's Church in the Parish of Hobart Town on 15 December 1830 and left for Sydney. He owned the publican's licence for the hotel Steam Packet on Windmill Street in Sydney on 1 August 1831. On 6 October 1845 Moses Solomon advertised in the *Sydney Morning Herald*, describing himself as 'Late of the Australian Hotel', Queens Wharf, Sydney, and of the Ship Inn, Liverpool, and announcing the opening of 'spacious premises, late the City Auction Mart, a few doors north of Hunter Street in George Street', and the 'Albion Inn and Hotel'. He invited the public to view his 'splendid and first rate commercial saloon which is fitted up in the English style. There is a private entrance to it for the accommodation of parties who may require to transact business'.

Petition 28/1647, in 4/1993, on 28 September 1828; CSO 1/295/7163, p. 161; *Sydney Monitor*, 25 September 1830, 12 February 1831; *Sydney (Morning) Herald*, 1 August 1831, 6 October 1845; CS Reports of Vessels Arrived 1830, 4/5201; *Hobart Town Gazette*, 13 April 1842.

SOLOMON, Moses

Harlequin, 1830; Free.
Married; Dealer.

Moses Solomon arrived in Van Diemen's Land on 4 March 1830. According to the *Hobart Town Gazette* of 13 April 1832: 'J. Parker and M. Solomons beg to inform the public that they have removed to the house in Elizabeth Street where they sell a choice selection of groceries'. Moses Solomon was recorded as arriving in Sydney in January 1831 from Hobart Town on the *Elizabeth* after eighteen months in Hobart Town, where he had worked as a boot- and shoemaker. He was accompanied by his wife, Mrs F. Solomon, and they travelled cabin class. He wrote that he hoped to open a shop in Sydney.

Moses Solomon worked as a publican in Sydney, first of the Britten's Hotel in George Street (1831–34), then the Stone Mason's Arms, Elizabeth Street, in 1837, the Steam Packet Hotel in Windmill Street in 1839, and the Ship Inn in Liverpool Street. His home, during all this time, appears to have been in George Street.

In August 1839 he was listed as an 'Innkeeper' of Liverpool, living in George Street. Solomon's assigned servant groom was withdrawn from his service when Solomon neglected to appear before the Bench to answer charges made against him by the prisoners, who said he had not given them rations and had punished them without legal authority.

'Moss Solomon', a slop seller at 277 George Street, was listed in *Low's Directory of the City and District of Sydney*, 1847.

CS Letters Received 1839, Police, 4/2466.1, 38/8559, in 4/5201; *Sydney Gazette*, 15 January 1833, 1 February 1834, 5 January 1837; *Sydney Monitor*, 12 February 1831, 7 April 1832.

SOLOMON, Moses (William)

b. London, d. 1869
Free.
2 children.

Moses Solomon changed his first name to William and moved to Western Australia, where he worked at the Custom's Office. He married Eliza (1813–1867). William Solomon died on 26 September 1869. Eliza had died on 28 March 1867.

Inquirer (WA), 29 September 1869, p. 2.

SOLOMON, Moss

b. London, 1796–1849
Alfred, 1841; Free.
Married; Dealer; 9 children.

Moss Solomon was the eldest son of Samuel Moss Solomon (q.v.) and Elizabeth (née Moses). Moss Solomon married twice. The children of Moss Solomon and

Betsy (née Myers) were Judah Moss (born 1818) (q.v.), Isabella (Solomon) (1820) (q.v.), Julia (Keesing) (1828) (q.v.), Rosetta (Daniels) (1829), and Leah (Marks) (1830) (q.v.). The children of Moss Solomon and his second wife, Leah (née Myers, Betsy's sister) (q.v.), were Samuel Moss (1835), Philip (1836) (q.v.), Kate (Salom) (1837), and Elias (1839) (q.v.).

Moss and Leah Solomon arrived in Sydney on 19 January 1841. They paid for their own passage. Accompanying them were some members of their family, including daughters Isabella and Kate and sons Samuel Moss and Philip. On 3 March 1841 the family sailed from Sydney to Adelaide by the brig *Dorset*, a ship owned by Vaiben and Emanuel Solomon (qq.v.) (who were the younger brothers of Moss). South Australia was in the middle of an economic depression and the family quickly travelled back to Sydney. When Moss died in Sydney on 4 February 1849, Leah Solomon and her family returned to Adelaide. Leah died at her home at North Terrace, Adelaide, at the age of sixty-four, 'the beloved mother of Mr Elias Solomon, Fremantle', and 'Mother of Mrs Salom, stepmother of Judah Moss Solomon and mother of Mrs John Daniels of North Adelaide'.

South Australian Advertiser, 5 January 1871.

SOLOMON, Moss Judah

b. Brisbane, 1843–1932
1 child.

The son of Judah Moss Solomon (q.v.) and Rachel Solomon (Rachael Cohen, q.v.), Moss Judah Solomon was born in Brisbane on 15 June 1843. He was the third free European child to be born in Brisbane. He was taken to Adelaide at the age of three.

At the age of seventeen he became an auctioneer in his father's business in Sydney. Moss Judah Solomon married twice. His first wife was Anna Benjamin, his first cousin once removed. His second marriage was to Fanny Bennet at the home of J. Daniels, North Adelaide. He went to the Northern Territory and opened auction rooms in Darwin in 1873. Solomon became a member of the first district council established in the Northern Territory. The federal electorate of Solomon in the Northern Territory is named for M. J. Solomon. He returned to Adelaide as an auctioneer and a trader in sugar and merchandise. He was president of the Adelaide Hebrew Congregation in 1870 and held that office in the congregation for a period of thirty-five years. He died in Adelaide in 1932. Fanny Solomon died on 7 June 1927.

Moss Judah Solomon and Anna (Benjamin) had a son, Ernest Philip Solomon, on 12 October 1872.

H. Munz, *Jews in South Australia*, p. 79f.

SOLOMON, Nathaniel

Free.
Married; 12 children.

Nathaniel Solomon appeared in the first voters' list in Sydney on 15 September 1842, with a shop and dwelling in George Street. His wife's name was Eva (q.v.).

SOLOMON, Philip

b. Southampton, 1814–1857
Craigevar, 1830; Free.
Single; Dealer; 7 children.

Philip Solomon was the son of a Navy Agent, David Solomon, of Southampton. Philip arrived on 21 December 1830 on the same ship as the 'Rev. I. Levy Jew Priest', in reality Aaron Levy (q.v.). Described as a 'settler', he was aged sixteen and travelled steerage. Solomon married Jane Benjamin, the daughter of Raphael Benjamin (q.v.), on 25 November 1840. The ceremony took place at the Bridge Street Synagogue in Sydney and Jacob Isaacs (q.v.) officiated. Philip Solomon was a committee member of the Sydney Synagogue in 1839 and gave £25 to the new York Street Synagogue building fund. Philip Solomon was listed as a voter in September 1842 with a shop and dwelling in George Street. He was a seat holder at the York Street Synagogue in 1845.

Solomon moved briefly to live at Market Place, Berrima. On 20 April 1840 he served as a juryman at the Berrima Assizes and, on 10 July 1841, gave £1 to help build a new church at West Bargo. On 22 August 1841 a son, Henry, was born in Berrima. Solomon signed a petition in Berrima asking that William Sherwin be made a Justice of Peace. On 9 March 1843 the *Sydney Morning Herald* reported that Philip Solomon had 'removed from Victoria Inn, Berrima, to become the licensee of the Elephant and Castle in King Street Sydney'.

In 1844 a daughter, Julia, was born in Sydney. In November 1844 Solomon was reported to be insolvent. His bankruptcy papers attest that the hotel had lost £8 or £9 each week. The family was arrested as they tried to leave the colony. Jane had been detained on board the *Thomas Lowy* with her eldest brother Samuel Benjamin. Jane said: 'It was dark. I went to board it [the ship] with my eldest brother Samuel Benjamin. He took my baby's cloak to my mother who had lent it to me'.

The *Sydney Morning Herald* reported, on 17 January 1845, that there had been a third meeting of creditors concerning the insolvency of Philip Solomon. On 29 January 1845 the same newspaper reported that he had been tried at the Supreme Court for trying to abscond to England after leaving his shop at Brickfield's Hill without paying £9 15s for goods he had purchased. The only assets he had left were three rings and twenty-one bed sheets. A jury sentenced him to twelve months imprisonment. The Supreme Court reserved judgment and the Chief Justice recommended a pardon.

On 7 July 1845 the *Sydney Morning Herald* noted that Solomon had commenced business in Solomon's Temple, at the corner of Clarence and Erskine streets, where he occupied newly erected premises. In that same week, Judah Moss Solomon (q.v.), 'late of Moreton Bay', took over premises in George Street opposite the police station as auctioneer and dealer. In that year 'P. Solomon' of Clarence Street in Sydney gave £10 to the York Street Synagogue at the time of its dedication.

The birth register of New South Wales lists the following children of Philip and Jane Solomon: Julia (born 1839), Henry (1841), David (1846), Joseph, Rebecca, Rachel and Phillipa. The Solomons went to California at the time of the gold rush in 1848, returning to Australia in 1851, when Solomon set up a general store in Maryborough, Victoria, with John Levy (q.v.). Philip Solomon died on 27 January 1857, aged forty-three, and was buried at the Melbourne General Cemetery. Jane Solomon died at Hawthorn in Melbourne on 30 October 1899.

Petition 4/2578.1; Ship Indent 4/5201; *Sydney Morning Herald*, 10 March 1843, 12 November 1844, 17 January 1845, 7 July 1845; *Australasian Chronicle*, 9 March 1843; The Family History of Dr Harry Shannon of Melbourne (typescript, 1976); Audrey van Hattem, *Time Was*, privately printed, Perth, 1998.

SOLOMON, Philip Moss

b. London, 1836–1917
1841; Free.
Single.

The son of Moss Solomon (q.v.) and Leah (née Myers) (q.v.), Philip arrived in Sydney with his parents and siblings on 19 January 1841. He married Julia Benjamin on 20 February 1867. He died in 1917.

SOLOMON, Phillip

b. London
Free.
Married; Dealer; 12 children.

Phillip Solomon and Sarah Phillips married in Sydney in July 1833—the third Jewish wedding to be registered by the Sydney Synagogue. They had a daughter, Elizabeth who was registered as a 'Hebrew' in Sydney in 1834. Their other children were: Rosetta (born 1835), Philip C. (1836), Frederick (1838), Caroline (1841), Anne (1842-died in infancy), Samuel (1844), Sarah (1845), Saul and Susannah (1846), Esther Queen (9 February 1849, in London), and Francis (23 December 1851, in Adelaide).

SOLOMON, Phillipa

Victoria, 1849; Free.
Married.

Phillipa was the wife of John Solomon (q.v.), an assisted migrant.

SOLOMON, Phoebe

b. 1827
Free.
Single.

Phoebe Solomon, aged nineteen, married Gaucher Burton Nathan (q.v.), aged twenty-nine, at Launceston on 17 June 1846.

SOLOMON, Rachael (vide: Rachael Barnett)

b. ca 1807, Sheerness
1839, Free

SOLOMON, Rebecca (née MOSS)

b. London, 1788–1864
Britomart, 1835; Free.
Married; 10 children.

Rebecca was the daughter of Michael and Elizabeth Moss. She married Samuel Solomon (q.v.) in 1814. Samuel Solomon was transported to New South Wales as a convict on the *Mangles* in 1833 for receiving stolen goods. Rebecca Solomon arrived on 1 February 1835 with nine children. The ship on which she and her children sailed was owned by Joseph Barrow Montefiore (q.v.), who supported her when she petitioned the Governor on 3 September 1835 to have her husband assigned to her. He was an assigned convict working in Port Macquarie for Major Innes JP.

> The Memorialist having always depended on the Industry of her husband for the support for herself and family consequently became embarrassed and ultimately destitute the knowledge of her forlorn situation induced several Philanthropic Individuals from compassion for her distress and being well acquainted with the circumstances of the case with which her husband was convicted to provide her with the means of paying her passage with her offspring with the expectation that the authorities here would permit him to labour for their wants … but her disappointment in that anticipation in accumulation her miseries has again thrust her upon the Benevolent persons who knew her character and family in England.

Major Innes testified: 'The husband was a forger and now is a cook and labourer. Conduct very good. I have no objection'. J. Barrow Montefiore testified that Rebecca was 'very industrious and respected'. The Colonial Secretary disagreed with the benevolent Major Innes. He wrote that Samuel Solomon had only been in the colony for two years and that the request could not be complied with, 'as it would amount to an exercise of indulgence before the legal period of probation' was over.

By 1836 Rebecca's husband was living in Sydney and had a shop there. The large Solomon family would become pioneers in 'Jews' Flat', near Cooma. Rebecca died on 24 March 1864 at Bathurst in New South Wales. Her children were: Henry (Harry) (born 1816) (q.v.), Elizabeth (1820) (q.v.), Samuel (1822) (Solomon Solomon, q.v.), Emma (q.v.) (1824), Julia (1826) (q.v.), Anna (1828), Morrice (1829) (Maurice Solomon, q.v.), Rosetta (1831), Charles (1833) (q.v.), and Sarah (1836), who was born in Sydney.

Rebecca Solomon, aged seventy-six, was buried in the Devonshire Street Jewish Cemetery, on 22 August 1864 and relocated to Rookwood cemetery in 1901

Petition in 4/2296, 35/7189, 3 September 1835.

SOLOMON, Rebecca

b. Sheerness, 1818–1874
Palambam, 1832; Free.
Single; 7 children.

The sixth child of Judah and Esther Solomon (qq.v.), Rebecca came out to Van Diemen's Land with her mother Esther and sister Sarah (q.v.). At the age of twenty-one she married the 26-year-old ship owner James Cook at Trinity Church in Hobart Town on 4 March 1839. Rebecca died in Bathurst (New South Wales) on 24 March 1874. She had seven children: Francis Wrentmore (born 14 May 1840), Esther (1 December 1841), Louisa Ann (6 October 1843), James (24 March 1845), Alice (28 April 1847), Walter (19 September 1848), and Emily (28 September 1850).

SOLOMON, Reuben

1827; Free.
Married; 9 children.

In 1827 Reuben and Sarah Solomon the newly-arrived settlers of Sydney, had a child who was named David, and whom they registered as a 'Hebrew'. Their other children were: Joseph (born 1830), Samuel (1831), Abraham (1832), Elizabeth (1833), Saul (1834), Moses (1837), Emanuel (1839) and an unnamed male child who was born in 1842.

SOLOMON, Reuben

b. London, 1804
Georgiana I (2), 1831; Convict; Sentenced to 14 years, Middlesex, 1830.
Single; Tailor; Height: 153 cm.

Reuben Solomon was convicted for stealing clothes on 9 December 1830. He had served a previous four-year sentence for the same offence. He had a ruddy, fair complexion, freckled, light brown hair, hazel/grey eyes. He could read and write. 'Jew.'

Reuben Solomon arrived in New South Wales on 27 July 1831 and was sent to the Hyde Park Barracks for one month. His initial assignment in 1831 was to Mr George Trevellyn, and then to Chief Justice Forbes at the Hunter Valley.

He received his ticket of leave in 1839 and a conditional pardon in 1842. On 12 July 1855 he stood trial at the Quarter Sessions at Bathurst, and was sentenced to five years labour on the roads.

Prisoner no. 1213-112, Indent list; TL 39/2409; CP 42/99.

SOLOMON, Rosetta

b. London, 1829–1861
1841; Free.
Single.

Rosetta Solomon arrived in Sydney on 19 January 1841 with her father, Moss Solomon (q.v.), and stepmother, Leah Solomon (q.v.). She married 'Mr' Daniels on 8 February 1854. She died in Adelaide on 23 April 1861.

SOLOMON, S. (Covety Solomon)

1788–1848
Convict.

'Covety' Solomon died, aged sixty, on 18 February 1848 and was buried in the Devonshire Street Jewish Cemetery in Sydney.

York Street Burial Register.

SOLOMON, Samuel (SOLOMONS)

b. Essex, 1774–1857
Mangles (6), 1833; Convict; Sentenced to life, Old Bailey, 1832.
Married; Umbrella-maker and salesman; Height: 163 cm; 8 children.

Dark, sallow complexion, black hair, dark chestnut eyes. A Jew. Whiskers joining under chin and turning grey. Lost one front tooth in his upper jaw. He could read and write. Samuel Solomon was the son of Moses Solomon of London, and a cousin of Mrs (Jacob) Josephson (Emma Josephson, q.v.).

Samuel was convicted at the Old Bailey on 6 September 1832 of stealing a bracket clock, valued at 10 shillings, and other household goods from a coffee house in Cornhill. In his own defence Solomon said: 'I am quite innocent of knowing it to be stolen. I bought it off Brown and it was in pawn at Mr Walter's in Aldersgate Street'. He told the court that he had eight children and that he had lived in the East End for twenty years. He was known as 'Honest Samuel or the Honest Jew'. Nine witnesses were brought in to the Old Bailey in order to testify to his good character. His age was given as fifty.

Samuel Solomon was initially placed on the *Phoenix* hulk on arrival in Sydney, being admitted on 7 May 1833, and then sent to the Hyde Park Barracks. On 3 September 1835 he was sent on to Port Macquarie. His behaviour had been 'good'.

On 3 September 1835 Rebecca Solomon (née Moss) (q.v.), who had arrived on the *Britomart*, petitioned the Governor on behalf of her husband, asking that he be assigned to her. He was a prisoner serving a life sentence. He had been an umbrella-maker and claimed to be a cook. He was assigned to Major Innes JP at Port Macquarie and was a 'special' there. She had nine children and had come free on the *Britomart* in February 1835. She had believed that her husband would be assigned to her when she arrived, and now found herself destitute: 'Her miseries have again thrown her upon the hands of benevolent persons who knew her character and her family in England previous to the disastrous circumstance'. Major Innes testified that Solomon's behaviour had been 'very good'. Joseph B. Montefiore (q.v.) asked, on her behalf, that Samuel be assigned to her because Rebecca was in need of help, 'her children being of too tender an age to contribute in any way towards their subsistence'. Montefiore added: 'I believe him [Samuel] to be a very industrious and respectable man'. Governor Bourke replied that Solomon would have to comply with the law, and that he had only served two years.

Several of Solomon's children settled at 'Reid's' or 'Reed's Flats', which was later named Bunyan, and was eight kilometres from the site of Cooma. The presence of the Solomon and Shannon families meant that the locals called the tiny settlement 'Jews' Flat'. Samuel Solomon bought the hotel the Squatters' Arms, established by Abraham Moses (q.v.), and developed a general store beside the public house that was managed by Samuel's son, Harry Solomon (Henry Solomon, q.v.). Solomon continued in business at Jews' Flat until September 1854, when the properties were transferred to his son Maurice (Morrice) Solomon (q.v.). Solomon moved to Sydney, but held an auctioneer's licence for the District of Cooma until 1858.

Solomon's children were Henry (Harry) (1816), who came to Australia after the rest of the family, Elizabeth (1820) (q.v.), Solomon (called Saul on the ship's indent) (1822) (q.v.), Emma (1824) (q.v.), Julia (1826) (q.v.), Anna (1828), Maurice (Morrice) (1829), Rosetta (1831) (q.v.), Charles (1833) (q.v.), and Sarah (1836), who was born in Sydney.

Samuel Solomon was buried by the Sydney Synagogue on 24 October 1857, at the age of eighty-two. Rebecca died on 21 August 1864. Authorisation for the removal of their graves to Rookwood was given by George J. Cohen of 10 Spring Street, Sydney.

OBSP, 1830–31, case 1824, pp. 758–9; *Phoenix* (hulk) Entrance Book 4/6282, no. 370; Petition 35/7189, 3 September 1835; Governors' Despatches, 30 August 1843, A1293-4/5208, p. 154; *Sydney Times*, 17 September 1836; HO 10/53; family research by Dinah Harvey, Sydney.

SOLOMON, Samuel

b. Sheerness, 1776–1864
Free.
Married; 1 child.

Samuel was the brother of Judah Solomon (q.v.), Joseph Solomon (q.v.), Henry (q.v.) and Isaac Solomon, and the father of Joseph ('Johnny') (q.v.), who was a pioneer settler of Melbourne. Samuel Solomon was buried by the Hobart Synagogue on 9 March 1864 at the age of eighty-eight.

SOLOMON, Samuel

b. Norwich, 1784
Admiral Gambier (2), 1811; Convict; Sentenced to 14 years, Old Bailey, 1810.
Single; Height: 152 cm; 1 child.

Samuel Solomon was a pickpocket who stole a watch (valued at £6) from a passerby at the New Inn, Shoreditch: 'He snatched the watch out of my fob'. Solomon was caught after a scuffle. He claimed, in his own defence, that he was 'very much in liquor'. He was initially sentenced at the Old Bailey on 11 April 1810 to transportation for life. He had brown hair, sallow complexion and light hazel eyes.

Samuel Solomon arrived in New South Wales in September 1811 and was soon sent on to Van Diemen's Land on the *Ruby*, arriving on 19 February 1812. By 2 October 1813 he appeared in the records of Van Diemen's Land when he was convicted of being drunk and disorderly and was placed in the gaol road gang. On 8 March 1814 he was sentenced to 100 lashes for breaking the doors and windows of Mrs Winch's house. Over the next ten years Solomon was punished twelve times for offences involving drunkenness, insolence and verbal abuse. As a consequence it was recorded that he received 225 lashes, several months in irons and a period sitting in the stocks. His police record ended on 30 March 1824 when he was sentenced, once again, to 100 lashes for 'abusing Constables Marr and B. Trainer on Saturday last and endeavoured to cause a Mob to assemble round them when taking Maurice Healey a runaway convict'. Solomon was returned to the Hobart Town Prisoners' Barracks for a month.

With his sentence due to expire, he was eventually handed his certificate of freedom on 9 December 1824. However, Samuel Solomon could not wait to leave the gaol and on 13 April 1824 he had appeared before the magistrates for having been absent from prison for several days. Solomon produced his piece of paper bearing the appropriate date and he was asked to find two sureties for himself before he was allowed to go free and return to New South Wales. In Sydney, Samuel and Elizabeth Solomon brought their son Benjamin to St Philip's to be baptised on 31 October 1825. Solomon appeared in the 1828 Census as a shoemaker working and living in Cambridge Street, Sydney. A second certificate of freedom was issued on 1 March 1830.

OBSP, 1810, case 168, p. 293 (the Old Bailey record gives his birth date as 1782; the 1828 Census indicates that he was born in 1784; and his certificate of freedom has a birth date of 1790); CF 4/4423; CON 31/38 S, no. 17; TL 13/2962; CF 30/86, in 4/4300 (there is a second CF, numbered 013/2962); *Hobart Town Gazette*, 16 April 1824, 23 April 1824.

SOLOMON, Samuel

b. Sheerness, 1799–1827
Prince Regent, 1827; Convict; Sentenced to 14 years, London, 1827.
Single; Silversmith; Height: 174 cm.

Dark sallow complexion, dark brown hair, brown eyes. Two marks on chin and small mark on left cheek. Could read and write. Jew. Samuel Solomon was transported for dealing in stolen goods. He was sentenced on 5 April 1827.

Samuel Solomon arrived in Sydney on 27 September 1827 and was assigned to the General Surveyor's Road Party. Solomon died on 8 December 1827, described by the authorities as a 'Jeweller aged twenty-eight', and was buried by St James' Church.

Ship Indent 4/4012, p. 217.

SOLOMON, Samuel Moss

b. London, 1770–1842
Enchantress, 1833; Free.
Married; Pencil Maker; 13 children.

The son of Moss Solomon and Julia (née Moses) of 30 Wentworth Street, Spitalfields, in East London, Samuel Moss Solomon married twice. His first wife was Elizabeth (Betsy) (née Moses), who was born on 30 October 1775 in London and who had eleven children, and his second wife, Esther (née Davis) (q.v.), who was born in 1775, and had two children. The children of the first marriage with links to Australia were Moss (q.v.), Vaiben (q.v.), Susan (who married Moses Benjamin, q.v.), Emanuel (q.v.), Hannah (Cohen) (q.v.), Sarah (Joshua, q.v.), Esther (who married Israel Myers, q.v.) and Phillip (q.v.). The children of the second marriage were Isaac (q.v.) and Elizabeth (who married Michael Cashmore) (q.v.).

Samuel Moss Solomon had invented the technique of manufacturing lead pencils. In Spitalfields in London he was known as 'Shlomo the pencil maker'. Arriving in Australia on 24 April 1833, he established an auction room in George Street. It was, according to J. M. Forde, not a large business. He came from England bearing a high rank in English Freemasonry and his Masonic apron is still preserved by the Grand Lodge in Adelaide. He served in the first Sydney Synagogue committee in July 1839 and gave £35 to the appeal for the new synagogue building in 1839. He stood for election to the synagogue's committee in September 1840. He was a seat holder in the Sydney Synagogue. He died, aged seventy-two, on 13 May 1842, and was buried at the Devonshire Street Jewish Cemetery in Sydney. His wife Esther had been born in Hammersmith on 1 January 1793, and died in Adelaide on 13 July 1875.

According to family tradition, the money that enabled the very large, multigenerational emigration of the Solomon family to Australia by the *Enchantress* came about through an inheritance of £1000 from the estate of a disowned son of Samuel Moss Solomon. After Vaiben and Emanuel Solomon were transported, this brother of the two convicts went to Jamaica, where he married a local woman and was cut off by the family. One Sunday afternoon, a carriage drew up at the family home in Spitalfields with a West Indian black woman, accompanied by her solicitor, bearing a cheque, which the family accepted.

Ship Indent 4/5204; Charles H. Bertie, *Old Sydney by Old Chum* [J. M. Forde], vol. 1; Trevor Cohen, 'The Honourable Vaiben Louis Solomon', *AJJHS*, vol. 8, no. 3 (1977), p. 98.

SOLOMON, Sarah

b. Sheerness
Ann, 1833; Free.
Married; 1 child.

Sarah Solomon, the wife of John Solomon (q.v.), arrived together with her son Israel (q.v.) and daughter-in-law Sarah (q.v.).

SOLOMON, Sarah

b. London, 1812
Ann, 1833; Free.
Married; 8 children.

The wife of Israel Solomon (q.v.), Sarah's children were Georgiana (1833), Rebecca (1835), Sarah (1838), Mary (1840), Leah (1842), Rosetta (1844), Eve (1846), and Rachael (1849).

SOLOMON, Sarah

b. Sheerness, 1819–1875
Free. Single.

Sarah was the youngest of the four children of Joseph Solomon (q.v.) of Evandale. On 4 January 1838 Sarah married Benjamin Walford (q.v.), the son of Barnard (Benjamin) Walford (q.v.), in Launceston. Sarah's father was dismayed that she had chosen to marry a man who regarded himself as Jewish even though the congregation in Hobart Town would not accept his status. Joseph Solomon gave his reluctant written consent to the marriage on 4 January 1838.

Walford had written to the government asking that the posting of banns be dispensed with:

> 'I request you will be pleased to forward me a licence for marriage with publication of Banns between Miss Sarah Solomon of Evandale and myself by the Rev. William H. Browne according to the rites and ceremonies of the United Church of England and Ireland.
>
> Signed Benjamin Walford. I am 21 free and unmarried.'

CSO 74/1, p. 90.

SOLOMON, Sarah

b. Sheerness, 1819–1881
Palambam, 1832; Free.
Single; 12 children.

The seventh and youngest child of Judah Solomon (q.v.) of Hobart Town and Esther (née Levy, Russell) (q.v.), Sarah came to Van Diemen's Land with her mother Esther and sisters Lydia (Benjamin, q.v.) and Rebecca (Barnett, q.v.). Sarah Solomon married her first cousin, Joseph Solomon (q.v.), otherwise known as 'Johnny' or Joseph III, the son of Samuel Solomon (q.v.), on 2 August 1838 in a Christian ceremony at Evandale, where her uncle Joseph Solomon (q.v.) lived. Joseph (Johnny) Solomon was one of the earliest settlers in the Port Phillip district. Sarah and Joseph had twelve children. Confusingly, the firstborn child (1839) was called Joseph; he died in Hobart at the age of fifteen in 1854. The birth places of the children tell the story of the family. Joseph was born in Hobart Town. Henry, born on 12 November 1840, died in Victoria on 6 April 1903. Alfred was born on 18 May 1844, and Charles in 1847 at Maidstone, Victoria. Louisa was born in 1848, and died in Hobart when she was five years old, on 3 September 1853. The other children were: Jessie (31 March 1850), Francis (2 August 1851), Esther (c. 1852, who died in infancy) in Hobart, Arthur (1 May 1854), Frances Elizabeth (1856), Albert Lionel (6 September 1856), and Walter Wilsmore (1859), who was born in Hobart and died at Maidstone on 10 January 1884.

Sarah died on 20 March 1881. Her husband Joseph died in Melbourne on 25 April 1890, aged seventy-one. They were buried in the Church of England section of the Melbourne General Cemetery in Carlton.

David F Solomon, 'From Convict to Colonist: Joseph Solomon of Evandale', in P. Elias and A. Elias (eds), in *A Few from Afar*, p. 69f.

SOLOMON, Sarah

b. London, 1823
Mermaid, 1828; Free.
4 children.

Sarah was the daughter of Ann and Isaac (Ikey) Solomon (qq.v.). She was the fifth child in the family. Her siblings were John (q.v.), Moses (q.v.), Anne (Nancy) (q.v.), David (q.v.), and Mark (q.v.). Sarah was the only child who remained 'loyal' to her father.

She rented a seat at the Hobart Synagogue in 1845, and her address was Norfolk Island Road. She claimed to have been the owner of a cottage in New Town Road from 1829. The raising of the level of the road had reduced the value of the cottage 'considerably', and on 15 July 1841 she asked the government for compensation.

Sarah Solomon married Godfrey Barnett Levy (George Levy, q.v.) 'draper', at her father's home in New Town Road in Hobart Town on 27 January 1847.

Correspondence, 8/2/408, AOT.

SOLOMON, Saul

b. London, 1812
Hooghly (4), 1834; Convict; Sentenced to 7 years, Southwark, 1834.
Single; Height: 175 cm.

Fresh complexion, dark hair, dark brown eyes, stout. Saul Solomon was convicted on the same day for the same crime as Solomon Solomons (q.v.), and was evidently sent out on the same ship. They were convicted of picking pockets.

The *Hooghly* arrived in Sydney on 18 November 1834. By the early 1840s the author of the *Registry of Flash Men* wrote of 'Saul Solomon of Pitt Street that he had the reputation of a thief'. On 7 October 1841 Saul Solomon was indicted for theft and acquitted. However, in August 1843 he was sent from New South Wales to Van Diemen's Land by the *Sir John Byng* with a ten-year sentence for 'stealing from the person'. He had been tried and sentenced at the Sydney Quarter Sessions on 1 August 1843 and arrived in Van Diemen's Land on 1 January 1844. A report in the Colonial Secretary's files reads: 'was originally a convict. Tried October 1841 for picking a pocket in an auction room but was acquitted. Had been in custody on suspicion of stealing—infamous house, dangerous character'.

In a petition from Saul Solomon in Launceston, dated 12 November 1849, it was stated that he had been tried at Sydney on 4 August 1843 and charged with robbing Mr McClachey of Mudgee. He was sentenced to be sent to the Port Arthur Penitentiary. At his trial he told a long story about having walked past Mr Rheuben's (q.v.) public house and discovering a £20 note. He claimed to be 'an injured man'. A witness against Solomon said that Solomon had 'sunk into the abyss of wretched mendacity'.

Prisoners Sent from New South Wales to Van Diemen's Land 4/4523; Sydney Quarter Sessions, 1 August 1843, CS Letters Received, Police Mounted, Recognition Book for 1843, 4/2697, no. 1050; Synagogue Petition, CO 280/157; CS 4/2879.1, 49/11944; CON 22/4, p. 306; *Sydney Morning Herald*, 18 January 1845; *Sydney Gazette*, 7 October 1841.

SOLOMON, Saul

b. 1818 Free.
Single; Dealer.

Solomon's name appeared on the Launceston Synagogue petition of 20 May 1843. On 17 October 1848 Solomon's haberdashery shop called the Red House, in Charles Street, Launceston, caught fire. It was a two-storey wooden building, which was completely destroyed. Solomon was insured and the damage was estimated to be in the vicinity of £2500.

Saul 'Solomons', aged thirty-five, married Julia Myers, aged thirty, in Hobart Town on 30 January 1853.

Sydney Morning Herald, 8 March 1843.

SOLOMON, Saul

b. London, 1818–1887
1843; Free.
Single; 6 children.

The son of Elias Solomon (q.v.) and Fanny (née Simmons), Saul married Elizabeth Murphy at Parramatta in 1847. Their six children were Fanny, Solomon, Nellie, Samuel, Elizabeth (born 1850) and Alice (1854). Saul died in Sydney on 16 January 1887.

SOLOMON, Serone

b. Berlin, 1809
Lady Kennaway (2), 1836; Convict; Sentenced to life, Liverpool, 1836.
Single; Cotton hawker and jeweller; Height: 165 cm.

Fresh ruddy complexion, with brown hair and reddish whiskers, hazel eyes, medium nose and mouth and chin. A Jew. Could read and write. Serone Solomon was sentenced for housebreaking at the Lancaster (Liverpool) Quarter Sessions on 18 June 1836. He had been previously convicted for stealing wearing apparel and money with two accomplices named Conners and Brown.

Solomon arrived in New South Wales on 18 January 1836 and was assigned to Mr D. Brady of Campbelltown. On 4 July 1838 he was sentenced to fifty lashes for giving false information to the police. On 30 November 1838 he received fifty additional lashes for being absent without leave from his prison gang and on 3 April 1839 he arrived at Norfolk Island, having been tried at the Sydney Supreme Court for 'robbery with fire arms', with a second life sentence and the proviso that he was not to be returned to New South Wales.

Solomon's time on Norfolk Island was tragic. On 16 July 1839, for neglect of work, he was given gaol on bread and water for one week. On 26 July, for neglect of work, he received twenty-five lashes. On 12 August, for appearing at muster in soiled clothes, he received three days in gaol on bread and water; on 11 September, for neglect of work, twenty-five lashes. On 18 October, for going to hospital on false pretences, he was sentenced to gaol on bread and water until further orders. On 22 November, for neglect of work, he was given seven days gaol on bread and water, and on 4 December, for neglect of work, twenty-four hours in gaol on bread and water. His name was included in the list of nine Jewish prisoners at Norfolk Island who Captain Maconachie hoped to help by requesting the Sydney Synagogue to send prayer books. On 24 February 1843 Solomon was absent from divine service and disobedient of orders. He was admonished on 28 April and 12 May 1843. Disobedience of orders and neglect of work resulted in one month in irons. One month's additional punishment was given for ovalling (changing the shape of) his irons, and he was admonished for destroying government property on

23 September 1845. For neglect of duty, he received solitary confinement for seven days.

On 26 November 1845 the convicts on Norfolk Island were sent to Van Diemen's Land on the *Lady Franklin*. His initial period of probation was spent in the chain gang at Lymington. On 14 July 1846 he was sentenced to four days solitary confinement for refusing to work. A ticket of leave was issued on 20 March 1849. On 27 March 1852 at Longford he was committed to trial and on 24 April he was found guilty of feloniously receiving a stolen brooch valued at £6. He was not allowed back into assigned service north of Oatlands after serving a sentence of three years hard labour in chains. On 6 May 1852, at Longford, he was sentenced to a further twelve months hard labour in chains for 'having secreted himself on the *Mariposa* with intent to escape'. Following his 'services at a fire' on 16 April 1855 a recommendation for official consideration was recorded on his dossier. On 14 May 1855, while an assigned servant in Hobart Town, Serone Solomon was punished with one month's hard labour for 'misconduct in being in a brothel'. A ticket of leave was reissued on 6 November 1855 and a conditional pardon on 6 May 1856.

'Sarony Solomon' appeared in the ledger of the Hobart Synagogue with a donation of sixteen shillings and sixpence in 1865.

CON 33/71, no. 17061; *Lady Kennaway* Printed Indent, 1836, p. 145, no. 36-2190; List of Prisoners at Norfolk Island, August 1844, ML, COD 2.

SOLOMON, Simon (Solomon SIMONS)

b. London, 1780–1875
Atlas (3), 1816; Convict; Sentenced to life, Old Bailey, 1815.
Single; Watchmaker; Height: 154 cm.

Dark pale complexion, black hair, dark eyes. Simon Solomon was transported to New South Wales on the Atlas (3) and then to Van Diemen's Land by the Kangaroo in 1816. Solomon had a sister who arrived as a convict on the Persian on 6 August 1827. At the Old Bailey, 'Solomon Simons', together with Thomas Smith, picked a pocket 'with violence'. Simons had been in custody before for picking pockets and riotous behaviour on the streets. He was sentenced to death on 10 May 1815 and then had his sentence commuted.

In Sydney on 3 September 1817 Simon Solomon was sentenced to extra labour for 'neglect of duty'. In 1821 and 1822 he was reprimanded no less than seven times for being absent from the muster and church, even though he held a ticket of leave.

A conditional pardon was issued to him on 7 September 1829 and an absolute pardon on 6 September 1836 (as listed in the *Hobart Town Courier*, 23 March 1838).

Simon Solomon, who was 'eighty-three years old, of Fingal', died on 2 October 1875.

CON 31/36; HO 10/1, no. 2; *OBSP*, 1814–15, case 594, p. 272; Ship Indent 4/4005, p. 181; *Hobart Town Gazette*, 18 October 1823; *Hobart Town Courier*, 23 March 1838; CP no. 104; AP no. 181.

SOLOMON, Simon

b. London, 1816
Lady Harewood (3), 1832; Convict; Sentenced to 7 years, Middlesex, 1831.
Single; Hawker; Height: 159 cm.

Ruddy dark complexion, brown hair, grey eyes. Thick nose. Can read. Simon Solomons was convicted for stealing a print, and sentenced on 1 December 1831. His uncle, Joseph Solomon (q.v.), had been sent to Australia in 1820.

The *Lady Harewood* arrived at Port Jackson on 5 August 1832. The name of Simon Solomons was entered in the Newcastle Gaol in 1832 and he was recorded as 'set at large' on 30 November 1838. The 1837 General Return of Convicts in New South Wales listed him as 'Simon Solomons', assigned to Mr William White of Merton. He was sent back to the Hyde Park Barracks to face the bench of magistrates on a charge of 'neglect'. He was sentenced to twenty-five lashes. Solomon was discharged from service 'to be married' on 30 November 1838. (There is no trace of this marriage in the colonial records.) A certificate of freedom was issued to him on 21 May 1839.

Lady Harewood Printed Indent, p. 85, no. 32-1564-91; Newcastle Gaol Entrance Book, 2/2006, no. 950, in 1838; CF 4/4348, 30/0750; Hyde Park Barracks Bench of Magistrates, X707.

SOLOMON, Simon (SOLOMONS) (Solomon SIMONS)

b. Bethnal Green, London, 1799
Morley (1), 1817; Convict; Sentenced to life, Old Bailey, 1816.
Single; Hawker; Height: 176 cm.

Dark complexion, black hair very thin on the top of his head, black eyes. His father, Jacob Solomon, was a hawker, who 'travels the country with hardware', according to his sister Catherine Solomon (q.v.), who arrived in Hobart Town as a convict on the Mermaid in 1828. On 17 May 1816, Simon Solomons and Isaac Jonas (q.v.) attacked and robbed a man who had just been with a prostitute in an alley near the churchyard of St Paul's. The victim chased his assailants, who were caught by three constables. On 29 May 1816 both boys were sentenced to death. The verdict was commuted and they were sent to Australia bracketed together on the same ship.

The convict transport ship *Morley* arrived in New South Wales on 10 April 1817 and Solomons was forwarded to Liverpool for assignment. Simon Solomon was sent to Van Diemen's Land on the *Cockburn* and was assigned to work as a servant to Mr Thornton who, on 7 March 1822, reported to the authorities that he had heard Solomon belligerently threaten to bring together several thousand convicts and rise up in rebellion against the authorities. Simon Solomon was sentenced to spend two months in the Hobart Town gaol gang and to receive fifty lashes. On 25 January 1821 Solomon had married Mary Gould, aged twenty-one. Mary had arrived as a prisoner on 29 August 1820 on the *Morley*. She had been convicted at the Old Bailey to fourteen years transportation for having forged bank notes in her possession. She was a very poor choice for a marriage partner, but they married nevertheless. Solomon had trained as a boxer in England and on 13 September 1822 he was found to have training weights in his possession, which were confiscated. On 25 June 1823 Solomon was reproved for assaulting William Garcia (q.v.) and on 29 April 1824 he was arrested for fighting and returned to the Public Works Department.

On 26 March 1825 Solomon asked for permission to visit New South Wales in order to pursue his boxing career, and then return to Hobart Town. Permission was granted. On 3 January 1827 (in Hobart Town) Mary Solomon was reprimanded for being found carousing at the Ship Inn 'at a late hour'. By 1828 she was 'out all night' and, on 4 May 1829, was judged to be living in a state of adultery. Mary

Solomons acquired a long record, for abusive behaviour, causing a riot, and being drunk.

On 13 April 1826 Solomon was again sentenced to fifty lashes and to be sent to Maria Island. We know that he remained in Hobart Town because, on 16 May 1826, as a result of his wife's complaints, he was bound over to keep the peace towards Mary Johnson and was fined £10. Solomon began to work as the gatekeeper at the Prisoners' Barracks. On 17 July 1826 he was sentenced to twenty-five lashes for allowing Abraham Jacobs (q.v.) to leave the barracks without proper permission and on 3 January 1827 was reprimanded for being absent from his duties at the gate. On 7 January 1829 Solomon was employed by Mrs Dinah Joseph (q.v.), only to be accused of taking from her premises £40 to £50 worth of goods while he was in her service. The informer could not be questioned, 'he being in such a bad state from a beating he had received from Solomon'. Solomon was a constable at the Hobart Town Prisoners' Barracks, but was in Mrs Joseph's service and was in the habit of purchasing goods at sales. The police suggested the accusation had been made to demonstrate that Mrs Joseph was in need of protection and should have her husband, Reuben Joseph (q.v.), assigned to her (*Hobart Town Courier,* 24 January 1829). However, on 28 March 1829, Solomon was found guilty of stealing forty-nine yards of cloth valued at twenty shillings. He was evidently sent back to prison for, on 1 August 1831, he was found at the public house of Barnard Walford (q.v.) while still a member of the hulk chain gang. Two years later, while still in government service, he was sentenced for having insulted an overseer, and on 8 February 1833 he was sent to Port Arthur for twelve months.

Solomon returned to Hobart Town and did his best to keep out of trouble even though, on 23 June 1836, he was reprimanded for drinking alcohol at a public house during divine service. By 1836 he held a ticket of leave. A conditional pardon was granted to him on 11 January 1839 and a free pardon on 6 April 1843. The 1842 Census of Hobart Town listed him as a tenant of 32 Brisbane Street, a shopkeeper, Jewish and married to Mary Smith, whose religion was 'C of E'. He held a hawker's licence, which expired in 1841 and 1843 for lack of payment. On 6 December 1843 Solomon was charged with neglect of duty while attached to the Public Works Department and was sent back to the prison at Port Arthur for a further six months.

CON 31/38, no. 169 S; CON 32/4, p. 322; CON 33/1, no. 109; CSO 1/367/8367; Ship Indent 4/4405; *Hobart Town Courier*, 24 January 1829, 18 January 1839; CP 1943; Free Pardon 31.

SOLOMON, Solomon

b. London, 1816–1901
1833; Free.
Married; Dealer.

Solomon Solomon married Isabella Isaac in London in 1842. She had been born in London on 5 April 1816 and died in Adelaide on 27 March 1901.

Pritchard Index.

SOLOMON, Solomon

b. Bath, Somerset, 1822–1900
Britomart, 1835; Free.
Single; 9 children.

The son of Samuel Solomon (q.v.) and Rebecca Solomon (née Moss) (q.v.), Solomon was erroneously listed on arrival with his mother and siblings as 'Saul'. Solomon married Rachel Abrahams (q.v.) at Sydney on 12 August 1840. Their children were: Lewis (Louis) (born 1842), Philip Charles (1843–1922), Esther (1846–1880), who married Nathan Cohen (q.v.), Michael Cleveland (1848), Rebecca (1850–1922), who married David Moses, Deborah (1853–1942), who married Nathan Cohen, Elizabeth (Bessie) (1855–1937), Samuel (1857–1914), and Caroline (1859–1944), born at Queanbeyan.

Solomon Solomon died at Eden, Twofold Bay, in New South Wales on 12 June 1900.

SOLOMON, Vaiben

b. London, 1798–1860
Lady Castlereagh, 1818; Convict; Sentenced to 7 years, County Durham, 1817.
Single; Pencil-maker; Height: 159 cm; 9 children.

Dark complexion, black hair, dark eyes. Vaiben Solomon was the older brother of Emanuel Solomon (q.v.) and the son of the pencil-maker Samuel Moss Solomon (q.v.) of Wentworth Street, Spitalfields. Vaiben was charged, along with his brother Emanuel, with breaking into a dwelling place (for which they were found not guilty) and with stealing coats and other clothes. They were both sentenced to death, though their sentences were duly commuted to transportation for seven years when they took advantage of an ancient ecclesiastical law allowing people who were able to read Psalm 81 to escape the death penalty. A family tradition relates that Vaiben's first name was originally Solomon, but that he acquired the nickname 'Fabian' from his brother Emanuel, and that name was corrupted to the more Jewish sounding 'Vaiben'. Almost every inhabitant of Wentworth Street, Wentworth Court, and the adjacent Bell Lane was Jewish.

The *Lady Castlereagh* arrived in New South Wales on 30 April 1818 and the Solomon brothers were both immediately sent to Van Diemen's Land. On 2 November 1819 Vaiben was punished with an extra week's work for the government in his own time for 'neglect of duty'. On 20 December 1819 he was found to have been disorderly at church and was sentenced by the magistrate, the Rev. Robert Knopwood, to extra labour for one week. Two days later he was sentenced for neglect of duty and given another week's work in his own time. On 22 May 1820 he was found to have been absent from Divine Service and sentenced to an extra month's work for the government and gaol at night. On 20 June 1820 he was acquitted of a charge of stealing a shirt from Mr Guest. On 28 August 1820 he received twenty-five lashes for being absent from the muster and Sunday service, for which he received twenty-five lashes. On 3 March 1821 Emanuel and Vaiben Solomon were found guilty of stealing the apparel of Mr William Copperwheat and sentenced to be sent to the penal settlement at Newcastle in New South Wales for three years That painful experience brought their career as convicts to an end and in 1824 they were free by servitude and living in Sydney. Vaiben Solomon was issued with a certificate of freedom on 5 August 1824.

On 3 June 1826 Vaiben Solomon married Mary Smith at St Philip's, Sydney. Mary changed her religion and her first name became 'Sarah'. David, born in 1828, the son of Vaiben and Sarah Solomon, was registered by his parents as a 'Hebrew'. In June 1832, when David died, his funeral became the second at the Devonshire Street Jewish Cemetery.

In July 1826 Vaiben applied to the government: 'That Petitioner has a relative David Myers [q.v.], a Prisoner per Ship *Almorah* in the year 1817 for the term of Fourteen Years who is a Watchmaker by Trade, is thirty-six years of age, and has lately arrived from Port Macquarie ... the said David Myers would be of great service to petitioner in Carrying on his business in King Street, Sydney'. The authorities suspected that Myers was not a relative and noted that Vaiben had met Myers at Port Macquarie.

Vaiben was listed as a dealer in George Street in the 1828 Census. His two-month-old son David was also listed. Vaiben and his brother Emanuel operated the Cheap Wholesale and Retail Warehouse at 74 George Street and, in 1833, opened the Australian Wine Vaults in George Street. A 'W. Solomon' was elected to the first committee that was established by a meeting of the Jews of Sydney on 10 September 1833. By 1836 he was working as a tailor and draper at 74 York Street.

Vaiben stood for a position on the committee of the board of management of the Sydney Synagogue in September 1840. He worked as a ship's agent in the 1840s in close partnership with his brother, who by then lived in Adelaide. Their formal partnership was dissolved in Sydney in 1844 but their friendship and business relationship—based on intercolonial trade—flourished.

Vaiben's children after David were Joseph (born 1830), Samuel (1831, who died in infancy), Abraham (1832), Elizabeth (1833), Saul (1834), Moses (1837), Edward Samuel (1839), Charles (1842) and Rosetta (1844).

Vaiben was a member of the Sydney Synagogue committee in 1837 and his family donated £140 to the congregation's building appeal in 1839. In August 1847 Mr Vaiben Solomon of Castlereagh Street refused to answer a summons to serve on a jury because the letter from the sheriff described him as a 'dealer' and not as a 'merchant'. He was fined £10. His honour was worth the price!

Vaiben Solomon died on 20 June 1860 at the age of sixty-one. He was buried at the Devonshire Street cemetery and later his body was transferred to Raphael's Ground.

E. S. Richards, 'The Fall and Rise of the Solomon Brothers', *AJJHS*, vol. 8, no. 2 (1975); Ship Indent 4/4006, p. 34; CS 4/3520, 27 July 1826; Petition, dated 10 July 1826, no. 109, 4/1817; 14/3520, CF 040/2469; 4/1966, letter 28/1369; CON 31/38; *Australian*, 15 July 1834, 26 September 1834, 29 September 1834, 2 June 1835, 28 April

1835, 6 May 1836, 22 October 1839, 6 April 1841, 23 September 1841; *South Australian Gazette*, 26 September 1838, 29 June 1839; *Sydney Gazette*, 12 August 1824, 3 December 1828, 1 April 1830, 11 December 1830, 1 October 1831; *Commercial Journal and Advertiser*, 11 May 1836, 22 June 1836, 3 August 1836.

SOLOMONS, Aaron

b. London, 1779–1866
I'Dire, 1841; Free.
Married; Tailor; 12 children.

The son of Phineas and Rose (née Asher), Aaron Solomons married Rachel Davis (daughter of Joseph Davis) on 29 July 1812 in London at the Great Synagogue. His second marriage was to Frances Asher (born 1803). Aaron Solomons' name is on the Launceston Synagogue petition list of 20 May 1843. The *Launceston Examiner* reported that on 9 February 1844 Aaron 'Solomon' preferred a complaint against Joseph Nathan (q.v.), who came to his shop and uttered threats against him. Nathan was bound over on a bond of £25 for six months. He called for a public meeting to consider founding a fund for the sick and the poor.

'A. & S. Solomons' bought the Launceston Emporium in Charles Street from David Benjamin (q.v.) in September 1846. David Benjamin then moved to Melbourne to join the more successful business managed by his younger brother, Solomon, and, in Launceston, the Solomons soon faced ruin. On 14 March 1849 Aaron Solomons appeared in the Insolvency Court. His creditors included Moses and Nathan (q.v.) of 'Nathan Moses and Co'. Solomon, who had a drapery store, had his furniture removed to the Frances and Pyles auction rooms. Solomon pleaded extreme poverty; he was destitute and his eight children were starving. The creditors refused to leave him any property. In an attempt to save his son from insolvency, Aaron denied that he had been in partnership with Saul who, he said, was answerable for goods worth £300. Saul had a bakery and pastry cook shop in Charles Street, which had been destroyed by fire. Aaron owed Nathan and Moses £500 and had received goods from them worth £400. Twelve months before, Solomons had fallen into difficulty with debts of £1400 and goods worth £800. The creditors had even taken away the baby's cradle.

The children of Aaron and Rachel were Saul (born 1822), and Nathaniel (1825) (q.v.). The children of Aaron and Frances were Phoebe (1826) (q.v.), who married (Isaacar) Bertram Nathan (q.v.), Leah (1832), Abigail (1834), who married Mark Capua in Adelaide on 7 April 1857, Isaac (1839), Louisa (1845), born in Launceston, Henry John, Miriam (1846), Rachael (1849), Joseph, and Sarah.

Aaron Solomons, of 177 Stephen Street, Melbourne, died on 29 June 1866, and was buried in the Jewish section of the Melbourne General Cemetery. Frances Solomons of 62 Russell Street, Melbourne, died on 3 August 1889 and was buried at the Melbourne General Cemetery.

Launceston Examiner, 9 February 1844, 14 May 1845, 17 March 1849; CO 280/157; *Cornwall Chronicle*, 3 October 1846.

SOLOMONS, Abraham

b. London, d. 1792
Albermarle, 1791; Convict; Sentenced to 7 years, Old Bailey, 1791.
Single; Labourer.

Abraham Solomons lived with his father, Isaac Solomons, at Garden Court, Whitechapel. Solomons appeared at the Old Bailey on two charges. He was acquitted on a charge of stealing a parcel from a coach as the witness failed to positively identify the thief. He was convicted for stealing a bundle of laundry from a washerwoman who knew the accused and spoke of having been robbed by 'the Jew boy Solomons'. His father declared at the trial: 'I am the unhappy father of this unfortunate young man. I live in Garden Court, Whitechapel. My chief employment is grafting silk stockings for gentlemen, my son lives with me but, of late, I cannot speak to his guilt or innocence; my wife died in childbed with seven children, he was employed all last summer by me ... I would rather give my voice for sending him abroad; he may make a bright man yet'. Solomons was sentenced on 12 July 1791, having been found guilty of stealing, but not violently.

Abraham Solomons arrived in New South Wales on 13 October 1791. He was buried by St Philip's in Sydney on 3 January 1792.

OBSP, 1789–90, case 57, p. 63, and case 59, p. 123; Burial Register, St Philip's, 1792.

SOLOMONS, Abraham

b. London, 1800
Morely (2), 1818; Convict; Sentenced to 7 years, Surrey Quarter Sessions, 1818.
Single; Furrier; Height: 160 cm.

Dark sallow complexion, black hair, dark eyes.

The *Morely* arrived in New South Wales on 18 November 1818 and on 24 November Solomons was forwarded to Liverpool for assignment on the *Lady Nelson*. On 6 November 1823 the *Sydney Gazette* announced that Abraham Solomons had absconded from service and, consequently, on 25 November 1823 Solomons was transported to Port Macquarie by the *Lady Nelson*. Abraham Solomons was listed as a government servant at Port Macquarie in 1825. He received a certificate of freedom on 10 May 1825. He was the purchaser of land in the District of Illawarra in 1837.

HO 10/20; Ship Indent 4/4006, p. 153; Land Correspondence 2/7982 (1837); CF 032/3656.

SOLOMONS, Eliza (Elizabeth)

b. London, 1816
Layton, 1833; Free.
Single; Servant.

Elizabeth Solomons was a 17-year-old bounty migrant from London, who arrived in Port Jackson on 17 December 1833. She appeared on the list of women employed from the lumber yard (where the new arrivals were allowed to gather in order to find a suitable employer). She was given a job by a Mr Vaiben Solomon (q.v.) of Hunter Street at the rate of six shillings a week.

Layton Indent 4/5205; List of Women Employed, 4/4325, p. 1.

SOLOMONS, Frederick

b. 1769
Surprize (1), 1790; Convict; Sentenced to 7 years, Old Bailey, 1788.
Single.

Frederick Solomons was sentenced for the theft of seven glazed framed prints valued at eight shillings. Together with two other men, Solomons stole the pictures from the shop window. They were chased through the streets. The other two men escaped and Solomons was found with the prints in his apron pockets. He claimed he had been asked to carry them, pleading 'I am as innocent as a child unborn'. On 2 April 1788, despite the evidence of three character witnesses, he was sentenced to seven years transportation.

Solomons came to Australia with the Second Fleet. In September 1791, a year after he had arrived, Solomons was sent to Norfolk Island. On 31 March 1793 he was given twenty-five lashes for 'answering to the name of another person on a muster at night'. On 6 November 1795 he sailed for Sydney on the *Supply*, but was back on Norfolk Island by the 1801 Muster. He does not appear in later colonial records.

Michael Flynn, *The Second Fleet*, p. 544; *OBSP*, 1787–88, case 296, p. 419; Norfolk Island Victualling Book, ML, A1958, p. 32a.

SOLOMONS, Hanna (Samuels)

Brothers, 1824; Convict.

Hannah Solomons married James Box at the Church of England, Parramatta, in 1833. This entry could well be a clerical error. A Hannah Samuels arrived as a convict on the *Brothers* in 1824 and was an assigned convict servant in Sydney.

SOLOMONS, Hannah

b. London, 1809
Princess Royal (2), 1829; Convict; Sentenced to 14 years, Old Bailey, 1828.
Single; Prostitute.

Hannah Solomons, a prostitute, robbed a client of £2 8s 6d. She was the sister of John Solomons (q.v.). Her client James Winter testified 'I am a lighterman. On Saturday, the 6th of September, I received three half crowns and two sovereigns. I had half a crown and one shilling besides. I went to a public houe, had a beefsteak, a pint of beer and a glass of gin with a fellow servant. I then came out and met (Hannah) Solomons who asked me to give her some gin, which I did. I was sober. I went to her lodgings in Bell Yard and gave her three shillings and six pence to get some supper. I sat in a chair and went to sleep. I had been up four nights and was very tired. I was awoke by Charles

Banks rumbling me over. I jumped up and said "You have robbed me". He went around the bed and gave something to Solomons who was sitting up in the bed. I went to seize him. He seized hold of me and got me down the siars, ill used me and turned me out. I called "Watch". Two watchmen went up the stairs into the same room with me. The prisoners were the both in bed. We could find nothing in the room. We took them to the watch-house'. Then returned and found my money in a silk handkerchief between the sacking and mattress. 'Hannah Solomons, aged twenty, was sentenced to transportation for fourteen years on 11 September 1828. Her accomplice was sentenced to six months in gaol.'

Hannah Solomons worked as an assigned servant in the District of Windsor and received a ticket of leave in 1832. She received permission to marry in 1837. The marriage was performed by the Rev. H. H. Bolard at St John's, Parramatta, and the groom was Charles Smith, aged twenty-five, who held a ticket of leave and had arrived on the *Surrey* (5). Hannah received her certificate of freedom on 2 May 1843.

OBSP 11 September 1828 case 1920. Principal Superintendent of Convicts, Ticket of Leave Butts, 15 November to 31 December 1832, 4/4086, 32/1165; Principal superintendent of Convicts, Registers of Exemption from Government Labour, 15 November 1832, 4/4062, 32/1165; Permission to Marry Book 4/4513, p. 16; CF 4/4382, 43/0694.

SOLOMONS, Isaac (SULLIVAN)

b. London, 1808
Florentia (1), 1828; Convict; Sentenced to 14 years, Old Bailey, 1827.
Single; Labourer; Height: 170 cm.

Isaac Solomons was a 19-year-old professional pickpocket who lived near Petticoat Lane and was arrested for stealing a watch. When he was caught he offered to refund its cost at five shillings a week. He defended himself by saying: 'I am no relation to Ikey Solomon' (Isaac Solomon, q.v.), 'and trust my name will not prejudice me'. He had a ruddy complexion, brown hair, hazel eyes and a slightly pock-pitted face. He could read. He had two previous convictions. Solomons was sentenced to transportation on 11 June 1827.

The *Florentia* arrived in Sydney on 3 January 1828 and Solomons was assigned to work for Mr John MacDonald in Parramatta. He was listed as a Jew in the 1828 Census. He was said to be aged twenty-two, and worked as a government servant on Road Gang no. 14 at Kissing Point. He was apprehended after absconding from Road Gang no. 30 on 21 April 1830 and was placed on the treadmill for three days. Later in the same year he absconded from Iron Gang no. 6, and was apprehended on 13 January 1831. Solomons worked as an assigned servant to Hugh O'Donnell in Parramatta from 1832 to 1840. On 4 May 1836 Isaac Solomons, alias Isaac Sullivan, asked for a new assignment. He wrote that he had 'served faithfully' and 'for nearly seven years I have been employed on the road in the District of Argyle and, at present employed thereon. Your Petitioner hereby prays that Your Excellency will be graciously pleased to order his being assigned to some master whereby he may derive a Knowledge of Agricultural and farming business which, at present is denied him'.

Sadly, Solomons of Road Party no. 4 was committed for trial on 26 July 1836 at the Hyde Park Barracks for being a 'runaway' and was remanded. However, according to the 1837 General Return of Convicts in New South Wales, he was still incarcerated in the 'House of Correction'. On 17 April 1839 he was admitted to the Parramatta Gaol for an unspecified offence and put on the treadmill as a punishment. A ticket of leave was issued in 1840 for the district of Liverpool. This was altered for Campbelltown on 20 April 1840 and on 5 December 1840 was changed for Maitland. He received a conditional pardon in 1841 and a certificate of freedom on 10 March 1842.

OBSP, 1826–27, case 1464, p. 562; Ship Indent 4/4013, p. 23; TL Register 4/4139–40/873; Bench of Magistrates, Hyde Park Barracks, X707; Parramatta Gaol Book 4/6533, no. 741; *Sydney Gazette*, 13 January 1831; CS 36/4146, 4/2309; Central Criminal Court 4/6448, for 12 November 1836; CP 41/1000; HO 10/52.

SOLOMONS, John (SOLOMON)

b. London, 1791
Mariner (1), 1816; Convict; Sentenced to 14 years, Old Bailey, 1815.
Single; Butcher; Height: 157 cm; 12 children.

Fair ruddy complexion, ruddy, pock-pitted. Brown hair, hazel eyes. John Solomons was tried on 6 December 1815. He had been tricked into selling twenty-four counterfeit replicas of 3-shilling pieces to an agent of the Bank of England. The transaction took place at Coventry Cross, Petticoat Lane. The City Constable, who made the arrest, said to the court: 'I held him tight as if it was highway robbery. I told him it was nearly as serious an affair. He said he did not care; they would not hang him; they could only transport him'.

John Solomons arrived in New South Wales on 11 October 1816. The 1828 Census gives us some information about John Solomons, who was most certainly Jewish but who appears to have abandoned his faith and become a 'Protestant'. He married Margaret H. Duncan at St Philip's Church on 22 February 1819. John 'Solomon' was listed as a 'dealer' living in Pitt Street, Sydney, with five children: George (aged nine), Hannah (aged seven), Mary Ann (aged five), Caroline (aged two and a half), and Joan (aged three months).

A ticket of leave was issued to him on 28 October 1817 for Sydney. John Solomons announced that he had 'removed to 4 King Street at the end of 1820'. On 12 May 1821 his household effects were put up for sale and he was called upon to show cause why he was not to be declared insolvent.

On 17 December 1827 the merchant Walter Jacob Levi (q.v.) appeared at the Supreme Court in Sydney on behalf of John Solomons: 'Last market day on Thursday morn John Solomon at a quarter past 5 came into the [Sydney] market to find his table gone. Mr Whitfield took hold of Solomon, took him by the collar and tore his jacket. Solomons had been a stall holder at the market for eight years. Whitfield did beat, bruise and wound and ill treat Solomon'.

A certificate of freedom was issued on 7 December 1829.

4/4425; Bigge Appendix, CO 201/118; TL 143/1223; CF 4/4299, 7 December 1829, 29/1048; *Sydney Gazette*, 17 December 1829; *Commercial Journal and Advertiser*, 23 September 1841; CF 4/4300.

SOLOMONS, Nathaniel (Nathan)

b. London, 1825–1900
1848; Free.
Married; Draper; 12 children.

The son of Aaron Solomons (q.v.) and Rachel (née Davis), and the brother of Saul Solomons (q.v.), Nathaniel Solomons had married Eva Sarah Van der Pohl (Isaacs) in Houndsditch, London, in 1843. Nathaniel and Eva arrived in Launceston with their two children, Rachel (born 1846) and Leah (1847), both of whom were born in London. Their next three children, Phoebe (1848), Rebecca (1849), and Isaac Henry (1850), were born in Launceston.

Nathan Solomons owned a drapery store in Launceston and on 6 October 1849 charged his assigned convict Abraham Cohen (alias Thomas Phillips) (q.v.) with stealing four pairs of trousers. Cohen was found 'not guilty'.

The family moved to Melbourne, where they had seven daughters: Katherine (Katie) (born 1855), Sarah (1857), Eva (1859), Julia (1861), Hannah (1864), Rebecca (1865), and Amelia (born in Ballarat, 2 February 1868).

Nathaniel died on 14 September 1900 at 'Rokeby', Herbert Street, Middle Park, and was buried at the Melbourne General Cemetery. His wife died at the Melbourne suburb of Albert Park on 28 July 1901.

SOLOMONS, Phoebe

1826–1847
Free.
Single.

Phoebe Solomons, the 16-year-old daughter of Aaron Solomons (q.v.), married 29-year-old Bertram Nathan (q.v.) in Launceston on 17 June 1846. She died in Launceston on 4 January 1847.

SOLOMONS, Rachael

b. 1826
Free.
Single.

Rachael Solomons (aged nineteen) married John Aaron in Launceston on 22 August 1845.

SOLOMONS, Samuel

b. London, d. 1853
Surprize (1), 1791; Convict; Sentenced to 7 years, Old Bailey, 1788.
1 child.

Samuel Solomons was tried on 10 December 1788. He had stolen 36 pounds weight of lead. A watchman found him behind the gate of the Aldgate Workhouse. He said: 'You old bloody bugger you won't find your own way out of here', and then took a short stick from under his coat. The prisoner ran out of Meeting House Yard and hid himself behind a 'necessary' (lavatory).

The convict transport ship *Surprize* lost thirty-eight of its prisoners on the way out to New South Wales and only 121 convicts landed alive. Samuel Solomons' sentence expired in 1795. He settled at the Hawkesbury and his name appeared on an 1806 petition from the inhabitants of the Hawkesbury District disputing John Macarthur's claim to speak on their behalf. The 1806 New South Wales Muster recorded that he was free by servitude and that he lived at Richmond Hill 'as a tenant with 49 acres of land with 6 growing wheat, 6 growing maize and 1 barley'. He was free by servitude and not being fed from the government stores. Solomons was listed in the 1811 New South Wales Muster. He received his certificate of freedom on 1 January 1811.

In 1820 he was listed as a tenant of Jane Pool with seven acres of land in the region. He was living with Sarah Eglington. They had one male child. Samuel Solomons was listed in the 1828 Census as being free by servitude and 'Protestant'. He was employed by Elizabeth Hill, Richmond. An absolute pardon was recommended in March 1839 and a conditional pardon was granted to him in August 1843. By 1841 Solomons and his 'wife' lived in Sydney at the corner of Liverpool Street and Kent Street. They were said to be 'very aged'. When rain flooded their cellar and their home wall began to crumble, they asked the authorities to build a buttress to support their home. Their petition was refused.

Samuel Solomons died on 4 July 1853 and was buried by the synagogue in the Jewish section of the Devonshire Street Cemetery.

OBSP, 1788–89, case 54, p. 38; HO 10/1, no. 2; HO10/5 Muster of 1811; Pardons Register 4/4427, p. 524; Petition 4/2535.4, 42/5460.1; New South Wales Muster, 12 August 1806; Petition 41/5460.1, June 1841, in 4/2535.4; Hawkesbury settler, 1806, A751, pp. 174, 179; Absolute Pardon recommended, 27 March 1839, A1220, pp. 545, 547; ML A1293 pp. 147–54; Certificate of Emancipation 1811, 4/4427, p. 524/5.

SOLOMONS, Samuel

b. London, 1795–1853
Prince of Orange (1), 1821; Convict; Sentenced to life, London, 1819.
Single; Tailor; Height: 160.5 cm; 3 children.

Pale complexion, sandy brown hair, grey eyes. Solomons robbed the Rev. Dr Roderick McLeod of a watch and chain. Solomons was of 'innocent appearance' on a moonlit night at 11 p.m., and made so many apologies for bumping into the clergyman that it put him off guard. Solomons ran down Petticoat Lane with the booty and was caught. He was sentenced to death at the London Gaol Delivery on 26 May 1819, and this was later commuted to transportation for life.

The *Prince of Orange* arrived in Sydney on 12 February 1821 and Samuel Solomons was forwarded to Parramatta for assignment. Solomons, aged thirty-six, was listed in the 1828 Census, and in the List of Convicts in New South Wales of November 1828, as a Jew and as a dealer in Goulburn Street, Sydney, and the holder of a ticket of leave. The Colonial Secretary noted that he was 'of Pitt St' and could receive an assigned convict servant. He was married to Elizabeth (aged thirty, holding a conditional pardon) with children Lewis aged five and Benjamin aged three. A ticket of leave was issued to him on 26 September 1828, a conditional pardon in 1834, and an absolute pardon, recommended on 1 March 1839 (no. 40), was granted on 14 May 1840.

Samuel Solomons moved to Sydney and was 'selling frocks and trousers etc at Polack's buildings opposite the Police Office' (according to the *Sydney Times*, 17 September 1836). Solomons had a business as general dealer at 18 York Street. On 6 July 1837 he advertised a furniture auction sale at 6 Polack's Building and then, through 1838 to 1842, he advertised auctions 'every Friday at 1 pm at the Sydney Cattle Market'. In September 1839 he was able to make a £15 donation to the appeal for the building of the new Sydney Synagogue. Samuel Solomons was declared insolvent in the crash of 1843 (*Sydney Morning Herald*, 28 August 1843), with debts of £397, outstanding debts of £123, and a deficiency of £263 12s.

He was active in the affairs of the Jewish community but resigned from the Sydney Synagogue Committee on 7 February 1840 due to 'the multiplicity of my affairs'. It is probable that his non-Jewish wife was proving an embarrassment. In 1839 Mr Samuel Solomons had given £5 to the York Street Synagogue on his own behalf and £5 for each of his male children, Master Lewis Solomons, Master Benjamin Solomons and Master William Solomons. Samuel Solomons was listed in the 1834 *General Post Office Directory* as living at the corner of Hunter and Castlereagh streets, Sydney.

OBSP, 1818–19, case 826, p. 315; HO 11/3; CS 4/4570, p. 33; TL Register 4/4061, dated 26 September 1828, 28/396; CP Register 4/4432-224, on 20 August 1835; Register of Exemptions 4/4062, p. 918; Governors' Despatches, ML, A1271, p. 222; Governors' Despatches, ML, A1220, p. 547, dated 1 March 1839; HO 10/52, AP 40.

SOLOMONS, Saul

b. London
Adelaide, 1834; Free.
Single; Clerk.

Saul Solomons came out as a free settler on the *Adelaide*, arriving in Sydney on 5 September 1834. James Simmons (q.v.) had chartered the entire ship and Saul Solomons was its only passenger and was probably employed by Simmons as his clerk.

Saul Solomons, 'dealer', of Parramatta, was declared insolvent on 10 March 1843. In 1849 Saul Solomons married Catherine Keegan at Scots Church in Sydney.

Indent 4/5207; *Sydney Morning Herald*, 10 March 1843.

SOLOMONS, Saul (SOLOMON)

b. London, 1822–1891
1840; Free.
Single; Draper; 6 children.

Saul Solomons came free to Van Diemen's Land. The 1842 Census shows that the family lived in a wooden house in Charles Street, Launceston, that was owned by Joshua Lyons (q.v.). Solomon gave two shillings and sixpence to a charitable appeal for the family of a district constable who had been shot by bushrangers on 9 June 1843. Saul signed the Launceston Synagogue petition of 20 May 1843 and father (Aaron Solomons, q.v.) and son formed a partnership 'A. & S. Solomons'. In 1846 they made the bad mistake of taking over the Launceston Emporium from David Benjamin (q.v.), who had decided to move to Melbourne. As the Emporium quickly sank into debt, Saul's own bakery business burnt down. As soon as it was possible Saul moved to South Australia with his family on the *Halcyon*, arriving on 28 February 1849.

On 20 November 1844 Solomons had married Miriam Barnett (q.v.), 'a shopkeeper' (born 1822 in London). It was Launceston's fifth Jewish wedding and Morris Whyte (Whyle, q.v.) officiated. Three of their six children were born in Launceston and three in Adelaide. They were Rachel Miriam (born 7 October 1845), Amelia (3 October 1846), Phoebe (11 March 1848), Baron Isaacar (8 May 1849), Henry Aaron (20 March 1851), and Matilda (Tillie) (18 June 1853). All six children lived out their lives in Adelaide and were eventually buried in Adelaide's West Terrace Jewish Cemetery. At the High Holydays in 1850 Saul Solomons was listed as a member of the committee of the Adelaide Hebrew Congregation.

Saul Solomons died in Adelaide on 8 March 1891. He had been a 'draper of Burra Burra House' for thirty-seven years. Miriam Solomons died on 5 August 1917, at the age of ninety-four.

CO 280/157; Pritchard Index.

SOLOMONS, Simon (SAULDS)

Salamander, 1790; Convict; Sentenced to 7 years, Old Bailey, 1789.
Single; Labourer.

According to the account of the trial a 'genteel' accomplice tricked a young servant who was carrying a box to leave his post and hail a coach. The servant returned only just in time to catch Simon Solomons who was running towards Aldgate with the deal box in which there was 70 shillings worth of soap. Solomons was sentenced on 9 September 1789.

Simon Solomons was transported with the Third Fleet on the *Salamander*, reaching Port Jackson on 1 August 1790. Solomons went on to Norfolk Island on the same ship. He left the island on 30 March 1793, having remained dependent on the government stores throughout the three years. From 1791 to 1796 he was listed as the owner of thirty acres of land at Parramatta. He was still in Sydney in August 1806 but did not appear in the 1811 Muster, and had probably returned to England.

OBSP, 1788–89, case 691, p. 818; Convict no. 365, in Norfolk Island Victualling Book, A1958, p. 33a; Magistrates Book 1/297, 1798; Registrar, General Dept. Files, series 1, p. 138; New South Wales Muster, 12 August 1806.

SOLOMONS, Solomon

b. London, 1794–1834
Marquis of Wellington, 1815; Convict; Sentenced to life, Old Bailey, 1814.
Single; Pedlar; Height: 166 cm; 6 children.

Dark sallow complexion, dark brown hair, hazel eyes. Solomon Solomons could neither read nor write English. He was sentenced on 20 April 1814 for stealing a watch and chain from a mathematical instrument maker. John Ripley gave evidence: 'I was walking down the Minories with a friend; we were arm in arm together; the prisoner stepped on the pavement, came round to my right hand and snatched my watch chain'. Mr James Grantham testified: 'We were walking down the Minories, Mr Ripley had hold of my arm, he let go and stumbled; the Jew ran off; I followed him and took him in custody; I never lost sight of him'. Solomons said: 'I was going in a great hurry to go to my aunt to let her know my mother was brought to bed; a gentleman called after me and took me in custody. I know nothing of it, no more than a new born infant'. He was sentenced at the London Gaol Delivery on 20 April 1814.

The *Marquis of Wellington* arrived in Sydney on 27 January 1815 and on 2 February Solomons was sent to Windsor for assignment. On 7 August 1816 Solomon Solomons was sent by the magistrate Rev. Cartwright to serve for three years at the penal settlement in Newcastle after he had 'continually' run away from the penal settlement. Between 1816 and 1820 Solomons was listed as an assigned convict servant to Joseph Thomas.

Solomons married Elizabeth Jones (who was a free settler) on 2 July 1821 at St Philip's in Sydney and one of his witnesses at the marriage, conducted by the Rev. William Cowper, was Abraham Levy (q.v.) and Maria Gardner. (The two chosen witnesses would be married to each other in mid 1824). By 1822 Solomons was working as a dealer in Sydney.

Solomon Solomons, 'a dealer', was imprisoned by the Governor's Court on 13 April 1823 for a demand to pay £50 (plus costs) to Robert Howe, who was described as Solomons' executor and administrator. Solomons signed his name in Hebrew script, the letters of which were then crudely copied on the court document. Solomons' signature must have been the first Hebrew letters on any Australian legal document.

On 8 April 1826 Solomons was reported and reprimanded for buying a bottle of gin from an unlicensed vendor. Worse was to come. The *Sydney Gazette* and the (Sydney) *Monitor* reported on 15 August 1826 that Solomon Solomons, holding a ticket of leave, had been apprehended in a 'House of Ill Fame' at 3 a.m., sitting around a card table and gambling. (The *Monitor* placed its report on its front page.) Ten days later his ticket of leave was cancelled.

John Macarthur wrote of Solomons that he was a 'Jew publican—lately deprived of his licence for keeping a disorderly house'. On 16 August 1826 Elizabeth Solomons petitioned the Colonial Secretary either to give her husband back his ticket of leave or to let him be assigned to her 'to support his three young infants'. The Rev. Cowper attested: 'This young woman is industrious, peaceable and sober and being moreover attentive to her three children, born in wedlock, is recommended'. Officialdom agreed with the plea: 'In consequence of this woman's good character, I will allow her husband to remain with her out of Barracks. He must attend church regularly with the other men and be informed if found gambling again he will be placed back in prison'.

In the 1828 Census Solomon Solomons' ticket of leave had not been returned, and he was described as Jewish and working in government service. However, in the List of Convicts in New South Wales in November 1828, he appeared as a dealer in Pitt Street. He lived with his wife Elizabeth, born in the colony, aged twenty-two. They had six children, all born in the colony: George (born 24 March 1822), William (13 October 1823), who died after falling into a well in 1825, John (6 February 1826), Michael (23 March 1828 to 1899), Solomon (3 April 1830), and William (1834–1882).

Family tradition says that Solomon died in 'a pub brawl' in 1834. Elizabeth subsequently married Lewis Barnett (q.v.).

OBSP, 20 April 1814; Ship Indent 4/4005; Sent to Newcastle 4/3495, 7 August 1816; CO 201/179, Letter to John Horton, 11 July 1826; Petitions from Wives of Convicts, 1826–27, 4/7084; TL Register 4/4060, TL 169/2303; *Australian*, 8 April 1826; *Monitor*, 25 August 1826; *Sydney Gazette*, 16 August 1826; Petition in CS 4/3504, p. 79; HO 10/33; family research by Jim Needs, Edgeworth, NSW, and Robin Guthrie, Sydney.

SOLOMONS, Solomon

b. London, 1796
Lady Castlereagh, 1818; Convict; Sentenced to life, Old Bailey, 1817.
Single; Butcher ('very little'); Height: 159 cm.

Fair ruddy complexion, dark brown hair, hazel eyes. Solomon Solomons was one of a gang of four or five men who 'hustled' around a man in Bacon Street in Bethnal Green. Solomons was seen to be the actual thief and was caught in the skirmish that followed the theft of the victim's wallet. He was condemned to death at the London Gaol Delivery on 21 May 1817 and the sentence was later commuted to transportation for life.

Solomon Solomons arrived in Sydney on 30 May 1818, and was sent on to Van Diemen's Land, arriving on 11 June 1818. His police dossier began on 4 July, when he was found to be drunk and disorderly and was ordered to work for the government for fourteen days in his own time. During the remainder of 1818 he received fifty lashes for two charges of disobeying an overseer and for neglect of duty. On 2 October 1819 he was found guilty of stealing a soldier's shirt and was sentenced to a further fifty lashes. For 'frequently losing government bullocks', he received twenty lashes on 13 December 1820. Two years later, on 8 May 1822, Solomons was given fifty lashes and three months in the chain gang for 'neglect of duty', and on 7 July 1826 he was convicted for the theft of a pair of shoes and a piece of canvas and sent to Maria Island to serve the first part of a three-year sentence. After an attempt to escape from the island, Solomons was sent to Macquarie Harbour on the island's west coast and to the dreaded penal colony on Sarah Island. It was a miracle he survived the experience.

On 9 November 1827, for 'neglect of duty', he received a further twenty-five lashes, and on 10 November 1927, for 'neglect of duty and refusing to work' on the day after being whipped, an additional twenty-five lashes was decreed. At Macquarie Harbour, on 15 December 1827, he was found guilty of 'wanton carelessness in letting a piece of wood fall upon a fellow prisoner', for which he received twenty-five lashes. On 5 January 1828, for 'neglect of duty and refusing to work', he received twenty-five lashes, and on 15 March 1828 he received eighteen lashes for 'neglect of duty'. On 26 March he was given eighteen lashes for 'refusing to work under false pretences'. On 3 May he received twenty-five lashes for 'neglect of duty', on 19 June, thirty-six lashes for 'stealing or having a stolen shirt in his possession', on 29 August, for 'refusing to work', twenty–five lashes. On 28 February 1829, for 'refusing to sit down in a Gang Boat going to the Small Island', he was put in irons for fourteen days, and on 5 June 1832, for 'neglect of duty', he received twenty-five lashes. He was returned to Hobart Town and on 4 February 1835 was sent to work with the Public Works Department at New Norfolk because of the 'filthiness in his ward' in Hobart Town.

Solomon Solomons received a ticket of leave on 23 September 1836, a conditional pardon on 18 January 1839, an absolute pardon in November 1840, and a free pardon on 24 December 1844, for 'Any Country Except Europe'. In recommending the pardon, the official report stated that 'Eight years had passed since he was charged with misconduct'. Solomons married, and apparently joined the Hobart Hebrew Congregation in 1845, renting seat no. 66.

OBSP, 1816–17, case 804, p. 280; Ship Indent 4/4002, p. 40; CON 13/1, p. 195; CON 31/38; CON 13/1, p. 73; CON 23/3; *Hobart Town Gazette*, 28 October 1826; *Hobart Town Courier*, 23 September 1836, 18 January 1839, 24 November 1840.

SOLOMONS, Solomon (Saul)

b. Portsmouth, 1814
Hooghly (4), 1834; Convict; Sentenced to 7 years, Southwark, 1834.
Single; Clothes dealer; Height: 169 cm.

Sallow, freckled complexion, black hair, chestnut eyes. Solomon Solomons was convicted on the same day, and of the same crime, as Saul Solomon (q.v.), and transported on the same ship. They were both convicted for picking pockets.

According to the 1837 General Return of Convicts in New South Wales Solomon Solomons was assigned to Mr J. Collett of Bathurst. Solomons received a ticket of leave in 1839. Solomon Solomons was charged at the Bathurst Police Magistrates Court on 17 June 1840 with receiving stolen property, and was returned to 'the service of the government'.

His ticket of leave was cancelled and he was briefly returned to government service. A certificate of freedom was issued on 8 April 1841. A second ticket of leave was issued in Sydney on 15 July 1842 and a conditional pardon was granted on 1 July 1843 (no. 224).

On 4 August 1843 Solomons was sentenced for theft (picking pockets) at the Sydney Quarter Sessions to ten years colonial servitude and was sent to Van Diemen's Land and to Port Arthur. A long series of breaches of discipline were recorded. On 5 July 1844 he was sentenced to four days in solitary confinement for 'insolence'. Three further sentences in solitary confinement followed. He was found to have a 'piece of yellow cloth in his possession' which extended a previous sentence of hard labour in chains by fourteen days. On 16 January 1846 he was found to have tobacco in his possession which earned him three months hard labour in chains. He was placed on probation from 1 June 1846 but on 6 July he was caught smoking and received seven days solitary confinement. In May 1848 he was allowed to proceed from the penitentiary at Port Arthur to Launceston. An application for a ticket of leave was refused even though it was said that he had 'saved the life of a child'. On 29 May 1849 he was caught 'out after hours' and sentenced to two months hard labour. A ticket of leave was issued 5 March 1850 on the condition that he would not go to Hobart Town. A conditional pardon was issued 3 February 1852 and a certificate of freedom 21 January 1856.

Hooghly Printed Indent, arrived 18 November 1834, p. 165; TL p. 508, of 1840 Governors' Despatches, ML, A1222; CS Out 4/3688, p. 130; Principal Superintendent of Convicts, TL Butts, 20 November 1838 to 1 February 1839, TL 39/44, 4/4125; CF 41/0453. (AOT) CON 35/1/2 p. 46.

SPENCER, Esther

b. London, 1775–1855
Indispensable, 1796; Convict; Sentenced to life, Old Bailey, 1794.
Married; Height: 163 cm; 13 children.

Dark complexion, dark hair, dark eyes. Jewess. Esther was convicted for stealing two silver pepper castors and three silver spoons, valued at £2 14s. She was seen entering the home of a tailor and was caught near Bethnal Green with the silver hidden in her apron pocket. Esther told the court: 'It is the first offence I ever did in my life. I hope you will forgive me'. She was sentenced to death on 16 July 1794, and this was later commuted to transportation for life.

The death certificate of Esther's daughter Cecilia (who died in Melbourne in 1896) states that Esther's real, or maiden, name was Salamon—a distinguished name in Anglo-Jewish history. Esther had thirteen children and three husbands in New South Wales. The first two children, by John Fitz (who arrived on the *Royal Admiral* in 1792), were Susannah, born 23 July 1797, and Joseph, born 29 December 1799. (There is a record in the colony's list of Birth, Marriages and Deaths of a Susanna Watson who was born in Sydney on 28 December 1798 and who was said to be the daughter of Michael Watson and Esther Spencer). Nine of Esther's children were fathered by Thomas Stubbs (who arrived on the *Albermarle*, 1791). They were: Mary Ann (born 28 May 1801), Thomas (18 May 1802), Sophia (8 June 1803), Cecilia (17 March 1805), Elizabeth (15 March 1808), Ann (14 June 1809), George (22 April 1811), John Emery (5 July 1812), and Godfrey (9 October 1814).

Stubbs died in 1815 at the age of forty-one and Esther became involved with Joseph Bigge, who had come free to the colony in 1809. They had two children, Robert (born 1816) and Louise (1817).

In the 1828 Census Esther Bigge was listed as a Protestant. In 1831 Esther Bigge of 20 Phillip Street, Sydney, wrote to the Colonial Secretary asking for a grant of land. By that time she had twenty-one grandchildren. Her husband died in 1833. She became 'the first to establish baths for the ladies of Sydney' and, in 1838, wrote that 'expense had not been spared to tender them deserving of the patronage hitherto bestowed on them'.

She died on 27 December 1855 at the age of seventy-nine and was buried in the Jewish section of Sydney's Devonshire Street Cemetery. The funeral was conducted by the Rev. Isaac Jacobs.

OBSP, 1794, case 447, no. 6; PRO 2730, p. 88; *Australian*, 11 October 1833; family information from June Walker (WA). Vic Death Registration Transcription Ref No 1896/14376. Biographic Database of Australia (information provided by Gary Luke).

SPYER, Joseph L.

d. 1841
Sydney Packet, 1833; Free.
Married.

Joseph Spyer arrived in Sydney on 3 February 1833 on the 83-ton *Sydney Packet*. His wife, Rosetta, was buried on 22 February 1841 in the Jewish section of the Lidcombe Cemetery and, on 1 March 1841, Joseph Spyer died and was 'buried in one tomb' with his wife.

Ship Indent 4/5204, arriving Port Jackson, 3 February 1833; *Sydney Gazette*, 5 February 1833.

SPYER, Lawrence Joseph (SPYERS)

1806–1881
Alexander Henry, 1828; Free.
Single; Merchant; 7 children.

The brother and partner of Stephen Spyer (q.v.), Lawrence Spyer arrived in Sydney on 28 May 1828. He was listed in the 1828 Census as a Jew, and a merchant in George Street with P. J. Cohen (q.v.), who came free to the colony. Spyer had arrived in New South Wales together with P.J.Cohen and the two young men formed a partnership. In April 1830, at the time of Passover, the first organised Jewish festival religious services in Australia were held at the premises of Cohen and Spyers. A year later the business had failed and on 31 March 1831 the partnership was declared to be insolvent.

Spyer went to Maitland to look after his brother's store. He married Julia de Metz on 30 December 1835. His brother Stephen married Rosetta de Metz.

In mid-1837 the Spyer brothers were placed in prison for three months by Samuel Lyons (q.v.) for money they owed to him.

Spyer joined the synagogue in September 1840 when he moved to Sydney and in September stood for election to the committee of management. A child, Sophia, was born on 10 August 1840, and Rosetta was born on 10 September 1841. Isabella was born in 1846, and Angelina in 1849. In all, the Spyers had seven children, five daughters and two sons.

On December 1842 'L & S Spyer merchants of Queens Place Sydney' asked the colonial administration for permission 'to import Champagne shipped by Messrs Jonas Phillips and Co in Philadelphia'. The firm L & S Spyer became one of the largest Jewish import-export businesses in Sydney during the mid-1840s, selling everything from turpentine and linseed oil to soda water bottles. They became representatives of the British Colonial Bank in 1843. In the 1850s the firm was joined by Henry and Joseph Spyer under the name of L. S. Spyer & Co., merchants, with their office at Wynyard Square. Lawrence Joseph Spyer was one of the four trustees for the New South Wales grant of land for a Jewish school in Sydney in 1850.

Lawrence Spyer died at Toorak in 1881. Julia Spyer died in Melbourne in 1883, aged sixty-seven.

CS Letters Received 1842, Miscellaneous, S–Y, 42/9140, December 1842, in 4/2579.3; *Australian*, 9 April 1830; *Sydney Gazette*, 19 May 1828, 31 March 1831, 19 May 1832, 30 December 1835; *Sydney Morning Herald*, 21 February 1843, 9 November 1843, 3 January 1845; Government Grants for Schools, 8 April 1850, series 197, p. 407.

SPYER, Stephen

Australia, 1830; Free.
Single; Dealer; 2 children.

Stephen Spyer travelled to New South Wales on the *Australia*, arriving on 16 April 1830, with the family of Michael Phillips (q.v.). In the *Sydney Gazette* of 19 May 1832, it was reported that: 'Mr Stephen Spyer of Maitland is about to leave the colony for a short period. Business will be conducted by Mr Michael Phillips of Sydney. His brother Mr Lawrence Spyer will look after his stores at Maitland'. Stephen Spyer returned to Sydney (cabin class) on the *Sovereign* on 26 May 1834, listed as a 'Merchant'.

On 16 June 1837 the *Sydney Gazette* told how the Spyer brothers were brought before the Supreme Court and sentenced to gaol for non-payment of debt: 'The claim was discharged after having been in gaol for three months under the benefit of the Insolvency Act. Mr Windeyer, counsel for Messrs Saul Lyons (q.v.) and others, opposed the discharge'. On 20 June 1837 a letter pointed out that it was Samuel Lyons (q.v.) and not Saul who opposed the release of the Spyer Brothers from gaol.

Stephen Spyer married Rosetta de Metz at the Sydney Synagogue on 8 January 1840. His brother Lawrence (q.v.) married Julia de Metz. On 18 July 1840 the Port Lincoln Hotel advertised in the *South Australian Register* that Mr Stephen Spyer had arrived from Sydney 'with goods such as bottled porter, sherry, rum and claret'. A son, Lawrence, was born in Sydney in 1840. On 25 July 1840 Spyer advertised that he was selling several properties, including the Port Lincoln Hotel itself. Rosetta died eight days after having given birth, on 22 February 1841. The baby, Joseph, died on 1 March and was buried with his mother at the Devonshire Street Jewish Cemetery. The tombstones of Rosetta and her son were removed to Raphael's Ground in 1901.

Spyer was included on the voters' list of Sydney in 1842. He owned Ultimo House and was a seat holder at the York Street Synagogue in 1845. Spyer returned to England to live and agreed to collect money in London for the Sydney Synagogue in 1845. On 11 October 1853 Stephen Spyer spent £2178 buying land in Sydney.

Ship Indent 4/5201, and 4/5206; *Sydney Gazette*, 19 May 1832, 16 June 1837, 20 June 1837; *Sydney Morning Herald*, 15 September 1842; *South Australian Gazette and Colonial Register*, 18 July 1840, 15 August 1840; Land Correspondence 2/7975 (11 October 1853).

STEINBOURNE, Aaron Moses (STEENBHOM)

b. Warsaw, Poland, c. 1825–1903
Lady Kennaway (3), 1851; Convict; Sentenced to 15 years, Central Criminal Court, 1845.
Single; Labourer; Height: 158 cm; 11 children.

Dark complexion, dark brown hair, black eyebrows, hazel eyes. Jew. Could read and write. 'Impediment in speech.' Aaron Steinbourne was transported for housebreaking and stealing jewellery and clocks from a private house at Lewisham. Following his conviction he spent time on the Justitia *hulk, where his behaviour was 'bad', and the* Warrior, *where he attempted to stab and strangle another prisoner. Apart from this lapse his behaviour was judged to be 'good otherwise'!*

Aaron Steinbourne arrived in Hobart Town on 28 May 1851 and was sent on to Norfolk Island. On 4 July 1851 he was admonished for 'neglect of duty'. On 9 December 1851 he was put in prison for one month for three counts of 'disobedience' and given twenty-five lashes for throwing a stone at a fellow prisoner. A long list of penalties for idleness and disobedience culminated on 19 April 1852 when he was punished for 'hunting and cutting up a duck' with a sentence of four months imprisonment. Steinbourne was transferred to Van Diemen's Land at the end of July 1852 and sent immediately to Port Arthur. On 22 November he was found guilty of disobedience of orders, for which his existing sentence of hard labour was extended by one month. On 3 September 1853 he was found in an officer's quarters 'under very suspicious circumstances' and his sentence was extended by three months. On 30 September he was sentenced to seven days in solitary confinement for 'insolence'. On 18 November he was found with suet and fat concealed among his rations. His existing sentence of hard labour was extended by four months. On 21 November he was sentenced to six months work in the stone quarry for having tea and sugar and fat concealed in his cell. Smoking a pipe 'improperly' brought six months solitary 'treatment'. On 28 February 1855 he was sentenced to fourteen days in solitary confinement for 'idleness and insolence'.

He finally obtained his ticket of leave on 21 October 1856 and a conditional pardon on 26 January 1858. In Hobart on 2 December 1858 in the Supreme Court he was found not guilty of a charge of 'attempting to commit sodomy'.

Aaron adopted the surname Steenbhom and married Rachel Symons on 16 November 1859 in the York Street synagogue. They opened a general goods store in Pitt Town and quickly fell into debt. During the next couple of years they travelled as dealers with a horse and cart in the districts of Berrima, Braidwood and Yass. In 1863 at Boorowa he was held up by the bushranger Ben Hall. After returning to Sydney Aaron's subsequent caeer as a shopkeeper in Darlinghurst was marked by one financial crisis after another.

Aaron and Rachel had eleven children. They were: Solomon Myer Aaron (1860–1927), Abraham Newyear (1862–1942), Rebecca Elizabeth (1865–1867), Sarah Esther (1867–1935), David Joseph (1870–1955), Ephraim Joshua (1872–1950), Menasseh Benjamin (1875–1953), Isaac Simon (1877–1878), Rebecca Leah (1878–1945), Jacob Emanuel (1881–1956), and Reuben Naphtali (1884–1963).

The sons were all apprenticed to various trades. Solomon was a shipping dealer based at Darling Harbour and served as hononorary auditor of the Montefiore Home and the Great Synagogue and secretary of the Grand Uniting Order of Oddfellows for twenty-five years. Abraham, Jacob and Menasseh were partners in one of the largest motor body building companies in New South Wales. In the mid 1920s Jacob succeeded in obtaining the old Darlinghurst Gaol for technical education. David was in Western Australia and officiated at the Kalgoorlie synagogue.

Aaron died in Sydney on 21 June 1903. Rachel died on 19 July 1919 at the age of seventy-seven. They are buried at Rookwood.

CON 33/102, no. 24245; CON 14/42; CON 18/52; family information supplied by Gary Luke, Sydney.

SULLIVAN, John

Free.

The *Sydney Gazette* reported on 17 March 1825 that: 'John Sullivan, a Jew, free, was apprehended under a violent suspicion of having stolen a canvas bag containing 300 Spanish dollars, from the office of the Colonial Treasurer between the hours of 11 and 12 this day whilst licences were being issued to the publicans. The circumstances were very strong against the prisoner'. Sullivan was committed to trial on 10 March 1825, found guilty, and discharged from custody on 28 September 1828.

In September 1839 John Sullivan pledged £5 to the building appeal of the proposed York Street Synagogue in Sydney.

T

TAYLOR, Thomas (Abraham MOSES) (Martin MOSS)

b. Stepney, 1800
Lotus, 1833; Convict; Sentenced to 7 years, Middlesex, 1832.
Cressy, 1843; Convict; Sentenced to 7 years, Central Criminal Court, 1843.
Married; Labourer and whaler; Height: 173 cm; 6 children (in England).

Fresh complexion, large head, black hair, black bushy whiskers, rather long face, hazel eyes, long thin nose, broad chin. Tattoo S. M. on inside left arm, small scars on both hands and wrists. Jew. Can read and write. Surgeon's report: 'Very useful on board ... gave great satisfaction'.

Abraham Moses was transported to Australia twice. The first time he arrived in Van Diemen's Land, he bore the name Martin Moss, and he came on the *Lotus* to Hobart Town on 16 May 1833. Moses, or Moss (and eventually Taylor), had been convicted at Middlesex on 29 November 1832 and sentenced to seven years transportation for having stolen two coats from the back of a cart guarded only by 'a boy'.

On 7 November 1835 (after his initial period of probation) Moss, an assigned servant to a Mr Tucker in Perth, was convicted for being drunk and for neglecting his work, and was returned to the service of the Crown. On 8 September 1836 he was sent to the cells for ten days for having been found gambling in the Colonial Hospital. On 21 September a further month's hard labour in chains was decreed. By 11 January 1837 he was once again working as an assigned convict servant when he was convicted of being drunk. On 8 August Martin Moss was convicted for misconduct, having been found in possession of a pencil case for which he could not account. He was given six months hard labour and sent to the Snake Banks Road Party at the discretion of the Lieutenant Governor. On 2 July 1838 he was found to have 'various articles in his possession for which he cannot satisfactorily account'. He was returned to government service and it was noted that he was not to be assigned again. However, by 4 November 1838, he had been assigned to Mr McDowell and was found to be drunk. He received seven days solitary confinement on bread and water. Martin Moss received his certificate of freedom in 1839 and returned to England.

He arrived back in Hobart Town on 20 August 1843, as a prisoner, with the new name 'Thomas Taylor'. By this time he was forty-three years old and reported that he had six children. He said that he had been transported for stealing meat valued at five shillings from a Public House on the Twyford Road. His previous conviction was for 'cart robbery':

> I served at Hobart Town and arrived by the *Lotus* in May 1833 in the name of 'Martin Moss' which is my proper name. I was in the service of Mr Dawson in Launceston. I obtained my freedom in 1839. I had been convicted [in Van Diemen's Land] for assault. I had separated from my wife and stated I am single at Gaol and went home as cook for Lieutenant Governor George Arthur in February 1841.

His wife's name was Sarah. His father, David, lived in Aldgate and was a 'corn doctor'. Taylor was sent to Port Arthur on 24 October 1843.

OBSP 29 November 1832, case 165. CON 33/40, no. 9750; CON 39/2, p. 112; CON 14/22, no. 4751; CON 18/37; CF 805.

TIETZNER, Wolff (TIEBZNER)

b. Courland, Prussia (Poland), 1811
Palmyra, 1846; Convict; Sentenced to 7 years, Central Criminal Court, 1845.
Single; Provision merchant; Height: 173 cm.

Fresh complexion, brown hair, black bushy whiskers, dark brown eyes, large nose. Jew. Can read and write German. Wolff Tielzner stole two casks of butter, biscuits, cheese and flour from a general dealer in provisions at Tower Hill. In "broken English" he had persuaded the store keeper to supply the captain of a fictitious ship with supplies.

No colonial offences were recorded against Tietzner. He was assigned to Moses Moses (q.v.) in Launceston in 1847. A ticket of leave was issued on 23 April 1850 and a conditional pardon on 23 July 1850.

OBSP 24 November 1845 case 123. CON 33/81, no. 18951; CON 14/36; CON 18/47.

TOLANO, Raphael

b. London, 1819–1896
Charles Kerr, 1837; Convict; Sentenced to 14 years, Central Criminal Court, 1836.
Single; Labourer; Height: 160 cm; 12 children.

Dark sallow complexion, black hair, hazel eyes. Small scar on left cheek. Could read and write. 'Hebrew'. The son of Joseph Tolano and Rebecca (née Romanel), Raphael Tolano was transported for picking pockets. He stole a handkerchief, valued at two shillings, in Newgate Street. He had served a previous sentence of six months, and was sentenced on 19 September 1836.

Raphael Tolano arrived in New South Wales on 9 October 1837 and was mustered at the Hyde Park Barracks the following week. At the end of that year the General Return of Convicts in New South Wales listed Tolano as a convict servant assigned to James R. Keay of Bathurst. A ticket of leave for the district of Bathurst was issued on 12 December 1843. Raphael Tolano 'of Bathurst' married Elizabeth Crabb (almost illiterate), the daughter of Emanuel Crabb (q.v.) at the Sydney Synagogue on 9 August 1848. On 1 October 1848 he received a conditional pardon.

When Joseph Simmons (q.v.) left his stores at Bathurst and Carcoar in order to return to Sydney in 1850, 'Ralph' Tolano was left in charge. When the gold rush began, Tolano took over the Beehive Store in 'the land of Ophir' and advertised that he would buy gold dust in exchange for goods. It was reported that he had quickly accumulated £500 worth of gold. He bought wool, sheepskins, hides, tallow and produce in exchange for goods.

In 1851 Tolano followed the gold rush to Turon and in September 1852 he gave evidence at a trial involving gold stolen from the Sydney Mail. He returned to Sydney and was listed in the 1855 *Waugh and Cox Directory of Sydney* at 391 George Street. On 32 May 1856 Tolano was granted a publican's licence for the Edinburgh Castle Hotel in Pitt Street and in April 1858 he received a licence for Skinner's Hotel.

By 1862 Tolano was the manager of the Royal Victorian Theatre and, later, the Prince of Wales Theatre, in Sydney. Joseph Jefferson, an itinerant American actor has left us a description of Tolano on stage:

> He was an under-sized, round shouldered little cockney, named Rolamo. Where he got this remarkably Italian appellation I cannot say, but if his ancestors belonged to the 'land of song' they must have strayed into the heart of Whitechapel just previous to the birth of their son and heir, as his dialect was strongly impregnated with the drawling twang of that locality. It is recorded of him that he never was known to put an h in the right place, and his talent for reversing the w and v almost amounted to genius. He had originally been lamplighter in the theatre, but by his industry and intelligence he rose to be its manager, and he was in the zenith of his fame when I arrived in Australia.

The children of Raphael and Elizabeth Tolano were Joseph, born at Bathurst (1849–1930), Moses Saul (1852), Rebecca (1856–1926), Phillip (1856–1923), Abraham (1857–1858), Rachel (1858, who died in infancy), Lewis Samuel (1859), Miriam (1862–1930), Sarah (1864), Catherine (1866), Rosetta, born in Brisbane (1869–1874), and Emanuel (1871), also born in Brisbane.

Raphael Tolano died on 2 November 1896 and was buried in the Jewish section of Rookwood Cemetery. Elizabeth died, aged eighty-two, on 19 May 1910.

Charles Kerr Printed Indent 9 October 1837, p. 161; *OBSP*, 1836, case 2038, p. 775; Pardon Register, 4/4182; TL 43/2792; CP 48/1896; M. Z. Forbes, 'The Jews of New South Wales and the Gold Rushes', *AJJHS*, vol. 12, no. 2 (1994), p. 291f; Kim Phillips, *One Family's Story*, Sydney, 1997.

U

UNDERWOOD, Elizabeth (née HARRIS)

b. Norfolk Island, 1794–1858
4 children.

Elizabeth Harris was the daughter of First Fleeters John Harris (q.v.) and Mary*, née Green, and the sister of Hannah Ritchie (q.v.). Elizabeth and Hannah were left in the care of James Larra (q.v.), who regarded the girls as his 'nieces'. On 17 June 1812 Elizabeth was married by the Rev. Samuel Marsden to Walter Lang, who had arrived the previous month from Calcutta. Lang died four years later, leaving Elizabeth a considerable fortune. Eight months after her husband's death she gave birth to a son, John George Lang (1816–1864), who would grow up to become Australia's first native-born novelist.

In 1829 Elizabeth Lang married Joseph Underwood, one of the wealthiest members of the colony. Joseph Underwood died in 1833, by which time Elizabeth had four daughters and was involved in a very large business empire.

Elizabeth Underwood, 'daughter of John and Matilda Harris', died in 1858 and was buried at Concord.

Nancy Keesing (Hertzberg), 'Israel Chapman in Fiction', *AJJHS*, vol. 6, no. 7 (1969), p. 411f; AG, pp. 47–9, 58, 59, 70.

*The convict records initially state that her name was 'Mary'. Later documents state that her name was 'Matilda'.

V

VALENTINE, Benjamin

b. London, 1802–1876
Marquis of Hastings (2), 1827; Convict; Sentenced to 7 years, Old Bailey, 1826.
Married; Coloured paper maker; Height: 145 cm; 3 children (in England).

Dark ruddy complexion, dark brown hair, brown eyes. He could read and write. Benjamin Valentine stole an iron weight weighing half a hundred weight and valued at four shillings from a hotel in Smithfield and was sentenced on 7 December 1826. He pleaded: 'I was in distress and one of my children was dying for want'. He had been convicted on two previous occasions.

On arrival in Sydney on 31 July 1827 Valentine was assigned to Mr George Morris, an innkeeper, of Sydney. He was listed on the 1828 Census as working with Road Party no. 14. He received a certificate of freedom on 30 December 1833.

Valentine became a respectable merchant and a prominent member of the Macquarie Street Synagogue. In 1870 he was appointed a trustee of the synagogue when there was a need to arrange compensation with the government regarding land that had been granted in Kent Street.

He was buried at the Lidcombe Cemetery (Raphael's Ground) on 22 March 1876.

By coincidence, a second 'Benjamin Valentine' was transported to Australia on the fourth voyage of the *Marquis of Hastings* as a convict transport ship, arriving in Hobart Town on 18 July 1839. He had been sentenced at Leeds on 11 October 1838 to ten years transportation for having embezzled £50 from a Mr Davis. He had a 'very bad' reputation in gaol and does not appear to have been Jewish.

OBSP, 1826–27, case 128, p. 62; Ship Indent 4/4012, p. 159; CON 31/44; CON 18/16; CF in 4/4319, 33/1360.

VALENTINE, Henry

b. London, 1809–1840
Manlius (1), 1827; Convict; Sentenced to 7 years, Old Bailey, 1827.
Butcher's boy; 1 child.

Henry Valentine was sentenced on 12 January 1827 as a pickpocket. He had been watched as he stole a handbag by cutting the strings of a woman's handbag containing a handkerchief, a bottle of smelling salts and half a crown. His religion given as 'Protestant'.

A 'Henry Valentine' arrived on the *Manlius* on 11 August 1827. His brother was Samuel Marks (q.v.), according to the *Registry of Flash Men*. On 5 December 1828 Henry Valentine appeared before the Bench of Magistrates on a charge of 'disrespectful conduct to his Master'. He was sentenced to twenty-five lashes. Valentine appeared in the *Registry of Flash Men*, which said that he was suspected of robbing Heydon, an auctioneer, and stealing his cash box. He was said to have lived at a house in Pitt Street with four prostitutes. He was caught at Parramatta and sentenced with Samuel Marks for the Heydon robbery. The 1837 General Return of Convicts in New South Wales listed him as the assigned convict servant of Mr W. Simpson of Maitland.

Valentine 'of the asylum' was buried by the Sydney Synagogue in the Devonshire Street Jewish Cemetery on 15 February 1840.

There is a birth register record that an 'unknown' child was born in Sydney to Henry Valentine on 16 February 1839 and was listed as an 'Israelite'. The child died at birth.

OBSP 11 January 1827 case 307. COD 120; Norfolk Island COD 2; W. A. Miles, *Registry of Flash Men*, 2/673.

VALENTINE, Henry

b. Aldgate, 1817
Waterloo, 1835; Convict; Sentenced to 14 years, Old Bailey, 1834.
Single; Errand boy; Height: 157 cm.

Fresh complexion, brown hair, oval face, high forehead, brown eyes, 'medium nose'. He had two pockmarks on his right cheek. Henry Valentine was convicted of 'picking a Lady's pocket'. He had served two three-month terms for similar offences. The surgeon reported that he was 'quiet and orderly' on board ship.

From 1835 to 1840 Valentine worked as an assigned servant in Launceston. In June 1835 he received six lashes on the breach for insolence to his overseer. In October 1835 he was sent to the treadmill for ten days for being out after hours. For neglect of duty and insolence he received thirty-six lashes in October 1837. On 31 January 1839 he received four months labour out of chains for neglect of duty, being drunk, disorderly and using indecent language. Valentine's assigned service was cancelled when, on 18 January 1840, he was caught at the 'Regatta Hotel contrary to orders'. He was sent to the Avoca District and 'not again' to be allocated service in Launceston. On 9 September 1840 he was sentenced to six months hard labour for having accused Mr Alford, his master, of perjury.

On 4 August 1842 Valentine was granted a ticket of leave. Three charges of being drunk followed in 1842, 1843 and 1845. At the Supreme Court, Launceston, he was found not guilty of assaulting John Martram and robbing him of twelve shillings (7 October 1845). His Launceston police record ends on 31 July 1848 when he was sent to the treadmill for one month for hawking goods without a licence.

Henry Valentine rented seat no. 54 in the Hobart Synagogue in 1845. He only paid £1 of its rental of £2 12s and the rest was written off as a bad debt. On 19 September 1846 he was found guilty of larceny under the sum of £5 and was given twelve months hard labour and it was recommended he be deprived of his ticket of leave and sent to Port Arthur. Henry Valentine's name appears against a donation in 1849 and he is mentioned as living near Launceston when the synagogue closed in the 1870s.

Allport Collection; *Waterloo* Indent, no. 85; VDL Papers, ML, A 1059-7, p. 28; CON 34/5, no. 85; CON 31/44; CON 18/21.

VALENTINE, Joshua

b. London, 1805
Norfolk (1), 1825; Convict; Sentenced to 7 years, Newgate, 1823.
Single; Confectioner; Height: 165 cm.

Florid complexion, a little pock-pitted, dark brown hair, hazel eyes. Joshua Valentine was tried and sentenced on 22 October 1823. He was 'Very well behaved' on the ship.

Valentine arrived in New South Wales on 18 August 1825 and was sent as an assigned convict servant to Major Ovens. He was not listed in the 1828 Census. Joshua Valentine received a ticket of leave in 1830 followed by a certificate of freedom on 8 December 1830, which was renewed on 11 May 1833.

Ship Indent 4/4009a; Principal Superintendent of Convicts 4/2115, 31/6670; TL 30/67; CF in 4/4303, and 4/4316; *Australian*, 24 December 1830.

VICTORSEN, Julius

b. Meta, Russia, 1816–1875
Ocean, 1849; Free.
Draper; 7 Children.

Julius Victorsen arrived in Adelaide from Hamburg on 15 September 1849 with his wife Rosetta (née Mendel, born c. 1817, in Elmshorne, Germany) and son Louis (born 25 July 1849). The Victorsens had married in 1848 in Altona (near Hamburg). They went to Clare in South Australia, where they founded a business, and they lived there for many years. The family moved from Clare to Glenelg in 1872 and Julius Victorsen died on 25 January 1875 at the age of fifty-nine.

Their children were Lewis (Louis) (1849), Manuel (1 April 1851, who died aged two), Mathilde (born 24 May 1852), Deborah (Theodora) (24 September 1853), Phillip (29 April 1855), Elijah (Edwin) (14 April 1857), and Hannah (Henrietta) (1 June 1861).

Pritchard Index.

W

WAINWRIGHT, Phoebe

b. London, 1810
David Scott, 1834; Free.
Single; Servant, actress; 1 child.

The *David Scott* was an immigrant ship bringing bounty migrants from London. It arrived in Sydney on 25 October 1834. Phoebe was described as a Jewess. She married a shoemaker named Charles Wilson. They had a child who was admitted to the Orphan School while Phoebe was placed on trial, on 4 March 1836, for stealing. She was found not guilty. At Darlinghurst in 1838 she was found guilty of obtaining money by false pretences and sentenced to six months in the Female Factory and then, in 1839, was sent to Van Diemen's Land for three years.

Police Department, Sydney, and Darlinghurst Gaol Entrance Book, 19 May 1835 to 28 February 1837, 4/6436, 4/6448, dated 4 March 1836; CS Letters Received 1839, Police, 4/2469.3, 39/10076, 25 February 1839.

WALFORD, Barnard (Bernard) (Benjamin)

b. Vienna, 1765–1828
Active, 1791; Convict; Sentenced to 7 years, Old Bailey, 1789.
Single; Engraver; 7 children.

Walford arrived in England in 1782. He stole a basket of laundry and was arrested in Petticoat Lane. He was described by his victim as 'a Jew in a brown coat with a white cape and his hair plaited with a bit of tape'. Walford explained: 'I am a foreigner. I come from Vienna. I have been in England seven years. I was taught English as a child'. He claimed to have rheumatism. His landlady, who was Jewish, and apparently living with him, said: 'He will not work. He sits down in a chair and says his limbs fail him'. Walford was sentenced at the Old Bailey on 28 October 1789.

Walford arrived in New South Wales on the Third Fleet by the *Active* in September 1791 and was sent to Norfolk Island on the *Reliance* on 13 February 1796. He was allowed to settle on Norfolk Island on the expiration of his sentence and was granted a farm allotment of 40 acres, of which 20 were cultivated. He married Jane Malloy, who already had two children by the time she met Walford. In 1807 Walford and his family were transferred to Van Diemen's Land and given land at

New Norfolk. In the 1809 Van Diemen's Land Muster, Walford was shown as the owner of 56 acres of land, one ewe, one goat, six pigs and six children!

Walford was mistakenly listed as 'Benjamin' Walford in the 1811 General Muster. He lived between Hobart Town and Browne's River (about three miles from Hobart). Barnard Walford became a baker in Liverpool Street, Hobart Town. In 1820 he handed over his business to his son Bernard (q.v.), while he became the licensee of the Turk's Head Inn (later the King's Head and the Joiners' Arms, which became the King George) in Murray Street. His son continued to hold the licence until 1842.

In 1817 Barnard Walford was brought before the magistrates on a charge of stealing a quantity of notes from William Morgan while he was drunk. Walford was acquitted, but was fined for retailing spirits without a licence. Between 1820 and 1827, Walford was the owner of the Adam and Eve in Liverpool Street and the King George in Murray Street.

On 21 May 1828 Walford wrote to the Lieutenant Governor offering 'heartfelt thanks for your goodness in being pleased to grant us a Piece of Land as a Burial Field. I feel more thankful that your grant has been approved of by the highest authority of the Church of England resident in these colonies'. Walford promised to send word of the Lieutenant Governor's kindness 'to our revered and highly respected Priest in England'. Before the year had ended, 'after a protracted illness' (*Hobart Town Gazette*, 27 September 1828), Walford died at the age of sixty-six, and became the first Jew to be buried in the Harrington Street Jewish Cemetery. His tombstone was later removed to the Jewish cemetery at Cornelian Bay.

Some of Walford's children appear to have considered themselves Jews. On 4 January 1838, in Launceston, Benjamin Walford married Sarah Solomon (q.v.), the daughter of Joseph Solomon (q.v.) of Evandale. Bernard Walford jnr (q.v.) applied on his deathbed to be buried as a Jew (16 July 1846), but this request was denied by the Hobart Hebrew Congregation. Walford's family consisted of Ann, born at Norfolk Island, 26 November 1791 (father unknown), Elizabeth, born 3 August 1794 (father unknown), Mary (1798), Bernard (1801), Rebecca (1803), Samuel (1805), Benjamin (Van Diemen's Land, 3 December 1809), Joseph (1812), and Isabella (1814).

OBSP, 1789–90, case 819, p. 964; Convict Indent COD/9; CSO 269, p. 168; List of Settlers on *Lady Nelson*, 9 November 1817, Piper Papers, vol. 1, p. 84f., A254; *Sydney Gazette*, 2 June 1810; *Hobart Town Gazette*, 24 February 1818, 19 June 1819, 2 September 1820, 11 November 1820, 31 March 1821, 28 April 1821, 10 May 1823; *Hobart Town Courier*, 14 June 1828; CO 201/52, General Muster, p. 2; CS Out 1/108/2633; CSO 1/269/6497; CSO Out 1543.1/530; CSO 1/269-6497, dated 21 May 1828; family history provided by Chris Simmons, UK, and Leslie Walford, Australia.

WALFORD, Benjamin

b. Van Diemen's Land, 1809–1885

The child of Barnard Walford (q.v.) and Jane Walford, Benjamin was born on 12 April 1809 at Launceston, two years after his parents arrival from Norfolk Island, and baptised on 3 December 1809. However, like his brother Bernard (q.v.),

Benjamin Walford clearly identified as a Jew. He married twice: His first wife was Sarah Solomon (q.v.), the daughter of Joseph Solomon (q.v.) of Evandale, and they married on 4 January 1838, despite the obvious disapproval of her father.

Walford wrote from Launceston to the Colonial Secretary: 'I request you will be pleased to forward me a licence for marriage without publication of Banns between Miss Sarah Solomon of Evandale and myself by the Rev. William Browne according to the rites and ceremonies of the United Church of England and Ireland. I am twenty-one and unmarried. Sarah is nineteen'. Joseph Solomon gave his consent on 4 January 1838, but stipulated in his will that Sarah would not share any of her inheritance until after Benjamin, her husband, was dead. As fate would have it, Sarah died first. Benjamin's second wife, Sarah Joseph, was probably the daughter of Reuben Joseph (q.v.). Benjamin Walford died in Sydney on 9 August 1885 at Glebe Point.

Family information from Chris Simmons (UK) and Leslie Walford (Australia).

WALFORD, Bernard (jnr)

b. Norfolk Island, 1801–1846

Bernard was the second child and first son of Barnard Walford (q.v.) and his wife Jane. In 1845 the 'young' Bernard Walford had paid for the placement of a tombstone in the Harrington Street Jewish cemetery on the grave of his father's faithful Jewish friend Michael Lee (q.v.). On 16 July 1846 Bernard Walford, who must have known he was dying, asked for permission to be buried in the Jewish cemetery in Hobart Town, which his father had obtained as a grant from the government. The synagogue existed by this time, and the board ungraciously refused his last request.

WARSCHAUER, Marcus (MOSES) (Mordecai MOSES)

b. Warsaw, 1777–1860

Moffatt (2), 1836; Convict; Sentenced to 14 years, Old Bailey, 1835.

Married; Dealer and Scripture reader; Height: 164 cm; 8 children.

Dark sallow complexion, brown hair mixed with grey, breast hairy, badly ruptured. Thomas Harris (q.v.), Marcus Warschauer and a non-Jewish printer named Ball were accused of forging Polish bank notes. Warschauer was arrested with a parcel of forged note plates in his possession at the Strand Coffee House. Both Harris and Warschauer were intensely involved in the affairs of the Duke's Place Synagogue. Warschauer was fifty-six years old at the time of his arrest. He had no previous convictions.

The parents of Marcus Warschauer, also known as Mordecai Moses, were Moses and Harriet Moses. The family had migrated to London prior to 1807 and his parents had adopted the English surname of Marsh. Marcus' first wife was Amelia Cohen, who bore five children. One of these was George Moss (q.v.), who migrated to New South Wales in 1831 and became the mainstay of the Sydney Jewish community. Amelia died in London c. 1819. In 1820 Mordecai Moses lived at 1 Harrow Alley, Houndsditch and was 'a dealer'. Warschauer's second wife was Abigail Barnett (Abigail Moses, q.v.), who followed her husband to Sydney and who brought with her three stepchildren, Alexander (Moses) (q.v.), Catherine Moss (q.v.) and Rosetta Moss (q.v.).

Mordecai Moses was appointed Keeper of the Jews' Burial Ground on application from Mr Michael Phillips (q.v.) to the Colonial Secretary on 24 November 1836. The Colonial Secretary wrote: 'I have examined the prisoner. He is a native of Poland and has but a very superficial knowledge of the English language—the last sixteen years of his life [has been spent] as a reader in a synagogue. I do not consider the man fit for private assignment'. In other words, Moses was officially exempted from assigned service. Moses was granted an allowance of ten shillings a week by the synagogue from 1 June 1838 to be sexton. (His allowance as 'acting *shamash*' had formerly been six shillings a week.) The Colonial Secretary Alexander McLeay told the Superintendent of Convicts that 'the former service of assignment of Mordecai Moses had been cancelled accordingly'. In gratitude Mordecai Moses wrote to the synagogue, 'My mind and my time shall be devoted to our House of God established in this distant clime'. He officiated at the marriage of his son George Moss in March 1840.

In 6 July 1841 Abigail died, and on her tombstone at the cemetery on Devonshire Street was inscribed 'the wife of an officer of the Sydney Synagogue and sexton of this ground'. She was aged fifty-two. Moses received a conditional pardon on 21 April 1844. In 1842 he had been appointed sexton (*shamash*) of the York Street congregation and an assistant reader at the synagogue. On 18 February 1850 Marcus Moses was granted a certificate of freedom. When he retired as sexton in 1857 a generous pension of £150 per annum was granted. He died aged eighty-five on 7 October 1860 at his residence Pitt Street, 'late second reader of the Sydney Synagogue'. The Hebrew inscription on his 'altar style' tombstone transferred to Rookwood placed in a prominent position of honour reads that he died on the night of Shimini Atzeret and buried on Simchat Torah 22 Tishri 5621 at the age of eighty-five. The English inscription adds 'A tribute of respect from the members of the York Street Synagogue to an old and faithful servant'

Abigail Moses was subsequently reinterred at the Rookwood Cemetery.

Moffatt Printed Indent, arrived 30 August 1836, p. 99; *OBSP*, 1835–36, cases 289–294, pp. 258–95; CS 4/2311, 36/2319, Miscellaneous Persons Out, p. 416, in 4/3682; CF 50/58; S 4/CP, 21 April 1844 in Governors' Despatches, ML, A1295; G. F. J. Bergman, 'The Bizarre Life of Mordecai Moses', *AJJHS*, vol. 8, no. 3 (1977), p. 100f. *Sydney Morning Herald* 10 October 1860.

WASSERMAN, Joseph

b. Frankfurt am Main, 1819
Duchess of Northumberland (1), 1843; Convict; Sentenced to 10 years, Central Criminal Court, 1842.
Single; Clerk; Height: 170 cm.

Fair complexion, hair brown, brown eyes, large nose, receding chin. Jew. Spoke English with a German accent. Could read and write. Guilty of larceny. Joseph Wasserman stole four gold watches and three gold chains from a shop in Leadenhall Street and was convicted of 'larceny'. His behaviour on board ship was 'remarkably quiet'. He was listed in the indent as 'Waserman'.

The *Duchess of Northumberland* arrived in Hobart Town on 18 January 1843. Wasserman was released from his first stage of probation on the Southport Road Gang on 18 July 1845. He worked as an assigned servant to two shopkeepers in Hobart Town until being assigned to work for Isaac Solomon (q.v.) of Liverpool Street on 11 February 1847. A ticket of leave was issued to Wasserman on 25 January 1848 and a conditional pardon on 27 November 1849. No colonial offences were recorded. He received permission to marry Charlotte Ellis in August 1848. The minister was the Rev. Palmer. Charlotte Ellis had come to the colony as a convict on the *Elizabeth and Henry* in June 1845.

CON 33/36; CON 52/2; CON 14/19; CON 18/34; CON 52/2; Permission to Marry Book, pp. 403, 349.

WHYLE, Morris (WYLE) (WHYTE)

b. Mecklenburg, 1806
Isabella I (5), 1833; Convict; Sentenced to 14 years, Liverpool, 1833.
Single; Hawker; Height: 162 cm.

Morris Whyle was convicted for receiving three stolen watches and four spoons at Liverpool, together with Asher Simons (q.v.), on 7 January 1833. The indent noted: 'The High Priest reports his family as very respectable in Germany'. His hulk report was 'Orderly'.

Whyle arrived in Van Diemen's Land on 14 November 1833. (He was listed in the Indent of the *Isabella I* as Morris 'Wyle'.) On 19 February 1834 he was charged with 'drawing obscene figures upon the kitchen wall'. He was an assigned convict to Mr Bates. He was then declared to be useless to his master and returned to Public Works. On 4 October 1836, while assigned to Mr Bryant, he was charged with suspicion of being an absconder. The charge was found to be untrue. On 24 December 1836 he was charged with being absent without leave. A ticket of leave was granted on 5 November 1839. On 22 March 1841 the ticket of leave was suspended because he was charged with 'Misconduct'. He received seven days hard labour. Whyle was granted a conditional pardon (no. 269) on 10 March 1842 and a certificate of freedom on 14 January 1847.

On 1 April 1842 Whyle officiated at the Jewish wedding of George Robinson (q.v.) to Sarah Phillips. It was the third Jewish wedding to be held in Launceston. In September 1843 Whyle signed a petition for clemency in favour of Isaac Jacobs (q.v.), who was in gaol for debt. His name also appeared on the Launceston Synagogue petition of May 1843. On 18 June 1844 Arthur Isaac Nathan (Asher Nathan, q.v.) officiated at Launceston's fourth Jewish wedding, when Morris Whyle married Alice Abrahams on 18 June 1844. He was aged thirty-eight and was a dealer and she was thirty-six and the widow of Henry Abrahams (q.v.). The marriage was witnessed by Godfrey Myers (q.v.), in the presence of Benjamin Francis (q.v.). Whyle then officiated at the next Jewish wedding in Launceston on 20 November 1844. On 29 June 1844 the *Launceston Examiner* reported that Morris Whyle had donated £5 for the Launceston Building Fund. He had become a partner in the Launceston firm Levy and Whyle, which operated from May 1844 to 18 February 1846. The *Launceston Examiner* (25 April 1846) reported that the entire stock worth £1300 was sold by Benjamin Francis.

Whyle, his wife and her son Henry Abrahams moved to Adelaide, South Australia, shortly after Whyle received his certificate of freedom. On 10 March 1849 the *South Australian Register* reported that there had been a law suit between Abrahams and Julius Amsberg, both formerly of Hamburg, with which Maurice Whyle, storekeeper at Hindley Street, formerly of Van Diemen's Land, where he was a convict, was involved as a witness. Whyle seems to have changed his name in South Australia and became known as 'Morris Whyte'. The London *Jewish Chronicle* reported that he had lent a Torah scroll to the newly formed Adelaide Hebrew Congregation for the High Holydays in 1850 and that he was a member of the congregation's committee.

Alice Whyle, 'wife of Morris', died in Adelaide on 7 July 1853 at the age of forty-five. She was described on her tombstone as the mother of Henry Abrahams.

CON 31/47; CON 27/6; MM 33/2; *Launceston Examiner*, 29 June 1844, 18 February 1846, 28 October 1846; *South Australian Gazette and Colonial Register*, 10 March 1849; *Jewish Chronicle* (London), 30 May 1851.

WILLIAMS, Henry

b. London, 1809
Champion, 1827; Convict; Sentenced to 7 years, Middlesex, 1827.
Single; Clerk; Height: 158 cm.

Ruddy complexion, brown hair, peculiar raised mark on right forehead. Jew. Could read and write. Henry Williams was sentenced to transportation for 'privately stealing'. He had stolen a cushion valued at ten shillings from a coach-maker. He had served a previous sentence of six months.

Henry Williams was listed in the 1828 Census as attached to the Engineers' Department in Parramatta. No religion was stated but he was listed as a Jew in the *Phoenix* entry book when he was admitted to the hulk on 17 May 1833 for being involved in a case of 'Highway Robbery'. He was sent on to the Hyde Park Barracks on 4 June 1833. A certificate of freedom was issued on 25 September 1834.

Ship Indent 4/4012, p. 245; *Phoenix* (hulk) Entry Book, 4/6282, no. 383; CF 4/4324, 34/1184.

WILLIAMS, Thomas

b. London, 1812
Bengal Merchant (3), 1836; Convict; Sentenced to 7 years, Old Bailey, 1835.
Single; Footman; Height: 157 cm.

Dark ruddy complexion, pock-pitted, brown hair and brown eyes. Jew. Could read and write. Thomas Williams had served four and three-quarter years in the hulks at Woolwich of an initial seven-year sentence for a previous conviction. He had the mark of a burn on the left side of his neck. He was sentenced at the Central Criminal Court on 6 April 1835 and transported for life for stealing a purse containing five shillings and sixpence from a gardener in a bar. Williams conducted a lengthy and lively defence of his case, arguing and examining witnesses.

Thomas Williams arrived in New South Wales on 9 December 1836, aged twenty-four. A certificate of freedom was issued on 30 March 1844.

Bengal Merchant Printed Indent, p. 126; *OBSP*, 1834–35, case 1095, p. 1062; CF 4/4390, 44/0466.

WILLIAMS, William (Abraham ABRAHAMS)

b. Lisbon, 1779–1856
Lord Eldon, 1817; Convict; Sentenced to life, Old Bailey, 1816.
Sail-maker; Height: 161 cm.

Dark yellow complexion, black hair, dark eyes. William Williams was sentenced at Middlesex on 30 October 1816 for 'privately stealing'. Williams entered a shop on the Strand and stole a pair of boots on display in the window. He ran into the street followed by the shopkeeper and the shopkeeper's son. The thief dropped the boots in the street.

The *Lord Eldon* arrived in New South Wales on 30 September 1817. On 17 July 1818 Williams (or Abrahams) was sent to Newcastle by the *Lady Nelson* for 'running away'. When he returned to Sydney he became an assigned convict servant to Aaron Barnett (q.v.) (who was listed as Erin Barnet). Barnett provided an attestation to Williams' good character in his application to gain a ticket of leave, which was issued on 1 December 1825. In the 1828 Census William Williams was listed as a Jew. He was aged forty-nine and held a ticket of leave. Williams was working as a confectioner at Samuel Cohen's (q.v.) shop at Clarence Terrace, Sydney. On 27 November 1834 Williams wrote from Parramatta asking for a conditional pardon. He admitted that he had been sent to Newcastle for one year. On 16 April 1827 he had been sentenced to spend four hours in the stocks after having been found drunk in the street on the Sabbath Day. The conditional pardon was slow in being issued. It was authorised in December 1837 but not issued until 1839. Williams was listed in the 1837 General Return of Convicts in New South Wales as sixty-seven years old and a resident of Parramatta with a ticket of leave.

The *Sydney Morning Herald* of 26 January 1843 reported that he had been declared insolvent with debts of £3792 and assets of £3655. He was discharged from bankruptcy on 16 February 1844. He died on 9 November 1856 and was buried by the Sydney Synagogue. He was described as a 'pensioner' and was said to be aged seventy-five.

Ship Indent 2/8266, p. 367; 4/4005, p. 361; Governors' Despatches, 1826, ML, A1196, p. 275, and A1217, p. 1005; TL 25/2105; CP 39/164; CS 4/1617.2, p. 270; 4/1717.2, pp. 270–2; CS 4/2296-35/159, 35/256, 35/254.

WILSON, Charles Abraham

b. Kent, 1806–1872
Lion, 1825; Free.
Single; 1 child.

Charles Wilson was a son of (Sarah) Emma Josephson (q.v.) and her first husband, Henry Wilson. His brother was also named Henry Wilson (q.v.). Family tradition says that Charles and Henry were the sons of a soldier killed in the Napoleonic Wars whose name originally had been Isaac Goodman. Goodman is said to have changed his name to Wilson when he converted to Christianity. Wilson's mother's surname had been changed from Mendoza to Moses. Emma Leah Moses (who later married Jacob Josephson) was his mother.

Charles Abraham Wilson appears to have been adopted by his stepfather, Jacob Josephson (q.v.). He was listed in the 1828 Census as twenty-two years of age and a lodger in the Josephson household in Castlereagh Street, Sydney. Wilson married Lydia Affriatt (q.v.) at St John's Church of England in Parramatta in 1835. They had a son, whom they named Charles Abraham Wilson.

Family research by Robert Wilson, Canada.

WILSON, Henry

b. London, 1814–1880
Sir G. Osborne, 1827; Free.
Single; 1 child.

The son of Henry Wilson (né Goodman) and Emma Josephson (q.v.), whose maiden name had been Mendoza (or Moses), Henry had been born in Bishopsgate Street, London, on 9 March 1814. He was the brother of Charles Abraham Wilson (q.v.) and Sarah Emma Wilson (q.v.). The children were adopted by their stepfather, Jacob Josephson (q.v.). Henry Wilson married Sarah Affriatt (q.v.) in Sydney on 4 May 1835, and they had a son, Charles Abraham Wilson (the same name was given to his first cousin, the son of Charles Abraham Wilson and Lydia, née Affriatt, q.v.).

Henry Wilson had the licence to operate the 'Valley Inn' in Sydney in the early 1840s.

Sarah Wilson died on 6 August 1910.

Family research by Robert Wilson, Canada.

WILSON, Sarah Emma

b. London, 1800
Thalia, 1823; Free.
Single.

Sarah was the daughter of (Sarah) Emma Josephson (q.v.), and the sister of Charles Abraham Wilson (q.v.) and Henry Wilson (q.v.). She married Barnett Levey (q.v.) in 1825.

WINEBERG, Henry

b. Poland
Free.
Dealer, jeweller.

In 1837 Henry Wineberg was authorised by the Sydney Synagogue to officiate at the wedding of Samuel Cohen and Rachel Nathan (qq.v.) in Port Macquarie. Henry Wineberg became a partner with Aaron Gainsborough (q.v.). The two men worked together in a jewellery business that flourished both in Sydney and in rural New South Wales. On 7 August 1844 the partnership was dissolved following a serious conflict. Wineberg accused Gainsborough of theft and assault. There was an inconclusive trial in Sydney in April 1845. Wineberg held the licence to the Crispin Arms Hotel in Clarence Street, Sydney.

The *Cumberland Times* reported the aftermath of the trial on 26 April 1845:

> Henry Wineberg brought before the Mayor, charged with wilful and gross perjury in having alleged one Aaron Gainsborg to be more of sinner than a Publican, and a capital hand at giving watches escape movements. Wineberg's then rather extraordinary absence of mind and which led to his new presence in body. A Doctor cannot find any traces of the blow he said he had received. Wineberg, who it was stated, required the utmost assistance to get him from his room to a cab and a chair to sit on while in Court, walked quickly away and was over Woolloomooloo Hill and far away, before Gainsbourg had hardly left the dock.

Another view of the event was given in the police report when Wineberg applied for naturalisation in 1845:

> Wineberg was connected with a robbery two years ago in Phillip Street when £100 of jewellery was taken … on 11 March he charged Gainsbourg with assault on the Parramatta Rd—the trial was in April—and Wineberg suddenly 'forgets' all the charges. Gainsbourg charged him with perjury but Wineberg still affected amnesia and was discharged. A search warrant revealed part of the stolen jewellery in Wineberg's possession.

The *Cumberland Times* reported that it was decided to 'postpone' the naturalisation.

Governors' Despatches, ML, A1237, p. 819, for 1845, A1200, p. 273, 9 March 1846; *Sydney Morning Herald*, 7 August 1844, 2 May 1845; *Cumberland Times*, 26 April 1845.

WINFIELD, Ann

b. 1829
Free.

The daughter of Caspar Marks (q.v.) Ann Winfield was buried as a Jew in Sydney in 1846, aged seventeen.

WOLF, Jacob

b. 1798
Emperor Alexander, 1833; Convict.
Labourer; Height: 155 cm.

Dark complexion, small head, dark brown to grey hair and thin on top, small face, brown eyes, long nose, large mouth, short chin, 'a Jew'. Sentenced at Leeds Quarter Sessions to 14 years transportation for receiving stolen goods. Married. Two children. Gaol report 'Bad'. Hulk report 'disorderly'. Stated this offence 'Buying stolen clothes'. Wife Catherine in London. Surgeon's report 'quiet and orderly' and 'never reported'.

Jacob Wolf arrived at Hobart Town on 12 August 1833. Wolf was sent to Port Arthur on 27 September 1833 and remained there until the end of 1834. His conduct record page is blank.

CON 18/1/6 reports that Wolf came by the *England*; CON 31/46; CON 27/1/6 no. 1603 reports that he came by the *Emperor Alexander* and was immediately sent on to Port Arthur.

WOLF, Sarah

Tory (1), 1845; Convict.

Sarah Wolf came to Van Diemen's Land as a convict on the *Tory*, arriving on 4 July 1845. She received official permission to marry the free settler William Worthy on 9 June 1848.

CON 52/2, p. 349; CON 41/6; CON 15/3; CON 19/5.

WOLFE, Emanuel

Palambam, 1833; Free.
Single; Printer.

Emanuel Wolfe gave his occupation as a printer in the ship's manifest. By 1839 the *Sydney Post Office Directory* listed him as a dealer in glass and earthenware with a shop and dwelling in Market Street. In 1845 Emanuel Wolfe appeared among the minor donors (fourteen shillings and sixpence) to the Hobart Synagogue. 'E & M Wolfe' of Hobart Town were the printers of the dedication service for the synagogues in Launceston and Hobart. The congregation paid Wolfe £10 14s for the booklet, which was in unvocalised Hebrew and English, and entitled *Dedication of the Hobart Synagogue*.

In the 1845 *Post Office Directory* there was a reference to the printing shop being in Liverpool Street in Hobart Town. However, in the *Bibliography of Australia*, Ferguson wrote: 'There is no record of E & M Wolfe being Hobart printers; the pamphlet was probably printed in Sydney'. This was certainly true of the *Order of Service Performed at the Consecration of the New Synagogue St John's St Launceston 1846*, because it bears the address Lower George Street. The two pamphlets are almost identical, but the complexity of the text and the style of the English translation testifies to the literate influence of Phineas Moss (q.v.) and indicates that the first booklet, at least, was printed in Van Diemen's Land.

A second pamphlet, *A Few Thoughts by a Member of the Bar*, was published by E & M Wolfe in Hobart Town in 1845.

In 1847 'E. Wolfe' of George Street, Sydney, published a *Lecture Delivered at the Sydney Synagogue by W. L. Lindenthal, Teacher of Hebrew and German Languages, Sydney*.

Emanuel's brothers, Morris (Moses Wolfe, q.v.) and Henry Wolfe (Wolff, q.v.), were both in Hobart Town in 1846. Emanuel left for Sydney later that year and

printed *The Rules and Catalogue of the Sydney Jewish Library and Hebraic Association* in 1848. His address, Lower George Street, appeared in the booklet.
Australian, 10 January 1835.

WOLFE, Isaac (WOOLF)

b. London, 1804
Medway (1), 1821; Convict; Sentenced to life, Richmond Quarter Sessions, 1820.
Single; Labourer; Height: 150 cm.

Brown hair, hazel eyes, a Jew. Isaac Wolfe was sixteen years old when he was sentenced at Richmond on 13 September 1820.

Isaac Wolfe arrived in Hobart Town on 13 March 1821. Wolfe's long convict dossier began when he was twenty-one years of age. On 5 July 1825, while at the Prisoners' Barracks in Hobart Town, he was sentenced to twenty-five lashes and a period of imprisonment on Maria Island for absenting himself from his work gang and having in his possession a loaf of bread 'without being able to give a satisfactory account of the same'. By 10 January 1826 he was back on the mainland and assigned to Mr Simpson, when he disobeyed an order of Simpson's and was returned to the Prisoners' Barracks. He was consigned to the Glenorchy Road Party and on 29 November 1826 was placed in the chain gang and given twenty-five lashes for 'beating and ill using Charles Penroy on Monday morning last'. Two weeks later, on 10 December 1826, he received another twenty-five lashes for having neglected his work on that morning. On 28 January 1828 he was part of the Black Snake Road Party when he was found to be absent from his hut at 12 o'clock on Saturday night, for which he received fifty lashes. On 22 July 1828 he was committed for trial for having stolen a waistcoat at the Prisoners' Barracks, together with five shillings from Angus Kennedy. He was found guilty. By 10 March 1830 he was an assigned servant to Mr H. Robson when he was given thirty lashes for 'disobedience of orders and insolence'. On 4 April 1834 he held a ticket of leave and was the assigned servant of Mr J. Welsh. The records do not specify his offence but his ticket of leave was cancelled by order of the Lieutenant Governor and he was ordered back to the penitentiary.

By the end of 1834 his ticket of leave had been restored only to be suspended again for four months for being repeatedly absent from the weekly muster. During this period of punishment he was sent to the Westbury Road Party. His ticket of leave had again been restored by the end of 1835. On 21 May 1836 he was sentenced to the treadmill for forty-eight hours for having been absent once again from the muster and from church. A conditional pardon was issued on 3 February 1838. On 16 March 1839 he was committed for trial in Launceston for larceny. The trial was held on 3 April and he was acquitted. He was given a conditional pardon on 4 February 1840. It is a wonder he was still alive following 155 lashes and almost twenty years as a convict.

CON 23/3; CON 31/45, no. 274, p. 102; *Colonial Times*, 19 August 1834; *Hobart Town Courier*, 22 August 1834; CP 38/1572; Prisoners Sent from Moreton Bay on 8 January 1840, in 4/6271; Prisoners Sent to Port Macquarie, 18 April 1835, in 4/3899.

WOLFE, John

Free.
Dealer.

John Wolfe was in gaol in Melbourne, having been convicted on 12 October 1842 for 'refusing to pay lawful wages'. He was to be released in December 1842.
42/9790, in 4/2589.2, 31 December 1842.

WOLFE, Moses (Morris) (Moses WOLFF)

Free.

The brother of Emanuel Wolfe (q.v.) and Henry Wolfe (Wolff, q.v.), Moses Wolfe's signature appeared on the Launceston Synagogue petition of 20 May 1843. In 1844 Moses, or Morris, Wolfe lived in Liverpool Street and owed the Hobart Synagogue eleven shillings for his 1844 membership subscription. He remained a member through 1845 and 1846, renting seat no. 48, and accumulating arrears of £4 10s before being written off as 'bad'.

WOLFE, Samuel (WULFF)

b. Copenhagen, 1810–1852
Portsea, 1838; Convict; Sentenced to 10 years, Central Criminal Court, 1838.
Watchmaker and jeweller; Height: 155 cm.

Dark, sallow, freckled, dark brown hair, brown eyes, slightly pock-pitted complexion. Hazel eyes. One tooth lost in front and marks of having been bled on arms. Ears pierced. Could read and write. Samuel Wolfe was convicted of 'unlawful pawning' on 24 February 1838. He had no previous convictions. Religion 'Protestant'.

Wolfe arrived in Sydney on 18 December 1838. Moses Lazarus (q.v.) wrote from Hobart Town to Colonial Secretary La Trobe in Melbourne stating that Lazarus hoped to open a jeweller's shop in Collins Street, in the new settlement of Melbourne, and asked for the assigned service of Samuel Wolfe, who, he said, was lately arrived in Hobart Town by the *Pyramus*. It was noted in the margin that he had arrived in Sydney in December 1838 on the *Portsea*.

Wolfe received a ticket of leave on 26 September 1843 at Geelong. On 25 April 1845 John Hunter Patterson at McIvor Creek, near Pyalong, engaged Samuel 'Wulff' to be a shepherd, and in early May sent him to Melbourne with a pony. Shortly after his arrival, on 19 July 1845, Samuel 'Wolff' appeared before the Supreme Court in Melbourne to plead guilty on a charge of obtaining money under false pretences by stealing a pony and attempting to sell it. Wolfe told the court that he was a foreigner and unacquainted with the law and was not aware that he had been guilty of any offence. His Honour Mr Therry said that he had shown considerable ingenuity in the law in the course of his defence. He had disposed of the horse very artfully. He had not sold it but had obtained money for it. He had arrived in the colony in a state of bondage and it was 'wonderful' after the chastisement he had endured, which transportation imposed, that he should have again sacrificed that liberty. He was sentenced to six months hard labour and, at the end of the sentence, was to be returned to assigned service.

Samuel 'Wolf' died in the Sydney Infirmary on 2 March 1852 and was buried by the Sydney Synagogue.

Ship Indent, X641, p. 196, no. 38-2327; VDL 39/126, Letter from M. Lazarus, on 22 October 1839; 2/8257, p. 307; *Port Phillip Patriot*, 21 July 1845; VPR, series 30P, Box 4-1-13A-4; TL 43/2275, in 4/4180.

WOLFF, Abraham

Regatta, 1844; Free.
Dealer.

'Messrs Wolf Senior and Junior' arrived steerage from London on the *Regatta* in November 1844. Abraham Wolff became a partner of Henry Horowitz (q.v.) and they worked as shopkeepers in Hobart Town. Their shared premises were at the corner of Harrington and Elizabeth streets, which they rented for £50 per annum. Wolff paid 28 shillings to the Hobart Synagogue in 1844 and rented seat no. 49 in the Hobart Synagogue in 1845–46. (The synagogue ledger spelt his name Wolff). Despite his donation, Henry was not listed in the synagogue's membership list. Abraham Wolff married Julia Phillips, the sister of Solomon Phillips (q.v.).

Hobart Town Courier, 29 May 1845.

WOLFF, Henry (WOLF) (WOLFE) (WOOLF)

b. London, 1823–1859
Isabella Watson, 1842; Free; Sentenced to 7 years, Sydney, 1842.
Single; Dealer; Height: 177 cm; 5 children.

Fresh complexion, dark hair, hazel eyes. Henry Wolff was the son of Mark and Matilda Wolff and a cousin of Wolff Lewis Pyke (q.v.). Mark Wolff was a chiropodist, who lived at 133 Leadenhall Street, London. On 10 February 1842 the *Sydney Free Press and Commercial Journal* reported that Henry 'Wolf 'had been convicted of embezzling a sum of money and had been sentenced at the Sydney Quarter Sessions to seven years transportation. He was initially sent to Norfolk Island and then transported to Van Diemen's Land, arriving on 8 March 1842. He said he was the brother of Emanuel Wolfe (q.v.) and Morris (Moses Wolfe, q.v.), who were both in Van Diemen's Land in 1846.

Henry Wolff was granted a ticket of leave on 29 September 1845. On 23 November 1846 Henry Wolff wrote to the Comptroller General, Hobarton: 'I respectfully beg to elicit your sanction to my marriage with Miss Grace Caspar of 21 Murray Street, a free person. My conduct during my residence in Hobart Town has been too guarded to cause the slightest displeasure. Henry Wolff by the *Isabella Watson* holding a ticket of leave'. Permission was granted. A copy of the letter is held by the synagogue. The marriage took place on 23 December 1846 (Jewish marriage no. 13) at his residence, 5 Lord's Buildings, Hobart Town. Grace Casper was twenty-one years of age and was the daughter of Ellis and Elizabeth Casper (qq.v.). The bridegroom was twenty-three years old. Henry Wolff was an enthusiastic supporter of the plan to build a Mikveh (ritual bath) in Hobart in the late 1840's.

In the *Hobart Town Directory and General Guide*, 1847, there is a three-quarter page advertisement for 'Henry Woolfs Select Academy for Young Gentlemen at 5 Lord's Buildings, Elizabeth Street. Latin, French and Dancing taught (if required). An evening school from half past seven to ten o'clock'. The principal would 'endeavour by means of kind and parental forbearance and attention to develop those emulative powers which in all children are more or less to be remarked'.

The Wolffs had five children. Edmund was born in Hobart Town on 10 December 1848. Alfred was born in Hamilton on 2 January 1850. On 15 July 1853 Alfred, the three-year-old child of Henry and Grace Wolff, was buried by the Hobart Synagogue. On 17 August 1853 the Hobart Synagogue recorded the birth and subsequent death of Frederick Benjamin Wolff. Matilda Eily (Emily) was born in 1855, and Henry was born in Melbourne in 1859.

Henry and Grace Wolff moved to Melbourne in time for the High Holydays in September 1855. Henry worked in partnership with his father-in-law, Ellis Casper. Henry and two of his children visited England in 1858–59, and arrived back in Melbourne at the time of a diphtheria epidemic. Henry died shortly after his return. He was buried in the Jewish section of the Melbourne General Cemetery at Carlton. His son, named Henry, died at the age of three weeks and was buried beside his father.

Grace married Jacob Silberberg in 1868 and died thirteen years later at the township of Macarthur in Victoria, on 14 October 1881, aged fifty-four.

Edmund Wolff, a law clerk, married Julia Osborne in 1867. Emily married her first cousin, George Levy (son of Sara and Samuel Levy), in 1876.

CON 37/1, p. 55; CON 16/1, p. 202; CON 52/2, p. 396; *Sydney Free Press and Commercial Journal*, 10 February 1841; Deportation Register 4/4523, p. 104; family research by Helen Andrea Wolff, in First Families 2001 (website).

WOOLF, Aaron

b. Riga, 1793
Layton (1), 1829; Convict; Sentenced to 7 years, Surrey, 1828.
Married; Jeweller and watchmaker; Height: 158 cm; 1 child.

Dark ruddy complexion, pock-pitted, dark black hair to grey, brown eyes, long nose, long double chin. Stout made, slightly pock-pitted. A Jew. Can read and write. Aaron Woolf was convicted for stealing fourteen gold patent watches valued at £143. He had no previous convictions. He was sentenced at Kingston on 27 December 1828.

Woolf arrived in Sydney on the *Layton* on 9 November 1829 and was assigned to work as a servant to George Barber, Argyle. On 7 December 1830 he was sentenced to seventy-five lashes for 'disobedience and outrageous conduct'. Described as a 'dealer', he was assigned in July 1832 to Daniel Rogers of Sydney. On 30 May 1833 he was sentenced to six months in irons for stealing a gold ring. On 31 December 1833 he received twelve months in irons for robbery. In the Sydney Gaol Recognition Book Woolf was described as 5'4" (162.5 cm), stout, swarthy with black hair and black eyes. On 25 April 1834 he was sentenced to thirty-six lashes for neglect of work. On 14 November 1836 he received twenty-five lashes for neglect of duty. A certificate of freedom was granted on 7 July 1838. His time of freedom was over quickly. On 24 October 1839 he was sentenced to ten years colonial transportation for stealing £18 from William Crane and arrived at Norfolk Island on 5 January 1840. The following month he was sent to gaol for two days for presenting himself at the hospital and pretending to be ill. In September 1843 he was found to have government leather in his possession and his sentence was lengthened. In the following year a small quantity of tobacco was found to be illegally in his possession and three months was added to his sentence.

Woolf's name was listed among the nine Jewish prisoners on Norfolk Island who applied to the Sydney Synagogue for prayer books. In October 1845 Woolf arrived in Van Diemen's Land on the *Lady Franklin* and was sent, during a six-month probation period, to the work gangs at Impression Bay on the Tasman Peninsula, at Port Macquarie (on Van Diemen's Land's west coast), and at Port Esperance.

On 23 March 1846 Woolf was again issued with a ticket of leave, and a certificate of freedom was issued on 24 October 1846. On 10 November that year the London Rabbinical Court (*Beth Din*) wrote to the congregation in Hobart Town asking for information about Woolf on behalf of his wife:

> a man by the name of Ze'ev the son of Aharon who was for many years transported from here to Sydney. Information has reached us that the said Wolf is now in Hobart Town, a policeman. His wife living here as a respectable woman wishes to know the truth. We therefore hope you will make every enquiry and will oblige us with every particular thereof to relieve the poor Woman from her anxiety.

4/4014, p. 255; CON 33/71 no. 16672; CON 16/3, p. 124; CON 33/71; Norfolk Island Book, 4/2698.1, no. 696; Gaol Recognition Book, 4/6298, no. 1218; *Sydney Gazette*, 27 September 1832; CF 38/577; *Australian*, 11 September 1838, p. 4; Letter from London *Beth Din*, 10 November 5607/1846.

WOOLF, Isaac

b. London, 1804
Mary II, 1822; Convict; Sentenced to life, Old Bailey, 1821.
Single; Errand boy; Height: 156 cm.

Pockmarked complexion, brown hair, hazel eyes (blind in right eye). Isaac Woolf was a pickpocket who was seen stealing from a police officer (by another policeman) in the midst of a crowd going into the East London Theatre. Woolf had stolen eight shillings.

Isaac Woolf was listed on the return of convicts discharged from the establishment in Emu Plains and sent to Port Macquarie on the *Sally* on 24 June 1823. He was listed in the 1828 Census as a shepherd to J. Macarthur, Voralga, Cookbundoon, and a 'Protestant'. He was granted a ticket of leave on 19 August 1834. At the General Sessions in Sydney on 17 November 1835, Woolf was convicted and sentenced to seven years colonial transportation for larceny—stealing half a chest of tea—and was sent by the *Governor Phillip* to Port Macquarie. He was then transferred to Moreton Bay, listed as a Jew. On 31 December 1838 Isaac Woolf was sentenced to twenty-five lashes for having lost several sheep to 'native dogs' from a herd he was guarding. On 19 March 1839 he was given fifty lashes for losing three sheep while in charge of the flock at Cooper Plains. Woolf was returned to Sydney on 8 January 1840 and appeared in the list of the 'Men in Irons'. Woolf was sent to the District of Berrima, where he received his ticket of leave on 14 October 1844. In November 1844 he was allowed to move to Goulburn.

OBSP, 1820–21, case 639, p. 328; Ship Indent 4/4009, p. 47; TL 44/2628, 14 October 1844, in 4/4194; 4/6445 p. 23; Chronological Register of Convicts at Moreton Bay, no. 2618; Prisoners Sent to Port Macquarie 4/3899, pp. 55, 412–13.

WOOLF, Mordecai (James)

b. Whitechapel, 1813
William Miles, 1828; Convict; Sentenced to 7 Years, Old Bailey, 1826.
Single; Silk weaver; Height 145.5 cm.

Fresh complexion, brown hair, brown eyes, slender build. His father Joseph Woolf was a weaver who lived at 11 West Street, Whitechapel. Mordecai was sentenced at the Old Bailey on 6 April 1826 to transportation for 'larceny'. He had broken into a house in Angle Court, Bartholomew Lane, and stolen three pairs of shoes. Despite his youth he had been in gaol twice before, the first time for house-breaking near the Guildhall and the second for vagrancy.

'James' Woolf arrived in Van Diemen's Land on 29 July 1828. He was a defiant prisoner. On 9 July 1832 he was given a six-week gaol term with hard labour for being found in Launceston without a pass. By November 1833 he was free by servitude. On 5 June 1837 he was brought before the Supreme Court in Hobart Town for having stolen a pair of stockings, and was sentenced to seven years in gaol, with three years of that sentence to be spent with the Grass Tree Hill Road Party. Woolf promptly absconded and was apprehended in a disorderly house in Goulburn Street. Because of this lapse, on 8 February 1838 his sentence was extended by a further three years and he was sent to Port Arthur for 'severe discipline'.

By this time Woolf was described as 169 cm tall, with a dark complexion, 'thick' whiskers, and 'a proud visage'. He had an aquiline nose, dark brown hair and a large mouth. He had a tattoo on the inside of his left arm of a soldier and a female with cup in hand. A round mark representing the world was tattooed on the back of his left hand. His behaviour at Port Arthur was so unruly that he was sent to Norfolk Island. He was listed among the nine Jewish prisoners at Norfolk Island who needed spiritual help from the Sydney Jewish congregation. Before prayer books could be dispatched Woolf had helped to organise a desperate attempt to escape from the island prison and joined a group of eight prisoners who seized a large six-oared whale boat and escaped. After three months of suffering they eventually reached Twofold Bay on the New South Wales coast, where they were promptly arrested by the captain of a local customs boat. They were sent to Sydney and, on 20 July 1840, were charged with absconding and with stealing a pair of white trousers. The seven escapees were tried and all but one received the death sentence for absconding. The court was lenient with Woolf. It was said that he had saved one of the crew from being murdered when the brig had been seized by the mutineers. He was therefore sentenced to be sent back to Norfolk Island, having been convicted of piracy, to serve a total of four years on the island with two years in chains. He was returned to Hobart Town in 1844, where he was listed as owing the Hobart Synagogue a pledge of seven shillings and sixpence, which (of course) remained unpaid.

At the Hobart Supreme Court on 22 January 1845 Woolf and five others were tried for 'robbery and putting in bodily fear'. The judge believed that 'Woolf was especially culpable inasmuch as his life had been spared before on conviction of piracy, but his Honour had no doubt under the present lenient administration their lives might be spared and they would be sent to Norfolk Island'. Woolf told his own heroic version of what happened next in the course of a petition for mercy. He had arrived on Norfolk Island in February 1845 on the *Lady Franklin*. Late in the evening of 12 April one of the government whale boats was wrecked on the reef and Woolf swam out to rescue some of the people in the water. He saved the convict storekeeper. He found the body of the chief constable and brought it back and four days later swam out to a whaler's boat beyond the reef with a rope and rescued the wreck. As a reward Woolf was sent back to Van Diemen's Land and to Port Arthur, where he was named as 'one of the most notorious prisoners at Port Arthur' in the 1848 Comptroller-General of Convicts' Report.

According to a note at the Tasmanian Archives, James Woolf of Norfolk Island married Sarah Jones on 22 October 1849. The witnesses at the wedding were Aaron and Jessie Price.

OBSP, 1826, case 588; CON 35/1; CON 34/2, no. 842; CON 44/3; *HRA*, series 1, vol. 22, p. 378; A Tale of Norfolk Island, Anon, Tract, 1845; CON 44/3, Petitions 1844; *Hobart Town Courier*, 8 February 1835, 30 January 1845, 23 February 1838, 28 June 1839; *Sydney Morning Herald*, 21 October 1842; CON 31/45, no. 841; I. Brand, *Escape from Port Arthur*; VDL Papers, ML, A1059.4; 1843 Recognition Book 4/5297, no. 1535.

WOOLFE, Michael (WOOLF)

b. London, 1825–1875
John Barry (5), 1839; Convict; Sentenced to 7 years, Old Bailey, 1838.
Single; Jeweller, errand boy; Height: 159 cm.

Dark pale complexion, freckled, brown hair, hazel eyes. No previous conviction. Jew. Michael Woolfe stole £200 worth of jewellery from his stepfather's and mother's shop in Oxford Street. He had been living away from home. His mother had attempted to set him up in a jewellery business when he was thirteen years old. The wife of a jeweller, a Mrs Ghost, seems to be partly responsible for Woolfe's thefts.

She was given a sentence of fourteen years transportation, while he was sentenced to seven years with a recommendation for mercy. The John Barry's *documents recorded that he was thirteen. However, the Old Bailey account gave his age as seventeen. Michael Woolfe was sentenced on 14 May 1838.*

Michael Woolfe arrived in Van Diemen's Land on 22 March 1839. Woolfe received a certificate of freedom on 15 February 1846. In 1866 a Michael 'Wolff' married Theresa Emma Waddlow in Melbourne.

OBSP, 1838, case 1309, p. 119; *John Barry* Printed Indent, p. 52; CF 46/0187.

WOOLFE, Samuel (WOLFE)

b. London, 1798
Ocean (2), 1818; Convict; Sentenced to 7 years, Old Bailey, 1817.
Single; Pen-cutter and quill manufacturer; Height: 166 cm.

Florid complexion, black hair, dark eyes. Woolfe was caught stealing an overcoat from a stage coach and sentenced at the London Gaol Delivery on 15 January 1817.

Woolfe arrived in New South Wales on 10 January 1818 and was granted a certificate of freedom on 15 January 1824.

OBSP, 1816–17, case 174, p. 71; Ship Indent 4/4005, p. 413; CF 4/4423, 029/1726.

WORMS, Henry

b. Frankfurt am Main, 1768
Medina, 1825; Convict; Sentenced to 14 years, Old Bailey, 1825.
Widower; Manufacturer and confectioner; Height: 161 cm; 8 children (in England).

Dark brown hair to grey, brown eyes, high temple, crooked teeth in upper mouth. Jew. Henry Worms was transported for receiving stolen goods. At the Fox and Peacock public house John Moriarty ordered a pint of porter and disappeared with the pewter pot. The landlord followed Moriarty and checked at the marine store shop of Henry Worms and heard the two men negotiating to acquire the stolen pot. A constable was summoned who searched the store and found Worms and his young son melting the pewter down. Henry Worms aged fifty-seven was sentenced to be transported for fourteen years. His son, Morris, aged fourteen was respited. Moriarty was sentenced to three months in prison. Henry Worms had been in gaol before. His behaviour was reported to be 'Orderly'.

Henry Worms arrived in Van Diemen's Land on 19 September 1825. On 25 June 1826 he was accused of profaning the Sabbath day by offering for sale cakes and lollypops at his house in Elizabeth Street. The complaint was dismissed. On 20 September 1826, as an assigned servant, he was absent from the Sunday muster and compulsory church service and was severely reprimanded. By 10 August 1830 Henry Worms held a ticket of leave. He was arraigned on a charge of assaulting James Gregory with the intent to commit an unnatural crime. He was confined to the police barracks, where he was found to be drunk. He was punished with ten days on the treadmill. On 7 June 1831 he was again drunk, and was sentenced to fifteen days on the treadmill. The *Colonial Times* then reported that Henry Worms,

'a Jew', who owned a pawnbroking shop and was a money lender in Hobart Town, was involved in the trial of Thomas Woolett, who had stolen a watch and had attempted to sell it to Worms. Henry's dossier ends abruptly with the word 'RUN'.
OBSP 13 January 1825, case 381. CON 31/45; CON 23/3, no. 662; MM33/1; *Colonial Times*, 15 June 1831.

WORTHY, Henry (JONES)

b. Bath, 1822
Hyderabad, 1845; Convict; Sentenced to 7 years, Somerset–Bath Quarter Sessions, 1844.
Single; Servant and groom; Height: 156 cm.

Fresh complexion, brown hair, brown eyes, hazel eyes, large nose. 'Jew'. Could read and write. Henry Worthy had been convicted before as a pickpocket. He was transported for stealing two fowls and two rabbits.

Worthy arrived at Norfolk Island on the *Hyderabad* on 20 February 1845. The first part of his sentence was spent at the penal colony there. Minor offences were recorded in his dossier. He was then sent to Van Diemen's Land, arriving on 1 May 1847, and was sent to the Port Arthur prison. He received his ticket of leave on 5 December 1848. A certificate of freedom was issued on 19 October 1852. He was tried at the Launceston Quarter Sessions on 12 February 1866 when he was accused of housebreaking and was acquitted. At the Police Court in Hobart on 4 June 1873 he was convicted of being 'idle and disorderly' and sentenced to three months imprisonment.
CON 33/86, Police, no. 20029; CON 14/29, p. 252.

Y

YATES, Saul

b. Liverpool, 1791–1867
1847; Free.
Married; Solicitor; 9 children.

Saul was the grandson of Rabbi Benjamin Ben Eliyakim Goetz of Strelizt. His father was sometimes referred to as 'the first rabbi of Liverpool' and earned his living as a seal engraver and was the city's 'Jews' High Priest'. Saul married Sarah Isaacs in London and their daughter Emily was born in London in 1840. The family is thought to have arrived in Australia around 1847. They settled in Goulburn. Saul Yates died in Goulburn 6 July 1867. Sarah died 1 August 1872 in Auckland. They had nine children: Alfred (1825), Julia and Samuel (1829), Rebecca and Edward (1833), Flora (1836), Leopold (1837), Emily (1840) and Benjamin (1843).

Saul Yates 'late of London; solicitor' was buried in the Goulburn Jewish Cemetery on 7 June 1860. Saul and Sarah's daughter, Emily, married Jacob Alexander (q.v.) of Goulburn. A son, Leopold, served as police magistrate in Yass and in 1860 presided at the opening of the Yass Court House. Leopold was appointed senior magistrate in Armidale, New South Wales in 1882.

YOULET, Abraham (Youler)

b. London, 1770–1842
Royal Admiral, 1792; Convict; Sentenced to 7 years, Old Bailey, 1791.
Single; Porter.

Abraham Youlet, aged twenty-one, was indicted at the Old Bailey for having stolen 149 pairs of stockings, silk cotton valued at £3 3s 6d, cotton night caps valued at twelve shillings and 12 000 pins, the goods of Thomas Flint. The goods were in a bag carried on the head of a boy servant. Youlet picked up the bag when it was dropped. The boy had been distracted because he was watching a public execution of eight prisoners outside the Old Bailey. Youlet produced character evidence from Isaac Phillips, who said that Youlet was his porter and was 'very honest'. Solomon Moses and John Tanner also appeared as character witnesses.

A letter written aboard the *Royal Admiral* at Cape of Good Hope dated 19 August 1792 by James Lacey tells the story of

> a Jew convict, who from his former bad conduct to his associates, met with continued taunts, and not having any other mode of revenge, informed Cap'n Bond that there had a plan been concerted on board of the hulks for the convicts to gain possession of the vessel, and in consequence eight men intirely [*sic*] innocent of that crime suffered a very severe punishment, but in a very short time he was detected, through the penetration of Mr Thompson, who fills the joint offices of gunner and inspector of the convicts, and in him the Jew underwent a descriptive in itself very severe, yet not anyways adequate to his deserts. The Jew had formerly been admitted on evidence, and on his depositions, several were transported, whom his dread of meeting in the settlement, as is supposed, and the aforementioned desire of revenge, actuated him to make the report of a fictitious meeting.

Youlet settled on the Hawkesbury, having arrived in New South Wales on 7 October 1792. On 15 April 1803 the Colonial Secretary included his name on the list of grants and leases registered by the administration and this registration was repeated on 6 September 1809. Youlet signed a petition to Governor Bligh. In the Bigge Appendix, 'Youler' was mentioned as being owed £72 1s 8d by the officers and settlers. On the map of the old Jewish Cemetery at Devonshire Street, which is held at Sydney's Great Synagogue, there is a note about Youlet's grave: 'Abraham Youel [*sic*], brother to Levey, Navy Agent Mount Terrace, London. Arrived Sydney by the Second Fleet and lived to upwards of ninety years of age. Died 2 August 1842'.

OBSP, 1791, no. 293, p. 435f.; *HRNSW,* vol. 2, p. 479f.; 9/2731, pp. 128, 188; Bigge Appendix, BT Box 12, p. 58.

YOUNG, George

Free; Tailor.

On 16 January 1845 George Young advertised that he was the agent for the intercolonial ship the *Dorset*. On 13 October 1847 'Young and Abrahams, Milliners and Dress Makers', advertised that they were in business opposite Mr William Samson's Auction Mart in Rundle Street.

South Australian Gazette and Colonial Register, 16 January 1845, 13 October 1847.

Z

ZADOCK, Aaron (ZADOK)

Free.
Single; Dealer.

Aaron Zadock was the brother of Colman Zadock (q.v.) and Ann Zadock (q.v.). On 13 October 1831 Zadock was summoned to the Supreme Court in Sydney by Henry Lazarus (q.v.) to answer a charge of insolvency. In early August 1832 Aaron Zadock of the Dolphin Hotel, Hyde Park, in Sydney advertised that he had 'only been in business a short while'. On Monday 13 August 1832 the *Sydney Herald* carried the announcement that 'Aaron Zadock of the Dolphin Hotel facing Hyde Park recommends his Hotel to Invalids from sickly climes'. The hotel was on the corner of Pitt Street and Elizabeth Street. On 5 October 1832 he had transferred the licence to John Head and was listed in the *Post Office Directory* as a 'General Dealer' in Cambridge Street. Aaron Zadock and Caroline Moses (Moss) were married on 30 April 1843 by the Sydney Synagogue.

Zadock moved to Illawarra in 1836 but, by 1847, the *Sydney Post Office Directory* listed him as a dealer living in Sussex Street. Aaron Zadock left Sydney by the barque *Victoria* bound for the Californian goldfields on 9 November 1849.

Sydney Monitor, 6 August 1832; *Sydney Gazette*, 13 October 1832; *Sydney Herald*, 13 August 1832; *Hill's Life in New South Wales*, 5 October 1832; *Australian*, 5 October 1832.

ZADOCK, Ann

1805–1850
Free.
Single.

Ann was the sister of Aaron and Colman Zadock (qq.v.). Ann died in Sydney on 21 October 1850 and, according to the York Street Synagogue records, an inquest was required to be held into the cause of her death.

ZADOCK, Colman (Kalman) (ZADOK)

1807–1852
Royal Admiral (2), 1833; Convict.
Single; Dealer.

The brother of Aaron Zadock (q.v.) and Ann Zadock (q.v.), Colman Zadock arrived in New South Wales on 26 October 1833. Zadock gave £10 to the Sydney Synagogue building fund in September 1839. On 26 February 1840 he married Elizabeth Solomon (q.v.) at the Sydney Synagogue. On 28 April 1842 Colman Zadock was listed as insolvent and in 1844 he applied (unsuccessfully) for the job of synagogue beadle with a salary of £25 per annum. However, Joel Joseph (q.v.) was elected. During the early 1840s Aaron and Colman Zadock were in business together and the *Shipping Gazette* recorded that on 8 November 1845 they had exported one case of earthenware goods and one case of drapery to Auckland. Colman Zadock died on 10 September 1852 at the Tarban Creek Lunatic Asylum. (The Sydney Synagogue Register of Deaths recorded that he died at the age of forty-five at his 'residence at Tarban Creek'.) Elizabeth died on 16 October 1854 at the age of thirty-three. Colman and Elizabeth Zadock were both buried in the Jewish section of the Devonshire Street cemetery and their tombstones removed to Rookwood in 1901.

Sydney Synagogue Minutes 1844, p. 134; *Sydney Gazette*, 23 April 1844; *Commercial Journal and Advertiser*, 1 April 1840; *Australian*, 8 March 1842.

Appendix

The Jews of Colonial Australia

Arrival

The statistics and the analysis that follows are based on the data that can be extrapolated from the biographical data in this book. It must be assumed that at least 10 per cent of 1365 Jews who came to Australia during this first colonial period grasped the opportunity to hide, or to ignore, their Jewish identity and quietly joined the Christian majority. In compiling the biographical dictionary a name might be known but not a birthplace. Twenty-one women are listed in their husbands' entries as no details other than their names and that they were 'free' settlers are known. Two convicts embarked for Australia and 'died at sea'. Converts both to and from Judaism have been included. Marital status will be noted for the convicts but not necessarily for the free settlers. Heights and physical descriptions are known for most convicts and not for free settlers. As we have fragmentary data the statistical total will vary. We know, for example, that at least 575 free Jewish settlers came to Australia in this period, and that between 1788 and 1850 more than 170 Jews moved to live in another colony for a significant period of time. These settlers have been counted in the 'other' colony's statistics even though they appear only once in the grand total of arrivals.

Migration patterns were not one way. The goal of almost every emancipist was to leave Australia and return to London. Similarly, financial success for the free settler frequently brought about the longed for chance to retire to England. During the colonial period four Jewish convicts were executed and 11 are known to have escaped. Thirty Jewish emancipists served their time and returned to England and 96 Jewish free settlers, together with their children, many of whom had been born in Australia, set sail for 'Home' in order to enjoy the capital amassed in the colonies.

There are 52 children who were born in the colonies, or who were brought to Australia by their parents, who have been given their own entries in the Biographical Dictionary because they were old enough to have established their own families or businesses before 1850.

The number of Jewish 'persons' registered by the colonial authorities in 1851 was 1887. There were 979 in New South Wales, 364 in Victoria, 100 in South Australia, nine in Western Australia and 435 in Van Diemen's Land.[1]

Table 1 Number of Jews in Australia, by region

New South Wales, 1788–1850	
Total male	756
Total female	231
Free male	339
Free female	198
Convict male	417
Convict female	33
Native born	31

Note: five convicts were sent direct to Norfolk Island.

Van Diemen's Land, 1804–1850	
Free male	114
Free female	59
Convict male	218
Convict female	15
Native born	21

South Australia, 1836–1850	
Free male	47
Free female	11

Victoria, 1834–1850	
Free male	67
Free female	14

Queensland, 1825–1850	
Free male	1
Free female	1
Convict male	3

Western Australia, 1829–1850	
Free male	8
Free female	2

The pattern of arrivals clearly shows the impact of the aftermath of the Napoleonic Wars. A. G. L. Shaw notes that from 1816 to 1825 the average number of convicts deported each year from the United Kingdom was 2600.[2] In the next ten years the number of deportees almost doubled. Three-fifths of all convicts sent to Australia were transported after 1830. At the same time it became known that economic conditions in the Australian colonies had begun to outstrip those experienced at home. In order to make transportation to Australia unappealing the authorities enforced a new and grim regime of judicial punishment, hard labour, strict silence, solitary confinement and secondary exile to brutal and isolated gaols.[3] Robson comments: 'The general picture of life for the convict in Van Diemen's Land was a dark one, though not as dark as it could have been. Yet on the island there existed one of the most amazing communities on the face of nineteenth century earth, importing some of the worst and most depraved criminals of Britain with which to increase the numbers of a society built on the rum traffic'.[4]

1 C. A. Price, *Jewish Settlers in Australia*, Appendix 1.
2 A. G. L. Shaw, p. 147.
3 A. G. L. Shaw, p. 140f.
4 L. L. Robson, p. 110.

By 1827 the number of free Jewish arrivals began to outnumber those sent to Australia as convicts. Transportation to New South Wales effectively finished by 1840 and, by then, a very large proportion of those who had been sent to Australia had served their time and had become emancipists who were no longer subject to the restrictions imposed upon the prisoners of the Crown. The small number of convicts who arrived between 1850 and 1853 reflects the dramatically diminished numbers sent to Tasmania following the discovery of gold on the mainland.

Following the arrival of the First Fleet, when eight of the 14 Jewish prisoners were female, very few Jewish women arrived in Australia as convicts. The general ratio of males to females among the free migrants was almost 4 to 1, but with the convict sample the ratio was 10 to 1. It has been estimated that women constituted 15 per cent of the total number of convicts transported to New South Wales and Van Diemen's Land.[5] Among the Jewish sample the percentage is even smaller. We can only speculate why this was so. Clearly, the males were out on the street 'living dangerously' and 'working' as pickpockets, purveyors of counterfeit coins and dealers in stolen goods. The teenagers and young men who were caught often worked in tandem, so that one would jostle or distract the victim while the other stole the pocket book or watch. Criminal groups were often 'mixed', with Jews and non-Jews on the prowl together. Tattooing is against Jewish legal and religious tradition (Leviticus 19:26) and yet a significant number of Jewish convicts wore identifying marks on the skin. Some names and initials had individual meaning, but the dots and darts tattooed on hands and arms were signs of membership in one of the criminal gangs of the metropolis.

Patterns of mortality for convicts and free settlers

The age distribution of both the free settlers and the convicts is bi-modal. The first peak in the ages of death in both is around fifty years of age. The death rates for male convicts were greater at around the age of fifty than they were for free settlers. In addition, more male free settlers than male convicts reached an advanced age. Male convicts were younger than the free settlers, less likely to be married, subject to harsh conditions and physical punishments and less likely to live beyond the age of fifty.

There were 429 households where both husband and wife were Jewish by birth. Acknowledging that it would be very difficult to find a Jewish partner in Australia, 136 of these marriages were contracted in the United Kingdom before setting sail. There were 203 marriages where one of the partners was Jewish. The letter files of the early congregations are filled with requests by the Jewish partners of these mixed marriages for their children to be recognised as Jewish. At least half the Jewish marriages performed in Sydney and Hobart Town were between cousins and, frequently, the brides were youngsters, aged between fourteen and seventeen. A total of 2048 children were born in these Jewish households.

5 L. L. Robson, p. 144.

Occupations and professions

The convicts' trades are self-descriptive and are taken from their dossiers and identity papers. The occupations of the free settlers were rarely identified on arrival and their choice of work became evident as they opened shops, advertised for trade or found employment. Some convicts, emancipists and free settlers described themselves by multiple occupations. We therefore have a convict who identified his 'trade' as 'tinman, tailor and brazier'. Another was an 'umbrella maker and salesman'. There was a 'watchmaker and baker', a 'dancing teacher and wizard', a 'cook, butcher and drover'.

Table 2 Listed occupations of Jews in Australia, 1788–1850

Occupation	*Convict*	*Free*
Boy	1	
Actor	1	
Apprentice	3	
Artist and dentist	1	
Attorney		2
Baker	4	3
Baker and groom	1	
Baker and jeweller	1	
Barber	3	1
Basketboy and weaver	1	
Blacklead pencil maker	2	
Bookbinder		1
Bricklayer	2	1
Brickmaker	2	
Broker	3	1
Butcher	14	3
Cab driver	1	
Cabinet-maker		1
Calico glazier	1	
Carpenter	1	5
Carter	5	
Chair-maker	1	
Chimney sweep	1	
Chiropodist		1
Cigar-maker	2	
Clergyman		1
Clerk	5	6
Clerk and hawker	1	
Clerk and shop assistant	1	
Clerk and shopman	1	
Clothes dealer	6	
Clothier		2
Coachman/groom	5	1
Compositor	1	
Confectioner	4	
Cook	2	
Cooper	1	1
Copperplate lithographer	1	
Corn cutter/dentist	1	
Costermonger	2	
Cotton hawker and jeweller	1	
Cotton spinner	1	
Cotton wick maker	1	
Dealer*	36	230
Dentist	1	1
Diamond dealer	1	
Die-maker	1	
Draper		10
Dressmaker	2	1
Dyer	2	1
Engraver	1	
Errand boy	14	1
Farrier		1
Fishmonger	6	1
Footman	1	
Fruitman/hawker	16	
Furrier	7	
Fustian dealer	1	
Gentleman	1	

Occupation	*Convict*	*Free*
Gentleman's servant	1	1
Gilder	1	
Glass cutter	11	1
Goldsmith		
Groom/coach keeper	6	
Hatter	8	
Hawker	34	2
Hebrew teacher	1	1
Housekeeper	2	1
Housemaid	2	2
Indoor servant	4	
Innkeeper		1
Ironmonger	1	
Jacket-maker	1	
Jeweller	7	7
Jeweller and music box maker	1	
Jeweller and watchmaker	5	3
'Jew merchant'	1	
Journeyman/ wheelwright	1	
Kitchen maid	1	
Labourer	77	3
Ladies shoemaker	1	
Lead pencil maker	1	
Linen draper	1	
Maid servant		1
Mantua-maker		2
Merchant		59
Musician	5	2
Needlewoman	2	
Nurse maid	1	1
Old clothes man	8	
Optician	1	
Orange seller	2	
Ornamental painter	1	
Ostrich feather maker		1
Parasol-maker		2
Pastry cook		2
Pawnbroker	1	
Pedlar	18	1
Pen/pencil-maker	7	1
Photographer, daguerreotype		1
Physician		1
Porter	5	
Printer		3
Prostitute	6	
Saddler	1	1
Sail-maker	2	
Sailor		2
Salesman	3	
Servant	6	11
Shoe and boot maker		1
Shoemaker	13	3
Shopkeeper	6	2
Silversmith	2	3
Skin dyer	1	
Slopseller	2	
Soldier	7	1
Solicitor		1
Spectacle-maker	1	
Stable boy	2	
Stage dancer	1	
Stockbroker	1	1
Straw bonnet maker	2	
Tailor	35	20
Teacher	2	
Tinman	1	
Tobacconist	2	
Trader	1	9

* Dealer includes those who also described themselves as labourers, butchers, fruit merchants, jewellers, scripture readers, clothiers, hawkers, carpenters, publicans, and school teachers.

There is a discernable and identifiable pattern. There are no agricultural workers, no tanners, no weavers, very few metal, wood, cane or cork workers, very few soldiers or sailors, one physician, and two lawyers. Membership of guilds and crafts required solemn oaths and declarations that were Christian. Apprentices worked on Saturday and often ate with the master's family, which would have caused the abrogation of Jewish food laws. Religiously observant Jews were therefore unable to learn traditional skilled trades. They were confined to the buying and selling of clothes, hawking trinkets, and dealing in promissory notes and cheap jewellery. Building on 'traditional' Jewish occupations learned in Poland, where the Jews formed the backbone of the middle class poised between prince and peasant, a significant number of the Jewish traders and merchants in Australia would become publicans and store keepers.

Places of birth

According to the sample studied by Robson, up until 1819 one-third of all those transported from England came from London, in the 1820s and 1830s one-quarter came from London, and after 1840 the proportion was one-fifth. Jewish convicts, however, do not follow this pattern and were overwhelmingly caught and convicted in London. More than 90 per cent of the Jews sent to Australia were tried in London, Newgate, Middlesex, and the Old Bailey, and this reflects the fact that the Jews of the United Kingdom lived in the capital. The origins of the Jewish free settlers are slightly more diverse.

Bibliography

Archives

New South Wales

Great Synagogue, Sydney (Bridge and York streets)

Letter Books; Minute Books, 1837–1860; Birth, Marriage and Death Registers; Plan of the Devonshire Street Cemetery, Jewish Section.

Mitchell Library, State Library of New South Wales

Bigge Appendix.
Bonwick Transcripts.
Campbell Town, Tasmania. List of Convicts 1821–1854. Assignment List of 106 Ships.
Census of New South Wales and Norfolk Island, 1823, 1824, 1825, 1841.
Certificates of Freedom, 1827–1867.
Colonial Secretary's Correspondence Papers, Index 1788–1825.
Colonial Secretary Register for Conditional Pardons 1791–1843.
County of Cumberland Bench Book, 1788–1821.
Darlinghurst Gaol Records 1815–1828.
Fitzroy Papers.
General Musters of New South Wales and Norfolk Island, 1805–1806 (subsequently published by Australian Biographical and Genealogical Record, Sydney, 1989).
General Musters of New South Wales, Norfolk Island and Van Diemen's Island, 1811, 1814, 1837 (subsequently published by Australian Biographical and Genealogical Record, Sydney, 1987).
Governors' Minutes and Memorandums.
Harbour Master, Daily Reports from Vessels Arriving at Port Jackson, 1820–1850.
Hawkesbury Benevolent Society (A625).
House of Correction (4/4569).
Index to Tasmanian Convicts 1821–1854.
Index of Vessels Arriving at Port Jackson, 1837–1850.
Land Correspondence (2/7799).
Land Purchases.
Letters of Denization.
List of Women who were employed from the Lumberyard.
Male Orphan Admission Book.

Marsden's Female Muster 1806: Musters of New South Wales and Norfolk Island 1805–1806 (subsequently published by the Australian Biographical and Genealogical Record, Sydney, 1989).
Musters and Lists, New South Wales and Norfolk Island, 1800–1802 (subsequently published by the Australian Biographical and Genealogical Record, Sydney, 1988).
Mutch, T. D., Index of Baptisms, Marriages and Deaths at St Philip's, Sydney, 1797–1956.
Newcastle Gaol Entrance and Description Books, 1832–1845 (2/2004).
Norfolk Island Victualling Book, Register of Persons Receiving Rations, 1792–1796 (A1958), 1802 (201/29), 1803–1812.
Old Forde card index.
Parramatta Gaol Record Book (4/6530, 4/6259).
Permission to Marry Books (CON 52/2), (4/4508–14) (Principal Superintendent of Convicts, Register of Convicts' Applications to Marry, Permission.
Petitions, Book of (4/1957).
Phoenix (hulk) Entrance Book (4/6282).
Piper Papers.
Port Macquarie Bench of Magistrates, Proceedings, 1830–1832.
Proceedings of the (Sydney) Bench of Magistrates.
Recognition Book Population Musters 1811, 1814, 1819.
Returns of Convicts 1810–1820.
St Philip's Register.
Supreme Court on Circuit, Quarter Sessions, 1824–1860.
Sydney Commercial Directory, 1851 (facsimile edition published as *Ford's Sydney Commercial Directory for the Year 1851: compiled with the greatest care up to 31 December 1850*).
Sydney and Norfolk Island Victualling List, 1788.
Transportation Register.
Windsor Bench of Magistrates.
York Street Synagogue, Report, Sydney, 1845 (subsequently published by Australian Jewish Historical Society as *Report of the Committee of the York Street (Sydney) Synagogue, Sydney, 1845*, Sydney, 1944).

Queensland

John Oxley Library, State Library of Queensland

Book of Trials, Moreton Bay, 1835–38.

Queensland State Archives

Chronological Register of Convicts at Moreton Bay (110/30).

South Australia

Adelaide Hebrew Congregation, Archives. Pritchard Index, South Australian Genealogy and Heraldry Society.

Tasmania

Allport Collection, State Library of Tasmania

Convict Ships Arriving in Van Diemen's Land, 1812–1853.
Elliston's *Hobart Town Almanack* and Ross's *Van Diemen's Land Annual*, Hobart Town, printed by William Gore Elliston, 1837.

Ross's *Van Diemen's Land Annual*, 1834, 1835–36, 1838, 1847, 1851–57.

General and Garrison Orders … Lieutenant-Governor (David Collins) of Port Phillip (from 16 October 1893 to 20 February 1804).

Archives Office of Tasmania

Baptisms, Marriages and Burials, VDL, 1803–1837.

Census Returns 1842–43, 1848, 1851–52 (microfilm no. 27).

Colonial Secretary's Office (VDL), Indexes to General Correspondence Records 1824–36, 1836–37, 1837–41 (3–7).

CON 14: Indents compiled on board the transports before arrival in Van Diemen's Land, 47 vols.

CON 15: Indents of Female Convicts 1842–1855, 8 vols.

CON 18: Descriptive Lists of Male Convicts 1828–1853, 56 vols.

CON 19: Descriptive Lists of Female Convicts 1828–1853, 14 vols.

CON 20: Descriptive Lists of Convicts Arriving on Minor Ships or Convicted Locally, 5 vols.

CON 22: Comprehensive Register of Convicts 1804–1853, 9 vols.

CON 23: Alphabetical Register of Male Convicts 1804–1839, 3 vols.

CON 31: Convict Records of Arrivals after 1827.

CON 33: Conduct Registers of Male Convicts, 1840–1853, 115 vols.

Launceston Police Books.

Launceston Police Register.

Population Musters, Van Diemen's Land, 1811, 1818, 1819, 1820, 1821.

Van Diemen's Land Pocket Almanack for the Year of Our Lord, 1824, 1825, 1829, 1831, 1833, Andrew Bent, Government Printer.

Hobart and Launceston Synagogue, Archives

Minute Books; Births, Marriages and Deaths (copy held at Archives Office of Tasmania).

Victoria

Melbourne Hebrew Congregation, Archives

Minute Books; Births, Marriages and Deaths.

State Library of Victoria

Port Phillip GPO Directory Tanner's *Melbourne Directory*, 1859. *New South Wales and Port Phillip Directory for 1839*

CD-ROM

Hyde Park Barracks Index. New South Wales Pioneers Index 1788–1918, Royal Melbourne Institute of Technology/Registry of Births, Deaths and Marriages, New South Wales, 1994.

Port Jackson Convicts Anthology, indexed by Lesley Uebel, 2001.

Rookwood Necropolis, Sydney, Australia, Old Jewish Section, Tombstones 1837–1984, Australian Jewish Genealogical Society, June 2004.

Tasmanian Convicts: The Complete List from the Original Records, Archives Office of Tasmania/ Genealogical Society of Victoria, 2000.

Tasmanian Pioneers Index 1803–1899, Royal Melbourne Institute of Technology/Archives Office of Tasmania, 1993.

Victorian Pioneers Index 1837–1888, Royal Melbourne Institute of Technology, rev. edn, 1994.

Newspapers and Periodicals

Adelaide Advertiser
Adelaide Observer
Adelaide Times
Atlas (Sydney)
Australasian Chronicle (Sydney)
Australian (Sydney)
Australian (Maitland)
Australian Israelite Bee of Australia, 1844
Bell's Life in Australia and Weekly Retrospect of All Events of Importance (Sydney)
Bell's Life in London and Sporting Chronicle, 1822–55
Citizen (NSW)
Colonial Observer (NSW)
Colonial Times Colonist (Sydney)
Commercial Journal and Advertiser (NSW)
Cornwall Chronicle (Launceston)
Cumberland Times & Western Advertiser Currency Lad (NSW)
Empire (NSW)
Gentleman's Magazine (UK)
Hebrew Standard (NSW)
Hobart Mercury
Hobarton Guardian or True Friend of Tasmania
Hobart Town Courier
Hobart Town Daily Advertiser
Hobart Town Gazette
Jewish Chronicle (London)
Jewish Herald
Launceston Advertiser
Launceston Examiner
London Chronicle
Macclesfield Courier
Maitland Mercury
Melbourne Morning Herald
Moreton Bay Courier
Morning Chronicle (NSW)
Morning Post and London Advertiser
Omnibus and Sydney Spectator
Port Phillip Gazette
Port Phillip Herald
Port Phillip Patriot
Sentinel (NSW)
South Australian
South Australian Almanack (also known as *Royal Almanack of South Australia)*
South Australian Gazette and Colonial Register
Sydney Chronicle
Sydney Free Press and Commercial Journal
Sydney Gazette and New South Wales Advertiser
Sydney General Trade List
Sydney Mail
Sydney Monitor

Sydney Morning Herald
Sydney Record Tamworth News Tasmanian and Austral-Asiatic Review
The Times (UK)
Van Diemen's Land Gazette and General Advertiser
Voice of Jacob (London)
Voice of Jacob (Sydney)

Books, Articles, Pamphlets

Agus, I. A., *The Heroic Age of Franco-German Jewry*, Yeshiva University Press, New York, 1969.

Agus, I. A., *Urban Civilization in Pre-Crusade Europe*, 2 vols, Yeshiva University Press, New York, 1965.

Aron, Joseph, and Judy Arndt, *The Enduring Remnant: The First 150 Years of the Melbourne Hebrew Congregation 1841–1991*, Melbourne University Press, Carlton, 1992.

Backhouse, James, *A Narrative of a Visit to the Australian Colonies*, London, 1843.

Barnett, R. D. 'Anglo-Jewry in the Eighteenth Century', in V. D. Lipman (ed.), *Three Centuries of Anglo-Jewish History*, published for the Jewish Historical Society of England by W. Heffer & Sons, Cambridge, 1961.

Bateson, Charles, *The Convict Ships, 1787–1868*, Brown, Son & Ferguson, Glasgow, 1969.

Baxter, Carol J. (ed.), *General Musters of New South Wales, Norfolk Island and Van Diemen's Land, 1811*, Australian Biographical and Genealogical Record/Society of Australian Genealogy, Sydney, 1987.

Bayley, William A., *Yass Municipal Centenary History*, Yass Municipal Council, 1973.

Ben-Sasson, H. H. (ed.), *A History of the Jewish People*, Harvard University Press, Cambridge, Mass., 1976.

Bermant, Chaim, *The Cousinhood: The Anglo-Jewish Gentry*, Eyre & Spottiswoode, London, 1971.

Bertie, Charles H., *Old Sydney by Old Chum* [J. M. Forde] (compiled from Forde's card index at the Mitchell Library), W. & F. Pascoe, Sydney, 1971.

Bigge, J. T., *Report of the Commissioner of Inquiry into the State of the Colony of New South Wales*, 3 vols, London, 1822 (Adelaide, 1966).

Blainey, Geoffrey, *A Land Half Won*, Macmillan, South Melbourne, 1980.

Blainey, Geoffrey, *The Tyranny of Distance*, Macmillan, South Melbourne, 1966.

Bolger, Peter F., *Hobart Town*, Australian National University Press, Canberra, 1973.

Brand, Ian, *Escape from Port Arthur*, Jason Publications, Tasmania, 1978.

Breward, Ian, *Australia: The Most Godless Place under Heaven?* Beacon Hill Books, Melbourne, 1988.

Butlin, N. G., C. W. Cromwell, and K. L. Suthern (eds), *General Return of Convicts in New South Wales, 1837*, Australian Biographical and Genealogical Record in association with the Society of Australian Genealogists, Sydney, 1987.

Cannon, Michael, *Old Melbourne Town Before the Gold Rush*, Loch Haven Books, Main Ridge, 1991.

Chapman, M., *The Humanist Jew: The Family of Elias and Rebecca Ellis—Early Anglo-Jewish Migrants to Australia*, Craftsmen Press, Hawthorn, 1981.

Chesney, K., *The Victorian Underworld*, Penguin, London, 1991.

Clark, C. M. H., *A History of Australia*, vol. 1, Melbourne University Press, Carlton, 1962.

Cobley, John, *The Crimes of the First Fleet Convicts*, Angus & Robertson, Sydney, 1970.

Cobley, John, *The Crimes of the* Lady Juliana Convicts, *1790*, Library of Australian History, Sydney, 1989.

Cobley, John, *Sydney Cove*, vol. 1 1788, vol. 2 1789–1790, vol. 3 1791–1792, vol. 4 1793–1795, vol. 5 1795–1800, Angus & Robertson, Sydney, 1963, 1980, 1983, 1986.

Colquhoun, P., *A Treatise on the Police of the Metropolis, explaining the various crimes ... which ... are felt as a pressure upon the Community, and suggesting remedies for their prevention. By a Magistrate*, C. Dilly, London, 1796.

Crook, G.T. (ed.), *The Complete Newgate Calendar*, 5 vols, Navarre Society, London, 1926.

Dowling (James), *Dowling's Select Cases, 1828 to 1844, Decisions of the Supreme Court of New South Wales*, ed. T. D. Castle, Frances Forbes Society for Australian Legal History, Sydney, 2005.

Eastley, Robyn, 'Using the Records of the Tasmanian Convict Department', *Tasmanian Historical Studies*, vol. 9, 2004.

Elias, Peter, and Ann Elias (eds), *A Few from Afar: Jewish Lives in Tasmania from 1804*, Hobart Hebrew Congregation, Hobart, 2003.

Ellis, A. S., *Elias and Rebecca Ellis: The Phillips Connections and Some of Their Descendants*, privately printed, 1974.

Elon, A., *The Pity of It All: A Portrait of German Jews, 1743–1933*, Allen Lane, London, 2002.

Encyclopedia Judaica, Keter Publishing, Jerusalem, 1978.

Endelman, T. M., *The Jews of Georgian England, 1714–1830: Tradition and Change in a Liberal Society*, Jewish Publication Society of America, Philadelphia, 1979.

Endelman, T. M., *Radical Assimilation in English Jewish History, 1656–1945*, Indiana University Press, Bloomington, 1990.

England, Parliament, House of Commons, *Report of the Select Committee on Transportation*, London, 1812.

Ettinger, S., '(Jews in) The Modern Period', in H. H. Ben-Sasson (ed.), *A History of the Jewish People*, Harvard University Press, Cambridge, Mass., 1976.

Falk, Barbara, *No Other Home: An Anglo-Jewish Story, 1833–1987*, Penguin Books, Ringwood, 1988.

Ferguson, (Sir) John Alexander, *Bibliography of Australia*, 7 vols, Angus & Robertson, 1941–69.

Ferguson, N., *The House of Rothschild: Money's Prophets, 1798–1848*, Penguin, London, 2000.

Flannery, Tim (ed.), *Watkin Tench 1788*, Text Publishing, Melbourne, 1996.

Flynn, Michael, *The Second Fleet: Britain's Grim Convict Armada of 1790*, Library of Australian History, Sydney, 1993.

Fowles, Joseph, *Sydney in 1848*, Facsimile Edition, Foreword by Moreton Herman, Ure Smith, Sydney, 1962.

Getzler, I., *Neither Toleration Nor Favour: The Australian Chapter of Jewish Emancipation*, Melbourne University Press, Carlton, 1970.

Gillen, M., *The Founders of Australia: A Biographical Dictionary of the First Fleet*, Library of Australian History, Sydney, 1989.

Goldman, Lazarus Morris, *The History of the Jews in New Zealand*, A. H. & A. W. Reed, Wellington, 1958.

Goldman, Lazarus Morris, *The Jews in Victoria in the Nineteenth Century*, privately printed, Melbourne, 1954.

Green, Geoffrey. L., *The Royal Navy and Anglo-Jewry, 1740–1820: Traders and Those who Served*, G. L. Green, London, 1989.

Griffin, G., and R. Howell, *Port Macquarie: The Windingsheet*, Port Macquarie Historical Society, 1996.

Griffiths, Arthur George Frederick, *The Chronicles of Newgate*, Chapman & Hall, London, 1884.

Hamling, Brian Frederick, *Maurice Coleman Davis of Karridale and Liveringa, Pioneer Builder and Pastoralist, 1835–1913*, Augusta Branch of the Royal Western Australian Historical Society, Perth, 1967.

Hawkins, J. B., *Australian Silver, 1800–1900*, National Trust of Australia, Sydney, 1973.

Historical Records of Australia, Series 1, 1788–1848, Governors' Despatches to and from England, ed. Frederick Watson, Parliamentary Library Committee, Government Printer, Sydney, 1914–1925.

Historical Records of New South Wales, vols 1, 2, ed. A. Britton, vols 3–7, ed. F. M. Bladen, Government Printer, Sydney, 1892–1901.

Hobart Town Directory and General Guide, J. Moore, 1847, 1852.

Holden, R., *Orphans of History: The Forgotten Children of the First Fleet*, Text Publishing, Melbourne, 2000.

Hyamson, A. M., *A History of the Jews in England*, Macmillan & Co, London, 1907.

Jacobs, J., *The Jews of Angevin England: Documents and Records from Latin and Hebrew Sources, Printed and Manuscript, for the First Time Collected and Translated*, David Nutt, London, 1893.

Johnson, Keith, and Malcolm Sainty, *Sydney Burial Ground, 1819–1901: Elizabeth and Devonshire Streets and History of Sydney's Early Cemeteries from 1788*, Library of Australian History, Sydney, 2001.

Jordan, Robert, *The Convict Theatres of Early Australia, 1788–1840*, Currency Press, Sydney, 2002.

Katz, D. S., *The Jews in the History of England, 1486–1850*, Clarendon Press, Oxford, 1996.

Katz, Jacob, *Out of the Ghetto: The Social Background of Jewish Emancipation, 1770–1870*, Schocken Books, New York, 1978.

Kerr, William, *Kerr's Melbourne Almanac and Port Phillip Directory for 1841*.

Knapp, A., and W. Baldwin, *The Newgate Calendar: comprising interesting memoirs of the most notorious characters who have been convicted of outrages on the laws of England since the commencement of the eighteenth century, with occasional anecdotes and observations, speeches, confessions*, J. Robins and Co., London, 1824–1828.

Kunz, Egon, *Blood and Gold: Hungarians in Australia*, Cheshire, Melbourne, 1969.

Lang, J. G., *Botany Bay, or True Tales of Early Australia*, Hobart, 1859 (London, 1861).

Lang, J. G., *The Forger's Wife or the Adventures of George Flower, the Celebrated Detective*, Sydney, 1855.

Learmonth, Noel F., *The Portland Bay Settlement: Being the History of Portland, Victoria, from 1800 to 1851*, Baulch Publications, Hawkesdale, 1983.

Lea-Scarlett, Errol, *Queanbeyan District and People*, Queanbeyan Municipal Council, 1968.

Lemcke, Geoffrey, *Reluctant Rebel: Lt Col. George Johnston, 1764–1823*, Geoffrey Lemcke, Willoughby, c. 1988.

Levi, J. S., *The Forefathers: A Dictionary of Biography of the Jews of Australia 1788–1830*, Australian Jewish Historical Society, Melbourne, 1976.

Levi, J. S., and G. F. J. Bergman, *Australian Genesis: Jewish Convicts and Settlers 1788–1860*, New Edition, Melbourne University Press, Carlton, 2002.

Linebaugh, P. *The London Hanged: Crime and Civil Society in the Eighteenth Century*, Penguin, London, 1991.

Lipman, V. D., 'The Development of London Jewry', in Salmond S. Levin (ed.), *A Century of Anglo-Jewish Life: Lectures to Commemorate the Centenary of the United Synagogue*, United Synagogue, London, 1973.

Lipman, V. D., *Three Centuries of Anglo-Jewish History*, published for the Jewish Historical Society of England by W. Heffer & Sons, Cambridge, 1961.

London Society for Promoting Christianity Among the Jews, *Annual Reports*, London, 1818–27.

Low, Francis, *City of Sydney Directory for MDCCCXLIV–V: containing names, places of business and residences of the principal inhabitants; the several government offices: public institutions and societies*, Sydney, 1844/45.

Low's Directory of the City and District of Sydney for MDCCCXLVII, Francis Low, Sydney, 1847.

McKay, Ann, *Journals of the Land Commissioners for Van Diemen's Land 1826–1828*, University of Tasmania and the Tasmanian Historical Association, Hobart, 1962.

Mahler, R., *A History of Modern Jewry 1780–1815*, Schocken Books, New York, 1971.

Meston, A. L., *The Half-castes of the Furneaux Group*, Queen Victoria Museum, Launceston, 1947.

Miles, William Augustus, *Registry of Flash Men*, digital facsimile edition produced by the Archives Office of New South Wales, 2002.

Mol, H., *Religion in Australia: A Sociological Investigation*, Thomas Nelson, Melbourne, 1971.

Moss, Phineas, *Calendar of all days and nights, Sabbaths and new moons, seasons, holydays and feasts, during the twelve months of the year. In the Hebrew and English Languages*, Hobart, 1853.

Mossenson, David, *Hebrew, Israelite, Jew: The History of the Jews of Western Australia*, University of Western Australia Press, Nedlands, 1990.

Mundy, Godfrey Charles, *Our Antipodes, or Residence and rambles in the Australian colonies: with a glimpse of the gold fields*, 3 vols, Richard Bentley, London, 1852.

Munz, Hirsch, *Jews in South Australia 1836–1936: An Historical Outline*, Adelaide, 1936.

Nathan, Lawrence D., *As Old as Auckland: The History of L. D. Nathan and Co. Ltd and of the David Nathan Family, 1840–1980*, Benton Ross, Takapuna, 1984.

Neal, D., *The Rule of Law in a Penal Colony: Law and Power in Early New South Wales*, Cambridge University Press, Cambridge, 1991.

Newman, Warren, and Lyall Green, *Tamworth: A Pictorial History*, Halbooks Publishing, Avalon, NSW, 1998.

New South Wales Almanac and Remembrancer of 1848, W. A. Coleman, Sydney, 1848.

New South Wales Calendar and General Post Office Directory, 1832, compiled by James Raymond, facsimile edition, Public Library of New South Wales, Sydney, 1966.

New South Wales Calendar and General Post Office Directory, 1833, Stephens & Stokes, King Street, Sydney, 1833.

O'Farrell, P., *The Catholic Church in Australia: A Short History*, Thomas Nelson, Melbourne, 1968.

Old Bailey Proceedings Online: The Whole Proceedings upon the King's Commission of the Peace, Oyer and Terminer, and Gaol Delivery for the City of London, and also the Gaol Delivery for the County of Middlesex, 1776–1834, University of Sheffield, University of Hertfordshire, oldbaileyonline.org, 2003.

Oldham, Wilfred, *The Land Policy of South Australia: From 1830–1842*, Public Library, Museum and Art Gallery of South Australia, G. Hassell & Son, Adelaide, 1917.

O'Shaughnessey, E. D. (ed.), *Australian Almanack and Sydney Directory for the Year of our Lord 1834*.

Parkes, (Sir) Henry, *Fifty Years in the Making of Australian History*, Turner & Henderson, Sydney, 1892.

Pelham, Camden (pseud.), *The Chronicles of Crime, or the Newgate Calendar*, 2 vols, London, 1841.

Pelham, Camden (pseud.), *The Newgate calendar containing the remarkable lives and trials of notorious criminals, past and present*, London, 1889.

Pfeffer, Jeremy I, From One End of the Earth to the Other: The London Bet Din, 1805–1855, and the Jewish Convicts Transported to Australia, Sussex Academic Press, Eastbourne (UK), 2008.

Philips, D., *William Augustus Miles (1796–1851): Crime, Policing and Moral Entrepreneurship in England and Australia*, History Department, University of Melbourne, Parkville, 2001.

Phillips, Kim, *One Family's Story*, privately published, Sydney, 1997.

Picciotto, J., *Sketches of Anglo-Jewish History*, 2 vols, Truebner & Co., London, 1875.

Polack, Joel S., *New Zealand: Being a Narrative of Travels and Adventures during a Residence in that Country between the Years 1831 and 1837*, 2 vols, Richard Bentley, London, 1838.

Porush, Israel, *The House of Israel*, Hawthorn Press, Melbourne, 1977.

Price, C. A., *Jewish Settlers in Australia*, Social Science Monograph of the Australian National University, Canberra, 1994 (first published in *AJJHS*, vol. 5, no. 8, 1964).

Recollections of 13 Years Residence in Norfolk Island and Van Diemen's Land, by Robert Jones Buckley, last Chief Gaoler at Norfolk Island, pamphlet, Sydney, 15 June 1823.

Rees, Sian, *The Floating Brothel: The Extraordinary Story of the* Lady Julian *and its Cargo of Female Convicts Bound for Botany Bay*, Hodder, Sydney, 2001.

Rivkin, Ellis, *The Shaping of Jewish History: A Radical New Interpretation*, Charles Scribner, New York, 1971.

Rivkin, Ellis, *The Unity Principle: The Shaping of Jewish History*, Behrman House, New York, 2003.

Robinson, Portia, *The Women of Botany Bay*, Macquarie Library, Sydney, 1988.

Robson, L. L., *The Convict Settlers of Australia: An Enquiry into the Origin and Character of the Convicts Transported to New South Wales and Van Diemen's Land 1787–1852*, Melbourne University Press, Parkville, 1965.

Roderick, Colin (ed.), *Jemmy Green in Australia*, Angus & Robertson, Sydney, 1955.

Roope, Colin, and Patricia Gregson, *An Organised Banditti: The Story Behind the 'Jewboy' Bushranger Gang*, Colin Roope and Patricia Gregson, Lake Macquarie, 2002.

Roth, Cecil, *Essays and Portraits in Anglo-Jewish History*, Jewish Publication Society of America, Philadelphia, 1962.

Roth, Cecil, *The Rise of Provincial Jewry: The Early History of the Jewish Community in the English Countryside, 1740–1840*, Jewish Monthly, London, 1950.

Rubinstein, Hilary L., *Chosen: The Jews in Australia*, Allen & Unwin, Sydney, 1987.

Rubinstein, Hilary L., *The Jews in Victoria 1835–1985*, Jewish Museum of Victoria/Allen & Unwin, Melbourne, 1986.

Rubinstein, S., *The Street Traders' Lot: London, 1851*, Sylvan Press, London, 1947.

Rubinstein, W. D., and H. L. Rubinstein, *The Jews in Australia: A Thematic History*, 2 vols, William Heinemann, Port Melbourne, 1991.

Rubinstein, W. D., et al., *The Jews in the Modern World: A History Since 1750*, Arnold (Hodder Headline Group), London, 2002.

Rushen, Elizabeth, *Single and Free: Female Migration to Australia, 1833–1837*, Australian Scholarly Publishing, Melbourne, 2003.

Russell, C., and H. S. Lewis, *The Jew in London: A Study of Racial Character and Present-day Conditions*, T. Crowell & Co., New York, 1901.

Sachar, H. M., *The Course of Modern Jewish History*, World Publishing Company, Cleveland, 1958.

Sachar, H. M., *Diaspora: An Inquiry into the Contemporary Jewish World*, Harper & Row, New York, 1985.

Sackville-O'Donnell, Judith, *The First Fagin: The True Story of Ikey Solomon*, Acland, Melbourne, 2002.

Sailman, M., *The Mystery Unfolded, or, an Exposition of the … Means Employed to Obtain Converts by the Agents of the London Society for Promoting Christianity among the Jews*, London, 1817.

Sainty, Malcolm R., and Keith A. Johnson (eds), *1828 Census of New South Wales, November 1828*, Library of Australian History, Sydney, 1980.

Salbstein, M. C. N., *The Emancipation of the Jews in Britain: The Question of the Admission of the Jews to Parliament, 1828–1860*, Fairleigh Dickinson University Press, Rutherford, NJ, 1982.

Shaftesley, J. M. (ed.), *Remember the Days: Essays in Honour of Cecil Roth*, Jewish Historical Society of England, London, 1966.

Shaw, A. G. L., *Convicts and the Colonies: A Study of Penal Transportation from Great Britain and Ireland to Australia and Other Parts of the British Empire*, Faber & Faber, London, 1966.

Shire, Angela (ed.), *Great Synagogue Marriage Registers, 1791–1850*, Frank J. Gent, Crediton, 2001.

Solomon, H. J., The Queer Colony, ms. on the Solomon Family, typescript. n.d.

Solomon, I. (Ikey), *Adventures, Memoirs from Trial, Transportation and Escape of … Isaac Solomon*, pamphlet, London, 1829.

Solomon, I. (Ikey), *The Life and Adventures of Isaac Solomon etc.*, pamphlet, London, 1830 (or 1831).

Solomon, I. (Ikey), *The Life and Exploits of Ikey Solomon etc.*, pamphlet, London, c. 1828.

Stenmark, Marea, *Sir David Martin: A Man of Courage and Dedication*, Simon & Schuster, East Roseville, 1996.

Stern, M. H., *Americans of Jewish Descent: A Compendium of Genealogy*, Hebrew Union College Press, Cincinnati, 1960.

Suttor T. L., *Hierarchy and Democracy in Australia, 1788–1870*, Melbourne University Press, Parkville, 1965.

Tardif, Phillip, *John Bowen's Hobart: The Beginning of European Settlement in Tasmania*, Tasmanian Historical Research Association Inc., Hobart, 2003.

Tipping, Marjorie, *Convicts Unbound: The Story of the* Calcutta *Convicts and their Settlement in Australia*, Viking O'Neil, South Yarra, 1988.

Tobias, J. J., *Prince of Fences: The Life and Crimes of Ikey Solomon*, Valentine Mitchell, London, 1974.

Tverksy-Steiner, Helen, *Abraham Jacob Solomon and Julia Solomon (née Isaacs)*, privately published, Adelaide, 2012.

Ward, Russel, *The Australian Legend*, Oxford University Press, Melbourne, 1958.

Wyatt, Ransome T., *The History of Goulburn*, Lansdowne Press, Sydney, 1972.

Index of Names

Note: b. = born; arr. = date of arrival in colonial Australia. The children of those listed are, whenever possible, named with their parents. If, by 1850, these descendants had established their own adult identity they are included in both the biographical texts and in the Index.